Administrative Law
and Regulatory Policy

Administrative Law and Regulatory Policy

Stephen G. Breyer
Richard B. Stewart
Professors of Law, Harvard Law School

Little, Brown and Company
Boston and Toronto

Library of Congress Catalog Card No. 78-71808

Second Printing

MV

Published simultaneously in Canada
by Little, Brown & Company (Canada) Limited
Printed in the United States of America

To Louis L. Jaffe
Teacher, Scholar, Colleague, Friend

Summary
of Contents

Table
of Contents

7. *Due Process Hearing Rights and the Positive State,* 593

10. *"Public Interest" Administrative Law: Representation and Disclosure,   1013*

Preface

The traditional course on Administrative Law primarily concerns the delegation of power to administrative agencies, the procedures that the law requires them to follow, the legal requirements for obtaining judicial review of agency decisions, and the standards applied during that review. Critics of this course persistently and increasingly raise two important objections:

First, isn't such a course too abstract? Too remote from the substantive essence of agency decisionmaking? Aren't efforts to generalize across decisions arising out of many different agencies and substantive fields misleading? Don't those decisions often reflect no more than court efforts to deal with distasteful agency action on a case-by-case basis, perhaps masked by appeals to procedural principle? In a word, is it possible to understand these court decisions without understanding the substantive work of the agency?

Second, doesn't concentration upon appellate court decisions mislead the student about what agencies do? The impact of judicial decisions upon agency work may often be slight; and court review may constitute only a small part of the work of the lawyers who practice before the agency. Should future lawyers not be given a broader understanding of the many other factors that affect the impact that agency action has upon the world? *

This casebook represents an effort to preserve the essential virtues of the traditional course while adapting it to meet these objections. The materials are organized along traditional procedural lines, as updated to reflect the vast change that has overtaken this body of law in recent years. At the same time the book uses notes and problems systematically to survey regulation, as broadly conceived to deal not only with prices and entry, but also with health, safety, and the environment. It shows the interaction between substance and procedure; and (particularly in Chapter 8) it describes some of the bureaucratic and political factors at work.

Thus, this casebook might be used in two different ways. The teacher who wishes to emphasize the "administrative process" rather than "administrative procedure" might use this book to do so. It will introduce the future practitioner to the substance of much regulation, its interplay with procedural rules, the agency seen as a bureaucratic institution, and the basic steps for obtaining court review. The teacher of the traditional course might teach that course from this book as well, using the substantive notes and comments as supplementary aids.

We recommend that those emphasizing the substantive regulatory aspects of the book in their courses refer to the Teachers Manual, which is based on our

---

* See R. Rabin, Perspectives on the Administrative Process 7-14 (1978).

teaching notes. The book's cases, questions, and problems are deliberately organized to elicit in class discussion the points and issues that the Manual contains.

The book provides sufficient material for a four-hour course. Those wishing to teach a three-hour course are advised to forgo selected substantive areas of regulation (such as utility rate regulation; food and drug regulation; FTC regulation of false advertising) or procedural topics (such as application of due process; privacy jurisdiction; Freedom of Information Act) or a combination thereof.

We wish to acknowledge the great debt we owe our predecessors, and we mention specifically Professors Clark Byse, Kenneth Culp Davis, Walter Gellhorn, and Louis Jaffe. Our work is obviously based upon their achievement. We particularly acknowledge our debt to Louis Jaffe, who, in mastering the intellectual problems of judicial review, laid the foundation upon which we erect our own view of administrative law. We also acknowledge our use of the work of many others too numerous to mention, though we wish to point out that the discussion of the Federal Trade Commission in Chapter 8 draws upon that in G. Robinson & E. Gellhorn, The Administrative Process (1974), though we put that discussion to somewhat different use.

We have dealt with the perennial problem of footnoting in casebooks as follows: all footnotes in a chapter are numbered consecutively from its beginning to its end. Thus footnotes belonging to cases within the chapter will not bear their original footnote numbers. The footnotes attached to cases are those written by the court unless the note itself specifically indicates that it was written by the editors.

We gratefully acknowledge the research assistance of Linda Agerter, Dee Carlson, Kenneth Kettering, Kenneth Kleinman, Diane Millman, Joseph Post, Richard Rose, Cass Sunstein, Victor Thuronyi, Jeffrey Wohl and Michael Young. Alan Morrison and Robert Pitovsky were generous in providing helpful comment and criticism. The unstinting work of our secretaries, Sue Campbell, Astrid Dodds, Cindy Dodge, Sarah Johnson, Karen Lee, Gayle McKeen, Angela O'Neill, and Shane Snowdon was indispensable and very much appreciated.

Stephen G. Breyer
Richard B. Stewart

Cambridge, Massachusetts
April, 1979

Acknowledgments

We wish to express our appreciation to the following authors, periodicals, and publishers for their permission to reproduce material from their publications:

Anthony, Toward Simplicity and Rationality in Comparative Broadcast Licensing Proceedings, 24 Stanford Law Review 1, 64-65, copyright 1971 by the Board of Trustees of the Leland Stanford Junior University. Reprinted with permission.

Breyer & MacAvoy, Energy Regulation by the Federal Power Commission (Studies in the Regulation of Economic Activity), Brookings Institution, 1974, pp. 66-68. Reprinted with permission.

Cox, Fellmeth & Scholz, "The Nader Report" on the Federal Trade Commission, copyright © 1969 by E. F. Cox, Robert C. Fellmeth, and John E. Scholz, Richard W. Baron Publishing Co., Inc. Reproduced with permission.

Cutler, Who Masters the Regulators? Oct. 18, 1978, Washington Post Corporation. Reproduced with permission.

Cutler & Johnson, Regulation and Political Process. Reprinted by permission of The Yale Law Journal Company and Fred B. Rothman & Company from *The Yale Law Journal*, Vol. 84, pp. 1409, 1413-1417.

Davis, K., Administrative Law Treatise, Vol. I, pp. 52-58. Copyright © 1978 by Kenneth Culp Davis. Reprinted with permission.

Fellmeth, The Interstate Commerce Omissions (Ralph Nader's Study Group Report), copyright © 1970 by the Center for the Study of Responsive Law. All rights reserved. Reprinted by permission of Viking Penguin Inc.

Friedman, What Price Guideposts? in Guidelines, Informal Controls, and the Marketplace, Shultz and Aliber, eds., pp. 18-24 (1966). University of Chicago Press. Reprinted with permission.

Gellhorn, Adverse Publicity by Administrative Agencies, 83 Harvard Law Review 1380, 1388-1390, 1408-1410 (1973). Copyright © 1973 by the Harvard Law Review Association. Reprinted with permission.

Harvard Center for Criminal Justice, Judicial Intervention in Prison Discipline. Reprinted by special permission of the Journal of Criminal Law, Criminology & Police Science, copyright © 1972 by Northwestern University School of Law, Vol. 63, No. 2.

Jaffe, The Independent Agency. Reprinted by permission of The Yale Law Journal Company and Fred B. Rothman & Company from *The Yale Law Journal*, Vol. 65, p. 1068.

Jaffe & Henderson, Judicial Review and the Rule of Law: Historical Origins, 72 Law Quarterly Review 345, 359-361. Reprinted with the permission of the publisher.

Jagger & Richards, You Can't Always Get What You Want, copyright © 1969 by Abkco Music, Inc. All rights reserved. Reprinted with permission.

Kahn, A., The Economics of Regulation, Vol. I, pp. 167-174. Copyright © 1970 by John Wiley & Sons, Inc. Reprinted with the permission of the publisher.

Morrison, Should the President Control the Regulators? Nov. 2, 1978, Washington Post Corporation. Reproduced with permission.

Note, Open Meeting Statutes: The Press Fights for the "Right to Know," 75 Harvard Law Review 1199, 1200-1203 (1962). Reprinted with permission.

Posner, R., The Behavior of Administrative Agencies, 1 Journal of Legal Studies 305, 328 (1972), University of Chicago Law School. Reprinted with permission.

Posner, R., The Federal Trade Commission, 37 University of Chicago Law Review 47, 82-89. Copyright © 1969, The University of Chicago. Reprinted with permission.

Ribicoff, Congressional Oversight and Regulatory Reform, 28 Administrative Law Review 415, published by the Section of Administrative Law, American Bar Association. Reprinted with permission.

Sloat, R., Comment, Government in the Sunshine Act: The Danger of Overexposure, 14 Harvard Journal on Legislation 620 (1977). Reprinted with permission.

Stigler, Private Vice and Public Virtue, 4 Journal of Law and Economics 1, 5-6 (1961), University of Chicago Law School. Reprinted with permission.

Scherer, Industrial Market Structure and Economic Performance, pp. 343-344, The Rand Corporation. Reprinted with permission.

Telser, Some Aspects of the Economics of Advertising, Journal of Business (1960), pp. 166, 169-170. Reprinted with the permission of The University of Chicago Press.

Thompson, M., Advertising and the FTC: The Role of Information in a Free Enterprise Economy. Copyright © 1974 by the Antitrust Law & Economics Review, Inc., P.O. Box 6134, Washington, D.C. Reprinted from Vol. 6, No. 4 (1973), by permission.

Wilson, J., The Dead Hand of Regulation. Reprinted with the permission of the author from The Public Interest, No. 25 (Fall 1971), pp. 39-58. Copyright © by National Affairs, Inc.

Administrative Law
and Regulatory Policy

1

Introduction: Administrative Government and Administrative Law

A. The Varieties of Administrative Agency

Modern government carries on a great variety of functions: it regulates private conduct; it taxes, it disburses money and goods to pensioners, welfare clients, and other recipients; and it directly provides such commonly used goods and services as national defense, police and fire protection, highways, and so on. Modern government is also preeminently administrative government. We may define administrative officials and employees as civilian government personnel who are engaged in implementing law and policy but are employed neither as legislators or legislative staff nor as judges or other personnel in the judicial system. Over 15 million administrative personnel employed by federal, state, and local government in the United States execute the multiple functions of the regulatory welfare state.

Administrative officials enjoy considerable lawmaking responsibility. For reasons elaborated in Chapter 2, legislatures have granted to administrators considerable discretion to decide questions of law and policy within more or less generous statutory constraints and guidelines. Agencies make law in different ways: in a manner closely analogous to courts through case-by-case adjudication on the basis of a trial-type record; in a legislative manner through promulgation of rules and regulations of general applicability; or through more informal patterns of decision and ordering. An *administrative agency* is an authority of government, other than a court or legislative body, with power to make and implement law in these various ways. The lawmaking output of administrative agencies far exceeds that of legislatures and courts in quantity, if not always in importance. For example, the formal regulations issued by federal administrative agencies annually fill tens of thousands of pages of small print in the Federal Register,[1] exceeding by a large

___

1. The Federal Register is an official U.S. government publication which appears five times each week and contains important federal administrative orders, announcements, and regulations.

multiple the statutes annually enacted by Congress. All of the federal courts together handle fewer than 200,000 cases annually. A single federal regulatory agency, the Interstate Commerce Commission, processed over 350,000 filings in 1976. Each year the Social Security Administration and the Internal Revenue Service dispose of tens of millions of claims. A large and increasing portion of lawyers' practice concerns administrative matters. We have tried in this book to provide an introduction to the administrative process for the student who expects to practice in, or wishes to know about, that area of the law.

What is the "administrative process"? Agencies come in many different shapes and sizes, with many different objectives, armed with many different sorts of legal authority. The materials in this book will provide exposure to a fair number of agencies. The following outline[2] may help you begin to think about similarities and differences among agencies.

1. Administrative Functions

The myriad functions discharged by administrative agencies can be classified into four broad categories that overlap in given cases but provide a useful point of reference:

Regulation of private conduct is a basic and expanding administrative function. Such regulation is often directed at commercial enterprises; examples include price, entry, and service regulation of electric utilities, railroads, airlines, and other carriers; environmental and consumer protection regulation; control of sale of liquor and prescription drugs; and regulation of terms and conditions of employment. Other forms of regulatory control, such as zoning, reach noncommercial activity as well.

Government exactions are also a traditional responsibility of administrative officials. Taxation and military conscription are the two most prominent examples.

Disbursement of money or other commodities is an administrative responsibility that has enjoyed dramatic growth in the past three decades. The payment of pensions to veterans and the dispensation of public lands under homestead and land-grant programs were established as administrative responsibilities early in the Republic. But only in this century have we witnessed the tremendous growth of the Social Security programs and other government systems of insurance, compensation, or assistance for the aged, the ill, the disabled, the unemployed, and the needy. While these payments are often made in cash, they may take other forms,

---

2. Here and elsewhere in this book we deal principally with the domestic activities of administrative agencies. The chief executive has been recognized to possess a considerable measure of inherent authority in the conduct of foreign affairs and international relations, see United States v. Curtiss-Wright Export Corp., 299 U.S. 304 (1936), and the exercise of administrative government in that field has occasioned less acute constitutional and other legal controversy than in domestic matters, where legislatures and courts have traditionally played a far more important role. However, general principles of administrative law have been extended to foreign-affairs functions touching importantly on the liberty or welfare of individuals. See, e.g., Kent v. Dulles, infra p. 258

such as food stamps. Subsidies to business enterprises, either directly through cash payments (to airlines or the merchant marine) or indirectly through "tax expenditure" provisions in the tax laws, are another important form of disbursement.

Direct government provisions of goods and services is a fourth type of administrative responsibility. Traditional examples include the maintenance of the Post Office; the construction of public works such as highways, dams, and navigation improvements; the provision of police, fire, and other protective services; and funding of public education. More recent additions include mass transit, communications satellite systems, government research and development programs, public hospitals, and public housing.

2. *Administrative Tools*

Administrative agencies employ a great variety of sanctions, incentives, and other tools to achieve their goals. In programs involving disbursements and direct government provision of goods and services, the authority to spend money is a basic tool of administration. In other instances, such as police protection and prison administration, the application or threat of physical force is involved. The richest mix of sanctions and incentives is characteristically found in regulatory programs fixing rates, prohibiting pollution, requiring installation of safety devices in automobiles, and so on. Some administrative agencies are empowered to control private conduct only by initiating court litigation. For example, the Antitrust Division of the Justice Department seeks to maintain competitive market conditions by initiating civil or criminal antitrust actions in the federal district courts. Police and prosecutors, while traditionally not thought of as administrative agencies, are now being recognized as authorities that can effectively make law by deciding which charges to prosecute. In other instances agencies are empowered to issue regulations proscribing conduct, but must initiate court proceedings to enforce them against an alleged violator. More typically, agencies are authorized to conduct administrative proceedings to determine whether a violation of statute or regulation has occurred and to impose sanctions or controls upon the violator, although in many cases ultimate coercive enforcement of such controls or sanctions can only be had through the courts.

For example, the Federal Trade Commission is authorized to issue cease and desist orders prohibiting persons from engaging in "unfair methods of competition" and "unfair and deceptive acts and practices" in commerce. The Commission can particularize the definition of prohibited conduct either through case-by-case adjudication resulting in an order against the respondent henceforth to cease and desist from the unlawful conduct or through the promulgation of general regulations which may subsequently be enforced through an administrative cease and desist proceeding. Violation of a cease and desist order makes the violator liable to substantial civil penalties (up to $10,000 per day of violation) or an injunction, but the FTC must apply to the courts for imposition of these sanctions. In the case of agencies, violation of administrative orders may give rise to criminal sanctions enforced through a prosecution by the Justice Department. Occasionally the administrative agency itself is given the power to assess civil penalties or financial liabilities on persons engaged in prohibited conduct, although ultimate enforcement of the assessment will normally require resort to the courts.

In special circumstances, regulatory officials may be empowered to impose immediate sanctions, such as the confiscation and destruction of adulterated food or drug products or the appointment of a conservator for a mismanaged bank. Administrative officials also enjoy discretionary powers that can be effectively utilized as a form of informal sanction. For example, the Securities Act of 1933, §8(a), 15 U.S.C. §77h(a), provides for a 20-day delay between SEC approval of a registration statement and prospectus for a new securities issue but empowers the Securities and Exchange Commission to accelerate the effective date of the approval. Because immediate approval of a registration statement and prospectus is a practical necessity for underwriters of new stock issues seeking to minimize their exposure to market fluctuations, by threatening to withhold acceleration the SEC can force issuers to conform to the Commission's view of what should be included in the registration statement or prospectus; judicial review of the Commission's position would come too late to be of practical value. Even highly informal agency activities, such as giving advice concerning the likely position that the agency will take with respect to the tax or regulatory treatment of a proposed transaction, have a highly important impact in shaping the conduct of taxpayers or regulated firms who wish to avoid the delay, expense, and risk of litigating with the agency an uncertain legal issue.

Licensing is another widely used regulatory technique that is characteristically employed to limit entry into a given field of activity or to enforce minimal qualifications of competence. Interstate airlines, interstate natural gas companies, stock exchanges, radio and television broadcasters and others must obtain permission in the form of a license from federal administrative authorities before undertaking their respective activities. State authorities exercise similar licensing powers over racetracks, lawyers, liquor stores, morticians, barbers, and so on. Licenses may be awarded to all those who meet minimal qualifications or may be limited to a fixed number and allocated on a first-come first-served basis or on the agency's assessment of the comparative qualifications of applicants or the needs of the public. Once issued, licenses may be transferred from one firm to another, as in the case of taxicab medallions or broadcast licenses, or transfer may be prohibited, as in the case of doctors and lawyers. The issuing agency typically enjoys the authority to revoke or suspend licenses or impose other sanctions for failure to meet standards of competence, service, or other aspects of performance defined by the agency. Although license revocation may characteristically be accomplished administratively, the ultimate sanction will be a civil or criminal action in court to punish or prevent a firm or person operating without a license.

Compensation awards are another tool utilized by administrative agencies. Examples include awards for injured employees by workmen's compensation commissions and awards by the Interstate Commerce Commission of reparations for excessive charges by rail carriers.[3] Administrative compensation schemes have often been established to provide more speedy, inexpensive, expert, or sympathetic processes of decision in lieu of court damage litigation. Such awards may have an indirect regulatory effect by inducing those subject to liability to change their conduct in order to avoid financial exposure.

Government programs to disburse or spend money may also have an important regulatory component. Preconditions on eligibility for government assistance payments may be designed to shape the conduct of recipients. For example, the "man in the house" rule, ultimately invalidated in King v. Smith, 392 U.S. 309 (1968), prohibited government assistance payments to single or separated mothers of dependent children who cohabited with a man. Tax expenditures, such as the provisions in §169 of the Internal Revenue Code for accelerated amortization by industry of pollution-control investments certified by environmental regulatory authorities, also have a regulatory component. There is also a regulatory aspect to the government's substantial position as an employer and purchaser of goods and services from private suppliers.[4] The widespread efforts during the late 1940s and early 1950s to eliminate from government employment persons with asserted communist sympathies undoubtedly had an effect on political expression and activities by government employees. Defense Department contract regulations give the Department extensive power over the financial practices and internal workings of defense contractors. Various statutory "blacklisting" provisions prohibit utilization of suppliers who violate federal regulations prohibiting employment discrimination or pollution.

Most administrative agencies characteristically combine many different tools and powers. The U.S. Environmental Protection Agency, for example, adjudicates violations of regulatory requirements giving rise to civil and criminal court sanctions and remedies; imposes civil penalties for violation of certain regulatory requirements; grants and revokes licenses for the marketing and use of pesticides; monitors and publicizes pollution levels throughout the nation; issues general regulations specifying required pollution-control measures; inspects polluters' records and operations; makes substantial grants for municipal waste-treatment plant construction and for environmental research; utilizes the environmental impact statement process of the National Environmental Policy Act to influence the environmental policies of other government agencies; and so on.

Another important tool of administrative control is the authority to investigate

---

3. A variant on traditional administrative compensation schemes is found in the Magnuson-Moss Act authorizing the Federal Trade Commission to promulgate regulations mandating the terms of consumer product warranties. Consumers are authorized to institute damage actions against manufacturers in federal district courts for violation of such regulations. See 15 U.S.C. §2319(d). In other contexts courts have implied a private right of action for damages for violation of administrative regulations. See Note, Implying Civil Remedies from Federal Regulatory Statutes, 77 Harv. L. Rev. 285 (1963).

4. The governmental sector as a whole in the United States employs over 15 million persons. The federal government alone buys more than $144 billion in goods and services annually from private contractors.

and disclose information. Administrative power to investigate is normally granted as an adjunct to other responsibilities, such as the enforcement of regulatory controls or the collection of taxes. But investigation can be utilized as a means of harassment or pressure, while threatened disclosure of unpopular or unsavory (if not necessarily unlawful) conduct can have an important deterrent effect. Some agencies, such as the Securities and Exchange Commission, have an explicit statutory power of forced disclosure of private conduct which is exercised by administrators for conduct-shaping purposes.

3. Structure and Organization

Administrative agencies vary considerably in their organizational structure and relation to other organs of government. Most administrative agencies share certain basic characteristics. Unlike courts, they have specialized responsibilities to implement and oversee government policy in some defined field. Unlike courts, many administrative agencies have large staffs organized along hierarchical bureaucratic lines. The specialized, bureaucratic character of agencies enables them to perform tasks for which courts are ill-suited: for example, to initiate, monitor, and coordinate the regulation of a given sector of the economy based on detailed experience of its particular characteristics, or to process large numbers of claims speedily at low cost.

Administrative agencies exist at every level of government: national, regional, state, county, municipal. This book will deal primarily with federal administrative agencies and federal administrative law because of their pervasive importance and because of the expository difficulties in dealing with the myriad of state and local variations. Even at the federal level there are notable differences in the constitution of administrative authorities. The President functions as an administrative agency when exercising designated lawmaking and law-enforcing responsibilities, such as the award of licenses to United States air carriers on international routes or the imposition of wage and price controls. More often, authority is delegated by statute or presidential order to subordinate officials.[5] Administrative responsibilities may be vested in the heads of the traditional departments of the federal government; for example, the Secretary of Agriculture has statutory authority to issue agricultural marketing orders, while the Secretary of the Interior issues regulations governing the use of national parks and other public lands. Such authority may be redelegated by the Secretary to subordinates within the department. In many instances a statute initially assigns lawmaking authority to a designated office or bureau within the traditional departments. For example, responsibility for aircraft safety is vested by statute in the Federal Aviation Agency within the Department of Transportation, while the Internal Revenue Service within the Treasury Department is given statutory authority to administer the federal income tax laws. Alter-

5. 3 U.S.C. §301 confers general authority in the President to delegate, subject to stated exceptions, to subordinate officials functions vested in him by law.

natively, Congress (or the President, by executive reorganization) may create administrative agencies outside the traditional departments with a single head who serves at the pleasure of the President. Examples include the Environmental Protection Agency, the General Services Administration (responsible for much of the government's purchases of supplies), and the Veterans Administration.

Finally, there are many versions of the so-called "independent" regulatory commission, typically composed of several members appointed by the President to serve for fixed terms, and charged with creating and implementing law and policy with a considerable degree of institutional autonomy; in some cases members of the agency may be removed by the President only for statutorily defined "cause." [6] Examples include the Interstate Commerce Commission (the first great federal regulatory agency); the Federal Reserve Board and Federal Trade Commission, both created before the First World War; and the "alphabet soup" agencies created during the New Deal and after — the Civil Aeronautics Board, the Federal Communications Commission, the Federal Maritime Commission, the National Labor Relations Board, the Securities and Exchange Commission, the Tennessee Valley Authority, and many others. These agencies have traditionally been located outside of the traditional departments; however, Congress recently created an "independent" multimember Federal Energy Regulation Commission located within the Department of Energy. Another structural variation is represented by the Occupational Safety and Health Review Commission, an "independent" agency which reviews the validity of workplace health and safety regulations promulgated by the Occupational Safety and Health Administration, which is located within the Labor Department and headed by an Assistant Secretary of Labor. Whether these differences in the formal structure of various agencies result in corresponding differences in their performance is a controversial question that we examine in Chapter 3.

In addition to these major regulatory agencies, which are relatively well known to administrative lawyers if not to the general public, there are more obscure agencies such as the American Battle Monuments Commission and the National Commission on Electronic Fund Transfer. Congress continues each year to create new agencies, often with major regulatory responsibilities. No one has ever attempted an exhaustive count of all the federal administrative authorities established by law, but the number probably exceeds a thousand. When the state, regional, and local authorities are added to the count, it runs to the hundreds of thousands.

4. Procedures

Administrative agencies also vary considerably in the decision-making procedures which they utilize. Regulatory agencies are often required by statute to act

6. See generally R. Cushman, The Independent Regulatory Commissions (1941). We explore the notion of the "independent commission" and the related problem of limitations on the presidential power in Chapter 2.

through formal case-by-case adjudication in which affected private parties enjoy the right to a trial-type hearing at which they and the commission's staff put in evidence through live witnesses subject to cross-examination; the agency's decision must be based exclusively on the record thus generated. Both regulatory and non-regulatory agencies are often authorized to promulgate regulations of general applicability, either through relatively informal procedures in which the public may be given published notice of the contents of a proposed regulation and the opportunity to submit written or oral comment or through the more formal, trial-type hearing procedures. Statutes and judicial decisions sometimes specify use of "hybrid" procedures by agencies which combine elements of the judicial trial-type hearing and more informal "legislative" processes. In many instances, statutes do not specify any formal decision-making requirements, although agencies may utilize, as a result of formal regulations or regular practice, standardized procedures such as the use of advisory committees, public hearings, circulation of draft regulations to interested persons, and so on. Formal decisionmaking procedures usually culminate in a written, publicly available administrative opinion or order stating the basis for the agency's decision.

The great bulk of administrative decisions are made through highly informal processes of information assembly, analysis, communication, and negotiation. Even where the formal procedures are provided by law, persons dealing with the government will ordinarily attempt in the first instance to resolve potential controversies through informal channels. Most agency decisions — even those of the major regulatory agencies — are never judicially reviewed (although the agency's and private parties' expectations as to how a court would rule if review were sought will be an important factor in their informal negotiation). Informal processes of decision are a necessity if the work of the government and society as a whole is to go on. If no government decision could be made except after elaborate procedural formalities and judicial review, the resulting delay, expense, and erosion of informal compromise would be intolerable. However, as we develop in subsequent chapters, the fairness and wisdom of informal administrative decisionmaking has always been distrusted in the United States, and this distrust has increased markedly in recent years, generating pressures for the expansion and elaboration of procedural formalities.

B. The Focus of This Book: Administrative Law and Regulation

The enormous variety and complexity characterizing "government administration" pose serious problems of choice and organization for those who wish to introduce the law student to the administrative process as a whole. What specifically should be taught and how should it be organized?

1. The Book's Content and Organization

We have approached the problem of choice by asking ourselves what we think a student who might practice administrative law ought to know as an introduction to the field. We concluded the following:

First, he should become familiar with administrative law — as classically taught. He should understand the broad, general principles applied by the courts in reviewing agency decisions including reviewing agency determination of law and fact and the procedures by agencies in making those determinations. The student should also know how to get into court in order to challenge agency decisions. Thus, he must understand such traditional principles as "reviewability," standing, ripeness, and exhaustion of remedies, which determine when or whether he can ask a court to review agency action.

Second, he should learn something about the substantive area of law or policy with which agencies deal. Obviously, one cannot deal comprehensively with "substantive law." We have selected a range of examples designed to introduce the student to the substance of "economic regulation," broadly conceived as governmental efforts to control firms' decisions about price, output, product quality, or production process. We have selected examples dealing with economic regulation because of its increasing pervasiveness, because many students will not take other courses specifically designed to teach it, and because such examples often well illustrate the interaction of "substance" and "procedure" that leads a court or an agency to reach a particular result.

Third, the student should have some acquaintance with the agency viewed as governmental bureaucracy. How does the agency work as a bureaucratic, government institution? Who are its personnel? How are they organized? How do they work? Moreover, the agency operates in a political environment. How are its actions affected by politics? By using the reform of the Federal Trade Commission as an example, we try in Chapter 8 to give the student some feeling for the way in which bureaucratic and political factors affect an agency's ability to carry out its statutory mission.

Fourth, the student should consider the recent efforts of courts to expand and revise traditional administrative law principles in order to impose greater controls on agencies' policymaking and exercise of discretion. In recent years there has been a growing sense that agencies have failed to discharge their substantive missions. In this book we examine various diagnoses of agency "failure" and the efforts of courts to remedy "failure" by expanding the availability of judicial review, imposing new procedural requirements on agency decisionmaking, and instituting other important changes in traditional administrative law doctrines.

In sum, we have tried to design a "traditional" administrative law course that integrates an important body of substantive subject matter while conveying a view of the agency as an operating governmental unit and of the courts as a possible instrument of redress for shortcomings in agency performance.

The book is basically organized in terms of administrative law topics; examples of various forms of substantive economic regulation are developed in the context of these topics. We begin in Chapter 2 with a discussion of the constitutional position of the administrative agency. Why and how did the departure from the traditional tripartite model of government occur? Why did the courts fail to use constitutional principles of separation of powers to prevent this departure? As we shall see, they did not; the "administrative state" was born, and hence we arrive at the question posed by Chapter 3: Have agencies proved capable of operating both efficiently and fairly? If not, what can be done about it? Chapter 3 emphasizes the policymaking discretion that administrative agencies enjoy as a result of their combining traditionally separated governmental powers and summarizes the current criticism of agencies' exercise of that discretion. It lists the wide variety of solutions proposed for problems of "agency failure" and notes that increased procedural protection for those affected (with increased court supervision) is only one type of remedy proposed. Throughout the remainder of the book, which explores the role of the courts and procedure, you will be asked to refer back to Chapter 3 and consider whether the particular form of court intervention or procedure is capable of dealing with the problems described.

The remaining chapters focus on the efforts of the courts to control administrative government. Chapter 4 deals with judicial review of the substantive validity of administrative decisions, including review of administrative fact-finding and law-making. Chapter 5 examines the extent to which courts have sought to channel administrative discretion by requiring agencies to adopt clear and detailed rules and policies that are consistently followed over time. Chapters 6 and 7 deal with procedural formalities in agency decisionmaking. Chapter 6 examines traditional due process requirements and more recent statutory and judge-made requirements governing the procedures employed by regulatory agencies. Chapter 7 reviews the "due process explosion." Chapter 8 examines the internal workings of an administrative agency (the Federal Trade Commission) as it attempts self-reform. Chapter 9 focuses on traditional doctrines governing the availability of judicial review. Chapter 10 looks at recent developments in administrative law, which may have been characterized as the development of a "public representation model."

2. *Administrative Law*

Administrative law consists of those legal rules and principles that define the authority and structure of administrative agencies, specify the procedural formalities that agencies employ, determine the validity of particular administrative decisions, and define the role of reviewing courts and other organs of government in their relation to administrative agencies.

Each particular field of administration has its corresponding substantive and adjective law. Labor law deals with the substantive principles and procedures utilized by the National Labor Relations Board and other administrative agencies with regulatory responsibility over labor relations. Environmental law deals similarly with the actions and procedures of the Environmental Protection Agency, the Nuclear Regulatory Commission, and other federal and state regulatory agencies with environmental responsibilities. The growth of the welfare state and the development of "public interest" advocacy has created whole new fields of law, such as welfare law, consumer protection law, and prison law. Administrative law as traditionally understood, however, deals with more general principles and rules that cut across the particular substantive fields and potentially embrace all forms of administrative activity.

Administrative law defined in this global sense is found primarily, although not exclusively, in the decisions of courts reviewing the validity of administrative actions in judicial proceedings instituted by private citizens.[7] The courts have evolved doctrines concerning the constitutional validity of administrative agencies, their powers and procedures, and the availability and extent of judicial review of the validity of administrative action; such doctrines are applicable to agencies operating in many different fields, ranging from regulation of private conduct to education and public assistance programs to defense contracting. Principles of administrative law also derived from the Constitution and statutes, the most notable example of which is the Administrative Procedure Act, the basis for numerous procedural cases.[8]

Administrative law is a particularly difficult and often an elusive subject for students precisely because of its generality and abstraction from the substantive and procedural law governing specific areas of administration. The global character of administrative law principles governing matters such as the scope of judicial review of agency fact-finding or the procedures to be employed in rule-making necessarily makes such principles broad and indeterminate. Moreover, courts, in applying these rather general principles, are sensitive to the identity of the agency whose action is challenged, the reputation and quality of its personnel, its overall mission and the practical difficulties which it faces in discharging that mission, the content of the particular action under challenge, and the respective equities of the agency and the affected private parties. The general principles of administrative law do not exhibit a smoothly consistent logical structure. They have evolved in an incremental fashion from the immersion by litigants and judges in disputes about particular substantive policies and agency programs. It is an important theme of this book that one cannot understand the significance of procedural requirements or principles of judicial review apart from the substantive responsibilities of particular agencies and the means available to those agencies for accomplishing their goals.[9]

7. Actions by states and local government units challenging federal regulations or restrictions on federal grants have become an important source of administrative law litigation in recent years.

8. The focus of this book will be on the development of administrative law by federal courts. Although state courts have played an important role in the evolution of administrative law, federal judiciary has, particularly in recent years, taken a leadership role. Moreover, the developing principles of administrative law and procedure vary to a considerable extent from state to state, and it would be impossible in a book of this compass to present an adequate or coherent overview of the many systems of state administrative law.

9. The difficulties which "lack of familiarity with relevant substantive problems" creates for students of administrative law are outlined in M. Shapiro, The Supreme Court and Administrative Agencies 107-108 (1968):

"... If administrative law is defined to exclude the substantive questions of transportation,

Practitioners of administrative law, who normally specialize in one or a few substantive areas of administration, are well equipped to appreciate this interplay between institutional structures, procedures, and substantive policy and the corresponding extent to which general administrative law principles are focused and redefined as they are applied to a given field of administration. Courts, particularly those with a heavy administrative law caseload, are also well equipped to understand the competing needs for accommodation to the particular realities of particular systems of administration and for maintenance and development of a general body of legal principles and doctrines that have currency throughout the administrative realm. Law students, who are often unversed in the working realities of many different schemes of administration, find it understandably difficult to grasp this interplay. In this book we have sought to meet this difficulty by focusing on particular substantive problems of administration by various agencies — such as the Federal Trade Commission, the Civil Aeronautics Board, and the Food and Drug Administration — as an integral part of our exposition of more general administrative law principles. These "case studies" in the administrative process should provide a sufficient background and understanding to begin to assess the impact (if any) of alternative procedural and institutional arrangements on real-world policy outcomes. They may also serve to generate a healthy skepticism about the viability of "administrative law" as a separate, generally applicable set of principles that apply across the board to the administrative process.

3. Economic Regulation

The substantive examples used throughout this book are not chosen at random. Rather, they are meant to illustrate certain typical problems that give rise to a demand for regulation and to illustrate certain major types of regulatory programs initiated to deal with those problems. Not every type of problem can be illustrated nor can all be treated in equal detail. Yet, the following "taxonomy" of regulation will help you understand the sense in which the substantive examples are meant to be typical.

---

communication, labor, fair trade, antitrust, patent and other law, which are the actual subjects of . . . decisions, then we are left with the various procedural vehicles emptied of the real freight of problems they have been used to haul and which determines when and in what direction they are set in motion. Moreover courts, with their eye on substance, are frequently careless of what procedural rule they use, how they phrase it, and whether today's use is consistent with yesterday's. The elimination of substantive policy concerns from administrative law reduces it to a formal, verbal, and ritualistic body of legal rhetoric divorced from the actual political phenomena which determine court-agency relations. . . . Perhaps most important, if courts, their eyes firmly fixed on substance, seek to make good policy by whatever procedural tools come to hand, whereas students of administrative law ignore whether the courts are making substantive sense and concern themselves only with neatness and consistency on matters of procedure, the result will be, and has been, that administrative lawyers see in the work of courts great confusion and contradiction. . . ."

a.   Problems Thought to Call for Regulation

One method of analyzing regulation is to view it as an attempt to solve various problems of "market" failure identified by economists. Such a view, popular with economists, treats the unregulated marketplace as the norm and assumes that those who advocate government intervention must justify it by showing that it is needed to achieve an important public objective that an unregulated marketplace cannot provide.[10]

Many market "defects" upon which demands for regulation have been based fall within one of the following categories:

(1) *The need to control monopoly power.* A traditional persistent rationale for price and profit regulation is based upon the need to control the exercise of economic power by a "natural monopolist." When economies of scale are so great as to make it inefficient for more than one firm to operate, that firm can increase its profits by restricting output and charging higher than competitive prices.[11]

Under these conditions, regulation aims in part at "allocating efficiency." To the extent that prices are set at levels which approximate those which would exist under competitive conditions, they more accurately reflect comparative costs in terms of real resources used. Consumers are not led, by an artificially (monopolistically set) high price for Product A, to substitute Product B (which in terms of real resources costs the economy more to produce). Essentially, unless prices are

---

10. In principle, some forms of "market failure" might be redressed through the courts. For example, courts could impose damage liability for pollution spillovers or enjoin dangerous levels of pollution. They might invalidate low wages as unconscionable. But court litigation is also plagued by imperfections and limitations that are especially pronounced in dealing with the problems of market failure that arise in an urban, industrialized society. Certain forms of market failure, such as air pollution or dangerously defective appliances, result in harms that are widespread but too small in the case of any individual to justify the expenses of a lawsuit to redress the harm. In some cases it may be thought necessary to prevent the occurrence of serious harms, such as those caused by unsafe drugs, through prophylacttic measures imposed in advance and continually policed; court damage awards are imposed after harm has occurred and the capacity of courts to devise comprehensive prophylactic injunctions and engage in ongoing monitoring and supervision is limited. Many forms of market failure — for example, the "spillover" problems generated by nuclear power generation and the disposal of nuclear wastes — call for centralized, specialized, technically knowledgeable administration of controls. Judges are laymen and generalists, and litigation is ad hoc and decentralized. By contrast, administrators can "concentrate their whole activity upon the problems of which the single case is merely an element," and bear responsibility for overall results. In many fields of "mass justice" — such as unemployment, disability, welfare or tax programs in which millions of claims must be processed annually — judicial procedures may be too dilatory and expensive. Also, judges have at times been charged with neglect of needed changes in the law to cope with "market failures" generated by industrialism because they were politically conservative and assertedly biased in favor of industry. Courts may have avoided attempted correction of "distributional failure," such as low wages, on the ground that such distributional issues are more appropriately addressed to the legislature.

Accordingly, much administrative regulation may be understood as an effort to redress allocational or distributional market failures which the courts have been unwilling or unable to redress.

11. "The competitive price" may be defined loosely as that price that would be set were the industry in fact capable of sustaining competition. As will become apparent in Chapter 4, the ambiguity of this definition is in part responsible for some of the difficulties facing classical regulation.

set so as to achieve "allocative efficiency," there is waste: raw materials might be combined to satisfy more fully consumer desires; instead, misled by faulty price signals, producers combine those raw materials into products that consumers want less. As long as one believes that, without regulation, the natural monopoly will raise prices substantially, one can reasonably argue that regulated prices will help to achieve "allocative efficiency" — that is to say, they will help to avoid wasting the world's limited supply of factors of production.[12]

The economic debate concerning whether regulated prices will avoid allocative waste is complex. But in any event, the rationale for regulation of monopoly power rests not only upon economic claims, but also upon political objectives such as fairer income distribution, avoiding discrimination in price or service among customers, and distrust of the social and political (as well as the economic) power of an unregulated monopolist.

We shall explore regulation of the "natural monopolist" in Chapter 4, using electricity production as an example.

(2) *The need to control windfall profits.* "Rents" as "windfall profits" may occur as the result of sudden increases in commodity prices. The profits may benefit any firm that holds a stock of that commodity or controls any nonduplicable low-cost source of supply.

Thus, those who owned large stocks of oil were in a position to obtain windfall profits when the OPEC countries raised the price of their new oil; those who had large stocks of coffee were in a similar position when the price of coffee went up; owners of old natural gas, if free to raise their prices, could obtain a windfall when the costs of finding new natural gas rose; and those who owned existing housing could reap windfall profits as long as construction costs rose faster than other costs. Such profits are common in competitive and noncompetitive industries alike. Ordinarily they are not regulated, but when they are large in amount and do not reflect any particular talent or skill on the part of producers, there may be a demand for regulation. The object of the regulation is to transfer allegedly undeserved profits from producers (or owners) of the scarce resource to consumers (or taxpayers).

We shall explore the subject of rent control in Chapter 5, using natural gas price regulation as an example.

(3) *The need to correct for "spillover" costs.* Regulation is frequently justified by the need to compensate for the fact that the price of a product does not reflect major costs that its production and use impose upon society.

Thus, the price of steel in the past did not reflect the "spillover" costs (sometimes referred to as "externalities") that its manufacture imposes in the form of air pollution. Neither the manufacturer nor the consumer bears these costs. As a

---

12. The subject of "allocational failure" and the "allocative efficiency" accounts for a large share of the discipline of economics. For a good introduction to these topics in the regulatory context, see A. Kahn, The Economics of Regulation (1971). See also B. Weisbrod et al., Public Interest Law: An Economic and Institutional Analysis ch. 2 (1978); R. Posner, Economic Analysis of Law chs. 9-13 (2d ed. 1977); R. Stewart & J. Krier, Environmental Law and Policy ch. 3 (1978).

result, the demand for steel will be greater than it would be if buyers had to pay for the cost of its adverse side effects.

Of course, the harmful effects of pollution result both from the steel company's production process and the fact that people live near the plant. In theory, steel users and pollution sufferers might agree to share the cost of pollution reduction through the installation of antipollution equipment if they could readily bargain among themselves. However, it is apparent that such bargaining is impracticable, and regulation in the presence of spillover costs is a way of correcting for that fact.

Environmental regulation is the most obvious example of regulation designed to deal with "spillover" problems. The substantive aspects of such regulation, though not examined in depth, will be touched upon in Chapter 4 and occasionally elsewhere.

(4) *The need to compensate for inadequate information.* For competitive markets to function well, consumers need information with which to evaluate competing products. This information is itself a commodity the supply of which will reflect costs and demand; however, the market for information is imperfect. Consumers as a class have an interest in obtaining information, but there is no satisfactory way for them to share the costs. Each is unwilling to pay enough for information from which all will benefit, but for which only some will pay. In addition, some products are so complex that individual consumers need the assistance of experts to evaluate them.

Government regulation is sometimes designed to compensate for inadequate information or to lower the costs to the consumer of obtaining adequate information. In particular, government action may be called for when (1) suppliers mislead consumers whose available legal remedies, such as private court actions, are expensive or impractical; (2) consumers cannot readily evaluate the information available, such as the potential effectiveness of a drug; or (3) the market on the supply side fails to furnish the information needed or demanded. In the last two instances, government may seek to provide more, or better, information or to require producers to supply the information, as in the case of the financial and other disclosures mandated by the SEC.

We shall discuss the SEC's work only briefly; but we shall examine regulation of advertising in detail in Chapter 8 and drug regulation in Chapter 6.

(5) *The need to eliminate "excessive" competition.* A commonly advanced justification for the regulation of airlines, trucking companies, and shipping firms is the asserted need to control "excessive," "destructive," or "unfair" competition. This argument is made in various ways, but underlying each is the view that if prices are too low most of the competing firms will go out of business. Only one or two firms will survive, and they will have a free rein in setting prices. Thus, products and services will end up being too costly.

One argument has historic roots. When airline regulation began in the mid-1930s, the airlines argued for protection against "excessive competition." Although they did not mention the large government subsidies they were then receiving, these subsidies may have led in part to their fear of "excessive" price-cutting. The subsidy program gave each airline an incentive to increase its size by cutting its prices well below cost, making up the resulting loss in revenues by means of the subsidy. Protection was provided in the form of minimum price regulation by the CAB. Similarly, minimum price regulation of trucking — which came about for several reasons — was in part a response to claims by the railroads that it was "unfair" to regulate them while leaving the unregulated truckers free to compete for the railroads' most lucrative business.

A second rationale for regulating excessive competition arises in the case of industries with large fixed costs and cyclical demand. The firms in the industry, pricing at incremental cost during an economic downswing, may find they have insufficient revenue to continue production. Yet, in some cases to close their plants is inefficient, since it is more expensive to reopen plants during the next upswing than to keep them open continuously. This rationale might be used to justify a "depression cartel" that sets price floors and allots market shares. It has not been used to justify existing regulation in the United States, except in agriculture.

A third rationale — articulated in the antitrust laws — relates to the possibility of "predatory" pricing. A dominant firm sets prices below variable costs, with the object of driving its rivals out of business and later raising its prices and recouping its lost profits before any new firms, attracted by the higher prices, enter the industry.

In Chapter 6 we shall examine the case of airline regulation, which — like trucking, ocean shipping, and milk production — has been argued for on the grounds of "excessive competition."

(6) *The need to alleviate scarcity.* It is sometimes argued that regulation is needed to allocate an item in short supply. Sudden and dramatic price increases or sudden supply failures (e.g., the oil boycott) lead to the claim that allocation through competitive market prices will cause too sudden or too serious a hardship on many users. It is important to bear in mind that a shortage may be the result of an ongoing regulatory program (as has been asserted in the case of natural gas). A shortage may also reflect a deliberate decision to abandon the market and use regulatory allocation to achieve "public interest" objectives, which are often neither clear nor specific (e.g., television licenses). We shall explore television and natural gas regulation in Chapter 5.

(7) *Other justifications.* In addition to the major justifications for economic regulation advanced above, there are others less commonly advanced. Sometimes, for example, a person other than the buyer makes purchasing decisions for him or helps to pay for his purchase or both. Market forces may then be distorted, generally causing greater consumption than if the buyer had to make the purchase and pay for it entirely by himself. Medical care is an example. When ethical or other institutional constraints or direct supervision by the physician fail to control the amount of such purchases, government regulation may be demanded in order to reduce the excessive use of medical resources.

Government intervention is occasionally justified on the ground that without it the firms in an industry would not produce their products in an economically efficient manner. Thus, European governments have sometimes intervened to overcome conservative business practices by "nationalizing" an industry, such as steel. And, regulatory agencies in the United States have sometimes sought to engage in industrywide "planning." [13]

Unequal bargaining power sometimes has been used as a rationale for regulating large firms in order to protect small firms with whom they deal. Examples include state regulations prescribing standard forms for insurance policies and the development by the courts of the "contract of adhesion" doctrine. In some instances Congress has granted small sellers an exemption from the antitrust laws, thereby allowing them to organize to deal more effectively with a large buyer. This was the justification offered for the antitrust exemption granted to agricultural and fishing cooperatives. It is also used to support both the exemption of trade unions from the antitrust laws and NLRB regulation to assure collective bargaining rights.

Finally, some kinds of regulation have an element of "paternalism." They are at least partially justified on the grounds that government has a certain obligation to protect individuals from their own irresponsibility. An example would be the requirement that motorcycle riders wear helmets (although, of course, arguments related to the public interest also support such a requirement). Similar motives play a significant role in such government decisions as the mandating of secondary school education.

You will find instances of regulation in this book in which some of these latter "rationales" are at work, but they will not be explored systematically in detail.[14]

It is important to bear in mind that many regulatory programs have multiple asserted justifications. With respect to regulation of workplace safety, for example, it can be argued that bargaining between employers and employees fails to take account of those interested parties not represented at the bargaining table, such as those other citizens who help to pay the costs of government health and disability programs. Therefore, bargaining alone may not result in adequate worker protection, and regulation through standard-setting is needed. This is a spillover rationale. On the other hand, one might believe that workers do not know enough about the risks of accidents to insist upon adequate safety expenditures. This is to argue that

---

13. In the 1920s, for example, the ICC tried a plan to consolidate the nation's railroad systems. See Transportation Act of 1920, Pub. L. No. 66-152, §406, 41 Stat. 456, 480-481 (1920); Public Utility Act of 1935, Pub. L. No. 74-333, 49 Stat. 803 (1935), gave the SEC the power to reduce the size of, and restructure, utility systems. In the 1960s the Federal Power Commission sought to reduce unit costs of electricity by urging private electric utilities to coordinate the planning and operation of generating and transmission facilities. See Federal Power Commission, National Power Survey (1964).

14. Administrative activities other than regulation may also be understood as responses to various kinds of shortcomings on the part of markets and courts. Many forms of government assistance payments are designed to redress the distributional failure of market arrangements to provide adequately for the poor or disabled. Direct government provision of many goods and services — such as national defense, police protection, and local highways — reflects the fact that the commodities involved are *collective* in character, in that (as a practical matter) they can not be furnished to one individual without simultaneously being made available to others. It is therefore infeasible for producers to provide such goods only to consumers who pay for them. Because of this "nonexcludability" feature the market will not provide sufficient quantities of collective goods. The government steps in to provide the collective good to all and utilizes the tax system to recoup the costs of doing so.

there is an information defect in the market. One might also feel that too few workers are adequately organized to bargain for the safety and health they need. This is the unequal bargaining power rationale. Finally, workers may overlook the likely seriousness of accidents and health hazards. If regulation is an effort to give them what they ought to want, it rests on a paternalistic rationale. Each rationale may, of course, suggest a different remedy. Identification of the most appropriate rationale will assist in choosing the regulatory tool best suited to the problem at hand.

b. The Classic Regulatory Tools

The great variety of regulatory problems makes it tempting to conclude that each program or system of regulation is unique. This is not the case, however. As indicated above, pp. 3-6, the tools at the agency's disposal can be categorized. More importantly, many different economic regulatory programs can be grouped into five classic types. They include (1) cost-of-service ratemaking, (2) allocation in accordance with a public interest standard, (3) standard-setting, (4) historically based price-setting, or allocation, and (5) screening or licensing.[15] Each of these types of regulation is typically accompanied by a particular set of significant characteristics. It should also be recognized that the various forms of classic regulation have certain characteristics in common, because almost all such programs are created, and operate, subject to the following four constraints:

First, the regulator and regulated industries are likely to have an adversary relationship, since the regulator will often be in a position to compel an industry to act in ways it would not choose to act.

Second, the regulator is an institutional bureaucracy operated by administrators or civil servants who prefer to design rules which they can administer with relative ease.

Third, new regulatory programs usually copy old ones. Thus, the framers of the Federal Aviation Act in 1937 [16] copied the language of the Motor Carrier Act of 1935, which in turn stemmed from the Interstate Commerce Act of 1887,[17] whose framers in turn modeled their statute on the British Railroad Act of 1845.[18] Those devising new programs have almost always been the prisoners of history.

Fourth, the regulatory agency decisions are subject to the requirements of administrative law, including the Administrative Procedure Act. Agencies can only make decisions of importance after (a) giving advance notice, (b) allowing affected parties an opportunity to present arguments and evidence for or against the proposed action through the device of "some kind of hearing," and (c) providing a public record of the reasons for their actions. Agencies must always act with an eye to being able to justify their decisions before a court of law, which may be asked to

15. Individualized screening typically involves licensing but licensing may also involve "allocation" or "standard setting."

16. 49 U.S.C. §§ 1373B, 1374B.

17. 49 U.S.C. §§ 2, 3(1).

18. 8 Vict. c. 20 (1845); 18 Vict. c. 31 (1854).

decide whether an agency's decision in a particular case was rational and reached through fair procedures.

In this book, you will explore in some detail instances of each of these typical modes of regulation. *Cost of service ratemaking* is the most commonly used method for regulating prices in a wide variety of individual industries, ranging from trucking and natural gas production to hospitals. It is examined in the context of electricity regulation in Chapter 4. *Allocation in accordance with a public interest standard is* commonly used when the government wishes to hand out a commodity or a permission which is in short supply. It is examined in the context of television regulation (Chapter 5). It is often used as well when the government allocates airline routes, trucking licenses, liquor licenses, or such commodities as natural gas. *Historically based price regulation* is examined in its most common context — a governmental effort to impose nationwide price controls (Chapter 2). This type of regulation has also been used to control oil prices and has been suggested as a method for controlling hospital costs. *Licensing as screening* is examined in the context of a drug regulation (Chapter 6). It is used when an agency must "clear" or certify a particular item as "safe" or fit to be sold. *Standard setting* is not examined specifically in any one context, but recurs throughout many of the examples used in the book.

In examining instances of these classic regulatory techniques, we have made an effort to stress significant characteristics of the mode, that is to say, features or difficulties that tend to recur whenever the particular form of regulation is applied. Thus, for example, cost of service ratemaking requires the regulator to determine a "rate base" — a feature that raises serious problems when this form of regulation is applied to an industry as complex as natural gas production.

Because the book is organized in terms of administrative law topics, it may be helpful here to list the extent to which we explore in some detail examples of regulation, first categorized by their principal rationale, and then by type of regulatory program used:

Rationale	Example	Chapter
monopoly power	electricity	4
rent control	natural gas	5
spillovers	environment	4
information defect	advertising	8
excessive competition	airlines	6
scarcity	television	6

Mode of Regulation		
cost of service ratemaking	electricity	4
historically based price regulation	economy wide price controls	2
public interest allocation	television	5
licensing as screening	drugs	6
standard setting	various	throughout

C. The Historical Development of Administrative Government and Administrative Law

As do so many other fields of jurisprudence, administrative law reflects history as much as or more than logic. What follows is a brief historical survey of the development of administrative law in response to the rise of administrative government. This survey should help you to understand the background of many present-day administrative law doctrines, place some of the older decisions in this book in context, and give you a preliminary grasp of some of the reasons why in the United States we have relied so heavily on the independent judiciary and the adversary process to control administrative power.

1. English Antecedents and the American Experience to 1875

The origins of American administrative law lie the common law courts of England. It was early established that officers of the Crown, such as bailiffs or sheriffs, were subject to damage liability if an aggrieved citizen could establish that the officer had committed what was prima facie a common law wrong (such as trespass or battery) which the officer was unable to justify by reference to statute or higher authority. This principle of accountability of government officials to damage suits in the regular courts of law was a fundamental element of the English lawyer's conception of the "rule of law".[19] But the common law damage remedy was often inadequate. The actions of government officials could not always be pigeonholed into the common-law forms of action. In addition, courts sensitive to the need for some administrative flexibility free from the overhanging threat of later damage liability built up doctrines of official privilege based upon the exercise of discretionary authority. Even if a plaintiff prevailed, the defendant official might be unable to satisfy the judgment out of his own pocket, or damages might not afford fully adequate relief.[20] In response to these and other limitations, the common law courts began in the seventeenth century to refashion old writs and develop new ones for the specific purpose of controlling official action. For example, the writ of mandamus was developed to require officials to grant or restore to citizens entitlements, such as the incumbency of a public office, owing to them as of right. The writ of prohibition was utilized to preclude administrative authorities from

19. W. Dicey, The Law of the Constitution 189 (8th edition 1915). Perhaps the most celebrated of decisions reflecting this principle is Dr. Bonham's Case, 8 Coke Rep. 107 (C.P. 1610), in which the London College of Physicians was found by Coke to lack authority to punish Bonham with imprisonment for practicing medicine in London without a license from the College, and were accordingly held liable in an action of trespass for false imprisonment brought by Bonham.

20. See generally L. Jaffe, Judicial Control of Administrative Action ch. 7 (1965).

exercising powers not within their jurisdiction. Courts refashioned the writ of certiorari to review particular decisions of administrative bodies and invalidate those decisions found to be without statutory warrant or otherwise in excess of the administrators' "jurisdiction." [21]

These writs were utilized by the common lawyers to control a growing variety of administrative functions, including the responsibility of local authorities for relief of the poor, the efforts of commissions to drain fens and other wetlands for agriculture, and the governance of the colleges of Oxford and Cambridge. Judicial review of administrative action was also available in cases where administrative officials resorted to courts to enforce their orders. The Chancellor's Court of Equity also began to develop the injunctive remedy as a means of controlling unlawful official action when an irreparable injury could be shown. But the common-law courts continued to play a leading role in checking official power.

This reliance upon the independent judiciary was not an inevitable solution to the need in modern government for an institution, in addition to the overworked legislature and chief executive, for controlling administrative action. Some Continental nations, such as Italy and France, have relied upon well-staffed and specialized tribunals, comprised of high-ranking civil servants and located within the administrative bureaucracy itself, to control the actions of administrators. Indeed, during the sixteenth and seventeenth centuries in England the Tudor and Stuart monarchs had developed powerful administrative tribunals, founded upon the asserted prerogative powers of the Crown, that were employed to control subordinate officials in their relation to the citizenry. These bodies — such as the Court of Star Chamber and the Court of High Commission — might well have evolved into a bureaucratic version of administrative justice analogous to the present French *Conseil d'Etat* or the Italian *Consiglio di Stato*. But this line of development was cut short in Britain by the Glorious Revolution of 1688, the political triumph of parliamentary government, and the related celebration of the independent judiciary as an important check on executive power.

The American colonies inherited the English system of common-law writs and the Chancellor's injunctive power as mechanisms for the control of administrative officials. This system of judicial remedies formed the central basis of administrative law in the state and federal courts during the first 100 years of the Republic.[22] The early history of American administrative law is a subject that has been little canvassed by scholars. The first treatises were not written until the beginning of the

21. See generally L. Jaffe, supra n. 20; E. Henderson, Foundations of English Administrative Law (1963); Jaffe & Henderson, Judicial Review and the Rule of Law; Historical Origins, 72 L.Q. Rev. 345 (1956).

22. The most celebrated American case involving the writ system is Marbury v. Madison, 5 U.S. (1 Cranch) 137 (1803). Marbury sought from the Supreme Court a writ of mandamus directing the Secretary of State to deliver to Marbury his commission as a federal magistrate. The case was decided by Chief Justice Marshall on the ground that a congressional statute, read by the Chief Justice as granting the Supreme Court original jurisdiction to issue writs in the nature of mandamus, was contrary to Article III of the Constitution and therefore invalid.

twentieth century,[23] and little sustained work on the earlier era has been done. Accordingly, our account here is necessarily impressionistic.

The era 1775-1875 is often viewed as one of relatively uninhibited laissez-faire. Certainly the role of administrative government in economic and social life was far less central than it is today. The publication of Adam Smith's Wealth of Nations in 1776 coincided with the progressive dismantlement in Britain of a pervasive system of mercantilist control of the national economy by the central government and regulation of local product and labor markets by guilds.[24] The principle of free and equal markets unfettered by government restrictions and grants of monopolistic "privilege" was a fundamental tenet in post-Revolutionary America. As a result, responsibility for the allocation of resources in the economy and the distribution of wages, rents, and profits was shifted from administrative officials to the marketplace and to the judges who formulated the rules of tort, property, and contract that defined the grounds and terms of market exchange.[25] The contemporary resurgence of administrative government, and the analysis of administrative intervention as a response to the "failure" of markets and courts, must be viewed against this background; as Professor Jaffe has reminded us, government during most eras of history has been "administrative" government.[26] The dominant role during the eighteenth and nineteenth centuries of the market and the judiciary as institutions for social and economic resource allocation may be but a brief and temporary interlude. Moreover, even during the heyday of laissez-faire, national and state governments in the United States played a substantial role in the economy.[27] For example, the federal government imposed taxes (principally tariffs, which had an important effect on external trade, and excise taxes); distributed the public lands to homesteaders and railroads; granted patents; paid military pensions; regulated relations with Indians; controlled immigration; regulated marine navigation and commerce; and operated the post office. State governments were even more active, promising (often with state funds) the construction of railroads, canals, turnpikes, and other transportation infrastructure and controlling commercial enterprises through hand-tailored corporate charters.

At the behest of aggrieved citizens, the courts adapted the traditional writs in an effort to exert a measure of control over the administrative officials responsible

23. See F. Goodnow, The Principles of the Administrative Law of the United States (1905); B. Wyman, The Principles of the Administrative Law Governing the Relations of Public Officers (1903). For somewhat later works see J. Dickinson, Administrative Justice and the Supremacy of Law in the United States (1927); E. Freund, Administrative Powers over Persons and Property: A Comparative Study (1928).

24. See Heckscher, Mercantilism (2d ed. 1955).

25. See J. Commons, Legal Foundations of Capitalism (1957); M. Horwitz, The Transformation of American Law, 1780-1860 (1977).

26. See L. Jaffe, Judicial Control of Administrative Action (1965). See also K. Polanyi, The Great Transformation (1944).

27. See O. & M. Handlin, Commonwealth: A Study in the Role of Government in the American Economy, Massachusetts 1774-1861 (1947, 1969); L. Hartz, Economic Policy and Democratic Thought, Pennsylvania 1776-1860 (1948). By "government" we here refer to intervention by the legislature or administrative authorities. The courts are, of course, a part of the government and common-law tort and property rules are a form of government intervention in the economy.

for these programs. From our perspective, the writ system appears a clumsy device, hedged with technicalities, and exhibiting surprising gaps in the availability of effective relief. In applying these remedies, the courts relied upon the concept of "jurisdiction" to establish a sharp distinction between those actions that were within administrators' authority, and therefore completely beyond further court review, from those actions that were in excess of "jurisdiction" and therefore subject to judicial invalidation. The doctrinal effort to draw a sharp division between the responsibilities of administrators and courts ignored the possibility, developed at great length in our own era, of a category of administrative discretion that is subject to limited and partial judical control and reexamination; however, the notion of "jurisdiction" was applied by judges with flexibility to achieve substantial justice in particular cases, and the writ system appears to have worked tolerably well — given the relatively limited intrusiveness of administrative powers in the early decades of the Republic.[28]

2. 1875–1930: The Rise of Regulation and the Traditional Model of Administrative Law

The decisive first step in the development of modern administrative law was the growth of administrative regulation of private economic activity in the latter half of the nineteenth century. This development first occurred at the state level, in the form of rate regulation of railroads, grain elevators, and other national monopolies.[29] The limitations of state regulation of interstate railroad operations[30] led to the establishment in 1887 of the first great federal regulatory agency, the Interstate Commerce Commission. The political explanation for the Commission's

---

28. See J. Dickinson, Administrative Justice and the Supremacy of Law 41-49 (1927). However, the common-law writs of certiorari and mandamus were not available in the federal courts outside of the District of Columbia because of Congress's failure to confer the requisite jurisdiction. The federal courts in the District of Columbia were an exception because they were regarded as successors to the common-law authority of the courts of Maryland. See McIntire v. Wood, 11 U.S. (7 Cranch) 503 (1813); Kendall v. United States, 37 U.S. (12 Pet.) 524 (1838).

29. The constitutionality of such regulations was sustained in Munn v. Illinois, 94 U.S. 113 (1876). However, federal courts developed the important constitutional principle that rate regulation must insure the regulated firm a reasonable return on capital, and that the federal judiciary would, as a matter of due process, review the reasonableness of the return afforded. See Chapter 4.

30. In the 1840s and 1850s the states attempted to control railroads through detailed statutory specification of rates and practices. But this proved impractical, and the states resorted to creation of administrative commissions to investigate and make recommendations to the legislature (the model in Massachusetts and many eastern states), or themselves regulate the railroads (the model in many midwestern states). However, state regulatory commissions were often ineffective, in part because of strict federal constitutional limitation on their power to regulate shipments involving interstate origins or destinations, imposed in Wabash, St. L. & P. Ry. v. Illinois, 118 U.S. 557 (1886), and in part because of the commissions' lack of resources and competence, their erratic political base, and the organized staying power of the railroads. See S. J. Buck, The Granger Movement (1913); R. Cushman, The Independent Regulatory Commissions 28-39 (1941); L. Friedman, A History of American Law 391-394 (1973).

creation and subsequent functioning is the subject of renewed controversy. A traditional view is that the Commission was created to protect shippers (especially small shippers) from the exercise of monopoly power and rate discrimination by larger carriers. Another view defined the problem of the "market failure" (which the Commission was created to solve) more broadly to include "destructive competition" and wasteful and duplicative services. On this view, the Commission was established not merely to shift income from railroads to shippers, but to vindicate a more general public interest in an efficient transportation system through planning by expert administrators. This view is reflected in the contemporary notion that the Commission is to be "independent" of politics, and composed of commissioners and staff expert in railroading.[31] A more recent "revisionist" view is that the Commission was created and administered to advance the interests of the railroads by protecting them against the rigors of competition.[32] Still other students have asserted that the Commission was not "captured" by the railroads but by shippers, and that shortsighted and inept regulation fatally weakened the railroads by destroying innovation and denying them needed revenues.[33] These conflicting views reflect interpretations of the politics of the administrative process, which could be replicated in the case of many other agencies, and which may represent the intellectual roots of the contemporary sense of administrative "failure" that we explore in Chapter 3.

Whatever the ultimate explanation for the creation of the Interstate Commerce Commission or other early regulatory bodies, such as the Federal Trade Commission (created in 1914 to enforce certain provisions of the antitrust laws and to prohibit "unfair methods of competition"), regulated firms repeatedly sought to block regulatory decisions by resort to the judiciary. The decisions of federal and state courts reviewing the actions of these early regulatory agencies laid the foundations of modern administrative law. In many instances the common-law writ system was supplanted by statutory provisions providing for judicial review of the regulatory body's decision. Many statutes also provided for a trial-type hearing before the regulatory agency in order to develop a factual record serving as the basis for agency action. When such statutory provisions were absent, courts often insisted upon a trial-type administrative hearing procedure as a requirement of constitutional due process.[34] Reviewing courts would then carefully scrutinize the agency's decision to determine whether, on the basis of the hearing record, the agency's factual findings were reasonable; whether the agency had acted within its statutory authority and had based its decision on legally relevant factors; and

31. See Illinois v. Chicago, R.I. & P. Ry., 218 U.S. 88, 102 (1910). For a brief history of the notion that public administration is an apolitical science, see M. Vile, Constitutionalism and the Separation of Powers 277-280 (1967).

32. See G. Kolko, Railroads and Regulation (1965). For criticism of Kolko's views as simplistic, see Purcell, Ideas and Interests: Businessmen and the Interstate Commerce Act, 54 J. Am. Hist. 561 (1967).

33. See A. Martin, Enterprise Denied: Origins of the Decline of American Railroads, 1897-1917 (1971).

34. See, e.g., Southern Ry. v. Virginia, 290 U.S. 190 (1933), discussed in Chapter 6, pp. 468-471 infra.

whether the decision was reasonable and not arbitrary in the particular circumstances.

The traditional model of administrative law which evolved from statutory enactments and judicial decisions was designed to control government intrusions into private liberty and property interests by relying on the judiciary to limit agency powers to those granted by the legislature. The traditional model had four essential elements:[35]

a. *The imposition of administratively determined sanctions on private persons must be authorized by the legislature through rules which control agency action.* This principle reflects the view that administrative officials possess no inherent powers over private liberty or property, and that official intrusions into such interests must be duly authorized by the legislature as the institutionalized mechanism of popular consent in representative government. Moreover, since the principle insists that any authority delegated by the legislature to administrator be defined and circumscribed through rules or standards that confine administrative discretion; this requirement promotes evenhanded treatment of private persons, limits officials' ability to exploit government powers for personal or arbitrary ends, and facilitates private planning.

b. *The decisional procedures utilized by the agency must tend to ensure agency compliance with authorizing legislative directives.* To ensure that agencies actually adhere to statutory authority and dispense evenhanded justice, agency procedures must be designed to promote the accurate, impartial, and rational application of legislative directives to given cases or classes of cases. In cases of enforcement of regulatory controls and sanctions, this requirement normally translated into trial-type hearings at which the person subject to regulation was entitled to present evidence and challenge the legal and factual basis of the agency's authority to act. The agency was then required to decide the matter exclusively on the basis of the record thus generated.[36]

c. *Judicial review must be available to ensure agency utilization of accurate and impartial decisionmaking procedures and agency compliance with legislative directives.*

d. *Agency decisional processes must facilitate the exercise of such judicial review.* One need not rely entirely upon judicial review to make certain the agency acts within its legislative mandate. Legislative oversight, media scrutiny, or internal bureaucratic checks might serve this purpose. But in our system we have placed heavy reliance on the independent judiciary to police official conformance to statutory authorization by reviewing both the factual and legal basis for administrative imposition of controls. This reliance on judicial review requires that agencies use procedures that will facilitate review, including development of an orderly administrative record and articulation by officials of the factual findings and legal conclusions which form the basis for agency actions.

35. For more extended discussion of the traditional model, see Stewart, The Reformation of American Administrative Law, 88 Harv. L. Rev. 1667, 1671-1676 (1975).
36. See, e.g., Wichita R.R. & Light Co. v. Public Util. Commn., 260 U.S. 48, 58 (1922); ICC v. Louisville & Nashville Ry., 227 U.S. 88, 93 (1913).

These four elements of the traditional model at least theoretically serve to limit and legitimate administrative power by functioning as a "transmission belt" to ensure that particular agency actions have been legislatively authorized. The courts, however, deployed these elements in a spirit that was often antagonistic or unsympathetic to administrative government.

Under the traditional model, judicial review of the validity of administrative action became an integral part of the regulatory process, and judges used review of agency fact-finding and legal determinations in order to exercise close and often exacting control over the agency's regulatory powers. For example, the statutory authority of the ICC was narrowly construed by reviewing courts in the initial years of the Commission's existence,[37] and the federal judiciary often paid little heed to the decisions of the Federal Trade Commission, viewing the agency as essentially a subordinate fact-finder.[38] While there were variations from judge to judge and decade to decade, the basic impact of hearing procedures and judicial review was to constrain the effective power of the new regulatory bodies to control private business conduct. This pattern undoubtedly reflected judicial distrust of administrative agencies, which threatened to circumvent traditional "separation of power" safeguards by combining the functions of the traditional branches. Also, regulatory agencies represented a large threat to established traditions which placed major reliance for resource allocation on private market exchange and the common-law decisions of courts — traditions which often favored business and allied financial interests.[39] The courts rarely struck down the leigslatures' creation of new administrative bodies on constitutional grounds; instead they exercised close review over particular agency decisions and procedures to hedge the exercise of administrative power. Congress and the states continued to create new regulatory agencies, even during the 1920s heyday of probusiness "normalcy."[40]

3. The New Deal

Franklin D. Roosevelt's New Deal created a host of new administrative agencies in Washington, sharply expanding the extent of intervention by the federal government in economic affairs and laying the foundations of a national welfare state. These developments responded to the dramatic collapse of the economy in the Great Depression, which seemed to demonstrate that the unregulated market could not be trusted to serve the social and economic welfare of the nation.

37. See, e.g., ICC v. Alabama Midland Ry., 168 U.S. 144 (1897); ICC v. Cincinnati, N.O. & T.P. Ry., 167 U.S. 479 (1897); Intermountain Rate Cases, 234 U.S. 476 (1914).
38. See generally G. Henderson, The Federal Trade Commission (1924).
39. See, e.g., M. Horwitz, The Transformation of American Law (1977).
40. For example, the Federal Power Commission was created in 1920, and the Federal Radio Commission (precursor of the FCC) in 1929. Important new administrative responsibilities were created by the Grain Futures Act of 1922, 42 Stat. 998; Railway Labor Act of 1926, 44 Stat. 577, 45 U.S.C. 151 et seq.; and Longshoremen's and Harbor Workers' Compensation Act of 1927, 44 Stat. 1424, 33 U.S.C. 901 et seq.

Congress responded obligingly to the President's call for new regulatory authorities to manage the economy, and a host of zealous lawyers and academics descended upon the nation's capitol with a strong belief in the inevitability and viability of centralized economic planning. The new administration's most ambitious effort at pervasive economic planning, the National Recovery Administration, fizzled and was eventually invalidated as unconstitutional by the Supreme Court.[41] But other, more discrete regulatory programs survived and grew, as a reconstituted Court ultimately sustained sweeping extensions of federal economic regulation under the commerce power. The Securities and Exchange Commission was created to regulate the nation's capital markets. The National Labor Relations Board was authorized to encourage the formation of unions and the development of collective bargaining in industry. The federal minimum wage and maximum hour legislation and a national program for state employment compensation also had an impact on labor markets. The Federal Communications Commission and the Civil Aeronautics Board were established to oversee important sectors of the economy. Extensive government intervention in agricultural pricing and output was undertaken, and government control over banking was extended. The basic rationale of these and other measures was to "save capitalism from itself" by correcting the most obvious failures of the unregulated market while avoiding the socialist alternative of direct government ownership of business enterprise.[42]

These new measures were bitterly assailed by many businessmen and leaders of the corporate bar, who contended that administrators exercised an essentially lawless discretion in a highly biased fashion. The Labor Board, for example, was attacked as blatantly antimanagement. It and other agencies were particularly criticized for combining prosecutorial and adjudicatory functions; lawyers representing business complained of prejudgment, one-sided fact-finding, and other departures from the judicial ideal of disinterested decisionmaking.[43] Critics of the administrative process, including the American Bar Association, sought to transfer the agencies' adjudicatory functions to independent tribunals and to impose detailed procedural checks and stringent judicial review on agency action.

On the other hand, defenders of the administrative process sought to justify the agencies' combination of functions and to minimize procedural formalities and judicial review, contending that the salvation of the economy required administrative controls involving expert knowledge, mixed powers, and discretionary manage-

41. See A.L.A. Schechter Poultry Corp. v. United States, 295 U.S. 495 (1935), infra p. 63.
42. Comprehensive and detailed government control of the economy was instituted during the Second World War in order to speed war production effort while holding down demand for consumer goods through price controls and rationing. However, these controls were largely dismantled at the conclusion of the war, although they were reintroduced briefly during the Korean conflict.
43. See, e.g., McGuire, Federal Administrative Decisions and Judicial Review Thereof; or Bureaucracy Under Control, 48 Va. State B.J. 301, (1936). Such criticism had been mounting even before the New Deal. See J. M. Beck, Our Wonderland of Bureaucracy: A Study of the Growth of Bureaucracy in the Federal Government, and Its Destructive Effect upon the Constitution (1932).

ment analogous to that exercised by business leaders. Successful administration was asserted to be incompatible with legalistic formalities and to involve technical issues beyond the undertaking of lay judges. In place of legalistic safeguards, defenders of the New Deal agencies relied upon the expert professionalism of administrators and political control by the President to contain potential abuses.[44]

During the earlier years of the New Deal, the federal courts often sided with critics of the new regulatory programs, invalidating many of the authorizing statutes as unconstitutional, narrowly construing the powers of other agencies, and closely scrutinizing particular regulatory decisions.[45] These decisions provoked vocal political criticism from Congress, the administration, and the press to the effect that the federal courts, and particularly the Supreme Court, were obstructing the popular will and thwarting the economic survival of the nation.[46] The President devised a "court-packing" plan to expand the membership of the Supreme Court with nominees of his own selection. While it did not ultimately succeed, the proposal's threat to the Court's autonomy persuaded several "swing" votes on the Court to shift, resulting in decisions that sustained the constitutional validity of New Deal administrative programs.[47] Attrition on the bench thereafter gave the President the opportunity to replace some of the most conservative members of the Court with individuals such as Hugo Black, a populist southern senator with a strong pro-New Deal voting record; William O. Douglas, former Chairman of the Securities and Exchange Commission; and Felix Frankfurter, public advocate and intellectual sparkplug of many New Deal programs. In a relatively short time, the Supreme Court (and with it, much of the lower federal judiciary) swung from almost undisguised hostility toward the new programs of administration to conspicuous deference. The availability of judicial review of administrative action was curtailed, and particular agency decisions were frequently sustained with judicial obeisance to the mysteries of administrative expertise.[48] The defenders of the administrative process appeared to have substantially succeeded in insulating their decisions from judicial check.

44. See, e.g., J. Landis, The Administrative Process (1938). See also President's Committee on Administrative Management, Report with Special Studies (1937). The latter publication, often called the Brownlow Report after its chairman, was the first in a series of official or semi-official studies of the administrative process in the federal government. It was particularly critical of Congress's creation of "independent" regulatory agencies, such as the ICC and FTC, partially insulated by statute from presidential control. It recommended abolition of multimember commissions (termed by it a "headless fourth branch" of government) and their replacement by agencies headed by single administrators directly accountable to the President. The Brownlow Report also criticized the agencies' combination of prosecuting and adjudicatory functions and recommended that the adjudicatory functions of regulatory agencies be transferred to an independent administrative tribunal. These recommendations were never carried out.

45. See, e.g., Railroad Retirement Board v. Alton R.R., 295 U.S. 330 (1935); Carter v. Carter Coal Co., 298 U.S. 238 (1936); Morgan v. United States, 298 U.S. 468 (1936).

46. See A. Schlesinger, The Politics of Upheaval 447-498 (1960).

47. See, e.g., NLRB v. Jones & Laughlin Steel Corp., 301 U.S. 1 (1937); Steward Machine Co. v. Davis, 301 U.S. 548 (1937).

48. See, e.g., Switchmen's Union v. National Mediation Board, 320 U.S. 297 (1943); NLRB v. Hearst Publications, Inc., 322 U.S. 111 (1944).

4. 1945–1965: The Administrative Procedure Act and the Maturation of the Traditional Model of Administrative Law

While the federal courts were becoming more deferential to the administrative process, critics of the New Deal gained political strength as the national sense of crisis that underwrote President Roosevelt's first term faded and the President's program showed far less than total success in reviving the economy. In 1940 Congress passed the Walter-Logan bill, which would have imposed standardized procedural requirements on federal agencies and mandated a broad availability and scope for judicial review of agency decisions. The bill, supported by the American Bar Association, was vetoed by President Roosevelt, who asserted that it represented "repeated efforts by a combination of lawyers who desire to have all the processes of government conducted through lawsuits and of interests which desire to escape regulation." However, the need for some form of legislation to respond to criticisms of the administrative process' fairness and to rationalize disparate administrative practices along more consistent lines was widely accepted.[49] In 1939, the President established the Attorney General's Committee on Administrative Procedure, chaired by Dean Acheson and composed of distinguished practitioners, judges, and academics. The Committee's report, issued in 1941,[50] was based on an extensive series of careful empirical studies of federal administrative agencies. A minority of the Committee recommended legislation that would create more standardized procedures for federal agencies; would require more searching judicial review; and would separate adjudicatory from prosecutorial functions.[51] The majority, while concurring in the need for standardizing legislation, favored greater scope for agency flexibility in organization and decisionmaking practices and sought to meet the "combination of functions" problem by creating independent hearing examiners to conduct adjudicatory hearings in the first instance. After protracted congressional consideration, a compromise measure was adopted in 1946 as the Federal Adminis-

---

49. In creating different agencies, Congress had given little apparent thought to consistency or functional logic in statutory provisions to be used by the agency or the availability and scope of judicial review. This haphazard performance continues to the present day. See generally Chapter 3. Development of greater consistency in such provisions could reduce confusion and uncertainty, save time for courts and practitioners, and promote more rational consideration of administrative law policies. Recall, however, the diversity of administrative agencies, and the related question whether it is sensible to attempt to devise a unified system of administrative law. Imposing a common procedural and institutional form on agencies with widely varying missions and operating environments could be seriously dysfunctional. In reviewing the provisions of the Administrative Procedure Act, discussed supra, you should consider how successfully it accommodates these competing considerations. You will note that, apart from provisions dealing with public availability of agency documents and decisionmaking, the APA has not been amended since its original enactment in 1946. Does this suggest that statutory codification is unwise, given the difficulties of enacting new legislation? Or does it show that the APA's provisions are sufficiently flexible to accommodate needed changes in the law?

50. Administrative Procedure in Government Agencies, S. Doc. No. 8, 77th Cong. 1st Sess. (1941).

51. See Pound, For the "Minority Report," 27 A.B.A.J. 664 (1941).

trative Procedure Act, now codified in 5 U.S.C. §§ 551 et seq.[52] The various provisions of the APA will be examined in greater detail in later chapters. Its principal elements are as follows:[53]

Section 2 of the Act, 5 U.S.C. §551, contains definitions establishing the Act's terms and coverage.[54] Section 3, 5 U.S.C. §552, establishes requirements for publication of certain rules and regulations in the Federal Register and requires agencies to make other important decisions and documents available to the public upon request. These provisions were subsequently amended in 1966, 1974, and 1976 to require that all documents in the agency's possession, with certain enumerated exceptions, be made available to members of the public; and to require, again with enumerated exceptions, that meetings of multimember agencies be open to the public. These provisions are discussed in Chapter 10.

Sections 4 through 8, 5 U.S.C. §§ 553-558, deal with the procedural formalities that agencies must observe in decisionmaking, and are discussed in detail in Chapters 5, 6, and 8. The purpose of the APA was to define and systematize such formalities, although particular statutes and agency regulations may impose different or additional requirements. The Act establishes a basic distinction between the promulgation of general regulations through rulemaking, and case-by-case decisions through adjudication. Subject to certain exemptions, the basic procedure provided by the APA for rulemaking in §553 consists of publication of proposed rules in the Federal Register, followed by opportunity for interested persons to submit written or oral comments on the proposed rules. However, where the relevant organic statute requires decision "on the record after opportunity for agency hearing," the APA provides in §§ 556-557 for modified trial-type hearing procedures in rulemaking. In cases of adjudication where the relevant organic statute requires an agency to decide "on the record after opportunity for agency hearing," the APA requires trial-type hearings conducted by independent "hearing examiners" (now called "administrative law judges"), followed by an appeal procedure to the head of the agency. Sections 554, 556-557 of the Act also mandate a partial separation of

52. Over the past 30 years the states have also codified administrative law principles in state administrative procedure acts. More than half of the states have adopted codes based on the Uniform Law Commissioners' Model State Administrative Procedure Act, first adopted in 1946 and revised in 1961. The Model Act resembles the federal APA in many respects. 13 Uniform Laws Annotated 347 (1978 pamphlet).

53. The text of the Act is reproduced in Appendix A. You should review the statute at this time to get a feel for its overall structure. Pay particular attention to the procedural requirements in 5 U.S.C. §§ 553-557 and to the judicial review provisions in §§ 701-706. You should be forewarned that the structure of the Act, particularly the procedural provisions, is intricate and often elliptical. Professor Jaffe has found it "inexpressibly complex, a Chinese puzzle compounded of particular circumstances and special cases." Jaffe, The American Administrative Procedure Act, 1956 Public Law 218, 219. Added difficulty has been created by the subsequent codification of the Act in 5 U.S.C. Technically, this codification eliminates need for references to the section of the Act as enacted, but many scholars and judges familiar with the Act in its original form still refer to the original section numbers.

54. Examine in particular the definition of "agency" in §551(1). Would it include the President? The FBI? The Office of Management and Budget? For discussion, see 1 B. Mezines, J. Stein & J. Gruff, Administrative Law §4.01 (1977). Is it sensible to create a single administrative code of such potentially sweeping generality? See n.49 supra.

functions between prosecuting staff and agency decisionmakers. These provisions were designed to meet criticisms of agency bias and combination of functions while stopping short of a total separation of adjudicatory and other regulatory functions. On the other hand, when the relevant organic statute fails to require that adjudication be conducted "on the record after opportunity for agency hearing," the APA does not impose any procedural requirements.

Section 10 of the Act, 5 U.S.C. §§ 701-706, deals with the availability, timing, form, and scope of judicial review. These provisions, which are discussed in Chapters 4 and 9, essentially codify preexisting judge-made principles of administrative law. However, §10(e), 5 U.S.C. §706, makes clear that reviewing courts not only must determine whether administrators complied with relevant statutes, but also must examine whether the agency's action was "arbitrary, capricious, an abuse of discretion." In cases of agency decision on the basis of a trial-type record, §706 also requires courts to determine whether the agency's fact-findings are supported by "substantial evidence" in the record as a whole.

In the 20 years following the enactment of the APA, the courts adhered to the Act's spirit of compromise between the extreme claims of the critics and the defenders of the new administrative process. The coverage of the APA's procedural safeguards was given a liberal construction.[55] Courts undertook a somewhat stiffer scrutiny of agency fact-finding than was characteristic in the later years of the New Deal.[56] Modest efforts were made to promote a degree of consistency in agency policy and avoid shifts in the law that might seriously prejudice expectation interests. Yet courts were careful to leave agencies a fair measure of discretion in the formulation and implementation of policy, and informal processes of communication and negotiation were left largely undisturbed. A cooperative accommodation between court and agency had evolved.

Studies of the administrative process multiplied during the postwar period. A Commission on Organization of the Executive Branch of the Government was twice convened under the chairmanship of former President Hoover. Its reports in 1949 and 1955 called for stronger presidential control over the "independent" commissions, greater use of principles of managerial efficiency, and streamlined procedural formalities in agency decisionmaking.[57] Students of the administrative process also expressed concern over the isolation of regulatory agencies from effective political control by the Chief Executive.[58] Other critics complained of agency failure to formulate clear and consistent policies.[59] Concern was expressed over the

55. See Wong Yang Sung v. McGrath, 339 U.S. 33 (1950), set out in Chapter 8, pp. 731-736 infra.

56. See Universal Camera Corp. v. NLRB, 340 U.S. 474 (1951), infra p. 170.

57. The second Hoover Commission report also recommended that regulatory agencies' adjudicatory responsibilities be lodged in a separate Administrative Court. This recommendation was never followed.

58. See M. Bernstein, Regulating Business by Independent Commission (1955); E. Redford, The President and the Regulatory Commissions (1960); J. Landis, Report on Regulatory Commissions (1960); J. Landis, Report on Regulatory Agencies to the President-Elect (1960).

59. See H. Friendly, The Federal Administrative Agencies: The Need for Better Definition of Standards (1962); Hector, Problems of the CAB and the Independent Regulatory Commissions, 69 Yale L.J. 931 (1960).

delay and high cost of administrative proceedings.[60] Congress investigated charges of corruption and undue influence in the regulatory process, particularly in the FCC's award of valuable broadcast licenses.[61] But there was no frontal attack on the very existence of the regulatory commissions. The general assumption was that marginal adjustments within the existing system would perfect the administrative state. This sense of stability was reinforced by the appearance of the first great treatises on modern administrative law.[62]

5. The Period Since 1965: Critique and Transformation of the Administrative Process

Basic public trust in the administrative process and the spirit of working partnership between agency and reviewing courts that had developed in the postwar period began to disintegrate after 1965. The work of administrative agencies came under increasingly sharp attack on several fronts, and courts began to impose more stringent and far-reaching controls on the administrative process.

Mounting criticism of the administrative process has had three distinct strands: First, consumer advocates such as Ralph Nader criticized the performance of traditional regulatory agencies on the grounds they had been "captured" by the very firms they were supposed to regulate and had failed to act vigorously to protect the interests of consumers, workers, and other supposed beneficiaries of regulatory programs.[63] The solutions offered by these critics to problems of agency indolence and "capture" include greater public openness in agency decisionmaking; increased participation by "public interest" advocates for consumer, environmental, and other interests in agency decisionmaking; more formal decisionmaking procedures; stricter judicial scrutiny of agency action or inaction, including judicial requirements that agencies take affirmative measures to protect the beneficiaries of regulatory policies; closer congressional scrutiny of agency policies; elimination of conflicts of interest by regulators with prior or subsequent ties to regulated firms; and (in some cases)

60. Landis, The Administrative Process — The Third Decade, 13 Ad. L. Rev. 17, 24-26 (1960).

61. See Subcommittee on Legislative Oversight of the House Committee on Interstate and Foreign Commerce, Independent Regulatory Commission, H.R. Rep. No. 2711, 85th Cong., 2d Sess. (1959). See also J. Landis, supra n.60.

62. See K. Davis, Administrative Law Treatise (1958), with supplements in 1970 and 1976; L. Jaffe, Judicial Control of Administrative Action (1965). Another important step in the study of the administrative process was the creation in 1964 of the Administrative Conference of the United States. The Conference, composed of practitioners, academics, and representatives of federal agencies, undertakes studies of federal administrative practices and procedures and makes recommendations for change.

63. See, e.g., R. Fellmeth, The Interstate Commission Omission: The Public Interest and the ICC (1970); James Turner, The Chemical Feast (1970). Theodore Lowi's influential book, The End of Liberalism (1969), attributed the "capture" phenomenon to Congress's unwillingness to choose among conflicting social goals and its consequent delegation of broad lawmaking responsibility to administrative fora in which well-organized and well-financed interests enjoy strategic advantages.

elimination or modification of regulatory programs that primarily benefit regulated firms.[64]

A second, and generally quite different line of criticism, has been directed against the regulatory agencies by economists and some businessmen. One version of this criticism holds that regulatory programs are characteristically created and administered for the benefit of strategically placed and well-organized special interests at the expense of the general public; that regulatory programs are inefficient and involve a serious welfare loss for the society as a whole or are at best ineffectual; and that efforts to "reform" the administrative process are likely to be ineffectual. Accordingly, it is urged, the best solution is to abolish administrative agencies. These critics admit that the market is an imperfect mechanism for making decisions on the allocation of goods and services and the distribution of wealth and income of the society, but assert that regulatory intervention is even more likely to "fail." [65] A second and milder version of this line of criticism holds that certain forms of administrative intervention are justified to correct serious forms of market failure, particularly when consumers' information about goods and services is highly imperfect, or when there are important spillover effects; or when the distribution of wealth and income that results from market exchange is inequitable. However, it is asserted that the tools customarily used by administrators to alter market behavior — such as regulatory prohibitions, licensing, and other legalistic controls — are inappropriate, clumsy, and excessively costly. These critics assert that the resulting "mismatch" between various forms of "market failure" and the tools used by administrators to deal with them often could be ameliorated by use of more appropriate tools, particularly of economic incentives. Rather than have a regulatory agency set a specific amount of permissible pollutants for each source,

64. See, e.g., T. Lowi, supra n.63; R. Fellmeth, supra n.63; Green & Nader, Economic Regulation vs. Competition: Uncle Sam the Monopoly Man, 82 Yale L.J. 871 (1973); Senate Committee on Government Operations, Study on Federal Regulation (six vols. 1977-1978); Subcommittee on Oversight and Investigations of the House Interstate and Foreign Commerce Committee, Federal Regulatory Reform (1976).

65. See, e.g., G. Stigler, The Citizen and the State: Essays in Regulation (1975); P. MacAvoy, ed., The Crisis of the Regulatory Agencies (1970); S. Breyer & P. MacAvoy, Energy Regulation by the Federal Power Commission (1974); Peltzman, An Evaluation of Consumer Protection Legislation: The 1962 Drug Amendments, 81 J. Pol. Econ. 1049 (1973); Posner, The Federal Trade Commission, 37 U. Chi. L. Rev. 47 (1969), excerpted in Chapter 3, p. 117 infra; Winter, Economic Regulation vs. Competition: Ralph Nader and Creeping Capitalism, 82 Yale L.J. 890 (1973).

However, some studies, continuing the tradition of the 1937 President's Committee on Administrative Management and the two Hoover Commissions, continued to assert that the major deficiencies in administrative performance could be corrected by structural reorganization and use of management efficiency techniques. See President's Advisory Council on Executive Reorganization, A New Regulatory Framework (1971) (popularly called the Ash Report). For criticism of this position, see R. Noll, Reforming Regulation: An Evaluation of the Ash Council's Proposals (1977); Symposium: Federal Regulatory Agencies, A Response to the Ash Report, 57 Va. L. Rev. 923 (1971).

During the Ford and Carter administrations some efforts were made, under the rubric of "regulatory reform," to implement some economists' criticisms of regulation. See Domestic Council Review Group on Regulatory Reform, The Challenge of Regulatory Reform (1976). A recent set of criticisms and suggestions is contained in American Bar Association Commission on Law and Economy, Federal Regulation: Roads to Reform (1978).

they would have administrators charge a fee for each pound of air or water pollution emitted, thereby affording greater flexibility to individual sources and insuring a given overall level of cleanup at cheaper cost. Rather than attempting to deal with the inequitable distributional impacts of market arrangements by minimum wages or rationing, they would urge government payment of wage or income subsidies.[66]

A third basic line of contemporary criticism has focused not on the agencies regulating private business, but on the administrative apparatus of the welfare and public service state. Welfare agencies, public housing authorities, school officials, and other dispensers of public benefits have not traditionally been subject to procedural formalities or judicial control to the same extent as administrators engaged in regulating private activity through coercive controls or financial penalties. Critics have asserted that the impact of these nonregulatory agencies on individual welfare and the dangers of arbitrary power are at least as great as in the case of traditional regulatory agencies. They have accordingly urged that administrative law safeguards — such as trial-type hearings or other procedural formalities and thorough judicial review — be extended to welfare recipients, public housing tenants, students, government employees, and so on.[67]

During the past ten years, the courts have responded to these various criticisms through a number of important developments.

First, they have extended the right to participate in agency decisions and to seek judicial review to welfare recipients, students, government contractors, and "public interest" representatives of consumers, environmentalists, the poor, and other loosely organized groups. By extending to these interests the same rights of participation and judicial redress formerly enjoyed by regulated firms, the courts have promoted the transformation of administrative law's basic purpose from one of limiting governmental power to protect private interests to an "interest representation model" in which all of the various interests with a stake in agency policy have acquired the right to participate in the formulation of agency policy through adversary procedures and secure judicial review of the balance struck by the agency among competing interests.[68]

Second, courts have extended the coverage and content of procedural formalities to require that actions formerly taken by administrators through informal means be more fully documented through a factual record, and that administrators employ procedural formalities that will give interested parties an effective chance to ascertain and rebut the factual and analytical bases for agency decisions. Federal courts have imposed greater procedural formalities on federal regulatory agencies

---

66. See, e.g., A. Kneese & C. Schultze, Pollution, Prices and Public Policy (1975); C. Schultze, The Public Use of Private Interest (1977).

67. See, e.g., Reich, Individual Rights and Social Welfare: The Emerging Legal Issues, 74 Yale L.J. 1245 (1965); Reich, The New Property, 73 Yale L.J. 733 (1964). See also K. Davis, Discretionary Justice (1969).

68. See Chapters 9 and 10, infra; Stewart, The Reformation of American Administrative Law, 88 Harvard L. Rev. 1669 (1975).

and on state and federal agencies involved in welfare and service functions such as education, administration of welfare programs, and public employment.[69]

Third, courts have effectively expanded judicial review by cutting back on traditional doctrines restricting its availability,[70] and have broadened the scope of judicial review by simultaneously insisting that agencies more fully explain and document their decisions and by scrutinizing more closely the factual and analytic bases for such decisions.[71]

Each of these developments has represented an evolutionary shift of traditional doctrines in favor of a greater measure of judicial control over agency decisionmaking. The limits of this development are still a matter of speculation and dispute. Procedural formalities and judicial review involve substantial costs in terms of resources and delay. Some critics maintain that these developments have been largely ineffectual in controlling the policy choices ultimately exercised by administrative officials.[72] Other critics — including, recently, the Supreme Court — have viewed these developments as an indirect form of judicial usurpation of "political" policy choices that should be made by legislative and administrative officials and not by courts.[73] Still other critics have emphasized the limited competence of courts to deal adequately with the complex and myriad problems of administrative government.[74]

The seeming stability of administrative law doctrines and principles that developed during the 1945-1965 period has thus been eroded. As in the New Deal period, judicial review of administrative action once again "gives a sense of battle." [75] How far is it possible to reconcile the exigencies of administrative government with judicial traditions of adversary hearings, impartial decisionmaking, and reasoned continuity in "the rule of law"? Given the expense, delay, and limited competencies of adversary litigation, is it any longer desirable or feasible to rely upon the courts as the primary protection of citizens against arbitrary or unlawful administrative action? If the courts cannot be relied upon to remedy the shortcomings of the administrative process, what alternative institutional mechanisms should be developed? How serious is the "failure" of the administrative process to live up to the high hopes of New Deal and later champions of government intervention? Can the "failures" of the administrative process be solved by alterations in institutional and procedural arrangements? By more specific and wiser directives from Congress? Or is "administrative failure" endemic? In again confronting these basic questions, the United States is finally coming to terms with itself as a matured version of the administrative state. For these reasons, we believe that the study of administrative law and policy is of particularly timely importance.

69. See Chapters 6 and 7, infra.
70. See Chapter 9, infra.
71. See Chapters 4, 5, and 10, infra.
72. See Sax, The (Unhappy) Truth about NEPA, 26 Okla. L. Rev. 239 (1973).
73. See Vermont Yankee Nuclear Power Corp. v. Natural Resources Defense Council, 435 U.S. 519 (1978), set out in Chapter 6.
74. See D. Horowitz, The Courts and Social Policy (1977).
75. See J. Landis, The Administrative Process 123 (1938).

2

The Uneasy Constitutional Position of the Administrative Agency

A. Introductory Note on Separation of Powers Principles

It has been a fundamental element of separation of powers doctrine as developed by Locke and Montesquieu and refined by Madison[1] that governmental intrusions on private liberty be authorized by general rules formulated by a politically responsible group of officials separate from the officials responsible for executing the rules.

Separation is necessary to ensure uniformity and impartiality in the application of sanctions. If the executing officials also had the power to decide when sanctions would be visited, enforcement policies might reflect the private advantage or prejudice of those officials; they would also be unpredictable. By contrast, requiring that the imposition of sanctions be governed by general rules fixed in advance by a distinct, politically responsible group of officials promises several safeguards. Because the rules are general and formulated by officials who may find it difficult to estimate how their own interests will be affected by the disposition of particular cases, there is a greater likelihood that the policies adopted will more nearly reflect a broad social judgment about desirable policy than the officials' own private advantage. This likelihood is enhanced if the officials in question must seek reelection. Moreover, the requirement that policies be general renders them more predictable, thus facilitating private planning and security. The principle of separation of lawmaking and law-applying powers also reduces the effective power which government can exert against citizens and reduces the possibility that the entire power of government could be taken over by any one faction.

Thus it follows, as a majority of the Court held in Youngstown Sheet & Tube Co. v. Sawyer,[2] that, outside of certain narrowly defined foreign affairs and military

---

1. For an excellent account of the evolution of separation of powers principles see M. J. C. Vile, Constitutionalism and the Separation of Powers (1967).
2. 343 U.S. 579 (1952), holding that the President, in the absence of congressional authorization, lacked constitutional power to order seizure and operation of the nation's steel mills in

situations, intrusions by executive officials on private liberty or property must be authorized by the legislature. Moreover, the doctrine against delegation of legislative power, reflected in court decisions, requires that such authorization take the form of rules that effectively control administrative decision. If a rule is too general or vague, there arises a danger that the executing officials will effectively control the imposition of sanctions, and the salutary elements of predictability and electoral responsibility will be impaired. On the other hand, if the legislative directives are too specific, there is the danger that the legislators will combine rulemaking and rule-applying functions by tailoring sanctions, thus impairing in a different fashion the safeguards of generality and predictability. Hence in United States v. Lovett,[3] the Court invalidated, as a violation of the Bill of Attainder Clause of the Constitution, a statute effectively removing certain named government employees (accused of disloyalty) from government employment, by directing that they be deprived of any compensation.

The Anglo-American separation of powers principle not only distinguishes between those who make general laws and those who implement and apply them, but also reserves a special role for an independent judiciary in this process. The courts have traditionally adjudicated controversies between private citizens, creating a sphere of judge-made private law apart from legislatively enacted public law. This practice further fragments effective governmental power and tends to preserve a distinct realm of private autonomy.[4] The courts have also traditionally exercised a reviewing function to ensure executive compliance with the applicable public law, policing executive officers' obedience to legislative commands and providing a further set of internal checks on governmental power used against the citizenry.

These traditional principles and practices have been threatened by the creation of administrative agencies which combine lawmaking, adjudicative, and executive functions. Agencies have been given the authority to promulgate legislative-type rules and simultaneously to apply these rules in given cases. They have been invested with the power to investigate and prosecute, and with the power to decide individual controversies. Responsibility for resolving disputes between private parties has been shifted from courts to agencies. In some cases legislatures have sought to exclude any judicial review of agencies' actions. The traditional allocation of prosecutorial and managerial functions to the executive in the implementation of law has been challenged by the legislative creation of agencies whose members are to a considerable degree independent of control by the Chief Executive.

The basic question addressed in this chapter is how courts can reconcile the combination of functions characteristic of modern administrative agencies with the separation of powers principles underlying the federal Constitution. The Constitution, after all, describes and distinguishes "legislative Powers" in Article I

---

order to resolve a labor dispute that had halted production of steel assertedly needed for purposes of national defense.

3. 328 U.S. 303 (1946).

4. See F. Hayek, Law, Legislation and Liberty: A New Statement of the Principles of Justice and Political Economy (1973).

(Congress), the "executive Power" in Article II (the President), and the "judicial Power" in Article III (the federal courts), but it contains no article authorizing administrative agencies.[5] While the Constitution does not mandate a "watertight" system of separation but does provide in some instances for sharing of power among different branches (consider the President's power to veto legislation), the Founders certainly never contemplated an institutional beast such as the Interstate Commerce Commission or the Federal Trade Commission. Yet, the "living" Constitution has often been interpreted by judges to accommodate the practical exigencies of an emerging nation. Defenders of the administrative process have rejected the historic principle of separation of powers as anachronistic in an urban, industrialized society, claiming, for example, that in order effectively to manage and control the complex modern economy government must emulate techniques of integrated, expert, hierarchical management practiced by business corporations. In 1938 Dean Landis wrote:

> If in private life we were to organize a firm for the operation of an industry, it would scarcely follow Montesquieu's lines. . . . Yet the problems of operating a private industry resemble to a great degree those entailed by its regulation.[6]

Does this mean that the courts should give constitutional carte blanche to the creation of new administrative bodies combining traditionally separated powers? Or should innovation be subject to some constitutional limits? If so, how should these limits be defined? These are the questions addressed in this chapter's materials.

B. The Agency's Power to Legislate

Article I, Section 1 of the Constitution, states that "all legislative powers . . . shall be vested in a Congress of the United States. . . ." Early cases stated that this legislative power, which the Constitution had delegated to Congress, could not be redelegated to others. As Justice Story put it, "The general rule of law is, that a delegated power cannot be delegated."[7] Justice Harlan, in Field v. Clark,[8]

5. The same issue respecting the separation of powers is raised by state constitutions. Among the most famous is Pt. 1, Art. 30 of the Constitution of the Commonwealth of Massachusetts, providing that "In the government of this Commonwealth, the legislative department shall never exercise the executive and judicial powers or either of them; The executive shall never exercise the legislative and judicial powers, or either of them; The judicial shall never exercise the legislative and executive, or either of them; to the end it may be a government of laws and not of men."
6. J. Landis, The Administrative Process 10 (1938).
7. Shankland v. Washington, 30 U.S. (5 Pet.) 390, 395 (1831).
8. 143 U.S. 649, 692 (1892).

wrote, "that Congress cannot delegate legislative power . . . is a principle universally recognized as vital to the integrity and maintenance of the system of government ordained by the Constitution."

Nonetheless, in 1897 in ICC v. Cincinnati, New Orleans & Texas Pacific Ry. the Court stated [9] that although the power to prescribe rules "in the future . . . is a legislative act, . . . Congress . . . might commit to some subordinate tribunal this duty." The Court went on to hold that the Interstate Commerce Act of 1887 did *not* give the ICC this "power to exercise the legislative function of prescribing rates which shall control in the future." Id. at 505-506. But when Congress later specifically granted this authority in the Hepburn Act (1906),[10] the courts simply assumed the constitutionality of its doing so.

Similar issues arose at the state level, as illustrated by the following case, which involved a state constitutional challenge to the Minnesota legislature's delegation of ratesetting authority to an administrative commission.

State ex rel. Railroad & Warehouse Commn. v. Chicago, M. & St. P. Ry.

38 Minn. 281, 37 N.W. 782 (1888)

[Groups of shippers complained to the Minnesota Railroad Commission that rates for milk carried on passenger trains to St. Paul and Minneapolis from Owatonna (71 miles/3¢ per gallon), from Faribault (56 miles/3¢ per gallon), from Northfield (43 miles/2½¢ per gallon), and from Farmington (30 miles/2½¢ per gallon) were unreasonably high. The Commission agreed with respect to the Owatonna and Faribault rates. It noted with approval that the Minnesota and Northwestern R.R. set a rate of 2½ cents per gallon regardless of distance. And it held that a rate of 2½ cents per gallon from all these towns would be equal and reasonable. The Commission then brought a mandamus action in the state court to compel the railroad to obey its order.]

MITCHELL, J. The questions here presented are — First, the construction, and second, the constitutionality, of chapter 10. [It creates the Railroad and Warehouse Commission.] It provides that all charges by any common carrier for the transportation of passengers and property shall be equal and reasonable. . . . [It requires carriers to file tariffs and charge only the rates contained in the tariff.] [I]n case the Commission shall at any time find that any part of the tariffs of rates, fares, charges, or classifications, so filed and published . . . are in any respect unequal or unreasonable, it shall have the power . . . to compel any common carrier to . . . adopt such rate, fare, charge, or classification as said Commission shall declare to be reasonable and equal; . . .

9. 167 U.S. 479, 494 (1897).
10. 34 Stat. 584.

[The court first held that under the statute it could issue a writ of mandamus at the Commission's request to enforce a Commission order.]

The next . . . question that arises on the construction of the act is as to the nature and extent of the powers granted to the Commission in the matter of fixing rates. . . . If language means anything, it is perfectly evident that the expressed intention of the legislature is that the rates recommended and published by the Commission . . . should be not simply advisory, nor merely prima facie equal and reasonable, but final and conclusive as to what are lawful or equal and reasonable charges; that, in proceedings to compel compliance with the rates thus published, the law neither contemplates nor allows any issue to be made or inquiry had as to their equality and reasonableness in fact. Under the provisions of the act, the rates thus published are the only ones that are lawful. . . . [In this respect the state act is unlike the federal Interstate Commerce Act, which allows the federal courts to review a Commission decision as to reasonableness.] This brings us to the question of the validity of the act, that is the authority of the legislature to confer such powers upon this Commission. That the legislature itself has the power to regulate railroad charges is now too well settled to require either argument or citation of authority. The history of the contest over this question is still fresh in the minds of all. Railways had become practically the public highway system of the country. The situation was anomalous, being the first instance in history where a public highway system was at the same time owned by private parties, and exclusively used by those who owned it. This condition of things, emphasized by the reckless railway management of 15 years ago, led to legislation assuming to regulate and limit railway charges for the transportation of persons and property. Entrenched behind the doctrine that a charter is a contract, the railroad companies denied the power of the legislatures to do this; claiming the right to charge what they pleased for their services, subject only to the common-law rule that these charges should be in themselves reasonable; and this they claimed was a question for judicial, and not legislative, determination. The dispute was submitted to the arbitrament of the courts. The decisions in the so-called "Granger Cases," over 11 years ago, resulted in a complete victory for the right of legislative control. It was there held that railway companies, being incorporated as common carriers for hire, and given extraordinary powers and special rights and privileges, in order that they might better serve the public, were engaged in a public employment, affecting the public interest, and therefore, unless protected by their charters, were subject to legislative control as to their rates of fare and freight; that for protection against wrong, under the form of legislative regulation, they must rely entirely upon the good faith of the people, and the wisdom and impartiality of the legislature. See Granger Cases, 94 U.S. 113-187. The result was so different from the preconceived ideas of the railway companies that they were slow to realize the full import of these decisions, and sometimes reluctant to accept the situation.

[Yet,] no modern civilized community could long endure that their public highway system should be in the uncontrolled, exclusive use of private owners. The only alternative was either governmental regulation, or governmental ownership of the roads. . . .

[The Court went on to hold that it was constitutional for a statute to deny the courts the power to review a determination, either by an agency or by the legislature, setting certain specific rates as reasonable.[11]]

This brings us to the only remaining question in the case. It is contended that the power to regulate rates, if it exists at all, is legislative, and therefore the act is void, because it delegates legislative power to a commission. This is really the most important question in the case. The constitution of the state vests all legislative power in a legislature, consisting of a senate and house of representatives. It is, of course, one of the settled maxims in constitutional law, that the power conferred upon the legislature to make laws cannot be delegated by that department to any other body. As was said by this court in State v. Young, 29 Minn. 551, 552, 9 N.W. Rep. 737: "It is a principle not questioned that except where authorized by the constitution, as in respect to municipalities, the legislature cannot delegate legislative power, cannot confer on any body or person the power to determine what shall be the law. The legislature only must determine what it shall be. In enacting a law, the legislature must pass on two things: *First*, on its authority to make the enactment; *second*, on the expediency of the enactment. It cannot refer either of these questions to the decision of any one else." But it is also true that it is often difficult to discriminate, in particular cases, between what is properly legislative, and what is or may be executive or administrative, duty. The authority that makes the laws has large discretion in determining the means through which they shall be executed; and the performance of many duties, which they may provide for by law, they may refer to some ministerial officer, specially named for the duty. Cooley, Const. Law, 114. It is not every grant of powers, involving the exercise of discretion and judgment, to executive or administrative officers, that amounts to a delegation of legislative power. The difference between the departments undoubtedly is that the legislative makes, the executive executes, and the judiciary construes, the law; but the maker of the law may commit something to the discretion of the other departments, and the precise boundary of this power is a subject of delicate and difficult inquiry, into which a court will not unnecessarily enter.... The principle is repeatedly recognized by all courts that the legislature may authorize others to do things which it might properly, but cannot conveniently or advantageously, do itself.... If this was not permissible, the wheels of government would often be blocked.... The statute books are full of legislation granting to officers large discretionary powers in the execution of laws, the validity of which has never been successfully assailed. We might mention as examples of this the grant of power to courts to adopt rules governing their own practice and process; the power given to boards for the control of public institutions to make contracts, fix prices, and adopt rules reasonably adapted to carry out the purposes of their creation. The power of taxation is legislative, but this does not require the legisla-

11. This holding was later reversed by the United States Supreme Court as inconsistent with the Due Process Clause of the Fourteenth Amendment. Chicago, M. & St. P. Ry. v. Minnesota, 134 U.S. 418(1890). The issue of preclusion of judicial review is examined further in Chapter 9, see pp. 896-921 infra.

ture itself to assess the value of each man's property, or determine his share of the tax. The exercise of the police power in requiring persons who follow certain occupations to obtain a license is legislative; but nothing is more common than to delegate to certain officers or boards the powers to ascertain and determine whether persons have the proper qualifications as to learning, skill, or moral character, and to grant or refuse a license accordingly as they may find the facts to be. The difference between the power to say what the law shall be, and the power to adopt rules and regulations, or to investigate and determine the facts, in order to carry into effect a law already passed, is apparent. The true distinction is between the delegation of power to make the law, which necessarily involves a discretion as to what it shall be, and the conferring of an authority or discretion to be exercised under and in pursuance of the law. . . . It seems to us that the authority and discretion conferred upon this Commission is of the latter kind. The legislature enacts that all freight rates and passenger fares should be just and reasonable. It had the undoubted power to fix these rates at whatever it deemed equal and reasonable; but what are equal and reasonable rates is a question depending upon an infinite and ever-changing variety of circumstances. What may be such on one road, or for one description of traffic, may not be such on or for another. What are reasonable one month may not be so the next. For a popular legislature that meets only once in two years, and then only for 60 days, to attempt to fix rates, would result only in the most ill-advised and haphazard action, productive of the greatest inconvenience and injustice, alike to the railways and the public. If such a power is to be exercised at all it can only be satisfactorily done by a board or commission, constantly in session, whose time is exclusively given to the subject, and who, after investigation of the facts, can fix rates with reference to the peculiar circumstances of each road, and each particular kind of business, and who can change or modify these rates to suit the ever-varying conditions of traffic. . . .

The legislature itself has passed upon the expediency of the law, and what it shall be. The Commission is entrusted with no authority or discretion upon these questions. It can neither make or unmake a single provision of law. It is merely charged with the administration of the law, and with no other power. Whether the charges of a railway in any particular case are or are not equal and reasonable is a fact left by the law for them to determine. . . .

Our opinion is that the act is not obnoxious to the objection made. Let the writ issue as prayed for.

Questions

1. Consider the following questions in relation to the *Chicago Railway* case:
   (a) Why should railroad rates be regulated at all?
   (b) Why should the legislature delegate the job of setting rates rather than setting them itself?
   (c) If it is going to delegate this power, why not delegate it to the courts?
   (d) Does delegation to an agency effectively dispose of the problems that you identified in answering *b* and *c* above?

2. The relevant distances and rates involved were as follows:

Towns	Distance from Minneapolis	Railroad's rates	Commission's rates
Owatonna	71	3 cents	2.5 cents
Faribault	56	3 cents	2.5 cents
Northfield	43	2.5 cents	2.5 cents
Farmington	30	2.5 cents	2.5 cents

(a) What factors should the agency take into account in determining whether these rates are equal and reasonable?

(b) Should a legislature be required to give specific statutory guidance as to what factors the agency should take into account? How?

(c) If the legislature does not give clear directives to administrators, on what basis are courts to review the legal validity of agency decisions?

C. The Agency's Power to Adjudicate

> The judicial Power of the United States shall be vested in one Supreme Court and in such inferior Courts as the Congress shall from time to time ordain. [U.S. Const. art. III, §1.]

Crowell v. Benson

285 U.S. 22 (1932)

Mr. Chief Justice HUGHES delivered the opinion of the Court.

This suit was brought in the District Court to enjoin the enforcement of an award made by Crowell, as deputy commissioner of the United States Employees' Compensation Commission, in favor of Knudsen and against Benson. The award was made under the Longshoremen's and Harbor Workers' Compensation Act and rested upon the finding of the deputy commissioner that Knudsen was injured while in the employ of Benson and performing service upon the navigable waters of the United States. The complainant alleged that the award was contrary to law for the reason that Knudsen was not at the time of his injury an employee of [Benson and his claim was not "within the jurisdiction" of the deputy commissioner and] . . . that the Act was unconstitutional. . . . The District Judge denied motions to dismiss and granted a hearing de novo upon the facts and the law, expressing the opinion that the Act would be invalid if not construed to permit such a hearing. The case was transferred to the admiralty docket, answers were filed presenting the issue as to the fact of employment, and the evidence of both parties having been heard, the District Court decided that Knudsen was not in the employ of the petitioner and restrained the enforcement of the award.... The decree was affirmed by the Circuit Court of Appeals....

The question of the validity of the Act may be considered in relation to (1) its provisions defining substantive rights and (2) its procedural requirements.

First. The Act has two limitations that are fundamental. It deals exclusively with compensation in respect of disability or death resulting "from an injury occurring upon the navigable waters of the United States" if recovery "through workmen's compensation proceedings may not validly be provided by State law," and it applies only when the relation of master and servant exists. "Injury," within the statute, "means accidental injury or death arising out of and in the course of employment," and the term "employer" means one "any of whose employees are employed in maritime employment, in whole or in part," upon such navigable waters. Employers are made liable for the payment to their employees of pre-scribed compensation "irrespective of fault as a cause for the injury." [But, there is no liability in the case of "any vessel under eighteen tons," nor shall compensation "be payable if the injury was occasioned solely by the intoxication of the employee or by the wilful intention of the employee to injure...himself or another."] The liability is exclusive.... The employer is required to furnish appropriate medical ...treatment. The compensation for temporary or permanent disability, total or partial, according to the statutory classification, and in case of the death of the employee, is fixed. As the Act relates solely to injuries occurring upon the navigable waters of the United States, it deals with the maritime law, applicable to matters that fall within the admiralty and maritime jurisdiction (Const. Art. III, §2; Nogueira v. N.Y., N.H. & H.R. Co., 281 U.S. 128, 138); and the general authority of the Congress to alter or revise the maritime law which shall prevail throughout the country is beyond dispute.... [T]he statute was designed to accomplish the same general purpose as the workmen's compensation laws of the States. In de-fining substantive rights, the Act provides for recovery in the absence of fault, classifies disabilities resulting from injuries, fixes the range of compensation in case of disability or death, and designates the classes of beneficiaries. In view of Federal power to alter and revise the maritime law, there appears to be no room for ob-jection on constitutional grounds to the creation of these rights, unless it can be found in the due process clause of the Fifth Amendment. But it cannot be said that either the classifications of the statute or the extent of the compensation pro-vided are unreasonable. Liability without fault is not unknown to the maritime law, and, apart from this fact, considerations are applicable to the substantive pro-visions of this legislation, with respect to the relation of master and servant, similar to those which this Court has found sufficient to sustain workmen's compensation laws of the States against objections under the due process clause of the Fourteenth Amendment.

Second. The objections to the procedural requirements of the Act relate to the extent of the administrative authority which it confers. The administration of the Act — "except as otherwise specifically provided" — was given to the United States Employees' Compensation Commission...which was authorized to estab-

lish compensation districts, appoint deputy commissioners, and make regulations.
... A claim for compensation must be filed with the deputy commissioner within
a prescribed period, and the deputy commissioner shall have full authority to hear
and determine all questions in respect to the claim. The deputy commissioner is
required to make, or cause to be made, such investigations as he deems to be
necessary and upon application of any interested party must order a hearing, upon
notice, at which the claimant and the employer may present evidence.... In conducting investigations and hearings, the deputy commissioner is not bound by
common law or statutory rules of evidence, or by technical or formal rules of procedure, except as the Act provides, but he is to proceed in such manner "as to
best ascertain the rights of the parties.".... Hearings before the deputy commissioner are to be public....

The Act further provides that if a compensation order is "not in accordance
with law," it "may be suspended or set aside, in whole or in part, through injunction proceedings, mandatory or otherwise, brought by any party in interest" against
the deputy commissioner.... Beneficiaries of awards, or the deputy commissioner,
may apply for enforcement to the Federal district court.[12]

As the claims which are subject to the provisions of the Act are governed by
the maritime law as established by the Congress and are within the admiralty
jurisdiction, the objection raised by the respondent's pleading as to the right to
a trial by jury under the Seventh Amendment is unavailing (Waring v. Clarke,
5 How. 441, 459, 460);... The other objections as to procedure invoke the due
process clause and the provision as to the judicial power of the United States.

(1) The contention under the due process clause of the Fifth Amendment relates to the determination of questions of fact. Rulings of the deputy commissioner
upon questions of law are without finality. So far as the latter are concerned, full
opportunity is afforded for their determination by the federal courts [on review].
... Moreover, the statute contains no express limitation attempting to preclude the
court, in proceedings to set aside an order as not in accordance with law, from
making its own examination and determination of facts whenever that is deemed
to be necessary to enforce a constitutional right properly asserted. See Ohio Valley
Water Co. v. Ben Avon Borough, 253 U.S. 287, 289, Ng Fung Ho v. White, 259
U.S. 276, 284, 285;... As the statute is to be construed so as to support rather
than to defeat it, no such limitation is to be implied. Apart from cases involving
constitutional rights... there can be no doubt that the Act contemplates that, as

---

12. The United States Employees' Compensation Commission estimates that the number
of employees who at times are engaged in employments covered by the Act is in excess of
300,000. Report for fiscal year ending June 30, 1931, p. 66.... During the last fiscal year the
injuries reported under the Act number 28,861, of which 156 were "fatal" cases. The total
number of cases disposed of during that year, including those brought forward from the preceding years, was 30,489, of which there were 13,261 "non-fatal" cases which caused no loss of time,
and 4,067 of such cases in which the duration of disability did not exceed seven days. Compensation payments were completed in 11,776 cases. Hearings held by deputy commissioners during the
fiscal year number 1,217, of which 905 involved compensation payments. At the end of the fiscal
year, there were 102 cases pending in federal district courts wherein the plaintiffs asked review
of compensation orders. Id., 68-70.

to questions of fact, ... the findings of the deputy commissioner, supported by evidence and within the scope of his authority, shall be final. To hold otherwise would be to defeat the obvious purpose of the legislation to furnish a prompt, continuous, expert and inexpensive method for dealing with a class of questions of fact which are peculiarly suited to examination and determination by an administrative agency specially assigned to that task. The object is to secure ... an immediate investigation and a sound practical judgment, and the efficacy of the plan depends upon the finality of the determinations of fact with respect to the circumstances, nature, extent and consequences of the employee's injuries and the amount of compensation that should be awarded. ... The use of the administrative method for these purposes, assuming due notice, proper opportunity to be heard, and that findings are based upon evidence, falls easily within the principle of the decisions sustaining similar procedure against objections under the due process clauses of the Fifth and Fourteenth Amendments.

The statute provides for notice and hearing; and an award made without proper notice, or suitable opportunity to be heard, may be attacked and set aside as without validity. The objection is made that, as the deputy commissioner is authorized to prosecute such inquiries as he may consider necessary, the award may be based wholly or partly upon an ex parte investigation and upon unknown sources of information, and that the hearing may be merely a formality. The statute, however, contemplates a public hearing and regulations are to require "a record of the hearings and other proceedings before the deputy commissioner." This implies that all proceedings by the deputy commissioner upon a particular claim shall be appropriately set forth, and that whatever facts he may ascertain and their sources shall be shown in the record and be open to challenge and opposing evidence. Facts conceivably known to the deputy commissioner, but not put in evidence so as to permit scrutiny and contest, will not support a compensation order. ... An award not supported by evidence in the record is not in accordance with law. But the fact that the deputy commissioner is not bound by the rules of evidence which would be applicable to trials in court or by technical rules of procedure, §23(a), does not invalidate the proceeding, provided substantial rights of the parties are not infringed.

(2) The contention [that the statute unconstitutionally bestows judicial power upon a nonjudicial body] ... presents a distinct question. In Murray's Lessee v. Hoboken Land and Improvement Co., 18 How. 272, 284, this Court, speaking through Mr. Justice Curtis, said: "To avoid misconstruction upon so grave a subject, we think it proper to state that we do not consider Congress can either withdraw from judicial cognizance any matter which, from its nature, is the subject of a suit at the common law, or in equity, or admiralty; nor, on the other hand, can it bring under the judicial power a matter which, from its nature, is not a subject for judicial determination."

The question in the instant case, in this aspect, can be deemed to relate only to determinations of fact. ... The Congress did not attempt to define questions of law, and the generality of the description leaves no doubt of the intention to reserve to the Federal court full authority to pass upon all matters which this

Court had held to fall within that category. There is thus no attempt to interfere with, but rather provision is made to facilitate, the exercise by the court of its jurisdiction to deny effect to any administrative finding which is without evidence, or "contrary to the indisputable character of the evidence," or where the hearing is "inadequate," or "unfair," or arbitrary in any respect. . . .

As to determinations of fact, the distinction is at once apparent between cases of private right and those which arise between the Government and persons subject to its authority in connection with the performance of the constitutional functions of the executive or legislative departments. The Court referred to this distinction in Murray's Lessee v. Hoboken Land and Improvement Co., supra, pointing out that "there are matters, involving public rights, which may be presented in such form that the judicial power is capable of acting on them, and which are susceptible of judicial determination, but which Congress may or may not bring within the cognizance of the courts of the United States, as it may deem proper." Thus the Congress, in exercising the powers confided to it, may establish "legislative" courts (as distinguished from "constitutional courts in which the judicial power conferred by the Constitution can be deposited") which are to form part of the government of territories or of the District of Columbia, or to serve as special tribunals "to examine and determine various matters, arising between the government and others, which from their nature do not require judicial determination and yet are susceptible of it." But "the mode of determining matters of this class is completely within congressional control. Congress may reserve to itself the power to decide, may delegate that power to executive officers, or may commit it to judicial tribunals." . . . Familiar illustrations of administrative agencies created for the determination of such matters are found in connection with the exercise of the congressional power as to interstate and foreign commerce, taxation, immigration, the public lands, public health, the facilities of the post office, pensions and payments to veterans.

The present case does not fall within the categories just described but is one of private right, that is, of the liability of one individual to another under the law as defined. But in cases of that sort, there is no requirement that, in order to maintain the essential attributes of the judicial power, all determinations of fact in constitutional courts shall be made by judges. On the common law side of the Federal courts, the aid of juries is not only deemed appropriate but is required by the Constitution itself. In cases of equity and admiralty, it is historic practice to call to the assistance of the courts, without the consent of the parties, masters and commissioners or assessors, to pass upon certain classes of questions, as, for example, to take and state an account or to find the amount of damages. While the reports of masters and commissioners in such cases are essentially of an advisory nature, it has not been the practice to disturb their findings when they are properly based upon evidence, in the absence of errors of law, and the parties have no right to demand that the court shall redetermine the facts thus found. In admiralty, juries were anciently in use not only in criminal cases but apparently in civil cases also. . . .

In deciding whether the Congress, in [allowing the deputy commissioner to determine the facts,] . . . has exceeded the limits of its authority to prescribe procedure in cases of injury upon navigable waters, regard must be had, . . . not to mere matters of form but to the substance of what is required. The statute has a limited application, being confined to the relation of master and servant, and the method of determining the questions of fact . . . is necessary to its effective enforcement. The Act itself, where it applies, establishes the measure of the employer's liability, thus leaving open for determination the questions of fact as to the circumstances, nature, extent and consequences of the injuries sustained by the employee for which compensation is to be made in accordance with the prescribed standards. Findings of fact by the deputy commissioner upon such questions are closely analogous to the findings of the amount of damages that are made, according to familiar practice, by commissioners or assessors; and the reservation of full authority to the court to deal with matters of law provides for the appropriate exercise of the judicial function in this class of cases. For the purposes stated, we are unable to find any constitutional obstacle to the action of the Congress in availing itself of a method shown by experience to be essential in order to apply its standards to the thousands of cases involved, thus relieving the courts of a most serious burden while preserving their complete authority to insure the proper application of the law.

(3) What has been said thus far relates to the determination of claims of employees within the purview of the Act. A different question is presented where the determination of fact are fundamental or "jurisdictional," [13] in the sense that their existence is a condition precedent to the operation of the statutory scheme. These fundamental requirements are that the injury occur upon the navigable waters of the United States and that the relation of master and servant exist. These conditions are indispensable to the application of the statute, not only because the Congress has so provided explicitly but also because the power of the Congress to enact the legislation turns upon the existence of these conditions.

In amending and revising the maritime law, the Congress cannot reach beyond the constitutional limits which are inherent in the admiralty and maritime jurisdiction.

In relation to these basic facts, [the existence of a master/servant relation[14] and the fact that the accident took place in navigable waters] the question is not the ordinary one as to the propriety of provision for administrative determinations. Nor have we simply the question of due process in relation to notice and hearing. It is rather a question of the appropriate maintenance of the federal judicial power in requiring the observance of constitutional restrictions. It is the question whether the Congress may substitute for constitutional courts, in which the judicial power of the United States is vested, an administrative agency — in this instance a single deputy commissioner — for the final determination of the existence of the facts upon which the enforcement of the constitutional rights of the citizen depend.

13. The term "jurisdictional," although frequently used, suggests analogies which are not complete when the reference is to administrative officials or bodies. . . . In relation to administrative agencies, the question is . . . whether it falls within the scope of authority validly conferred.

14. Ed. note: The Court was doubtful whether Congress could constitutionally impose strict liability in the absence of a master/servant relationship.

The recognition of the utility and convenience of administrative agencies for the investigation and finding of facts within their proper province, and the support of their authorized action, does not require the conclusion that there is no limitation of their use, and that the Congress could completely oust the courts of all determinations of fact by vesting the authority to make them with finality in its own instrumentalities or in the Executive Department. That would be to sap the judicial power as it exists under the Federal Constitution, and to establish a government of a bureaucratic character alien to our system, wherever fundamental rights depend, as not infrequently they do depend, upon the facts, and finality as to facts becomes in effect finality in law. . . .

In cases brought to enforce constitutional rights, the judicial power of the United States necessarily extends to the independent determination of all questions, both of fact and law, necessary to the performance of that supreme function. The case of confiscation is illustrative, the ultimate conclusion almost invariably depending upon the decisions of questions of fact. This court has held the owner to be entitled to "a fair opportunity for submitting that issue to a judicial tribunal for determination upon its own independent judgment as to both law and facts." Ohio Valley Water Co. v. Ben Avon Borough, supra.

Jurisdiction in the Executive to order deportation exists only if the person arrested is an alien, and while, if there were jurisdiction, the findings of fact of the Executive Department would be conclusive, the claim of citizenship "is a denial of an essential jurisdictional fact" both in the statutory and the constitutional sense, and a writ of habeas corpus will issue "to determine the status." Persons claiming to be citizens of the United States "are entitled to a judicial determination of their claims," said this Court in Ng Fung Ho v. White, [259 U.S. at 285] and in that case the cause was remanded to the Federal District Court "for trial in that court of the question of citizenship."

In the present instance, the argument that the Congress has constituted the deputy commissioner a fact-finding tribunal is unavailing, as the contention makes the untenable assumption that the constitutional courts may be deprived in all cases of the determination of facts upon evidence even though a constitutional right may be involved . . . [w]hen fundamental rights are in question, this Court has repeatedly emphasized "the difference in security of judicial over administrative action." Ng Fung Ho v. White, supra. . . .

[The Court held the statute constitutional because it construed the statute to allow the federal court to determine for itself the existence of these fundamental or jurisdictional facts.]

Upon what record is the determination to be made? There is no provision of the statute which seeks to confine the court in such a case to the record before the deputy commissioner or to the evidence which he has taken. . . . As the question is one of the constitutional authority of the deputy commissioner as an administrative agency, the court is under no obligation to give weight to his proceedings pending the determination of that question. . . . We think that the essential independence of the exercise of the judicial power of the United States in the enforcement of constitutional rights requires that the Federal court should determine such an issue upon its own record and the facts elicited before it.

The argument is made that there are other facts besides the locality of the injury and the fact of employment which condition the action of the deputy commissioner.... But we think that there is a clear distinction between cases where the locality of the injury takes the cases out of the admiralty and maritime jurisdiction, or where the fact of employment being absent there is lacking under this statute any basis for the imposition of liability without fault, and those cases which fall within the admiralty and maritime jurisdiction and where the relation of master and servant in maritime employment exists. It is in the latter field that the provisions for compensation apply and that ... the determination of the facts relating to the circumstances of the injuries received, as well as their nature and consequences, may appropriately be subjected to the scheme of administration for which the Act provides....

We are of the opinion that the District Court did not err in permitting a trial de novo on the issue of employment. Upon that issue the witnesses who had testified before the deputy commissioner and other witnesses were heard by the District Court. The writ of certiorari was not granted to review the particular facts but to pass upon the question of principle. With respect to the facts, the two courts below are in accord, and we find no reason to disturb their decision.

Decree affirmed.

Mr. Justice BRANDEIS, dissenting....

The primary question for consideration is not whether Congress provided, or validly could provide, that determinations of fact by the deputy commissioner should be conclusive upon the district court. The question is: Upon what record shall the district court's review of the order of the deputy commissioner be based? ...

[Why, asks Justice Brandeis, are "constitutional facts" different from any other fact? Why can Congress not give an administrative agency the power to determine constitutional facts just as any other fact — or at least the power to collect the evidence upon which the fact will be determined?

[Justice Brandeis challenged the Court's requirement of a totally new evidentiary hearing before the District Court in order to create a record supplanting that developed at the administrative hearing. He pointed out that such a procedure would involve duplication and delay, and asserted that nothing in the Constitution prevented Congress from assigning to administrative agencies the exclusive power to collect the record evidence upon which factual issues would be determined, even if these facts were labeled "constitutional" or "jurisdictional." The Justice noted that before 1913, federal equity courts did not take *any* evidence in open court, nor did admiralty courts. Rather, evidence was taken by a Master — just like the Deputy Commissioner here. The Justice also addressed the question of the standard for judicial review of agency fact-finding on the basis of the administrative record. He asserted that neither the Due Process Clause nor any other provision in the Constitution requires de novo judicial review of the questions whether the injury occurred in or on navigable waters and whether an employer-employee relation existed, and challenged the logic of singling out these issues from statutory prerequisites for liability and according them special de novo treatment as "constitutional" or "jurisdictional" issues.]

The holding that the difference between the procedure prescribe by the Longshoremen's Act and these historic methods of hearing evidence transcends the limits of congressional power when applied to the issue of the existence of a relation of employment, as distinguished from that of the circumstances of an injury or the existence of a relation of dependency, seems to me without foundation in reality. Certainly, there is no difference to the litigant.

[Even if the employment relation is a "constitutional" issue,] I see no reason for making special exception as to issues of constitutional right, unless it be that under certain circumstances, there may arise difficulty in reaching conclusions of law without consideration of the evidence as well as the findings of fact.

[Justice Brandeis concluded that the administrative proceedings here provided sufficient safeguards to obviate the need for de novo judicial review of facts.]

... Trial de novo of the existence of the employer-employee relation is not required by the Judiciary Article of the Constitution. The mere fact that the Act deals only with injuries arising on navigable waters, and that independently of legislation such injuries can be redressed only in courts of admiralty, obviously does not preclude Congress from denying a trial de novo. For the Court holds that it is compatible with the grant of power under Article III to deny a trial de novo as to most of the facts upon which rest the allowance of a claim and the amount of compensation. . . . I see no basis for a contention that the denial of the right to a trial de novo upon the issue of employment is in any manner subversive of the independence of the federal judicial power. Nothing in the Constitution, or in any prior decision of this Court to which attention has been called, lends support to the doctrine that a judicial finding of any fact involved in any civil proceeding to enforce a pecuniary liability may not be made upon evidence introduced before a properly constituted administrative tribunal, or that a determination so made may not be deemed an independent judicial determination. Congress has repeatedly exercised authority to confer upon the tribunals which it creates, be they administrative bodies or courts of limited jurisdiction, the power to receive evidence concerning the facts upon which the exercise of federal power must be predicated, and to determine whether those facts exist. The power of Congress to provide by legislation for liability under certain circumstances subsumes the power to provide for the determination of the existence of those circumstances. It does not depend upon the absolute existence in reality of any fact. . . .

By the Longshoremen's Act, Congress created fact-finding and fact-gathering tribunals, supplementing the courts and entrusted with power to make initial determinations in matters within, and not outside, ordinary judicial purview. The purpose of these administrative bodies is to withdraw from the courts, subject to the power of judicial review, a class of controversies which experience has shown can be more effectively and expeditiously handled in the first instance by a special and expert tribunal. The proceedings of the deputy commissioners are endowed with every substantial safeguard of a judicial hearing. Their conclusions are, as a matter of right, open to reexamination in the courts on all questions of law; and, we assume for the purposes of this discussion, may be open even on all questions of the weight of the evidence. . . .

The "judicial power" of Article III of the Constitution is the power of the federal government, and not of any inferior tribunal. There is in that Article nothing which requires any controversy to be determined as of first instance in the federal district courts. The jurisdiction of those courts is subject to the control of Congress. Matters which may be placed within their jurisdiction may instead be committed to the state courts. If there be any controversy to which the judicial power extends that may not be subjected to the conclusive determination of administrative bodies or federal legislative courts, it is not because of any prohibition against the diminution of the jurisdiction of the federal district courts as such, but because, under certain circumstances, the constitutional requirement of due process is a requirement of judicial process. An accumulation of precedents, already referred to, has established that in civil proceedings involving property rights determination of facts may constitutionally be made otherwise than judicially; and necessarily that evidence as to such facts may be taken outside of a court. I do not conceive that Article III has properly any bearing upon the question presented in this case.

. . . To permit a contest de novo in the district court of an issue tried, or triable, before the deputy commissioner will, I fear, gravely hamper the effective administration of the Act. The prestige of the deputy commissioner will necessarily be lessened by the opportunity of relitigating facts in the courts. The number of controverted cases may be largely increased. Persistence in controversy will be encouraged. And since the advantage of prolonged litigation lies with the party able to bear heavy expenses, the purpose of the Act will be in part defeated.

. . . [T]he judgment of the Circuit Court should be reversed and the case remanded.

Notes and Questions

1. Why might Congress delegate the power to assess accident liability to an agency instead of a court?

2. What constitutional problems might arise when adjudicatory functions, formerly exercised by the courts are delegated to an agency?

   (a) How does the Chief Justice deal with these questions: Is the delegation adequately specific? Can Congress provide for liability without fault? Must it provide for a jury trial?

   (b) What "due process" problems does this delegation raise? How does the Chief Justice deal with them?

   (c) What "separation or powers" problems does this delegation raise? To what extent do the "due process" answers successfully resolve them?

3. How does Justice Brandeis deal with the separation of powers issues? Does he adequately distinguish Ng Fung Ho? Would his approach allow Congress to

transfer all of the civil business of the federal district courts to administrative agencies?

4. What are the implications of *Crowell* for the scope of judicial review of agency decisions? Does the Constitution require that courts review all questions of law presented in agency decisions? If so, how should "questions of law" be defined in this context? Is the Chief Justice's model of agencies as nothing more than subordinate fact-finders accurate or desirable?

5. *Crowell* indicates that there are certain types of controversies (disputes of "private right") whose resolution may not be withdrawn entirely from the courts and given exclusively to administrative agencies. (In Chapter 9, infra pp. 916-921, we examine more generally the question whether and in what circumstances judicial review is constitutionally required.) The Supreme Court has also held that certain issues are "administrative" in character and many not be assigned to Article III courts for ultimate resolution. In Federal Radio Commn. v. General Electric Co., 281 U.S. 464 (1930), the Court held that it might not constitutionally be given final authority to award a radio license or determine the terms of the license; license awards were found to be an "administrative" function. See also Keller v. Potomac Elec. Co., 261 U.S. 428 (1923) (public utility ratemaking an administrative function). The continuing vitality of these decisions is at least doubtful given the broad lawmaking discretion often exercised by courts in implementing statutes such as the antitrust laws. For discussion see L. Jaffe, Judicial Control of Administrative Action 103-109 (1965).

1. The Subsequent History of the "Jurisdictional Fact" Doctrine

The "jurisdictional fact" doctrine of *Crowell* has suffered much criticism, and doubts have often been expressed by judges[15] and commentators[16] alike as to its continued vitality. However, the Supreme Court has declined invitations to extend the doctrine[17] and lower courts almost uniformly confine the doctrine to the two specific jurisdictional findings listed in *Crowell*: the finding of employment and the finding that the injury occurred upon navigable waters. Lower courts have also

---

15. Justice Frankfurter's comment in a concurrence to Estep v. United States, 327 U.S. 114 (1946), is typical: "In view of the criticism which that doctrine as sponsored by Crowell v. Benson . . . brought forth and of the attritions of that case through later decisions, one had supposed that the doctrine had earned a deserved repose." Id at 142.

16. See, e.g., Dickinson, Crowell v. Benson: Judicial Review of Administrative Determinations of Questions of "Constitutional Fact," 80 U. Pa. L. Rev. 1055 (1932); Schwartz, Does the Ghost of Crowell v. Benson Still Walk?, 98 U. Pa. L. Rev. 163 (1949).

17. E.g., whether claimant is a dependent widow or mistress, L'Hote v. Crowell, 54 F.2d 212, rev'd per curiam, 286 U.S. 528 (1932); whether injury arose out of and in the course of employment, Voehl v. Indemnity Ins. Co., 288 U.S. 162 (1933); O'Keeffe v. Smith Associates, 380 U.S. 359 (1965); whether death was accidental or suicidal, Del Vecchio v. Bowers, 296 U.S. 280 (1935); and whether decedent was a member of the crew, South Chicago Coal & Dock Co. v. Bassett, 309 U.S. 251 (1940).

construed *Crowell* to give the trial court discretion concerning whether to conduct a trial de novo.[18] Which, then, is more significant? The fact that the Court has declined the opportunities to overrule *Crowell*, thereby perhaps reserving the holding as an ace in the hole for some future contingency,[19] or the fact that it has interred the doctrine, for all practical purposes, by not reversing the lower court decisions? [20]

The jurisdictional fact doctrine may still retain some vitality when important personal interests are involved. In *Crowell*, Chief Justice Hughes relied in part on Justice Brandeis' opinion for the Court in Ng Fung Ho v. White,[21] which held that, in habeas corpus proceedings to test the validity of a deportation order, the petitioner was entitled to a de novo judicial trial on claim of citizenship. The Court stated that the government could not constitutionally deport a citizen; administrative denial of a claim of citizenship was therefore "a denial of an essential jurisdictional fact." [22] Brandeis apparently regretted this choice of language, and in *Crowell* he sought to distinguish *Ng Fung Ho* on the ground that the statute in question there did not provide for an administrative hearing and judicial review on the basis of the administrative record. He stated, "No question arose [in *Ng Fung Ho*] as to whether Congress might validly have provided for review exclusively upon the record made in the executive department; nor as to the scope of review which might have been permissible upon such record." [23] Consider also that *Ng Fung Ho* asserted that "To deport one who ... claims to be a citizen obviously deprives him of liberty. ... It may result also in loss of both property and life, or of all that makes life worth living." 259 U.S. at 284.

Deportation orders are now subject to review in the United States courts of appeals on the record of the administrative hearing, and the Attorney General's findings of fact are made conclusive "if supported by reasonable, substantial and probative evidence on the record considered as a whole. ...." 8 U.S.C. §1105a. However, if the petitioner claims to be a national of the United States and "a genuine issue of material fact as to nationality is presented," the proceedings must be transferred to the district court "for hearing de novo of the nationality claim." 8 U.S.C. §1105a(a)(5). The Supreme Court apparently still believes that an alien

---

18. The Ninth Circuit, for example, has consistently ruled that a trial de novo is not required as to navigable waters where there is no real issue of fact and no new evidence is to be presented which is not already in·the administrative record. Western Boat Bldg. Co. v. O'Leary, 198 F.2d 409 (9th Cir. 1952); Morrison Knudsen Co. v. O'Leary, 288 F.2d 542 (9th Cir.), *cert denied*, 368 U.S. 817 (1961). Compare Associated Indemnity Corp. v. Shea, 455 F.2d 913, 914-915 n.2 (5th Cir. 1972), where the court asserted that the standard for review of all agency findings under the Longshoremen's Act is now the substantial evidence rule. This case led a district court to deny a de novo hearing where the finding that the injury occurred on navigable waters was questioned. See also Rockport Yacht & Supply Co. v. Hollis, 371 F. Supp. 1229 (S.D. Tex. 1973).

19. L. Jaffe, Judicial Control of Administrative Action 651 (1965).

20. See K. Davis, Administrative Law Treatise §§ 29.08, 29.09 (1958).

21. 259 U.S. 276 (1922).

22. Id. at 284.

23. 285 U.S. 22, 90, n.26a (1932).

who raises a citizenship claim during a deportation hearing is entitled to a judicial determination of that claim.[24]

A related doctrine retains limited vitality and should be mentioned. In Ohio Valley Water Co. v. Ben Avon Borough,[25] the Supreme Court enunciated the "constitutional fact" doctrine. It held that the Due Process Clause required a full judicial trial when a utility raised a claim of confiscation, asserting that municipal limitations on its rates deprived it of revenues adequate to yield a profit, and thereby took its property for public use without payment of just compensation. The court must determine both the law and the facts on its own independent judgment, and the prior hearings conducted by the agency seemingly are for naught. *Ben Avon* will be considered later, but it should be noted here that the case has had a powerful influence on state decisions. Massachusetts continued to follow the *Ben Avon* doctrine, primarily as an interpretation of the state constitution.[26] Some eight states expressly follow *Ben Avon*, and at least nine others profess some degree of adherence to the doctrine.[27]

The state cases are also useful for comparison on the separation of powers notion,[28] upon which *Crowell* is partly founded. In 1957 in State ex rel. Hovey Concrete Products Co. v. Mechem,[29] the New Mexico Supreme Court was called upon to determine the constitutionality of the state's new Workmen's Compensation Act, which vested authority in an administrative agency to adjudicate claims. The court found the Act unconstitutional, reasoning that the judicial power under the state constitution extended to all determinations of rights and liabilities between individuals. The legislature, however, could confer " 'quasi-judicial' power on administrative boards for the protection of the rights and interest of the public in general

---

24. See Agosto v. Immigration & Naturalization Service, 436 U.S. 748 (1978); Hampton v. Mow Sun Wong, 426 U.S. 88, 118 (Rehnquist, J., dissenting) (1976).

25. 253 U.S. 287 (1920).

26. See New England Tel. & Tel. Co. v. Department of Public Utilities, 360 Mass. 443, 275 N.E.2d 493 (1971); Opinion of the Justices, 328 Mass. 679, 106 N.E.2d 259 (1952).

27. See Glick, Independent Judicial Review of Administrative Rate-Making: The Rise and Demise of the *Ben Avon* Doctrine, 40 Fordham L. Rev. 305, 313-314 (1971). The New York Court of Appeals initially held that the doctrine should be followed until expressly overruled, Staten Island Edison Corp. v. Maltbie, 296 N.Y. 374, 73 N.E.2d 705 (1947), but dictum in a later case indicated the court's opinion that de novo review had been transformed into a substantial evidence test. Mount St. Mary's Hospital v. Catherwood, 26 N.Y.2d 493, 509, 260 N.E.2d 508, 520, 311 N.Y.S.2d 863, 875 (1971). Taking the hint, the Appellate Division specifically rejected both *Ben Avon* and *Staten Island* and concluded that a public utility has no right to a judicial trial de novo. New York Tel. Co. v. Public Service Commn., 36 App. Div. 2d 261, 320 N.Y.S.2d 280 (3d Dept. 1971), *rev'd on other grounds*, 29 N.Y.2d 164, 272 N.E.2d 554, 324 N.Y.S.2d 53 (1971).

28. See, e.g., In re Opinion of the Justices, 87 N.H. 492, 179 A. 334, 110 A.L.R. 319 (1933) (motor vehicle accident plan would be unconstitutional if an administrative agency were empowered to adjudicate questions of "legal right between private parties"); Laisne v. State Board of Optometry, 19 Cal. 2d 821, 123 P.2d 457 (1942) (revocation of license required opportunity to present new evidence in a trial de novo); Bixby v. Pierno, 4 Cal. 3d 130, 481 P.2d 242, 93 Cal. Rptr. 234 (1971) (court must exercise its independent judgment when a "vested, fundamental right" is at stake).

29. 63 N.M. 250, 316 P.2d 1069 (1951).

whose orders are not to be overruled if supported by substantial evidence." [30] The New Mexico version of the separation of powers is apparently quite rigid, for when the legislature tried to require a judicial trial de novo of a proceeding which was historically administrative in nature (authorization to change location of a water well), the court also declared that scheme unconstitutional.[31]

Perhaps the key question surrounding the jurisdictional and constitutional fact doctrines is the proper role of judicial review. Requiring a new trial in order to determine ultimate questions of fact might well paralyze the administrative process. Attempts to distinguish which factual situations may be subjected to trial de novo will ultimately collapse, as Justice Brandeis pointed out. Nevertheless, there are some decisions which the Supreme Court regards as so important that it is unwilling to defer to the judgment of administrative agencies or even to that of juries, in some cases. Consider the following areas of the law: libel of public figures,[32] obscenity,[33] and admissibility of "voluntary" confessions.[34] In each of these areas the Supreme Court has felt compelled to substitute its own independent judgment as to the facts in particular cases, and has explicitly admitted as much on occasion.[35] The Court is obviously uncomfortable about its role in such cases, and can cure the dilemma by fashioning a prophylactic rule, as in Miranda v. Arizona, or by appointing some alternative decisionmaker, as in Miller v. California. As yet, there appears to be no final solution to the problem of review of administrative findings of jurisdictional or constitutional facts.[36]

---

30. 316 P.2d at 1070.

31. Fellows v. Shultz, 81 N.M. 496, 469 P.2d 141 (1970).

32. Cantrell v. Forest City Publishing Co., 419 U.S. 245 (1974); Gertz v. Robert Welch, Inc., 418 U.S. 323 (1974); Rosenbloom v. Metromedia, Inc., 403 U.S. 29 (1971) and cases at 30 n.1; Monitor Patriot Co. v. Roy, 401 U.S. 265 (1971); Time, Inc. v. Pape, 401 U.S. 279, 293-294 (1971) (Harlan, J., dissenting); New York Times Co. v. Sullivan, 376 U.S. 254 (1964).

33. Miller v. California, 413 U.S. 15 (1973) ("If a state law that regulates obscene material is thus limited, as written or construed, the First Amendment values . . . are adequately protected by the ultimate power of appellate courts to conduct an independent review of constitutional claims when necessary." Id. at 25); Paris Adult Theatre v. Slaton, 413 U.S. 49, 101-102 (1973) (Brennan, J., dissenting) (First Amendment requires independent review by appellate courts of the constitutional fact of obscenity); "Memoirs" v. Massachusetts, 383 U.S. 413 (1966); Roth v. United States, 354 U.S. 476 (1957). In Redrup v. New York, 386 U.S. 767 (1967), the Court began the practice (which continued until *Miller*) of per curiam reversals of convictions for dissemination of materials that at least five members of the Court, applying their separate tests, deemed not to be obscene. Some 31 cases were disposed of in this fashion. Paris Adult Theatre v. Slaton, 413 U.S. at 82-83 & n. 8 (Brennan, J., dissenting) (1973).

34. Miranda v. Arizona, 384 U.S. 436 (1966); Escobedo v. Illinois, 378 U.S. 478 (1964); Payne v. Arkansas, 356 U.S. 560 (1958); Watts v. Indiana, 338 U.S. 49 (1949); Ashcraft v. Tennessee, 322 U.S. 143 (1944); Lisenba v. California, 314 U.S. 219 (1941); Chambers v. Florida, 309 U.S. 227 (1940).

35. See, e.g., Ashcraft v. Tennessee, 322 U.S. 143 (1944) (Court's duty to make an independent examination of the coerced confession could not be "foreclosed by the finding of a court, or the verdict of a jury, or both").

36. See Strong, Judicial Review: A Tri-dimensional Concept of Administrative-Constitutional Law, 69 W. Va. L. Rev. 249 (1967); Strong, The Persistent Doctrine of "Constitutional Fact," 46 N.C.L. Rev. 223 (1967).

2. The Seventh Amendment as a Limitation on the Agency's Power to Adjudicate

In the famous case of NLRB v. Jones & Laughlin Steel Corp., 301 U.S. 1 (1937), the NLRB found Jones & Laughlin guilty of discriminating against union members — an unfair labor practice — and ordered reinstatement and back pay. The company challenged the constitutionality of the National Labor Relations Act, but the Court upheld it as within the commerce power. The opinion also touched briefly on the Seventh Amendment question:

> Respondent complains that the Board not only ordered reinstatement but directed the payment of wages for the time lost. . . . It is argued that the requirement is equivalent to a money judgment and hence contravenes the Seventh Amendment with respect to trial by jury. The Seventh Amendment provides that "In suits at common law, where the value in controversy shall exceed twenty dollars, the right of trial by jury shall be preserved." The Amendment thus preserves the right which existed under the common law when the Amendment was adopted. Thus it has no application to cases where recovery of money damages is an incident to equitable relief even though damages might have been recovered in an action at law. It does not apply where the proceeding is not in the nature of a suit at common law.
>
> The instant case is not a suit at common law or in the nature of such a suit. The proceeding is one unknown to the common law. It is a statutory proceeding. Reinstatement of the employee and payment for time lost are requirements imposed for violation of the statute and are remedies appropriate to its enforcement. The contention under the Seventh Amendment is without merit.[37]

In Curtis v. Loether, 415 U.S. 189 (1974), the Court held that the Seventh Amendment requires a jury trial in an action for money damages under the Civil Rights Act of 1968 (making it illegal to discriminate in renting a house). Petitioner argued that a jury trial was *not* required because her cause of action was created by statute, not by the common law. The Court replied:

> Whatever doubt may have existed should now be dispelled. The Seventh Amendment does apply to actions enforcing statutory rights, and requires a jury trial upon demand, if the statute creates legal rights and remedies, enforceable in an action for damages in the ordinary courts of law.
>
> NLRB v. Jones & Laughlin Steel Corp., 301 U.S. 1 (1937), relied on by petitioner, lends no support to her statutory-rights argument. The Court there upheld the award of backpay without jury trial in an NLRB unfair practice proceeding, rejecting a Seventh Amendment claim on the ground that the case involved a "statutory proceeding" and "not a suit at common law or in the nature of such a suit." Id., at 48. Jones & Laughlin merely stands for the proposition that the Seventh Amendment is generally inapplicable in admin-

37. 301 U.S. 1, 48-49 (1937).

istrative proceedings, where jury trials would be incompatible with the whole concept of administrative adjudication and would substantially interfere with the NLRB's role in the statutory scheme. . . . [This case upholds] congressional power to entrust enforcement of statutory rights to an administrative process or specialized court of equity free from the strictures of the Seventh Amendment. But when Congress provides for enforcement of statutory rights in an ordinary civil action in the district courts, where there is obviously no functional justification for denying the jury trial right, a jury trial must be available if the action involves rights and remedies of the sort typically enforced in an action at law.

We think it is clear that a damages action under §812 is an action to enforce "legal rights" within the meaning of our Seventh Amendment decisions. . . .[38]

Compare Atlas Roofing Co. v. Occupational Safety and Health Review Commn., 430 U.S. 442 (1977), rejecting a Seventh Amendment defense to administrative imposition of monetary penalties for regulatory violations. The Court asserted that ". . . when Congress creates new statutory 'public rights,' it may assign their adjudication to an administrative agency with which a jury trial would be incompatible, without violating the Seventh Amendment's injunction that jury trial is to be 'preserved' in 'suits at common law.'" 430 U.S. at 455.

Does Jones & Laughlin, as glossed by Curtis and Atlas, mean that Congress may validly nullify the Seventh Amendment by transferring the entire civil business of the federal district courts to administrative agencies?

D. The Nondelegation Doctrine

1. The Traditional Model

As we develop further in Chapter 3, contemporary administrative law to a large extent reflects the efforts of judges to deal with the problem of agency "failure" by seeking ways to assert control over the procedures or the outcome of agency decisionmaking. This fact is ironic in light of the great legal battles of the 1930s — battles that succeeded in freeing the agencies from stringent judicial review.

After Crowell v. Benson, it was apparent that there were very few constitutional checks on Congress's power to create agency powers to legislate and adjudicate. Yet the courts retained potentially significant powers of review. The traditional model of judicial review — as articulated in Crowell — suggested that the courts had considerable control over the work of the agencies. They could check the agencies through the application of the following classical doctrines:

(a) Nondelegation. The courts could strike down too broad a delegation of power from Congress to the agency.

38. 415 U.S. 189, 194-195 (1974).

(b) Review of Fact. The courts could review the fact-finding of the agencies to see whether the agencies' factual conclusions were supported by the record.

(c) Review of Law. The courts could review the decision to see that it stayed strictly within the limits set out in statutes enacted by Congress.

(d) Compliance with Proper Procedure. The courts could call upon the Constitution, statutes, and the common law to prescribe agency procedure.

Many of the cases we shall study involve the application of these four traditional principles. We shall see how the growing need to rely upon administrative policy discretion and specialized experience tended to weaken them, leaving the courts with few weapons with which to control agency activity. And we shall see how courts in recent years have sought to revive these doctrines or to find substitutes for them.

In this section, we shall examine one of these major principles of control — the doctrine of nondelegation. We shall examine its use, its gradual abandonment, and its transformation into alternative (and in some respects weaker) doctrines of control. The weakening of the nondelegation doctrine has coincided with increasingly broad delegations by legislatures of lawmaking powers to agencies, creating vast administrative discretion.

2. The Nondelegation Doctrine — Pre-1935 Supreme Court Decisions

Prior to its 1935 decisions in Panama Refining Co. v. Ryan, 293 U.S. 388 (1935), and A. L. A. Schechter Poultry Corp. v. United States, 295 U.S. 495 (1935), the Supreme Court had consistently sustained congressional statutes against the charge that they invoved an unlawful delegation of legislative power to executive officials.

The Brig Aurora, 11 U.S. (7 Cranch) 382 (1813), sustained a statute which revived certain previously expired statutory provisions upon a determination by the President that either Great Britain or France had ceased violating the neutral commerce of the United States. The Court found nothing objectionable in conditioning such revival on an executive determination.

Field v. Clark, 143 U.S. 649 (1892), relied upon the Brig Aurora case to uphold a statute which provided for imposition of a retaliatory tariff schedule on imports from nations which imposed duties on American products which the President "may deem to be reciprocally unequal and unreasonable." The President, the Court held, was not given legislative authority by the statute because his powers were limited to ascertaining a matter of "fact" — the imposition by foreign nations of "reciprocally unequal and unreasonable" tariffs — upon which the legislative provision for retaliatory tariff schedules was contingent.

The "contingency" rationale proved inadequate in United States v. Grimaud, 220 U.S. 506 (1911), which sustained a statute giving the Secretary of Agriculture broad authority to "make provision for the protection against destruction and depradations upon the public forests and forest reservations" including authority to adopt "such rules and regulations . . . to regulate [the reservations'] occupancy and use, and to preserve the forests thereof from destruction." Violation of the regulations was made a criminal offense. The Court held that the statute did not delegate legislative authority but merely gave the Secretary a "power to fill up the details."

An even more generous standard was applied in J. W. Hampton, Jr. & Co. v. United States, 276 U.S. 394 (1928), which upheld a statute giving the President power to revise the tariff duties specified in the statute whenever he determined that such revision was necessary to "equalize the costs of production in the United States and the principal competing country." While the Court justified the President's powers under the statute by reference to the contingency theory of Field v. Clark and the "filling up the details" principle of Grimaud, it rested on the broader ground that "If Congress shall lay down by legislative act an intelligible principle to which the person or body authorized to [take action] is directed to conform, such legislative action is not a forbidden delegation of legislative power." The Court found that the notion of adjusting tariffs to "equalize the costs of production" constituted an "intelligible principle." (Does it?)

3. Panama Refining and Schechter

(a) The major piece of legislation, designed to help ease the depression, enacted during President Roosevelt's first "100 days" in office was the National Industrial Recovery Act of 1933. Its object was to have representatives on management and labor in each industry meet and develop codes of "fair competition." In practice this procedure was meant to stabilize wages and prices with the hope that, by arresting price and wage declines, business confidence would be restored and workers' purchasing power maintained. Many saw the Act in broader terms as the vehicle for inaugurating comprehensive national planning of the economy, which they believed necessary to ensure future economic growth. Critics feared the development of a "corporate state" suggesting a parallel with the philosophy of Mussolini.

The NIRA, 48 Stat. 195 (1935), provided in part the following (emphasis added):

DECLARATION OF POLICY

Section 1. A national emergency productive of widespread unemployment and disorganization of industry, which burdens interstate and foreign commerce, affects the public welfare, and undermines the standards of living of the American people, is hereby declared to exist. It is hereby declared to be the policy of Congress to remove obstructions to the free flow of interstate and foreign commerce which tend to diminish the amount thereof; and to provide for the general welfare by promoting the organization of industry for the purpose of cooperative action among trade groups, to induce and maintain united action of labor and management under adequate governmental sanctions and supervision, to eliminate unfair competitive practices, to promote the fullest possible utilization of the present productive capacity of industries, *to avoid undue restriction of production* (except as may be temporarily required), to increase the consumption of industrial and agricultural products by increasing purchasing power, to reduce and relieve unemployment, to improve standards of labor, and otherwise to rehabilitate industry and to conserve natural resources.

Section 2. (a) To effectuate the policy of this title, the President is hereby authorized to establish such agencies ... as he may find necessary, to prescribe their authorities, duties, responsibilities, and tenure ...

(b) The President may delegate any of his functions and powers under this title to such officers, agents, and employees as he may designate or appoint ...

CODES OF FAIR COMPETITION

Section 3. (a) Upon the application to the President by one or more trade or industrial associations or groups, the President may approve a *code or codes of fair competition* for the trade or industry or subdivision thereof, represented by the applicant or applicants, if the President finds (1) that such associations or groups impose no inequitable restrictions on admission to membership therein and are truly representative of such trades or industries or subdivisions thereof, and (2) that *such code or codes are not designed to promote monopolies or to eliminate* or oppress small enterprises and will not operate to discriminate against them, and will tend to effectuate the policy of this title: *Provided,* That such code or codes shall not permit monopolies or monopolistic practices: *Provided further,* That where such code or codes affect the services and welfare of persons engaged in other steps of the economic process, nothing in this section shall deprive such persons of the right to be heard prior to approval by the President of such code or codes. The President may, as a condition of his approval of any such code, impose such conditions (including requirements for the making of reports and the keeping of accounts) for the protection of consumers, competitors, employees, and others, and in furtherance of the public interest, and may provide such exceptions to and exemptions from the provisions of such code, as the President in his discretion deems necessary to effectuate the policy herein declared.

(b) After the President shall have approved any such code, the provisions *of such code shall be the standards of fair competition* for such *trade or industry or subdivisions thereof.* Any violation of such standards in any transaction in or affecting interstate or foreign commerce shall be deemed an unfair method of competition in commerce within the meaning of the Federal Trade Commission Act....

(b) "In the course of its short life from August, 1933, to February, 1935, the Administration formulated and approved 546 codes and 185 supplemental codes filling 18 volumes and 13,000 pages; 685 amendments and modifications to these codes. It issued over 11,000 administrative orders interpreting, granting exemptions from, and establishing classifications under the provisions of individual codes; 139 administrative orders bearing generally upon administrative procedure. These codes of so-called fair competition were not uniform in content. They contained regulations of the greatest variety of practices. Most of them had *minimum wage* and *hour* provisions. One or another of them had provisions *for minimum price* or prohibition *against sales below 'cost'* (cost being a generalized figure which might be much above actual cost); provisions *controlling or restricting* production sometimes directly, sometimes by concealed devices; provisions *prohibiting exceptional* discounts, rebates and other *devices of price competition;* provisions regulating advertising, sales techniques, etc." [39]

As a practical matter, a draft of each code would be written and presented to the government by a few powerful groups in each major industry. Other firms and interests would be notified, and a final draft would emerge out of negotiations among the parties.

(c) Panama Refining Co. v. Ryan, 293 U.S. 388 (1935), involved a challenge to the NIRA's Petroleum Code. The challengers won the major portion of their case when it was discovered that the official version of the code, through a mistake, set oil production quotas, but contained no sentence making a violation of oil production quotas unlawful. (The fact that government lawyers had difficulty finding the official version led to the creation of the Federal Register and the requirement that agency documents, to be valid, must be published there. See 49 Stat. 500 (1935)).

The President, however, had also issued an Executive Order under §9(c) of the NIRA. This section stated that "the President is authorized to prohibit the transportation in interstate commerce" of oil produced in violation of state-imposed production quotas. The majority of the Court held this section unconstitutional because it did not provide a standard governing *when* the President was to exercise the authorized power. Justice Cardozo, the sole dissenter, argued that NIRA §1 delineated many such standards. Chief Justice Hughes replied that that was just the problem: NIRA §1 provided too many conflicting standards with no indication how the President was to choose among them. Nor had the President indicated how he had so chosen.[40]

A. L. A. Schechter Poultry Corp. v. United States

295 U.S. 495 (1935)

Mr. Chief Justice HUGHES delivered the opinion of the Court.

Petitioners . . . were convicted in the . . . Eastern District of New York on eighteen counts of an indictment charging violations of what is known as the "Live Poultry Code." . . . By demurrer to the indictment . . . the defendants contended (1)

39. L. Jaffe & N. Nathanson, Administrative Law, Cases and Materials 52 (4th ed. 1976) (emphasis added).

40. The Connolly Hot Oil Act, Pub. L. No. 74-14, §3, 49 Stat. 30 (1935), remedies this defect by providing a standard: "Whenever the President finds that the amount of petroleum products moving in interstate commerce is so limited as to be the cause . . . of a lack of parity between supply . . . and demand" he can forbid the interstate movement of "hot" oil. What does this standard mean?

that the Code had been adopted pursuant to an unconstitutional delegation by Congress of legislative power; ...

The defendants are slaughterhouse operators. Schechter Poultry Corporation and Schechter Live Poultry Market are corporations conducting wholesale poultry slaughterhouse markets in Brooklyn, New York City. . . . They buy the poultry for slaughter and resale. After the poultry is trucked to their slaughterhouse markets in Brooklyn, it is there sold, usually within twenty-four hours, to retail poultry dealers and butchers who sell directly to consumers. The poultry purchased from defendants is immediately slaughtered, prior to delivery, by *schochtim* in defendants' employ. . . .

The "Live Poultry Code" [is a code of "fair competition" for those in the New York area live poultry industry. It] was promulgated under §3 of the National Industrial Recovery Act. . . . [and] was approved by the President on April 13, 1934. . . .

The Code ... provides that no employee, with certain exceptions, shall be permitted to work in excess of forty (40) hours in any one week, and that no employee, save as stated, "shall be paid in any pay period less than at the rate of fifty (50) cents per hour." ... The minimum number of employees, who shall be employed by slaughterhouse operators, is fixed. . . .

Provision is made for administration through an "industry advisory committee," to be selected by trade associations and members of the industry, and a "code supervisor" to be appointed, with the approval of the committee, by agreement between the Secretary of Agriculture and the Administrator for Industrial Recovery. . . .

The seventh article, containing "trade practice provisions," prohibits various practices which are said to constitute "unfair methods of competition." ...

Of the eighteen counts of the indictment upon which the defendants were convicted, . . . ten counts were for violation for the requirement (found in the "trade practice provisions") [that a wholesale seller could not allow a buyer to select particular chickens. Rather they had] . . . "to accept the run of any half coop, coop, or coops." ... [It was charged] that the defendants in selling to retail dealers and butchers had permitted "selections of individual chickens taken from particular coops and half coops."

. . . [One other count] charged the sale to a butcher of an unfit chicken. . . .

We recently had occasion to review the pertinent decision and the general principles which govern ... [the question of delegating legislative power], Panama Refining Co. v. Ryan, 293 U.S. 388. The Constitution provides that "All legislative powers herein granted shall be vested in a Congress of the United States, which shall consist of a Senate and House of Representatives." Art. I, §1.

And the Congress is authorized "To make all laws which shall be necessary and proper for carrying into execution" its general powers. Art. I, §8, par. 18. The Congress is not permitted to abdicate or to transfer to others the essential legislative functions with which it is thus vested. We have repeatedly recognized the necessity of adapting legislation to complex conditions involving a host of details with which the national legislature cannot deal directly. We pointed out in the *Panama Com-*

pany case that the Constitution has never been regarded as denying to Congress the necessary resources of flexibility and practicality, which will enable it to perform its function in laying down policies and establishing standards, while leaving to selected instumentalities the making of subordinate rules within prescribed limits and the determination of facts to which the policy as declared by the legislature is to apply. But we said that the constant recognition of the necessity and validity of such provisions, and the wide range of administrative authority which has been developed by means of them, cannot be allowed to obscure the limitations of the authority to delegate, if our constitutional system is to be maintained. Id., p. 421.

Accordingly, we look to the statute to see whether Congress has overstepped these limitations, whether Congress in authorizing "codes of fair competition" has itself established the standards of legal obligation, thus performing its essential legislative function, or, by the failure to enact such standards, has attempted to transfer that function to others.... As to the "codes of fair competition," under §3 of the Act, the question is ... whether there is any adequate definition of the subject to which the codes are to be addressed.

What is meant by "fair competition" as the term is used in the Act? Does it refer to a category established in the law, and is the authority to make codes limited accordingly? Or is it used as a convenient designation for whatever set of laws the formulators of a code for a particular trade or industry may propose and the President may approve ... as being wise and beneficent provisions for the government of the trade or industry in order to accomplish the broad purposes of rehabilitation, correction and expansion which are stated in the first section of Title I?

The Act does not define "fair competition." "Unfair competition," as known to the common law, is a limited concept. In recent years, its scope has been extended....

The Federal Trade Commission Act (§5) introduced the expression "unfair methods of competition," which were declared to be unlawful. What are "unfair methods of competition" are thus to be determined in particular instances, upon evidence, in the light of particular competitive conditions and of what is found to be a specific and substantial public interest. To make this possible, Congress set up a special procedure. A Commission, a quasi-judicial body, was created....

In providing for codes, the National Industrial Recovery Act dispenses with this administrative procedure and with any administrative procedure of an analogous character. But the difference between the code plan of the Recovery Act and the scheme of the Federal Trade Commission Act lies not only in procedure but in subject matter. We cannot regard the "fair competition" of the codes as antithetical to the "unfair methods of competition" of the Federal Trade Commission Act. The "fair competition" of the codes has a much broader range and a new significance....

For a statement of the authorized objectives and content of the "codes of fair competition" we are referred repeatedly to the "Declaration of Policy" in §1 of Title I of the Recovery Act.... That declaration embraces a broad range of objectives....

Under §3, whatever "may tend to effectuate" these general purposes may be

included in the "codes of fair competition." . . . [T]he purpose is clearly disclosed to
authorize new and controlling prohibitions through codes of laws which would
embrace what the formulators would propose, and what the President would
approve, or prescribe, as wise and beneficient measures for the government of trades
and industries in order to bring about their rehabilitation, correction and development, according to the general declaration of policy in §1. . . .

The Government urges that the codes will "consist of rules of competition
deemed fair for each industry by representative members of that industry — by the
persons most vitally concerned and most familiar with its problems." Instances are
cited in which Congress has availed itself of such assistance; as e.g., in the exercise
of its authority over the public domain, with respect to the recognition of local
customs or rules of miners as to mining claims, or, in matters of a more or less
technical nature, as in designating the standard height of drawbars. But would it
be seriously contended that Congress could delegate its legislative authority to trade
or industrial associations or groups so as to empower them to enact the laws they
deem to be wise and beneficent for the rehabilitation and expansion of their trade
or industries? Could trade or industrial associations or groups be constituted legislative bodies for that purpose because such associations or groups are familiar with
the problems of their enterprises? And, could an effort of that sort be made valid
by such a preface of generalities as to permissible aims as we find in §1 of Title I?
The answer is obvious. Such a delegation of legislative power is unknown to our law
and is utterly inconsistent with the constitutional prerogatives and duties of
Congress.

The question, then, turns upon the authority which §3 of the Recovery Act
vests in the President to approve.

If the codes have standing as penal statutes, this must be due to the effect of
the executive action. But Congress cannot delegate legislative power to the President to exercise an unfettered discretion to make whatever laws he thinks may be
needed or advisable for the rehabilitation and expansion of trade and industry.

Accordingly we turn to the Recovery Act to ascertain what limits have been
set to exercise of the President's discretion. *First*, the President, as a condition of
approval, is required to find that the trade or industrial associations or groups which
propose a code, "impose no inequitable restrictions on admission to membership"
and are "truly representative." . . .

Second, the President is required to find that the code is not "designed to
promote monopolies or to eliminate or oppress small enterprises and will not
operate to discriminate against them." . . . But these restrictions leave virtually untouched the field of policy envisaged by §1. . . . The Act provides for the creation by
the President of administrative agencies to assist him, but the action or reports of
such agencies, or of his other assistants . . . have no sanction beyond the will of the
President, who may accept, modify or reject them as he pleases. Such recommendations or findings in no way limit the authority which §3 undertakes to vest in
the President with no other conditions than those there specified. And this authority
relates to a host of different trades and industries, thus extending the President's

discretion to all the varieties of laws which he may deem to be beneficial in dealing with the vast array of commercial and industrial activities throughout the country. . . .

Section 3 of the Recovery Act is without precedent. It supplies no standards for any trade, industry or activity. It does not undertake to prescribe rules of conduct to be applied to particular states of fact determined by appropriate administrative procedure. Instead of prescribing rules of conduct, it authorizes the making of codes to prescribe them. For that legislative undertaking, §3 sets up no standards, aside from the statement of the general aims of rehabilitation, correction and expansion described in §1. In view of the scope of that broad declaration, and of the nature of the few restrictions that are imposed, the discretion of the President in approving or prescribing codes, and thus enacting laws for the government of trade and industry throughout the country, is virtually unfettered. We think that the code-making authority thus conferred is an unconstitutional delegation of legislative power. . . .

Mr. Justice CARDOZO, concurring.

The delegated power of legislation which has found expression in this code is not canalized within banks that keep it from overflowing. It is unconfined and vagrant. . . .

Here, in the case before us, is an attempted delegation not confined to any single act nor to any class or group of acts identified or described by reference to a standard. Here in effect is a roving commission to inquire into evils and upon discovery correct them.

. . . If codes of fair competition are codes eliminating "unfair" methods of competition ascertained upon inquiry to prevail in one industry or another, there is no unlawful delegation of legislative functions when the President is directed to inquire into such practices and denounce them when discovered. . . .

But there is another conception of codes of fair competition, their significance and function, which leads to very different consequences. . . . By this other conception a code is not to be restricted to the elimination of business practices that would be characterized by general acceptance as oppressive or unfair. It is to include whatever ordinances may be desirable or helpful for the well-being or prosperity of the industry affected. In that view, the function of its adoption is not merely negative, but positive; the planning of improvements as well as the extirpation of abuses. What is fair, as thus conceived, is not something to be contrasted with what is unfair or fraudulent or tricky. The extension becomes as wide as the field of industrial regulation. If that conception shall prevail, anything that Congress may do within the limits of the commerce clause for the betterment of business may be done by the President upon the recommendation of a trade association by calling it a code. This is delegation running riot. No such plenitude of power is susceptible of transfer. The statute, however, aims at nothing less, as one can learn both from its terms and from the administrative practice under it.

. . . It sets up a comprehensive body of rules to promote the welfare of the industry, if not the welfare of the nation, without reference to standards, ethical or commercial, that could be known or predicted in advance of its adoption. One of the new rules, the source of ten counts in the indictment, is aimed at an established practice, not unethical or oppressive, the practice of selective buying. . . .

4. Post-Schechter *Delegation — The Example of Price Controls*

This example of economic regulation concerns economywide price controls. Such controls have typically been authorized by statutes that raise delegation problems. You should consider both the nature of price controls (how do they work?) *and* the courts' reaction to the delegation problem. What is the connection between the two?

Galbraith, Wage and Price Controls

Hearings Before the House Comm. on Banking and Currency on H.R. 17880, 91st Cong., 2d Sess. 6 (1970)

[Professor J. K. Galbraith argued for the adoption of wage and price controls as follows.]

Let me begin by summarizing matters relating to the economy as they now stand. First, unemployment is now at 5 percent of the labor force and in fact considering the lag in the statistics, and the nature of the statistics themselves, the underenumeration of those who are not seeking work, who have withdrawn from the labor force because they found the search for jobs hopeless, probably somewhat higher. Production has been stable or declining for many months. Inflation is at a record rate and duration since the years immediately following World War II. The housing industry despite a housing shortage is, as the chairman pointed out, deeply depressed. The financial markets have just had their most severe break in 40 years.

We have this disenchanting combination of circumstances because a theory of economic management has been tried, fully tried and found wanting. It is always unwise to put theory to a test if it is unsound. The theory was that control of the monetary supply, as most eloquently advocated by Prof. Milton Friedman of the University of Chicago, could, if combined with a reasonable restrictive fiscal policy bring stable prices and without unduly depressive effects on the economy. This doctrine discounted the ability of large corporations and strong unions to shove up prices and wages under conditions even of severe monetary and fiscal restraint. The proponents of this view are men who believe deeply in the market. Not remarkably among men of deep belief, they substitute faith for reality. Though this may be theologically commendable, it can be very hard on the other people who must suffer for their faith.

Wages do shove up prices and prices do pull up wages in the modern highly organized economy. Monetary restraint, while it works rather ruthlessly for the smaller businessman, works very well for the larger businessman, and especially as

I have noted for the home construction industry, does not so directly affect General Motors, General Electric, United States Steel or the other very large corporations. These firms have large cash flows, are favored visitors at the banks and can pass their higher interest rates on to the public. This is precisely the part of the economy which gives leadership on the wage-price spiral. As Dr. McCracken pointed out yesterday in Europe, farm prices, prices of services generally at the moment are stable or even coming down, but prices in the organized sector of the economy — prices in the sector of the economy where large corporations bargain with strong unions — are still going up. In saying a year ago last January that it had no concern for wages and prices the administration may well have done as much to promote inflation as it accomplished in the ensuing 18 months to control it. . . .

Within the framework of its approved measures, monetary and fiscal policy, there is nothing that the administration can now do. The inflation with its punishing impact on those with fixed incomes, on the public services, and on those who are promised a real dollar-for-dollar return on their savings, that punishment still continues. To ease interest rates and relax further on the budget — some relaxation of the budget is inevitable from falling revenues — would accelerate this inflation. To continue the present policy is to continue for some period the present remarkable combination of inflation and recession. We have long known, Mr. Chairman, that under some circumstances you can have your cake and eat it too. We are now learning from this combination of inflation and recession that you cannot have your cake and not be able to buy it either.

To tighten up sufficiently on money and the budgets to end inflation would, we now know, require a very serious recession. So, disagreeable as may be the prospect, there must be a search for a new line of policy. . . .

If the economic problem is serious, and it is, the responding action must be serious. Wage claims now in prospect provide for the present inflation, the expected increase in inflation, a safety margin for unexpected inflation and beyond that for a hoped-for increase in real wages. These wage claims will be disinflated only if there is a firm promise to the unions of price stability. Nothing can now be accomplished by the most massive deployment of public oratory, whatever the added component of mild jawboning, strong jawboning, billingsgate or old-fashioned competitive hog-calling. Nor are these dignified devices for conducting the affairs of the modern State. Nor do they become either useful or effective by calling them income policy, which is the present fashion.

The proper course is, under legislative authorization, as this title recommends, to freeze all prices and wages as of some recent date. I think, myself, this should be for a period of about 6 months.

This assures all concerned that the spiral, the wage price spiral, has been brought to an end. Where prices and wages are set by the market rather than by corporate and union power, there is no need to continue the freeze. This means that all retail prices, all farm prices, all wages not covered by collective bargaining contracts, all prices of firms employing fewer than 100 or possibly even 1,000 workers should be promptly released from control. The point is important and I would like to stress it. Where neither corporations nor unions have power to shove up prices and wages, the Government obviously doesn't need to prevent the shoving. That is what we are concerned with here. Some of these prices and wages will rise, and some of them will fall, but that will be in response to a market decision.

One needs to control through public action those prices and wages that are subject to strong private control.

The 6 months should be used in working out with corporations and unions a more permanent system of restraint. Here I depart in my recommendation more than slightly from that in the legislation. This includes the elimination of inequities resulting from arbitrary imposition of any freeze. Different unions in particular will be caught in various contractual states in their bargaining and the difference between a union that has just completed bargaining for a wage increase and one that has not yet got it is indefensible. This sort of thing will have to be ironed out. There will have to be provision for the further wage increases that can be tolerated that are consistent with expected gains in productivity and therefore not damaging to price stability. From this stage on we should notice that the wage increases that the worker gets will be real. If the policy is to be equitable and even defensible there must also be provision in industries of exceptionally high profits for either price reductions or surrender of excess profits. One cannot have a policy that holds wages in line but does nothing about such profits.

I would also suggest that executive salaries should also be frozen and it would be good for the Congress to suspend the unfortunate bonanza which the last tax bill gave to earned income, as it is called, in the upper executive salary brackets.

Once price and wages are under control, interest rates can be drastically reduced. These interest rates now include a large percentage for expected inflation. . . . Price and wage controls are not pleasant. . . .

The limited controls that I have advocated paralleling those in the second title of this bill will not be pleasant to administer — the administrative problem must be taken seriously. But these controls, when the public interest is weighed, are by far the least unpleasant, by far the most practical of the various courses of action available.

They should not require a vast administrative organization in this limited form. One should notice that only a few hundred collective bargaining contracts and a few thousand larger corporations will be under surveillance.

Corporations can be accorded freedom for individual price adjustments within a general level of return. There are other simplifications of the same sort that are possible. Let me point out again that all one is concerned with here is stopping the gross spiral of large wage increases and large price increases to cover them. We are not concerned with establishing precise price stability.

For all of this, no great organization is needed. A few hundred people would suffice. . . .

Still, I do not want to minimize the task. It requires much more effort than doing nothing. But public officials are paid to work and try harder, especially where it saves in public suffering.

Friedman, What Price Guideposts?

G. Shultz, & R. Aliber, Guidelines, Informal Control, and the Marketplace: Policy Choices in a Full Employment Economy (1966)

[Professor Friedman has a different view of the matter.]

The distinction between inflation and deflation, important as it is, is less important than the distinction between open inflation, one in which prices are free to rise without governmental price controls, and suppressed inflation, one in which the government attempts to suppress the manifestations of the inflationary pressure by controlling prices, including prices not only of products but also of factor services (i.e., wage rates, rents, interest rates) and of foreign currencies (i.e., exchange rates).

Open inflation is harmful. It generally produces undesirable transfers of income and wealth, weakens the social fabric, and may distort the pattern of output. But if moderate, and especially if steady, it tends to become anticipated and its worst effects on the distribution of income are offset. It still does harm, but, *so long as prices are free to move*, the extremely flexible private enterprise system will adapt to it, take it in stride, and continue to operate efficiently. The main dangers from open inflation are twofold: first, the temptation to step up the rate of inflation as the economy adapts itself; second, and even more serious, the temptation to attempt cures, especially suppression, that are worse than the disease.

Suppressed inflation is a very different thing. Even a moderate inflation, if effectively suppressed over a wide range, can do untold damage to the economic system, require widespread government intervention into the details of economic activity, destroy a free enterprise system, and along with it, political freedom. The reason is that suppression prevents the price system from working. The government is driven to try to provide a substitute that is extremely inefficient. The usual outcome, pending a complete monetary reform, is an uneasy compromise between official tolerance of evasion of price controls and a collectivist economy. The greater the ingenuity of private individuals in evading the price controls and the greater the tolerance of officials in blinking at such evasions, the less the harm that is done; the more law-abiding the citizens, and the more rigid and effective the governmental enforcement machinery, the greater the harm.

A dramatic illustration of the difference between open and suppressed inflation is the contrast between the experience of Germany after World War I and after World War II. This happens to be one of those beautiful examples that history turns up for us from time to time in which experience is almost in the nature of a controlled experiment, because the difference in the character of the monetary phenomena is so great compared to differences in other relevant respects. After World War I, Germany had an open inflation of extremely large magnitude. It is difficult for us to contemplate the kind of inflation Germany experienced at that time because it is so extreme. A student of mine, Phillip Cagan, wrote a doctoral dissertation on hyperinflation in different countries, which has become something of a classic. He had the problem of how to define hyperinflation. He defined it as beginning when prices started to rise at the rate of more than 50 per cent a month. In the German hyperinflation after World War I, there were periods when prices rose not 50 per cent a month but doubled every week and some occasions on which they were doubling every day. Indeed, it got to the point that firms started to pay their employees their wages three times a day — after breakfast, lunch, and dinner, so that they could go out and spend them before they lost their value. That was really a whopping inflation, yet it went on for something like three years.

The inflation did untold harm to Germany. The impoverishment of the middle classes, the arbitrary redistribution of income, and the frantic instability unquestionably helped to lay the groundwork for Hitler's emergence later. Looked at, however, from the purely technical point of view of its effect on production, the astounding thing is that until the last six months of the inflation, total output in Germany never declined. Indeed, Germany was one of the few countries in the world that did not experience a great depression in 1920-21, when prices in the gold standard part of the world dropped by 50 per cent. Total output remained up. Why? Because the inflation was open. Prices were allowed to rise freely and hence the price system could still be used to allocate resources. Of course, after a time people started to use all sorts of escalation devices to link their contracts to the value of the mark in the foreign exchange market, which was also a free market price, and so on. The price system, however, could work even under those handicaps.

After World War II, Germany was under inflationary pressure as a result of an increase in the quantity of money during the war and the fixation of prices. By our usual standards, the pressure was substantial. If prices had been allowed to rise freely immediately after the war, the price level would probably have quadrupled. That is a large price rise. But it is negligible by comparison with the price rise after World War I which has to be described in terms of factors like 10 to the 10th power. The price rise after World War II, however, was suppressed. Ordinarily, it is extremely difficult to suppress a price rise of that magnitude, to enforce price control when the market price would be four times the controlled price. But there were certain especially favorable circumstances from the point of view of enforcing price control in Germany at that time. Germany was occupied by the armed forces of Britain, France, and the United States, and the occupation forces enforced price control.

The result of suppressing inflation was that output in Germany was cut in half. The price system was not allowed to function. People were forced to revert to barter. Walter Eucken in an article describing this period tells the story of people who worked in a factory making pots and pans. They would work there for two or three days and then they would be given their pay in the form of aluminum saucepans. They would take the saucepans and spend the rest of the week scouring the countryside trying to find some farmer who would be willing to trade a few potatoes or other produce for the saucepans. That is not a very efficient way to organize resources. It was so inefficient that something had to be done and something was done. People developed their own forms of money. Cigarettes came into use as money for small transactions and cognac for large transactions — the most liquid money I have ever come across. But even with these expedients, suppressed inflation cut output in half from the level at the immediate end of the war.

In 1948 as you know, the so-called German miracle began. It was not a very complicated thing. It amounted to introducing a monetary reform, eliminating price control, and allowing the price system to function. The extraordinary rise in German output in the few years following this reform was not owing to any miracle of German ingenuity or ability or anything like that. It was the simple, natural result of allowing the most efficient technique people ever found for organizing resources to work instead of preventing it from working by trying to fix prices here, there, and everywhere.

Although this is the most dramatic example, numerous other examples can be cited of a less extreme kind. In the immediate postwar period, I visited Europe and spent some time in Britain and France. Both countries at that time had widespread price controls. But there was an important difference. The people of Britain were relatively law-abiding, the people of France were not. The result was that Britain was being strangled by the law obedience of her people and France was being saved by the black market.

The reason suppressed inflation is so disastrous, as these examples suggest, is that the price system is the only technique that has so far been discovered or invented for efficiently allocating resources. If that is prevented from operating, something else must be substituted. What do we substitute? It is always some kind of clumsy physical control. . . .

The United States had widespread experience with the results of price and wage controls during World War II, and New York City's housing difficulties are a current reminder of their long-reaching effects, since New York is the only city in the land that still has rent controls as a heritage of the war. The memory of this experience leads government officials to disavow any intention of imposing explicit price and wage controls. But voluntary controls are no improvement, except as they are more readily evaded. Let them be abided by, and the consequences will be the same.

Economic Stabilization Act of 1970

Pub. L. No. 91-379, 84 Stat. 799 (1970)

TITLE II — COST OF LIVING STABILIZATION

§201. *Short title.* This title may be cited as the "Economic Stabilization Act of 1970."

§202. *Presidential authority.* (a) The President is authorized to issue such orders and regulations as he may deem appropriate to stabilize prices, rents, wages, and salaries at levels not less than those prevailing on May 25, 1970. Such orders and regulations may provide for the making of such adjustments as may be necessary to prevent gross inequities.

§203. *Delegation.* The President may delegate the performance of any function under this title to such officers, departments, and agencies of the United States as he may deem appropriate.

§204. *Penalty*. Whoever willfully violates any order or regulation under this title shall be fined not more than $5,000.

§205. *Injunctions*. Whenever it appears to any agency of the United States, authorized by the President to exercise the authority contained in this section to enforce orders and regulations issued under this title, that any person has engaged, is engaged or is about to engage in any acts or practices constituting a violation of regulation or order under this title, it may in its discretion bring an action, in the proper district court of the United States, or the proper United States court of any territory or other place subject to the jurisdiction of the United States to enjoin such acts or practices and upon a proper showing a permanent or temporary injunction or restraining order shall be granted without bond. Upon application of the agency, any such court may also issue mandatory injunctions commanding any person to comply with any regulation or order under this title.

§206. *Expiration*. The authority to issue and enforce orders and regulations under this title expires at midnight February 28, 1971, but such expiration shall not affect any proceeding under section 204 for a violation of any such order or regulation, or for the punishment for contempt committed in the violation of any injunction under section 205, committed prior to March 1, 1971.

House Committee Report on Economic Stabilization Act

H.R. 91-1330, 91st Cong., 2d Sess. (1970)

... Many economists, many Members of Congress, some of whom have introduced legislation similar to title II of H.R. 17880, labor leaders, the AFL-CIO, mayors of some of our Nation's largest cities, and others have called on the Congress to provide discretionary standby authority to the President to impose wage, price, rent, and salary controls to combat and break the back of inflation and the inflation psychology which pervades our thinking and our economy.

A Gallup poll conducted in the middle of June clearly indicates the wishes of the American people in this matter. This poll concluded that if the question on wage and price controls "were put to the people of the Nation in the form of a referendum, . . . they would . . . vote in favor of mandatory controls."

Many Members of Congress have received letters and an overwhelming response to questionnaires which they have sent their constituents favoring the institution of wage and price controls on an equitable basis at this time. . . .

It is the firm opinion of the majority of the members of your committee that if the Congress, in its wisdom, enacts this legislation, the President will have all of the necessary weapons needed to control inflation. . . .

Those members of your committee who argued against this title during committee hearings and voted against this title during the executive sessions, argued that legislation providing for wage and price freezes should be mandated by the

Congress if the Congress desires this authority, and not left up to the discretion of the President. The majority of your committee argued that this is an obvious ploy to detract attention from the fact that this responsibility must reside with the President and within the executive branch. The Congress itself is neither constituted or organized to take on this function. It is not a legislative function, both in terms of appropriate timing in instituting the controls and removing them, since only the Executive can determine the appropriate time for instituting the controls and removing them, and only the Executive is equipped to determine and establish the necessary rules and regulations to carry out the law once imposed.

The majority of your committee who voted for title II of H.R. 17880 deemed it highly improper for the Congress to mandate such authority. In supporting this proposal it was argued that one could easily envision the possibility that, once having imposed wage-price-salary-rent freezes, a few months hence it would be necessary to remove them in whole or in part. But if the Congress had mandated such action through to the termination date of February 28, 1971, as set forth in the bill, it could well be days or weeks before such action would be rescinded by the Congress if needed, and indeed, the Congress itself may not be in session when it would be appropriate to remove such controls. . . .

Executive Order No. 11,615 Providing for Stabilization of Prices, Rents, Wages, and Salaries

36 C.F.R. 600 (Aug. 15, 1971)

Whereas, in order to stabilize the economy, reduce inflation, and minimize unemployment, it is necessary to stabilize prices, rents, wages, and salaries: and

Whereas, the present balance of payments situation makes it especially urgent to stabilize prices, rents, wages, and salaries in order to improve our competitive position in world trade and to protect the purchasing power of the dollar:

Now, Therefore, by virtue of the authority vested in me by the Constitution and statutes of the United States, including the Economic Stabilization Act of 1970 (P.L. 91-379, 84 Stat. 799), as amended, it is hereby ordered as follows:

Sec. 1. (a) Prices, rents, wages, and salaries shall be stabilized for a period of 90 days from the date hereof at levels not greater than the highest of those pertaining to a substantial volume of actual transactions by each individual, business, firm or other entity of any kind during the 30-day period ending August 14, 1971, for like or similar commodities or services. If no transactions occurred in that period, the ceiling will be the highest price, rent, salary, or wage in the nearest preceding 30-day period in which transactions did occur. No person shall charge, assess, or receive, directly or indirectly, in any transaction prices or rents in any form higher than those permitted hereunder, and no person shall, directly or indirectly, pay or agree to pay in any transaction wages or salaries in any form, or to use any means to obtain payment of wages and salaries in any form, higher than those permitted hereunder, whether by retroactive increase or otherwise.

(b) Each person engaged in the business of selling or providing commodities or services shall maintain available for public inspection a record of the highest prices or rents charged for such or similar commodities or services during the 30-day period ending August 14, 1971.

(c) The provisions of sections 1 and 2 hereof shall not apply to the prices charged for raw agricultural products.

Sec. 2. (a) There is hereby established the Cost of Living Council which shall act as an agency of the United States and which is hereinafter referred to as the Council.

(b) The Council shall be composed of the following members: The Secretary of the Treasury, the Secretary of Agriculture, the Secretary of Commerce, the Secretary of Labor, the Director of the Office of Management and Budget, the Chairman of the Council of Economic Advisers, the Director of the Office of Emergency Preparedness, and the Special Assistant to the President for Consumer Affairs. The Secretary of the Treasury shall serve as Chairman of the Council and the Chairman of the Council of Economic Advisers shall serve as Vice Chairman. The Chairman of the Board of Governors of the Federal Reserve System shall serve as adviser to the Council.

(c) Under the direction of the Chairman of the Council a Special Assistant to the President shall serve as Executive Director of the Council, and the Executive Director is authorized to appoint such personnel as may be necessary to assist the Council in the performance of its functions.

Sec. 3. (a) Except as otherwise provided herein, there are hereby delegated to the Council all of the powers conferred on the President by the Economic Stabilization Act of 1970.

(b) The Council shall develop and recommend to the President additional policies, mechanisms, and procedures to maintain economic growth without inflationary increases in prices, rents, wages, and salaries after the expiration of the 90-day period specified in Section 1 of this Order.

(c) The Council shall consult with representatives of agriculture, industry, labor and the public concerning the development of policies, mechanisms, and procedures to maintain economic growth without inflationary increases in prices, rents, wages, and salaries.

(d) In all of its actions the Council will be guided by the need to maintain consistency of price and wage policies with fiscal, monetary, international and other economic policies of the United States.

(e) The Council shall inform the public, agriculture, industry, and labor concerning the need for controlling inflation and shall encourage and promote vo'untary action to that end.

Sec. 4. (a) The Council, in carrying out the provisions of this Order, may (i) prescribe definitions for any terms used herein, (ii) make exceptions or grant exemptions, (iii) issue regulations and orders, and (iv) take such other actions as it determines to be necessary and appropriate to carry out the purposes of this Order.

(b) The Council may redelegate to any agency, instrumentality or official of the United States any authority under this Order, and may, in administering this Order, utilize the services of any other agencies, Federal or State, as may be available and appropriate.

(c) On request of the Chairman of the Council, each Executive department or agency is authorized and directed, consistent with law, to furnish the Council with available information which the Council may require in the performance of its functions.

(d) All Executive departments and agencies shall furnish such necessary assistance as may be authorized by section 214 of the Act of May 3, 1945 (59 Stat. 134; 31 U.S.C. §691).

Sec. 5. The Council may require the maintenance of appropriate records or other evidence which are necessary in carrying out the provisions of this Order, and may require any person to maintain and produce for examination such records or other evidence, in such form as it shall require, concerning prices, rents, wages, and salaries and all related matters. The Council may make such exemptions from any requirement otherwise imposed as are consistent with the purposes of this Order. Any type of record or evidence required under regulations issued under this Order shall be retained for such period as the Council may prescribe.

Sec. 6. The expenses of the Council shall be paid from such funds of the Treasury Department as may be available therefor.

Sec. 7. (a) Whoever willfully violates this Order or any order or regulation issued under authority of this Order shall be fined not more than $5,000 for each such violation.

(b) The Council shall in its discretion request the Department of Justice to bring actions for injunctions authorized under Section 205 of the Economic Stabilization Act of 1970 whenever it appears to the Council that any person has engaged, is engaged, or is about to engage in any acts or practices constituting a violation of any regulation or order issued pursuant to this Order.

Richard Nixon

The White House
August 15, 1971

Amalgamated Meat Cutters v. Connally

337 F. Supp. 737 (D.D.C. 1971)

[The Meat Cutters Union challenged the Economic Stabilization Act on grounds of excessive delegation.

In an important opinion by Judge LEVENTHAL, the three-judge court sustained the constitutionality of the Act. The opinion first lays down a standard for determining whether a given delegation of legislative power is permissible:]

[T]here is no forbidden delegation of legislative power "if Congress shall lay down by legislative act an intelligible principle" to which the official or agency must conform.

Concepts of control and accountability define the constitutional requirement. The principle permitting a delegation of legislative power, if there has been sufficient demarcation of the field to permit a judgment whether the agency has kept within the legislative will, establishes a principle of accountability under which compatibility with the legislative design may be ascertained not only by Congress but by the courts and the public. That principle was conjoined in *Yakus*[41] with a recognition that the burden is on the party who assails the legislature's choice of means for effecting its purpose, a burden that is met only if we could say that there is an absence of standard for the guidance of the Administrator's action so that it would be impossible in a proper proceeding to ascertain whether the will of Congress has been obeyed.

[The court then concluded that the Act, read in light of its background, legislative history, and prior regulatory programs to control wages and prices, did furnish an "intelligible principle" by which a court could police its implementation. It stressed that "the standards of a statute are not to be tested in isolation" and derive "meaningful content from the purpose of the Act, its factual background, and the statutory context." Congress, the court found, contemplated a broad freeze of prices and wages, whose timing must necessarily be left to executive discretion, to halve "cost-push" inflation and check accompanying "inflationary psychology." The court also found significance in the limited duration of the authority granted the President.

The Meat Cutters Union contended, however, that, despite the limited duration of the delegated power, the delegation was invalid because it afforded the President a "blank check" for controlling domestic affairs that is intolerable in our constitutional system. The Union stressed the absence in the Act of a requirement, found in earlier price and wage control programs, that controls be "fair and equitable," and argued that the Act therefore gave the President power arbitrarily to prefer certain social and economic constituencies at the expense of others. It pointed to the exemption from control in Executive Order 11,615 of the prices of raw agricultural products as an example of such an arbitrary preference. To this argument the court replied as follows:]

If the Act gives the President authority to be unfair and inequitable, as the Union claims, this legislative vessel may indeed founder on a constitutional rock. But we do not reach this constitutional issue because we do not think the Act can be given the extremist interpretation offered by the Union.

We take this view not only because of the doctrine that statutes are to be construed so as to avoid serious constitutional questions, but more directly because we do not think it can sensibly or fairly be said that this extremist approach was

41. Ed. note: Yakus v. United States, 321 U.S. 414 (1944), upheld a broad delegation to the Office of Price Administration during World War II empowering it to control prices and rents so as "to stabilize prices and to prevent speculative, unwarranted, and abnormal increases in prices and rents." The Administration was to establish prices that were "generally fair and equitable," giving consideration "so far as practicable" to prices between October 1 and October 15, 1941. In sustaining the delegation as constitutional, the Court relied in part on the fact that the OPA had, through regulations and guidelines, developed greater specificity in the criteria used to fix prices and rents.

what was intended by the legislature. As we have already shown there is no lack of specificity in the constitutional sense in the standards of the Act for the initiation of controls, either in particular industries or sectors the economy, or in the general wage-price freeze.

The problem that now concerns us is whether the Act has sufficient specificity to avoid the constitutional condemnation, of excessive "blank check" authority to the President, as to the period following the initial general price-wage freeze.

We do not think it can be said that the possibility of controls beyond the initial freeze was left without any standard other than the President's unfettered discretion, including the discretion to be unfair and inequitable. This is not a case where Congress indicated an intention to leave the matter wholly to the discretion of the President without any possibility of judicial review. The ultimate standard for follow-on controls replacing the freeze is a standard of fairness and equity. This standard of removal of "gross inequities" is voiced as an authority of the President in §202 of the Act. . . . We think there is fairly implicit in the Act the duty to take whatever action is required in the interest of broad fairness and avoidance of gross inequity, although presumably his range of discretion means there may be inequities that a President may remove that he is not compelled by law to remove.

This conclusion is supported by constitutional consideration and historic context. The 1942 statute on prices specifically articulated the "generally fair and equitable" standard. But the broad equity standard is inherent in a stabilization program. It was incorporated into the 1942 wage control measures providing for stabilization of wages and salaries. Fairness and equity are also furthered by the requirement that the Executive develop implementing standards, with deliberate criteria replacing the fortuities of a freeze.

It is not our purpose or function at this time to define the contours of the standard of broad fairness and avoidance of gross inequity. That would be appropriate if the taking or omission of specific action were challenged. But we reiterate that we cannot accept the contention of the Government that the court must pass on the constitutionality of the Act without any conception of its content. We take the intermediate course and rule that our judgment has two parts: first, that the statute does at least contain a standard of broad fairness and avoiding gross inequity, — leaving to the future the implementation of that standard; second, that this statute is not unconstitutional as an excessive delegation of power by the legislature to the Executive for the limited term of months contemplated by Congress to follow the initiating general freeze.

. . . Another feature that blunts the "blank check" rhetoric is the requirement that any action taken by the Executive under the law, subsequent to the freeze must be in accordance with further standards as developed by the Executive. This requirement, inherent in the Rule of Law and implicit in the Act, means that however broad the discretion of the Executive at the outset, the standard once developed limits the latitude of subsequent Executive action.

The importance in present context of this self-limiting aspect of Executive and agency discretion is brought out in Yakus v. United States, supra. After noting that the Constitution does not demand the impossible, that the essentials of the legislative function are preserved with a determination of legislative police, Chief Justice Stone continues: "It is no objection that the determination of facts and the inferences to be drawn from them in the light of the statutory standards and declaration of policy call for the exercise of judgment, and for the formulation of subsidiary administrative policy within the prescribed statutory framework."

The crucial paragraph of the opinion specifically relies on the reasoning of Executive administration as helping to supply the requisite specificity and precision: "[T]he standards prescribed by the present Act, with the aid of the 'statement of the considerations' required to be made by the Administrator, are sufficiently definite and precise to enable Congress, the courts and the public to ascertain whether the Administrator, in fixing the designated prices, has conformed to those standards. . . . Hence we are unable to find in them an unauthorized delegation of legislative power."

The requirement of subsidiary administrative policy, enabling Congress, the courts and the public to assess the Executive's adherence to the ultimate legislative standard, is in furtherance of the purpose of the constitutional objective of accountability. This 1970 Act gives broadest latitude to the Executive. Certainly there is no requirement of formal findings. But there is an ongoing requirement of intelligible administrative policy that is corollary to and implementing of the legislature's ultimate standard and objective. This requirement is underscored by the consideration that the exercise of wide discretion will probably call for "imaginative interpretation," leaving the courts to see whether the Executive, using its experience. "has fairly exercised its discretion within the vaguish, penumbral bounds" of the broad statutory standard.

In view of the administration of the prior two stabilization programs the Government cannot sensibly contend that the requirement of development of administrative standards is unattainable or would reduce to a futility the legislative objective of controlling inflation.

[Finally, the court discussed the pertinence of the *Schechter* decision:]

In *Schechter*, which held invalid the provisions of the National Industrial Recovery Act that authorized the fixing of codes of fair conduct, the "function of formulating the codes was delegated, not to a public official responsible to Congress or to the Executive, but to private individuals engaged in the industries to be regulated." Yakus v. United States, supra, 321 U.S. at 424; . . . The "corporate state" aspects of the Blue Eagle codes that emerged in practice were made possible and reinforced by a legal context of authority to prescribe "codes of fair competition" that covered the entire range of economic life, going beyond even the broad subject matter before us.

Schechter has fairly been described as a ruling that administered "the hemlock of excessive delegation" in a case of "delegation run riot." We think the extremist pattern then before the Court cannot fairly be analogized to the anti-inflation statute, limited in life and' passed in a context of experiences with similar legislation, that is before us for consideration.

Plaintiff's motion for injunctive relief must be denied.

The following are typical regulations designed to deal with problems arising in the administration of price controls. They were issued pursuant to amendments of the Economic Stabilization Act and are set out in Title 6 of the Code of Federal Regulations.

CHAPTER III   PRICE COMMISSION
PART 300   PRICE STABILIZATION
SUBPART A   GENERAL

§300.5 *Definitions*. . . . "Price increase" means an increase in the unit price of a property or service or a decrease in the quality of substantially the same property or services.

"Profit margin" means the ratio that operating income (net sales less cost of sales and less normal and generally recurring costs of business operations, determined before nonoperating items, extraordinary items, and income taxes) bears to net sales as reported on the person's financial statement prepared in accordance with generally accepted accounting principles consistently applied. . . .

§300.11 *General rule.* (a) No person may charge a price with respect to any sale or lease of an item of property or a service after November 13, 1971, which exceeds the base price (or other price authorized under this part) for that item of property or that service. . . .

§300.12 *Manufacturers.* A manufacturer may charge a price in excess of the base price only to reflect increases in allowable costs that it incurred since the last price increase in the item concerned, or that it incurred after January 1, 1971, whichever was later, and that it is continuing to incur, reduced to reflect productivity gains, and only to the extent that the increased price does not result in an increase in its profit margin over that which prevailed during the base period. . . .

§300.13 *Retailers and wholesalers.* (a) General. A retailer or wholesaler may charge a price in excess of the base price whenever its customary initial percentage markup after November 13, 1971, with respect to property sold, is equal to or less than its last customary initial percentage markup before November 14, 1971, or, at its option, its customary initial percentage markup during its last fiscal year ending before August 15, 1971. However, the increased price may not result in an increase in its profit margin over that which prevailed during the base period. . . .

§300.409 *New property and new services.* . . . (b) Base price determination. A person offering a new property or a new service shall determine its base price as follows:

(1) Net operating profit markup — Manufacturer or service organization. A manufacturer or service organization shall apply the net operating profit markup it received on the most nearly similar property or service it sold or leased to the same market during the freeze base period to the total allowable unit costs of the new property or service. For the purposes of this subparagraph, "net operating profit market" means the ratio which the selling price bears to the total allowable unit costs of the property or service.

(2) Customary initial percentage markup — Retailer or wholesaler shall apply the customary initial percentage markup it received on the most nearly similar property or service it sold to the same market during the freeze base period to the allowable unit costs of the new property.

(3) Average price of comparable property or services. If the person did not offer a similar property or service for sale or lease to a particular market during the freeze base period, the base price for sales or leases to that market shall be the average price received in a substantial number of current transactions in that market by other persons selling or leasing comparable property or services in the same marketing area.

(4) Customary pricing practice. If none of the methods provided in subparagraphs (1) through (3) of this paragraph can be used and the new property or new service is not reasonably comparable to any property or service previously sold or leased by any person within the same marketing area or being sold or leased by the person concerned in current transactions in the same market, he may use any customary pricing practice he used during the freeze base period, or, if the person did not sell or lease any property or service before August 15, 1971, he may use any other pricing practice commonly used by other persons engaging in comparable business with the same market.

ECONOMIC STABILIZATION REGULATIONS

CHAPTER I   COST OF LIVING COUNCIL

PART 101   COVERAGE, EXEMPTIONS AND CLASSIFICATION OF
ECONOMIC UNITS

§101.11 *Price category I firms; prenotification and reporting requirements.* (a) A price category I firm is:

(1) a firm with annual sales or revenues of $100 million of more....

(b) Each price category I firm shall submit a prenotification to the Price Commission of each proposed price adjustment in accordance with regulations issued by the Price Commission.

(c) No proposed price adjustment shall be put into effect by any price category I firm unless such price adjustment has been approved or permitted to take effect in accordance with regulations issued by the Price Commission....

Questions[42]

1. The Federal Emergency Price Control Act of 1942 imposed criminal sanctions on "Any person who willfully violates any provision of section 4 of this Act." Section 4(a) in turn provided that "It shall be unlawful ... for any person to sell or deliver any commodity ... in violation of any regulation or order under section 2." Section 2 authorized the Price Administrator (head of the OPA) to establish such maximum prices "as in his judgment will be generally fair and equitable and

42. Compare the following fact situation to that in M. Kraus & Bros. v. United States, 327 U.S. 614 (1946).

will effectuate the purposes of this Act," and stated that "Regulations, orders, and requirements under this Act may contain such provisions as the Administrator deems necessary to prevent the circumvention or evasion thereof."

In December 1942, the Administrator issued Regulation 269, establishing maximum prices for poultry. Section 5 of this regulation, entitled "Evasion," read:

"Price limitations set forth in this Revised Maximum Price Regulation No. 269 *shall not be evaded* whether by direct or indirect methods in connection with any offer, solicitation, agreement, sale, delivery, purchase or receipt of, or relating to, the commodities prices of which are herein regulated, alone or in conjunction with any other commodity, or by way of commission, service, transportation, or other charge, or discount, premium, or other privilege or other trade understanding or otherwise."

During the Thanksgiving season in 1943, while Regulation 269 was still in effect, the Krause Poultry Company was engaged in the wholesale poultry business. In a criminal proceeding brought against Krause, it was alleged that the company had forced several of its retailer customers to purchase chicken feet and/or chicken skins along with and as a condition of the sale of poultry to them, and thus had violated the regulation. At trial the evidence showed that several butchers who had ordered dressed chicken from the defendant also received chicken feet and chicken skins without previous order or solicitation by them and that they were billed for both the poultry and the parts. The price of the poultry was not in excess of the ceiling price for dressed chicken plus the ceiling prices for chicken feet and chicken skin. Most of the retailer customers testified that they sold a small amount of the chicken parts and gave the rest away, while one testified that he was forced to dump all the parts.

Krause, while not denying that the sale of poultry was conditioned on the "tie-in sale" of the parts, tried to introduce testimony that there was a demand for these parts and that they did have value. The trial court rejected this effort, and Krause was convicted.

On appeal Krause argued that the Price Control Act was invalid under the nondelegation doctrine, which holds that "Congress cannot delegate any part of its legislative power except under the limitation of a prescribed standard." [43]

(a) Do the pre-*Panama Refining* cases require the Court to sustain the Act?

(b) Does *Schechter* or *Panama Refining* require the Court to invalidate the Act? Consider in this respect the discussion in *Schechter* seeking to distinguish the prohibition of "unfair methods of competition" in §5 of the Federal Trade Commission Act, whose constitutional validity has been upheld by the Court, from the NIRA's requirement of "fair competition," which the Court invalidated. On what basis can the two statutes be distinguished? Which does the 1942 Act more closely resemble?

2. If the Court upholds the constitutionality of the 1942 Act, must it then uphold the constitutionality of the 1970 Price Stabilization Act? Was *Meat Cutters* rightly decided?

43. United States v. Chicago, M., St. P. & P. R.R., 282 U.S. 311, 324 (1931).

3. If *Krause* does not succeed on its claim that the 1942 Act constitutes an unconstitutional delegation of legislative power, are there any other defenses that it might assert?

4. Are the purposes of the nondelegation doctrine served, despite the broad statutory language of the Act, if price control commissions administer the Act under specific, administratively created, regulations? To what extent is it possible to write such regulations? Consider the price regulations printed above. What sort of regulations could adequately deal with the following problems?

(a) The determination of profits: Widget Toys has annual gross revenues of $100,000, an investment of $100,000, a wage bill of $50,000, and profits of $10,000. Its work force wants a wage increase of $10,000. Under the regulations, what incentive does Widget have to resist? Should profits be figured as a percentage of sales or of investment?

(b) New product: Jones has invented a vastly improved "safe" pesticide. He has secured a patent and wishes to begin production.

(c) Special cases: Brown's clothing store has been losing money steadily for the past three years. He must raise his prices to survive.

(d) New demand: The opening of nuclear power plants has significantly increased the demand for bethelium, a metal now produced by only two small American refiners. Deposits of the ore are scattered throughout the Rocky Mountain basin.

(e) Consider the Krause chicken case: Krause's second ground for appeal is that the statute does not apply to his conduct. How should the court decide this claim? What methods, other than a regulation such as Regulation 269, might the Price Commission use to deal with the problem of evasion?

Note: Post-*Schechter* Doctrine

There has been no federal case since *Schechter* invalidating legislation on the ground of overly broad delegation. To the contrary, in addition to *Meat Cutters,* other decisions have upheld other delegations that seem fairly extreme. Yakus v. United States, 321 U.S. 414 (1944), relied upon in *Meat Cutters,* upheld a World War II price control statute authorizing the Office of Price Administration "to stabilize prices and to prevent speculative, unwarranted, and abnormal increases in prices and rents." In Lichter v. United States, 334 U.S. 742 (1948), the Supreme Court sustained the validity of the Renegotiation Act, which provided for the recovery of "excessive profits" by government officers. When originally enacted, the law made no effort to guide the officers' determination of what was "excessive"; a later amendment contained a host of often conflicting "considerations" for the administrator to take into account.

In United States v. Southwestern Cable Co., 392 U.S. 157 (1968), the Court upheld a regulation of the Federal Communications Commission forbidding Community Antenna Television Systems to rebroadcast certain television signals outside of a particular area. The Court sustained the Commission's authority to regulate CATV under the statutory provision making the Communications Act of 1934 applicable to "all interstate and foreign communication by wire or radio"; it held that the Commission could make rules reasonably ancillary to its responsibilities to regulate television, although the only standard governing the Commission in its exercise of this power lies in the Commission's authority to issue "such rules and regulations . . . not inconsistent with law" as "public convenience, interest or necessity requires." 47 U.S.C. §303(r). For another interesting (and extreme) example of delegation, see Arizona v. California, 373 U.S. 546 (1963) (upholding Secretary of Interior's power to allocate water from interstate river among various states). The Court has continued to sustain broad delegations concerning foreign relations and trade. See Federal Energy Administration v. Algonquin SNG, Inc., 426 U.S. 548 (1976).

On the other hand, state courts have occasionally applied the nondelegation doctrine to invalidate legislation.[44] And, in one recent case, the Supreme Court indicated (in dicta) that the nondelegation doctrine may have life when delegations of the taxing power are at issue. National Cable Television Assn. v. United States, 415 U.S. 336 (1974).

E. The Relation of the Executive to the Administrative Agencies

1. Introduction

Much administrative law has grown out of the relationship between the courts and the "independent" federal administrative agencies. The Interstate Commerce Commission, established in 1887, is ordinarily considered the first such agency. Its several members are appointed by the President; however, their terms do not coincide with his. They were intended to be experts who would independently administer the Interstate Commerce Act. The independent agency model was copied when the Federal Trade Commission was created in 1914. The "independent agency" grew in popularity during the New Deal period, which saw the establishment of the Civil Aeronautics Board, the National Labor Relations Board, the Securities Exchange Commission, and the Federal Power Commission. Many others have been created since. What is the "constitutional position" of the independent agencies? Are they, as a 1937 presidential commission wrote, "in reality miniature independent governments, ... a headless 'fourth branch' of the Government"?[45] The notion that these agencies are constitutionally "special" arose out of several cases dealing with separation of powers and the President's power to remove appointed officials.

Before turning to those cases, it is helpful to refer to the categorization set out by Mr. Justice Jackson in his concurrence in Youngstown Sheet & Tube Co. v.

44. See K. Davis, Administrative Law Treatise §§ 2.07-2.11 (1958).
45. Report of the President's Committee on Administrative Management 36 (1937).

Sawyer, 343 U.S. 579, 634-638 (1952) (holding President Truman's seizure of the steel mills to avert a strike unconstitutional):

> We may well begin by a somewhat over-simplified grouping of practical situations in which a President may doubt, or others may challenge, his powers, and by distinguishing roughly the legal consequences of this factor of relativity.
>
> 1. When the President acts pursuant to an express or implied authorization of Congress, his authority is at its maximum, for it includes all that he possesses in his own right plus all that Congress can delegate. In these circumstances, and in these only, may he be said (for what it may be worth) to personify the federal sovereignty....
>
> 2. When the President acts in absence of either a congressional grant or denial of authority, he can only rely upon his own independent powers, but there is a zone of twilight in which he and Congress may have concurrent authority, or in which its distribution is uncertain....
>
> 3. When the President takes measures incompatible with the expressed or implied will of Congress, his power is at its lowest ebb, for then he can rely only upon his own constitutional powers minus any constitutional powers of Congress over the matter. Courts can sustain exclusive presidental control in such a case only by disabling the Congress from acting upon the subject. A presidential claim to a power at once so conclusive and preclusive must be scrutinized with caution, for what is at stake is the equilibrium established by our constitutional system....

Myers v. United States

272 U.S. 52 (1926)

[Myers was appointed Postmaster for a four-year term at Portland, Oregon, under a statute providing that postmasters "shall be appointed and may be removed by the President and with the advice and consent of the Senate." President Wilson removed him from office, prior to the expiration of this term, without the consent of the Senate. In this suit for back pay, the government claimed Myers' removal was lawful because it is unconstitutional to limit the President's power to remove an executive branch official by requiring the Senate's agreement.

The Court agreed with the government. Chief Justice Taft wrote that the power to remove subordinates is inherently part of the executive power, which Article II, §1, of the Constitution vests "in a President of the United States."

Chief Justice TAFT wrote:]

Made responsible under the Constitution for the effective enforcement of the law, the President needs as an indispensable aid to meet it the disciplinary influence upon those who act under him of a reserve power of removal.... The highest and most important duties which his subordinates perform are those in which they act for him. In such cases they are exercising not their own but his discretion....

In all such cases, the discretion to be exercised is that of the President in determining the national public interest and in directing the action to be taken by his executive subordinates to protect it. In this field his cabinet officers must do his will. He must place in each member of his official family, and his chief executive subordinates, implicit faith. The moment that he loses confidence in the intelligence, ability, judgment, or loyalty of any one of them, he must have the power to remove him without delay. To require him to file charges and submit them to the consideration of the Senate might make impossible that unity and co-ordination in executive administration essential to effective action.

The duties of the heads of departments and bureaus in which the discretion of the President is exercised and which we have described are the most important in the whole field of executive action of the Government. There is nothing in the Constitution which permits a distinction between the removal of the head of a department or a bureau, when he discharges a political duty of the President or exercises his discretion, and the removal of executive officers engaged in the discharge of their normal duties. The imperative reasons requiring an unrestricted power to remove the most important of his subordinates in their most important duties must, therefore, control the interpretation of the Constitution as to all appointed by him.

But this is not to say that there are not strong reasons why the President should have a like power to remove his appointees charged with other duties than those above described. The ordinary duties of officers prescribed by statute come under the general administrative control of the President by virtue of the general grant to him of the executive power, and he may properly supervise and guide their construction of the statutes under which they act in order to secure that unitary and uniform execution of the laws which Article II of the Constitution evidently contemplated in vesting general executive power in the President alone. Laws are often passed with specific provision for the adoption of regulations by a department or bureau head to make the law workable and effective. The ability and judgment manifested by the official thus empowered, as well as his energy and stimulation of his subordinates, are subjects which the President must consider and supervise in his administrative control. Finding such officers to be negligent and inefficient, the President should have the power to remove them. Of course there may be duties so peculiarly and specifically committed to the discretion of a particular officer as to raise a question whether the President may overrule or revise the officer's interpretation of his statutory duty in a particular instance. Then there may be duties of a quasi-judicial character imposed on executive officers and members of executive tribunals whose decisions after hearing affect interests of individuals, the discharge of which the President can not in a particular case properly influence or control. But even in such a case he may consider the decision after its renditions, as a reason for removing the officer, on the ground that the discretion regularly entrusted to that officer by statute has not been on the whole intelligently or wisely exercised. Otherwise he does not discharge his own constitutional duty of seeing that the laws be faithfully executed.

[The Chief Justice conceded that Congress could limit the power of the

President to remove inferior officers — say, by creating a Civil Service, with removal only for cause. But it can do so only because the Constitution, Article II, §2, allows Congress to "vest the appointment of such inferior officers as they think proper, in the President alone, in the courts of law, or in the heads of departments." In any event, Congress had not vested "in the President alone" the power to appoint Myers; hence his appointment must be considered a major one, and his removal must, constitutionally, be left to the discretion of the President.]

[Justices Holmes, Brandeis, and McReynolds dissented.

Justice HOLMES wrote:]

...The arguments drawn from the executive power of the President, and from his duty to appoint officers of the United States (when Congress does not vest the appointment elsewhere), to take care that the laws be faithfully executed, and to commission all officers of the United States, seem to me spiders' webs inadequate to control the dominant facts.

We have to deal with an office that owes its existence to Congress and that Congress may abolish tomorrow. Its duration and the pay attached to it while it lasts depend on Congress alone. Congress alone confers on the President the power to appoint to it and at any time may transfer the power to other hands. With such power over its own creation, I have no more trouble in believing that Congress has power to prescribe a term of life for it free from any interference than I have in accepting the undoubted power of Congress to decree its end. I have equally little trouble in accepting its power to prolong the tenure of an incumbent until Congress or the Senate shall have assented to his removal. The duty of the President to see that the laws be executed is a duty that does not go beyond the laws or require him to achieve more than Congress sees fit to leave within his power.

Humphrey's Executor v. United States

295 U.S. 602 (1935)

[The Federal Trade Commission was created in 1914 to enforce (concurrently with the Justice Department) certain provisions of the antitrust laws and to define and eliminate "unfair methods of competition." Proponents of the bill wanted "a nonpartisan organization, which moves absolutely free from the interference of either Congress or the President." [46] In its early years the Commission brought few major cases. President Franklin D. Roosevelt believed that his predecessors had deliberately appointed commissioners who did not believe in the legislative purposes of the Trade Commission Act. He therefore sought to replace Commissioner Humphrey. He felt that, in doing so, he would be able to make the Commission act more effectively.]

Mr. Justice SUTHERLAND delivered the opinion of the Court....

William E. Humphrey...was nominated by President Hoover...as a mem-

46. 51 Cong. Rec. 11235 (1914).

ber of the Federal Trade Commission, and was confirmed.... He was commissioned for a term of seven years expiring September 25, 1938;... On July 25, 1933, President Roosevelt addressed a letter to the commissioner asking for his resignation, on the ground "that the aims and purposes of the Administration with respect to the work of the Commission can be carried out most effectively with personnel of my own selection," but disclaiming any reflection upon the commissioner personally or upon his services. The commissioner replied, asking time to consult his friends. After some further correspondence upon the subject, the President on August 31, 1933, wrote the commissioner expressing the hope that the resignation would be forthcoming and saying: "You will, I know, realize that I do not feel that your mind and my mind go along together on either the policies or the administering of the Federal Trade Commission, and, frankly, I think it is best for the people of this country that I should have a full confidence." The Commissioner declined to resign; and on October 7, 1933, the President wrote him: "Effective as of this date you are hereby removed from the office of Commissioner of the Federal Trade Commission."

Humphrey never acquiesced in this action, but continued thereafter to insist that he was still a member of the commission, entitled to perform its duties and receive the compensation provided by law. [In this suit for back pay the Court of Claims certified two questions to the Supreme Court:]

> 1. Do the provisions of section 1 of the Federal Trade Commission Act, stating that "any commissioner may be removed by the President for inefficiency, neglect of duty, or malfeasance in office," restrict or limit the power of the President to remove a commissioner except upon one or more of the causes named? [The Supreme Court answered yes.]
> If the foregoing question is answered in the affirmative, then —
> 2. If the power of the President to remove a commissioner is restricted or limited as shown by the foregoing interrogatory and the answer made thereto, is such a restriction or limitation valid under the Constitution of the United States?

...To support its contention that the removal provision of §1... is an unconstitutional interference with the executive power of the President, the government's chief reliance is Myers v. United States, 272 U.S. 52.... [T]he narrow point actually decided was only that the President had power to remove a postmaster of the first class, without the advice and consent of the Senate as required by act of Congress. In the course of the opinion of the court, expressions occur which tend to sustain the government's contention, but these are beyond the point involved and, therefore, do not come within the rule of stare decisis. In so far as they are out of harmony with the views here set forth, these expressions are disapproved....

The office of a postmaster is so essentially unlike the office now involved that the decision in the Myers case cannot be accepted as controlling our decision here. A postmaster is an executive officer restricted to the performance of executive functions. He is charged with no duty at all related to either the legislative or judicial power. The actual decision in the *Myers* case finds support in the theory that such an officer is merely one of the units in the executive department and, hence, inherently subject to the exclusive and illimitable power of removal by the Chief Executive, whose subordinate and aid he is.... [T]he necessary reach of the decision goes far enough to include all purely executive officers. It goes no farther; — much less does it include an officer who occupies no place in the executive department and who exercises no part of the executive power vested by the Constitution in the President.

The Federal Trade Commission is an administrative body created by Congress to carry into effect legislative policies embodied in the statute in accordance with the legislative standard therein prescribed, and to perform other specified duties as a legislative or as a judicial aid. Such a body cannot in any proper sense be characterized as an arm or an eye of the executive. Its duties are performed without executive leave and, in the contemplation of the statute must be free from executive control.... [T]he commission acts in part quasi-legislatively and in part quasi-judicially....

The fundamental necessity of maintaining each of the three general departments of government entirely free from the control or coercive influence, direct or indirect, of either of the others, has often been stressed and is hardly open to serious question.

The power of removal here claimed for the President falls within this principle, since its coercive influence threatens the independence of a commission, which is not only wholly disconnected from the executive department, but which, as already fully appears, was created by Congress as a means of carrying into operation legislative and judicial powers, and as an agency of the legislative and judicial departments....

The result of what we now have said is this: Whether the power of the President to remove an officer shall prevail over the authority of Congress to condition the power by fixing a definite term and precluding a removal except for cause, will depend upon the character of the office; the *Myers* decision, affirming the power of the President alone to make the removal, is confined to purely executive officers; and as to officers of the kind here under consideration, we hold that no removal can be made during the prescribed term for which the officer is appointed, except for one or more of the causes named in the applicable statute.

Weiner v. United States

357 U.S. 349 (1958)

Mr. Justice FRANKFURTER delivered the opinion of the Court.

This is a suit for back pay, based on petitioner's alleged illegal removal as a member of the War Claims Commission.... By the War Claims Act of 1948, Congress established that Commission with "jurisdiction to receive and adjudicate according to law," claims for compensating internees, prisoners of wars, and religious organizations, and who suffered personal injury or property damage at the hands of the enemy in connection with World War II. The Commission was to be composed of three persons, at least two of whom were to be members of the bar, to be appointed by the President, by and with the advice and consent of the Senate. The Commission was to wind up its affairs not later than three years after the expiration of the time for filing claims, . . . and Congress made no provision for removal of a Commissioner.

Having been duly nominated by President Truman, the petitioner . . . took office on June 8, following. On his refusal to heed a request for his resignation, he was, on December 10, 1953, removed by President Eisenhower. . . .

Controversy pertaining to the scope and limits of the President's power of removal fills a thick chapter of our political and judicial history. The long stretches of its history . . . were laboriously traversed in Myers v. United States, 272 U.S. 52. . . . Speaking through a Chief Justice who himself had been President, the Court did not restrict to the immediate issue before it, the President's inherent power to remove a postmaster, obviously an executive official. . . . [T]he Court announced that the President had inherent constitutional power of removal also of officials who have "duties of a quasi-judicial character . . . whose decisions after hearing affect interests of individuals, the discharge of which the President can not in a particular case properly influence or control." Myers v. United States, supra, at 135. This view of presidential power was deemed to flow from his "constitutional duty of seeing that the laws be faithfully executed." Ibid.

The assumption was short-lived. . . . In Humphrey's Executor v. United States, 295 U.S. 602 [the Court] narrowly confined the scope of the Myers decision to include only "all purely executive officers." 295 U.S., at 628. The Court explicitly "disapproved" the expressions in Myers supporting the President's inherent constitutional power to remove members of quasi-judicial bodies. . . .

Humphrey's case was a cause célèbre — and not least in the halls of Congress. And what is the essence of the decision in Humphrey's case? It drew a sharp line of cleavage between officials who were part of the Executive establishment and were thus removable by virtue of the President's constitutional powers, and those who are members of a body "to exercise its judgment without the leave or hindrance of any other official or any department of the government," 295 U.S., at 625-626, as to whom a power of removal exists only if Congress may fairly be said to have conferred it. This sharp differentiation derives from the difference in functions between those who are part of the Executive establishment and those whose tasks require absolute freedom from Executive interference. . . .

Thus, the most reliable factor for drawing an inference regarding the President's power of removal in our case is the nature of the function that Congress vested in the War Claims Commission. What were the duties that Congress confided to this Commission? . . . .

. . . The Commission was established as an adjudicating body with all the paraphernalia by which legal claims are put to the test of proof, with finality of determination "not subject to review by any other official of the United States or by any court by mandamus or otherwise.". . . .

... Congress could, of course, have given jurisdiction over these claims to the District Courts or to the Court of Claims. The fact is that it chose to establish a Commission to "adjudicate according to law" the classes of claims defined in the statute did not alter the intrinsic judicial character of the task with which the Commission was charged. . . . If, as one must take for granted, the War Claims Act precluded the President from influencing the Commission in passing on a particular claim, a fortiori must it be inferred that Congress did not wish to have hang over the Commission the Damocles' sword of removal by the President for no reason other than he preferred to have on that Commission men of his own choosing. . . . Judging the matter in all the nakedness in which it is presented, namely, the claim that the President could remove a member of an adjudicatory body like the War Claims Commission merely because he wanted his own appointees on such a Commission, we are compelled to conclude that no such power is given to the President directly by the Constitution, and none is impliedly conferred upon him by statute simply because Congress said nothing about it. The philosophy of *Humphrey's Executor*, in its explicit language as well as its implications, precludes such a claim.

The judgment is reversed.

Questions

1. The President is precluded by the statutes which create the civil service system from removing most civil servants without cause. Why under *Myers* is this limitation on the President's power constitutional? Are you convinced by *Myers'* reasoning?

2. Is *Humphrey's Executor* limited in its application to the "independent agencies"?

(a) Section 5 of the Department of Transportation Act, 80 Stat. 835 (1966), established "within the Department a [five-member] National Transportation Safety Board" which investigates accidents and hears appeals in cases involving, for example, revocations of licenses to fly. The statute states that the President shall appoint its members to five-year terms, with the Senate's advice and consent, and can remove them only for "inefficiency, neglect of duty or malfeasance." Is this limitation on his removal power constitutional? [47]

(b) The Administrator of the Federal Aviation Administration makes initial decisions to award or to revoke a license to fly. Prior to 1968 the FAA was an "independent agency" in the sense of being located outside of any of the traditional departments. It was then transferred to the Department of Transportation. The statute is silent as to the Administrator's term of office or removal. Can the President remove him without cause?

(c) The Secretary of Agriculture has authority under the Packers & Stockyards

---

47. In 1975 Congress, perhaps concerned by this point, changed the statute to make the Board "an independent agency of the United States." Pub. L. No. 93-633, §303(a) 88 Stat. 2166, 2167, 49 U.S.C. §1902 (1975). Aside from these few words the statute remains basically the same. Why should the word "independent" make a constitutional difference?

Act of 1921 to determine, after hearing, whether a packer is guilty of enumerated unlawful practices. And he can prescribe, after a hearing, just and reasonable rates. His authority under this Act is similar to that of, say, the CAB in relation to airline rates. Can Congress constitutionally enact a statute prohibiting the President from removing the Secretary without cause?

3. Professor Davis writes that the Government Manual "treats as independent any agency outside the eleven executive departments." That is one test. But a more meaningful test is presence or absence of power of the President to discharge the agency head or heads without cause." [48] Do you agree? If not, what is the test of whether an agency is "independent"? Does such a characterization help decide constitutional separation of powers issues? Consider the following:

Note: The "Independent" Agencies

The traditional and prominent independent agencies are the CAB, FCC, FMC, FRB, FTC, ICC, NLRB, NRC, and SEC.[49] Do these "alphabet" agencies enjoy a constitutional position somehow distinct from other bureaucratic units more clearly within the executive branch?

1. *From a stictly legal point of view:*

(a) Whether the agency is or is not within an executive department is not determinative of whether Congress can limit the President's power to remove an agency head without cause, is it? Do the cases mean to distinguish agencies on the basis of their positions in an organizational chart? Might not Congress, as with the Transportation Safety Board, limit the President's power to remove the heads of some "executive offices" as it has done with his power to remove the heads of certain of these "independent" agencies? [50]

(b) Is the President legally prevented from "dictating policy" to an "independent" agency? If so, he is also often prevented from doing so in the case of units within the executive branch. The President cannot dictate policy to any unit insofar as that policy runs counter to the statute under which the unit operates. But, more importantly, certain units within the executive branch exercise delegated authority under statute, free from presidential interference. It seems unlikely, for example, that the President could directly overrule the FAA's decision not to grant a license to fly — despite the fact that the FAA is part of the Department of Transportation — for Congress has delegated the authority to license to the Administrator, not to the President. Moreover, Congress stated that the Administrator "shall not submit his decisions for the approval of, nor be bound by, the decisions or recommenda-

48. K. Davis, Administrative Law of the Seventies §1.09 (1976).

49. Civil Aeronautics Board, Federal Communications Commission, Federal Maritime Commission, Federal Reserve Board, Federal Trade Commission, Interstate Commerce Commission, National Labor Relations Board, Nuclear Regulatory Commission, Securities Exchange Commission.

50. Moreover the Environmental Protection Agency, General Services Administration, and National Aeronautics and Space Administration are "independent" organizationally, yet their heads serve at the President's pleasure.

tions of, any committee, board, or other organization created by Executive Order." [51]

2. *From a practical point of view:*

(a) Regardless of what the statute says, the President can often determine who will run an "independent" agency.[52] Unfilled vacancies, resignations, and "throwing in the towel" often allow a new President quickly to gain control of an administrative body. Although FCC commissioners are appointed for seven-year terms, one of those commissioners is by virtue of executive reorganization provisions selected by the President as chairman — a far more important job. And he serves as *chairman* at the President's pleasure[53] — a fact that may make him susceptible to the President's policy views. Alternatively, there are executive department officials that the President, for political reasons, cannot remove from office (consider J. Edgar Hoover at the FBI or Frances Knight at the Passport Office). Thus these officials can serve and make policy almost totally insulated from the President's views. This insulation is not necessarily detrimental. Consider how disturbed one would be if the President told his Attorney General whom to prosecute. These examples should simply point out that "organizational position" does not necessarily correspond with "policy independence" either legally or practically.

(b) The President has other means available to affect the policies of "independent agencies." The Department of Justice, for example, frequently intervenes in agency proceedings. Except in a few limited situations, the Department will also represent the agency in court, and thus may influence its views. Further, the President controls budget requests. Since the Budget and Accounting Act of 1921, agency budget requests must be reviewed — along with all executive department requests — by the Office of Management and Budget, which may modify them.[54]

Moreover, the President retains some control over the selection of high-level agency personnel. Some agencies have an unwritten policy of consulting with the White House over high-level appointments, especially where the chairman is politically indebted to the President or a White House sponsor.[55] The power to allocate "supergrades," the highly paid positions without which an agency is virtually immobilized, is vested in the Civil Service Commission, the members of which are all appointed by the President.[56] This power over personnel is not inconsiderable and has been used to coerce an "independent" agency.[57]

Finally, the President can influence agency policy and structure through his control over the introduction of substantive legislation and through reorganization

---

51. 49 U.S.C. §1341(a) (1970).

52. Moreover, legislation governing the FMC, FCC, and SEC contains no express limitation on the President's removal powers.

53. Legislation has been proposed to change this situation by making appointments to a chairmanship subject to Senate confirmation. See Staff of S. Comm. on Governmental Affairs, 5 Study on Federal Regulation 41, 95th Cong, 1st Sess. (1977).

54. 31 U.S.C. §§ 16 et seq. There are a few exceptions. See 15 U.S.C. §2076(k) (Consumer Product Safety Commission).

55. See W. Cary, Politics and the Regulatory Agencies 13 (1967).

56. See 15 U.S.C. §§ 1101, 1103.

57. See Dixon, The Independent Commissions and Political Responsibility, 23 Ad. L. Rev. 1, 10 (1975).

of the government. All legislation proposed by the President or the agencies must be cleared through the Office of Management and Budget, though often an agency will independently approach a member of Congress with suggestions. In recent years the Congress has authorized sweeping powers to the President to reorganize the government, subject to veto by either house. President Nixon used this power to transfer to himself the power to select the ICC Chairman, who had previously been elected by the entire Commission. At the same time, the Chairman was given authority over personnel, the distribution of business, and expenditures.[58] President Nixon also created the EPA through reorganization.[59]

On the other hand, Congress, executive branch officials, and the public often refer to certain agencies, such as the ICC or CAB as "independent." Presumably, the Solicitor General pays them greater deference than an executive department when he formulates a legal position for the government; OMB may treat their budget requests or legislative recommendations with greater respect. Consider, for example, the controversy surrounding an Executive Order, proposed by President Carter, which required each government agency to give advance notice of its agenda, to analyze the impact of major regulatory proposals, and to conduct periodic reviews of existing regulations. The White House would have applied the order to the "independent" as well as to "executive branch" agencies. Several important senators promptly objected that the President lacked the authority to exercise control over the independent agencies (citing *Humphrey's Executor*). The President backed down, stating that "a confrontation with Congress over the applicability of the order to the independent regulatory agencies would only detract from the important reform steps being taken." Therefore, he asked the chairman of [the independent] agencies to voluntarily apply the policies and procedures of the Executive Order. He asked the chairman to report their progress to him and to the Congress." [60]

Perhaps "independence" is a state of mind. But is it a doctrine of law?

2. The Legislative Veto

An issue that tests both the separation of powers doctrine and the theory that "independent" agencies enjoy a special status in this regard involves the constitutionality of the legislative veto. This "veto" consists of a clause in a statute which allows a rule or an action of the President, of an executive department, or an

58. Reorg. Plan No. 1 of 1969, 3 C.F.R. 1066 (1966-1970 Compilation), reprinted in 49 U.S.C. §11 app., at 195 (1970) and in 83 Stat. 859 (1969).
59. Reorg. Plan No. 3 of 1970, 3 C.F.R. 1072 (1966-1970 Compilation), reprinted in 5 U.S.C. app., at 609 (1970), and in 84 Stat. 2086 (1970). Under the Reorganization Act of 1977, a reorganization plan may not have the effect of "creating a new executive department, abolishing or transferring an executive department or independent regulatory agency, or all the functions thereof, or consolidating two or more executive departments or two or more independent regulatory agencies, or all the functions thereof."
60. See Executive Order 12044, 43 Fed. Reg. 12661, 12670 (1978); Cohen, A Fight over Independence, National Journal, Dec. 31, 1977, at 2016.

"independent" agency, to take effect only if it is not "vetoed" by a resolution passed by both houses of Congress,[61] or by one house of Congress,[62] or by a committee,[63] or even by a single committee chairman.[64] The Legislative Appropriation Act of 1932,[65] which granted reorganization authority to the President, was the first important act to contain a "one-house veto" provision. Since then more than 300 legislative vetoes have been inserted in more than 200 Acts of Congress — *the vast majority of these since* 1970.[66] Every President since 1932 has argued that these veto provisions are unconstitutional,[67] but the Supreme Court has not ruled on their constitutionality.[68]

a. The Legality of the Veto

Those opposed to the veto argue their case on both technical and pragmatic grounds. Technically speaking, they claim that the legislative veto must be an exercise of legislative, executive, or judicial power, for the Constitution delegates none other to the federal government. If the power is executive or judicial, Congress cannot exercise it, for, with a few specifically mentioned exceptions,[69] the Constitution grants Congress only *legislative* power.[70] If the power is legislative, it must be exercised in the constitutionally prescribed manner. Article I, §1, vests "all legislative powers . . . in a Congress . . . which shall consist of a Senate and a House of Representatives" and . . . "all legislation must be passed by *both* houses." More-

61. See, e.g., Motor Vehicle & School Bus Safety Amendments of 1974, 15 U.S.C. §14106 (d)(1) (standards with respect to "air bags" promulgated by Secretary ineffective if both houses of Congress adopt resolution of disapproval).

62. See, e.g., the legislative veto in the Federal Salary Act of 1967, 2 U.S.C. §359(B), 81 Stat. 624, 644 (1967).

63. See, e.g., Dept. of Interior and Related Agencies Appropriations for Fiscal Year 1976, Pub. L. No. 94-165, tit. II, 89 Stat. 977, 993-994 (1975) (forestry service cannot close a regional office without consent of congressional committees on appropriations and agriculture).

64. See, e.g., Supplemental Appropriation Act for 1953, Pub. L. No. 82-547, §1413, 66 Stat. 637, 661 (1952) (Budget Director can amend a Budget Circular only with approval of the Chairman of the House Appropriations Committee).

65. 47 Stat. 382 (1932).

66. See Miller & Knapp, The Congressional Veto: Preserving the Constitutional Framework, 52 Ind. L.J. 367, 371 (1977).

67. See Watson, Congress Steps Out: A Look at Congressional Control of the Executive, 63 Calif. L. Rev. 983, 1002-1029 (1975).

68. The Court might have decided the issue in Buckley v. Valeo, 424 U.S. 1 (1976), but it avoided it. Justice White, in a concurrence, expressed the view that the legislative veto is constitutional. A contrary view was expressed in dissent by Judge McKinnon in Clark v. Valeo, 559 F.2d 642, 678 (D.C. Cir.), *aff'd sub nom.* Clark v. Kimmit, 431 U.S. 450 (1977). A closely divided Court of Claims sustained the validity of a one-house veto provision in a statute conferring upon the President authority to provide salary increases for federal judges. Atkins v. United States, 556 F.2d 1028 (Ct. Cl. 1977), *cert. denied,* 434 U.S. 1009 (1978). Its opinion was narrowly drawn by reference to the subject of government salaries and the particular features of the statute at issue. For discussion, see McGowan, Congress, Court, and Control of Delegated Power, 77 Colum. L. Rev. 1119 (1977).

69. E.g., the power to confirm presidential appointments.

70. See Buckley v. Valeo, n.68 supra; Springer v. Philippine Islands, 277 U.S. 189 (1928).

over, since the "presentation clause" (Art. 1, §7, cl. 3) specifically requires that "every order, Resolution, or Vote to which the Concurrence of" the two Houses "may be necessary" must be "presented to the President" for his signature or veto, a legislative act — such as the "veto" — is invalid without such presidential participation.

On pragmatic grounds, these opponents claim that legislative vetoes cause delay and uncertainty, and, most importantly, they vest too much power in one house, one committee, or one committee chairman. If a broad delegation of authority contains a legislative veto, the details of that authority would be filled, not by the administrative process nor by the legislative process (involving both houses and the President). Rather they may be developed by a single house (or a single committee) vetoing (or threatening to veto) contrary proposals made by the Executive. The one-house veto thus can exemplify that very delegation of legislative authority to subgroups within Congress — its exercise unchecked by the need to secure the approval of the Congress as a whole — that the principles of presidential participation and of bicameralism were intended to prevent.

Opponents also point to other devices within the power of Congress that can be used to check executive exercise under broadly delegated powers. For one thing, Congress can provide that the legislation delegating authority expire in a short time. Thus, to continue to exercise the authority, the President would have to seek the approval of both houses of Congress by requesting the enactment of new legislation. Alternatively, Congress can tailor its statutes more specifically, limiting the power that it fears the Executive will exercise in an undesirable way. Further, Congress can require the President, before taking action, to consult with congressional representatives, whose views will carry significant political weight. Congress can also delegate the power at issue to an appropriately constituted commission for final decision. Finally (as in the case of the Federal Rules of Civil Procedure), Congress can provide that implementation of the executive action will be delayed until it has time to consider it and to enact legislation preventing the Executive's action from taking effect. While these alternative "checks" give less power to the houses of Congress, they also avoid giving a single house (or committee) the power to decide on its own, for example, who shall and who shall not receive a tax rebate or be deported.[71]

The supporters of the veto dismiss the arguments based on the Constitution's language as overly technical. They claim that the "necessary and proper" clause gives Congress adequate authority to delegate legislative power to a single house or single committee. More importantly, they view the "veto" as a practical and desirable check on the growing power of the President. They note that except for Congress, the size of which is limited to a certain number of senators and representatives, government has increased exponentially since 1787. The knowledge

71. See Chadha v. Immigration & Naturalization Service, No. 77-1702 (9th Cir., argued Apr. 10, 1978). The Immigration and Naturalization Act gives the Attorney General authority to allow certain aliens to remain within the country unless, in an individual case, one house of Congress should pass a resolution to the contrary. 8 U.S.C. §1254(c)(2). As a practical matter, the Immigration Subcommittee Chairman wields this power.

explosion has made it virtually impossible for Congress to cope with the needs of the electorate. The replacement of a limited government with the welfare state has changed the role of our institutions, necessitating flexible responses to the problems of the time. The rise of the "Imperial Presidency" and the abuses of recent administrations make it imperative that Congress reassert its rightful position in the separation of powers scheme of the Constitution. Congress finds it difficult to generate detailed expert factual information and is therefore generally captive to whatever the Executive wishes to tell its members. Finally, there is a "rocking the boat" argument — if the congressional veto is held unconstitutional, enormous uncertainty will surround all of the statutes with such a provision.[72]

b. Applying the Legislative Veto to Independent Agencies

Congressman Levitas, Testimony Concerning H.R. 12048

Before House Rules Comm. (unpublished, June 1, 1976)

Legislation to control the administrative rulemaking process was the first bill I introduced upon coming to Congress last year. . . . Such legislation has drawn 140 cosponsors, which clearly indicates overwhelming sentiment in this Congress — among Republicans and Democrats, liberals, and conservatives, representing all parts of the country — for legislation aimed at bringing the bureaucracy back under control. . . .

Not surprisingly, the public is angry and frustrated, too often feeling that they have no choice but to obey a burdensome, costly, and perhaps ridiculous regulation promulgated by bureaucrats they do not know, have not elected, and cannot remove. . . .

Mr. Chairman, it is our duty to see that the public is given an input, through their elected representatives, in the promulgation of these rules. This is basic to restoring citizen confidence in government. . . .

This legislation sets an outside time limit of 90 calendar days (of continuous session) from the time of promulgation for congressional consideration of a rule. A rule shall not become effective if within 90 calendar days both houses adopt a concurrent resolution of disapproval, or if within 60 calendar days of promulgation one house adopts a resolution of disapproval and that resolution is not disapproved by the other house within 30 calendar days following its transfer to that body.

72. On the subject of the legislative veto, see Bruff & Gelhorn, Congressional Control of Administrative Regulation: A Study of Legislative Vetoes, 90 Harv. L. Rev. 1369 (1977); Ginnae, The Control of Federal Administration by Congressional Resolutions and Committees, 66 Harv. L. Rev. 569 (1953); Providing Reorganization Authority to the President: Hearings on H.R. 3131 Before a Subcommittee of the House Committee on Government Operations, 95th Cong., 1st Sess. 76 (statement of Prof. Tribe), 134 (statement of Prof. Philip B. Kurland) 1977); Miller & Knapp, supra n.66; McGowan, supra n.68; Stewart, Constitutionality of the Legislative Veto, 13 Harv. J. Legis. 593 (1976); Watson, supra n.67.

The procedure can be more expeditious than this. If, after 60 calendar days no committee of either house has reported or been discharged from further consideration of a concurrent disapproval resolution and neither house has adopted a resolution, the rule may go into effect immediately.

This legislation also gives the promulgating agency another chance to consider a regulation that Congress may deem questionable; either house may adopt a resolution of reconsideration within 90 calendar days after the date the rule was promulgated, which will prevent the rule from going into effect and will send the rule back to the agency, giving that agency 60 calendar days within which to re-promulgate the rule or withdraw it. If the agency does not act within 60 calendar days, the rule shall lapse. This same reconsideration procedure is also applicable to rules which were in effect at the time this becomes law.

If after 60 calendar days of promulgation no committee of either house has reported or been discharged from further consideration of a resolution or recon-sideration, the rule may go into effect at the end of this period, and if within 60 days a committee has reported or been discharged from further consideration of such a resolution, it may go into effect not sooner than 90 calendar days. Addition-ally, 180 days after passage of a resolution for reconsideration of a rule which has taken effect, the rule shall lapse unless repromulgated by the agency....

Mr. Chairman, I do not want to close without meeting one of the main objec-tions lodged against this legislation, viz., that Congress is incapable of dealing with the thousands of regulations promulgated annually. Some suggest vast numbers of additional staffers will have to be hired if this bill becomes law. This allegation is misleading and false. Already, for example, each committee of the House has a review and investigations subcommittee with the responsibility of monitoring a particular function of the bureaucracy. Also, the staff of these subcommittees al-ready review the activities of federal agencies every day and they already read and review the rules promulgated by the agencies. The problem is they can't do anything about them. As for workload, already over 14,000 bills and resolutions have been introduced since the beginning of the 94th Congress. This amount is almost twice the number of all rules and regulations promulgated in 1974. Only those bills and resolutions which were important and necessary have been acted on by a committee and eventually received full House attention. Such would be the case with those regulations that are affected under H.R. 12048.

Additionally, this criticism ignores what will perhaps be the greatest benefit from this legislation. The real benefit of this legislation will not be found in those few regulations which the Congress actually vetos, or directs the agencies to reconsider. Rather, it will be in the establishment of the unquestioned realization in each agency that they cannot promulgate regulations with impunity. They will be made to realize that they are accountable. And, Mr. Chairman, I believe it is axiomatic that we begin to see more carefully drafted regulations emerge from the bureaucracy; we will begin to see more attention paid to views of citizens during the comment period; we will begin to see a more responsive Executive Branch. This, then, will be the real benefit of this legislation. It will not destroy the administrative process, it will make it more responsive and the American public will be the winner.

Public Citizen Litigation Group, Testimony[73]

Before Senate Govt. Operations Comm. (May 20, 1976)

... In order to help the Committee appreciate these difficulties, we have tried to hypothesize a situation in which a mythical agency has decided to issue a rule and wants to put it into effect, and then to attempt to dramatize for the Committee some of the problems that the agency will encounter. In this dramatization, Mr. Robertson will assume the role of agency Chairman and I will assume that of the agency's General Counsel.

CHAIRMAN: What a great day! The Commission has finally reached unanimous agreement on the airline overbooking rule, and voted to issue it at once.

GENERAL
  COUNSEL: We have been working on this for years, but it's worth it because the rule is really a good one. . . .

CH: How soon can we put the rule in force?

GC: I don't know.

CH: What do you mean, you don't know. You are our lawyer. What does the law say?

GC: That's the problem. It doesn't say.

CH: But it must say.

GC: Let me try to explain. You see, Congress has been unhappy with some of the rules we have issued — not only our rules, but other agencies' as well. They now want to look them over before they go into force. So we have to wait 90 days for them to go into effect, to give Congress that opportunity. . . .

CH: So, why don't we just put in a date 90 days from today?

GC: It is a little more complicated than that. You see, the statute says 90 days continuous session, and that doesn't mean 90 calendar days. For instance, if either House is in adjournment for more than three days at a time, then those days off don't count. . . .

GC: I forgot to tell you about something else.

CH: What is that?

GC: If we don't make it by the end of this Congress, we have to start all over again next year since the continuous session rule is halted when Congress adjourns *sine die*. But there is a possibility that this could take less than the 90 days.

CH: It is terribly confusing. What is Congress going to do with these rules when we send them over?

GC: Well, they are going to review them on the merits.

CH: But we did that here. We had all kinds of public proceedings.

73. Improving Congressional Oversight of Federal Regulatory Agencies, Hearings before the Senate Government Operations Comm., 94th Cong., 2d Sess. 166-172 (1976) (statement of Alan B. Morrison and Reuben B. Robertson).

GC: But they are going to do it again.

CH: You mean that industry, the consumer groups, and all the federal agencies are going to get a second bite at the apple?

GC: It is worse than that, even — they don't even have to show up here at all. They can save their guns for Congress.

CH: Well, what standards are there by which the Congress might overrule us?

GC: There aren't any. They can do it for any reason — political, legal, constitutional, or simply because they don't like the agency.

CH: Well, is it at least an up-or-down vote?

GC: No, as I mentioned before, they can send it back and order reconsideration.

CH: Reconsideration? But we have already had extensive proceedings to reconsider the proposed rule.

GC: That doesn't matter. If either House passes a resolution for reconsideration, we have only 60 days to act or the rule automatically dies. And within those 60 days, we can either withdraw the rule or repromulgate it — with or without changes.

CH: Suppose we do repromulgate it. Have we finally completed the process?

GC: No way. The whole congressional review process starts over. . . .

CH: Well, can Congress pick and choose part of the rule — disapprove some of it and let the rest stay?

GC: Not as I understand this statute, although some of the other proposals would have allowed it. But I'm certain that the Congress could, if it wanted, let us know what aspects of the rule bother it.

CH: How will they possibly know what part we need, and whether we would have passed the rule at all absent the part that Congress doesn't like?

GC: They can always ask us. And in fact, we are probably going to have to defend the rule.

CH: You mean that we are going to have to send all our experts up to the Hill to explain to Congress and their staffs — in both Houses — why we did what we did?

GC: I'm afraid so. Probably the Commissioners will also be asked to testify.

CH: How can they possibly do this? Don't they understand that there are 60,000 pages of rules in the Federal Register every year — not to mention the hundreds of pages of backup materials for each rule — and that there are ten feet of the Code of Federal Regulations? Isn't Congress already so overworked that it can't get done everything on its agenda? Why do they want to do this?

GC: I really don't have any idea.

CH: Say, what about those statutes that Congress is writing, telling us we have to promulgate certain rules within fixed times? Is this one of those cases?

GC: No, this isn't.

CH: Well, just what are we supposed to do in those cases? I guess if you send the rule to Congress in the time prescribed, you are OK.

CH: Sort of makes a mockery of those firm statutory deadlines doesn't it?

GC: I won't dispute that one with you.

CH: Tell me about review of these rules by the courts. How does that fit in?

GC: Well, in the first place, it really gives everyone a third bite of the apple.

CH: I understand that. What I want to know is, when are the court proceedings to take place?

GC: I was kind of wondering about that myself. The law is not at all clear. Our statute says if you don't like a final rule we have issued, you must petition the court for review within 60 days. Once that is done, the cases tend to move right along, since the judges don't like all this criticism about backlogs.

CH: Anybody who doesn't like our rule for any reason can appeal it in court, at the same time as they stir up opposition in Congress. Are we going to have to spend a lot of time writing court briefs while Congress is reviewing the matter?

GC: Seems sort of silly, doesn't it? On the other hand, it seems sort of silly to wait until Congress gets finished, and then add court delay on top of that.

CH: You know, almost every time we put a rule into effect, somebody is asking us or the court for a stay. Isn't it going to be pretty hard to object to another delay after all of these delays?

GC: That is not the part of my job I think I am going to relish. It certainly undercuts all of our efforts to eliminate regulatory delay, which has been such a source of criticism.

CH: One more question and I will let you go back to work. Why are we bothering to issue any rules at all?

GC: Maybe that is the whole point of the statute.

Before making up your mind about the wisdom of the proposals such as the legislative veto or deciding how much independence from the President agencies ought to have, read Section D of Chapter 3, which considers proposals that would make the agencies less independent either of Congress or of the President.

3

The Problem of
Administrative
Discretion

The object of this chapter is to acquaint you with some of the criticism of the administrative process — criticism based upon the claim that the agency has not exercised its discretion wisely. The chapter will then survey a range of proposals aimed at improving agency performance. Some of these would seek to limit agency discretion to increase the likelihood that it will be soundly exercised.

The chapter's theme is administrative discretion. Does the administrator exercise too wide a discretion? How can he be led to exercise it more wisely? This theme is sounded throughout the rest of this book and throughout the body of opinions making up much of modern administrative law.

A. The Concentration of Unchecked Power

The materials in the preceding chapter illustrate the basic fact that courts have declined to interpose significant constitutional checks on the legislature's creation of administrative agencies that combine, in an unprecedented manner and degree, power traditionally distributed among the three branches recognized in the federal Constitution and most state constitutions. Agencies have been permitted to exercise delegated legislative power, to assume responsibility for adjudication formerly performed by courts, and to exercise prosecutorial and managerial functions while isolated from direct control by the chief executive. This circumstance has created two basic difficulties at the level of constitutional or political theory.

The first difficulty is one of accountability or legitimacy. The amalgam that is the administrative agency enjoys no constitutional status, nor does it enjoy the modes of validation that invest the three traditional branches. Unlike legislators and the Chief Executive, administrators are not elected by the citizenry and are not held accountable to the electorate. Nor do they enjoy the life tenure, insulation from partisan politics, and traditional professional commitment to an ideal of principled decisionmaking that serve to legitimate the judicial power. In the words of President Franklin Roosevelt's Committee on Administrative Management, they are effectively a "headless 'fourth branch' " of government.[1] One scholar has found that, because of these and other factors, the administrative process in the United States has suffered from a near-perpetual crisis of legitimacy that has eroded public confidence in administrators and hindered the effective discharge of their duties.[2]

During the New Deal, champions of the administrative process supposed that there was an objective "public interest" that could be ascertained and implemented by expert administrators, skilled and experienced, provided they were given generous powers. Today we are less certain that "experts" will determine and execute what is in the "public interest." We are apt to be skeptical of the existence of an objective "public interest," and view most important issues of administrative policy as a choice among competing economic interests and social values. Because technical experts have no special claim to wisdom in such choices, the current tendency to view administrative issues as problems of social choice has exacerbated the problem of agency legitimacy.[3]

A second basic problem is that administrative agencies *combine* powers previously distributed among the three traditional branches. As already noted, the constitutional separation of powers among the traditional branches was never watertight (see Chapter 2.E supra). But agencies such as the Federal Trade Commission meld prosecuting, legislating, judging, and managing functions in a far more complete and systematic fashion than the original structure of the Constitution would admit. The Framers' purpose in separating the powers of government among the various branches can be viewed from two perspectives.[4] On the other hand, it serves to interpose internal checks on the exercise of governmental authority in order to diminish the total effective power that the government can exert against the citizenry — to prevent tyranny. Administrative agencies in the United States have not threatened a societywide administrative dictatorship because their powers, while combined, have generally been limited to defined industries such as regulation of railroads) or subject matter (such as deceptive or anticompetitive trade practices).[5] However, those subject to administrative regulation have often complained bitterly of the tyranny of administrators who are at the same time prosecutor, judge, and jury. In addition, the administrative combination tends to erode the certainty,

---

1. Report of the President's Committee on Administrative Management 36 (1937). The Committee's criticism was directed in particular at the independent regulatory commissions, but experience teaches that agencies nominally accountable to the President often enjoy considerable de facto autonomy.

2. Freedman, Crisis and Legitimacy in the Administrative Process, 27 Stan. L. Rev. 1041 (1975).

3. See Stewart, The Reformation of American Administrative Law, 88 Harv. L. Rev. 1667, 1682-1685 (1975).

4. For a far more complete historical and theoretical analysis of the separation of powers principles, see M. Vile, Constitutionalism and the Separation of Powers (1967); G. Wood, The Creation of the American Republic 1776-1787 (1969).

5. A notable exception to this generalization is the National Recovery Administration, created early in the New Deal and invested with sweeping powers over the economy. See Chapter 2, pp. 61-67 supra.

predictability, and impartiality arguably inherent in a system in which one group of men and women makes laws and another applies them.

A further purpose of the separation of powers among the branches is to diffuse governmental decisionmaking authority, thus rendering it more difficult for some private interest group to capture the machinery of government in order to advance its economic or social welfare at the expense of other interest groups. Madison, in The Federalist No. 10, eloquently portrays society as an amalgam of "factions" or interest groups competing for wealth. If "men were angels, there would be no need of government," but man's acquisitive appetite requires the restraint of civil authority. However, the creation of government gives rise to the fresh danger that it will be taken over by one faction in order to extort wealth from another. The separation of powers within government, as well as the decentralization of power through a federal structure of government, were calculated to minimize the danger of "capture" of the government machinery by a powerful faction or interest group, and to promote the adoption of policies broadly acceptable to a wide range of social and economic interests.

Administrative agencies threaten this system of safeguards by combining powers in ways that threaten to short-circuit the checks relied upon by Madison. Administrators often have the power to exercise governmental authority so as to benefit directly specific social or economic groups. Agencies often reallocate wealth, not only directly, as in the administration of the Internal Revenue Code or the administrative allocation of scarce welfare resources such as public housing, but also indirectly through regulatory policies that favor some consumers or firms at the expense of others.[6] Because agency decisionmaking is not highly visible and is not direcly subject to the electoral check, there is a danger that the redistributive authority of agencies will be exercised in favor of a limited group of organized interests with a special stake in an agency's policies.

The requirement that agencies hold hearings in which parties affected by the agency's action can be represented by counsel may be viewed as an effort to regularize this struggle for advantage within a legislative "adversary" framework. However, it has often been asserted that wealthy and well-organized interests are favored in this form of struggle, resulting in "capture" of the agency by regulated or client firms.[7] Another view is that the efforts of various private groups to advance their interests through the administrative process to a large degree simply offset one another, and that the considerable social resources involved in formal administrative proceedings, fees of lawyers and experts, and costly delays are a deadweight loss serving no useful purpose.

But what heed can we give these objections to the administrative process if it is a practical necessity of modern government? James Landis asserted that "The administrative process is, in essence, our generation's answer to the inadequacy of

6. See Posner, Taxation by Regulation, 2 Bell J. Econ. & Mgmt. Sci. 22 (1971); Peltzman, Toward a More General Theory of Regulation, 19 J. Law & Econ. 211 (1976).
7. See the discussion in Posner, Theories of Economic Regulation, 4 Bell J. Econ. & Mgmt. Sci. 335 (1973).

the judicial and legislative processes." [8] Has not the verdict of history vindicated that view? There are at present some 87 *major* regulatory agencies in the federal government alone,[9] and hundreds of thousands more in state and local government. Congress has in the last six years authorized three to five major new regulatory programs each year.

Is it possible to abolish administrative agencies and return to the tripartite frame of government celebrated in the eighteenth century? If not, is it possible to serve the basic purposes of the Founders through alternative institutional arrangements? Are there potential mechanisms in a large, industrialized society in an era of "positive" government, to afford the administrative process a greater measure of formal accountability and legitimacy and promote the basic purposes underlying the Framers' separation of powers? Or are these ideals merely anachronistic vestiges of an earlier era, wholly unrealistic and inappropriate today? You should bear these fundamental questions in mind throughout the materials that follow.

B. Criticisms of the Regulatory Process

Few students of the subject today would share Dean Landis' optimism about the potential use of the administrative agency. Federal administrative agencies have been subjected to an increasing barrage of criticism emanating from a variety of philosophical and political positions. Economists are concerned with the inefficiency, waste, and shortages they see caused by certain forms of regulation. Businessmen complain of unreasonable administrative burdens and lack of coordination among agencies. Consumer groups complain that regulation is ineffective. All this criticism centers around the charge that the agencies have failed effectively to discharge their mission of regulating given sectors of the economy to promote the public interest. The excerpts which follow are intended to give you a modest sampling of views on agency "failure." [10] You should assess critically the differences of opinion in the excerpts on whether the agencies have "failed," the nature of the "failure," and the locus of responsibility for "failure." You should also consider what solutions might appropriately be devised to remedy these perceived failures. In particular, is "failure" attributable to the anomalous constitutional position of the agencies, which exercise combined powers without formal accountability? Can "failure" be eliminated by altered institutional arrangements or modifications in

8. Landis, The Administrative Process 46 (1938).

9. The Challenge of Regulatory Reform, Report to the President from the Domestic Council Review Groups on Regulatory Reform 47-58 (1977). This count excludes agencies which establish criteria for eligibility to receive federal grants or which determine design or engineering standards for government purchases, and also excludes vast numbers of nonregulatory agencies.

10. The excerpts here reflect the views of legislators, executive branch adviser groups, and commentators outside government. Later in these materials we will encounter similar views by judges that agencies have failed their responsibilities, and assess the judicial response.

judicial doctrines? Or do criticisms of administrative "failure" simply reflect a disagreement with Congress's policy judgments in directing agencies to deal with social problems, in which case the only remedy is to change those congressional policies through the political process?

Bernstein, Testimony[11]

84th Cong., 2d Sess., pt. 1, vol. 1, at 60-64 (1956)

A review of American regulatory experience since the 1880's reveals the principal characteristics of the independent commission:

The general public knows very little and cares very little about independent commissions. Public concern with regulation usually declines sharply after the establishment of a commission. The regulatory problems are themselves so intricate and complex that they defy easy comprehension. The lawyers, moreover, have succeeded in turning regulation into a highly technical, legalistic process that presumably lies outside the layman's area of experience. And finally, attempts to take regulation out of politics by assigning regulatory responsibilities to commissions have failed to insulate regulation from politics, but they have removed the commissions from the public spotlight and have allowed public support for regulation to wither and die.

Commissions operate in hostile environments, and their regulatory policies become conditional upon the acceptance of regulation by the regulated groups. In the long run, a commission is forced to come to terms with the regulated groups as a condition of its survival.

The vaunted independence of regulatory commissions is a device to escape popular politics. It facilitates maximum responsiveness of a commission to the demands and interests of regulated groups. It provides maximum freedom from exposure to popular political forces. It tends to alienate the commission from sources of political strength in Congress and the Presidency. It reduces the effectiveness of regulation.

... [Commissions] gradually lose their sense of mission. In their mature stage, their concept of the public interest is hardly distinguishable from the view of the dominant regulated interests.

... The principal rationale for the creation of independent commissions has been the restriction of certain abusive business practices. The administrative apparatus employed by the commissions centered upon the case-by-case consideration of separate issues and problems in a manner closely approximating the behavior of a judge and jury in a court of law. As regulation was patterned more and more upon the judicial model and commissioners looked upon themselves increasingly as administrative judges, they tended to become passive and judge-like in the exercise

11. Hearings Before the Antitrust Subcomm. of the House Judiciary Comm. on Monopoly Problems in Regulated Industries, Statement of Marver S. Bernstein, Dean, Woodrow Wilson School of Public and International Affairs, Princeton University.

of their regulatory functions. They waited for cases and parties to present themselves; they did not seek out cases or make independent investigations and inquiries. They gradually allowed the private parties to control their flow of business by confining themselves to the cases brought before them. They lost their initiative to the private parties subject to regulation. They became dependent upon parties adversely affected by regulation or by the behavior of the regulated business firms for knowledge of alleged violations. Gradually their preoccupation with individual cases made them incapable of planning their work effectively, and they lost their capacity to promote the public interest aggressively. They could not plan their activities and allowed backlogs of cases to develop and increase.

Not only did the case method and judicial model place the commissions on the defensive, but the method itself became grossly disadvantageous to small firms. It required a special lawyer's vocabulary, expensive legal counsel, and specialized knowledge of complex matters to carry a case before the commission. The procedure was involved and complicated. While it was designed in part to protect private parties against arbitrary and capricious action by the Government, it also generated extraordinary delays in disposing of cases and was inordinately expensive for small firms and small businessmen. Inevitably, the heavy reliance of the commission upon the judicial hearing procedure helped the large firm and hindered the small firm. . . .

. . . As an independent agency affecting a limited clientele, it operates in relative obscurity. Most commissions prefer to approach their regulatory programs as matters entirely separate from the current course of political and economic development. Independence to them means freedom from presidential supervision and freedom to operate as wholly separate and independent entities. The atmosphere in which they operate, therefore, is not the kind of atmosphere that is congenial to the promotion of vigorous competition. In their effort to escape popular politics, they emphasize their friendly relation to the dominant regulated groups. The maintenance of the position of these dominant regulated groups becomes, in the eyes of the commission, the rock upon which the public interest rests.

For these reasons it is impossible to avoid the conclusion that regulation of particular industries by independent commissions tends to destroy rather than promote competition.

Jaffe, The Independent Agency — A New Scapegoat

(Book Review of M. Bernstein, Regulating Business by Independent Commission) 65 Yale L.J. 1068 (1956)

The Independent Regulatory Commission is under heavy attack. The offense is being led by non-lawyers, among whom are Professor Marver S. Bernstein of Princeton and Professor Horace M. Gray of the University of Illinois. The Independent Commission has, as a matter of fact, been the bête noire of political scientists for many years, but the present attack is more comprehensive, more circumstantial and more effective. The independent agency has on the other hand been the darling of the lawyer, but some of them are beginning to be fickle. There can be no question in my mind that a re-evaluation of the role of the independent agency is indicated. I think it is clear, as Professor Bernstein's book demonstrates, that the case for the independent agency has been grossly overstated. But the present attack goes far beyond deflation. It makes the agencies a scapegoat. The battle against them is being fought with slogans: "industry-oriented," "politically irresponsible," etc. Lawyers shouted "Hosanna" in 1938 and saw the Promised Land revealed by Joseph ("Moses") Eastman.[12] Now it is the turn of the Jeremiahs: the Promised Land has become a place of abominations. The agencies have betrayed reform and abandoned decency. Perhaps it is inevitable that Thought and History should move in this violently dialectic fashion, swinging from illusion to disillusion, from battlecry to battlecry, from slogan to slogan. These oscillatory lunges may be necessary to unsettle the vast mass of social inertia; but I think that we academicians should deal somewhat more subtly, more justly if you will, with causes and effects, with the description and evaluation of social consequence, and finally, with judgment.

Americans are a people not notably endowed with the historic sense. They are given to enthusiasm, and that is good because enthusiasm moves mountains. But enthusiasts are prone to violent disillusion: mountains are sometimes stubborn, and even when they yield the view on the other side may be displeasing. Although certainly exaggerated, the hopes set upon administrative agencies and particularly independent agencies were more completely realized than anyone had a right to expect, and it is just this which is part of the trouble. We find ourselves with vaguely felt and undefinable challenges. We are miserably bereft of a program for reform. The independent agency, ironically enough, is a microcosm of our present prosperous predicament — liking not what we see, we attribute our malaise to "industry-orientation" or some other half truth. . . .

The campaign by the political scientists against the independent agency has proceeded on both constitutional and political grounds. The Constitution, it is argued, requires that all executive functions be subject to presidential control. The President's Committee on Administrative Management somewhat rashly, but picturesquely, called the independent agency "the headless fourth branch." They were forthwith accused by lawyers of conceptualism. Lawyers have been partial to these agencies. Liberal lawyers until their current disillusion believed that reforms could be more effectively realized outside of politics. In the fruitfully naive view of that era, "expertness" was envisaged as an objective force which if left to itself would inevitably produce reform. Conservative lawyers preferred the independent agency because it emphasized judicialization. This they hoped would act, if not at once at least in time, as a brake on power. And all lawyers could find common ground for their preference in the value set on formally rationalized action and on continuity. But the autonomy of "expertness" as an objective de-

12. Ed. note: Eastman was a member of the ICC in the 1920s and 1930s and was a prominent champion of the administrative process.

terminant of policy is, I am afraid, an illusion. Policy-making *is* politics. Policy should, to be sure, be fairly and decently made; it should have continuity and dependability. But nothing that I have seen shows that these criteria are less honored and observed in executive agencies, at least when they are required by statute to observe procedural protections. . . .

In reply to this argument, lawyers have maintained that the notion of presidential coordination is a myth. No man or organization representing him is capable of coordinating the multifarious conflicts entrusted to government resolution. A certain amount of unresolved conflict is inevitable, perhaps valuable. It attests to the fundamentally indeterminate, pluralistic character of our complex system. Though these things may be true, they do not seem to me to be an adequate answer. The question is not of complete coordination, but of the availability of the power to coordinate policy in a given area at a given time. The practical difficulties of coordination hardly warrant, except for strong and well-considered reasons, the creation of additional obstacles. . . .

The political argument is based on an attempt to document the charge that the independent agency, having no duly constituted master, is falling under the domination of private interests, characteristically the interests whose activities it is supposed to regulate. This is the so-called phenomenon of the industry-oriented agency. . . . It is to my mind not a little curious that the critics limit their examination of this phenomenon to the independent agency. I would suppose that it was necessary first to establish the executive agencies as the norm and then to show how the independent agencies tend to depart from that norm. Yet anyone who follows the activities of the Department of Agriculture, for example, comes to feel (though this too is no doubt an exaggeration) that the Department is a glorified farmer's lobby. An examination of the milk licensing activities suggests the enormous power of the farm cooperatives. It is certainly not my thesis that all departments, nor for that matter all independent agencies, are industry-oriented; but the current demonstration with respect to the independent agency is neither scientific nor scrupulous.

The distortion in the attack goes much deeper. As I see it the critics' real quarrel, if they would but recognize and admit it, is with Congress. The Interstate Commerce Commission, so much used as an example, is attacked for proceeding along the lines of its congressional mandate and at the same time for failing to create a mandate which neither Congress nor anyone else has been able to formulate. The Commission is criticized for being "railroad minded" and monopolistic. But can anyone find in the legislation of 1935 and 1940 an intention to establish competition as the presumptive norm of transportation regulation? Joseph Eastman, the intellectual godfather of that legislation, insisted that "free-for-all competition has never worked successfully, either here or elsewhere. It has been tried and found wanting." "Constructive coordination" is to be preferred to "destructive competition." The ICC is "to find the work which each form of transportation can do best and endeavor to build up a national transportation system in which the various agencies will function with more regard to correlation and less to competition and with a minimum of waste." Everyone seems to be

agreed that the railroads and the large truckers were the dominant forces in pro-
curing that legislation. Was this in the name of competition? When somewhat
later the Supreme Court came close to holding that railroad rate conferences were
a violation of the antitrust laws, Congress immediately immunized them. Was
this another indication of a congressional mandate for competition? . . . The record
indicates that the ICC has liberally authorized a vast increase in trucking facilities.
The statistics show that the rate of growth in common carrier trucking has
enormously exceeded that in railroading. It is indeed arguable that trucks have
been permitted to take traffic from the railroads, even though our highways are
overburdened and rail transportation is less expensive. Under the jurisprudence of
the ICC the doctrine of protecting established "shares" of the traffic is now
working as much in favor of the trucks as of the railroads. This kind of policy may
be as doubtful as you please, but it is hard to see how an agency with a mandate
to "coordinate" can fail to arrive at some such doctrine.

The greatest weakness of the critics, to my mind, is that they have failed to
face honestly and wholeheartedly the most serious difficulty facing regulation today.
That difficulty is the radical lack of a meaningful statutory policy in many of the
areas where the independent agencies function. In some cases the policy has become obsolete. The coordination theory of the 1930's, for example, was based on
the economic defeatism of that era. It was assumed that our economy had become
static, and that therefore the economic problem was one primarily of allocating
resources. Eastman was prepared to find what each means of transportation could
do best, as if that were a discoverable quantity in a static world. Yet the tremendously dynamic character of our economic system has substantially altered most
of the traditional premises for resolving the transportation problems. The constant
engineering changes, the breakup of old monopolistic situations because of new
modes of carriage, the tremendous increase in freights — all of these raise questions
both as to the desirability and feasibility of close regulation.

In radio the situation is somewhat different, for there never has been a statutory policy. The FCC was simply told to go ahead and regulate in "the public
interest." I have studied for some years the attempts of the Commission to deal,
in the absence of a congressional or popular mandate, with the baffling and mani-
fold complexities in that field. The Commission has lacked foresight, has often
been timid and has sometimes been subservient, but to my mind this is the result
of the absence of congressional guidance. I conclude that it is much easier to
criticize than to come up with an administrative program that could command
support. It was long ago pointed out by Herbert Croly, as Professor Bernstein re-
minds us, that regulation creates a basic problem because it divides the responsibility for management. The gist of the difficulty, as I see it, is that the regulator
accepts no responsibility for the ultimate success of the enterprise, yet his interference discourages entrepreneurial initiative and diminishes the sense of responsibility. If the regulator is given a clear mandate to remove a perceived evil, he has
an adequate and limited basis for validating his interference with management, and
management has a basis for calculating the effects of the interference. But in the
absence of a clear mandate, it is not only inevitable, but appropriate that regulation

take the form of an accommodation in which industry is the senior partner. This is the essence of "industry-orientation."

There is very little in our history, I think, to indicate that an executive agency will be much different from an independent agency in periods when public opinion or statutory policy is slack, indeterminate, or lacking in conviction. The odds are that it will respond in much the same way to the climate of opinion.... It is, I think, demonstrable that when a new reform is to be undertaken, an independent agency may provide a hard-hitting, single-minded authority, oblivious to the immediate partisan requirements of the Administration. The Labor Board proved this up to the hilt. In time, the immediate problem solved, the agency loses its zest and settles into routine. What institution does not? It may be a shade easier at this later stage to infuse the executive agency with a new spirit, for in the absence of an adequate congressional mandate, there is perhaps a better chance that the executive will be able to evolve and gain support for a fresh approach. But if one has a "set" in favor of vigorous regulation, it is pretty much a matter of chance whether he will find it in executive or independent agencies....

I would agree with Professor Bernstein that we cannot look to the agencies for new thinking. In the early stages of its history while still engaged in dealing with the specific problem ("the evil") that brought it into being, the independent agency can be relied upon to fight for a program in and out of Congress. But once it has reduced the urgency of the problem and has, as it were, created its own world, it is apt to become a defender of the status quo. It looks upon its work and finds it good. We must therefore look elsewhere for new policy — to the President, to one of the executive departments, to Congress and its committees. The independent agency may even throw its force against the presidential initiative and provide leadership for the status quo....

One may, then, follow Professor Bernstein's argument that the merits of the independent agency have been exaggerated. But when he loads upon it all of the frustrations of his Utopian yearning, he is transcending analysis and providing himself with a sacrificial scapegoat.

[For a more recent restatement of Professor Jaffe's views, see Jaffe, The Illusion of the Ideal Administration, 86 Harv. L. Rev. 1183 (1973).]

Fellmeth et al., The Interstate Commerce Omission

(The Nader Report on the ICC) 311-325 (1970)

FINDINGS

THE COMMISSION (1)

Commission appointments have been made almost solely on the basis of political considerations, resulting in a Commission that is unqualified and weak.

Every Commissioner has a political sponsor. The position, despite its critical importance, has become a political payoff, an elephant's graveyard for political hacks.

The only three Commissioners with any experience received their experience from the industry side.

There is no evidence that any of the Commissioners are even capable of developing that "sharpness" between regulators and regulated which is a prerequisite to regulation in the public interest.

The ICC is now primarily a forum at which private transportation interests settle their disputes.

The ICC chooses to define policy through its massive caseload, asserting itself directly only through a mere dozen or so rule-making proceedings each year.

Only if the settlement of special interest disputes over the allocation of the transportation market complements the needs of the public, is the public interest served.

Costs of making and presenting a case (aside from ICC filing fees) are substantial — even for the minor expansion of operating authority — and thus prohibitive for the public and for small businesses.

As a passive forum, the ICC has failed to provide for any useful mechanism for the representation of the public interest in the development of the record.

The Commission's upper staff has a collective personality of extreme conservatism, with all policy recommendations made from within the framework of conditions extant in the 1930's.

The average tenure in the ICC of Bureau Directors is thirty-one years.

Any suggestion to encourage some competition is met with stock answers: "The result would be chaos," or "We remember the 1930's."

Further precluding the possibility of a public interest perspective is the Commission's relationship with industry — which can be generously described as "intimate."

Two hundred twenty trips by Commissioners in three years. According to one Commissioner, 25 per cent of expenses paid by industry.

Pleasure cruises, with industry jets standing by for the Commissioner's use.

An incredible waste of time with 1 million words in three years of speeches written for industry by ICC staff, and extensive travel to meet with industry executives (all well represented in Washington) in the surface transportation meccas of Puerto Rico, Hawaii, and the Bahamas.

The ICC has numerous advisory groups to help set policy at the initial, formative stages within the agency — including not one consumer or consumer representative.

Job interchange levels between the ICC and industry have grown, with "deferred bribes" becoming the norm.

Many officials admit they receive job offers from industry while in government employ.

In the past decade all but one Commissioner who has left the agency has ended up working for a carrier or a carrier association directly, or indirectly as an ICC Practitioner. Many of these men are unqualified in the field and have been chosen because of their connections back in the agency, or as a reward.

A high rate of job interchange at the middle and lower staff levels is more understandable than at the top levels, since most young attorneys view the ICC as a training ground for later transportation industry practice.

Congressional oversight has not affected agency policy.

Hearings are considered "part of the game," and hostile questions are a necessary part of the hearing process.

Congressional oversight committees are understaffed.

Transportation industry investment in the campaigns of Congressmen, particularly on the House side, is substantial.

Much legislation recommended by the ICC originates with industry....

The ICC has failed to consider the import of major rail mergers on the shipping public, despite the legal requirement to do so, and has generally rubber-stamped merger requests.

The ICC has constructed substantial barriers to entry into the transportation industry, barriers which protect the inefficient.

Carriers are not granted certification so long as existing carriers are potentially able to carry the traffic.

Offering more efficient, faster service, more responsive to the needs of shippers, is not considered relevant to certification.

The offer of lower rates to shippers cannot be considered as a factor in determining the adequacy of existing service under present ICC procedure.

The great bulk of the ICC's caseload consists of requests by carriers for the privilege of expanding their respective ICC-protected markets into new commodities and along new routes.

ICC justifications for providing entry protection for each carrier have no basis in fact....

ICC regulatory policies have in fact increased concentration, made intramodal collusive pricing easier, reduced incentives for increased efficiency, facilitated rate discrimination, and lessened service competition.

Most evidence and studies indicate the desirability of a deregulated market system.

The ICC's minimum rate powers are used to protect inefficient carriers and modes from competition....

Report of the President's Advisory Council on
Executive Organization, A New Regulatory Framework[13]

pp. 4-7 (1971)

FINDINGS

The regulatory commissions are not sufficiently accountable for their actions to either the Congress or the President because of the degree of their independence and remoteness in practice from those constitutional branches of government. Regulatory activities, therefore, are not adequately supported and are not effectively coordinated with national policy goals.

Inherent deficiencies in the commission form of organization prevent the commissions from responding effectively to changes in industry structure, technology, economic trends, and public needs.

Deficiencies in the performance of the regulatory commissions are partly due to the difficulty of attracting highly qualified commissioners and retaining executive staff. Even able administrators have difficulty in serving as coequals on collegial commissions.

— While there are notable exceptions, it is difficult to attract to regulatory positions men of skill in administration and breadth of perspective largely because of the procedures and traditions associated with appointment to the regulatory commissions.

— Given these traditions and the shared responsibility of the collegial form, it is not likely that commission positions will generate greater interest in the future.

Certain judicial activities of the commissions conflict with their policymaking responsibilities and generate an organizational environment inimical to regulatory efficiency and constructive response to industry and the public.

— Many commissions engage excessively in case-by-case adjucation as a basis for policy formulation rather than using less formal procedures such as exchanges of written or oral information, informal regulatory guidance, or rulemaking.

— The judicial cast of agency review proceedings places too great an emphasis on legal perspectives to the detriment of economic, financial, technical, and social perspectives. One result is a high level of legal skill among agency professionals and commissioners, but generally insufficient capability in other disciplines.

— The judicial cast of agency review proceedings delays final administrative determinations and invites dilatory appeals.

13. The Council, consisting of five businessmen and the former Dean of the Harvard Business School, was chaired by Roy L. Ash, then Chairman of Litton Industries, and later Director of the Office of Management and Budget.

— Overjudicialization encumbers the time and energies of commissioners and staff, causes undue case backlogs, imposes high costs upon litigants, prevents anticipatory action through rulemaking, deters informal settlements, and precludes coordination of agency policy and priorities with those of the executive branch.

Certain functional responsibilities are inappropriately distributed among the various commissions.

— Responsibility for regulation of transportation is distributed among the ICC, CAB, and FMC, impeding formulation of broader regulatory policy covering the several transportation modes and coordination within the Department of Transportation, and thus forestalling consistency in national transportation policy.
— Responsibility for promotion of transportation, vested in some regulatory commissions, conflicts with the regulatory activity of those agencies.
— Combination of antitrust enforcement and consumer protection in the FTC deprives that agency of a central purpose, fostering an uncertainty of emphasis as between its functions, inordinate delay, and preoccupation with routine matters.
— Regulation of public utility holding companies by the SEC is no longer best performed by that agency. Regulatory expertise regarding public utility holding companies rests with the FPC.

RECOMMENDATIONS

To assure coordination of regulatory matters with national policy goals, to improve the management efficiency of regulatory functions, to improve accountability to the Congress and the executive branch, and to increase the probability of superior leadership for regulatory activities, the transportation, power, securities, and consumer protection regulatory functions should be administered by single administrators, appointed by the President. These functions should be performed by agencies respectively designated: Transportation Regulatory Agency, Federal Power Agency, Securities and Exchange Agency, and Federal Trade Practices Agency.

— The authority and responsibility attending the single administrator form should enable the agencies to attract and retain the most highly qualified administrators and executive staffs.
— Unambiguous placement of authority for agency policy and operations in a single administrator should increase accountability to both the Congress and the President.
— Agency work should be expedited by utilizing more effective administrative techniques made possible by one-man management of agency activities.

The communications regulatory function and the antitrust enforcement function should, as now, be carried out by multimember bodies for reasons supervening the advantages of a single administrator. The FCC should be reduced in size from seven to five members, to serve 5-year terms.

To prevent the overjudicialization of agency procedures and attitudes and to assure comprehensive and anticipatory policymaking, internal agency review of proceedings should be limited in time and focused primarily on the consistency of the decision with agency policy. Appeals from final agency decisions should be heard by an Administrative Court of the United States.

— The Administrative Court should review appeals by an aggrieved party from final agency determinations of the transportation, securities and power agencies. Decisions of the antitrust, trade practices, and communications agencies would be reviewed in the Federal courts as they are today.
— The court should consist of as many as 15 judges, appointed by the President and confirmed by the Senate for terms sufficiently long as to attract men of quality. We suggest 15-year staggered terms, with judges sitting in three-man panels for each case reviewed by the court.

Certain functional responsibilities of the agencies should be realigned.

— To reflect the increasing interdependence of the structure, economics, and technology of the technology of the transportation modes, regulatory responsibilities of the ICC, CAB, and the FMC should be combined within a new Transportation Regulatory Agency.
— To correct the conflict inherent in performing regulatory and promotional functions in the same agency, the promotional subsidy-granting activities of the CAB should be transferred to the Department of Transportation.
— To assure that each of its missions is more effectively performed, the FTC's consumer protection responsibilities should be vested in a new Federal Trade Practices Agency and its antitrust enforcement responsibilities should be vested in a new Federal Antitrust Board. The Board should consist of a chairman and two economist members, each appointed by the President with the consent of the Senate.
— To provide an organizational placement which better reflects current realities, the regulatory responsibilities of the SEC under the Public Utility Holding Company Act should be transferred to the Federal Power Agency.

Posner, The Federal Trade Commission

37 U. Chi. L. Rev. 47, 82-89 (1969)

III. THE CAUSES OF REGULATORY FAILURE

If the Commission's prior critics are to be believed — and there is no reason to doubt the descriptive accuracy of their studies — the Commission's performance has been gravely deficient throughout its entire history. In the light of this extraordinary record, the critics' determination to regard the agency's failings as accidental and readily remediable, their faith that minor changes in organizational structure or personnel or procedures will turn the trick, does not convince. With failings so palpable and the correctives so obvious and relatively easy to implement, why has nothing been done? The answer is that many of the suggested correctives *have* been applied [14] and have had little effect, because they were addressed to unimportant symptoms rather than to the underlying causes. We are now in a position to discuss some of those causes. The foremost one is that the administrative process appears to have no constructive contribution to make to combatting either fraud or monopoly. When it is introduced into these areas the principal effect is to create undesirable biases and inefficiencies in the formulation and application of policy.

In addition, the ability of the FTC to promote the public interest is impaired by its dependence on Congress. Whatever the legal or constitutional merits of the view that the FTC is an "arm of Congress," the phrase describes the political realities accurately. Why many agencies both inside and outside the Executive Branch are extremely subservient while others, such as the Department of Justice, are not is something of a mystery. A part of the answer, perhaps, is that the size and complexity of the federal government preclude the establishment of an effective presidential presence other than at a few key points. Elsewhere power gravitates to Congress. Now Congress is organized in a manner calculated to protect and foster parochial economic interests at the expense of the larger consumer interest. Each Congressman represents a particular geographical area, often quite small. The welfare of his constituents may depend disproportionately on a few key industries. The promotion of these industries becomes one of his most important duties as a representative of the district. The consequent distortions in economic legislation are aggravated by the fact that power is unevenly distributed among the members of Congress. An important committee chairman has a great deal of power to advance the interests of businesses located in his district, however unimportant those interests may be from a national standpoint. Moreover, in bidding for the favor of members of Congress, consumers are at a disadvantage in comparison with trade associations, labor unions, and other more familiar pressure groups. Consumers form too large, diffuse, and heterogeneous a group to organize effectively for the presentation of demands to their representatives. It is hardly surprising that so much of our economic legislation is protectionist in character.

14. For example, the Commission now writes opinions in virtually all adjudicative matters; opinion writing is now the responsibility of each Commssoner's office, rather than of a central pool of opinion writers; the rules of practice and procedure have been vastly improved; Commission meeting procedures have been placed on a more efficient basis; the Commission has experimented with new administrative techniques, such as the trade regulation rule; litigation has been deemphasized in favor of greater reliance on rulemaking and informal compliance techniques; consent-order procedures have been instituted; the position of the Chairman has been strengthened; the Bureau of Economics has been strengthened in recent years; and an Office of Program Review has been created.

The arm, like the torso, seems guided more by solicitude for parochial interests than by consideration for the general welfare. The Trade Commission has acquired a constituency of business groups that includes numerous associations of retail dealers, food brokers, wholesale grocers, auto-parts jobbers, and others. It promotes their interests, as we have seen, with little regard for the larger social interest in competition and efficiency. This is a pattern one would expect of an arm of Congress, and, rooted as it seems to be in the structure of our governmental system, the exhortations of critics are unlikely to change it. Why the Commission's constituency consists of small-business rather than big-business groups, heavily concentrated in distribution rather than in manufacturing, is a fascinating and important question. Perhaps it is because a typical such group — we may instance the National Association of Retail Druggists — has certain attributes favorable to the exertion of political influence not shared by most large manufacturers or chain stores. It has numerous members in every congressional district, and not only are they numerous but they constitute a prosperous, vocal, and on both counts influential segment of every community. . . .

Another obstacle to radical improvement of the FTC arises from the structure of incentives operating on the members and staff of the Commission. It is a familiar proposition in economics that when individuals are unable to appropriate the social gain resulting from an undertaking the allocation of resources to it will be deficient. If farmers are not permitted to own the crops that they grow, they will lack incentive to sow — others being free to reap — and an adequate supply of food will not be forthcoming. The failure to apply similar reasoning to the analysis of governmental undertakings, a failure just beginning to be remedied,[15] has concealed serious deficiencies in the governmental process.

Let us adopt the plausible assumption that people who work for an administrative agency, whether as members of the agency or as its staff, are not a race apart; that the differences between them and people in private life in respect of probity, high-mindedness, freedom from material concerns, self-abnegation, and the like are on the whole unimportant. We assume, and rightly so, that businessmen are primarily motivated by hope or private gain, and I am suggesting only that a similar assumption be indulged of civil servants. That is not to say that civil servants are corrupt. In the vast majority of cases they pursue their private gain within the limits of the legally permissible. Private gain, moreover, is not to be equated solely with money, but includes leisure, security, prestige, power, serenity, and other goods, and the optimum mixture of these goods varies from individual to individual. But we must not be misled by the rhetoric of public service to suppose that the personnel of the FTC differ fundamentally as to motivation and incentives from those of Procter and Gamble.

There would be no reason for dismay at this were there some mechanism by

15. See A. Downs, Inside Bureaucracy (1966); J. Hirshleifer, J. De Haven & J. Milliman, Water Supply: Economics, Technology, and Policy 82-86 (1960); Stigler, The Regulation of Industry (April 10, 1969, mimeo).

which the private gain of FTC commissioners and staff could be aligned with the social gain yielded by consumer-protection activities. But there is not. The output of a regulatory agency, unlike the output of a private firm, is not sold in any market, and not being sold, cannot be priced. As a result, unless the mission of the agency is quite straightforward — I instance the Internal Revenue Service — it is impossible, within broad limits, to determine whether the resources being devoted to the regulatory activity are too few or too many. Worse, it means that regulators lack objective criteria against which to measure the efficiency of regulation. The absence of such criteria, in turn, makes it difficult to design a system of rewards for success and punishments for failure that would equate the regulators' self-interest to the social interest in effective regulation. Unlike businessmen, whose social product is measured with reasonable precision by profit-and-loss statements, or professionals, whose performance can usually be measured with tolerable accuracy by reference to widely accepted professional standards, the performance of regulators is extremely difficult to evaluate, which makes it possible for them in many instances to bend their regulatory duties to the service of personal interest. . . .

Whatever its limitations, the analysis is at least relevant as a reminder of what should be obvious anyway, that the personal goals of FTC members and staff (power is shared between these groups, not concentrated exclusively in the hands of the commissioners) influence the character and direction of the Commission's activity. What are those goals? In an unpublished paper, George J. Stigler proposes as a reasonable assumption that regulators act so as (a) to retain their jobs and (b) to obtain greater appropriations for their agency as a way of increasing personal power (and frequently remuneration as well). This assumption seems reasonable in regard to commissioners who seek reappointment and those staff members who make a career of government service. The self-interest of such individuals would appear to dictate the avoidance of controversy and the conciliation of well organized economic interests and influential Congressmen. Such policies are inconsistent with the determined and effective pursuit of consumer interests.

Not every commissioner or staff member, to be sure, makes a career of government service. Among the 15 FTC commissioners appointed since 1949 who are not present incumbents, the average tenure was less than 4 years, which is much less than a full term (7 years). The majority of these commissioners left the agency to join private law firms. The turnover among staff is also high, and most of those who leave enter the private practice of law too. A commissioner concerned with his future success at the bar will have no greater incentive to promote the consumer interest fearlessly and impartially than one whose guiding principles are job retention and agency aggrandizement. He will receive no bonus upon entry (or reentry) into private practice for the vigorous championing of the consumer interest. The gratitude of consumers — indulging the improbable assumption that such a thing exists — cannot be translated into a larger practice. On the other hand, the enmity of the organized economic interests, the trade associations and trade unions, that a zealous pursuit of consumer interests would engender may do him some later harm, while making his tenure with the Commission more tense and demanding than would otherwise be the case. Exceptional people may rise to the challenge but they are unlikely ever to constitute a sizable fraction of commissioners.

The picture is much the same with regard to those members of the staff who do not intend to make the Commission a career. The principal attraction of Commission service to lawyers who wish to use it as a steppingstone to private practice lies in the opportunities it affords to gain trial experience of an amount and at a level of responsibility usually denied young men in private firms. . . .

Given the absence of any mechanism for effectively conforming the private interests of FTC personnel to the social interest in consumer protection, it is hardly surprising that over the years the FTC has devoted its principal efforts to bringing that . . . do not promote any coherent public policy, at the behest of corporations, trade associations, and trade unions whose motivation is at best to shift the costs of their private litigation to the taxpayer and at worst to harass competitors. By taking the part of well organized economic pressure groups, representing established firms and their employees, rather than of new entrants, foreigners, or the unorganized and largely silent consumer, the FTC commissioners and staff have minimized the friction and work that a genuine dedication to consumer interests would have entailed. By concentrating on trivial fraud cases they have created the illusion of tangible results, while minimizing controversy, acquiring litigation experience, and stimulating demand for lawyers experienced in Trade Commission cases. And by concentrating its antitrust activities not in monopolistic or oligopolistic industries, but in the most competitive industries in the American economy, such as food, textiles, and retail and wholesale distribution, and by applying antitrust principles to shield the well organized economic blocs in those industries (such as food brokers and retail gasoline dealers) from the competitive gale, the Commission has curried favor with the politically influential.

IV. What Is To Be Done

There are mounting indications that the operational efficiency and overall effectiveness of the Commission are, by any standard, extremely low at present. . . . To many, its comparative inefficiency will seem scandalous, but one could regard it as the agency's saving grace. A recent study of the Commission criticized it for the diminution of its enforcement activities in the last few years; it might instead have commended it. One would be deeply concerned about an institution that pursued with skill, tenacity, and dispatch the anticompetitive policies that are the Commission's stock-in-trade in both the restraint-of trade and deceptive-practice areas. Perhaps a more efficient management would reconsider those policies, but I doubt it. If the analysis presented in this article is correct, there is no salutary role for a federal trade commission. What is required is not redirection, but reduction. Few bureaucrats, however, can bring themselves to preside over the contraction or liquidation of their bureau.

I would urge that more attention be given ... to reliance on market processes, and on the system of judicial rights and remedies that provides the framework of transactions in the market, as an alternative to the Trade Commission. A comparison of institutional arrangements reveals some interesting contrasts between courts and the Commission. One is in regard to capacity for modernization and reform. During the more than 50 years that the FTC has been adrift in its backwater, enormous strides in reducing the cost and efficacy of judicial processes have been made. Judicial procedure has been radically simplified; small claims courts have been created; new rights of action have been declared — recently, at the state level, in one of the areas where the FTC has been floundering (protection against fraud); and Neighborhood Legal Services have been created to assure meaningful legal remedies for poor people. One can criticize some of these developments, and certainly much remains to be done. In particular, it is shocking that successful litigants are generally unable to recover their legal expenses from the losing party. Still, it is interesting that the updating of the judicial process should be proceeding more rapidly than the reform of the administrative process.

A particularly important source of strength in the judicial process is the prestige that judges enjoy in our society. It is significant that judicial appointment is normally a terminal appointment rather than a steppingstone. In the federal court system, certainly, it is rare for judges to leave the bench for private practice. This is not to imply that members of administrative agencies should be given life tenure. Considering the caliber of the appointees, which is unlikely to be improved materially by such a system, the results would be disastrous. For reasons apparently deeply rooted in the attitudes of lawyers, it is impossible to attract many first-rate people to a long-term, let alone lifetime, career as a member of an administrative agency. Until those attitudes change, life tenure for agency members is out of the question and judicial enforcement of rules against fraud will continue to have this marked advantage over administrative: In striving to establish a proper balance between the rights of sellers and consumers, judges, with rare exception, are not going to be influenced by considerations of the impact of their decision upon a future career at the bar.

In the real world, a choice among institutional arrangements for dealing with social problems is a choice among highly imperfect alternatives. A free market backed up by private judicial remedies will not eliminate all frauds, nor will the Antitrust Division acting through the courts eliminate all restraints of trade. It does not follow, however, that the administrative process is a sound alternative or supplement to these approaches. On what evidence we have, the costs of having a federal trade commission appear to exceed the benefits.

[For other economics-oriented studies of regulatory agencies concluding that they do more harm than good, or are ineffective, see Noll, Peck, & McGowan, Economic Aspects of Television Regulation (1973); Breyer & MacAvoy, Energy Regulation by the Federal Power Commission (1974); Civil Aeronautics Board Practices and Procedures, Report of the Sucommittee on Administrative Practice and Procedure of the Senate Committee on the Judiciary (1975).]

Senate Report on the Consumer Protection Organization Act [16]

S. Rep. No. 92-1100, 92d Cong., 2d Sess. 8-14 (1972)

NEED FOR CONSUMER REPRESENTATION

Title II of this bill establishes a Consumer Protection Agency as an independent, nonregulatory agency. Four basic principles form its foundation:

(1) The CPA is an advocate for the interests of consumers;
(2) The CPA is a nonregulatory agency;
(3) The CPA is an independent agency; and
(4) The CPA is not the sole representative of the interests of consumers.

A Consumer Advocate. — The committee believes that it is necessary to create an agency to represent the interests of consumers before other Federal agencies and courts. Such an advocate is necessary because the interests of consumers have lacked the continuing effective representation that other interests have had before Federal agencies and courts. This imbalance in representation has resulted in a system of Federal regulation which has frequently given inadequate consideration to the interests of consumers.

The committee recognizes that despite the existence of hundreds of regulatory programs and the passage of much new consumer protection legislation, consumers are not yet receiving the protection which they need and have been promised. Committees of Congress, Federal agencies, special commissions, consumer organizations, responsible business organizations, and newspapers every day document the failure of Federal programs to meet the needs of consumers.

It has been widely argued that one reason for the failure of regulatory agencies to protect consumers adequately is that they have been too heavily influenced by the industries they are supposed to regulate. The committee recognizes that, to some degree, a close relationship between regulatory agencies and regulated industries is inevitable. This is true for many reasons.

First, industry often requires a close relationship with a regulatory agency. Regulatory policies can be a major factor in the success or failure of a business enterprise.

Second, industry has the resources to maintain effective advocates. Many businesses are in a position to employ the best talent available in presenting their views to regulatory agencies.

Third, a regulatory agency may often need a close relationship with industry. In order to do its job well an agency must be familiar with the industry it is to regulate. This proximity usually results in daily contact between the agency and representatives of industry.

Fourth, the law mandates that the arguments of industry be heard. Constitu-

16. Although the bill covered in the Report passed the House in substantially the form described, a similar bill was filibustered in the Senate near the close of the Ninety-second Congress. Successive efforts to enact a consumer advocate agency bill failed, and it was defeated in the House of Representatives in 1978 — a defeat which many supporters felt was final.

tional and statutory requirements guarantee a regulated industry the right to seek to have its views heard in the agency's decision-making process and the right to appeal an adverse determination to the courts.

Fifth, many regulators are former businessmen, and vice versa. The value of an employee with Government experience to an industry and the corresponding value of an employee experienced in industry to an agency have worked to maximize mutual understanding and cooperation between regulatory agencies and regulated industries.

The committee does not regard the familiar close relationship between regulatory agencies and regulated industries as harmful per se to the public interest. Similar relationships exist in our judicial system between the bench and members of the bar without producing any systematic denial of justice. It is detrimental to the public interest, however, when the close relationship between a regulatory agency and a regulated industry is not balanced by effective representation of other affected interests.

It is this imbalance of representation which this bill seeks to redress.

Theoretically, access to an agency's decisionmaking process is open to consumers as well as to industry, but for many reasons consumers have not been able to have their interests adequately represented before decisionmakers.

First, the consumer interest is fragmented. Every consumer is exposed to thousands of different products and services. Government approved price increases may require a consumer to pay 2 or 3 percent more for a given product or service. That amount may not be significant to an individual consumer. Almost certainly, it will not be sufficient to justify his hiring an advocate to protest to a regulatory agency. For the seller, however, that 2 or 3 percent, multiplied by the number of products sold, may well be significant; it may represent millions of dollars. Consequently, it may be in the seller's interest to spend substantial resources to participate in regulatory decisions concerning that item, whereas it would not be economically feasible for any individual consumer to do so.

Second, professional representation is expensive.

Third, the tax laws facilitate the representation of business interests. No one produces his income as a consumer. If a consumer hires an advocate to represent his interests as a consumer, the expense is not related to the production of income and is therefore not tax deductible. When an industry hires an advocate to represent its interests, however, the cost is related to the production of income and is therefore deductible.

For these and other reasons, the interests of consumers have never been represented adequately in the regulatory process. Representative Rosenthal stated the problem graphically in his testimony on S. 1177.

> There has been an empty chair for the consumer everywhere: the public utility companies have their hearings for rate increases, and they are supported by lawyers, economic investigators, and very skillful people, and the other seat for the consumer has obviously been empty. We have had an empty seat for some 30-odd years here in Washington. . . .

   In the FDA's lengthy proceeding to set standards for the content of orange juice, for example, many businesses were well represented by their advocates; but no one was an advocate for the interests of consumers. When the Department of Agriculture established the sanitation standards of meat and poultry plants, the industry is well represented by its advocates, but no one is an advocate for the interests of consumers. When the ICC set rates for the transportation of goods, shippers and carriers are well represented by their advocates; but no one is an advocate for the interests of consumers.

   The committee believes that the vast majority of Federal regulators are honest and conscientious, and will respond to a reasonable argument on the merits, presented in an effective manner. The major purpose of this bill is to make possible that kind of representation for consumers. It is the view of the committee that the best way to achieve this purpose is the establishment of a Federal agency to advocate the interests of consumers.

   The need for effective consumer advocacy cannot be satisfied merely by making improvements in existing Federal regulatory agencies. Congress has created many new regulatory agencies and programs in response to a conspicuous catastrophe or to meet an aroused public demand. Too often, however, Congress has failed to provide the funds needed to carry out regulatory programs well and neglected its responsibility to see that the agencies it had created were doing an effective job. As public pressure subsided and congressional interest was drawn elsewhere, too many regulatory programs have become ineffective.

   Congress should improve the regulatory agencies by providing the necessary new authority, resources, and organization, as well as by overseeing the manner in which they carry out their statutory responsibilities. But, improving the regulatory agencies, while an important task, is not an alternative to creating a consumer advocate to appear before these agencies. The adversary system — the keystone of American justice — requires that all affected interests have a fair opportunity to express their views. As long as one interest lacks an effective means of presenting its position, no agency decisionmaker, however honest and competent, can be expected to take full and accurate account of that interest.

   A nonregulatory agency....

   The committee strongly believes that the CPA should be entirely nonregulatory. A regulatory agency must consider the entire public interest. It must make judgments by balancing one interest and one argument against another.

   A consumer advocate, on the other hand, is not designed to be an impartial arbiter. In the same manner as a lawyer retained to represent the interests of a business before a regulatory agency, the CPA will represent the interests of consumers. The CPA is counsel for consumers, not a judge deciding cases.

   An independent agency. — The committee believes that, in addition to being nonregulatory, the CPA must also be independent within the executive branch. An effective consumer advocate must be able to argue his case on the merits in support of the interests he is protecting. By the nature of its function as an advocate, the CPA will continually be taking positions in controversial matters. The committee feels that it is essential to insulate the CPA from day-to-day political pressures within the executive branch.

Diversity of consumer interests. — The CPA will not be able to represent all interests of all consumers. The committee recognizes the wide diversity of consumer interests and understands that in any one case, a number of different consumer interests may be involved. Furthermore, these interests may potentially conflict with one another. For example, if automobile safety standards are imposed requiring the installation of new equipment, the cost of automobiles may rise, and the interest of consumers in having automobiles available at a low price may suffer. At the same time, the interests of consumers in having safe automobiles may be enhanced. Or consider the hexacholorophine controversy. One group of consumers, interested primarily in maintaining a sterile, therapeutic environment, will favor continued use of the chemical, while another group, more concerned with possible harmful side effects, will argue for strict limitations or total exclusion of its use. Consumers in one part of the country may have an interest in favoring one policy which would not be in the interest of consumers in another part of the country. Or consumers in one income level may have interests different from the interests of consumers at other levels.

The committee does not expect the CPA to resolve such conflicts. Using its best judgment, the CPA will usually determine which side to represent. In some cases, however, the consumer interest may lie simply in presenting all relevant information to an agency on different sides of the same question.

The CPA's decision to advocate one consumer interest will not in any way reduce the rights of others to advocate different consumer interests. The CPA is not intended to preempt the consumer representation field.

Questions: Why can't agencies like the FTC be counted upon to represent the interests of consumers? If a consumer advocate agency, why not similar agencies for the poor, environmentalists, minority groups, etc.? To what extent might the criticisms of "failure" directed at traditional agencies apply as well to a consumer advocate agency?

Senate Report on CAB Practices and Procedures[17]

94th Cong., 1st Sess. 19-20 (1975)

CONCLUSIONS AND RECOMMENDATIONS

... In summary form, the subcommittee has concluded the following:

1. Many of the Board's procedures fail to meet commonly accepted standards of fairness and openness. In some instances major policies have been determined

17. Report of the Subcomm. on Administrative Practice and Procedure of the Senate Comm. on the Judiciary.

without a prior opportunity for the public fully to present arguments and alternatives. In other instances, individuals have been hurt as a result of procedurally unsound Board action. This conclusion applies, in particular, to the Board's route award procedures, the route moratorium, the "motion for expedited hearing," intervention by the Chairman's office in route cases, the "minimum charter rate" experience, the capacity restricting agreements, charter rule enforcement, the Air Europe case, and the campaign contribution investigation.

2. Board regulation has not effectively brought about the low-fare service that is technically feasible and that consumers desire. Instead it has sought primarily to protect the regulated scheduled airline industry and to promote regularly scheduled air service.

3. Air service can be made available to the American public at significantly lower prices. Increased competition is likely to bring about the provision of such service. The major alternatives to increased reliance upon competition, namely, stricter ratemaking standards, discount fares, and capacity restricting agreements, are less likely to prove effective.

4. To some extent the Board's failings reflect the inherent difficulty of applying classical rate and entry regulation to a competitive, economically volatile industry. Classical ratemaking sets fares that equal costs (including a reasonable profit). Yet the Board's experience suggests it is extremely difficult, if not impossible, to develop a cost-based ratemaking system that uses fair procedures and keeps fares in such an industry low.

Classical entry regulation substitutes for impersonal market forces, which tolerate bankruptcies and allow the efficient, aggressive, or superior firms to survive, personal quasijudicial decisions by regulators, who inevitably feel responsible for the "health" of the firms they regulate, who tend to see "fair" decisions as those that treat with rough equality the various industry claimants before them, and who thus seek industry stability and improved service. Given the difficulty of fashioning a set of consistent standards for awarding routes that will meet these objectives, that will conform to statutory requirements, and that will help to keep fares low, it is not surprising that the Board has tended to avoid hearings, to rely on informal negotiation, and, when denying route applications, to substitute for substantive criteria, procedural ones, which are less open to outside criticism or review.

Finally, the classical regulatory response to defects in regulation is to create more regulation. The Board's response to the problem of excess capacity was to introduce capacity restricting agreements. Yet, to do so in this highly competitive, complex industry brought the consumer the worst of both worlds, high prices and poor service.

This is not to say that inherent defects are the only cause of the CAB's failings. These may, for example, also reflect the human tendency to listen more closely to representatives, such as those for the industry, who are powerful, well-informed, and can reward regulators with future jobs or contracts. Or they may reflect the variety of political forces that the regulator must often take into account. Nor is it to say that classical regulation is always undesirable. In the case of some industries, it may be necessary. Yet classical regulation is not an appropriate tool for dealing with the problems of the airline industry. Defects in airline regulation run so deep that major change is required. Rather, reliance upon strong safety regulation, the antitrust laws to prevent predatory behavior, and the competitive process is more appropriate. Thus, a program of gradual, measured change toward increased reliance upon competition is called for.

The subcommittee's recommendations are designed to move gradually towards a system that increasingly relies upon competition, rather than classical regulation, to bring about low fares.

Wilson, The Dead Hand of Regulation

The Public Interest, Fall 1971, at 39-58

After decades of public and journalistic neglect, the government agencies that set prices, control entry, and regulate conduct in many of our most important industries have suddenly found themselves in the limelight. Owing to the efforts of Ralph Nader and other advocates of "consumerism," a considerable segment of attentive opinion has become convinced that the prosaic, often arcane decisions of these little understood commissions are not always in the public interest. Such a view is correct, and for dramatizing the fact we owe Nader and the others a debt of gratitude.

But dramatic confrontations between "raiders" and "bureaucrats," however useful in creating an issue, are not so useful in understanding the issue. Persons easily convinced that the government is not acting rightly tend to assume that it is because the government is not righteous; if industries are being regulated wrongly, then (in this view) it must be because bad people are doing the regulating. It would be unfortunate if the resolution of the regulatory issue were framed in terms of the moralistic premises that first gave rise to it.

It would be all the more unfortunate considering that a number of scholars, chiefly economists, have developed over the last ten years a substantial set of analytical tools and empirical findings which, taken together, constitute an impressive contribution to our knowledge of what happens when the government tries to intervene in the economy. Yet compared to the enormous influence of those economists who have developed ways of managing our tax, fiscal, and monetary policies, the influence exercised by the regulatory economists has been negligible.

The problems of regulatory agencies go beyond price setting ... and involve issues ranging from allocation (e.g., deciding who will get a television broadcast license) through the approval of business practices (e.g., deciding which firms may merge and which may not) to the control of what may or may not be broadcast (e.g., deciding whether radio stations will be allowed to editorialize or whether television stations show too much violence or too many commercials). In evaluating these and other kinds of government regulations, there are two standards one may employ — efficiency and equity. By "efficiency" I mean that a given regulatory policy achieves a desirable objective at minimal cost; by "equity" I mean that the regulatory policy, whether efficient or not, treats those subject to it fairly — that is, treats like cases alike on the basis of rules known in advance and applicable to all.

Until the end of the 1950's the many criticisms of regulatory commissions were generally based on rather narrow or truncated versions of these two criteria. Those concerned with efficiency tended to emphasize the problem of who would determine what the desirable social objective should be and thus to whom regulatory agencies would be accountable. This in general was the concern of the Hoover Commission and of the political scientists who complained that the commissions were a "headless fourth branch" of government and were being "captured" by the very industries they were supposed to regulate. Typical of the reform proposals of such commentators, most of whom accepted without much question the desirability of regulation, were suggestions that the commissions have "stronger leadership," "clearer mandates," "popular support," and "effective management." Rarely did any of these authors say to what concrete ends that leadership and popular support should be directed or what should be contained in the clear mandate. And as for industry influence over commissions, the best answer came from Louis Jaffe of the Harvard Law School: Whether a commission does or does not serve the ends of industry is much less important than whether it serves the correct ends, and these may or may not be what industry wants.

Critics concerned with equity, who on the whole were less favorably disposed to the idea of administrative regulation at all, concentrated their fire on the administrative procedures of the commissions, and sought by various legal and judicial remedies to insure that parties appearing before the commissions would receive ample notice, a fair hearing, an opportunity for review, and the other elements of due process as then conceived. The culmination of this movement was the passage of the Administrative Procedures Act of 1946. Though its proponents, mostly lawyers, hailed it as marking a new era in administrative law, the new era did not arrive. In the opinion of most observers, the influence of the act was marginal, and such effect as it did have was generally in the direction of making regulation slower and more costly rather than fairer.

Indeed, insofar as it sought to treat affected parties more justly, the act was doomed from the start, for it was based on a fundamental misconception of much of the regulatory process. Adjudication, as it occurs in a court of law, is (in the words of Lon Fuller) an "institutionally protected opportunity to present proofs and arguments" to support a claim of right deriving from some previously agreed to standard. This is what we do, for example, when we sue a person for failure to pay a debt. But most regulatory commissions do not have such standards, nor do most of their clients have a "right" to (for example) a vacant television license, an airline route, or a particular price for long-distance telephone calls. In deciding who shall receive the license or fly the route or what the price shall be, the agency has no single solution to which the affected parties can direct their arguments. Equity or justice in cases of this sort does not consist so much in providing the opportunities for court-like speeches as in enunciating and adhering to a reasonable standard, applicable to all, that will permit the affected parties to conduct themselves free of the fear of capricious governmental action.

THE EFFECTS OF REGULATION

The economists have cut through much (though as we shall see, not all) of the fuzzy rhetoric and empty reforms addressed to these issues and have asked instead the simple question, "What effect does a regulatory policy have and, given certain goals, how can that effect be improved?" The first thing to decide was whether regulatory policies, especially in the rate-fixing area, *had any effect at all.* Everyone, of course, assumed that they had. Why else would businessmen complain so much about these rates and an aroused public demand even lower ones? The landmark study on this issue has been the effort of George J. Stigler and Claire Freidland to determine whether or not state control over the prices that electric utilities could charge had any effect on what prices they did charge. They compared the rates charged by utilities in states with regulation to those charged in states without it during the period (before 1937) when there was a significant number of unregulated states. In calculations for various years from, 1912 to 1937, the existence of regulation had no significant effect. Nor was there in unregulated as opposed to regulated states any evidence of greater price discrimination (between, for example, domestic and industrial consumers) or of differences in utility profit levels as measured by stockholder experience. Stigler and Friedland explain their findings by the absence of long-run monopoly power in the hands of electric companies (they face competition from other energy sources) and the inability of a regulatory body to determine what rates ought to be relative to costs, or even to learn what the costs are.

That the incompetence of the agency as much as the nature of the industry may make price regulation so chancy a phenomenon will suggest to some readers what it has suggested to several generations of reformers: the need to have "better" commissions, perhaps ones staffed with economists as able as Professor Stigler. After all, what is required is simply to set prices so as to provide a "reasonable return on investment." But as Felix Frankfurter and Henry Hart pointed out over 35 years ago, a fair and defensible determination of the rate base is maddeningly hard to make. Initial capital investment obviously will not do, as the value of the plant has no doubt appreciated since it was built. Replacement cost seems a better alternative, until one realizes that estimating it for an electric light or telephone company requires a kind of economic science fiction almost impossible to justify. What is the cost of "replacing" a utility that grew with the surrounding community's growth from village to metropolis and now exists in such close interconnection with the people it serves that to "replace" it would require virtually replacing the community itself? And in any case, assessing the value of a company can take (and has taken) years, hardly an arrangement conductive to regular and flexible adjustments in rates to meet changing economic conditions.

Just because it is hard to fix rates does not mean that rates are not fixed. They are, and often with quite significant results to the consumer. This is perhaps best illustrated in the field of transportation. Anyone who buys an airplane ticket or ships his furniture to another city is paying a price that is affected by, and sometimes uniquely determined by, a government agency. Merton J. Peck of Yale has studied the results of this process for shippers and Richard E. Caves has studied it with respect to airlines. Both conclude that prices would be lower to the consumer if they were not regulated.

WHO HAS CAPTURED WHOM

Scholars as diverse as the radical historian Gabriel Kolko and the conservative economist George Stigler offer a simple explanation for the behavior of these and other regulatory agencies: They have been captured by, or were created to serve the interests of, the industries they are supposed to regulate. To Kolko, business regulation, like all other "reform" efforts in American government, has had the intended effect of making secure the control over wealth exercised by the dominant economic class. To Stigler, any industry with sufficient political influence will use the coercive power of the state to limit entry into the industry and thus to restrict competition.

There are examples of regulation that seem to have no other explanations than those. The benefits given to the petroleum industry by import quotas and tax-depletion allowances represent an enormous subsidy (perhaps as much as $5 billion a year). The CAB has not allowed the formation of a new trunk airline since it was created in 1938. At one time the butter producers virtually suppressed the use of margarine by obtaining laws that forbade coloring margarine to look like butter. Plenty of other instances could no doubt be added.

But just as striking are the cases contrary to the theory of industry capture. The Federal Power Commission can hardly be called the tool of the natural gas producer interests; until recently it has set well-head prices below what the producers would like and indeed what the public interest probably requires. If the ICC was once dominated by the railroads, it is not today. So generous has that agency been to the chief rivals of the railroads, the truckers and barge lines, that today the rail industry favors deregulation altogether.

Indeed, there may well be as many industries that have been "captured" by their regulatory agency as agencies captured by the industry. But the term "capture" reflects a simplistic view of the politics of regulation. Though there have been very few good studies of agency politics, what probably happens is this: An agency is established, sometimes with industry support and sometimes over industry objections, and then gradually creates a regulatory climate that acquires a life of its own. Certain firms will be helped by some of the specific regulatory decisions making up this climate, others will be hurt. But the industry as a whole will adjust to the climate and decide that the costs of shifting from the known hazards of regulation to the unknown ones of competition are too great; it thus will come to defend the system. The agencies themselves will become preoccupied with the details of regulation and the minutiae of cases in whatever form they first inherit them, trying by the slow manipulation of details to achieve various particular effects that happen to commend themselves from time to time to various agency members. In a burst of academic masochism, Paul MacAvoy recently read all 1,041 pages in Volume 42 of the Federal Power Commission Reports, and concluded that it is hard to find any consistent policy preference concealed in their bureaucratic and ponderous language;

hints appear here and there in the few important cases, but it would be hard to call them a "policy." The net effects of the FPC's actions often are clear, but whether they are intended, and if so on what grounds, is not clear.

Louis Jaffe has probably stated the political situation more accurately — the agencies are not so much industry-oriented or consumer-oriented as *regulation-oriented*. They are in the regulation business, and regulate they will, with or without a rationale. If the agencies have been "captured" by anybody, it is probably by their staffs who have mastered the arcane details of rate setting and license granting.

In any event, most regulatory agencies have been doing pretty much what Congress has asked of them. Congress never intended that competition should govern in transportation, and the ICC has seen to it that it hasn't. Indeed, if any agency has been "captured" by its clients, it has been, under certain presidents, the National Labor Relations Board; but again, this is exactly what Congress intended in the Wagner Act. (Curiously, academic criticism of business domination of regulatory agencies rarely extends to organized labor influence in the NLRB.) The Securities and Exchange Commission has had a running feud with much of Wall Street, just as Congress hoped it would. Indeed, if any single political force benefits from economic regulation, it is Congress — or more accurately, those key Congressional committee and subcommittee chairmen with a substantive interest in, or appropriations responsibilities over, the regulatory agencies. The FCC has been reluctant to make any change in its controls over cable communications without checking with key Senators, and the NLRB regularly hears from members of the House Education and Labor Committee about matters pending before it.

But even Congressional intervention, like industry control, is not in itself a problem; everything depends on the ends toward which such intervention or control is directed. The problem of efficiency, in short, is not wholly a problem of clientelism, political meddling, or agency incompetence; in substantial part it is a problem of the nature of the tasks which we have given the agencies. These tasks probably could not be performed well even in theory, and amid the practical realities of confused ends and ambiguous standards they are, through the fault of no one in particular, performed abominably.

EQUITY

The economic analyses thus far described have rather little to say explicitly about the problem of equity. . . .

Not that people are generally indifferent to considerations of justice and fair play; far from it. But they tend to limit their concern to victimized individuals and groups with whom they have sympathy. Those who publish books and articles rarely, if ever, argue that a person should be subject to arbitrary arrest, or that ex post facto laws should be tolerated, or that demonstrations should be allowed or forbidden at the pleasure of an administrator. Or do they? Consider the following statement, written by a man who was later to become a Justice of the United States Supreme Court:

> Unless the police officer has effective bargaining power, little can be expected. He must have sanctions or desired favors which he can trade for changes in behavior. . . . He may be asked to exercise his discretion, for example, to allow a certain demonstration to take place. Then, if the need of the demonstrators is sufficiently urgent, a trade may be consummated. In return for the favor of the police officer, the demonstrators may change their speeches and leaflets in accordance with the police officers' conception of equity and justice.

I venture that most readers would find this statement shocking and odious. The idea that the right to demonstrate should be subject to arbitrary powers and the content of the demonstration modified by the capacity of a policeman to bargain with the demonstrators seems the height of unfairness.

Now, I must confess that the Justice-to-be (Abe Fortas, as it turns out) did not exactly say this. Instead, Fortas was writing, in 1937, about how the staff of the SEC should behave. His exact words were as follows:

> Unless the administrator has effective bargaining power, little can be expected. He must have sanctions or desired favors which he can trade for changes in practices. . . . He may be asked to exercise his discretion, for example, to accelerate the effective date of registration [of a new security]. Then, if the need of the registrant is sufficiently urgent, a trade may be consummated. In return for the favor of the administrator, the registrant may amend his practices in accordance with the administrator's conception of equity and justice.

Most people, other than securities registrants, would find this statement at worst to be a candid but scarcely shocking glimpse into the real-life behavior of bureaucrats. Political scientists would probably cite this approvingly as an example of how the informal use of "necessary" administrative discretion can lead to the more "effective management" of the economy. I am perfectly aware, of course, that there are differences, perhaps decisive ones, between free speech and securities registration; but I think it behooves all who unhesitatingly condemn the first quotation and approve the second to think through rather carefully just what these differences may be and why speech should have near-absolute protection and commerce near-zero protection.

Whether or not we place the interests of the firm on the same plane as the interests of the writer or speaker, it seems clear (again, hardly anyone has examined the problem) that a person or corporation subject to regulation cannot in many cases know in advance where he stands, nor expect to be treated tomorrow by the same rule that governed his actions today. The theory of regulation advanced in the earlier part of this paper — that it tends to be an ad hoc, particularistic process, affected, but not determined, by a policy habit or inclination — suggests not only that agencies will not operate on the basis of general rules, but that they will go to some pains to avoid developing such rules.

There are two reasons for this. One is that the greater the codification of substantive policy, the less the power the agency can wield over any client in the particular case. As Michel Crozier has argued with respect to bureaucracy generally, power depends in part on uncertainty — I have power over you to the extent you cannot be sure in advance what my reactions to your behavior will be.

The second reason for avoiding codification is related to the first: The agency and its staff wish to be able to achieve particular goals in particular cases. Though the goals may be ambiguous and the cases all different, the general desire to realize a particular state of affairs is more important to the agency than the desire simply to insure that the rules are followed.... [I]t is as if the baseball umpire desired not just to see that the game was played fairly, but also that a certain number of runs were scored (so the fans would be happy), a certain number of pitches thrown (so the pitcher would get a good workout), and a certain price charged by the owners (so they would be either happy or unhappy, depending on his intentions).

THE UNLIKELIHOOD OF CHANGE

Neither industry nor the agencies have much need to fear major reforms, or at least reforms that reduce the item-by-item discretionary regulation that now exists. Quite the contrary. The reform impulse, except among economists who specialize in the problems of better use of regulated resources, is now of an entirely different sort — increased regulation, increased discretion, more numerous challenges to existing corporate practices....

... The most articulate segment of public opinion has recently become aroused by the issue of "consumerism," and this almost surely will lead to demands for increasing the power and aggressiveness of the regulatory agencies. There is, of course, no necessary contradiction between a desire to protect the consumer and the desire to use scarce resources more efficiently; the efforts of the Federal Trade Commission or the Food and Drug Administration to insure that false and misleading claims are not made for products and that harmful substances are not sold to unwitting buyers are in principle unobjectionable. Indeed, one of the ironies of economic regulation is that it has generally existed with respect to those tasks it can do only poorly (such as setting rates and prices and controlling market entry) and has not existed, or has been indifferently managed, with respect to those tasks it could do well (such as controlling the effects of business activity on third parties or on the environment). Reducing the emission of noxious fumes or preventing the sale of a harmful drug is conceptually and perhaps administratively easier than deciding what allocation of television licenses will be in "the public interest" or what price levels are "reasonable"; yet until recently Congress has encouraged the agencies to do the latter but not the former. In so far as the contemporary concern for ecology and public health redresses this balance, it is all to the good.

But it is unlikely that the desire to improve and perfect human affairs will stop there. An effort will be made to "'protect" the consumer by setting the price he can pay or forbidding him to buy certain products of whose dangers he is fully aware. Moreover, enhancing the powers or stimulating the activity of regulatory agencies for whatever reasons will lead the agencies themselves to enlarge their

mandate and extend their influence. Consumer advocates, including as they do
many of those most skeptical on other grounds of the manageability of large government organizations, should be the last to suppose that bigger consumer-protection agencies will work as intended; but of course, they are among the first to
suppose it.

C.   Alternative Remedies for Regulatory "Failure"

The problems with, and criticisms of, regulation and agency performance have
spawned a host of suggestions for change or "reform." Many of the cases studied
in this course can be best understood as representing an effort by judges to deal
with agency failings — though in doing so the judges must work within a narrow
framework of institutional and legal constraints.

Before turning to the many different legal doctrines developed as part of the
judicial effort to oversee government agencies, you should consider some of the
major alternative analyses of what is wrong with government regulatory agencies
and how their failings might be overcome. These analyses have led to a variety of
suggestions for reform, which can be roughly grouped as follows: (1) changes in
substantive policy; (2) improved regulatory personnel; (3) increased control by
Congress; (4) increased control by the Executive; (5) changes in agency structure;
(6) the development of new institutions. As you consider specific problems of
specific agencies throughout the course, you should try to determine the extent
to which changes in procedure would help, whether improved structure or personnel or closer supervision is required, or whether significant substantive policy
change is needed.

1.   Substantive Policy Change: "Deregulation" and "Mismatch"

There are those who argue that most agency failings can be traced to the
agency's legislative mandate. It has been given a job that it cannot do, or cannot
do well.

Consider, for example, the Civil Aeronautics Board, prior to the recent Airline Deregulation Act of 1978. (See Chapter 6.) The Board was told to regulate
the prices and profits of air carriers and to control entry into the industry. Yet the
industry itself is highly competitive, consisting of ten major domestic carriers and
many smaller carriers. Moreover, the economics of the industry are volatile. Board
critics argue that there was no practical way for an agency to determine proper
prices for firms in such an industry. Inevitably the agency would have to set fixed
prices that prevent firms from competing in price. The firms instead would compete in service, with better meals, wider seats, more frequent schedules, and emptier
planes. The result, from the consumer's point of view, was undesirable high prices

as he was offered more expensive service than he wanted. The only practical solution, according to these critics, was not to regulate at all, but to return to a free marketplace and allow competition to determine prices, the range of service offered, and which firms offer it. Similarly, some have claimed that the many criticisms of the performance of the Interstate Commerce Commission, the Federal Power Commission, the Federal Maritime Commission, or the Federal Trade Commission stem from the fact that these agencies should not be regulating at all.

This school of thought advocates widespread "deregulation." In many areas, it sees the defects of government regulation as outweighing those of the marketplace. Although unregulated workplaces, or automobiles, may be unsafe, regulated workplaces or automobiles are likely to be no safer and to be far more expensive to boot.

It is difficult, however, to accept widespread deregulation as a solution. For one thing, there are many categories of cases where administrative regulation seems clearly warranted by considerations of allocational efficiency. For example, some administrative control of bona fide natural monopolies is often thought to be inescapable. Collectively managed controls may also be necessary to deal effectively with many types of economic externalities. While the problems of air and water pollution might theoretically be dealt with entirely through private liability rules administered by the courts, the difficulties and drawbacks involved in implementing such a scheme have led responsible observers to endorse systems that depend at least in part on centralized and specialized administrative direction as an essential element in dealing with the problems of environmental degradation. And in a complex industrial society permeated by technological changes with significant second- and third-order consequences, one may come to the same judgment in many other fields, such as broadcasting.[18] Moreover, existing regulatory systems have developed strong supporters among interest groups who have benefitted from, or relied upon, existing regulation. Regardless of the irrationality of ICC trucking regulations, many shippers may have located factories or warehouses relying upon their continued existence. They, as well as many truck owners and workers, would oppose any sudden major change in the substantive rules.

A somewhat more sophisticated critique is sounded by those who blame many regulatory problems upon a basic mismatch between the objective of a regulatory

---

18. The finite nature of all the radiomagnetic spectrum and the problem of broadcast interference call for some system of allocating frequencies. However, a program of regulation through licensure, directed in part at program content, is not inevitable. Periodic auctions of broadcast licenses, or the creation of transferable property rights in the spectrum, are allocational alternatives that might better serve existing viewer tastes without the troublesome prospect of governmental control over program content. But there are countervailing considerations. The preference-shaping impact of television on audiences, especially children, may afford a ground for governmental regulation based on considerations independent of efficiency. The limited number of channels may generate a "bunching" effect, concentrating programming content into areas desired by large groups with congruent interests, leaving significant segments of the population without service. Moreover, the "fairness doctrine," requiring stations to present contrasting sides of controversial issues of public importance, implicates larger social concerns that might not necessarily be served adequately by alternatives to regulation. The choice between regulation and alternatives geared to market mechanisms is thus fairly debatable.

program and the tools used to achieve that objective. This approach attempts to classify several different types of economic problems, with which an unregulated market and a court system of private litigation allegedly cannot cope, that give rise to a demand for regulation. As we have already noted in Chapter 1, Section B.3.a supra, these include:

(a) "Natural monopoly" — the need to control the prices and profits of a firm like the telephone company in an industry where it is wasteful to have more than one firm;

(b) Rent control — the desire to transfer large unearned windfalls from, say, producers (or landlords) to consumers (or renters);

(c) Spillovers — the problem of a commodity or production process imposing costs (such as pollution) on the community which costs are not reflected in the price that buyers must pay for the product;

(d) Inadequate information — the inability of consumers to obtain enough information to make reasonable buying decisions;

(e) Various others — such as the need to rationalize efficiently small firms into larger production units, the need to compensate for the fact that the purchaser of a good (say medical care) does not himself pay for it, or the alleged need to prevent "excessive competition" or "predatory behavior."

There are also a number of weapons at the government's disposal that it might use to deal with these problems: (1) It can attack them through more aggressive antitrust law enforcement designed to make the unregulated marketplace work more effectively. (2) It can use classic systems of regulation, which include "cost of service" ratemaking, allocation systems, or the writing of standards for products or workplaces. (3) It can impose taxes or provide subsidies designed either to transfer income or to discourage (or encourage) the use of a particular product or production process. (4) It can use systems of arbitration or collective bargaining or mediation to achieve agreed-upon changes. (5) It can itself provide information. (6) It can itself operate a "nationalized" industry.

According to the "mismatch" view, the major source of regulatory problems arises from a failure to match properly the weapon with the problem it is seeking to overcome. The weapon which should be selected is that which will interfere the least with the private marketplace and which will rely to the maximum feasible extent upon incentives, rather than administrative rules, to cure the problem at hand. Thus, the problems of airlines or trucking might be better dealt with through increased antitrust enforcement. (This view has been accepted in the case of airlines, which were recently "deregulated." See Chapter 6.) The problem necessitating natural gas regulation — windfall producer profits — would have been better dealt with through taxes. Environmental problems might be ameliorated through increased use of tax, or other incentive, devices. And, many problems of industrial safety would be better dealt with through collective bargaining or increased information. Instead, the overuse of classic "command and control" regulatory techniques, in which administrators attempt to mandate specific private conduct in each of these areas, has led to many of the criticisms already noted. Many of the problems you will consider throughout the course fall within the "mismatch" matrix sketched above. You might try to determine the extent to which regulatory problems reflect a correctable "mismatch." See Breyer, Analyzing Regulatory Failure: Mismatches, Less Restrictive Alternatives, and Reform, 92 Harv. L. Rev. 549 (1979).

Two difficulties with the mismatch approach are: (1) the detailed knowledge of the industry or agency usually needed before a specific, detailed improved mandate can be devised; and (2) the difficulty of obtaining the political consensus needed to enact major substantive change.

Government programs whose basic aim is to redistribute income or wealth have also been criticized for employing clumsy or inappropriate tools. The federal government, for example, administers dozens of programs to confer benefits on various classes of beneficiaries. Sometimes these benefits take the form of cash — aid for families with dependent children, unemployment compensation, disability payments. But in many instances the benefits are distributed in kind — low-cost housing, food stamps, special educational programs for the disadvantaged, day care facilities for working mothers, Medicaid. These often overlapping programs give rise to a vast, complex bureaucracy. Critics like Milton Friedman would sweep away this system of special programs and benefits with a single system of cash payments based on income; the very poorest would get the highest payments, and payments would diminish proportionately as income rises, ceasing altogether at some legislatively fixed poverty level. Such "negative income tax" proposals would eliminate the need for many administrators and would assertedly lead to a more rational and equitable system of benefits. But the entire approach has been criticized as ignoring the special needs of various groups in the population. Moreover, the proposal has been opposed by beneficiary groups (some of whom would receive less under a negative income tax than under existing programs, especially when they are eligible for benefits under several programs); by members of Congress (many of whom have in part built their careers on specialized benefit programs); and by existing agencies (many of which would be abolished).

2. Improving the Quality of Regulators

A second view blames agency failure in large part upon poor quality personnel. Proposals growing out of this view are designed to secure the appointment of personnel who will do a better job.

a. Attracting Better Personnel

The prime key to the improvement of the administrative process is the selection of qualified personnel. Good men can make poor laws workable; poor men will wreak havoc with good laws. [Landis, Report on Regulatory Agencies to the President-elect 66 (1960).]

Most students of the administrative process see room for tremendous personnel improvement, but there is little agreement on how to remedy the situation. Most of the suggestions for improvement fall into the following five general categories:

(1) *Setting up an Office of Appointments within the White House.* The leading proponents of establishing an appointments office in the White House, with a director reporting directly to the President, believe it would improve appointee quality by (a) making the appointments process more visible and thereby encouraging greater public participation; (b) making certain that recruitment does not occur haphazardly without adequate time devoted to it; and (c) encouraging the development of standards and criteria for the selection of commissioners and agency heads. These standards might make it more difficult for a President to select personnel on the basis of political connections, and would make more likely selection on the basis of competence, experience, honesty, and philosophical compatibility with the agency's mission. Critics of this proposal are uncertain how such standards would be developed, whether the White House office could develop them, whether, if it did, the standards would produce better candidates, and whether a White House office is likely to prove immune to political pressures.

(2) *Establishing a congressional committee to develop appointment standards.* Because the job of developing appropriate and specific appointment standards is so difficult, Common Cause believes the task should be performed by a special congressional committee. The chief criteria to be applied in the development of these standards should be: (a) unquestioned honesty and proof that the candidate has never used public office for his private gain, (b) administrative competence, (c) commitment to enforce the major policies of the agency, and (d) belief in the basic principles of regulatory accountability. Coupled with enforcement of the standards which this committee develops, the Senate, in the confirmation process, must engage in broad and extensive questioning of every nominee designed to bring out his expertise, views, past record, and any potential conflicts of interest. To facilitate the process and to guarantee increased public participation, the Senate should postpone any confirmation vote on a particular candidate until two weeks after the close of the hearing and three days after a full report has been issued by the appropriate committee.

(3) *Creating an independent qualifications board.* Common Cause has also suggested that every presidential appointee be reviewed by a nonpartisan qualification board. The existence of such an entity would encourage the chief executive to make better appointments out of fear of being embarrassed by adverse comments; moreover, such a board might help the President search for possible appointees — or at least screen out incompetent candidates.[19]

(4) *Increasing the status and attractiveness of agency positions.* Some ob-

---

19. See generally Regulatory Reform — Vol. 1: Quality of Regulators: Hearings Before the Subcommittee on Oversight and Investigations of the House Comm. on Interstate and Foreign Commerce, 94th Cong., 1st Sess. (1975).

servers believe that the salary and status of the agency jobs are inadequate to attract first-class administrators. The Ash Council recommended agency heads have more power and authority. Others have proposed lifetime tenure for commissioners. Still others propose higher salaries. Some have suggested a massive advertising campaign to publicize the jobs, explaining how complex and interesting they are. Common Cause has advocated the creation of a public interest talent bank.[20]

The chairman of a major commission now earns a salary of nearly $60,000, comparable to that of a cabinet undersecretary. Moreover, the chairman of the FCC, for example, enjoys considerable power and prestige. Other members have slightly lower salaries and enjoy considerably less power. Of course, whether the salary and position is adequately attractive may depend upon whom one wishes to attract; $60,000 may seem enormous to a civil servant or professor, yet inadequate to a successful lawyer or top business executive. Still there may be other features of the job that discourage business applicants. Consider:

> [A] majority of business executives are uncomfortable and unsuccessful in the federal government's topmost political, policy making posts as department heads and assistant secretaries. They are unaccustomed to and sometimes resentful of the interests of the legislative branch in administrative affairs. They are unfamiliar with the necessity for clearance and coordination with numerous other departments. They are irritated by public scrutiny of their actions and by rigid controls exercised over recruitment of personnel, the budgeting of funds and the procurement of supplies and equipment. [John McDonald, The Business in Government, Fortune, July 1954, at 69.]

> In Washington, your ability to articulate your accomplishments in a way that is memorable and persuasive generally counts more than the objective standards of efficiency and success as we know them in business. [Peter Peterson, former Secretary of Commerce.]

(5) *Increasing agency visibility.* One of the best ways to attract top-quality personnel is for an agency to be known as an exciting place where things are happening. A well-publicized need for reform plus the opportunity to bring it about attracted excellent personnel to the Federal Trade Commission in 1969 (see Chapter 8, Section C.2, infra). Yet, there is no obvious way to institutionalize this particular attractive feature.

The notion that "better people" will overcome the problems of agency failure has been criticized on two grounds: (1) "Better people" is always a solution to any institutional problem, but the number of "better people" is limited. Even if we successfully identified and attracted them to the administrative agencies, is it obvious that society would be better off than if they were running, for example,

---

20. See generally Hearings, Quality of Regulators, supra n.19; and The Federal and Executive Service: Hearings on H.R. 3807 before the Subcomm. on Manpower and Civil Service of the House Comm. on Post Office and Civil Service, 92d Cong., 2d Sess. (1972).

medical clinics, disarmament conferences, or IBM? (2) There is no suggestion for any institutional mechanism that promises to be more successful than at present in identifying and attracting "'better people." Who are they?

b. The Revolving Door

Popular wisdom identifies a partial cause of regulation's failure with the fact that many regulators have a financial stake in the well-being of the industry or firms that they regulate. This stake may consist of the ownership of stock in companies affected by regulatory action. It may arise out of hoped-for future employment, for many commissioners and agency staff leave the agency for work in (or for) regulated industry or law firms or other professional groups that serve industry. Or, it may arise out of past associations and loyalties, for staff and commissioners often come from regulated companies or their law firms as well.

Common Cause, in an empirical study of this problem, found:

— 518 employees in eleven agencies were found to have financial interests that conflicted, or appeared to conflict, with their official duties; 619 employees in these agencies who were required by agency regulations to file financial statements had failed to do so;

— 52 percent (or 22) of the 42 regulatory commissioners who were appointed during fiscal years 1971-1975 came from companies regulated by their agency, or from such companies' law firms;

— 48 percent (or 17) of the 36 commissioners who left during this five-year period went to work for regulated industries or their law firms;

— 5 of the 6 commissioners appointed to the Federal Trade Commission during the five-year period came from FTC-regulated companies or their law firms, and all 5 who left during this period took jobs with such companies or firms;

— 52.5 percent (or 73) of the top 139 employees of the Energy Research and Development Administration (ERDA) used to work for private enterprises in the energy field, and 75 percent of these employees came from ERDA contractors;

— 72 percent (or 307) of the top 429 employees of the Nuclear Regulatory Commission (NRC) had been employed by private energy enterprises, and 90 percent (or 279) of these 307 employees came from enterprises holding NRC licenses or contracts. Common Cause research also showed that 192 of these 279 employees came from firms that, in addition to having dealings with NRC, also had contracts with ERDA;

— 65 percent of NRC's 162 consultants were working both for NRC and for private enterprises that were recipients of NRC licenses or contracts;

— 35 percent (or 23) of 66 top Interior Department (DOI) officials had been employed by private enterprises involved in energy activities, and 52 percent (or 12) of these 23 employees came from private enterprises which have leases from DOI or received contracts from the Department;

— 20 of 29 former top agency officials who took industry jobs had, after leaving government, contacted officials in their former agency on policy matters or specific proceedings;
— 1406 Defense Department officers and employees left the Department between 1969 and 1973 to take jobs with defense contractors, and 379 of these employees went to work for contractors that they dealt with while in office or that were under their official jurisdiction;
— 11 of the 12 lawyers who, over the preceding five years, left the General Counsel's office of the Food and Drug Administration to take nongovernmental jobs went to work for regulated companies or their law firms.

Whether or not these findings are sufficiently typical to warrant their intended implication, most observers recognize that a "conflict of interest" problem exists and is significant.

Reformers have typically proposed three types of approach:

(1) *Public financial disclosure.* Executive branch officials would be required to file annual public financial disclosure statements stating all of their sources of income, including gifts, honorariums, and other items, as well as their net worth, including all property, companies, and organizations in which they held any financial interest. At present such statements are required of all top officials; some would like to see this reporting requirement extended below the level of political appointees to top agency and executive staff as well.

(2) *Divestiture.* Some critics of the administrative process would like to see a rule requiring all top officials and employees to divest, unless granted a specific exemption, all financial interests in any company or organization which is affected in any way by any proceeding in which they participate. Such a requirement now applies to judges in the sense that a federal judge must "disqualify himself" whenever he knows "that he . . . or his spouse or minor child . . . has a financial interest in the subject matter in controversy . . . or any other interest that could be substantially affected by the outcome of the proceeding." 28 U.S.C. §455.

(3) *Postemployment restrictions.* Some have suggested requiring employees working for the government to sign contracts agreeing that for two years after he leaves the government he will not work, represent, or accept any compensation from any company or organization that was affected by proceedings in which he personally participated. Former employees might also be required to file a report of their current occupation and place of employment.

Common Cause suggests that, to enforce standards of the sort suggested, and to prevent other conflicts of interest:

— Agencies should hire "ethics counselors" (with authority to grant an occasional exception).
— A high level committee would handle the special cases of top officials.
— An executive committee would review financial statements within a fixed time deadline.
— The Civil Service Commission would enforce the rules by suspending any employee who violates them.

Proposals have also been made to clarify and expand the restrictions; the Code of Professional Responsibility limits on private practice by former government lawyers regarding matters which the lawyer dealt with or had supervisory responsibility for during his government employment. For example, if a lawyer was involved in drafting regulations for an agency, is she precluded from later defending a private client against enforcement of the same regulations? What if she was the General Counsel of the agency and was not personally involved in the drafting? A particularly controversial issue is whether the disqualification of a former government lawyer should extend to all of the other lawyers in her firm.[21]

Why have these suggestions not been welcomed by all those who believe in good government? Some point out that an effort to apply them strictly may make it that much more difficult to attract the "highly qualified" personnel who reformers typically claim are needed. Will top professionals accept jobs in the government if doing so requires them to sell all their investments, pay the resulting taxes, and reinvest in government securities? Of course, public interest lawyers, professors, and many others may not have such investments and thus would not be affected. But does this fact not suggest why "conflict of interest" proposals are frequently viewed not as "neutral" good government suggestions but rather as weighted towards one end of the political spectrum?

Others are concerned about privacy. What are the implications for privacy of working in an office where everyone — and the general public — knows one's net worth from day to day?

The most serious problem these proposals raise, however, concerns the government's need for expertise. The factual information base needed to carry on the many regulatory activities, ranging from determining how pollution controls ought to be implemented to how energy should be allocated, is enormous. Administrators possessing detailed knowledge of the industry — those familiar with its workings, problems, and standards — can often move far more quickly and effectively than those coming fresh to the problem. (For example, it took the National Highway Transportation Safety Administration more than seven years to determine what tire characteristics should appear on a tire's label and how they should be measured. The standard might never have been developed had the job of doing so not been placed in the hands of an agency official who had previously worked for a tire company for 35 years.) Those familiar enough with the industry to possess the necessary qualifications for appointment to many agencies are likely to have had some prior industry connection. Moreover, if younger employees cannot look for future employment in the regulated industry or the law firms that serve it, will they seek jobs in regulatory agencies? Must they choose between permanent government careers and careers totally outside it?

The questions are meant to show how "revolving door" proposals imply major change in the nature of the Civil Service. They may well move the country in the

---

21. See Former Government Attorneys in Private Practice — Final Legal Ethics Committee Proposal for Comment, 3 District Lawyer 44 (1978); Note, Ethical Problems for the Law Firm of a Former Government Attorney: Firm or Individual Disqualification?, 1977 Duke L.J. 512.

direction of a more professional, more permanent Civil Service less open to penetration or "leavening" by temporary appointees from business or the professions — rather more like the French or British models. Whether it is possible to do so, whether it is desirable, whether such a Civil Service would become too powerful; whether it would be technically ignorant; whether it would prove more skilled and efficient — all are questions that you should begin to form an opinion about as you learn more about some of the concrete problems facing agency decision-makers.

3. *Increased Congressional Control of the Agencies*

Many critics of agency performance, including numerous senators and congressmen, believe that increased congressional supervision of the agencies would lead to improved performance. Some, but not all, proposals for increased congressional control should be considered in conjunction with proposals for substantive change. After all, only Congress can change an agency's legislative mandate. Other proposals, however, involve mechanisms for closer supervision and oversight of the daily work of an agency.

Most such proposals represent variations on the following themes:

(a) *Improved liaison.* Congress might hire special liaison personnel responsible to Congress itself and place them within the agencies.

"Liaison personnel located within regulatory agencies may provide Congress with access to valuable information. At present, Congress usually gets only an agency's official view of its activities — a view which may filter out unfavorable, though potentially important, information. With liaison personnel stationed physically within an agency's confines, Congress may be better able to find out just how it functions. Such an arrangement might also facilitate communication between congressional and agency staffs.

"The idea of having liaison personnel in regulatory agencies may or may not be objectionable to the agencies, but it should be noted that twelve of the executive agencies now have more than 500 congressional liaison officers, many of whom use congressional office space.

"Development of a close relationship between the liaison officer and the agency, however, may lead to co-option of the officer if measures are not taken to prevent it. Other problems arise: To whom would the liaison personnel report? How would the Congress efficiently utilize the information provided by a liaison officer?

"Of course, Congress has agencies such as the GAO that can maintain liaison with regulatory agencies. Legislators and staff also maintain formal and informal liaison with agency officials. Placing liaison officers within the agencies, though, may improve upon these existing relationships." [22]

22. Ribicoff, Congressional Oversight and Regulatory Reform, 28 Ad. L. Rev. 415, 423 (1976).

In evaluating the proposal, ask yourself, what precisely is the liaison officer supposed to do? Does it matter whether he is hired by the agency or by Congress?

(b) *Increased use of oversight.* Different congressional committees tend to exercise jurisdiction over the work of a particular regulatory agency. Thus the Aviation Subcommittee of the Senate Commerce Committee is concerned with the CAB; the Health Subcommittee will review the work of the FDA; and the Energy Subcommittee of the Interior Committee will review the work of the FPC.

For the most part, these subcommittees and committees exercise *legislative* jurisdiction; they consider proposals for new laws, and they may hold hearings designed to determine how particular provisions of old laws are being implemented. They will also review the budget authorization request of an agency.[23]

Occasionally, a committee or subcommittee undertakes a fundamental review of an agency's work, designed not with particular legislation in mind, but rather to see how well the agency is performing. Such reviews are rare. And the committee with general legislative authority is often so closely in touch with the agency that it does not need, or does not wish, general oversight hearings. For example, the first general review of the CAB's work was conducted in 1975, not by the Senate Commerce Committee Aviation Subcommittee, but by the Administrative Practices Subcommittee of the Judiciary Committee — a subcommittee that has only general oversight and virtually no legislative jurisdiction.

Some have argued that oversight hearings should be conducted more frequently, particularly by committees not directly responsible for the agency, for the latter may be biased in the agency's favor. The Ninety-third Congress required all large committees to set up separate subcommittees with responsibility for oversight work.

(c) *Special office for regulatory agency oversight.* "The idea is not without its problems, however. Even if it were implemented, there is no guarantee that additional oversight will be done unless committee chairmen take steps to insure it. Also, unless the reports of the oversight committee are readable and concise, the full committee members may well ignore the subcommittee's efforts. Finally, the establishment of separate oversight committees may wrongly imply that oversight is a 'pure notion.' As Walter Oleszek indicates, '[o]versight involves actions of a legislative, investigative and fiscal character, and to suggest that all oversight can be done by a specific subcommittee that lacks wide-ranging authority may not be a practicable idea.' " [24]

"[Some have proposed] that Congress create a special office to review regulatory agency activities. Such an office would presumably be an independent source of information on regulations issued by the agencies. It is also a potential source of additional expertise.

"Although Congress does need more information and expertise concerning the activities of the regulatory agencies, creation of a new office presents some

23. Appropriations committees also engage in oversight, but such review is rarely global or systematic. See M. Kirst, Government Without Passing Laws (1969).

24. Ribicoff, n.22 supra, at 425.

difficulties. Congress has recently created two new offices: the Congressional Budget Office and the Office of Technology Assessment. There is, of course, the danger the Congress will create its own mini-bureaucracy to cope with each of its problems. It might be better to devise ways for the standing committees with oversight responsibilities to develop the expertise themselves, rather than to rely on a new office. On the other hand, a new office may be better able to develop a comprehensive view of government regulation than any particular committee. The Government Operations study will review this type of proposal." [25]

One example of this sort of proposal is contained in S. 2878, 94th Cong., 2d Sess. (1976), proposed by Senators Javits and Muskie. The bill would establish an Office of Regulatory Oversight, which would be managed by a board of six congressmen, six senators and one staff director. The director would have a large staff, including outside consultants. The office would do the following:

(1) It would evaluate the work of existing agencies. It would identify the impact of regulation on particular industries and sectors; and it would determine which parts of the economy are underregulated and which overregulated. It would produce biannual reports on the work of each agency.

(2) It would provide any information about agency work needed by other congressional committees.

(3) Upon the request of a congressional committee, it would review any rule proposed by any agency and describe its likely effect. After obtaining the President's opinion, Congress, by joint resolution, might alter the rule.

(4) It would screen appointments and report on the qualification of nominees.

(5) It would recommend specific substantive and procedural improvements in agency work.

In addition, S. 2878 requires each agency to setup advisory councils with members from business, labor, consumer, public interest, and government groups. The councils would also screen nominees and promulgate conflict of interest regulations.

Obviously, the bill is far too ambitious in its hopes for the office; it has given the office the responsibility for "good government" itself. But, the issue remains whether the existence or creation of such an office would help bring about better performance by creating a small staff sufficiently knowledgeable and visible to criticize agency work productively.

(d) *Sunset legislation.* This type of legislation would terminate an agency's life after a given period of years, unless its mandate were specifically renewed by Congress. This approach was followed with respect to the Federal Energy Administration, originally created in 1974 by a law which provided the Administration would cease to exist after June 30, 1976. Colorado and Florida have enacted sunset laws and other states are considering them. The object of these proposals is to *force* the Executive and Congress to review the work of agencies and to enact reforms.

25. Id. at 424.

Two bills typify the various approaches to the problem. S. 2812, 94th Cong., 1st Sess. (1975) provides that every year for a five-year period the President would submit to Congress a plan for maintaining or reforming regulation of specified sectors of the economy. Within six months, the appropriate congressional committee would have to report a bill embodying any changes it wishes to make in existing regulation. If Congress neither enacted the committee's bill nor passed a resolution disapproving the President's plan, the plan would become law automatically three months later. If the President's plan was rejected, Congress would have to pass a substitute within a further six months or the agency would disappear and its regulations would become null and void.

Senate 3318, 94th Cong., 2d Sess. (1976) is more limited in scope. Congress would establish a specific schedule for terminating several regulatory agencies: the CAB, FAA, OSHA, FEA, ICC, and FMC. To avoid termination, these agencies would have to convince Congress that continued existence is justified. The bill is intended as a pilot project.

Note that sunset laws work by using the normal legislative presumption in favor of the status quo. It is harder to enact legislation than to defeat it. They require enactment to *preserve* an agency's life rather than to abolish it.

(e) *Zero-based budgeting.* This type of proposal requires an agency to justify its entire budget every few years.

"Customarily, the officials in charge of an established program have to justify only the increase which they seek above last year's appropriation. In other words, what they are already spending is usually accepted as necessary, without examination. Substantial savings could undoubtedly be realized if [it were required that] every agency . . . make a case for its entire appropriation request each year, just as if its program or programs were entirely new. Such budgeting procedure may be difficult to achieve, partly because it will add heavily to the burdens of budget-making, and partly also because it will be resisted by those who fear that their pet programs would be jeopardized by a system that subjects every . . . activity to annual scrutiny of its costs and results." [26]

Senate 2925, 94th Cong., 2d Sess. (1976) provides for quadrennial program review. Each budget must: (1) identify those government programs with the same or similar objectives with cost/effectiveness comparisons; (2) examine the extent to which programmatic goals have been achieved with specific analysis of variances; (3) specify in quantitative terms the program objectives over the next four years; and (4) examine the impact of each program on the national economy. Each budget submitted must be "zero-based"; each item must be defended line by line. A basic problem with this approach is that global reexamination of an agency's entire budget is a demanding task; often neither the data nor the the analytical tools required are available. In the face of limited information, time, and resources, both agencies and Congress may inevitably fall back on some form of incremental review.

(f) *Concurrent transmittal of budget proposals to Congress and OMB.* "Cur-

---

26. Address of Arthur Burns, Dec. 2, 1969, Plaza Hotel, New York, N.Y.

rently the Budget and Accounting Act of 1921 forbids independent agencies from submitting their own budgets to Congress. The Act requires that the budgets and requests of regulatory agencies be submitted to the Bureau of the Budget (now Office of Management and Budget). The budgets and requests for appropriations are then included in the budget that the President submits to Congress each year.

"Although one author contends that the Act is 'no more than an implementing tool to carry out the President's responsibility and duty to see that the laws are faithfully executed,' there is some merit to the charge that the Executive Branch has used the Act in ways not anticipated by Congress in order to gain control over the independent agencies. As A. Everett MacIntyre explains:

> When an agency submits its budget to the Bureau of the Budget [now OMB] each item contained therein must be extensively justified, and agency members and personnel may be asked for further elaborations during the course of personal interviews. An agency's proposed appropriations request is reviewed by the Bureau of the Budget, which follows policies and priorities established by the President and not necessarily by Congress. To the extent they coincide congressional intent will be fulfilled; to the extent they differ congressional intent will, of necessity, take a back seat.

In 1975, regulatory commission budget requests were reduced by approximately 4 to 24 percent. By cutting funds for different programs OMB engages in the establishment of priorities for regulation. Thus, 'what was intended as a purely housekeeping measure not infrequently has become an instrument of control over policy.'

"At least two bills currently before Congress would require independent regulatory agencies to submit their budget proposals to Congress at the same time the proposals are submitted to OMB. One of the primary purposes of these bills is to provide more information to Congress." [27]

A related proposal would prevent the President from requiring agencies to submit comments on legislative proposals to OMB for editing.[28] Thus Congress would receive the agency's "unexpurgated" opinions.

How much difference such proposals would make is debatable because in practice under the existing system congressmen sympathetic to expansion of the agency's resources and authority can often elicit an unexpurgated version of the agency's position.

(g) *Congressional veto of agency regulations.* "Perhaps the most controversial proposal for improved congressional oversight is the congressional 'veto' of agency rules. In its simplest form, such a proposal would allow either or both Houses of

27. Ribicoff, n.22 supra, at 422.
28. 7 U.S.C. §4a(h)(1970), for example, prevents any executive official from requiring the Commodity Futures Trading Commission to "submit its legislative recommendations, or testimony, or comments on legislation, to any officer or agency of the United States for approval, comments or review prior to [their] ... submission ... to the Congress." See also 15 U.S.C. §2076(k)(1)(1976) (Consumer Product Safety Commission).

Congress to disapprove an agency rule by simple or concurrent resolution within 60 or 90 days of the promulgation of the rule.

"Proponents of the legislative veto of agency regulations argue that such a provision is needed in order for Congress to reassert control over the regulatory process. They contend that the veto will be a valuable tool in making sure that agencies do not overstep their proper bounds. As a tool that is less cumbersome than the usual legislative process, it is, therefore, more attractive to legislators. Even if the veto is used only sparingly, it is argued that it will help assure the elected representatives of the people a say in important regulatory policy matters.

"Opponents of the proposal contend that it will create great administrative burdens for Congress. Thousands of regulations are promulgated each year, and it would be a great task to review each regulation within the suggested 60 or 90 day time period. Furthermore, there would be increased delay in the regulatory process because each regulation — even if it were not the subject of congressional interest — would be held up for the required 'laying over' period. Critics also argue that the legislative veto could be abused by well-financed and well-organized special interest groups. These groups might bypass the normal administrative processes in favor of what they consider a friendlier and more easily manipulated forum — the Congress. A regulation totally consistent with the substance and spirit of the law could be overturned by a resolution passed on a voice vote by a handful of members who may happen to be on the floor at that time." [29]

For additional discussion of the legislative veto, see Chapter 2, Section E.2, supra.

4. Increased Presidential Control of the Agencies

Some critics doubt that Congress has the ability or desire to police the agencies. The President himself, they argue, should be given additional power to control them. Consider the arguments advanced by Lloyd N. Cutler.

Cutler, Who Masters the Regulators?

Washington Post, Oct. 18, 1978

Every school child learns about the separation of powers. The federal government has three branches — legislative, executive, judicial. Right? Wrong.

Oh yes, we forgot the regulatory branch. The ICC, the CAB, the FCC, the SEC, the FTC, the NLRB, the FEC, the CPSC and about a dozen other agencies operate under laws that make them independent of the legislative and executive branches. So there are really four branches. Right? Wrong, because each of these

29. Ribicoff, n.22 supra, at 426-427.

independent agencies is also independent of every other agency. So that makes about 23 branches? Careful, you may well be wrong again.

For there is a new theory abroad in the land that even regulatory agencies *within* the executive branch are also independent of the president and of one another. There are over 60 such agencies, many of them parts of a Cabinet department. According to this new theory, the president — the chief executive of the nation and the head of the executive branch — does not have the last word over what any of these agencies can do. Indeed, he cannot even have the first word. He is not supposed to intervene in their regulatory actions at all. Whatever you may have learned in civics class, the new theory denies that the president is in charge of the whole executive branch.

The new theory rejects any such unitary concept of the executive branch on both legal and policy grounds. The legal issue is now being tested in the case of OSHA's cotton-dust standards. It raises one of the most important constitutional questions of modern times.

OSHA is part of the Department of Labor. It was created by a 1975 statute to set standards for health and safety in the workplace. It proposed issuing a standard governing the permissible level of "cotton dust" in textile mills, where excessive levels have led to the widespread occupational disease called "brown lung." The proposed levels were challenged by the textile industry because they require expensive equipment and their technical feasibility is doubted. Charles Schultze, chairman of President Carter's Council of Economic Advisers, became concerned that the proposed levels and technical requirements would have an unduly inflationary impact, and he persuaded the president that certain modifications would provide a better balance between the nation's occupational health and anti-inflation goals. He wrote to Secretary of Labor Marshall, proposing these modifications with the president's approval. Secretary Marshall objected to the modifications, and in a meeting with both his Cabinet aides, the president worked out a compromise. That compromise was embodied in the final regulation, over the objection of the Textile Workers Union. The Union has now appealed OSHA's regulation to the courts on a variety of grounds. One ground is that the president's intervention was illegal, because the OSHA statute vests the power to issue the regulation in the secretary of labor, and the president could not lawfully instruct the secretary how to exercise his statutory discretion.

This case capsulizes a basic problem of our federal government today, a problem that has recently been examined by the American Bar Association's Commission on Law and the Economy, headed by one of the nation's most distinguished lawyer-statesmen, John J. McCloy. As the McCloy Commission noted, we have adopted a wide variety of economic and social goals — such as checking inflation, spurring economic growth, reducing unemployment, improving workplace health and safety, cleaning up the environment and closing the energy gap. We are only beginning to realize that many of these goals directly conflict with one another, and that even in a country as richly endowed as ours, all of them compete for the same limited resources. We cannot pursue them all in full measure at the same time.

A critical task of modern democratic government is to make wise balancing choices among proposed courses of action that pursue one or more of these conflicting and competing objectives.

We have delegated each of our conflicting and competing goals to a different regulatory agency, sometimes even dividing a single goal (e.g., employment discrimination) among a number of overlapping and competing agencies. Each agency has limited responsibility for balancing a proposed action in pursuit of its primary goal against adverse impacts on the pursuit of other goals. Each agency asserts an independence from the political process, and from the other agencies, that weakens the national ability to make balancing choices, or to hold anyone accountable when choices are made badly or not at all.

Many of our regulatory agencies were created under laws that make them expressly independent of both the president and the Congress. While others like OSHA are merely part of an executive branch department, their governing laws vest the power to issue regulations in the secretary of the department rather than the president. To confuse matters further, some of these laws expressly require presidential review and approval of particular actions by the secretary, perhaps implying that he is not authorized to modify or disapprove other actions.

As a result, many of the interest groups who support the single missions of particular regulatory agencies, as well as many members of Congress and others who mistrust an "imperial" presidency, regard presidential intervention in the regulations issued by executive branch agencies as illegal, or at least undesirable. Where Harry Truman was fond of saying, "The buck stops here," they prefer a regulatory system in which the buck stops nowhere. And for a variety of political reasons, presidents have in fact been loath to step into regulatory issues. Indeed, a number of President Carter's aides regard his recent encounter with cotton dust as politically costly to him. . . .

In this lawyer's opinion, the president does indeed possess the ultimate constitutional power over the content and the timing of regulations issued by executive branch agencies, so long as the action taken is within the agency's statutory authority. As a matter of political theory and policy, the president ought to assert such power whenever he deems it necessary to make an important balancing choice among conflicting and competing national goals.

Article II of the Constitution vests the executive power in "a president." It does not authorize the Congress to distribute some of that power to the president's subordinates free of presidential control. Its principal reference to executive departments is to the power of the president to "require the opinion, in writing, of the principal officer in each of the executive departments" — language that implies he is not bound to accept any such "opinion." It is the president, not any of his executive branch subordinates, who is constitutionally empowered to "take care that the laws be faithfully executed."

The Constitution adopts Montesquieu's brilliant theory of the separation of powers among the principal branches of government. The basic argument for the theory is the need for each of the three main branches to check and balance the other two. That argument does not justify the indefinite number of sub-separations of power *within* the executive branch that are implicit in the notion that the Congress may delegate specific compartments of power to separate officers of that branch, and at the same time deny the president the power to supervise their actions. . . .

When major balancing decisions must be made, only elected officials and their immediate staffs can provide the requisite overview and coordination, and stand accountable at the polls for the results. The Congress cannot perform these tasks by legislating the details of one regulatory decision after another; that is why Congress delegated much of this power to executive branch agencies in the first place. The president is the elected official most capable of making the needed balancing decisions as critical regulatory issues arise within his own executive branch, while the most appropriate and effective role for Congress is to review and, where necessary, curb particular presidential interventions.

Should the president decide to take up the gauntlet, he should do so openly. He should observe appropriate procedural safeguards of public notice and opportunity for comment. He should comply with any applicable *ex parte* rules that would apply to the agency itself. He should confine his actions to the relatively few truly critical occasions when a balance needs to be struck between conflicting and competing national goals. . . .

Lloyd Cutler and David Johnson have proposed the following:

Cutler & Johnson, Regulation and the Political Process

84 Yale L.J. 1395, 1414-1417 (1975)

As a first step to bring the decisions and policies of the independent agencies within the continuing control of both elected branches of government, and to require the elected branches to assume continuing responsibility for the work of their offspring, we suggest a statute that would authorize the President to modify or direct certain agency actions, and to set priorities among competing statutory goals, subject to a one-house congressional veto and to expedited judicial review. Our proposed statute would have the following principal features:

(1) The President would be authorized to direct any regulatory agency (a) to take up and decide a regulatory issue within a specified period of time, or (b) to modify or reverse an agency policy, rule, regulation or decision (with the exception noted in paragraph 4 below). Such action could be taken only by Executive Order published in the Federal Register, setting forth presidential findings that the action or inaction of an agency on a regulatory issue (or a conflict in the actions or policies of various agencies) threatened to interfere with or delay the achievement of an important national objective, and stating the reasons for such findings.

(2) No such Order could be issued until 30 days after publication of a notice in the Federal Register stating the President's intention to consider doing so and inviting written comments from interested members of the public thereon. All such comments would be maintained in a public docket file. No public hearing would be required. The President and his staff would be barred from receiving oral presentations from interested persons (except where the affected agency's own ex parte rules would bar such a presentation to the agency itself), but a public record of those attending any such informal meeting and a summary of what took place would have to be kept.

(3) Any such Executive Order would not take effect for 60 legislative days, and would not take effect at all if within such 60-day period either house of Congress adopted a resolution setting it aside.

(4) No such Order could be issued with respect to any agency selection among competing applicants for the grant or renewal of a particular license or privilege or any subsequent revocation of such a particular license or privilege.

(5) Any agency order resulting from such an Executive Order would be subject to judicial review for conformity with the statutory powers governing such agency, except that the President's determination of relative priority among statutory goals of the particular agency and of other government agencies would be deemed conclusive if a rational basis therefor is set out in the Executive Order. Judicial review of agency orders resulting from such Executive Orders would be expedited in accordance with a specified statutory timetable not exceeding 180 days for all proceedings up to and including the filing of appeals or petitions for review in the Supreme Court.

President Nixon, Conversations[30]

[Consider the following excerpts from a discussion in President Nixon's office, including a telephone call by President Nixon to Deputy Attorney General Richard Kleindienst:]

Beginning at 3:03 P.M. on the afternoon of April 19, 1971 the President met with White House Special Assistant Ehrlichman and George Shultz, Director of the Office of Management and Budget. The antitrust actions against ITT were among the subjects discussed. Ehrlichman said that the deadline for the ITT-Grinnell appeal [an appeal by the government from an adverse court decision in a government-filed suit to set aside an ITT merger with Grinnell] was the following day and he reported that, despite his attempts to give the Justice Department "signals," the appeal was being pursued. The President then telephoned Kleindienst and ordered him to drop the appeal. After the telephone conversation the President

30. Hearings pursuant to H.R. Res. 803 Before the House Comm. on the Judiciary, 93d Cong., 2d Sess., book V, pt. 1, at 311-320, 346-378; book VIII, at 321-323 (1974); as edited by H. Linde & G. Bunn, Legislative and Administrative Processes (1977).

expressed his concern that Assistant Attorney General for the Anti-Trust Division McLaren's actions with respect to conglomerates were contrary to the Administration's antitrust policy.

EHRLICHMAN: We are going to see the Attorney General tomorrow, and by then it may be too late, in a sense, —

PRESIDENT: Hm. Honestly?

EHRLICHMAN: ITT case, where God knows we have made your position as clear as we could to Mr. what's-his-name over there.

PRESIDENT: McLaren.

EHRLICHMAN: And, uh, John [Mitchell, the then Attorney General and the President's former law partner] has said because ITT is involved, he's not involved because he's got a conflict of interest going back to the old law firm. Richard Kleindienst, uh, uh, has been supervising McLaren's work. It's the *Grinnell* case. It involves an attack on, uh, conglomerates, on a theory which specifically had been contemplated by the Johnson Administration and laid aside as too anti-business.

PRESIDENT: Kleindienst is in this? [*Picks up telephone.*]

How long before that [unintelligible] do you expect a moritorium?

EHRLICHMAN: Well, they filed a notice of appeal. If we do not file a statement of jurisdiction by tomorrow the case is dead, and, uh, —

PRESIDENT: Who?

EHRLICHMAN: The Justice Department.

PRESIDENT: They're not going to file.

EHRLICHMAN: Well, I thought that was your position.

PRESIDENT: Oh, hell.

EHRLICHMAN: I've been trying to give, I've been trying to give them signals on this, and, uh, they've been horsing us pretty steadily. Uh, uh, Geneen [President of ITT] . . .

PRESIDENT: I don't want to know anything about the case. I don't want to know about Geneen. I've met him and I don't know — I don't know whether ITT is bad, good, or indifferent. But there is not going to be any more antitrust actions as long as I am in this chair. . . .

EHRLICHMAN: All right. There's this other one that you are going to talk to John about tomorrow on the networks.

PRESIDENT: Well, I don't want him to do that, for other reasons.

EHRLICHMAN: Well, that's right. This, that's —

PRESIDENT: These are all coming together.

EHRLICHMAN: This is the wrong time.

PRESIDENT: We wanted to do that at another time. . . . [*Picks up telephone.*] Yeah.

Hi, Dick, how are you?

Fine, fine. I'm going to talk to John tomorrow about my general attitude on antitrust, and in the meantime, I know that he has left with you, uh, the IT&T thing because apparently he says he had something to do with them once.

Well, I have, I have nothing to do with them, and I want something clearly understood, and, if it is not understood, McLaren's ass is to be out within one hour. The IT&T thing — stay the hell out of it. Is that clear? That's an order.

The order is to leave the goddamned thing alone. Now, I've said this, Dick, a number of times, and you fellows apparently don't get the me——, the message over there. I do not want McLaren to run around prosecuting people, raising hell about conglomerates, stirring things up at this point. Now, you keep him the hell out of that. Is that clear?

Or either he resigns. I'd rather have him out anyway. I don't like the son-of-a-bitch.

The question is, I know, that the jurisdiction — I know all the legal things, Dick, you don't have to spell out the legal — . . .

That's right. Don't file the brief.

Your — my order is to drop the goddamn thing. Is that clear?

Okay. [*Hangs up.*]

SCHULTZ: From the standpoint of the economics of it, uh, I would be the last to say we should not continue, uh, to, uh, pursue the antitrust laws in the proper way, but, the, uh — I think the conglomerates have taken a bum rap.

PRESIDENT: This is, this is the problem. The problem is McLaren's a nice little fellow who's a good little antitrust lawyer out of Chicago. Now he comes in and all these bright little bastards that worked for the Antitrust Department for years and years and years and who hate business with a passion — any business — have taken him over.

. . . There's simply a question of tactically, they've gone off on a kick, that'll make them big goddamn trust busters. That was all right fifty years ago. Fifty years ago maybe it was a good thing for the country. It's not a good thing for the country today. That's my views about it, and I am not — We've been, been through this crap. They've done several of them already about — They have raised holy hell with the people that we, uh, uh — Well, Geneen, hell, he's no contributor. He's nothing to us. I don't care about him. So you can — I've only met him once, twice — uh, we've, I'm just, uh — I can't understand what the trouble is.

EHRLICHMAN: Well, —

PRESIDENT: It's McLaren, isn't it?

EHRLICHMAN: McLaren has a very strong sense of mission here.

PRESIDENT: Good — Jesus, he's — Get him out. In one hour. . . .

And he's not going to be a judge, either. He is out of the goddamn government. You know, just like that regional office man, in, San Francisco. I put an order in to Haldeman today that he be fired today. . . .

Oh, I know what McLaren is, he believes this.

EHRLICHMAN: Yeah.

PRESIDENT: I know. Who the hell — he wasn't elected [unintelligible].

EHRLICHMAN: That's the point —

PRESIDENT: He is here by sufferance.

EHRLICHMAN: That's the point.

PRESIDENT: And he is not going to stay one, uh, another minute. Not a minute. . . .

Compare the following excerpt from another conversation:

SPECIAL ASSISTANT
JOHN DEAN: The [Washington] Post, as you know, has got a real large team that they've assigned to do nothing but this [Watergate case].

Couldn't believe they put Maury Stans' [a Nixon cabinet member and later a Nixon fund raiser] story about his libel suit, which was just playing so heavily on the networks last night, and in the evening news, they put it way back on about page eight of the Post. . . .

PRESIDENT NIXON: I expect that. That's all right. We've [unintelligible].

SPECIAL ASSISTANT
H. R. HALDEMAN: The Post is —

PRESIDENT: The Post has asked — it's going to have its problems.

DEAN: The networks, the networks are good with Maury coming back three days in a row and —

PRESIDENT: That's right. Right. The main thing is the Post is going to have damnable, damnable problems out of this one. They have a television station —

DEAN: That's right, they do.

PRESIDENT: And they're going to have to get it renewed.

HALDEMAN: They've got a radio station, too.

PRESIDENT: Does that come up too? The point is, when does it come up?

DEAN:	I don't know. But the practice of nonlicensees filing on top of licensees has certainly gotten more —
PRESIDENT:	That's right.
DEAN:	More active in the, in the area.
PRESIDENT:	And it's going to be goddamn active here.

What difference in the propriety of President Nixon's actions, if any, do you find between the *ITT* example and the *Post* example? Are the Watergate tapes still relevant to our institutional problems? How? Abuses of office can be found in the legislative and judicial branch as well as the executive, can't they?

Consider the following reply to the Cutler essay, bearing in mind the potential relevance of the Nixon tapes.

Morrison, Should the President Control the Regulators?

Washington Post, Nov. 2, 1978

Lloyd Cutler's Oct. 18 op-ed article "Who Masters the Regulators?" forcefully argues that the President should have the right to control any decision made by any part of the executive branch. The debate surrounding his position has taken on new importance because President Carter asserted in his anti-inflation speech of Oct. 24 that he will in fact use the power of his office to prevent the issuance of regulations that he considers inflationary. While the matter may end up in court, there are, it seems to me, strong policy as well as legal reasons why presidential control of regulatory decisions should be denied.

The article contains three separate views of the current situation. First, it suggests, as the president apparently assumes, that the president now has the authority to do what he did in the cotton-dust case — change the decision made of the Department of Labor. The difficulty with that analysis is that Congress has specifically given him that authority in areas such as international aviation routes, pay of government officials, the issuance of passports and the requirements for obtaining a job in the federal civil service. The absence of such authority in the field of occupational health strongly suggests that Congress did not intend the president to be the final decision-maker there.

Second, Cutler concludes that, to the extent that the president does not have such authority, the statute is unconstitutional. To sustain that position, it would be necessary to overcome language in a 1926 decision of the Supreme Court, in which Chief Justice William H. Taft observed that, "Of course there may be duties so peculiarly and specifically committed to the discretion of a particular officer as to raise a question whether the president may overrule or revise the officer's interpretation of his statutory duty in a particular instance."

Although it ruled unconstitutional a provision requiring the consent of the Senate before an important federal officer could be fired by the president, the court in the quoted language, as well as in other portions of that and subsequent opinions, has been seen as indicating that a statute that precluded presidential interference with decisions by his own cambinet members would be upheld. Thus, while the president could have fired Secretary Ray Marshall for his decision in the cotton-dust case, he does not have the right to change what the secretary concluded was required by the facts and the law.

Third, Cutler's views can be seen as a plea to change the law and specifically authorize presidential decisionmaking throughout the executive branch. While that position is surely a debatable one, it seems to me unwise for a variety of reasons.

Before looking at some of those reasons, it might be useful to spend a minute examining what took place in the cotton-dust case itself, since the article appears to endorse the White House's role there. The statute at issue gives the secretary of labor the authority to issue final health and safety standards, including standards limiting the amount of cotton dust in the air in textile factories. The agency's rules require that a hearing be held and that the decision be based on the record compiled by it. In those hearings, any agency of the government or member of the public can — and in this case the White House's Council on Wage and Price Stability did — submit comments about the standard, including its alleged inflationary impact.

But the White House was not satisfied to have its views considered like everyone else's. Thus, after the record was closed, and at the final stages of the process, the White House staff began a series of meetings with officials of the Occupational Safety and Health Administration in an effort to persuade them to revise their views on the basis of data submitted by the White House. That data was untested, its source is uncertain, and there was no opportunity for the workers, whose lives are directly affected by breathing cotton dust, to comment on it.

Because the White House proceedings were conducted in secret, the precise basis for the White House's request for modification is not entirely clear. If, as it appears, general inflationary considerations were at the heart of the objections, it is open to serious question as to whether those concerns are legally relevant under a statute that already requires that standards be "feasible," which the courts have construed to include both economic and technical feasibility. Congress was well aware of the costs of providing adequate standards, and it rejected an approach that would have put dollar values on the health of working men and women in this country. Thus, if there is to be a change in the law, it must be Congress, and not the president, who makes it. Moreover, even if those considerations are relevant, is it fair to make those arguments without giving the opponents a chance to analyze the data and reply?

More generally, is it really desirable to set the White House up as a new Inflationary Advocacy Agency? In light of economic forecasts emanating from the White House in the past, there is the serious question of whether any White House is technically competent to perform that service. Any such activity would require a significant expansion of the White House staff to take on such complex issues beyond the additional 100 economists added by President Carter to police wage and price increases.

No doubt it will be argued that the White House will only need to be involved in a few cases. The difficulty is that it will be impossible to decide which are those few appropriate cases without a large staff to make preliminary determinations.

More important, the question of which cases to enter will become a political football, with every lobbyist in town calling the White House asking for an opportunity to explain why his case is the single one that requires presidential supervision. Doesn't the White House have enough problems without adding a whole new layer of difficulties on top?

_____

Who has the better of the debate, Cutler or Morrison? On issues of law? (Review the discussion in Chapter 2, pp. 92-95 supra.) On questions of policy? [31] What are the strengths and drawbacks of presidential intervention as compared to congressional veto proposals? [32]

5. Altering Agency Structure

Many critics believe that agency performance can be significantly improved by changing agency structure. More specifically, the structure of the independent agencies has been criticized on such grounds as (1) adjudication and management functions should not be combined; (2) multimember boards cannot manage effectively; and (3) independence from the President breeds irresponsibility. In 1937, the President's Committee on Administrative Management observed:

> For the purposes of management, boards and commissions have turned out to be failures. Their mechanism is inevitably slow, cumbersome, wasteful, and ineffective, and does not lend itself readily to cooperation with other agencies. Even strong men on boards find that their individual opinions are watered down in reaching board decisions. When freed from the work of management, boards are, however, extremely useful and necessary for consultation, discussion, and advice; for representation of diverse views and citizen opinion; for quasi-judicial action; and as a repository for corporate powers.
> The conspicuously well-managed administrative units in the Government are almost without exception headed by single administrators.

The First Hoover Commission[33] concluded that chairmen are "to frequently merely presiding officers at commission meetings. No one has been responsible for planning and guiding the general program of commission activity." Finding that administra-

---

31. See also American Bar Association Commission on Law and the Economy, Federal Regulation: Roads to Reform (Exposure Draft 1978), which inclines to the Cutler view, although several members of the Commission issued separate opinions expressing the view advocated by Morrison.

32. See also Byse, Comments on a Structural Reform Proposal: Presidential Directives to Independent Agencies, 29 Ad. L. Rev. 157 (1977).

33. Commission on Organization of the Executive Branch of the Government (1947-1949).

tion by plural executives was universally regarded as inefficient, it noted that it was very difficult for a bureau chief to report to five or more masters. The Second Hoover Commission[34] reached similar conclusions, as did the Landis Report in 1960. As a result of the Landis work, the agencies' structure was somewhat changed. The power of the chairman was increased and his term redefined so that he serves as chairman at the pleasure of the President.

The most recent thorough study of agency structure is that of the Ash Commission in 1972.[35] Excerpts from its report are reproduced p. 115 supra, and p. 786 infra. The Commission made four major suggestions for agency reform: (a) The multimember commission structure should be changed; each agency should be headed by a single administrator, directly responsible to the President. (b) The jurisdiction of the present agencies should be altered. (c) Internal review of decisions within the agency should be sharply circumscribed. (d) A new administrative court should be established to review most administrative decisions.

We shall consider these suggestions and other proposals for changing agency structure in more detail in Chapter 8, p. 781 infra. Consider also the implications for agency performance of the scope of the agency's responsibilities. In what ways might the proneness to "failure" of an agency (such as the CAB) charged with regulating many aspects of a particular industry's performance differ from that of an agency (such as the FTC or EPA) charged with regulating a particular aspect of the behavior of business generally?

6. New Institutions

Various suggestions have been made to create new institutions that will improve agency performance — some by providing greater technical capabilities, others by forcing the agencies to focus more directly on the problems of consumers as ordinary citizens. The following types of proposals are typical:

(a) An administrative court. The Ash Council recommended creating a separate court — like the tax court — whose sole function would be to review the decisions of the securities, energy, and transportation agencies. The judges would develop substantive expertise and thus find it easier to determine when a decision was arbitrary. A single expert court would also encourage the development of a uniform body of administrative law; it would reduce procedural differences among agencies; and it might handle cases more expeditiously. Ash proposed a court of 15 judges, appointed for 15-year terms, serving in panels of three.[36]

(b) A technical review board. Many agency decisions are based upon collection and analysis of technical data. Many judges feel that they lack sufficient

34. Commission on Organization of the Executive Branch of the Government (1953-1955).
35. President's Advisory Council on Executive Organization, A New Regulatory Framework: Report on Selected Independent Agencies (1971).
36. A Commerce Court, composed of federal circuit judges on special assignment, was created in 1910 to review decisions of the Interstate Commerce Commission but was abolished within three years. See 1 I. Sharfman, The Interstate Commerce Commission 52-70 (1935). A specialized court to review environmental controversies was proposed and rejected in the early 1970s. See Comment, Attorney General's Report Rejects Establishing an Environmental Court, 4 Envtl. L. Rptr. 10019 (1974).

knowledge of economics, statistics, computers, engineering, or science to know whether the agency has reasonably evaluated the information that is possessed. In fact, many agencies themselves are dominated by lawyers and lack the skills needed to develop and to evaluate technocratic arguments.

A technical review board, composed of experts in technical disciplines, might serve as advisors to judges or to agencies. They would not present evidence, but would help organize and evaluate evidence presented by others. It might offer this advice formally, giving the parties a chance to criticize, or informally, like a law clerk.[37]

(c) *The ombudsman.* Ombudsmen have proved successful in many foreign countries, several states, and a handful of American cities. Traditionally the ombudsman can react to citizen complaints or act on his own initiative. He can investigate, criticize, publicize, and recommend changes in any administrative action, procedure, or practice. But he does not have the power to change or modify any administrative act himself.[38]

Ombudsmanlike functions are performed at the federal level, but not by an ombudsman. The power to examine agency procedures and practices, for example, rests in the hands of —

(1) the Administrative Conference of the United States, an agency which studies other agencies and issues lengthy reports and makes many proposals for reform each year;

(2) the Office of Management and Budget, which considers the effectiveness of an agency's performance when it reviews the requested budgets; and

(3) committees of Congress, which conduct budget reviews and investigate agency malpractices.

The power to investigate and prosecute criminal misbehavior on the part of public officials belongs to the Department of Justice. When the Department's activities themselves were at issue, an office of Special Prosecutor was created.

The power and the obligation to investigate in response to citizen complaints — to cut through agency red tape, produce action, and correct individual instances of injustice — rest in the hands of 100 senators and 435 congressmen. A major function of each congressional office is to handle these complaints. Staff are assigned to forward complaints from constituents to agencies with requests for speedy action or response. Congressional inquiries are given top priority within the agencies. Of course, the congressional offices may not be so careful as an ombudsman to separate legitimate from unjustified complaints. Correcting a wrong can often look much like doing a constituent a favor. Yet, this very fact means that the congressman's service, in correcting wrongs, helps him build a political base within his constituency; it brings him political power. Is it likely then that he would want to give up some of the source of his power to an ombudsman?

(d) *The Consumer Protection Agency and other special-purpose advocacy*

---

37. See B. Ackerman et al., The Uncertain Search for Environmental Quality 147-161 (1974).

38. See generally W. Gellhorn, When Americans Complain (1966); W. Gellhorn, Ombudsmen & Others (1966); Frank, State Ombudsman Legislation in the United States, 29 U. Miami L. Rev. 397 (1975).

agencies. For several years congressional supporters of a Consumer Protection Agency have come close to securing its creation. The major function of such an agency would be to represent the consumer point of view in proceedings before most federal agencies, Congress, and the courts. It would also gather information and make recommendations for legislation and other changes in Congress that would benefit consumers. See the excerpt from a Senate Report favoring the creation of such an agency, pp. 123-126 supra.

Supporters of such legislation argue that consumers are often underrepresented before agencies that make decisions that significantly affect them. All special interests organize and secure representation, for each member of a special interest knows he can be affected significantly by its outcome. Consumers, however, are far harder to organize; there are more of them, communication is more difficult and expensive, and no one consumer is likely to be hurt as much by any individual decision. The object of the CPA is to redress this representational balance.

Those opposed to the Agency argue that agencies already are instructed to represent the public interest and that that interest should be no different from that of the consumer. How is the CPA to decide whether natural gas prices should stay low or should increase to provide more gas? Which is in the consumer's interest? The decision is no easier for the CPA than the FPC, and the FPC is more qualified to make it. Moreover, the head of the CPA will have great political power and authority; his independence does not offer adequate assurance that his power will be used responsibly. Finally, if there are problems with agencies, these stem from the growth of administration; there is too much bureaucracy; and one cannot effectively deal with the problem of "too many agencies" by creating yet another.

If a special advocate agency for consumers is justified, what about similar agencies for other interest groups? To some extent existing government agencies with other functions — such as the Environmental Protection Agency and the Departments of Commerce, Labor, and Agriculture — play a broader advocate role within government for their "constituents." Should other interests — the handicapped prisoners, bus riders — also be provided with an advocate agency?

(e) *Public disclosure.* To what extent might public disclosure of agency information and deliberations serve as an effective and desirable check on agency discretion by subjecting agency decisionmaking to media publicity and public scrutiny? An affirmative answer is implicit in the federal Freedom of Information Act, which requires (with certain exceptions) disclosure by federal agencies to "any person" of agency documents, and the Government Sunshine Act, which requires that meetings of multimember federal agencies be open to the public. These statutes, and judicial decisions interpreting their requirements, are examined in Chapter 10.

D. The Role of the Courts in Controlling Administrative Action — A Transitional Note

In this chapter we have surveyed various forms of criticism of the agencies' exercise of their considerable policymaking discretion and examined a variety of potential legislative/executive solutions to the problem of discretion, ranging from abolition of the agencies to the creation of new forms of oversight.

In practice, however, the principal burden of reviewing and controlling administrative decisions has fallen to the courts. As we will see in Chapter 9, the courts have in recent years expanded their role through a number of doctrinal changes that have facilitated the invocation of judicial review. Moreover, it is likely that judges and lawyers will for the forseeable future continue to play a central role in controlling administrative power.

In the following chapters we examine how judges have traditionally performed their reviewing role, and how they have developed new techniques of control in response to the developing criticism of administrative failure.

In Chapter 4 we examine the courts' review of the legal and factual bases for agency action. The essential question here is the scope of judicial review in the context of broad statutory delegations. If courts simply restrict themselves to ensuring that agencies operate within the broad bounds of statutory authority, then agencies will enjoy a considerable measure of uncontrolled discretion. If, on the other hand, courts select the dispositive rule or policy whenever the statute is vague or general, courts would be assuming policymaking functions which they are often ill-equipped to decide, which involve "political" tradeoffs, and which have arguably been reserved by the legislature for agencies rather than courts. We will also consider whether there is a viable third alternative, under which courts would examine whether agencies, in exercising their discretion, adequately considered all relevant factors and rationally explained their choices, but with the ultimate power of choice being left to the agencies.

In Chapter 5 we examine a different approach to the problem of agency discretion along lines advocated by Professor Davis, in which courts seek to require that agencies adopt relatively precise and intelligible rules or standards and follow them consistently. Professor Davis argues that it is unwise and largely futile to attempt to force the legislature to specify policy in detail, and that instead courts should require agencies to do so through adoption of consistently applied rules, principles, and standards that would narrow the agency's effective discretion, render the exercise of government power more predictable, and facilitate outside review and oversight.

In Chapters 6 and 7 we examine a third approach to the problem of agency discretion — the imposition of formal procedural requirements for agency decisionmaking designed to improve the quality of that decisionmaking and to assure input by those governed by the administrator's policy choices.

As you learn of the many procedural requirements embodied in judicial decisions and seek to evaluate their efficacy, you should ask two separate sets of questions. First, you should ask whether they are likely to cure the sorts of problems that have led agency critics to criticize that particular agency as unfair or ineffective. Second, you should ask whether the procedure is desirable in its own right, regardless of its impact on agency effectiveness. It is probable that more procedures will be found justified on the second ground than the first. In any event, judicial attempts to improve agency performance by mandating improved procedures constitutes much of the basic subject matter of this course.

Chapter 8, focusing on agency structures, examines the partial separation of adjudicatory from investigating and prosecuting functions within the agency. It also considers the requirement that agencies adhere to some extent to principles of decisionmaking impartiality applicable in judicial proceedings, and the possibilities for internal reform by agencies themselves.

Finally, in Chapter 10 we examine the courts' extension of a number of traditional doctrines to develop an "interest representation" model of administrative law that transforms agency proceedings and judicial review into a surrogate political process in which all of the interests with a recognized stake in agency policies may be represented.

None of these various approaches is necessarily inconsistent with any other, and they may often be complementary. For example, procedural formalities generate an evidentiary record that in turn facilitates more searching judicial review of the decision. But each represents a different point of emphasis in the judicial effort to control administrative power. You should critically evaluate these various approaches in terms of their success in meeting some of the central concerns raised in this chapter. To what extent are these various judicial responses likely to correct agency "failure"? Are they likely to exacerbate certain forms of agency "failure" because of the delays, resource costs, and adversary posture generated by decisional formalities and judicial review? To what extent do they create a viable conceptual structure that serves to legitimate the exercise of governmental authority by administrative agencies? Do the most basic problems with the administrative process relate to fundamental choices of substantive policy that can only be initiated and carried out by the legislature and the executive?

4

The Scope of Judicial Review— Questions of Fact and Law

A. Review of Questions of Fact

1. *The Universal Camera Litigation*

NLRB v. Universal Camera Corp. (I)

179 F.2d 749 (2d Cir. 1950)

Before L. HAND, Chief Judge, and SWAN and FRANK, Circuit Judges.
L. HAND, Chief Judge.

This case arises upon a petition to enforce an order of the Labor Board, whose only direction that we need consider was to reinstate with back pay a "supervisory employee," named Chairman, whom the respondent discharged on January 24, 1944, avowedly for insubordination. If the Board was right, the discharge was in fact for giving testimony hostile to the respondent at a hearing conducted by the Board to determine who should be the representative of the respondent's "maintenance employees." [1] Chairman was an assistant engineer, whose duties were to supervise the "maintenance employees," and he testified at the hearing in favor of their being recognized as a separate bargaining unit. The respondent opposed the recognition of such a unit, and several of its officers testified to that effect, among whom were Shapiro, the vice-president, Kende, the chief engineer, and Politzer, the "plant engineer." The examiner, who heard the witnesses, was not satisfied that the respondent's motive in discharging Chairman was reprisal for his testimony; but on review of the record a majority of the Board found the opposite, and on August 31, 1948, ordered Chairman's reinstatement. The respondent argues (1) that the

---

1. Ed. note: Discharge of an employee for testimony at an NLRB hearing, which is made an unfair labor practice by the National Labor Relations Act, is remediable by a Board order of reinstatement with back pay.

majority's findings are subject to a more searching review under the New Act than under the Old; (2) that in the case at bar the findings cannot be supported, because they are not supported by "substantial evidence"; and (3) that its liability to Chairman, if any, ended with the passage of the New Act.

The substance of the evidence was as follows. On November 30, 1943, Chairman and Kende testified at the hearing upon representation, after which Kende told Chairman that he [Chairman] had "perjured" himself; and on the stand in the proceeding at bar Kende testified that Chairman "was either ignorant of the true facts regarding the organization within the company . . . or . . . he was deliberately lying, not in one instance, but in many instances, all afternoon"; and "that there was definite doubt regarding his suitability for a supervisory position of that nature." The examiner believed the testimony of Chairman that two other employees, Goldson and Politzer, had cautioned him that the respondent would take it against him, if he testified for the "maintenance employees"; and Kende swore that he told another employee, Weintraub — the personnel manager — that he thought Chairman was a Communist. After Politzer reported to him on December second or third that this was a mistake, Kende told him to keep an eye on Chairman. From all this it is apparent that at the beginning of December Kende was hostile to Chairman; but he took no steps at that time to discharge him.

Nothing material happened until the very end of that month, when Chairman and Weintraub got into a quarrel, about disciplining a workman, named Kollisch. Chairman swore that Weintraub demanded that he discharge Kollisch for loafing; and Weintraub swore that he only demanded that Chairman put Kollisch to work. In any event high words followed; Chairman told Weintraub that he was drunk; Weintraub brought up a plant guard to put Chairman out of the premises, and the quarrel remained hot, until one, Zicarelli, a union steward, succeeded in getting the two men to patch up an apparent truce. Two days later Weintraub saw Politzer and told him that he had heard that Politzer was looking into Chairman's statement that Weintraub was drunk, and on this account Weintraub asked Politzer to discharge Chairman. Politzer testified that he answered that Chairman was going to resign soon anyway, and this the examiner believed. He did not, however, believe Politzer's further testimony that Chairman had in fact told Politzer that he was going to resign; he thought that Politzer either was mistaken in so supposing, or that he had made up the story in order to quiet Weintraub. Probably his reason for not believing this part of Politzer's testimony was that he accepted Chairman's testimony that ten days later Politzer intimated to Chairman that it would be well for him to resign, and Chairman refused. Whatever the reason, Weintraub did not, after his talk with Politzer, press the matter until January 24, 1944, when, learning that Chairman was still in the factory, he went again to Politzer and asked why this was. When Politzer told him that Chairman had changed his mind, Weintraub insisted that he must resign anyway, and, upon Politzer's refusal to discharge him, they together went to Kende. Weintraub repeated his insistence that Chairman must go, giving as the reason that his accusation of drunkenness had undermined Weintraub's authority. Kende took Weintraub's view and Politzer wrote out an order of dismissal. No one testified that at this interview, or any time after

December first, any of the three mentioned Chairman's testimony at the representation hearing.

As we have said, the examiner was not satisfied that the Board had proved that Chairman's testimony at the representation proceeding had been an actuating cause of his discharge; but, not only did the majority of the Board reverse his ruling as to that, but they also overruled his finding that Politzer had told Weintraub on January first that Chairman was going to resign. They then found that Kende and Weintraub had agreed to bring about Chairman's discharge, at some undefined time after December first, because of Chairman's testimony; and that Weintraub's complaint on January 24 was a cover for affecting that purpose. Whether these findings were justified is the first, and indeed the only important, question of fact; and as a preliminary point arises the extent of our review.

This has been the subject of so much uncertainty that we shall not try to clarify it; but we must decide what change, if any, the amendment of 1947 [2] has made. Section 10(e) now reads that the findings "shall be conclusive" "if supported by substantial evidence on the record considered as a whole"; and the original was merely that they should be conclusive, "if supported by evidence." In National Labor Relations Board v. Pittsburgh Steamship Company the Supreme Court refused to say whether this had made any change, and remanded the case to the court of appeals to decide the point in the first instance. Of the four decisions which have discussed it, two have held that no change, or no material change, was made, one has held that the amendment was intended "to give the courts more latitude on review," but did not decide how much; and the fourth merely held that it did not make the review a "hearing de novo." (Since the opinion in the last was written by the same judge who wrote the first, it is to be read as deciding that there was no change.) It is true that there were efforts, especially in the House, to give to courts of appeal a wider review than before; but the Senate opposed these, and, so far as concerns the adjective, "substantial," it added nothing to the interpretation which the Supreme Court had already put upon the earlier language. The most probable intent in adding the phrase, "on the record considered as a whole," was to overrule what Congress apparently supposed — perhaps rightly — had been the understanding of some courts: i.e. that, if any passage could be found in the testimony to support a finding, the review was to stop, no matter how much other parts of the testimony contradicted, or outweighed, it. . . . It appears to us that, had it been intended to set up a new measure of review by the courts, the matter would not have been left so at large. We cannot agree that our review has been "broadened"; we hold that no more was done than to make definite what was already implied.

Just what that review was is another and much more difficult matter — particularly, when it comes to deciding how to treat a reversal by the Board of a finding of one of its own examiners. Obviously no printed record preserves all the evidence, on which any judicial officer bases his findings; and it is principally on that account that upon an appeal from the judgment of a district court, a court of

2. Ed. note: The 1947 Taft-Hartley Amendments to the National Labor Relations Act.

appeals will hesitate to reverse. Its position must be: "No matter what you saw of the witnesses and what else you heard than these written words, we are satisfied from them alone that you were clearly wrong. Nothing which could have happened that is not recorded, could have justified your conclusion in the face of what is before us." That gives such findings great immunity, which the Rules extend even to the findings of masters, when reviewed by a district judge. The standing of an examiner's findings under the Labor Relations Act is not plain; but it appears to us at least clear that they were not intended to be as unassailable as a master's. The Old Act provided for "examiners";[3] but they did not have to make reports, and, although §10(c) of the New Act requires them to do that, it does not undertake to say how persuasive their findings are to be. On the other hand, §8(a) of the Administrative Procedure Act provides that "on appeal from or review of" the decision of an "officer" who has presided at a hearing, "the agency shall . . . have all the powers which it would have in making the initial decision." It is clear that these words apply to the decisions of the "agency" upon the evidence; but nothing is said as to what effect the "agency" must give to the "officer's" findings; except that, if the text be read literally, it could be argued that the "agency" was to disregard it. The reports in Congress do not help very much. The Senate Report merely said that the findings "would be of consequence, for example, to the extent that material facts in any case depend on the determination of the credibility of witnesses as shown by their demeanor or conduct at the hearing." The House Report was the same, *in ipsissimus verbis*, although it did add that "in a broad sense the agencies reviewing powers are to be compared with that of courts under §10(a) of the bill." That would have made them as conclusive upon an "agency" as the "agency's" findings are upon a court; and it is safe to say that the words will not bear so much. When the same question came up under the Old Act, the courts left the answer equally uncertain. The Seventh Circuit in A. E. Staley Manufacturing Company v. National Labor Relations Board said that, "where it" (the Board) "reaches a conclusion opposite to that of an Examiner, we think the report of the latter has a bearing on the question of substantial support and materially detracts therefrom"; and that has in substance received the approval of the Eighth Circuit, and of the Sixth, as well as a recent reaffirmation by the Seventh itself. All this leaves the question in confusion. On the one hand we are not to assume that the Board must accept the finding, unless what is preserved in the record makes it "clearly erroneous." That would assimilate examiners to masters, and, if that had been intended, we should expect a plainer statement. On the other hand, the decisions we have cited certainly do mean that, when the Board reverses a finding, it shall count in the court's review of the Board's substituted finding. . . . On the whole we find ourselves unable to apply so impalpable a standard without bringing greater perplexity into a subject already too perplexing. The weight to be given to another person's conclusion from evidence that has disappeared, depends altogether upon one's confidence in his judicial powers. The decision of a child of ten would count for nothing; that of an experienced master would count for

---

3. Rule 53(e)(2), Federal Rules of Civil Procedure.

much. Unless we are to set up some canon, universally applicable, like that of Rule 53(a)(2), each case in this statute will depend upon what competence the Board ascribes to the examiner in question.... We hold that, although the Board would be wrong in totally disregarding his findings, it is practically impossible for a court, upon review of those findings which the Board itself substitutes, to consider the Board's reversal as a factor in the court's own decision. This we say, because we cannot find any middle ground between doing that and treating such a reversal as error, whenever it would be such, if done by a judge to a master in equity.

The foregoing discussion is relevant in the case at bar for the following reason. One ground why the evidence failed to convince the examiner of any agreement between Kende and Weintraub to discharge Chairman, was that he thought it quite as likely that the quarrel between Weintraub and Chairman at the end of December still rankled in Weintraub's mind, and induced him to insist upon Chairman's discharge on January 24, 1944. It became important in this view to explain why Weintraub waited for over three weeks; and this the examiner did explain because he believed that Politzer had told Weintraub that Chairman was going to resign. When the majority of the Board refused to accept this finding, they concluded that, since this left Weintraub's delay unexplained, his motive was to be related back to the quarrel of Kende and Chairman on November 30. We should feel obliged in our turn to reverse the reversal of this finding, if we were dealing with the finding of a judge who had reversed the finding of a master, because the reasons given do not seem to us enough to overbear the evidence which the record did not preserve and which may have convinced the examiner. These were (1) that the examiner did not believe all that Politzer had said; and (2) that the finding was "irreconcilable with the other related facts and all the other evidence bearing on Politzer's behavior and attitude." It is no reason for refusing to accept everything that a witness says, because you do not believe all of it; nothing is more common in all kinds of judicial decisions than to believe some and not all. Nor can we find "other related facts" which were "irreconcilable" with believing that Politzer told Weintraub that Chairman was going to resign. Indeed, Chairman himself swore that on January 11, Politzer suggested to him that he resign, which affirmatively serves to confirm the examiner's findings that Politzer told Weintraub that Chairman would resign in order to placate him. However, as we have said, we think that we are altogether to disregard this as a factor in our review, which we should confine to the bare record; and on that we cannot say that Politzer's testimony had to be believed, in the face of Chairman's denial that he ever told him that he would resign.

There remains the question whether, with this explanation of Weintraub's delay missing, there was "substantial evidence" that the cause of Chairman's discharge was his testimony; and on that the Board had the affirmative; so that it is not enough that Kende and Weintraub might have agreed to find a means of getting rid of Chairman, or that Kende unassisted might have been awaiting an opportunity. Once more, if this was the finding of a judge, we should be in doubt whether it was sufficiently supported. When Weintraub went to Politzer on January 24, 1944, with his complaint at Chairman's continued presence in the factory, and when the two went to Kende because Politzer would not discharge Chairman, if Weintraub was acting in accordance with an agreement between Kende and himself, he was concealing the facts from Politzer. So too was Kende at the ensuing interview; indeed, we must assume that the two had arranged beforehand to keep Politzer in the dark, else Weintraub could scarcely have relied upon Kende to play his part. This appears to us to be constructed substantially out of whole cloth, so improbable is it that they should have gone to such devious means to deceive Politzer. On the other hand, although it is possible that Kende had been waiting for a proper occasion, independently of Weintraub, and that he seized upon Wein-traub's complaint, being secretly actuated by his old grievance, we do not read the majority's decision as distinctly indicating that they meant so to find. But, if they did, unless we assume that Weintraub's complaint was trumped up ad hoc, to deceive Politzer, it becomes the merest guess that Kende did not find it alone a sufficient reason for his action, and reverted to his concealed spite.

Nevertheless, in spite of all this we shall direct the Board's order to be enforced. If by special verdict a jury had made either the express finding of the majority that there was an agreement between Kende and Weintraub, or the alternate finding, if there be one, that Kende without Weintraub's concurrence used Weintraub's complaint as an excuse, we should not reverse the verdict; and we understand our function in cases of this kind to be the same. Such a verdict would be within the bounds of rational entertainment. When all is said, Kende had been greatly outraged at Chairman's testimony; he then did propose to get him out of the factory; he still thought at the hearings that he was unfit to remain; and he had told Weintraub to keep watch on him. We cannot say that, with all these circumstances before him, no reasonable person could have concluded that Chairman's testimony was one of the causes of his discharge, little as it would have convinced us, were we free to pass upon the evidence in the first instance. . . .

An enforcement order will issue.

SWAN, Circuit Judge (dissenting).

In National Labor Relations Board v. A. Sartorius & Co., 2 Cir., 140 F.2d 203, 205 we said that "if an administrative agency ignores all the evidence given by one side in a controversy and with studied design gives credence to the testimony of the other side, the findings would be arbitrary and not in accord with the legal requirement." I think that is what the majority of the board has done in the case at bar. I would reverse its finding of motive and deny enforcement of the order.

Universal Camera Corp. v. NLRB

340 U.S. 474 (1951)

Mr. Justice FRANKFURTER delivered the opinion of the Court.

The essential issue raised by this case and its companion, Labor Board v. Pittsburgh Steamship Co., . . . is the effect of the Administrative Procedure Act and the legislation colloquially known as the Taft-Hartley Act on the duty of Courts of Appeals when called upon to review orders of the National Labor Relations Board.

The Courts of Appeals for the Second Circuit granted enforcement of an order directing, in the main, that petitioner reinstate with back pay an employee found to have been discharged because he gave testimony under the Wagner Act and cease and desist from discriminating against any employee who files charges or gives testimony under that Act. The court below, Judge Swan dissenting, decreed full enforcement of the order. 179 F.2d 749. Because the views of that court regarding the effect of the new legislation on the relation between the Board and the Courts of Appeals in the enforcement of the Board's orders conflicted with those of the Court of Appeals for the Sixth Circuit, we brought both cases here. 339 U.S. 951 and 339 U.S. 962. The clash of opinion obviously required settlement by this Court.

I

Want of certainty in judicial review of Labor Board decisions partly reflects the intractability of any formula to furnish definiteness of content for all the impalpable factors involved in judicial review. But in part doubts as to the nature of the reviewing power and uncertainties in its application derive from history, and to that extent an elucidation of this history may clear them away.

The Wagner Act provided: "The findings of the Board as to the facts, if supported by evidence, shall be conclusive." Act of July 5, 1935, §10(e), 49 Stat. 449, 454, 29 U.S.C. §160(e). This Court read "evidence" to mean "substantial evidence," Washington, V. & M. Coach Co. v. Labor Board, 301 U.S. 142, and we said that "[s]ubstantial evidence is more than a mere scintilla. It means such relevant evidence as a reasonable mind might accept as adequate to support a conclusion." Consolidated Edison Co. v. Labor Board, 305 U.S. 197, 229. Accordingly, it "must do more than create a suspicion of the existence of the fact to be established. . . . it must be enough to justify, if the trial were to a jury, a refusal to direct a verdict when the conclusion sought to be drawn from it is one of fact for the jury." Labor Board v. Columbian Enameling & Stamping Co., 306 U.S. 292, 300.

The very smoothness of the "substantial evidence" formula as the standard for reviewing the evidentiary validity of the Board's findings established its currency. But the inevitably variant applications of the standard to conflicting evidence soon brought contrariety of views and in due course bred criticism. Even though the whole record may have been canvassed in order to determine whether the evidentiary foundation of a determination by the Board was "substantial," the phrasing of this Court's process of review readily lent itself to the notion that it was enough that the evidence supporting the Board's result was "substantial" when considered by itself. It is fair to say that by imperceptible steps regard for the fact-finding function of the Board led to the assumption that the requirements of the Wagner Act were met when the reviewing court could find in the record evidence which, when viewed in isolation, substantiated the Board's findings. Compare

Labor Board v. Waterman Steamship Corp., 309 U.S. 206; Labor Board v. Bradford Dyeing Assn., 310 U.S. 318; and see Labor Board v. Nevada Consolidated Copper Corp., 316 U.S. 105. This is not to say that every member of this Court was consciously guided by this view or that the Court ever explicitly avowed this practice as doctrine. What matters is that the belief justifiably arose that the Court had so construed the obligation to review.

Criticism of so contracted a reviewing power reinforced dissatisfaction felt in various quarters with the Board's administration of the Wagner Act in the years preceding the war. The scheme of the Act was attacked as an inherently unfair fusion of the functions of prosecutor and judge. Accusations of partisan bias were not wanting. The "irresponsible admission and weighing of hearsay, opinion, and emotional speculation in place of factual evidence" was said to be a "serious menace." No doubt some, perhaps even much, of the criticism was baseless and some surely was reckless. What is here relevant, however, is the climate of opinion thereby generated and its effect on Congress. Protests against "shocking injustices" and intimations of judicial "abdication" with which some courts granted enforcement of the Board's orders stimulated pressures for legislative relief from alleged administrative excesses.

The strength of these pressures was reflected in the passage in 1940 of the Walter-Logan Bill. It was vetoed by President Roosevelt, partly because it imposed unduly rigid limitations on the administrative process, and partly because of the investigation into the actual operation of the administrative process then being conducted by an experienced committee appointed by the Attorney General. It is worth noting that despite its aim to tighten control over administrative determinations of fact, the Walter-Logan Bill contented itself with the conventional formula that an agency's decision could be set aside if "the findings of fact are not supported by substantial evidence."

The final report of the Attorney General's Committee was submitted in January, 1941. The majority concluded that "[d]issatisfaction with the existing standards as to the scope of judicial review derives largely from dissatisfaction with the fact-finding procedures now employed by the administrative bodies." Departure from the "substantial evidence" test, it thought, would either create unnecessary uncertainty or transfer to courts the responsibility for ascertaining and assaying matters the significance of which lies outside judicial competence. Accordingly, it recommended against legislation embodying a general scheme of judicial review.[4]

---

4. Referring to proposals to enlarge the scope of review to permit inquiry whether the findings are supported by the weight of the evidence, the majority said:

"Assuming that such a change may be desirable with respect to special administrative determinations, there is serious objection to its adoption for general application.

"In the first place there is the question of how much change, if any, the amendment would produce. The respect that courts have for the judgments of specialized tribunals which have carefully considered the problems and the evidence cannot be legislated away. The line between 'substantial evidence' and 'weight of evidence' is not easily drawn — particularly when the court is confined to a written record, has a limited amount of time, and has no opportunity further to question witnesses on testimony which seems hazy or leaves some lingering doubts unanswered. 'Substantial evidence' may well be equivalent to the 'weight of evidence' when a tribunal in

Three members of the Committee registered a dissent. Their view was that the "present system or lack of system of judicial review" led to inconsistency and uncertainty. They reported that under a "prevalent" interpretation of the "substantial evidence" rule "if what is called 'substantial evidence' is found anywhere in the record to support conclusions of fact, the courts are said to be obliged to sustain the decision without reference to how heavily the countervailing evidence may preponderate — unless indeed the stage of arbitrary decision is reached. Under this interpretation, the courts need to read only one side of the case and, if they find any evidence there, the administrative action is to be sustained and the record to the contrary is to be ignored." Their view led them to recommend that Congress enact principles of review applicable to all agencies not excepted by unique characteristics. One of these principles was expressed by the formula that judicial review could extend to "findings, inferences, or conclusions of fact unsupported, upon the whole record, by substantial evidence." So far as the history of this movement for enlarged review reveals, the phrase "upon the whole record" makes its first appearance in this recommendation of the minority of the Attorney General's Committee. This evidence of the close relationship between the phrase and the criticism out of which it arose is important, for the substance of this formula for judicial review found its way into the statute books when Congress with unquestioning — we might even say uncritical — unanimity enacted the Administrative Procedure Act.[5]

One is tempted to say "uncritical" because the legislative history of that Act hardly speaks with that clarity of purpose which Congress supposedly furnishes courts in order to enable them to enforce its true will. On the one hand, the sponsors of the legislation indicated that they were reaffirming the prevailing "substantial evidence" test. But with equal clarity they expressed disapproval of the manner in which the courts were applying their own standard. The committee reports of both houses refer to the practice of agencies to rely upon "suspicion, surmise, implication, or plainly incredible evidence," and indicate that courts are to exact higher standards "in the exercise of their independent judgment" and on consideration of "the whole record."

Similar dissatisfaction with too restricted application of the "substantial evidence" test is reflected in the legislative history of the Taft-Hartley Act. The bill as reported to the House provided that the "findings of the Board as to the facts shall be conclusive unless it is made to appear to the satisfaction of the court either (1) that the findings of fact are against the manifest weight of the evidence,

---

which one has confidence and which had greater opportunities for accurate determination has already so decided.

"In the second place the wisdom of a general change to review of the 'weight of evidence' is questionable. If the change would require the courts to determine independently which way the evidence preponderates, administrative tribunals would be turned into little more than media for transmission of the evidence to the courts. It would destroy the values of adjudication of fact by experts or specialists in the field involved. It would divide the responsibility for administrative adjudications." Final Report, 91-92.

5. Ed. note: The Court quoted the provisions on the scope of judicial review contained in the APA, 5 U.S.C. §706(2).

or (2) that the findings of fact are not supported by substantial evidence." The bill left the House with this provision. Early committee prints in the Senate provided for review by "weight of the evidence" or "clearly erroneous" standards. But, as the Senate Committee Report relates, "it was finally decided to conform the statute to the corresponding section of the Administrative Procedure Act where the substantial evidence test prevails. In order to clarify any ambiguity in that statute, however, the committee inserted the words 'questions of fact, if supported by substantial evidence *on the record considered as a whole....*'"

It is fair to say that in all this Congress expressed a mood. And it expressed its mood not merely by oratory but by legislation. As legislation that mood must be respected, even though it can only serve as a standard for judgment and not as a body of rigid rules assuring sameness of application. Enforcement of such broad standards implies subtlety of mind and solidity of judgment. But it is not for us to question that Congress may assume such qualities in the federal judiciary.

From the legislative story we have summarized, two concrete conclusions do emerge. One is the identity of aim of the Administrative Procedure Act and the Taft-Hartley Act regarding the proof with which the Labor Board must support a decision. The other is that now Congress has left no room for doubt as to the kind of scrutiny which a Court of Appeals must give the record before the Board to satisfy itself that the Board's order rests on adequate proof....

Whether or not it was ever permissible for courts to determine the substantiality of evidence supporting a Labor Board decision merely on the basis of evidence which in and of itself justified it, without taking into account contradictory evidence or evidence from which conflicting inferences could be drawn, the new legislation definitely precludes such a theory of review and bars its practice. The substantiality of evidence must take into account whatever in the record fairly detracts from its weight. This is clearly the significance of the requirement in both statutes that courts consider the whole record....

To be sure, the requirement for canvassing "the whole record" in order to ascertain substantiality does not furnish a calculus of value by which a reviewing court can assess the evidence. Nor was it intended to negative the function of the Labor Board as one of those agencies presumably equipped or informed by experience to deal with a specialized field of knowledge, whose findings within that field carry the authority of an expertness which courts do not possess and therefore must respect. Nor does it mean that even as to matters not requiring expertise a court may displace the Board's choice between two fairly conflicting views, even though the court would justifiably have made a different choice had the matter been before it de novo. Congress has merely made it clear that a reviewing court is not barred from setting aside a Board decision when it cannot conscientiously find that the evidence supporting that decision is substantial, when viewed in the light that the record in its entirety furnishes, including the body of evidence opposed to the Board's view.

There remains, then, the question whether enactment of these two statutes has altered the scope of review other than to require that substantiality be determined in the light of all that the record relevantly presents. A formula for judicial review of administrative action may afford grounds for certitude but cannot assure certainty of application. Some scope for judicial discretion in applying the formula can be avoided only by falsifying the actual process of judging or by using the formula as an instrument of futile casuistry. It cannot be too often repeated that judges are not automata. The ultimate reliance for the fair operation of any standard is a judiciary of high competence and character and the constant play of an informed professional critique upon its work.

Since the precise way in which courts interfere with agency findings cannot be imprisoned within any form of words, new formulas attempting to rephrase the old are not likely to be more helpful than the old. There are no talismanic words that can avoid the process of judgment. The difficulty is that we cannot escape, in relation to this problem, the use of undefined defining terms.

Whatever changes were made by the Administrative Procedure and Taft-Hartley Acts are clearly within this area where precise definition is impossible. Retention of the familiar "substantial evidence" terminology indicates that no drastic reversal of attitude was intended.

But a standard leaving an unavoidable margin for individual judgment does not leave the judicial judgment at large even though the phrasing of the standard does not wholly fence it in. The legislative history of these Acts demonstrates a purpose to impose on courts a responsibility which has not always been recognized. Of course it is a statute and not a committee report which we are interpreting. But the fair interpretation of a statute is often "the art of proliferating a purpose," Brooklyn National Corp. v. Commissioner, 157 F.2d 450, 451, revealed more by the demonstrable forces that produced it than by its precise phrasing. The adoption in these statutes of the judicially-constructed "substantial evidence" test was a response to pressures for stricter and more uniform practice, not a reflection of approval of all existing practices. To find the change so elusive that it cannot be precisely defined does not mean it may be ignored. We should fail in our duty to effectuate the will of Congress if we denied recognition to expressed Congressional disapproval of the finality accorded to Labor Board findings by some decisions of this and lower courts, or even of the atmosphere which may have favored those decisions.

We conclude, therefore, that the Administrative Procedure Act and the Taft-Hartley Act direct that courts must now assume more responsibility for the reasonableness and fairness of Labor Board decisions than some courts have shown in the past. Reviewing courts must be influenced by a feeling that they are not to abdicate the conventional judicial function. Congress has imposed on them responsibility for assuring that the Board keeps within reasonable grounds. That responsibility is not less real because it is limited to enforcing the requirement that evidence appear substantial when viewed, on the record as a whole, by courts invested with the authority and enjoying the prestige of the Courts of Appeals. The Board's findings are entitled to respect; but they must nonetheless be set aside when the record before a Court of Appeals clearly precludes the Board's decision from being justified by a fair estimate of the worth of the testimony of witnesses or its informed judgment on matters within its special competence or both.

From this it follows that enactment of these statutes does not require every Court of Appeals to alter its practice. Some — perhaps a majority — have always applied the attitude reflected in this legislation. To explore whether a particular court should or should not alter its practice would only divert attention from the application of the standard now prescribed to a futile inquiry into the nature of the test formerly used by a particular court.

Our power to review the correctness of application of the present standard ought seldom to be called into action. Whether on the record as a whole there is substantial evidence to support agency findings is a question which Congress has placed in the keeping of the Courts of Appeals. This Court will intervene only in what ought to be the rare instance when the standard appears to have been misapprehended or grossly misapplied.

II

Our disagreement with the view of the court below that the scope of review of Labor Board decisions is unaltered by recent legislation does not of itself, as we have noted, require reversal of its decision. The court may have applied a standard of review which satisfies the present Congressional requirement.

The decision of the Court of Appeals is assailed on two grounds. It is said (1) that the court erred in holding that it was barred from taking into account the report of the examiner on questions of fact insofar as that report was rejected by the Board, and (2) that the Board's order was not supported by substantial evidence on the record considered as a whole, even apart from the validity of the court's refusal to consider the rejected portions of the examiner's report.

The latter contention is easily met. It is true that two of the earlier decisions of the court below were among those disapproved by Congress. But this disapproval, we have seen, may well have been caused by unintended intimation of judicial phrasing. And in any event, it is clear from the court's opinion in this case that it in fact did consider the "record as a whole," and did not deem itself merely the judicial echo of the Board's conclusion. The testimony of the company's witnesses was inconsistent, and there was clear evidence that the complaining employee had been discharged by an officer who was at one time influenced against him because of his appearance at the Board hearing. On such a record we could not say that it would be error to grant enforcement.

The first contention, however, raises serious questions to which we now turn.

III

The Court of Appeals deemed itself bound by the Board's rejection of the examiner's findings because the court considered these findings not "as unassailable as a master's." [6] 179 F.2d at 752. They are not. Section 10(c) of the Labor Man-

---

6. Rule 53(e)(2), Fed. Rules Civ. Proc., gives finality to the findings of a master unless they are clearly erroneous.

agement Relations Act provides that "If upon the preponderance of the testimony taken the Board shall be of the opinion that any person named in the complaint has engaged in or is engaging in any such unfair labor practice, then the Board shall state its findings of fact...." 61 Stat. 147, 29 U.S.C. (Supp. III) §160(c). The responsibility for decision thus placed on the Board is wholly inconsistent with the notion that it has power to reverse an examiner's findings only when they are "clearly erroneous." Such a limitation would make so drastic a departure from prior administrative practice that explicitness would be required.

The Court of Appeals concluded from this premise "that, although the Board would be wrong in totally disregarding his findings, it is practically impossible for a court, upon review of those findings which the Board itself substitutes, to consider the Board's reversal as a factor in the court's own decision. This we say, because we cannot find any middle ground between doing that and treating such a reversal as error, whenever it would be such, if done by a judge to a master in equity." 179 F.2d at 753. Much as we respect the logical acumen of the Chief Judge of the Court of Appeals, we do not find ourselves pinioned between the horns of his dilemma.

We are aware that to give the examiner's findings less finality than a master's and yet entitle them to consideration in striking the account, is to introduce another and an unruly factor into the judgmatical process of review. But we ought not to fashion an exclusionary rule merely to reduce the number of imponderables to be considered by reviewing courts.

The Taft-Hartley Act provides that "The findings of the Board with respect to questions of fact if supported by substantial evidence on the record considered as a whole shall be conclusive." 61 Stat. 148, 29 U.S.C. (Supp. III) §160(e). Surely an examiner's report is as much a part of the record as the complaint or the testimony. According to the Administrative Procedure Act, "All decisions (including initial, recommended, or tentative decisions) shall become a part of the record...." §8(b), 60 Stat. 242, 5 U.S.C. §1007(b). We found that this Act's provision for judicial review has the same meaning as that in the Taft-Hartley Act. The similarity of the two statutes in language and purpose also requires that the definition of "record" found in the Administrative Procedure Act be construed to be applicable as well to the term "record" as used in the Taft-Hartley Act.

It is therefore difficult to escape the conclusion that the plain language of the statutes directs a reviewing court to determine the substantiality of evidence on the record including the examiner's report. The conclusion is confirmed by the indications in the legislative history that enhancement of the status and function of the trial examiner was one of the important purposes of the movement for administrative reform.

This aim was set forth by the Attorney General's Committee on Administrative Procedure:

> In general, the relationship upon appeal between the hearing commissioner and the agency ought to a considerable extent to be that of trial court to appellate court. Conclusions, interpretations, law, and policy should, of

course, be open to full review. On the other hand, on matters which the hearing commissioner, having heard the evidence and seen the witnesses, is best qualified to decide, the agency should be reluctant to disturb his findings unless error is clearly shown.

Apparently it was the Committee's opinion that these recommendations should not be obligatory. For the bill which accompanied the Final Report required only that hearing officers make an initial decision which would become final in the absence of further agency action, and that agencies which differed on the facts from their examiners give reasons and record citations supporting their conclusion. This proposal was further moderated by the Administrative Procedure Act. It permits agencies to use examiners to record testimony but not to evaluate it, and contains the rather obscure provision that an agency which reviews an examiner's report has "all the powers which it would have in making the initial decision." [7]

But this refusal to make mandatory the recommendations of the Attorney General's Committee should not be construed as a repudiation of them. Nothing in the statutes suggests that the Labor Board should not be influenced by the examiner's opportunity to observe the witnesses he hears and sees and the Board does not. Nothing suggests that reviewing courts should not give to the examiner's report such probative force as it intrinsically commands. To the contrary, §11 of the Administrative Procedure Act contains detailed provisions designed to maintain high standards of independence and competence in examiners. Section 10(c) of the Labor Management Relations Act requires that examiners "shall issue . . . a proposed report, together with a recommended order." Both statutes thus evince a purpose to increase the importance of the role of examiners in the administrative process. High standards of public administration counsel that we attribute to the Labor Board's examiners both due regard for the responsibility which Congress imposes on them and the competence to discharge it.

The committee reports also make it clear that the sponsors of the legislation thought the statutes gave significance to the findings of examiners. Thus, the Senate Committee responsible for the Administrative Procedure Act explained in its report that examiners' decisions "would be of consequence, for example, to the extent that material facts in any case depend on the determination of credibility of witnesses as shown by their demeanor or conduct at the hearing." The House Report reflects the same attitude; and the Senate Committee Report on the Taft-Hartley Act likewise indicates regard for the responsibility developing on the examiner.

We do not require that the examiner's findings be given more weight than in reason and in the light of judicial experience they deserve. The "substantial evi-

7. §8(a), 60 Stat. 242, 5 U.S.C. §1007(a). The quoted provision . . . was added by the Senate Judiciary Committee. The Committee . . . gave no explanation for this particular change . . . It is likely that the sentence was intended to embody a clause in the draft prepared by the Attorney General's Committee, which provided that on review of a case decided initially by an examiner an agency should have jurisdiction to remand or to "affirm, reverse, modify, or set aside in whole or in part the decision of the hearing commissioner, or itself to make any finding which in its judgment is proper upon the record."

dence" standard is not modified in any way when the Board and its examiner disagree. We intend only to recognize that evidence supporting a conclusion may be less substantial when an impartial, experienced examiner who has observed the witnesses and lived with the case has drawn conclusions different from the Board's than when he has reached the same conclusion. The findings of the examiner are to be considered along with the consistency and inherent probability of testimony. The significance of his report, of course, depends largely on the importance of credibility in the particular case. To give it this significance does not seem to us materially more difficult than to heed the other factors which in sum determine whether evidence is "substantial."...

We therefore remand the cause to the Court of Appeals. On reconsideration of the record it should accord the findings of the trial examiner the relevance that they reasonably command in answering the comprehensive question whether the evidence supporting the Board's order is substantial. But the court need not limit its reexamination of the case to the effect of that report on its decision. We leave it free to grant or deny enforcement as it thinks the principles expressed in this opinion dictate.

Judgment vacated and cause remanded.

Mr. Justice BLACK and Mr. Justice DOUGLAS concur with parts I and II of this opinion but as to part III agree with the opinion of the court below....

NLRB v. Universal Camera Corp. (II)

190 F.2d 429 (2d Cir. 1951)

Before SWAN, Chief Judge, and FRANK and L. HAND, Circuit Judges.
L. HAND, Circuit Judge.

By a divided vote we decided this appeal last year upon the same record that is now before us, holding that the Board's order should be "enforced." The Supreme Court vacated our order and remanded the cause to us for reconsideration in two particulars. The first was that, although the amendment of the old act was in terms limited to adding that courts of appeal should scrutinize the whole record on reviewing findings of the Board, its implications were more extended. The second was that in considering whether the Board's findings were adequately supported by the evidence we were not altogether to disregard the findings of its examiner. As to the first, the Court agreed that in the case at bar we had based our review upon the whole record, but it held that the amendment had been a resultant of prolonged discussion in both Houses; and, although in form it did no more than incorporate what had always been the better practice — our own included — it was intended to prescribe an attitude in courts of appeal less complaisant towards the Board's findings than had been proper before; not only were they to look to the record as a whole, but they were to be less ready to yield their personal judgment on the facts; at least less ready than many at times had been. Presumably that does not extend to those issues on which the Board's specialized experience equips it with major premises inaccessible to judges, but as to matters of common knowledge we are to use a somewhat stiffer standard. Just where the Board's specialized experience ends it may no doubt be hard to say; but we are to find the boundary and beyond it to deem ourselves as competent as the Board to pass upon issues of fact. We hold that all the issues at bar are beyond the boundary and for that reason we cannot accept the Board's argument that we are not in as good a position as itself to decide what witnesses were more likely to be telling the truth in this labor dispute.

Upon the second issue we had said that we could find no practical mesne between giving the findings of an examiner the immunity which a court must give to those of a master, and saying that, although the Board should no doubt treat them as having some evidentiary value, it was impossible for us to measure what that ought to be; and that therefore we would decide the appeal, as though there had been no findings. Although this went too far, again it is plain that the weight which we should insist that the Board should give them must be left at large; except that we must count them for something, and particularly when — as indeed we said at length in our first opinion — they were based on that part of the evidence which the printed words do not preserve. Often that is the most telling part, for on the issue of veracity the bearing and delivery of a witness will usually be the dominating factors, when the words alone leave any rational choice. Perhaps as good a way as any to state the change effected by the amendment is to say that we are not to be reluctant to insist that an examiner's findings on veracity must not be overruled without a very substantial preponderance in the testimony as recorded.

In the case at bar the examiner came to the conclusion that Chairman's discharge on January 24, 1944, was not because of his testimony two months before. He believed that Politzer had told Weintraub, a day or two after Weintraub's quarrel with Chairman at the end of December, that Chairman had said he was going to resign; and, although he did not believe that Chairman had in fact said so, he found that Politzer either thought he had, or told Weintraub that he had in the hope of soothing over their quarrel. We see nothing improbable in this story, nor can we find any contradiction of it in Chairman's testimony that on January 11th Politzer asked him if he were going to resign. Indeed, if Politzer had got the impression that Chairman was going to resign, Politzer might very naturally have followed it with an inquiry which to Chairman appeared like opening up a new subject. Be that as it may, we are satisfied, as we were before, that there was enough to justify the conclusion that, when Weintraub complained that Chairman was undermining his influence in the factory, Politzer put him off, presumably in the hope that time might soften his animosity. Hence, even were the Board's argument more cogent than it is, we can no longer agree that it was free to overrule the examiner's conclusion that Weintraub's delay in complaining to Kende was because he had been waiting for Chairman to resign. Once this is accepted as true, it becomes incredible that Chairman's dismissal on January 24, 1944, was in fulfillment of any joint plan between Kende and Weintraub. In our first opinion we gave our reasons for thinking so; and, as we read the Board's brief, it does not argue the contrary.

However, it does argue that, even if Kende and Weintraub had had no such joint plan, the case against the respondent was proved, for it was enough if Kende independently and of his own motion seized upon Weintraub's complaint to vent his personal spleen upon Chairman. It is of course true that no one can be sure what may have actuated Kende at least in part; nothing is more difficult than to disentangle the motives of another's conduct — motives frequently unknown even to the actor himself. But for that very reason those parts of the evidence which are lost in print become especially pregnant, and the Board which had no access to them should have hesitated to assume that the examiner was not right to act upon them. A story may indeed be so unreasonable on its face that no plausibility in its telling will make it tenable, but that is seldom true and certainly was not true here. In appeals from the Board we have over and over again refused to upset findings which in cold type seemed to us extremely doubtful just because we were aware that we could not know what may have been the proper deciding factors. However limited should be the regard which the Board must give to the findings of its examiner, we cannot escape the conclusion that the record in the case at bar was such that the following findings of the examiner should have turned the scale; "the undersigned is not persuaded that Kende based his decision upon any animus against Chairman for testifying rather than on an evaluation of Weintraub's request based upon the merits." Indeed, it is at least doubtful whether the Board meant to overrule that finding except as it was involved in its own finding that Kende and Weintraub had had a joint plan to oust Chairman. That it may not have meant more appears from the statement in note seven of its opinion: "the absence of direct and detailed evidence of such a conspiracy . . . does not militate against our conviction that it was actually because of Chairman's testimony at the Board hearing and only ostensibly because of the resurrected December 30th episode that Weintraub and Kende brought about Chairman's discharge. On the evidence before us we have no substantial doubt" (surely a very curious assurance) "that discrimination occurred." Be that as it may, upon a reexamination of the record as a whole, and upon giving weight to the examiner's findings — now in compliance with the Court's directions as we understand them — we think that our first disposition of the appeal was wrong, and we hold that the Board should have dismissed the complaint.

Order reversed; complaint to be dismissed.

FRANK, Circuit Judge (concurring).

Recognizing, as only a singularly stupid man would not, Judge Hand's superior wisdom, intelligence and learning, I seldom disagree with him, and then with serious misgivings. In this instance, I have overcome my misgivings because I think that his modesty has moved him to interpret too sweepingly the Supreme Court's criticism of our earlier opinion written by him. I read the Supreme Court's opinion as saying that we had obeyed the new statute with but one exception: We had wholly disregarded the examiner's finding which the Board rejected.

The Supreme Court . . . said of our earlier opinion that "it is clear" that this court "in fact did consider the 'record as a whole,' and did not deem itself merely the judicial echo of the Board." In interpreting the new statute, the Court relied upon and quoted Senator Taft's statement, "It does not go quite so far as the power given to a circuit court of appeals to review a district-court decision." And the

Court, after saying that the new statute was not intended to "negative the function of the Labor Board" with reference to "findings within . . . a specialized field of knowledge," significantly added the following: "Nor does it mean that even as to matters not requiring expertise a court may displace the Board's choice between two . . . conflicting views, even though the court would justifiably have made a different choice had the matter been before it."

I think, then, that we must thus conclude: (1) Except that we did not consider the examiner's findings which differed from the Board's, we had not in this case disobeyed the new statute; (2) that statute does not put us, vis à vis the Board, in the same position we occupy with respect to a trial court; (3) even as to matters within the area of the Board's so-called "expertise," we may not try Board cases de novo.

Concerning our error in disregarding the examiner's findings, Judge Hand, as I understand him, interprets as follows the Supreme Court's ruling: The Board may never reject an examiner's findings if it rests on his evaluation of the credibility of oral testimony unless (1) that rejection results from the Board's rational use of the Board's specialized knowledge or (2) the examiner has been absurdly naive in believing a witness. This, I think, is somewhat more restrictive of the Board's powers than the Supreme Court suggested, for it said: "The responsibility for decision thus placed on the Board is wholly inconsistent with the notion that it has power to reverse an examiner's findings only when they are 'clearly erroneous.'"

I would also, by way of caution, add this qualification (to which, judging from his opinions elsewhere, I gather Judge Hand will not demur): An examiner's finding binds the Board only to the extent that it is a "testimonial inference," or "primary inference," i.e., an inference that a fact to which a witness orally testified is an actual fact because that witness so testified and because observation of the witness induces a belief in that testimony. The Board, however, is not bound by the examiner's "secondary inferences," or "derivative inferences," i.e., facts to which no witness orally testified but which the examiner inferred from facts orally testified by witnesses whom the examiner believed. The Board may reach its own "secondary inferences," and we must abide by them unless they are irrational; in that way, the Board differs from a trial judge (in a juryless case) who hears and sees the witnesses, for, although we are usually bound by his "testimonial inferences," we need not accept his "secondary inferences" even if rational, but, where other rational "secondary inferences" are possible, we may substitute our own. Since that is true, it is also true that we must not interfere when the Board adopts either (1) its examiner's "testimonial inferences" and they are not absurd, or (2) his rational "secondary inferences."

Except as noted above, I concur.

2. Background Notes on Universal Camera

Behind the labor legislation of the 1930s lay a long history of judicial hostility to the economic weapons used by labor in its struggle to organize. If an employer could convince a court that a strike or boycott had "unlawful objectives" or used "unlawful means," the court would order it enjoined. Critics claimed that the term "unlawful" was used broadly by the courts to denote not something contrary to law but any objective which the courts disapproved. The creation of the National Labor Relations Board under the Wagner Act of 1935 was in part a response to this widely acknowledged judicial hostility toward union activity. Faced with an avowed government policy of actively promoting unionization and collective bargaining through reliance on a Labor Board staffed by "enthusiasts burning with zeal for organized labor," many courts exercised great restraint in overturning findings by the Board. A series of ambiguous Supreme Court decisions created confusion among the lower courts concerning whether they should consider the entire record when ascertaining the substantiality of the Labor Board's position or only that evidence favorable to the Board's decision.[8]

No opinion of the Supreme Court explicitly stated that the substantiality of evidence was to be determined by examining only evidence that supported the Board decision, nor did all lower courts interpret the Court's decisions to require this. However, on oral argument in NLRB v. Pittsburgh Steamship Co., 340 U.S. 498 (1951), the companion case to *Universal Camera*, Justice Frankfurter indicated his view that in fact the Supreme Court had been using the more deferential standard. Quoting from NLRB v. Nevada Consolidated Copper Corp., 316 U.S. 105 (1942), he said " 'since upon examination of the record, we cannot say that the finding of fact of the Board is without support in the evidence' — that means if I find something in the evidence which supports it, my case is at an end. That is what I thought I had been doing." To which the government counsel who was arguing fervently that the Court had been using the whole record test all along could only reply, "I cannot contradict your Honor." [9]

It is difficult to believe, however, that courts literally looked at only those portions of the record favorable to the Board. Suppose a record contained evidence that (a) an employee testified in favor of a union at a Labor Board hearing and (b) the employer subsequently discharged him. Would a court have sustained a Board finding of an unfair labor practice if the employer introduced evidence showing that (c) ten years lapsed between the time of testimony and discharge and (d) the employee was repeatedly drunk in the six months prior to discharge? Doesn't the reasonableness of inferring certain facts from given evidence inevitably depend upon the presence or absence of other relevant evidence? Perhaps courts did not literally look only at evidence favorable to the Board but were simply very deferential to the Board's fact-finding.[10]

8. Compare Consolidated Edison Co. v. NLRB, 305 U.S. 197 (1938), with NLRB v. Waterman Steamship Corp., 309 U.S. 206 (1940).

9. Jaffe, Judicial Review: Substantial Evidence on the Whole Record, 64 Harv. L. Rev. 1233, 1236 (1951) Compare Consolidated Edison Co. v. NLRB, 305 U.S. 197 (1938), with NLRB v. Bradford Dyeing Assn., 310 U.S. 318 (1940), and Medo Photo Supply Corp. v. NLRB, 321 U.S. 678 (1944).

10. See Stason, "Substantial Evidence" in Administrative Law, 89 U. Pa. L. Rev. 1026 (1941); Jaffe, Judicial Review: Substantial Evidence on the Whole Record, 64 Harv. L. Rev. 1233 (1951); Medo Photo Supply Corp. v. NLRB, 321 U.S. 678 (1944); Eastern Coal Corp. v. NLRB, 176 F.2d 131 (4th Cir. 1949).

3. Judicial Review of Agency Fact-Finding

(a) Why should there be any judicial review of fact-finding by administrative agencies? The advantages of specialized fact-finding experience was an important reason for the creation of many administrative agencies. The concern of the courts is to preserve the integrity of the statutes and other rules of law. Why not leave fact-finding to the agencies, reserving only questions of law for reviewing courts? American courts have habitually reviewed the sufficiency of evidence to support agency fact-finding, and the Supreme Court in Crowell v. Benson went so far as to suggest that review of the sufficiency of the evidence was required by due process. See p. 47 supra.[11] But why?

The obvious answer is that if administrative agencies were totally free to find whatever facts they pleased, without regard to the evidence or the reasonableness of inferences that might be drawn from the evidence, agencies could so alter the operation of statutes or legal rules as to effectively change their meaning. For example, if the NLRB were free to "find," regardless of the evidence presented, that *any* employee discharge was motivated by anti-union bias, the National Labor Relations Act would be transformed into a legal guarantee of employee tenure. On the other hand, if the Board were free to "find" a lack of anti-union motivation in discharges, no matter how blatant the evidence of such animus, the intended purposes of the Act would be destroyed. Accordingly, if courts are effectively to review the fidelity and impartiality with which administrative agencies apply statutes or legal rules, they must also review agency fact-finding.

This does not mean that the courts should ordinarily decide each relevant factual issue de novo. Quite apart from the circumstance that some relevant evidence (the demeanor of witnesses) does not appear in the printed record, de novo judicial fact-finding would destroy many of the reasons for creating administrative agencies in the first place. Speedy and cheap administrative resolution of controversies would be threatened. The capability of administrative agencies to draw specialized inferences based on their experience would be lost. The burden on reviewing courts imposed by millions of such administrative cases would be intolerable. Administrative agencies would become little more than evidence gatherers, and most decisional responsibility would be shifted to the judiciary.

Accordingly, in a system such as ours that relies upon administrative adjudication backed by judicial review, neither the extreme of total judicial deference to agency fact-finding, nor the opposite extreme of de novo fact-finding by reviewing courts is ordinarily acceptable. The problem is to define middle ground between these extremes. The "substantial evidence" standard adopted in the APA and Taft-Hartley Act represents one attempt to formulate such an intermediate position. But it is not easy to determine in the abstract precisely what the "substantial evidence" standard requires of a court reviewing administrative fact-finding.

(b) The problem of judicial review of agency fact-finding parallels similar

11. See also Vajtauer v. Commissioner of Immigration, 273 U.S. 103 (1927).

issues involved when judges review fact-finding by juries, or appellate courts review fact-finding by trial judges.

One might ask what factors should lead a reviewing court to give greater (or lesser) deference to fact-finding by administrative agencies as compared to either trial judges or juries. Some courts have equated the substantial evidence test with the standard used for the grant or denial of directed verdicts.[12] In the oral argument for NLRB v. Pittsburgh Steamship Co., 340 U.S. 498 (1951), however, Justice Frankfurter explicitly rejected the analogy to the jury verdict standard:

> When you deal with a jury, you introduce a popular element into the adminis-
> tration of law. I would give a jury myself every possible leeway to believe in
> plausible stories, but when you deal with these matters where it is not a
> question of a jury, and with all due regard to the expertise and expertness of
> the NLRB, judges also have a good deal of experience in the world with these
> matters. . . .[13]

Frankfurter suggests that judges give administrative agencies less leeway to find facts than they give juries. Yet might the opposite conclusion be equally well defended? Might Congress not have intended the agency to introduce a "popular" element as well as expertise into fact-finding?

Should reviewing courts give greater leeway to agencies than they give to trial judges' fact-findings, which will be set aside if "clearly erroneous"? On the one hand, agencies can draw upon specialized experience which trial judges lack. On the other hand, there is a greater danger that an agency with a strongly defined mission, such as the Labor Board, will "bend" the evidence in order to support outcomes which it prefers on grounds of general policy. How should these considerations be balanced? As the *Universal Camera* opinions indicate, it has generally been accepted that "substantial evidence" represents a narrower standard of review, permitting administrators greater discretion in fact-finding than that accorded to trial judges under the "clearly erroneous" standard.

Does the selection of the label "substantial evidence" instead of the label "clearly erroneous" have any practical significance in terms of how reviewing courts decide specific cases? Circuit Judge Leventhal commented in International Brotherhood of Electrical Workers v. NLRB, 448 F.2d 1127, 1142 (D.C. Cir. 1971):

> I had originally thought that this was the case dreamed of by law school pro-
> fessors, a case where I could conscientiously say that although I considered
> the findings "clearly erroneous" so that I would have voted to reverse if the
> decision had been rendered by a trial court, nevertheless there was support in
> "substantial evidence" so that I should vote to affirm because the determina-

12. This formulation was cited with approval in *Universal Camera* and subsequent Supreme Court decisions such as Consolo v. Federal Maritime Commn. 383 U.S. 607 (1966).

13. Jaffe, Judicial Review: Substantial Evidence on the Whole Record, 64 Harv. L. Rev. 1233, 1246 (1951). See also Stern, Review of Findings of Administrators, Judges and Juries: A Comparative Analysis, 58 Harv. L. Rev. 70 (1944).

tion was made by an administrative agency. On further reflection I do not see "substantial evidence" supporting the agency's determination.[14]

(c) Should the stringency of judicial review of agency fact-finding vary depending on what is at stake in the decision? In NLRB v. Walton Mfg. Co., 369 U.S. 404 (1962), the Supreme Court disapproved the apparent practice by the Fifth Circuit Court of Appeals of requiring a greater weight of evidence to support Board orders imposing back pay awards on employers than in cases where the Board's relief was wholly prospective since such awards "may impoverish or break an employer." [15]

(d) Both before and after *Universal Camera*, reviewing courts have shown deference to agency findings about the credibility of witnesses. For example, in NLRB v. Marchus Trucking Co., 286 F.2d 583 (2d Cir. 1961), the court characterized witness' statments as "synthetic" but it nonetheless allowed the hearing examiner and Board to accept them. It held that it would overturn the agency's belief in a witness's oral testimony only if "on its face it is hopelessly incredible," or if the demeanor of the witness, which was not accessible to the reviewing court, could not conceivably sustain the agency's evaluation. 286 F.2d at 589.[16]

Whether one believes such decisions go too far[17] in insulating administrative fact-finding from judicial review depends upon how important one believes demeanor is as evidence in assessing credibility. In considering *Universal Camera* on remand, Judge Learned Hand indicated that demeanor is often "the most important part" but other judges have thought demeanor less weighty than the inherent probability of testimony in the light of general human experience, the interest of the witness in the case, and other background circumstances. For example, in Farmers Cooperative v. NLRB, 208 F.2d 296 (8th Cir. 1953), the court overturned

14. Note that the reviewing function is placed primarily in the district or circuit courts of appeal, not the Supreme Court. In *Universal Camera*, Justice Frankfurter wrote: "Whether on the record as a whole there is substantial evidence to support agency findings is a question which Congress has placed in the keeping of the Courts of Appeal. This Court will intervene only in what ought to be the rare instance when the standard appears to have been misapprehended or grossly misapplied." 340 U.S. at 491. He added, in NLRB v. Pittsburgh S.S. Co., 340 U.S. 498 (1951), decided the same day: "This is not the place to review a conflict of evidence nor to reverse a Court of Appeals because in its place we would find the record tilting one way rather than the other. . . ." 340 U.S. at 503. This circumstance raises further questions about the practical significance of abstract doctrinal analysis by the Supreme Court concerning the appropriate scope of review.

15. 369 U.S. at 406, citing NLRB v. Tex-O-Kan, 122 F.2d 433, 438. See, e.g., NLRB v. Pittsburgh S.S. Co., 340 U.S. 498 (1951).

16. See also NLRB v. Pittsburgh S.S. Co, 337 U.S. 656 (1949). In NLRB v. Walton Mfg. Co., 369 U.S. 404 (1962), the Supreme Court considered the position of the Fifth Circuit that in reinstatement cases involving back pay awards the Board should not disbelieve, on the basis of generalized suspicion, sworn employer testimony that grounds other than union activity were the basis of dismissal. The Court disapproved this position, citing authority to the effect that a witness's demeanor may persuade the trier that the truth is the opposite of his testimony.

17. Dissenting in *Walton*, Justice Frankfurter stated that the majority had in effect made the Board's determination of witness credibility "absolute and unreviewable," 369 U.S. at 417. Professor Davis criticizes both Frankfurter's reading of the majority opinion and his position that the Board cannot disbelieve a witness in the absence of impeachment or contradiction. See K. Davis, Administrative Law Treatise §29.06 (1970 Supp.).

an order by the Labor Board which had been based upon the testimony of one Dudley, a discharged employee whom the hearing examiner had credited despite adverse testimony from other employees and management. The court found that Dudley's "self-interest and bias were obvious." [18]

(e) To what extent can courts review fact-finding which the agency justifies on the basis of its superior ability to draw inferences from evidence in a field where it is technically expert or has specialized experience? A reviewing judge might on this basis sustain agency factual findings that the judge himself would not be prepared, on the basis of his lay experience, to infer from the evidence in the record. Thus in NLRB v. Stow Mfg. Co., 217 F.2d 900 (2d Cir. 1954), Judge Learned Hand found not even a "scintilla" of evidence to justify the Board's conclusion that company practices had turned employees against the union, but nevertheless sustained the agency "because we are to attribute to the Board an acquaintance with phenomena in this field, out of which it was reasonable to draw the conclusion that such practices in fact ordinarily do cause a change of votes." 217 F.2d at 905. Recall also Judge Hand's emphasis in his second *Universal Camera* opinion on the "Board's specialized experience [which] equips it with major premises inaccessible to judges." But if agency claims of "expertise" could always fill otherwise fatal gaps in the evidence, judicial review could easily become "a mere feint." [19] Yet it is obviously difficult for judges who lack technical training to determine the validity of factual inferences drawn by specialized administrative agencies with respect to scientific or other technical issues.[20]

For most judges, the greater the apparent importance of specialized agency experience in evaluating data, the greater the deference they will accord to agency factual conclusions. Conversely, Judge Hand, in his opinion on remand in *Universal Camera*, asserted that where the Board's specialized experience is not relevant, judges should "deem themselves as competent as the Board to pass upon issues of fact." Does this mean that a reviewing court should decide de novo all factual issues which do not relate to the agency's specialized experience?

---

18. 208 F.2d at 304. See also United States ex rel. Exarchou v. Murff, 265 F.2d 504 (2d Cir. 1959) (rejecting hearing officer's disbelief that a divorced man and divorced woman could live with each other without sexual intercourse); Nagle v. Eizaguirre, 41 F.2d 735 (9th Cir. 1930) (setting aside deportation order based on testimony of a prostitute because her testimony revealed her to be "as devoid of veracity as of virtue" and having "not the slightest regard for the legal or moral sanction of an oath"). See also Sahm, Demeanor Evidence: Elusive and Intangible Imponderables, 47 A.B.A.J. 580 (1961).

19. Cf. Mar Gong v. Brownell, 209 F.2d 448 (9th Cir. 1954). The trial judge had denied a Chinese immigrant's claim of U.S. citizenship based on the immigrant's uncorroborated testimony that his father had been naturalized. The trial judge relied on his general experience in immigration cases, concluding that Chinese immigrants seeking citizenship on such a basis generally did not testify truthfully. The Court of Appeals reversed, concluding that rejection of the immigrant's claims must be based on the evidence received in the case at hand rather than the generalized experience of the trier.

20. Some have proposed alternatives to judicial review for controlling the "quality" of administrative fact-finding on technical questions. For example, a Policy Review Board within the executive branch, independent of the various administrative agencies and staffed by economists, scientists, mathematicians, and other experts, might review the technical issues in important agency decisions. See B. Ackerman, S. Ackerman, J. Sawyer & D. Henderson, The Uncertain Search for Environmental Quality 147-161 (1974); see Chapter 3.

(f) It is not always easy to distinguish between agency fact-finding and policy-making. In Environmental Defense Fund v. EPA, 548 F.2d 998 (D.C. Cir. 1976), the manufacturer challenged EPA's interim suspension of the pesticides Heptachlor and Chlordane pending a full proceeding on whether manufacture and distribution of the pesticides should be permanently cancelled. The hearing examiner had recommended against suspension, being "hesitantly unwilling at this time to find that Heptachlor and Chlordane are conclusively carcinogens in laboratory animals." The EPA administrator, however, ordered suspension, finding that the hearing examiner had erroneously required a conclusive rather than a probable showing of animal carcinogenicity and deciding that in any event the evidence showed that Heptachlor and Chlordane were animal carcinogens. The reviewing court found that there was sufficient evidence to support the existence of a substantial likelihood of carcinogenic hazard from the use of the pesticides, and sustained the suspension order. Was the court deferring to an instance of specialized agency fact-finding or of agency policy discretion? Does the answer make a difference to the amount of discretion that the agency ought to enjoy?

(g) In addition to the factors already discussed, reviewing courts may, as a practical matter, give agencies greater, or lesser, "leeway" to find facts depending on the court's confidence in the agency, the judge's reaction to the underlying merits of the decision, the judge's confidence in her own ability to deal with technical matters, and the sheer bulk of the record. The same court in the same year may display wide variations in the deference accorded to agency findings, depending on the agency and issues involved.[21] In *Universal Camera*, Justice Frankfurter asserted that Congress, by adopting the "substantial evidence on the whole record" standard of review, expressed a "mood" concerning the function of reviewing courts. Given the number of different factors that affect the deference paid by courts to agency fact-finding, one must wonder whether one can speak more definitively than in terms of a "mood."

(h) As we shall see, in addition to adjudicating particular controversies, agencies also make policy by laying down broad rules of general applicability in formal or informal rulemaking proceedings or in the course of adjudication. Different agencies may decide, for example, the extent to which cable television systems should be allowed to offer competition to over-the-air broadcasters; how much proof of safety and efficacy should be required to market new drugs; or what rules should determine "disability" for determining eligibility for assistance payments for those too disabled to work. These and many other "legislative" decisions made by agencies involve considerable analysis and interpretation of factual material as well as value choice. The extent to which courts will review the factual basis for such decisions — whether the scope of judicial review is the same as in the context of particular adjudications — is an issue which will be raised later in this book.

---

21. Compare SEC v. New England Electric System, 390 U.S. 207 (1968) (deference to findings of Securities and Exchange Commission), with Baltimore & Ohio R.R. v. Aberdeen & Rockfish R.R., 393 U.S. 87 (1968) (ICC findings set aside).

4. The Relevance of Hearing-Examiner Findings

(a) The difficulties in defining the appropriate scope of judicial review of agency fact-finding were exacerbated by the creation of independent hearing examiners.[22] The APA created the office of hearing examiner to receive evidence and make initial findings (subject to review and modification by agency heads) primarily in response to the claims that it was unfair to have all adjudications decided by the agency commissioners themselves; they might be biased in a particular case because they combined policymaking, investigative, prosecutorial, and adjudicatory responsibilities.

Where the agency heads affirm the hearing examiner's fact-findings, no special reviewing difficulties are presented. But what is a reviewing court to do when the agency rejects the hearing examiner's findings? If the reviewing court gives no weight to the hearing examiner's conclusions, the agency heads would have little incentive to pay heed to the findings of hearing examiners, who would tend to lose their effectiveness as a check on the possible "bias" of the commissioners. Hearing examiners might become only evidence collectors; the real decision would occur later, with wasteful duplication of effort by private parties and the prosecuting staff of the agency. Of course, commissioners would likely give weight to the opinions of hearing examiners in routine cases, for the commissioners are pressed for time, and, in any event, they know the examiner has "lived with" the case. Yet in important cases they might be tempted to "redecide" the lot.

On the other hand, if courts gave near conclusive weight to the factual conclusions of hearing examiners, some of the special virtues of administrative fact-finding could be largely destroyed. The hearing examiner is more limited than the commissioner in his ability to draw inferences from the views of agency staff, for commissioners can more readily consult staff experts.[23] More importantly, it is perfectly proper for agency heads to use individual cases to elaborate on, or to change, agency policy. Since it is not always easy to distinguish discretion to draw specialized inferences of fact-finding from discretion to make law or policy, forced reliance on the hearing examiner's factual findings could unduly cabin administrators' policymaking discretion. Finally, the agency heads usually know the hearing examiner and are familiar with his biases. They thus may know when one of his factual findings is likely to be wrong.

Caught between these competing policies, reviewing courts can follow the course suggested by the Supreme Court in *Universal Camera* — giving the hearing examiner's findings some undefined weight as a relevant part of the record, setting aside the agency's decision if it does not meet the substantial evidence test. Courts have also sometimes remanded for further proceedings rather than attempt to choose among competing findings by the hearing examiner and the agency heads.

22. Such hearing examiners now hold the title "Administrative Law Judge."
23. In Lorain Journal Co. v. FCC, 351 F.2d 824 (D.C. Cir.), *cert. denied*, 383 U.S. 967 (1965), the court relied in part on the Commissioners' business experience and access to agency staff in affirming a finding contrary to that of the trial examiner.

They have done so when the agency heads did not explicitly state their reasons for overturning the hearing examiner's decision,[24] and when they overturned the hearing examiner without considering the testimony that he had considered.[25]

(b) The problem of what weight to give to hearing examiners' findings that have been reversed by the agency heads is particularly acute where witness credibility is an issue. The hearing examiner has observed the demeanor of witnesses; the agency heads and reviewing court have not. But, as we have already noted, the credibility of testimony is not solely a function of the witness's demeanor but also of that testimony's inherent plausibility.

On remand in *Universal Camera*, Judge Hand asserted that the findings of a hearing examiner based on witness demeanor are not to be overruled by an agency without "a very substantial preponderance [of contrary evidence] in the testimony as recorded." However, in FCC v. Allentown Broadcasting Corp., 349 U.S. 358 (1955), the Supreme Court reversed a Court of Appeals decision that had used the Hand formula to set aside agency action. The Supreme Court stated that the formula was unduly restrictive and was tantamount to the "clearly erroneous" standard which it disapproved in *Universal Camera*. In the *Allentown* case, an applicant from Allentown and an applicant from Easton were competing for a radio broadcasting license on the same frequency. The hearing examiner had awarded a license to the Allentown applicant, doubting the Easton applicant's ability to serve the community because of its witnesses' evasiveness. The Commission, however, granted the license to the Easton applicant, stressing that Easton presently had the one license while Allentown had three, also concluding that the Easton's need for additional locally originating programs was decisive. The Supreme Court found that the Commission's conclusion was supported by "substantial evidence" considering the whole record that had to be weighed, the programming promised by the various applicants, the need of the respective communities, and the concentration of Easton media as well as the evasiveness of witnesses. Thus, the decisive issue may not have been credibility and the substantiality of evidence supporting particular fact-findings but rather the Commission's discretion to weigh various policy factors without being tied to the one factor for which credibility was an issue.[26] Where fact-findings based on credibility were more clearly central to

24. Retail Store Employees Union v. NLRB, 360 F.2d 494 (D.C. Cir. 1965).

25. Cinderella Career and Finishing Schools v. FTC, 425 F.2d 583 (D.C. Cir. 1970).

26. For similar decisions using the "substantial evidence" standard to sustain an agency reversal of a hearing examiner where policy judgments seem to predominate over credibility or other purely factual issues, see Lorain Journal Co. v. FCC, 351 F.2d 824 (D.C. Cir.), *cert. denied*, 383 U.S. 967 (1965) (in determining whether a newspaper was exercising unlawful "control" over a broadcasting station it is "for the Commission to measure the force of the various vectors and to chart the resultant in the parallelogram of forces" Id. at 828); American Federation of Television and Radio Artists v. NLRB, 395 F.2d 622 (D.C. Cir. 1968) (the Board's determination that collective bargaining had reached an impasse "does not rest on a divergent view of credibility of witnesses as to evidentiary facts so much as a different overall judgment as to the proper inferences to be drawn from the largely undisputed evidence" Id. at 628).

We explore in Chapter 6, pp. 522-530, some of the reasons why courts use the substantial evidence standard, which is properly limited to review of fact-finding, in order to sustain or set aside agency conclusions on law and policy.

the result, reviewing courts have relied upon contrary findings by hearing examiners in setting aside agency determinations.[27]

The cases do not clearly delineate the extent to which an agency is free to reject a hearing examiner's factual conclusions, including those of credibility, by relying upon the agency's specialized experience with practices in a given field of administration or the hearing examiner's lack of it. In Environmental Defense Fund v. EPA, 489 F.2d 1247 (D.C. Cir. 1973), the reviewing court sustained EPA's prohibition of most uses of DDT pesticide despite a contrary decision by the hearing examiner. The agency relied in part on the fact that the hearing examiner, a former coal mine accident specialist, had no special experience with pesticides.

5. Burdens of Persuasion and Burdens of Production

(a) The "burden of persuasion" with respect to a factual issue falls upon the party who will lose on that issue unless the relevant evidence sufficiently preponderates in his favor to meet a given "standard of proof." The "burden of production" with respect to an issue falls upon the party who must bring forward some evidence on that issue in order to avoid an adverse decision on that issue; but once *some* evidence has been produced, either he or the other party may have the burden of persuading the trier of fact of the proposition's truth or falsity.

(b) The "standard of proof" that a trier of fact will use to determine whether a "burden of persuasion" has been met is quite a different thing from the "standard of review" used by a court in reviewing the decision of the trier of fact. This is obvious in the typical criminal case. To convict a defendant, the prosecution must persuade the jury of his guilt beyond "a reasonable doubt." But, to sustain a guilty verdict, an appellate court need not itself be convinced of guilt beyond "a reasonable doubt." It need only be convinced that a jury could have reasonably believed so.

This distinction played an important role in Woodby v. Immigration and Naturalization Service, 385 U.S. 276 (1966). A resident alien, the wife of an American soldier, was ordered deported because she had engaged in prostitution. In reaching this conclusion, the Board of Immigration Appeals had not specifically considered the persuasion burden defining the degree of certainty with which deportability must be established. The Court of Appeals noted that §106(a)4 of the Immigration and Naturalization Act states that a deportation order, "if supported by reasonable, substantial, and probative evidence on the record considered as a whole, shall be conclusive," and §242(b)(4) of the Act provides that "no decision of deportability shall be valid unless it is based upon reasonable, substantial, and probative evidence." It concluded that the burden on the government was to establish deportability by "reasonable, substantial and probative evidence on the record as a whole," and that this burden had been satisfied. The Supreme Court, however,

27. For example, in Dobbs Houses, Inc. v. NLRB, 325 F.2d 531 (5th Cir. 1963), the court set aside the agency's finding of an unfair labor practice based on the subsequent testimony of employees at the hearing where the hearing examiner had reached a contrary conclusion on the basis of statements contemporaneous with the events in question. See also Retail Store Employees Union v. NLRB, 360 F.2d 494 (D.C. Cir. 1965).

decided that "these two statutory provisions are addressed not to the degree of proof required at the administrative level in deportation proceedings, but to a quite different subject — the scope of judicial review." In the absence of a statutory provision defining the burden of persuasion at trial, the Court, noting that the persuasion burden was a question traditionally left to the judiciary to resolve, chose to require that the government prove its allegations by "clear, unequivocal, and convincing evidence." The Court decided that this persuasion burden, which was the same one it had required in denaturalization and expatriation cases, was appropriate, since "[t]he immediate hardship of deportation is often greater than that inflicted by denaturalization, which does not, immediately at least, result in expulsion from our shores. And many resident aliens have lived in this country longer and established stronger family, social, and economic ties here than some who have become naturalized citizens." [28]

(c) The Administrative Procedure Act §556(d) provides that "Except as otherwise provided by statute, the proponent of a rule or order has the burden of proof." It is not clear whether "burden of proof" means "burden of persuasion" or "burden of production." The legislative history is ambiguous.[29] The difference is often important. Yet, the ambiguity may be desirable, for it allows courts to use traditional judicial factors — access to the evidence, place of the issue in the statutory scheme, etc. — in allocating the relevant burdens.

Consider, for example, cases involving a claim for disability compensation under the Social Security Act. Courts agreed that the ultimate burden of persuasion on "disability" falls on the claimant. To show "disability" a claimant must show not only an inability to continue former work, but also inability to perform *any* type of work.[30] But, recognizing the difficulties which claimants would have in producing evidence on that question, some courts ruled that the claimant need only to come forward with evidence that he could not perform his *former* job; the burden then shifted to the Secretary to produce evidence that work existed in the claimant's geographic area that he or she could perform and for which the claimant would be hired.[31] In 1967 Congress amended the Social Security Act to ease the burden the courts had placed on the Secretary; for example, evidence that a claimant could perform work that existed generally in the *national* economy would be sufficient to defeat the claim for disability. But the courts continued to place the burden of production on this issue upon the Secretary, despite indications of congressional displeasure with past court rulings.[32] Similarly, courts have held,

28. 385 U.S. at 276. See Jaffe, Administrative Law: Burden of Proof and Scope of Review, 79 Harv. L. Rev. 914 (1966) (comment on *Woodby* while in the Second Circuit); Note, Standard of Proof in Deportation Proceedings, 18 Stan. L. Rev. 1237 (1966).

29. See, e.g., H.R. Rep. No. 1980, 79th Cong., 2d Sess. 270 (1946).

30. Celebrezze v. Bolas, 316 F.2d 498 (5th Cir. 1966); Thomas v. Celebrezze, 331 F.2d 541 (4th Cir. 1964).

31. Torres v. Celebrezze, 349 F.2d 342 (1st Cir. 1965); Cooke v. Celebrezze, 365 F.2d 425 (4th Cir. 1966); Tigner v. Gardner, 356 F.2d 647 (5th Cir. 1966).

32. See Meneses v. Secretary of HEW, 442 F.2d 803 (D.C. Cir. 1971); Liebman, The Definition of Disability in Social Security and Supplemental Security Income: Drawing the Bounds of Social Welfare Estates, 89 Harv. L. Rev. 833 (1976).

despite the APA's language, that the burden of proving affirmative defenses rests upon an opponent rather than a proponent of an order when this allocation is supported by the basic purposes of a statutory scheme.[33] Moreover, courts that have read the APA to place the burden of persuasion on an order's "proponent" may find that the person who initiates the proceeding is not the "true" proponent.[34]

A further source of flexibility in allocating burdens arises out of the APA's exception, "where otherwise provided by statute." This exception has been put to good use in environmental litigation where gaps in data or scientific knowledge about health or environment make burden of proof rules important. Thus, in Environmental Defense Fund v. EPA, 548 F.2d 998 (D.C. Cir. 1976), cert. denied sub nom. Jelsicol Chem. Corp. v. EPA, 431 U.S. 925 (1977), a manufacturer challenged the EPA's suspensions of the marketing of the pesticides Heptachlor and Chlordane. EPA regulations state that "[a]t the hearing, the proponent of suspension [e.g., the EPA staff] shall have the burden of going forward to present an affirmative case for suspension. However, the ultimate burden of persuasion shall rest with the proponent of the registration [e.g., the manufacturer]." 40 C.F.R. §164.212(g) (1976). The Court of Appeals approved the regulation, and held that this case fell into the APA §556(d) exception as being "otherwise provided by statute" because the policies underlying the substantive statute dictated that the persuasion burden should rest on the plaintiff registrant to show that benefits exceed risks. The court added that, in any event, the burden of proof which the APA casts on the "proponent" is the burden of coming forward with evidence, and not the ultimate burden of persuasion.[35]

6. The Use of Hearsay Testimony

Either by statute or through judicial decision, hearsay evidence has generally been held admissible in administrative proceedings. In addition, §556(d) of the APA provides that "[a]ny oral or documentary evidence may be received. . . ."

Some courts have held, however, that hearsay evidence — standing alone — is not sufficient to support an administrative decision. In Carroll v. Knickerbocker Ice

33. See NLRB v. Mooney Aircraft, 366 F.2d 809 (5th Cir. 1966) (unlawfully discharged employees' "wilful loss of earnings," (i.e., not looking for other work) is an affirmative defense with the burden of producing evidence on the employer). But see NLRB v. Mastro Plastics, 354 F.2d 170 (2d Cir. 1965), cert. denied 384 U.S. 972 (1966) (Board must produce employees to testify about loss of earnings since it is within their special knowledge).

34. Thus, in Foster v. Seaton, 271 F.2d 836 (D.C. Cir. 1959), the Interior Department instituted proceedings challenging Foster's claim to ownership interests in government lands based on his asserted discovery of valuable mineral deposits; the government contended that no such deposits had been found by him. The court held that the government need only produce evidence on their point: the burden of persuasion fell on Foster, for he was the "true proponent" of a rule or order.

35. See also National Realty & Const. Co. v. OSHA, 489 F.2d 1257 (D.C. Cir. 1973), discussing production and persuasion burdens under the Occupational Health and Safety Act, 29 U.S.C. §§ 654 et seq.

Co., 218 N.Y. 435, 113 N.E. 507 (1916), the court, setting aside an award of death benefits, wrote "still in the end, there must be a residuum of legal (i.e., nonhearsay) evidence to support the claim before an award can be made," 113 N.E. 507, 509, and in Consolidated Edison Co. v. NLRB, 305 U.S. 197 (1932), the Supreme Court said that, while the administrative board was by statute not bound by technical rules of evidence, "this assurance of a desired flexibility in administrative proceedings does not go so far as to justify orders without a basis in evidence having rational probative force. Mere uncorroborated hearsay or rumor does not constitute substantial evidence." [36]

Recently, however, in Richardson v. Perales, 402 U.S. 389 (1971), in sustaining the denial by the Social Security Administration of a claim for disability benefits, the Supreme Court seems to have disposed of Carroll's "residuum rule." The only testimony presented at the administrative hearing was by Perales, his doctor, and a fellow employee, all supporting Perales' claim. The agency, in denying the claim, relied on hospital records and the written reports of four examining physicians. The Court of Appeals overturned the administrative decision, ruling that hearsay uncorroborated by oral testimony could not constitute substantial evidence when the hearsay was directly contradicted by the testimony of live medical witnesses and by the claimant in person. The Supreme Court upheld the agency. It emphasized that the reports were impartial, consistent, and based on personal examinations by competent physicians. The Court also noted that Perales had not exercised his right to subpoena the examining physicians in order to cross-examine them. In addition, the Court pointed to the "sheer magnitude of the administrative burden" and the desirability of informal procedures in administrative hearings. "The matter comes down to the question of the procedure's integrity and fundamental fairness. . . ." 402 U.S. at 410. Three dissenters voted to reserve the administrative decision on the grounds that evidence which had not been tested by cross-examination "is of no value," that uncorroborated hearsay does not constitute "substantial evidence" under the APA, and that the agency's reliance on written reports was therefore an impermissible "cutting of corners."

Professor Davis says that "[p]ost-Perales cases seem to support the view that no rule should exist that evidence inadmissible in a jury case may not be substantial, but that substantiality should be determined by appraising it in its full context." [37] Nonetheless, given the emphasis in Perales on the claimant's failure to exercise his right to subpoena the reporting physicians, and on the reliability of mutually consistent medical reports, can the residuum rule and its counterparts be said to be entirely defunct in the federal courts? [38]

36. 305 U.S. 197, 230. See also cases holding the hearsay evidence unreliable: National Council of American-Soviet Friendship v. Subversive Activities Control Board, 322 F.2d 375 (D.C. Cir. 1963) (determination that organization was a Communist front); Bridges v. Wixon, 326 U.S. 135 (1945) (deportation of labor leader because of alleged Communist Party membership); and Reilly v. Pinkus, 338 U.S. 269 (1949) (forbidding use of mail because of alleged fraud in weight-reducing scheme).

37. K. Davis, Administrative Law Treatise §14.11 (1967 Supp.).

38. See Browne v. Richardson, 468 F.2d 1003 (1st Cir. 1972), and Reil v. United States, 456 F.2d 777 (Ct. Cl. 1972).

7. *Alternative Standards of Review*

The substantial evidence test is the dominant standard for judicial review of factual determinations by agencies. It is specified in the APA and in many other statutes governing particular agencies. But there are statutes that call for a different test. In some instances, the statutory standard broadens the scope of judicial review, as in the Commodity Exchange Act, 7 U.S.C. §8, which states that administrative findings shall be conclusive if "supported by the weight of the evidence." Under this standard, the reviewing court supposedly weighs the evidence to determine whether its judgment as to the preponderance of the evidence matches that of the agency. But if the court continues to defer to administrative expertise and credibility findings, the end result may not differ significantly from the result produced under the substantial evidence test.[39]

The APA also provides that reviewing courts shall determine whether agency findings are "unwarranted by the facts to the extent that the facts are subject to trial de novo by the reviewing court." [40] In Citizens To Preserve Overton Park v. Volpe, 401 U.S. 402 (1971), reproduced infra p. 276, the Supreme Court stated that de novo review is authorized by the APA only when "the action is adjudicatory in nature and the agency factfinding procedures are inadequate" or "when issues that were not before the agency are raised in a proceeding to enforce nonadjudicatory agency action," and indicated that these situations would occur only rarely. Since review de novo can make much of the administrative process superfluous, reviewing courts have rarely made de novo factual determinations in the absence of specific statutory authorization.

Overton Park has created confusion regarding the appropriate scope of review in informal rulemaking and adjudication. The APA "substantial evidence" standard applies only to formal "on the record" rulemaking or adjudication (see §706(2)(E)). Since it presumes review on the basis of all of the relevant evidence, the substantial evidence standard in any event would be inappropriate in informal decisionmaking, which does not generate a trial-type record containing all of the relevant evidence. Some scholars have maintained that the de novo review provision in §706(2)(F) was designed to apply broadly in such cases, on the supposition that reviewing courts would themselves hear evidence and decide the relevant facts in order to review the legal validity of the informal action.[41] Since this view was largely fore-

---

39. See General Foods Corp. v. Brannan, 170 F.2d 220 (7th Cir. 1948); Great Western Food Distributors v. Brannan, 201 F.2d 476 (7th Cir.) *cert. denied*, 345 U.S. 997 (1953).

40. Courts are directed to exercise de novo review in some state workmen's compensation acts, Ohio Rev. Code §4123.519 (1975). De novo review is also provided in the Immigration and Nationality Act of 1961, 8 USC §§ 1251 et seq. (when the petitioner asserts a substantial claim to citizenship), the Equal Employment Opportunity Act of 1972, 42 U.S.C. §2000e-16 (when a federal employee alleges discrimination in employment opportunities), Food Stamp Act, 7 U.S.C. §2022 (in challenge by a retail food store or wholesale food concern of its disqualification from participating in the food stamp program); and the Federal Coal Mine Health & Safety Act of 1969, 30 U.S.C. §§ 801 et seq. (on the amount of the penalty assessed against a mine operator).

41. See Nathanson, Probing the Mind of the Administrator: Hearing Variations and Standards of Judicial Review Under the Administrative Procedure Act and Other Federal Statutes, 75 Colum. L. Rev. 721, 763-764 (1975).

closed by *Overton Park*'s reading of §706[2][F], reviewing courts have used the "arbitrary and capricious" standard of review specified in §706[2][A] to review informal fact-finding. Although, as we shall see, the "arbitrary and capricious" provision was basically designed as a standard for agency conclusions on law and policy, the "arbitrary and capricious" test has, for want of any other plausible alternative, been seized upon by judges in reviewing agency fact-finding as well.[42] The scope of the standard in this new context remains unclear.[43]

Some statutes narrow the scope of review of agency fact-finding or seek to foreclose it entirely, often through a provision that the findings of an agency shall be "final." The courts, however, have strained against preclusion of judicial review, especially where personal liberties are at stake. Despite such finality language, the judicial revision of finality provisions has been particularly noticeable in immigration and draft cases.[44]

(a) The history of the scope of review in immigration cases has been turbulent. The "finality language" in immigration statutes was originally held to preclude judicial review altogether,[45] but the Supreme Court later held that questions of law were open to reviewing courts.[46] Then in Vajtauer v. Commissioner of Immigration, 273 U.S. 103 (1927), where aliens had been arrested and ordered deported on charges that they had advocated overthrowing the government, the Court stated that deportation without a fair hearing or on charges unsupported by any evidence is a denial of due process. The ultimate question was whether "the warrant of deportation was supported by any evidence" that the alien advocated a violent overthrow of government. Id. at 106. While the "any evidence" standard implies a narrower scope of review than the substantial evidence test, many commentators believe that following *Vajtauer* the courts in practice applied a scope of review indistinguishable from the substantial evidence standard in the APA. However, in Heikkila v. Barber, 345 U.S. 229 (1953), the Court denied that the substantial evidence test was the appropriate standard of review in deportation cases and held that due process only required the less demanding "any evidence" test. In 1961 the immigration statute was amended explicitly to make deportation orders reviewable by the substantial evidence test.[47]

(b) In Estep v. United States, 327 U.S. 114 (1946), the Supreme Court decided that the statutory provision making decisions of the local draft board "final" precluded the customary scope of review, but the courts could consider whether a local board had acted outside its "jurisdiction." The board would exceed its juris-

42. Although the opinion is ambiguous on this score, *Overton Park* seems to suggest that the "arbitrary and capricious" standard applies to review of questions of fact as well as of law.
43. See p. 511 infra (*Vermont Yankee*).
44. Congressional efforts explicitly to preclude judicial review of questions of law as well as issues of fact are explored in Chapter 9, Section B.3.
45. Lem Moon Sing v. United States, 158 U.S. 538 (1895).
46. Gegiow v. Uhl, 239 U.S. 3 (1915).
47. See 2 Gordon & Rosenfield, Immigration Law and Procedure; Note, Deportation and Exclusion: A Continuing Dialogue Between Congress and the Courts, 71 Yale L.J. 760 (1962); Jaffe, Judicial Review: Question of Fact, 69 Harv. L. Rev. 1020 (1956); Developments in the Law: Immigration and Nationality, 66 Harv. L. Rev. 643 (1953).

diction "only if there is no basis in fact for the classification which it gave the registrant." Id. at 122. This "no basis in fact" standard was used in Dickinson v. United States, 346 U.S. 389 (1953), to overturn the denial of Dickinson's claim to a minister's exemption. The Court agreed that it could not apply the substantial evidence standard because of the statute's finality provision. But it nevertheless insisted "that there be some proof that is incompatible with the registrant's proof of exemption." After examining the record the Court concluded that the board had not overcome the registrant's prima facie case for exemption.[48]

In 1967 Congress incorporated the "no basis in fact" formula into §10(b)(3) of the Military Selective Service Act of 1967. In several subsequent cases the courts, though noting the narrow scope of review of agency fact-finding, overturned board decisions on the ground that they were inadequately explained or otherwise procedurally defective.[49]

Professor Davis doubts that in practice there is much of a distinction between the "no basis in fact" and the substantial evidence standards. He states that "Perceptive judges can hardly be expected to sustain an order because it has basis in fact if that basis does not seem to them to be substantial." The only difference he thinks possible is where isolated evidence may sustain a finding without review of the whole record.[50]

(c) No statute specifically addresses the scope of judicial review of federal civil service determinations. But the courts have shown an increasing willingness to apply a substantial evidence standard of review to administrative determinations respecting government employment.[51]

Questions

1. Should a reviewing court reverse the following findings of fact if made by a judge? a jury? an administrative agency?

(a) A workman's compensation proceeding turns on whether the dead man first had a heart attack and then fell from a ladder or whether he first fell and then had a heart attack. The only evidence on this point is that he was found dead of a heart attack at the bottom of the ladder. The fact-finder finds that his fall came first and compensation is awarded.

48. In Witmer v. United States, 348 U.S. 375 (1955), unlike Dickinson, the registrant could not make out a prima facie case for exemption on objective facts alone. The Court thus found a basis in fact for the board's denial of the claim in Witmer's inconsistent statements.

49. See Clay a.k.a. Ali v. United States, 403 U.S. 698 (1971); Fein v. Selective Service System, 405 U.S. 365 (1972).

50. K. Davis, Administrative Law Treaties §29.07 (1958 & 1970 Supp.).

51. Compare McTiernan v. Gronouski, 337 F.2d 31 (2d Cir. 1964), and Brown v. Zuckert, 349 F.2d 461 (7th Cir. 1965), cert. denied, 382 U.S. 998 (1966), with Finfer v. Caplin, 344 F.2d 38 (2d Cir.), cert. denied, 382 U.S. 883 (1965), Meehan v. Macy, 392 F.2d 822 (D.C. Cir. 1968), and Charlton v. United States, 412 F.2d 390 (3d Cir. 1969). See also Guttman, The Development and Exercise of Appellate Powers in Adverse Action Appeals, 19 Am. U.L. Rev. 323 (1970); Johnson & Stoll, Judicial Review of Federal Employee Dismissals and Other Adverse Actions, 57 Cornell L. Rev. 178 (1972).

(b) In the case above, assume that the proceeding is a malpractice claim against a doctor for allowing a patient to return to work too soon. If the heart attack preceded the fall, liability would be found. The fact-finder finds that the heart attack came first and awards damages. Does it matter if the agency has the power to revoke the physician's license?

(c) A workmen's compensation proceeding turns in part on whether the dead man died as a result of a 300-pound cake of ice falling upon him as he unloaded it from a truck on Jan. 15, 1958. The evidence on this point consists of: testimony by his wife and doctor that, just before dying of delirium tremens, the dead man told them that the ice fell on him; testimony by fellow workers, who were with him all day on Jan. 15, that they saw no cake of ice fall upon him; and undisputed testimony by doctors that there were no bruises upon his body. The fact-finder finds that the ice fell and awards compensation.[52]

2. Reconsider *Universal Camera*:

(a) Suppose the Board had justified its decision as follows: "Based on our experience in many proceedings and labor relations generally, discharge of employees following employee testimony favorable to the union is almost invariably attributable to the employer's anti-union motives. Testimony by supervisory personnel that the discharge was for other reasons is almost always an effort to disguise its real purpose." Should a reviewing court then have sustained the Board's order?

(b) Why should the reviewing court in this case have given any weight to the hearing examiner's findings? How much weight should his findings have?

(c) Might the *Universal Camera* case have been simplified for the Board and for the Court if either had paid more attention to defining appropriate rules for burden of proof and less attention to the question of scope of review? How might such rules have been defined?

3. Do you believe that it is possible to delineate clearly and consistently the appropriate roles of hearing examiner, agency, and reviewing court in relation to an issue of fact?

4. Section 8(a)(3) of the National Labor Relations Act prohibits an employer from discriminating "in regard to hire or tenure of employment . . . to encourage or discourage membership in any labor organization." The Enderby Machine Tool Company was charged with a violation of this section in the discharge of four employees, and a hearing on the complaint was held before an NLRB trial examiner. At this hearing, the General Counsel introduced evidence that the International Association of Machinists had begun an organizing drive at the Enderby plant, that Jonathan Enderby (president and sole stockholder) had made a number of anti-union speeches on company time, and that Enderby had asked a number of employees whether they belonged to the union. Four of those who answered that they were union members were discharged within the next week.

52. See Carroll v. Knickerbocker Ice Co., 218 N.Y. 435, 113 N.E. 507 (1916).

Enderby's case in rebuttal consisted primarily of his own testimony. He testified that although he was opposed to the union and said so to his employees, he
had never made any threats. He also stated that some twelve employees other
than the four in question had told him that they belonged to the union, and
none of these employees had been discharged. Finally, he stated that his reason
for discharging the four in question was their record of repeated lateness in reporting for work. Time clock records were introduced for each of the four showing at
least one late arrival after the organizing drive began and several additional late-
nesses during the preceding months. A foreman testified for the company that each
of the four had been warned against repeated tardiness before the organizing
campaign began.

(a) The trial examiner found a §8(a)(3) violation and ordered the four reinstated with back pay. He specifically stated that he "disbelieved the testimony of
Mr. Enderby, based on my observations of him as a witness." He also stated that
the rest of the evidence was trivial and without other evidence, Enderby's testimony
"proved nothing."

The Board reversed and ordered the complaint dismissed. It stated that the
General Counsel had not made a prima facie case, since he had only offered circumstantial evidence. It also stated that there was no objective basis for disbelief
of Enderby's testimony, especially in light of the objective documentary evidence
and the uncontradicted testimony of the foreman regarding prior warnings. It also
stated that the Board considered it to be "significant that the General Counsel
never made an attempt to rebut the documentary evidence."

What argument can each side make on a petition for reconsideration of the
Board's determination? (The General Counsel is not authorized to secure review
of Board decisions rejecting an unfair labor practice charge, and the employees
likewise do not, ordinarily, have the right to secure review.)

(b) The trial examiner found there was no §8(a)(3) violation and ordered the
complaint dismissed: "I have carefully considered the testimony of Mr. Enderby,
and based on my personal observation of him, I concluded that he has told the
truth regarding his motive. In support of this, I found considerable support in the
accompanying documentary evidence." In addition, the trial examiner also stated
that he considered the General Counsel's case to be insufficient as a matter of law
to establish a prima facie case, since all of the evidence was circumstantial.

The Board reversed and ordered the employees reinstated with back pay. Initially it observed that the trial examiner had applied an incorrect burden of proof.
On the merits, it stated that the story put forth by Mr. Enderby was inherently
implausible: "Based on our experience, we have concluded that the tactics employed here are precisely the kind of activities which employers use to halt union
organizing drives." It also discounted the weight of the documentary evidence,
finding that it was relatively weak in its probative value. It also observed that the
employer was the one who ought to have put in the rest of the relevant documents.

In Enderby's petition to review the Board's decision, what arguments are available to each side?

B. The "Constitutional Fact" Doctrine: The Example of Ratemaking

1. Introductory Note

Recall the debate in Crowell v. Benson between Chief Justice Hughes and Justice Brandeis about whether there are special "constitutional facts" or "jurisdictional facts" that a litigant can ask a court to redetermine de novo. The Chief Justice felt that the existence of "navigable waters" was one such question, and he argued that in Ng Fung Ho even Justice Brandeis had conceded the need for special review of findings of fact that led to deportation.

The argument about the proper role of judicial review of "jurisdictional" or "constitutional" fact has been much influenced by the subject matter of the cases that raised the issue. In the 1930s and 1940s most of these cases involved public utility ratemaking. The legal question was whether prices set by an administrative body (a rate commission) allowed the utility to earn a rate of return high enough to avoid "confiscation." A rate was "confiscatory" if it was so low that it constituted a "taking" of the company's property — a taking made unlawful by the Fourteenth Amendment's prohibition of deprivation of "property without due process of law." The underlying institutional issue was whether the courts should independently determine whether a particular rate of return was confiscatory or whether they should give weight to an administrative judgment that it was not.

An understanding of ratemaking in this controversy is important for two distinct reasons. First, *cost of service ratemaking*, used to set electricity rates, is also used almost without exception when the government seeks to set prices in any particular industry. Thus a student of the administrative process should be familiar with how this system works and with a few of the typical problems that arise when it is applied.

Second, only by understanding the details of how ratemaking works can one assess the comparative competencies of court and agency in determining a "fair," "proper," or "adequate" level for rates. And these comparative competencies arguably should play a role in determining the extent of factual review — at least as much of a role as a characterization of an issue as "jurisdictional" or "constitutional." But you can make up your own mind about this assertion after reviewing the ratemaking process and the courts' efforts to control it.

2. The Natural Monopoly

The classic case for rate regulation is the "natural monopoly." Natural monopoly in the economic sense exists when there is a relation between the size of the market and the size of the most efficient firm such that one firm of efficient size can produce all the market can take at a remunerative price and can continually expand its capacity at less cost than that of a new firm entering the business.

Changing technology, population growth, and the like may either create or eliminate natural monopolies. Developments in transportation over the years eliminated many local monopolies — in effect, local markets were merged into much larger markets. Mass production techniques tend in the direction of monopoly, but often new innovations will reverse the trend and by and large, in highly developed countries like the United States, few industries fall in the natural monopoly category. Generally speaking, they consist almost entirely of the so-called "public utilities" such as telephone and telegraph, local distribution of power, gas, and water, and electric power generation. When monopoly is the problem, the purpose of government ratemaking is of course to impose *maximum* prices to protect the public from monopolistic exploitation. Similarly, a variety of collateral controls over costs and quality of product is usually thought necessary in an endeavor to provide a substitute for the forces of competition.[53]

3. Cost of Service Ratemaking

In principle, ratemaking might be thought to have as its object the setting of prices equal to those that the firm would set if it did not have monopoly power; i.e., to replicate a "competitive price." In practice, maximum prices are set through a "cost of service" method. Whether this method leads to a "competitive" price is for you to judge.

"Cost of service" ratemaking is designed to set prices that will provide the regulated firm with revenues just sufficient to cover its costs (which include a reasonable profit). First the regulator determines the firm's probable future costs. These include:

— Operating costs (labor, raw materials, administration, etc.);
— Taxes;
— Depreciation of the equipment used to supply the commodity (buildings, generators, etc.);
— The cost of capital (or profit). This cost is determined by multiplying a "fair rate of return" (r) times invested capital, or "rate base" (RB). One method of determining the rate base is to take original investment and subtract depreciation. RB for period T_5, for example, equals the sum of all investment up to T_5 minus the sum of all depreciation up through T_4.

The sum of these four items yields the firm's revenue requirement.

Ordinarily, the ratemaker determines these costs by looking at historical costs in the last period of operations for which company records are available — called the "test period." Costs in the coming period are assumed to equal those in the test period.

The ratemaker then sets prices for period, say T_5, designed to yield the revenue requirement. Ordinarily it is assumed that the quantity sold in the coming period

53. D. C. Bok & D. F. Turner, Economic Regulation (unpublished mimeograph materials, 1977).

will remain roughly the same as that in the test period, regardless of price. Thus prices are set so that price (p) in the time period 5 (T_5) times quantity (q) in time period 5 equals the revenue requirement in time period 5 (i.e., $p_5 \times q_5 = RR_5$). And q_5 is taken to be roughly the same as q_4. Where these assumptions plainly are unwarranted — where, for example, demand will undoubtedly increase during the next year — the regulator will try to make appropriate adjustments if doing so is administratively feasible.

4. Statutes That Govern Ratemaking

The following provisions, taken from the Natural Gas Act, are typical of both state and federal legislative mandates authorizing agencies to control the maximum prices charged by natural monopolies. The provisions reproduced here give the Federal Power Commission the power to set the rates of large interstate gas pipelines.

Sec. 4.... (c) Under such rules and regulations as the Commission may prescribe, every natural-gas company shall file with the Commission . . . schedules showing all rates and charges for any transportation or sale subject to the jurisdiction of the Commission, and the classifications, practices, and regulations affecting such rates and charges, together with all contracts which in any manner affect or relate to such rates, charges, classifications, and services.

(d) Unless the Commission otherwise orders, no changes shall be made by any natural-gas company in any such rate, charge, classification, or service, or in any rule, regulation, or contract relating thereto, except after thirty days' notice to the Commission and to the public. . . .

(e) Whenever any such new schedule is filed the Commission shall have authority . . . to enter upon a hearing concerning the lawfulness of such rate, charge, classification, or service; and, pending such hearing and decision thereon, the Commission . . . may suspend the operation of such schedule . . . but not for a longer period than five months beyond the time when it would otherwise go into effect; and after full hearings . . . the Commission may make such orders with reference thereto as would be proper in a proceeding initiated after it had become effective. If the proceeding has not been concluded and an order made at the expiration of the suspension period . . . the proposed change of rate, charge, classification or service shall go into effect. Where increased rates or charges are thus made effective, the Commission may . . . order such natural-gas company to refund, with interest, the portion of such increased rates or charges by its decision found not justified. At any hearing involving a rate or charge sought to be increased, the burden of proof to show that the increased rate or charge is reasonable shall be upon the natural gas company. . . .

Sec. 5. (a) Whenever the Commission . . . shall find that any rate, charge, or classification demanded, observed, charged, or collected by any natural-gas company in connection with any transportation or sale of natural gas, subject to the Commission, or that any rule, regulation, practice, or contract affecting such rate, charge, classification is [unlawful,] the Commission shall determine the just and reasonable rate, charge, classification, rule, regulation, practice, or contract to be thereafter observed and in force, and shall fix the same by order . . .[54]

5. Determining the Rate Base; The Role of the Courts

The following cases will give you a rough idea of the controversy that surrounded ratemaking in the first half of the century. Consider whether modern courts have simply abandoned their efforts to control agency ratemaking, and if so, why. For additional background, consult Henderson, Railway Valuation and the Courts, 33 Harv. L. Rev. 902, 1031 (1920).

Smyth v. Ames

169 U.S. 466 (1898)

[In 1893 the Nebraska state legislature passed a statute imposing maximum rates on intrastate shipments of goods by railroads operating in the state. These rates averaged 29.5 percent less than the rates that had been charged in the immediately preceding years. Evidence accepted by the lower court indicated that if these rates had been charged during the years 1891-1893, the railroads, except in four instances, would not have recovered their operating expenses on intrastate shipments, let alone obtain a contribution to interest on bonded debt or return to stockholders. The lower court declared that application of the statutory rates in such circumstances was an unconstitutional deprivation of property without due process of law. In affirming, the Supreme Court commented in part as follows.]

Mr. Justice HARLAN delivered the opinion of the Court:

. . . If a railroad corporation has bonded its property for an amount that exceeds its fair value, or if its capitalization is largely fictitious, it may not impose upon the public the burden of such increased rates as may be required for the purpose of realizing profits upon such excessive valuation or fictitious capitalization; and the apparent value of the property and franchises used by the corporation, as represented by its stocks, bonds and obligations, is not alone to be considered when determining the rates that may be reasonably charged. . . .

A corporation maintaining a public highway, although it owns the property it employs for accomplishing public objects, must be held to have accepted its rights, privileges and franchises subject to the condition that the government creating it, or the government within whose limits it conducts its business, may by legislation protect the people against unreasonable charges for the services rendered by it. It cannot be assumed that any railroad corporation, accepting franchises,

54. 15 U.S.C. §§ 717c, 717d.

rights and privileges at the hands of the public, ever supposed that it acquired, or that it was intended to grant to it, the power to construct and maintain a public highway simply for its benefit, without regard to the rights of the public. But it is equally true that the corporation performing such public services and the people financially interested in its business and affairs have rights that may not be invaded by legislative enactment in disregard of the fundamental guarantees for the protection of property. The corporation may not be required to use its property for the benefit of the public without receiving just compensation for the services rendered by it. How such compensation may be ascertained, and what are the necessary elements in such an inquiry, will always be an embarrassing question. As said in the case last cited: "Each case must depend upon its special facts; and when a court, without assuming itself to prescribe rates, is required to determine whether the rates prescribed by the legislature for a corporation controlling a public highway are, as an entirety, so unjust as to destroy the value of its property for all the purposes for which it was acquired, its duty is to take into consideration the interests both of the public and of the owner of the property, together with all other circumstances that are fairly to be considered in determining whether the legislature has, under the guise of regulating rates, exceeded its constitutional authority, and practically deprived the owner of property without due process of law.... The utmost that any corporation operating a public highway can rightfully demand at the hands of the legislature, when exerting its general powers, is that it receive what, under all the circumstances, is such compensation for the use of its property as will be just both to it and to the public."

We hold, however, that the basis of all calculations as to the reasonableness of rates to be charged by a corporation maintaining a highway under legislative sanction must be the fair value of the property being used by it for the convenience of the public. And in order to ascertain that value, the original cost of construction, the amount expended in permanent improvements, the amount and market value of its bonds and stock, the present as compared with the original cost of construction, the probable earning capacity of the property under particular rates prescribed by statute, and the sum required to meet operating expenses, are all matters for consideration, and are to be given such weight as may be just and right in each case. We do not say that there may not be other matters to be regarded in estimating the value of the property. What the company is entitled to ask is a fair return upon the value of that which it employs for the public convenience. On the other hand, what the public is entitled to demand is that no more be exacted from it for the use of a public highway than the services rendered by it are reasonably worth. But even upon this basis, and determining the probable effect of the act of 1893 by ascertaining what could have been its effect if it had been in operation during the three years immediately preceding its passage, we perceive no ground on the record for reversing the decree of the Circuit Court. On the contrary, we are of opinion that as to most of the companies in question there would have been, under such rates as were established by the act of 1893, an actual loss in each of the years ending June 30, 1891, 1892, and 1893; and that, in the exceptional cases above stated, when two of the companies would have earned something above operating expenses, in particular years, the receipts or gains, above operating expenses, would have been too small to affect the general conclusion that the act, if enforced, would have deprived each of the railroad companies involved in these suits of the just compensation assured to them by the Constitution. Under the evidence there is no ground for saying that the operating expenses of any of the companies were greater than necessary.

Ohio Valley Water Co. v. Ben Avon Borough

253 U.S. 287 (1920)

Mr. Justice McREYNOLDS delivered the opinion of the court.

Acting upon a complaint charging plaintiff in error, a water company, with demanding unreasonable rates, the Public Service Commission of Pennsylvania instituted an investigation and took evidence. It found the fair value of the company's property to be $924,744 and ordered establishment of a new and lower schedule which would yield seven per centum thereon over and above operating expenses and depreciation.

Claiming the Commission's valuation was much too low and that the order would deprive it of a reasonable return and thereby confiscate its property, the company appealed to the Superior Court. The latter reviewed the certified record, appraised the property at $1,324,621.80, reversed the order and remanded the proceeding with directions to authorize rates sufficient to yield seven per centum of such sum.

The Supreme Court of the State reversed the decree and reinstated the order saying — "The appeal [to the Superior Court] presented for determination the question whether the order appealed from was reasonable and in conformity with law, and in this inquiry was involved the question of the fair value, for rate making purposes, of the property of appellant, and the amount of revenue which appellant was entitled to collect. In its decision upon the appeal, the Superior Court differed from the commission as to the proper valuation to be placed upon several items going to make up the fair value of the property of the water company for rate making purposes." It considered those items and held that as there was competent evidence tending to sustain the Commission's conclusion and no abuse of discretion appeared, the Superior Court should not have interfered therewith. "A careful examination of the voluminous record in this case has led to the conclusion that in the items wherein the Superior Court differed from the commission upon the question of values, there was merely the substitution of the former's judgment for that of the commission, in determining that the order of the latter was unreasonable."

Looking at the entire opinion we are compelled to conclude that the Supreme Court interpreted the statute as withholding from the courts power to determine the question of confiscation according to their own independent judgment when the action of the Commission comes to be considered on appeal.

The order here involved prescribed a complete schedule of maximum future rates and was legislative in character.... In all such cases, if the owner claims confiscation of his property will result, the State must provide a fair opportunity for submitting that issue to a judicial tribunal for determination upon its own independent judgment as to both law and facts; otherwise the order is void because in conflict with the due process clause, Fourteenth Amendment....

Here the insistence is that the Public Service Company Law as construed and applied by the Supreme Court has deprived plaintiff in error of the right to be so heard; and this is true if the appeal therein specifically provided is the only clearly authorized proceeding where the Commission's order may be challenged because confiscatory. Thus far plaintiff in error has not succeeded in obtaining the review for which the Fourteenth Amendment requires the State to provide....

[Reversed.]

Missouri ex rel. Southwestern Bell Tel. Co. v. Public Serv. Commn.

262 U.S. 276 (1923)

[The company appealed from an order of the Missouri Supreme Court affirming the rates set by the state commissions. The company had submitted evidence showing: reproduction cost new, $35 million; reproduction cost less depreciation, $31.3 million; book cost (original investment), $22.8 million. The Commission determined book value by taking book cost and subtracting depreciation; it adjusted upward for the value of intangibles and arrived at a rate base of $20.4 million.

The Supreme Court held that the value must be at least $25 million. The increased price of building, for example, made the existing plant worth more than its original cost. That fact must be taken into account. Justice McREYNOLDS wrote for the Court:]

... Obviously, the Commission undertook to value the property without according any weight to the greatly enhanced costs of material, labor, supplies, etc., over those prevailing in 1913, 1914 and 1916. As matter of common knowledge, these increases were large. Competent witnesses estimated them as 45 to 50 per centum....

In the Minnesota Rate Cases, 230 U.S. 352, 454, this was said: "The making of a just return for the use of the property involves the recognition of the fair value if it be more than its cost. The property is held in private ownership and it is that property, and not the original cost of it, of which the owner may not be deprived without due process of law."... Estimates for to-morrow cannot ignore prices of to-day.

Witnesses for the Company asserted — and there was no substantial evidence to the contrary — that excluding cost of establishing the business the property was worth at least 25% more than the Commission's estimates, and we think the proof shows that for the purposes of the present case the valuation should be at least $25,000,000....

[Justice Brandeis, together with Justice Holmes, concurred in the result, but launched a sweeping attack on Smyth v. Ames. That case, they claimed, led commissions to try to determine "present value" of a utility plant, for it guaranteed investors a reasonable return on that "value." The result was that commissioners sought to determine the "reproduction cost" of a plant — a difficult task. Justice BRANDEIS discussed Smyth v. Ames as follows]:

... The compensation which the Constitution guarantees an opportunity to earn is the reasonable cost of conducting the business. Cost includes not only operating expenses, but also capital charges. Capital charges cover the allowance ... for the use of the capital; ... the allowance for risk incurred; and enough more to attract capital. The reasonable rate to be prescribed by a commission may allow an efficiently managed utility much more. But a rate is constitutionally compensatory, if it allows to the utility the opportunity to earn the cost of the service as thus defined.

To decide whether a proposed rate is confiscatory, the tribunal must determine both what sum would be earned under it, and whether that sum would be a fair return. The decision involves ordinarily the making of four subsidiary ones:

1. What the gross earnings from operating the utility under the rate in controversy would be. (A prediction.)

2. What the operating expenses and charges, while so operating, would be. (A prediction.)

3. The rate-base, that is, what the amount is on which a return should be earned. (Under Smyth v. Ames, an opinion, largely.)

4. What rate of return should be deemed fair. (An opinion, largely.)

A decision that a rate is confiscatory (or compensatory) is thus the resultant of four subsidiary determinations. Each of the four involves forming a judgment, as distinguished from ascertaining facts. And as to each factor, there is usually room for difference in judgment. But the first two factors do not ordinarily present serious difficulties. The doubts and uncertainties incident to prophecy, which affect them can often be resolved by a test period; ... The doubts and uncertainties incident to the last two factors can be eliminated, or lessened, only by redefining the rate base, called value, and the measure of fairness in return, now applied under the rule of Smyth v. Ames. The experience of the twenty-five years since that case was decided has demonstrated that the rule there enunciated is delusive. . . . [I]t is essential that the rate base be definite, stable, and readily ascertainable; and that the percentage to be earned on the rate base be measured by the cost, or charge, of the capital employed in the enterprise. It is consistent with the Federal Constitution for this Court now to lay down a rule which will establish such a rate base and such a measure of the rate of return deemed fair. In my opinion it should do so.

The rule of Smyth v. Ames sets the laborious and baffling task of finding the present value of the utility. It is impossible to find an exchange value for a utility, since utilities, unlike merchandise or land, are not commonly bought and sold in the market. Nor can the present value of the utility be determined by capitalizing its net earnings, since the earnings are determined, in large measure, by the rate which the company will be permitted to charge; and, thus, the vicious circle would be encountered. So, under the rule of Smyth v. Ames, it is usually sought to prove the present value of a utility by ascertaining what it actually cost to construct and install it; or by estimating what it should have cost; or by estimating what it would cost to reproduce, or to replace, it. To this end an enumeration is made of the component elements of the utility, tangible, and intangible. Then the actual, or the proper, cost of producing, or of reproducing, each part is sought. And finally, it is estimated how much less than the new each part, or the whole, is worth. That is, the depreciation is estimated. Obviously each step in the process of estimating the cost of reproduction, or replacement, involves forming an opinion, or exercising judgment, as distinguished from merely ascertaining facts. And this is true, also, of each step in the process of estimating how much less the existing plant is worth, than if it were new. There is another potent reason why, under the rule of Smyth v. Ames, the room for difference in opinion as to the present value of a utility is so wide. The rule does not measure the present value either by what the utility cost to produce; or by what it should have cost; or by what it would cost to reproduce, or to replace it. Under that rule the tribunal is directed, in forming its judgment, to take into consideration all those and also, other elements, called relevant facts.

Obviously "value" cannot be a composite of all these elements. Nor can it be arrived at on all these bases. They are very different; and must, when applied in a particular case, lead to widely different results. The rule of Smyth v. Ames, as interpreted and applied, means merely that all must be considered. What, if any, weight shall be given to any one, must practically rest in the judicial discretion of the tribunal which makes the determination. Whether a desired result is reached may depend upon how any one of many elements is treated. It is true that the decision is usually rested largely upon records of finacial transactions, on statistics and calculations. But as stated in Louisville v. Cumberland Telegraph & Telephone Co., 225 U.S. 430, 436, "every figure . . . that we have set down with delusive exactness" is "speculative."

The efforts of courts to control commissions' findings of value have largely failed. The reason lies in the character of the rule declared in Smyth v. Ames. The rule there stated was to be applied solely as a means of determining whether rates already prescribed by the legislature were confiscatory. . . . But the commissions used it as a guide for making, or approving, rates. And the tendency developed to fix as reasonable, the rate which is not so low as to be confiscatory. . . . The result, inherent in the rule itself, is arbitrary action, on the part of the rate regulating body. For the rule not only fails to furnish any applicable standard of judgment, but directs consideration of so many elements, that almost any result may be justified. . . .

At first reproduction cost was welcomed by commissions as evidence of present value. Perhaps it was because the estimates then indicated values lower than the actual cost of installation. [But when construction prices rose, commissions became reluctant to base value on replacement cost, for doing so would have meant rate increases.]

The adoption of the amount prudently invested as the rate base and the amount of the capital charge as the measure of the rate of return would give definiteness to these two factors involved in rate controversies which are now shifting and treacherous, and which render the proceedings peculiarly burdensome and largely futile. Such measures offer a basis for decision which is certain and stable. The rate base would be ascertained as a fact, not determined as matter of opinion. It would not fluctuate with the market price of labor, or materials, or money. It would not change with hard times or shifting populations. It would not be distorted by the fickle and varying judgments of appraisers, commissioners, or courts. It would, when once made in respect to any utility, be fixed, for all time, subject only to increases to represent additions to plant, after allowance for the depreciation included in the annual operating charges. The wild uncertainties of the present method of fixing the rate base under the so-called rule of Smyth v. Ames would be avoided; and likewise the fluctuations which introduce into the enterprise unnecessary elements of speculation, create useless expense, and impose upon the public a heavy, unnecessary burden. . . .

. . . The most serious vice of the present rule for fixing the rate base is not the existing uncertainty; but that the method does not lead to certainty. Under it, the value for rate-making purposes must ever be an unstable factor. Instability is a standing menace of renewed controversy. The direct expense to the utility of maintaining an army of experts and of counsel is appalling. The indirect cost is far greater. The attention of officials high and low is, necessarily, diverted from the constructive tasks of efficient operation and of development. The public relations of the utility to the community are apt to become more and more strained. And a victory for the utility, may in the end, prove more disastrous than defeat would have been. The community defeated, but unconvinced, remembers; and may refuse aid when the company has occasion later to require its consent or cooperation in the conduct and development of its enterprise. Controversy with utilities is obviously injurious also to the public interest. The prime needs of the community are that facilities be ample and that rates be as low and as stable as possible. The community can get cheap service from private companies, only through cheap capital. It can get efficient service, only if managers of the utility are free to devote themselves to problems of operation and of development. It can get ample services through private companies, only if investors may be assured of receiving continuously a fair return upon the investment. . . .

The rule by which the utilities are seeking to measure the return is, in essence, reproduction cost of the utility or prudent investment, whichever is the higher. . . . [But if] the aim were to ascertain the value (in its ordinary sense) of the utility property, the enquiry would be, not what it would cost to reproduce the identical property, but what it would cost to establish a plant which could render the service, or in other words, at what cost could an equally efficient substitute be then produced. Surely the cost of an equally efficient substitute must be the maximum of the rate base, if prudent investment be rejected as the measure.

[Justice Brandeis concluded that the actual dollar amount of investment should determine the rate base. He concurred in the judgment of reversal, however, on the ground that the state commission had set too low a figure for the book value of the utility's investments.]

Justice Brandeis' position was rejected in McCardle v. Indianapolis Water Co., 272 U.S. 400 (1926). After reviewing the facts, the Court held (Brandeis, J., dissenting) that in view of the increased value of its land and other property, a utility must, under the Constitution, be allowed to value its rate base at $19 million, though its historical cost was $15 million.

St. Joseph Stock Yards Co. v. United States

298 U.S. 38, 49-53 (1936)

Chief Justice Hughes delivered the opinion of the Court:

... *The scope of judicial review upon the issue of confiscation....* Here, a large capital investment is involved and the main issue is as to the alleged confiscation of that investment.

A preliminary question is presented by the contention that the District Court, in the presence of this issue, failed to exercise its independent judgment upon the facts. 11 F. Supp. pp. 326-328. See Ohio Valley Water Co. v. Ben Avon Borough, 253 U.S. 287, 289.... The District Court thought that the question was still an open one under the Packers and Stockyards Act, and expressed the view that, even though the issue is one of confiscation, the court is bound to accept the findings of the Secretary if they are supported by substantial evidence and that it is not within the judicial province to weigh the evidence and pass upon the issues of fact....

... The fixing of rates is a legislative act. In determining the scope of judicial review of that act, there is a distinction between action within the sphere of legislative authority and action which transcends the limits of legislative power. Exercising its rate-making authority, the legislature has a broad discretion. It may exercise that authority directly, or through the agency it creates or appoints to act for that purpose in accordance with appropriate standards. The court does not sit as a board of revision to substitute its judgment for that of the legislature or its agents as to matters within the province of either.... When the legislature itself acts within the broad field of legislative discretion, its determinations are conclusive. When the legislature appoints an agent to act within that sphere of legislative authority, it may endow the agent with power to make findings of fact which are conclusive, provided the requirements of due process which are specially applicable to such an agency are met, as in according a fair hearing and acting upon evidence and not arbitrarily. Interstate Commerce Comm'n v. Louisville & Nashville R. Co., 227 U.S. 88, 91.... In such cases, the judicial inquiry into the facts goes no further than to ascertain whether there is evidence to support the findings, and the question of the weight of the evidence in determining issues of fact lies with the legislative agency acting within its statutory authority.

But the Constitution fixes limits to the rate-making power by prohibiting the deprivation of property without due process of law or the taking of private property for public use without just compensation. When the legislature acts directly, its action is subject to judicial scrutiny and determination in order to prevent the transgression of these limits of power. The legislature cannot preclude that scrutiny and determination by any declaration or legislative finding. Legislative declaration or finding is necessarily subject to independent judicial reviews upon the facts and the law by courts of competent jurisdiction to the end that the Constitution as the supreme law of the land may be maintained. Nor can the legislature escape the constitutional limitation by authorizing its agent to make findings that the agent has kept within that limitation. Legislative agencies, with varying qualifications, work in a field peculiarly exposed to political demands. Some may be expert and impartial, others subservient. It is not difficult for them to observe the requirements of law in giving a hearing and receiving evidence. But to say that their findings of fact may be made conclusive where constitutional rights of liberty and property are involved, although the evidence clearly establishes that the findings are wrong and constitutional rights have been invaded, is to place those rights at the mercy of administrative officials and seriously to impair the security inherent in our judicial safeguards. That prospect, with our multiplication of administrative agencies, is not one to be lightly regarded. It is said that we can retain judicial authority to examine the weight of evidence when the question concerns the right of personal liberty. But if this be so, it is not because we are privileged to perform our judicial duty in that case and for reasons of convenience to disregard it in others. The principle applies when rights either of person or of property are protected by constitutional restrictions. Under our system there is no warrant for the view that the judicial power of a competent court can be circumscribed by any legislative arrangement designed to give effect to administrative action going beyond the limits of constitutional authority. This is the purport of the decisions above cited with respect to the exercise of an independent judicial judgment upon the facts where confiscation is alleged. The question under the Packers and Stockyards Act is not different from that arising under any other act, and we see no reason why those decisions should be overruled.

But this judicial duty to exercise an independent judgment does not require or justify disregard of the weight which may properly attach to findings upon hearing and evidence. On the contrary, the judicial duty is performed in the light of the proceedings already had and may be greatly facilitated by the assembling and analysis of the facts in the course of the legislative determination. Judicial judgment may be none the less appropriately independent because informed and aided by the sifting procedure of an expert legislative agency. Moreover, as the question is whether the legislative action has passed beyond the lowest limit of the permitted zone of reasonableness into the forbidden reaches of confiscation, judicial scrutiny must of necessity take into account the entire legislative process, including the reasoning and findings upon which the legislative action rests. We have said that "in a question of ratemaking there is a strong presumption in favor of the conclusions reached by an experienced administrative body after a full hearing." Darnell v. Edwards, 244 U.S. 564, 569. The established principle which guides the court in the exercise of its judgment on the entire case is that the complaining party carries the burden of making a convincing showing and that the court will not interfere with the exercise of the rate-making power unless confiscation is clearly established. Los Angeles Gas Corp. v. Railroad Commission, 289 U.S. 287, 305. . . .

FPC v. Hope Natural Gas Co.

320 U.S. 591, 601-603 (1944)

[Mr. Justice Douglas delivered the opinion of the Court.]

. . . When we sustained the constitutionality of the National Gas Act in the *Natural Gas Pipeline Co.* case, we stated that the "authority of Congress to regulate the prices of commodities in interstate commerce is at least as great under the Fifth Amendment as is that of the States under the Fourteenth to regulate the prices of commodities in intrastate commerce." 315 U.S. p. 582. Rate-making is indeed but one species of price-fixing. Munn v. Illinois, 94 U.S. 113, 134. The fixing of prices, like other applications of the police power, may reduce the value of the property which is being regulated. But the fact that the value is reduced does not mean that the regulation is invalid. Block v. Hirsh, 256 U.S. 135, 155-157; Nebbia v. New York, 291 U.S. 502, 523-539 and cases cited. . . . The heart of the matter is that rates cannot be made to depend upon "fair value" when the value of the going enterprise depends on earnings under whatever rates may be anticipated.

We held in Federal Power Commission v. Natural Gas Pipeline Co., that the Commission was not bound to the use of any single formula or combination of formulae in determining rates. Its rate-making function, moreover, involves the making of "pragmatic adjustments." . . . And when the Commission's order is challenged in the courts, the question is whether that order "viewed in its entirety" meets the requirements of the Act. . . . Under the statutory standard of "just and reasonable" it is the result reached not the method employed which is controlling. It is not theory . . . but the impact of the rate order which counts. If the total effect of the rate order cannot be said to be unjust and unreasonable, judicial inquiry under the Act is at an end. The fact that the method employed to reach that result may contain infirmities is not then important. . . .

From the investor or company point of view it is important that there be enough revenue not only for operating expenses but also for the capital costs of the business. These include service on the debt and dividends on the stock. . . . By that standard the return to the equity owner should be commensurate with returns on investments in other enterprises having corresponding risks.

The extent to which the Court, under *Hope*, was willing to accept a Commission determination may be indicated by Market St. Ry. v. Railroad Commission,

324 U.S. 548 (1945). The book value of company property was $42 million; its reproduction value $25 million, the face value of its outstanding securities $38 million, and its salvage value $8 million. The Commission reduced fares from 7 cents to 6 cents. It claimed that a 6-cent fare would earn the company a return of 6 percent on $8 million — the salvage value. The Supreme Court held this order constitutional, arguing that the firm faced a profitless future under any rate structure; thus the property's only value was as salvage. If the Commission was right in believing a fare reduction would lead to a "traffic increase, . . . it would earn [a return] on the salvage value. . . . If expectations of increased traffic were unfounded, it could probably not earn a return from any rate that could be devised." . . . 324 U.S. at 568.

Questions

In the following problems, keep two points in mind. First, decisions about a proper rate base or rate of return are interrelated. Both help to determine the size of a certain pile of money, namely the profit, $r \times RB$, which is available for distribution (a) to bondholders and then (b) to stockholders. (Of course a portion of the stockholders' share may be reinvested in the company where it will earn further returns for the stockholders.) Thus, determining a proper rate base and rate of return are matters subsidiary to the main question: how big should that pile of money be?

Second, in a certain sense it is impossible for shareholders to earn more than a competitive rate of return. Does this sound surprising? If so, consider the fact that the market for capital is a large and highly competitive one. If the "competitive price" of capital is 9 percent, what will happen if the regulator allows the firm to earn profits that would provide its shareholders with a 10 percent return? The price of the share will simply rise. Conversely, a return lower than 9 percent will cause the share price to fall. The return as a percentage of the market price of the share will continue to equal the "cost of capital," but existing shareholders will receive a windfall gain, or loss. One can thus view the problem of preventing a regulated firm from earning monopoly returns as a problem of preventing its *current* shareholders from earning unjustified windfall gains; and the problem of securing them a "fair" return, one of preventing its *current* shareholders from suffering unjustified windfall losses.

Ben Avon states that courts must make an *independent* determination of the facts when a firm claims that a commission-set rate is "confiscatory." It is no wonder, then, that courts and commissions looked to Supreme Court opinions for guidance as to how to set rates. Smyth v. Ames was highly influential when it declared that in determining the rate base, "the present as compared with the original cost of construction" must be taken into account.

1. Suppose that Electricity Company is organized in year one with a capital investment of $20 million, including $10 million raised from the sale of equity. Assume that the cost of equity capital is 7 percent. By year ten, inflation has doubled the value of the physical plant and equipment. Should the equity shareholders be allowed a 7 percent return (a) on their *original* investment, or (b) on

the *present worth* of the items that their investment was used to buy? Put differently, should profits be allowed to rise to the point where the present price of shares doubles? Consider the following arguments:

> It is unfair to the shareholders to keep their dollar return constant, for the value of money has fallen by 50 percent. Moreover, not to allow their return to rise will make it difficult to raise new capital.

> The company must be allowed more earnings so that it can keep some aside to help pay for the more expensive new equipment that will be needed to replace existing equipment when it wears out.

What do you think of these arguments? Can you think of others that are relevant?

2. Suppose that deflation cut the value of Electricity Company's investment in half. Should the shareholders still be allowed to earn a 7 percent return on their original investment? Or should profits be cut to the point where the market value of their shares falls by 50 percent? If profits are not cut, will utility customers not be charged prices that are closer to what a monopoly, rather than a competitive, firm would charge them? How will this fact affect their use of electricity?

3. Suppose that, due to changing residential patterns in the city, Electricity's plant site is now worth ten times what it was worth in year one. Should profits be allowed to rise to reflect this increased value of its investment in plant? If they are not allowed to do so, what action might Electricity Company take to increase returns to shareholders? I.e., how should it decide whether to sell its plant and build a new one?

4. If "reproduction cost" is an appropriate standard of valuation, how should it be determined? The American Society of Civil Engineers (in 1916) stated that "estimates of the cost of reproduction should be based on the assumption that the identical property is to be reproduced, rather than a substitute property." Does this view make sense? Why did Justice Brandeis oppose the use of this standard?

5. Do you favor use of a "reproduction cost" or "historical cost" standard for measuring the rate base? Why? (Commissions now almost universally use "historical cost" for measuring the rate base.)

6.　Determining the Rate of Return

The rate of return and the rate base are related in that multiplying them produces a pile of money — profits — that will be distributed to investors. The basic regulatory question is how large that pile is to be. To decide, for administrative reasons, that the rate base will normally equal historical net investment does not by itself determine the rate of return. In determining that rate, commissions are moved by three sets of considerations: (1) the need to be fair to investors; (2) the need to attract roughly that amount of investment that competitive market considerations would dictate; and (3) the need for administrative simplicity.

Part of the commissions' problem can be readily solved. Those who have invested in fixed income securities can be paid the coupon rate of interest. Persons buying 8 percent bonds will be paid back 8 percent per year on the dollars they invested; and the utility will be allowed to earn enough profit to pay them, so long as it can do so. Unregulated firms in competitive markets would treat their bondholders no differently; such a payment is fair; it is readily calculable; and it is consistent with valuing the rate base — the plant and equipment that the borrowed money was used to purchase — at historical cost.

The more difficult problem is that of calculating a fair return on equity. That is to say, how large should the profit pool be, over and above the amount needed to pay bondholders? To put the same question differently, what price should the company be allowed to charge so that the return it earns on its total investment (valued at historical cost) after subtracting the amount paid to bondholders (and the amount of book value their investment represents) leaves enough to pay a "fair" or "proper" return to equityholders on their investment (which should equal the remainder of the firm's book value)?

Since the accounting concepts involved make this question appear more confusing than necessary, consider a simple balance sheet. The firm has borrowed $10 million — $6 million in debt and $4 million in equity. It has invested that money in plant and equipment worth $10 million. The debt carries different coupon rates of interest — half at 6 percent and half at 8 percent — because the money was raised at different times. The rate of return allowed the firm on its $10 million book value must be sufficient to allow it to pay its bondholders $420,000 ($180,000 plus $240,-000). The issue is how much higher the rate ought to be so that a proper return will be earned on shareholders' equity.[55] The "rate of return" that the regulator allows the firm on its $10 million will simply equal this figure, averaged proportionately with the others. (Thus if shareholders should earn 10 percent, $400,000 will have to be earned for them; $820,000 will have to be earned in total; and the allowed rate of return will equal 8.2 percent):

Net Assets (RB)   *Net Worth*

	investment	*cost*
$10 million	stock	$4 million
	6% bonds	$3 million
	8% bonds	$3 million

$$\text{rate of return:} \quad 6\% \times 30\% \; RB = 1.8\% \quad (6\% \text{ bonds})$$
$$8\% \times 30\% \; RB = 2.4\% \quad (8\% \text{ bonds})$$
$$\underline{10\% \,(?) \times 40\% \; RB = 4.0\% \quad (\text{stock})}$$
$$\text{allowed } r \text{ on RB} \qquad = \qquad 8.2\%$$

55. Depreciation over time does not change this example. If $10 million were raised initially but the plant has been depreciated down to $6 million, $4 million has been raised from consumers as a "depreciation" charge. That $4 million either was returned to investors as a "return of capital" diminishing the historical amount they have invested, or it was kept by the firm and reinvested for them. If the latter, the historical investment by the firm remains at $10 million though part of it is in new equipment.

At first, one might grasp at the following deceptively simple standard to measure the "proper" rate of return to equityholders: "pay equityholders precisely that amount that will induce them to put up necessary[56] investment and no more." To pay more would permit unnecessary profits to investors; to pay less would not raise the money.

This rule must be modified, however, for a firm might pay more without increasing profits to new investors or pay less but still raise the money. This is so because the securities market is itself competitive and prices of securities fluctuate. Thus, if a regulated firm seeks $2 million in new investment, and if the competitive rate of return (considering comparative risk and attractiveness of other securities on the stock exchange) for its shares is 10 percent, the firm can still attract $2 million by offering 8 percent. The shares will simply fall in price, so that the return to the investor on his *purchase price* will still be 10 percent. That is to say, the $160,000 the firm was offering as a return will buy it only $1.6 million in investment; to obtain the additional $400,000, it will have to offer more shares; and, when it does so, the extra money it pays as a return will have to come from the pockets of existing shareholders. Assume, for example, that the firm owns plants worth $2 million and has 20,000 shares of stock; it pays its shareholders 8 percent ($160,000). If the competitive rate of return is 10 percent, it will find that to raise $2 million more it has to sell many more than 20,000 new shares. If the regulator allows only 8 percent return, it will allow a total profit pool (on $4 million) of $320,000. This must be sufficient to pay 10 percent on the market value of all shares, old and new. Thus the shares' total market value must be $3.4 million. To raise the new $2 million will require issuing enough new shares so that the new shareholders own the firm's assets in the ratio of 2 to 2.3. Thus the firm, to raise $2 million, will have to issue 33,333 shares, which will each sell at $60; the value of the old shares will also sink to $60; and the old shareholders will own less than two-fifths of the company, though they advanced as much money as the new shareholders. The above example is meant to show that money sometimes can be raised at a lower than market rate by "diluting the equity" of existing investors. Conversely, if higher than competitive rates of return are offered to new investors, the price of the shares will be bid up; the total market value of the shares will exceed their book value (as in the above example total market value of all shares was *less* than book value); and existing shareholders will earn a windfall profit (instead of incuring a windfall loss).

Thus our initial standard, "pay equity investors the minimum they insist upon to put up the money," is insufficiently specific unless one adds, "provided that there is no dilution of existing equity (nor any increase in the value of existing equity)."

---

56. Note that if historical investment reflected the actual current value of the investment (which it probably does not), and if the price to consumers accurately reflected costs, this rule would automatically determine the level of new investment at precisely that level at which consumers were willing to pay its cost — the level that a free market would set — for a regulator would find he could not obtain enough funds from consumers at prices equal to costs to pay for more investment than that. In practice, however, the regulator and utility must make very rough estimates of increases in consumer demand, costs of new supply, and then just how much new supply consumers would pay for, thereby determining the level of "necessary" interest.

That is to say, one should seek to pay a return to equity equal to the market price of new investment in the regulated firm. That price will keep the market value of the firm's shares equal to the book value of the investment they represent.

One should note that this standard, while specific and fair, does not necessarily reflect what would occur in competitive markets. In competitive markets, existing share prices of any individual firm might rise above book value or sink below it. Economic considerations such as the increased (or decreased) value of existing plant may bring about windfall gains or losses to shareholders — a matter discussed in the preceding subsection (B.5). Unusual efficiency (or inefficiency) on the part of a firm's management could also cause a firm's profits, and stock prices, to rise (or to fall). This matter will be considered in the next subsection. Here, let us assume that the goal of earning a return on equity that reflects the market price of new investment in the firm is reasonable, and ask how the commission is to determine that price.

1. *The "comparable earnings" method.* The traditional method of determining a proper return on equity is for the commission to examine rates of return in "comparable" industries. Of course, this procedure requires the regulator to determine what industries are "comparable."

Consider two examples. A staff expert for the FPC determines the appropriate return for a pipeline transmission company by placing it in terms of risk on a scale of comparability consisting of (a) industrials in general as a background, (b) companies in defensive industries which, like utilities, are comparably least affected by economic cyclicality, (c) utilities as a whole, and (d) other pipelines.

An industry expert in airline rate hearings in the early 1970s argued that between 1958 and 1969 electric utilities earned between 10 and 14 percent on the book value attributable to common stock; between 1965 and 1969 gas pipelines earned 15 percent; truckers earned 15 percent; and food processors earned more; therefore airlines, being subject to more risk, should earn 18 percent.

Comparisons may help to set outer limits, yet, as these examples suggest, they could not possibly point to a precise a rate of return. For one thing, the industries being compared may themselves earn higher than competitive returns. The fact that gas pipeline shares between 1965 and 1969 sold at nearly twice their book value suggests that the return earned by the firm was more than needed to induce the investment. For another thing, to compare one regulated industry to another is circular if the practice of doing so is generally adopted by the regulators.

Finally, the return needed to induce investment depends upon risk; but risks vary widely between industries and over time. Those truckers earning 15 percent were the successful truckers who remained in business. To what extent should that risk be discounted by the possibility of business failure? And how should the resulting figure be compared with the airline industry, where *no* major firm has been allowed to fail since 1938, when regulation began (though, of sixteen original firms, six have been allowed to merge into the remaining ten)? Moreover, risks for shareholders are not the same as those for firms, for shareholders can diversify their portfolios. To what extent should the regulator take this fact into account? While one industry may be perceived as more risky or less risky than another, there is no precise way to translate this observation into a specific amount of more (or less) profit needed to attract capital into the regulated firm.

2. *The "discounted cash flow"* (DCF) *method* has the virtue of forcing the regulator to ask the relevant question: "What is the minimum return that must be paid (without dilution) to equity investors to obtain their capital?" This method seeks to determine what a firm must pay equityholders now or in the future by looking at what they have insisted upon being paid in the past.

One can determine what rate of return a shareholder now earns by comparing the price of the share with the stream of profits that it is expected to yield its owners. The rate that "discounts" this stream — that makes it equal to the present share price — is the investment's current "rate of return." The regulator would then set the regulated firm's allowable rate of return equal to that number; thus investors would expect a stream of profits from the regulated firm precisely equal to what they might earn elsewhere.

But how is one to determine the "stream of profits" that an investment was expected to yield its owner? That stream is *not* determined by looking at the existing dividend and assuming it will continue to be paid each year, for most investors expect dividends per share to grow over time, both from reinvested earnings and from other factors. Nor can "expected profits" be determined by looking at the firm's present total earnings (dividend plus retained earnings) and assuming they will continue to be earned each year, for, in fact, investors expect them to vary, and to grow, over time. One can, however, view the expected stream of profits as equal to current dividends *as adjusted* for expected growth (or decline) in dividends.[57] But can one go further? Can one try to measure investors' subjective assessment of expected growth in dividends or earnings? If so, one would know the growth they expect, and thus their total expected return. Some economists and ratemaking experts have sought to measure this highly subjective expectation.

Most commonly, the rate expert prepares elaborate models correlating, for example, the dividend-price ratio of many different stocks in the stock market with a series of objectively measurable factors that might be related to expected growth such as *past* average growth in earnings, or dividends, or book equity, or revenue, or net plant. He then finds that some combination of these factors correlates well with increasing price-dividend ratios. That is to say, he finds the greater the past average growth in, say, net plant, etc., the lower the dividend a buyer will accept when buying a, say, $20 share. After working out the precise correlation of his "bundle" of factors with the price-dividend ratio, he announces that the "bundle" (or more accurately some numerical operation on the "bundle," such as .127 times past plant growth plus 1.837 times past income growth, etc.) equals factor g or expected growth, which investors are paying for, along with dividends, when they buy their shares. Then, by measuring the "bundle" for the regulated firm in the past, the expert tells us what investors expected as a return, and by comparing

---

57. Of course, owners are interested in capital gains, as well. But the capital gain ought to reflect no more than the new owner's expectation of a stream of dividends (though at some point it may reflect the firm's liquidation value).

the "bundle" plus dividends with the share price of the regulated firm's stock, the expert knows what subjective rate of return investors insisted upon. By extrapolating the "bundle" features into the future, the expert will estimate what rate of return the firm must earn to give equityholders that same subjective rate of return on their investment in the future as they insisted upon in the past.

There are several serious problems with this approach. First, and most obviously, attempts to correlate measurable variables with investors' expectations of growth in earnings or dividends must be imprecise. So many different factors affect those expectations and their importance may change so radically over time, that despite past successes with the model, one must be uncertain whether the factors it uses comprise all, or all the more important, factors, that determined expectations of future growth in earnings or dividends.

Second, can one safely assume that those objective features that led investors to predict a certain growth rate in the past will continue to do so in the future? Changes in general economic conditions, in expectations about the stock market, and in expectations about government regulatory or tax policy, may all change the way in which the investor translates a history of, say, past growth in net plant into expected future growth in earnings.

Third, the total expected return that investors will insist upon to hold shares in the firm may change radically[58] with changes in economic conditions, government policy, or stock market expectations.[59]

Fourth, commissions using the DCF model should keep in mind the fact that regulatory policy will itself affect investors' expected return. And a commission cannot be certain precisely how the market will translate an allowed rate of return from the firm into an expected return to the shareholder. Thus, airline shareholders may have insisted upon an expected 16 percent in the 1960s. Yet, if the CAB therefore changes its regulatory policy to allow the firms to earn 16 percent on equity, that policy will itself affect earning expectations; the industry may become less risky; and, as a result, investors may require less than 16 percent.

3. *Conclusions.* This discussion is meant to suggest that setting a rate of return cannot, even in principle, be reduced to an exact science. To spend hours of hearing time considering elaborate "rate of return" models is of doubtful value; and suggestions of a proper rate — carried out to several decimal places — give an

---

58. This fact casts doubt on the usefulness of one plan (see Note, An Earnings-Price Approach to Fair Rate of Return in Regulated Industries, 20 Stan. L. Rev. 287 (1968)) for the setting of a rate of return: the authors of that plan point out that a regulator can tell if he has allowed shareholders too high or too low a return *in the past*: If the market price of shares rises above book value, a greater return was offered than needed to attract dollars equal to the book value of investment, and the contrary if market value sinks below book value. Yet, the suggestion that the regulator should then raise or lower the rate of return accordingly is of limited value, *for market conditions and investor demands change.* Thus a 9 percent allowed rate of return from 1974 to 1977 may have been too high and share prices may exceed book value, yet for 1978 to 1981, it could be too low. If so, a regulator lowering the rate in 1977 would compound his error, not correct it.

59. Indeed, if one could determine precisely which observable, measurable historical features comprise the investor's expectation of g, could one not easily determine which shares on the stock market are undervalued, buy them, announce one's results, and make a fortune?

air of precision that must be false. All this is assuming one accepts the standard: "give the investor just that return he will insist upon to make his investment and no more." Such a standard would equate book and market investment values. Yet suppose regulators met the standard. What incentive would a firm have to become more efficient? We next turn to that subject.

Questions

Assume that we are trying to allow investors a fair return on their original investment — i.e., the "book value" of the company's assets.

1. Electricity Company has been earning $10 per share for the past two years. The book value of each share is $100. The market price of each share has risen to $150. The staff of the regulatory commission argues that the commission should allow the company a return of only $7 per share, which, the staff claims, is the cost of capital. How should the company reply?

2. Electricity Company points out to the commission that in other states electricity companies earn 10 percent on book value. What should the staff reply?

3. Suppose that Electricity Company argues that it has consistently earned more than 7 percent because it is more efficient than most other companies and has continuously reduced costs. Should it be allowed to earn $10 per share in the future? More? Less?

7. Control of Operating Expenses

(a) Since rates must be set to cover operating expenses as well as return on capital, regulatory commissions have obvious reasons for wishing to review expenses to make sure that they are not unnecessary or too high. The absence of competition, coupled with a right to a "fair rate of return" makes it less likely that utility managements will make "efficient" decisions unless some substitute for competitive pressure can be brought to bear. Regulatory scrutiny of expenditures is one way of attempting to supply a substitute.

Moreover, a policy of regulatory scrutiny and disallowance of expenses in setting rates is likely to make stockholder scrutiny more intensive, thus further promoting the goal of efficiency and at the same time reducing the burden on the regulatory board. In the absence of any regulation, or if rate regulation were unaccompanied by scrutiny of expenses, stockholders might have little interest in examining management expenditures, believing that the greater part of any waste could be passed off to consumers in the form of higher prices. They will in all likelihood be much more concerned if, because of disallowance, the wasteful expenditures come entirely out of their own pockets.

Nevertheless, there are obvious difficulties, practical if not theoretical, which limit the effectiveness of regulatory intervention in management decisions. A commission obviously cannot participate in day-to-day decisions; neither can it review in detail all decisions that have been made. Excessive review and reversal of management decisions might do more harm than good by paralyzing the very management initiative and imagination that should be promoted.

Thus, the proper division of responsibilities between management and regulatory commission is a very complex question, and few clear lines seem to have emerged from commission practice and court decisions over the years. The general principle seems to be a presumption against interference. In Missouri et rel. Southwestern Bell Tel. Co. v. Public Service Commn., 262 U.S. 276, 289 (1923), the Supreme Court cited the following rule with approval: "The Commission is not the financial manager of the corporation and it is not empowered to substitute its judgment for that of the directors of the corporation; nor can it ignore items charged by the utility as operating expenses unless there is an abuse of discretion in that regard by corporate officers."

It is obviously easier for courts and commissions to examine whether certain types of expenditures, e.g., for political advertising, are legitimate than to review whether certain legitimate expenditures, e.g., for salaries, are excessive in amount. In Pacific Tel. & Tel. v. Public Utilities Commn., 62 Cal. 2d 634, 401 P.2d 353, 44 Cal. Rptr. 1 (1965), for example, the Commission decided "to exclude from operating expenses for rate fixing purposes all amounts claimed for [charitable] . . . contributions. . . . It may be emphasized that the commission's declared future policy does not purport to prohibit the utility from making contributions but only precludes charging against its ratepayers."

On the other hand, the Federal Power Commission, in United Gas Pipeline Co., 31 F.P.C. 1180, 1189-1190, 54 P.U.R.3d 285, 295 (1964), wrote that "contributions of a reasonable amount to recognized and appropriate charitable institutions constitute a proper operating expense. Corporations have an obligation to the communities in which they are located and they are expected to recognize this obligation. It is our opinion that these contributions have an important relationship to the necessary costs of doing business."

(b) Consider the following two cases, both of which concern advertising. In Southwestern Electric Power Co. v. FPC, 304 F.2d 29 (5th Cir.), cert. denied sub nom. Alabama Power Co. v. FPC, 371 U.S. 924 (1962), sixty-three electricity companies sought court review of an FPC order that forbade them to classify "political" advertising expenses as "operating expenses." Any such expenditures had to be charged to profit:

> The eight advertisements here involved, most of them illustrated, are similar in that they develop this theme: a substantial portion of the sums paid for electricity by customers of private electric light and power companies goes for taxes; people who get their electricity from federal government electric systems have included in their bills either nothing for taxes or else a very small amount, since, generally speaking, the government systems are not taxed; you who use private power pay taxes used to help build the federal plants; in effect you are helping to pay the electric bills of those who buy the public power; this is unfair tax favoritism. The advertisements then conclude with inquiries, varying

from "Don't you think something ought to be done about this unfair tax favoritism?" to "Don't you think this unfair tax favoritism needs thorough study and discussion?" 304 F.2d at 32.

The companies argued that the content of the advertisement was true and it was designed to counter the widespread publicity provided by those favoring "public power." The court then continued:

> Assuming that the Commission had authority to give special treatment in its system of accounts to these particular expenditures, what is the basis for requiring them to be charged to income and is this within the authority of the Commission?
>
> The answer given by the Commission to this question was as follows: ". . . The political expenditures of utilities fall into a peculiar category. By their nature, such expenditures obviously have a doubtful relationship to rendering utility service. . . . The function of electric utilities and licensees under the Power Act is . . . to render public service in a business affected with a public interest; and it is fair and reasonable to require customers to pay the expenses properly incurred by the companies in rendering this service. However, on matters which are politically controversial, differences of opinion may and frequently do exist between the companies and their customers, between management and the rate payer. The classification generally of political expenditures to operating accounts might seem to imply that such expenditures must in due course and without further question be paid by the rate payer. Such an implication would be unwarranted and possibly unfair, in view of the fact that on politically controversial matters, the opinions of management and the rate payer may differ decidely. Thus this accounting classification, while isolating and identifying these controversial expenditures, appropriately avoids any implication that the companies are entitled without a further showing to charge against the rate payer the cost of political programs favored by the companies but possibly opposed by those who must pay the costs of supporting these enterprises.". . .
>
> We cannot disturb this determination of the Commission or hold its conclusions to be an abuse of discretion if there be a rational basis for its conclusions and warrant in the record for its judgment. It cannot be said that the Commission's conclusion here lacked a rational basis. . . .[60]

Compare the advertising at issue in Southern California Gas Co., 35 P.U.R. 3d 300 (Cal. P.U.C. 1960), involving the sales promotion expenses of a local gas distributor. The Commission observed:

> Advertising by public utilities frequently has been opposed by customer witnesses in rate proceedings, but the commission always has recognized the value of advertising and sales promotion by utilities. We consistently have allowed reasonable amounts for such purposes. . . .

60. 304 F.2d at 41-43. Compare Pacific Tel. & Tel. v. Public Utilities Commn., 62 Cal. 2d 634, 401 P.2d 353, 44 Cal. Rptr. 1 (1965) (a $17,000 lobbying expense was disallowed).

Applicant states the purpose of its sales promotion activities is to attain the full economic utilization of its facilities by (1) obtaining new gas customers, (2) retaining present customers, (3) encouraging the increased use of gas, and (4) developing and promoting new uses of gas which will result in a well-balanced load. Other reasons shown in this record for sales promotion activities include: (1) To maintain and secure improvement in load factor, (2) to maintain applicant's competitive position with the electric utilities, (3) to maintain and improve applicant's public relations, (4) to educate the public in better use of gas, (5) to compete generally for the consumer's dollar, and (6) to lower the cost of financing through making the applicant better known to the investors and security holders. . . .

[The Commission found that the firm's $6.5 million advertising expense, about 2.3 percent of its operating revenues, was a] reasonable allowance for sales promotion activities in the test year to be borne by the ratepayer. . . . Our action herein is not to be construed as limiting the amount applicant may spend for sales promotion in the test year or in any other period. Such determination is for the applicant to make. Our determination herein relates solely to the reasonable allowance of sales promotion expenses to be included in gas rates of this applicant to be borne by its ratepayers.[61]

(c) Compare Latourneau v. Citizens Util. Co., 125 Vt. 38, 209 A.2d 307 (1965), in which the court reversed [62] the Commission's disallowance of a $70,000 salary paid to a president who spends an average of two days a week on company affairs. The court held that this amount was not "out of line" with salaries paid presidents of other utilities.[63]

8. Efficiency in Production

In addition to direct disallowance of expenses, regulators have tried other methods of encouraging the firm to use and develop efficient, cost-saving production techniques.

First, regulators have relied upon the "rate-setting lag" to provide an incentive for efficient production. If the prices that are set in year one will remain in effect for at least three or four years, the firm will be able to keep any extra profits it makes in the interim. Thus, it will try to lower its costs to generate extra profit. If its costs are rising — due to inflation — the lag between the time it applies for a rate increase and the time it is granted may put extra pressure on the firm to hold down costs to avoid losses.

---

61. 35 P.U.R. 3d 300, 309-313. In People's Gas Light & Coke Co. v. Slattery, 373 Ill. 31, 25 N.E.2d 482 (1939), the court upheld a commission's disallowance of losses incurred by a gas utility on sales of gas appliances which it sold to promote the sale of gas.

62. The courts also reversed a commission decision not to allow litigation expenses as part of operating expenses. See Driscoll v. Edison Light & Power Co., 307 U.S. 104 (1939).

63. Entertainment, club memberships, etc., have usually been allowed as operating expenses where reasonable.

How well this crude incentive system works is debatable. For one thing, commissions do not set rates at regular intervals. Rather, commission-initiated rate investigations are rare; commissions ordinarily consider rates when firms seek approval of newly filed tariffs that will raise rates. When costs are rising, a firm will have little incentive to hold them down (say, during a potential test year), for it must provide evidence of high costs to obtain the rate increase. When costs are falling, the firm's desire to increase productivity and cut costs still more will be tempered by its fear of earning sufficient profit to provoke a rate investigation by the commission. For another thing, a "lag" at best produces incentives to find short-run productivity savings. Investment in research that will produce only long-run savings, for example, is discouraged, for the regulator is far more likely to take such savings into account in determining costs; thus, the benefits of research will flow directly to the consumer, not to the firm. In general, the incentive systems produced by varying regulatory "lags" are complex and quite different from those of a competitive market.

Second, regulators have tried to take increased efficiency into account when setting a rate of return. Firms judged to be more efficient are given a "bonus," by being allowed extra profit above the "cost of capital." Or, sometimes the "cost of capital" is determined on an industry, rather than a firm, basis, allowing firms of above average efficiency to earn more and others less. This system was formalized in the District of Columbia, where a sliding scale was adopted, permitting a firm that earned more than the allowed rate of return in period x to obtain a small increase in the *allowed* rate of return for the next period. Yet how could the commission determine whether the profit increase was due to increased efficiency or to other factors? Moreover, what was the commission to do about inflation, which would make invisible any efficiency saving? More generally, how should a commission determine how much the bonus should be? If it uses industry averages, how does it know whether below average performances flow from below average efficiency or from an uncontrollable feature of firm life (e.g., a worse route structure for an airline)? Do firm managers believe receipt of the bonus is predictable? Such questions suggest the imprecision inherent in the "bonus" method. Still, some informal "reward" in the rate of return for special efficiency has been fairly popular among state commissions, which feel that it represents a practical, though crude, way to lower production costs. Of course, such a system makes still more imprecise the "scientific, precise" methods of ascertaining the cost of capital described earlier. Regulators have also occasionally provided more direct monetary incentives for increased production efficiency by paying bonuses directly to workers — a system that has roughly the same virtues and drawbacks with regulated as with unregulated firms.

Third, commissions have sometimes sought to define performance standards which firms are required to meet, by, for example, disallowing costs in excess of those set by the standard. There are several obvious difficulties with this approach. Which company practices are to be the subject of such standards? Who will draw them up? How will they be applied and enforced? Obviously, the more detailed the standard, the more complex its drafting and administration. But the more general it is, the more difficulty the commission will have in using it to force any change in the firm's behavior. At some point, the detail would be sufficiently great to require the commission to possess such expertise about the firm that the commission would be nearly as qualified as management to run the company. If so, one might ask, why duplicate experts? Why not nationalize the firm and have the commission run it? (Of course, nationalization has its own problems.) This tension — between the fact that information and skill rest primarily within the firm and the fact that greater motivation to achieve a given social goal (here, cost-cutting) is generated within the commission — is common to the setting of standards through an adversary process.

Questions

1. Should contributions to charity be included in allowable operating expenses? Why or why not? Who bears the cost of charitable contributions by unregulated private corporations? Is that an appropriate test to apply to regulated companies?

2. With regard to advertising expenses:

(a) Is advertising for the purpose of increasing sales distinguishable from charitable contributions? In what respects?

(b) Should advertising and other promotion expenses be limited to "reasonable" amounts? If so, what is the test of "reasonableness"?

(c) Electric and gas utilities commonly are in substantial competition. What effect if any should be given to this fact in determining the reasonableness of advertising expenditures?

(d) Is it appropriate to treat "political advertising" differently from ordinary advertising? What about expenses incurred in lobbying for or against legislation affecting the regulated company's interests?

3. Electricity Company has borrowed $500 million which it is using to build a new atomic plant due to begin service in 1979. The company is paying $50 million for this money in annual interest charges. Should its present rates increase to cover this interest cost?

9. The Test Year

Commissions determine future operating costs by looking to past costs; and the rates so determined remain in effect for some time though operating costs may well have changed. Thus, if prices increase after rates have been set (as in the electricity industry in the early 1970s), the company will earn a lower return than the commission has allowed. If prices fall (as in gas pipelines in the mid-1970s) the companies may charge a higher than competitive price and earn excess profits.

Commissions base their costs upon a test year because of their need for certainty and their need to avoid unresolvable factual disputes that threaten lengthy proceedings, arbitrary decisions, and court reversals. Although test-year prices will differ from future prices, at least they are known. One thereby avoids what would be endless and unresolvable arguments about what future costs will probably be.

Commissions make some effort to adjust for known inflation. Thus, the Civil Aeronautics Board allowed the industry to *annualize* the costs incurred at the end of the test year instead of averaging costs throughout the entire year. And some public utilities commissions allow firms to assume higher future labor costs, at least if those costs are already the subject of a negotiated contract. Fuel adjustment clauses allow utilities to pass through fuel cost increases as they are incurred. Still, using test-year costs often leads to prices different from those that would be set with competition.

The difference between regulated and competitive prices is aggravated by the tendency of commissions to use "test year" quantities in determining how changes in price levels will affect firm revenues. If a firm's revenue requirement increases by $1 million, the regulator is likely to divide the $1 million by the quantity sold during the test year and raise unit prices by the result. Such a calculation assumes that the price change will not itself affect the number of units sold — a most unreasonable assumption.

Why then have regulators only rarely tried to take account of how demand responds to changes in price? Partly because estimating demand elasticities is so difficult. ("Elasticity" means the percentage change in demand divided by the percentage change in price.) For example, after extensive hearings the CAB determined that elasticity of demand for airline travel equalled $-.7$. This number assumes that as price falls (rises), demand will rise (fall) less than proportionately. Academic economists strongly criticized the result, claiming that a figure of -1.2 or -1.0 would reflect the response of demand more accurately. They noted, for example, that when Pacific Southwest Airlines entered the Sacramento-Los Angeles market in 1967 offering a 25 percent reduction in fares, traffic over the route doubled. Yet, as to each piece of evidence showing high elasticity, arguments can be made that it is a "special case." Thus, for example, the PSA experience may reflect the increased demand for air travel in general or the increase in the importance of Sacramento, rather than its price cut. In the words of one experienced airline financial analyst, "There has never been a study which satisfactorily removed the nonprice determinants of demand while successfully freezing the price determinants for a sufficiently long period of time to produce results which could be deemed extrapolatable. . . ." [64]

A second response is that in other regulated industries, such as electricity, it may be reasonable to assume that demand is highly inelastic. Thus, use of the test year's quantity figures may provide as accurate a result as more elaborate, inevitably controversial, demand estimates would have done. Thus, using a demand estimate based on a "test year," like basing costs on a test year (with rough adjustments) frequently represents what is, administratively speaking, the least bad alternative.

64. Statement of Harry A. Kimbriel, Oversight of Civil Aeronautics Board Practices and Procedures, Hearings Before the Subcommittee on Administrative Practice and Procedures of the Senate Committee on the Judiciary, 94th Cong., 1st Sess. 2237 (1975).

Questions

1. Are past "test year" costs strong evidence as to future costs? Will "test year" quantities stay the same as prices change? If not, why do commissions tend to stick to "test year" figures?

2. Suppose that rates are set for Natural Gas Pipeline Co. In 1962, operating costs decline. What, as a practical matter, is likely to happen to Gas Pipeline Co.'s rates? Why?

3. Is regulation likely to produce prices that, in general, replicate those that would be set were there competition in the industry?

4. You are now in a position to judge the ability of the courts to review the "constitutional facts" that may show confiscation. First ask, in light of St. Joseph Stockyards and then Hope, what has happened to the Ben Avon doctrine? Why? Second consider the Hope standard: "it is the result reached not the method employed that is controlling." Does this standard leave the courts with any significant power of review?

5. Proposition: "The Hope standard is absurd. If any part of rate setting should be subject to review it is the method employed, not the result reached. Almost any result can be justified on the basis of some system or other. What is important is to see that the agency acts fairly, rationally, and consistently. The courts ought to review the method employed, with these criteria in mind." Argue for and against this proposition.

C. Review of Questions of Law

Addison v. Holly Hill Fruit Products, Inc.

322 U.S. 607 (1944)

Mr. Justice FRANKFURTER delivered the opinion of the Court. . . .

[The Fair Labor Standards Act, 52 Stat. 1060, requires employers to pay a fixed minimum wage. The Act exempts certain employers from this requirement. Among those exempted are employers whose employees are engaged in the canning of agricultural products, provided that the canning plant is located "within the area" of agricultural production. The exact language of this exemption states that it applies to those "within the area of production (as defined by the Administrator), engaged in . . . canning of agricultural . . . commodities for market . . ."

On October 20, 1938, the Administrator defined "area of production," to include an individual engaged in canning "if the agricultural . . . commodities are obtained by the establishment where he is employed from farms in the immediate locality and the number of employees in such establishment does not exceed seven."

Holly Hill, a citrus fruit cannery, employs 200 workers. It is located in Davenport, Florida, a town of 650 people. Some of its employees sued for payments under the minimum wage law. The District Court held in their favor. The Court of Appeals reversed, holding that Holly Hill was exempt. It found the limitations of the exemptions to those firms employing seven or fewer workers unlawful, and without this numerical limitation Holly Hill fell within the statutory exemption.

The Supreme Court must determine whether the Administrator's regulation is lawful. Thus the Court must decide if the Administrator could lawfully include in the definition of "area of production" the condition that the number of employees in the establishment not exceed seven.]

. . . In short, when Congress exempted "any individual within the area of production (as defined by the Administrator)" (§13(a)(10)), did it authorize the Administrator not only to designate territorial bounds for the purposes of exemption but also to except establishments from such exemption according to the number of workers employed.

Congress provided for eleven exemptions from the controlling provisions relating to minimum wages or maximum hours of the Fair Labor Standards Act. Employment in agriculture is probably the most far-reaching exemption. Closely related to it is the exemption which is our immediate concern — those workers engaged in processes necessary for the marketing of agricultural products and employed "within the area of production" of such commodities. Such was the phrase and such its conjunction with the exemption for agriculture of which it formed an integral part as the bill passed both Houses, except that the enumerated exempted employments subsidiary to agriculture varied in the two bills. The parenthetical qualification "(as defined by the Administrator)" emerged from the conference committee of the two Houses.

The textual meaning of "area of production" is thus reinforced by its context: "area" calls for delimitation of territory in relation to the complicated economic factors that operate between agricultural labor conditions and the labor market of enterprises concerned with agricultural commodities and more or less near their production. The phrase is the most apt designation of a zone within which economic influences may be deemed to operate and outside of which they lose their force. In view, however, of the variety of agricultural conditions and industries throughout the country, the bounds of these areas could not be defined by Congress itself. Neither was it deemed wise to leave such economic determination to the contingencies and inevitable diversities of litigation. And so Congress left the boundary-making to the experienced and informed judgment of the Administrator. Thereby Congress gave the Administrator appropriate discretion to assess all the factors relevant to the subject matter, that is, the fixing of minimum wages and maximum hours.

In delimiting the area the Administrator may properly weigh and synthesize all such factors. So long as he does that and no more, judgment belongs to him and not to the courts. For Congress has cast upon him the authority and the duty to define the "area of production" of agricultural commodities with reference to which exemption in subsidiary employments may operate. But if Congress intended to allow the Administrator to discriminate between smaller and bigger establishments within the zone of agricultural production, Congress wholly failed to express its purpose. Where Congress wanted to make exemption depend on size, as it did in two or three instances not here relevant, it did so by appropriate language. Congress referred to quantity when it desired to legislate on the basis of quantity.

Congressional purpose as manifested by text and context is not rendered doubtful by legislative history. Meagre as that is, it confirms what Congress has formally said. The only extrinsic light cast on Congressional purpose regarding "area of production" is that cast by the sponsors of this provision for enlarging the range of agricultural exemptions. Senator Schwellenbach frankly stated that the largest apple packing plant in the world would be exempt if the "work done in that plant is as described in the amendment." 81 Cong. Rec. 7877. And in the House, Representative Biermann, while explaining his amendment in somewhat Delphic terms, did indicate plainly enough that he had in mind not differences between establishments within the same territory but between rural communities and urban centers: "may I say that all over this country it has been recognized that there should be a labor differential between the large city and the little town." 83 Cong. Rec. 7401.

From such light as Congress gave us beyond its words, it would appear that in giving exemption to an "area of production," without differentiating as between establishments within such area, Congress might well have considered that a large plant within an area should not be given an advantage over small plants in competing for labor within the same locality, while at the same time it gave the Administrator ample power, in defining the area to take due account of the appropriate economic factor in drawing the geographic lines. In any event, Congress did not leave it to the Administrator to decide whether within geographic bounds defined by him the Act further permits discrimination between establishment and establishment based upon the number of employees. The determination of the extent of authority given to a delegated agency by Congress is not left for the decision of him in whom authority is vested.

The wider a delegation is made by Congress to an administrative agency the more incomplete is a statute and the ampler the scope for filling in, as it is called, its details. But when Congress wants to give wide discretion it uses broad language. . . . In the Fair Labor Standards Act, Congress legislated very differently in relation to the problem before us. . . . Congress did not prescribe or proscribe generally and then give broad discretion for administrative relief as in the Interstate Commerce Act or for remedies as in the National Labor Relations Act. Congress did otherwise. It dealt with exemptions in detail and with particularity, enumerating not less than eleven exempted classes based on different industries, on different occupations within the same industry (the classification in some instances to be defined by the Administrator, in some made by Congress itself, in others subject to definition by other legislation), on size and on areas. In short the Administrator was not left at large. . . .

We should of course be faithful to the meaning of a statute. But after all Congress expresses its meaning by words. If legislative policy is couched in vague language, easily susceptible of one meaning as well as another in the common speech of men, we should not stifle a policy by a pedantic or grudging process of construction. To let general words draw nourishment from their purpose is one thing. To draw on some unexpressed spirit outside the bounds of the normal meaning of words is quite another. . . .

Legislation introducing a new system is at best empirical, and not infrequently administration reveals gaps or inadequacies of one sort or another that may call for amendatory legislation. But it is no warrant for extending a statute that experience may disclose that it should have been made more comprehensive. "The natural meaning of words cannot be displaced by reference to difficulties in administration." Commonwealth v. Grunseit (1943) 67 C.L.R. 58, 80. For the ultimate question is what has Congress commanded, when it has given no clue to its intentions except familiar English words and no hint by the draftsmen of the words that they meant to use them in any but an ordinary sense. The idea which is now sought to be read into the grant by Congress to the Administrator to define "the area of production" beyond the plain geographic implications of that phrase is not so complicated nor is English speech so poor that words were not easily available to express the idea or at least to suggest it. After all, legislation when not expressed in technical terms is addressed to the common run of men and is therefore to be understood according to the sense of the thing, as the ordinary man has a right to rely on ordinary words addressed to him.

The details with which the exemptions in this Act have been made preclude their enlargement by implication. While the judicial function in construing legislation is not a mechanical process from which judgment is excluded, it is nevertheless very different from the legislative function. Construction is not legislation and must avoid "that retrospective expansion of meaning which properly deserves the stigma of judicial legislation." Kirschbaum Co. v. Walling, 316 U.S. 517, 522. To blur the distinctive functions of the legislative and judicial processes is not conducive to responsible legislation.

We agree therefore with the Circuit Court of Appeals in holding invalid the limitations as to the number of employees within a defined area. [Justice Frankfurter went on to ask whether, if the regulation was invalid, the employees were or were not exempt. He concluded that the District Court should hold the case until the administrator wrote a new regulation.]

[A concurring opinion by Mr. Justice ROBERTS is omitted.]

Mr. Justice RUTLEDGE, with whom Mr. Justice BLACK and Mr. Justice MURPHY concur, dissenting:

In my opinion the Administrator has defined "area of production" in a valid manner, and therefore the employee petitioners should prevail. . . .

The basic issue, as the case was presented, is whether the Administrator can include in the definition not only spacial limits but also a limit upon the number of employees in exempted establishments. . . .

[The Administrator] insists it, or an equivalent limitation on size of the plant, must be included, unless any definition he may make is to work havoc with some major policy of the Act, either by exempting large numbers of industrial employees or by creating disturbances of competitive situations, both for farmers and for canners and packers, which the statute expressly sought to avoid.

The Administrator's task is highly complex. It involves defining exemptions for employees throughout the nation engaged in "handling, packing, storing, ginning, compressing, pasteurizing, drying, preparing in their raw or natural state, or canning of agricultural or horticultural commodities for market, or in making cheese or butter or other dairy products." §13(a)(10). All these operations follow immediately upon harvest and removal from the field or milking. All can be done on the farm and frequently are done there, but may be done elsewhere, often in factories. All consist in the first stages of preparation for market.

But whether the specified operations will be done on the farm, as part of the farm work or away from it, and in either small neighborhood establishments or in larger industrial plants, will depend upon a variety of factors as great as that which comprehends the whole vast process of starting the nation's crops, over 300, on their respective marketing courses. The initial steps in marketing such widely different products as cotton and apples; tobacco and milk; potatoes and citrus fruits; legume crops, wheat, corn and other grains, on the one hand, and tomatoes, strawberries, truck garden products, etc., on the other, are within the delegation.

The mere enumeration of these instances indicates some of the variables involved. Others add to the difficulty. Highly perishable crops, as fruits and vegetables, require immediate action in these stages of handling. Cotton, grains, root crops, etc., less perishable, may wait longer on the farm, some for months, before these processes become necessary. Some crops are highly concentrated for production in a few regions, such as citrus fruits in Florida, Southern Texas, and Southern California, but are marketed on a nation-wide scale. Others have regional areas of production, like cotton in the South, celery in Michigan, tobacco in the border states and a few northern regions, yet depend on the national market. Still others have regions of greater or less concentration, but are grown all over the nation, like wheat and other grains, apples, potatoes, etc.

Obviously, "area of production," in the sense of where the commodity is produced for purposes of commercial marketing, will vary from the whole nation, in the case of the more common grains, fruit crops and root crops, down to a few highly concentrated regions or areas in the case of others more dependent upon special climatic and soil combinations. And between the extremes of nation-wide and highly localized production are all ranges of sectional and regional production areas. . . .

It follows necessarily that the Administrator's power is discretionary and the important questions are to what extent and in what manner may his discretion work. Neither subdivision (a)(10) nor §13 as a whole supplies these answers. The section itself does not supply all the standards necessary for definition of the term. At most it affords direction to exempt some but not other employees engaged in the specified activities and that those exempted must be within the "area of production." This necessarily includes some region where the commodity is produced. But since that region is an unknown quantity and so also is the question what employees within it are to be exempted, solutions must be found either in other provisions of the statute or in the legislative history, unless the delegation is to fall for want of standards.

The statute itself furnishes clear guides for directing the Administrator. He is confined, as has been noted, by subsection (a)(10) to employees engaged in the specified initial operations of marketing. They must work within some producing region. Apart from the exemption they are within the Act's coverage, but close to the major line it draws between farm workers, who are excluded from, and industrial labor, which is within its coverage. Depending, not upon what they do, but upon where and how they do this work, they would fall on one side or the other of this line and within or without the incidence of the evils the Act sought to eradicate. . . .

The broad line between farming and industry runs throughout the Act. It is the statute's basic line of policy between coverage and noncoverage. The line not only is pertinent to each of the statute's provisions but, where the contrary is not clearly and unambiguously stated, it is controlling. There can be no assumption that Congress intended employees in one group to be transferred to or treated as being in the other where no such clear mandate can be found.

In determining what Congress intended by the delegation, it is crucial to keep in mind that, whatever decision the Administrator may make and by whatever criteria, the effect of his action must be to put some employees on one side of this line and others on the opposite side. That consequence he cannot escape. And, because he cannot avoid it, the line is pertinent and material to his choice, as it is to all others he must make in performing his duties. It is the statute's lodestar. The distinction between farming and industry is the essence of his determination. An "area of production" determined without reference to this distinction would contradict, not enforce, the statute's basic policy. . . .

. . . [The Administrator] could not escape the question of size. . . .

The legislative history discloses one object of the exemption as originally proposed was to protect small farmers, who are unable to perform these operations at the farm and therefore are dependent upon whatever nearby establishments may exist, whether large or small. Various members of the Senate and of the House sponsored amendments for this purpose. As the bills went to conference each contained flat exemptions, substantially covering the activities now specified in §13(a)(10). But the debates in both houses show that even the sponsors of the various amendments differed or were doubtful concerning whether the amendments would give exemption to large plants. There was general agreement that small ones should be relieved from coverage. Senator Reynolds went further and proposed several amendments to relieve all small plants from the Act's provisions, not merely those engaged in the limited operations specified in the bills or §13(a)(10). These were defeated. And there was vigorous demand, from the sponsor of the bill in the Senate and others, for restricting the scope of the amending exemptions to small plants. These differences were not settled on the floor of either house. But when the bills came to conference, they were resolved by changing the flat exemptions into discretionary ones to be defined by the Administrator.

Since the delegation feature did not appear until the conference report and there is little in that report or in the debates upon it to add light, the previous discussions are wholly inconclusive, except in one respect. This was to show that there was great variety and complexity of opinion, and that this revolved around the question of size. That question continued unresolved up to conference and was resolved there, not by decision either way, but by reference to the Administrator. It must be taken therefore that the purpose was to give him discretion to make the necessary choices between the conflicting viewpoints as the facts of particular situations would give occasion for doing. And, it would seem, the preponderance of sentiment in favor of exempting small plants, but not large ones, except in occasional instances where this would be necessary to protect the small farmer, well could be taken as his guiding light. The legislative history, therefore, in so far as it sheds light at all, clearly is not inconsistent with what the Administrator has done, but on the contrary supports it. . . .

Nothing prevents the Administrator from drawing the lines as he thinks best, unless the suggestion of the specially concurring opinion is followed that they must be drawn in regular circles or squares. The courts have no business to tell him where to put them. . . . I do not believe that Congress, when it gave the Administrator his complicated task and authorized him to consider all the relevant and complex economic factors, not only denied him the power to execute those considerations in his action, but compelled him to frustrate them in defining "area of production." The Court does not deny the Administrator may consider the size of the plant, and make this even the crucial factor in his decision. Yet it would only impede or defeat his judgment, formed on proper considerations, as well as the statute's purposes, to require him to state the exemption, not simply in the terms best chosen to express his meaning clearly and definitely, but in others couched in pure though tortured geography. According to his experience and confirmed judgment, shared by successive administrators and never reversed or modified, to require the latter method of formulation would make his task well nigh impossible or, if not that, incapable of being discharged without doing violence to the Act's major purposes and standards.

. . . "Area of production" as used in §13(a)(10) means an exemption, limited to persons performing the specified operations within a producing region, but selected from all so situated by an exercise of the Administrator's judgment in accordance with the statute's prime objects and chief limitations, among which necessarily is the size of the plant. If that is so, I see no good reason for forbidding the Administrator to say so. . . .

Mourning v. Family Publications Service, Inc.

411 U.S. 356 (1973)

[The Truth in Lending Act requires merchants who regularly extend credit to disclose the amount of the finance charge "to each person to whom consumer credit is extended and upon whom a finance charge is or may be imposed. . . ." Sec. 121. The Act also provides: "The [Federal Reserve] Board shall prescribe regulations to carry out the purposes of [the Act]. These regulations may contain such

... provisions ... as in the judgment of the Board are necessary or proper to effectuate the purposes of [the Act], to prevent ... evasion ... or to facilitate compliance." Sec. 105. The Board issued a regulation requiring disclosure whenever credit is offered to a customer "for which either a finance charge is ... imposed *or which ... is ... payable in more than four installments.*" Regulation Z (emphasis added).

Plaintiff signed a contract under which defendant promised to deliver four magazines each month for five years and plaintiff promised to pay $3.45 per month for 2½ years. Plaintiff then refused to pay and sued for statutory damages (including attorney's fees) on the ground that defendant had not complied with Regulation Z.

The Supreme Court (5 to 4) reinstated the District Court's grant of summary judgment to plaintiff. It rejected defendant's claim that the underlined words in Regulation Z went beyond the Board's statutory authority for no "finance charge" was necessarily involved.]

Mr. Chief Justice BURGER delivered the opinion of the Court:

... The standard to be applied in determining whether the Board exceeded the authority delegated to it under the Truth in Lending Act is well established under our prior cases. Where the empowering provision of a statute states simply that the agency may "make ... such rules and regulations as may be necessary to carry out the provisions of this Act," we have held that the validity of a regulation promulgated thereunder will be sustained so long as it is "reasonably related to the purposes of the enabling legislation." Thorpe v. Housing Authority of the City of Durham, 393 U.S. 268, 280-281 (1969)....

... [W]e cannot agree with the conclusion of the Court of Appeals that the Board exceeded its statutory authority in promulgating the Four Installment Rule. Congress was clearly aware that merchants could evade the reporting requirements of the Act by concealing credit charges. In delegating rulemaking authority to the Board, Congress emphasized the Board's authority to prevent such evasion....

... The burdens imposed on creditors are not severe, when measured against the evils which are avoided. Furthermore, were it possible or financially feasible to delve into the intricacies of every credit transaction, it is clear that many creditors to whom the rule applies would be found to have charged for deferring payment, while claiming they had not. That some other remedial provision might be preferable is irrelevant. We have consistently held that where reasonable minds may differ as to which of several remedial measures should be chosen, courts should defer to the informed experience and judgment of the agency to whom Congress delegated appropriate authority....

Respondent contends, however, that the Four Installment Rule must be abrogated since it is "inconsistent" with portions of the enabling statute. The purported conflict arises because the statute specifically mentions disclosure only in regard to transactions in which a finance charge is in fact imposed, although the rule requires disclosure in some cases in which no such charge exists. Respondent argues that, in requiring disclosure as to some transactions, Congress intended to preclude the Board from imposing similar requirements as to any other transactions....

Since the deterrent effect of the challenged rule clearly implements the objectives of the Act, respondent's contention is reduced to a claim that the rule is void because it requires disclosure by some creditors who do not charge for credit and thus need not be deterred. The fact that the regulation may affect such individuals does not impair its otherwise valid purpose. . . .

. . . In Village of Euclid v. Ambler Realty Co., 272 U.S. 365, 388-389 (1926), the Court held that, in defining a class subject to regulation, "[t]he inclusion of a reasonable margin to insure effective enforcement, will not put upon a law, otherwise valid, the stamp of invalidity." . . . Nothing less will meet the demands of our complex economic system. Where, as here, the transactions or conduct which Congress seeks to administer occur in myriad and changing forms, a requirement that a line be drawn which insures that not one blameless individual will be subject to the provisions of an act would unreasonably encumber effective administration and permit many clear violators to escape regulation entirely. That this rationale applies to administrative agencies as well as to legislatures is implicit in both *Gemsco* and *American Trucking Assns*. In neither case was every individual engaged in the regulated activity responsible for the specific consequences the agency sought to eliminate.

[Mr. Justice POWELL argued in dissent that this was not a "credit transaction." Three other justices thought summary judgment was error because whether a "credit transaction" was involved raised a question of fact.]

Skidmore v. Swift & Co.

323 U.S. 134 (1944)

Mr. Justice JACKSON delivered the opinion of the Court.

Seven employees of the Swift and Company packing plant at Fort Worth, Texas, brought an action under the Fair Labor Standards Act to recover overtime, liquidated damages, and attorneys' fees, totalling approximately $77,000. . . .

It is not denied that the daytime employment of these persons was working time within the Act. Two were engaged in general fire-hall duties and maintenance of fire-fighting equipment of the Swift plant. The others operated elevators or acted as relief men in fire duties. They worked from 7:00 A.M. to 3:30 P.M., with a half-hour lunch period, five days a week. They were paid weekly salaries.

Under their oral agreement of employment, however, petitioners undertook to stay in the fire hall on the Company premises, or within hailing distance, three and a half to four nights a week. This involved no task except to answer alarms, either because of fire or because the sprinkler was set off for some other reason. No fires occurred during the period in issue, the alarms were rare, and the time required for their answer rarely exceeded an hour. For each alarm answered the employees were paid in addition to their fixed compensation an agreed amount, fifty cents at first, and later sixty-four cents. The Company provided a brick fire hall equipped with steam heat and air-conditioned rooms. It provided sleeping quarters, a pool table, a domino table, and a radio. The men used their time in sleep or amusement as they saw fit, except that they were required to stay in or close by the fire hall and be ready to respond to alarms. It is stipulated that "they agreed to remain in the fire hall and stay in it or within hailing distance, subject to call, in event of fire or other casualty, but were not required to perform any specific tasks during these periods of time, except in answering alarms." The trial court . . . said as a "conclusion of law" that "the time plaintiffs spent in the fire hall subject to call to answer fire alarms does not constitute hours worked, for which overtime compensation is due them under the Fair Labor Standards Act, as interpreted by the Administrator and the Courts," and in its opinion observed, "of course we know pursuing such pleasurable occupations or performing such personal chores, does not constitute work." The Circuit Court of Appeals affirmed.

. . . [N]o principle of law found either in the statute or in Court decisions precludes waiting time from also being working time. We have not attempted to, and we cannot, lay down a legal formula to resolve cases so varied in their facts as are the many situations in which employment involves waiting time. Whether in a concrete case such time falls within or without the Act is a question of fact to be resolved by appropriate findings of the trial court. Walling v. Jacksonville Paper Co., 317 U.S. 564, 572. This involves scrutiny and construction of the agreements between the particular parties, appraisal of their practical construction of the working agreement by conduct, consideration of the nature of the service, and its relation to the waiting time, and all of the surrounding circumstances. Facts may show that the employee was engaged to wait, or they may show that he waited to be engaged. His compensation may cover both waiting and task, or only performance of the task itself. Living quarters may in some situations be furnished as a facility of the task and in another as a part of its compensation. The law does not impose an arrangement upon the parties. It imposes upon the courts the task of finding what the arrangement was.

We do not minimize the difficulty of such an inquiry where the arrangements of the parties have not contemplated the problem posed by the statute. But it does not differ in nature or in the standards to guide judgment from that which frequently confronts courts where they must find retrospectively the effect of contracts as to matters which the parties failed to anticipate or explicitly to provide for.

Congress did not utilize the services of an administrative agency to find facts and to determine in the first instance whether particular cases fall within or without the Act. Instead, it put this responsibility on the courts. . . . But it did create the office of Administrator, impose upon him a variety of duties, endow him with powers to inform himself of conditions in industries and employments subject to the Act, and put on him the duties of bringing injunction actions to restrain violations. Pursuit of his duties has accumulated a considerable experience in the problems of ascertaining working time in employments involving periods of inactivity and a knowledge of the customs prevailing in reference to their solution. From these he is obliged to reach conclusions as to conduct without the law, so that he should seek injunctions to stop it, and that within the law, so that he has no call to interfere. He has set forth his views of the application of the Act under different circumstances in an interpretative bulletin and in informal rulings. They provide a practical guide to employers and employees as to how the office representing the public interest in its enforcement will seek to apply it. Wage and Hour Division, Interpretative Bulletin No. 13.

The Administrator thinks the problems presented by inactive duty require a flexible solution, rather than the all-in or all-out rules respectively urged by the parties in this case, and his Bulletin endeavors to suggest standards and examples to guide in particular situations. In some occupations, it says, periods of inactivity are not properly counted as working time even though the employee is subject to call. Examples are an operator of a small telephone exchange where the switchboard is in her home and she ordinarily gets several hours of uninterrupted sleep each night; or a pumper of a stripper well or watchman of a lumber camp during the off season, who may be on duty twenty-four hours a day but ordinarily "has a normal night's sleep, has ample time in which to eat his meals, and has a certain amount of time for relaxation and entirely private pursuits." Exclusion of all such hours the Administrator thinks may be justified. In general, the answer depends "upon the degree to which the employee is free to engage in personal activities during periods of idleness when he is subject to call and the number of consecutive hours that the employee is subject to call without being required to perform active work." "Hours worked are not limited to the time spent in active labor but include time given by the employee to the employer. . . ."

The facts of this case do not fall within any of the specific examples given, but the conclusion of the Administrator, as expressed in the brief amicus curiae, is that the general tests which he has suggested point to the exclusion of sleeping and eating time of these employees from the workweek and the inclusion of all other on-call time: although the employees were required to remain on the premises during the entire time, the evidence shows that they were very rarely interrupted in their normal sleeping and eating time, and these are pursuits of a purely private nature which would presumably occupy the employees' time whether they were on duty or not and which apparently could be pursued adequately and comfortably in the required circumstances; the rest of the time is different because there is nothing in the record to suggest that, even though pleasurably spent, it was spent in the ways the men would have chosen had they been free to do so.

There is no statutory provision as to what, if any, deference courts should pay to the Administrator's conclusions. And, while we have given them notice, we have had no occasion to try to prescribe their influence. The rulings of this Administrator are not reached as a result of hearing adversary proceedings in which he finds facts from evidence and reaches conclusions of law from findings of fact. They are not, of course, conclusive, even in the cases with which they directly deal, much less in those to which they apply only by analogy. They do not constitute an interpretation of the Act or a standard for judging factual situations which binds a district court's processes, as an authoritative pronouncement of a higher court might do. But the Administrator's policies are made in pursuance of official duty, based upon more specialized experience and broader investigations and information than is likely to come to a judge in a particular case. They do determine the policy which will guide applications for enforcement by injunction on behalf of the Government. Good administration of the Act and good judicial administration alike require that the standards of public enforcement and those for determining private rights shall be at variance only where justified by very good reasons. The fact that the Administrator's policies and standards are not reached by trial in adversary form does not mean that they are not entitled to respect. This Court has long given considerable and in some cases decisive weight to Treasury Decisions and to interpretative regulations of the Treasury and of other bodies that were not of adversary origin.

We consider that the rulings, interpretations and opinions of the Administrator under this Act, while not controlling upon the courts by reason of their authority, do constitute a body of experience and informed judgment to which courts and litigants may properly resort for guidance. The weight of such a judgment in a particular case will depend upon the thoroughness evident in its consideration, the validity of its reasoning, its consistency with earlier and later pronouncements, and all those factors which give it power to persuade, if lacking power to control. . . .

[Reversed.]

Note: Interpretive and Legislative Rules

A distinction is sometimes made between "interpretive" rules and "legislative" rules. In Gibson Wine Co. v. Snyder, 194 F.2d 329, 331 (D.C. Cir. 1952), the court described interpretive rules as "statements as to what the administrative officer thinks the statute or regulation means," while legislative rules "create law, usually [implementing] an existing law." Professor Davis states that the key distinction between them is whether the agency "in issuing the Regulation was exercising delegated power to make rules having force of law." If so, the rule is "legislative." Administrative Law of the Seventies §5.03-1 (1976). Under this approach a rule would be "legislative" even if (as in *Mourning*) it construes or amplifies a statutory term, so long as it represents an exercise of delegated lawmaking authority. On the other hand, a rule might (because of an absence of delegated lawmaking authority) be "interpretive" even though it did not construe or interpret a statutory term.

How does one tell whether the agency has been delegated the authority to issue "rules having the force of law"? Moreover, what turns on this or any other distinction between "legislative" and "interpretive" rules? Some have thought the deference due the agency by the court may be different for legislative as opposed to interpretive rules. Thus, Professor Davis, for example, argues that "the distinction is important because courts often substitute judgment as to the content of an interpretive rule but almost always (theoretically always) refrain from substituting judgment as to the content of a legislative rule." He goes on to argue that legislative rules can be reviewed only for "arbitrariness." [65] You should also note that the Ad-

---

65. K. Davis, Administrative Law Treatise §5.03 (1958). The Supreme Court, in General Electric Co. v. Gilbert, 429 U.S. 125 (1976), cites *Skidmore* with approval as to the deference to be given "interpretive rules." The Court suggested that it would grant still more deference to rules the agency is authorized by statute to promulgate.

ministrative Procedure Act, 5 U.S.C. §553(a)(3)(A), exempts from its "notice and comment" rulemaking procedures "interpretive rules [and] general statements of policy."

Others have stated that "attempts to draw a hard and fast line between 'interpretive' and 'substantive' regulations have been rather unrewarding." Rather "specific regulations promulgated pursuant to a general statutory delegation of authority must be treated as authoritative, whether labelled 'substantive' or 'interpretive,' especially in areas where the agency possesses expertise not shared by the courts." National Nutritional Foods Assn. v. Weinberger, 512 F.2d 688, 696 (2d Cir.), *cert. denied,* 423 U.S. 827 (1975).

Can Professor Davis's approach be reconciled with *Holly Hill?* With *Skidmore?* Are *Holly Hill* and *Mourning* consistent? Should the distinction between "legislative" and "interpretive" rules be abandoned?

NLRB v. Hearst Publications, Inc.

322 U.S. 111 (1944)

Mr. Justice RUTLEDGE delivered the opinion of the Court.

These cases arise from the refusal of respondents, publishers of four Los Angeles daily newspapers, to bargain collectively with a union representing newsboys who distribute their papers on the streets of that city. Respondents [contend] that they were not required to bargain because the newsboys are not their "employees" within the meaning of that term in the National Labor Relations Act. . . .

[The NLRB, after hearings,] concluded that the regular full-time newsboys selling each paper were employees within the Act [and Hearst was ordered to bargain with them.] . . .

[T]he Circuit Court of Appeals, one judge dissenting, set aside the Board's orders. Rejecting the Board's analysis, the court independently examined the question whether the newsboys are employees within the Act, decided that the statute imports common-law standards to determine that question, and held the newsboys are not employees.

The findings of the Board disclose that the Los Angeles Times and the Los Angeles Examiner, published daily and Sunday, are morning papers. Each publishes several editions which are distributed on the streets during the evening before their dateline, between about 6:00 or 6:30 P.M. and 1:00 A.M., and other editions distributed during the following morning until about 10:00 o'clock. The Los Angeles Evening Herald and Express, published every day but Sunday, is an evening paper, which has six editions on the presses between 9:00 A.M. and 5:30 P.M. The News, also published every day but Sunday, is a twenty-four hour paper with ten editions.

The papers are distributed to the ultimate consumer through a variety of channels, including . . . newsboys who sell on the streets of the city and its suburbs. . . .

The newsboys work under varying terms and conditions. They may be "bootjackers," selling to the general public at places other than established corners, or they may sell at fixed "spots." They may sell only casually or part-time, or full-time; and they may be employed regularly and continuously or only temporarily. The units which the Board determined to be appropriate are composed of those who sell full-time at established spots. Those vendors, misnamed boys, are generally mature men, dependent upon the proceeds of their sales for their sustenance, and frequently supporters of families. Working thus as news vendors on a regular basis, often for a number of years, they form a stable group with relatively little turnover, in contrast to schoolboys and others who sell as bootjackers, temporary and casual distributors. . . .

The newsboys' compensation consists in the difference between the prices at which they sell the papers and the prices they pay for them. The former are fixed by the publishers and the latter are fixed either by the publishers or, in the case of the News, by the district manager. In practice the newsboys receive their papers on credit. They pay for those sold either sometime during or after the close of their selling day, returning for credit all unsold papers. Lost or otherwise unreturned papers, however, must be paid for as though sold. Not only is the "profit" per paper thus effectively fixed by the publisher, but substantial control of the newsboys' total "take home" can be effected through the ability to designate their sales areas and the power to determine the number of papers allocated to each. While as a practical matter this power is not exercised fully, the newsboys' "right" to decide how many papers they will take is also not absolute. In practice, the Board found, they cannot determine the size of their established order without the cooperation of the district manager. And often the number of papers they must take is determined unilaterally by the district managers.

In addition to effectively fixing the compensation, respondents in a variety of ways prescribe, if not the minutiae of daily activities, at least the broad terms and conditions of work. This is accomplished largely through the supervisory efforts of the district managers, who serve as the nexus between the publishers and the newsboys. The district managers assign "spots" or corners to which the newsboys are expected to confine their selling activities. Transfers from one "spot" to another may be ordered by the district manager for reasons of discipline or efficiency or other cause. Transportation to the spots from the newspaper building is offered by each of respondents. Hours of work on the spots are determined not simply by the impersonal pressures of the market, but to a real extent by explicit instructions from the district managers. Adherence to the prescribed hours is observed closely by the district managers or other supervisory agents of the publishers. Sanctions, varying in severity from reprimand to dismissal, are visited on the tardy and the delinquent. . . .

. . . [R]espondents . . . urge that on the entire record the [newsboys] cannot be considered their employees. They base this conclusion on the argument that by common-law standards the extent of their control and direction of the newsboys' working activities creates no more than an "independent contractor" relationship and that common-law standards determine the "employee" relationship under the Act. They further urge that the Board's selection of a collective bargaining unit is neither appropriate nor supported by substantial evidence.

I

The principal question is whether the newsboys are "employees." Because Congress did not explicitly define the term, respondents say its meaning must be determine by reference to common-law standards. . . .

. . . Few problems in the law have given greater variety of application and conflict in results than the cases arising in the borderland between what is clearly an employer-employee relationship and what is clearly one of independent, entrepreneurial dealing. . . .

. . . It is enough to point out that, with reference to an identical problem, results may be contrary over a very considerable region of doubt in applying the distinction, depending upon the state or jurisdiction where the determination is made. . . .

Mere reference to these possible variations as characterizing the application of the Wagner Act in the treatment of persons identically situated in the facts surrounding their employment and in the influences tending to disrupt it, would be enough to require pause before accepting a thesis which would introduce them into its administration. . . .

. . . Both the terms and the purposes of the statute, as well as the legislative history, show that Congress had in mind no such patchwork plan for securing freedom of employees' organization and of collective bargaining. . . .

II

Whether, given the intended national uniformity, the term "employee" includes such workers as these newsboys must be answered primarily from the history, terms and purposes of the legislation. . . .

Congress, on the one hand, was not thinking solely of the immediate technical relation of employer and employee. It had in mind at least some other persons than those standing in the proximate legal relation of employee to the particular employer involved in the labor dispute. It cannot be taken, however, that the purpose was to include all other persons who may perform service for another or was to ignore entirely legal classifications made for other purposes. Congress had in mind a wider field than the narrow technical legal relation of "master and servant," as the common law had worked this out in all its variations, and at the same time a narrower one than the entire area of rendering service to others. The question comes down therefore to how much was included of the intermediate region between what is clearly and unequivocally "employment," by any appropriate test, and what is as clearly entrepreneurial enterprise and not employment.

It will not do, for deciding this question as one of uniform national application, to import wholesale the traditional common-law conceptions or some distilled essence of their local variations as exclusively controlling limitations upon the scope of the statute's effectiveness. . . .

Congress . . . sought to find a broad solution, one that would bring industrial peace by substituting, so far as its power could reach, the rights of workers to self-organization and collective bargaining for the industrial strife which prevails where these rights are not effectively established. Yet only partial solutions would be provided if large segments of workers about whose technical legal position such local differences exist should be wholly excluded from coverage by reason of such differences. Yet that result could not be avoided, if choice must be made among them and controlled by them in deciding who are "employees" within the Act's meaning. Enmeshed in such distinctions, the administration of the statute soon might become encumbered by the same sort of technical legal refinement as has characterized the long evolution of the employee-independent contractor dichotomy in the courts for other purposes. The consequences would be ultimately to defeat, in part at least, the achievement of the statute's objectives. Congress no more intended to import this mass of technicality as a controlling "standard" for uniform national application than to refer decision of the question outright to the local law.

The Act, as its first section states, was designed to avert the "substantial obstructions to the free flow of commerce" which result from "strikes and other forms of industrial strife or unrest" by eliminating the causes of that unrest. . . . Hence the avowed and interrelated purposes of the Act are to encourage collective bargaining and to remedy the individual worker's inequality of bargaining power by "protecting the exercise . . . of full freedom of association, self-organization, and designation of representatives of their own choosing, for the purpose of negotiating the terms and conditions of their employment or other mutual aid or protection." 49 Stat. 449, 450.

The mischief at which the Act is aimed and the remedies it offers are not confined exclusively to "employees" within the traditional legal distinctions separating them from "independent contractors." Myriad forms of service relationship, with infinite and subtle variations in the terms of employment, blanket the nation's economy. Some are within this Act, others beyond its coverage. Large numbers will fall clearly on one side or on the other, by whatever test may be applied. But intermediate there will be many, the incidents of whose employment partake in part of the one group, in part of the other, in varying proportions of weight. And consequently the legal pendulum, for purposes of applying the statute, may swing one way or the other, depending upon the weight of this balance and its relation to the special purpose at hand. . . .

It is not necessary in this case to make a completely definitive limitation around the term "employee." That task has been assigned primarily to the agency created by Congress to administer the Act. Determination of "where all the conditions of the relation require protection" involves inquiries for the Board charged with this duty. Everyday experience in the administration of the statute gives it familiarity with the circumstances and backgrounds of employment relationships in various industries, with the abilities and needs of the workers for self-organization and collective action, and with the adaptability of collective bargaining for the peaceful settlement of their disputes with their employers. The experience thus acquired must be brought frequently to bear on the question who is an employee under the Act. Resolving that question, like determining whether unfair labor practices have been committed, "belongs to the usual administrative routine" of the Board. Gray v. Powell, 314 U.S. 402, 411.

... Undoubtedly questions of statutory interpretation, especially when arising in the first instance in judicial proceedings, are for the courts to resolve, giving appropriate weight to the judgment of those whose special duty is to administer the questioned statute. Norwegian Nitrogen Products Co. v. United States, 288 U.S. 294.... But where the question is one of specific application of a broad statutory term in a proceeding in which the agency administering the statute must determine it initially, the reviewing court's function is limited. Like the commissioner's determination under the Longshoremen's & Harbor Workers' Act, that a man is not a "member of a crew" (South Chicago Coal & Dock Co. v. Bassett, 309 U.S. 251) or that he was injured "in the course of employment" (Parker v. Motor Boat Sales, 314 U.S. 244) and the Federal Communications Commission's determination that one company is under the "control" of another (Rochester Telephone Corp. v. United States, 307 U.S. 125), the Board's determination that specified persons are "employees" under this Act is to be accepted if it has "warrant in the record" and a reasonable basis in law.

In this case ... the Board concluded that the newsboys are employees. The record sustains the Board's findings and there is ample basis in the law for its conclusion....

Mr. Justice ROBERTS, dissenting:

... I think it plain that newsboys are not "employees" of the respondents within the meaning and intent of the National Labor Relations Act. When Congress, in §2(3), said "The term 'employee' shall include any employee, ..." it stated as clearly as language could do it that the provisions of the Act were to extend to those who, as a result of decades of tradition which had become part of the common understanding of our people, bear the named relationship. Clearly also Congress did not delegate to the National Labor Relations Board the function of defining the relationship of employment so as to promote what the Board understood to be the underlying purpose of the statute. The question who is an employee, so as to make the statute applicable to him, is a question of the meaning of the Act and, therefore, is a judicial and not an administrative question....

... There is a general and prevailing rule throughout the Union as to the indicia of employment and the criteria of one's status as employee. Unquestionably it was to this common, general, and prevailing understanding that Congress referred in the statute and, according to that understanding, the facts stated in the opinion below, and in that of this court, in my judgment, demonstrate that the newsboys were not employees of the newspapers....

See also Gray v. Powell, 314 U.S. 402, 412 (1941), cited in *Hearst*, where the Court sustained an agency's determination that a particular firm's activities were subject to regulation by the Department of the Interior, stating that "Where, as here, a determination has been left to an administrative body, this delegation will be respected and the administrative conclusion left untouched. Certainly, a finding on congressional reference that an admittedly constitutional act is applicable to a particular situation does not require such further scrutiny. Although we have here no dispute as to the evidentiary facts, that does not permit a court to substitute its judgment for that of the Director. It is not the province of a court to absorb the administrative functions to such an extent that the executive or legislative agencies become mere fact-finding bodies deprived of the advantages of prompt and definite action."

After *Hearst* Congress amended the statute to define "employee" so as not to include "an individual having the status of an independent contractor." 29 U.S.C. §152(3). Does this show that *Hearst* misconstrued the statute?

Packard Motor Car Co. v. NLRB

330 U.S. 485 (1947)

Mr. Justice JACKSON delivered the opinion of the Court.

The question presented by this case is whether foremen are entitled as a class to the rights of self-organization, collective bargaining, and other concerted activities as assured to employees generally by the National Labor Relations Act. . . .

. . . Foremen carry the responsibility for maintaining quantity and quality of production, subject, of course, to the overall control and supervision of the management. Hiring is done by the labor relations department, as is the discharging and laying off of employees. But the foremen are provided with forms and with detailed lists of penalties to be applied in cases of violations of discipline, and initiate recommendations for promotion, demotion and discipline. All such recommendations are subject to the reviewing procedure concerning grievances provided in the collectively-bargained agreement between the Company and the rank-and-file union.

The foremen as a group are highly paid and, unlike the workmen, are paid for justifiable absence and for holidays, are not docked in pay when tardy, receive longer paid vacations, and are given severance pay upon release by the Company.

These foremen determined to organize as a unit of the Foremen's Association of America, an unaffiliated organization which represents supervisory employees exclusively. Following the usual procedure, after the Board had decided that "all general foremen, foremen, assistant foremen, and special assignment men employed by the Company at its plants in Detroit, Michigan, constitute a unit appropriate for the purposes of collective bargaining within the meaning of Section 9(b) of the Act," the Foremen's Association was certified as the bargaining representative. The Company asserted that foremen were not "employees" entitled to the advantages of the Labor Act, and refused to bargain with the union. After hearing on charge of unfair labor practice, the Board . . . [determined that foremen were employees and ordered the Company to bargain].

The issue of law as to the power of the National Labor Relations Board under the National Labor Relations Act is simple and our only function is to determine whether the order of the Board is authorized by the statute.

The privileges and benefits of the Act are conferred upon employees, and §2(3) of the Act, so far as relevant, provides "The term 'employee' shall include any employee. . . ." 49 Stat. 450. The point that these foremen are employees both in the most technical sense at common law as well as in common acceptance of the term, is too obvious to be labored. The Company, however, turns to the Act's definition of employer, which it contends reads foremen out of the employee class and into the class of employers. Section 2(2) reads: "The term 'employer' includes any person acting in the interest of an employer, directly or indirectly. . . ." 49 Stat. 450. The context of the Act, we think, leaves no room for a construction of this to deny the organizational privilege to employees because they act in the interest of an employer. Every employee, from the very fact of employment in the master's business, is required to act in his interest. He owes to the employer faithful performance of service in his interest, the protection of the employer's property in his custody or control, and all employees may, as to third parties, act in the interests of the employer to such an extent that he is liable for their wrongful acts. A familiar example would be that of a truck driver for whose negligence the Company might have to answer.

The purpose of §2(2) seems obviously to render employers responsible in labor practices for acts of any persons performed in their interests. It is an adaptation of the ancient maxim of the common law, respondeat superior, by which a principal is made liable for the tortious acts of his agent and the master for the wrongful acts of his servants. Even without special statutory provision, the rule would apply to many relations. But Congress was creating a new class of wrongful acts to be known as unfair labor practices, and it could not be certain that the courts would apply the tort rule of respondeat superior to those derelictions. Even if it did, the problem of proof as applied to this kind of wrongs might easily be complicated by questions as to the scope of the actor's authority and of variance between his apparent and his real authority. Hence, it was provided that in administering this act the employer, for its purposes, should be not merely the individual or corporation which was the employing entity, but also others, whether employee or not, who are "acting in the interest of an employer."

. . . Though the foreman is the faithful representative of the employer in maintaining a production schedule, his interest properly may be adverse to that of the employer when it comes to fixing his own wages, hours, seniority rights or working conditions. He does not lose his right to serve himself in these respects because he serves his master in others. And we see no basis in this Act whatever for holding that foremen are forbidden the protection of the Act when they take collective action to protect their collective interests.

The company's argument is really addressed to the undesirability of permitting foremen to organize. It wants selfless representatives of its interest. It fears that if foremen combine to bargain advantages for themselves, they will sometimes be governed by interests of their own or of their fellow foremen, rather than by the company's interest. There is nothing new in this argument. It is rooted in the misconception that because the employer has the right to wholehearted loyalty in the performance of the contract of employment, the employee does not have the right to protect his independent and adverse interest in the terms of the contract itself and the conditions of work. But the effect of the National Labor Relations Act is otherwise, and it is for Congress, not for us, to create exceptions or qualifications at odds with its plain terms.

Moreover, the company concedes that foremen have a right to organize. What it denies is that the statute compels it to recognize the union. In other words, it wants to be free to fight the foremen's union in the way that companies fought other unions before the Labor Act. But there is nothing in the Act which indicates that Congress intended to deny its benefits to foremen as employees, if they choose to believe that their interests as employees would be better served by organization than by individual competition. . . .

We are invited to make a lengthy examination of views expressed in Congress while this and later legislation was pending to show that exclusion of foremen was intended. There is, however, no ambiguity in this Act to be clarified by resort to legislative history, either of the Act itself or of subsequent legislative proposals which failed to become law.

Counsel also would persuade us to make a contrary interpretation by citing a long record of inaction, vacillation and division of the National Labor Relations Board in applying this Act to foremen. If we were obliged to depend upon administrative interpretation for light in finding the meaning of the statute, the inconsistency of the Board's decisions would leave us in the dark. But there are difficult questions of policy involved in these cases which together with changes in Board membership, account for the contradictory views that characterize their history in the Board. . . .

. . . We are not at liberty to be governed by those policy considerations in deciding the naked question of law whether the Board is now, in this case, acting within the terms of the statute. . . .

The judgment of enforcement is affirmed.

Mr. Justice DOUGLAS, with whom THE CHIEF JUSTICE and Mr. Justice BURTON concur, dissenting.

First. Over thirty years ago Mr. Justice Brandeis, while still a private citizen, saw the need for narrowing the gap between management and labor, for allowing labor greater participation in policy decisions, for developing an industrial system in which cooperation rather than coercion was the dominant characteristic. In his view, these were measures of therapeutic value in dealing with problems of industrial unrest or inefficiency.

The present decision may be a step in that direction. It at least tends to obliterate the line between management and labor. It lends the sanction of federal law to unionization at all levels of the industrial hierarchy. It tends to emphasize that the basic opposing forces in industry are not management and labor but the operating group on the one hand and the stockholder and bondholders on the other. The industrial problem as so defined comes down to a contest over a fair division of the gross receipts of industry between these two groups. The struggle for control or power between management and labor becomes secondary to a growing unity in their common demands on ownership.

I do not believe this is an exaggerated statement of the basic policy questions which underlie the present decision. For if foremen are "employees" within the meaning of the National Labor Relations Act, so are vice-presidents, managers, assistant managers, superintendents, assistant superintendents — indeed, all who are on the payroll of the company, including the president; all who are commonly referred to as the management, with the exception of the directors. If a union of vice-presidents applied for recognition as a collective bargaining agency, I do not see how we could deny it and yet allow the present application. But once vice-presidents, managers, superintendents, foremen all are unionized, management and labor will become more of a solid phalanx than separate factions in warring camps. Indeed, the thought of some labor leaders that if those in the hierarchy above the workers are unionized, they will be more sympathetic with the claims of those below them, is a manifestation of the same idea.

I mention these matters to indicate what tremendously important policy questions are involved in the present decision. My purpose is to suggest that if Congress, when it enacted the National Labor Relations Act, had in mind such a basic change in industrial philosophy, it would have left some clear and unmistakable trace of that purpose. But I find none.

Second. "Employee" ... is used in opposition to the term "employer." An "employer" is defined to include "any person acting in the interest of an employer." §2(2). The term "employer" thus includes some employees. And I find no evidence that one personnel group may be both employers and employees within the meaning of the Act. Rather, the Act on its face seems to classify the operating group of industry into two classes; what is included in one group is excluded from the other.

It is not an answer to say that the two statutory groups are not exclusive because every "employee" while on duty — whether driving a truck or stoking a furnace or operating a lathe — is "'acting in the interest" of his employer and is then an "employer" in the statutory sense. The Act was not declaring a policy of vicarious responsibility of industry. It was dealing solely with labor relations. It put in the employer category all those who acted for management not only in formulating but also in executing its labor policies.

Foremost among the latter were foremen. Trade union history shows that foremen were the arms and legs of management in executing labor policies. In industrial conflicts they were allied with management. Management indeed commonly acted through them in the unfair labor practices which the Act condemns. When we upheld the imposition of the sanctions of the Act against management, we frequently relied on the acts of foremen through whom management expressed its hostility to trade unionism.

Third. The evil at which the Act was aimed was the failure or refusal of industry to recognize the right of workingmen to bargain collectively. In §1 of the Act, Congress noted that such an attitude on the part of industry led "to strikes and other forms of industrial strife and unrest" so as to burden or obstruct interstate commerce. We know from the history of the decade that the frustrated efforts of workingmen, of laborers, to organize led to strikes, strife, and unrest. But we are pointed to no instances where foremen were striking; nor are we advised that managers, superintendents, or vice-presidents were doing so. . . .

If foremen were to be included as employees under the Act, special problems would be raised — important problems relating to the unit in which the foremen might be represented. Foremen are also under the Act as employers. That dual status creates serious problems. An act of a foreman, if attributed to the management, constitutes an unfair labor practice; the same act may be part of the foreman's activity as an employee. In that event the employer can only interfere at his peril. The complications of dealing with the problems of supervisory employees strongly suggest that if Congress had planned to include them in its project, it would have made some special provision for them. But we find no trace of a suggestion that when Congress came to consider the units appropriate for collective bargaining, it was aware that groups of employees might have conflicting loyalties. . . .

Fourth. When we turn from the Act to the legislative history, we find no trace of Congressional concern with the problems of supervisory personnel. The reports and debates are barren of any reference to them, though they are replete with references to the function of the legislation in protecting the interests of "laborers" and "workers." . . .

Sixth. The truth of the matter is, I think, that when Congress passed the National Labor Relations Act in 1935, it was legislating *against* the activities of foremen, not on their behalf. Congress was intent on protecting the right of free association — the right to bargain collectively — by the great mass of workers, not by those who were in authority over them and enforcing oppressive industrial policies. Foremen were instrumentalities of those industrial policies. They blocked the wage earners' path to fair collective bargaining. To say twelve years later that foremen were treated as the victims of that antilabor policy seems to me a distortion of history.

If we were to decide this case on the basis of policy, much could be said to support the majority view. But I am convinced that Congress never faced those policy issues when it enacted this legislation. I am sure that those problems were not in the consciousness of Congress. A decision on those policy matters cuts deep into our industrial life. It has profound implications throughout our economy. It involves a fundamental change in much of the thinking of the nation on our industrial problems. The question is so important that I cannot believe Congress legislated unwittingly on it. Since what Congress wrote is consistent with a restriction of the Act to workingmen and laborers, I would leave its extension over supervisory employees to Congress. . . .

———

After the *Packard* decision, Congress, in the Taft-Hartley Act, amended the statute to exclude from the definition of employee "any individual employed as a supervisor." 61 Stat. 138 (1947). Despite the amendment, controversy over definition continues. In NLRB v. Bell Aerospace Co., 416 U.S. 267 (1974), the Supreme

Court (5 to 4) reversed a Board ruling that would have allowed buyers with authority to negotiate small contracts to organize. The Board reasoned that Congress meant to exclude only those involved in formulating and implementing labor relations policies. But the Court held the exclusion to apply to all those clearly within the management hierarchy.

Questions

1. The Taft-Hartley Act provides that a labor organization cannot be certified as a collective bargaining agent unless "each officer of such labor organization and officers of any national or international labor organization of which it is an affiliate or constituent unit" certifies that he is not a member of the Communist party. The officers of the local unit of the Textile Workers Union and the national officers of this union did so certify but not the officers of the CIO (Congress of Industrial Organizations). The employer refused to bargain with the union. The Textile Union was a member of the CIO, which is a federation of so-called national and international unions. The Board held that the CIO was not a national or international labor organization within the meaning of the Act, and, therefore, the certification of its officers was not necessary to qualify the Textile Union as a bargaining agent. The Board argued that in labor circles the CIO and AFL were regarded not as "unions" but as "federations." Highland Park, a firm that does not wish to bargain with the Textile Workers, appeals the Board's decision (the effect of which is to require bargaining) to the courts. What result?

2. Assume that the statute read in relevant part "and the officers of any national or international labor organization (*as defined by the Board*) of which it is an affiliate or constituent unit." What arguments can Highland Park make on appeal? To what extent is it helped by *Holly Hill?* What will the Board argue in reply?

3. Assume that the words italicized in Question 2 do *not* appear in the statute, but the Board has promulgated a regulation which states that the statute does not apply to the CIO or other "labor federations." To what extent is Highland Park's position strengthened? To what extent does Skidmore v. Swift help the Board?

4. Assume that the statute reads as in Question 1 above and no regulation has been promulgated. Is the Board's determination that the statute does not apply to the CIO a "finding of fact"? If it is a "matter of law" must the court, not the Board, decide the matter (see APA §§ 10(a), 10(e))? What arguments will Highland Park make? How does *Hearst* help the Board? (Can *Hearst* be distinguished from *Packard?*)

5. The Court in *Packard* notes the decisional vacillation of the Board on the question in issue. Might the case have been differently decided if the Board had, over many years, consistently held that supervisory personnel were not "employees"? Why? [66]

66. Cf. SEC v. Sloan, 436 U.S. 103 (1978).

O'Leary v. Brown-Pacific-Maxon, Inc.

340 U.S. 504 (1951)

Mr. Justice FRANKFURTER delivered the opinion of the Court.

In this case we are called upon to review an award of compensation under the Longshoremen's and Harbor Workers' Compensation Act. Act of March 4, 1927, 44 Stat. 1424, as amended, 33 U.S.C. §901 et seq. The award was made on a claim arising from the accidental death of an employee of Brown-Pacific-Maxon, Inc., a government contractor operating on the island of Guam. Brown-Pacific maintained for its employees a recreation center near the shoreline, along which ran a channel so dangerous for swimmers that its use was forbidden and signs to that effect erected. John Valak, the employee, spent the afternoon at the center, and was waiting for his employer's bus to take him from the area when he saw or heard two men, standing on the reefs beyond the channel, signaling for help. Followed by nearly twenty others, he plunged in to effect a rescue. In attempting to swim the channel to reach the two men he was drowned.

A claim was filed by his dependent mother. . . . In due course, the Deputy Commissioner found as a "fact" that "at the time of his drowning and death the deceased was using the recreational facilities sponsored and made available by the employer for the use of its employees and such participation by the deceased was an incident of his employment, and that his drowning and death arose out of and in the course of said employment. . . ." Accordingly, he was awarded a death benefit of $9.38 per week. Brown-Pacific and its insurance carrier thereupon petitioned the District Court to set aside the award. That court denied the petition on the ground that "there is substantial evidence . . . to sustain the compensation order." On appeal, the Court of Appeals for the Ninth Circuit reversed. It concluded that "The lethal currents were not a part of the recreational facilities supplied by the employer and the swimming in them for the rescue of the unknown man was not recreation. It was an act entirely disconnected from any use for which the recreational camp was provided and not in the course of Valak's employment." . . . We granted certiorari, 340 U.S. 849, because the case brought into question judicial review of awards under the Longshoremen's Act in light of the Administrative Procedure Act.

The Longshoremen's and Harbor Workers' Act authorizes payment of compensation for "accidental injury or death arising out of and in the course of employment." . . . As we read its opinion the Court of Appeals entertained the view that this standard precluded an award for injuries incurred in an attempt to rescue persons not known to be in the employer's service, undertaken in forbidden waters outside the employer's premises. We think this is too restricted an interpretation of the Act. Workmen's compensation is not confined by common-law conceptions of scope of employment. . . . The test of recovery is not a causal relation between the nature of employment of the injured person and the accident. Thom v. Sinclair, [1917] A.C. 127, 142. Nor is it necessary that the employee be engaged at the time of the injury in activity of benefit to his employer. All that is required is that the "obligations or conditions" of employment create the "zone of special danger" out of which the injury arose. Ibid. A reasonable rescue attempt, like pursuit in aid of an officer making an arrest, may be "one of the risks of the employment, an incident of the service, foreseeable, if not foreseen, and so covered by the statute." Matter of Babington v. Yellow Taxi Corp., 250 N.Y. 14, 17, 164 N.E. 726, 727; Puttkammer v. Industrial Comm'n, 371 Ill. 497, 21 N.E.2d 575. This is not to say that there are not cases "where an employee, even with the laudable purpose of helping another, might go so far from his employment and become so thoroughly disconnected from the service of his employer that it would be entirely unreasonable to say that injuries suffered by him arose out of and in the course of his employment." Matter of Waters v. Taylor Co., 218 N.Y. at 252, 112 N.E. at 728. We hold only that rescue attempts such as that before us are not necessarily excluded from the coverage of the Act as the kind of conduct that employees engage in as frolics of their own.

The Deputy Commissioner treated the question whether the particular rescue attempt described by the evidence was one of the class covered by the Act as a question of "fact." Doing so only serves to illustrate once more the variety of ascertainments covered by the blanket term "fact." Here of course it does not connote a simple, external, physical event as to which there is conflicting testimony. The conclusion concerns a combination of happenings and the inferences drawn from them. In part at least, the inferences presuppose applicable standards for assessing the simple, external facts. Yet the standards are not so severable from the experience of industry nor of such a nature as to be peculiarly appropriate for independent judicial ascertainment as "questions of law."

Both sides conceded that the scope of judicial review of such findings of fact is governed by the Administrative Procedure Act.... The standard, therefore, is that discussed in Universal Camera Corp. v. Labor Board.... It is sufficiently described by saying that the findings are to be accepted unless they are unsupported by substantial evidence on the record considered as a whole. The District Court recognized this standard.

When this Court determines that a Court of Appeals has applied an incorrect principle of law, wise judicial administration normally counsels remand of the cause to the Court of Appeals with instructions to reconsider the record. Compare Universal Camera Corp. v. Labor Board, supra. In this instance, however, we have a slim record and the relevant standard is not difficult to apply; and we think the litigation had better terminate now. Accordingly we have ourselves examined the record to assess the sufficiency of the evidence.

We are satisfied that the record supports the Deputy Commissioner's finding. The pertinent evidence was presented by the written statements of four persons and the testimony of one witness. It is, on the whole, consistent and credible. From it the Deputy Commissioner could rationally infer that Valak acted reasonably in attempting the rescue, and that his death may fairly be attributable to the risks of the employment. We do not mean that the evidence compelled this inference; we do not suggest that had the Deputy Commissioner decided against the claimant, a court would have been justified in disturbing his conclusion. We hold only that on this record the decision of the District Court that the award should not be set aside should be sustained.

Reversed.

Mr. Justice MINTON, with whom Mr. Justice JACKSON and Mr. Justice BURTON join, dissenting.

Liability accrues only if [there is] . . . some connection between the death and the employment. Not in any common-law sense of causal connection but in the common-sense, everyday, realistic view. The Deputy Commissioner knew that, so he found as a *fact* that "at the time of his drowning and death the deceased was using the recreational facilities sponsored and made available by the employer for the use of its employees and such participation by the deceased was an incident of his employment. . . ." This finding is false and has no scintilla of evidence or inference to support it.

I am unable to understand how this Court can say this is a fact based upon evidence. It is undisputed upon this record that the deceased, at the time he met his death, was outside the recreational area in the performance of a voluntary act of attempted rescue of someone unknown to the record. There can be no inference of liability here unless liability follows from the mere relationship of employer and employee. The attempt to rescue was an isolated, voluntary act of bravery of the deceased in no manner arising out of or in the course of his employment. The only relation his employment had with the attempted rescue and the following death was that his employment put him on the Island of Guam.

I suppose the way to avoid what we said today in Universal Camera Corp. v. Labor Board . . . is to find facts where there are no facts, on the whole record or any piece of it. . . . [The Court seems to indicate there is some room left for voluntary] acts of the employees outside the course of their employment for which the employer may not be liable. There surely are such areas, but this case does not recognize them. The employer is liable in this case because he is an employer.

I would affirm the judgment of the Court of Appeals.

O'Keeffe v. Smith, Hinchman & Grylls Associates

380 U.S. 359 (1965)

PER CURIAM.

Robert C. Ecker drowned during a Saturday outing while boating on a South Korean lake. At the time of his death he was employed at a defense base in South Korea by the respondent, Smith, Hinchman & Grylls Associates, a government contractor. . . .

Based upon the . . . stipulated facts, the Deputy Commissioner of the Bureau of Employees' Compensation, United States Department of Labor, petitioner herein, determined "that the accident and the subsequent death of the decedent arose out of and in the course of employment." He therefore awarded death benefits . . . The employer . . . then brought this action . . . to set aside . . . the enforcement of this compensation award. The District Court affirmed the compensation award. . . . [T]he Court of Appeals for the Fifth Circuit summarily reversed. . . .

The petition for writ of certiorari is granted and judgment of the Court of Appeals is reversed. . . .

In cases decided both before and after the passage of the Administrative Procedure Act . . . the Court has held that the [statute limits] . . . the scope of judicial review of the Deputy Commissioner's determination that a "particular injury arose out of and in the course of employment." Cardillo v. Liberty Mutual Ins. Co., 330 U.S. 469, 477-478; O'Leary v. Brown-Pacific-Maxon, Inc., 340 U.S. 504, 507-508.

"It matters not that the basic facts from which the Deputy Commissioner draws this inference are undisputed rather than controverted. . . . It is likewise immaterial that the facts permit the drawing of diverse inferences. The Deputy Commissioner alone is charged with the duty of initially selecting the inference which seems most reasonable and his choice, if otherwise sustainable, may not be disturbed by a reviewing court. . . . Moreover, the fact that the inference of the type here made by the Deputy Commissioner involves an application of a broad statutory term or phrase to a specific set of facts gives rise to no greater scope of judicial review. . . ." Cardillo v. Liberty Mutual Ins. Co., supra, at 478.

The rule of judicial review has therefore emerged that the inferences drawn by the Deputy Commissioner are to be accepted unless they are irrational or "unsupported by substantial evidence on the record . . . as a whole." O'Leary v. Brown-Pacific-Maxon, Inc., supra, at 508. . . .

. . . [Under] *Brown-Pacific-Maxon* . . . [a]ll that is required is that the "obligations or conditions" of employment create the "zone of special danger" out of which the injury arose. . . . [T]he Court in *Brown-Pacific-Maxon* drew the line only at cases where an employee had become "so thoroughly disconnected from the service of his employer that it would be entirely unreasonable to say that injuries suffered by him arose out of and in the course of his employment." This standard is in accord with the humanitarian nature of the Act as exemplified by the statutory command that "[i]n any proceeding for the enforcement of a claim for compensation under this chapter it shall be presumed, in the absence of substantial evidence to the contrary . . . [t]hat the claim comes within the provisions of this chapter." §20(a).

In this case, . . . [t]he District Court . . . held "that the Deputy Commissioner was correct in his finding that the conditions of the deceased's employment created a zone where the deceased Ecker had to seek recreation under exacting and unconventional conditions and that therefore the accident and death of the decedent arose out of and in the course of employment."

We agree that the District Court correctly affirmed the finding of the Deputy Commissioner. While this Court may not have reached the same conclusion as the Deputy Commissioner, it cannot be said that his holding that the decedent's death, in a zone of danger, arose out of and in the course of his employment is irrational or without substantial evidence on the record as a whole. The decedent was hired to work in the exacting and unconventional conditions of Korea. His transportation over and back was to be at the employer's expense, and while there he was considered to be working on a 365-day-per-year basis, subject to call at the job site at any time, and quite often he worked Saturdays and Sundays and at other times outside the working day. The employer considered decedent and all other employees at this hazardous overseas base to be "in the course of regular occupation from the time they leave the United States until their return." Finally, the employer provided neither housing nor recreational activities for its employees, but expected them to live, while necessarily in the country to perform its work, under the exacting and dangerous conditions of Korea. The employer paid decedent's rent and provided him with a per diem expense allowance for each day of the year, including weekends and holidays, to cover the necessary living expenses in the Korean economy. The accident here occurred on an outing for a short period of time on a lake located only 30 miles from the employer's job site. In the words of the District Court, "It was reasonable to conclude that recreational activities contributed to a higher efficiency of the employer's work and that when conducted in the restricted area of employment, on a work day, so to speak, and in a manner not prohibited by the employer, such activity was an incident of the employment."

The dissent . . . [would reverse the determination that the accident involved was] within the "zone of special danger." As *Brown-Pacific-Maxon* made clear, it is just this type of determination which the statute leaves to the Deputy Commissioner subject only to limited judicial review. Indeed, this type of determination, depending as it does on an analysis of the many factors involved in the area of the employment, would seem to be one peculiarly for the Deputy Commissioner. . . .

Reversed.

Mr. Justice HARLAN, whom Mr. Justice CLARK and Mr. Justice WHITE join, dissenting.

Ecker was employed in Seoul, Korea, as an assistant administrative officer for Smith, Hinchman & Grylls Associates, Inc., an engineering management concern working under contracts with the United States and Korean Governments. His duties were restricted to Seoul where he was responsible for personnel in the stenographic and clerical departments. He was subject to call at the job site at any time, but the usual work week was 44 hours, and employees were accustomed to travel far from the job site on weekends and holidays for recreational purposes. Ecker did not live at the job site; he was given an allowance to live on the economy in Seoul. On his Memorial Day weekend he went to a lake 30 miles east of Seoul where a friend of his (not a co-employee) had a house. Ecker intended to spend the holiday there with his friend and another visitor. Their Saturday afternoon project was to fill in the beach in front of the house with sand, but none was readily available. In order to obtain it the three crossed the lake in a small aluminum boat to a sandy part of the shore. There they filled the boat with a load of sand, intending to transport it back to the house. The return trip, however, put Archimedes' Principle to the test; in the middle of the lake the boat capsized and sank. Two of the three men drowned, including Ecker.

The Longshoremen's and Harbor Workers' Compensation Act, . . . provides workmen's compensation for any "accidental injury or death arising out of and in the course of employment. . . ." The Court holds, per curiam, that Ecker died in the course of his employment. I see no meaningful interpretation of the statute which will support this result except a rule that any decision made by a Deputy Commissioner must be upheld. That interpretation, although meaningful, is unsupportable.

O'Leary v. Brown-Pacific-Maxon, Inc., 340 U.S. 504, . . . was intended to mean only that where the employer had placed a facility for employees in an especially dangerous location and thus had created a danger of accidents, a "reasonable rescue attempt" could be "one of the risks of the employment." This was made crystal clear by the caveat: "We hold only that rescue attempts such as that before us are not necessarily excluded from the coverage of the Act as the kind of conduct that employees engage in as frolics of their own." Ibid.

. . . Mr. Justice Frankfurter wrote both *Universal Camera* and *Brown-Pacific-Maxon*, and delivered the opinions on the same day. Reliance upon *Universal Camera* in *Brown-Pacific-Maxon* shows beyond doubt that the Court was not establishing a rule that *any* compensation award by a Deputy Commissioner would be automatically upheld, for it was the whole purpose of *Universal Camera* to effectuate congressional intent that the courts *expand* their scope of review over administrative decisions.

I read *Brown-Pacific-Maxon* to mean that . . . [t]he cases in which this limited review of the administrator's decision is appropriate are those in which one application of the statute to the external facts of the case effectuates the judicially recognizable purpose of the statute as well as another. Dominion over the broad or clear purposes of the statute thus remains firmly in the courts' hands, while within the confines of such statutory purposes, administrators are left discretion to provide the intimate particularizations of statutory application. [In] *Brown-Pacific-Maxon* . . . [e]ither result [that the job did or did not bring the decedent near a specially dangerous channel] would have been consistent with the statutory purpose of compensating all job-connected injuries on the actual job site and, additionally, those injuries off the job site which result from the "special" dangers of the employment. In the sense that both results would have been supportable, the review of the choice actually made by the Deputy Commissioner was treated as review of a finding of fact.

In the case before us, the Deputy Commissioner's ruling is not consistent with the statutory purpose. The injury did not take place on the actual job site, and it did not arise out of any special danger created by the job. In so sense can it be said that Ecker's job created any "special" danger of his drowning in a lake, or more particularly, of his loading a small boat with sand and capsizing it. Nothing indicates that the lake was rougher, the boat tippier, or the sand heavier than their counterparts in the United States. If there were "exacting and unconventional conditions" in Korea it does not appear that the lake, boat, or sand was one of them. There is nothing more than a "but for" relationship between the accident and the employment. To permit the award of compensation to stand reads the "job-connected" emphasis right out of the statute. . . .

Whether the injury is compensable should depend to some degree on the cause of the injury as well as the time of day, location, and momentary activity of the employee at the time of the accident. I would distinguish between a case in which Ecker smashed his hand in a filing cabinet while at the office and one in which he tripped over a pebble while off on a weekend hike. In the first case Ecker's injury would have arisen out of and in the course of his employment, whereas the statute would not apply to the second case unless the injury were traceable to some special danger peculiar to the employment, which was clearly not the case. Thus, if while off on that same weekend hike Ecker stepped on a mine left over from the Korean conflict, a different result could follow.

This view of the statute makes far more sense to me than the view adopted by the Court. . . .

Mr. Justice Douglas, dubitante.

The problems under this Act should rest mainly with the Courts of Appeals. What we said in Universal Camera Corp. v. Labor Board, 340 U.S. 474, 490, of review by Courts of Appeals of decisions of the National Labor Relations Board, should be applicable here:

"Reviewing courts must be influenced by a feeling that they are not to abdicate the conventional judicial function. Congress has imposed on them responsibility for assuring that the Board keeps within reasonable grounds. That responsibility is not less real because it is limited to enforcing the requirement that evidence appear substantial when viewed, on the record as a whole, by courts invested with the authority and enjoying the prestige of the Courts of Appeals. The Board's findings are entitled to respect; but they must nonetheless be set aside when the record before a Court of Appeals clearly precludes the Board's decision from being justified by a fair estimate of the worth of the testimony of witnesses or its informed judgment on matters within its special competence or both."

Applying that test I would not be inclined to reverse a Court of Appeals that disagreed with a Deputy Commissioner over findings as exotic as we have here.

Questions

1. Is the issue in *Smith Associates* and *Brown-Pacific-Maxon* one of "fact" or of "law"? How did you decide this question?

2. If the issue is one of law, are there reasons why the courts might defer to the commissioner's judgment? What are they?

3. If the issue is one of law, the Supreme Court must be wrong to speak of the "substantial evidence" standard (but note that in *Smith Associates* the Court couples that term with the standard of "irrationality").

4. Consider the following two cases:

(a) Miss Williams was in the company of a gentleman friend in a pickup truck parked at the end of a breakwater on Guam at 11 P.M. The friend testified that he had been showing her the lights in the harbor. Another driver lost control of his truck, crashed into Williams's truck, and injured her. A commissioner's finding that the injuries were *not* received in the "scope of employment," upheld by the District Court, was *reversed* by the Court of Appeals. Self v. Hanson, 305 F.2d 699 (9th Cir. 1962).

(b) Mr. Takara was one of forty employees sent to Guam to do emergency repair work in 1962. After 12 days of work, he and some friends, wishing an evening out, set off from the jobsite and headed for a nearby restaurant. They decided not to take a company bus but hitchhiked instead. While trying to thumb a ride back to the job site at 9:30 P.M., Takara was hit by a truck. A commissioner's finding that injuries were not received in "the scope of employment," upheld by the District Court, was *reversed* by the Court of Appeals, (relying in part on the Supreme Court's favorable citation of *Self* in *Smith Associates*). Takara v. Hanson, 369 F.2d 392 (9th Cir. 1966).

Are *Takara* and *Self* consistent with *Smith Associates* and *Brown-Pacific-Maxon* or did the Ninth Circuit misread those two cases? Is there any way those cases can be reconciled?

Note

Under *Universal Camera* one would expect to find the "substantial evidence" test applied to findings of fact by an agency. Yet, we shall see that in many cases courts use that standard to test the validity of rules promulgated by an agency or even to determine the correctness of an agency's decision on a matter of law — a matter within the delegated power of the agency to determine. One can find two possible reasons for such a use of the standard (apart from confusion).

First, some courts may be reluctant to admit that agencies are legally empowered to determine questions of law. (Why?) By using a substantial evidence test, the reviewing court implies the question is one of fact — or of "mixed fact and law" — and hence within the agency's power to decide.[67]

Second, some courts may fear that agencies have been given too much discretion to promulgate rules and to determine major questions of policy. Apparently under the APA, unless Congress specifically states to the contrary, most major policy decisions within the statute's confines must be upheld unless they are "arbitrary, [or] capricious," i.e., unless they are "irrational." §10(e). Fearing that the standard, as these words have come to mean, gives the agency far too much leeway, courts have sometimes sought to control agency decisions of law and policy — despite the fact that the use of such a standard wrongly suggests the agency is deciding a question of fact rather than making policy. By seeming to pin the basis for disagreement with the agency upon evidentiary questions, the court avoids conspicuous abrogation of policymaking powers that ordinarily belong to the agency. This is but one of the ways in which courts have tried to deal with the problem of agency discretion — a matter to which we shall soon turn.

You have seen how courts can approach reviewing questions of law with very different degrees of deference granted to the agency making the decision under review. Does this not remind you of the very different degrees of deference shown by reviewing courts to agency ratemaking decisions — decisions which have been viewed by the courts as involving "questions of fact"? You should begin to question

---

67. See generally the comprehensive treatment by Professor Jaffe, Judicial Review, Questions of Law, 69 Harv. L. Rev. 239 (1955).

the extent to which a division of issues into "fact" and "law" will tell us about the probable attitude of (or deference likely to be shown by) a reviewing court.

What is the appropriate division of lawmaking responsibility between administrative agencies and reviewing courts? Do the decisions in this section establish a consistent pattern?

D. Direct Judicial Control of Administrative Discretion

1. Limiting Agency Discretion Through "Creative" Statutory Construction

Kent v. Dulles

357 U.S. 116 (1958)

Mr. Justice DOUGLAS delivered the opinion of the Court.

This case concerns two applications for passports, denied by the Secretary of State. One was by Rockwell Kent, who desired to visit England and attend a meeting of an organization known as the "World Council of Peace" in Helsinki, Finland. The Director of the Passport Office informed Kent that issuance of a passport was precluded by §51.135 of the Regulations promulgated by the Secretary of State on two grounds:[68] (1) that he was a Communist and (2) that he had had "a consistent and prolonged adherence to the Communist Party line." The letter of denial specified in some detail the facts on which those conclusions were based. . . .

[Kent subsequently refused to submit, as required by the passport regulations, an affidavit that he was not then and never had been a member of the Communist Party, and his application was denied for failure to satisfy this requirement. Dr. Walter Briehl, a psychiatrist, was similarly denied a passport for refusal to sign an affidavit disclaiming membership in the Communist Party following preliminary findings by the Department that he had been a Party member and a member of

---

68. 22 C.F.R. §51.135 provides:

"In order to promote the national interest by assuring that persons who support the world Communist movement of which the Communist Party is an integral unit may not, through use of United States passports, further the purposes of that movement, no passport, except one limited for direct and immediate return to the United States, shall be issued to:

"(a) Persons who are members of the Communist Party or who have recently terminated such membership under such circumstances as to warrant the conclusion — not otherwise rebutted by the evidence — that they continue to act in furtherance of the interests and under the discipline of the Communist Party:

"(b) Persons, regardless of the formal state of their affiliation with the Communist Party, who engage in activities which support the Communist movement under such circumstances as to warrant the conclusion — not otherwise rebutted by the evidence — that they have engaged in such activities as a result of direction, domination, or control exercised over them by the Communist movement;

"(c) Persons, regardless of the formal state of their affiliation with the Communist Party, as to whom there is reason to believe, on the balance of all the evidence, that they are going abroad to engage in activities which will advance the Communist movement for the purpose, knowingly and wilfully of advancing that movement."

various "Communist front" organizations. In each case the applicant filed an action for declaratory relief, which was denied by the District Court. The Court of Appeals affirmed the District Court's action.]

A passport not only is of great value — indeed necessary — abroad; it is also an aid in establishing citizenship for purposes of re-entry into the United States. . . . But throughout most of our history — until indeed quite recently — a passport, though a great convenience in foreign travel, was not a legal requirement for leaving or entering the United States. See Jaffe, The Right to Travel: The Passport Problem, 35 Foreign Affairs 17. Apart from minor exceptions . . . it was first made a requirement by §215 of the Act of June 27, 1952, 66 Stat. 190, 8 U.S.C. §1185, which states that, after a prescribed proclamation by the President, it is "unlawful for any citizen of the United States to depart from or enter, or attempt to depart from or enter, the United States unless he bears a valid passport." And the Proclamation necessary to make the restrictions of this Act applicable and in force has been made.

Prior to 1952 there were numerous laws enacted by Congress regulating passports and many decisions, rulings, and regulations by the Executive Department concerning them. . . . [I]n 1856 Congress enacted what remains today as our basic passport statute. Prior to that time various federal officials, state and local officials, and notaries public had undertaken to issue either certificates of citizenship or other documents in the nature of letters of introduction to foreign officials requesting treatment according to the usages of international law. By the Act of August 18, 1856, 11 Stat. 52, 60-61, 22 U.S.C. §211a, Congress put an end to those practices. This provision, as codified by the Act of July 3, 1926, 44 Stat., Part 2, 887, reads, "The Secretary of State may grant and issue passports . . . under such rules as the President shall designate and prescribe for and on behalf of the United States, and no other person shall grant, issue, or verify such passports."

. . . [F]or most of our history a passport was not a condition to entry or exit.

It is true that, at intervals, a passport has been required for travel. [Restrictions were] imposed during the War of 1812 and during the Civil War. A . . . restriction, which was the forerunner of that contained in the 1952 Act, was imposed by Congress in 1918.

The Act of May 22, 1918, 40 Stat. 559, made it unlawful, while a Presidential Proclamation was in force, for a citizen to leave or enter the United States "unless he bears a valid passport." . . . That statute was invoked by Presidential Proclamation No. 1473 on August 8, 1918 . . . which continued in effect until March 3, 1921. . . .

The 1918 Act was effective only in wartime. It was amended in 1941 so that it could be invoked in the then-existing emergency. 55 Stat. 252. It was invoked by Presidential Proclamation No. 2523, November 14, 1941, 55 Stat. 1696. That emergency continued until April 28, 1952. Congress extended the statutory provisions until April 1, 1953. [The President also renewed the Proclamation of Emergency.] It was during this extension period that the Secretary of State issued the Regulations here complained of.

Under the 1926 Act and its predecessor a large body of precedents grew up which repeat over and again that the issuance of passports is "a discretionary act" on the part of the Secretary of State. The scholars, the courts, the Chief Executive, and the Attorneys General, all so said. This long-continued executive construction should be enough, it is said, to warrant the inference that Congress had adopted it. . . . But the key to that problem, as we shall see, is in the manner in which the Secretary's discretion was exercised, not in the bare fact that he had discretion.

The right to travel is a part of the "liberty" of which the citizen cannot be deprived without due process of law under the Fifth Amendment. . . . Freedom of movement across frontiers in either direction, and inside frontiers as well, was a part of our heritage. Travel abroad, like travel within the country, may be necessary for a livelihood. It may be as close to the heart of the individual as the choice of what he eats, or wears, or reads. Freedom of movement is basic in our scheme of values. . . .

Freedom of movement also has large social values. As Chafee [Z. Chafee, Three Human Rights in the Constitution of 1787 (1956)] put it, "Foreign correspondents and lecturers on public affairs need firsthand information. Scientists and scholars gain greatly from consultations with colleagues in other countries. Students equip themselves for more fruitful careers in the United States by instruction in foreign universities. Then there are reasons close to the core of personal life — marriage, reuniting families, spending hours with old friends. Finally, travel abroad enables American citizens to understand that people like themselves live in Europe and helps them to be well-informed on public issues. An American who has crossed the ocean is not obliged to form his opinions about our foreign policy merely from what he is told by officials of our government or by a few correspondents of American newspapers. Moreover, his views on domestic questions are enriched by seeing how foreigners are trying to solve similar problems. In many different ways direct contact with other countries contributes to sounder decisions at home." Id., at 195-196. And see Vestal, Freedom of Movement, 41 Iowa L. Rev. 6, 13-14.

Freedom to travel is, indeed, an important aspect of the citizen's "liberty." We need not decide the extent to which it can be curtailed. We are first concerned with the extent, if any, to which Congress has authorized its curtailment.

The difficulty is that while the power of the Secretary of State over the issuance of passports is expressed in broad terms, it was apparently long exercised quite narrowly. So far as material here, the cases of refusal of passports generally fell into two categories. First, questions pertinent to the citizenship of the applicant and his allegiance to the United States had to be resolved by the Secretary, for the command of Congress was that "No passport shall be granted or issued to or verified for any other persons than those owing allegiance, whether citizens or not, to the United States." 32 Stat. 386, 22 U.S.C. §212. Second, was the question whether the applicant was participating in illegal conduct, trying to escape the toils of the law, promoting passport frauds, or otherwise engaging in conduct which would violate the laws of the United States. . . .

The grounds for refusal asserted here do not relate to citizenship or allegiance on the one hand or to criminal or unlawful conduct on the other. Yet, so far as relevant here, those two are the only ones which it could fairly be argued were adopted by Congress in light of prior administrative practice. One can find in the records of the State Department rulings of subordinates covering a wider range of activities than the two indicated. But as respects Communists these are scattered rulings and not consistently of one pattern. We can say with assurance that whatever may have been the practice after 1926, at the time the Act of July 3, 1926, was adopted, the administrative practice, so far as relevant here, had jelled only around the two categories mentioned. We, therefore, hesitate to impute to Congress, when in 1952 it made a passport necessary for foreign travel and left its issuance to the discretion of the Secretary of State, a purpose to give him unbridled discretion to grant or withhold a passport from a citizen for any substantive reason he may choose.

More restrictive regulations were applied in 1918 and in 1941 as war measures. We are not compelled to equate this present problem of statutory construction with problems that may arise under the war power. Cf. Youngstown Sheet & Tube Co. v. Sawyer, 343 U.S. 579. . . .

Since we start with an exercise by an American citizen of an activity included in constitutional protection, we will not readily infer that Congress gave the Secretary of State unbridled discretion to grant or withhold it. If we were dealing with political questions entrusted to the Chief Executive by the Constitution we would have a different case. But there is more involved here. . . . [A]s we have seen, the right of exit is a personal right included within the word "liberty" as used in the Fifth Amendment. If that "liberty" is to be regulated, it must be pursuant to the law-making functions of the Congress. Youngstown Sheet & Tube Co. v. Sawyer, supra. And if that power is delegated, the standards must be adequate to pass scrutiny by the accepted tests. Where activities or enjoyment, natural and often necessary to the well-being of an American citizen, such as travel, are involved, we will construe narrowly all delegated powers that curtail or dilute them. . . .

Thus we do not reach the question of constitutionality. We only conclude that §1185 [Act of 1952] and §211a [Act of 1856] do not delegate . . . the . . . authority exercised here.

Reversed.

Mr. Justice CLARK, with whom Mr. Justice BURTON, Mr. Justice HARLAN, and Mr. Justice WHITTAKER concur, dissenting. . . .

. . . [T]he Court . . . determines (1) that the Secretary's denial of passports in peacetime extended to only two categories of cases, those involving allegiance and those involving criminal activity, and (2) that the Secretary's wartime exercise of his discretion, while admittedly more restrictive, has no relevance to the practice which Congress can be said to have approved in 1952. Since the present denials do not involve grounds either of allegiance or criminal activity, the Court concludes that they were beyond the pale of congressional authorization. Both of the propositions set out above are vital to the Court's final conclusion. Neither of them has any validity: the first is contrary to fact, and the second to common sense.

The peacetime practice of the State Department indisputably involved denial of passports for reasons of national security. The Report of the Commission on Government Security (1957), 470-473, summarizes the Department's policy on granting passports to Communists by excerpts from State Department documents. Shortly after the 1917 Russian Revolution, the Department "became aware of the scope and danger of the world-wide revolutionary movement and the attendant purpose to overthrow all existing governments, including our own." Thereafter "passports were refused to American Communists who desired to go abroad for indoctrination, instruction, etc. *This policy was continued until 1931....*" (Emphasis added.) From 1931 "until World War II no persons were refused passports because they were Communists." After World War II, "[a]t first passports were refused," but upon reconsideration of the matter in 1948, "the decision was made that passports would be issued to Communists and supporters of communism who satisfied the Department that they did not intend, while abroad, to engage in the promotion of Communist activities." At the same time, however, it was decided that "passports should be refused to persons whose purpose in traveling abroad was believed to be to subvert the interest of the United States." Later in 1948 the policy was changed to give Communist journalists passports even though they were "actively promoting the Communist cause." Nearly two years later, in September 1950, the latter leniency was reversed, after it was pointed out "that the Internal Security Act of 1950 clearly showed the desire of Congress that no Communists should be issued passports of this Government." The matter was referred to the Department's Legal Adviser, "who agreed that it was the duty of the State Department to refuse passports to all Communists, including journalists."

Other evidence of peacetime denials for security reasons is more scattered, but nevertheless existent. . . .

An even more serious error of the Court is its determination that the Secretary's wartime use of his discretion is wholly irrelevant in determining what discretionary practices were approved by Congress in enactment of §215. In a wholly realistic sense there is no peace today and there was no peace in 1952. . . .

Were this a time of peace, there might very well be no problem for us to decide, since petitioners then would not need a passport to leave the country. The very structure of §215 is such that either war or national emergency is prerequisite to imposition of its restrictions.

Indeed, rather than being irrelevant, the wartime practice may be the only relevant one, for the discretion with which we are concerned is a discretionary control over international travel. Yet only in times of war and national emergency has a passport been required to leave or enter this country, and hence only in such times has passport power necessarily meant power to control travel.

Finally, while distinguishing away the Secretary's passport denials in wartime, the majority makes no attempt to distinguish the Secretary's practice during periods when there has been no official state of war but when nevertheless a presidential proclamation of national emergency has been in effect, the very situation which has prevailed since the end of World War II. Throughout that time, as I have pointed out, the Secretary refused passports to those "whose purpose in traveling abroad was believed to be to subvert the interest of the United States." Numerous specific instances of passport denials on security grounds during the years 1947-1951 were reported in a February 1952 law review article, nearly half a year prior to passage of §215. Note, Passport Refusals for Political Reasons, 61 Yale L.J. 171.

... The majority's resolution of the authority question prevents it from reaching the constitutional issues raised by petitioners, relating to claims of unlawful delegation of legislative power, violation of free speech and association under the First Amendment, and violation of international travel under the Fifth Amendment. In view of that, it would be inappropriate for me, as a dissenter, to consider those questions at this time.... Accordingly, I would affirm on the issue of the Secretary's authority to require the affidavits involved in this case, without reaching any constitutional questions.

Questions on Kent v. Dulles

1. How can the Court possibly read such a broad grant of authority ("under such rules as the President shall designate and prescribe") as limiting the Secretary's power to deny the issuance of passports to cases of disloyalty or illegality? Is the Court claiming that, despite the broad language of the statute, Congress intended to grant a much narrower discretion? Which Congress's intent is controlling? The 1856 Congress that enacted the statute? The 1926 Congress that codified it (along with many other statutes) as part of the United States Code? The 1952 Congress that extended the President's authority to require possession of a passport as a condition of exit or entry?

2. Is the Court's position rather that Congress's intent is irrelevant, because the Executive's consistent exercise of the passport power in specified ways has operated to circumscribe the power delegated? Why should administrative practice redefine the extent of a delegated power? Wouldn't such a doctrine threaten necessary administrative flexibility?

Even if past administrative practice were controlling, isn't the dissent persuasive in claiming that past practice supports the denial of passports in this case?

3. Is the Court's rationale that general grants of authority will not empower administrators to curtail constitutionally recognized liberties — that a clear and explicit statement of intent to grant such authority is required as a matter of due process? What would justify such a judge-made "clear statement" rule of statutory construction?

4. Why didn't the Court invalidate the entire passport statute as an unconstitutional delegation of legislative power due to lack of any standards? [69] Why might the approach actually taken in *Kent* be preferable to total invalidation?

---

69. Compare Aptheker v. Secretary of State, 378 U.S. 500 (1964), where the Court invalidated, as a violation of Fifth Amendment due process, §6 of the 1950 Subversive Activities Control Act making it unlawful for any member of an organization specified by the Attorney General as Communist to apply for or hold a passport. The Court emphasized the overly broad nature of the prohibition, which disregarded a member's actual knowledge of the organization's purposes, his/her committment to its aims, and the purpose of his/her particular travel abroad.

Zemel v. Rusk

381 U.S. 1 (1965)

Mr. Chief Justice WARREN delivered the opinion of the Court....

Prior to 1961 no passport was required for travel anywhere in the Western Hemisphere. On January 3 of that year, the United States broke diplomatic and consular relations with Cuba. On January 16 the Department of State eliminated Cuba from the area for which passports were not required, and declared all out-standing United States passports (except those held by persons already in Cuba) to be invalid for travel to or in Cuba "unless specifically endorsed for such travel under the authority of the Secretary of State."...

[Plaintiff, a citizen holding a valid passport, applied for and was denied validation of his passport for travel to Cuba for the purpose of informing himself about affairs in Cuba. Plaintiff then brought an action before a three-judge district court challenging the constitutionality of the 1926 Passport Act, §215 of the Immigration and Nationality Act of 1952, and the State Department's restrictions on travel to Cuba. The District Court ruled for the government.]

We think that the Passport Act of 1926, 44 Stat. 887, 22 U.S.C. §211a (1958 ed.), embodies a grant of authority to the Executive to refuse to validate the passports of United States citizens for travel to Cuba. That Act provides, in pertinent part: "The Secretary of State may grant and issue passports . . . under such rules as the President shall designate and prescribe for and on behalf of the United States. . . ." This provision is derived from §23 of the Act of August 18, 1856. . . . The legislative history of the 1926 Act and its predecessors does not, it is true, affirmatively indicate an intention to authorize area restrictions. However, its language is surely broad enough to authorize area restrictions, and there is no legislative history indicating an intent to exclude such restrictions from the grant of authority; these factors take on added significance when viewed in light of the fact that during the decade preceding the passage of the Act, the Executive had imposed both peacetime and wartime area restrictions. [The Court cites examples of the imposition of area restrictions.] The use in the 1926 Act of language broad enough to permit executive imposition of area restrictions, after the Executive had several times in the recent past openly asserted the power to impose such restrictions under predecessor statutes containing substantially the same language, supports the conclusion that Congress intended in 1926 to maintain in the Executive the authority to make such restrictions.

This construction of the Act is reinforced by the State Department's continued imposition of area restrictions during both times of war and periods of peace since 1926 [citing examples].

Even if there had been no passport legislation enacted since the 1926 Act, the post-1926 history of executive imposition of area restrictions, as well as the pre-1926 history, would be of relevance to our construction of the Act. The interpretation expressly placed on a statute by those charged with its administration must be given weight by courts faced with the task of construing the statute. . . . [Also,] in 1952

Congress, substantially reenacting laws which had been passed during the First and Second World Wars, provided that after the issuance of a presidential proclamation of war or national emergency, it would be unlawful to leave or enter the United States without a valid passport. Section 215 of the Immigration and Nationality Act of 1952, 66 Stat. 190, 8 U.S.C. §1185 (1958 ed.). The Solicitor General urges that in view of the issuance in 1952 of a presidential proclamation of national emergency which is still outstanding, travel in violation of an area restriction imposed on an otherwise valid passport is unlawful under the 1952 Act. The correctness of this interpretation is a question we do not reach on this appeal. . . . But whether or not the new legislation was intended to attach criminal penalties to the violation of area restrictions, it certainly was not meant to cut back upon the power to impose such restrictions. Despite 26 years of executive interpretation of the 1926 Act as authorizing the imposition of area restrictions, Congress in 1952, though it once again enacted legislation relating to passports, left completely untouched the broad rulemaking authority granted in the earlier Act.

This case is therefore not like Kent v. Dulles, . . . where we were unable to find, with regard to the sort of passport refusal involved there, an administrative practice sufficiently substantial and consistent to warrant the conclusion that Congress had implicitly approved it. . . .

[The Court rejected claims, based on the Due Process Clause of the Fifth Amendment and on the First Amendment, that the area restrictions infringed plaintiff's constitutional rights, distinguishing *Kent* on the ground that the restriction on Zemel's passport did not "result from an expression or association on his part" and that he was "not being forced to choose between membership in an organization and freedom to travel."]

Finally, appellant challenges the 1926 Act on the ground that it does not contain sufficiently definite standards for the formulation of travel controls by the Executive. It is important to bear in mind, in appraising this argument, that because of the changeable and explosive nature of contemporary international relations, and the fact that the Executive is immediately privy to information which cannot be swiftly presented to, evaluated by, and acted upon by the legislature, Congress — in giving the Executive authority over matters of foreign affairs — must of necessity paint with a brush broader than that it customarily wields in domestic areas. . . .

This does not mean that simply because a statute deals with foreign relations, it can grant the Executive totally unrestricted freedom of choice. However, the 1926 Act contains no such grant. We have held, Kent v. Dulles, . . . and reaffirm today that the 1926 Act must take its content from history: it authorizes only those passport refusals and restrictions "which it could fairly be argued were adopted by Congress in light of prior administrative practice." Kent v. Dulles. . . . So limited, the Act does not constitute an invalid delegation.

[The Court declined to determine whether Zemel would be subject to criminal prosecution if he were to travel to Cuba without a passport validated for that country.]

Affirmed.

Mr. Justice BLACK, dissenting.

Article I of the Constitution provides that *"All* legislative Powers herein granted shall be vested in a Congress of the United States, which shall consist of a Senate and House of Representatives." (Emphasis supplied.) ... Since Article I ... vests, "All legislative Powers" in the Congress, and no language in the Constitution purports to vest any such power in the President, it necessarily follows, if the Constitution is to control, that the President is completely devoid of power to make laws regulating passports or anything else. And he has no more power to make laws by labeling them regulations than to do so by calling them laws. I cannot accept the Government's argument that the President has "inherent" power to make regulations governing the issuance and use of passports. ... We emphatically and I think properly rejected a similar argument advanced to support a seizure of the Nation's steel companies by the President. Youngstown Sheet & Tube Co. v. Sawyer, 343 U.S. 579. And regulation of passports, just like regulation of steel companies, is a lawmaking — not an executive, law-enforcing — function.

Nor can I accept the Government's contention that the passport regulations here involved are valid "because the Passport Act of 1926 in unequivocal words delegates to the President and Secretary a general discretionary power over passports. ..." That Act does provide that "the Secretary of State may grant and issue passports, and cause passports to be granted, issued, and verified in foreign countries ... under such rules as the President shall designate and prescribe. ..." Quite obviously, the Government does not exaggerate in saying that this Act "does not provide any specific standards for the Secretary" and "delegates to the President and Secretary a general discretionary power over passports" — a power so broad, in fact, as to be marked by no bounds except an unlimited discretion. It is plain therefore that Congress has not itself passed a law regulating passports; it has merely referred the matter to the Secretary of State and the President in words that say in effect, "We delegate to you our constitutional power to make such laws regulating passports as you see fit." The Secretary of State has proceeded to exercise the power to make laws regulating the issuance of passports by declaring that he will issue them for Cuba only to "persons whose travel may be regarded as being in the best interests of the United States," as he views those interests. For Congress to attempt to delegate such an undefined lawnmaking power to the Secretary, the President, or both, makes applicable to this 1926 Act what Mr. Justice Cardozo said about the National Industrial Recovery Act: "This is delegation running riot. No such plenitude of power is susceptible of transfer." A.L.A. Schechter Poultry Corp. v. United States, 295 U.S. 495, 553 (concurring opinion). See also Panama Ref. Co. v. Ryan, 293 U.S. 388; cf. Kent v. Dulles, 357 U.S. 116, 129.

Our Constitution has ordained that laws restricting the liberty of our people can be enacted by the Congress and by the Congress only. I do not think our Constitution intended that this vital legislative function could be farmed out in large blocks to any governmental official, whover he might be, or to any governmental department or bureau, whatever administrative expertise it might be thought to have. The Congress was created on the assumption that enactment of this free country's laws could be safely entrusted to the representatives of the people in Congress, and to no other official or government agency. The people who are called on to obey laws have a constitutional right to have them passed only in this constitutional way. . . . I think the 1926 Act gives the lawmaking power of Congress to the Secretary and the President and that it therefore violates the constitutional command that "All" legislative power be vested in the Congress. I would therefore reverse the judgment.

[Justice DOUGLAS, in a dissent joined by Justice GOLDBERG, found that the area restriction was a violation of Zemel's First Amendment rights "to know, to converse with others, to consult with them, to observe social, physical, political and other phenomena abroad as well as at home. . . ."

Justice GOLDBERG in a separate dissent also asserted that Congress had not authorized the executive to impose area restrictions. He found that the legislative history demonstrated that the 1852 statute, codified in 1926, was "designed solely to centralize authority in the hands of the Secretary of State in order to overcome the abuses and chaos caused by the fact that prior to the passage of the statute numerous unauthorized persons issued passports and travel documents." In addition, he found that the administrative practices relied upon by the majority were less consistent, persuasive, and relevant than the administrative practices relied upon by Mr. Justice Clark in his *Kent* dissent.]

Questions on *Zemel* and the Limits of Clear Statement Doctrine

1. Can *Zemel* be successfully distinguished from *Kent*? [70]
2. Should courts frequently utilize principles of clear statement in order to construe statutory delegations narrowly? Would this be a better way of limiting agency discretion than attempting to force greater legislative specificity through use of the nondelegation doctrine? What do *Kent* and *Zemel* together suggest might be the problem with broader use of clear statement principles?

The clear statement principle has two ingredients. First, the court must identify a given category of interests whose infringement by an administrative agency must be explicitly authorized. Second, the court must determine whether such explicit authorization has been granted in a given case.

How should the category of interests protected by clear statement principles be defined? In *Kent* a constitutionally protected liberty interest was involved. But wasn't a liberty interest also involved in *Zemel*? Should the principle of clear state-

___

70. In United States v. Laub, 385 U.S. 475 (1967), the Court decided a question reserved in *Zemel*, holding that travel in violation of an area restriction was not made a criminal offense by the 1952 Act making it unlawful for a citizen to "depart from or enter . . . the United States unless he bears a valid passport." Is this holding consistent with the Court's reasoning in *Zemel*? In Lynd v. Rusk, 389 F.2d 940 (D.C. Cir. 1967), the court held that the Secretary of State could not refuse to issue a passport to an applicant who refused to give assurances that he would not travel to designated areas where his passport was not valid but did agree not to use his passport for travel to such areas.

ment extend to interests that do not enjoy constitutional status? Consider, for example, Judge Leventhal's conclusion that the statute in *Meatcutters*, supra p. 79, did not authorize wage and price controls that were unfair or inequitable. Is this not an application of clear statement principles to economic regulation?

Beyond the problem of identifying those interests to which clear statement principles apply is the problem of deciding when Congress has spoken with sufficient explicitness to satisfy the requirement of clear statement. Was there such explicitness in *Zemel?* Does the degree of explicitness required depend on the "importance" (however measured) of the interest involved?

3. Is there a danger that freewheeling use by courts of clear statement principles could represent a usurpation by the courts of the lawmaking discretion which Congress has delegated to the agencies? Given the current widespread criticism of agency "failure," should *all* delegations of authority to administrators be narrowly construed? In the past, the courts often stretched legislative grants of authority to enable agencies to deal with all related aspects of a regulatory problem, but there are now signs of a shift in judicial attitudes.[71]

Hampton v. Mow Sun Wong

426 U.S. 88 (1976)

Mr. Justice STEVENS delivered the opinion of the Court.

Five aliens, lawfully and permanently residing in the United States, brought this litigation to challenge the validity of a policy, adopted and enforced by the Civil Service Commission and certain other federal agencies, which excludes all persons except American citizens and natives of American Samoa from employment in most positions subject to their respective jurisdictions. . . .

[Congress, in the Civil Service Act, 5 U.S.C. §3301, delegated to the President the power to "(1) prescribe such regulations for the admission of individuals into the civil service in the executive branch as will best promote the efficiency of that service; [and] (2) ascertain the fitness of applicants as to age, health, character, knowledge, and ability for the employment sought."

The President, acting under this grant of authority as well as the "authority vested in [him] by the Constitution," promulgated Executive Order No. 10577, 19 Fed. Reg. 7521 (Nov. 22, 1954), in which he authorized the Civil Service Com-

71. For an example of a broad construction of agency power to enable it to exercise comprehensive regulatory authority, see United States v. Southwestern Cable Co., 392 U.S. 157 (1968), sustaining the FCC's power to regulate the origination of programming by cable television systems as reasonable ancillary to the Commission's long-standing statutory power to regulate over-the-air broadcasting. Thereafter the FCC used this new authority to protect existing over-the-air broadcasters from the competition of the new cable technology. These FCC policies were invalidated in Home Box Office, Inc. v. FCC, 567 F.2d 9 (D.C. Cir.), cert. denied, 434 U.S. 829 (1977), where the court held that the agency's authority to regulate cablecasting must be narrowly construed because of the infringements on constitutionally protected free speech involved.

mission "to establish standards with respect to citizenship, age, education . . . and for residence and other requirements which applicants must meet to be admitted to or rated in examinations." Acting pursuant to this authority, the Commission adopted regulations barring aliens from employment in most federal Civil Service positions.]

The complaint alleged that there are about four million aliens living in the United States; they face special problems in seeking employment because our culture, language, and system of government are foreign to them; about 300,000 federal jobs become available each year, but noncitizens are not permitted to compete for those jobs except in rare situations when citizens are not available or when a few positions exempted from the competitive civil service are being filled. Plaintiffs further alleged that the advantage given to citizens seeking federal civil service positions is arbitrary and violates the Due Process Clause of the Fifth Amendment to the United States Constitution and Executive Order No. 11,478, 3 C.F.R. 803 (1966-1970 comp.), which forbids discrimination in federal employment on the basis of "national origin." The complaint sought declaratory and injunctive relief. . . .

[The District Court ruled for the defendants, members of the U.S. Civil Service Commission and officials of federal agencies (the General Services Administration, the Department of Health, Education, and Welfare, and the Post Office) that had refused to hire plaintiffs. The Court of Appeals reversed, holding that the broad ban on employment of aliens violates the equal protection principles contained in the Due Process Clause of the Fifth Amendment. In so ruling, it relied in part on the Supreme Court's decisions in Sugarman v. Dougall, 413 U.S. 634 (1973), and In re Griffiths, 413 U.S. 717 (1973), invalidating as violative of equal protection state laws excluding aliens from state government employment and admission to the state bar, respectively.

The Supreme Court discussed arguments by the federal government defendants that *Sugarman* and *Griffiths* were inapposite, because considerations of national and international policy not relevant to state employment decisions might justify a refusal by the federal government to employ aliens.]

. . . We agree with the petitioners' position that overriding national interests may provide a justification for a citizenship requirement in the federal service even though an identical requirement may not be enforced by a State.

We do not agree, however, with the petitioners' primary submission that the federal power over aliens is so plenary that any agent of the National Government may arbitrarily subject all resident aliens to different substantive rules than those applied to citizens. . . .

The rule enforced by the Commission has its impact on an identifiable class of persons who, entirely apart from the rule itself, are already subject to disadvantages not shared by the remainder of the community. Aliens are not entitled to vote and, as alleged in the complaint, are often handicapped by a lack of familiarity with our langage and customs. The added disadvantage resulting from the enforcement of the rule — ineligibility for employment in a major sector of the economy — is of sufficient significance to be characterized as a deprivation of an interest in liberty.[72] Indeed, we deal with a rule which deprives a discrete class of persons of an interest in liberty on a wholesale basis. By reason of the Fifth Amendment, such a deprivation must be accompanied by due process. It follows that some judicial scrutiny of the deprivation is mandated by the Constitution.

Respondents argue that this scrutiny requires invalidation of the Commission rule under traditional equal protection analysis. . . . However, it is not necessary to resolve respondents' substantive claim, if a narrower inquiry discloses that essential procedures have not been followed.

When the Federal Government asserts an overriding national interest as justification for a discriminatory rule which would violate the Equal Protection Clause if adopted by a State, due process requires that there be a legitimate basis for presuming that the rule was actually intended to serve that interest. If the agency which promulgates the rule has direct responsibility for fostering or protecting that interest, it may reasonably be presumed that the asserted interest was the actual predicate for the rule. That presumption would, of course, be fortified by an appropriate statement of reasons identifying the relevant interest. Alternatively, if the rule were expressly mandated by the Congress or the President, we might presume that any interest which might rationally be served by the rule did in fact give rise to its adoption.

In this case the petitioners have identified several interests which the Congress or the President might deem sufficient to justify the exclusion of noncitizens from the federal service. They argue, for example, that the broad exclusion may facilitate the President's negotiation of treaties with foreign powers by enabling him to offer employment opportunities to citizens of a given foreign country in exchange for reciprocal concessions — an offer he could not make if those aliens were already eligible for federal jobs. Alternatively, the petitioners argue that reserving the federal service for citizens provides an appropriate incentive to aliens to qualify for naturalization and thereby to participate more effectively in our society. They also point out that the citizenship requirement has been imposed in the United States with substantial consistency for over 100 years and accords with international law and the practice of most foreign countries. Finally, they correctly state that the need for undivided loyalty in certain sensitive positions clearly justifies a citizenship requirement in at least some parts of the federal service, and that the broad exclusion serves the valid administrative purpose of avoiding the trouble and expense of classifying those positions which properly belong in executive or sensitive categories.

The difficulty with all of these arguments except the last is that they do not identify any interest which can reasonably be assumed to have influenced the Civil

72. See Board of Regents v. Roth, 408 U.S. 564 [Ed. note — the *Roth* case is discussed in Chapter 7, pp. 620-628]. See also the statement for the Court by Mr. Justice Hughes in Truax v. Raich, 239 U.S. 33 (1915), a case dealing with the employment opportunities of aliens:

"... It requires no argument to show that the right to work for a living in the common occupations of the community is of the very essence of the personal freedom and opportunity that it was the purpose of the Amendment to secure. . . . If this could be refused solely upon the ground of race or nationality, the prohibition of the denial to any person of the equal protection of the laws would be a barren form of words. . . ." 239 U.S. 33 at 41.

Service Commission, the Postal Service, the General Service Administration, or the Department of Health, Education, and Welfare in the administration of their respective responsibilities or, specifically, in the decision to deny employment to the respondents in this litigation. We may assume with the petitioners that if the Congress or the President had expressly imposed the citizenship requirement, it would be justified by the national interest in providing an incentive for aliens to become naturalized, or possibly even as providing the President with an expendable token for treaty negotiating purposes; but we are not willing to presume that the Chairman of the Civil Service Commission, or any of the other original defendants, was deliberately fostering an interest so far removed from his normal responsibilities. Consequently, before evaluating the sufficiency of the asserted justification for the rule, it is important to know whether we are reviewing a policy decision made by Congress and the President or a question of personnel administration determined by the Civil Service Commission.

It is perfectly clear that neither the Congress nor the President has ever *required* the Civil Service Commission to adopt the citizenship requirement as a condition to eligibility for employment in the federal civil service. On the other hand, in view of the fact that the policy has been in effect since the Commission was created in 1883, it is fair to infer that both the Legislature and the Executive have been aware of the policy and have acquiesced in it. In order to decide whether such acquiescence should give the Commission rule the same support as an express statutory or Presidential command, it is appropriate to review the extent to which the policy has been given consideration by Congress or the President, and the nature of the authority specifically delegated to the Commission.

[After reviewing several appropriations statutes providing for compensation for employment of specified classes of aliens, the Court concluded] that the Appropriations Acts cannot fairly be construed to evidence either congressional approval or disapproval of the specific Commission rule challenged in this case.

Our review of the relevant Executive orders leads us to a similar conclusion with respect to the President's responsibility for the rule. . . .

It is the business of the Civil Service Commission to adopt and enforce regulations which will best promote the efficiency of the federal civil service. That agency has no responsibility for foreign affairs, for treaty negotiations, for establishing immigration quotas or conditions of entry, or for naturalization policies. Indeed, it is not even within the responsibility of the Commission to be concerned with the economic consequences of permitting or prohibiting the participation by aliens in employment opportunities in different parts of the national market. On the contrary, the Commission performs a limited and specific function.

The only concern of the Civil Service Commission is the promotion of an efficient federal service. In general it is fair to assume that its goal would be best served by removing unnecessary restrictions on the eligibility of qualified applicants for employment. With only one exception, the interests which the petitioners have put forth as supporting the Commission regulation at issue in this case are not matters which are properly the business of the Commission. That one exception is the administrative desirability of having one simple rule excluding all noncitizens when it is manifest that citizenship is an appropriate and legitimate requirement for some important and sensitive positions. Arguably, therefore, administrative convenience may provide a rational basis for the general rule.

For several reasons that justification is unacceptable in this case. The Civil Service Commission, like other administrative agencies, has an obligation to perform its responsibilities with some degree of expertise, and to make known the reasons for its important decisions. There is nothing in the record before us, or in matter of which we may properly take judicial notice, to indicate that the Commission actually made any considered evaluation of the relative desirability of a simple exclusionary rule on the one hand, or the value to the service of enlarging the pool of eligible employees on the other. Nor can we reasonably infer that the administrative burden of establishing the job classifications for which citizenship is an appropriate requirement would be a particularly onerous task for an expert in personnel matters; indeed, the Postal Service apparently encountered no particular difficulty in making such a classification. Of greater significance, however, is the quality of the interest at stake. Any fair balancing of the public interest in avoiding the wholesale deprivation of employment opportunities caused by the Commission's indiscriminate policy, as opposed to what may be nothing more than a hypothetical justification, requires rejection of the argument of administrative convenience in this case.

In sum, assuming without deciding that the national interests identified by the petitioners would adequately support an explicit determination by Congress or the President to exclude all noncitizens from the federal service, we conclude that those interests cannot provide an acceptable rationalization for such a determination by the Civil Service Commission. . . .

The judgment of the Court of Appeals is affirmed.

Mr. Justice BRENNAN, with whom Mr. Justice MARSHALL joins, concurring.

I join the Court's opinion with the understanding that there are reserved the equal protection questions that would be raised by congressional or Presidential enactment of a bar on employment of aliens by the Federal Government.

Mr. Justice REHNQUIST, with whom THE CHIEF JUSTICE, Mr. Justice WHITE, and Mr. Justice BLACKMAN join, dissenting.

The Court's opinion enunciates a novel conception of the procedural due process guaranteed by the Fifth Amendment, and from this concept proceeds to evolve a doctrine of delegation of legislative authority which seems to me to be quite contrary to the doctrine established by a long and not hitherto questioned line of our decisions. Neither of the Court's innovations is completely without appeal in this particular case, but even if we were to treat the matter as an original question I think such appeal is outweighed by the potential mischief which the doctrine bids fair to make in other areas of the law.

At the outset it is important to recognize that the power of the federal courts is severely limited in the areas of immigration and regulation of aliens. . . . [N]either an alien nor a citizen has any protected liberty interests in obtaining federal employment. Cafeteria Workers v. McElroy, 367 U.S. 886, 896-899 (1961). Nor in the absence of some form of statutory tenure is a Government employee entitled to a hearing prior to discharge, for "government employment, in the absence of legislation, can be revoked at the will of the appointing officer." Id. . . .

. . . [W]hile positing an equal protection problem, the Court does not rely on an equal protection analysis, conceding that "overriding national interests may provide a justification for a citizenship requirement in the federal service even though an identical requirement may not be enforced by a State." . . . Thus the Court seems to agree that the Equal Protection Clause does not provide a basis for invalidating this denial of *federal* civil service employment. The Court instead inexplicably melds together the concepts of equal protection and procedural and substantive due process to produce the following holding: "[T]he added disadvantage resulting from the enforcement of the rule — ineligibility for employment in a major sector of the economy — is of sufficient significance to be characterized as a deprivation of an interest in liberty. Indeed, we deal with a rule which deprives a discrete class of persons of an interest in liberty on a wholesale basis. By reason of the Fifth Amendment, such a deprivation must be accompanied by due process." . . .

The meaning of this statement in the Court's opinion is not immediately apparent. As already noted, there is no general "liberty" interest in either acquiring federal employment or, in the absence of a statutory tenure, in retaining it . . .

There is a liberty interest in obtaining public employment which is protected against procedural deprivation in certain circumstances, as the Court's citation to Board of Regents v. Roth, 408 U.S. 564 . . . indicates. But the cases cited in that passage from *Roth* . . . are distinguishable from the present case in at least two respects. In the first place they were both efforts by States, not to deny *public* employment, but to go further and proscribe the right to practice one's chosen profession in the *private* sector of the economy. Even more importantly, the vice found in each of those cases was the failure of the State to grant a "full prior hearing". . . .

But in the case presently before the Court, there is simply no issue which would require a hearing in order to establish any matter of disputed fact. All of the respondents freely concede that they are aliens. Their claim is not that they were entitled to a hearing in order to establish the fact that they were citizens, or to establish some other relevant fact; indeed they request no hearing for any purpose. Petitioners assert that due to respondents' alienage they are barred from federal employment, and respondents simply contend that they may not be.

Yet the Court does not decide this issue, but proceeds instead to hold that procedural due process includes not only a shield against arbitrary action but a scalpel with which one may dissect the administrative organization of the Federal Government. "When the Federal Government asserts an overriding national interest as justification for a discriminatory rule which would violate the Equal Protection Clause if adopted by a State, due process requires that there be a legitimate basis for presuming that the rule was actually intended to serve that interest." . . . What the Court seems to do is to engraft notions of due process onto the case law from this Court dealing with the delegation by Congress of its legislative authority to administrative agencies.

In two cases decided in the October Term 1934 the Court held that Congress "is not permitted to abdicate or to transfer to others the essential legislative functions with which it is ... vested" by Art. I, §1, of the Constitution. Schecter Corp. v. United States, 295 U.S. 495, 529. Panama Refining Co. v. Ryan, 293 U.S. 388. Nothing in either of those opinions, the only cases in which delegations to administrative agencies have been struck down, suggested any reliance upon the Due Process Clause of the Fifth Amendment, and it seems a fair statement to say that the Court has not seen fit during the 40 years following these decisions to enlarge in the slightest their relatively narrow holdings.

Not only is such reliance unjustified by prior decisions of this Court as to the scope of the due process guarantee, but it flies in the face of those cases which hold that the manner in which policies concerning aliens are made within the political branches of the government is not subject to judicial scrutiny. . . .

The solid ground by which such procedures may properly be challenged is to argue that there was an improper delegation of authority, which has not previously been thought to depend upon the procedural requirements of the Due Process Clause.

The Court, while not shaping its argument in these terms, seems to hold that the delegation here was faulty. Yet, it seems to me too clear to admit of argument that under the traditional standards governing the delegation of authority the Civil Service Commission was fully empowered to act in the manner in which it did in this case.

[Justice Rehnquist reviews the legislation authorizing the President to establish qualifications for Civil Service employment, the President's delegation of that authority to the Commission, and the Commission's exercise of that authority through regulations disqualifying aliens.]

Both Congress and the President thus took a power which they possessed and, instead of exercising it directly, chose to delegate it. This is the process by which all federal regulations are promulgated and to forbid it would be to necessarily dismantle the entire structure of the Executive Branch. But the majority does not challenge the procedure as to all cases. Rather, the challenge seems to be leveled only at policies which "raise ... constitutional questions. . . ." In those cases it becomes necessary for the agency, which was concededly acting within the scope of its delegated power, to provide reasons which will justify its actions in the eyes of the courts.

But, as previously discussed, such a holding overlooks the basic principle that a decision to exclude aliens from the civil service is a political decision reserved to Congress, the wisdom of which may not be challenged in the courts. Once it is determined that the agency in question was properly delegated the power by Congress to make decisions regarding citizenship of prospective civil servants, then the reasons for which that power was exercised are as foreclosed from judicial scrutiny as if Congress had made the decision itself. The fact that Congress has delegated a power does not provide a back door through which to attack a policy which would otherwise have been immune from attack.

For this Court to hold ... that the agency chosen by Congress, through the President, to effectuate its policies, has "no responsibility" in that area is to interfere in an area in which the Court itself clearly has "no responsibility": the organization of the Executive Branch. Congress, through the President, obviously *gave* responsibility in this area to the Civil Service Commission. The wisdom of that delegation is not for us to evaluate. ...

Questions on Hampton v. Mow Sun Wong

1. Why didn't *Hampton* employ the analysis utilized in Kent v. Dulles? If there is a constitutionally recognized "liberty" interest in the opportunity for government employment,[73] a broad statutory delegation should not be read to confer authority on the Executive to infringe that interest; any such infringement should be specifically and explicitly authorized by Congress.

2. Following the *Hampton* decision, the President issued an order disqualifying aliens from the Civil Service.[74] Is his action valid? Under the Kent v. Dulles approach suggested in the preceeding question? Under the *Hampton* approach?

3. Where an agency adduces a policy justification for action taken by it under a broad statutory delegation, how does a reviewing court determine whether that policy consideration is a "proper concern" of that agency that "can reasonably be assumed to have influenced" its decision? Suppose, for example, that the President's order delegating authority to the Civil Service Commission had directed it to consult with the State Department and the Immigration and Naturalization Service before promulgating regulations involving aliens, and that the Commission had engaged in such consultation before promulgating the regulation at issue in *Hampton*. What result? [75]

4. Note that *Hampton* acknowledges administrative convenience to be a proper concern of the Commission, but holds that "any fair balancing of the public interest" precludes disqualification of all aliens because of administrative difficulties in classifying those sensitive positions from which aliens could clearly be excluded. What is the source of the Court's authority to impose its views on the "fair balancing of the public interest" upon the Commission?

73. The question whether there is a "liberty" interest in government employment is considered in Chapter 7, p. 627, Note 2.

74. Executive Order No. 11,935, 41 Fed. Reg. 37301 (1976), order sustained, Vergara v. Hampton, 47 U.S.L.W. 1041 (7th Cir., Aug. 24, 1978).

75. For analysis of the *Hampton* decision see L. Tribe, American Constitutional Law 1137-1146 (1978). Professor Tribe finds that the decision adopts a principle of "structural due process" under which basic or fundamental private interests may not be infringed by government except through institutional processes of decision which ensure considered and responsible determination that important countervailing government interests justify the infringement.

Might the decision be analyzed in the terms of the more traditional approach that reviewing courts will not defer to an agency's resolution of competing policies where the agency has no relevant "expertise"?

Citizens to Preserve Overton Park, Inc. v. Volpe

401 U.S. 402 (1971)

Opinion of the Court by Mr. Justice MARSHALL, announced by Mr. Justice STEWART.

The growing public concern about the quality of our natural environment has prompted Congress in recent years to enact legislation designed to curb the accelerating destruction of our country's natural beauty. We are concerned in this case with §4(f) of the Department of Transportation Act of 1966, as amended, and §18(a) of the Federal-Aid Highway Act of 1968, 82 Stat. 823, 23 U.S.C. §138 (1964 ed. Supp. V) (hereafter, §138). These statutes prohibit the Secretary of Transportation from authorizing the use of federal funds to finance the construction of highways through public parks if a "feasible and prudent" alternative route exists. If no such route is available, the statutes allow him to approve construction through parks only if there has been "all possible planning to minimize harm" to the park.

Petitioners, private citizens as well as local and national conservation organizations, contend that the Secretary has violated these statutes by authorizing the expenditure of federal funds for the construction of a six-lane interstate highway through a public park in Memphis, Tennessee. Their claim was rejected by the District Court, which granted the Secretary's motion for summary judgment, and the Court of Appeals for the Sixth Circuit affirmed. After oral argument, this Court granted a stay that halted construction and, treating the application for the stay as a petition for certiorari, granted review. 400 U.S. 939. We now reverse the judgment below and remand for further proceedings in the District Court.

Overton Park is a 342-acre city park located near the center of Memphis. The park contains a zoo, a nine-hole municipal golf course, an outdoor theater, nature trails, a bridle path, an art academy, picnic areas, and 170 acres of forest. The proposed highway, which is to be a six-lane, high-speed, expressway, will sever the zoo from the rest of the park. Although the roadway will be depressed below ground level except where it crosses a small creek, 26 acres of the park will be destroyed. The highway is to be a segment of Interstate Highway I-40, part of the National System of Interstate and Defense Highways. I-40 will provide Memphis with a major east-west expressway which will allow easier access to downtown Memphis from the residential areas on the eastern edge of the city.

Although the route through the park was approved by the Bureau of Public Roads in 1956 and by the Federal Highway Administrator in 1966, the enactment of §4(f) of the Department of Transportation Act prevented distribution of federal funds for the section of the highway designated to go through Overton Park until the Secretary of Transportation determined whether the requirements of §4(f) had been met. Federal funding for the rest of the project was, however, available; and the state acquired a right-of-way on both sides of the park. In April 1968, the Secretary announced that he concurred in the judgment of local officials that I-40 should be built through the park. And in September 1969 the state acquired the right-of-way inside Overton Park from the city. Final approval for the project — the route as well as the design — was not announced until November 1969, after Congress had reiterated in §138 of the Federal-Aid Highway Act that highway construction through public parks was to be restricted. Neither announcement approving the route and design of I-40 was accompanied by a statement of the Secretary's factual findings. He did not indicate why he believed there were no feasible and prudent alternative routes or why design changes could not be made to reduce the harm to the park.

Petitioners contend that the Secretary's action is invalid without such formal findings and that the Secretary did not make an independent determination but merely relied on the judgment of the Memphis City Council. They also contend that it would be "feasible and prudent" to route I-40 around Overton Park either to the north or to the south. And they argue that if these alternative routes are not "feasible and prudent," the present plan does not include "all possible" methods for reducing harm to the park. Petitioners claim that I-40 could be built under the park by using either of two possible tunneling methods, and they claim that, at a minimum, by using advanced drainage techniques the expressway could be depressed below ground level along the entire route through the park including the section that crosses the small creek.

Respondents argue that it was unnecessary for the Secretary to make formal findings, and that he did, in fact, exercise his own independent judgment which was supported by the facts. In the District Court, respondents introduced affidavits, prepared specifically for this litigation, which indicated that the Secretary had made the decision and that the decision was supportable. These affidavits were contradicted by affidavits introduced by petitioners, who also sought to take the deposition of a former Federal Highway Administrator who had participated in the decision to route I-40 through Overton Park.

The District Court and the Court of Appeals found that formal findings by the Secretary were not necessary and refused to order the deposition of the former Federal Highway Administrator because those courts believed that probing of the mental processes of an administrative decisionmaker was prohibited. And, believing that the Secretary's authority was wide and reviewing courts' authority narrow in the approval of highway routes, the lower courts held that the affidavits contained no basis for a determination that the Secretary had exceeded his authority.

We agree that formal findings were not required. But we do not believe that in this case judicial review based solely on litigation affidavits was adequate.

A threshold question — whether petitioners are entitled to any judicial review — is easily answered. Section 701 of the Administrative Procedure Act, 5 U.S.C. §701 (1964 ed. Supp. V), provides that the action of "each authority of the government of the United States," which includes the Department of Transportation, is subject to judicial review except where there is a statutory prohibition on review or where "agency action is committed to agency discretion by law." In this case, there is no indication that Congress sought to prohibit judicial review and there is most certainly no "showing of 'clear and convincing evidence' of a . . . legislative intent" to restrict access to judicial review. Abbott Laboratories v. Gardner, 387 U.S. 136, 141 (1967). . . .

Similarly, the Secretary's decision here does not fall within the exception for action "committed to agency discretion." This is a very narrow exception. Berger, Administrative Arbitrariness and Judicial Review, 65 Col. L. Rev. 55 (1965). The legislative history of the Administrative Procedure Act indicates that it is applicable in those rare instances where "statutes are drawn in such broad terms that in a given case there is no law to apply." S. Rep. No. 752, 79th Cong., 1st Sess., 26 (1945).

Section 4(f) of the Department of Transportation Act and §138 of the Federal-Aid Highway Act are clear and specific directives. Both the Department of Transportation Act and the Federal-Aid to Highway Act provide that the Secretary "shall not approve any program or project" that requires the use of any public parkland "unless (1) there is no feasible and prudent alternative to the use of such land, and (2) such program includes all possible planning to minimize harm to such park. . . ." This language is a plain and explicit bar to the use of federal funds for construction of highways through parks — only the most unusual situations are exempted.

Despite the clarity of the statutory language, respondents argue that the Secretary has wide discretion. They recognize that the requirement that there be no "feasible" alternative route admits of little administrative discretion. For this exemption to apply the Secretary must find that as a matter of sound engineering it would not be feasible to build the highway along any other route. Respondents argue, however, that the requirement that there be no other "prudent" route requires the Secretary to engage in a wide-ranging balancing of competing interests. They contend that the Secretary should weigh the detriment resulting from the destruction of parkland against the cost of other routes, safety considerations, and other factors, and determine on the basis of the importance that he attaches to these other factors whether, on balance, alternative feasible routes would be "prudent."

But no such wide-ranging endeavor was intended. It is obvious that in most cases considerations of cost, directness of route, and community disruption will indicate that parkland should be used for highway construction whenever possible. Although it may be necessary to transfer funds from one jurisdiction to another, there will always be a smaller outlay required from the public purse when parkland is used since the public already owns the land and there will be no need to pay for right-of-way. And since people do not live or work in parks, if a highway is built on parkland no one will have to leave his home or give up his business. Such factors are common to substantially all highway construction. Thus, if Congress intended these factors to be on an equal footing with preservation of parkland there would have been no need for the statutes.

Congress clearly did not intend that cost and disruption of the community were to be ignored by the Secretary. But the very existence of the statutes indicates that protection of parkland was to be given paramount importance. The few green havens that are public parks were not to be lost unless there were truly unusual factors present in a particular case or the cost or community disruption resulting from alternative routes reached extraordinary magnitudes. If the statutes are to have any meaning, the Secretary cannot approve the destruction of parkland unless he finds that alternative routes present unique problems.

Plainly, there is "law to apply" and thus the exemption for action "committed to agency discretion" is inapplicable. But the existence of judicial review is only the start: the standard for review must also be determined. For that we must look to §706 of the Administrative Procedure Act, 5 U.S.C. §706. . . . [A] "reviewing court shall . . . hold unlawful and set aside agency action, findings, and conclusions found" not to meet six separate standards.[76] In all cases agency action must be set aside if the action was "arbitrary, capricious, an abuse of discretion, or otherwise not in accordance with law" or if the action failed to meet statutory, procedural, or constitutional requirements. . . . In certain narrow, specifically limited situations, the agency action is to be set aside if the action was not supported by "substantial evidence." And in other equally narrow circumstances the reviewing court is to engage in a de novo review of the action and set it aside if it was "unwarranted by the facts.". . .

Petitioners argue that the Secretary's approval of the construction of I-40 through Overton Park is subject to one or the other of these latter two standards of limited applicability. First, they contend that the "substantial evidence" standard of §706(2)(E) must be applied. In the alternative, they claim that §706(2)(F) applies and that there must be a de novo review to determine if the Secretary's action was "unwarranted by the facts." Neither of these standards is, however, applicable.

Review under the substantial-evidence test is authorized only when the agency action is taken pursuant to a rulemaking provision of the Administrative Procedure Act itself, 5 U.S.C. §553 . . . or when the agency action is based on a public adjudicatory hearing. See 5 U.S.C. §§ 556, 557 . . . The Secretary's decision to allow the expenditure of federal funds to build I-40 through Overton Park was plainly not an exercise of a rulemaking function. . . . And the only hearing that is required by either the Administrative Procedure Act or the statutes regulating the distribution of federal funds for highway construction is a public hearing conducted by local officials for the purpose of informing the community about the proposed project and eliciting community views on the design and route. 23 U.S.C. §128 . . . The hearing is nonadjudicatory, quasi-legislative in nature. It is not designed to produce a record that is to be the basis of agency action — the basic requirement for substantial-evidence review. . . .

Petitioner's alternative argument also fails. De novo review of whether the Secretary's decision was "unwarranted by the facts" is authorized by §706(2)(F) in only two circumstances. First, such de novo review is authorized when the

---

76. [The Court quotes the language of §706, including the concluding provision that:] "In making the foregoing determinations the Court shall review the whole record or those parts of it cited by a party, and due account shall be taken of the rule of prejudicial error."

action is adjudicatory in nature and the agency factfinding procedures are inadequate. And, there may be independent judicial factfinding when issues that were not before the agency are raised in a proceeding to enforce nonadjudicatory agency action. H.R. Rep. No. 1980, 79th Cong., 2d Sess. Neither situation exists here.

Even though there is no de novo review in this case and the Secretary's approval of the route of I-40 does not have ultimately to meet the substantial-evidence test, the generally applicable standards of §706 require the reviewing court to engage in a substantial inquiry. Certainly, the Secretary's decision is entitled to a presumption of regularity. . . . But that presumption is not to shield his action from a thorough, probing, in-depth review.

The court is first required to decide whether the Secretary acted within the scope of his authority. . . . This determination naturally begins with a delineation of the scope of the Secretary's authority and discretion. L. Jaffe, Judicial Control of Administrative Action 359 (1965). As has been shown, Congress has specified only a small range of choices that the Secretary can make. Also involved in this initial inquiry is a determination of whether on the facts the Secretary's decision can reasonably be said to be within that range. The reviewing court must consider whether the Secretary properly construed his authority to approve the use of parkland as limited to situations where there are no feasible alternative routes or where feasible alternative routes involve uniquely difficult problems. And the reviewing court must be able to find that the Secretary could have reasonably believed that in this case there are no feasible alternatives or that alternatives do involve unique problems.

Scrutiny of the facts does not end, however, with the determination that the Secretary has acted within the scope of his statutory authority. Section 706(2)(A) requires a finding that the actual choice made was not "arbitrary, capricious, an abuse of discretion, or otherwise not in accordance with law.". . . To make this finding the court must consider whether the decision was based on a consideration of the relevant factors and whether there has been a clear error of judgment. . . . Although this inquiry into the facts is to be searching and careful, the ultimate standard of review is a narrow one. The court is not empowered to substitute its judgment for that of the agency.

The final inquiry is whether the Secretary's action followed the necessary procedural requirements. Here the only procedural error alleged is the failure of the Secretary to make formal findings and state his reason for allowing the highway to be built through the park.

Undoubtedly, review of the Secretary's action is hampered by his failure to make such findings, but the absence of formal findings does not necessarily require that the case be remanded to the Secretary. Neither the Department of Transportation Act nor the Federal-Aid Highway Act requires such formal findings. Moreover, the Administrative Procedure Act requirements that there be formal findings in certain rulemaking and adjudicatory proceedings do not apply to the Secretary's action here. See 5 U.S.C. §§ 553(a)(2), 554(a). . . . And, although formal findings may be required in some cases in the absence of statutory directives when the nature of the agency action is ambiguous, those situations are rare. . . . Plainly, there is no ambiguity here; the Secretary has approved the construction of I-40 through Overton Park and has approved a specific design for the project. . . .

That administrative record is not, however, before us. The lower courts based their review on the litigation affidavits that were presented. These affidavits were merely "post hoc" rationalizations . . . which have traditionally been found to be an inadequate basis for review. . . . SEC v. Chenery Corp., 318 U.S. 80, 87 (1943). And they clearly do not constitute the "whole record" compiled by the agency: the basis for review required by §706 of the Administrative Procedure Act. . . .

Thus it is necessary to remand this case to the District Court for plenary review of the Secretary's decision. That review is to be based on the full administrative record that was before the Secretary at the time he made his decision. But since the bare record may not disclose the factors that were considered or the Secretary's construction of the evidence it may be necessary for the District Court to require some explanation in order to determine if the Secretary acted within the scope of his authority and if the Secretary's action was justifiable under the applicable standard.

The court may require the administrative officials who participated in the decision to give testimony explaining their action. Of course, such inquiry into the mental processes of administrative decisionmakers is usually to be avoided. United States v. Morgan, 313 U.S. 409, 422 (1941). And where there are administrative findings that were made at the same time as the decision, as was the case in Morgan, there must be a strong showing of bad faith or improper behavior before such inquiry may be made. But here there are no such formal findings and it may be that the only way there can be effective judicial review is by examining the decisionmakers themselves. See Shaughnessy v. Accardi, 349 U.S. 280 (1955).

The District Court is not, however, required to make such an inquiry. It may be that the Secretary can prepare formal findings . . . that will provide an adequate explanation for his action. Such an explanation will, to some extent, be a "post hoc rationalization" and thus must be viewed critically. If the District Court decides that additional explanation is necessary, that court should consider which method will prove the most expeditious so that full review may be had as soon as possible.

Reversed and remanded.

[Mr. Justice BLACK, joined by Mr. Justice BRENNAN, filed a separate opinion concluding that the Secretary had obviously not paid attention to the statutory requirements regarding the routing of highways through parks, and that the entire matter should be remanded to the Secretary for "hearings that a court can review" and for findings by the Secretary.

Mr. Justice BLACKMUN filed a concurring opinion, while Mr. Justice DOUGLAS took no part in the consideration or disposition of the case.

On remand, the District Court decided to make a "thorough, probing, in depth review" of the Secretary's decision rather than remanding to the Secretary for fresh proceedings and administrative findings. On the basis of extensive hearings, including submission of personel affidavits of the Secretary, testimony by some of his assistants, and numerous documentary exhibits, the court concluded that the

Secretary had not given serious consideration to alternative routes, as required by the Supreme Court's decision. However, the court concluded, on the basis of extensive factual evidence, that the Secretary could reasonably decide either way on the question whether there was a feasible and prudent alternative available "without his decisions being arbitrary or capricious or without committing a clear error of judgment," and that if he chose to select the park routing, the statutory requirement of "all possible planning to minimize harm to such park" would be satisfied. Accordingly, the case was remanded to the Secretary for an exercise of his discretion to choose among alternative routings. Citizens to Preserve Overton Park, Inc. v. Volpe, 335 F. Supp. 873 (W.D. Tenn. 1972). Subsequently the Secretary disapproved the Overton Park route without identifying a "prudent and feasible" alternative. This action was invalidated by the District Court at the behest of state highway officials contending that the Secretary could not disapprove a given route without specifying alternatives, 357 F. Supp. 846 (W.D. Tenn. 1973), but on appeal the Secretary's action was sustained, 494 F.2d 1212 (6th Cir. 1974).]

Notes and Questions on *Overton Park*

1. The Supreme Court's *Overton Park* opinion addresses several important questions, including the availability of judicial review of discretionary administrative decisions, the various means of developing a record for judicial review of informal administrative action, and the scope of judicial review of the merits. We are concerned only with the last question here; the availability of judicial review and the problem of a record will be discussed subsequently, see pp. 477-530 and 859-1012 infra.

2. Note that *Overton Park* structures judicial review of the events as a two-step process: first, a court is to decide whether the Secretary acted within the scope of his statutory authority; second, even though the Secretary is acting within his statutory authority, the court must review the particular choice made in order to determine whether it "'was based on a consideration of relevant factors" and was not "arbitrary, capricious, an abuse of discretion." [77] What is the distinction be-

---

77. Immediately following reference to the "arbitrary and capricious" standard of the APA, the Court indicated that the question was whether the agency has made "a clear error of judgment." This statement has generated some confusion, and considerable criticism, because the "clear error" standard has traditionally been used by appellate courts to review discretionary decisions by trial judges (such as the grant of a preliminary injunction). It has been widely assumed that the "arbitrary and capricious" standard applicable to review of agency decision was more deferential than the "clear error" standard applicable to trial courts, yet the Supreme Court seemed to equate the two standards. Scholarly commentary has concluded that this seeming equation was probably inadvertent, and that the traditional distinction between the two standards (which, like the various standards of judicial review of fact-finding, are largely expressions of "mood,") should be maintained. See Nathanson, Probing the Mind of the Administrator: Hearing Variations and Standards of Judicial Review under the Administrative Procedure Act and Other Federal Statutes, 75 Colum L. Rev. 721 (1975).

Query: *Should* reviewing courts be more deferential to the discretionary policy choices of administrators than of trial judges?

tween these two inquiries? Does the Court's position imply that statutes may authorize arbitrary and capricious action by administrators?

3. In discussing the scope of the Secretary's authority, the Supreme Court lays down a rule narrowly restricting his power to approve highway routings through parks to a few cases where "truly unusual factors" were present or "the cost or community disruption resulting from alternative routes reached extraordinary magnitudes." Otherwise, the Court found the statutory language to be "a plain and explicit bar to the use of federal funds for construction of highways through parks." Is this a sound construction of the statute? The legislative history[78] shows that the statutory provisions in question were regarded as far more of a compromise between pro-highway and anti-highway forces than the Court's opinion admits. Might the Court's construction of the statute to "tilt" in favor of parks nonetheless have been justified in order to provide a counterweight to the apparent biases of highway agencies? In order to protect "underrepresented" environmental interests? [79]

In what ways does the technique utilized in *Overton Park* to control agency discretion resemble and differ from the techniques utilized in *Kent* and *Hampton*? To the extent that innovative construction of statutes to limit the discretion of mission-oriented agencies is a legitimate and desirable judicial technique, how widespread is its potential application?

Note: Environmental Protection and the Administrative Process

Measures to protect the natural environment have played a major role in the expansion and modification of the administrative process in recent years. Many new administrative agencies, such as the Environmental Protection Agency and its counterparts at the state level, have been created. At the same time, as *Overton Park* illustrates, many traditional agencies with missions other than environmental quality have been required by statutes and reviewing courts to give increased attention to environmental concerns.[80]

Why are government measures to protect environmental quality needed? The answer lies in the "spillover" quality of environmental harms. A factory polluting a stream or a motorist polluting the air imposes harms — health, aesthetic, economic — on others. The fact that part of the costs of such activities are not borne

---

78. See H.R. Rep. No. 1584, 90th Cong., 2d Sess. (1968); S. Rep. No. 1340, 90th Cong., 2d Sess. (1968), as reprinted in 3 U.S. Code Cong. & Admin. News at 3482 (1968); 114 Cong. Rec. 19914-19917 (1968); U.S. Code Cong. & Admin. News 3538 (1968); 114 Cong. Rec. 23706-23708, 24029, 24032-24038 (1968).

79. For discussion, see Stewart, The Development of Administrative and Quasi-Constitutional Law in Judicial Review of Environmental Decisionmaking: Lessons from the Clean Air Act, 62 Iowa L. Rev. 714-722, 733-740 (1977).

80. Particularly noteworthy is the National Environmental Policy Act of 1969, 42 U.S.C. §§ 4321 et seq., requiring that agencies proposing action that threatens significant environmental harm prepare a detailed impact statement describing the environmental consequences of the proposed action and of alternatives to it.

by the actor (which economists term a problem of external costs) encourages the actor to engage in more pollution than he would if all the costs of pollution were borne by him. The presence of spillover harms creates a form of "market failure" resulting in a higher level of pollution than would be the case if the costs of all spillover harms were internalized to those generating them.[81]

Conceivably, the problem of environmental degradation might be handled through private litigation in the courts. Excessive pollution could be curtailed indirectly by the threat of damage awards to victims of pollution or directly through the award of injunctions. In practice, however, court litigation has not proved adequate to deal with environmental degration in a modern industrialized society. The requirement of establishing causation is very difficult to satisfy when plaintiff's injury (e.g., cancer) could have many causes other than defendant's emissions. The inadequacies of judicial machinery are accentuated where the harm suffered by any given individual is small or consists of a low risk that she will suffer some future harm (as in the case of latent health injury), or where the harm (such as smog in Los Angeles) is caused by many actors.[82] In order to provide remedies that are prophylactic and operate on a more comprehensive scale, legislatures have empowered administrative agencies to issue regulations and orders requiring pollution sources to adopt controls or prohibiting certain forms of environmental degradation by private actors.[83]

Actions by government can also cause "spillovers" that impair environmental

81. Two caveats must be entered here. First, it is not logically inevitable that polluters be assigned responsibility for the damage caused by pollution. For damage to occur, the presence of persons suffering damage is also necessary. The damage is caused by the congruence of pollution and other activities, and the assignment of responsibility for the damage is a matter of social policy; in some instances it may be preferable to hold the "victims" responsible, as where a developer builds around a heretofore isolated airport or other polluting facility. For discussion, see R. Stewart & J. Krier, Environmental Law and Policy chs. 3 & 4 (2d ed. 1978); Coase, The Problem of Social Cost, 3 J. Law & Econ. 1 (1960); Calabresi, Transaction Costs, Resource Allocation and Liability Rules — A Comment, 11 J. Law & Econ. 67 (1968).

Second, if only a few people were involved, the problem of excessive pollution might be resolved by bargaining. For example, if only one polluter and the receptor (person suffering pollution damage) were involved, the receptor could bribe the pollutor to control his emissions. But when many polluters and receptors are involved, the costs of bargaining and "free rider" effects make privately negotiated solutions impractical.

82. For discussion, see R. Stewart & J. Krier, Environmental Law & Policy ch. 4 (2d ed. 1978).

83. Economists have criticized reliance on "command and control" regulation of pollution on the ground that it is unnecessarily cumbersome and costly. Administrative regulations tend to be rigid and uniform in character, requiring the same degree of control from various sources even though one source could reduce its emissions far more cheaply than another. In order to achieve environmental quality at less cost, economists urge the use of emission fees or taxes on pollution, or creation of transferrable pollution rights that could be bought and sold at a price determined by market forces. See A. Kneese & C. Schultze, Pollution, Prices and Public Policy (1975). Thus far, however, legislatures have shown little disposition to authorize such market-type incentives in lieu of traditional regulatory controls, in part because economists and others have not adequately addressed the practical problems in implementing them. See Roberts & Stewart, Book Review (W. F. Baxter, People or Penguins: The Case for Optimal Pollution (1974); B. A. Ackerman et al., The Uncertain Search for Environmental Quality (1974)), 88 Harv. L. Rev. 1644 (1975).

quality. For example, government construction of a highway through a park not only destroys some parkland but also lessens the aesthetic appeal of the remaining parkland. Spillovers may also be generated by government research and development promotion of new techcnologies (such as the "breeder" nuclear reactor) that generate environmental hazards (such as highly radioactive nuclear wastes). Government development of natural resources owned by it — such as timber in national forests or oil in outer continental shelf lands — may also cause environmental harms.

Ideally, the government would carefully weigh the environmental costs of any proposed action and balance them against the expected benefits before going ahead. In practice, however, Congress delegates great discretion over such decisions to administrative agencies whose developmental mission may lead them to chronically overestimate the benefits of proposed action and disregard and downplay the environmental costs involved. For example, the basic mission of the Highway Bureau is to build highways at lowest cost, while the basic mission of the Atomic Energy Commission was to promote the development of nuclear power. The mission orientation of such agencies — which may be accentuated by constant lobbying from industry and other organized client interests with a major stake in the agency's promotion of its mission — leads to a form of "bureaucratic externality" in which the agency tends to ignore or discount the adverse effects of its choices on values or goals that are not central to its mission.[84]

Bureaucratic tunnel vision is by no means limited to agencies with developmental missions. Agencies whose prime mission is to protect the environment or health — such as the Environmental Protection Agency and the Occupational Health and Safety Administration — often tend to downplay or disregard the economic costs which protective regulations impose on industry and consumers.

The rising concern with environmental quality has created strong pressures on traditional doctrines of judicial review of administrative action. Industry and others subject to administrative controls to protect health and the environment claim that controls are unreasonable or excessively costly, and have called upon the courts to scrutinize closely decisions by environmental regulatory agencies. At the same time, environmental advocates have scored the disregard of environmental spillovers by government agencies with developmental missions, and have asked courts to abandon traditional principles of deference to the exercise of administrative discretion in order to force such agencies to adopt policies more favorable to environmental concerns.

---

84. In 1974, the Atomic Energy Commission was reorganized in an effort to eliminate the conflict between its promotional mission and its statutory responsibility to regulate the safety of nuclear power; the Commission's promotional mission was transferred to a new Energy Research and Development agency (which has since been absorbed into the Department of Energy), and its regulatory responsibilities vested in a Nuclear Regulatory Commission (NRC). However, such reorganizations may not accomplish a great deal, at least in the short run. The staff of the NRC was largely drawn from the AEC; in the view of many critics, they still maintain a bias in favor of promoting nuclear power.

Question

The Federal Highways Act provides for a program of federal grants-in-aid to the states to facilitate "the prompt and early completion of the National System of Interstate and Defense Highways," 23 U.S.C. §101(b). The routes of the system "to the greatest extent possible, shall be selected by joint action of the state highway departments of each state and the adjoining states subject to the approval of the Secretary of Transportation." The Federal Government pays 90 percent of the cost.

This controversy concerns a stretch of highway to be part of Interstate Route 87 in New York State. There were two proposed routes: one, the Chestnut Ridge route which was approved and is now attacked by certain public interest groups and towns; and a more westerly route. Chestnut Ridge is 8.8 miles, the westerly route is 9.5 miles. When the route was first proposed in 1960, Chestnut Ridge was estimated to cost $14.5 million, the westerly route $18.8 million. McMorran, New York Superintendent of Public Works, first proposed to the Bureau of Roads of the Department of Transportation the Chestnut Ridge route. At a public hearing many expressed opposition; others favored it. A further hearing was held in February 1962 on both plans. One thousand attended a meeting which lasted from 1:30 P.M. to 5:00 A.M. the following morning. McMorran now concluded that the westerly route best met "the social, cultural and economic requirements of Westchester County, and the needs of the Interstate System generally." Nevertheless the Bureau of Roads chose Chestnut Ridge while conceding that the other was preferable from "a purely planning standpoint" though it believed that opponents of Chestnut Ridge exaggerated the difference between the two routes in this respect. Thereafter meetings and conferences went on until the final decision in 1966. The question was twice referred to the then-Secretary of the Interior. A study was made by that Department's Bureau of Outdoor Recreation. It concluded that the westerly route was "least damaging to the existing and future open space needs of the county," so that the additional expense of $4.3 million was justified. Nevertheless the Bureau of Roads persisted in its choice of Chestnut Ridge, which in 1965 it defended before the Subcommittee on Public Roads of the Senate Committee on Public Works. The Secretary of Transportation approved Chestnut Ridge.

Both routes traverse country of great natural beauty. On both there are wildlife sanctuaries. If the westerly route were adopted a privately owned sanctuary of 46 acres would be destroyed and a nearby public park adversely affected. Chestnut Ridge would run between two privately owned sanctuaries — one of 254 acres, the other of 105 — but only 9.3 acres would be taken. The Department of the Interior and the New York Commissioner of Construction prefer the westerly route. The engineers of the Road Bureau think their concern is exaggerated.

The town of Bedford prefers the westerly route because Chestnut Ridge would bisect the town. Opinion in the village of Mt. Kisco is divided but a majority favors the westerly route. The towns of North Castle and New Castle are less affected but prefer Chestnut Ridge. Fewer individual property owners will be affected by Chestnut Ridge.

In the meantime, construction costs have risen so that the respective construction costs are $26.9 million for the westerly route and $21.2 million for Chestnut Ridge (some experts would estimate the present difference in construction costs between the two as less). The present evidence on land acquisition costs does not clearly indicate that land costs for one route would be cheaper than for the other. Costs are continuing to rise pending a final resolution of the controversy.

In reliance upon the choice of the Chestnut Ridge route by the Bureau of Roads and that Bureau's commitment of federal funds, the state has entered into a $26 million construction contract based upon the Chestnut Ridge route. The contractor has spent over $9 million under the contract for labor, materials, and equipment. The state has spent over $1 million in engineering the Chestnut Ridge route, has made offers of $2 million to acquire property rights on the Chestnut Ridge route, and has reached agreement on property acquisitions on that route totaling $200,000.

The Federal Highways Act states that "local needs, to the extent practicable, suitable, and feasible, shall be given equal consideration with needs of interstate commerce." 23 U.S.C. §101(b). A project, among other things, is "to conform to the particular needs of each locality." 23 U.S.C. §109(a). The Act declared it to be the national policy that "in carrying out the provisions of this title, the Secretary shall use maximum effort to preserve Federal, State, and local government park-lands and historic sites and the beauty and historic value of such lands and sites." 23 U.S.C. §138. Regulations adopted by the Secretary under the Act provide that "The conservation and development of natural resources, the advancement of economic and social values and the promotion of desirable land utilization, as well as the existing and potential highway traffic and other pertinent criteria are to be added to a federal-aid system. . . ." 23 C.F.R. §1.6(c) (now repealed; see Fed. Reg. 33142).

Plaintiffs — the town of Bedford, a civic association of Bedford residents, two wildlife sanctuaries whose property will be adversely affected by the proposed Chestnut Ridge route, individuals whose property would be taken by that route, and the Road Review League, "a nonprofit association which concerns itself with community problems, primarily those involving the location of highways" — brought suit in federal district court against the Secretary of Transportation, challenging the selection of the Chestnut Ridge route.

The court concluded that engineering and cost considerations clearly favored the shorter Chestnut Ridge route, which would also displace fewer individual property owners, but found it clear that under the Act the choice was not to be made solely on the basis of engineering considerations or the number of affected landowners. It found that the evidence on "planning" considerations (effect on existing land use) preponderated in favor of the western route, and noted that both the Interior Department and the New York Commissioner of Conservation considered the western route preferable from a conservation viewpoint. The court also characterized a Road Bureau official's view that an interstate highway would enhance the landscape through which it passed as "so bizarre as to be almost irrational." However, the judge found that the Road Bureau's conclusion that conservation and aesthetic factors indicated no clear preference for either route was not contrary to the "overwhelming weight" of the evidence, "despite the fact that if I had been in its place I might have evaluated it differently." The judge noted that a number of factors "seem to me to weigh more heavily in favor of the westerly route than" the agency thought. In conclusion, the judge emphasized that the selection of the appropriate route turned on a number of factors, and that some favored the westerly route and others the Chestnut Ridge. Asserting that "the court cannot substitute its own judgment for that of the agency," the court found that the agency's choice was not "plainly wrong," and held in favor of the agency.[85]

Plaintiffs appeal. What result?

2. Alternative Approaches to Judicial Review of Agency Discretion

The previous subsection illustrates a variety of techniques of statutory construction that courts have utilized to narrow agency discretion or force agencies to give weight to certain values or interests which they are otherwise prone to disregard or discount. However, the materials in that subsection should also suggest that there are definite limits to the use of such techniques. In many instances (probably most), where statutes contain a broad delegation of discretion to agencies, the use of clear statement principles or other techniques of statutory construction to limit or structure agency decisions in a broad category of cases would neither be justified nor wise. Very often agency decisions must be based on an ad hoc assessment of a particular situation in light of a number of competing values, interests, or other factors, and the governing statute cannot plausibly be construed to require that this particularistic assessment reach one and only one result. But such decisions are very often important ones, and there may be legitimate concern that in making them administrators may act carelessly, give excessive weight to particular interests or goals, or otherwise exercise their discretion unwisely. To what extent can judicial review serve to meet these concerns by promoting "better" decisions in such cases? In cases where statutory construction to limit the general dimensions of agency discretion is not feasible, what techniques can courts utilize?

In this subsection we examine several such techniques; subsequent chapters examine others, such as requiring procedural formalities in administrative decisionmaking or requiring consistency in the application of agency policies.

a. The "Arbitrary and Capricious" Standard

The APA §706(2)(A) directs reviewing courts to set aside "agency action, findings, and conclusions" found to be "arbitrary, capricious, an abuse of discretion." Why isn't this adequate and appropriate authority for courts to invalidate particular agency exercises of discretion which the judges deem unsound or inequitable?

85. See Road Review League v. Boyd, 270 F. Supp. 650 (S.D.N.Y. 1967).

Despite the potential breadth of the "arbitrary and capricious" standard, courts during the past 30 years have been extremely reluctant to utilize it to overturn particular agency decisions. This reluctance is reflected in the District Court's decision in the highway routing problem, supra p. 286, and in *Overton Park's* admonition that the "ultimate standard of review" under the arbitrary and capricious standard is a "narrow one" and that a reviewing court "is not empowered to substitute its judgment for that of the agency."

In the thousands of federal court decisions annually reviewing federal administrative action, only a comparative handful invalidate agency action on this ground.[86] Litigants attempting to persuade a reviewing court that the balance struck by an agency among relevant factors is "arbitrary and capricious" must be prepared to persuade the court that the agency's decision has no rational basis whatsoever. Given the artfulness of agency opinion writers, the skills of government lawyers, and the plausibility of agency claims of "expertise," this is a very difficult burden to carry.[87]

Environmentalists have argued that this tradition of judicial deference should be abandoned in environmental cases. See Sive, Some Thoughts of an Environmental Lawyer in the Wilderness of Administrative Law, 70 Colum. L. Rev. 612 (1970), which points out that government governs the use of most of our physical resources, both the natural and the man-made components of our environment. The governing is largely by administrative agencies. He asserts that a litigant attempting to show that administrative decisions lack a "rational basis" or "substantial evidence" to support them "has a difficult task," a task exacerbated by the limited resources available to environmental litigants who are typically in the position of "a David

---

86. For examples of the infrequent instances where a reviewing court has invalidated an agency policy choice as arbitrary and capricious, see Natl. Assn. of Independent TV Producers and Distributors v. FCC, 516 F.2d 526 (2d Cir. 1975) (rapid FCC implementation of new network programming rules invalidating longer phase-in period required); National Tire Dealers and Retreaders Assn. v. Brinegar, 491 F.2d 31 (D.C. Cir. 1974) (invalidating requirement of permanent retread labeling on all retreaded tires); CBS v. FCC, 454 F.2d 1018 (D.C. Cir. 1971) (FCC administration of "equal time" requirements for political broadcasts). There are signs that courts in recent years have been somewhat more willing to invalidate agency decisions as "arbitrary and capricious" than previously, a development which may reflect the recent tide of criticism of agency "failure," and growing skepticism of administrative claims of "expertise." See, e.g., Aqua Slide 'N' Dive Corp. v. Consumer Product Safety Comm., 569 F.2d 831 (5th Cir. 1978) (invalidating CPSC safety regulations for pool slides); Home Box Office, Inc. v. FCC, 567 F.2d 9 (D.C. Cir.), cert. denied, 434 U.S. 829 (1977) (invalidating FCC restrictions on ability of cablecasters to compete with established over-the-air broadcasters). See also Hampton v. Mow Sun Wong, supra p. 268, in which the Supreme Court flatly rejected administrative convenience as an adequate justification for blanket disqualification of aliens from government employment. Although the Court did not use the words "arbitrary and capricious," that is the effect of its ruling.

87. As noted above in Section B of this chapter, reviewing courts may use the substantial evidence standard for review of agency fact-finding as a means for overturning particular instances of discretionary lawmaking by agencies which courts regard as unsound. The use of the "substantial evidence" standard for this purpose is abetted by the courts' use of the "law"/"fact" distinction to characterize as questions of "fact" issues that are analytically questions of law. Why should courts be so reluctant to utilize the "arbitrary and capricious" standard directly to invalidate agency lawmaking while they more often set aside through the more indirect "substantial evidence" standard?

challenging a Goliath." This situation, Sive argues, leaves promotion-oriented government agencies substantially free to pursue policies that seriously degrade the environment. Accordingly, the traditional deference to agency discretion should be altered in favor of more aggressive review in order to "neutralize the effluents of affluence," prevent "the asphalt jungle from supplanting most of the still green part of our one earth," and "enable courts to decree in judgments the basic ecological principle that one community's toilet is another's faucet."

However, courts generally have refused to heed such pleas and declined to apply the "arbitrary and capricious" standard with special right in order to protect environmental interests.[88]

Questions

1. Why have courts been so reluctant to utilize the "arbitrary and capricious" standard more aggressively? Why shouldn't a judge substitute her judgment for that of an agency on an ad hoc issue of policy when the judge believes that the agency's choice is unwise or inequitable? Who is better qualified to evaluate competing social values, a relatively disinterested, generalist judiciary, or a specialized administrative agency with the danger of bias that a particularized mission creates?

2. Consider the Sive excerpt, which indicates that courts sometimes use the "substantial evidence" test to review agency policy choices. If a more intrusive, less deferential version of the "arbitrary and capricious" standard (or "substantial evidence" standard applied to policy choices) were adopted, should it be employed across the board in all cases, or should it be limited to certain types of administrative decisions or to the protection of certain classes of interests affected by agency decisions? For example, can the arguments for more searching judicial review be limited to cases where government projects such as highways threaten the environment? What of administrative decisions touching on health and safety or the interests of consumers or the poor? What of pollution control regulations claimed by industry to be unjustifiedly rigorous and costly?

3. Senator Bumpers introduced legislation (S. 2408, 94th Cong., 1st Sess. (1975)) that would replace the first sentence of APA §706 with the following:

> To the extent necessary to decision and when presented, the reviewing court shall de novo decide all relevant questions of law, interpret constitutional and statutory provisions, and determine the meaning or applicability of the terms of an agency action. There shall be no presumption that any rule or regulation of any agency is valid, and whenever the validity of any such regulation is drawn in question in any court of the United States or of any State, the court shall not uphold the validity of such challenged rule or regulation unless such validity is clearly and convincingly shown. . . .

88. See, e.g., Natural Resources Defense Council v. Nuclear Regulatory Commn., 580 F.2d 698 (D.C. Cir. 1978); Environmental Defense Fund, Inc., v. Costle, 11 E.R.D. 1209 (D.C. Cir. 1978).

How would this provision change existing standards of judicial review? Would it change the result in the highway routing problem? Should it be adopted?

b. "Remand" Techniques

Another prominent environmental advocate, Professor Joseph Sax, has opposed the courts' flatly substituting their judgment on policy questions for that of the agency, claiming that this would make the courts into "Environmental Czars." Instead, building on "public trust" doctrines in property law, he would have the courts set aside agency action that threatened serious environmental harm that was not explicitly authorized by statute.[89] Since the agency would have to return to Congress to obtain explicit authorization in order for the agency action to go forward, Professor Sax believes that his proposal would "remand" the policy issue for decision to the politically most responsible branch of government.[90]

Questions: How would courts decide when environmental harms were sufficiently serious and when legislative authorization was insufficiently specific to trigger the "remand" technique? What would be the practical effect if courts used a "remand" technique freely, forcing administrators to apply regularly to Congress for authorization for particular projects or decisions? Recall that the Bureau of Roads in the highway routing problem, supra p. 286, successfully defended its choice of routes before the Subcommittee on Public Roads of the Senate Public Works Committee.

c. The "Adequate Consideration" or "Hard Look" Approach

While generally declining invitations to substitute their judgment for that of agencies with respect to particular exercises of discretion or to engage in frequent "remands" of policy issues to the legislature by construing agency authority narrowly, courts in recent years have sought to develop a middle way between the Sive and Sax proposals and the more traditional practices of extensive deference to agency discretion. They have done so by requiring agencies to consider in their proceedings and opinions all of the relevant policies and factors bearing on discretionary policy choices, and sometimes by scruitinizing closely the logical and factual

---

89. See J. Sax, Defending the Environment 175-192 (1971).
90. Reconsider, in the light of the Sax proposal, the decisions in Kent v. Dulles, supra p. 258, and Hampton v. Mow Sun Wong, supra p. 268. Do these decisions involve a "remand" technique? For an example of a "remand" to the legislature of a controversial environmental issue, see Wilderness Society v. Morton, 479 F.2d 842 (D.C. Cir. 1973) (barring construction of the trans-Alaska pipeline). The subsequent history of the controversy is reflected in Wilderness Society v. Morton, 495 F.2d 1026 (D.C. Cir. 1974), rev'd sub nom. Alyeska Pipeline Service Co. v. Wilderness Society, 421 U.S. 240 (1975). Cf. TVA v. Hill, 98 S. Ct. 2279 (1978), refusing to exempt ongoing projects from the Endangered Species Act's prohibition of federal projects endangering rare species; the decision has provoked congressional proposals to amend the Act.

bases for the choices made, while leaving to the agency the ultimate selection of policy so long as it has a considered and rational basis.

This approach has been explained by Judge Leventhal of the District of Columbia Circuit Court of Appeals, who asserts that reviewing courts must determine whether the agency has taken a "hard look" at the relevant evidence and policy alternatives, and has made a reasoned exercise of its discretion in a given case.[91] The "hard look" approach requires agencies to develop an evidentiary record reflecting the factual and analytical basis for their decisions,[92] to explain in considerable detail their reasoning, and to give "adequate consideration" to the evidence and analysis submitted by private parties.

There is a crucial difference between the sanction imposed by courts under the "arbitrary and capricious" standard and that imposed under the "hard look" or "adequate consideration" doctrine. When an agency decision is judged so irrational as to be arbitrary and capricious, that decision will be invalidated and the agency will normally be permanently foreclosed from implementing its choice. However, under the "hard look" or "adequate consideration" approach, the court does not condemn the agency's policy choice as irremediably irrational, but simply concludes that the agency has not adequately justified its choice; the normal remedy is a remand for further proceedings in which the agency may attempt to buttress its original policy choice with more extensive analysis and explanation.[93] Under the "arbitrary and capricious" standard, the court effectively substitutes its judgment for that of the agency on the reasonableness of a substantive policy choice. Under the "hard look" or "adequate consideration" approach, it reviews whether the agency has adequately reviewed all relevant factors and considerations and made a reasoned choice.[94]

The development of the "hard look" or "adequate consideration" approach was considerably encouraged by the Supreme Court's *Overton Park* decision; al-

91. See Leventhal, Environmental Decisionmaking and the Role of the Courts, 122 U. Pa. L. Rev. 509, 511 (1974).

92. Development of an adequate record to prevent judicial review under the "hard look" approach may require agencies to employ procedures going beyond those imposed in the APA or other relevant statutes. We explore this problem and the related questions of the courts' authority to mandate the use of additional procedures, in Chapter 6, pp. 477-530 infra.

93. However, judges sometimes run the two approaches together by asserting that a policy choice made without sufficient analysis or reasoned explanation is inherently "arbitrary and capricious." See NRDC v. NRC, 547 F.2d 633, 661, (D.C. Cir. 1976) (concurring opinion of Tamm, J.), *remanded sub nom.* Vermont Yankee Nuclear Corp. v. NRDC, 435 U.S. 519 (1978).

94. For a sample of judicial invocation of the "hard look" approach to set aside agency action and remand for further proceedings, see South Terminal Corp. v. EPA, 504 F.2d 646 (1st Cir. 1974) (failure to develop sufficient data to justify controls on auto pollution); Palisades Citizens Assn. v. CAB, 420 F.2d 188 (D.C. Cir. 1969) (for failure to consider environmental interests in helicopter routing); Texas v. EPA, 499 F.2d 289 (5th Cir. 1974) (lack of agency justification for pollution controls); Environmental Defense Fund v. Ruckelshaus, 439 F.2d 584 (D.C. Cir. 1971) (agency failure to institute proceedings on continued use of potentially carcinogenic pesticide). See generally Stewart, The Development of Administrative and Quasi-Constitutional Law in Judicial Review of Environmental Decisionmaking: Lessons from the Clean Air Act, 62 Iowa L. Rev. 713, 733-740 (1977).

though stating that the ultimate substantive standard of review under the "arbitrary and capricious" standard is narrow, the Court emphasized that courts reviewing agency discretion should engage in a "searching and careful inquiry" into the agency's "consideration of the relevant factors" and the factual foundations of its policy choice. See pp. 280-281 supra. Another landmark decision in the development of this approach to review of discretion is the following case.

Scenic Hudson Preservation Conf. v. FPC (I)

354 F.2d 608 (2d Cir. 1965)

HAYS, Circuit Judge:

In this proceeding the petitioners are the Scenic Hudson Preservation Conference, an unincorporated association consisting of a number of non-profit, conservationist organizations, and the towns of Cortlandt, Putnam Valley and Yorktown. Petitioners ask us, pursuant to §313(b) of the Federal Power Act, 16 U.S.C. §825(b), to set aside ... [an] order of March 9, 1965 granting a license to the intervener, the Consolidated Edison Company of New York, Inc., to construct a pumped storage hydroelectric project on the west side of the Hudson River at Storm King Mountain in Cornwall, New York. ...

A pumped storage plant generates electric energy for use during peak load periods, using hydroelectric units driven by water from a headwater pool or reservoir. The contemplated Storm King project would be the largest of its kind in the world. Consolidated Edison has estimated its cost, including transmission facilities, at $162,000,000. The project would consist of three major components, a storage reservoir, a powerhouse, and transmission lines. The storage reservoir, located over a thousand feet above the powerhouse, is to be connected to the powerhouse, located on the river front, by a tunnel 40 feet in diameter. The powerhouse, which is both a pumping and generating station, would be 800 feet long and contain eight pump generators.

Transmission lines would run under the Hudson to the east bank and then underground for 1.6 miles to a switching station which Consolidated Edison would build at Nelsonville in the Town of Philipstown. Thereafter, overhead transmission lines would be placed on towers 100 to 150 feet high and these would require a path up to 125 feet wide through Westchester and Putnam Counties for a distance of some 25 miles until they reached Consolidated Edison's main connections with New York City.

During slack periods Consolidated Edison's conventional steam plants in New York City would provide electric power for the pumps at Storm King to force water up the mountain, through the tunnel, and into the upper reservoir. In peak periods water would be released to rush down the mountain and power the generators. Three kilowatts of power generated in New York City would be necessary to obtain two kilowatts from the Cornwall installation. When pumping the powerhouse would draw approximately 1,080,000 cubic feet of water per minute from the Hudson, and when generating would discharge up to 1,620,000 cubic feet of water per minute into the river. The installation would have a capacity of 2,000,000 kilowatts, but would be so constructed as to be capable of enlargement to a total of 3,000,000 kilowatts. The water in the upper reservoir may be regarded as the equivalent of stored electric energy; in effect, Consolidated Edison wishes to create a huge storage battery at Cornwall. See Federal Power Commission, National Power Survey 120-21 (1964).

The Storm King project has aroused grave concern among conservationist groups, adversely affected municipalities and various state and federal legislative units and administrative agencies.

To be licensed by the Commission a prospective project must meet the statutory test of being "best adapted to a comprehensive plan for improving or developing a waterway," Federal Power Act §10(a), 16 U.S.C. §803(a). In framing the issue before it, the Federal Power Commission properly noted: "[W]e must compare the Cornwall project with any alternatives that are available. If on this record Con Edison has available an alternative source for meeting its power needs which is better adapted to the development of the Hudson River for all beneficial uses, including scenic beauty, this application should be denied."

If the Commission is properly to discharge its duty in this regard, the record on which it bases its determination must be complete. The petitioners and the public at large have a right to demand this completeness. It is our view, and we find, that the Commission has failed to compile a record which is sufficient to support its decision. The Commission has ignored certain relevant factors and failed to make a thorough study of possible alternatives to the Storm King project. While the courts have no authority to concern themselves with the policies of the Commission, it is their duty to see to it that the Commission's decisions receive that careful consideration which the statute contemplates. . . .

The Storm King project is to be located in an area of unique beauty and major historical significance. The highlands and gorge of the Hudson offer one of the finest pieces of river scenery in the world. The great German traveler Baedeker called it "finer than the Rhine." Petitioners' contention that the Commission must take these factors into consideration in evaluating the Storm King project is justified by the history of the Federal Power Act. . . .

Section 10(a) of the Federal Power Act, 16 U.S.C. §803(a), reads:

§803. Conditions of license generally.

All licenses issued under sections 792, 793, 795-818, and 820-823 of this title shall be on the following conditions: . . .

(a) That the project adopted . . . shall be such as in the judgment of the Commission will be best adapted to a comprehensive plan for improving or developing a waterway or waterways for the use or benefit of interstate or foreign commerce, for the improvement and utilization of water-power development, and for other beneficial public uses, including recreational purposes; and if necessary in order to secure such plan the commission shall have au-

thority to require the modification of any project and of the plans and specifications of the project works before approval.

"Recreational purposes" are expressly included among the beneficial public
uses to which the statute refers. The phrase undoubtedly encompasses the conservation of natural resources, the maintenance of natural beauty, and the preservation
of historic sites. . . . All of these "beneficial uses," the Supreme Court has observed,
"while unregulated, might well be contradictory rather than harmonious." Federal
Power Comm. v. Union Electric Co., 381 U.S. 90, 98 (1965). . . . In licensing a
project, it is the duty of the Federal Power Commission properly to weigh each
factor. . . .

[The court concluded that petitoners had standing to secure judicial review of
the Commission's decision. The issue of standing to secure judicial review of administrative action is examined in Chapters 9 and 10 infra.]

The Federal Power Act §313(b), 16 U.S.C. §825l(b), reads in part:

> (b) If any party shall apply to the court for leave to adduce additional
> evidence, and shall show to the satisfaction of the court that such additional
> evidence is material and that there were reasonable grounds for failure to
> adduce such evidence in the proceedings before the Commission, the court
> may order such additional evidence to be taken before the Commission and
> to be adduced upon the hearing in such manner and upon such terms and
> conditions as to the court may seem proper.

The Commission in its opinion recognized that in connection with granting a
license to Consolidated Edison it "must compare the Cornwall project with any
alternatives that are available." There is no doubt that the Commission is under a
statutory duty to give full consideration to alternative plans. . . .

In the present case, the Commission heard oral argument on November 17,
1964, on the various exceptions to the Examiner's report. On January 7, 1965 the
testimony of Mr. Alexander Lurkis, as to the feasibility of an alternative to the
project, the use of gas turbines, was offered to the Commission by Hilltop Cooperative of Queens, a taxpayer and consumer group. The petition to intervene and
present this new evidence was rejected on January 13, 1965 as not "timely." It was
more than two months after the offer of this testimony, on March 9, 1965, that the
Commission issued a license to Consolidated Edison. When Mr. Lurkis's testimony
was subsequently reoffered by the petitioners on April 8, 1965, it was rejected because it represented "at best" a "disagreement between experts." On the other hand,
we have found in the record no meaningful evidence which contradicts the proffered
testimony supporting the gas turbine alternative.

Mr. Lurkis is a consulting engineer of thirty-nine years experience. He has
served as Chief Engineer of the New York City Bureau of Gas and Electric, in
charge of a staff of 400, and as Senior Engineer of the New York City Transit
Authority, where he supervised the design and construction of power plants. The
New York Joint Legislative Committee on Natural Resources, after holding hear-

ings on the Storm King project on November 19 and 20, 1964, summarized Mr. Lurkis's testimony as follows:

> Mr. Alexander Lurkis . . . presented a detailed proposal for using gas turbines. This, he claimed, would meet the alleged peaking need of Con Ed and result in a saving for its customers of $132,000,000. The Committee has learned that similar gas turbine installations are now in use or proposed for use by a number of progressive electric utilities throughout the nation. In addition to meeting the alleged peak power needs and saving money for the ratepayer, the gas turbines proposed by Mr. Lurkis would have the following advantages:
>
> (1) Permit the company greater flexibility in meeting the power needs of its service area. Admittedly, technological developments in power production are changing and improving this field at such a rapid rate that it may well be entirely revolutionized in 10 to 15 years. There are obvious advantages in the gas turbine installations. Small installations can be added as needed to meet demand. This, in contrast to a single, giant, permanent installation such as Con Ed proposes at Storm King Mountain, which would tie the technology and investment of one company to a method of power production that might be obsolete in a few years.
>
> (2) Keep the power production facilities within New York City. This would not only avoid the desecration of the Hudson Gorge and Highlands, but also, would eliminate the great swathe of destruction down through Putnam and Westchester Counties and their beautiful suburban communities. [Preliminary Report at 6.] . . .

Aside from self-serving general statements by officials of Consolidated Edison, the only testimony in the record bearing on the gas turbine alternative was offered by Ellery R. Fosdick. Fosdick's hastily prepared presentation considered turbines driven by steam and liquid fuel as well as gas; his direct testimony occupied less than ten pages of the record. Fosdick's testimony was too scanty to meet the requirement of a full consideration of alternatives. Indeed, under the circumstances, we must conclude that there was no significant attempt to develop evidence as to the gas turbine alternative; at least, there is no such evidence in the record.

The Commission argues that petitioners made "no attempt to secure additional testimony." Yet the record indicates that more than two months before the license was granted the Commission summarily rejected the offer of Mr. Lurkis's testimony. . . .

Especially in a case of this type, where public interest and concern is so great, the Commission's refusal to receive the Lurkis testimony, as well as proffered information on fish protection devices and underground transmission facilities, exhibits a disregard of the statute and of judicial mandates instructing the Commission to probe all feasible alternatives. Michigan Consolidated Gas Co. v. Federal Power Comm., 108 U.S. App. D.C. 409, 283 F.2d 204, 224, 226, *cert. denied*, 364 U.S. 913 . . . (1960); City of Pittsburgh v. Federal Power Comm., 99 U.S. App. D.C. 113, 237 F.2d 741 (1956).

The Federal Power Commission argues that having intervened "petitioners cannot impose an affirmative burden on the Commission." But, as we have pointed out, Congress gave the Federal Power Commission a specific planning responsibility. See Federal Power Act §10(a), 16 U.S.C. §803(a). The totality of a project's immediate and long-range effects, and not merely the engineering and navigation aspects, are to be considered in a licensing proceeding. As Commissioner Ross said in his dissent:

> I do feel the public is entitled to know on the record that no stone has been left unturned. How much better it would be if the public is clearly advised under oath and cross examination that there truly is no alternative? The thread running through this case has been that the applicant is entitled to a license upon making a prima facie case. My own personal regulatory philosophy compels me to reject this approach. This Commission of its own motion, should always seek to insure that a full and adequate record is presented to it. A regulatory commission can insure continuing confidence in its decisions only when it has used its staff and its own expertise in manner not possible for the uninformed and poorly financed public. With our intimate knowledge of other systems and to a lesser extent of their plans, it should be possible to resolve all doubts as to alternative sources. This may have been done but the record doesn't speak. Let it do so.

In this case, as in many others, the Commission has claimed to be the representative of the public interest. This role does not permit it to act as an umpire blandly calling balls and strikes for adversaries appearing before it; the right of the public must receive active and affirmative protection at the hands of the Commission.

This court cannot and should not attempt to substitute its judgment for that of the Commission. But we must decide whether the Commission has correctly discharged its duties, including the proper fulfillment of its planning function in deciding that the "licensing of the project would be in the overall public interest." The Commission must see to it that the record is complete. The Commission has an affirmative duty to inquire into and consider all relevant facts. . . .

In addition to the Commission's failure to receive or develop evidence concerning the gas turbine alternative, there are other instances where the Commission should have acted affirmatively in order to make a complete record.

The Commission neither investigated the use of interconnected power as a possible alternative to the Storm King project, nor required Consolidated Edison to supply such information. . . .

In its March 9 opinion the Commission postponed a decision on the transmission route to be chosen until the May 1965 hearings were completed. Inquiry into the cost of putting lines underground was precluded because the May hearings were limited to the question of overhead transmission routes. The petitioners' April 26, 1965 motion to enlarge the scope of the May hearing was denied. The Commission insisted that the question of underground costs had been "extensively considered." We find almost nothing in the record to support this statement. . . .

Consolidated Edison witnesses testified that the Storm King project would result in annual savings of $12,000,000 over a steam plant of equivalent capacity.

Given these savings, the Commission should at least have inquired into the capital and annual cost of running segments of the transmission line underground in those areas where the overhead structures would cause the most serious scenic damage. We find no indication that the Commission seriously weighed the aesthetic advantages of underground transmission lines against the economic disadvantages.

At the time of its original hearings, there was sufficient evidence before the Commission concerning the danger to fish to warrant further inquiry....

On remand, the Commission should take the whole fisheries question into consideration before deciding whether the Storm King project is to be licensed.

The Commission should reexamine all questions on which we have found the record insufficient and all related matters. The Commission's renewed proceedings must include as a basic concern the preservation of natural beauty and of national historic shrines, keeping in mind that, in our affluent society, the cost of a project is only one of several factors to be considered. The record as it comes to us fails markedly to make out a case for the Storm King project on, among other matters, costs, public convenience and necessity, and absence of reasonable alternatives. Of course, the Commission should make every effort to expedite the new proceedings.

Petitioners' application, pursuant to Federal Power Act §313(b), 16 U.S.C. §825l(b), to adduce additional evidence concerning alternatives to the Storm King project and the cost and practicality of underground transmission facilities is granted.

The licensing order of March 9 and the two orders of May 6 are set aside, and the case remanded for further proceedings.

Questions on Scenic Hudson I

1. Why didn't the court simply set aside the agency's decision as arbitrary and capricious on the ground that the environmental harms which the project would cause outweighed the benefits of the project, particularly when alternative sources of electricity are considered?

2. What is the source of the court's authority to remand the case for more complete evidentiary development and consideration of alternative power sources and environmental impacts?

3. Are *Scenic Hudson* and Hampton v. Mow Sun Wong, supra p. 268, consistent? *Scenic Hudson* requires detailed consideration by the Commission of factors, such as environmental impacts, that are not a central part of the agency's mission or comparative expertise. *Hampton,* on the other hand, indicates that discretionary choices by an agency may not be sustained on the basis of factors that are not its prime or proper responsibility. Can the two decisions be reconciled? [95] If not, which is sounder?

95. Suppose, for example, that the Commission in *Scenic Hudson* had refused to approve the project because of its adverse environmental impacts. Would *Hampton* require a reviewing court to reverse? Cf. NAACP v. FPC, 425 U.S. 662 (1976), rejecting claims that the "public interest, convenience and necessity" standard in the Federal Power Act for regulation of certain power-generating and transmission activities authorizes the FPC to regulate racial practices in hiring by firms engaged in such activities.

4. Why shouldn't the Commission have been permitted to reject the gas turbine alternative on the basis of its specialized experience rather than reopening lengthy trial-type proceedings on the basis of a proposed alternative submitted only after the original hearings had closed? Is the "hard look" approach consistent with the spirit of the "substantial evidence" standard of review of agency fact-finding?

5. Should the "hard look" or "adequate consideration" standard of review be applied to all agency decisions? Only to those involving complex technical issues? Only to those threatening "preferred" or "underrepresented" values? [96]

d. Problems in Implementing the "Hard Look" or "Adequate Consideration" Standard

How do reviewing courts determine whether an agency has taken a "hard look" or given an "adequate consideration" to alternative policy choices and to evidence, analysis, and values relevant to its exercise of discretion? In *Scenic Hudson (I) the* court found that the Commission had failed to develop an adequate record or to give a sufficient decisional explanation with respect to the gas turbine alternative and certain environmental impacts. But what if the agency does develop a comprehensive record and fully discusses relevant considerations in its opinion? Will the court also give close scrutiny to the merits of the justifications offered by the agency for choosing the alternative over others? Consider the following decision.

Scenic Hudson Preservation Conf. v. FPC (II)

453 F.2d 463 (2d Cir. 1971),
rehearing en banc denied by equally divided court, id. at 494,
cert. denied, 407 U.S. 926 (1972)

HAYS, Circuit Judge:

By Opinion No. 584, dated August 19, 1970, the Federal Power Commission granted a license to Consolidated Edison Company of New York, Inc., to construct, operate, and maintain a pumped storage project along the western shore of the Hudson River at Cornwall, New York. Eight parties[97] have filed petitions pursuant

96. For example, would you agree with Chief Judge Bazelon's assertion in Environmental Defense Fund, Inc. v. Ruckleshaus, 439 F.2d 584, 598 (D.C. Cir. 1971), that "fundamental personal interests in life, health and liberty" have "a special claim to judicial protection, in comparison with the economic interests at stake in a ratemaking or licensing proceeding"?

97. All of the petitioners except Palisades Interstate Park Commission object to the licensing order of the Federal Power Commission in toto. The Palisades Interstate Park Commission opposes only the site 2 alternative which calls for the location of the powerhouse within Palisades Interstate Park. The objection of petitioner City of New York is based on the aqueduct and air pollution question alone. The Izaak Walton League of America rests its objection primarily on the fisheries question and other environmental factors. All other petitioners raise virtually all the issues discussed in this opinion. Intervenor Consolidated Edison Company of New York, Inc., supports the Commission's order, as does intervenor Town of Cornwall.

to Section 313(b) of the Federal Power Act, 16 U.S.C. §185*l*(b) (1964) seeking to set aside this order on various grounds. The issues raised by these petitions are both complex and important, involving, as they do, the conflict between the needs of a highly technological society and the increased awareness of environmental considerations.

The opinion and order of the Federal Power Commission presented here for review follow by five years the earlier remand by this court in Scenic Hudson Preservation Conference v. Federal Power Commission, 354 F.2d 608 [Scenic Hudson I]. . . . In the intervening period extensive hearings have been held, two decisions have been rendered by a Hearing Examiner and the Commission has issued its own opinion.

The new proceedings have produced a project that is different in some ways from the project that was before this court in 1965.

The functional elements of the project remain the same. It is still to be the largest pumped storage plant in the world and its principal function, to provide energy for peak load periods, is unchanged. The proposed location is the same as that previously proposed . . .

. . . However, unlike the project presented in 1965, which provided for a powerhouse that was 80 percent underground, the powerhouse now licensed by the Commission is to be entirely underground. . . .

. . . Eight discharge tunnels from the reversible pump-turbine and motor generation units would convey water between each turbine and an open tailrace leading to the river. The tailrace with abutments at both ends would run 685 feet along the river. A fish protective device is to be located in front of the tailrace intake.

The third major facet of the project relates to transmission facilities. Submarine cable installations and spare pipes would transmit the energy generated in the powerhouse under the Hudson River and would continue underground on the east side of the river for approximately 1.6 miles to a point out of sight of the river. At this point overhead transmission would commence and would continue for approximately 9.2 miles through Putnam County to Con Edison's existing Pleasant Valley-Millwood-Sprain Brook transmission right of way. Changes have been made in the proposed route and the towns of Cortlandt, Putnam Valley and Yorktown, which challenged the route before this court in 1965, no longer do so. . . .

A visitor's information center and picnic and parking facilities, proposed in the original project for the powerhouse site, have been eliminated. In their place, a 57 acre, mile-long park is to be constructed along the riverfront. Additional recreational facilities are to be provided at a 36 acre scenic overlook inland from the project with access from the existing State Highway 9-W. . . .

The petitions in this case are occasioned by the "grave concern" aroused among conservationist groups by the Storm King project. Scenic Hudson, supra, at 612. The petitions allege lack of compliance with the terms of our earlier remand, absence of substantial evidence to support the Commission's findings, and failure to comply with statutory mandates. We find, however, that the Commission has fully complied with our earlier mandate and with the applicable statutes and that its findings are supported by substantial evidence. In view of the extensive powers delegated to the Commission and the limited scope of review entrusted to this court, it is our duty to deny the petitions. . . .

In the Federal Power Act Congress granted the Commission "sweeping authority and a specific planning responsibility." The Act "was the outgrowth of a widely supported effort on the part of conservationists to secure the enactment of a complete scheme of national regulation which would promote the comprehensive development of the nation's water resources." *Scenic Hudson*, supra, at 613 and authorities cited there.

The scope of review of the Commission's exercise of its authority and responsibility is narrowly limited. The Act, §313(b), provides that "[t]he finding of the Commission as to the facts, if supported by substantial evidence, shall be conclusive." 16 U.S.C. §825*l*(b). In assessing the factual contentions raised in the petitions, this court's authority "is essentially narrow and circumscribed." Permian Basin Area Rate Cases, 390 U.S. 747, 766 (1968). . . . The licensing of projects such as the Storm King plant and the evaluation of their environmental impact has been entrusted to "the informed judgment of the Commission, and not to the preferences of reviewing courts." Id. at 767 . . .

Petitioners would have us reject these familiar principles because, they argue, different standards ought to prevail with respect to issues arising in an environmental context. There is an effort to find a basis for this position in our earlier remand in *Scenic Hudson* and in cases which have taken a similar approach. See e.g., Citizens to Preserve Overton Park, Inc. v. Volpe. . . .

To read these cases as sanctioning a new standard of judicial review for findings on matters of environmental policy is to misconstrue both the holdings in the cases and the nature of our remand in *Scenic Hudson*. An element common to all these cases was the failure of an agency or other governmental authority to give adequate consideration to the environmental factors in the situations with which they were presented. In Citizens to Preserve Overton Park, Inc. v. Volpe, supra, 401 U.S. at 416, . . . for example, the Court remanded the case to the district court to determine whether the Secretary of Transportation's decision "was based on a consideration of the relevant factors." The Court pointed out that "[a]lthough this inquiry into the facts is to be searching and careful, the ultimate standard of review is a narrow one. The court is not empowered to substitute its judgment for that of the agency." Id. . . .

In our opinion in *Scenic Hudson*, supra, remanding the 1965 orders of the Commission, we were careful to make it clear that we were raising no question of change in the basic standard of administrative review and that the purpose of our remand was only to require the proper performance of its functions by the Commission. We said: "While the courts have no authority to concern themselves with the policies of the Commission, it is their duty to see to it that the Commission's decisions receive that careful consideration which the statute contemplates." Id. at 612 of 354 F.2d. . . . "This court cannot and should not attempt to substitute its judgment for that of the Commission. But we must decide whether the Commission has correctly discharged its duties. . . . The Commission must see to it that the record is complete." Id. at 620.

Where the Commission has considered all relevant factors, and where the challenged findings, based on such full consideration, are supported by substantial evidence, we will not allow our personal views as to the desirability of the result reached by the Commission to influence us in our decision. We now turn therefore to an examination of whether our remand has been complied with, where there is substantial evidence to support the Commission's decisions on the issues remanded and other challenged issues, and whether the Commission has complied with all applicable statutory requirements. . . .

The proceedings on remand involved 100 hearing days, the testimony of some sixty expert witnesses, and the introduction of 675 exhibits. The record comprises more than 19,000 pages. Both the Hearing Examiner and the Commissioners arranged with the parties to visit the proposed site and the surrounding area before rendering their decisions.

On August 19, 1970, the Commission issued its decision. In its opinion the Commission reviewed the power needs of the area served by Con Ed and considered possible alternatives to the Storm King project in terms of reliability, cost, air and noise pollution, and overall environmental impact. Concluding that there was no satisfactory alternative, the Commission evaluated the environmental effects of the project itself. It held that the scenic impact would be minimal, that no historic site would be adversely affected, that the fish would be adequately protected and that the proposed park and scenic overlook would enhance recreational facilities. The Commission found that further undergrounding of transmission lines would result in unreliability in the delivery of power and would be too costly. The Commission determined that construction of the project would entail no appreciable hazard to the Aqueduct.

We find that the proceedings of the Commission and its report meet the objections upon the basis of which we remanded the earlier determination. Examination of the Commission's conclusions and the evidence on which the conclusions are based establishes that the Commission has complied with our instructions and that the evidence supporting the Commission's conclusions amply meets the statutory requirement of substantiality.

[The court then considered the Commission's opinion and the proceedings in detail, finding that there was an adequate consideration of alternatives and that the Commission's findings were support by substantial evidence.]

We do not consider that the five years of additional investigation which followed our remand were spent in vain. The petitioners performed a valuable service in that earlier case, and later before the Commission. By reason of their efforts the Commission has reevaluated the entire Cornwall project. The modifications in the project reflect a heightened awareness of the conflict between utilitarian and aesthetic needs. Whether the project as it now stands represents a perfect balance of these needs is not for this court to decide. Since the Commission has fully performed the duties and responsibilities imposed upon it, it is our obligation to deny the petitions in all respects.

[Judge OAKES dissented and would have set aside the Commission's order on the grounds (1) that the FPC had failed adequately to consider the threat posed by the project to underground aqueducts supplying water to New York City from the Catskill Aqueduct; (2) that the FPC failed adequately to consider the effects on New York City of the project, which will require 1.4 KWH of pumping energy to be generated during off-peak hours by existing fossil fuel electrical generating systems in New York City in order to furnish 1 KWH of electrical energy from the project during peak hours; (3) that the FPC's findings with respect to environmental impact were insufficient to satisfy the requirements of the National Environmental Policy Act.]

The opinions of the majority and of Judge Oakes are well worth reviewing in their entirety.

The Storm King pumped storage project was subsequently the subject of additional litigation challenging the project's impact on fish in the Hudson. See Hudson River Fisherman's Association v. FPC, 498 F.2d 827 (2d Cir. 1974); and prohibiting the dumping of rock and other fill material in the Hudson without a federal permit, see Scenic Hudson Preserv. Conf. v. Callaway, 499 F.2d 127 (2d Cir. 1974). Consolidated Edison eventually abandoned the project because of mounting costs, a deterioration in Consolidated Edison's financial position, and changing power needs. For an account of the *Scenic Hudson* litigation, which portrays it as a case of litigious obstructionism by wealthy environmentalists, see Tucker, Environmentalism and the Leisure Class, Harper's, Dec. 1977, at 49.

Questions on Scenic Hudson II

1. What was accomplished by the five years of delay and additional proceedings following *Scenic Hudson I*? Did it result in "better" Commission decision-making? [98] If so, at what cost?

2. Unless reviewing courts are prepared to review critically the wisdom of the agency's choice, does the "adequate consideration" or "hard look" requirement accomplish anything beyond requiring agencies to develop voluminous records and write exhaustively long opinions? [99] Or will close scrutiny of the merits of discretionary agency choices inevitably invite a "court to substitute its judgment for that of the agency"? Would that be undesirable?

Note on Ethyl Corp. v. EPA

How competent are the courts to apply a "hard look" or "adequate consideration" approach to review agency policy choices involving complex technical issues?

---

98. Do you suppose that the Commission modifed the project (as described in *Scenic Hudson II*) because it believed, after fuller consideration, that the modifications were wise, or because it believed that concessions to environmentalists and towns were necessary to avoid other adverse court decisions?

99. The value of lengthy records and long opinions is particularly suspect in light of the fact that top agency decisionmakers often do not read the record and generally do not write the agency's opinions. For discussion, see pp. 760-769 infra.

The problem is discussed in concurring opinions filed by Chief Judge Bazelon and Judge Leventhal in Ethyl Corp. v. EPA, 541 F.2d 1 (D.C. Cir. 1976, en banc), *cert. denied*, 426 U.S. 941 (1976). The Environmental Protection Agency (EPA) is authorized to prohibit the use of additives in motor vehicle fuel if it determines that their use "will endanger the public health or welfare." EPA adopted regulations substantially eliminating the use in gasoline of lead additives (designed to increase octane ratings and improve engine efficiency), asserting that clinical tests and epidemiological data on the health of persons exposed to different lead levels in everyday living established that airborne lead attributable to emissions from automobiles using leaded gas was a health hazard. The scientific and medical evidence was voluminous, often conflicting, and hardly clear-cut. A panel of the Court of Appeals initially set aside the EPA's action for want of adequate proof that lead additives caused illness. On reconsideration en banc, the EPA's action was sustained by a 5-to-4 vote. The majority opinion by Judge Wright emphasized that the determination whether the evidence established a health hazard was in considerable degree a "legislative-type policy judgment," but the majority opinion also reviewed the relevant medical and scientific evidence in great detail, as did the principal dissenting opinion. It is worth glancing at the opinions, which total some 118 pages in the Federal Reporter, in order to appreciate the extent and detail of their examination of medical, chemical, statistical and other technical issues.

Concurring in the majority opinion, Chief Judge Bazelon (joined by Judge McGowan) expressed these views:

> I agree with the court's construction of the statute that the Administrator is called upon to make "essentially legislative policy judgments" in assessing risks to public health. But I cannot agree that this automatically relieves the Administrator's decision from the "procedural . . . rigor proper for questions of fact." Quite the contrary, this case strengthens my view that[100] ". . . in cases of great technological complexity, the best way for courts to guard against unreasonable or erroneous administrative decisions is not for the judges themselves to scrutinize the technical merits of each decision. Rather, it is to establish a decision-making process that assures a reasoned decision that can be held up to the scrutiny of the scientific community and the public."

100. Chief Judge Bazelon expressed this view in International Harvester Co. v. Ruckelshaus, 478 F.2d 615, 652 (1973) (Bazelon, C.J., concurring).

[*International Harvester* reviewed the denial by EPA of automobile manufacturers' request for a postponement of deadlines for reducing automobile emissions of all pollutants on the ground that the requisite control technology was not available. The court, in an opinion by Judge Leventhal, set aside EPA's decision and remanded for further proceedings, finding, after an elaborate review of technical evidence and analysis, that EPA had not adequately justified its conclusion that the requisite technology was available. Judge Bazelon concurred in the result, but based his vote on the EPA's failure to utilize additional procedural formalities. He took issue with the majority's detailed review of technical matters:

"Socrates said that wisdom is the recognition of how much one does not know. I may be wise if that is wisdom, because I recognize that I do not know enough about dynamometer extrapolations, deterioration factor adjustments, and the like to decide whether or not the government's approach to these matters was statistically valid. Therein lies my disagreement with the majority." 478 F.2d at 650-651.]

This record provides vivid demonstration of the dangers implicit in the contrary view, ably espoused by Judge Leventhal, which would have judges "steeping" themselves "in technical matters to determine whether the agency 'has exercised a reasoned discretion.'" It is one thing for judges to scrutinize FCC judgments concerning diversification of media ownership to determine if they are rational. But I doubt judges contribute much to improving the quality of the difficult decisions which must be made in highly technical areas when they take it upon themselves to decide, as did the panel in this case, that "in assessing the scientific and medical data the Administrator made clear errors of judgment." The process of making a de novo evaluation of the scientific evidence invites judges of opposing views to make plausible-sounding, but simplistic, judgments of the relative weight to be afforded various pieces of technical data.

... But this is a temptation which, if not resisted, will not only impose severe strains upon the energies and resources of the court but also compound the error of the panel in making legislative policy determinations alien to its true function. . . .

Because substantive review of mathematical and scientific evidence by technically illiterate judges is dangerously unreliable, I continue to believe we will do more to improve administrative decision-making by concentrating our efforts on strengthening administrative procedures. [541 F.2d at 66-67.]

Judge Leventhal replied as follows:

[Judge Bazelon's] opinion — if I read it right — advocates engaging in no substantive review at all, whenever the substantive issues at stake involve technical matters that the judges involved consider beyond their individual technical competence. . . .

Taking the opinion in its fair implication, as a signal to judges to abstain from any substantive review, it is my view that while giving up is the easier course, it is not legitimately open to us at present. In the case of legislative enactments, the sole responsibility of the courts is constitutional due process review. In the case of agency decision-making the courts have an additional responsibility set by Congress. Congress has been willing to delegate its legislative powers broadly — and courts have upheld such delegation[101] — because there is court review to assure that the agency exercises the delegated power within statutory limits, and that it fleshes out objectives within those limits by an administration that is not irrational or discriminatory. Nor is that envisioned judicial role ephemeral, as *Overton Park* makes clear.

Our present system of review assumes judges will acquire whatever technical knowledge is necessary as background for decision of the legal questions. It may be that some judges are not initially equipped for this role, just as they may not be technically equipped initially to decide issues of obviousness and infringement in patent cases. If technical difficulties loom large, Congress may push to establish specialized courts. Thus far, it has proceeded on the assumption that we can both have the important values secured by generalist

101. Amalgamated Meat Cutters & Butcher Workmen v. Connally, 337 F. Supp. 737 (D.D.C. 1971) (3-judge court).

judges and rely on them to acquire whatever technical background is necessary.

The aim of the judges is not to exercise expertise or decide technical questions, but simply to gain sufficient background orientation. Our obligation is not to be jettisoned because our initial technical understanding may be meager when compared to our initial grasp of FCC or freedom of speech questions. When called upon to make de novo decisions, individual judges have had to acquire the learning pertinent to complex technical questions in such fields as economics, science, technology and psychology. Our role is not as demanding when we are engaged in review of agency decisions, where we exercise restraint, and affirm even if we would have decided otherwise so long as the agency's decisionmaking is not irrational or discriminatory.

The substantive review of administrative action is modest, but it cannot be carried out in a vacuum of understanding. Better no judicial review at all than a charade that gives the imprimatur without the substance of judicial confirmation that the agency is not acting unreasonably. Once the presumption of regularity in agency action is challenged with a factual submission, and even to determine whether such a challenge has been made, the agency's record and reasoning has to be looked at. If there is some factual support for the challenge, there must be either evidence or judicial notice available explicating the agency's result, or a remand to supply the gap. . . .

On issues of substantive review, on conformance to statutory standards and requirements of rationality, the judges must act with restraint. Restraint, yes, abdication, no. [541 F.2d at 68-69.] [102]

e. Concluding Note on the Functions of Judicial Review

Administrative choices often involve both technical complexities in the collection and evaluation of data and social value judgments in weighing competing policy choices. Moreover, these two aspects of policy choice are often inextricably intertwined. For example, in the *Ethyl* case, supra, a decisionmaker's assessment of the relevant evidence on the effects of lead additives would likely be strongly influenced by how that decisionmaker views the importance of protecting susceptible individuals from health hazards versus the financial burdens on gasoline companies (and ultimately consumers) of removing lead from gasoline, and by the

---

102. Ed. note: An approach similar to Judge Leventhal's was articulated in Essex Chemical Corp. v. Ruckleshaus, 486 F.2d 427, 434 (D.C. Cir. 1973):

"In subjecting the Administrator's actions to review we apply a test of reasonableness. . . . The judgment of the Administrator is to be weighted against his statutory function and limitations, the record searched to determine if indeed his decisions and reasons therefore are themselves reasoned, and at that point our function terminates. Our 'expertise' is not in setting standards for emission control but in determining if the standards as set are the result of reasoned decisionmaking. Yet, even this limited function requires that we foray into the technical world to the extent necessary to ascertain if the Administrator's decision is reasoned. While we must bow to the acknowledged expertise of the Administrator in matters technical we should not automatically succumb thereto, overwhelmed as it were by the utter 'scientificity' of the expedition."

decisionmaker's attitude toward risk and uncertainty in the face of serious inadequacy in the data.

A court potentially serves both as a "quality control" mechanism in improving the technical soundness of agency decisions, and as a generalist forum for reassessing administrative choices among competing social values. The "output" of government agencies in promoting environmental quality, safer products, and the like, is rarely easily measured. The indirect costs imposed by administrative requirements on private actors are also difficult to ascertain. Moreover, governmental institutions other than courts rarely have a sustained interest in and responsibility for monitoring the quality of particular agency decisions. That responsibility has primarily fallen to the courts, which have traditionally been available as of right to persons adversely affected by administrative action. Having no special competence to assess the ultimate costs and benefits of administrative decisions, courts (in the absence of controlling statutory directives restricting agency choice) have attempted to enhance the quality of agency decisions through controls on the decisionmaking process. As developed in subsequent materials, they have fashioned procedural devices to ensure input of evidence and argument to the agency from relevant affected interests. And through the "adequate consideration" or "hard look" approach to reviewing the agency's decision and the justifications offered for it, they have sought to promote reasoned and careful agency evaluation and choice.

Some agency lawyers, as well as "public interest" and private practice lawyers practicing before agencies believe that the prospect of searching judicial review of the substantive grounds for agency policy choices has had a highly beneficial impact on the quality of agency decisionmaking.[103]

However, there continue to be worrisome doubts about the competence of the courts to perform this "quality control" function when technical issues are involved. Scientists and other specialists are often far less complimentary about the effects of intrusive judicial review than are lawyers. One possible response to these difficulties is to increase the technical competence of reviewing courts. Leventhal,

---

103. See Pedersen, Formal Records and Informal Rulemaking, 85 Yale L.J. 38, 59-60 (1975).

"The effect of detailed factual review by the courts on the portion of the agency subject to it is entirely beneficial. It is a great tonic to a program to discover that even if a regulation can be slipped or wrestled through various layers of internal or external review without significant change, the final and most prestigious reviewing forum of all — a circuit court of appeals — will inquire into the minute details of methodology, data sufficiency and test procedure and will send the regulations back if these are lacking. The effect of such judicial opinions within the agency reaches beyond those who were concerned with the specific regulations reviewed. They serve as a precedent for future rule-writers and give those who care about well-documented and well-reasoned decisionmaking a lever with which to move those who do not.

"I see no way to relieve the courts, ultimately, of a substantial burden of factual inquiry. Courts alone have the time, the influence, and the freedom from ceremonial and 'political' considerations that are necessary to a thorough, dispassionate and effective review of extremely complex and controversial matters."

See also Stewart, The Development of Administrative and Quasi-Constitutional Law in Judicial Review of Environmental Decisionmaking: Lesson from the Clean Air Act, 62 Iowa L. Rev. 713, 731-732, 738-740 (1977).

Environmental Decisionmaking and the Role of the Courts, 122 U. Pa. L. Rev. 509 (1974), surveys some of the alternative means of doing so, including the creation of specialized reviewing courts; the employment by judges of "science clerks" and other technically trained assistants; and the availability of panels of eminent scientists, selected by a body such as the National Academy of Sciences, with whom judges could meet informally to discuss the general background of the scientific issues in a case. Another proposal has been to create a "Science Court" to which reviewing courts could refer scientific issues for decision by a panel of eminent scientists based on the adversary presentations of other scientists favoring one side or another of the issue.[104] What drawbacks do you see in these various alternatives? [105]

Other commentators have focused less on the courts' lack of technical competence to review closely discretionary policy choices than the danger that such review will become a vehicle for judges to impose their subjective values on the administrative process. The "adequate consideration" and "hard look" approaches to review are inevitably elastic, and these critics fear that they would inevitably be selectively applied by judges to uphold agency policies which the judges personally found acceptable and to block or delay policies which the judges disliked. The very fact that the control exerted over policy outcomes through a "hard look" approach would be more veiled and indirect than use of the straightforward "arbitrary and capricious" standard could increase the danger that such control would be based on inarticulate and unexamined judicial policy preferences. These critics would condemn such control by judges over administrative policies both on the ground that it is likely to produce bad outcomes because judges lack relevant experience and information, and on the ground that it is contrary to democratic principles of decisionmaking.[106]

Critics such as Professor Joseph Sax take a still different view. He believes that efforts by courts to impose judicial models of reasoned decisionmaking on bureaucratic agencies have very little effect on substantive policy outcomes, which are largely determined by the agency's mission, the strength of regulated or client interests, and current congressional attitudes.[107] On this view, judicial efforts to ensure a "hard look" by agencies at all relevant options and considerations represent a costly ritual, a time-consuming charade that might as well be abandoned.

Conceivably the function of quality control over discretionary agency policies could be transferred from courts to a nonjudicial body, such as the Congress Office of Technology Assessment or an executive branch authority independent of the agencies subject to review. Consider a proposal to create a Policy Review Board

104. See The Science Court Experiment: An Interim Report, 193 Science, Aug. 20, 1976, at 653.
105. For discussion, see Bazelon, Coping with Technology Through the Legal Process, 62 Cornell L. Rev. 817 (1977).
106. See Breyer, Vermont Yankee and the Courts' Role in the Nuclear Energy Controversy, 91 Harv. L. Rev. 1833 (1978); Wright, The Courts and the Rulemaking Process: The Limits of Judicial Review, 59 Cornell L. Rev. 375 (1974).
107. See Sax, The (Unhappy) Truth About NEPA, 26 Okla. L. Rev. 239 (1973).

in the executive branch that would consist of scientists, economists, engineers, systems analysts, and other specialists, and would review the technical soundness and breadth of major administrative decisions.[108] Such a body could bring technically informed judgments to bear in scrutinizing administrative choices. An alternative model is provided by Continental systems which rely on tribunals (such as the French *Conseil d'Etat* or the Italian *Cosiglio di Stato*) located within the administrative branch and composed of senior civil servants, to exercise a supervisory, "quality control" function.

Questions: What advantages and drawbacks would you foresee in the Continental approach? Why is the United States unique in relying so heavily on the general-purpose judiciary to control administrative officials?

108. See B. Ackerman et al., The Uncertain Search for Environmental Quality 147-161 (1974).

Judicial Requirements of Clarity and Consistency

A. Requiring Agencies to Narrow Their Discretion Through Adoption of Specific Rules

Boyce Motor Lines, Inc. v. United States

342 U.S. 337 (1952)

Mr. Justice CLARK delivered the opinion of the Court.

The petitioner is charged with the violation of a regulation promulgated by the Interstate Commerce Commission under 18 U.S.C. §835.[1] The Regulation provides:

"Drivers of motor vehicles transporting any explosive, inflammable liquid, inflammable compressed gas, or poisonous gas shall avoid, so far as practicable, and, where feasible, by prearrangement of routes, driving into or through congested thoroughfares, places where crowds are assembled, street car tracks, tunnels, viaducts, and dangerous crossings."

The statute directs that "[w]hoever knowingly violates" the Regulation shall be subject to fine or imprisonment or both.

The indictment, in counts 1, 3, and 5, charges that petitioner on three separate occasions sent one of its trucks carrying carbon bisulphide, a dangerous and in-

---

1. 18 U.S.C. §835:

"The Interstate Commerce Commission shall formulate regulations for the safe transportation within the limits of the jurisdiction of the United States of explosives and other dangerous articles, including flammable liquids, flammable solids, oxidizing materials, corrosive liquids, compressed gases, and poisonous substances, which shall be binding upon all common carriers engaged in interstate or foreign commerce which transport explosives or other dangerous articles by land, and upon all shippers making shipments of explosives or other dangerous articles via any common carrier engaged in interstate or foreign commerce by land or water.

"Such regulations shall be in accord with the best-known practicable means for securing safety in transit, covering the packing, marking, loading, handling while in transit, and the precautions necessary to determine whether the material when offered is in proper condition to transport."

flammable liquid, through the Holland Tunnel, a congested thoroughfare. . . . On the third of these trips the load of carbon bisulphide exploded in the tunnel and about sixty persons were injured. The indictment further states that "there were other available and more practicable routes for the transportation of said shipment, and . . . the [petitioner] well knew that the transportation of the shipment of carbon bisulphide . . . into the . . . Holland Tunnel was in violation of the regulations promulgated . . . by the Interstate Commerce Commission. . . ." There is no allegation as to the feasibility of prearrangement of routes, and petitioner is not charged with any omission in that respect.

The District Court dismissed those counts of the indictment which were based upon the Regulation in question, holding it to be invalid on the ground that the words "so far as practicable, and, where feasible" are "so vague and indefinite as to make the standard of guilt conjectural." 90 F. Supp. 996, 998. The Court of Appeals for the Third Circuit reversed, holding that the Regulation, interpreted in conjunction with the statute, establishes a reasonably certain standard of conduct. 188 F.2d 889. . . .

A criminal statute must be sufficiently definite to give notice of the required conduct to one who would avoid its penalties, and to guide the judge in its application and the lawyer in defending one charged with its violation. But few words possess the precision of mathematical symbols, most statutes must deal with untold and unforeseen variations in factual situations, and the practical necessities of discharging the business of government inevitably limit the specificity with which legislators can spell out prohibitions. Consequently, no more than a reasonable degree of certainty can be demanded. Nor is it unfair to require that one who deliberately goes perilously close to an area of proscribed conduct shall take the risk that he may cross the line.

In Sproles v. Binford, 286 U.S. 374 (1932), these principles were applied in upholding words in a criminal statute similar to those now before us. Chief Justice Hughes, speaking for a unanimous court, there said:

" 'Shortest practicable route' is not an expression too vague to be understood. The requirement of reasonable certainty does not preclude the use of ordinary terms to express ideas which find adequate interpretation in common usage and understanding. . . . The use of common experience as a glossary is necessary to meet the practical demands of legislation."

The Regulation challenged here is the product of a long history of regulation of the transportation of explosives and inflammables. Congress recognized the need for protecting the public against the hazards involved in transporting explosives as early as 1866. The inadequacy of the legislation then enacted led to the passage, in 1908, of the Transportation of Explosives Act, which was later extended to cover inflammables. In accordance with that Act, the Commission in the same year issued regulations applicable to railroads. In 1934 the Commission exercised its authority under the Act to promulgate regulations governing motor trucks, including the Regulation here in question. In 1940 this Regulation was amended to substantially its present terminology. That terminology was adopted only after more than three years of study and a number of drafts. The trucking industry participated extensively in this process, making suggestions relating to drafts submitted to carriers and their organizations, and taking part in several hearings. The Regulation's history indicates the careful consideration which was given to the difficulties involved in framing a regulation which would deal practically with this aspect of the problem presented by the necessary transportation of dangerous explosives on the highways.

The statute punishes only those who knowingly violate the Regulation. This requirement of the presence of culpable intent as a necessary element of the offense does much to destroy any force in the argument that application of the Regulation would be so unfair that it must be held invalid. That is evident from a consideration of the effect of the requirement in this case. To sustain a conviction, the Government not only must prove that petitioner could have taken another route which was both commercially practicable and appreciably safer (in its avoidance of crowded thoroughfares, etc.) than the one it did follow. It must also be shown that petitioner knew that there was such a practicable, safer route and yet deliberately took the more dangerous route through the tunnel, or that petitioner willfully neglected to exercise its duty under the Regulation to inquire into the availability of such an alternative route.

In an effort to give point to its argument, petitioner asserts that there was no practicable route its trucks might have followed which did not pass through places they were required to avoid. If it is true that in the congestion surrounding the lower Hudson there was no practicable way of crossing the River which would have avoided such points of danger to a substantially greater extent than the route taken, then petitioner has not violated the Regulation. But that is plainly a matter for proof at the trial. We are not so conversant with all the routes in that area that we may, with no facts in the record before us, assume the allegations of the indictment to be false. We will not thus distort the judicial notice concept to strike down a regulation adopted only after much consultation with those affected and penalizing only those who knowingly violate its prohibition.

We therefore affirm the judgment of the Court of Appeals remanding the cause to the District Court with directions to reinstate counts 1, 3, and 5 of the indictment.

Affirmed.

Mr. Justice JACKSON, with whom Mr. Justice BLACK and Mr. Justice FRANKFURTER join, dissenting.

Congress apparently found the comprehensive regulation needed for the transportation of explosives and inflammables too intricate and detailed for its own processes. It delegated the task of framing regulations to the Interstate Commerce Commission and made a knowing violation of them criminal. Where the federal crime-making power is delegated to such a body, we are justified in requiring considerable precision in its exercise. Kraus & Bros. v. United States, 327 U.S. 614, 621-622.

This regulation does not prohibit carriage of explosives. It presupposes that they must be transported, and, therefore, attempts to lay down a rule for choice of routings. Petitioner was admonished to avoid congested thoroughfares, places where crowds are assembled, streetcar tracks, tunnels, viaducts and dangerous crossings. Nobody suggests that it was possible to avoid all of these in carrying this shipment from its origin to its destination. Nor does the regulation require that all or any of them be avoided except "so far as practicable." I do not disagree with the opinion of Chief Justice Hughes and the Court in Sproles v. Binford, 286 U.S. 374, that, in the context in which it was used, " 'shortest practicable route' is not an expression too vague to be understood." A basic standard was prescribed with definiteness — distance. That ordinarily was to prevail, and, if departed from, the trucker was to be prepared to offer practical justifications.

But the regulation before us contains no such definite standard from which one can start in the calculation of his duty. It leaves all routes equally open and all equally closed. The carrier must choose what is "practicable," not, as in the Sproles case, by weighing distance against obstacles to passage. We may, of course, take judicial notice of geography. Delivery of these goods was impossible except by passing through many congested thoroughfares and either tunnels, viaducts or bridges. An explosion would have been equally dangerous and equally incriminating in any of them. What guidance can be gleaned from this regulation as to how one could with reasonable certainty make a choice of routes that would comply with its requirements?

It is said, however, that definiteness may be achieved on the trial because expert testimony will advise the jury as to what routes are preferable. Defects in that solution are twofold: first, there is no standard by which to direct, confine and test the expert opinion testimony and, second, none to guide a jury in choosing between conflicting expert opinions.

It is further suggested that a defendant is protected against indefiniteness because conviction is authorized only for knowing violations. The argument seems to be that the jury can find that defendant knowingly violated the regulation only if it finds that it knew the meaning of the regulation he was accused of violating. With the exception of Screws v. United States, 325 U.S. 91, which rests on a very particularized basis, the knowledge requisite to knowing violation of a statute is factual knowledge as distinguished from knowledge of the law. I do not suppose the Court intends to suggest that if petitioner knew nothing of the existence of such a regulation its ignorance would constitute a defense.

This regulation prescribes no duty in terms of a degree of care that must be exercised in moving the shipment. The utmost care would not protect defendant from prosecution under it. One can learn his duty from such terms as "reasonable care" or "high degree of care." Of course, one may not be sure whether a trier of fact will find particular conduct to measure up to the requirements of the law, but he may learn at least what he must strive for, and that is more than he can learn from this regulation.

This question is before this Court on the indictment only. In some circumstances we might feel it better that a case should proceed to trial and our decision be reserved until a review of the conviction, if one results. But a trial can give us no better information than we have now as to whether this regulation contains sufficiently definite standards and definition of the crime. An acquittal or disagreement would leave this unworkable, indefinite regulation standing as the only guide in a matter that badly needs intelligible and rather tight regulation. It would remain, at least to some extent, as an incoherent barrier against state enactment or enforcement of local regulations of the same subject. Would it not be in the public interest as well as in the interest of justice to this petitioner to pronounce this vague regulation invalid, so that those who are responsible for the supervision of this dangerous traffic can go about the business of framing a regulation that will specify intelligible standards of conduct?

Notes and Questions

1. The Congressional statute referred to in *Boyce* states that the Interstate Commerce Commission "shall formulate regulations for the safe transport . . . of explosives . . . in accordance with the best known practicable means for securing safety in transit." Knowing violations of the Commission's regulations are criminal offences. Acting under the authority of this statute, the Commission promulgated a regulation that provided that "drivers [of explosives] . . . shall avoid so far as practicable . . . driving into or through congested thoroughfares, places where crowds are assembled, streetcar tracks, tunnels, viaducts and dangerous crossings."

2. Note that the Commission has been authorized to promulgate regulations, the violation of which is made by statute a criminal offense. The constitutionality of this arrangement is well established. See, e.g., United States v. Grimaud, 220 U.S. 506 (1911). However, it is accepted that agencies themselves may not be delegated authority to determine whether or not violation of their regulations is a crime; only the legislature may authorize criminal sanctions.

The majority opinion seems to assume that the only relevant function of specific rules and standards is to give "fair warning" to those subject to sanctions. It is persuaded that specific standards to provide fair warning are not required in this case because the statute requires a finding of "knowing" violation of the regulations before sanctions may be imposed. Does this argument persuade you? Is the regulation sufficiently precise to allow for criminal liability? What specifically must the trucking firm driver "know" in order to be convicted?

3. Why did Congress not lay down a standard of liability itself? Why did it delegate this power to an agency?

4. Did Congress intend the ICC to enact a regulation that does little more than reiterate the language of the statute? What alternative methods of dealing with the dangerous cargo problem were open to the ICC?

5. Does the ICC's regulation represent an unwarranted concession to industry?

6. If the dissent's approach were followed, how would reviewing courts determine whether the standards or regulations adopted by an agency were sufficiently specific?

1. Due Process Requirements That Agencies Formulate Standards

Soglin v. Kauffman

418 F.2d 163 (7th Cir. 1969)

[Plaintiffs, students at the University of Wisconsin and members of Students for a Democratic Society, were charged by defendant University officials with "misconduct" consisting of physical obstruction of University buildings in order to prevent representatives of Dow Chemical Company from conducting job interviews. Defendants instituted disciplinary proceedings to expel plaintiffs, who brought a declaratory judgment action under 28 U.S.C. §1343,[2] contending that "misconduct" is an unduly vague standard and that disciplinary proceedings for "misconduct" therefore violate the due process clause of the Fourteenth Amendment.]

... [D]efendants argue that "misconduct" represents the inherent power of the University to discipline students and that this power may be exercised without the necessity of relying on a specific rule of conduct. This rationale would justify the ad hoc imposition of discipline without reference to any preexisting standards of conduct so long as the objectionable behavior could be called misconduct at some later date. No one disputes the power of the University to protect itself by means of disciplinary action against disruptive students. Power to punish and the rules defining the exercise of that power are not, however, identical. Power alone does not supply the standards needed to determine its application to types of behavior or specific instances of "misconduct." As Professor Fuller has observed: "The first desideratum of a system for subjecting human conduct to the governance of rules is an obvious one: there must be rules." Fuller, Law and Morality, p. 46 (2d printing, 1965).... The use of "misconduct" as a standard in imposing the penalties threatened here must ... fall for vagueness. The inadequacy of the rule is apparent on its face. It contains no clues which could assist a student, an administrator or a reviewing judge in determining whether conduct not transgressing statutes is susceptible to punishment by the University as "'misconduct."

Pursuant to appropriate rule or regulations, the University has the power to maintain order by suspension or expulsion of disruptive students. Requiring that such sanctions be administered in accord with preexisting rules does not place an unwarranted burden upon university administrations. We do not require university codes of conduct to satisfy the same rigorous standards as criminal statutes. We only hold that expulsion and prolonged suspension may not be imposed on students by a university simply on the basis of allegations of "misconduct" without

---

2. 28 U.S.C. §1343(3) provides original jurisdiction in the federal district courts of actions to "redress the deprivation under color of any State law, statute, ordinance, regulation, custom or usage, of any right, privilege or immunity secured by the Constitution of the United States or by any Act of Congress providing for equal rights of citizens or of all persons within the jurisdiction of the United States ..." The substantive correlative of this jurisdictional provision is found in 42 U.S.C. §1983. For a discussion of §1983, see p. 629 infra.

reference to any preexisting rule which supplies an adequate guide. The possibility of the sweeping application of the standard of "misconduct" to protected activities does not comport with the guarantees of the First and Fourteenth Amendments. The desired end must be more narrowly achieved.

[The judgment of the district court ruling that disciplinary proceedings based on a standard of "misconduct" were unconstitutional was affirmed.]

Hornsby v. Allen

326 F.2d 605 (5th Cir. 1964)

Before TUTTLE, Chief Judge, JONES, Circuit Judge, and JOHNSON, District Judge.

TUTTLE, Chief Judge:

Appellant Mrs. Hornsby is an unsuccessful applicant for a license to operate a retail liquor store in Atlanta, Georgia. She brings this action under 28 U.S.C. §1343 to redress an alleged deprivation of civil rights and under 28 U.S.C. §2201 to obtain a declaration of her rights. The Mayor, the City Clerk, and the Aldermen of Atlanta are defendants. In her complaint, Mrs. Hornsby alleges that although she met all the requirements and qualifications, as to moral character of the applicant and proposed location of the store, prescribed for the holder of a retail liquor dealer's license, her application was denied "without a reason therefor" by the Mayor and Board of Aldermen. This action is characterized as "arbitrary, unreasonable, unjust, capricious, discriminatory" and in contravention of the due process and equal protection clauses of the 14th Amendment. The complaint also charges that a system of ward courtesy was followed in the issuance of liquor licenses; under this system licenses allegedly would be granted only upon the approval of one or both of the aldermen of the ward in which the store was to be located. This too is said to constitute a violation of the 14th Amendment.

The defendants' motion to dismiss was granted by the court below on the ground that the complaint only concerned a political question which was not covered by the due process provisions of the 14th Amendment. . . .

Since licensing consists in the determination of factual issues and the application of legal criteria to them — a judicial act — the fundamental requirements of due process are applicable to it. Due process in administrative proceedings of a judicial nature has been said generally to be conformity to fair practices of Anglo-Saxon jurisprudence . . . , which is usually equated with adequate notice and a fair hearing. . . .

We find in this case that Mrs. Hornsby's allegations, if borne out by the evidence, are sufficient to show a violation of her 14th Amendment rights. If her application actually was denied because the delegation from her ward decided, from their own knowledge of the circumstances, that Mrs. Hornsby should not be issued a liquor license, then she was deprived of the hearing which due process requires, since she could not discover the claims of those opposing her and subject their evidence to cross-examination. In addition, Mrs. Hornsby was not afforded an opportunity to know, through reasonable regulations promulgated by the board, of the objective standards which had to be met to obtain a license.

The proper question to be determined upon the hearing of this case in the district court is not whether the plaintiff below is entitled under the law to a liquor license. The determination of whether she should be granted one is a function of the Aldermanic Board. The role of the courts is to ascertain whether the manner in which this determination was or is made accords with constitutional standards of due process and equal protection. We are of the opinion that the complaint alleged sufficient facts to show that the denial of appellant's application for a license did not meet these standards and, since done under color of state statute, constituted a violation of 42 U.S.C. §1983.

It follows that the trial court must entertain the suit and determine the truth of the allegations. If it develops that no ascertainable standards have been established by the Board of Aldermen by which an applicant can intelligently seek to qualify for a license, then the court must enjoin the denial of licenses under the prevailing system and until a legal standard is established and procedural due process provided in the liquor store licensing field.

The judgment is reversed.

[A dissenting opinion by Judge JONES is omitted.]

Holmes v. New York City Housing Authority

398 F.2d 262 (2d Cir. 1968)

Before HAYS, ANDERSON and FEINBERG, Circuit Judges.

ANDERSON, Circuit Judge:

This class action was brought on September 9, 1966 by 31 named plaintiffs on behalf of themselves and all others similarly situated under the Civil Rights Act, 42 U.S.C. §1983, and the Federal Constitution, challenging the procedures employed by the defendant New York City Housing Authority in the admission of tenants to low-rent public housing projects administered by it in New York City. The jurisdiction of the district court is predicated upon 28 U.S.C. §1343(3).

Each year the Authority receives approximately 90,000 applications out of which it is able to select an average of only 10,000 families for admission to its public housing projects. In doing so the Authority gives preference to certain specified classes of candidates, e.g., "site residents," families in "emergency need of housing," "split famiiles," "doubled up and overcrowded families."....

In federal-aided projects the Authority is required to allocate the remaining apartments among non-preferenec candidates in accordance with "an objective scoring system" which is designed to facilitate comparison of the housing conditions of these applicants.... For state-aided projects, however, there is no similar regulation and we assume that this is also the case with local-aided projects. The plaintiffs in this action are all non-preference candidates seeking admission to any of the public housing projects run by the defendant.

In the complaint the named plaintiffs allege that although they have filed with the Authority a total of 51 applications for admission to its housing facilities, 36 in 1965 or earlier, and some as long ago as 1961, none has been advised in writing at any time of his eligibility, or ineligibility, for public housing.

The complaint cites numerous claimed deficiencies in the admissions policies and practices of the Authority. Regulations on admissions (other than those pertaining to income level and residence) are not made available to prospective tenants either by publication or by posting in a conspicuous public place. Applications received by the Authority are not processed chronologically, or in accordance with ascertainable standards, or in any other reasonable and systematic manner. All applications, whether or not considered and acted upon by the Authority, expire automatically at the end of two years. A renewed application is given no credit for time passed, or precedence over a first application of the same date. There is no waiting list or other device by which an applicant can gauge the progress of his case and the Authority refuses to divulge a candidate's status on request. Many applications are never considered by the Authority. If and when a determination of ineligibility is made (on any ground other than excessive income level), however, the candidate is not informed of the Authority's decision, or of the reasons therefor.

The complaint charges that these procedural defects increase the likelihood of favoritism, partiality, and arbitrariness on the part of the Authority, and deprive the plaintiffs of a fair opportunity to petition for admission to public housing, and to obtain review of any action taken by the Authority. The deficiencies are alleged to deprive applicants of due process of law in violation of the Fourteenth Amendment to the Federal Constitution.

Clearly there is sufficient in the complaint to state a claim for relief under §1983 and the due process clause. One charge made against the defendant, which has merit at least in connection with state-aided projects where the Authority has adopted no standards for selection among non-preference candidates, is that it thereby failed to establish the fair and orderly procedure for allocating its scarce supply of housing which due process requires. It hardly need be said that the existence of an absolute and uncontrolled discretion in an agency of government vested with the administration of a vast program, such as public housing, would be an intolerable invitation to abuse. See Hornsby v. Allen, 326 F.2d 605, 609-610 (5 Cir. 1964). For this reason alone due process requires that selections among applicants be made in accordance with "ascertainable standards," id. at 612, and, in cases where many candidates are equally qualified under these standards, that further selections be made in some reasonable manner such as "by lot or on the basis of the chronological order of application." Hornsby v. Allen, 330 F.2d 55, 56 (5 Cir. 1964) (on petition for rehearing). Due process is a flexible concept which would certainly also leave room for the employment of a scheme such as the "objective scoring system" suggested in the resolution adopted by the Authority for federal-aided projects. . . .

[A dissenting opinion by Judge HAYS is omitted.]

Notes and Questions

1. Note that in *Soglin, Hornsby,* and *Holmes* federal courts are reviewing the validity of state administrative action. In cases such as *Boyce,* involving federal agencies, federal courts may find that the administrator's conduct (including the failure to adopt more specific standards) violates the statute creating the agency or the provisions of the APA. (Would any provisions in the APA require the administrative adoption of standards had *Holmes* or *Hornsby* or *Soglin* involved federal agencies?) But where state administrative action is involved, federal courts are bound, under the principle of Erie R.R. v. Tompkins, 304 U.S. 64 (1938), by state court interpretations of state law, including the agency's conformance with state statutes. Unless there is an overriding federal statute governing the action of state officials (such as federal statutory requirements regarding the disposition by states of federal grants-in-aid), the only federal claims normally available for challenging state administrative action are those based on the federal Constitution. Accordingly, challenges to state administrative action in federal court often assume a constitutional form — typically, a claim that state officials transgressed the Due Process Clause of the Fourteenth Amendment and 42 U.S.C. §1983.[3]

2. Why does the Constitution require state agencies (or federal agencies) to develop and adhere to standards when neither criminal sanctions (as in *Boyce*) nor civil sanctions (such as a fine or forfeiture) are involved? *Soglin* is perhaps explicable as involving a form of "punishment" directed at activities with First Amendment overtones. But *Hornsby* and *Holmes* involved government allocation of scarce resources or opportunities. Why does the federal Constitution require that this allocation be accomplished through judicial models of standards and reasoned decision? Are standards required by principles of equal protection? Cf. Yick Wo v. Hopkins, 118 U.S. 356 (1886) (systematic exercise of laundry-licensing authority to discriminate against persons of oriental extraction violates equal protection).

3. Suppose that in *Holmes* and *Hornsby* the state had argued that, in the state's judgment, the key to liquor licensing or allocating scarce public housing tenancies is the character and fitness of the applicant, and that these qualifications can only be ascertained through essentially subjective personal judgments by state administrators? If standards are required, what standards might these agencies adopt?

4. Does it follow from *Soglin* that the prohibition in section 5 of the Federal Trade Commission Act of "unfair methods of competition" is unconstitutional?

---

3. As developed in later materials (see Chapter 7, Parts B & C infra), there has in recent years been a "due process explosion" as federal judges have imposed a variety of formal procedural requirements on state administrators based on due process and §1983. Note that if there is a substantial federal law claim for challenging state action, state law claims may also be presented in federal court under the principle of pendent jurisdiction.

The Fifth Amendment subjects federal officials to due process requirements as well. But in reviewing federal administrative action, federal courts may find a violation of the APA or some other federal statute and avoid the need to reach constitutional issues.

Can *Boyce* be reconciled with *Hornsby* and *Holmes?* Of what relevance is the doctrine against delegation of legislative power? [4]

5. Another potential distinction between *Boyce,* and *Hornsby* and *Holmes,* is offered by Professors Gellhorn and Robinson, Perspectives on Administrative Law, 75 Colum. L. Rev. 771, 792-793 (1975). They argue that procedural requirements — such as agency adoption of specific rules or standards — can only be understood and justified as a means of securing underlying substantive rights. On their view, the *Hornsby* and *Holmes* rulings are based on an implicit underlying right to a fair and evenhanded system for allocation of scarce governmental benefits. They argue that decisions such as *Holmes* are not authority for requiring specific rules in other areas of administration where no substantive entitlement exists. We explore the relation between substantive entitlements and procedural rights in greater detail in Chapter 7.

2. Administrative Formulation of Standards as a Substitute for the Delegation Doctrine

K. Davis, 1 Administrative Law Treatise (2d ed.) (1978)

208-09, 211-12, 213-15

(a) The basic purpose of the traditional non-delegation doctrine is unsatisfactory and should be changed. It should no longer be either to prevent delegation of legislative power or to require meaningful statutory standards. The purpose should be to do what can be done through such a doctrine *to protect private parties against injustice on account of unnecessary and uncontrolled discretionary power.*

Instead of saying that delegations are unlawful or that delegations are unlawful unless accompanied by meaningful standards, the courts should affirmatively assert that delegations are lawful and desirable, as long as the broad legislative purpose is discernible and as long as protections against arbitrary power are provided. Courts should assert that congressional formulation and enactment of the content of the Code of Federal Regulations would mean worse government, not better government, because Congress is and should be geared to major policies and main outlines, and administrators are better qualified to legislate the relative details, often including even major policy determinations. The courts should recognize that

---

4. See Chapter 2 supra. The prevailing view is that the federal doctrine against standardless delegations of legislative power does not apply to the states. See Freund, The Supreme Court and Civil Liberties, 4 Vand. L. Rev. 533, 537 n.31 (1951). But cf. Sweezy v. New Hampshire, 354 U.S. 234 (1957). The holding in cases like *Hornsby* and *Holmes* that due process requires standards for administrative action is to some degree a functional surrogate for the nondelegation doctrine, although it permits standards to be supplied by administrators as well as legislators.

administrative legislation through the superb rulemaking procedure that is rapidly developing usually provides better protection to private interests than congressional enactment of detail.

The change in the basic purpose is essential because the underlying problem is broader than control of delegation; the problem is to provide effective protection against administrative arbitrariness. Solving that problem requires protection not only against delegated power but also against undelegated power, especially the enormous undelegated power of selective and sometimes discriminatory enforcement, an undelegated power which is typically exercised without either statutory or administrative standards, without procedural safeguards prescribed by statutes or by administrative rules or by reviewing courts, and without judicial review.

(b) Safeguards are usually more important than standards, although both may be important. The criterion for determining the validity of a delegation should be the totality of the protection against arbitrariness, not just the one strand having to do with statutory standards.

For instance, a delegation *without standards* of power to make rules in accordance with proper rulemaking procedure and a delegation *without standards* of power to work out policy through case-to-case adjudication based on trial-type hearings should normally be sustained, whenever the general legislative purpose is discernible. The risk of arbitrary or unjust action is much greater from informal discretionary action, but even there the protection from safeguards is likely to be more effective than protection from standards. For instance, if one administrator in exercising discretionary power without hearings used a system of open findings, open reasons, and open precedents, but another who is also acting without hearings never states findings or reasons and never uses precedents as a guide, the delegation to the first administrator is much more deserving of judicial support than the delegation to the second. . . .

(c) The crucial consideration is not what the statute says but what the administrators do. The safeguards that count are the ones the administrators use, not the ones mentioned in the statute. The standards that matter are the ones that guide the administrative determination, not merely the ones stated by the legislative body. The test should accordingly be *administrative* safeguards and standards, not *statutory* safeguards and standards.

The alteration in the nondelegation doctrine in this respect can be a rather small one: The courts should continue their requirement of meaningful standards, except that when the legislative body fails to prescribe the required standards for discretionary action in particular cases, the administrators should be allowed to satisfy the requirement by prescribing them within a reasonable time.

When an administrator is making a discretionary determination affecting a private party, standards which have been adopted through administrative rulemaking are just as effective in confining and guiding the discretionary determination as would be standards stated in the statute. They are not only as effective but in one important aspect they are better. The weakness of a judicial requirement of *statutory* standards is that legislators are often unable or unwilling to supply them. The strength of a judicial requirement of *administrative* standards is that, with the right kind of judicial prodding, the administrators can be expected to supply them. To the extent that the objective is to require standards to guide discretionary determinations in cases affecting particular parties, that objective can be better attained through judicial insistence that administrators create the standards through rule-making than by judicial insistence upon statutory standards. Legislative bodies should clarify their purposes to the extent that they are able and willing to do so, but when they choose to delegate without standards, the courts should uphold the delegation whenever the needed standards to guide particular determinations have been supplied through administrative rules or policy statements. . . .

(d) Another strength in the idea that the courts should require administrative standards whenever statutory standards are inadequate is that the idea opens the way for courts to give more attention to the manner in which administrators confine and structure their discretionary power. The requirement of administrative standards will and should naturally grow into a somewhat larger requirement — that administrators must do what they reasonably can do to develop and to make known the needed confinements of their discretionary power through not only standards but also principles and rules. In other words, the nondelegation doctrine will evolve into a broad system of judicial protection against unnecessary and uncontrolled discretionary power.

When standards are lacking to guide the exercise of discretionary power in individual cases, courts should in appropriate circumstances require administrative rulemaking to provide the standards, the guides, the rules, the limits, and the procedures. The movement during the 1970s toward judicially required administrative rulemaking has been a strong one. . . .

The best tool for the courts to use to accomplish the proper purposes of the nondelegation doctrine probably is judicially required rulemaking.

(e) Shifting the nondelegation doctrine to a judicially-enforced requirement that administrators must do what they reasonably can do to develop and to make known the needed confinements of their discretionary power through standards, principles, and rules, as well as to structure their power through procedural safeguards, will open the way for a judicial requirement that will reach not only delegations of power but also assumptions of undelegated power, including especially the enormous power of selective enforcement.

In broad perspective, the American legal system has become one in which courts usually strive to protect citizens against injustice at the hands of any public officers except enforcement officers. No one has planned the exception. No one would. It is the product of long-term drift. Injustice at the hands of *any* public officer should be subject to judicial correction, whenever the issues are appropriate for judicial determination. This means, more specifically, that injustice from police, prosecutors, regulatory agencies, licensing agencies, and any other administrators in the exercise of initiating and prosecuting powers should be subject to judicial correction.

The ideal of "equal justice under law" can and should be extended to the initiating and prosecuting functions, so as to correct an outstanding flaw in the basic system of American justice.

Notes and Questions

1. Substituting a requirement of administrative standards for the nondelegation doctrine as a means of limiting administrative discretion would avoid serious political confrontations like that provoked by the *Schechter* decision. Courts have traditionally exercised an important role in controlling administrative officials, and requiring administrators to crystallize their discretion in standards would be consonant with judicial traditions of promoting predictability and impartiality in the application of governmental sanctions.

But how much certainty and predictability is either feasible or desirable in the context of administrative action? Recall that one of the reasons for creation of administrative agencies was the perceived need for self-starting, prophylactic initiatives to deal with rapidly changing economic and social problems. To the extent that administrators are charged with management of given sectors of the economy, isn't a business model of decisionmaking more appropriate than a judicial one? Consider also that highly specific rules might invite circumvention and evasion through creation of "loopholes," and that political constraints and disagreements, both within and without the agency, may prevent it from reaching a firm position on controversial issues of policy.

Professor Davis acknowledges the need for flexibility, and asserts that in differing contexts it will be appropriate to develop rules of varying degrees of specificity in order "to locate the optimum degree of structuring in each respect for each discretionary power." [5] But how well equipped are reviewing courts to identify this "optimum" in the face of agency claims in given contexts that specific rules are not feasible or desirable? Consider Professor Davis's proposal in light of the *Boyce* decision, supra. See also Stewart, The Reformation of American Administrative Law, 88 Har. L. Rev. 1667, 1698-1702 (1975), which asserts that Professor Davis's proposal contains many of the drawbacks of the nondelegation doctrine it is designed to replace because it requires courts to second-guess the judgments of "front-line" decisionmakers as to how far it is wise and feasible to develop more specific policies in a given field of government, and whether it is politically possible to achieve agreement on any specific policy.

2. Even if agencies can be forced to adopt more specific rules, will "better" policies emerge? Recall that an important criticism of agency "failure" is that agencies "tilt" their exercise of discretion in favor of well-organized regulated firms or client interests. Justice Harlan asserted that the doctrine against delegation of legislative power serves two basic purposes:

> *First,* it insures that fundamental policy decisions in our society will be made not by an appointed official but by the body immediately responsible to the people. *Second,* it prevents judicial review from becoming merely an exercise at large by providing the courts with some measure against which to judge the official action that has been challenged.[6]

5. K. Davis, Discretionary Justice: A Preliminary Inquiry 99 (1969).
6. Arizona v. California, 373 U.S. 546, 626 (1963) (Harlan, J., dissenting).

Professor Davis's proposal for "structuring" administrative discretion may serve the second goal. Will it make any contribution to the first goal of assuring that the content of government policies is fairly responsive to the citizenry as a whole? See Stewart, supra.

3. The final paragraphs in the Davis excerpt reflect his belief that the principle of structuring discretion by requiring administrators to adopt specific rules or standards should be extended to the exercise of prosecutorial discretion by regulatory agencies and, especially, by criminal prosecutors and the police. This position is elaborated by Professor Davis in his Discretionary Justice (1969), Police Discretion (1975), and Administrative Law in the Seventies (1976), which emphasize the largely uncontrolled discretion exercised by police in deciding to intervene, stop, frisk, interrogate, search, and arrest, and by prosecutors in deciding whether to prosecute, what charges to bring, what plea bargains to accept, whether to oppose release from custody pending trial, and what sentences to recommend. He also criticizes the pervasiveness of unstructured and unreviewed discretion in other sectors of the criminal justice system, including prison administration and parole decisions. Professor Davis asks:

> The American system of administrative law purports to be one in which officers may not exercise governmental power which has not been lawfully delegated to them, and in which the exercise of delegated power is presumed to be judicially reviewable. . . . Why, then, do we assume that we must allow the police to exercise undelegated power which is usually unreviewable? Why do the main principles of administrative law not apply to the police? Why is lawlessness of the police with respect to selective enforcement normal and expected? Is it because those lawyers who are educated in administrative law are uninterested in the police, and because those lawyers who or concerned with the criminal process are generally uneducated in administrative law?
>
> The police are administrators — all 420,000 of them. Their departments are in all respects administrative agencies — all 40,000 of them. The law that controls or fails to control them is clearly administrative law. . . .[7]

Professor Davis's critique of discretion has been matched by rising public dissatisfaction with the criminal justice system and a growing conviction by many commentators and government officials that excessive administrative discretion is an important root of the problem.[8] For a useful review indicating that police discretion is still largely unchecked, but cautioning against excessive reliance on the

---

7. K. Davis, Administrative Law in the Seventies 116 (1976).

8. See, e.g., Amsterdam, Perspectives on the Fourth Amendment, 58 Minn. L. Rev. 349 (1974), which argues that police searches and arrests should be held invalid under the Fourth Amendment unless they are conducted in accordance with reasonably specific rules, promulgated by the legislature or police authorities, that would limit police practices to ensure protection of Fourth Amendment privacy values. Professor Amsterdam believes that this approach would control police practices more effectively than case-by-case application of the exclusionary rules in individual prosecutions; would promote equal treatment of persons subject to arrest or search; and would facilitate public scrutiny and review of police practices and policies.

judiciary to control official discretion, see Vorenberg, Narrowing the Discretion of Criminal Justice Officials, 1976 Duke L. J. 651.

Traditionally, the decisions of prosecutors and administrative authorities whether or not to institute criminal prosecutions or civil actions for enforcement or imposition of liabilities have not been subjected to judicial scrutiny.[9] What might explain this tradition?

Courts have also been traditionally reluctant to review the decisions of regulatory agencies whether to initiate administrative proceedings.[10] But recently, in response to the growing sense of agency "failure," courts have required agencies to justify failures to institute enforcement actions against regulated firms where such failure has been attacked by consumer or environmental groups or racial minorities who are the prime beneficiaries of the regulatory scheme.[11] Increasingly, courts have found that failures to act are unjustified, and have held that agency initiation of enforcement proceedings is mandated by relevant statutes.[12]

Can the courts' willingness to demand explanations and review and limit the prosecutorial discretion exercised by regulatory agencies be reconciled with their continuing refusal to do so with respect to prosecutorial discretion in the criminal justice system?

4. Professor Davis seems to believe that the use of more precise standards will lead to "fairer" decisions. Is this true? How should administrators deal with the need for exceptions and for tempering the rigors of "law" with "equity"?

9. In the criminal context, a third party normally cannot complain of a prosecutor's refusal to proceed against an alleged offender. See Linda R. S. v. Richard D., 410 U.S. 614 (1973) (abandoned wife may not secure judicial review of prosecutor's failure to proceed against husband for nonsupport). A person against whom proceedings are initiated can normally challenge the prosecutor's decision to charge only upon a showing that it was "deliberately based upon an unjustifiable standard such as race, religion, or other arbitrary classification." Oyler v. Boles, 368 U.S. 448 (1962).

10. For example, when an agency commences proceedings against one firm in an industry, challenging its adherence to practices common to the entire industry, courts have stated that the agency's action may be judicially challenged if shown by the target firm to be "plainly arbitrary and capricious"; but the firm has the burden of establishing arbitrary action, and courts normally sustain the agency. See FTC v. Universal-Rundle Corp., 387 U.S. 244 (1967); Moog Industries v. FTC, 355 U.S. 411 (1958). Also, courts have traditionally declined to interfere with administrative decisions not to institute proceedings, except in rare cases where the refusal to proceed was found to violate a controlling statute. For example, the Supreme Court has held that the NLRB cannot refuse to exercise jurisdiction over all cases involving union employees or the hotel industry where the relevant statute provides for limitation by the Board of its jurisdiction over labor relations based solely on the dollar amount of interstate business involved. See Office Employees Intl. Union v. NLRB, 353 U.S. 313 (1957); Hotel Employees Local No. 225 v. Leedom, 358 U.S. 99 (1958).

11. See, e.g., Medical Committee for Human Rights v. SEC, 432 F.2d 659 (D.C. Cir. 1970), vacated as moot, 404 U.S. 403 (proxy regulations); EDF v. Ruckleshaus, 439 F.2d 584 (D.C. Cir. 1971) (regulation of unsafe pesticides).

12. See, e.g., Davis v. Romney, 490 F.2d 1360 (3d Cir. 1974) (FHA enforcement of requirement that federally insured housing meets local code requirements); Adams v. Richardson, 480 F.2d 1159 (D.C. Cir. 1973) (en banc) (HEW enforcement of Civil Rights Act Title VI); Rockbridge v. Lincoln, 449 F.2d 567 (9th Cir. 1971) (Interior Department regulations to protect Indians).

3. Restrictions on Agency Use of Rules to Limit Discretion: Is There a Requirement of Individualized Decision?

Fook Hong Mak v. Immigration and Naturalization Service

435 F.2d 728 (2d Cir. 1970)

FRIENDLY, Circuit Judge:

Petitioner Fook Hong Mak, a fifty year old, married male alien, is a citizen of the Republic of China. In April 1968 he was admitted to the United States without a visa, pursuant to §101(a)(15)(C) and §214 of the Immigration and Nationality Act of 1952 and the Regulations thereunder, 8 C.F.R. §214.2(c)(1), as a nonimmigrant alien "in immediate and continuous transit through the United States." He was on a journey from Hong Kong to South America, in the course of which an eight day lay-over in this country had been authorized. When the INS discovered that he was still here six months later, it began a deportation proceeding. Conceding deportability, Fook Hong Mak sought two forms of discretionary relief — adjustment of status to that of an alien lawfully admitted for permanent residence under §245 or, failing that, voluntary departure under §244(e).

Section 245, so far as here material, reads as follows:

> (a) The status of an alien, other than an alien crewman, who was inspected and admitted or paroled into the United States may be adjusted by the Attorney General, in his discretion and under such regulations as he may prescribe, to that of an alien lawfully admitted for permanent residence if (1) the alien makes an application for such adjustment, (2) the alien is eligible to receive an immigrant visa and is admissible to the United States for permanent residence, and (3) an immigrant visa is available to him at the time his application is approved. . . .
>
> (c) the provisions of this section shall not be applicable to any alien who is a native of any country of the Western Hemisphere or of any adjacent island named in Section 101(b)(5).

Acting under the authority specifically delegated to him by the Immigration and Nationality Act, the Attorney General adopted a regulation, 8 C.F.R. §214.2(c), which in its present form provides:

> §214.2 Special requirements for admission, extension, and maintenance of status.
>
> The general requirements in §214.1 are modified for the following nonimmigrant classes: . . .
>
> (c) Transits — (1) Without visas. An applicant for admission under the transit without visa privilege must establish that he is admissible under the immigration laws; that he has confirmed and onward reservations to at least the next country beyond the United States, and that his departure from the United States will be accomplished within ten calendar days after his

arrival.... The privilege of transit without a visa may be authorized only under the conditions that the carrier, without the prior consent of the Service, will not refund the ticket which was presented to the Service as evidence of the alien's confirmed and onward reservation, *that the alien will not apply for extension of temporary stay or for adjustment of status under Section 245 of the Act,* and that at all times he is not aboard an aircraft which is in flight through the United States he shall be in the custody directed by the district director.[13] (Emphasis supplied.)

Conceding that Fook Hong Mak met the three numbered requirements of §245(a) and that the presence in the United States of his wife and children, at least one of whom is a citizen, made even temporary departure somewhat of a hardship, the Board of Immigration Appeals, affirming the Special Inquiry Officer, found that the italicized condition of the Regulation precluded consideration of his application for such relief. It granted the alternative request for voluntary departure, which will enable the petitioner to apply from abroad for entry as an immigrant. Fook Hong Mak says that whether or not the Board would have been justified in denying his application for adjustment of status on the merits, the Attorney General's self-imposed restriction on the consideration of it is unlawful.

We are unable to understand why there should be any general principle forbidding an administrator, vested with discretionary power, to determine by appropriate rulemaking that he will not use it in favor of a particular class on a case-by-case basis, if his determination is founded on considerations rationally related to the statute he is administering. The legislature's grant of discretion to accord a privilege does not imply a mandate that this must inevitably be done by examining each case rather than by identifying groups. The administrator also exercises the discretion accorded him when, after appropriate deliberation, he determines certain conduct to be so inimical to the statutory scheme that all persons who have engaged in it shall be ineligible for favorable consideration, regardless of other factors that otherwise might tend in their favor. He has then decided that one element is of such determinative negative force that no possible combination of others could justify an affirmative result. By the same token he could select one characteristic as entitling a group to favorable treatment despite minor variables. Nothing in this offends the basic concept that like cases should be treated similarly and unlike ones differently. The administrator has simply determined that the one paramount element creates such "likeness" that other elements cannot be so legally significant

---

13. While the Regulation in question was codified under §214 in the Code of Federal Regulations, the authority under which it was issued derives not only from §214 of the Act, whereby "[t]he admission to the United States of any alien as a nonimmigrant shall be for such time and under such conditions as the Attorney General may by regulations prescribe," but also from §103, charging the Attorney General with "the administration and enforcement of this chapter and all other laws relating to this chapter" including the establishment of "such regulations . . . as he deems necessary for carrying out his authority," and §245, providing for the adjustment of status of aliens "in his discretion and under such regulations as he may prescribe."

as to warrant a difference in treatment. This may be an even "juster justice" than to accord different treatment because of trivial differences of fact; at least it is competent for the administrator to think so. The leading student of the problem has recently counseled: "When legislative bodies delegate discretionary power without meaningful standards, administrators should develop standards at the earliest feasible time, and then, as circumstances permit, should further confine their own discretion through principles and rules." Davis, Discretionary Justice: A Preliminary Inquiry 55 (1969)....

We have stated ... recently, in United States ex rel. Stellas v. Esperdy, 366 F.2d 266, 269-270 (2 Cir. 1966), *vacated and remanded* at the INS' suggestion, *on a point not here material*, 388 U.S. 462 (1967): "... the Attorney General may govern the exercise of his discretion by written or unwritten rules; indeed it would be remarkable if he did not. Any such decision is an application of facts to principles. All this regulation does is provide a substitute for the exercise of discretion on a case by case basis. But there has been an exercise of discretion; ... We know of no rule which requires a case by case approach; the Attorney General certainly may proceed by regulation."

The Attorney General's determination that aliens who had obtained admission without a visa as being "in immediate and continuous transit through the United States," §101(a)(15)(C), should not be eligible to apply for adjustment of status under §245 was reasonably related to the statutory scheme. Both the definition and other provisions of the Immigration and Nationality Act, notably §238(d) which authorizes the Attorney General to enter into contracts with transportation lines guaranteeing that such passage will occur, show that Congress authorized the Attorney General to accord the unusual benefit of admission as a nonimmigrant and without a visa only because quick departure was assured. It was reasonable for the Attorney General to conclude that aliens admitted on so fleeting a basis were not within the spirit of §245 and thus could not deserve favorable exercise of his discretion, even if they came within the letter. He could properly have thought also that to entertain such applications in any case would encourage aliens to obtain admission under the pretense that they were in "immediate and continuous transit" and then stay on for years, as Fook Hong Mak has managed to do, thereby upsetting the balance of benefit and burden that Congress had envisioned. He could have thought further that affording such encouragement might create such burdens for transportation lines that had contracted to assure the departure of such aliens as to make them reluctant to do so and in the long run thus impede the facility of international travel which the privilege of transit without visa was intended to enhance....

Petitioner argues that however the matter might otherwise stand, the Attorney General's blanket exclusion of transits without visas from consideration for status adjustment under §245 was unauthorized because that section itself states two exceptions — alien crewmen and aliens who are natives of any country of the Western Hemisphere or any adjacent island named in §101(b)(5). But it is fallacious to reason that because Congress *prevented* the Attorney General from exercising any discretion in favor of those groups, which Congress had found to have abused the privileges accorded them, it meant to *require* him to exercise it in favor of everyone else on a case-by-case basis even if experience should convince him of the existence of another group with similar potentialities or actualities of abuse. . . . Having expressed its judgment that two categories should be ineligible for the exercise of discretion, Congress left it open to the Attorney General to determine whether the applications of all other aliens seeking status adjustment under §245 should be evaluated on the merits of each case or whether some categories were susceptible to handling on a less individualized basis. . . .

The petition to review is denied.

Asimakopoulos v. Immigration and Naturalization Service

445 F.2d 1362 (9th Cir. 1971)

HUFSTEDLER, Circuit Judge:

Petitioners seek review of a decision of the Board of Immigration Appeals (the "Board") denying their petition for suspension of deportation under 8 U.S.C. §1254(a)(1). We reverse and remand. . . .

[Petitioner aliens, husband and wife, had entered the United States in 1961 and 1962, respectively, as visitors and students. Admission for these purposes is deemed a "protected status" in the terminology of the Immigration Service. Deportation proceedings were eventually initiated after petitioners had overstayed or otherwise violated the terms of their admission. Meanwhile, they had married and had two sons born in the United States. Private bills in Congress to naturalize petitioners had failed of passage.]

In 1969, petitioners successfully moved to reopen the deportation proceedings in order to apply for suspension of deportation under 8 U.S.C. §1254(a)(1). The special inquiry officer and the Board denied relief. Neither the special inquiry officer, nor the Board, nor the Service has ever questioned the fact that petitioners have met all of the requirements for eligibility for suspension of deportation set forth in section 1254(a)(1), which section provides that

the Attorney General may, in his discretion, suspend deportation and adjust the status to that of an alien lawfully admitted for permanent residence, in the case of an alien who applies to the Attorney General for suspension of deportation and —

(1) is deportable under any law of the United States except the provisions specified in paragraph (2) of this subsection; has been physically present in the United States for a continuous period of not less than seven years immediately preceding the date of such application, and proves that during all of such period he was and is a person of good moral character; and is a person whose deportation would, in the opinion of the Attorney General, result in

extreme hardship to the alien or to his spouse, parent, or child, who is a citizen of the United States or an alien lawfully admitted for permanent residence. . . .

Denial of relief was predicated on [the prior decision of the Service in Matter of Lee (B.I.A. 1966), 11 I. & N. Dec. 649], holding that the Board would not exercise its discretion in favor of an alien applying for suspension of deportation who had been in this country in a protected status unless the alien could show "particularly strong equities" favoring him.

[The rule announced by the Board in *Lee* had been based on a portion of a 1965 House Judiciary Committee Report, H.R. Rep. No. 1167, 89th Cong., 1st Sess. (1965), on a Joint Resolution vetoing decisions by the Attorney General to suspend the deportation of individual aliens under §1254(a)(1). (8 U.S.C. §1254(c) authorizes this congressional veto procedure). The Report stated in broad terms that suspension of deportation should not ordinarily be granted to aliens admitted in protected status, such as students and visitors, because they were especially likely to overstay the terms of entry and exercise delaying tactics against deportation in order to seek relief under §1254(a)(1). Relying on the Report, *Lee* announced that in order to qualify for suspension of deportation, protected status aliens would not only have to meet the requirements of §1254(a)(1), but must in addition show "particularly strong equities." The Court, apparently reacting to what it perceived to be improper or unwise congressional intrusion, held that the Report did not justify the *Lee* rule because the resolution to which the Report was directed only concerned the deportation of specific aliens and did not mandate a general change in the standards for suspension of deportation. In addition, the Report reflected only the views of the Committee, not Congress as a whole.]

We overturn *Lee* and the decision of the Board in this case on an additional ground. Although eligibility for suspension does not compel the granting of the requested relief . . . eligibility does trigger the exercise of discretion. . . . The standard announced in Matter of Lee effectively precludes the exercise of discretion in many cases in which the applicant would otherwise qualify for relief. The Board's failure to exercise discretion is reversible error. . . . Accordingly, reliance on a test that prevents the exercise of discretion is also reversible error. . . . We do not express any opinion about the manner in which the Attorney General or his delegates should exercise the discretion committed to him.

The judgment is reversed and the cause is remanded for further proceedings not inconsistent with the views herein expressed.

Notes and Questions

1. Who has the more persuasive position, Judge Friendly or Judge Hufstedler? Are there any differences in the relevant statutes that would justify the difference in result?

The immigration statutes typically emphasize the discretionary nature of the authority granted to the INS, in part to avoid the impression of granting any "rights" to aliens and to limit accordingly the scope of judicial review. Ironically, this feature of the statutes was relied upon in *Asimakopoulos* to sustain the alien's position.[14]

2. *Asimakopoulos* and *Fook Hong Mak* reflect a more general conflict in administrative law and practice between consistent treatment, which would be promoted through categorical rules, and individuation of agency decisions by tailoring them to the particular circumstances of each case. Is the procedural ruling in *Asimakopoulos* based on an implicit underlying right to individual consideration? If so, in what other types of administrative proceedings would such a right apply? [15]

Would a requirement of individuation impose undue burdens on the administrative process in circumstances where claims in the thousands (e.g., the INS) or millions (e.g., Social Security benefits) must be processed annually? Given the comparative infrequency of judicial review, what steps could be taken to ensure that individuation does not become a license for arbitrary, biased, or inconsistent administrative decisionmaking?

3. Once an agency adopts general rules to decide cases, may it depart from them in individual cases where they might be inappropriate? [16]

B. Requiring Agencies to Explain Their Decisions and the Requirement of Consistency in Adjudication

1. The Chenery Litigation

Note: The Public Utility Holding Company Act

The Public Utility Holding Company Act of 1935, 15 U.S.C. §§ 79 et seq., gave the Securities and Exchange Commission sweeping authority to reorganize and simplify the complex corporate structure typical of many of the public utility empires assembled by financial entrepreneurs in the 1920s. By constructing a series of parent-subsidiary relations in which the parent corporations owned a controlling interest in the voting equity of the subsidiary, and through lavish use of nonvoting common or preferred stock and bonds to finance the entire structure, entrepreneurs

---

14. Can the difference in result in the two cases be explained on the ground that the rule enforced in *Fook Hong Mak* had been promulgated through notice and comment rulemaking in which all interested persons could participate, while the principle applied in *Asimakopoulos* had been formulated in a prior adjudication? For criticism of the *Asimakopoulos* decision, see K. Davis, Administrative Law of the Seventies 421-424 (1976). For a more general review of discretionary decisionmaking by the Immigration and Naturalization Service, see Sofaer, Judicial Control of Informal Discretionary Adjudication and Enforcement, 72 Colum. L. Rev. 1293 (1972).

15. For discussion, see Tribe, Structural Due Process, 10 Harv. C.R.-C.L. L. Rev. 269 (1975).

16. See Note, Violations by Agencies of Their Own Regulations, 87 Harv. L. Rev. 629, 645-647 (1974). We consider this issue in greater detail at pp. 445-458 infra.

with a comparatively modest equity investment in the parent holding company located at the apex of a pyramid of corporate relations could control the entire pyramid and the vast industrial properties it comprised. These arrangements afforded the controlling entrepreneurs two significant opportunities for profit. First, the control group could cause subsidiary utility operating companies to enter into contracts with service or supply firms dominated by the control group on terms unduly favorable to the latter. Second, the control group's common stock investment in the utility pyramid was highly leveraged, because most of the financing was provided by preferred stock or bonds entitled to no more than a specified return. If the collective enterprise prospered financially (as most enterprises did during the 1920s), then the control group's investment might be multiplied in value many times over. On the other hand, if the enterprise failed, the control group's investment would be wiped out, but its loss would be minor compared to that of preferred stockholders and bondholders who had contributed the bulk of the capital at risk.

The violent decline of the stock market in 1929 caused many of these highly leveraged pyramids to collapse quickly, triggering other financial failures that accelerated the advent of the Great Depression.

During the first Roosevelt administration, these practices became a prime target of congressional investigations. The activities of Samuel Insull in pyramiding utility properties in the Midwest were a particular focus of attack. Against the background of these investigations, Congress in 1935 enacted the Public Utility Holding Company Act, which imposed a "death sentence" on surviving holding company arrangements by requiring geographical integration and financial reorganization and simplification of public utility corporate structures under the direction of the SEC.[17]

The Act requires public utility holding companies to register with the SEC, which is empowered to impose reorganization terms on registered companies. However, voluntary reorganizations, subject to SEC approval, are also provided for and encouraged. Section 7 of the Act authorizes the SEC to approve the issuance of new securities pursuant to a voluntary reorganization unless the Commission finds that "the terms and conditions of the issue or sale of the security are detrimental to the public interest or the interest of investors or consumers." Section 11 authorizes the submission of voluntary reorganization plans "[i]n accordance with such rules and regulations or order as the Commission may deem necessary or appropriate in the public interest or for the protection of investors or consumers," and authorizes the Commission to approve such a plan if it finds the plan to be "fair and equitable to the persons affected by such plan."

17. For background reading on the origins of the Act and its early administration, see Michael Parrish, Securities Regulation and the New Deal (1970); William O. Douglas, Democracy and Finance (1940); Ferdinand Pecora, Wall Street Under Oath (1939). In the 1933 Securities Act and the 1934 Securities Exchange Act, Congress required companies issuing new securities through interstate commerce and companies whose securities are traded on a national securities exchange to disclose for the benefit of investors financial information concerning the issuer, including information on its financial structure and performance, interlocking corporate relations, and company contracts or supplier relations in which the issuer's executives or directors are financially interested. In light of these disclosure requirements, why was the Public Utility Holding Company Act necessary?

SEC v. Chenery Corp. (I)

318 U.S. 80 (1943)

Mr. Justice FRANKFURTER delivered the opinion of the Court.

[Respondents Chenerys were officers, directors and controlling shareholders of Federal Water Service Corporation (Federal), a public utility holding company (whose assets consisted of controlling shares in a variety of public utility corporations) subject to reorganization under the Public Utility Holding Company Act. From 1937 to 1940 respondents negotiated with the SEC over the terms of a proposed voluntary reorganization which called for the merger of Federal and certain affiliated corporations into a single new corporation with one class of common stock. The Chenerys were unsuccessful in persuading the SEC to authorize holders of class B common stock of Federal (a controlling but junior class of shares owned by the Chenerys) to exchange these shares for the common of the reorganized company. Participation was limited to holders of Federal's preferred stock and class A common, with the preferred shareholders being allocated 94.7 percent of the common in the reorganized company. During the period 1937-1940, while the reorganization plan was being negotiated, the Chenerys purchased from brokers in the over-the-counter market 12,407 shares of Federal's preferred stock. Had the Chenerys been permitted to participate in the reorganization by exchanging these shares for common stock in the reorganized company, they would have been entitled to more than 10 percent of the reorganized company's common, representing a controlling block of shares. The price at which the Chenerys purchased the preferred was substantially less than the book value of the equivalent common of the reorganized company. The Chenerys purchased the preferred in part for the purpose of continuing their management of the enterprise.]

In ascertaining whether the terms of issuance of the new common stock were "fair and equitable" or "detrimental to the interests of investors" within §7 of the Act, the Commission found that it could not approve the proposed plan so long as the preferred stock acquired by the respondents would be permitted to share on a parity with other preferred stock. The Commission did not find fraud or lack of disclosure, but it concluded that the respondents, as Federal's managers, were fiduciaries and hence under a "duty of fair dealing" not to trade in the securities of the corporation while plans for its reorganization were before the Commission. . . .

Accordingly, the plan was thereafter amended to provide that the preferred stock acquired by the respondents, unlike the preferred stock held by others, would not be converted into stock of the reorganized company, but could only be surrendered at cost plus 4 percent interest. The Commission, over the respondents' objections, approved the plan as amended, and it is this order which is now under review. . . .

The Commission did not find that the respondents as managers of Federal acted covertly or traded on inside knowledge, or that their position as reorganization managers enabled them to purchase the preferred stock at prices lower than they would otherwise have had to pay, or that their acquisition of the stock in any way prejudiced the interests of the corporation or its stockholders. To be sure, the new stock into which the respondents' preferred stock would be converted under the plan of reorganization would have a book value — which may or may not represent market value — considerably greater than the prices paid for the preferred stock. But that would equally be true of purchases of preferred stock made by other investors. The respondents, the Commission tells us, acquired their stock as the outside world did, and upon no better terms. . . .

Applying by analogy the restrictions imposed on trustees in trafficking in property held by them in trust for others, Michoud v. Girod, 4 How. 503, 557, the Commission ruled that even though the management does not hold the stock of the corporation in trust for the stockholders, nevertheless the "duty of fair dealing" which the management owes to the stockholders is violated if those in control of the corporation purchase its stock, even at a fair price, openly and without fraud. The Commission concluded that "honesty, full disclosure, and purchase at a fair price do not take the case outside the rule."

In reaching this result the Commission stated that it was merely applying "the broad equitable principles enunciated in the cases heretofore cited," namely, Pepper v. Litton, 308 U.S. 295; Michoud v. Girod, 4 How. 503, 557; Magruder v. Drury, 235 U.S. 106, 119-20, and Meinhard v. Salmon, 249 N.Y. 458, 164 N.E. 545. Its opinion plainly shows that the Commission purported to be acting only as it assumed a court of equity would have acted in a similar case. Since the decision of the Commission was explicitly based upon the applicability of principles of equity announced by courts, its validity must likewise be judged on that basis. The grounds upon which an administrative order must be judged are those upon which the record discloses that its action was based.

In confining our review to a judgment upon the validity of the grounds upon which the Commission itself based its action, we do not disturb the settled rule that, in reviewing the decision of a lower court, it must be affirmed if the result is correct "although the lower court relied upon a wrong ground or gave a wrong reason." Helvering v. Gowran, 302 U.S. 238, 245. The reason for this rule is obvious. It would be wasteful to send a case back to a lower court to reinstate a decision which it had already made but which the appellate court concluded should properly be based on another ground within the power of the appellate court to formulate. But it is also familiar appellate procedure that where the correctness of the lower court's decision depends upon a determination of fact which only a jury could make but which has not been made, the appellate court cannot take the place of the jury. Like considerations govern review of administrative orders. If an order is valid only as a determination of policy or judgment which the agency alone is authorized to make and which it has not made, a judicial judgment cannot be made to do service for an administrative judgment. For purposes of affirming no less than reversing its orders, an appellate court cannot intrude upon the domain which Congress has exclusively entrusted to an administrative agency.

If, therefore, the rule applied by the Commission is to be judged solely on the basis of its adherence to principles of equity derived from judicial decisions, its order plainly cannot stand.

[After reviewing the judicial precedent relied upon by the SEC, the Court found that such precedent did not prohibit reorganization purchases in the circumstances presented here, and accordingly did not support the SEC's prohibition of the Chenerys' participation in the reorganization.]

Determination of what is "fair and equitable" calls for the application of ethical standards to particular sets of facts. But these standards are not static. In evolving standards of fairness and equity, the Commission is not bound by settled judicial precedents. Congress certainly did not mean to preclude the formulation by the Commission of standards expressing a more sensitive regard for what is right and what is wrong than those prevalent at the time the Public Utility Holding Company Act of 1935 became law. But the Commission did not in this case proffer new standards reflecting the experience gained by it in effectuating the legislative policy. On the contrary, it explicitly disavowed any purpose of going beyond those which the courts had theretofore recognized. Since the Commission professed to decide the case before it according to settled judicial doctrines, its action must be judged by the standards which the Commission itself invoked. . . .

But the Commission urges here that the order should nevertheless be sustained because "the effect of trading by management is not measured by the fairness of individual transactions between buyer and seller, but by its relation to the timing and dynamics of the reorganization which the management itself initiates and so largely controls." Its argument lays stress upon the "strategic position enjoyed by the management in this type of reorganization proceeding and the vesting in it of statutory powers available to no other representative of security holders." It contends that these considerations warrant the stern rule applied in this case since the Commission "has dealt extensively with corporate reorganizations, both under the Act, and other statutes entrusted to it," and "has, in addition, exhaustively studied protective and reorganization committees," and that the situation was therefore "peculiarly within the Commission's special administrative competence." . . .

But the difficulty remains that the considerations urged here in support of the Commission's order were not those upon which its action was based. The Commission did not rely upon "its special administrative competence"; it formulated no judgment upon the requirements of the "public interest or the interest of investors or consumers" in the situation before it. Through its preoccupation with the special problems of utility reorganizations the Commission accumulates an experience and insight denied to others. Had the Commission, acting upon its experience and peculiar competence, promulgated a general rule of which its order here was a particular application, the problem for our consideration would be very different. Whether and to what extent directors or officers should be prohibited from buying or selling stock of the corporation during its reorganization, presents problems of policy for the judgment of Congress or of the body to which it has delegated power to deal with the matter. Abuse of corporate position, influence, and access to information may raise questions so subtle that the law can deal with them effectively only by prohibitions not concerned with the fairness of a particular transaction. But before transactions otherwise legal can be outlawed or denied their usual business consequences, they must fall under the ban of some standards of conduct prescribed by an agency of government authorized to prescribe such standards — either the courts or Congress or an agency to which Congress has delegated its authority. Congress itself did not proscribe the respondents' purchases of preferred stock in Federal. Established judicial doctrines do not condemn these transactions. Nor has the Commission, acting under the rule-making powers delegated to it by §11(e), promulgated new general standards of conduct. It purported merely to be applying an existing judge-made rule of equity. The Commission's determination can stand, therefore, only if it found that the specific transactions under scrutiny showed misuse by the respondents of their position as reorganization managers, in that as such managers they took advantage of the corporation or the other stockholders or the investing public. The record is utterly barren of any such showing. Indeed, such a claim against the respondents was explicitly disavowed by the Commission. . . .

Judged, therefore, as a determination based upon judge-made rules of equity, the Commission's order cannot be upheld. Its action must be measured by what the Commission did, not by what it might have done. It is not for us to determine independently what is "detrimental to the public interest or the interest of investors or consumers" or "fair or equitable" within the meaning of §§ 7 and 11 of the Public Utility Holding Company Act of 1935. The Commission's action cannot be upheld merely because findings might have been made and considerations disclosed which would justify its order as an appropriate safeguard for the interests protected by the Act. There must be such a responsible finding. . . . There is no such finding here.

Congress has seen fit to subject to judicial review such orders of the Securities and Exchange Commission as the one before us. That the scope of such review is narrowly circumscribed is beside the point. For the courts cannot exercise their duty of review unless they are advised of the considerations underlying the action under review. If the action rests upon an administrative determination — an exercise of judgment in an area which Congress has entrusted to the agency — of course it must not be set aside because the reviewing court might have made a different determination were it empowered to do so. But if the action is based upon a determination of law as to which the reviewing authority of the courts does come into play, an order may not stand if the agency has misconceived the law. In either event the orderly functioning of the process of review requires that the grounds upon which the administrative agency acted be clearly disclosed and adequately sustained. "The administrative process will best be vindicated by clarity in its exercise." Phelps Dodge Corp. v. Labor Board, 313 U.S. 177, 197. What was said in that case is equally applicable here: "We do not intend to enter the province that belongs to the Board, nor do we do so. All we ask of the Board is to give clear indication that it has exercised the discretion with which Congress has empowered it. This is to affirm most emphatically the authority of the Board." Ibid.

In finding that the Commission's order cannot be sustained, we are not imposing any trammels on its powers. We are not enforcing formal requirements. We are not suggesting that the Commission must justify its exercise of administrative discretion in any particular manner or with artistic refinement. We are not sticking in the bark of words. We merely hold that an administrative order cannot be upheld unless the grounds upon which the agency acted in exercising its powers were those upon which its action can be sustained.

The cause should therefore be remanded to the Court of Appeals with directions to remand to the Commission for such further proceedings, not inconsistent with this opinion, as may be appropriate.

So ordered.

Mr. Justice DOUGLAS took no part in the consideration and decision of this case.

Mr. Justice BLACK, with whom Mr. Justice REED and Mr. Justice MURPHY concur, dissenting.

... The conclusions of the Court with which I disagree are those in which it holds that while the Securities and Exchange Commission has abundant power to meet the situation presented by the activities of these respondents, it has not done so. This conclusion is apparently based on the premise that the Commission has relied upon the common law rather than on "new standards reflecting the experience gained by it in effectuating legislative policy," and that the common law does not support its conclusion; that the Commission could have promulgated "a general rule of which its order here was a particular application," but instead made merely an ad hoc judgment; and that the Commission made no finding that these practices would prejudice anyone.

The Commission's actual finding was that "The plan of reorganization herein considered, like the previous plans filed with us over the past several years, was formulated by the management of Federal, and discussions concerning the reorganization of this corporation have taken place between the management and the staff of the Commission over the past several years"; that C. T. Chenery purchased 8,618 shares of preferred stock during this period; that other officers and directors of the concerns involved acquired 3,789 shares during the same period; that for this stock these respondent fiduciaries paid $328,346.89 and then submitted their latest reorganization plan, under which this purchased stock would have a book value in the reorganization company of $1,162,431.90. In the light of these and other facts the Commission concluded that the new plan would be "unfair, inequitable, and detrimental, so long as the preferred stock purchased by the management at low prices is to be permitted to share on a parity with other preferred stock." The Commission declined to give "effectiveness" to the proposed plan and entered "adverse findings" against it under §§ 7(d)(1) and 7(d)(2) of the controlling Act, resting its refusal to approve on this statement: "We find that the provisions for participation by the preferred stock held by the management result in the terms of issuance of the new securities being detrimental to the interests of investors and the plan being unfair and inequitable."

The grounds upon which the Commission made its findings seem clear enough to me....

While I consider that the cases on which the Commission relied give full support to the conclusion it reached, I do not suppose, as the Court does, that the Commission's rule is not fully based on Commission experience. The Commission did not "explicitly disavow" any reliance on what its members had learned in their years of experience, and of course they, as trade experts, made their findings that respondent's practice was "detrimental to the interests of investors" in the light of their knowledge. That they did not unduly parade fact data across the pages of their reports is a commendable saving of effort since they meant merely to announce for their own jurisdiction an obvious rule of honest dealing closely related to common law standards. Of course, the Commission can now change the form of its decision to comply with the Court order. The Court can require the Commission to use more words; but it seems difficult to imagine how more words or different words could further illuminate its purpose or its determination. A judicial requirement of circumstantially detailed findings as the price of court approval can bog the administrative power in a quagmire of minutiae. Hypercritical exactions as to findings can provide a handy but an almost invisible glideway enabling courts to pass "from the narrow confines of law into the more spacious domain of policy." Phelps Dodge Corp. v. Labor Board, 313 U.S. 177, 194.

That the Commission has chosen to proceed case by case rather than by a general pronouncement does not appear to me to merit criticism. The intimation is that the Commission can act only through general formulae rigidly adhered to. In the first place, the rule of the single case is obviously a general advertisement to the trade, and in the second place the briefs before us indicate that this is but one of a number of cases in which the Commission is moving to an identical result on a broad front. But aside from these considerations the Act gives the Commission wide powers to evolve policy standards, and this may well be done case by case. . . .

Federal Water Service Corp. (The SEC Decision on Remand)

18 S.E.C. 231 (1945)

[On remand, The Commission denied a motion by the Chenerys to amend the reorganization plan to permit them to participate in the reorganization and held that they must exchange the shares purchased pending reorganization at cost plus 4 percent interest. The Commission expressly disclaimed reliance on judicial precedent and based its ruling on its experience with reorganizations and the need to protect investors.]

THE POWERS OF A HOLDING COMPANY MANAGEMENT UNDER THE ACT

It has been our experience under the Act that the normal influence of a holding company management pervades the entire system down to the lowest tier of operating companies. For example, in this case, directly and through control of Operators (the holder of all of Federal's Class B stock), the interveners controlled a utility system of 42 subholding and operating companies which operated water, gas, electric and other properties in 13 states and one foreign country. In this system the interveners occupied over 100 directorships, 35 presidencies, 20 vice presidencies and 6 treasurerships; one intervener was chairman of the board of 11 companies, another was general counsel for 17 companies and a third was a consulting engineer for 16 companies. With respect to Federal itself the interveners included three directors, the president, six vice presidents, the secretary and the treasurer.

The management of a holding company under the Act, through its pervasive control over the financial, operational and accounting policies of the parent and its operating subsidiaries, is in a position to initiate and shape market movements. It can determine whether and when subsidiary earnings are to be drawn up into the holding company or withheld or obscured within the accounts of the subsidiaries. Through such determinations it can affect substantially the corporate income of the holding company, reduce or increase an impairment of capital, and ultimately affect its ability to pay dividends. These are important factors affecting the market prices of the holding company's outstanding securities, and even affecting the ultimate allocation of new securities among the various classes of security holders. . . .

The combination of these multiple powers in the management while a reorganization is under consideration places at its command a formidable battery of devices that would enable it, if it should choose to use them selfishly, to affect in material degree the ultimate allocation of new securities among the various existing classes, to influence the market for its own gain, and to manipulate or obstruct the reorganization required by the mandate of the statute. If, in this setting, the management enters upon a stock purchase program there is inevitably the temptation, as well as the opportunity, to shape the reorganization proceeding so as to encourage public selling on the market at low prices. . . .

CONFLICTING INTERESTS ARISING FROM STOCK PURCHASE PROGRAM BY MANAGEMENT DURING THE REORGANIZATION UNDER THE ACT

If in any case we had proof that reorganization managers had actually purchased future control at bargain prices *intentionally* created or maintained by their own acts, plainly we would be unable to find fair and equitable a plan of reorganization which embodied provisions allowing them to reap the benefits.

But even where proof of intentional wrongdoing is lacking, should the answer be substantially different? We think not. Where the management embarks upon a stock purchase program during a reorganization, it places its personal interests actively at odds with the interests of other stockholders it represents in the reorganization. Where that occurs, and the management thereafter submits a plan by which it would realize substantial benefits through stock acquired during its purchase program, it asks us to make what in effect is a positive finding that its realization of such benefits is fair and equitable to all persons affected by the plan. In such circumstances we do not believe the statute limits our power and duty to withhold approval solely to cases in which someone is able to establish by affirmative evidence that actual misconduct accompanied such a conflict of interests. It is the responsibility of the proponents of the plan to satisfy us that the plan is fair and equitable under Section 11(e). An affirmative determination of that kind cannot appropriately be left to rest upon conjecture. . . .

Turning now to the case before us the salient fact is, as the interveners have stated, that their primary object in buying the preferred stock of Federal was to obtain the voting power that was accruing to that stock through the reorganization, and to profit from their investment therein. This stock they had purchased in the market at prices that were depressed in relation to what they anticipated would be, and what in fact was, the earning and asset value of its reorganization equivalent. We think we need look no further than this. . . .

THE NECESSITY FOR PREVENTIVE MEASURES AND THE REASONS FOR THE MEASURE APPLIED IN THIS CASE

The problem before us is, therefore, one of temptations combined with powers of accomplishment. Since the achieving of personal gain through the use of fiduciary power is unfair, we believe the incentive to misuse such power must be removed so that the potentialities of harm to investors and the public will to that extent be eliminated. For the reasons we have already given, we deem it impossible to do less. . . .

Those who sold out cannot be helped in these proceedings. Despite that fact, they are persons who have been affected by the development and consummation of this plan. If there were affirmative proof that the managers intentionally had taken advantage of them, we would be unable to approve as fair and equitable, or as not detrimental to investors, a plan that would confirm to the managers all benefits of the transactions by which they did so. But, even lacking such proof, in the face of the conflict of interest disclosed by this record, we cannot, for the reasons we have described, achieve the positive conviction of fairness to them that we deem essential if the integrity of the reorganization process under this Act is to be maintained above reasonable suspicion.

As to the public stockholders who remain, we cannot make the affirmative finding required by Section 11(e) that the plan is "fair and equitable to the persons affected thereby" in the face of so many questions about fairness and equity which we believe no amount of testifying can completely and satisfactorily answer.

REASONS FOR ACTION BY ORDER RATHER THAN BY GENERAL RULE

The position of the interveners comes down to this: that approving a plan limiting them to their cost plus 4 percent interest is unfair to them because when they made their purchases they expected to perpetuate their control and make a profit, and that our order operates, according to their claim, retroactively to prevent the realization of their expectations. But this is true only in the sense that the decision of any case of first impression may have an effect not foreseen or foreseeable. The effects of our decision upon the expectations of the interveners must be weighed against the interests of others, and we think that a contrary decision would be unfair and detrimental to the interests of investors and to the public interest itself.

Moreover in this case the interveners, when they bought the preferred stock of Federal, were not acting wholly in a legal vacuum. As reasonable men they must at least have known that they were running some risk that their purchase program might not achieve its purpose. . . .

The interveners urge that we have no alternative but to act first by general rule or published statement of policy if we are to act at all in a matter of this kind. The Supreme Court indicated the advisability of promulgating a general rule, though we do not understand its opinion to hold that the absence of a preexisting rule is fatal to the decision we have reached. Now that we have had the question sharply focused in this and other cases before us, and have had an extensive period in which to consider the problems involved, we may well decide that a general rule, with adequately flexible provisions, would be both practicable and desirable; but we do not see how the promulgation of such a rule now or later would affect our duty to act by order in this case in deciding whether this plan is fair and equitable and meets the other standards of the Act. We therefore reserve for further consideration the question whether or not a rule should be adopted.

SEC v. Chenery Corp. (II)

332 U.S. 194 (1947)

Mr. Justice MURPHY delivered the opinion of the Court.

The latest order of the Commission definitely avoids the fatal error of relying on judicial precedents which do not sustain it. This time, after a thorough re-examination of the problem in light of the purposes and standards of the Holding Company Act, the Commission has concluded that the proposed transaction is inconsistent with the standards of §§ 7 and 11 of the Act. It has drawn heavily upon its accumulated experience in dealing with utility reorganizations. And it has expressed its reasons with a clarity and thoroughness that admit of no doubt as to the underlying basis of its order.

The argument is pressed upon us, however, that the Commission was foreclosed from taking such a step following our prior decision. It is said that, in the absence of findings of conscious wrongdoing on the part of Federal's management, the Commission could not determine by an order in this particular case that it was inconsistent with the statutory standards to permit Federal's management to realize a profit through the reorganization purchases. All that it could do was to enter an order allowing an amendment to the plan so that the proposed transaction could be consummated. Under this view, the Commission would be free only to promulgate a general rule outlawing such profits in future utility reorganizations; but such a rule would have to be prospective in nature and have no retroactive effect upon the instant situation.

We reject this contention, for it grows out of a misapprehension of our prior decision and of the Commission's statutory duties. We held no more and no less than that the Commission's first order was unsupportable for the reasons supplied by that agency. But when the case left this Court, the problem whether Federal's management should be treated equally with other preferred stockholders still lacked a final and complete answer. It was clear that the Commission could not give a negative answer by resort to prior judicial declarations. And it was also clear that the Commission was not bound by settled judicial precedents in a situation of this nature. 318 U.S. at 89. Still unsettled, however, was the answer the Commission might give were it to bring to bear on the facts the proper administrative and statutory considerations, a function which belongs exclusively to the Commission in the first instance. The administrative process had taken an erroneous rather than a final turn. Hence we carefully refrained from expressing any views as to the propriety of an order rooted in the proper and relevant considerations. . . .

It is true that our prior decision explicitly recognized the possibility that the Commission might have promulgated a general rule dealing with this problem under its statutory rule-making powers, in which case the issue for our consideration would have been entirely different from that which did confront us. 318 U.S. 92-93. But we did not mean to imply thereby that the failure of the Commission to anticipate this problem and to promulgate a general rule withdrew all power from that agency to perform its statutory duty in this case. To hold that the Commission had no alternative in this proceeding but to approve the proposed transaction, while formulating any general rules it might desire for use in future cases of this nature, would be to stultify the administrative process. That we refuse to do.

Since the Commission, unlike a court, does have the ability to make new law prospectively through the exercise of its rule-making powers, it has less reason to rely upon ad hoc adjudication to formulate new standards of conduct within the framework of the Holding Company Act. The function of filling in the interstices of the Act should be performed, as much as possible, through this quasi-legislative promulgation of rules to be applied in the future. But any rigid requirement to that effect would make the administrative process inflexible and incapable of dealing with many of the specialized problems which arise. See Report of the Attorney General's Committee on Administrative Procedure in Government Agencies, S. Doc. No. 8, 77th Cong., 1st Sess., p. 29. Not every principle essential to the effective administration of a statute can or should be cast immediately into the mold of a general rule. Some principles must await their own development, while others must be adjusted to meet particular, unforeseeable situations. In performing its important functions in these respects, therefore, an administrative agency must be equipped to act either by general rule or by individual order. To insist upon one form of action to the exclusion of the other is to exalt form over necessity.

In other words, problems may arise in a case which the administrative agency could not reasonably foresee, problems which must be solved despite the absence of a relevant general rule. Or the agency may not have had sufficient experience with a particular problem to warrant rigidifying its tentative judgment into a hard and fast rule. Or the problem may be so specialized and varying in nature as to be impossible of capture within the boundaries of a general rule. In those situations, the agency must retain power to deal with the problems on a case-to-case basis if the administrative process is to be effective. There is thus a very definite place for the case-by-case evolution of statutory standards. And the choice made between proceeding by general rule or by individual, *ad hoc* litigation is one that lies primarily in the informed discretion of the administrative agency. See Columbia Broadcasting System v. United States, 316 U.S. 407, 421.

Hence we refuse to say that the Commission, which had not previously been confronted with the problem of management trading during reorganization, was forbidden from utilizing this particular proceeding for announcing and applying a new standard of conduct. Cf. Federal Trade Commission v. Keppel & Bro., 291 U.S. 304. That such action might have a retroactive effect was not necessarily fatal to its validity. Every case of first impression has a retroactive effect, whether the new principle is announced by a court or by an administrative agency. But such retro-activity must be balanced against the mischief of producing a result which is contrary to a statutory design or to legal and equitable principles. If that mischief is greater than the ill effect of the retroactive application of a new standard, it is not the type of retroactivity which is condemned by law. See Addison v. Holly Hill Co., 322 U.S. 607, 620.

[The Court then summarized the reasons given by the Commission for its decision on remand.]

We are unable to say in this case that the Commission erred in reaching the result it did. The facts being undisputed, we are free to disturb the Commission's conclusion only if it lacks any rational and statutory foundation. In that connection, the Commission has made a thorough examination of the problem, utilizing statutory standards and its own accumulated experience with reorganization matters. In essence, it has made what we indicated in our prior opinion would be an informed, expert judgment on the problem.

... The "fair and equitable" rule of §11(e) and the standard of what is "detrimental to the public interest or the interest of investors or consumers" under §7(d)(6) and §7(e) were inserted by the framers of the Act in order that the Commission might have broad powers to protect the various interests at stake. 318 U.S. at 90-91. The application of those criteria, whether in the form of a particular order or a general regulation, necessarily requires the use of informed discretion by the Commission. The very breadth of the statutory language precludes a reversal of the Commission's judgment save where it has plainly abused its discretion in these matters. ... Such an abuse is not present in this case.

[The Court reversed the judgment of the Court of Appeals, which had set aside the Commission's denial of the Chenerys' application for amendment of the reorganization plan. Justice Burton concurred in the result, and Chief Justice Vinson and Justice Douglas did not participate in the decision.]

Mr. Justice JACKSON, dissenting.

The Court by this present decision sustains the identical administrative order which only recently it held invalid. SEC v. Chenery Corp., 318 U.S. 80. As the Court correctly notes, the Commission has only "recast its rationale and reached the same result." ... There being no change in the order, no additional evidence in the record and no amendment of relevant legislation, it is clear that there has been a shift in attitude between that of the controlling membership of the Court when the case was first here and that of those who have the power of decision on this second review.[18]

I feel constrained to disagree with the reasoning offered to rationalize this shift. It makes judicial review of administrative orders a hopeless formality for the litigant, even where granted to him by Congress. It reduces the judicial process in such cases to a mere feint. While the opinion does not have the adherence of a majority of the full Court, if its pronouncements should become governing principles they would, in practice, put most administrative orders over and above the law.

The essential facts are few and are not in dispute. This corporation filed with the Securities and Exchange Commission a voluntary plan of reorganization. While the reorganization proceedings were pending sixteen officers and directors bought on the open market about 7½% of the corporation's preferred stock. Both the Commission and the Court admit that these purchases were not forbidden by any law, judicial precedent, regulation or rule of the Commission. Nevertheless, the Commission has ordered these individuals to surrender their shares to the corporation at cost, plus 4% interest, and the Court now approves that order.

It is helpful, before considering whether this order is authorized by law, to reflect on what it is and what it is not. It is not conceivably a discharge of the Commission's duty to determine whether a proposed plan of reorganization would be "fair and equitable." It has nothing to do with the corporate structure, or the classes and amounts of stock, or voting rights or dividend preferences. It does not remotely affect the impersonal financial or legal factors of the plan. It is a personal deprivation denying particular persons the right to continue to own their stock and to exercise its privileges. Other persons who bought at the same time and price in the open market would be allowed to keep and convert their stock. Thus, the order is in no sense an exercise of the function of control over the terms and relations of the corporate securities.

Neither is the order one merely to regulate the future use of property. It literally takes valuable property away from its lawful owners for the benefit of other private parties without full compensation and the Court expressly approves the taking. . . . Admittedly, the value above cost, and interest on it, simply is taken from the owners, without compensation. No such power has even been confirmed in any administrative body.

It should also be noted that neither the Court nor the Commission purports to adjudge a forfeiture of this property as a consequence of sharp dealing or breach of trust. The Court says, "The Commission admitted that the good faith and personal integrity of this management were not in question; . . . ." And again, "It was frankly admitted that the management's purpose in buying the preferred

18. Ed. note: Between *Chenery I* and *Chenery II*, Justice Roberts and Chief Justice Stone left the Court, and three new Justices — Vinson, Burton, and Rutledge — joined it. The two departing Justices had both joined in the majority opinion in *Chenery I*; of the three new Justices, one (Vinson) didn't participate in *Chenery II*, and another (Burton) concurred in the result.

stock was to protect its interest in the new company. It was also plain that there was no fraud or lack of disclosure in making these purchases.". . .[19]

As there admittedly is no law or regulation to support this order, we peruse the Court's opinion diligently to find on what grounds it is now held that the Court of Appeals, on pain of being reversed for error, was required to stamp this order with its approval. We find but one. That is the principle of judicial deference to administrative experience. That argument is five times stressed in as many different contexts. . . .

What are we to make of this reiterated deference to "administrative experience" when in another context the Court says, "Hence we refuse to say that the Commission, *which had not previously been confronted with the problem of management trading during reorganization*, was forbidden from utilizing this particular proceeding for announcing and applying *a new standard of conduct*."? (Emphasis supplied.)

The Court's reasoning adds up to this: The Commission must be sustained because of its accumulated experience in solving a problem with which it had never before been confronted!

Of course, thus to uphold the Commission by professing to find that it has enunciated a "new standard of conduct" brings the Court squarely against the invalidity of retroactive law-making. But the Court does not falter. "That such action might have a retroactive effect was not necessarily fatal to its validity.". . . "But such retroactivity must be balanced against the mischief of producing a result which is contrary to a statutory design or to legal and equitable principles." (Par. 17.) Of course, if what these parties did really was condemned by "statutory design" or "legal and equitable principles," it could be stopped without resort to a new rule and there would be no retroactivity to condone. But if it had been the Court's view that some law already prohibited the purchases, it would hardly have

19. Ed. note: In view of the assertions by the majority and the dissent that the SEC found no fraud or bad faith by the Chenerys, consider the following excerpt from the SEC's brief in *Chenery II*, pp. 44-46, quoted in L. Jaffe & N. Nathanson, Administrative Law 223 (4th ed. 1976):

"The Commission in its present opinion has explained the wholly argumentative meaning which it had intended to convey by the so-called 'admissions' of fair dealing on the part of Federal's managers, as referred to in this Court's prior opinion. . . . What the Commission meant in its original opinion, and what its counsel in briefs and argument upon review had assumed, was merely that the inflexible rule of equity on which it originally relied did not even permit inquiry into the question whether the transactions of the reorganization managers here were characterized by 'honesty, full disclosure and purchase at a fair price.'

"It should be noted that the opinion of the court below not only ignores the Commission's explanation of why it actually made no findings whatever on the subject of the good or bad faith of Federal's managers, but instead emphasizes again and again, without any foundation in the record, what it terms affirmative findings that "petitioners' purchases of stock were in all respects fair, honest and aboveboard, resulting neither in any unjust enrichment to themselves nor harm to other stockholders or the public' . . . , and that 'the result was neither unfair nor inequitable to the persons affected by the plan' . . . The Commission has made no such findings.

"Thus the Commission rested not only on the ground that undiscoverable abuse may have occurred, but that, in some respects, abuse was inevitable as a result of the purchase program."

been necessary three sentences earlier to hold that the Commission was not prohibited "from utilizing this particular proceeding for announcing and applying a *new standard of conduct.*". . . (Emphasis supplied.)

I give up. Now I realize what Mark Twain meant when he said, "The more you explain it, the more I don't understand it.". . . .

The truth is that in this decision the Court approves the Commission's assertion of power to govern the matter *without* law, power to force surrender of stock so purchased whenever it will, and power also to overlook such acquisitions if it so chooses. The reasons which will lead it to take one course as against the other remain locked in its own breast, and it has not and apparently does not intend to commit them to any rule or regulation. This administrative authoritarianism, this power to decide without law, is what the Court seems to approve in so many words: "The absence of a general rule or regulation governing management trading during reorganization did not affect the Commission's duties. . . ." This seems to me to undervalue and to belittle the place of law, even in the system of administrative justice. It calls to mind Mr. Justice Cardozo's statement that "Law as a guide to conduct is reduced to the level of mere futility if it is unknown and unknowable."

Mr. Justice FRANKFURTER joins in this opinion.

Note: Aftermath of the Chenery Decisions

Following the *Chenery* decisions, the SEC approved two public utility holding company reorganization plans in which management was permitted to participate on the basis of securities in the company purchased pending reorganization.

In Cities Service Co., 26 S.E.C. 678 (1947), the Commission permitted management that had, between 1938 and 1944,[20] purchased securities of the company in the market pending reorganization, to participate fully in a reorganization plan affording them substantial profits on their purchases. The Commission stated that its earlier decision in *Federal Water Service* had been based on "the particular circumstances of the case" and that "we did not undertake to prescribe a standard of conduct generally applicable to trading by officers and directors." [21]

20. Recall that the SEC's first decision in *Federal Water Service* was made in 1941, and the decision on remand in 1945.

21. 26 S.E.C. at 687. The Commission asserted that *Cities Service* was distinguishable from *Federal Water Service* on several grounds: (a) some of the purchases were made before the need for reorganization of the company became apparent; (b) given the nature of the company's financial organization and performance, the approximate structure of the ultimate reorganization was forseeable to informed investors, and the practical ability of management to manipulate current share prices by variations in reorganization proposals was therefore less than in *Federal Water Service*; (c) management here, unlike the Chenerys, had purchased shares for individual investment and not as part of a concerted plan to maintain managing control of the reorganized enterprise. In conclusion, the Commission stated that it was considering issuing a prophylactic regulation dealing with the problem of management purchases in order to avoid the burdens of case-by-case determinations mired in "largely subjective questions of intention and motivation," but that meanwhile management should be warned that trading in their companies was "dangerous to the reorganization process" and "that in light of this warning we will feel much freer in the future to resolve borderline cases against the persons engaged in such trading activities than would be warranted in cases of first impression." 26 S.E.C. at 695.

In American States Utilities Corp., 26 S.E.C. 718 (1947), the Commission also permitted controlling officers and directors to profit through participation in a reorganization plan on the basis of market purchases of the company's securities between 1940 and 1945, pending reorganization. The Commission rejected its staff's argument that *Federal Water Service* stood for an absolute prohibition on management purchases pending reorganization.[22]

Meanwhile, following *Chenery II*, the fourth reorganization plan for Federal Water Service Corp. was finally approved by the SEC. The Chenerys filed objections, claiming that *Chenery II* had sustained the Commission on the understanding that it had adopted a broad prophylactic rule prohibiting all stock purchases by management pending reorganization; that *Cities Service Co.* and *American States Utilities Corp.* demonstrated that the Commission had not adopted such a rule; and that *Federal Water Service* was a far weaker case for prohibiting management purchases than either *Cities Service Co.* or *American States Utilities* because management in the latter cases had been warned by the former litigation of the Commission's disfavor of management purchases, whereas the Chenerys had received no such warning at the time of their purchases. The District Court agreed with the Chenerys' contention and would have concluded that the SEC's approval of the Federal Water Service reorganization plan was unlawful because the plan was not "fair and equitable" as to the Chenerys. However, the court found that it was precluded from so ruling by the Supreme Court's *Chenery II* decision, which it held to be "res judicata, or, at least, the law of the case" on the question of the Chenerys' participation in the reorganization.[23]

Notes and Questions: *Chenery* and the Requirement That Agencies Explain Their Decisions

We deal here with the *Chenery I* requirement that agencies explain their decisions and the evaluation, in *Chenery II* and other decisions, of the adequacy of such explanations. Two other issues presented in the *Chenery* litigation — the problem of unfair "retroactivity" in agency decisions, and the choice between rulemaking and adjudication in formulation of policy — are discussed later in this chapter.

1. What error was committed by the SEC in its first decision? Since the Supreme Court concedes that the substantive result reached by the SEC — prohibiting the Chenerys from exchanging their newly purchased shares for stock in the reorganized company — is probably within its statutory authority, why didn't the Court uphold the agency's action? What, realistically, will be accomplished by remanding for further proceedings?

---

22. It distinguished *American States* from *Federal Water Service* on the grounds (a) there was no concerted plan of purchases to perpetuate management control and (b) the timing of the purchases made it unlikely that they were connected with management's role in the submission and negotiation of reorganization plans.

23. In re Federal Water & Gas Corp., 87 F. Supp. 289 (D. Del. 1949), *aff'd*, 188 F.2d 100 (3d Cir.), *cert. denied*, 341 U.S. 953 (1951).

When a lower court reaches the right result for the wrong reason, appellate courts generally do not remand for further proceedings, but affirm the lower court's decision after supplying the proper rationale. Why should not courts reviewing administrative action follow this practice?

2. Did the SEC, in its decision on remand from the Supreme Court's first *Chenery* decision, adequately explain its result? Review the controlling provisions of the Act and consider the various potential grounds that might justify the Commission in denying the Chenerys' participation in the reorganized company. If the SEC on remand failed adequately to justify its action, why didn't the Supreme Court in its second *Chenery* decision remand again?

Suppose that the Commission's decisions in *Cities Service Co.* and *American States Utilities Co.* had been handed down before *Chenery II*. Should they have led the Court to hold that the Commission had not adequately explained its decision on remand in the *Chenery* litigation? If the agency need not be consistent from one case to the next in the reasons it gives for its decisions, what is the point of requiring the agency to give reasons in the first place?

3. In recent years reviewing courts, responding to the developing sense of agency "failure," have displayed considerable rigor in applying the requirement that agencies explain their decisions.[24] The requirement of detailed explanation has been extended to informal adjudication, see, e.g., Citizens to Preserve Overton Park, Inc. v. Volpe, supra p. 276; and to informal rulemaking, see, e.g., Kennecott Copper Co. v. EPA, 462 F.2d 846 (D.C. Cir. 1972).

4. What is the source of the courts' authority to demand detailed explanations by agencies of their decisions?

You should consider the interrelation between judicial requirements of detailed explanation and judicial review of agency action as arbitrary and capricious. While detailed findings may often not be necessary to enable a reviewing court to determine whether an agency obeyed relevant statutory directives and acted within the general scope of its authority, it would often be impossible for a court to determine whether an agency's discretionary balancing of relevant factors in given circumstances was plainly unreasonable in the absence of a full explanation.[25] See, e.g., *Scenic Hudson I* supra p. 293.

24. See, e.g., Scenic Hudson Preservation Conf. v. FPC (I), 354 F. 2d 608 (2d Cir. 1965), *cert. denied*, 384 U.S. 941 (1966), supra p. 293; Office of Communications of United Church of Christ v. FCC, 359 F.2d 994 (D.C. Cir. 1966), 425 F.2d 543 (D.C. Cir. 1969) (after remand), infra pp. 1014-1021, 1040-1042; International Harvester Co. v. Ruckleshaus, 478 F.2d 615 (D.C. Cir. 1973); Appalachian Power Co. v. Train, 545 F.2d 1351 (4th Cir. 1976).

25. In Kennecott Copper Co. v. EPA, 462 F.2d 846 (D.C. Cir. 1972), the court found that the Agency's explanation for the adoption of an air pollution standard through informal notice and comment rulemaking was inadequate. The court conceded that the EPA's explanation satisfied the requirement in §553 of the APA that agencies engaged in informal rulemaking furnish a "concise general statement" of the basis and purpose of the regulations adopted. But the court stated that "Inherent in the responsibility entrusted to this court is a requirement that we be given sufficient indication of the basis on which the Administrator [adopted the standard] so that we may consider whether it embodies an abuse of discretion or error of law.

"The provision for statutory judicial review contemplates some disclosure of the basis of the agency's action. Citizens to Preserve Overton Park v. Volpe, . . . Securities and Exchange Commission v. Chenery Corp., . . .

"There are contexts, . . . contexts of fact, statutory framework and nature of action, in

Moreover, the requirement of detailed explanations, supported by facts and logic, can itself be viewed as a technique for controlling administrative discretion by helping to ensure agency consideration of all relevant factors and permitting more careful analysis and decision. Judge Friendly expresses this view in Chenery Revisited: Reflections on Reversal and Remand of Administrative Orders, 1969 Duke L.J. 199, 209-210:

> Thus the *Chenery* Court was saying to the SEC: "Here, instead of doing something traditional, as you wrongly believed, you are venturing into terra incognita. Principles of equity do not compel the ruling you made, although the statute permits you to make it. Have you given enough thought to your choice? Are you entirely sure the evil calls for any remedy, let alone the drastic one you have chosen? Would compulsory disclosure of dealings be a preferable alternative to forfeiture of profits? Have you sufficiently considered the propriety of applying the rule to parties who acted without knowledge that you would impose it, as against using your rule-making authority?" These were questions worth asking. Even if the Chenery Court had scant doubt how they would be answered in the instant case, such a declaration to the agencies, indicating that decisions based on a wrong reason generally cannot be expected to stand even though a reviewing court can discern the possibility of a right one, should improve the administrative process in general.

Judge Friendly goes on to discuss cases in which he believes that remands for more adequate agency explanations have significantly improved administrative decision-making. Such cases, he believes, refute the view that remands simply invite "the mechanical regurgitation of 'canned' findings . . ." [26]

Others take a less favorable view of the impact of judicial attention to detailed agency statements and explanations, concluding that in most instances it merely forces agencies to rationalize decisions reached on other grounds and leads to time-consuming remand proceedings that accomplish little or nothing except to satisfy judicial instincts for tidiness and order. For example, Professor Joseph Sax has challenged the view that decisions will be improved if administrators "articulate the standards and principles that govern their discretionary decisions in as much detail as possible":

> I cannot imagine a more dubious example of wishful thinking. I know of no solid evidence to support the belief that requiring articulation, detailed findings or reasoned opinions enhances the integrity or propriety of the administrative decisions. I think the emphasis on the redemptive quality of procedural reform is about nine parts myth and one part coconut oil.

which the minimum requirements of the Administrative Procedure Act may not be sufficient. In the interest of justice, cf. 28 U.S.C. §2106, and in aid of the judicial function, centralized in this court, of expeditious disposition of challenges to standards, the record is remanded for the Administrator to supply an implementing statement that will enlighten the court as to the basis on which he reached the . . . standard. . . ." 462 F.2d at 849-850.

26. Similar optimism concerning the value of detailed explanations is in Environmental Defense Fund, Inc. v. Ruckelshaus, 439 F.2d 584, 597-598 (D.C. Cir. 1971) (Bazelon, C.J.).

Professor Sax concludes that agencies are unlikely to change established policies reflecting institutional biases unless they receive specific substantive directives from Congress.[27]

5. In many cases where courts remand agency decisions because of inadequacies in the explanations given, one is left with the impression that the judges are motivated less by a conviction that this practice will improve the quality of agency decisionmaking than by a desire to set aside results they disfavor without conspicuously overruling the agency's choice as arbitrary and capricious.[28] This practice produces costly and time-consuming remand proceedings. In some cases, the agency reaches the same result, only to be reversed again by the reviewing court.[29] In other cases, courts may accept the agency's decision on remand, but their action may be influenced by the additional costs and court-agency confrontations that might be provoked by a second remand.[30]

2. The Requirement That Agencies Explain Inconsistent or Deviant Decisions

Contractors Transport Corp. v. United States

537 F.2d 1160 (4th Cir. 1976)

BUTZNER, Circuit Judge:

Contractors Transport Corporation petitions for review of an Interstate Commerce Commission order which denied Contractors' application for a certificate of convenience and necessity under 49 U.S.C. §307 to transport iron and steel articles from Roanoke and Troutville, Virginia, to Delaware, Kentucky, Maryland, West Virginia, and the District of Columbia. . . . [The ICC granted a competing application by Russell Transfer, Inc.]

Referring to Contractors' and Russell's applications, the commission noted: "These proceedings involve the same origins, similar commodities, essentially the same destination States and, in one instance, the same shipper, therefor they have been consolidated and will be disposed in this report and order." . . . George Transfer & Rigging Company, which held a certificate covering most of the areas for which Contractors sought authority . . . filed no protest against Russell.

The commission concluded that the evidence established a need for transportation service in the areas covered by the applications and that each applicant had proved a prima facie case. It held, however, that George was adequately and

27. Sax, The (Unhappy) Truth about NEPA, 26 Okla. L. Rev. 239 (1973).
28. See, e.g., Appalachian Power Co. v. Train, 545 F.2d 1351 (4th Cir. 1976); Office of Communications of United Church of Christ v. FCC, 359 F.2d 994 (D.C. Cir. 1966).
29. See Office of Communications of United Church of Christ v. FCC, 425 F.2d 543 (D.C. Cir. 1969).
30. See Chenery II, p. 342 supra; Scenic Hudson Preservation Conf. v. FPC (II), 453 F.2d 463 (2d Cir. 1971), and id. at 482 (Oakes, J., dissenting), supra pp. 298, 302.

efficiently meeting transportation needs from Roanoke and Troutville to points in Delaware, Kentucky, Maryland, West Virginia, and the District of Columbia. Accordingly, it denied Contractors' application to serve those states. On the other hand, without reference to the adequacy of George's service, the commission granted Russell's application to carry articles of iron and steel from Roanoke and Troutville to a number of points, including Maryland, West Virginia, and the District of Columbia.

The Motor Carrier Act leaves determinations of public convenience and necessity to the commission's discretion, and the scope of judicial review under the arbitrary and capricious standard is narrow. . . . There must be, however, a rational basis for the agency's action. . . . Patently inconsistent application of agency standards to similar situations lacks rationality and is arbitrary. . . . A reviewing court is powerless to supply an explanation for apparent inconsistencies in an agency's decision. SEC v. Chenery Corp. [II]. Thus, the grounds for an agency's disparate treatment of similarly situated applicants must be reasonably discernible from its report and order. . . .

The commission's decision does not meet these requirements. Under substantially similar circumstances, Contractors and Russell received markedly different treatment. The commission stated no basis for its uneven disposition of the two applications, nor did it indicate why George's existing service was adequate to exclude Contractors, but not Russell, from serving destinations in Maryland, West Virginia, and the District of Columbia.

The Commission's order denying Contractors' application must be vacated and the case remanded to the commission for reconsideration. If the commission does not alter its decision, it should explicitly state its reasons for the apparently inconsistent treatment of Contractors and Russell.

Brennan v. Gilles & Cotting, Inc.

504 F.2d 1255 (4th Cir. 1974)

WINTER, Circuit Judge:
Following the collapse of a scaffolding which caused the death of two workers on the payroll of Southern Plate Glass Company (Southern), a subcontractor of Gilles & Cotting, Inc. (Gilles), the Secretary of Labor issued citations against Southern and Gilles for "serious violations" of the safety regulations governing scaffolds. Southern did not contest its liability, but Gilles challenged the citation against it and the accompanying proposed fine of $550. The administrative judge decided both that the fatal scaffolding assembly had been constructed in violation of safety regulations properly promulgated pursuant to the Occupational Safety and Health Act of 1970 (OSHA), and that under the statute Gilles was responsible for the violations. Though he found that Gilles was answerable because its payroll employees had access to the zones of danger created by the scaffold, the principal

basis of his decision was a broader holding that Gilles, as general contractor, was liable under the Act for safety violations hazardous to employees of subcontractors.

On review, the [Occupational Safety and Health Review] Commission, in a split decision, reversed. Stating that no payroll employee of Gilles was "affected" by the scaffold's hazardous condition and concluding that Gilles should not be jointly responsible for the hazard which Southern's scaffolding created for Southern's workers, the majority exonerated Gilles. The Secretary appealed.

We conclude that, under OSHA, the Commission was empowered to decide both of the questions of whether a general contractor should be concurrently responsible for the safety of subcontractor workers as a joint employer and of whether proof of employee *access* to the zones of danger created by a safety violation, short of proof of *presence* in the zones of danger, will suffice to support a citation either way. We therefore affirm the Commission's decision that a general contractor is not jointly responsible for the safety of subcontractor workers. However, we must remand the second issue of access versus presence, since the Commission's decision was . . . an unexplained departure from the rule of decision followed in other OSHA cases that access alone is sufficient to make out a violation. . . .

. . . On the facts of this case, Gilles' responsibility for the scaffold as a direct employer of its own payroll workers turns on a question of law crucial to the enforcement of the Act: whether employee *access* to the zones of danger created by a safety violation suffices to support a citation or whether proof of actual presence is required. . . .

While the choice between access and actual exposure is committed to the Commission's discretion, and indeed would seem to be determinative of Gilles' liability in this case, the opinion of the Commission majority does not expressly decide the question, much less provide the thoroughgoing statement of reasons the issue deserves. . . .

. . . [W]hile administrative agencies can change previously announced policies, . . . and can fashion exceptions and qualifications, they must explain departures from agency policies or rules apparently dispositive of a case. . . .

Notes and Questions

1. The requirements of consistency imposed in *Contractors Transport* and *Gilles & Cotting* seem more rigorous than those employed by courts in the past, and reflect the growing judicial insistence on agency explanations for their decisions.[31]

2. Might the decision in *Contractors Transport* reflect relevant differences among the carriers involved (such as quality of management) that can not easily

31. See also the *Takara* and *Self* decisions summarized at p. 256 supra. But see Butz v. Glover Livestock Commn. Co., 411 U.S. 182 (1973) (Department of Agriculture allowed to suspend registration of stockyard operator for negligent short-weighting despite line of agency decisions saying that such a sanction could only be imposed for "intentional and flagrant misconduct").

be "proved" by record evidence? [32] If so, doesn't the nominally "procedural" requirement of "consistency" impose substantive limits on the agency's discretion?

3. Should an agency be permitted to defend inconsistencies of the sort revealed in *Gilles & Cotting* on the ground that there had been intervening changes in the agency's membership?

4. The Federal Trade Commission seeks to prevent misleading and deceptive advertising. One of the more trivial questions in this area that has caused confusion over the years is whether it is — in the words of §5 of the FTC Act — a prohibited "unfair method of competition" or an "unfair or deceptive act or practice" to represent that a thing is "free" when the customer has to buy something else in order to get it. The Commission in 1953 issued its opinion in the *Black* case, declaring that "the businessmen of the United States are entitled to a clear and unequivocal answer to this question," and then stating:

> Until such time as either the Congress of the United States amends Section 5 of the Federal Trade Commission Act, or until an appellate court of the United States clearly interprets the existing provisions of Section 5 of the Federal Trade Commission Act to mean otherwise, our position in this matter is as follows:
>
> The use of the word "free" in advertising to describe any article is considered by the Commission to be an unfair or deceptive act or practice under the following circumstances:
>
> (1) When all of the conditions, obligations, or other prerequisites to the receipt and retention of the "free" article of merchandise are not clearly and conspicuously explained or set forth at the outset so as to leave no reasonable probability that the terms of the advertisement or offer might be misunderstood; or
>
> (2) When, with respect to the article required to be purchased in order to obtain the "free" article, the offerer either (1) increases the ordinary and usual price; or (2) reduces the quality; or (3) reduces the quantity or size of such article of merchandise.

For a number of years the Mary Carter Paint Company has represented that it will give a "free" can of paint with every can purchased. The company maintained that the purchase price was equivalent to the price of a single can of competing brands of comparable grade and quality and that the customer could not buy a single can of Mary Carter paint for a lower price even if he did not want the free can. The Commission, in a §5 proceeding against Mary Carter, held that even if these contentions were correct, the company had violated that section by its "free" offer. The *Black* decision was not overruled; rather the rule of the case was explained as having "a necessary corrollary" that "a person can offer as 'free' an article which may be obtained upon the purchase of another article only if the article required to be purchased has an established market price." No such price existed in this case because the only price that had been in effect for many years

---

32. Might the difference in result in the SEC decision reviewed in *Chenery* and its subsequent decisions in *Cities Service* and *American States Utilities* be explained on such a ground?

was for two cans. The fact that the customer did not have to take the second can was irrelevant. The lack of any established market price for one can of paint (the prices of other brands of paints not being germane) made the offer deceptive. The company was ordered to cease and desist from representing

> (a) that any amount is respondent's usual and customary retail price of any merchandise when said amount is in excess of the price at which such merchandise is customarily and usually sold by respondents at retail in the regular course of business; or
> (b) that any article of merchandise is being given free or as a gift when such is not the fact.

On Mary Carter's petition for judicial review of the order, what result?

3. Requiring Consistency to Safeguard Expectations — The Problems of "Retroactive" Adjudication

As the decisions in the previous section illustrate, consistency may be required in order to promote more rational administrative decisionmaking. But consistency serves other goals as well. Agency evolution of case-by-case adjudication creates a danger that the governing legal rules will be altered after the relevant events occurred, creating potentially harsh and inequitable defeat of expectations generated by the preexisting law. However, the automatic assumption that every instance of change in legal rules through adjudication is unfairly "retroactive" is not always warranted. The change may have been foreseeable, the magnitude of the reliance interest may be negligible, etc. One must in each case consider the nature, extent, and legitimacy of the expectation interests claimed to have been defeated by an adjudicatory change in the law. Consider, for example, the *Chenery* litigation. Did the SEC's decisions, represent harsh "retroactive" lawmaking, as claimed by the Chenerys and Justice Jackson?

When case-by-case evolution of policy does work unforeseen changes in the law that defeat substantial and legitimate expectation interests, should the courts require consistency in agency adjudication in order to protect expectation interests? Where would reviewing courts derive the power to preclude "retroactive" agency lawmaking in adjudication? [33] Courts themselves, of course, have long been engaged in "retroactive" adjudicatory lawmaking.

Even if courts do have authority to preclude agencies from changing the law through adjudication when important expectation interests would be defeated, on

---

33. While the Constitution prohibits ex post facto criminal legislation, Congress retains considerable freedom to alter the legal consequences of past events where only civil liability is in issue. See, e.g., Lichter v. United States, 334 U.S. 742 (1948) (renegotiation and capture of excess profits on contracts with government); Flemming v. Nestor, 363 U.S. 603 (1960) (termination of accrued Social Security benefits). See generally Hochman, The Supreme Court and the Constitutionality of Retroactive Legislation, 73 Harv. L. Rev, 692 (1960).

what occasions should such authority be exercised? What about the need for flexibility and change in agency policies? In some cases the courts have invalidated the practice of "retroactive" adjudication, and in others sustained it. Are the differences in result attributable to the subjective, ad hoc reactions of the judges in question, or does a consistent pattern emerge? Consider the following:[34]

NLRB v. GUY F. ATKINSON CO., 195 F.2d 141 (9th Cir. 1952), involved an action brought by the NLRB to enforce an order declaring the respondent company guilty of an unfair labor practice for discharging one of its employees, Herves, for not paying union dues. The lawfulness of his discharge therefore hinged on the validity of a closed shop agreement between the Atkinson Co. and the AFL Building Trades Department. The Board held that the agreement was invalid, relying on two changes in policy adopted in Board decisions handed down after Herves' discharge. First, the Board had held that a union chosen by a majority of employees and recognized by the employer at a time when employment was small could not continue as the exclusive bargaining representative when employment had greatly expanded (in the absence of a new election or evidence of support by a majority of the new work force). This ruling was applied to Atkinson and the AFL, Atkinson's work force having greatly expanded since its initial recognition of the AFL. Second, at the time of the Atkinson-AFL agreement and Herves' discharge, the Board was following a decisional policy of not exercising jurisdiction over the building and construction trades. This policy was reversed in subsequent decisions, and the Board applied the new policy in the instant case. The court set aside the Board's order requiring Herves' reinstatement with back pay.

"We think it apparent that the practical operation of the Board's change of policy, when incorporated in the order now before us, is to work hardship upon respondent altogether out of proportion to the public ends to be accomplished. The inequity of such an impact of retroactive policy making upon a respondent innocent of any conscious violation of the [Wagner] act, and who was unable to know, when it acted, that it was guilty of any conduct of which the Board would take cognizance, is manifest. It is the sort of thing our system of law abhors." 195 F.2d at 149.

NLRB v. LOCAL 176, UNITED BROTHERHOOD OF CARPENTERS, 276 F.2d 583 (1st Cir. 1960). The court sustained a Board adjudicatory change of policy that outlawed previously permitted union hiring hall arrangements tending to favor union members, but refused to enforce an order, based on the changed policy, against the union requiring it to refund dues paid by members. The court noted that the unions' conduct "was recognized as unlawful only after it had occurred," and that "a disgorgement order would seem to be an ex post facto penalty." 276 F.2d at 586.

34. Discussed in somewhat greater detail in L. Jaffe & N. Nathanson, Administrative Law: Cases and Materials 269-276 (4th ed. 1976).

NLRB v. E & B BREWING CO., 276 F.2d 594 (6th Cir. 1960), *cert. denied,* 366 U.S. 908 (1961). The NLRB ordered reinstated one of E & B's employees who had been terminated, at the insistence of the Union, on the grounds that he had been hired in violation of the "hiring hall" provisions of the Union's labor contract with E & B. The NLRB's disapproval of such hiring hall provisions as per se unfair labor practices overruled a line of earlier Board decisions, which tolerated them. Held, the NLRB's new policy was impermissibly retroactive in that it "work[ed] hardship . . . altogether out of proportion to the public ends to be accomplished," in requiring reinstatement with a hearing. 276 F.2d at 600, citing NLRB v. Guy F. Atkinson Co., 195 F.2d 141, 149 (9th Cir. 1952).

LEEDOM v. IBEW, 278 F.2d 237 (D.C. Cir. 1960). In a 1953 decision the NLRB adopted a rule that "during the life of any bargaining agreement with a term up to five years, no representation proceedings could be instituted by a labor organization not a party to that contract, provided a substantial part of the industry involved was covered by contracts of a similar term." In a 1958 case the Board shortened its "contract bar" rule to two years, and required a representation election at the behest of a competing union even though a three year contract between the existing union and the employer had 10 months to run. The Board's action was sustained.

"The Board does not deny that the [respondent] Union may have relied upon the [original bar rule then in effect] when negotiating the contract. Nor does it gainsay that retroactive application of the new bar may work a hardship upon the Union. Rather it points out that periodic adjustments in the contract bar rules are necessary to [achieve statutory objectives]. It further contends that immediate application of its revised rule was necessary to prevent 'an administrative monstrosity' . . . In weighing these opposing claims, we think the balance falls in favor of the Board." 278 F.2d at 241-242.

NLRB v. APW PRODUCTS, 316 F.2d 899 (2d Cir. 1963). The Board in a prior adjudication had adopted a "tolling rule." Under this rule, if a trial examiner refused to reinstate an employee who had brought charges of discrimination against his or her employer, and if the Board reversed the trial examiner, the employee would not be entitled to back pay for the period between the trial examiner's decision and the Board's decision. In this case the Board, reversing its hearing examiner, ordered reinstatement and also revoked its tolling rule, awarding back pay for the entire period since discharge. The Board's action was upheld by the court, although the court noted:

"It is not apparent why in the ten months that the Examiner's report was before it, the Board could not have found means to inform the parties — and other interested persons — that overruling of its tolling rule was being considered and to give them some opportunity to express their views." 316 F.2d at 906.

NLRB v. MAJESTIC WEAVING CO., 355 F.2d 854 (2d Cir. 1966). Majestic negotiated with the Union before a majority of its employees had affiliated themselves with the Union. The Board found this to be "unlawful assistance to a union" in violation of 29 U.S.C. §158(a)(2), overruling a prior longstanding decision. The court ruled against the Board on the grounds that Majestic was not adequately notified before the hearing of the substantive claims to be advanced by the Board. In dictum, the court (noting that the Board had required the employer to refund to employees dues paid to the Union) added:

"Although courts have not generally balked at allowing administrative agencies to apply a rule newly fashioned in an adjudicative proceeding to past conduct, a decision branding as 'unfair' conduct stamped 'fair' at the time the party acted, raises judicial hackles considerably more than a determination that merely brings within the agency's jurisdiction an employer previously left without, . . . or shortens the period in which a collective bargaining agreement may bar a new election, . . . or imposes a more severe remedy for conduct already prohibited. . . ." 355 F.2d at 860.

H. & F. BINCH CO. PLANT OF NATIVE LACES AND TEXTILE DIV. OF INDIAN HEAD, INC. v. NLRB, 456 F.2d 357 (2d. Cir. 1972). The court upheld a Board order directing reinstatement with back pay of strikers who had unconditionally applied for reinstatement upon departure of those hired during the strike to replace them. Following decisions in other circuits, it rejected the employer's argument that the Board's decision requiring that strikers be rehired reflected a change of policy that should not be "retroactively" enforced through a back pay award. While noting that "it is indeed surprising that the Board should so consistently have refused to utilize its rule-making powers," the court found that the decision "was hardly a great surprise" in view of other decisions eroding employers' freedom in refusing to rehire strikers. The court found it appropriate to "weigh the hardship" in imposing liability on the employer for conduct that had not previously been proscribed against denial to employees of "important rights that are now recognized to have been properly theirs," concluding that it would "await a stronger case before we refuse to give retroactive force to a Board order because it was founded on a decision enunciating a stricter rule of conduct for employers or unions than the Board had previously imposed."

Questions

1. William Budd, an employee of the Vendetta Company, was subpoenaed by the NLRB in 1969 to testify in an unfair labor practice proceeding against the company. Shortly after giving his testimony, Budd was discharged by the company without any explanation. An unfair labor practice complaint was filed against the company under §8(a)(4) of the NLRA, which prohibits discharge of an employee because "he has filed charges or given testimony under this Act." The Board has jurisdictional requirements limiting the cases in which it would hear charges of unfair labor practices to those involving firms whose revenues exceed a given amount. In 1970, while this proceeding was pending, the Board in a series of case decisions (which did not involve Vendetta and concerned allegations of unfair labor practices

other than §8(a)(4) violations) and press releases adopted new and stricter jurisdictional requirements under which Vendetta's annual volume (from 1965 to 1970
large enough to exceed the Board's dollar minimum then in effect) became too
small to fall within the Board's general jurisdictional boundaries. On this basis, the
Board decided to dismiss the proceeding against Vendetta without reaching the
merits of the case. Budd seeks judicial review of the Board's decision. What result?

2. Acting pursuant to its authority under §9 of the NLRA, the NLRB directed an election among the employees of the A company. There were two competing unions, B and C, and the company manifested its support of B by threatening to close down if C won the election and by threatening to fire those employees
who supported C. (These acts are plainly unfair labor practices under §8 and
therefore subject to the Board's remedial powers.) The election was held; B won;
and C filed objections on the ground that A's preelection conduct prevented a
fair election from being held. While these objections were pending, A entered
into a collective bargaining agreement with B. (If the first election was subject
to invalidation because of A's conduct and a second election warranted, A's entry
into a contract with B would constitute unlawful assistance of a labor organization
under §8.) Fourteen months after the election the objections were still pending,
and the Board in another case overruled the following two long-standing policies:
(1) that a union was deemed to have waived any objections to an employer's preelection conduct if it passed up an opportunity to file objections to that conduct
prior to the election; and (2) that the Board would not rule on the merits of any
objections to an election, no matter when they were filed, where more than a year
had lapsed since that election. Several additional months have passed and a new
NLRB proceeding has been instituted against A seeking to have its contract with B
declared to constitute unlawful assistance under §8. The questions now before the
Board are whether it should apply its newly announced policies so as (1) to declare
that A's recognition of B is an unfair labor practice and to enjoin continued
recognition and (2) to set aside the election and order a new one. How should
the Board rule on these questions? If it does apply the new policies, what should a
reviewing court do? Consider APA §706.

4. Requiring Consistency in Agency Adjudication: The FCC and Allocation in the "Public Interest"

a. Introduction

This section will explore the principle of inconsistency in agency adjudication
in the context of the Federal Communications Commission control of broadcast
licenses. This is an example of an important form of regulation: the allocation of
a commodity in short supply in accordance with a "public interest" standard.

"Public interest" allocation typically is used to deal with problems with the
following characteristics: (1) There are more qualified applicants seeking valuable
goods that the agency controls than there are goods to go around. This is typically

true of applicants for television licenses, trucking rights, airline routes, and scarce natural gas. It is typically untrue of those seeking to become television repairmen or chiropodists. In the latter cases, licensing is designed to enforce minimum standards of service quality. (2) While the agency can set minimum standards to weed out the unqualified, it cannot choose among those remaining on the basis either of a market or a designedly random standard. In some cases, such as communications, the statute is inconsistent with auction or lottery; in others, such as airlines, an auction or lottery would run counter to other major agency policies.

The systems used by the FCC, the CAB, and others to award licenses, routes, etc. in accordance with a "public interest" standard have worked as follows. First, the agency (usually through rulemaking) defines the product to be given out. The CAB, for example, has had to decide which city-pairs to combine into a "route," and the FCC must decide how much of the electromagnetic spectrum will be awarded to an applicant. Second, the agency (again through rulemaking) promulgates minimum qualifications — such as legal, financial or technical qualifications — which will be applied by the staff. Third, the agency will choose among qualified applicants on the basis of evidence produced in a lengthy, complex, "comparative" adjudicatory hearing, at which the competing parties can present evidence and argument about the criteria for choosing among the applicants and the extent to which they meet those criteria. Fourth, the agency later must determine whether to renew the rights it has awarded and what advantages, if any, to give the incumbent in the adjudicatory "renewal" proceedings.

Note: Broadcasting Regulation

The need for government regulation of broadcasting is commonly explained by the limited amount of electromagnetic "space" available. The electromagnetic spectrum has a wide variety of uses, ranging from astronomy to citizen band radio. To avoid interference, that spectrum must be allocated among uses, and to avoid interference among, say, broadcasters who use a portion of that spectrum, each must be restricted to a particular frequency.

When commercial radio was in its infancy in the 1920s, the Department of Commerce made licenses available to whoever applied. Broadcasters using the same frequency in overlapping areas caused interference and static. Congress responded to the resulting demand for regulation with the Radio Act of 1927 and the Federal Communications Act of 1934. The latter Act, like much of preceding regulatory legislation, gave broad authority to a multimember administrative commission, which was to allocate the spectrum, assign frequencies, determine the power and location of transmitters, and award broadcast licenses to applicants insofar as doing so would serve "the public convenience, interest and necessity."

The statutory provisions governing the awarding of licenses are contained in 47 U.S.C. §§ 307-310:

> Sec. 307. (d) No license granted for the operation of a broadcasting station shall be for a longer term than three years and no license so granted

for any other class of station shall be for a longer term than five years, and any license granted may be revoked as hereinafter provided. Upon the expiration of any license, upon application therefor, a renewal of such license may be granted from time to time for a term of not to exceed three years in the case of broadcasting licenses, and not to exceed five years in the case of other licenses, if the Commission finds that public interest, convenience, and necessity would be served thereby. . . . Consistently with the foregoing provisions of this subsection, the Commission may by rule prescribe the period or periods for which licenses shall be granted and renewed for particular classes of stations, but the Commission may not adopt or follow any rule which would preclude it, in any case involving a station of a particular class, from granting or renewing a license for a shorter period than that prescribed for stations of such class if, in its judgment, public interest, convenience, or necessity would be served by such action.

APPLICATIONS FOR LICENSES

Sec. 308. (a) The Commission may grant construction permits and station licenses, or modifications or renewals thereof, only upon written application therefor received by it. . . .

(b) All applications for station licenses, or modifications or renewals therefor, shall set forth such facts as the Commission by regulation may prescribe as to the citizenship, character, and financial, technical, and other qualifications of the applicant to operate the station; the ownership and location of the proposed station and of the stations, if any, with which it is proposed to communicate; the frequencies and the power desired to be used; the hours of the day or other periods of time during which it is proposed to operate the station; the purposes for which the station is to be used; and such other information as it may require. . . .

ACTION UPON APPLICATIONS; FORM OF AND CONDITIONS ATTACHED TO LICENSES

Sec. 309. (a) Subject to the provisions of this section, the Commission shall determine, in the case of each application filed with it to which section 308 of this title applies, whether the public interest, convenience, and necessity will be served by the granting of such application, and, if the Commission, upon examination of such application and upon consideration of such other matters as the Commission may officially notice, shall find that public interest, convenience, and necessity would be served by the granting thereof, it shall grant such application. . . .

(d) (1) Any party in interest may file with the Commission a petition to deny any application. . . . The petition shall contain specific allegations of fact sufficient to show . . . that a grant of the application would be prima facie inconsistent with subsection (a) of this section. Such allegations of fact shall, except for those of which official notice may be taken, be supported by affidavit of a person or persons with personal knowledge thereof. The applicant shall be given the opportunity to file a reply in which allegations of fact or denials thereof shall similarly be supported by affidavit.

(2) If the Commission finds on the basis of the application, the pleadings filed, or other matters which it may officially notice that there are no substantial and material questions of fact and that a grant of the application would be consistent with subsection (a) of this section, it shall make the grant, deny the petition, and issue a concise statement of the reasons for denying the petition, which statement shall dispose of all substantial issues raised by the petition. If a substantial and material question of fact is presented or if the Commission for any reason is unable to find that grant of the application would be consistent with subsection (a), it shall proceed as provided in subsection (e) of this section.

(e) If, in the case of any application to which subsection (a) of this section applies, a substantial and material question of fact is presented or the Commission for any reason is unable to make the finding specified in such subsection, it shall formally designate the application for hearing on the ground or reasons then obtaining and shall forthwith notify the applicant and all other known parties in interest of such action and the grounds and reasons therefor, specifying with particularity the matters and things in issue but not including issues or requirements phrased generally. . . .

(h) Such station licenses as the Commission may grant shall be in such general form as it may prescribe, but each license shall contain, in addition to other provisions, a statement of the following conditions to which such license shall be subject: (1) The station license shall not vest in the licensee any right to operate the station nor any right in the use of the frequencies designated in the license beyond the term thereof nor in any other manner than authorized therein. . . .

Sec. 310. (d) No construction permit or station license, or any rights thereunder, shall be transferred, assigned, or disposed of in any manner, voluntarily or involuntarily, directly or indirectly, or by transfer of control of any corporation holding such permit or license, to any person except upon application to the Commission and upon finding by the Commission that the public interest, convenience, and necessity will be served thereby. Any such application shall be disposed of as if the proposed transferee or assignee were making application under section 308 of this title for the permit or license in question; but in acting thereon the Commission may not consider whether the public interest, convenience, and necessity might be served by the transfer, assignment, or disposal of the permit or license to a person other than the proposed transferee or assignee.

b. The Comparative Hearing

As long as unallocated frequency space exceeded demand, the FCC's licensing problems were limited to determining the applicant's ability to meet minimal technical, financial and legal requirements. Once space became more limited, however, the FCC had to choose among several minimally qualified applicants.[35]

35. The FCC, like other agencies in similar circumstances, found it difficult to define precisely the product that it was going to allocate. It proceeded to do so by developing master allocation plans.

Initially the FCC proceeded on the basis of "first come, first served." It examined applicants serially, awarding the license to A, unless competitors B and C could show A was not minimally qualified. If A was awarded the license, B would be granted a hearing prior to denial; but, as a practical matter, the award to A precluded an award to conflicting applicants B or C.

(1) *The Ashbacker Principle*

Ashbacker Radio Corp. v. FCC

326 U.S. 327 (1945)

Mr. Justice Douglas delivered the opinion of the Court.

The primary question in this case is whether an applicant for a construction permit under the Federal Communications Act . . . is granted the hearing to which

---

To develop a plan for allocating spectrum space to local areas is difficult. AM signals, for example, curve over the horizon (which FM signals do not). Thus a strong signal broadcast on AM will interfere with local signals on the same frequency across the country. To what extent should space be reserved for stations able to broadcast nationally and to what extent should the power of individual stations be limited to allow several stations in geographically separate communities to use the same frequency?

Similarly, how should the television spectrum be divided among communities? Thirteen channels were originally set aside for VHF broadcasting, but because of possible interference, only seven can be received at any particular place. In allocating channels the FCC had to choose between (1) allowing all viewers to receive seven different channels, and (2) allowing many individual localities to originate programs. To give every viewer a choice of seven stations, the seven stations would have to be national or regional with each of the seven broadcasting a single program nationwide at any one time. Alternatively, the FCC could allow, say Peoria, Illinois to possess stations that originated their own programs, but the two or three stations located in Peoria would interfere with Chicago stations on the same frequency. Thus Chicago's allocation would be cut from seven to four or five. Since many Chicago viewers could not pick up Peoria (despite the fact that Peoria's stations would interfere with Chicago's use of the same frequency), Chicago viewers would be left with a choice of four channels instead of seven.

In creating its master plan, the FCC by and large opted for "local origination" over "maximum viewer choice." In doing so, it may have been aided by the Communications Act's command to distribute licenses so as to provide "equality of radio broadcasting service" to "each of the states," §307(b). Yet, this decision has been severely criticized, for it leaves many viewers with only three choices. That fact, in turn, has helped create three national networks, and increased the difficulty of creating a fourth. See R. Noll, M. Peck & J. McGowan, Economic Aspects of Television Regulation (1973).

The master plan does not end the problem of "defining the product" (determining precisely *what* is to be awarded an applicant), for it is still possible that Smith's and Jones's applications for a license to broadcast from town A could interfere with Brown's and White's applications to broadcast from B; that would depend on the power of the transmitters and their precise proposed locations. In such instances, the Commission *first* determines which town, (A or B) should receive the service. It *then* decides which of the applicants, say Smith or Jones, should provide the service.

But it does so by holding a single big hearing in which the parties can argue both questions at once. Brown, for example, may argue that he is much better than Smith or Jones and this vast difference in quality overcomes the fact that A has only two stations while B has three. In other words, the questions of *what* is to be allocated and *who* is to receive it, often are, or can be, interrelated.

he is entitled by §309(a) of the Act, where the Commission, having before it two applications which are mutually exclusive, grants one without a hearing and sets the other for hearing.

In March 1944 the Fetzer Broadcasting Company filed with the Commission an application for authority to construct a new broadcasting station at Grand Rapids, Michigan, to operate on 1230 kc with 250 watts power, unlimited time. In May 1944, before the Fetzer application had been acted upon, petitioner filed an application for authority to change the operating frequency of its station WKBZ of Muskegon, Michigan, from 1490 kc with 250 watts power, unlimited time, to 1230 kc. The Commission, after stating that the simultaneous operation on 1230 kc at Grand Rapids and Muskegon "would result in intolerable interference to both applicants," declared that the two applications were "actually exclusive." The Commission, upon an examination of the Fetzer application and supporting data, granted it in June 1944 without a hearing. On the same day the Commission designated petitioner's application for hearing. Petitioner thereupon filed a petition for hearing, rehearing and other relief directed against the grant of the Fetzer application. The Commission denied this petition, stating,

"The Commission has not denied petitioner's application. It has designated the application for hearing as required by Section 309(a) of the Act. At this hearing, petitioner will have ample opportunity to show that its operation as proposed will better serve the public interest than will the grant of the Fetzer application as authorized June 27, 1944. Such grant does not preclude the Commission, at a later date from taking any action which it may find will serve the public interest. . . ."

Our chief problem is to reconcile two provisions of §309(a) where the Commission has before it mutually exclusive applications. . . .

. . . It is plain that §309(a) not only gives the Commission authority to grant licenses without a hearing, but also gives applicants a right to a hearing before their applications are denied. We do not think it is enough to say that the power of the Commission to issue a license on a finding of public interest, convenience or necessity supports its grant of one of two mutually exclusive applications without a hearing of the other. For if the grant of one effectively precludes the other, the statutory right to a hearing which Congress has accorded applicants before denial of their applications becomes an empty thing. We think that is the case here.

. . . Congress has granted applicants a right to a hearing on their applications for station licenses. Whether that is wise policy or whether the procedure adopted by the Commission in this case is preferable is not for us to decide. We only hold that where two bona fide applications are mutually exclusive the grant of one without a hearing to both deprives the loser of the opportunity which Congress chose to give him. . . .

Mr. Justice FRANKFURTER, dissenting.

. . . There is nothing in the Communications Act that restricts the Commission in translating its duty to further the public interest as it did in the particular situation before it. In granting Fetzer's application and setting the denial of the petitioner's down for a hearing after fully canvassing the situation, the Commission brought itself within the explicit provisions of the Communications Act and applied them with that flexibility of procedure which Congress has put into the Commission's own keeping. [Moreover], [a]dministrative practice indicates that where there are conflicting applications, the Commission has granted some without hearing where it thought the public interest best served by that procedure, while setting others for hearing where the public interest so demanded. Fetzer made a clear showing to the agency designated for the purpose by Congress that the public interest would be served by the grant of its application. The same agency found no basis in public interest for Ashbacker's application. Certainly it is wholly consonant with the scheme of the legislation and the powers given to the Commission that, upon denial of the Ashbacker application after a finding that it would not and Fetzer would serve the public interest, the burden be cast on Ashbacker to show that it would serve the public interest better than would Fetzer. . . .

Note: Scope of the Ashbacker Hearing

While *Ashbacker* stands for the proposition that qualified applicants must be given a *meaningful* hearing, it is uncertain how extensive that hearing must be. On the one hand, the Supreme Court in United States v. Storer Broadcasting Co., 351 U.S. 192 (1956), significantly limited the extent of an applicant's hearing right by allowing the FCC to deny a hearing to applicants which its rules automatically disqualified. The FCC had adopted "multiple-ownership" rules limiting the number of media interests that any one licensee could control. Storer had reached its limit under the rules and was denied its application for an additional station without a hearing. The Supreme Court held that the rules were reasonable, the FCC had power to adopt them, and, since they automatically disqualified Storer, there was nothing to have a hearing about. "We do not think Congress intended the Commission to waste time on applications that do not state a valid basis for a hearing," 351 U.S. at 205.

On the other hand, in an earlier case, Johnston Broadcasting v. FCC, 175 F.2d 351 (D.C. Cir. 1949), the Court of Appeals cast some doubt on the Commission's ability to limit the issues that can be raised at a comparative hearing. In addition, the opinion explores some of the difficulties inherent in the process. The Court held that the Commission had adequately considered the merits of the two contenders. In doing so, it wrote:

A choice between two applicants involves more than the bare qualifications of each applicant. It involves a comparison of characteristics. Both A and B may be qualified, but if a choice must be made, the question is which is the better qualified. Both might be ready, able and willing to serve the public interest. But in choosing between them, the inquiry must reveal which would better serve that interest. So the nature of the material, the findings and the bases for conclusion differ when (1) the inquiry is merely whether an applicant is qualified and (2) when the purpose is to make a proper choice between two qualified applicants. To illustrate, local residence may not be an essential to qualification. But as between two applicants otherwise equally able, local residence might be a decisive factor. . . .

Findings must be made in respect to every difference, except those which are frivolous or wholly unsubstantial, between the applicants indicated by the evidence and advanced by one of the parties as effective. . . . The final conclusion must be upon a composite consideration of the findings as to the several differences, pro and con each applicant.

. . . The Commission cannot ignore a material difference between two applicants and make findings in respect to selected characteristics only. Neither can it base its conclusion upon a selection from among its findings of differences and ignore all other findings. It must take into account all the characteristics which indicate differences, and reach an over-all relative determination upon an evaluation of all factors, conflicting in many cases. In its judgment upon this evaluation, the Commission has wide discretion.

We say that the required findings need go no further than the evidence and the proposals of the parties. . . . When the minimum qualifications of both applicants have been established, the public interest will be protected no matter which applicant is chosen. From there on the public interest is served by the selection of the better qualified applicant, and the private interest of each applicant comes into play upon that question. Thus, the comparative hearing is an adversary proceeding. The applicants are hostile, and their respective interests depend not only upon their own virtues but upon the relative shortcomings of their adversaries. We think, therefore, that the Commission is entitled to assume that in such a proceeding the record of the testimony will contain reference to all the facts in respect to which a difference between the parties exists, and that the parties will urge, each in his own behalf, the substantial points of preference. The Commission need not inquire, on its own behalf, into possible differences between the applicants which are not suggested by any party, although in its discretion it may do so. . . .

(2) The Selection Process Up to 1965

Let us examine the procedure developed by the FCC in picking the winning applicant in the case of conflicting applications.

The FCC has promulgated criteria setting forth minimal qualifications. Its staff applies those criteria to weed out unqualified applicants. The FCC requires applicants to complete an elaborate formal application, which elicits information relevant to criteria such as the following:

legal qualifications: citizenship; history of any violations of law; compliance with rules concerning cross-ownership (owning more than one TV or radio station or newspaper), compliance with other ownership rules; etc.

financial qualifications: source of capital, amount of capital; estimated costs, revenues, construction expenses, etc.

proposed program service: efforts made to determine community needs (surveys); proposed programming, amount of time devoted to public service, news, etc.; proposed method of operating the station.

engineering qualifications: frequency, transmitter height, terrain, antenna, etc.

As is apparent, these criteria are complex, yet they are so administered that they are likely to produce more than one qualified applicant for television or radio frequencies with significant commercial value.[36]

Where several applicants meet these minimal criteria the agency enters into an elaborate hearing procedure, the object of which is to help the FCC determine which applicant is the "best." During such a hearing, each applicant, represented by counsel, argues that it is "good," and its competitors are "bad."

Prior to 1965, the Commission announced that it would take the following into account in determining the comparative merits of competing applicants:

The extent to which the station would *be locally owned.*

The extent to which *management and ownership* is integrated, i.e., do the owners themselves participate in management?

The extent to which owners have *diverse backgrounds.*

The extent to which owners have *participated in civic affairs.*

Proposed program policies.

The carefulness of operational planning.

Relative likelihood of the station *carrying out* the *program proposals* that it promises.

Broadcast experience.

Past broadcast record.

The adequacy of technical facilities.

The background and qualifications of *staff.*

The *character* of the *applicants* as revealed, for example, by past violations of law.

The *areas* and *populations* to be served.

Avoiding *concentration of media control;* i.e., does the applicant already own a radio station, a television station, or a newspaper?

The FCC indicated that certain of these criteria were much more important than others, but it did not indicate how much more. Each applicant was given preferences or demerits — pluses, minuses, or neutrals — as to each criterion. Although there were not any clear set of criteria indicating how the factors were to be weighted, the FCC compared preferences and demerits and announced a winner. See K. Jones, Licensing of Major Broadcast Facilities by the FCC 48-50 (1962).

(3) *Consistency in FCC Decisionmaking: The Biscayne Case*

The *Biscayne* case, which follows, typifies some of the problems inherent in the FCC's procedures and the regulatory task it has undertaken. Four applicants

36. If there is only one such applicant, the criteria can be administered by the staff. Authority is delegated to the head of the broadcast bureau to decide most issues, and his decision will be reviewed only in unusual instances.

sought a license to operate an unallocated television channel in the Miami area. Each met the FCC's minimum requirements. A comparative hearing opened in February 1954. The FCC reached a decision in January 1956. Court challenges and remands delayed the proceedings further and a final award was made in 1962.

The FCC, in its 1956 decision, held that the four applicants were equal in three categories of comparison ("civic participation," "program proposals," and "engineering capacity'). In "local ownership" Biscayne ranked second; in "diversification" it ranked last. On the other hand, its "past broadcast experience" was good, and it had the best proposal for the "integration of management and ownership."

Biscayne's competitors pointed out, however, that Biscayne's General Manager, Niles Trammel, was formerly president and chairman of the board of the National Broadcasting Company (NBC) and, after retiring retained a consulting relationship under contract with NBC. This contract, they alleged, created a conflict of interest, which, under past FCC decisions, warranted a demerit. The Commission did not assess a demerit and awarded the license to Biscayne.

The Commission stated on this point in conclusion 35 of its opinion:

In view of the advisory area in which Mr. Trammell will perform services for NBC — general policy problems, station problems, sales policies, talent, film and related matters — and the further fact that the terms of the contract provide that Mr. Trammell shall do nothing in conflict with NBC interests, we are told that we must conclude in view of past decisions of the Commission that Biscayne's position as a free competitor in the broadcast field is disturbed. . . . We point out that his contract is an independent contractor's arrangement under which, on request, Mr. Trammell gives advice from time to time or makes contacts for NBC on the basis of his past knowledge and experience. The contract fee [$25,000 per year], while substantial, is in the nature of an honorarium, as well as a means whereby NBC retains a link with the knowledge and experience of one of its former officials and prevents that former official from communicating trade secrets to others. Unlike the facts in the prior cases of conflict of interests upon which the Commission has passed, we have here in Mr. Trammell, an individual who is no longer an official of a network, who cannot act for that network in any decisive manner and who can decide none of its policies. It is thus distinguishable from Abilene Broadcasting Company, 3 [P & F Radio Reg. Rep.] 1684, decided December 31, 1947, in which Abilene Broadcasting Company was penalized because its 30% stockholder Cagle was also president, director and general manager (and 10% stockholder) of Texas State Network, Inc., which had 16 affiliated radio stations in Texas, one of which was KRBC, the only existing station in Abilene (and which would be a competitor of the applicant). The Commission said that, as a stockholder in the network Cagle would be interested in building up KRBC, an affiliate of the network, which would interfere with his obligation to build up the station applied for. Nor is the present situation like that obtaining in WJPS, Inc. 3 [P & F Radio Reg. Rep.] 1314 (1947). There the Commission ruled that the fact that a 25% stockholder in an applicant corporation was also the vice-president of the American Broadcasting Company is an important consideration in deciding which of two comparative applications should be preferred. The dissimilarity lies, as has been observed, in the severance of Mr. Trammell's control over network operation which occurred when he resigned from the NBC network. Mr. Trammell's status is no longer that of an officer or employee of a network. The situation of an agent serving two principals whose interests may not always coincide is therefore absent. In the narrow advisory area that remains we, like the Examiner, note the testimony of Mr. Trammell recorded herein that in the event of possible impairment of his efficiency as an officer of Biscayne by virtue of consultant duties he would terminate the consultant relationship. It is our judgment that the consultant contract should have no adverse effect upon the application of Biscayne in this proceeding.[37]

Biscayne's competitors appealed to the courts. They argued in the Court of Appeals that, under its past cases, the FCC was obliged to assess a demerit against Biscayne, and given the closeness of the contest, a demerit would swing the balance against it.

Sunbeam Television Corp. v. FCC

243 F.2d 26 (D.C. Cir. 1957)

FAHY, Circuit Judge. . . .
The Commission determined that a consultant contract which Mr. Trammell, the President, Director and General Manager of Biscayne, had with the National Broadcasting Company, . . . "should have no adverse effect upon the application of Biscayne in this proceeding." We think this was error. [The court went on to discuss the details of Mr. Trammell's $25,000 contract with NBC, and his central role in the Biscayne organization.]
The failure to give any adverse effect to Mr. Trammell's association with NBC, in considering the comparative qualifications of Biscayne, was a departure from the Commission's established policy that it is desirable for local television stations and network organizations to be independent of each other, and thus to assure that networks can freely compete for affiliation with local stations, and local stations freely compete for network affiliation. This policy is found in the Commission's decisions. In Abilene Broadcasting Co., 3 Pike & Fischer RR 1684, adverse significance was attached to the fact that a substantial stockholder of the applicant was an officer and director of a network, a part of which was in competition with the applicant. In WJPS, Inc., 3 Pike & Fischer [Radio Reg. Rep.] 1314, the Commission regarded the fact that a substantial stockholder of the applicant was also vice president of American Broadcasting Company, a network, "an important consideration in deciding which of two mutually exclusive applications should be preferred."
. . . The Commission now differentiates these cases, relying on ". . . the severance of Mr. Trammell's control over network operation which occurred when he

37. 11 P & F Radio Reg. Rep. 1113, 1160-1161 (1956).

resigned from the NBC network. Mr. Trammell's status is no longer that of an officer or employee of a network. The situation of an agent serving two principals whose interest may not always coincide is therefore absent."

A person under contract to do nothing in conflict with a particular network of the scope of NBC, from which he receives compensation of $25,000 per annum, considered with other provisions of the contract to which we have referred, is contractually bound to the interests of the network, though not by the ordinary employee-employer or officer-company relationship. He is an agent "serving two principals whose interests may not always coincide." Mr. Trammell's relationship with NBC is of a character that is not unlikely to affect Biscayne's choice of network affiliation, and NBC's choice of a local outlet in the Miami area.

Though Biscayne was not necessarily disqualified by this conflict of interest of its President, the error in refusing to consider it as adverse to Biscayne cannot be said to be insubstantial. The comparative qualifications of the competing applicants made the choice between them a close one. This is emphasized by the decided advantage of the other applicants with respect to diversification of media of mass communication, long considered important because of the public interest in non-concentration of control over, and of the sources of, media of communication. The Commission held "there can be no question that each of the other three applicants is entitled to a preference over Biscayne on this factor." The importance of this preference given to the appellants over Biscayne is intrinsically obvious. But the importance of Biscayne's own preferences based on the broadcast experience and past records of its principals is not so obvious. In considerable part these preferences appear to have arisen from Biscayne's concentration of media of mass communication, which is itself an adverse rather than a preferential factor. It thus appears that two of Biscayne's three preferences arose from conditions which might on reconsideration cause the Commission to accord them less weight than it accords the preferences of appellants. In any event we cannot say that had the Commission also considered adversely to Biscayne the Trammell arrangements with NBC the decision would have been the same. . . .

Reversed and the case remanded for further proceedings not inconsistent with this opinion.

Federal Communications Commission: In re Application of Biscayne Television Corp.

22 F.C.C. Reports 1464 (1957)

DECISION [ON REMAND]

(ADOPTED: JUNE 20, 1957)

. . . 4. The Commission readopts so much of conclusion 35 of its original decision as remains after striking the last three sentences thereof and [substituting] . . . , to-wit:

"Mr. Trammell's position is, to a limited extent — namely his contractual obligation to NBC — that of an agent serving two principals whose interests may not always coincide. Previous Commission cases cited by exceptors to the initial decision dealt, in each instance, with the presence in an applicant of a stockholder who was an important officer in a network organization. In the circumstances the Commission was concerned — though not to the extent of disqualifying the applicant — with the possibility of network dominance as it might be influenced by the official position in the network of such stockholder of the applicant. Mr. Trammell's status as an agent of NBC, effected through the medium of a contract under which he can be called upon to advise NBC on matters set forth in this decision, is of less serious concern to the Commission than the relationships involved in the referenced proceedings since Mr. Trammell's NBC agency status is advisory and not executive. . . . At the time of this hearing, . . . there were 3 television stations operating in the Miami area, and 2 others were allocated and in hearing status (including this channel 7). . . . In the situation here present the public is assured of the availability of the three national networks programs over approximately equivalent facilities, assuming that each of the networks desires an affiliate in the area and that the stations allocated desire an affiliation, matters over which the Commission has no jurisdiction. The Commission therefore concludes — upon full consideration of the facts as they appear of record with respect to the Trammell contract, as set out in the decision, including the consideration that such contract is of a consulting nature which presents a situation in no way carrying the duties and powers present in an officer-company relationship; the fact that in actual operation the contract has led to only infrequent contacts between Mr. Trammell and NBC and that the record indicates that this will continue to be the situation; Mr. Trammell's uncontradicted testimony that he will not allow any activities under such consultant contract to interfere with or impede his duties with and responsibilities to Biscayne and that he would relinquish the agreement if called upon thereunder to perform acts inconsistent with his responsibilities to Biscayne — that the adverse considerations which attach as a result of the contractural arrangement do not involve substantial questions of public policy. . . . Nevertheless a possible conflict of interest, latent in the consultant arrangement which according to the record has now about 2½ years yet to run, exists. That the other Biscayne principals were fully apprised of the arrangement does not remove the matter from the boundaries of Commission concern. To sum up the matter, the Commission is of the view that the consulting arrangement, though not one of major concern on the basis of the considerations set forth, supra, involves an undesirable aspect on the basis of which a demerit should be visited upon Biscayne."

. . . 6. The Commission strikes conclusion 45 in toto and . . . adopts the following, to wit:

"45. The applicants before us have been found and concluded to be substantially equal in several areas of comparison: programming, program policies and preparation of proposals, studios, equipment, staffing, and civic participation. Slight differences have been noted in local residence and in diversification of occupation of principals. In local residence, East Coast and Sunbeam make showings which are better than those of Biscayne and South Florida; however, the showings of the latter two applicants are substantial, and the percentage superiority of East Coast and Sunbeam therefore is of cumulative force only, yielding only a minor preference. With respect to the diversification of business and professional endeavors of the principals of the applicants, Biscayne suffers in comparison with its competitors, but this factor is of lesser strength in comparison with the other factors in which differences are found. In integration of ownership with management, the Commission is impressed with the showing made by Biscayne as distinctly superior to that of any other applicant. Here stressed is the meaningful character of the integration shown by Biscayne, in terms of strong experience for the responsibility vested coupled with demonstrated civic responsiveness. Also, Biscayne has been given a preference on the factor encompassing the broadcast experience of its principals in Miami, the particular area here involved, . . . a vital element in the assurance of effectuation of proposals. Finally, the past broadcast records of WIOD and WQAM, traceable to important principals of Biscayne have been found to be good records on an overall basis and superior in some respects. Thus, on three significant factors Biscayne excels; on another its showing has been good, but slightly inferior to two other applicants; on a fifth factor, secondary in significance, it defers to the other applicants. We note as adverse to Biscayne the matter of the consulting contract. In diversification of communications interests, an important factor in the circumstances of this case, all other applicants obtain a clear preference over Biscayne. The task of evaluation, then, is to determine whether this last factor, coupled with the minor preferences noted against Biscayne on 2 other factors, and the demerit arising from the consulting arrangement, shall overcome the superiorities achieved by Biscayne in 3 significant elements. The Commission is satisfied that the balance is with Biscayne. All things considered, it has demonstrated, in our judgment, qualifications that surpass those of the competitors. The only elements of any consequence detracting from its superior showing are its diversification disadvantage and the demerit referred to. These comparative detractions do not overcome Biscayne's substantial superiority on the basis of its overall proposals herein. It is concluded, upon reconsideration, that Biscayne is the most qualified of the four parties which sought this channel, to provide a service in the public interest, convenience and necessity. Our decision therefore is that the grant should be affirmed to Biscayne. . . ."

Questions

1. On what basis did the FCC decide that a license should be awarded to Biscayne?

2. Why did the *Biscayne* court concern itself with the matter of the FCC's consistency? Were the FCC's distinctions of past cases not persuasive? In any event, why should the FCC be precluded from changing its mind about the relative importance it places upon certain possible conflicts of interest, or, for that matter, about any other factor that goes into determining the "public interest, convenience, and necessity"?

3. Suppose one of Biscayne's competitors had sought judicial review of the

Commission's decision on remand. How should the court of appeals decide the case?

(4) Criticism of the FCC's Use of Standards and the FCC's Effort to Develop Precise Criteria

The FCC has long been criticized for failure to develop a coherent set of standards that will allow consistent adjudication of conflicting licensing applications. The Landis Commission, for example, stated that the FCC "seems incapable of policy planning. . . , of fashioning procedures that are effective to deal with its problems." Judge Friendly quotes a Senate Committee's conclusion that the FCC resolves comparative proceedings "through an arbitrary set of criteria whose application . . . is shaped to suit the cases of the moment." Indeed, Judge Friendly, while recognizing the difficulties involved, criticizes the FCC as well for its failure to develop a "better definition of standards." [38]

The problem has not been that the FCC had too few standards, but rather that it has had too many. The FCC has not indicated how the pluses and minuses it awards are to be added or compared. Is a negative on "broadcast experience" more important than a negative on "past broadcast record"? And how do both compare with "concentration"? In other words, it is better to be a new applicant for a television station without prior experience, an applicant that owns a radio station in a nearby community with a good record, or one that owns a television station in a distant community with an average record? Moreover, how does one determine *how* good a broadcast record must be to warrant a plus? The FCC indicated that certain criteria were more important than others, but it explained neither how awards of credit were to be scaled within a single criterion nor how credits and demerits in different categories were to be compared.

Those who have studied the FCC's comparative hearing process complain that these problems are not simply theoretical. After exhaustively examining comparative hearing procedures, one scholar characterized them as "unpredictable, excessively discretionary, complex and baffling, deficiently consonant with the rule of law, and producing results that seem inconsistent from case to case." [38a] The lack of definite standards deprives applicants of sufficient notice, allows retroactive application of new policy, prevents the growth of precedent and leads to a cynical public suspicious of a "corrupt" commission. One scholar claims, for example, that the only fact that explains FCC awards over a period of many years is that the FCC consistently awarded licenses to applicants who supported the presidential candidate who was successful.[38b]

---

38. H. Friendly, The Federal Administrative Agencies: The Need for Better Definition of Standards 53-73 (1962).

38a. Anthony, Towards Simplicity and Rationality in Comparative Broadcast Licensing Proceedings, 24 Stan. L. Rev. 1, 39 (1971).

38b. Schwartz, Comparative Television and the Chancellor's Foot, 47 Geo. L.J. 655 (1959).

Before giving way to total cynicism, however, one should consider the nature of the problem with which the FCC must deal. It must award licenses in the "public interest," but how precisely is it to define that vague term? The criteria used by the Commission suggest that it is interested in obtaining diversity of media ownership, local ownership, and also "good programming."

The concern with programming suggests a serious dilemma. Surely a Commission asked to award licenses in the public interest must have "good programming" as some kind of objective; to ignore programming entirely would make a mockery of its mission. Yet efforts to consider the type or quality of the programming an applicant is likely to offer encounter three serious difficulties.

First, the applicants are likely to promise whatever sorts of programming the commission requires, yet later depart from the prior promises. A sample of 35 comparative hearing cases between 1952 and 1965, for example, reveals that winning applicants *proposed* dedicating an average of 31.5 percent of their time to live local broadcasting. They *actually* devoted less than 12 percent of their time to such programs. The difficulty of enforcing program promises arises in part out of the FCC's tendency to grant renewal applications, and its limited ability to prevent winning applicants from transferring their licenses to others.[38c]

Second, the Commission must take account of restrictions on censorship, arising out of both the First Amendment and the Communications Act. The court in *Johnston Broadcasting* confirmed the Commission's power to take programming into account, for it noted that "in a comparative consideration, it is well recognized that comparative service to the listening public is the vital element and programs are the essence of that service." [38d] Yet the Commission is reluctant to act in ways that might even arguably be characterized as violating the free speech protected by the First Amendment or constituting "censorship" forbidden by §326 of the Act.

Third, and perhaps most important, there is neither a clear consensus about what constitutes good (or bad) programming nor is there a clear consensus about the possibility of making such judgments. Decisions on what constitutes good programming — like those concerning ethics, taste, and aesthetics — can be discussed rationally (within limits) but there is greater difficulty in reaching agreement and greater danger in governmental enforcement of unagreed-upon conclusions than in the case of many other political, economic, or social matters. Thus, it would be almost universally acknowledged that a station that runs the same grade B film — called "20,000 Buckets of Blood" — eleven times each week is doing a poor job of programming and *not* simply because of the repetition involved. Yet it seems foolhardy to enter the dispute about what constitutes "good programming for children" with the hope of a clear, precise, consensus solution. As a result, one sees sense in an interpretation of Congress's mandate that Commission decisions have *something* to do with the quality of programming; but precisely *what* and how is uncertain.

The Commission might approach this problem by relying heavily on subjective judgment in awarding licenses. That is to say, it might view the evidence as to the

38c. See Moline Television Corp., 31 F.C.C.2d 263, 272 (1971).
38d. Johnston Broadcasting Co. v. FCC, 175 F.2d 351, 359 (D.C. Cir. 1949).

quality of the persons owning and managing the station, their proposals, their connections with the community, their past records, etc. and simply judge intuitively and instinctively, weighing all the factors, which applicant is likely to do the best job. (And "best job" in part means providing the viewer with "good programs." And, "good programs" means more than just "local programs" or even "news" and "public affairs.") This type of procedure, while not commonly used by lawyers, is commonly used by managers, particularly when filling job vacancies. Formal minimal criteria are supplemented by general, somewhat subjective, criteria related to "qualifications" to select the "best" person for the job.

On the other hand, the suggestion typically made in light of the serious criticisms raised above is that the Commission should develop and formalize its selection criteria, making them more objective, to minimize the role of subjective judgment, and to choose the applicant whom application of the formal criteria automatically selects.[39] The FCC moved towards such an approach in 1965 when, stung by criticism of irrationality, unfairness, inconsistency, and favoritism, it announced the selection of new criteria. The two primary criteria to be applied are "diversification of control of the media" and "integration of ownership and management." Such factors as local residence, participation in civic affairs, and previous broadcast experience are treated as subsidiary to the "integration" issue; the extent to which owners participate in management is paramount. Other factors, such as program proposals, past broadcast record, engineering qualifications, and character, while still relevant, are explicitly downgraded in importance. (It is also still open to the parties to request consideration of other factors.) [40]

The FCC's policy statement has been characterized as "a change in the philosophies of license allocations away from predictions of programming intent and toward structural policies." [41] The Commission has constructed an objective model of the type of station most likely to program in the public interest — a station without owners who have interests in other stations or newspapers, but whose owners come from the locality to be served, stay in touch with civic leaders, and run the station themselves. The applicant who comes closest to this "structural" model will be awarded the license.

There are three major difficulties with the 1965 approach. First, the standards remain highly subjective. Scaling is difficult within each category. To measure the "concentration" factor, for example, one must weigh such subsidiary factors as number of stations owned, degree of ownership, nearness to the station applied for, importance of the stations, etc. How these subsidiary factors should be measured and weighed, and how they should affect the award of a preference, is unclear. Nor does the Commission state how integration and concentration are to be balanced. Moreover, since these "major" factors may appear to the candidates as evenly

39. For an excellent analysis of the FCC's standards and an argument for the use of more precise ones, see Anthony, Towards Simplicity and Rationality in Comparative Broadcast Licensing Proceedings, 24 Stan. L. Rev. 1 (1971).
40. FCC Policy Statement on Comparative Broadcast Hearings, 1 F.C.C.2d 393 (1965).
41. Comment, Comparing the Incomparable: Towards a Structural Model for FCC Comparative Broadcast License Renewal Hearings, 43 U. Chi. L. Rev. 573 (1976).

balanced, the "minor" factors reassume major importance and the parties seek to raise a host of subsidiary issues.

Second, the "major factors" do not seem to have determined the outcome of specific cases. Professors Noll, Peck, and McGowan examined the FCC's awarding of 16 new television broadcast licenses since 1965. The 45 applications for the licenses were ranked in terms of the factors mentioned in the 1965 policy statement. After regressing these factors against the award of the license, they found local ownership, local origination of programming, and news and public affairs programming to be *negatively* correlated with the award of the license, while ownership of other broadcast facilities was slightly *positively* correlated. In other words, the greater the degree of an applicant's local ownership, local origination, or public affairs programming, the *less* likely he would receive the award; while cross-ownership made the award *more* likely — just the opposite of what one would expect from the policy statement. (Newspaper ownership, however, ran in the expected direction, making an award most *unlikely*).[41a]

Third, if the criteria had been made still more specific and if they had been rigorously applied, would they not have yielded an absurd result? An owner of however little experience, managing his own station would have been preferred over an absentee owner no matter how experienced the manager he hired. The owner of a small Albuquerque newspaper presumably could not open a station in Utica, N.Y., while General Motors would be perfectly game to operate the largest station in Detroit. Moreover, the standards used seem to bear little relation to the development of "quality" programs.

Commissioner Hyde summarized the argument for *less* definite standards in dissenting from the 1965 Policy Statement. The statement, he (perhaps unnecessarily) feared,

> would press applicants into a mold . . . thus deterring perhaps better qualified applicants from applying; it would preclude significant consideration of material differences among applicants and result in automatic preferences of applicants slavishly conforming to the mold and eventually for the Commission to decide cases on trivial differences among applicants. . . .

He adds:

> I know of no two where the underlying facts [or] . . . differences among applicants are identical. Therefore, the significance to be given in each decision to each difference and to each criterion must of necessity vary and must necessarily be considered in context with the other facts of the individual cases. . . .
>
> . . . [T]he Commission is . . . placing legislative-like restrictions upon . . . the responsibility Congress intended it to [perform] with broad discretion. It

41a. See R. Noll, M. Peck & J. McGowan, Economic Aspects of Television Regulation (1973).

would appear we do not trust Commissioners to exercise judgement with as much discretion as Congress intended to repose in the agency.[41b]

In a nutshell, greater specificity might lead to *fairer* results but would the results carry out the statute's objective as well? Before trying to answer this question, consider the FCC's experience with renewal applications.

c.   The Renewal Problem

(1) *Background*

The Communications Act explicitly states that broadcasters do *not* obtain any vested right to their licenses, which expire every three years. Yet some expectation of renewal is perhaps reasonable in view of the millions of dollars, as well as the time and effort of employees and suppliers, invested in a station. Such an expectation may also encourage a broadcaster to invest in developing a market, or in "public interest" programming. When a license expires after three years, the licensee applies for renewal. At this point, other applicants may file and demand a comparative hearing.

The FCC first faced the question of whether to give an advantage (or how much advantage to give) to an incumbent in Hearst Radio (WBAL), 15 F.C.C. 1149 (1951). The Commission wrote that "excellent performance as a licensee will be given favorable consideration where we find a reasonable likelihood that such performance will continue." This standard, and the WBAL case, would seem reasonable were it not for the fact that the Commission found WBAL's programming unbalanced and suffering from "an overabundance of commercial programs and commercial religious programs" — until a few months before the hearing, when it reformed. The Commission added:

> The determining factor in our decision is the clear advantage of continuing the established and excellent service now furnished by WBAL, and which we find to be in the public interest, when compared to the risks attendant on the execution of proposed programming of the competing applicant, excellent though the proposals may be.

Rightly or wrongly, the industry took *WBAL* as indicating a policy of "the incumbent wins." In any event, prior to the Commission's 1969 decision in *WHDH*, infra (which technically did not involve a renewal but was interpreted by the industry as an abrupt departure from an automatic renewal policy), only one television renewal was denied over the applicant's objection.[42] In fact no regular

---

41b. 1 F.C.C.2d at 400, 401, 404.
42. Abel, Clift, & Weiss, Station License Revocation and Denials of Renewals, 1934-69, 14 J. Broadcasting 411 (1970).

television renewal applicant faced a comparative hearing in the 1950s and 1960s.[43] Even in the early 1970s, the only major failure to renew consisted of the revocation of Alabama Educational Television's eight licenses, for pursuing racist policy, 50 F.C.C.2d 461 (1975). (Four other denials had taken place for technical reasons).[44]

One can explain the FCC's failure to deny renewal applications on two obvious grounds. For one thing, it reflects to some extent a reasonable view of the merits. It is desirable to encourage market development through broadcaster investment. Stability increases the profitability of long-term investment. Still, it is difficult to see how the merits could justify quite so favorable a policy. Are there not *some* stations which only maximize short-run profits? Is the "competitive spur" theory — that license insecurity encourages better programming — *totally* without merit?

One might supplement the "merits" with political factors. The results reflect to some extent the political power of the existing broadcasters. After the *WHDH* decision, Congress threatened to enact legislation that would have greatly reduced the Commission's authority to deny license renewal. Moreover, even without congressional action, the Chairman of the Senate Communications Subcommittee, who favored the broadcasters' position, has the power to "reward" or "punish" Commissioners through his Committee's review of appropriations, his ability to conduct oversight hearings, and his ability to make politically visible those of the Commissioners' actions likely to prove politically rewarding or embarrassing.

There is, however, another set of factors that should be taken into account — factors more deeply embedded in the "public interest" allocation system itself, and which will be seen at work in other agencies (such as the CAB):

First, the policy would seem to reflect a tendency (common to all administrative or legal institutions) to protect a person's reliance upon reasonable expectations. Note that such a tendency cannot affect the workings of a marketplace, for the market impersonally destroys firms, workers, and investment so that others may prosper. But regulation substitutes for an impersonal marketplace human beings who can be held responsible for what occurs, and who feel inclined to protect the reasonable reliance of the regulated.

In the case of broadcasting the *amount* of reliance can be great. Not only has the TV station owner invested possibly millions of dollars in obtaining a license and developing programs, community contracts, etc., but also employees have invested their time in developing careers with the station. Suppliers and customers as well have a vested interest in the broadcaster retaining his license. But is the reliance reasonable? Of course, the statute proclaims that licenses might not be renewed; it specifically denies the existence of a property right in a license — but years of automatic renewal have created contrary expectations. More importantly, is there *any* feasible way to prevent such expectations from arising? [45]

43. Geller, The Comparative Renewal Process in Television: Problems and Suggested Solutions, 61 Va. L. Rev. 471, 477 (1975).

44. Abel, Clift, & Weiss, supra n. 42, as updated by personal communication with the authors.

45. Compare the inexperienced climber who seeks to scale El Capitan in the face of repeated warnings by a forest ranger that he will not risk the lives of rescuers should the climber

Second, once it is conceded that investment, or reliance, or incumbency, is to be given *some* advantage, how is the agency to decide *how much* advantage to give it? The agency's inherent inability to specify how various relevant factors are to be weighted makes it difficult to specify how all *other* factors are to be compared with that of the incumbency. Moreover, incumbency carries with it not only the reliance (and political and pragmatic) features just mentioned but also the fact that the average incumbent has actually produced programs that are acceptable to the community it serves; the challenger is inevitably associated with uncertainty and risk. And the Commission knows that all it knows about the challenger is based upon an advocates' hearing, which must involve distortion of the truth. It would seem natural that, insofar as the Commission judges who is likely to do the "best" job, to favor the applicant who has already performed adequately over those who have not, whose selection would inevitably involve risk and whose abilities are basically unknowable.

Third, the problem is exacerbated by the amorphous and problematic criteria utilized by the Commission in comparative hearings. The application of indeterminate criteria to choose among a set of initial applicants may not be unfair, for it is no worse than a random lottery; yet, its fairness is questionable when an existing licenseholder (with some equity attaching to possession) is involved, for random selection no longer seems justified. Then, unless the criteria can be justified as likely to produce a better broadcaster, their use to supplant a present broadcaster seems unjustified.

Greater Boston Television Corp. (WHDH) v. FCC

444 F.2d 841 (D.C. Cir. 1970)

LEVENTHAL, Circuit Judge: . . .

The initial proceeding to select a licensee to operate on Channel 5 in Boston began in 1954 with consideration of four mutually exclusive applications. Three years later, the Commission announced the granting of the application of WHDH, Inc., a wholly owned subsidiary of the corporate publisher of the Boston Herald-Traveler newspaper. 22 F.C.C. 767. The station began broadcasting in the same year. While the decision was on appeal in this court, it came to the court's attention that the Commission's award might be subject to an infirmity by virtue of improper ex parte contacts with the Chairman of the Commission. Retaining jurisdiction, we remanded to the Commission for an evidentiary hearing.

. . . [It turned out that] Mr. Robert Choate of WHDH, Inc., had . . . [com-

---

get into trouble. The climber knows full well, that no matter *what* the ranger says, if he gets stuck a rescue party *will* be sent out; and he is right. Is he not *reasonable* (though monstrous) to rely on this *expectation*? Certain expectations cannot easily be destroyed by prior announcements. No matter what Congress or the FCC say, firms and individuals will invest time, effort, and money to obtain and develop broadcasting rights, and once that is done, administrators whose policies will affect that investment are likely to feel *some* obligation to protect it.

municated with the] Chairman of the FCC [ex parte at a private lunch and sought to discuss relevant legislation pending before Congress]. The Chairman, however, rebuffed Mr. Choate's attempt at discussion, and later called public attention to the matter in testimony before the House Committee on Legislative Oversight.

... The Commission ... discerned a meaningful and improper, albeit subtle, attempt to influence the Commission, and condemned it as an effort that "does violence to the integrity of the Commission's processes." ... The Commission concluded that while the original grant to WHDH was not void ab initio, it was voidable and action should be taken to set it aside.... [It allowed] WHDH to continue broadcasting on Channel 5 [but on special temporary authority]....

[In the meantime it] ... held new hearings, this time among three of the four original applicants. On September 25, 1962, it again awarded a construction permit to WHDH. 33 F.C.C. 449. It ascribed a demerit to WHDH because of Choate's improper approaches to the Commission Chairman. In the same order it made a grant to WHDH of an operating license for only four months — stating that it was exercising its discretion to grant a license for such a short term, as contrasted with the 3-year term permissible and normally provided, because it believed this in the public interest due to "the inroads made by WHDH upon the rules governing fair and orderly adjudication." [It then started to hold "renewal hearings" at which WHDH was opposed by BBI, Charles River, and Greater Boston TV]....

Meanwhile, the grant of the 4-month license had been appealed to this court.... On December 21, 1963, while this appeal was pending, Mr. Choate died. We remanded again to determine what effect his death would have on the awards. Being aware of the impending comparative hearings on the renewal of WHDH's temporary license, we authorized the Commission to combine the renewal proceedings with the proceedings, on remand, for reconsideration of the award of the construction permit and the 4-month operating license, both to be conducted on a comparative basis assessing the public interest in the light of the absence of Mr. Choate.

The consolidated comparative proceeding authorized by this court began in May, 1964....

On August 10, 1966, [the] Hearing Examiner issued an exhaustive Initial Decision, in favor of granting the renewal by WHDH....

On January 22, 1969, [after reviewing the applicants in accordance with its 1965 criteria *used for initial license applicants*] the Commission reversed the Hearing Examiner's decision, and entered an order denying the application of WHDH and granting that of BBI....

Reaction to the Commission's decision was swift. One distinguished commentator characterized it as a "spasmodic lurch toward 'the left.' " The television industry began organizing its forces to seek legislative reversal of what seemed to be a Commission policy ... that placed all license holders on equal footing with new applicants every time their three-year licenses came up for renewal.

[On May 19, 1969, the Commission wrote a supplementary opinion which stated that its *WHDH* decision] was not an ordinary renewal case since "unique events and procedures ... place WHDH in a substantially different posture from the conventional applicant for renewal of broadcast license." The FCC noted that WHDH's operation, although conducted some 12 years, has been for the most part under temporary authorizations. It did not receive a license to operate a TV station until September 1962, and then for only 4 months, because of the Commission's concern with the "inroads made by WHDH upon the rules governing fair and orderly adjudication." ...

While the Commission's decision was on appeal to this court, the legislative pressure continued to build. A bill, introduced by Senator Pastore, Chairman of the Communications Subcommittee of the Senate Commerce Committee, proposed to require a two hearing procedure, wherein the issue of renewal would be determined prior to and to the exclusion of the evaluation of new applications. On January 15, 1970, the Commission issued a new Policy Statement, which, while retaining the single hearing approach, provided that the renewal issue would be determined first, in a proceeding in which new applicants would be able to appear to the extent of calling attention to the license holder's failings. ... Only upon a refusal to renew would full comparative hearings be held.

The Policy Statement set forth that a licensee with a record of "solid, substantial service" to the community, without serious deficiencies, would be entitled to renewal notwithstanding promise of superior performance by a new applicant. This was said to provide predictability and stability of broadcast operations, yet to retain the competitive spur since broadcasters will wish to ensure that their service is so "substantial" as to avoid the need for comparative proceedings.

The Commission expressly stated that its policy statement "is inapplicable, however, to those unusual cases, generally involving court remands, in which the renewal applicant, for sui generis reasons, is to be treated as a new applicant." ... In such case the license holder cannot obviate the comparative analysis called for by the established [i.e., the 1965] Policy Statement. ...

WHDH's central contention rests on [its claim that it is involved in a *renewal* proceeding and therefore the Commission cannot judge it according to criteria applicable to *new* applicants. It admits that under the "new applicant" criteria its case is weak].

On that basis it is undeniable that a strong preference would be available to BBI in view of the "integration" and "diversity" criteria. ...

[WHDH claims that] [t]he application of the criteria in the 1965 Policy Statement constitute[s] an improper refusal to honor the established policy of promoting broadcast license stability. ...

If the case were before us solely on the Decision adopted by the Commission on January 22, 1969 — susceptible of the construction that the 1965 Policy Statement was applicable to all renewal proceedings — we would be presented with a different question. While ... this statute does not reflect the same concern for "security of certificate" that appears in other laws, there would be a question whether the Commission had unlawfully interfered with legitimate renewal expectancies implicit in the structure of the Act. In addition, a question would arise whether administrative discretion to deny renewal expectancies, which must exist under any standard, must not be reasonably confined by ground rules and standards — a contention that may have increased significance if First Amendment problems are presented on renewal application by a newspaper affiliate, including the possibility that TV proceedings may come to involve overview of newspaper operations....

Fortunately, the present posture of this case permits us to refer to these problems as matters that are not involved in our decision. The Commission's opinion of May 19, 1969, entered on reconsideration, expressly puts this case in a special and unique category because of the past history of WHDH.

This interpretation of its action is underscored by the 1970 Policy Statement on Comparative Hearings Involving Renewal Applicants. This Statement in essence carries forward the general policy on renewals expressed in Hearst Radio, Inc. (WBAL), 15 F.C.C. 1149 (1951), on which WHDH places substantial reliance. The Commission's 1970 statement puts its policy thus (see 22 F.C.C.2d at 425): "[I]f the applicant for renewal of license shows in a hearing with a competing applicant that its program service during the preceding license term has been substantially attuned to meeting the needs and interests of its area, and that the operation of the station has not otherwise been characterized by serious deficiencies, he will be preferred over the newcomer and his application for renewal will be granted. His operation is not based merely upon promises to serve solidly the public interest. He has done so. Since the basic purpose of the act — substantial service to the public — is being met, it follows that the considerations of predictability and stability, which also contribute vitally to that basic purpose, call for renewal."

The permissibility of the general policy continued by this Statement is not in issue since that is not challenged, if anything it is relied on, by WHDH. Assuming its validity, the Commission's failure to apply the policy to WHDH is not error.

The Commission's 1970 Policy Statement carries a proviso ... indicating that it is inapplicable to "those unusual cases, generally involving court remands, in which the renewal applicant, for sui generis reasons, is to be treated as a new applicant." In such cases the applicant's record will be examined, but subject to the comparative analysis called for by the 1965 Policy Statement.

We think the distinction drawn by the Commission, in both this case and the 1970 statement, providing for special consideration of certain renewal applicants, as in remand cases, as if they were new applicants, to be reasonable both generally and in its application to the case before us....

... WHDH was not expressly informed in advance that the comparison ... was the criteria normally used for a new application devoid of any elements of renewal. But this did not affect the range of proof which any party might tender or contest....

There being no impediment in the content or shape of the record due to lack of fair notice, certainly we cannot say the Commission was unreasonable when in the last analysis it used the tainted overtures of WHDH as a reason for fresh consideration of all applicants, without any special advantage to WHDH by virtue of its operation under lawful but temporary authority....

Affirmed.

(2)   *The FCC's Efforts to Formulate Renewal Policy*

In re Policy Statement on Comparative Hearings Involving Regular Renewal Applicants

22 F.C.C.2d 424 (Jan. 1970)

In 1965 the Commission issued a policy statement on comparative broadcast hearings which is applicable to hearings to choose among qualified new applicants for the same broadcast facilities. See "Policy Statement on Comparative Broadcast Hearings," 1 F.C.C.2d 393. We believe that we should now issue a similar statement as to the comparative hearing where a new applicant is contesting with a licensee seeking renewal of license. . . . There has, however, been considerable controversy on this issue, as shown by the hearings on S. 2004 now going forward before the Senate Subcommittee on Communications. . . .

[This bill, sponsored by Senator Pastore, chairman of the Subcommittee, together with 21 other Senators and 118 representatives, would amend the Communications Act to introduce a two-stage procedure in renewals. The first stage would only involve the existing licensee and its past performance; if its performance were found to be "in the public interest," the license would be automatically renewed, and the second stage comparative hearing, in which competing applicants might participate, would never be held.]

The statutory scheme calls for a limited license term. This permits Commission review of the broadcaster's stewardship at regular intervals to determine whether the public interest is being served; it also provides an opportunity for new parties to demonstrate in public hearings that they will better serve the public interest. It is this latter aspect of the statutory scheme with which we deal here. . . .

The public interest standard is served, we believe, by policies which insure that the needs and interests of the listening and viewing public will be amply served by the community's local broadcast outlets. Promotion of this goal, with respect to competing challenges to renewal applicants, calls for the balancing of two obvious considerations. The first is that the public receive the benefits of the statutory spur inherent in the fact that there can be a challenge, and indeed, where the public interest so requires, that the new applicant be preferred. The second is that the comparative hearing policy in this area must not undermine predictability and stability of broadcast operation.

The institution of a broadcast service requires a substantial investment, particularly in television, and even where the investment is small it is likely to be relatively large to the person making it. It would disserve the public interest to reward good public service by a broadcaster by terminating the authority to continue that service. If the license is given subject to withdrawal despite a record of such good service, it will simply not be possible to induce people to enter the field and render what has become a vital public service. Indeed, rather than an incentive to qualified broadcasters to provide good service, it would be an inducement to the opportunist who might seek a license and then provide the barest minimum of service which would permit short run maximization of profit, on the theory that the license might be terminated whether he rendered a good service or not. The broadcast field thus must have stability, not only for those who engage in it but, even more important, from the standpoint of service to the public.

We believe that these two considerations call for the following policy — namely, that if the applicant for renewal of license shows in a hearing with a competing applicant that its program service during the preceding license term has been substantially attuned to meeting the needs and interests of its area, and that the operation of the station has not otherwise been characterized by serious deficiencies, he will be preferred over the newcomer and his application for renewal will be granted. His operation is not based merely upon promises to serve solidly the public interest. He has done so. Since the basic purpose of the act — substantial service to the public — is being met, it follows that the considerations of predictability and stability, which also contribute vitally to that basic purpose, call for renewal. . . .

If on the other hand the hearing record shows that the renewal applicant has not substantially met or served the needs and interests of his area, he would obtain no controlling preference. On the contrary, if the competing new applicant establishes that he would substantially serve the public interest, he should clearly be preferred over one who was given the opportunity to do so but chose instead to deliver less than substantial service to the public. In short, the past record of the renewal applicant is still the critical factor, but here it militates against renewal and in favor of the new applicant, provided that the latter establishes that he would solidly serve the public interest.

. . . [W]e recognize that the terms "substantially" and "minimally" lack mathematical precision. However, the terms constitute perfectly appropriate standards. Thus, the word "substantially" is defined as "strong; solid; firm; much; considerable; ample; large; of considerable worth or value; important" (Webster's New World Dictionary College Edition, p. 1454); the word "minimal" carries the pertinent definition, "smallest permissible" (id. at p. 937). However, application and evolution of the standards would again be left to the hearing process. The renewal applicant would have a full opportunity to establish that his operation was a "substantial" one, solidly meeting the needs and interests of his area, and not otherwise characterized by serious deficiencies. He could, of course, call upon community leaders to corroborate his position. On the other hand, the competing party would have the same opportunity in the hearing process to demonstrate his allegation that the existing licensee's operation has been a minimal one. And he, too, can call upon community leaders to testify to this effect if that is, indeed, the case. The programming performance of the licensee in all programming categories (including the licensee's response to his ascertainments of community needs and problems) is thus vital to the judgment to be made. . . .

Two other points deserve stress in this respect. First, . . . the renewal applicant will not have to demonstrate that his past service has been "exceptionally" or "unusually" worthy. Were that the criterion, only the exceptional or unusual renewal applicant would win a grant of continued authority to operate, and the great majority of the industry would be told that even though they provide strong, solid service of significant value to their communities, their licenses will be subject to termination. As stated at the outset, such a policy would disserve the public interest. . . .

Second, the renewal applicant must run upon his past record in the last license term. . . .

[T]he renewal applicant, seeking to obtain the benefits of this policy, cannot properly supply minimal service during the first 2 years of his license term and then upgrade during the third year because of the imminence of possible challenge. . . .

We recognized that there can be concern whether this policy will prevent a new applicant willing to provide a superior service from supplanting an existing licensee who has broadcast a substantial, but less impressive, service. But, as stated, there are obvious risks in accepting promises over proven performance at a substantial level, and we see no way, other than the one we have taken, adequately to preserve the stability and predictability which are important aspects of the overall public interest. . . .

DISSENTING OPINION OF COMMISSIONER NICHOLAS JOHNSON

The issues surrounding citizen participation in the license renewal process are among the most complex and significant before the FCC.

The nature of the American political process is such that any efforts to regulate broadcasting by either Congress or this Commission must constitute a negotiated compromise of sorts. That the broadcasting industry today is perhaps the most powerful Washington lobby in our Nation's history is generally acknowledged. Popular reform movements always start with a substantial disadvantage. For none is that more true than for those groups trying to improve the contribution of television to the quality of American life. But, then, the stakes are higher.

There is no question but that the American people have been deprived of substantial rights by our action today. There is also no question that the results could be much worse — given the commitment of the broadcasting industry on this issue, and the introduction of legislation (such as S. 2004) by 22 Senators and 118 Representatives. . . .

There is a germ of legitimate concern in the broadcasters' position. (1) It is inequitable that a broadcaster who has made an exceptional effort to serve the needs of his community, and whose programming is outstanding by any measure, should be subjected to the expense and burden of lengthy hearings merely because some fly-by-night chooses to take a crack at his license. (2) When evaluating a competing application in a renewal case, a record of outstanding performance by the licensee obviously should be given considerable weight. (3) It is far better to provide consistent national standards for station ownership by general rulemaking (with divestiture if necessary) than to involve them on the case-by-case happenstance of which stations' licenses happen to be challenged. (4) There are some public benefits from stability for those broadcasters who take their responsibilities seriously.

What the public loses by this statement can be summarized in the word "competition." The theory of the 1934 Communications Act was that the public would be served by the best licensees available. No licensee would have a right to have his license renewed. Each would be open to the risk that a competing applicant would offer a service preferable in some way, and thereby win the license away. The FCC was to choose the best from among the applications before it, whether the incumbent's record was mediocre or excellent. This is the principle of the marketplace: the public is assured the best products by opening the market to all sellers, comparing their products, and rewarding the best with the greater sales. The analogy in broadcasting is the competing application. The FCC is the public's proxy. It is we who must make the choice among competitors; it is the public that receives the benefits (or burdens) of our choice....

I cannot avoid reference, in passing, to the significance of this particular kind of necessary compromise with broadcasting's power. The record of Congress and the Commission over the years shows their relative powerlessness to do anything more than spar with America's "other government," represented by the mass media....

I have considerable sympathy and respect for my colleagues' commendable and good faith effort to resolve this conflict between formidable political power and virtually unrepresented public interest. They have tried. They really have. And it is not at all clear to me that more than they have done would have been politically possible, or could have withstood political appeal. It is not even clear that today's effort is secure.

Thus it is, with no feelings save understanding, frustration and sorrow, that I dissent.

In re Formulation of Policies Relating to the Broadcast Renewal Applicant, Stemming from the Comparative Hearing Process

27 F.C.C.2d 580 (Feb. 1971)

NOTICE OF INQUIRY

[The purpose of the inquiry was to define the level of "substantial" service that would enable a renewal applicant to avoid a comparative hearing.]

Clearly, any possible guidelines must be general in nature.... However, [we shall] in this inquiry . . . focus on two critically important areas, and give some prima facie indication of what constitutes substantial performance in these areas. The areas are local programming, and programming designed to contribute to an informed electorate. The reason for focus on these two areas is obvious. The congressional scheme of TV allocations is based on local outlets.... If a television station does not serve in a substantial manner as a local outlet — if it is, in effect, a network spigot or mere purveyor of nonlocal film programming, it is clearly not meeting its crucial role. Similarly, we have stated that the reason we have allotted so much spectrum space to broadcasting is because of the contribution which it can make to an informed electorate.... If a broadcaster does not make such a contribution in a substantial fashion, he is again undermining the basic allocations scheme....

With this as necessary background, we now set out the following proposed figures as representing *substantial* service:

(i) With respect to local programming, a range of 10-15% of the broadcast effort (including 10-15% in the prime time period, 6-11 P.M., when the largest audience is available to watch).

(ii) The proposed figure for news is 8-10% for the network affiliate, 5% for the independent VHF station (including a figure of 8-10% and 5%, respectively in the prime time period).

(iii) In the public affairs area, the tentative figure is 3-5%, with, as stated, a 3% figure for the 6-11 P.M. time period.

These figures are, of course, tentative ones set forth for comment by the interested parties.

There are a number of obvious considerations as to the above inquiry. First, as stated, it does not constitute the complex picture as to whether a station is rendering substantial service. Thus, it does not deal with every programming category. We believe that not every category is susceptible to the drawing of general guidelines. For example, there may be substantial agricultural interest in one area, and virtually none in another. As to such variables, only individual inspection, perhaps in the hearing process, could definitively delineate whether substantial service was being rendered in every respect. This point merits emphasis; we have no intention, now or at any future time, to try to delineate that X% of time need be devoted to a particular programming area such as agriculture, religious, etc. Second, even as to the two general areas where we think we can usefully set forth overall guidelines, ... we point out that the guidelines, if adopted, would not be a requirement that would automatically be definitive, either for or against the renewal applicant. Thus, if the applicant did not meet these guidelines, he could still argue in a comparative hearing that his service was substantial. . . .

CONCURRING OPINION OF COMMISSIONER NICHOLAS JOHNSON

... [T]he Commission is now obliged to deal, in some fashion, with the creation of a definition of "substantial performance."

Thus, while I cannot relax and enjoy it, I can at least bring myself to confront the inevitable. Accordingly, I concur in the issuance of this Notice of Inquiry.

As I see it, we have two basic alternatives: (1) A "common law" case-by-case evolution of "substantial performance," or (2) an effort at general definition and promulgation as a general policy statement or rule.

The latter approach clearly has the advantages of (1) administrative ease, reducing our hearings and processing load substantially, and (2) reducing the sense of insecurity and instability in the industry when standards are vague, unarticulated or unknown.

If general guidelines are to be used, we then reach the following issues.

First, there is a fundamental conceptual issue regarding the nature of "substantial." Is the FCC to determine levels of programming performance (or other criteria) which, if met, constitute "substantial" performance? Is it theoretically —

and practically — possible for *all* licensees to be "substantial" performers?

Or does "substantial" refer to the "best" performers — necessarily a comparative evaluation?

The industry's arguments at the time (and later before this Commission), and the concern of public interest groups, I had always assumed the latter standard was what was desired and anticipated.

If the comparative approach is to be used, we must then address some crucial "details." What percentage of the broadcasters can be found to have demonstrated "substantial performance" — 2%, 10%, 25%, 50%, 80%? . . .

But once that has been resolved, we confront the question of criteria. Are news, public affairs and local programming the only quantifiable measures? . . .

In short, . . . there are a great many questions.

I concur in the proposition that we have to move. . . . I'm open to suggestions on where we go.

DISSENTING STATEMENT OF COMMISSIONER ROBERT WELLS

. . . I fear that setting quantitative standards will be the impetus for licensees to play this numbers game to satisfy the Commission. If this occurs, the licensee will not be discharging his responsibility to operate the station in the public interest. If this country is to enjoy truly diverse programming, we must leave some measure of flexibility to the licensee. This policy will leave fewer decisions to management.

We are naive if we think that the licensee of a television station that is worth millions of dollars will take any chances on falling below our numerical floor. If by meeting or exceeding these numbers he is practically assured of license renewal, there can be no doubt as to the course he will follow. By meeting these requirements, he will have precluded the possibility of the public being in a position to have a meaningful impact on his performance.

I realize that handling renewals on a case-by-case basis is not the most expeditious way to discharge our responsibilities. But, after all, the function of this agency is to render judgment, not necessarily to set hard and fast rules. True, there will be leeway for some judgment under the proposal that the majority has sanctioned. It will be minimal compared to the latitude which both the broadcaster and the public have a right to expect. We have taken the easy road.

Citizens Communications Center v. FCC (CCC I)

447 F.2d 1201 (D.C. Cir. 1971)

J. Skelly WRIGHT, Circuit Judge:

Appellants and petitioners in these consolidated cases challenge the legality of the "Policy Statement on Comparative Hearings Involving Regular Renewal Applicants," 22 F.C.C.2d 424, released by the Federal Communications Commission on January 15, 1970, and by its terms made applicable to pending proceedings. Briefly stated, the disputed Commission policy is that, in a hearing between an incumbent applying for renewal of his radio or television license and a mutually exclusive applicant, the incumbent shall obtain a controlling preference by demonstrating substantial past performance without serious deficiencies. Thus if the incumbent prevails on the threshold issue of the substantiality of his past record, all other applications are to be dismissed without a hearing on their own merits. . . .

. . . The Communications Act itself says nothing about a presumption in favor of incumbent licensees at renewal hearings; nor is an inability to displace operating broadcasters inherent in government management, as is established by the fact that in its early years of regulation the Federal Radio Commission often refused to renew licenses.

Nonetheless, the history of Commission decision and of the decisions of this court reflected until recently an operational bias in favor of incumbent licensees. . . .

Then, in the very controversial *WHDH* case, the Commission for the first time in its history, in applying comparative criteria in a renewal proceeding, deposed the incumbent and awarded the frequency to a challenger. [The court also referred to the introduction of S. 2004.]

Superimposed full length over the preceding historical analysis of the "full hearing" requirement of Section 309(e) of the Communications Act is the towering shadow of *Ashbacker*. . . . Although *Ashbacker* involved two original applications, no one has seriously suggested that its principle does not apply to renewal proceedings as well. . . .

. . . [T]he Commission's 1970 Policy Statement implicitly accepts *Ashbacker* as applicable to renewal proceedings. To circumvent the *Ashbacker* strictures, however, it adds a twist: the Policy Statement would limit the "comparative" hearing to a single issue — whether the incumbent licensee had rendered "substantial" past performance without serious deficiencies. If the examiner finds that the licensee has rendered such service, the "comparative" hearing is at an end and, barring successful appeal, the renewal application must be granted. Challenging applicants would thus receive no hearing at all on their own applications, contrary to the express provision of Section 309(e) which requires a "full hearing."

In *Ashbacker* the Commission had promised the challenging applicant a hearing on his application after the rival application was granted. The Supreme court in *Ashbacker* said that such a promise was "an empty thing." At least the Commission here must be given credit for honesty. It does not make any empty promises. It simply denies the competing applicants the "full hearing" promised them by Section 309(e) of the Act. Unless the renewal applicant's past performance is found to be insubstantial or marred by serious deficiencies, the competing applications get no hearing at all. The proposition that the 1970 Policy Statement violates Section 309(e), as interpreted in *Ashbacker*, is so obvious it need not be labored. . . .

Early after *Ashbacker* this court indicated what a "full hearing" entailed. In Johnston Broadcasting Co. v. FCC, 175 F.2d 351, 356-357 (1949), we explained that the statutory right to a full hearing included a decision upon all relevant criteria: "A choice between two applicants involves more than the bare qualifications of each applicant. It involves a comparison of characteristics. Both A and B may be qualified, but if a choice must be made, the question is which is the better qualified.... The Commission cannot ignore a material difference between two applicants and make findings in respect to selected characteristics only...."

We do not dispute, of course, that incumbent licensees should be judged primarily on their records of past performance. Insubstantial past performance should preclude renewal of a license. The licensee, having been given the chance and having failed, should be through.... At the same time, *superior* performance should be a plus of major significance in renewal proceedings.[46] Indeed, as *Ashbacker* recognizes, in a renewal proceeding, a new applicant is under a greater burden to "make the comparative showing necessary to displace an established licensee." 326 U.S. at 332.... But under Section 309(e) he must be given a chance. How can he ever show his application is comparatively better if he does not get a hearing on it? The Commission's 1970 Policy Statement's summary procedure would deny him that hearing.[47]

The suggestion that the possibility of nonrenewal, however remote, might chill uninhibited, robust and wide-open speech cannot be taken lightly. But the Commission, of course, may not penalize exercise of First Amendment rights. And the statute does provide for judicial review. Indeed, the failure to promote the full exercise of First Amendment freedoms through the broadcast medium may be a consideration against license renewal. Unlike totalitarian regimes, in a free country there can be no authorized voice of government. Though dependent on government for its license, independence is perhaps the most important asset of the renewal applicant.

The Policy Statement purports to strike a balance between the need for "predictability and stability" and the need for a competitive spur.... Unfortunately, instead of stability the Policy Statement has produced rigor mortis. For over a year

46. The court recognizes that the public itself will suffer if incumbent licensees cannot reasonably expect renewal when they have rendered superior service. Given the incentive, an incumbent will naturally strive to achieve a level of performance which gives him a clear edge on challengers at renewal time. But if the Commission fails to articulate the standards by which to judge superior performance, and if it is thus impossible for an incumbent to be reasonably confident of renewal when he renders superior performance, then an incumbent will be under an unfortunate temptation to lapse into mediocrity, to seek the protection of the crowd by eschewing the creative and the venturesome in programming and other forms of public service. The Commission in rulemaking proceedings should strive to clarify in both quantitative and qualitative terms what constitutes superior service.... Along with elimination of excessive and loud advertising and delivery of quality programs, one test of superior service should certainly be whether and to what extent the incumbent has reinvested the profit on his license to the service of the viewing and listening public. We note with approval that such rulemaking proceedings may soon be under way. News Notes, 39 U.S.L. Week 2513 (March 16, 1971).

47. Since one very significant aspect of the "public interest, convenience, and necessity" is the need for diverse and antagonistic sources of information, the Commission simply cannot make a valid public interest determination without considering the extent to which the ownership of the media will be concentrated or diversified by the grant of one or another of the applications before it.... The Supreme Court itself has on numerous occasions recognized the distinct connection between diversity of ownership of the mass media and the diversity of ideas and expression required by the First Amendment....

now, since the Policy Statement substantially limited a challenger's right to a full comparative hearing on the merits of his own application, not a single renewal challenge has been filed. . . .

Wherefore it is ORDERED: (1) that the Policy Statement, being contrary to law, shall not be applied by the Commission in any pending or future comparative renewal hearings; (2) that the Commission's order of July 21, 1970 denying petitioners' petition for reconsideration of the Policy Statement and refusing to institute rule making proceedings is reversed; and (3) that these proceedings are remanded to the Commission with directions to redesignate all comparative renewal hearings to which the Policy Statement was deemed applicable to reflect this court's judgment.

[Judge McKINNON's concurring opinion is omitted.]

Note that Judge Wright lists five factors for determining whether an incumbent license-holder had performed in a "superior" manner: (1) elimination of loud and excessive advertising; (2) delivery of quality programs; (3) reinvestment of profits; (4) diversity; and (5) independence from governmental influence.

In re Formulation of Policies Relating to the Broadcast Renewal Applicant, Stemming from the Comparative Hearing Process

31 F.C.C.2d 443 (Aug. 1971)

FURTHER NOTICE OF INQUIRY

. . . This Further Notice . . . is called for in light of the recent decision of the United States Court of Appeals for the District of Columbia Circuit in Citizens Communications Center v. FCC. . . .

The essence of that decision is that in a comparative hearing involving a regular renewal applicant, the Communications Act and Ashbacker Radio Corp. v. FCC, 326 U.S. 327 (1945), require a single full hearing in which the parties may develop evidence and be adjudged on all relevant criteria.

[T]he Court stressed that . . . incumbent licensees should be judged primarily on their records of "past performance . . . ," and that "[i]nsubstantial past performance should preclude renewal of a license . . . [while] [a]t the same time, *superior* performance should be a plus of major significance in renewal proceedings." . . . Further, the Court states that it ". . . recognizes that the public itself will suffer if incumbent licensees cannot reasonably expect renewal when they have rendered superior service." . . . It urges the Commission to strive to clarify in rulemaking proceedings what constitutes superior service, and notes "with approval that such rulemaking proceedings may soon be underway." . . . The proceedings referred to are, of course, the instant proceedings in this Docket.

We believe that while the Court disapproved the procedure set up in the Renewal Policy Statement, and emphasized the need for a more flexible weighing of the good and bad points of both the renewal applicant and the new applicant, it did not intend to overturn the policy that "a plus of major significance" should be awarded to a renewal applicant whose past record warrants it or to undercut the purpose of the present proceeding to seek out and quantify, at least in part, that degree of performance. We therefore continue to propose for the comment of interested persons the percentage guidelines set forth in our prior Notice. It appears to us that they would prima facie indicate the type of service warranting a "plus of major significance" in the comparative hearing. That is the standard at whose recognition we are directing our efforts. We recognize that particular labels can be misleading. Thus, we used the term "substantial service" in the sense of "strong, solid" service — substantially above the mediocre service which might just minimally warrant renewal ... We believe that the Court may have read this use of "substantial" service as meaning minimal service meeting the public interest standard ... and therefore employed the term "superior" service to make clear that it had in mind a contrast with mediocre service — as it put it ..., a "lapse into mediocrity, to seek the protection of the crowd." In short, we believe that it is unnecessary to further refine the label. What rather counts are the guidelines actually adopted to indicate the "plus of major significance" — the type of service which, if achieved, is of such nature that one can "... reasonably expect renewal."

[The FCC goes on to invite interested parties to submit comments and proposed guidelines for evaluating incumbents and notes that one of the issues considered will be whether] in any proposed area a guideline is appropriate or whether the matter is one best left to the full hearing, where its significance can be adjudged in the particular circumstances.

Thus, the important factor of diversification of control of media of mass communications is one which must be evaluated on the facts of each case. This, we think, is the thrust of the Court's statement that, "Diversification is a factor properly to be weighed and balanced with other important factors, including the renewal applicant's prior record, at a renewal hearing." ... It is, we think, impossible to formulate any general standard here since, as the Court has indicated, the matter turns upon the facts of the diversification issue and the renewal applicant's record. ...

CONCURRING OPINION OF COMMISSIONER NICHOLAS JOHNSON

... I have some disagreement with the particular views outlined by my colleagues in this further notice as well.

... [T]he court unanimously suggested specific criteria for use in determining whether an incumbent had performed in a "superior" manner and was therefore entitled to a plus in the overall weighing process of a comparative hearing. These include:

(1) Elimination of excessive and loud advertising
(2) Delivery of quality programs

(3) The extent to which the incumbent has reinvested the profit from his license to the service of the viewing and listening public

(4) Diversification of ownership of mass media

(5) Independence from government influence in promoting First Amendment objectives

Several of these criteria deserve discussion but two merit particular treatment. My colleagues seem to minimize the importance of the diversification issue in their analysis. . . .

. . . The court [also] suggested that reinvestment of profits "to the service of the listening and viewing public" would "certainly" be one test. I disagree with my colleagues that this is a question to be left "to the hearing process." In my view it goes to the heart of the Commission's discomfiture caused by the court's decision in this case.

It is a commonplace that the Communications Act bars property rights in the license held by the broadcaster as a public trustee. But it is also clear that this "law" has been ignored by the Commission over the years. When a license is transferred for $20 million, 80-90% of the value of the transfer is made up of the opportunity to broadcast — the *property* that is the license. The value of the transfer depends on the medallion value of the broadcasting permit. The "forfeiture" that occurs when an incumbent loses to a new competitor is precisely that property value that the Act says shall not be created. The 1952 amendments to the Act simply accentuated this dilemma by insuring a free market in the buying and selling of licenses, subject only to Commission regulation. 47 U.S.C. 310(b) (1964). An oligopolistic industry (especially in television), profit maximizing behavior, virtually automatic renewal, and a Commission permissive to the buying and selling of licenses have combined to make an industry with very large profits which were then translated into capital gains as licenses were sold. Profits which were very large, as compared with the original investment to secure a license, then appear "normal" to a licensee who has bought his way in by paying the full price for a license where the profit stream expectations have been capitalized. It is against this background of illicit property rights, and requirements for high profits, that the court's suggestion that profits be turned back into service rests. The licensee is trapped between his desire (1) to profit-maximize, either to meet the required return on his investment, or to enhance the value of his present investment, and (2) his need to insure his license against challenge through performance — performance which will require him to forego some profits. If the Commission permits challengers to be considered on their merits, as the law and the courts now require, then incumbent licensees will have to put more resources into service in order to insure themselves against successful challenge. Since not all this increment in service is consistent with full profit-maximizing behavior, profits and capital values will be reduced. But this is exactly the result the temporary grant of a license to use a public resource was meant to achieve. If granting of licenses was simply to authorize the accumulation of maximum profits by the licensee, it is difficult to see why the grant was temporary, or why comparative hearings were required to choose the applicant who would provide the *"best possible* service" rather than *"substantial* service."...

Citizens Communications Center v. FCC (CCC II)

463 F.2d 822 (D.C. Cir. 1972)

Per Curiam:

Alleging failure on the part of the Federal Communications Commission to comply with the mandate of this court in these proceedings, petitioners ask for further relief in the form of clarification of the mandate and/or mandamus to the Commission. We deny the petition for mandamus and grant the petition for clarification to the extent indicated herein.

In its opinion in this case issued June 11, 1971, this court held that the Commission's 1970 Renewal Policy Statement is "contrary to law." That Statement, therefore, is null and void and may not be used by the Commission for any purpose. The essence of our opinion is that in cases involving a renewal application the Communications Act and Ashbacker Radio Corp. v. FCC... require a single full comparative hearing in which all applicants may develop evidence and have their applications judged on all relevant criteria, including plans for integration of minority groups into station operation. In so holding, this court specifically rejected the Commission's finding that "substantial service" by the license holder warranted practically automatic renewal. We did say that *"superior* performance should be a plus of major significance in renewal proceedings,"... [a]nd we suggested specific criteria for use in determining whether an incumbent had performed in a "superior" manner....

While we suggested further that the Commission, in rule making proceedings, "clarify in both quantitative and qualitative terms what constitutes superior service,"... we did not intend that that suggestion be included in the court's mandate. The Commission at this time, pending acquisition of additional experience in this area, apparently prefers to proceed on a case-by-case basis in comparative renewal hearings to develop the criteria suggested by petitioners and by this court as appropriate for rule making. This court at this time will not require the Commission to proceed by rule making since that judgment is one basically for the Commission.

Since *Citizens Communications Center II*, the FCC has brought one contested renewal case to a conclusion. In that case, the Commission (overturning its hearing examiner's decision *not* to renew) awarded the license to the incumbent. RKO General, 44 F.C.C.2d 926 (1973), *aff'd sub nom.* Fidelity Television, Inc. v. FCC, 515 F.2d 684 (D.C. Cir.), *cert. denied,* 423 U.S. 926 (1975). The hearing examiner had found the incumbent's (KHJ-TV's) programming deficient. The Commission agreed that "in comparison with the three other independent UHF television stations in the market, KHJ-TV during this period had the highest percentage of entertainment programs, the lowest percentage in news and discussion categories and the lowest percentages of live programming."

Nonetheless, the Commission found several good points and concluded that KHJ-TV's performance was "within the bounds of average performance expected of all licensee's, thus warranting neither a preference nor a demerit." And, on balance, it concluded that the license should be renewed. Critics of the Commission's decision (including Chief Judge Bazelon in dissent on review) complained that the Commission downplayed RKO's (KHJ-TV's parent) record of antitrust violations while highlighting the fact that a competitor had not reported the small stock interest one of its shareholders held in a suburban shopping newspaper. And one commentator concluded: "In the final analysis KHJ-TV won solely because it was the incumbent; it had neither a good record nor integration nor diversification nor anything else in its favor." [47a]

In Cowles Florida Broadcasting, 37 P & F Radio Reg. Rep. 1487 (1976), the Commission also granted renewal, leading a dissenting Commissioner to state that the case "should set to rest my lingering fears that the Commission intends to use the comparative process to dislodge incumbent licensees." Id. at 1556.

In 1976 the Commission recommended to Congress that it end comparative renewal proceedings and effectively grant tenure to existing stations as long as they perform reasonably well.[47b] Then, in 1977, it terminated its efforts to develop renewal "standards" and returned to its pre-Citizens Communications case-by-case procedures, examining "all elements of the licensee's past performance that bear upon its service in the public interest." [47c]

Questions

Comparative Initial Awards

1. Consider the 1965 policy statement and Commissioner Hyde's dissent. Do you believe the 1965 standards are sufficiently precise as to provide fair notice and to allow outside observers (or courts) to judge whether they are being consistently applied?

2. Consider the following suggestion by Professor Anthony to make the 1965 standards more specific by making explicit a numerical system for scaling and comparison:[48]

47a. Geller, The Comparative Renewal Process in Television: Problems and Suggested Solutions, 61 Va. L. Rev. 471, 495 (1975).

47b. See Report of the Federal Communications Commission to the Congress of the United States re the Comparative Renewal Process (1976).

47c. Report and Order, Docket 19154, F.C.C. 77-204, 69-022 (March 9, 1977) at 16.

48. Anthony, Towards Simplicity and Rationality in Comparative Broadcast Licensing Proceedings, 24 Stan. L. Rev. 1, 64-65 (1971).

ILLUSTRATION OF THE RECOMMENDED SYSTEM FOR CHOOSING AMONG
COMPETING APPLICANTS

SUBJECTS FOR EVALUATION:

Diversification and Past Broadcast Record.

STANDARDS:

DIVERSIFICATION:

2 points credit: Awarded to any applicant that (i) does not have more
than X percent interest in, or exercise a substantial operating influence on,
any medium defined in (a) or (b) below; and (ii) is not more than X percent
owned by, or subject to the substantial operating influence of, persons who
have more than X percent interest in or who exercise substantial control over any
medium defined in (a) or (b) below: (a) Any broadcast station or daily newspaper or CATV system or other medium of similar significance located within
100 miles of the community for which the license is sought or within the
same state. (b) Any national or regional medium of communication that has
a substantial circulation in the area to be served.

3 points credit: Awarded to any applicant that has no substantial media
interests at all.

PAST BROADCAST RECORD:

1 point credit: Awarded to any applicant that has, or in which a certain
proportion of the principals have, a "satisfactory" past broadcast record, as defined.

4 points credit: Awarded to any applicant that has, or in which a certain
proportion of the principals have, an "outstanding" past broadcast record, as
defined.

PRIORITIES (RANKING):

Category	Total Points	Diversification Credit	Past Broadcast Record Credit
A	7	No substantial media interests (3)	Outstanding record (4)
B	6	No substantial interest in nearby or national media (2)	Outstanding record (4)
C	4	No substantial media interests (3)	Satisfactory record (1)
		or	
		(No credit)	Outstanding record (4)

Category	Total Points	Diversification Credit	Past Broadcast Record Credit
D	3	No substantial interest in nearby or national media (2)	Satisfactory record (1)
		or	
		No substantial media interests (3)	(No credit)
E	2	No substantial interest in nearby or national media (2)	(No credit)
F	1	(No credit)	Satisfactory record (1)
G	0	(No credit)	(No credit)

RULES FOR AWARD:

The license in each case will be granted to the applicant who places in the highest-ranking category on the basis of credits awarded by application of the standards. If more than one applicant places in the highest category, one of them will be chosen by lot.

Evaluate this proposal in terms of (a) its likely fairness, and (b) its likely effectiveness in selecting the "best" applicant.

Renewals

3. "Judge Wright in *Citizens Communications* considered *Ashbacker* but he forgot about *Storer*. A hearing is not required when there is nothing to have a hearing about."

Argue for, and then against, this proposition.

4. What is the likely effect of the *Citizens Communications* opinion upon the FCC's efforts to develop "renewal" criteria? Are the standards that the court suggests workable? What are their major weaknesses? Evaluate the court's approach in terms of its probable ability to produce (a) a fairer system; (b) a system with increased First Amendment protection; (c) a system that will provide better programs.

Alternate Systems of Allocation

5. A system for determining who will broadcast presumably can be judged in terms of (at least) its fairness, its consistency with First Amendment considerations, and its ability to bring about good programming. Several alternative systems have been suggested. They include:

— A lottery among minimally qualified applicants;

— An auction among minimally qualified applicants with an award to the highest bidder (or other systems that increase use of the free market);[49]

49. See Vany, Eckert, Meyers, O'Hara & Scott, A Property System for Market Allocation of the Electromagnetic Spectrum: A Legal-Economic-Engineering Study, 21 Stan. L. Rev. 1499 (1969).

— Entry of new competition such as CATV system users, who would broadcast by cable, and charge the viewer for programs;
— Increased reliance on public broadcasting.

In light of what you have read, what do you think of the desirability or feasibility of some of these alternatives?

C. Rulemaking Versus Adjudication as Means for Developing Agency Policy

1. Introduction

Rulemaking and adjudication are paradigms of lawmaking whose distinguishing features can be briefly stated. Rulemaking consists in the promulgation of generally applicable requirements or standards governing future conduct. Adjudication consists in determining the legal consequences of past events in a particular controversy between specific parties. (Adjudication sometimes involves the enforcement in a given case of a previously promulgated general rule, although it can also involve case-by-case evolution of norms by the decisionmaker.)

These paradigms, however useful and familiar, oversimplify. For example, while it is customarily said that rulemaking is prospective and adjudication retrospective, the actual impact of these alternative decisional modes on expectation interests varies widely. A regulation that is nominally prospective in effect may defeat important expectation interests. Consider, for example, the promulgation by the SEC, after the Chenerys had purchased additional stock but before formal reorganization proceedings, of a regulation prohibiting any participation in reorganized companies by management on the basis of interim stock purchases.[50] However, there is no a priori reason why regulations need be prospective even in form; Congress has enacted statutes changing the legal consequences of past events,[51] and there appears no reason in principle why it might not delegate such authority to administrative agencies, although a reviewing court would undoubtedly demand quite explicit evidence of such delegation. On the other hand, adjudication often eventuates in prospective remedies, such as an injunction or declaratory judgment, and even an award of damages based on past events may not disturb expectation interests if based upon settled legal doctrine, or if the emergence of a new decisional rationale was clearly foreseeable.

50. Suppose the SEC had adopted such regulations after the reorganization application had been filed. The applicability of newly promulgated administrative regulations to pending administrative adjudications turns on the intent of the regulations and the agency's statutory authority. In many instances courts have held that new regulations do apply to pending cases. See, e.g., Thorpe v. Housing Authority of City of Durham, 393 U.S. 268 (1969).

51. See Hochman, The Supreme Court and the Constitutionality of Retroactive Legislation, 73 Harv. L. Rev. 692 (1960).

Again, regulations are typically thought of as precise, detailed, and inflexible directions for conduct, while adjudicatory decisions are often thought to be based on fluid and evolving standards whose precise content varies with the facts of each particular case. In practice, however, regulations often contain vague and open-ended standards. Consider, for example, the regulations issued by the ICC in the *Boyce* case, p. 311 supra. Professor Davis, arguing in favor of greater agency use of rulemaking and against the view that rulemaking requires an agency to commit itself, perhaps prematurely, to a detailed policy of broad application, argues that regulations can be just as fuzzy, tentative, and flexible as any adjudicatory rationale.[51a]

On the other hand, in adjudication judges often develop quite precise and rigid rules of broad applicability. The Rule in Shelly's Case and the Rule Against Perpetuities are famous historical examples. More recently, the federal courts have adopted and consistently applied for many years the rule that price-fixing agreements among horizontal competitors constitute a per se violation of the antitrust laws. See, e.g., United States v. Socony-Vacuum Oil Co., 310 U.S. 150 (1940).

In the materials that follow, bear these variations in mind and beware the dangers of oversimplified contrast between rulemaking and adjudication.

Agency Rulemaking Authority. Many administrative agencies are empowered to decide particular cases through adjudication and also to engage in rulemaking. The nature and scope of statutory provisions granting rulemaking authority vary widely. In some cases, the agency is authorized to prescribe standards of conduct, and sanctions are provided for violation of agency regulations.[52] In other instances, portions of the statutory scheme cannot become operative until after the agency has exercised a delegated authority to issue regulations. See Addison v. Holly Hill Fruit Products, p. 226 supra. The agency may be given rulemaking authority to resolve doubtful cases, or to prevent circumvention of statutory commands. See Mourning v. Family Publications Service, Inc., supra p. 232. In still other instances, the organic statute contains a "catchall" provision authorizing the agency to issue such regulations as may be necessary to carry out the purposes of the statute, creating debate whether the agency has been authorized to prescribe substantive standards of private conduct or whether its power to issue regulations is limited to internal administration and procedure. The following case involves this question.

National Petroleum Refiners Assn. v. FTC

482 F.2d 672 (D.C. Cir. 1973)

WRIGHT, Circuit Judge.

This case presents an important question ... whether the Federal Trade Commission, under its governing statute, 15 U.S.C.A. §§ 41 et seq., and specifically 15

51a. K. Davis, Discretionary Justice: A Preliminary Inquiry 59-63 (1969).
52. E.g., Federal Clean Air Act §§ 111, 113, 42 U.S.C. §§ 7411, 7413.

U.S.C.A. §46(g), is empowered to promulgate substantive rules of business conduct or, as it terms them, "Trade Regulation Rules." The effect of these rules would be to give greater specificity and clarity to the broad standard of illegality — "unfair methods of competition in commerce, and unfair or deceptive acts or practices in commerce" — which the agency is empowered to prevent. 15 U.S.C.A. §45(a). Once promulgated, the rules would be used by the agency in adjudicatory proceedings aimed at producing cease and desist orders against violations of the statutory standard. The central question in such adjudicatory proceedings would be whether the particular defendant's conduct violated the rule in question.

The case is here on appeal from a District Court ruling that the Commission lacks authority under its governing statute to issue rules of this sort. . . . Specifically at issue in the District Court was the Commission's rule declaring that failure to post octane rating numbers on gasoline pumps at service stations was an unfair method of competition and an unfair or deceptive act or practice. . . .

As always, we must begin with the words of the statute creating the Commission and delineating its powers. Section 5 directs the Commission to "prevent persons, partnerships, or corporations . . . from using unfair methods of competition in commerce and unfair or deceptive acts or practices in commerce." Section 5(b) of the Trade Commission Act specifies that the Commission is to accomplish this goal by means of issuance of a complaint, a hearing, findings as to the facts, and issuance of a cease and desist order. . . .

. . . Section 6(g) of the Act, 15 U.S.C.A. §46(g), states that the Commission may "[f]rom time to time . . . classify corporations and . . . make rules and regulations for the purpose of carrying out the provisions of section 41 to 46 and 47 to 58 of this title."

According to appellees, however, this rule-making power is limited to specifying the details of the Commission's non-adjudicatory, investigative and informative functions spelled out in the other provisions of Section 6 and should not be read to encompass substantive rule-making in implementation of Section 5 adjudication. . . .

[After an analysis of the Act's statutory language, legislative history, and of court decisions that the court found relevant, the court sustained the FTC's claim to "substantive" rulemaking power, discounting earlier statements by FTC commissioners (concurred in by most commentators) that it did not enjoy such power.]

Thus there is little question that the availability of substantive rule-making gives any agency an invaluable resource-saving flexibility in carrying out its task of regulating parties subject to its statutory mandate. More than merely expediting the agency's job, use of substantive rule-making is increasingly felt to yield significant benefits to those the agency regulates. Increasingly, courts are recognizing that use of rule-making to make innovations in agency policy may actually be fairer to regulated parties than total reliance on case-by-case adjudication.

. . . [U]tilizing rule-making procedures opens up the process of agency policy innovation to a broad range of criticism, advice and data that is ordinarily less likely to be forthcoming in adjudication. Moreover, the availability of notice before promulgation and wide public participation in rule-making avoids the problem of singling out a single defendant among a group of competitors for initial imposition of a new and inevitably costly legal obligation. . . .

Such benefits are especially obvious in cases involving initiation of rules of the sort the FTC has promulgated here. The Commission's statement of basis and purpose indicated that the decision to impose the obligation of octane rating disclosure on gasoline dealers entailed careful consideration of automobile engine requirements, automobile dealers' practices in instructing purchasers how to care for their engines, consumer gasoline purchasing habits, and costs to gasoline dealers. In addition, the Commission had to choose exactly what kind of disclosure was the fairest. In short, a vast amount of data had to be compiled and analyzed, and the Commission, armed with these data, had to weigh the conflicting policies of increasingly knowledgeable consumer decision-making against alleged costs to gasoline dealers which might be passed on to the consumer. True, the decision to impose a bright-line standard of behavior might have been evolved by the Commission in a single or a succession of adjudicatory proceedings, much as the Supreme Court has imposed per se rules of business behavior in antitrust cases. See, e.g., United States v. Topco Associates, Inc., 405 U.S. 596 (1972) (horizontal territorial restraints); United States v. Socony-Vacuum Oil Co., 310 U.S. 150 (1940) (price fixing). But evolution of bright-line rules is often a slow process and may involve the distinct disadvantage of acting without the broad range of data and argument from all those potentially affected that may be flushed out through use of legislative-type rule-making procedures. And utilizing rule-making in advance of adjudication here minimizes the unfairness of using a purely case-by-case approach requiring "compliance by one manufacturer while his competitors [engaging in similar practices] remain free to violate the Act." Weinberger v. Bentex Pharmaceuticals, Inc., . . . 412 U.S. at 653. . . .

[Problems of delay and inefficiency] . . . have plagued the Trade Commission down to the present. . . . There is little disagreement that the Commission will be able to proceed more expeditiously, give greater certainty to businesses subject to the Act, and deploy its internal resources more efficiently with a mixed system of rule-making and adjudication than with adjudication alone. With the issues in Section 5 proceedings reduced by the existence of a rule delineating what is a violation of the statute or what presumptions the Commission proposes to rely upon, proceedings will be speeded up. For example, in an adjudication proceeding based on a violation of the octane rating rule at issue here, the central question to be decided will be whether or not pumps owned by a given refiner are properly marked. Without the rule, the Commission might well be obliged to prove and argue that the absence of the rating markers in each particular case was likely to have injurious and unfair effects on consumers or competition. Since this laborious process might well have to be repeated every time the Commission chose to proceed subsequently against another defendant on the same ground, the difference in administrative efficiency between the two kinds of proceedings is obvious. Furthermore, rules, as contrasted with the holdings reached by case-by-case adjudication, are more specific as to their scope, and industry compliance is more likely simply because each company is on clearer notice whether or not specific rules apply to it.

Moreover, when delay in agency proceedings is minimized by using rules, those violating the statutory standard lose an opportunity to turn litigation into a profitable and lengthy game of postponing the effect of the rule on the current practice. As a result, substantive rules will protect the companies which willingly comply with the law against what amounts to the unfair competition of those who would profit from delayed enforcement as to them. This, too, will minimize useless litigation and is likely to assist the Commission in more effectively allocating its resources. In addition, whatever form rules take, whether bright-line standards or presumptions that are rebuttable, they are likely to decrease the current uncertainty many businesses are said to feel over the current scope and applicability of Section 5. . . .

Any fears that the agency could successfully use rule-making power as a means of oppressive or unreasonable regulation seem exaggerated in view of courts' general practice in reviewing rules to scrutinize their statement of basis and purpose to see whether the major issues of policy pro and con raised in the submissions to the agency were given sufficient consideration. . . . The Commission is hardly free to write its own law of consumer protection and antitrust since the statutory standard which the rules may define with greater particularity is a legal standard. Although the Commission's conclusions as to the standard's reach are ordinarily shown deference, the standard must "get [its] final meaning from judicial construction." FTC v. Colgate-Palmolive Co., 380 U.S. 374, 385 (1965). . . .

In sum, we must respectfully register our disagreement with the District Court's painstaking opinion. Its result would render the Commission ineffective to do the job assigned by Congress. . . . We hold that under the terms of its governing statute, and under Section 6(g), 15 U.S.C.A. §46(g), in particular, the Federal Trade Commission is authorized to promulgate rules defining the meaning of the statutory standards of the illegality the Commission is empowered to prevent.

Questions on *National Petroleum Refiners*

1. The court's analysis of the relevant legislative history and precedent on the questions of the FTC's "substantive" rulemaking power is lengthy and has therefore been omitted. Details of the arguments pro and con can be obtained by reading the Court of Appeals' opinion in full and by consulting the opinion of the District Court, 340 F. Supp. 1343 (D.D.C. 1972). It is fair to conclude that when Congress adopted the Federal Trade Commission Act in 1914, it did not anticipate that the FTC would wield "substantive" rulemaking powers. Given the more established place of agencies today and the exigencies of modern administration, should the Act nonetheless be construed as granting such power when reasonably necessary for accomplishment of the Commission's mission? [53]

2. Why was the Commission so anxious to establish that it had authority to issue "substantive" regulations, infractions of which would constitute "unfair

---

53. Cf. Purex v. Proctor & Gamble Co., 308 F. Supp. 584 (C.D. Cal. 1970), aff'd, 453 F.2d 288 (9th Cir. 1971), cert. denied, 405 U.S. 1065 (1971) (FTC cease and desist order held a "final judgment or decree" within §5(a) of the 1914 Clayton Act, and therefore entitled to weigh as "prima facie evidence" in subsequent civil proceeding).

competition" in violation of the Act? Why couldn't the Commission, in the context of a particular adjudicatory proceeding against gasoline distributors, adopt a per se decisional rule that failure to post octane ratings is an instance of "unfair competition," and apply that rule in subsequent adjudications? Or why couldn't the FTC espouse a rule in a press release, or a speech by the Chairman, or an advisory opinion to a firm subject to its jurisdiction and simply follow that rule in all subsequent formal cases? How might the strategic position of the FTC and of regulated firms differ under such approaches in comparison to rulemaking?

Note: Agency Choice Between Rulemaking and Adjudication as Means of Policy Formation

Where an agency has been invested with both adjudicatory and rulemaking authority, it must decide in the first instance whether to develop law and policy through one procedural mode or the other.[54] Traditionally, many agencies — particularly the "independent" regulatory commissions — placed preponderant reliance on case-by-case adjudication to articulate and evolve administrative policy. This practice was subjected to sharp criticism by distinguished commentators, who urged much greater reliance on rulemaking.[55] The main grounds of criticism, some of which are reflected in the *National Petroleum Refiners* opinion, have been that reliance on case-by-case adjudication creates uncertainty and inconsistency; that rulemaking procedures are superior for formulating policy of general applicability because they facilitate input to the decision by all those affected; and that rulemaking encourages agencies to make clear choices among alternative policies, promoting both the efficacy and political accountability of the agency.[56]

Recently there has been a dramatic shift toward greater use of rulemaking by many agencies. However, as reflected in the materials that follow, this shift is less attributable to the persuasiveness of the commentators who have championed rulemaking than to resource constraints and other factors that have made rule-

---

54. The emphasis here is on means for innovation and change in the content of agency policy — a frequent necessity for administrative agencies beset by constant changes in the field they must control and in the demands made upon them. The enforcement of established agency policy, whether expressed in regulations or decisional law, must ultimately proceed through adjudication.

55. See K. Davis, Discretionary Justice: A Preliminary Inquiry 52-96 (1969); H. Friendly, The Federal Administrative Agencies: The Need for Better Definition of Standards (1962); Wright, book review of Discretionary Justice: A Preliminary Inquiry by Kenneth Culp Davis (1971), 81 Yale L.J. 575 (1972).

56. For a vigorous defense of policymaking through rulemaking rather than adjudication, see the FTC's Trade Regulation Rules on "Unfair or Deceptive Advertising and Labelling of Cigarettes in Relation to the Health Hazards of Smoking," 29 Fed. Reg. 8324, 8365-8373 (1964), *partially vacated due to superseding congressional statute, without modification of findings or conclusions,* 30 Fed. Reg. 9484 (1965). Robinson, The Making of Administrative Policy: Another Look at Rulemaking and Adjudication and Administrative Procedure Reform, 118 U. Pa. L. Rev. 485, 529-539 (1970), asserting that the choice between rulemaking and adjudication is a factor of minor significance in the agencies' failure to articulate clear, sound policies, citing as evidence frequent instances of agency "failure" by the FCC despite its heavy reliance on rulemaking in many aspects of its administration.

making comparatively more attractive from the viewpoint of bureaucratic self-interest.

What are the comparative advantages of rulemaking and adjudication from the viewpoint of administrators? Of the public? Of those regulated by the agency? Suppose you were SEC staff counsel at the time of the Chenery reorganization proceedings, and had been asked by the Commission to make a recommendation as to whether the SEC should deal with the problem of management stock purchases pending reorganization through case-by-case decisions of reorganization applications or by general regulations. What factors would you consider and what would you recommend?

The following may serve as a preliminary outline of relevant considerations:

Procedures. As developed more fully in Chapter 6, there are differences between the procedures employed in formal adjudication by regulatory agencies and those governing rulemaking. Adjudication to enforce regulatory controls frequently (but by no means always) involves the use of trial-type proceedings involving specific parties, oral testimony, cross-examination, and decisions exclusively on the basis of the hearing record. Rulemaking typically (but by no means always) involves more informal "notice and comment" procedures in which the agency publishes proposed regulations in the Federal Register and any member of the public may submit written comments on the proposal. The proceeding is regarded as "legislative" in character, and traditionally the agency need not base its decision exclusively on the materials published by it and the written comments. Consider the resource implications of these alternative procedures from the agency's viewpoint. Also consider the differences in the "data bases" likely to be generated by adjudication as opposed to rulemaking. Which would be more suitable for the development of policies of general applicability?

The Degree of Agency Commitment to New Policies. Despite Professor Davis's insistence that regulations can be as flexible and open-ended as adjudicatory rationales, the promulgation of regulations of general applicability has traditionally been viewed as committing an agency more specifically and more permanently to a given policy than case-by-case adjudication. Why might administrators wish to avoid such commitments? On the other hand, might use of detailed regulations make for greater effectiveness in the agency's discharge of its responsibilities? Recall again the *Boyce* case, p. 311 supra.

Retroactivity/Prospectivity. Bearing in mind all of the caveats discussed at p. 398 supra, accomplishing changes in legal rules through rulemaking rather than adjudication is likely to interfere less with expectation interests. Why might an agency nonetheless prefer use of adjudication in a situation such as that presented in the *Chenery* decisions?

Scope of Judicial Review. What differences might there be in the scope of judicial review when an agency announces a new rule through generally applicable regulations promulgated without a trial-type record as compared to its adoption in a particular adjudication with specific facts revealed in the record? Consider in this respect the procedures typically utilized in enforcement, in adjudication and in rulemaking.

Consistency and Uniformity vs. Individuation. Policy formulations through rulemaking could be expected to promote more consistent and evenhanded treatment of similarly situated individuals than case-by-case development of policy through adjudication. But, as indicated at p. 232 supra, in many contexts uniformity may be less important than individuation; adjudication affords broader scope for tailoring decisions to the particular circumstances of each case.

Clarity and Publicity. Professor Shapiro argues that rulemaking affords administrators less scope to "hide the ball" through an often murky path of case-by-case adjudication whose direction and net significance can be understood, if at all, only by specialist lawyers who closely monitor the agency in question.[57] By contrast, rulemaking encourages the agency to articulate policy in a more crystallized fashion that can be more readily understood and evaluated by a broader segment of the public.

Fairness to Parties Participating in the Adjudicative Proceeding. The FTC Trade Regulation Rule on cigarette advertising, 29 Fed. Reg. 8324, 8367 (1964), notes: "If the tribunal in an adjudicative proceeding is too intent upon fashioning rules for future guidance, the task of rendering a fair result on the record before it may be slighted. Since the task of assessing individual liability on the basis of past practices and the task of fashioning rules of general application for future guidance are different, it has been argued that a tribunal which seeks to lay down broad rules in deciding individual cases may frequently fail to do complete justice to the parties before it."

This problem has been found to exist in NLRB adjudications. See Peck, The Atrophied Rule-Making Powers of the National Labor Relations Board, 70 Yale L.J. 729, 758-759 (1961).

Planning. If adjudication is relied on as a vehicle for policy formulation, agencies may have less control over the content and evolution of their policies, since policies will only be announced when cases which can realistically serve as vehicles for them happen to come before the agency.[58] In addition, reliance on adjudication may encourage administrators to "muddle through" on a case-by-case basis, focusing on the special facts of each proceeding, and to neglect a more global "planning" approach to the problems faced by the agency which rulemaking may encourage.[59] On the other hand, lack of knowledge, disagreements within the agency, or political constraints may make case-by-case "muddling through" the only feasible course. Consider in this respect the FCC's efforts to develop criteria for initial broadcast license grants and renewals, supra pp. 362-398.

Questions: The Rulemaking/Adjudication Issue in Chenery

Reread those portions of the *Chenery* decisions by the Supreme Court and the SEC that discuss whether the Commission should deal with the problem of manage-

57. See Shapiro, The Choice of Rulemaking or Adjudication in the Development of Administrative Policy, 78 Harv. L. Rev. 921 (1965).

58. However, as Professor Shapiro points out: "But many agencies, like the FTC, have the power to initiate cases as well as to decide them, and these agencies can exercise virtually the same degree of planning in the commencement of adjudicatory proceedings as they can in rulemaking." Shapiro, id. at 932.

59. See L. Jaffe, Judicial Control of Administrative Action 20 (1965).

ment stock purchases during reorganization by rulemaking or by adjudication.[60] Then consider the following questions in light of the preceding comparison of the respective advantages and disadvantages of the two modes of procedure.

1. Why did the SEC elect to deal with the management purchase problem through adjudication?

2. Is it true, as urged in Justice Jackson's *Chenery II* dissent, that *Chenery I* required the SEC to utilize rulemaking if it wished to go beyond judicial precedent prohibiting management stock purchases pending reorganization? If Justice Jackson is correct, why didn't the Court in *Chenery I* dismiss the case rather than remanding?

3. Did the Commission on remand from *Chenery I* give any meaningful reasons for its reliance on adjudication rather than rulemaking to deal with the problem of management stock purchases? If not, doesn't *Chenery I* require a second remand requiring the Commission to explain its choice?

4. What justification does the Court advance in *Chenery II* for refusing to disturb the SEC's choice of adjudication rather than rulemaking? Note that the Court (following the SEC's opinion on this point) discusses the problem of retroactive effect with the claim that "Every case of first impression has a retroactive effect, whether the new principle is announced by a court or an administrative agency," p. 344 supra. How relevant is this assertion in the context of administrative proceedings in which the agency, unlike a court, has the option of making changes in the law through rulemaking?

5. Does *Chenery II* mean that agencies enjoy complete discretion in choosing to develop policy through adjudication or rulemaking? Given that most commentators urge greater use of rulemaking as fairer and more likely to yield sound policies, why shouldn't courts exercise greater control over agencies' use of one procedure or another?

2. The APA and Agency Choice Between Rulemaking and Adjudication

Two parts of the APA have potential application to an agency's choice between rulemaking and adjudication.

Section 706 of the Act requires reviewing courts to set aside agency action that is contrary to statute or "arbitrary, capricious, an abuse of discretion." Conceivably there might be cases in which an agency had been given general authority to proceed by rulemaking or adjudication, but the statute explicitly or implicitly requires the

---

60. Are there other ways that the SEC might have attempted to deal with the problem of management stock purchases pending reorganization other than issuing general regulations specifying when purchases would be permitted, or determining, on a case-by-case basis in the context of particular reorganization plans, the permissibility of such purchases after they had already occurred? See Note, SEC v. Chenery Corp.: A Case Study in Administrative Technique, 62 Harv. L. Rev. 478 (1949).

agency to determine certain matters by one procedure or the other.[61] Normally, however, the relevant statute will provide no guidance on the choice, and review must be had under the "arbitrary and capricious" standard. As indicated by the *Bell Aerospace* decision reproduced below, courts have generally refused to utilize this standard to control agency choice of procedures, continuing the pre-APA deference to agency discretion reflected in *Chenery II*.

However, other sections of the APA specifically define "rulemaking" and "adjudication" for APA purposes, and specify the procedures to be utilized in the two forms of lawmaking. For definitions, see §551(4), (5), (6), (7), (8), (9). Note that "adjudication" is residually defined to include "licensing" and anything that is not "rulemaking." "Rule" is defined, inter alia, as "the whole or part of an agency statement of general or particular applicability designed to implement, interpret or prescribe law or policy . . ." [62]

The procedures for rulemaking are specified in §553; the norm is notice and comment rulemaking. In cases of adjudication required by the relevant statute to be based on a record after agency hearing, the trial-type procedures of §§ 554, 556, and 557 must be employed.

This system of classification raises the question whether certain forms of lawmaking are, as a matter of APA definition, exclusively "rulemaking" or exclusively "adjudication" that can only be accomplished through the corresponding APA procedures. If so, the combination of APA definitions and procedural specifications might constrain agency choices between alternative procedures quite independently of "arbitrary and capricious" review. This question is presented in the decision which follows.

NLRB v. Wyman-Gordon Co.

394 U.S. 759 (1969)

Mr. Justice Fortas announced the judgment of the Court and delivered an opinion in which The Chief Justice, Mr. Justice Stewart, and Mr. Justice White join.

On the petition of the International Brotherhood of Boilermakers and pursuant to its powers under §9 of the National Labor Relations Act, 49 Stat. 453, 29 U.S.C. §159, the National Labor Relations Board ordered an election among the production and maintenance employees of the respondent company. In connection with the election, the Board ordered the respondent to furnish a list of the names and addresses of its employees who could vote in the election, so that the unions could

61. After reading Morton v. Ruiz, infra p. 415, consider whether it might be based on a requirement in the Snyder Act that BIA limitations of eligibility be accomplished only through rulemaking.

62. Consider in particular the reference to statements of "particular applicability." Does this mean that FTC cease and desist orders or NLRB directions to bargain in given cases are instances of rulemaking? Does it include back pay awards or money judgments in given cases? If so, "rulemaking" would swallow up most of what we would customarily regard as adjudication.

use the list for election purposes. The respondent refused to comply with the order, and the election was held without the list. Both unions were defeated in the election.

The Board upheld the unions' objections to the election because the respondent had not furnished the list, and the Board ordered a new election. The respondent again refused to obey a Board order to supply a list of employees, and the Board issued a subpoena ordering the respondent to provide the list or else produce its personnel and payroll records showing the employees' names and addresses. The Board filed an action in the United States District Court for the District of Massachusetts seeking to have its subpoena enforced or to have a mandatory injunction issued to.compel the respondent to comply with its order.

The District Court held the Board's order valid and directed the respondent to comply. 270 F. Supp. 280 (1967). The United States Court of Appeals for the First Circuit reversed. 397 F.2d 394 (1968). The Court of Appeals thought that the order in this case was invalid because it was based on a rule laid down in an earlier decision by the Board, Excelsior Underwear Inc., 156 N.L.R.B. 1236 (1966), and the *Excelsior* rule had not been promulgated in accordance with the requirements that the Administrative Procedure Act prescribes for rule-making, 5 U.S.C. §553. We granted certiorari to resolve a conflict among the circuits concerning the validity and effect of the *Excelsior* rule. 393 U.S. 932 (1968).

I

The *Excelsior* case involved union objections to the certification of the results of elections that the unions had lost at two companies. The companies had denied the unions a list of the names and addresses of employees eligible to vote. In the course of the proceedings, the Board "invited certain interested parties" to file briefs and to participate in oral argument of the issue whether the Board should require the employer to furnish lists of employees. 156 N.L.R.B., at 1238. Various employer groups and trade unions did so, as amici curiae. After these proceedings, the Board issued its decision in *Excelsior*. It purported to establish the general rule that such a list must be provided, but it declined to apply its new rule to the companies involved in the *Excelsior* case. Instead, it held that the rule would apply "only in those elections that are directed, or consented to, subsequent to 30 days from the date of [the] Decision." Id., at 1240, n. 5....

Section 6 of the National Labor Relations Act empowers the Board "to make ..., in the manner prescribed by the Administrative Procedure Act, such rules and regulations as may be necessary to carry out the provisions of this Act." 29 U.S.C. §156....

[The Court then summarized the notice and comment procedures of the APA, 5 U.S.C. §553.]

The rule-making provisions of that Act, which the Board would avoid, were designed to assure fairness and mature consideration of rules of general application. See H.R. Rep. No. 1980, 79th Cong., 2d Sess., 21-26 (1946); S. Rep. No. 752, 79th Cong., 1st Sess., 13-16 (1945). They may not be avoided by the process of making rules in the course of adjudicatory proceedings. There is no warrant in law for the

Board to replace the statutory scheme with a rule-making procedure of its own invention. . . . The "rule" created in *Excelsior* was not published in the Federal Register, which is the statutory and accepted means of giving notice of a rule as adopted; only selected organizations were given notice of the "hearing," whereas notice in the Federal Register would have been general in character; under the Administrative Procedure Act, the terms or substance of the rule would have to be stated in the notice of hearing, and all interested parties would have an opportunity to participate in the rule making. . . .[63]

. . . There is no question that, in an adjudicatory hearing, the Board could validly decide the issue whether the employer must furnish a list of employees to the union. But that is not what the Board did in *Excelsior*. The Board did not even apply the rule it made to the parties in the adjudicatory proceeding, the only entities that could properly be subject to the order in that case. Instead, the Board purported to make a rule: i.e., to exercise its quasi-legislative power.

Adjudicated cases may and do, of course, serve as vehicles for the formulation of agency policies, which are applied and announced therein. See H. Friendly, The Federal Administrative Agencies 35-62 (1962). They generally provide a guide to action that the agency may be expected to take in future cases. Subject to the qualified role of stare decisis in the administrative process, they may serve as precedents. But this is far from saying, as the Solicitor General suggests, that commands, decisions, or policies announced in adjudication are "rules" in the sense that they must, without more, be obeyed by the affected public.

In the present case, however, the respondent itself was specifically directed by the Board to submit a list of the names and addresses of its employees for use by the unions in connection with the election. This direction, which was part of the order directing that an election be held, is unquestionably valid. See, e.g., NLRB v. Waterman S.S. Co., 309 U.S. 206, 226 (1940). Even though the direction to furnish the list was followed by citation to "Excelsior Underwear Inc., 156 NLRB No. 111," it is an order in the present case that the respondent was required to obey. Absent this direction by the Board, the respondent was under no compulsion to furnish the list because no statute and no validly adopted rule required it to do so.

Because the Board in an adjudicatory proceeding directed the respondent itself to furnish the list, the decision of the Court of Appeals for the First Circuit must be reversed.[64]

63. Ed. note: The Board has never utilized the Act's rule-making procedures. It has been criticized for contravening the Act in this manner. See, e.g., 1 K. Davis, Administrative Law Treatise §6.13 (Supp. 1965); Peck, The Atrophied Rule-Making Powers of the National Labor Relations Board, 70 Yale L.J. 729 (1961).

64. Mr. Justice Harlan's dissent argues that because the Board improperly relied upon the *Excelsior* "rule" in issuing its order, we are obliged to remand. He relies on SEC v. Chenery Corp., 318 U.S. 80 (1943). To remand would be idle and useless formality. *Chenery* does not require that we convert judicial review of agency action into a ping-pong game. In *Chenery*, the Commission had applied the wrong standards to the adjudication of a complex factual situation, and the Court held that it would not undertake to decide whether the Commission's result might have been justified on some other basis. Here, by contrast, the substance of the Board's command is not seriously contestable. There is not the slightest uncertainty as to the outcome of a proceeding before the Board, whether the Board acted through a rule or an order. It would be meaningless to remand.

II

The respondent also argues that it need not obey the Board's order because the requirement of disclosure of employees' names and addresses is substantively invalid. This argument lacks merit. . . .

III

[The Court also held that the Board's requirement that a list be furnished could be enforced by subpoena.]

The judgment of the Court of Appeals is reversed, and the case is remanded to the District Court with directions to reinstate its judgment.

It is so ordered.

Mr. Justice BLACK, with whom Mr. Justice BRENNAN and Mr. Justice MARSHALL join, concurring in the result.

I agree with Parts II and III of the prevailing opinion of Mr. Justice Fortas, holding that the *Excelsior* requirement that an employer supply the union with the names and addresses of its employees prior to an election is valid on its merits and can be enforced by a subpoena. But I cannot subscribe to the criticism in that opinion of the procedure followed by the Board in adopting that requirement in the *Excelsior* case, 156 N.L.R.B. 1236 (1966). Nor can I accept the novel theory by which the opinion manages to uphold enforcement of the *Excelsior* practice in spite of what it considers to be statutory violations present in the procedure by which the requirement was adopted. Although the opinion is apparently intended to rebuke the Board and encourage it to follow the plurality's conception of proper administrative practice, the result instead is to free the Board from all judicial control whatsoever regarding compliance with procedures specifically required by applicable federal statutes. . . . Apparently, under the prevailing opinion, courts must enforce any requirement announced in a purported "adjudication" even if it clearly was not adopted as an incident to the decision of a case before the agency, and must enforce "rules" adopted in a purported "rule making" even if the agency materially violated the specific requirements that Congress has directed for such proceedings in the Administrative Procedure Act. I for one would not give judicial sanction to any such illegal agency action.

In the present case, however, I am convinced that the *Excelsior* practice was adopted by the Board as a legitimate incident to the adjudication of a specific case before it, and for that reason I would hold that the Board properly followed the procedures applicable to "adjudication" rather than "rule making."

[Justice Black notes that the NLRB has been given both adjudicatory and rule-making powers.] . . . No language in the National Labor Relations Act requires that the grant or the exercise of one power was intended to exclude the Board's use of the other.

Nor does any language in the Administrative Procedure Act require such a conclusion. The Act does specify the procedure by which the rule-making power is to be exercised. . . . In this same statute, however, Congress also conferred on the affected administrative agencies the power to proceed by adjudication, and Congress specified a distinct procedure by which this adjudicatory power is to be exercised. . . . Thus, although it is true that the adjudicatory approach frees an administrative agency from the procedural requirements specified for rule making, the Act permits this to be done whenever the action involved can satisfy the definition of "adjudication" and then imposes separate procedural requirements that must be met in adjudication. Under these circumstances, so long as the matter involved can be dealt with in a way satisfying the definition of either "rule making" or "adjudication" under the Administrative Procedure Act, that Act, along with the Labor Relations Act, should be read as conferring upon the Board the authority to decide, within its informed discretion, whether to proceed by rule making or adjudication. Our decision in SEC v. Chenery Corp., 332 U.S. 194 (1947), though it did not involve the Labor Board or the Administrative Procedure Act, is nonetheless equally applicable here. As we explain in that case, "the choice made between proceeding by general rule or by individual, *ad hoc* litigation is one that lies primarily in the informed discretion of the administrative agency." Id., at 203.

In the present case there is no dispute that all the procedural safeguards required for "adjudication" were fully satisfied in connection with the Board's *Excelsior* decision, and it seems plain to me that that decision did constitute "adjudication" within the meaning of the Administrative Procedure Act, even though the requirement was to be prospectively applied. . . .

The prevailing opinion seems to hold that the *Excelsior* requirement cannot be considered the result of adjudication because the Board did not apply it to the parties in the *Excelsior* case itself, but rather announced that it would be applied only to elections called 30 days after the date of the *Excelsior* decision. But the *Excelsior* order was nonetheless an inseparable part of the adjudicatory process. . . . [T]he Board did not feel that it should upset the Excelsior Company's justified reliance on previous refusals to compel disclosure by setting aside this particular election.

Apart from the fact that the decisions whether to accept a "new" requirement urged by one party and, if so, whether to apply it retroactively to the other party are inherent parts of the adjudicatory process, I think the opposing theory accepted by the Court of Appeals and by the prevailing opinion today is a highly impractical one. In effect, it would require an agency like the Labor Board to proceed by adjudication only when it could decide, *prior* to adjudicating a particular case, that any new practice to be adopted would be applied retroactively. Obviously, this decision cannot properly be made until all the issues relevant to adoption of the practice are fully considered in connection with the final decision of that case. If the Board were to decide, after careful evaluation of all the arguments presented to it in the adjudicatory proceeding, that it might be fairer to apply the practice only prospectively, it would be faced with the unpleasant choice of either starting all over again to evaluate the merits of the question, this time in a "rule-making" proceeding, or overriding the considerations of fairness and applying its order retroactively anyway, in order to preserve the validity of the new practice and avoid duplication of effort. I see no good reason to impose any such inflexible requirement on the administrative agencies.

For all of the foregoing reasons I would hold that the Board acted well within its discretion in choosing to proceed as it did, and I would reverse the judgment of the Court of Appeals on this basis.

Mr. Justice Douglas, dissenting. . . .

I am willing to assume that, if the Board decided to treat each case on its special facts and perform its adjudicatory function in the conventional way, we should have no difficulty in affirming its action. The difficulty is that it chose a different course in the *Excelsior* case and, having done so, it should be bound to follow the procedures prescribed in the Act as my Brother Harlan has outlined them. When we hold otherwise, we let the Board "have its cake and eat it too." . . . [I]t is no answer to say that the order under review was "adjudicatory." For as my Brother Harlan says, an agency is not adjudicating when it is making a rule to fit future cases. A rule like the one in *Excelsior* is designed to fit all cases at all times. It is not particularized to special facts. It is a statement of far-reaching policy covering all future representation elections.

It should therefore have been put down for the public hearing prescribed by the Act.

The rule-making procedure performs important functions. It gives notice to an entire segment of society of those controls or regimentation that is forthcoming. It gives an opportunity for persons affected to be heard.

This is a healthy process that helps make a society viable. The multiplication of agencies and their growing power make them more and more remote from the people affected by what they do and make more likely the arbitrary exercise of their powers. . . .

It has been stated that "the survival of a questionable rule seems somewhat more likely when it is submerged in the facts of a given case" then when rule making is used. See Shapiro, The Choice of Rulemaking or Adjudication in the Development of Administrative Policy, 78 Harv. L. Rev. 921, 946-947 (1965). Moreover, "agencies appear to be freer to disregard their own prior decisions than they are to depart from their regulations." Id., at 947. Failure to make full use of rule-making power is attributable at least in part to "administrative inertia and reluctance to take a clear stand." Id., at 972.

Rule making is no cure-all; but it does force important issues into full public display and in that sense makes for more responsible administrative action.

I would hold the agencies governed by the rule-making procedure strictly to its requirements and not allow them to play fast and loose as the National Labor Relations Board apparently likes to do.

Mr. Justice Harlan, dissenting.

The language of the Administrative Procedure Act does not support the Government's claim that an agency is "adjudicating" when it announces a rule which it refuses to apply in the dispute before it. The Act makes it clear that an agency "adjudicates" only when its procedures result in the "formulation of an *order*." 5 U.S.C. §551(7). (Emphasis supplied.) An "order" is defined to include "the whole or a *part* of a final disposition ... of an agency *in a matter other than rule making....*" 5 U.S.C. §551(6). (Emphasis supplied.) This definition makes it apparent that an agency is not adjudicating when it is making a rule, which the Act defines as "an agency statement of general or particular applicability and *future effect....*" 5 U.S.C. §551(4). (Emphasis supplied.) Since the Labor Board's *Excelsior* rule was to be effective only 30 days after its promulgation, it clearly falls within the rule-making requirements of the Act.

Nor can I agree that the natural interpretation of the statute should be rejected because it requires the agency to choose between giving its rules immediate effect or initiating a separate rule-making proceeding. An agency chooses to apply a rule prospectively only because it represents such a departure from pre-existing understandings that it would be unfair to impose the rule upon the parties in pending matters. But it is precisely in these situations, in which established patterns of conduct are revolutionized, that rule-making procedures perform the vital functions that my Brother Douglas describes so well in a dissenting opinion with which I basically agree.

Given the fact that the Labor Board has promulgated a rule in violation of the governing statute, I believe that there is no alternative but to affirm the judgment of the Court of Appeals in this case. If, as the plurality opinion suggests, the NLRB may properly enforce an invalid rule in subsequent adjudications, the rule-making provisions of the Administrative Procedure Act are completely trivialized....

[Justice Harlan also argued that *Chenery I* required denial of the subpoena because the Board, in issuing it, had relied solely on the *Excelsior* decision.]

Since the major reason the Board has given in support of its order is invalid, *Chenery* requires remand.... The prevailing opinion explains its departure from our leading decisions in this area on the ground that: "There is not the slightest uncertainty as to the outcome of [this] proceeding" on remand. Ante, n.6, at 767. I can perceive no justification whatever for this assertion. Since the *Excelsior* rule was invalidly promulgated, it is clear that, at a minimum, the Board is obliged on remand to recanvass all of the competing considerations before it may properly announce its decision in this case.[65] We cannot know what the outcome of such a reappraisal will be....

I would affirm the judgment of the Court of Appeals.

Notes and Questions

1. Consider first the plurality opinion by Justice Fortas, which finds that the Board engaged in APA "rulemaking" in *Excelsior* without following the appropriate procedures, yet sustains a subsequent Board order based on the *Excelsior* rule,

---

65. ... I would go further and require the Board to initiate a new rule-making proceeding where, as here, it has previously recognized that the proposed new rule so departs from prior practices that it cannot fairly be applied retroactively. In the absence of such a proceeding, the administrative agency must be obliged to follow its earlier decisions which did not require employers to furnish *Excelsior* lists to unions during organizing campaigns.

on the ground that the subsequent order can be independently sustained as a valid adjudication. Is this rationale consistent with *Chenery I*? What deterrent is there for the Board in the future to evade APA rulemaking requirements by repeating the *Excelsior/Wyman-Gordon* strategy? [66]

2. Consider now Justice Black's concurring opinion, which denies that the Board in *Excelsior* was engaged in "rulemaking" for APA purposes. Who has the better of the statutory analysis on this point, Justice Black or Justice Harlan? Justice Black seems concerned about the possibility that an agency might start down the adjudicatory path and then conclude in the process of final decision that any change should be prospective; if prospective changes were regarded as notice and comment "rulemaking," then an agency would have at that point to begin all over again with a new set of procedures. But how plausible is Justice Black's concern in this case, which is (as we shall see) but one instance of the NLRB's frequent use of adjudicatory cases as vehicles for the announcement of precise rules of general application? In any event, how great is the burden on the agency of commencing fresh rulemaking proceedings when the possibility of prospective application becomes clear?

There is a more general question as to the desirability of prospective overruling in adjudication by courts or agencies.[67] Agencies, of course, often have the alternative of making law prospectively through rulemaking. Does this alternative cut for or again the use by agencies of prospective overruling in adjudication?

3. Why is *Excelsior* analyzed as if it were enunciating a rule? Why can't it be given some weight purely as a precedent? Its prospective nature? The fact that it is of general applicability? [68] Just why is the NLRB so anxious to avoid rulemak-

---

66. What do you make of Justice Fortas' suggestion that "comments, decisions, or policies announced in adjudication" are not " 'rules' in the sense that they must, without more, be obeyed by the affected public" (p. 409 supra)? Is the Justice suggesting that the law embodied in regulations is more "binding" than that embodied in adjudicatory decisions? If so, is his position sound? If the Board hadn't cited *Excelsior*, would its decision be set aside for failure to give adequate reasons? Suppose the Board simply reiterated the rationale of *Excelsior* without mentioning that decision by name?

67. For discussion in the context of judicial adjudication, see Mishkin, The High Court, The Great Writ, and the Due Process of Time and Law, 79 Harv. L. Rev. 56 (1965); Schwartz, Retroactivity, Reliability, and Due Process: A Reply to Professor Mishkin, 33 U. Chi. L. Rev. 719 (1966).

68. See Robinson, The Making of Administrative Policy: Another Look at Rulemaking and Adjudication in Administrative Procedure Reform, 118 U. Pa. L. Rev. 485, 512 (1970): ". . . *Wyman-Gordon* can and should be analyzed and understood primarily with reference to the particular practice of the NLRB involved. The vice of the practice lies not in the fact that the Board has used adjudication to develop labor relations policy; nor in the fact that in particular cases principles have developed which go beyond the immediate case and must in some sense be 'obeyed' by other parties. The real trouble, rather, lies in the fact that the Board has not even purported to develop its policy rules as an incident to its litigation of cases, but has virtually singled out individual cases as vehicles in which to consider and promulgate general policy rules which are largely independent of the facts and issues of the particular case. In some instances, it may not be unfair to say that individual cases have been manipulated or at least distorted for the ulterior ends of rulemaking."

See also Retail, Wholesale and Dept. Store Union v. NLRB, 466 F.2d 380 (D.C. Cir. 1972) (*Wyman-Gordon* does not preclude "perspective overruling" by the Board in adjudication so long as the changed rule is applied to the case in which it is announced).

ing and to utilize adjudication as a vehicle of policy change? [69] Do any of the various *Wyman-Gordon* opinions suggest any limits on this practice so long as the Board applies the new policy adopted to the case before it?

Morton v. Ruiz

415 U.S. 199 (1974)

[Ruiz, a full-blooded unassimilated Papago Indian living 15 miles from a reservation, and maintaining close ties with it, was denied general assistance benefits under the Snyder Act by the Bureau of Indian Affairs (BIA). The BIA contended that the Snyder Act and appropriations under it had limited benefits to Indians living on reservations. Alternatively, BIA relied upon a provision in the BIA Manual (a collection of internal agency management directives not published in a form available to the general public), stating that "Eligibility for general assistance is limited to Indians living on reservations . . ." BIA referred to this provision in its letter to Ruiz denying benefits.

The Court, in a unanimous opinion by Justice Blackmun, initially rejected BIA's statutory argument, concluding, in the light of the legislative history, that Congress had authorized assistance for Indians such as Ruiz who lived "near" reservations as well as those living on the reservations. However, the Court concluded that the BIA might enjoy some residual discretion in defining the class of eligible recipients, particularly if appropriations were not sufficient to provide adequate benefits to all those potentially eligible under the statute. The Court then considered whether this discretion had been validly exercised by BIA to limit eligibility to those living on reservations.]

Assuming, arguendo, that the Secretary rationally could limit the "on or near" appropriation to include only the smaller class of Indians who lived directly "on" the reservation . . . the question that remains is whether this has been validly accomplished. The power of an administrative agency to administer a congressionally created and funded program necessarily requires the formulation of policy and the making of rules to fill any gap left, implicitly or explicitly, by Congress. In the area of Indian affairs, the Executive has long been empowered to promulgate rules and policies,[70] and the power has been given explicitly to the Secretary and

---

69. Prior to *Wyman-Gordon*, the Board had apparently never utilized its rulemaking powers in defining and implementing the substantive provisions of the Labor Act. Since that decision it has changed certain jurisdictional rules through rulemaking. See R. Gorman, Basic Text on Labor Law: Unionization and Collective Bargaining 16-17 (1976). For a useful discussion of the problems involved in the NLRB's adjudicative approach to policy formulation, see Bernstein, The NLRB's Adjudication-Rulemaking Dilemma Under the Administrative Procedure Act, 79 Yale L.J. 571 (1970); K. Kahn, The NLRB and Higher Education: The Failure of Policymaking Through Adjudication, 21 U.C.L.A. L. Rev. 63 (1973); Shapiro, The Choice of Rulemaking or Adjudication in the Development of Administrative Policy, 78 Harv. L. Rev. 921, 944-957 (1965).

70. "The President may prescribe such regulations as he may think fit for carrying into effect the various provisions of any act relating to Indian affairs." 25 U.S.C. §9.

This provision relates back to the Act of June 30, 1834, §17, 4 Stat. 738.

his delegates at the BIA.[71] This agency power to make rules that affect substantial individual rights and obligations carries with it the responsibility not only to remain consistent with the governing legislation, but also to employ procedures that conform to the law. No matter how rational or consistent with congressional intent a particular decision might be, the determination of eligibility cannot be made on an ad hoc basis by the dispenser of the funds.

The Administrative Procedure Act was adopted to provide, inter alia, that administrative policies affecting individual rights and obligations be promulgated pursuant to certain stated procedures so as to avoid the inherently arbitrary nature of unpublished ad hoc determinations. That Act states in pertinent part:

> Each Agency shall separately state and currently publish in the Federal Register for the guidance of the public — ...
> (D) substantive rules of general applicability adopted as authorized by law, and statements of general policy or interpretations of general applicability formulated and adopted by the agency. [5 U.S.C. §552(a)(1).]

The sanction added in 1967 by Pub. L. 90-23, 81 Stat. 54, provides:

> Except to the extent that a person has actual and timely notice of the terms thereof, a person may not in any manner be required to resort to, or be adversely affected by, a matter required to be published in the Federal Register and not so published. ...

In the instant case the BIA itself has recognized the necessity of formally publishing its substantive policies and has placed itself under the structure of the APA procedures. The 1968 introduction to the Manual reads:

> *Code of Federal Regulations:* Directives which relate to the public, including Indians, are published in the Federal Register and codified in 25 Code of Federal Regulations (25 CFR). These directives inform the public of privileges and benefits available; eligibility qualifications, requirements and procedures; and of appeal rights and procedures. ...

Unlike numerous other programs authorized by the Snyder Act and funded by the annual appropriations, the BIA has chosen not to publish its eligibility requirements for general assistance in the Federal Register or in the CFR. This continues to the present time. The only official manifestation of this alleged policy of restricting general assistance to those directly on the reservations is the material in the Manual which is, by BIA's own admission, solely an internal-operations brochure intended to cover policies that "do not relate to the public." Indeed, at oral argument the Government conceded that for this to be a "real

---

71. "The Commissioner of Indian Affairs shall, under the direction of the Secretary of the Interior, and agreeably to such regulations as the President may prescribe, have the management of all Indian affairs and of all matters arising out of Indian relations." 25 U.S.C. §2.

legislative rule," itself endowed with the force of law, it should be published in the Federal Register. . . .

Where the rights of individuals are affected, it is incumbent upon agencies to follow their own procedures. This is so even where the internal procedures are possibly more rigorous than otherwise would be required. Service v. Dulles, 354 U.S. 363, 388 (1957); Vitarelli v. Seaton, 359 U.S. 535, 539-540 (1959). The BIA, by its Manual, has declared that all directives that "inform the public of privileges and benefits available" and of "eligibility requirements" are among those to be published. The requirement that, in order to receive general assistance, an Indian must reside directly "on" a reservation is clearly an important substantive policy that fits within this class of directives. Before the BIA may extinguish the entitlement of these otherwise eligible beneficiaries, it must comply, at a minimum, with its own internal procedures.

The overriding duty of our Federal Government to deal fairly with Indians wherever located has been recognized by this Court on many occasions. See, e.g., Seminole Nation v. United States, 316 U.S. 286, 296 (1942); Board of County Comm'rs v. Seber, 318 U.S. 705 (1943). [I]t is essential that the legitimate expectation of these needy Indians not be extinguished by what amounts to an unpublished ad hoc determination of the agency that was not promulgated in accordance with its own procedures, to say nothing of those of the Administrative Procedure Act. The denial of benefits to these respondents under such circumstances is inconsistent with "the distinctive obligation of trust incumbent upon the Government in its dealings with these dependent and sometimes exploited people." Seminole Nation v. United States, 316 U.S., at 296; see Squire v. Capoeman, 351 U.S. 1 (1956). Before benefits may be denied to these otherwise entitled Indians, the BIA must first promulgate eligibility requirements according to established procedures.

Notes and Questions

(1) Does the Court hold that BIA limitations on eligibility for general assistance must be accomplished through rulemaking rather than adjudication? If so, is the decision consistent with *Chenery II*? Is the Court simply announcing a special rule for Indians?

Alternatively, does the Court leave open the possibility that BIA might have dealt with the eligibility problem on a case-by-case basis, holding only that (a) BIA had elected to deal with the issue through general regulations and had invoked these regulations to deny assistance to Ruiz, and (b) that accordingly BIA was required to follow APA requirements and the policy stated in its manual [72] of publishing such regulations in the Federal Register and CFR? Does this mean

---

72. We examine below, pp. 445-458, the principle that agencies must follow their own regulations. Why should BIA be required to follow the statement in the introduction to its manual that directives relating to eligibility would be published in the Federal Register and codified in CFR, when the manual itself has not been made publicly available?

Does *Ruiz* rest on an implicit substantive requirement of a fair general system for the allocation of limited government benefits? Cf. *Hornsby* and *Holmes*, supra pp. 317, 318.

that all internal agency directives and guidelines must be published in the Federal Register?

(2) Even if the BIA violated the APA by not publishing the regulation, why isn't its denial of assistance to Ruiz sustainable under *Wyman-Gordon*? [73]

NLRB v. Bell Aerospace Co.

416 U.S. 267 (1974)

[The NLRB certified as an appropriate unit for collective bargaining 25 Bell Aerospace employees who served as buyers in Bell's purchasing and procurement department, determining prices and specifications for supplies and the selection of supplies to Bell. At a subsequent election directed by the Board, a majority of the buyers voted to be represented by a union. In reliance upon prior decisions, including Packard Motor Co. v. NLRB, supra p. 244, Bell opposed certification on the ground that the buyers were "managerial employees" and therefore not subject to the Act. However, the Board ruled that even if the buyers were "managerial employees," they were subject to the Act, asserting that the Act extended to all "managerial employees" except those whose participation in a labor organization would create a conflict of interest with their job responsibilities, and that no such conflict was present here. In so ruling, the Board overturned a long line of prior NLRB decisions holding that "managerial employees" were not subject to the Act, including several decisions specifically refusing to certify buyers as a collective bargaining unit on the ground that they were, in effect, "managerial employees."

The Second Circuit Court of Appeals refused to enforce the Board's order requiring Bell to negotiate with the buyers' union. The Court found, based on the legislative history and the purposes of the Act, that it did not cover any "managerial employees," and that the Board's ruling to the contrary was erroneous. However, the Court also found that the Board enjoys a measure of discretion in classifying buyers as either "managerial" or nonmanagerial employees, and that since the Board had, because of its construction of the Act, not clearly focussed on the question of classification in this case, Bell's buyers might be found to be nonmanagerial employees and therefore subject to the Act. Nonetheless, the Court concluded that in light of prior Board decisions classifying buyers as "managerial," it would be unfair to permit the Board to reclassify buyers as "nonmanagerial" through adjudication, and that any such change could only be accomplished by rulemaking; it accordingly dismissed the case rather than remanding for further proceedings.

The Supreme Court, in an opinion by Justice Powell with four Justices dissenting, agreed with the Court of Appeals' construction of the Act as not governing "managerial employees" and also agreed with its conclusion that the Board could rationally categorize buyers as either "managerial" or "nonmanagerial." However, the Court disagreed with the Second Circuit's conclusion that a reclassification of

73. For a broadside attack on the Morton v. Ruiz decision, see Davis, Administrative Law Surprises in the *Ruiz* Case, 75 Colum. L. Rev. 823 (1975).

buyers from "managerial to "nonmanagerial" could only be accomplished through rulemaking. Excerpts from the Court's opinion on this point, which was joined by all of the Justices, follow:]

The Court of Appeals also held that, although the Board was not precluded from determining that buyers or some types of buyers were not "managerial employees," it could do so only by invoking its rulemaking procedures under §6 of the Act, 29 U.S.C. §156.[74]

A similar issue was presented to this Court in its second decision in SEC v. Chenery Corp., 332 U.S. 194 (1947) (*Chenery II*).[75] There, the respondent corporation argued that in an adjudicative proceeding the Commission could not apply a general standard that it had formulated for the first time in that proceeding.

[The Court then quoted at length from the language of *Chenery II*.] The Court concluded that "the choice made between proceeding by general rule or by individual, ad hoc litigation is one that lies primarily in the informed discretion of the administrative agency." Id., at 203.

The views expressed in *Chenery II* and *Wyman-Gordon* make plain that the Board is not precluded from announcing new principles in an adjudicative proceeding and that the choice between rulemaking and adjudication lies in the first instance within the Board's discretion. Although there may be situations where the Board's reliance on adjudication would amount to an abuse of discretion or a violation of the Act, nothing in the present case would justify such a conclusion. Indeed, there is ample indication that adjudication is especially appropriate in the instant context. As the Court of Appeals noted, "[t]here must be tens of thousands of manufacturing, wholesale and retail units which employ buyers, and hundreds of thousands of the latter." 475 F.2d, at 496. Moreover, duties of buyers vary widely depending on the company or industry. It is doubtful whether any generalized standard could be framed which would have more than marginal utility. The Board thus has reason to proceed with caution, developing its standards in a case-by-case manner with attention to the specific character of the buyers' authority and duties in each company. The Board's judgment that adjudication best serves this purpose is entitled to great weight.

The possible reliance of industry on the Board's past decisions with respect to buyers does not require a different result. It has not been shown that the adverse consequences ensuing from such reliance are so substantial that the Board should be precluded from reconsidering the issue in an adjudicative proceeding. Furthermore, this not a case in which some new liability is sought to be imposed on individuals for past actions which were taken in good-faith reliance on Board pronouncements. Nor are fines or damages involved here. In any event, concern about such consequences is largely speculative, for the Board has not yet finally determined whether these buyers are "managerial."

74. Section 6 provides:
"The Board shall have authority from time to time to make, amend, and rescind, in the manner prescribed by the Administrative Procedure Act, such rules and regulations as may be necessary to carry out the provisions of this subchapter." 29 U.S.C. §156.
75. *Chenery II* did not involve §4 of the APA, 5 U.S.C. §553, but is nevertheless analogous.

It is true, of course, that rulemaking would provide the Board with a forum for soliciting the informed views of those affected in industry and labor before embarking on a new course. But surely the Board has discretion to decide that the adjudicative procedures in this case may also produce the relevant information necessary to mature and fair consideration of the issues. Those most immediately affected, the buyers and the company in the particular case, are accorded a full opportunity to be heard before the Board makes its determination.

The judgment of the Court of Appeals is therefore affirmed in part and reversed in part, and the cause remanded to that court with directions to remand to the Board for further proceedings in conformity with this opinion.

It is so ordered.

Notes and Questions

1. Can *Bell Aerospace* be reconciled with Morton v. Ruiz? Does it show that the latter is a "sport" decision?

2. Does *Bell Aerospace* give agencies complete discretion to utilize adjudication rather than rulemaking in formulating and changing policy (at least so long as the agency eschews prospective overruling of the *Wyman-Gordon* type)? Consider Chisholm v. FCC, 538 F.2d 349 (D.C. Cir. 1976), *cert. denied*, 429 U.S. 890 (1976), in which the FCC utilized an adjudicatory proceeding to overturn well-established and long-standing principles (also established through adjudication) that had narrowly defined the scope of a provision in the Communications Act exempting "bona fide news events" from the Act's "equal time" requirement that broadcasters who make time available to one candidate for political election must make equal time available to all other candidates. In overruling prior decisions, the Commission held that presidential press conferences, press conferences by other candidates, and candidates' debates sponsored by nonbroadcast organizations could qualify for exemption. Relying on *Bell Aerospace*, a majority of the court rejected the contention of petitioners that the change must be accomplished by rulemaking, noting that petitioners had been afforded ample opportunity in the Commission's adjudicatory proceedings to submit their views. (Rep. Shirley Chisholm, the Democratic National Committee, and the National Organization of Women had opposed the change because it would permit media coverage of President Ford's press conferences without triggering the "equal time" requirement.)

Judge Wright dissented, contending (1) that *Bell Aerospace* involved a situation where (as the Supreme Court pointed out) rulemaking was inappropriate because of the many different conditions of buyers' employment, whereas here the FCC has established a uniform new general "rule" for which rulemaking was appropriate; (2) that rulemaking might encourage a broader submission of views; (3) that the legislative history of the Communications Act indicated that Congress had expected the Commission to utilize rulemaking to define the scope of the equal time requirement.

See also the decision in *Citizens Communications Center II*, supra p. 394, permitting the FCC to develop license renewal criteria through adjudication rather than rulemaking.

3. An Example of Rate Setting Through Rulemaking: The FPC, "Area" Ratesetting, and "Rent Control"

We shall now consider the Federal Power Commission's efforts to control the price at which producers of natural gas sell their product. The example is instructive for two reasons. First, the underlying substantive economic problem is that of controlling "rents" or windfall profits that might be earned by producers. The problems that an agency faces when it tries to control rents are similar whether the producer is a natural gas producer or the owner of city housing.

Second, the courts revealed in *Permian Basin* (infra) a willingness to allow the FPC broad discretion when "innovative" procedures were arguably needed to get the job done. This fact may reflect the existence of broad authority for the agency to choose its methods of procedure. On the other hand, it may reflect no more than sympathy with the agency's efforts to develop a workable price control system (or a lack of sympathy with agency delay). Advocates of this view would point to *CATCO* (also discussed below) and the restrictions the Court placed on the agency's power to *refuse* to set a price. You must compare the two cases to determine the extent to which court "sympathy" with substantive agency objectives can affect the breadth of the procedural discretion the agency is allowed.

These few cases ought also to give you a picture of how agency and court, action and reaction, combine to produce a regulatory regime in which buyers and sellers must actually operate.

a. Background

The natural gas industry has three basic segments: production, transmission, and distribution. Production takes place for the most part in the South and Southwest. Producers sell most gas to interstate pipeline companies (transmission segment), which transport it from Louisiana, Texas, Oklahoma, and the Gulf of Mexico to all other parts of the United States. The pipeline companies resell most gas to local distributing companies (distribution segment) which bring it directly to local homes and businesses.

Distributing companies and pipeline companies are generally considered to have the characteristics of natural monopolies. State utility commissions regulate the former; the Federal Power Commission (now the Energy Regulatory Commission within the Department of Energy) regulates the latter. In each instance the regulator applies traditional cost of service ratemaking principles, along the lines discussed supra at pp. 201-202.

Since the 1950s there has been considerable argument about whether natural gas producers should be regulated as well. While some facts about producers and production are disputed, there is general agreement on the following:

(1) The cost of extracting gas from existing wells and keeping them in working order is only a very small part of total gas production cost. The largest part of gas production cost is accounted for by exploration expense and by interest pay-

ments. Interest payments are high because discovered gas reserves will be sold gradually over a twenty-year period. The capital investment necessary to find those reserves is, in theory, recovered over those twenty years. There is also a loss of several years from the time investment in exploration is made until it begins to produce a return.

(2) Before World War II, gas was discovered and exploited mainly as a by-product of the search for oil. Before 1950 almost all gas produced was oil well gas. But by 1960 about half of all gas came from gas wells; and by 1970 more than three-quarters of all gas came from wells that produce only gas and which were found in the search for gas itself. Thus most gas costs today can be treated as costs of gas itself (plus liquids — such as propane — that the gas contains).

(3) There are more than 3500 producers of natural gas, producing in five or six major fields. About twenty of these producers account for more than half of all gas production. In the early 1960s, the five largest producers accounted for about half the production in the Permian Basin (a Texas-New Mexico field). In the Texas Gulf, the four largest producers accounted for slightly more than one-quarter of new reserves. It is not difficult to enter the industry, for the initial investment required of a small producer is low. Most economists have claimed that, judged by its structure and entry conditions, field production of natural gas is more competitive than most American industries.

(4) Beginning in the 1950s the price of natural gas in the field began to rise. The cost of finding new gas has continually increased to the point where gas that sold for 15¢ to 20¢ per Mcf (thousand cubic feet) 20 years ago would sell for ten times as much today.

The rapid increases in price in the 1950s led to a strong demand for regulation. Initially those advocating regulation claimed that the producers possessed "monopoly power." Yet, the market facts make it difficult to rest a claim for regulation on that ground. Nonetheless, there are other grounds on which regulation might rest.

Regulation of Windfall Profits. The major argument for regulating the prices of oil and natural gas has rested on the claimed desirability of preventing producers from obtaining unearned windfall "rents." Any firm or individual possessing an existing stock of a product whose cost is rapidly increasing will obtain windfalls — and this fact is independent of the state of competition in the market. Anyone, for example, who hoarded coffee costing $1 per pound is now able to sell that coffee at $3-4 per pound, despite a highly competitive coffee market, simply because the price of new coffee has risen to that level. Similarly, the value of old domestic oil, which may have cost $3-5 per barrel before the embargo, rose to $12-14 per barrel after 1974. And the value of a large fixed supply of old natural gas rose from, say, $0.15-0.21 per Mcf (thousand cubic feet) to $1.50-3.00 per Mcf as a result of the increase in the cost of producing additional supplies.

Large increases in the costs of a product coupled with a large stock of older, cheaper products have typically given rise to a demand for regulation. Prices, it is claimed, should be kept down (a) to avoid giving large windfalls to producers in the form of extra profits and (b) instead to give any such windfalls to the consumer in the form of lower prices. Rent control of housing is one common form of this type of regulation.

The Classic Regulatory System. The effort to regulate rents has called forth a complex ratesetting system. Obviously, the prevention of windfalls simply by keeping the price of *all* the product uniformly low — say, if the price of coffee were held to $1 per pound or oil to $2 per barrel or gas to $0.20 per Mcf — could create a serious shortage of that product, for new product costs more than that to produce. On the other hand, to keep prices uniformly and sufficiently high to elicit additional supply is equivalent to no regulation at all. The result — developed by the FPC in the 1960s — is a "tiered" pricing system, which sets different prices for different vintages of product. For example, the price of old gas is held at, say, $0.20 per Mcf, whereas the price of new gas is allowed to rise — high enough, in principal, to encourage new production.

The use of a tiered price control system immediately raises two major questions. One should ask of any such system:

(1) How is the "high" price determined? And how does one know that it is high enough to elicit sufficient new supply?

(2) Who gets the lower-priced product? Obviously, all users want it. But, because users cannot be allowed to bid for it, as prices would then simply rise to the "high" level, *how* is that lower-priced product allocated?

The FPC tried to solve these two problems through classic "cost of service" ratemaking, which involved an effort to determine the actual costs of thousands of producers. After years of hearings, they promulgated a set of prices that most observers believe were too low, helped to produce a shortage, and inevitably led to the allocation of gas primarily on the basis of historical use. The shortage was exacerbated by the fact that intrastate gas was unregulated, so producers sold new gas in the same state it was produced, and business moved south to obtain it. The oil regulators have dealt with the allocation problem through a complex "entitlement" system that, in effect, precludes a shortage by subsidizing the importation of foreign oil. (Rent control of housing usually does not involve trying to control rents of new housing; older, low-priced housing is allocated on an historical basis.)

We shall now examine in greater detail the system of rules that the FPC developed and the legal constraints within which it operated. Doing so will shed some light on the virtues and vices of setting rates by rulemaking as well as on the extent to which a court can control the ratemaking process through judicial review. At this point you should review the ratefixing provisions of the Natural Gas Act, p. 202 supra.

The Permian Basin Area Rate Cases

390 U.S. 747 (1968)

Mr. Justice HARLAN delivered the opinion of the Court.

These cases stem from proceedings commenced in 1960 by the Federal Power Commission under §5(a) of the Natural Gas Act, ... to determine maximum just and reasonable rates for sales in interstate commerce of natural gas produced in the Permian Basin. ... The Commission conducted extended hearings[76] [utilizing formal rulemaking procedures under APA §§ 556-557], and in 1965 issued a decision that both prescribed such rates and provided various ancillary requirements. On petitions for review, the Court of Appeals for the Tenth Circuit sustained in part and set aside in part the Commission's orders. Because these proceedings began a new era in the regulation of natural gas producers, we granted certiorari and consolidated the cases for briefing and extended oral argument. ... For reasons that follow, we ... sustain in their entirety the Commission's orders.

I

The circumstances that led ultimately to these proceedings should first be recalled. The Commission's authority to regulate interstate sales of natural gas is derived entirely from the Natural Gas Act of 1938. The Act's provisions do not specifically extend to producers or to wellhead sales of natural gas, and the Commission declined until 1954 to regulate sales by independent producers[77] to interstate pipelines. Its efforts to regulate such began only after this Court held in 1954 that independent producers are "natural-gas compan[ies]" within the meaning of §2(6) of the Act. Phillips Petroleum Co. v. Wisconsin, 347 U.S. 672. The Commission has since labored with obvious difficulty to regulate a diverse and growing industry under the terms of an ill-suited statute.

The Commission initially sought to determine whether producers' rates were just and reasonable within the meaning of §§ 4(a) and 5(a) by examination of each producer's costs of service. Although this method has been widely employed in various rate-making situations, it ultimately proved inappropriate for the regulation of independent producers. Producers of natural gas cannot usefully be classed as public utilities. They enjoy no franchises or guaranteed areas of service. They are intensely competitive vendors of a wasting commodity they have acquired only by costly and often unrewarded search. Their unit costs may rise or decline with the vagaries of fortune. The value to the public of the services they perform is measured by the quantity and character of the natural gas they produce, and not by the resources they have expended in its search; the Commission and the consumer alike are concerned principally with "what [the producer] gets out of the ground, not ... what he puts into it. ..." FPC v. Hope Natural Gas Co., 320 U.S. 591, 649 (separate opinion). The exploration for and the production of natural gas are thus "more erratic and irregular and unpredictable in relation to investment than any phase of any other utility business." Id., at 647. Moreover, the number

76. There were some 384 parties before the Commission, including 336 gas producers. Hearings began on October 11, 1961, and closed on September 10, 1963. The final transcript includes more than 30,000 pages. The examiner's decision was issued on September 17, 1974. The Commission heard three days of oral argument, and issued its decision on August 5, 1965. A supplementary opinion denying applications for rehearing was issued on October 4, 1965.

77. Independent producers are those that do "not engage in the interstate transmission of gas from the producing fields to consumer markets and [are] not affiliated with any interstate natural-gas pipeline company." Phillips Petroleum Co. v. Wisconsin, 347 U.S. 672, 675.

both of independent producers and of jurisdictional sales is large,[78] and the administrative burdens placed upon the Commission by an individual company costs-of-service standard were therefore extremely heavy.[79]

In consequence, the Commission's regulation of producers' sales became increasingly laborious, until, in 1960, it was described as the "outstanding example in the federal government of the breakdown of the administrative process." [80] The Commission in 1960 acknowledged the gravity of its difficulties, and announced that it would commence a series of proceedings under §5(a) in which it would determine maximum producers rates for each of the major producing areas. One member of the Commission has subsequently described these efforts as "admittedly ... experimental. ...." These cases place in question the validity of the first such proceeding.[81]

... The Commission in *Phillips* asserted that it possesses statutory authority both to determine and to require the application throughout a producing area of maximum rates for producers' interstate sales. It averred that the adoption of area maximum rates would appreciably reduce its administrative difficulties, facilitate effective regulation, and ultimately prove better suited to the characteristics of the natural gas industry. ...

The rate structure devised by the Commission for the Permian Basin includes two area maximum prices. The Commission provided one area maximum price for natural gas produced from gas wells and dedicated to interstate commerce after January 1, 1961. It created a second, and lower, area maximum price for all other natural gas produced in the Permian Basin. The Commission reasoned that it may employ price functionally, as a tool to encourage discovery and production of appropriate supplies of natural gas. It found that price could serve as a meaningful incentive to exploration and production only for gas-well gas committed to interstate commerce since 1960; the supplies of associated and dissolved gas, and of previously committed reserves of gas-well gas, were, in contrast, found to be relatively unresponsive to variations in price. The Commission expected that its adoption of separate maximum prices would both provide a suitable incentive to exploration and prevent excessive producer profits.

78. The Commission in its second *Phillips* opinion stated that there were then 3,372 independent producers with rates on file; these producers had on file 11,091 rate schedules and 33,231 supplements to those schedules. There were, at the moment of the Commission's opinion, 570 producers involved in 3,278 rate increase filings awaiting hearings and decisions. 24 F.P.C., at 545.

79. The Commission stated in its second *Phillips* opinion that "if our present staff were immediately tripled, and if all new employes would be as competent as those we now have, we would not reach a current status in our independent producer rate work until 2043 A.D. — eighty-two and one half years from now." 24 F.P.C., at 546. It added that if "the plan of rate regulation ... here announced is not lawful," it would follow that "as a practical matter, adequate regulation of producers appears to be impossible under existing law." Id. at 547.

80. Landis, Report on Regulatory Agencies to the President-Elect, printed for use of the Senate Committee on the Judiciary, 86th Cong., 2d Sess., 54. . . .

81. We are informed that four other area proceedings are pending in various stages before the Commission. These, in combination with the present proceeding, reach some 90% of the sales of natural gas subject to the Commission's jurisdiction. Brief for the Federal Power Commission 14-15.

The Commission declined to calculate area rates from prevailing field prices. Instead, it derived the maximum just and reasonable rate for new gas-well gas from composite cost data, obtained from published sources and from producers through a series of cost questionnaires. This information was intended in combination to establish the national costs in 1960 of finding and producing gas-well gas; it was understood not to reflect any variations in cost peculiar either to the Permian Basin or to periods prior to 1960. The maximum just and reasonable rate for all other gas was derived chiefly from the historical costs of gas-well gas produced in the Permian Basin in 1960; the emphasis was here entirely local and historical. The Commission believed that the uncertainties of joint cost allocation made it difficult to compute accurately the cost of gas produced in association with oil.[82] It held, however, that the costs of such gas could not be greater, and must surely be smaller, than those incurred in the production of flowing gas-well gas. In addition, the Commission stated that the exigencies of administration demanded the smallest possible number of separate area rates.

Each of the area maximum rates adopted for the Permian Basin includes a return to the producer of 12% on average production investment, calculated from the Commission's two series of cost computations. The Commission assumed for this purpose that production commences one year after investment, that gas wells deplete uniformly, and that they are totally depleted in 20 years. The rate of return was selected after study of the returns recently permitted to interstate pipelines, but, in addition, was intended to take fully into account the greater financial risks of exploration and production. The Commission recognized that producers are hostages to good fortune; they must expect that their programs of exploration will frequently prove unsuccessful, or that only gas of substandard quality will be found. . . .

The Commission derived from these calculations the following rates for the Permian Basin. Gas-well gas, including its residue, and gas-cap gas, dedicated to interstate commerce after January 1, 1961, may be sold at 16.5¢ per Mcf (including state production taxes) in Texas, and 15.5¢ (excluding state production taxes) in New Mexico. Flowing gas, including oil-well gas and gas-well gas dedicated to interstate commerce before January 1, 1961, may be sold at 14.5¢ per Mcf (including taxes) in Texas, and 13.5¢ per Mcf (excluding taxes) in New Mexico. . . .

II

The parties before this Court have together elected to place in question virtually every detail of the Commission's lengthy proceedings. It must be said at the outset that, in assessing these disparate contentions, this Court's authority is essentially narrow and circumscribed.

Section 19(b) of the Natural Gas Act provides without qualification that the "finding of the Commission as to the facts, if supported by substantial evidence,

---

82. Joint costs "are incurred when products cannot be separately produced. . . ." M. Adelman, The Supply and Price of Natural Gas 25 (1962). . . .

shall be conclusive." More important, we have heretofore emphasized that Congress has entrusted the regulation of the natural gas industry to the informed judgment of the Commission, and not to the preferences of reviewing courts. A presumption of validity therefore attaches to each exercise of the Commission's expertise, and those who would overturn the Commission's judgment undertake "the heavy burden of making a convincing showing that it is invalid because it is unjust and unreasonable in its consequences." FPC v. Hope Natural Gas Co., [320 U.S. 591]. We are not obliged to examine each detail of the Commission's decision; if the "total effect of the rate order cannot be said to be unjust and unreasonable, judicial inquiry under the Act is at an end." Ibid.

Moreover, this Court has often acknowledged that the Commission is not required by the Constitution or the Natural Gas Act to adopt as just and reasonable any particular rate level; rather, courts are without authority to set aside any rate selected by the Commission which is within a "zone of reasonableness." FPC v. Natural Gas Pipeline Co., 315 U.S. 575, 585. No other rule would be consonant with the broad responsibilities given to the Commission by Congress; it must be free, within the limitations imposed by pertinent constitutional and statutory commands, to devise methods of regulation capable of equitably reconciling diverse and conflicting interests. It is on these premises that we proceed to assess the Commission's orders. . . .

We turn first to questions of the Commission's constitutional and statutory authority to adopt a system of area regulation and to impose various supplementary requirements. The most fundamental of these is whether the Commission may, consistently with the Constitution and the Natural Gas Act, regulate producers' interstate sales by the prescription of maximum area rates, rather than by proceedings conducted on an individual producer basis. . . .

It is plain that the Constitution does not forbid the imposition, in appropriate circumstances, of maximum prices upon commercial and other activities. . . . See, e.g., Tagg Bros. v. United States, 280 U.S. 420; Bowles v. Willingham, 321 U.S. 503. No more does the Constitution prohibit the determination of rates through group or class proceedings. This Court has repeatedly recognized that legislatures and administrative agencies may calculate rates for a regulated class without first evaluating the separate financial position of each member of the class; it has been thought to be sufficient if the agency has before it representative evidence, ample in quantity to measure with appropriate precision the financial and other requirements of the pertinent parties. . . .

No constitutional objection arises from the imposition of maximum prices merely because "high cost operators may be more seriously affected . . . than others," Bowles v. Willingham, supra, at 518, or because the value of regulated property is reduced as a consequence of regulation. FPC v. Hope Natural Gas Co., supra, at 601. Regulation may, consistently with the Constitution, limit stringently the return recovered on investment, for investors' interests provide only one of the variables in the constitutional calculus of reasonableness. . . .

It is, however, plain that the "power to regulate is not a power to destroy," . . . and that maximum rates must be calculated for a regulated class in conformity with the pertinent constitutional limitations. Price control is "unconstitutional . . . if arbitrary, discriminatory, or demonstrably irrelevant to the policy the legislature is free to adopt. . . ." Nebbia v. New York, 291 U.S. 502, 539. Nonetheless, the just and reasonable standard of the Natural Gas Act "coincides" with the applicable constitutional standards, FPC, v. Natural Gas Pipeline Co., supra, at 586, and any rate selected by the Commission from the broad zone of reasonableness permitted by the Act cannot properly be attacked as confiscatory. Accordingly, there can be no constitutional objection if the Commission, in its calculation of rates, takes fully into account the various interests which Congress has required it to reconcile. We do not suggest that maximum rates computed for a group or geographical area can never be confiscatory; we hold only that any such rates, determined in conformity with the Natural Gas Act, and intended to "balanc[e] . . . the investor and the consumer interests," are constitutionally permissible. FPC v. Hope Natural Gas Co., supra, at 603.

One additional constitutional consideration remains. The producers have urged, and certain of this Court's decisions might be understood to have suggested, that if maximum rates are jointly determined for a group or area, the members of the regulated class must, under the Constitution, be proffered opportunities either to withdraw from the regulated activity or to seek special relief from the group rates. We need not determine whether this is in every situation constitutionally imperative, for such arrangements have here been provided by the Commission, and we cannot now hold them inadequate.

The Commission declared that a producer should be permitted "appropriate relief" if it establishes that its "out-of-pocket expenses in connection with the operation of a particular well" exceed its revenue from the well under the applicable area price. 34 F.P.C., at 226. It did not indicate which operating expenses would be pertinent for these calculations.[83] The Commission acknowledged that there might be other circumstances in which relief should be given, but declined to enumerate them. It emphasized, however, that a producer's inability to recover either its unsuccessful exploration costs or the full 12% return on its production investment would not, without more, warrant relief. It announced that in many situations it would authorize abandonment under §7(b) . . . rather than an exception to the area maximum price. Finally, the Commission held that the burden would be upon the producer to establish the propriety of an exception, and that it therefore would not stay enforcement of the area rates pending disposition of individual petitions for special relief. . . .

For the reasons indicated, we find no constitutional infirmity in the Commission's adoption of an area maximum rate system for the Permian Basin.

We consider next the claims that the Commission has exceeded the authority given it by the Natural Gas Act. The first and most important of these questions is whether, despite the absence of any constitutional deficiency, area regulation is in-

---

83. The Court of Appeals remarked that "[o]ut-of-pocket expenses are not defined and we do not know what they include." 375 F.2d, at 30. It is certainly true that the Commission proffered no definition, but we cannot regard this as a fatal omission.

consistent with the terms of the Act. The producers that seek reversal of the judgments below offer three principal contentions on this question. First, they emphasize that the Act uniformly employs the singular to describe those subject to its requirements: §4(a), for example, provides that rates received by "any natural-gas company" must be just and reasonable. It is urged that the draftsman's choice of number indicates that each producer's rates must be individually computed from evidence of its own financial position. We cannot infer so much from so little; we see no more in the draftsman's choice of phrase than that the Act's obligations are imposed severally upon each producer.

Reliance is next placed upon one sentence in the Report of the House Committee on Interstate and Foreign Commerce, which in 1937 recommended passage of the Natural Gas Act. The Committee remarked that the "bill provides for regulation along recognized and more or less standardized lines." H.R. Rep. No. 709, 75th Cong., 1st Sess., 3. It added that the bill's provisions included nothing "novel." Ibid. We find these statements entirely inconclusive, particularly since, as the Committee doubtless was aware, regulation by group or class was a recognized administrative method even in 1937. Compare Tagg Bros. vs. United States, supra; New England Divisions Case, supra....

Surely the Commission's broad responsibilities therefore demand a generous construction of its statutory authority.[84]

Such a construction is consistent with the view of administrative rate making uniformly taken by this Court. The Court has said that the "legislative discretion implied in the rate making power necessarily extends to the entire legislative process, embracing the method used in reaching the legislative determination as well as that determination itself." Los Angeles Gas Co. v. Railroad Comm'n, 289 U.S. 287, 304. And see San Diego Land & Town Co. v. Jasper, 189 U.S. 439, 446. It follows that rate-making agencies are not bound to the service of any single regulatory formula; they are permitted, unless their statutory authority otherwise plainly indicates, "to make the pragmatic adjustments which may be called for by particular circumstances," FPC v. Natural Gas Pipeline Co., supra, at 586....

There are, moreover, other factors that indicate persuasively that the Natural Gas Act should be understood to permit area regulation. The Act was intended to create, through the exercise of the national power over interstate commerce, "an agency for regulating the wholesale distribution to public service companies of natural gas moving interstate"; Illinois Gas Co. v. Public Service Co., 314 U.S. 498, 506; it was for this purpose expected to "balanc[e] ... the investor and the consumer interests." FPC v. Hope Natural Gas Co., supra, at 603. This Court has repeatedly held that the width of administrative authority must be measured in part by the purposes for which it was conferred; ...

The Commission has asserted, and the history of producer regulation has confirmed, that the ultimate achievement of the Commission's regulatory purposes may

---

84. We obtain additional assistance from §6; it provides that the Commission "shall have power to perform any and all acts, and to prescribe ... such orders, rules, and regulations as it may find necessary or appropriate to carry out the provisions of this" Act. 15 U.S.C. §717a.

easily depend upon the contrivance of more expeditious administrative methods. The Commission believes that the elements of such methods may be found in area proceedings. "[C]onsiderations of feasibility and practicality are certainly germane" to the issues before us. Bowles v. Willingham, supra, at 517. We cannot, in these circumstances, conclude that Congress has given authority inadequate to achieve with reasonable effectiveness the purposes for which it has acted. . . .

Mr. Justice DOUGLAS, dissenting.

What the Court does today cannot be reconciled with the construction given the Natural Gas Act by FPC v. Hope Natural Gas Co., 320 U.S. 591, 602. In that case we said, in determining whether a rate had been properly found to be "just and reasonable" under the Act, that (1) "it is the result reached not the method employed which is controlling"; (2) it is "not theory but the impact of the rate order which counts"; (3) "If the total effect of the rate order cannot be said to be unjust and unreasonable, judicial inquiry under the Act is at an end."

The area rate orders challenged here are based on averages.[85] No single producer's actual costs, actual risks, actual returns, are known.

The "result reached" as to any producer is not known.

The "impact of the rate order" on any producer is not known.

The "total effect" of the rate order on a single producer is not known.

Group regulation of rates is not, of course, novel. It has at times been authorized. The Federal Aviation Act of 1958, §1002(e), 72 Stat. 789, 49 U.S.C. §1482(e), permits it. . . . Under the War Power, extensive price regulation on a group basis was sustained. Bowles v. Willingham, 321 U.S. 503, 517-519. The Interstate Commerce Commission has undertaken it, as revealed by the Divisions of Revenue cases. New England Divisions Case, 261 U.S. 184; . . . The requirement in the Divisions of Revenue cases is that the group evidence be "typical in character, and ample in quantity, to justify the finding made in respect to each division of each rate of every carrier." 261 U.S., at 196-197. In other words, where the rates fixed will recover the

---

85. In its effort to determine costs of production, the Commission sent out questionnaires (Appendices A, B, and C), to 458 producers in the Permian Basin area. . . . Appendices B and C inquired as to production costs; Appendix A covered drilling costs. . . .

The Commission's staff used response to these questionnaires to develop a composite cost of service study. [W]eighted cost averages were computed — i.e., the replies on Appendix B were given a weight proportional to the volume Mcf covered by these responses.

In establishing the rate for new gas-well gas, the Commission elected to proceed by determining costs on a national, rather than an area, basis. . . . It used the Permian questionnaire responses, however, as "a vital source of information," employing them in determining various components of the final national average cost. . . . The Commission also turned to various "well-recognized and authoritative industry data sources [which] were utilized by various witnesses in the proceeding." Id., at 191.

Various adjustments were made because of factors such as atypical years of the Permian questionnaire data being disproportionate to the national figures. . . .

The Commission's rate for flowing gas was based primarily on the questionnaire data which had been compiled by the staff into a composite cost of service study. The Commission in this instance based the ceiling price on Permian Basin area costs, although it used nationwide data in determining exploration and development costs. See 34 F.P.C., at 212-218. And, although the term "flowing gas" was defined to include casinghead gas [from oil wells], residue gas derived therefrom, and old gas-well gas, the Commission used only the costs of the old gas-well gas in determining the area rate. . . .

typical group cost of service, the individual producer's right to a minimum of its operating expenses and capital changes is protected. Cost of service includes operating expenses and capital charges. FPC v. Natural Gas Pipeline Co., 315 U.S. 575, 607 (concurring opinion). With that protection I can see no reason why group rates may not be sanctioned here. But more is required than the Commission undertook to do in these cases.

In the present cases the Commission found averages; but there are no findings as to the typicality and representative nature of those averages.[86] We certainly cannot take judicial notice that the averages are typical. Mr. Justice Brandeis in the leading Divisions of Revenue case said that "averages are apt to be misleading" and they cannot be accepted "as a substitute for typical evidence." 265 U.S. at 291....

An average cost is not only apt to be "misleading" it may indeed not be representative of any producer....

The average per capita income of a Middle East kingdom is said to be $1,800 a year. But since one man — or family — gets most of the money, $1,800 a year describes only a mythical resident of that country.

The 12% return allowed by the Commission and computed on an average-cost basis may likewise have no relation whatever to the reality of the actual costs of any producer.

One producer's cost, though, varying from year to year, may average out at $1 per Mcf. Another's may average out at 5¢ per Mcf. Does that make 52.5¢ per Mcf representative of either producer, even if the 52.5¢ per Mcf is stable over the entire period of years? ...

The Commission will allow individual application for relief from these new rates. But it has not prescribed the terms and conditions on which relief will be granted. It has said, however, that an individual producer must show more than that its cost of service is greater than the averages on which the rate is based. 34 F.P.C., at 180.

In a regulated industry there is no constitutional guarantee that the most inefficient will survive. Hegeman Farms Corp. v. Baldwin, 293 U.S. 163, 170-171....

Although we assume that the Act authorizes group rate-making, we cannot disregard the basic structure of the Act, patterned on the "conventional standards of rate-making" (FPC v. Hope Natural Gas Co., supra, at 616) and providing in §§ 4(a) and 5(a) that all rates of *"any"* natural gas company be "just and reasonable." Beyond the group is the single producer; beyond the community of producers

---

86. Nor did the Commission discuss the distribution of the data within the grouping being considered — that is, matters of the concentration, symmetry, and uniformity of the data....

Perhaps for a group as large and diversified as that involved in this case, typical and representative averages cannot be computed.... Perhaps the Commission could have subdivided the group until it arrived at groupings whose members possessed essentially similar characteristics. Cf. United States v. Borden Co., 370 U.S. 460, 469. This would not mean that the Commission would in effect be returning to an individual-producer regulatory method; rather, the Commission could stop the subdivision at that point where group averages became typical and representative. But, as this case now stands, the Commission has not made the necessary findings; and, of course, this Court lacking the required expertise, cannot undertake to supply those findings for the Commission, nor is it our function to do so.

is the individual. The ultimate thrust of the Act reaches the individual producer; and unless we know what the group rate in final analysis does to it or disables it from doing we cannot perform our duty on judicial review. . . .

b.   The Legal Basis for Allowing an Area Rate That May "Confiscate" Property

We have previously seen the Supreme Court insist upon close judicial scrutiny of facts directly relevant to a plausible claim of unconstitutional action by an agency. Specifically, under *Ben Avon*, supra p. 204, this tendency toward strict review was exercised to determine whether an authorized rate unconstitutionally "confiscated" a firm's investment. *Hope Natural Gas*, supra p. 212, indicated a shift in direction, but did that case leave the agency free to reduce the value of an individual's investment to zero? And to offer only "administrative convenience" as a justification for doing so? That is what *Permian Basin* seems to suggest, for a rate that allows an "average" return on investment will likely allow some producers *no* return. Let us examine the cases relied upon by the Court to support this result to see whether it flowed logically from prior law.

TAGG BROS. v. UNITED STATES, 280 U.S. 420 (1930)

[The case involved a challenge to an order of the Secretary of Agriculture, under the Packers and Stockyards Act, setting maximum rates for marketing agencies. In relevant part, Justice Brandeis stated for the Court:]

The contention that the Act, if construed as authorizing the order assailed, is void under the due process clause, is likewise unsound. It rests upon the fact that the services for which the Secretary's order fixes the charges are practically the personal services of brokers. Some of the market agencies are corporations; some partnerships; some are individually owned. The capital needed in the conduct of their business is small. It is said that the business is wholly one of skill and labor, and that the commission man's only implements of trade are a horse on which he rides in the stockyards and a desk on which he keeps his accounts. . . .

The argument is that to prescribe a common maximum of earning power for commission men, who differ between themselves in the length of their experience, their relative aptitude for the work and their individual industry, is to penalize the skillful for the benefit of the unskillful; that in legislative price-fixing there are vital distinctions, from the constitutional standpoint, between property and the use of property, on the one hand, and personal services, on the other; that property originates with the State and reverts to the State, whereas, liberty — freedom to contract as to personal services — is a pre-requisite to the very organization of a government of the people; that it is impossible to ascertain what is a fair return for personal services because liberty, unlike property, has no actual or theoretical equivalent in money; that while property may be taken for a public use upon payment of just compensation, liberty — personal services — may not be so taken except in time of war or as a punishment for crime; that, since personal services can not be taken for a public use, they cannot be said to be dedicated to a public use or devoted to a public service; ... The constitutionality of the power conferred does not rest upon so narrow a ground. There is nothing in the nature of monopolistic personal services which makes it impossible to fix reasonable charges to be made therefor; and there is nothing in the Constitution which limits the Government's power of regulation to businesses which employ substantial capital. ...

ACKER v. UNITED STATES, 298 U.S. 426 (1936)

Acker v. United States also involved the Packers and Stockyards Act. The Court, per Justice Roberts, held that the issue of whether a rate for personal services was reasonable did not involve the issue of confiscation.

THE NEW ENGLAND DIVISIONS CASE, 261 U.S. 184 (1923)

[In the New England Divisions Case, the Court considered the lawfulness of ICC rules that governed the division of joint fares among railroads participating in portions of a single long carriage. Justice Brandeis wrote for the Court:]
... It is asserted that the order is necessarily based upon the theory that, under §15(6), the Commission has authority to fix divisions as between groups of carriers without considering the carriers individually; that Congress did not confer such authority; and that, hence, the order is void. Whether Congress did confer that authority we have no occasion to consider; for it is clear that the Commission did not base its order upon any such theory. The order directs a 15 percent increase in the divisions to the several New England lines. It is comprehensive. But it is based upon evidence which the Commission assumed was typical in character, and ample in quantity, to justify the finding made in respect to each division of each rate of every carrier. Whether the assumption was well founded will be discussed later. Here we are to consider merely, whether Congress authorized the method of proof and of adjudication pursued, and whether it could authorize it, consistently with the Constitution. ...

NEW YORK v. UNITED STATES, 331 U.S. 284 (1947)

[In New York v. United States, the Court rejected a claim that certain ICC rate orders were "confiscatory." Justice Douglas wrote for the Court:]
... [C]orrect practice requires that, where the opportunity exists, all pertinent evidence bearing on the [reasonableness of rates set by the] Commission should be submitted to it in the first instance and should not be received by the District Court as though it were conducting a trial de novo. The reason is plain enough. These problems of transportation economics are complicated and involved. For example, the determination of transportation costs and their allocation among various types of traffic is not a mere mathematical exercise. Like other problems in cost account- ing, it involves the exercise of judgment born of intimate knowledge of the par-

ticular activity and the making of adjustments and qualifications too subtle for the uninitiated. Moreover, the impact of a particular order on revenues and the ability of the enterprise to thrive under it are matters for judgment on the part of those who know the conditions which create the revenues and the flexibility of managerial controls. For such reasons, we stated in Board of Trade v. United States, 314 U.S. 534, 546:

> The process of rate making is essentially empiric. The stuff of the process is fluid and changing — the resultant factors that must be valued as well as weighed. Congress has therefore delegated the enforcement of transportation policy to a permanent expert body and has charged it with the duty of being responsive to the dynamic character of transportation problems.

Thus we think that if the additional evidence was necessary to pass on the issue of confiscation, the cause should have been remanded to the Commission for a further preliminary appraisal of the facts which bear on that question. . . .

[The Court held that since further rate proceedings before the Commission were contemplated, carriers would have an appropriate opportunity to introduce evidence before the ICC to show that the operational impact of its rate orders was confiscatory; the Court refused to set aside the ICCs orders.]

BOWLES v. WILLINGHAM, 321 U.S. 503 (1944)

[This case involved the constitutionality of a system of controlling housing rents during wartime. Justice Douglas wrote:]

It is said . . . that §2(b) of the Act is unconstitutional because it requires the Administrator to fix maximum rents which are "generally fair and equitable." The argument is that a rental which is "generally fair and equitable" may be most unfair and inequitable as applied to a particular landlord and that a statute which does not provide for a fair rental to each landlord is unconstitutional. During the first World War the statute for the control of rents in the District of Columbia provided machinery for securing to a landlord a reasonable rental. Block v. Hirsh, 256 U.S. 135, 157. . . . And under other price-fixing statutes such as the Natural Gas Act of 1938, Congress has provided for the fixing of rates which are just and reasonable in their application to particular persons or companies.

. . . Congress departed from that pattern when it came to the present Act. It has been pointed out that any attempt to fix rents, landlord by landlord, as in the fashion of utility rates, would have been quite impossible. Wilson v. Brown, 137 F.2d 348, 352-354. Such considerations of feasibility and practicality are certainly germane to the constitutional issue. . . .

Moreover, there would be no constitutional objection if Congress as a war emergency measure had itself fixed the maximum rents in these areas. We are not dealing here with a situation which involves a "taking" of property. . . . There is no requirement that the apartments in question be used for purposes which bring them under the Act. Of course, price control, the same as other forms of regulation, may reduce the value of the property regulated. But, as we have pointed out in the *Hope Natural Gas Co.* case (320 U.S. p. 601), that does not mean that the regulation is unconstitutional. [See] Block v. Hirsh, 256 U.S. 135 (1921)....A member of the class which is regulated may suffer economic losses not shared by others. His property may lose utility and depreciate in value as a consequence of regulation. But that has never been a barrier to the exercise of the police power.... Indeed, the decision in Munn v. Illinois, 94 U.S. 113, the pioneer case in this Court, involved a legislative schedule of maximum prices for a defined class of warehouses and was sustained on that basis. We need not determine what constitutional limits there are to price-fixing legislation. Congress was dealing here with conditions created by activities resulting from a great war effort. Yakus v. United States, supra. A nation which can demand the lives of its men and women in the waging of that war is under no constitutional necessity of providing a system of price control on the domestic front which will assure each landlord a "fair return" on his property.

BLOCK v. HIRSH, 256 U.S. 135 (1921)

Mr. Justice Holmes delivered the opinion of the court.

This is a proceeding brought by defendant in error, Hirsh, to recover possession of the cellar and the first floor of a building on F Street in Washington, which the plaintiff in error, Block holds after the expiration of a lease to him.... Block declined to surrender the premises, relying upon the Act of October 22, 1919, c. 80, Title II — "District of Columbia Rents"; ...

By Section 109 of the Act the right of a tenant to occupy ... any building ... is to continue notwithstanding the expiration of his term, ... so long as he pays the rent.... The statute [declares that this provision] is made necessary by emergencies growing out of the war.... As emergency legislation the Title is to end in two years unless sooner repealed....

[The issue is whether this rent control statute is constitutional.] Under the police power the right to erect buildings in a certain quarter of a city may be limited to from eighty to one hundred feet. Welch v. Swasey, 214 U.S. 91. Safe pillars may be required in coal mines. Plymouth Coal Co. v. Pennsylvania, 232 U.S. 531. Billboards in cities may be regulated. St. Louis Poster Advertising Co. v. St. Louis, 249 U.S. 269. Watersheds in the country may be kept clear. Perley v. North Carolina, 249 U.S. 510. These cases are enough to establish that a public exigency will justify the legislature in restricting property rights in land to a certain extent without compensation. But if to answer one need the legislature may limit height to answer another it may limit rent. We do not perceive any reason for denying the justification held good in the foregoing cases to a law limiting the property rights now in question if the public exigency requires that. The reasons are of a different nature but they certainly are not less pressing. Congress has stated the unquestionable embarrassment of Government and danger to the public health in the existing condition of things. The space in Washington is necessarily monopolized in comparatively few hands, and letting portions of it is as much a business as any other. Housing is a necessary of life. All the elements of a public interest justifying some degree of public control are present. The only matter that seems to us open to debate is whether the statute goes too far. For just as there comes a point at which the police power ceases and leaves only that of eminent domain, it may be conceded that regulations of the present sort pressed to a certain height might amount to a taking without due process of law. . . .

The main point against the law is that tenants are allowed to remain in possession at the same rent that they have been paying, unless modified by the Commission established by the act, and that thus the use of the land and the right of the owner to do what he will with his own and to make what contracts he pleases are cut down. But if the public interest be established the regulation of rates is one of the first forms in which it is asserted, and the validity of such regulation has been settled since Munn v. Illinois, 94 U.S. 113. It is said that a grain elevator may go out of business whereas here the use is fastened upon the land. The power to go out of business, when it exists, is an illusory answer to gas companies and waterworks, but we need not stop at that. The regulation is put and justified only as a temporary measure. . . . A limit in time, to tide over a passing trouble, well may justify a law that could not be upheld as a permanent change.

Machinery is provided to secure to the landlord a reasonable rent. §106. It may be assumed that the interpretation of "reasonable" will deprive him in part at least of the power of profiting by the sudden influx of people to Washington caused by the needs of Government and the war, and thus of a right usually incident to fortunately situated property. . . . But while it is unjust to pursue such profits from a national misfortune with sweeping denunciations, the policy of restricting them has been embodied in taxation and is accepted. . . .

[The constitutionality of the statute was sustained.]

c. The Origin of Field Price Regulation

If prior law is inadequate to explain *Permian Basin*, consider the history of FPC efforts to regulate gas field prices.

Phillips Petroleum Co. v. Wisconsin

347 U.S. 672 (1954)

Mr. Justice MINTON delivered the opinion of the Court. . . .

The Power Commission is authorized by §4 of the Natural Gas Act to regulate the "rates and charges made, demanded, or received by any natural-gas company for or in connection with the transportation or sale of natural gas subject to the jurisdiction of the Commission. . . ." "Natural-gas company" is defined by §2(6) of the Act to mean "a person engaged in the transportation of natural gas in interstate commerce, or the sale in interstate commerce of such gas for resale." The jurisdiction of the Commission is set forth in §1(b) as follows:

> The provisions of this Act shall apply to the transportation of natural gas in interstate commerce, to the sale in interstate commerce of natural gas for resale for ultimate public consumption for domestic, commercial, industrial, or any other use, and to natural-gas companies engaged in such transportation or sale, but shall not apply to any other transportation or sale of natural gas or to the local distribution of natural gas or to the facilities used for such distribution or to the production or gathering of natural gas.

Petitioners admit that Phillips [a natural gas producer without any interstate pipeline ownership] engages in "the sale in interstate commerce of natural gas for resale," as, of course, they must. . . . They contend, however, that the affirmative grant of jurisdiction over such sales in the first clause of §1(b) is limited by the negative second clause of the section. In particular, the contention is made that the sales by Phillips are a part of the "production or gathering of natural gas" to which the Commission's jurisdiction expressly does not extend.

We do not agree. In our view, the statutory language, the pertinent legislative history, and the past decisions of this Court all support the conclusion of the Court of Appeals that Phillips is a "natural-gas company" within the meaning of that term as defined in the Natural Gas Act, and that its sales in interstate commerce of natural gas for resale are subject to the jurisdiction of and regulation by the Federal Power Commission.

The Commission found that Phillips' sales are part of the production and gathering process, or are "at least an exempt incident thereof." This determination appears to have been based primarily on the Commission's reading of legislative history and its interpretation of certain decisions of this Court. Also, there is some testimony in the record to the effect that the meaning of "gathering" commonly accepted in the natural-gas industry comprehends the sales incident to the physical activity of collecting and processing the gas. Petitioners contend that the Commission's finding has a reasonable basis in law and is supported by substantial evidence of record and therefore should be accepted by the courts, particularly since the Commission has "consistently" interpreted the Act as not conferring jurisdiction over companies such as Phillips. See Gray v. Powell, 314 U.S. 402; Labor Board v. Hearst Publications, Inc., 322 U.S. 111. We are of the opinion, however, that the finding is without adequate basis in law, and that production and gathering, in the sense that those terms are used in §1(b), end before the sales by Phillips occur. . . .

In general, petitioners contend that Congress intended to regulate only the interstate pipeline companies since certain alleged excesses of those companies were the evil which brought about the legislation. If such were the case, we have difficulty in perceiving why the Commission's jurisdiction over the transportation *or* sale for resale in interstate commerce of natural gas is granted in the disjunctive. It would have sufficed to give the Commission jurisdiction over only those natural-gas companies that engage in "transportation" or "transportation *and* sale for resale" in interstate commerce, if only interstate pipeline companies were intended to be covered....

Rather, we believe that the legislative history indicates a congressional intent to give the Commission jurisdiction over the rates of all wholesales of natural gas in interstate commerce, whether by a pipeline company or not and whether occurring before, during, or after transmission by an interstate pipeline company. There can be no dispute that the overriding congressional purpose was to plug the "gap" in regulation of natural-gas companies resulting from judicial decisions prohibiting, on federal constitutional grounds, state regulation of many of the interstate commerce aspects of the natural-gas business. A significant part of this gap was created by cases holding that "the regulation of wholesale rates of gas and electrical energy moving in interstate commerce is beyond the constitutional powers of the States." ... The committee reports on the bill that became the Natural Gas Act specifically referred to two of these cases and to the necessity of federal regulation to occupy the hiatus created by them. Thus, we are satisfied that Congress sought to regulate wholesales of natural gas occurring at both ends of the interstate transmission systems....

Regulation of the sales in interstate commerce for resale made by a so-called independent natural-gas producer is not essentially different from regulation of such sales when made by an affiliate of an interstate pipeline company. In both cases, the rates charged may have a direct and substantial effect on the price paid by the ultimate consumers. Protection of consumers against exploitation at the hands of natural-gas companies was the primary aim of the Natural Gas Act.... Attempts to weaken this protection by amendatory legislation exempting independent natural-gas producers from federal regulation have repeatedly failed, and we refuse to achieve the same result by a strained interpretation of the existing statutory language.

[Justices BURTON, CLARK, and DOUGLAS dissented.]

As you may have guessed from *Phillips,* prior to 1954 the Commission neither expected nor intended to regulate the field price of natural gas. After *Phillips* and after a congressional bill reversing *Phillips* was vetoed by President Eisenhower, the Commission set to work.

Breyer & MacAvoy, Energy Regulation by the Federal Power Commission

pp. 66-68 (1974)

The Federal Power Commission first tried to regulate gas producers as if they were public utilities allowed to earn "fair return on fair value." The procedure was the same as for setting gas pipeline prices, with the agency judging the "costs of service" and allowing prices sufficient for a company to recover these costs but no more. This way of regulating prices seemed to promise that no producing company would earn more than a reasonable return on its capital — or at least that companies with unusually low costs would, instead of receiving windfalls, have to pass them on as lower prices. This method also seemed to avoid the risk of serious shortages. If production costs were to increase and there was demand for higher-cost reserves, then under this regulation the supply would be available at higher (cost-justified) prices. . . .[87]

The very numbers of producers of natural gas created overwhelming difficulties in rate-of-return regulation. In 1954 there were more than 5,000 producers, and by 1960 more than 2,900 applications for increased rates were awaiting FPC action. The individual case approach to regulation required findings on costs, including joint costs attributable to gas, and on the allowable rate of return and rate base for the hundreds of companies involved in the 2,900 suspended applications. This would have taken an intolerable amount of time. The decision in the first producer case — the *Phillips* case — took 82 hearing days, and 235 exhibits and 10,626 pages of testimony went into the record. Although further cases might have been handled in shorter time with less legal material, differences from case to case in joint costs and degrees of riskiness, and therefore in allowable rates of return, were obviously going to require numerous individual decisions. By 1960 the Federal Power Commission had completed only 10 of these cases. The remaining backlog led the Landis Commission, appointed by President Kennedy to study the regulatory agencies, to conclude that "without question,' the Federal Power Commission represents the outstanding example of "breakdown of the administrative process." Sheer glut caused the abandonment of the procedure of finding individual costs of service.

87. [C]osts of natural gas posed several extraordinary difficulties. Joint expenditures on *exploration* may yield joint production of petroleum and natural gas, separate production, or no production — some gas from oil wells, some from gas wells, in addition to many dry holes. Expenditures on *separate development* of gas fields yield gas with liquids of a number of types, and expenditures on *gas refining* yield both "dry" gas and salable liquid. Outlays to produce jointly two products complicate the regulatory process because there is no direct way to decide whether or to what extent a specific dollar should be considered to be the "cost of gas production" or the "cost of liquid production."

. . . The distinct regulatory problem for gas has been that oil prices are not regulated by the Federal Power Commission. Therefore the commission had to find the exact costs of one of the joint products or else had to try for indirect regulation of the earnings on the unregulated sales of liquids.

The commission's efforts at exactitude were not successful. Attempts were made to apply various accounting techniques for allocating joint costs so as to find precise gas costs. One method allocated joint costs according to the ratio of separable costs of oil production to separable costs of gas production. A second method allocated joint costs in accordance with the number of thermal units (BTUs) contained respectively in the oil and gas produced. A third method, recognizing that BTUs of oil and gas might not be of equal value, multiplied the BTUs by a factor representing relative value (a circular procedure, since value determined cost, cost determined price, and price determined value). None of these procedures had much to do with the price that gas would command under competitive conditions. An economic analyst could not find long-term marginal costs of a single product by using them; nor could he produce with them an estimate of the historical average costs for that product. On the contrary, these accounting methods created the illusion of separable costs when in truth the costs were intermingled and could not be separated. To let rate base figures compiled on any of the conventional theories of rate-making govern a rate for natural gas is little better than to draw figures out of a hat.

d. Regulation of Producer Prices Under §7 of the Natural Gas Act

A further method that the Commission used to control field prices after 1954 relied upon §7 of the Natural Gas Act. Section 7 stated that no firm can build or extend facilities to transport natural gas interstate unless it "shall first have . . . obtained from the Commission a certificate [of] . . . public convenience and necessity. . . ." Moreover, the Commission may "attach to the issuance of the certificate . . . such reasonable . . . conditions as the public convenience and necessity may require." Section 7 effectively prevents producers of new gas from selling that gas interstate without Commission approval. And the Commission decided to grant its permission only on the condition that the firm sell the gas below a certain maximum price.

One might ask how the Commission was to know what that price should be, for determining costs on an individual firm basis seemed too time-consuming, and area rate proceedings had not yet been started. The answer is that the Commission could *roughly* estimate a proper price. Then, if that price was too low, the company would file for a rate increase. Under §4 (see Ch. 4.B supra) the increase would have to be granted after a six-month suspension; but the increase would be subject to §4's requirement of rebate once the Commission finally and formally determined the true, reasonable price. (The Commission could, of course, investigate the firm's rates under §5 (see Ch. 4.B supra) even if no rate was initially set by the Commission. But under §5 the firm's price would stay in effect during the rate proceeding and there was no requirement of eventual rebate.)

This §7 system arose out of the *CATCO* cases. Continental Oil and Tidewater Oil proposed to dedicate a large amount of offshore gas to the interstate market — "the largest reserve ever committed to one sale." It proposed to charge 21.4 cents per Mcf, about 3.5 cents higher than the prevailing field rate. Initially the FPC hearing examiner decided to grant certificates without a rate provision. The Commission reversed the examiner, first ordering him to take evidence on "what rates the public convenience and necessity requires," 17 F.P.C. 563 (1957). CATCO then told the FPC that "they could not present sufficient evidence at the hearing contemplated by the Commission's order within any reasonable period . . . and they could not afford to commence construction until at least the initial rate question is resolved." The FPC revoked its remand and set the initial rate itself at 18 cents per Mcf, 17 F.P.C. 732 (1957). The Commission then granted a rehearing at the request of the interstate pipeline company, (Tennessee Gas Transmission Co.), which proposed to purchase and transport the gas, and which feared that CATCO would not sell if the price was at 18 cents. The Commission wrote (17 F.P.C. 880, 881-882 (1957)):

> In its application for rehearing filed June 4, 1957, Tennessee Gas has stated that it had been advised that the CATCO companies were unwilling to accept the permanent certificates of public convenience and necessity granted by the [FPC's last] order because they objected to the pricing and other conditions specified in the order, and that they would terminate the con-

tracts so that the large supply of gas contained in the off-shore reserves of the CATCO companies would not become available to the customers of Tennessee Gas. . . . They indicated . . . that if they failed to obtain certificates without price conditions which they considered objectionable, they would seek to dispose of their gas elsewhere than to Tennessee Gas and the interstate market [i.e., the unregulated intrastate market].

In the present status of the case we are left with the difficult problem of how to assure the delivery of this gas to the large market served by Tennessee Gas, and at the same time protect the consumers from an unreasonably high price. In reaching a solution to this problem we are moved by the primary consideration that the public served through the Tennessee Gas system is greatly in need of increased supplies of natural gas. Further, it appears to us, important as is the issue of price, that as far as the public is concerned, the precise charge that is made initially is less important than the assurance of this great supply of gas. In view of these circumstances and the fact that the record does not show that the 21.4-cent rate is necessarily excessive, we agree with the presiding examiner that this certificate proceeding under Section 7 of the Natural Gas Act should not assume the character of a rate proceeding under Section 5(a). We are of the opinion that, in the circumstances of this case, in view of the great demand for gas by customers of Tennessee Gas, the price consideration should not be made the prime determinant of what the public convenience and necessity require. By virtue of the authority conferred upon us by Sections 4 and 5 of the Natural Gas Act and the proposal to modify the contracts made by the CATCO companies, we are of the opinion that we will be able to adequately protect the public interest with respect to the matter of price. In order, therefore, to insure that deliveries of gas by the four CATCO companies to Tennessee Gas will commence as promptly as possible, we will grant permanent certificates to them by this order without any condition affecting the initial price of 21.4 cents per Mcf.

However, because the 21.4-cent price, as we have heretofore observed, is higher than Tennessee Gas is paying under any other contract, it should be subject to prompt investigation under Section 5(a) as to its reasonableness. . . .

Distributing companies, intervenors in the CATCO proceeding, sought judicial review, leading to the following Supreme Court Decision.

Atlantic Refining Co. v. Public Service Commn. [*CATCO*]

360 U.S. 378 (1959)

Mr. Justice CLARK delivered the opinion of the Court.

In view of this framework in which the Commission is authorized and directed to act, the initial certificating of a proposal under §7(e) of the Act as being required by the public convenience and necessity becomes crucial. This is true because the delay incident to determination in §5 proceedings through which initial certificated rates are reviewable appears nigh interminable. Although Phillips Petroleum Co. v. Wisconsin, 347 U.S. 672, was decided in 1954, cases instituted under §5 are still in the investigative stage. This long delay, without the protection of refund, as is possible in a §4 proceeding, would provide a windfall for the natural gas company with a consequent squall for the consumers. This the Congress did not intend. Moreover, the fact that the Commission was not given the power to suspend initial rates under §7 makes it the more important, as the Commission itself [said in its first decision], that "this crucial sale should not be permanently certificated unless the rate level has been shown to be in the public interest." 17 F.P.C. 563, 575.

This is especially true where, as here, the initial price will set a pattern in an area where enormous reserves of gas appear to be present.... The Commission has found that the transaction here covers the largest reserve ever committed to interstate commerce in a single sale. Indications are that it is but a puff in comparison to the enormous potentials present under the seabed of the Gulf. The price certificated will in effect become the floor for future contracts in the area. This has been proven by conditions in southern Louisiana where prices have now vaulted from 17 cents to over 23 cents per Mcf. New price plateaus will thus be created as new contracts are made and unless controlled will result in "exploitation" at the expense of the consumer, who eventually pays for the increases in his monthly bill.

It is true that the Act does not require a determination of just and reasonable rates in a §7 proceeding as it does in one under either §4 or §5. Nor do we hold that a "just and reasonable" rate hearing is a prerequisite to the issuance of producer certificates. What we do say is that the inordinate delay presently existing in the processing of §5 proceedings requires a most careful scrutiny and responsible reaction to initial price proposals of producers under §7. This is the more important during this formative period when the ground rules of producer regulation are being evolved.

There is, of course, available in such a situation, a method by which the applicant and the Commission can arrive at a rate that is in keeping with the public convenience and necessity. The Congress, in §7(e), has authorized the Commission to condition certificates in such manner as the public convenience and necessity may require. Where the proposed price is not in keeping with the public interest because it is out of line or because its approval might result in a triggering of general price rises or an increase in the applicant's existing rates by reason of "favored nation" clauses or otherwise, the Commission in the exercise of its discretion might attach such conditions as it believes necessary.

This is not an encroachment upon the initial rate-making privileges allowed natural gas companies under the Act, ... but merely the exercise of that duty imposed on the Commission to protect the public interest in determining whether the issuance of the certificate is required by the public convenience and necessity, which is the ... standard in §7 applications. In granting such conditional certificates, the Commission does not determine initial prices nor does it overturn those agreed upon by the parties. Rather, it so conditions the certificate that the consuming public may be protected while the justness and reasonableness of the price fixed by the parties is being determined under other sections of the Act. Section 7 procedures in such situations thus act to hold the line awaiting adjudication of a just and reasonable rate.... On the other hand, if unconditional certificates are issued where the rate is not clearly shown to be required by the public convenience and necessity, relief is limited to §5 proceedings, and, as we have indicated, full protection of the public interest is not afforded.

Our examination of the record here indicates that there was insufficient evidence to support a finding of public convenience and necessity prerequisite to the issuance of the permanent certificates. The witnesses tendered developed little more information than was included in the printed contracts. As the proposed contract price was higher than any paid by Tennessee, including offshore production in the West Delta area of Louisiana, it is surprising that evidence, if available, was not introduced as to the relative costs of production in the two submerged areas. Moreover the record indicates that the proposed price was some 70% higher than the weighted average cost of gas to Tennessee; still no effort was made to give the "reason why." More damaging was the evidence that this price was greatly in excess of that which Tennessee pays from any lease in southern Louisiana. . . . Nor was the evidence as to whether the certification of this price would "trigger" increases in leases with "favored nation" clauses convincing, and the claim that it would not lead to an increase in rates by Tennessee was not only unsupported but was already proven unfounded.[88]

Nor do we find any support whatever in the record for the conclusory finding on which the order was based that "the public served through the Tennessee Gas system is greatly in need of increased supplies of natural gas." . . .

[Affirmed and remanded.]

The Commission's response to the CATCO *decision.* After CATCO, the FPC issued a general policy statement containing its roughly determined ceiling prices. 24 F.P.C. 812-820 (1960). "Provisional" ceiling prices were set area by area. In the Permian Basin, for example, they ranged from 11 cents to 17 cents per Mcf; in Louisiana, from 13.7 cents to 16.6 cents; and in Texas from 11 cents to 18 cents.

In arriving at these price levels, the Commission wrote, it considered "cost information from all decided and pending cases, existing and historical price structures, volumes of production, trends in production, price trends in the various areas over a number of years, trends in exploration and development, trends in demands, and the available markets for the gas."

". . . [Although the price levels set were only 'guidelines'] [f]or the present, and in the absence of compelling evidence calling for other action for us, proposed initial sales of natural gas by independent producers which include rates higher than those indicated shall be denied a certificate or certificated only upon the condition that lower rates be filed."

The Commission also announced the beginning of its area rate proceedings: "The new area rate determinations resulting from such proceedings will represent

---

88. Tennessee has subsequently filed an application with the FPC requesting higher rates designed to produce some $19,000,000 additional annual revenue. Tennessee Gas Transmission Co., Docket G-17166.

final determinations of just rates for the areas involved as of the date of the decision and for prior periods."

Questions

1. Consider the factors leading the Court to its *Permian Basin* result.

(a) Did the *Permian Basin* Court deal adequately with the claim of "confiscation"? After that decision, what remains of the doctrine?

(b) Use of classical cost of service ratemaking applied on a firm-by-firm basis would have avoided any "confiscation" problem. Why did the FPC not use it? What is the substantive impact of the FPC's decision to deal with the problem of natural gas producer prices through rulemaking?

(c) The Commission used a complex "tier" method of regulation, setting different prices for "old" gas and "new" gas, for oil well gas and gas well gas. Why did it do so? What difficulties did the Commission encounter in setting those rates? What dangers does such a system pose for the consumer?

2. Examine critically the justifications adduced by the Court for its construction of the statute in *Phillips*. How persuasive are they? Did the Court abrogate to itself discretionary issues of policy that should have been left to the agency?

3. Is *Atlantic Refining* (CATCO) hopelessly inconsistent with *Permian Basin*? Argue both sides of this question.

4. Can you now understand why a natural gas shortage has been created?

5. On September 1, 1971 the legislature of the State of Ames adopted legislation enabling towns and cities to control rents. The Act reads in part as follows:

> *Section 1: Findings:* Inflation and war have produced a housing shortage, high rents, and abnormally high profits on investment in housing. The purpose of this Act is to alleviate the currently severe shortage of housing and to lower abnormally high rents. It is designed to secure an adequate, but not an exorbitant, return on the investment an owner has actually made in his property, while lowering rents that are currently too high.
>
> *Section 2:* This Act shall take effect in any city or town which accepts its provisions.
>
> *Section 4:* At the time of acceptance the city or town shall appoint a Rent Control Administrator. The Administrator in accordance with reasonable administrative procedures shall have the power to issue orders and to promulgate regulations to effectuate the purposes of this Act.
>
> *Section 5: Maximum rent:* No person shall charge a rent higher than the rent determined by the Administrator to be reasonable. In determining a reasonable rent the Administrator shall take into account the owner's need to earn a fair return on investment and to cover all necessary costs; he shall also seek to prevent the charging of rents that yield excessive profits. The Administrator, in his discretion, may reduce rents to a level equal to the rent charged an occupant six months prior to the acceptance of this Act by the city or town.
>
> *Section 8:* Any person who knowingly charges more than the maximum lawful rent shall be guilty of a class 1 misdemeanor. Any tenant of any person charging more than the maximum lawful rent may recover any excess paid plus $200 liquidated damages in a civil action.

The Langdell City Council is considering adopting a rent control ordinance under the authority of this enabling act. Assume that you are representing either a landlord or a tenant group. You are to appear before a special meeting of the town council. You are to consider the three or four most important problems that are likely to arise if rent control is adopted. Can regulations be written or procedures be devised to deal adequately with these problems? If so, briefly describe them.

D.   Consistency in Applying Regulations: "An Agency Must Follow Its Own Rules"

1.   Introduction: Rate Structures

We have already examined the problem of consistency in agency adjudication. Here we examine the question of consistency where an agency elects to develop policy through rulemaking. The *Arizona Grocery* case, which follows, is famous for its enunciation of a basic principle of administrative law, namely, that an agency must follow its own rules. The case also embodies a classical problem of ratemaking: how rates are to be structured so that each customer pays an appropriate share of fixed costs or overhead. We shall consider both aspects of the case here. As shall become apparent, an appreciation of the substantive regulatory issue helps to determine the proper disposition of the procedural issue.

2.   Economic Background

Recall the discussion of cost of service ratemaking at pp. 201-202 supra. There we considered how the regulator determined the firm's "revenue requirement," i.e., how much money it would need to cover its costs, including a reasonable profit. Here we shall consider one of the problems that arises when the regulator sets prices designed to yield revenues that equal that requirement. One obvious problem is determining how the prices that one sets affect demand for the product. Obviously the revenues generated by a price increase depend upon the *extent* to which the increase leads to a fall in sales. Yet, accurate information about this relationship — demand elasticity — is notoriously difficult for the agency to develop.

A further set of problems can be grouped under the heading "rate structure." These problems concern the relationship among the various prices the regulated firm charges for its various products sold to different customers, sold at different places, or sold at different times. Typical of such problems are those concerning joint costs (which include fixed or overhead costs) incurred in providing a number of different products. For example, the cost of constructing and maintaining the roadbed is a joint cost of all services performed by railroads in transporting passengers and various commodities. The problem of joint costs is especially acute in an industry, such as the railroad industry, with relatively high fixed overhead costs (land, terminal facilities, and track) and relatively low incremental costs.

In such an industry, prices set equal to the incremental cost of increasing production or services by another unit will not earn enough revenue to cover fixed overhead costs, including the payment of return to investors for the use of their money to purchase land, trackage, and other fixed-cost items. A long-run policy of incremental or marginal cost pricing will therefore not be possible in such an industry.

Here one might ask two preliminary but important questions. First, why should prices be set equal to incremental cost? To answer this question in detail, with appropriate qualifications, would require a lengthy essay on welfare economics. Briefly, when prices throughout the economy equal incremental costs (as is the case in most competitive industries), consumers face a relative set of prices that tells them the true cost to the economy of consuming a bit more of A or a bit less of B — a fact that tends to make buying and selling choices economically efficient. Where the prices of some commodities are set equal to incremental costs and the prices of other commodities are not, consumers are given a misleading set of price signals that can lead to consumption and production decisions that are economically inefficient. Suppose that the price ($1) of one product (A) is far in excess of its incremental cost ($.50), while the price of other products is equal to their incremental cost ($.75), which is somewhat higher than that of A. Consumers would compare the price of A with that of B and C and choose relatvely more of B and C, even though (1) they would prefer relatively more of A if its price were set equal to incremental cost, and (2) it would cost society less in terms of resources expended to produce relatively more A, and less B and C.

Whether one ought always to price at incremental costs — particularly in a world where differences between cost and price may vary among industries — is much debated. But the ability of such prices to inform the public about the true economic cost of buying a bit more or less of the regulated product — and thus direct buying decisions toward the cheapest way to satisfy preferences — is a strong point in their favor.

Second, one might ask, if fixed investment is very high and incremental costs are low, should we regulate, or should we nationalize, the firm? This question is worth considering for the light it sheds upon a proper rate structure. Consider a famous example: a bridge that costs, say, $10 million to build, but which will last forever. Assume the resource cost of one person's crossing — the wear and tear on the bridge — is 5 cents. To charge more than 5 cents will prevent some potential users from crossing, leading them to spend their money on less preferred alternatives that cost society more to produce. Yet, if the bridge owner charges only 5 cents, how is he to pay back the investors who put up $10 million to build the bridge? The answer, the argument goes, is nationalization. If the government invests $10 million, needed bridges will be built, while as long as it charges a toll of only 5 cents once the bridge is built, no one will be unnecessarily discouraged from using it.

Nationalization, however, has problems of its own. Consider two common ones related to allocation and efficiency:

(a) How is the government to know where to build bridges? Unless bridge users were *prepared* to pay not only 5 cents, but also *enough additional money to pay the investment cost*, it was wasteful to build the bridge. The investment funds should have been spent on other projects which the public wanted more. A private investor will build bridges only where users can, and will, pay enough to cover investment costs. The government can try to replicate (or improve upon) the private investor's decision by asking the civil service to work out a cost/benefit calculus related to each project and invest only in those which show an adequate social return. But will such studies produce results as accurate as those flowing from the discipline imposed upon investors by the knowledge that users must in fact pay sufficient tolls if the investment is to be recovered? (Critics of the work of the Army Corps of Engineers typically argue not.)

(b) Are nationalized industries less efficiently operated than those run by private firms? Do they run the risk of undue political interference? Ambrose Bierce defined a lighthouse as a building near a seashore containing a large lantern and a friend of a politician.

The point to be noted here is that regulation, a step short of nationalization, will not, and is not designed to, yield prices that equal incremental costs. Even when regulation works perfectly, it cannot cure the "inefficiency" caused by a private firm's need to cover average costs when (because of large fixed costs) they are greater than incremental costs. Rather, regulation must aim to set prices that allow fixed investment — investment in rights-of-way or railway beds, representing unrepeatable expenditure — to be paid for or recovered. Doing so will lead to a certain amount of allocative waste compared to the ideal.

Now let us turn to the regulator's "rate structure" problem. Suppose in our bridge hypothetical that the bridge is built by private enterprise. Suppose further that, in order to provide investors a return on the capital invested to build the bridge, an extra $1 million must be raised annually, over and above the revenues generated by a 5-cent toll to cover incremental operating expenses. How should tolls be set to raise the needed extra revenue?

At first one might think, "charge everyone the same," for each obtains the same service from the bridge, namely one crossing. Yet to charge each crosser equally (say, 10 cents) can have several pernicious effects. For one thing, some potential crossers, willing to pay, say 8 cents, but not 10 cents, for bridge crossing, will stay at home — a pity, in that the economy could give them what they value at 8 cents, for an economic expenditure of only 5 cents worth of additional resources. For another thing, they might buy something else for 8 cents, say, a ride in a ferryboat, and thereby require the economy to use 8 cents worth of resources giving them *less* satisfaction than *might* have been given them (through bridge crossing) with an economic expenditure of only 5 cents worth of extra resources. And one can imagine the waste involved if a host of 8-cent-cost ferryboats appear, attracting passengers from the 5-cent-bridge because of its 10-cent price.

To minimize this waste, economists have sometimes advocated charging prices that reflect an allocation of fixed costs in inverse relation to elasticity of demand. That is to to say, those to whom bridge use is worth more will be charged a higher proportion of fixed costs; those to whom it is worth less will be charged less, and, as a result, are less likely to stop using the bridge or switch to a ferryboat. The resulting pattern of resource use it more likely to resemble what it would have been if prices were set equal to incremental cost. The Interstate Commerce Commission, for example, has traditionally had railroads charge more for shipping valuable items than for shipping inexpensive ones, presumably because a small extra charge is less likely to affect the shipping behavior of those who send expensive items.

Aside from a theoretical point — that this type of pricing does not always minimize economic waste — this effort to minimize waste when allocating fixed costs often founders on administrative obstacles. As previously mentioned, to measure demand elasticities is extremely difficult. But this difficulty is compounded by efforts to classify customers or services into administerable categories that correspond, even roughly, to demand elasticities. Thus, for example, the ICC's system of varying rates according to value of the product shipped may bear only a distant relation to the "inverse demand elasticity" it is supposed to represent. Do shippers of diamonds, in fact, care less about transportation cost per pound than shippers of salt? Perhaps so, for transportation is a smaller proportion of final selling price. But their willingness to do so may also depend in large part, not upon the proportion of transportation costs in final value, but on the state of competition in the diamond market and the availability of alternative transport. If diamond selling is fiercely competitive, to the point where sellers look for any and every cost-saving device, and if equally good truck transport is readily available, even a small increase in rail prices will lead diamond sellers to use trucks, while a monopolistic salt industry which does not have alternative modes of transport readily available to it may be willing to pay quite high rail prices before it would use other modes of transport.

A simplified example will help to explain the form in which this problem arises in the *Arizona Grocery* case, which we consider below. Assume that a railroad builds a track connecting A, B, and C. Assume that the track costs $5 million. Assume further that, once the track is built, it costs an additional $2 million to buy special cars for carrying oil from A through B to C. Suppose that points A and C are connected by a river, plied by barge lines. The *incremental cost* of carrying the oil by rail from A to C is $2 million — the amount needed for cars and upkeep — the amount that the railroad would save by refusing to carry oil from A to C. The *fully allocated* cost of carrying the oil by rail from A to C, however, includes a "fair" portion of the overhead necessary to supply any rail transport between A and C whatsoever. In particular, it includes a proportionate share of the cost of the railbed — a sunk cost that need never be incurred again. Let us assume that that "fair share" of the overhead is $1 million. In that case, the fully allocated cost

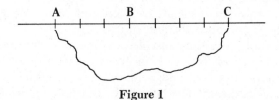

Figure 1

of carrying oil between A and C for the railroad is $3 million, the incremental cost is $2 million.

Suppose that a barge can carry oil from point A to point C at a cost of $2.5 million. Should the railroad be allowed to cut its price for carrying oil from A to C, let us say, to $2.2 million — a price near incremental cost? Or should the ICC insist that it keep its price in the range of $3 million?

The major economic arguments for allowing the railroad to cut its price are the following:

First, unless the railroad cuts its price, all oil will be carried by barge. That means that the portion of fixed costs previously borne by the A to C oil shippers will no longer be borne by them; the fares the railroad charges other shippers will therefore have to rise to recover the additional amount of fixed cost. In our example, if the railroad cut its prices to $2.2 million, the oil shippers will still contribute $200,000 to overhead. If these shippers are lost to the barge lines because the railroad is not allowed to cut its prices, this $200,000 will have to be made up by other railroad customers.

Second, since the railroad fixed costs are in place — the roadbed will never have to be built again — the extra resources that the economy must put forth to carry the oil from A to C by rail amount to $2 million worth of resources. To carry that same amount from A to C by barge, however, requires an extra $2.5 million worth of resources. Thus we can do the same job and have $500,000 worth of resources left over if the shipper sends his oil by rail.

These economic arguments are well known and widely accepted.[89] Other economic arguments, however, suggest that in some circumstances the ICC should not allow the railroad to cut price to incremental cost. First, suppose that the barge line's cost of $2.5 million includes a fee of $1 million that the barge line must pay to the government to cover the cost of initially improving the river or digging a canal. If those costs are nonrepeatable, that fee of $1 million also represents payment for a fixed cost and the true incremental cost for barge line carriage is $1.5 million — in other words, the barge line's incremental costs are lower than the railroad's, but it may not be legally possible for the barge line to lower its prices to its own incremental costs. In such a situation it may be economically sensible for the ICC to prevent the railroads from charging a fee equal to the railroad's incremental cost — when that cost is greater than the barge line's incremental cost but less than the barge lines' fully allocated cost. Second, transport by barge may serve some other social purpose; for example, it may help provide for national defense, add to the scenic beauty of the countryside, or help people in some other way not reflected in the price charged for the service. In order to serve this other social goal, the Commission, pursuant to its statutory authority, may impose a rate structure to ensure that the goods move by barge rather than by rail.

Finally, one should consider the plight of an oil-using widget producer located

89. See, e.g., A. Kahn, 1 The Economics of Regulation 162-166; id., vol. 2 at 23-24, 85; Baumol & Walton, Full Costing, Competition and Regulatory Practice, 82 Yale L. J. 639 (1973).

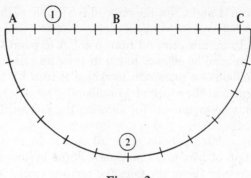

Figure 2

at B in competition with a similar oil-using widget producer located at C. If the railroad is allowed to cut its price for oil transport to C due to riverboat competition, the B producer will often end up paying a higher price for oil than the C producer (though incremental costs of shipment are lower), and widget producers will tend to locate at C, not B. The source of this discrimination is that fixed costs must be collected from someone, and we often must ask B to make a larger contribution than C in order to prevent a rail/barge shipping misallocation; in doing so, we create a B/C producer-location misallocation. It may be some comfort to you (but not to B) to realize that even if the regulator keeps the C rail prices high, B is not helped. Oil will then go by barge to C and so will the oil-using widget makers.

Does the situation change any if, instead of a barge, another rail line runs between A and C? In this case, allowing rail line #1 to lower its A-C price to incremental costs not only hurts B, but also seems unnecessary. It is unlikely that the incremental costs for the A-C oil on line #2 will be much below line #1; indeed, they are likely to be higher. Moreover, the regulator can control the prices of each. Thus, a refusal to let #1 lower its A-C price and raise its A-B price is unlikely to end up with oil shippers using a higher incremental cost mode of transport. The discriminatory harm to B is not counterbalanced by so clear an allocative good.

3. The ICC's Ratemaking Powers

The Supreme Court held in ICC v. Cincinnati Ry., 167 U.S. 479 (1897), that the 1887 Interstate Commerce Act's grant of power to the ICC to condemn rates as unreasonable only empowered it to award reparations for the past and did not grant the ICC power to prescribe rates for the future. In the Hepburn Act of 1906, Congress specifically bestowed this power on the Commission. Since then the ICC's basic powers over railroad rates have been similar to those found in many economic regulatory statutes. All rates must be set forth in published tariffs. The standards applied to judge the lawfulness of rates are whether they are "just and reasonable" and "nondiscriminatory."

In the Transportation Act of 1920 the ICC was empowered to prescribe *minimum* as well as maximum rates; this power was granted to enable the ICC to prevent "destructive" or predatory competition through low rates that might drive competing carriers out of business. The Commission's rate regulation authority was subsequently extended to motor carriers and water carriers (barges).

There are four basic types of relief which the Commission affords through its rate regulation authority:

(a) Most rates are reviewed when the carrier files a tariff seeking to *change* a rate (for a given commodity between given points). A competing carrier or a shipper may then ask the ICC to *suspend* the proposed rate (which it may do for seven months) while it determines its lawfulness. If the proceeding is not completed within seven months, the rate takes effect subject to a refund obligation if it is later found to have been too high. (Compare the FPC's statute at p. 202 supra.)

(b) The ICC in one proceeding may (at the behest of carriers, shippers, or on its own motion) investigate the costs or revenues of all railroads in a region, or in the whole country, and make a blanket adjustment in all rates in order to increase (or to limit) the total revenue carriers receive.

(c) Shippers or competitors may challenge specific individual *existing* rates (as opposed to the *proposed* rates involved in paragraph (a)), and request that a different rate be prescribed for the future.

(d) Shippers may challenge an existing rate as unreasonably high and seek reparations (damages) equal to the difference between the rate they have been charged and a "reasonable" rate, as determined by the Commission. Such reparation proceedings are often joined with a request of the type described in paragraph (c); in such cases the shipper seeks reparations for the past and an order by the Commission setting the appropriate rate for the future.[90]

4. The Arizona Grocery Case

In 1920, railroads maintained a rate of $1.045 per hundred pounds on sugar from California points to Phoenix, Arizona. Shippers contended that the rates were unreasonably high; the Commission awarded reparations based on a rate of 96.5 cents and directed the railroads to charge a rate no higher than 96.5 cents in the future. The railroads subsequently established rates at or below 96.5 cents. In 1922, Phoenix merchants challenged the then-existing San Francisco rates as unreasonable, and sought reparations. In 1925, the ICC ordered that the rate from San Francisco to Phoenix be reduced to 73 cents, seemingly because the rate from

90. If the shipper seeks only reparations, he may seek to bypass the Commission (whose reparation awards can only be enforced in court proceedings, in which they represent "prima facie evidence" of the facts) and directly seek damages in a court action. Such efforts create problems of "primary jurisdiction" which are discussed in Chapter 9.

San Francisco to Chicago had fallen to 84 cents. The Commission also awarded reparations on San Francisco to Phoenix shipments on or after July 1, 1922; the amount of reparations was based on the difference between the rates charged by the railroads and 73 cents. In Traffic Bureau of Phoenix Chamber of Commerce v. Atchison, Topeka & Santa Fe Ry. Co., 95 I.C.C. 244, 248 (1925), a dissenting Commissioner argued:

> Some of these complainants came before us in June, 1920, attacking the rates on sugar, in carloads, from California refineries to Phoenix and asking for reparation, just as they do here. . . . We found the rate unreasonable to the extent that it exceeded 96.5 cents, which we then prescribed for the future. . . . They now come by complaint filed November 3, 1922, and allege that a rate on the same traffic of 96 cents, 0.5 cent lower than that so prescribed, has been unreasonable since February 17, 1921, four months prior to our former decision, and again ask reparation. Meantime, on July 26, 1922, we had found not unreasonable a rate of 96.5 cents, minimum 60,000 pounds, from California refining points to destinations in Nevada and Utah for hauls ranging from 419 to 823 miles, as compared with the hauls here considered ranging from 489 to 800 miles over the Santa Fe, and 451 to 921 miles over the Southern Pacific. Nevada Public Commission v. S.P. Co., 73 I.C.C. 240. That rate also was reduced by the carriers to 96 cents. The general 10 per cent reduction of July 1, 1922, brought this reasonable rate down to 86.5 cents and later, in the general sugar readjustment, the carriers established to Phoenix a rate of 84 cents, minimum 60,000 pounds. All of these were lower than what we had found reasonable and prescribed.
>
> The majority do not reverse those decisions. They do not show change in circumstances and conditions but refer to them as "fully set out" in Phoenix Chamber of Commerce v. Director General, supra. And yet they find unreasonable rates lower than the rate prescribed in that case. . . .
>
> The rate of 84 cents, minimum 80,000 pounds, established January 11, 1924, as a result of our findings in Sugar Cases of 1922, 81 I.C.C. 448, is necessary if California sugar, concededly far exceeding the local demands, is to find a market in the Middle West in competition with sugar from refineries on the Atlantic seaboard and Gulf of Mexico.
>
> For the average distance of 625 miles to Phoenix this 84-cent rate earns 26.8 mills per ton-mile, which compares favorably with 27.3 mills per ton-mile under the average present rate of 82 cents from California refineries to destinations in Nevada and Utah considered in the Nevada case, supra, for an average distance of 600 miles. There the annual movement was shown to be 79 carloads and here less than 100. The majority ignore these comparisons but rest on others less pertinent. . . .
>
> The reasonableness of the basis prescribed is not self-demonstrative. Nor is this failure of demonstration supplied by the evidence of record, by the comparison with the Memphis-Southwestern scale, injected by the majority, or by the necessities of the case. Under such circumstances the complaint should be dismissed. I am authorized by Chairman Aitchison and Commissioners Esch and Lewis to say that they concur in this expression of dissent.

Arizona Grocery Co. v. Atchison, Topeka & Santa Fe Ry.

284 U.S. 370 (1932)

Mr. Justice ROBERTS delivered the opinion of the Court.

This case turns upon the power of the Interstate Commerce Commission to award reparations with respect to shipments which moved under rates approved or prescribed by it.

[The Court recited the history of the proceedings before the ICC.]

The respondents objected that they should not be required to pay reparations on shipments which moved under rates approved or prescribed by the Commission as reasonable. To this that body replied, "We reserve the right, upon a more comprehensive record, to modify our previous findings, upon matters directly in issue before us as to which it clearly appears that our previous findings would not accord substantial justice under the laws which we administer. We have such a case here. For the first time the record before us is comprehensive in the evidence which it contains upon the reasonableness of the rates assailed. Upon this record we reach the conclusion that the rate prescribed in the first Phoenix case, during the period embraced in these complaints, was unreasonable and that a lower rate would have been reasonable during that period. If we are within our authority in finding that a lower rate would have been reasonable, then it must follow that shippers who paid the freight charges at the higher rate paid charges which were unreasonable, and are entitled to reparation. . . ."

The carriers having failed to pay the amount awarded, the petitioner sued therefor in the District Court, and recovered judgment. The Circuit Court of Appeals reversed. . . .

The exaction of unreasonable rates by a public carrier was forbidden by the common law. Interstate Commerce Comm. v. Baltimore & Ohio R. Co., 145 U.S. 263, 275. The public policy which underlay this rule could, however, be vindicated only in an action brought by him who paid the excessive charge, to recover damages thus sustained. Rates, fares, and charges were fixed by the carrier, which took its chances that in an action by the shipper these might be adjudged unreasonable and reparation be awarded.

But we are here specially concerned with the Interstate Commerce Act of 1887 and with some of the changes or supplements adopted since its original enactment. That Act did not take from the carriers their power to initiate rates — that is, the power in the first instance to fix rates, or to increase or to reduce them. . . . In order to render rates definite and certain and to prevent discrimination and other abuses, the statute required the filing and publishing of tariffs specifying the rates adopted by the carrier, and made these the *legal* rates, that is, those which must be charged to all shippers alike. Any deviation from the published rate was declared a criminal offense, and also a civil wrong giving rise to an action for damages by the injured shipper. Although the Act thus created a legal rate, it did not abrogate, but expressly affirmed, the common-law duty to charge no more than a reasonable rate, and left upon the carrier the burden of conforming its charges to that standard. In other words, the legal rate was not made by the statute a lawful rate — it was lawful only if it was reasonable. Under §6 the shipper was bound to pay the legal rate; but if he could show that it was unreasonable he might recover reparation.

The Act altered the common law by lodging in the Commission the power theretofore exercised by courts, of determining the reasonableness of a published rate. If the finding on this question was against the carrier, reparation was to be awarded the shipper, and only the enforcement of the award was relegated to the courts. In passing upon the issue of fact the function of the Commission was judicial in character; its action affected only the past, so far as any remedy of the shipper was concerned, and adjudged for the present merely that the rate was then unreasonable; no authority was granted to prescribed rates to be charged in the future. Indeed, after a finding that an existing rate was unreasonable, the carrier might put into effect a new and slightly different rate and compel the shipper to resort to a new proceeding to have this declared unreasonable. Since the carrier had complete liberty of action in making the rate, it necessarily followed that upon a finding of unreasonableness, an award of reparation should be measured by the excess paid, subject only to statutory limitations of time. . . .

The Hepburn Act and the Transportation Act [of 1920] evince an enlarged and different policy on the part of Congress. The first granted the Commission power to fix the maximum reasonable rate; the second extended its authority to the prescription of a named rate, or the maximum or minimum reasonable rate, or the maximum and minimum limits within which the carriers' published rate must come. When under this mandate the Commission declares a specific rate to be the reasonable and lawful rate for the future, it speaks as the legislature, and its pronouncement has the force of a statute. This Court has repeatedly so held with respect to the fixing of specific rates by state commissions; and in this respect there is no difference between authority delegated by state legislation and that conferred by Congressional action.

But it is suggested that the mere setting of limits by Commission order leaves the carrier free to name any rate within those limits, and, as at common law, it must at its peril publish a reasonable rate within the boundaries set by the order; that as it has the initiative it must take the burden, notwithstanding the Commission's order, of maintaining the rate at a reasonable level, and will be answerable in damages if it fails so to do. This argument overlooks the fact that in declaring a maximum rate the Commission is exercising a delegated power legislative in character; that it may act only within the scope of the delegation; that its authority is to fix a maximum or minimum *reasonable* rate; for it is precluded by the statute from fixing one which is unreasonable, which by the statute is declared unlawful. If it were avowedly to attempt to set an unreasonably high maximum its order would be a nullity.

The report and order of 1921 involved in the present case declared in terms that 96.5 cents was, and for the future would be, a reasonable rate. There can be no question that when the carriers, pursuant to that findings, published a rate of 96 cents, the legal rate thus established, to which they and the shipper were bound to conform, became by virtue of the Commission's order also a lawful — that is, a reasonable — rate.

Specific rates prescribed for the future take the place of the legal tariff rates theretofore in force by the voluntary action of the carriers, and themselves become the legal rates. As to such rates there is therefor no difference between the legal or published tariff rate and the lawful rate. The carrier cannot change a rate so prescribed and take its chances of an adjudication that the substituted rate will be found reasonable. It is bound to conform to the order of the Commission. If that body sets too low a rate, the carrier has no redress save a new hearing and the fixing of a more adequate rate for the future. It cannot have reparation from the shippers for a rate collected under the order upon the ground that it was unreasonably low. This is true because the Commission, in naming the rate, speaks in its quasi-legislative capacity. The prescription of a maximum rate, or maximum and minimum rates, is as legislative in quality as the fixing of a specified rate. . . .

As respects its future conduct the carrier is entitled to rely upon the declaration as to what will be a lawful, that is, a reasonable, rate; and if the order merely sets limits it is entitled to protection if it fixes a rate which falls within them. Where, as in this case, the Commission has made an order having a dual aspect, it may not in a subsequent proceeding, acting in its quasi-judicial capacity, ignore its own pronouncement promulgated in its quasi-legislative capacity and retroactively repeal its own enactment as to the reasonableness of the rate it has prescribed. . . .

It could repeal the order as it affected future action, and substitute a new rule of conduct as often as occasion might require, but this was obviously the limit of its power, as of that of the legislature itself.

The argument is pressed that this conclusion will work serious inconvenience in the administration of the Act; will require the Commission constantly to re-examine the fairness of rates prescribed, and will put an unbearable burden upon that body. If this is so, it results from the new policy declared by the Congress, which, in effect, vests in the Commission the power to legislate in specific cases as to the future conduct of the carrier. But it is also to be observed that so long as the Act continues in its present form, the great mass of rates will be carrier-made rates, as to which the Commission need take no action except of its own volition or upon complaint, and may in such case award reparation by reason of the charges made to shippers under the theretofore existing rate.

Where the Commission has, upon complaint and after hearing, declared what is the maximum reasonable rate to be charged by a carrier, it may not at a later time, and upon the same or additional evidence as to the fact situation existing when its previous order was promulgated, by declaring its own finding as to reasonableness erroneous, subject a carrier which conformed thereto to the payment of reparation measured by what the Commission now holds it should have decided in the earlier proceeding to be a reasonable rate.

The judgment is affirmed.

Mr. Justice HOLMES and Mr. Justice BRANDEIS think that the judgment should be reversed for the reasons stated by Judge Hutcheson in the concurring opinion in Eagle Cotton Oil Co. v. Southern Ry. Co., 51 F.2d 443, 445.

[In that opinion, Judge Hutcheson asserted that the ICC should not be precluded from awarding reparations under a rate it had previously approved or promulgated, and that this approach was consonant with the basic spirit of the Interstate Commerce Act, which allowed carriers considerable flexibility in adjusting rates, subject to limited intervention by the ICC. Judge Hutcheson contrasted the federal Act with many state systems of railroad rate regulation (some of which require all rates to be approved by the relevant regulatory commission), which preclude shipper reparations under commission-approved rates, leaving shippers the sole remedy of "a seasonable application for a change of rate before any damage had been suffered."]

Notes and Questions

1. In 1960 Shipper A brings a reparations proceeding before the ICC, charging that Railroad's $1/lb. rate for widgets from Cambridge to Tuxedo Park in 1958-1960 was unreasonably high; the Commission awards reparations on finding that a reasonable rate was $.80/lb.

(a) May Shipper A bring a second proceeding in 1962, seeking reparations for the 1958-1960 period on the basis that a reasonable rate was $.60? Is it relevant that a competitor (Shipper B) would be free to bring such a proceeding?

(b) May Shipper A bring a proceeding in 1962 seeking reparations for the 1960-1962 period on the basis that a reasonable rate was $.60?

Should the answer to (b) be any different if the Commission in a 1960 proceeding entered an order prescribing $.80/lb. as a maximum reasonable rate for the future?

2. *Arizona Grocery* is normally cited for the proposition that an agency must follow its own rules (until they are properly changed). Was that point disputed in the case? What was the argument between the majority and the dissenters about?

3. Why *should* agencies be required to follow their own regulations unless and until those regulations are changed or withdrawn? Why shouldn't the agency be free to depart from a regulation in individual cases in order to exercise the sort of flexibility that agencies enjoy in case-by-case adjudication?

4. (a) Which rule would be the wiser: a rule that makes an ICC-prescribed fare automatically a "reasonable" fare; or a rule that makes an ICC-prescribed fare determinative that no higher fare is "reasonable," but not determinative as to whether equal or lower fares are "reasonable" — in other words, a rule that keeps the railroads "at risk" when they set rates equal to or lower than the ICC rate?

(b) Assume that in 1920 the Santa Fe's carload rate for 100 pounds of sugar from San Francisco to St. Paul was $1.50 and the rate from San Francisco to Phoenix was $1.04. In 1921 Santa Fe reduces the St. Paul rate to $.95.

(1) Phoenix sugar buyers protest to the Commission. They point to §1 of the Interstate Commerce Act, which provides that "it shall be unlawful for any common carrier ... to charge [more] ... for a shorter than for a longer distance

over the same line or route in the same direction [except on special authorization by the Interstate Commerce Commission]." And they add that "If the rates to St. Paul are remunerative, then clearly rates to Phoenix are excessive." Santa Fe claims that the $.95 rate is necessary to allow San Francisco sugar to compete with New Orleans sugar brought up the Mississippi by barge. The cost per pound of sugar in New Orleans and in San Francisco is identical. Should the Commission raise the St. Paul fare? Should it lower the Phoenix fare?

(2) A clock manufacturer who ships from San Francisco to Phoenix complains to the Commission that the rates for comparable shipments of sugar, whether measured by weight or by volume, are ten times lower. What response, before the Commission, are the railroads likely to make?

Note: The Principle That Agencies Must Follow Their Own Regulations

There are numerous cases reaffirming the general proposition on which *Arizona Grocery* has been thought to stand: that "an administrative ruling until changed binds both the outside world and the agency." In fact, a public interest plaintiff obtained a ruling from a District of Columbia court that the firing of Archibald Cox in the famous "Saturday night massacre" was unlawful. The Department of Justice had promulgated regulations that restricted the government's power to fire Mr. Cox. Although the President, or the Attorney General, might have withdrawn or modified those regulations, neither had done so. Hence they were legally binding. See Nader v. Bork, 366 F. Supp. 104 (D.D.C. 1973). Gardner v. FCC, 530 F.2d 1086 (D.C. Cir. 1976), invalidated the Commission's failure to adhere to long-established procedures even though they had not been formalized in regulations.

However, exceptions to the general rule have sometimes been permitted where the regulations in question relate to internal agency procedures or where a rule is waived to afford more lenient treatment of a person.[91] What objections could there be to allowing an agency to waive a regulation in order to treat a particular individual more leniently?

Problem: The Federal Alcohol Administration (now the Alcohol and Tobacco Tax Division) was a division of the Treasury Department charged with statutory responsibility for insuring that the packaging and labeling of certain alcoholic beverages was adequately informative and not in any way deceptive or misleading. Pursuant to this authority, the division in 1935 promulgated a regulation defining "straight bourbon whiskey" and "straight corn whiskey" in identical terms. In 1938, the division amended the regulation to require a substantially higher percentage of corn grain in the fermented mash for "straight corn whiskey." In June 1936, certain whiskey was distilled by the Hiram Company under conditions which brought it within the then effective definition of straight corn whiskey and later

91. See Berger, Do Regulations Really Bind Regulators?, 62 Nw. U. L. Rev. 137 (1967); Sofaer, Judicial Control of Informal Discretionary Adjudication and Enforcement, 72 Colum. L. Rev. 1293 (1972); Note, Violation by Agencies of Their Own Regulations, 87 Harv. L. Rev. 629 (1974).

that year was sold to the Walker Company. In late 1937, Walker bottled the whiskey and affixed labels describing the contents as straight corn whiskey. In 1938, after the amended regulation was adopted, Walker proposed to ship the bottles in interstate commerce. The contents did not satisfy the amended definition of straight corn whiskey. The governing statute instructed division officers to prevent the release from bottling plants of distilled spirits that did not comply with the packaging and labeling regulations, and made it unlawful to introduce any such product into interstate commerce.

Should or must the division permit the shipment of the bottles?

E.   Estoppel and Res Judicata

1.   Estoppel

(a) In the first edition of his Administrative Law Treatise (1958) Professor Davis wrote:

> Although the courts have developed a doctrine of equitable estoppel, under which one who makes a representation to another who reasonably relies to his detriment is estopped to deny truth of the representation or to gain by taking a position inconsistent with the representation, the courts usually hold that the doctrine of equitable estoppel does not apply to the government. [Id. at 491.]

Indeed, in 1947 the District of Columbia wrote of the "well settled doctrine that res judicata and equitable estoppel do not ordinarily apply to decisions of administrative tribunals." Churchill Tabernacle v. FCC, 160 F.2d 244, 246 (D.C. Cir. 1947). Professor Davis traced the origin of this doctrine back to sovereign immunity and the notion that "the King cannot be estopped for it cannot be presumed the King would do wrong to any person." [92] He argued strongly that the doctrine was outmoded and was gradually being replaced by decisions that estopped government agencies.

In Federal Crop Ins. Corp. v. Merrill, 332 U.S. 380 (1947), the Supreme Court refused to estop the government under the following circumstances: (1) Plaintiffs applied for crop insurance, told the government's County Committee that their wheat was "reseeded," were told the wheat was insurable, and paid the premium. (2) Unbeknownst to plaintiffs *and* to the local government agents, an agency regulation prohibited insuring reseeded wheat. The Court held that the government did *not* have to pay when the crop failed.

Professor Davis contrasts *Merrill* with Moser v. United States, 341 U.S. 41 (1951). A statute provided that an alien who sought exemption from the draft could never become a U.S. citizen. Moser (a Swiss citizen living in the United States) wanted a draft exemption. He asked the Swiss legation if the exemption

92. Halsbury, Laws of England 248 (1956), quoting from Bacon's abridgements.

would bar him from becoming a U.S. citizen. The Swiss legation told him it would *not*. The legation presumably relied on misinformation from the State Department. Moser relied on this representation, asked for and received the exemption. He later applied for citizenship; a decision denying him citizenship was overturned by the Supreme Court, which held that he had not "knowingly and intentionally waived his rights."

Moser did not mention estoppel directly, and it involved citizenship, perhaps a special area.[93] But by the time of Professor Davis's 1970 Supplement, he could find many lower court cases holding the government estopped. The Court of Claims held a government contracting officer's delay in contesting an "adjustment" made by a private contractor "constituted a waiver" by the government to claims that the work could have been done in another manner, resulting in savings to the government. The Court wrote: "[W]hen the government is acting in its proprietary capacity, it may be estopped by an act of waiver in the same manner as a private contractor." Roberts v. United States, 357 F.2d 938, 945-946 (Ct. Cl. 1966). The courts had also held the Commissioner of Internal Revenue estopped in tax cases where denial of the estoppel would have been particularly unfair.[94]

By 1976, Professor Davis could write of the traditional "nonestoppel" doctrine: "The opposite ... now has almost uniform [case] ... support.... The doctrine of equitable estoppel does apply to the government." Administrative Law of the Seventies 399 (1976). Thus the courts estopped the government from claiming land that formed part of a national forest because it had (wrongly) told plaintiff the land was outside the forest and plaintiff had invested $350,000 in managing it. United States v. Georgia-Pacific Co., 421 F.2d 92 (9th Cir. 1970). And, the government was not allowed to recover soil bank money paid to plaintiffs (in violation of regulations) because a government officer had helped plaintiffs draw up their leaseholds so they would qualify. United States v. Lazy FC Ranch, 481 F.2d 985 (9th Cir. 1973). Still, there are cases refusing to estop the government. In Montilla v. United States, 457 F.2d 978 (Ct. Cl. 1972), Montilla retired from the Army, having been led to believe by a superior officer that he qualified for retirement pay. He did not, and despite his statement that he had been misled and would have remained in the Army to qualify, the Court of Claims held that *Merrill* controls.

(b) Assume that the government can be estopped. Are the factors that determine whether "estoppel" should apply the *same* when the government is a party as when only private parties are involved?[95] Consider the question in the context of the following:

Problem: A zoning ordinance of Los Angeles County permitted automobile wrecking yards in a certain locality, provided they were licensed by the County Licensing Office and had an eight-foot fence around them. In 1968 the ordinance was amended to prohibit auto wrecking yards in the area, but an "automatic

93. Remember Ng Fung Ho v. White, 259 U.S. 276 (1922), supra p. 55.
94. See, e.g., Schuster v. Commissioner, 312 F.2d 311 (9th Cir. 1962); Simmons v. United States, 308 F.2d 938 (5th Cir. 1962).
95. For discussion, see Newman, Should Official Advice be Reliable? Proposals as to Estoppel and Related Doctrines in Administrative Law, 53 Colum. L. Rev. 374 (1953).

exception" was granted for any then existing use "if such existing use is not in violation of this or any other ordinance or law." The Crunch Company had operated an auto wrecking yard in the area for several years without a fence or a license, but did obtain a license from the County License Office in 1968, after the amended ordinance was adopted. The license stated that it could not be transferred without approval of the License Office and expired, subject to renewal, in 1971.

In 1970, the Shredd Company proposed to buy the yard and wrote to the License Office to inquire about its status. No reply was received, and a Shredd representative went to the License Office to pursue the inquiry. A License Office employee checked the files and told the Shredd representative that Crunch had an "automatic exception" under the 1968 ordinance and that approval of a transfer and renewal of the license would be "just a formality." Shredd then purchased the business from Crunch, but the License Office refused to approve the transfer because (a) for several years Crunch had violated the law by operating without a license, and (b) the property was still in violation because of the absence of a fence. Thus the grandfather clause of the zoning ordinance was said to be inapplicable. Shredd offered to build the required fence, but to no avail. Shredd now brings an action in an state court against the License Commissioner to compel approval of the transfer. What result?

2. Res Judicata

Again, the interesting question is whether basic principles of res judicata apply in any different way when a suit is not between private parties but involves the government as well.

Consider the following basic principles as put by the American Law Institute, Restatement of Judgments:

§1. Personal Judgments

Where a reasonable opportunity has been afforded to the parties to litigate a claim before a court which has jurisdiction over the parties and the cause of action, and the court has finally decided the controversy, the interests of the State and of the parties require that the validity of the claim and any issue actually litigated in the action shall not be litigated again by them.

§68. Questions of Fact

(1) Where a question of fact essential to the judgment is actually litigated and determined by a valid and final judgment, the determination is conclusive between the parties in a subsequent action on a different cause of action, except as stated in §§ 69, 71 and 72.

(2) A judgment on one cause of action is not conclusive in a subsequent action on a different cause of action as to questions of fact not actually litigated and determined in the first action.

§70. Questions of Law

Where a question of law essential to the judgment is actually litigated and determined by a valid and final personal judgment, the determination is not conclusive between the parties in a subsequent action on a different cause of action, except where both causes of action arose out of the same subject matter or transaction; and in any event it is not conclusive if injustice would result.

Note how the courts have decided the following cases:

(a) A Maryland Board of County Commissioners, sitting as the Zoning Board, changed the zoning status of a 47-acre parcel of land in 1964 from "restricted to detached one family houses" to "suitable for garden apartments." The owners of the land had twice previously sought changes in the zoning and after having been turned down a second time by the Board in 1961 (on a proposal similar to this one) had unsuccessfully appealed to the courts.

Those protesting the latest decision appealed to the courts which overturned the Board's decision on grounds of res judicata. The facts had not changed sufficiently since the last application to warrant rezoning, reasoned the court; hence the Board's decision is arbitrary and capricious. The Board acts as an adjudicatory agency exercising power delegated from the legislature and therefore cannot act arbitrarily.

A dissent argued that res judicata did not apply because the rezoning action was "legislative" and not "judicial." It noted that even without res judicata, Maryland's "mistake/change" rule (which allowed piecemeal zoning changes only on strong evidence for an original mistake or substantial change in conditions) might apply, but either these were sufficient changes or the rule was too strict for such legislative decisionmaking. Woodlawn Area Citizens Assn. v. Board of County Commrs., 241 Md. 187, 216 A.2d 149 (1966).

(b) In 1929 the Federal Trade Commission found Raladam guilty of an unfair trade practice in misrepresenting the weight-reducing properties of his product "Mermola." The Supreme Court set aside the finding on the ground that the evidence did not show that Raladam's competitors were injured (a statutory prerequisite at that time). The FTC began the case again, introduced evidence of harm to competitors, found Raladam guilty, and rejected a claim of res judicata. The Supreme Court affirmed. FTC v. Raladam Co., 316 U.S. 149 (1942).

(c) An administrative hearing was held to determine whether to dismiss a policeman for accepting money from a gambler. At a first hearing the gambler would not testify and the Commissioner held the charges unproved. Then Gross decided to testify and a new hearing was held. The courts held that res judicata did not bar the new hearing. Evans v. Monaghan, 306 N.Y. 312, 118 N.E.2d 452 (1954).

(d) Plaintiff owned a chain of retail liquor stores. He also had a wholesaler's license and he sold considerable liquor at wholesale to his own retail stores. A statute said that a wholesale license should be revoked unless the wholesaler carried on a bona fide wholesale business and "sale by a wholesale licensee to himself as a retail licensee" is not bona fide.

In the 1950s the Licensing Board decided *not* to revoke plaintiff's license because plaintiff bought large quantities of liquor, had made substantial investment, and had relied on a prior administrative construction suggesting this was adequate to keep the license. The Board warned, however, that it might change its view if there were a future showing that the holding of the license presents "a situation which is contrary to the public welfare and morals and detrimental to the public interest."

In the early 1960s the Board revoked plaintiff's wholesale license because plaintiff sold only to himself. The courts rejected plaintiff's claim of res judicata. It reasoned that only collateral estoppel might apply and it did not because "factors, i.e., public interest and effect upon third parties, strongly indicate that the prior determination of the board should not preclude" reexamination of the statute and applying the correct interpretation to plaintiff. Louis Stores, Inc. v. Department of Alcoholic Beverage Controls, 57 Cal. 2d 740, 371 P.2d 758 (1962).

(e) The Patent Office rejected an application by plaintiff on the ground of "obviousness." The plaintiff applied again and submitted new evidence. The new evidence overcame the objection, but the Patent Office still denied on grounds of res judicata. The courts overturned the Patent Office decision, Application of Herr, 377 F.2d 610 (C.C.P.A. 1967).

Questions

1. Which of the above five cases do you believe were correctly decided? Why?

2. The Van Kirkland Underwriting Company agreed to underwrite a securities issued by the Edsel Vacuum Cleaner Company. The underwriting agreement between Van Kirkland and Edsel contained a clause releasing Van Kirkland from its obligations if at the time scheduled for issuance of the security any lawsuit was pending challenging the issue's legality. Such a lawsuit was filed, and Van Kirkland refused to proceed. Believing that Van Kirkland may have procured the suit to be instituted in order to avoid its obligations, the SEC began an investigation and asked certain attorneys for Van Kirkland to appear and testify. The attorneys refused, on the basis of the lawyer-client privilege, and the SEC brought an action in a federal district court to compel their appearance. After considering the SEC's investigative record, the court dismissed the complaint, holding that no prima facie showing of fraud had been made out that would justify overriding the attorney-client privilege. Several months later, the SEC instituted an administrative proceeding to consider whether Van Kirkland's broker-dealer registration should be suspended or revoked, and whether the company should be expelled or suspended from membership in the National Association of Securities Dealers, because of alleged fraud in connection with the Edsel matter. Van Kirkland, alleging that the SEC had no evidence not presented to the court in the prior action, sues in federal court to enjoin the Commission from reexamining the question of fraud. On the Commission's motion to dismiss for failure to state a claim, what result?

6

Hearing Requirements in Economic Regulation and Taxation

In this chapter we examine requirements that agencies exercising traditional functions of taxation and economic regulation follow formal procedures in adjudication or rulemaking. In Chapter 7, we examine the application of procedural requirements to the additional functions exercised by the modern welfare state — most notably the allocation of advantageous opportunities such as government employment; public education; and welfare, disability, and retirement benefits.[1]

These procedural requirements have five basic sources:[2]

1. The organic statute creating an agency or vesting it with additional powers often specifies applicable procedures.

2. The agency may have adopted procedural regulations, which it must follow in accordance with the *Arizona Grocery* principle.

3. The Administrative Procedure Act provides procedural requirements of general applicability.

4. The courts, as will be shown, have created "federal common law" imposing procedural requirements on agencies; these requirements, based neither on specific statutory provisions nor the Constitution, are designed to facilitate judicial review.[3]

5. Judicially defined constitutional requirements of due process may also be applicable.

In any particular case you should carefully consider the applicability of each of these sources of procedural law. You should also take care to examine the particular type of procedures that might be required. Beware of oversimplified labels like the term "hearing." A "verbal coat of many colors," the term "hearing" is used by courts and commentators to refer to a wide variety of procedural requirements,

---

1. In Chapter 7 we also examine the judicial extension of procedural safeguards to "enclaves," such as prisons, that traditionally had operated with great autonomy.

2. We refer here to requirements created under federal law. There are analogous state law requirements governing state agencies, which are also subject to the federal due process requirements of the Fourteenth Amendment and to any applicable federal statutes or regulations.

3. The requirement, developed in *Chenery* and subsequent cases, that agencies articulate a sustainable justification for their discretionary decisions, is an example.

ranging from the notice and comment procedures typically required in rulemaking by federal agencies, to "legislative" hearings where interested persons are invited to express views orally to a decisionmaker and respond to questions, to full trial-type procedures with oral presentation of evidentiary testimony, cross-examination by counsel, and decision on the basis of a formal record. The term "hearing" is often unavoidably convenient, but you should always identify the particular type of "hearing" in question.

Lastly, you should consider why insistence on procedural formalities has always played such an important role in American administrative law.[4] Does this suggest that procedural requirements could be viewed as a functional substitute for detailed legislative specification of policy choices? Consider other goals that procedural formalities might serve: promoting accuracy in agency fact-finding; securing agency conformance to statutory directives; enhancing the quality of agency policy judgments; permitting persons affected by decisions to have their say; facilitating judicial review. Are there other purposes that might be relevant?

A.   Traditional Due Process Requirements

1.   *The Requirement of a Trial-Type Hearing*

Londoner v. Denver

210 U.S. 373 (1908)

[Plaintiffs, owners of property in Denver, challenged the assessment of a tax against them to cover the costs of paving a public street upon which their property fronted. Relevant Colorado statutes provided that the Board of Public Works might, after notice and opportunity for hearing, order the paving of a street upon petition of a majority of the owners of property fronting thereon. However, before taking effect, this order had to be approved and implemented through adoption, by the Denver City Council, of an ordinance authorizing the paving. Following completion of the paving, the Board was directed to determine the total cost of the work and apportion it among the properties fronting on the street. This assessment was again required to be approved by the City Council by adoption of an implementing ordinance. The statutes provided that, before taking such action, the Council must provide notice and opportunity to file written objections. The statutes also provided that the determinations by the Council of the propriety of the improvement and assessment orders should be conclusive and binding on the Colorado courts.

---

4. In Britain far less emphasis has been placed on procedural formalities as a means of controlling agency action. See generally B. Schwartz & H. Wade, Legal Control of Government: Administrative Law in Britain and the United States (1972).

In the instant case, after the paving had been ordered by the Board, approved by the Council, and completed, and after the Board had recommended assessments but before action by the City Council, plaintiffs filed with the Council written objections to the proposed assessment, contending, among other matters, (1) that the authorization of the improvement was invalid because a petition by a majority of affected property owners had not been filed, and the Council had not afforded a hearing on that issue; (2) the paving had not been properly completed; (3) the apportionment of costs was improper and not in proportion to the benefits afforded by the paving to the respective property owners; (4) the hearing procedures afforded by the Council with respect to the assessment were inadequate. The City Council then approved the proposed assessment without affording any further opportunity for plaintiffs to be heard.

After the Colorado courts rejected their challenge to the Council's action, the Supreme Court entertained plaintiffs' claims that the Council's action violated the due process clause of the Fourteenth Amendment. The Court, in an opinion by Justice Moody, rejected all of the plaintiffs' challenges to the merits of the Council's actions and to its authority under Colorado law, and addressed the procedural validity of the Council's actions. The Court first considered whether the Council's action in authorizing the improvements without notice and opportunity for hearing violated due process:]

... We think it does not. The proceedings, from the beginning up to and including the passage of the ordinance authorizing the work did not include any assessment or necessitate any assessment, although they laid the foundation for an assessment, which might or might not subsequently be made. Clearly all this might validly be done without hearing to the landowners, provided a hearing upon the assessment itself is afforded.

[The Court next considered whether the Council's approval of the assessments without opportunity for an oral hearing was constitutional.]

In the assessment, apportionment and collection of taxes upon property within their jurisdiction the Constitution of the United States imposes few restrictions upon the States. In the enforcement of such restrictions as the Constitution does impose this court has regarded substance and not form. But where the legislature of a State, instead of fixing the tax itself, commits to some subordinate body the duty of determining whether, in what amount, and upon whom it shall be levied, and of making its assessment and apportionment, due process of law requires that at some stage of the proceedings before the tax becomes irrevocably fixed, the taxpayer shall have an opportunity to be heard, of which he must have notice, either personal, by publication, or by a law fixing the time and place of the hearing.... It must be remembered that the law of Colorado denies the landowner the right to object in the courts to the assessment, upon the ground that the objections are cognizable only by the [City Council].

If it is enough that, under such circumstances, an opportunity is given to submit in writing all objections to and complaints of the tax to the [Council], then there was a hearing afforded in the case at bar. But we think that something more than that, even in proceedings for taxation, is required by due process of law. Many requirements essential in strictly judicial proceedings may be dispensed with in proceedings of this nature. But even here a hearing in its very essence demands that he who is entitled to it shall have the right to support his allegations by argument however brief, and, if need be, by proof, however informal. . . .

It is apparent that such a hearing was denied to the plaintiffs in error. . . . The assessment was therefore void, and the plaintiffs in error were entitled to a decree discharging their lands from a lien on account of it. . . .

Judgment reversed.

The CHIEF JUSTICE and Mr. Justice HOLMES dissent.

Questions

1. Why does the Fourteenth Amendment require notice and opportunity for hearing when an administrative arm of the state assesses a tax? The Court implicitly concedes that no such requirement would apply if the state legislature had directly assessed the tax. Why should there be any federal constitutional limitations on the discretion of a state legislature to delegate certain of its responsibilities to administrative agencies unencumbered by procedural safeguards?

2. Why is oral presentation of evidence and argument before a state administrative decisionmaker required by the federal Constitution? Why was the opportunity to make written submissions that was afforded inadequate?

Bi-Metallic Investment Co. v. State Board of Equalization

239 U.S. 441 (1915)

Mr. Justice HOLMES delivered the opinion of the court.

This is a suit to enjoin the State Board of Equalization and the Colorado Tax Commission from putting in force, and the defendant Pitcher as assessor of Denver from obeying, an order of the boards increasing the valuation of all taxable property in Denver forty percent. The order was sustained and the suit directed to be dismissed by the Supreme Court of the State. . . . The plaintiff is the owner of real estate in Denver and brings the case here on the ground that it was given no opportunity to be heard and that therefore its property will be taken without due process of law, contrary to the Fourteenth Amendment of the Constitution of the United States. That is the only question with which we have to deal. There are suggestions on the one side that the construction of the state constitution and laws was an unwarranted surprise and on the other that the decision might have been placed, although it was not, on the ground that there was an adequate remedy at law. With these suggestions we have nothing to do. They are matters purely of state law. The answer to the former needs no amplification; that to the latter is that the allowance of equitable relief is a question of state policy and that as the Supreme Court of the State treated the merits as legitimately before it, we are not to speculate whether it might or might not have thrown out the suit upon the preliminary ground.

For the purposes of decision we assume that the constitutional question is presented in the baldest way — that neither the plaintiff nor the assessor of Denver, who presents a brief on the plaintiff's side, nor any representative of the city and county, was given an opportunity to be heard, other than such as they may have had by reason of the fact that the time of meeting of the boards is fixed by law. On this assumption it is obvious that injustice may be suffered if some property in the county already has been valued at its full worth. But if certain property has been valued at a rate different from that generally prevailing in the county the owner has had his opportunity to protest and appeal as usual in our system of taxation, Hagar v. Reclamation District, 111 U.S. 701, 709, 710, so that it must be assumed that the property owners in the county all stand alike. The question then is whether all individuals have a constitutional right to be heard before a matter can be decided in which all are equally concerned — here, for instance, before a superior board decides that the local taxing officers have adopted a system of undervaluation throughout a county, as notoriously often has been the case. . . .

Where a rule of conduct applies to more than a few people it is impracticable that every one should have a direct voice in its adoption. The Constitution does not require all public acts to be done in town meeting or an assembly of the whole. General statutes within the state power are passed that affect the person or property of individuals, sometimes to the point of ruin, without giving them a chance to be heard. Their rights are protected in the only way that they can be in a complex society, by their power, immediate or remote, over those who make the rule. If the result in this case had been reached as it might have been by the State's doubling the rate of taxation, no one would suggest that the Fourteenth Amendment was violated unless every person affected had been allowed an opportunity to raise his voice against it before the body entrusted by the state constitution with the power. In considering this case in this court we must assume that the proper state machinery has been used, and the question is whether, if the state constitution had declared that Denver had been undervalued as compared with the rest of the State and had decreed that for the current year the valuation should be forty percent higher, the objection now urged could prevail. It appears to us that to put the question is to answer it. There must be a limit to individual argument in such matters if government is to go on. In Londoner v. Denver, 210 U.S. 373, 385, a local board had to determine 'whether, in what amount, and upon whom' a tax for paving a street should be levied for special benefits. A relatively small number of persons was concerned, who were exceptionally affected, in each case upon individual grounds, and it was held that they had a right to a hearing. But that decision is far from reaching a general determination dealing only with the principle upon which all the assessments in a county had been laid.

Judgment affirmed.

Notes and Questions

1. Note the grounds upon which Justice Holmes seeks to distinguish Londoner v. Denver. Are they persuasive? Would the result have been different if a class ac-

tion procedure had been available to streamline the representation of large numbers of persons in agency proceedings?

2. Professor Davis has asserted that the key in determining whether a trial-type hearing is required is whether the controversy turns on "adjudicative facts" or "legislative facts." Professor Davis explains the distinction as follows:

> ...Adjudicative facts are the facts about the parties and their activities, businesses, and properties. Adjudicative facts usually answer the questions of who did what, where, when, how, why, with what motive or intent; adjudicative facts are roughly the kind of facts that go to a jury in a jury case. Legislative facts do not usually concern the immediate parties but are general facts which help the tribunal decide questions of law and policy and discretion.
>
> Facts pertaining to the parties and their businesses and activities, that is, adjudicative facts, are intrinsically the kind of facts that ordinarily ought not to be determined without giving the parties a chance to know and to meet any evidence that may be unfavorable to them, that is, without providing the parties an opportunity for trial. The reason is that the parties know more about the facts concerning themselves and their activities than anyone else is likely to know, and the parties are therefore in an especially good position to rebut or explain evidence that bears upon adjudicative facts. Yet people who are not necessarily parties, frequently the agencies and their staffs, may often be the masters of legislative facts. Because the parties may often have little or nothing to contribute to the development of legislative facts, the method of trial often is not required for the determination of disputed issues about legislative facts.[5]

Does Professor Davis's distinction explain the difference in result between *Londoner* and *Bi-Metallic*? Even if "legislative" facts are involved, why shouldn't the affected parties be entitled to a trial-type hearing to put in evidence concerning these facts? You should consider the utility and predictive value of Professor Davis's distinction throughout the materials that follow, including those dealing with statutory and judge-made common-law requirements as well as requirements of constitutional due process.

3. Note that in *Londoner*, statutes precluded review of the agency's decision in the state courts, whereas in *Bi-Metallic* a taxpayer could challenge the validity of any tax eventually imposed in the courts. Does this explain the difference in result?

Southern Ry. v. Virginia

290 U.S. 190 (1933)

Mr. Justice McREYNOLDS delivered the opinion of the Court.

This appeal questions the validity of Ch. 62, Acts General Assembly of Vir-

5. K. Davis, 1 Administrative Law Treatise §7.02 (1958).

ginia, 1930; Michie's Code 1930, §3974a. Pertinent portions are in the margin.[6] The claim is that enforcement of the Act as construed by the State Supreme Court, would deprive appellant of property without due process of law and thus violate the XIV Amendment.

Purporting to proceed under the challenged chapter, the Highway Commissioner, without prior notice, advised appellant that in his opinion public safety and convenience required elimination of the grade crossing near Antlers; also, he directed construction there of an overhead passage according to accompanying plans and specifications. Replying, the Company questioned the Commissioner's conclusion upon the facts, denied the validity of the Act, and refused to undertake the work.... The Commission ... directed the Railway to construct the overhead. The Supreme Court construed the statute and approved this action.

As authoritatively interpreted the challenged Act permits the Highway Commissioner — an executive officer — without notice or hearing to command a railway company to abolish any designated grade crossing and construct an overhead when, in his opinion, necessary for public safety and convenience. His opinion is final upon the fundamental question whether public convenience and necessity require the elimination, unless what the [Virginia] Supreme Court denominates "arbitrary" exercise of the granted power can be shown. Upon petition, filed within sixty days, the Corporation Commission may consider the proposed plans and approve or modify them, but nothing more. The statute makes no provision for review by any court. But the Supreme Court has declared that a court of equity may give relief under an original bill where "arbitrary" action can be established.

As construed and applied, we think the statute conflicts with the XIV Amendment.

Certainly, to require abolition of an established grade crossing and the outlay of money necessary to construct an overhead would take the railway's property in a very real sense. This seems plain enough both upon reason and authority....

If we assume that by proper legislation a State may impose upon railways the duty of eliminating grade crossings, when deemed necessary for public safety and convenience, the question here is whether the challenged statute meets the requirements of due process of law. Undoubtedly, it attempts to give an administrative officer power to make final determination in respect of facts — the character of a crossing and what is necessary for the public safety and convenience — without

6. Ch. 62, Acts General Assembly of Virginia 1930, p. 74. (Michie's Code §3974a).
"... Whenever the elimination of an existing crossing at grade of a State road by a railroad, or a railroad by a State road, and the substitution therefor of an overhead ... crossing becomes, in the opinion of the state highway commissioner, necessary for public safety and convenience, ... the state highway commissioner shall notify in writing the railroad company ... upon which the existing crossing at grade ... is, ... stating particularly the point at which ... the existing grade crossing is to be eliminated ... and that the public safety or convenience requires that the crossing be made ... above ... the tracks of said railroad, or that the existing grade crossing should be eliminated or abolished, and a crossing constructed above ... the tracks of said railroad, ... and shall submit to said railroad company plans and specifications of the proposed work.... It shall thereupon be the duty of the railroad company to provide all equipment and materials and construct the overhead ... crossing, ... in accordance with the plans and specifications submitted by the state highway commissioner...."

notice, without hearing, without evidence; and upon this *ex parte* finding, not subject to general review, to ordain that expenditures shall be made for erecting a new structure. The thing so authorized is no mere police regulation.

In Interstate Commerce Comm'n v. Louisville & N.R. Co., 227 U.S. 88, 91, replying to the claim that a Commission's order made without substantial supporting evidence was conclusive, this Court declared:

"A finding without evidence is arbitrary and baseless. And if the Government's contention is correct, it would mean that the Commission had a power possessed by no other officer, administrative body, or tribunal under our Government. It would mean that where rights depended upon facts, the Commission could disregard all rules of evidence, and capriciously make findings by administrative fiat. Such authority, however beneficently exercised in one case, could be injuriously exerted in another; is inconsistent with rational justice, and comes under the Constitution's condemnation of all arbitrary exercise of power. . . ."

The claim that the questioned statute was enacted under the police power of the State and, therefore, is not subject to the standards applicable to legislation under other powers, conflicts with the firmly established rule that every state power is limited by the inhibitions of the XIV Amendment. . . .

Counsel submit that the Legislature, without giving notice or opportunity to be heard, by direct order might have required elimination of the crossing. Consequently, they conclude the same end may be accomplished in any manner which it deems advisable, without violating the Federal Constitution. But if we assume that a state legislature may determine what public welfare demands and by direct command require a railway to act accordingly, it by no means follows that an administrative officer may be empowered, without notice or hearing, to act with finality upon his own opinion and ordain the taking of private property. There is an obvious difference between legislative determination and the finding of an administrative official not supported by evidence. In theory, at least, the legislature acts upon adequate knowledge after full consideration and through members who represent the entire public.

Chapter 62 undertakes to empower the Highway Commissioner to take railway property if and when he deems it necessary for public safety and convenience. It makes no provision for a hearing, and grants no opportunity for a review in any court. This, we think, amounts to the delegation of purely arbitrary and unconstitutional power unless the indefinite right of resort to a court of equity referred to by the court below affords adequate protection. . . .

This Court has often recognized the power of a State, acting through an executive officer or body, to order the removal of grade crossings; but in all these cases there was the right to a hearing and review by some court. . . .

After affirming appellant's obligation to comply with the Commissioner's order, the court below said: "The railroad is not without remedy. Should the power vested in the Highway Commissioner be arbitrarily exercised, equity's long arm will stay his hand." But, by sanctioning the order directing the Railway to proceed, it, in effect, approved action taken without hearing, without evidence, without opportunity to know the basis therefor. This was to rule that such action was not necessarily "arbitrary." There is nothing to indicate what that court would deem arbitrary action or how this could be established in the absence of evidence or hearing. In circumstances like those here disclosed no contestant could have fair opportunity for relief in a court of equity. There would be nothing to show the grounds upon which the Commissioner based his conclusion. He alone would be cognizant of the mental processes which begot his urgent opinion.

The infirmities of the enactment are not relieved by an indefinite right of review in respect of some action spoken of as arbitrary. Before its property can be taken under the edict of an administrative officer the appellant is entitled to a fair hearing upon the fundamental facts. This has not been accorded. The judgment below must be reversed. The cause will be remanded for further proceedings not inconsistent with this opinion.

Reversed.

The CHIEF JUSTICE, Mr. Justice STONE and Mr. Justice CARDOZO dissent upon the ground that there has been a lawful delegation to the State Highway Commissioner of the power to declare the need for the abatement of a nuisance through the elimination of grade crossings dangerous to life and limb; that this power may be exercised without notice or a hearing . . . provided adequate opportunity is afforded for review in the event that the power is perverted or abused; and that such opportunity has been given by the statutes of Virginia as construed by its highest court.

Notes and Questions

1. What if the Highway Commissioner had been given statutory authority to issue regulations to implement the Act, had promulgated a regulation requiring elimination of grade crossings at all locations at which an accident had occurred during the past year, and had then applied the regulation to require elimination of a particular grade crossing at which several accidents had occurred during the past year? Would a hearing be constitutionally required at any point?

2. As procedures for summary judgment illustrate, see F.R.C.P. 56, even in court adjudication a trial-type evidentiary hearing need not be held if the relevant facts are not in dispute. The same principle applies to administrative adjudication.[7] Would a trial-type hearing have been required if it were undisputed that several accidents had occurred at the crossing in question during the past year, and the Commissioner justified his action by asserting that the public convenience and necessity required elimination of a grade crossing at any site at which an accident

7. See Weinberger v. Hynson, Westcott & Dunning, Inc., 412 U.S. 609 (1973). However, as in court proceedings, opportunity for submission on issues of law must be afforded. The question is whether the submission must be oral or may be only written. In contrast to *Londoner*, the Supreme Court in FCC v. WJR, The Goodwill Station, 337 U.S. 265 (1949), held that oral argument before the FCC was not constitutionally required on a station's challenge to the grant of a license that would assertedly cause interference with its broadcasting. The Court held that the opportunity to submit written briefs was sufficient, stating that "the right to oral argument as a matter of procedural due process varies from case to case in accordance with differing circumstances."

had occurred during the previous year? Is the "legislative/adjudicative" fact distinction relevant?

3. Can *Bi-Metallic*, *Londoner*, and *Southern Ry.* all be reconciled under the principle that a hearing is required in adjudication but not in rulemaking?

4. What purposes does *Southern Ry.* assume might be served by a hearing? Should a hearing be constitutionally required in cases where the administrator's decision is purely a discretionary one? [8]

5. Justice Holmes in *Bi-Metallic* argues that an agency need not hold a hearing because the legislature would not be required to do so in taking similar action, while Justice McReynolds in *Southern Ry.* rejects the legislative analogy. Which position is the more persuasive? Are they inconsistent?

6. The majority in *Southern Ry.* seems to concede that a hearing before the agency might not be required if more extensive review of the merits of the Commissioner's decision were available in the state courts. In what ways might judicial review serve as a substitute for an agency hearing? Is it a completely adequate substitute? If the agency fails to hold a hearing and generates no record of the relevant evidence, how can the court review agency fact-finding? [9] Do the due process justifications for requiring a hearing suggest that *both* an agency hearing *and* judicial review of the merits is constitutionally required?

2. Summary Administrative Action: The Timing of a Hearing

North American Cold Storage Co. v. Chicago

211 U.S. 306 (1908)

[A Chicago ordinance prohibited cold storage houses from storing food unfit for human consumption, and authorized summary seizure and destruction by city health officers of unfit food so stored. Defendants, Chicago health officials, ordered complainant storage warehouse to deliver up for destruction assertedly putrid poultry. Upon refusal of the warehouse to comply, defendants threatened summary

8. See Jackson County Public Water Supply Dist. No. 1 v. State Highway Commn., 365 S.W.2d 553 (Mo. 1963), where the State Highway Commission directed certain highway improvements necessitating relocation of the Water District's mains and required the District to bear the costs of relocation despite the latter's claim that it could not afford to do so. The court found that the allocation of costs was a matter committed by statute to the Commission's discretion, and that therefore the District was not entitled to a trial-type hearing on the issue of relocation cost allocation under a state administrative procedure act providing for such a hearing where "legal rights, duties or privileges are at stake."

Cf. State v. Weinstein, 322 S.W.2d 778 (Mo. 1959), where a water company challenged the State Highway Commission's order directing relocation of its pipelines on the ground that relocation was not necessitated by the Commission's building plans. Asserting that the case turned on "adjudicative facts," the court held that a trial-type hearing was required pursuant to the state administrative procedure act. Is *Jackson County* therefore to be explained on the ground that only "legislative" facts were involved there, or is there another basis for distinction?

9. See Citizens to Preserve Overton Park, Inc. v. Volpe, supra p. 276.

destruction of stored goods deemed by them to be unfit and prohibited further deliveries to the warehouse. Complainants applied for an injunction prohibiting the stoppage of deliveries and the threatened destruction. The lower federal court dismissed for want of jurisdiction.]

Mr. Justice PECKHAM . . . delivered the opinion of the court. . . .

The general power of the State to legislate upon the subject embraced in the above ordinance of the city of Chicago, counsel does not deny. . . . Nor does he deny the right to seize and destroy unwholesome or putrid food, provided that notice and opportunity to be heard be given the owner or custodian of the property before it is destroyed. We are of opinion, however, that provision for a hearing before seizure and condemnation and destruction of food which is unwholesome and unfit for use, is not necessary. . . . The right to so seize and destroy is, of course, based upon the fact that the food is not fit to be eaten. Food that is in such a condition, if kept for sale or in danger of being sold, is in itself a nuisance, and a nuisance of the most dangerous kind, involving, as it does, the health, if not the lives, of persons who may eat it. A determination on the part of the seizing officers that food is in an unfit condition to be eaten is not a decision which concludes the owner. The ex parte finding of the health officers as to the fact is not in any way binding upon those who own or claim the right to sell the food. If a party cannot get his hearing in advance of the seizure and destruction he has the right to have it afterward, which right may be claimed upon the trial in an action brought for the destruction of his property, and in that action those who destroyed it can only successfully defend if the jury shall find the fact of unwholesomeness as claimed by them. . . .

Complainant, however, contends that there was no emergency requiring speedy action for the destruction of the poultry in order to protect the public health from danger resulting from consumption of such poultry. It is said that the food was in cold storage, and that it would continue in the same condition it then was for three months, if properly stored, and that, therefore, the defendants had ample time in which to give notice to complainant or the owner and have a hearing of the question as to the condition of the poultry, and as the ordinance provided for no hearing, it was void. But we think this is not required. The power of the legislature to enact laws in relation to the public health being conceded, as it must be, it is to a great extent within legislative discretion as to whether any hearing need be given before the destruction of unwholesome food which is unfit for human consumption. If a hearing were to be always necessary, even under the circumstances of this case, the question at once arises as to what is to be done with the food in the meantime. Is it to remain with the cold storage company, and if so under what security that it will not be removed? To be sure that it will not be removed during the time necessary for the hearing, which might frequently be indefinitely prolonged, some guard would probably have to be placed over the subject-matter of investigation. What is the emergency which would render a hearing unnecessary? We think when the question is one regarding the destruction of food which is not fit for human use the emergency must be one which would fairly appeal to the reasonable discretion of the legislature as to the necessity for a prior hearing, and in that case its decision would not be a subject for review by the courts. As the owner of the food or its custodian is amply protected against the party seizing the food, who must in a subsequent action against him show as a fact that it was within the statute, we think that due process of law is not denied the owner or custodian by the destruction of the food alleged to be unwholesome and unfit for human food without a preliminary hearing. . . .

Affirmed.

Mr. Justice BREWER dissents.

Questions

1. Why wouldn't impoundment of the food pending an administrative hearing on the issue of contamination adequately protect the government's interest here? More generally, how can a court evaluate the government's interest in summary action and weigh it against the hearing rights of persons threatened with summary action?

2. Note that the Court suggests that the availability of a subsequent tort action adequately protects the owner. Does it? What would the test of liability be? What are plaintiff's chances of collecting any judgment that it might win? [10]

Bowles v. Willingham

321 U.S. 503 (1944)

[The Emergency Price Control Act of 1942 authorized the Administrator of the Office of Price Administration (OPA) by regulations or order to "establish such maximum rent or maximum rents . . . as in his judgment will be generally fair and equitable and will effectuate the purposes of the Act." In 1942 the Administrator issued regulations governing rentals in designated areas of the country where defense activities threatened inflationary pressures on rents. The regulations froze all rents in effect on April 1, 1941. Rents for accommodations first rented after that date were frozen at the level of the initial rental charge, except that the OPA Rent Director might reduce such rents if he determined that they were in excess of those generally prevailing as of April 1, 1941. OPA rent regulations and orders were subject to judicial review in an Emergency Court of Appeals created by the Act, which provided that no "regulation, order, or price schedule shall be enjoined or set aside in whole or in part, unless the complainant establishes to the satisfaction of the court that the regulation, order, or price schedule is not in accordance with the law or is arbitrary and capricious."

The present case involved the application of OPA's defense rental regulations to Mrs. Willingham, who owned three apartments in Macon, Georgia, first rented in July and August 1941, for a total rental of $137.50 per month. Pursuant to the

---

10. In Chapter 9, we explore in greater detail the liability of officials in damages for commissions of torts or other violations of law and the reach of judge-made doctrines of official immunity from liability.

regulations, the Rent Director proposed to reduce the maximum rental to $90 on the grounds that the rents charged by her were in excess of those generally prevailing on April 1, 1941.

After rejecting the claim that the statute constituted an unconstitutional delegation of legislative power, the claim that it represented an unconstitutional "taking" of property and certain other issues, the Court, in an opinion of Mr. Justice DOUGLAS, considered the claim that the Act violated due process because it failed to provide for a hearing before rent control regulations and orders became effective.]

It is finally suggested that the Act violates the Fifth Amendment because it makes no provision for a hearing to landlords before the order or regulation fixing rents becomes effective. Obviously, Congress would have been under no necessity to give notice and provide a hearing before it acted, had it decided to fix rents on a national basis the same as it did for the District of Columbia. See 55 Stat. 788. We agree with the Emergency Court of Appeals (Avant v. Bowles, 139 F.2d 702) that Congress need not make that requirement when it delegates the task to an administrative agency. In Bi-Metallic Investment Co. v. State Board, 239 U.S. 441, . . . Mr. Justice Holmes, speaking for the Court, stated, p. 445: "Where a rule of conduct applies to more than a few people it is impracticable that every one should have a direct voice in its adoption. The Constitution does not require all public acts to be done in town meeting or an assembly of the whole. General statutes within the state power are passed that affect the person or property of individuals, sometimes to the point of ruin, without giving them a chance to be heard. Their rights are protected in the only way that they can be in a complex society, by their power, immediate or remote, over those who make the rule." We need not go so far in the present case. Here Congress has provided for judicial review of the Administrator's action. To be sure, that review comes after the order has been promulgated; and no provision for a stay is made. But . . . that review satisfies the requirements of due process. As stated by Mr. Justice Brandeis for a unanimous Court in Phillips v. Commissioner, 283 U.S. 589, 596-597: "Where only property rights are involved, mere postponement of the judicial inquiry is not a denial of due process, if the opportunity given for the ultimate judicial determination of the liability is adequate. . . . Delay in the judicial determination of property rights is not uncommon where it is essential that governmental needs be immediately satisfied." . . . Congress was dealing here with the exigencies of wartime conditions and the insistent demands of inflation control. . . .

Congress chose not to fix rents in specified areas or on a national scale by legislative fiat. It chose a method designed to meet the needs for rent control as they might arise and to accord some leeway for adjustment within the formula which it prescribed. At the same time, the procedure which Congress adopted was selected with the view of eliminating the necessity for "lengthy and costly trials with concomitant dissipation of the time and energies of all concerned in litigation rather than in the common war effort." S. Rep. No. 931, 77th Cong., 2d Sess., p. 7. To require hearings for thousands of landlords before any rent control order could be made effective might have defeated the program of price control. Or Congress might well have thought so. National security might not be able to afford the luxuries of litigation and the long delays which preliminary hearings traditionally have entailed."

[A concurring opinion by Justice RUTLEDGE and a dissenting opinion by Justice ROBERTS are omitted.]

Notes and Questions

1. Justice Douglas relies upon *Bi-Metallic* to argue that no hearings need be held before general OPA regulations become effective. But does *Bi-Metallic* support the denial of a hearing before entry of a particular rent order directed at a single person, such as the proposed order reducing Mrs. Willingham's rental to $90? [11]

2. Suppose a court later determined that the rent fixed by the OPA was unreasonably low. Could Mrs. Willingham, relying on the court's suggestion in *North American Cold Storage*, recover damages from OPA officials equal to the difference between the rent fixed and a reasonable rent? [12]

3. The federal taxing authorities have exercised the authority, without prior notice and hearing to the taxpayer, to demand instant payment by a taxpayer of deficiency assessments upon an administrative determination that collection is in immediate jeopardy (because the taxpayer may convey away his assets, go into hiding, etc.), and summarily seize and sell the taxpayer's property if payment is not made at once. This procedure was sustained against due process challenge in Phillips v. Commissioner of Internal Revenue, 283 U.S. 589 (1931) (relied upon in *Willingham*), on the grounds that the practice was long established and that the taxpayer could challenge the propriety of the assessment in subsequent judicial proceedings.[13]

11. Other issues in the *Willingham* decision are covered at p. 434, supra.

In 150 East 47th Street Corp. v. Creedon, 162 F.2d 206 (Emer. Ct. App. 1947), which dealt solely with an OPA rent reduction order for a single apartment, the court believed that "[*Willingham*] was focused on the legislative character of the basic rent regulation, affecting thousands of persons. A proceeding looking to an individual reduction order, in which the standards set forth in an adjustment provision of the regulation are applied to a particular set of facts relating to a single landlord, is quasi-judicial in character; and here it is obviously more appropriate to afford an opportunity for a hearing — not necessarily formal in character — before the reduction order becomes effective." [162 F.2d at 210.]

However, the court found that entry of an individual rent order without notice and hearing was constitutional where the statute and regulations provided that the order would be stayed if the landlord deposited the disputed portion of the rent in escrow pending judicial review of the order's validity. Would the entry of an individual rent order be constitutional in the absence of a stay provision?

12. Rate regulatory authorities such as the ICC, FPC, and CAB are given statutory authority to suspend proposed rate increases by regulated firms for specified periods of time (e.g., up to seven months in the case of the ICC) pending administrative determination of the reasonableness of the proposed increases. Judicial review of the suspensory power's exercise is either narrow or precluded altogether. For a review of the exercise of this power by federal agencies, together with a recommendation that agencies give more detailed explanation for their decisions on suspension, see Spritzer, Uses of the Summary Power to Suspend Rates: An Examination of Federal Regulatory Agency Practices, 120 U. Pa. L. Rev. 39 (1971).

13. Potential doubts about *Phillips'* continued validity may be reflected in Laing v. United States, 423 U.S. 161 (1976), a jeopardy assessment case in which a majority of the Court con-

4. There is precedent for summary administrative action in a wide variety of regulatory contexts. Some examples follow; for a general discussion, see Freedman, Summary Action by Administrative Agencies, 40 U. Chi. L. Rev. 1 (1972). Consider in each of these cases whether the availability of subsequent judicial review would provide an adequate remedy if the agency's action were unlawful:

Fahey v. Mallonee, 332 U.S. 245 (1947), sustained the action, taken without notice and hearing, of the Federal Home Loan Administration in appointing a conservator to assume control of a savings and loan association that was assertedly being managed in "unlawful, unauthorized, and unsafe manner." The Court stressed that summary measures of this sort were traditional in control of banking, "one of the longest regulated and most closely supervised of public callings."

Ewing v. Mytinger & Casselberry, 339 U.S. 594 (1950), dealt with the Food and Drug Administration's statutory authority to seize, without hearing, articles which the Administrator finds probable cause to believe to be "misbranded" and dangerous to health, fraudulent, or misleading to consumers. Following seizure, the articles must be brought before a federal court for condemnation, at which point the manufacturer or owner is entitled to a full hearing. In this case, the FDA had simultaneously and in different areas of the country made ten seizures (and threatened additional seizures) of a "Nutrilite Food Supplement" distributed by Mytinger & Casselberry; the FDA did not claim that the product was harmful to health, but asserted that its labeling was misleading and that the product was therefore "misbranded." Mytinger & Casselberry asserted that the seizures would destroy its business before opportunity for trial. A three-judge district court, finding that there was no emergency justifying immediate action to protect the public, held that before seizures could be instituted, Mytinger & Casselberry was entitled to an administrative hearing on whether there was probable cause to believe that the product was misbranded. The Supreme Court reversed, analogizing the FDA's seizure actions to the initiation of a criminal prosecution by a prosecutor or grand jury, which can also cause severe harm to reputation or business pending a judicial determination of the merits. The Court also held that Congress might extend the remedy of summary seizure traditional in the protection of public health to instances of misleading labeling. Justices Frankfurter and Jackson dissented, asserting that the District Court might review whether the FDA had abused its discretion by instituting multiple seizures.[14]

---

strued the Internal Revenue Code to require that sale of the seized property be delayed in order to permit opportunity for judicial review of the underlying assessment. Justice Brennan, concurring, expressed doubts about the constitutionality of traditional jeopardy assessment procedures. Three dissenters asserted the continued validity of *Phillips* and disagreed with the majority's statutory construction. See also Boyd v. United States, 439 F. Supp. 907 (E.D. Pa. 1977); Parrish v. Daly, 350 F. Supp. 735 (S.D. Ind. 1972).

14. In addition to denying Mytinger & Casselberry the right to a preseizure administrative hearing, the Court held that FDA's institution of seizures was not subject to judicial review. Is this still good law?

B.   The Procedural Requirements of the APA and the Interplay Between Rulemaking and Adjudication

1.   *Introductory Note on the Procedural Provisions of the APA*

While the APA's procedural requirements may (and often are) supplemented or overridden by specific provisions in particular statutes, they have, since 1946, provided the basic structure of procedures for federal administrative agencies.[15]

The APA's requirements are geared to the fundamental distinction between rulemaking and adjudication. You should at this point reread §551(4)-(9), and review the earlier note on the APA's definition of "rulemaking" and "adjudication," pp. 406-407 supra.

Notice and comment rulemaking. The basic procedure for rulemaking is the notice and comment procedure provided in §553. Its basic ingredients are:

(1) general notice of proposed rulemaking in the Federal Register, specifying the time and place of the rulemaking proceedings, the legal authority relied upon for their issuance, and the content or subject matter of the proposed rules;[16]

(2) opportunity for "interested persons" to comment upon the proposed rules by written submissions and, at the option of the agency, opportunity for oral argument;

(3) issuance, when rules are finally promulgated, of "a concise general statement of their basis and purpose."

(4) provision, in the case of "substantive" rules, that they shall not be effective in less than 30 days after promulgation.

In framing "notice and comment" procedures, the intent of the APA draftsmen was to emulate the model of legislative hearings. The purpose of the procedure is to enlighten the decisionmaker by exposure to the viewpoints of interested persons,[17] and to enable them to have a say. Following the analogy to legislative practice the courts adhered to the traditional notion that in making its final decision, an agency is not required to base its decision on the written comments submitted or

---

15. In the materials which follow in this chapter, you will wish to consider whether the categories provided in the APA defining various types of administrative action and applicable procedures are sound. Should these categories be redrawn, and, if so, how? Alternatively, is it desirable to attempt a general codification of procedural requirements that must apply to a very wide range of different agencies and activities? Should the definition of appropriate procedures be left to Congress on an agency-by-agency basis, or to the courts on a case-by-case basis? You should appreciate that a completely ad hoc approach to decisional procedures would be undesirable, but the appropriate balance between general codification and individual tailoring is an issue of continuing importance.

16. However, such notice may be dispensed with if those subject to the proposed rule are personally served or have actual notice.

17. In practice, any member of the public is permitted to submit written comments to an agency and thus qualifies as an "interested person," but when oral argument is afforded by an agency, it is normally limited to those few persons or organizations most directly affected by the proposed rule.

whatever materials might be included in the notice of proposed rulemaking. Rather, the agency was permitted to base its decision on "information available in its own files," and upon its general "knowledge and expertise." Notice and comment rulemaking was thus not "on the record." [18]

Section 553 contains many exceptions allowing agencies to avoid the basic notice and comment requirement.[19] Under §553(a), military and foreign affairs functions and rules relating to "agency management or personnel or to public property, loans, grants, benefits or contracts" are excluded altogether from the requirements of §553. The latter exception, which includes many highly important functions of modern government (such as management of public lands, the award of government contracts, and the administration of welfare, disability, educational and other grants and loans) has been sharply attacked, and its repeal has been urged by the Administrative Conference of the United States.[20]

Under §553(b)(A) and (B), the requirement of Federal Register notice (and the corresponding §553(c) requirement of opportunity for notice and comment) does not apply (except when notice or hearing is required by relevant statute) to "interpretive rules, general statements of policy, or rules of agency organization, procedure, or practice," or when the agency for good cause finds that notice and comment procedure is impracticable, unnecessary, or contrary to the public interest. Agency determinations of "good cause" are judicially reviewable for abuse of discretion.[21]

The exception for "interpretive or "procedural" rules and "general statements of policy" has proven far more troubling. The APA does not define the terms in question. The exception for "interpretive" rules implies a contrast to "legislative" rules, echoing the confused distinction between "interpretive" and "legislative" rules in determining the scope of judicial review of agency lawmaking. See p. 238 supra. The tendency of reviewing courts in recent years has been largely to disregard these various labels in favor of a functional approach that focuses on whether the

---

18. California Citizens Band Assn. v. United States, 375 F.2d 43, 54 (9th Cir.), *cert. denied*, 389 U.S. 844 (1967). In short, notice and comment rulemaking traditionally was not "on the record," since it does not generate an exclusive set of evidentiary materials upon which the decision is based, any more than the oral hearings of a congressional committee and the letters that it receives constitutes the exclusive basis for its recommendations. See Auerbach, Informal Rule Making: A Proposed Relationship Between Administrative Procedures and Judicial Review, 72 Nw. U.L. Rev. 15, 23-24 (1977).

19. However, rules that are excepted from the notice and comment procedures of §553 may nonetheless be subjected to requirements of Federal Register publication or public availability under §552. For example, §552(a)(1)(C), (D) requires agencies to publish in the Federal Register "rules of procedure" and "substantive rules of general applicability adopted as authorized by law, and statements of general policy or interpretations of general applicability formulated and adopted by the agency."

20. See Administrative Conference Recommendation No. 16, Administrative Conference 1969 Annual Report 45 (1970); Bonfield, Public Participation in Federal Rulemaking Relating to Public Property, Loans, Grants, Benefits, or Contracts, 118 U. Pa. L. Rev. 540 (1970). See also Sinaiko, Due Process Rights of Participation in Administrative Rulemaking, 63 Calif. L. Rev. 886 (1975), arguing that in some circumstances the Constitution may require notice and comment procedures.

21. E.g., Detroit Edison Co. v. EPA, 496 F.2d 244 (6th Cir. 1974); Akron, C. & Y. R.R. v. United States, 370 F. Supp. 1231 (D. Md. 1974).

rules in question are sufficiently important and controversial to merit the safeguards of notice and comment procedures.[22]

The requirement of a thirty-day waiting period before "substantive" rules become effective, which was designed to permit an opportunity for those affected to urge reconsideration, does not apply to rules granting or recognizing exemptions or relieving restrictions, "interpretive" rules and "statements of policy," or where the agency otherwise provides for good cause found and published with the rule.

On the record rulemaking. In cases where a relevant statute provides that "rules . . . be made on the record after opportunity for an agency hearing," §553(c) requires that an agency engaged in rulemaking utilize the more formal procedures of §§ 556 and 557 in lieu of opportunity for written comment. These more formal procedures — called "formal" or "on the record" rulemaking — in contradistinction to "informal" or "notice and comment" rulemaking — normally include the taking of evidence by an administrative law judge or other hearing officer through adversary trial-type proceedings, an initial or recommended decision by that officer based on the evidence presented, followed by opportunity for an appeal procedure before the agency heads on the basis of the record compiled by the hearing officer. However, §556(a) provides that in such rulemaking "an agency may, when a party will not be prejudiced thereby, adopt procedures for the submission of all or part of the evidence in written form." [23]

An essential difference between notice and comment rulemaking and "on the record" rulemaking, as traditionally understood, is that only the latter generates an exclusive evidentiary record upon which the agency's decision can be reviewed by a court. Accordingly, §706(2)(E) provides for court review of the substantiality of the evidence supporting agency findings only in proceedings subject to §§ 556 and 557 (or where a particular statute requires on the record procedures). The APA "substantial evidence" test does *not* apply to notice and comment rulemaking, and this omission is supported by powerful considerations of logic. As made clear in *Universal Camera*, the substantial evidence test requires the court to assess agency fact-findings *on the basis of the record as a whole*, including all of the evidence before the agency that might tend to support or undermine its conclusions. But in traditional notice and comment procedures, there is no "record" encapsulating all of the relevant evidence. Since agencies have traditionally been free to base their decisions on whatever knowledge or material they deem relevant, without presenting the same as evidence or disclosing it to those submitting comments, it is difficult to

---

22. See, e.g., Rodway v. Department of Agriculture, 514 F.2d 809 (D.C. Cir. 1975); National Motor Freight Traffic Assn. v. United States, 268 F. Supp. 90 (D.D.C. 1967). But see Energy Reserves Group, Inc. v. Department of Energy, 447 F. Supp. 1135, 47 U.S.L.W. 2319 (Temp. Emerg. Ct. App. 1978); Eastern Kentucky Welfare Rights Org. v. Simon, 506 F.2d 1278 (D.C. Cir. 1974), *aff'd on other grounds*, 426 U.S. 26 (1976). For discussion, see Warren, Notice Requirements in Administrative Rulemaking: An Analysis of Legislative and Interpretive Rules, 29 Ad. L. Rev. 367 (1977); Note, A Functional Approach to the Applicability of Section 553 of the Administrative Procedure Act to Agency Statements of Policy, 43 U. Chi. L. Rev. 430 (1976); K. Davis, Administrative Law of the Seventies §§ 6.01-7 to 6.01-10 (1976).

23. Section 557 also permits an agency in rulemaking to dispense with an initial or recommended decision by the hearing officer, but it is normal agency practice to require such a decision.

understand how a substantial evidence standard of review could be applied by a reviewing court to informal rulemaking.

On the record adjudication. As in rulemaking, the procedural requirements of the APA in adjudication vary sharply depending on whether or not the specific statute conferring substantive authority on the agency requires it to be exercised "on the record after opportunity for agency hearing." If the relevant statute requires an "on the record" decision after opportunity for hearing, the requirements of §554 apply (with stated exceptions listed in §554(a)). Section 554(c)(2) in turn invokes the requirements of §§ 556 and 557. "On the record" or "formal" adjudication is accordingly subject to the trial-type procedures provided in §§ 554, 556, and 557. The procedures governing "on the record" adjudication are normally more rigorous than those governing "on the record" rulemaking. For example, §554(d), which applies to most instances of formal adjudication but not to formal rulemaking, requires separation within the agency of prosecuting and investigative functions from decisionmaking functions. Section 556(d) permits use of documentary presentation of evidence (when parties will not be prejudiced thereby) in formal rulemaking but not in formal adjudication (except where the agency is determining claims for money or benefits or applications for initial licenses). You should at this point review carefully the provisions of §§ 554, 556, and 557.

Informal adjudication. In instances where the relevant statute does not require that adjudicatory decisions be made "on the record after opportunity for agency hearing," the APA as such provides no procedures that must be followed. The lack of APA procedures for "informal adjudication" is quite significant when one recalls that §551(6), (7) defines "adjudication" broadly to include "the whole or a part of a final disposition . . . of an agency in a matter other than rulemaking but including licensing." Because "adjudication" is a residual category that encompasses all agency dispositions other than rulemaking, it includes such matters as decisions on grants, contract awards, and other actions that might not intuitively be thought of as "adjudication." For example, the approval of a federally funded highway location in *Overton Park*, p. 276 supra, was an instance of adjudication. As *Overton Park* illustrates, the absence of formal procedures in informal adjudication poses difficulties for courts attempting to review the merits of the underlying decision.

2. The Extent of "On the Record" Rulemaking Requirements

United States v. Florida East Coast Ry. Co.

410 U.S. 224 (1973)

Mr. Justice REHNQUIST delivered the opinion of the Court.

Appellees, two railroad companies, brought this action in the District Court for the Middle District of Florida to set aside the incentive per diem rates established by appellant Interstate Commerce Commission in a rulemaking proceeding. . . . They challenged the order of the Commission on both substantive and procedural grounds. The District Court sustained appellees' position that the Commission had failed to comply with the applicable provisions of the Administrative Procedure Act, 5 U.S.C. §551 et seq., and therefore set aside the order without dealing with the railroads' other contentions. The District Court held that the language of §1(14)(a) [24] of the Interstate Commerce Act, 24 Stat. 379, as amended, 49 U.S.C. §1(14)(a), required the Commission in a proceeding such as this to act in accordance with the Administrative Procedure Act, 5 U.S.C. §556(d) ["formal rulemaking"], and that the Commission's determination to receive submissions from the appellees only in written form was a violation of that section because the appellees were "prejudiced" by that determination within the meaning of that section.

Following our decision last Term in United States v. Allegheny-Ludlum Steel Corp., 406 U.S. 742 (1972), we noted probable jurisdiction. . . . We here decide that the Commission's proceeding was governed only by §553 of that Act, and that appellees received the "hearing" required by §1(14)(a) of the Interstate Commerce Act. We, therefore, reverse the judgment of the District Court. . . .

I. BACKGROUND OF CHRONIC FREIGHT CAR SHORTAGES

This case arises from the factual background of a chronic freight-car shortage on the Nation's railroads. . . . Judge Friendly, writing for a three-judge District Court in the Eastern District of New York in the related case of Long Island R. Co. v. United States, 318 F. Supp. 490, 491 (E.D.N.Y. 1970), described the Commission's order as "the latest chapter in a long history of freight-car shortages in certain regions and seasons and of attempts to ease them." Congressional concern for the problem was manifested in the enactment in 1966 of an amendment to §1(14)(a) of the Interstate Commerce Act, enlarging the Commission's authority to prescribe per diem charges for the use by one railroad of freight cars owned by another. . . .

In December 1967, the Commission initiated the rulemaking procedure giving

24. Section 1(14)(a) provides:
"The Commission may, after hearing, on a complaint or upon its own initiative without complaint, establish reasonable rules, regulations, and practices with respect to car service by common carriers by railroad subject to this chapter, including the compensation to be paid and other terms of any contract, agreement, or arrangement for the use of any locomotive, car, or other vehicle not owned by the carrier using it (and whether or not owned by another carrier), and the penalties or other sanctions for nonobservance of such rules, regulations, or practices. In fixing such compensation to be paid for the use of any type of freight car, the Commission shall give consideration to the national level of ownership of such type of freight car and to other factors affecting the adequacy of the national freight car supply, and shall, on the basis of such consideration, determine whether compensation should be computed solely on the basis of elements of ownership expense involved in owning and maintaining such type of freight car, including a fair return in value, or whether such compensation should be increased by such incentive element or elements of compensation as in the Commission's judgment will provide just and reasonable compensation to freight car owners, contribute to sound car service practices (including efficient utilization and distribution of cars), and encourage the acquisition and maintenance of a car supply adequate to meet the needs of commerce and the national defense. The Commission shall not make any incentive element applicable to any type of freight car the supply of which the Commission finds to be adequate and may exempt from the compensation to be paid by any group of carriers such incentive element or elements if the Commission finds it to be in the national interest."

rise to the order that appellees here challenge. It directed Class I and Class II line-haul railroads to compile and report detailed information with respect to freight-car demand and supply at numerous sample stations for selected days of the week during 12 four-week periods, beginning January 29, 1968. . . .

[The Commission instituted rulemaking proceedings with the expectation that a formal §556 evidentiary hearing would be required. However, a Senate subcommittee held oversight hearings in which the ICC's delay in implementing the 1966 Amendments was sharply criticized.]

Judge Friendly, describing the same event in Long Island R. Co. v. United States, supra, said: "'To say that the presentation was not received with enthusiasm would be a considerable understatement. Senators voiced displeasure at the Commission's long delay at taking action under the 1966 amendment, engaged in some merriment over what was regarded as an unintelligible discussion of methodology . . . and expressed doubt about the need for a hearing. . . . But the Commission's general counsel insisted that a hearing was needed . . . and the Chairman of the Commission agreed. . . ." 318 F. Supp., at 494.

The Commission, now apparently imbued with a new sense of mission, issued in December 1969 an interim report. . . . The Commission concluded, however, that in view of the 1966 amendment it could impose additional "incentive" per diem charges [above the level needed to provide boxcar owners with an adequate return on investment] to spur prompt return of existing cars and to make acquisition of new cars financially attractive to the railroads. It did so by means of a proposed schedule that established such charges on an across-the-board basis for all common carriers by railroads subject to the Interstate Commerce Act. Embodied in the report was a proposed rule adopting the Commission's tentative conclusions and a notice to the railroads to file statements of position within 60 days. . . .

Both appellee railroads filed statements objecting to the Commission's proposal and requesting an oral hearing, as did numerous other railroads. In April 1970, the Commission, without having held further "hearings," issued a supplemental report making some modifications in the tentative conclusions earlier reached, but over-ruling in toto the requests of appellees.

The District Court held that in so doing the Commission violated §556(d) of the Administrative Procedure Act, and it was on this basis that it set aside the order of the Commission.

II. APPLICABILITY OF ADMINISTRATIVE PROCEDURE ACT

In United States v. Allegheny-Ludlum Steel Corp., supra, we held that the language of §1(14)(a) of the Interstate Commerce Act authorizing the Commission to act "after hearing" was not the equivalent of a requirement that a rule be made "on the record after opportunity for an agency hearing" as the latter term is used in §553(c) of the Administrative Procedure Act. Since the 1966 amendment to §1(14)(a), under which the Commission was here proceeding, does not by its terms add to the hearing requirement contained in the earlier language, the same result should obtain here unless that amendment contains language that is tantamount to such a requirement. Appellees contend that such language is found in the provisions of that Act requiring that: "[T]he Commission shall give consideration to the national level of ownership of such type of freight car and to other factors affecting the adequacy of the national freight car supply, and shall, on the basis of such consideration, determine whether compensation should be computed. . . ." While this language is undoubtedly a mandate to the Commission to consider the factors there set forth in reaching any conclusions as to imposition of per diem incentive charges, it adds to the hearing requirements of the section neither expressly nor by implication. We know of no reason to think that an administrative agency in reaching a decision cannot accord consideration to factors such as those set forth in the 1966 amendment by means other than a trial-type hearing or the presentation of oral argument by the affected parties.

Both of the district courts that reviewed this order of the Commission concluded that its proceedings were governed by the stricter requirements of §§ 556 and 557 of the Administrative Procedure Act, rather than by the provisions of §553 alone. The conclusion of the District Court for the Middle District of Florida, which we here review, was based on the assumption that the language in §1(14)(a) of the Interstate Commerce Act requiring rulemaking under that section to be done "after hearing" was the equivalent of a statutory requirement that the rule "be made on the record after opportunity for an agency hearing." Such an assumption is inconsistent with our decision in *Allegheny-Ludlum,* supra.

The District Court for the Eastern District of New York reached the same conclusion by a somewhat different line of reasoning. That court felt that because §1(14)(a) of the Interstate Commerce Act had required a "hearing," and because that section was originally enacted in 1917, Congress was probably thinking in terms of a "hearing" such as that described in the opinion of this Court in the roughly contemporaneous case of ICC v. Louisville & Nashville R. Co., 227 U.S. 88, 93 (1913). The ingredients of the "hearing" were there said to be that "[a]ll parties must be fully apprised of the evidence submitted or to be considered, and must be given opportunity to cross-examine witnesses, to inspect documents and to offer evidence in explanation or rebuttal." Combining this view of congressional understanding of the term "hearing" with comments by the Chairman of the Commission at the time of the adoption of the 1966 legislation regarding the necessity for "hearings," that court concluded that Congress had, in effect, required that these proceedings be "on the record after opportunity for an agency hearing" within the meaning of §553(c) of the Administrative Procedure Act.[25]

Insofar as this conclusion is grounded on the belief that the language "after hearing" of §1(14)(a), without more, would trigger the applicability of §§ 556 and

---

25. Ed. note: However, the District Court for the Eastern District of New York, in Long Island R. Co. v. United States, 318 F. Supp. 490 (E.D.N.Y. 1970), concluded that the Commission's failure to afford an opportunity for oral testimony, cross-examination, or oral argument was not a violation of the APA's "on the record" rulemaking requirements because §556(a) permits the use "when a party will not be prejudiced thereby [of] procedures for the submission of all or part of the evidence in written form," and the court found no prejudice from the use of documentary procedures in the proceeding.

557, it, too, is contrary to our decision in *Allegheny-Ludlum*, supra. The District Court observed that it was "rather hard to believe that the last sentence of §553(c) was directed only to the few legislative sports where the words 'on the record' or their equivalent had found their way into the statute book." 318 F. Supp., at 496. This is, however, the language which Congress used, and since there are statutes on the books that do use these very words, see, e.g., the Fulbright Amendment to the Walsh-Healey Act, 41 U.S.C. §43a, and 21 U.S.C. §371(e)(3), the regulations provision of the Food and Drug Act, adherence to that language cannot be said to render the provision nugatory or ineffectual. We recognized in *Allegheny-Ludlum* that the actual words "on the record" and "after . . . hearing" used in §553 were not words of art, and that other statutory language having the same meaning could trigger the provisions of §§ 556 and 557 in rulemaking proceedings. But we adhere to our conclusion, expressed in that case, that the phrase "after hearing" in §1(14)(a) of the Interstate Commerce Act does not have such an effect.

III. "HEARING" REQUIREMENT OF §1(14)(a) OF THE INTERSTATE COMMERCE ACT

Inextricably intertwined with the hearing requirement of the Administrative Procedure Act in this case is the meaning to be given to the language "after hearing" in §1(14)(a) of the Interstate Commerce Act. . . .

[The Court indicated that even if the language of §1(14)(a) did not trigger the formal rulemaking requirements of §§ 556 and 557 of the APA, it might by its own force require greater procedural formalities than the ICC provided.]

The term "hearing" in its legal context undoubtedly has a host of meanings. Its meaning undoubtedly will vary, depending on whether it is used in the context of a rulemaking-type proceeding or in the context of a proceeding devoted to the adjudication of particular disputed facts. It is by no means apparent what the drafters of the Esch Car Service Act of 1917, 40 Stat. 101, which became the first part of §1(14)(a) of the Interstate Commerce Act, meant by the term.

[The Court discounted statements made at the time of the 1966 amendments to §1(14)(a) that the Commission could only exercise its authority after a "hearing," because the speakers did not specify that the contemplated "hearing" must include oral testimony, cross-examination, and oral argument. The Court also referred to the documentary procedures authorized in APA §556(d) as an indication that the term "hearing" need not include these ingredients.]

. . . Although appellees have asserted no claim of constitutional deprivation in this proceeding, some of the cases they rely upon expressly speak in constitutional terms, while others are less than clear as to whether they depend upon the Due Process Clause of the Fifth and Fourteenth Amendments to the Constitution, or upon generalized principles of administrative law formulated prior to the adoption of the Administrative Procedure Act.

[The Court then sought to distinguish ICC v. Louisville & Nashville R. Co., 227 U.S. 88 (1913):]

. . . The type of proceeding there, in which the Commission adjudicated a complaint by a shipper that specified rates set by a carrier were unreasonable, was sufficiently different from the nationwide incentive payments ordered to be made by all railroads in this proceeding so as to make the *Louisville & Nashville* opinion inapplicable in the case presently before us.

The basic distinction between rulemaking and adjudication is illustrated by this Court's treatment of two related cases under the Due Process Clause of the Fourteenth Amendment. In Londoner v. Denver, cited in oral argument by appellees, 210 U.S. 373 (1908), the Court held that due process had not been accorded a landowner who objected to the amount assessed against his land as its share of the benefit resulting from the paving of a street. Local procedure had accorded him the right to file a written complaint and objection, but not to be heard orally. This Court held that due process of law required that he "have the right to support his allegations by argument however brief, and, if need be, by proof, however informal." Id., at 386. But in the later case of Bi-Metallic Investment Co. v. State Board of Equalization, 239 U.S. 441 (1915), the Court held that no hearing at all was constitutionally required prior to a decision by state tax officers in Colorado to increase the valuation of all taxable property in Denver by a substantial percentage. The Court distinguished *Londoner* by stating that there a small number of persons "were exceptionally affected, in each case upon individual grounds." Id., at 446.

Here, the incentive payments proposed by the Commission in its tentative order, and later adopted in its final order, were applicable across the board to all of the common carriers by railroad subject to the Interstate Commerce Act. No effort was made to single out any particular railroad for special consideration based on its own peculiar circumstances. Indeed, one of the objections of appellee Florida East Coast was that it and other terminating carriers should have been treated differently from the generality of the railroads. But the fact that the order may in its effects have been thought more disadvantageous by some railroads than by others does not change its generalized nature. Though the Commission obviously relied on factual inferences as a basis for its order, the sources of these factual inferences was apparent to anyone who read the order of December 1969. The factual inferences were used in the formulation of a basically legislative-type judgment, for prospective application only, rather than in adjudicating a particular set of disputed facts.

The Commission's procedure satisfied both the provisions of §1(14)(a) of the Interstate Commerce Act and of the Administrative Procedure Act, and were not inconsistent with prior decisions of this Court. We, therefore, reverse the judgment of the District Court, and remand the case so that it may consider those contentions of the parties that are not disposed of by this opinion.

It is so ordered.

Mr. Justice Powell took no part in the consideration or decision of this case.

Mr. Justice Douglas, with whom Mr. Justice Stewart concurs, dissenting.

The present decision makes a sharp break with traditional concepts of procedural due process. The Commission order under attack is tantamount to a rate order. Charges are fixed that nonowning railroads must pay owning railroads for boxcars of the latter that are on the tracks of the former. This is the imposition on carriers by administrative fiat of a new financial liability. I do not believe it is within our traditional concepts of due process to allow an administrative agency to saddle anyone with a new rate, charge, or fee without a full hearing that includes the right to present oral testimony, cross-examine witnesses, and present oral argument. That is required by the Administrative Procedure Act, 5 U.S.C. §556(d); §556(a) states that §556 applies to hearings required by §553. Section 553(c) provides that §556 applies "[w]hen rules are required by statute to be made on the record after opportunity for an agency hearing." A hearing under §1(14)(a) of the Interstate Commerce Act fixing rates, charges, or fees is certainly adjudicatory, not legislative in the customary sense.

The question is whether the Interstate Commerce Commission procedures used in this rate case "for the submission of . . . evidence in written form" avoided prejudice to the appellees so as to comport with the requirements of the Administrative Procedure Act.[26]

. . . [Appellee] Seaboard argued that it had been damaged by what it alleged to be the Commission's sudden change in emphasis from specialty to unequipped boxcars and that it would lose some $1.8 million as the result of the Commission's allegedly hasty and experimental action. Florida East Coast raised significant challenges to the statistical validity of the Commission's data[27] and also contended that its status as a terminating railroad left it with a surfeit of standard boxcars which should exempt it from the requirements to pay incentive charges. . . .

. . . I believe that "prejudice" was shown when it was claimed that the very basis on which the Commission rested its finding was vulnerable because it lacked statistical validity or other reasoned basis. At least in that narrow group of cases, prejudice for lack of a proper hearing has been shown.

Both Long Island R. Co. v. United States, 318 F. Supp. 490 (E.D.N.Y. 1970), and the present case involve challenges to the Commission's procedures establishing incentive per diem rates. In *Long Island*, however, the railroad pointed to no specific challenges to the Commission's findings. . . .

The more exacting hearing provisions of the Administrative Procedure Act, 5 U.S.C. §§ 556-557, are only applicable, of course, if the "rules are required by statute to be made on the record after opportunity for an agency hearing." Id., §553(c).

United States v. Allegheny-Ludlum Steel Corp., 406 U.S. 742, was concerned strictly with a rulemaking proceeding of the Commission for the promulgation of "car service rules" that in general required freight cars, after being unloaded, to be returned "in the direction of the lines of the road owning the cars." Id., at 743.

26. 5 U.S.C. §556(d) provides that a "sanction may not be imposed" without a full hearing, including cross-examination. But §556(d) makes an exception which I submit is not relevant here. It provides: "In rule making . . . an agency may, *when a party will not be prejudiced thereby*, adopt procedures for the submission of all or part of the evidence in written form." (Emphasis added.)

27. Florida East Coast argues, for example, that the Commission's finding of a boxcar shortage may be attributable to a variety of sampling or definitional errors, asserting that it is unrealistic to define boxcar deficiencies in such a manner as "to show as a 'deficiency' the failure to supply a car on the day requested by the shipper no matter when the request was received." The Government's contention that a 24-hour standard was not used seems unresponsive to this argument. See 337 I.C.C. 217, 221.

We sustained the Commission's power with respect to these two rules on the narrow ground that they were wholly legislative. We held that §1(14)(a) of the Interstate Commerce Act, requiring by its terms a "hearing," "does not require that such rules 'be made on the record' " within the meaning of §553(c). Id., at 757. We recognized, however, that the precise words "on the record" are not talismanic, but that the crucial question is whether the proceedings under review are "an exercise of legislative rulemaking" or "adjudicatory hearings." Ibid. The "hearing" requirement of §1(14)(a) cannot be given a fixed and immutable meaning to be applied in each and every case without regard to the nature of the proceedings.

The rules in question here established "incentive" per diem charges to spur the prompt return of existing cars and to make the acquisition of new cars financially attractive to the railroads. Unlike those we considered in *Allegheny-Ludlum*, these rules involve the creation of a new financial liability. Although quasi-legislative, they are also adjudicatory in the sense that they determine the measure of the financial responsibility of one road for its use of the rolling stock of another road.

The majority finds ICC v. Louisville & Nashville R. Co., 227 U.S. 88, "sufficiently different" as to make the opinion in that case inapplicable to the case now before us. I would read the case differently, finding a clear mandate that where, as here, ratemaking must be based on evidential facts, §1(14)(a) requires that full hearing which due process normally entails.... I would agree with the District Court in *Long Island* R. Co., supra, at 497, that Congress was fully cognizant of our decision in *Louisville & Nashville* R. Co. when it first adopted the hearing requirement of §1(14)(a) in 1917. And when Congress debated the 1966 amendment that empowered the Commission to adopt incentive per diem rates, it had not lost sight of the importance of hearings. Questioned about the effect that incentive compensation might have on terminating lines, Mr. Staggers, Chairman of the House Committee on Interstate and Foreign Commerce and floor manager of the bill, responded: "I might say to the gentleman that this will not be put into practice until there have been *full hearings* before the Commission and all sides have had an opportunity to argue and present their facts on the question." 112 Cong. Rec. 10443 (emphasis added). Nor should we overlook the Commission's own interpretation of the hearing requirement in §1(14)(a) as it applies to this case. The Commission's order initiating the rulemaking proceeding notified the parties that it was acting "under authority of Part I of the Interstate Commerce Act (49 U.S.C. §1, et seq.); more particularly, section 1(14)(a) and the Administrative Procedure Act (5 U.S.C. §§ 553, 556, and 557)." Clearly, the Commission believed that it was required to hold a hearing on the record.

Accordingly, I would hold that appellees were not afforded the hearing guaranteed by §1(14)(a) of the Interstate Commerce Act and 5 U.S.C. §§ 553, 556, and 557, and would affirm the decision of the District Court.

Notes and Questions on Florida East Coast

1. The Supreme Court's decision must be understood against the background of two developments not mentioned in the opinion.

First is the pronounced increase in the use of rulemaking procedures in recent years, particularly by regulatory agencies that had formerly relied extensively upon case-by-case adjudication to develop policy. Some of the reasons underlying this shift include the flexibility of rulemaking procedures; their greater suitability in eliciting the views of a variety of interested persons and in resolving issues of policy and "legislative fact"; and the encouragement they provide agencies to focus upon and crystallize issues of general importance rather than case-by-case "muddling through." [28] Probably the most important factor in this shift from the viewpoint of the agencies themselves was the desire to escape the long delays and resource burdens involved in formulating policy through formal adjudication.

Second, developing experience with the use of formal, on the record procedures in rulemaking persuaded many observers that such formalities were inordinately cumbersome and time-consuming, and offered few advantages over more informal, notice and comment rulemaking procedures.[29] Special notoriety was given to the requirements in the Food, Drug and Cosmetic Act §371(e) that the FDA use "on the record" rulemaking procedures in establishing standards of identity for foods, requirements for labeling of foods for special dietary purposes, and other specified requirements. Of sixteen such proceedings during the 1960s, not one was completed in less than two years, and the average elapsed time between first proposal and final order was four years. Two proceedings lasted more than ten years. In one of the two, the main issue was whether it would "promote honesty and fair dealing in the interest of consumers" to require that peanut butter contain at least 90 percent peanuts (as proposed by the FDA) or 87 percent peanuts (as proposed by the industry). The proceedings were prolix, and their utility doubtful. For example, the first government witness consumed an entire day in presenting a survey of cookbook and patent peanut butter formulations and in being cross-examined on missing recipes as well as on his personal preferences in peanut butter. The other mammoth hearing, Foods for Special Dietary Uses, considered whether the diet of the average American is reasonably adequate in vitamins and minerals, and took 247 days of testimony to produce 32,405 pages of transcript.[30]

28. See Judge Wright's opinion in the *National Petroleum Refiners* decision, p. 398 supra, and the other commentators whose views are summarized at p. 403 supra.

29. See Hamilton, Rulemaking on a Record by the Food and Drug Administration, 50 Texas L. Rev. 1132 (1972); Hamilton, Procedures for the Adoption of Rules of General Applicability: The Need for Procedural Innovation in Administrative Rulemaking, 60 Calif. L. Rev. 1276 (1972).

30. See generally Hamilton, Rulemaking on a Record by the Food and Drug Administration, 50 Tex. L. Rev. 1132, 1142-1150 (1972).

Against the background of this experience at the FDA and analogous experience at other agencies, the Administrative Conference of the United States in 1972 adopted a recommendation that ordinarily Congress should not require mandatory procedural requirements in rulemaking other than notice and comment, and should never require "trial-type procedures for resolving questions of policy or of broad or general fact." Recommendation 72-5, Recommendations and Reports of the Administrative Conference of the United States (1970-1972) 66. Moreover, the potential availability of trial-type hearings can be a potent bargaining threat that the regulated industry can utilize to secure the adoption, through a process of informal negotiations and compromise, of regulations more acceptable to it.

Nonetheless, some lawyers defend formal procedures in rulemaking on the ground that a regulator "ought to appear publicly, if there is a challenge, and put on the table, subject to cross-examination, the facts on which he grounds his proposal." Austern, Food Standards: The Balance Between Certainty and Innovation, 24 Food Drug Cosmetic L.J. 440, 451 (1969).

Against this background, the Supreme Court would have been understandably reluctant to saddle agency rulemaking with the trial-type procedures discredited by studies at the FDA and other agencies.

2. Even if formal rulemaking procedures are often counterproductive, did the Supreme Court give too much weight to "functional" considerations in construing the "after hearing" language of §1(14)(a)? [31] To what extent should the understanding of Congress in 1917 be disregarded in light of current attitudes toward administrative procedures and the slow pace of the ICC in implementing the 1966 amendment to §1(14)a? Should we ignore the intent of Congress in 1917 and look to Congress's procedural expectation in 1966? [32] Even here, Judge Friendly argues powerfully in his *Long Island R. Co.* opinion that Congress probably contemplated use of trial-type hearings. Should the Court give less weight to Congress's often nebulous procedural expectations than to its clear purpose to eliminate freight car shortages expeditiously?

3. Even if "functional" considerations are entitled to considerable weight, it is not clear that they justify the decision in *Florida East Coast*. Sections 556 and 557 provide considerable flexibility in streamlining "on the record" proceedings in order to accommodate flexibility and a need for expedition. Recall that §556(d) permits agencies engaged in rulemaking to require documentary submission of evidence when the parties will not be prejudiced thereby, and that §557 permits the agency to omit the time-consuming practice of an initial or recommended decision by the hearing officer. Additional possibilities for expedition are suggested in §556(e), which contemplates agency use of an official notice procedure, subject to a party's opportunity for rebuttal.[33] It would thus appear that on the record rulemaking could be streamlined to the following essentials: all evidence, rulings and decisions must be included in a documentary record which must be made available to the parties, who must be afforded the opportunity to submit documentary evidence and argument and object to a tentative decision issued by the agency. Professor Nathanson argues that, given these possibilities for streamlining formal rule-

---

31. Judge Friendly, in his opinion in Long Island R. Co. v. United States, 318 F. Supp. 490 (E.D.N.Y. 1970) (which reviewed the same ICC action at issue in *Florida East Coast*), and in his article, "Some Kind of Hearing", 123 U. Pa. L. Rev. 1267, 1305-1315 (1975), argues powerfully that when Congress enacted the "after hearing" language in 1917 it contemplated use of a trial-type evidentiary hearing of the sort which the Supreme Court had recently described in ICC v. Louisville & Nashville R.R., 227 U.S. 88 (1913). Professor Nathanson concurs in Judge Friendly's view, asserting that "[i]f there is any well-established point of reference for the Section 553(c) phrase 'required to be made on the record after opportunity for hearing,' it would be the rulemaking provisions of the Interstate Commerce Act as consistently interpreted by the Commission and the Supreme Court prior to *Florida East Coast* . . ." Nathanson, Probing the Mind of the Administrator: Hearing Variations and Standards of Judicial Review under the Administrative Procedure Act and Other Federal Statutes, 75 Colum. L. Rev. 721, 733 (1975).

32. Recall the comparable issue in Kent v. Dulles whether, in construing the statutory delegation of passport authority to the Secretary of State, the Court should look to the Congress that originally enacted the provision in 1856, the Congress that codified the delegation in 1926, or more contemporary Congresses that had authorized the requirement of a passport for entry or exit. See pp. 258-263, *supra*.

33. See the materials on official notice, pp. 530-539, *infra*.

making procedures, there is no justification for reading statutory "hearing" procedures with undue narrowness in order to avoid the provisions of APA §§ 556-557, and that *Florida East Coast* is unsound.[34] On the other hand, one may well ask why agencies, such as the FDA, that are clearly subject to formal rulemaking requirements have not utilized the streamlining possibilities suggested above. May not agencies legitimately fear that any departures from the trial-type norm — in particular, denial of the right to cross-examine — may be successfully attacked as prejudicial on judicial review? [35]

4. How far does *Florida East Coast* go in restricting the applicability of APA "on the record" requirements to agency rulemaking? Do §§ 556 and 557 apply only where the relevant statute repeats the talismanic §553(c) phrase "on the record after opportunity for an agency hearing"? [36] The Court's opinion leaves open the possibility that "other statutory language having the same meaning could trigger the provisions of §§ 556 and 557," but lower courts have understood *Florida East Coast* as making the terms "on the record" and "hearing" "virtually . . . a touchstone test" of formal rulemaking requirements. Mobil Oil Corp. v. FPC, 483 F.2d 1238 (D.C. Cir. 1973).

5. Note that *Florida East Coast* discusses potential constitutional objections to its interpretation of the Interstate Commerce Act by referring to the *Londoner/Bi-Metallic* distinction between rulemaking and adjudicating. Does this mean that there can never be a constitutional right to some form of trial-type procedure in rulemaking? Suppose the ICC's regulations, while drafted in general terms, happened to apply to only one carrier or turned on sharply focused and disputed facts, such as the cost of new boxcars. Would due process require trial-type procedures in such a case? [37] Would these circumstances lead the court to alter its construction of the Act? Can the meaning of the term "after hearing" in §1(14)(a) vary depending on the issues involved in various rulemaking proceedings? Consider in this respect the position espoused by Justice Douglas in dissent. Does it introduce too much procedural uncertainty in comparison to the majority's emphasis on the APA statutory terms "hearing" and "on the record," and on the formal distinction between rulemaking and adjudication?

34. See Nathanson, Probing the Mind of the Administrator: Hearing Variations and Standards of Judicial Review Under the Administrative Procedure Act and Other Federal Statutes, 75 Colum. L. Rev. 721, 738-739 (1975).

35. Consider in this respect Justice Douglas's dissent in *Florida East Coast*. What guidance does it afford agencies in deciding whether or not they must afford a right to present oral testimony and to cross-examine?

36. Is it relevant whether the particular statute in question was enacted before or after the 1946 APA? If so, how should one classify the statutory provision in *Florida East Coast*, first enacted in 1917 but amended in 1966?

37. For contrasting views on whether the promulgation of regulations applicable to only one person constitutes "rulemaking," compare Law Motor Freight, Inc. v. CAB, 364 F.2d 139 (1st Cir. 1966), *cert. denied*, 387 U.S. 905 (1967), with ABC Air Freight Co. v. CAB, 391 F.2d 295 (2d Cir. 1968), *appeal after remand*, 419 F.2d 154 (1969), *cert. denied*, 397 U.S. 1006 (1970), and Philadelphia Co. v. SEC, 175 F.2d 808 (D.C. Cir. 1948), *dismissed as moot*, 337 U.S. 901 (1949). See also Sinaiko, Due Process Rights of Participation in Administrative Rulemaking, 63 Calif. L. Rev. 886 (1975).

3. The Interplay Between Rulemaking and Adjudication

The shift by agencies from adjudication to rulemaking in evolving basic regulatory policies has been given added impetus by *Florida East Coast*, which largely eliminated earlier fears that rulemaking could only be carried out through cumbersome trial-type procedures like those used in the FDA peanut butter case.[38]

This shift to notice and comment rulemaking has created serious difficulties for litigants seeking to challenge the factual bases for agency decisions. Because most regulatory statutes require a trial-type hearing in adjudication resulting in sanctions or controls on private behavior, adjudication, even when used as a vehicle to develop new policy, was normally based upon an extensive evidentiary record that could be utilized on review to challenge the agency's action. By contrast, traditional notice and comment rulemaking did not produce an evidentiary record, and an agency could base its determinations on whatever materials it believed relevant without disclosing such materials to those subject to the rule or to the reviewing court. In these circumstances judicial review of the validity of an agency rule was necessarily quite modest; a rule would be sustained if it did not transgress relevant statutory directives, was not irrational on its face, and was supportable by some state of facts that the agency might plausibly allege to exist.[39] Lacking the opportunity to ferret out and challenge the evidence supposedly supporting the agency's action, the position of a litigant attacking a rule adopted after notice and comment was not an enviable one.

In this subsection and the one which follows, we examine the efforts of regulated firms and other private litigants to counteract the strategic disadvantage which they suffered by reason of agencies' shift from formal adjudication to informal rulemaking. This section deals with their contention that, after an agency adopted a general regulation through rulemaking and sought to apply or enforce it in a given case, the respondent should be afforded a trial-type hearing to elicit and challenge the evidentiary basis for the general regulation.

FPC v. Texaco, Inc.

377 U.S. 33 (1964)

Mr. Justice Douglas delivered the opinion of the Court.

The Federal Power Commission in its regulation of independent producers[40]

38. See, e.g., Phillips Petroleum Co. v. FPC, 475 F.2d 842 (10th Cir. 1973); Bell Tel. Co. v. FCC, 503 F.2d 1250 (3d Cir. 1974), *cert. denied sub nom.* American Tel. & Tel. Co. v. FCC, 422 U.S. 1026 (1975); Associated Elec. Co-op., Inc. v. Morton, 507 F.2d 1167 (D.C. Cir. 1974), *cert. denied,* 423 U.S. 830 (1975); National Assn. of Food Chains, Inc. v. ICC, 535 F.2d 1308 (D.C. Cir. 1976).

39. E.g., Superior Oil Co. v. FPC, 322 F.2d 601, 619 (9th Cir. 1963), *cert. denied,* 377 U.S. 922 (1964). In earlier decisions, courts had analogized judicial review of agency regulations to that of legislative statutes, concluding that the agency was no more required to support its measures by evidence of record than was the legislature. E.g., Assigned Car Cases, 274 U.S. 564 (1927).

40. See Natural Gas Act, 52 Stat. 821-833, as amended, 15 U.S.C. §§ 717-717w; Phillips Petroleum Co. v. Wisconsin, 347 U.S. 672.

of natural gas has required them to file their contracts as rate schedules. This was done by regulations which evolved as a result of a series of rule-making proceedings. The pertinent regulations presently provide that only certain pricing provisions in the contracts of independent producers are "permissible," any other being "inoperative and of no effect at law." The regulations go on to say that any contract executed on or after April 2, 1962, containing price-changing provisions other than the "permissible" ones, "shall be rejected" so far as producer rates are concerned,[41] that a producer's application for a certificate of public convenience and necessity under §7 of the Natural Gas Act "shall be rejected" if any contract submitted in support of it contains any of the forbidden provisions, and that, so far as pipeline certificates are concerned, any producer contract executed after that date which has that infirmity "will be given no consideration in determining adequacy" of a pipeline company's gas supply.

[The regulations, which were designed to eliminate the use of "escalator" clauses adjusting the contract price for gas to current (higher) prices for newly delivered gas, were adopted in conformance with APA §553 notice and comment procedures.] No oral argument was had but an opportunity was afforded for all interested parties to submit their views in writing; and the two respondents in this case — Texaco and Pan American — along with others, did so.

Later, each respondent submitted an application for a certificate of public convenience and necessity under §7 of the Natural Gas Act, to supply natural gas to a pipeline company. Section 7 provides, with exceptions not presently material, that the Commission "shall set" such an application "for hearing." Since, however, the applications disclosed price clauses that are not "permissible" under the regulations, the Commission without a hearing rejected the applications. . . . Petitions for review were filed with the Court of Appeals, which set aside the order of the Commission. 317 F.2d 796. It held that while the regulations are valid as a statement of Commission policy, they cannot be used to deprive an applicant of the statutory hearing granted those who seek certificates of public convenience and necessity. . . .

The main issue in the case is whether the "hearing" granted under [APA §553] is adequate, so far as the price clauses are concerned, for purposes of §7 of the Natural Gas Act. We think the Court of Appeals erred, . . . and that the statutory requirement for a hearing under §7 does not preclude the Commission from particularizing statutory standards through the rule-making process and barring at the threshold those who neither measure up to them nor show reasons why in the public interest the rule should be waived.

41. Section 154.93 defines the "permissible" provisions:

"(a) Provisions that change a price in order to reimburse the seller for all or any part of the changes in production, severance, or gathering taxes levied upon the seller;

"(b) Provisions that change a price to a specific amount at a definite date; and

"(c) Provisions that, once in five-year contract periods during which there is not provision for a change in price to a specific amount (paragraph (b) of this subsection), change a price at a definite date by a price-redetermination based upon and not higher than a producer rate or producer rates which are subject to the jurisdiction of the Commission, are not in issue in suspension or certificate proceedings, and, are in the area of the price in question. . . ."

In [United States v. Storer Broadcasting Co., 351 U.S. 192 (1956)] the Federal Communications Commission, pursuant to its general rule-making authority, limited permissible multiple ownership for radio and television stations. Storer, which had seven radio stations and five television stations, was under that rule automatically disqualified for further licensing. To surmount that barrier it argued that the Act required a license to issue where the public interest would be served and that before an application could be denied, a hearing must be held. We said: "We read the Act and Regulations as providing a 'full hearing' for applicants who have reached the existing limit of stations, upon their presentation of applications conforming to Rules 1.361(c) and 1.702, that set out adequate reasons why the Rules should be waived or amended. The Act, considered as a whole, requires no more. We agree with the contention of the Commission that a full hearing, such as is required by §309(b) ... would not be necessary on all such applications. As the Commission has promulgated its Rules after extensive administrative hearings, it is necessary for the accompanying papers to set forth reasons, sufficient if true, to justify a change or waiver of the Rules. We do not think Congress intended the Commission to waste time on applications that do not state a valid basis for a hearing. If any applicant is aggrieved by a refusal, the way for review is open." 351 U.S., at 205.

In the present case, as in *Storer*, there is a procedure provided in the regulations whereby an applicant can ask for a waiver of the rule complained of.[42] Facts might conceivably be alleged sufficient on their face to provide a basis for waiver of the price-clause rules and for a hearing on the matter. Cf. Atlantic Refining Co., 28 F.P.C. 469; 29 F.P.C. 384. But no such attempt was made here by Pan American, the only respondent to which the present point has any immediate applicability.

The rule-making authority here, as in *Storer*, is ample to provide the conditions for applications under §4 or §7. Section 16 of the Natural Gas Act gives the Commission power to prescribe such regulations "as it may find necessary or appropriate to carry out the provisions of this Act." We deal here with a procedural aspect of a rate question and with a certificate question that is important in effectuating the aim of the Act to protect the consumer interest. . . .

To require the Commission to proceed only on a case-by-case basis would require it, so long as its policy outlawed indefinite price-changing provisions, to repeat in hearing after hearing its conclusions that condemn all of them. There would be a vast proliferation of hearings, for as a result of Phillips Petroleum Co. v. Wisconsin, 347 U.S. 672, there are thousands of individual producers seeking applications. . . . We see no reason why under this statutory scheme the processes of regulation need be so prolonged and so crippled.

Pan American finally argues that the "hearing" accorded it under §[553] of the Administrative Procedure Act did not comply with that Act nor with the

---

42. Regulation §1.7(b), 18 C.F.R. (Cum. Supp. 1963), §1.7(b), provides in relevant part: "A petition for the issuance, amendment, waiver, or repeal of a rule by the Commission shall set forth clearly and concisely petitioner's interest in the subject matter, the specific rule, amendment, waiver, or repeal requested, and cite by appropriate reference the statutory provision or other authority therefor. . . ."

Natural Gas Act [because it did not receive a formal "on the record" adjudicatory hearing prior to rejection of its application]. What the Commission did in these cases, however, is not an "adjudication," not "an order," not "licensing" within the meaning of §[551]. Whether Pan American can qualify for a certificate of public convenience and necessity has never been reached. It has only been held that its application is not in proper form because of the pricing provisions in the contracts it tenders. No decisions on the merits have been reached. The only hearing to which Pan American so far has been entitled was given when the regulations in question were adopted pursuant to §[553] of the Administrative Procedure Act.

Reversed.

[Mr. Justice STEWART dissented from the Court's disposition of the hearing issue, relying upon the opinion of the Court of Appeals below, 317 F.2d 796, 804-807, which argued that denying Texaco the opportunity for hearing at which it could elicit and challenge relevant evidence effectively deprived Texaco of meaningful judicial review of the Commission's action.]

Notes and Questions on *Texaco*

1. On recalling the earlier materials on FPC regulation of natural gas producer prices, pp. 421-445 supra, you will recognize the *Texaco* case as a key step in the FPC's effort to ease the burdens of regulating producer prices in general and price increases in particular by switching to rulemaking from adjudication in formulating basic policy.

2. How is it possible for Justice Douglas to conclude that the Commission's action in *Texaco* was not "adjudication" under the APA and accordingly that the trial-type procedures of §§ 554, 556, and 557 were inapplicable? Recall that the APA defines adjudication to encompass all agency dispositions other than rulemaking, and specifically to include licensing. The FPC's denial of the particular applications tendered by Texaco and Pan American was certainly not rulemaking; it was plainly the denial of the licenses sought by the applicants.

Even if it were accepted that the FPC's action constituted "adjudication" and that the Natural Gas Act triggered the formal adjudicatory requirements of §§ 554, 556, and 557, the Commission's denial of a hearing in this case could still be upheld because of the absence of material disputed facts. An agency, no less than a court, should be permitted to utilize "summary judgment" procedures and dispense with an evidentiary hearing when there are no material facts in dispute and the matter can be disposed of on the law alone.[43] In *Texaco*, there was no dispute that the FPC's regulations required the FPC to deny the producers' applications. Since the sole issue raised by the producers was whether a hearing was required on the denial of their applications, administrative summary judgment was proper.

43. See, e.g., Sun Oil Co. v. FPC, 256 F.2d 233 (5th Cir.), *cert. denied*, 358 U.S. 872 (1958), sustaining the Commission's revocation of Sun's certificate to market natural gas without oral or evidentiary hearing on the ground that there was no "fact question involved and hence no evidence would have been material" and that the matter turned on issues of policy or law as to which neither the statute nor due process required opportunity for oral (as opposed to written) argument.

This logic still does not meet Justice Stewart's concern that the producers be given an opportunity to test the factual bases for the Commission's rule. But if each producer were entitled to an evidentiary hearing whenever a general regulation was applied to it, the advantages of rulemaking would be completely destroyed. Is there a solution to this dilemma?

3. To what extent was or should the Court's ruling be based on the FPC's provisions for waiver of its regulation in individual cases? What would an applicant have to establish in order to obtain a waiver?

American Airlines, Inc. v. CAB

359 F.2d 624 (D.C. Cir.) (en banc),
cert. denied, 385 U.S. 843 (1966)

LEVENTHAL, Circuit Judge:

On August 7, 1964, the Civil Aeronautics Board, two members dissenting, issued a "policy" regulation (PS-24), providing that only all-cargo carriers may provide "blocked space service" — essentially the sale of space on flights at whole-sale rates, when "blocked" or reserved by the user on an agreement to use a specified amount of space. . . .

[The CAB's "blocked space" regulation was adopted through notice and comment procedures, and the carriers were also afforded oral argument before the Board. Prior to adoption of the regulation, all carriers could offer "blocked" space. The regulations limited blocked space service to all-cargo carriers on the theory that this policy would best promote the development of air cargo services. "Combination" carriers, offering passenger and cargo service, filed proposed tariffs offering blocked space cargo service. These applications were summarily rejected by the Board on the basis of the regulations.]

Petitioners claim that §401(g) of the Federal Aviation Act, 49 U.S.C. §1371(g), [which authorizes the Board after "notice and hearings" to alter, amend, or modify existing certificates authorizing carriers to engage in air transportation] assures them an "adjudicatory hearing" because the Board action [in promulgating and applying the regulations] amounts to a modification or suspension of existing rights under their certificates of public convenience and necessity.

In essence, petitioners' argument is the same as the thesis this court accepted ten years ago in the *Storer* case, only to be reversed by the Supreme Court. . . .

Petitioners argue that the *Storer* doctrine is restricted to regulations affecting future applications for new licenses or certificates, whereas here the CAB regulation affected rights under existing certificates. . . .

. . . However, the *Storer* doctrine is not to be revised or reshaped by reference to fortuitous circumstances. It rests on a fundamental awareness that rulemaking is a vital part of the administrative process, particularly adapted to and needful for sound evolution of policy in guiding the future development of industries subject to intensive administrative regulation in the public interest, and that such rulemaking is not to be shackled, in the absence of clear and specific Congressional requirement, by importation of formalities developed for the adjudicatory process and basically unsuited for policy rule making. . . .

We are not here concerned with a proceeding that in form is couched as rule making, general in scope and prospective in operation, but in substance and effect is individual in impact and condemnatory in purpose. The proceeding before us is rulemaking both in form and effect. There is no individual action here masquerading as a general rule. We have no basis for supposing that the Board's regulation was based on a sham rather than a genuine classification. The classes of carriers were analyzed both functionally and in terms of capacity for furthering the promotional purposes of the Act. The class of combination carriers is not accorded the same rights as the class of all-cargo carriers, but the difference is in no sense a punishment for sins of commission or omission. . . .

[The court noted that in the rulemaking proceedings leading to adoption of the regulations, the Board had afforded the carriers oral argument as well as the opportunity to file written comments.]

However, there is no basis on the present record for concluding that additional procedures were requisite for fair hearing. We might view the case differently if we were not confronted solely with a broad conceptual demand for an adjudicatory-type proceeding, which is at least consistent with, though we do not say it is attributable to, a desire for protracted delay. Nowhere in the record is there any specific proffer by petitioners as to the subjects they believed required oral hearings, what kind of facts they proposed to adduce, and by what witnesses, etc. Nor was there any specific proffer as to particular lines of cross-examination which required exploration at an oral hearing.

The particular point most controverted by petitioners is the effect of the CAB regulation on their business. The issue involves what Professor Davis calls "legislative" rather than "adjudicative" facts. It is the kind of issue involving expert opinions and forecasts, which cannot be decisively resolved by testimony. It is the kind of issue where a month of experience will be worth a year of hearings. . . .

To avoid any possible misapprehension, our affirmance of the Board's action is without prejudice to the right of the combination carriers to reopen the question of their exclusion upon a showing that the Boards' assumptions could not reasonably continue to be maintained in the light of actual experience, that their overall cargo business was significantly impaired, or that the air freight market had sufficiently expanded so that the promotion of the air cargo industry through blocked space reduced rates would not be imperiled by their participation. . . .

Affirmed.

WASHINGTON, Senior Circuit Judge, did not participate in this decision.

BURGER, Circuit Judge, with whom DANAHER and TAMM, Circuit Judges, join (dissenting):

. . . I have trouble seeing how a "regulation" which turns identical certificates into ones which place the licensees in entirely distinct carrier roles, carrying different types of cargo for different types of shippers, can be said to be anything less than an amendment of outstanding certificates. This much is clear, for it is undisputed that after the "regulation" Petitioners could not lawfully engage in the same carriage as their all-cargo competitors. Indeed the Board concedes that its action has excluded Petitioners from performing the kind of carriage which they were originally certificated to perform and in which they have made large investments of capital. I therefore dissent from the majority's conclusion that an adjudicatory hearing was not required. As I see it this is nothing more than a transparent device to favor some carriers at the expense of others. . . .

. . . [T]he CAB's result here is reached by a rule which has different impacts upon members of the same basic category. When the Board makes such a differentiation, the proceedings inescapably become highly adversary in character, especially where the final determination purports to rest upon asserted differences in capabilities and potentialities as between individual carriers. The rulemaking procedure's lack of direct testimony of witnesses, cross-examination, and other features of adjudicatory hearings is totally inadequate for the testing of such competing considerations, both factual and inferential.

. . . A general dissatisfaction with the "rigors" of procedural safeguards should not lead to dispensing with them in a case where they are most appropriate, nor to amending the statute judicially. . . .

Notes and Questions

1. *American Airlines* carries one step further the essential principle of *Texaco* — that a trial-type hearing is not required in the application of a validly adopted regulation in individual adjudication where there is no factual dispute that the regulations apply — by approving its use to diminish rights under a preexisting license. Does this extension raise any additional statutory or constitutional problems beyond those involved in *Texaco*? See also Air Line Pilots Assn. v. Quesada, 276 F.2d 892 (2d Cir. 1960) (sustaining an FAA regulation lowering the maximum flying age of pilots on scheduled airlines to age 60, in effect amending pilots' existing licenses); WBEN, Inc. v. United States, 396 F.2d 601 (2d Cir.), *cert. denied,* 393 U.S. 914 (1968) (upholding application without hearing of FCC regulations restricting operations of previously licensed radio broadcasters); Note, The Agency Use of Rulemaking to Deny Adjudications Apparently Required by Statute, 54 Iowa L. Rev. 1086 (1969).

2. While reluctant to impose blanket hearing requirements that would stifle agency experimentation through "protracted delay," the majority in *American Airlines* is sensitive to the possibility that particular issues might be illuminated through additional procedures beyond notice and opportunity for comment. How would a reviewing court determine when such procedures would be required? Would they be required in the original rulemaking proceedings, or when a regulation was applied to a particular firm or individual?

3. The FTC from time to time issues trade regulation rules. It states that:

> Where a trade regulation rule is relevant to any issue involved in an adjudicative proceeding thereafter instituted, the Commission may rely upon the rule

to resolve such issue, provided that the respondent shall have been given fair hearing on the legality and propriety of applying the rule to the particular case.

In 1964, after notice and a hearing at which adoption of oral and written evidence was considered, the FTC promulgated the following rule:

> [I]n connection with the sale, offering for sale, or distribution in commerce . . . of cigarettes it is an unfair or deceptive act or practice within the meaning of section 5 of the Federal Trade Commission Act . . . to fail to disclose, clearly and prominently, in all advertising and on every pack, box, carton or other container in which cigarettes are sold to the consuming public that cigarette smoking is dangerous to health and may cause death from cancer and other diseases.

In 1969, the Tarfree Company was organized and began to market Tarfree cigarettes. It claimed in its advertising to have the lowest tar and nicotine content of any cigarette containing tobacco, and failed to place any health warning in either its advertising or its labeling. The FTC brought a §5 proceeding against this company, alleging that it had failed to include the required warnings and that the name of the brand and the claims made for it were deceptive. The FTC introduced evidence showing that Tarfree violated the rule. What sorts of claims might Tarfree make in response?

4. The Development of Hybrid Rulemaking Procedures

The increased resort by agencies to rulemaking for development of basic policy, together with *Florida East Coast* and the *Texaco-American Airlines* line of decisions, threatened effectively to insulate important agency decisions from judicial review by depriving litigants of the opportunity to elicit and challenge underlying evidentiary materials.[44] Concern that greater agency use of notice and comment rulemaking would greatly diminish judicial control of agency decisionmaking has been heightened by the developing perception of agency "failure" and the perceived need for more effective outside scrutiny of agency decisions.

As we have already indicated in Chapter 4, concern with agency "failure" has led to more searching judicial review of discretionary policy decisions, in which administrators are required to explain in detail the grounds for their decisions. Re-

---

44. The problem of developing an evidentiary basis for challenging agency rules was exacerbated by a growing tendency, described in greater detail in Chapter 9, pp. 960-992 infra, to "preenforcement" review of regulations. Under this practice, a person subject to a regulation may challenge its validity before it is actually applied to her in an adjudicatory proceeding. In this posture, a litigant could not raise the *Texaco-American Airlines* claim to a trial-type adjudicatory hearing to test the basis for a regulation when it is enforced.

viewing courts will closely examine the evidentiary support for these explanations. However, this "hard look" approach to judicial review would be gravely compromised if agencies were free to utilize notice and comment procedures that did not generate a reviewable record of relevant evidence.[45]

The draftsmen of the APA apparently contemplated that courts reviewing agency rules adopted through notice and comment or other less formal procedures would themselves hear evidence and develop a factual record to judge the validity of the rule.[46] But there are many difficulties in this approach. In many instances, relevant statutes provide for judicial review in courts of appeals, which have no regular evidence-gathering machinery.[47] Post-decision assembly of a record invites post hoc rationalization by the agency. Moreover, the function of procedural safeguards is not only to provide a record for judicial review, but to enlighten and shape the agency's exercise of its discretion by assuring input of evidence and views by interested persons. This latter function would be largely destroyed if formal evidentiary procedures were postponed to the stage of judicial review; moreover, practicalities dictate that in most cases there will be no judicial review.

In lieu of developing the relevant facts independently, courts require agencies to develop an evidentiary base for their regulation through "hybrid" rulemaking procedures that are less formal than a full-fledged trial-type hearing but more substantial than §553 notice and comment requirements. In this subsection we examine the respective development of hybrid procedures by Congress and by reviewing courts.

45. For example, in order to avoid the delays involved in case-by-case determination of safety issues in the context of individual proceedings to license particular nuclear generating plants, the AEC (and its successor, the Nuclear Regulatory Commission) shifted to notice and comment rulemaking to resolve issues such as reactor safety or fuel recycling on a generic basis. However, this shift has deprived environmental groups of opportunities for cross-examination to probe and test the assumptions and data behind nuclear safety decisions. For discussion, see J. Lieberman, Generic Hearings: Preparation for the Future, 16 Atomic Energy L.J. 141 (1974); Notes, The Use of Generic Rulemaking to Resolve Environmental Issues in Nuclear Power Plant Licensing, 61 Va. L. Rev. 869 (1975). See also the *Vermont Yankee* litigation, pp. 516-522, infra.

46. See Nathanson, Probing the Mind of the Administrator: Hearing Variations and Standards of Judicial Review under the Administrative Procedure Act and Other Federal Statutes, 75 Colum. L. Rev. 721, 755-759 (1975); Williams, "Hybrid Rulemaking" under the Administrative Procedure Act: A Legal and Empirical Analysis, 42 U. Chi. L. Rev. 401, 418-424 (1975); Auerbach, Informal Rule Making: A Proposed Relationship Between Administrative Procedures and Judicial Review, 72 Nw. U.L. Rev. 15, 23-24 (1977).

47. But see the Hobbs Act, 28 U.S.C. §§ 2341-2351, 2353, which provides for direct court of appeals review for the actions of a number of federal agencies, including the FCC, the Secretary of Agriculture, and the Federal Maritime Commission, but authorizes the court of appeals to direct a district court to take evidence where an agency "hearing is not required by law and a genuine issue of material fact is presented." This authority was utilized by a court of appeals in Lake Carriers Assn. v. United States, 414 F.2d 567 (6th Cir. 1969).

In Quaker Action Group v. Morton, 516 F.2d 717 (D.C. Cir. 1975), the constitutionality of regulations limiting demonstrations in front of the White House was challenged by an injunction action in the district court, which heard elaborate evidence on relevant factual issues, paving the way for a careful court of appeals decision. Should this practice be more widely emulated in cases of preenforcement review brought initially in the district court, or is *Quaker Action Group* special because of the First Amendment issues presented on the merits?

a.   Congressional Specification of Hybrid Procedures

Many of the regulatory statutes enacted by Congress during the 1970s explicitly grant rulemaking power to administrators, but hedge its exercise with specific procedural requirements that go beyond §553 notice and comment procedures without requiring oral trial-type hearings in every case.

The Federal Trade Commission Improvement Act of 1974 (Magnuson-Moss Act), 15 U.S.C. §57(a), provides a good example of statutory hybrid procedures. It confirms the result in National Petroleum Refiners Assn. v. FTC, supra p. 339, by explicitly granting the Commission rulemaking authority to define with specificity acts or practices which are "unfair or deceptive." In promulgating such regulations, the FTC is directed to utilize notice and comment procedures, subject to additional, statutorily defined "informal hearing" practices under which an "interested person is entitled . . . to present his position orally or by documentary submission (or both)." If "the Commission determines that there are disputed issues of material fact it is necessary to resolve," it must afford parties the opportunity to file "rebuttal submissions," and "such cross-examination of persons as the Commission determines (i) to be appropriate, and (ii) to be required for a full and true disclosure with respect to such issues." However, the Commission is authorized to impose time limitations on oral presentations, to itself conduct the cross-examination on behalf of parties, or require that persons having common interests appoint one representative for purposes of cross-examination. 15 U.S.C. §57(a). Transcripts of oral presentations and cross-examination, as well as all written submissions, together with the rule, the Commission's decision, "and any other information which the Commission considers relevant to such rule," constitute the record on review,[48] and the court is directed to use a "substantial evidence" standard of review of facts.

A somewhat different model is provided in the Occupational Health and Safety Act of 1970, 29 U.S.C. §651 et seq. The statute requires that proposed health and safety standards be published in the Federal Register; any interested person may then file "written objections to the rule, stating the grounds thereof, and requesting a public hearing on such objections." 29 U.S.C. §655(b)(3). The Secretary must then provide a "public hearing," which has generally been interpreted to mean a legislative-type hearing at which interested persons can present argument but not testimonial evidence or cross-examination.[49]

Other rulemaking formalities beyond notice and opportunity for comment required by recent statutes include consultation with specific officials or organiza-

---

48. See Kestenbaum, Rulemaking Beyond APA: Criteria for Trial-Type Procedures and the FTC Improvements Act, 44 Geo. Wash. L. Rev. 679 (1976).

49. See Angel v. Butz, 487 F.2d 260, 263 (10th Cir. 1973), cert. denied, 417 U.S. 967 (1974). Promulgated standards are subject to a "substantial evidence" standard of review in the Courts of Appeals. 29 U.S.C. 660. Analogous procedures are provided in the Consumer Products Safety Act. See Scalia & Goodman, Procedural Aspects of the Consumer Product Safety Act, 20 U.C.L.A. L. Rev. 899 (1973).

tions,[50] creation of and consultation with advisory committees,[51] and shared responsibility with other agencies for promulgating rules.[52]

b. Judicial Development of Hybrid Rulemaking Procedures on the Basis of Specific Statutory Provisions

Mobil Oil Corp. v. FPC

483 F.2d 1238 (D.C. Cir. 1973)

Before LEVENTHAL and WILKEY, Circuit Judges, and JAMESON, Senior District Judge for the District of Montana.

WILKEY, Circuit Judge:

[In many cases, extraction of natural gas also produces hydrocarbons in a liquefiable form. These liquid or liquefiable products are sometimes transported in natural gas pipelines primarily designed to transport the gaseous product. In these proceedings, the Commission asserted the authority to set rates for the transport of liquid or liquefiable products as necessarily ancillary to its statutory authority to set "just and reasonable" rates for the transportation of natural gas in interstate commerce, since the rates for natural gas would depend upon the allocation of overhead and joint operating costs to liquid and liquefiable products transported in the same pipeline.

The Commission had previously dealt with this problem on a case-by-case basis by determining that a certain percentage of joint costs that it allocated to liquid or liquefiable hydrocarbons could not be charged to natural gas transportation.

The present proceedings were initiated by a Federal Register notice stating that the Commission was contemplating issuance of a "general policy" on the allocation of joint costs, without specifying further what the content of such policy might be. The comments submitted by various pipelines and state authorities were also general. At an informal conference, certain pipelines submitted data on joint cost allocation from pending proceedings to establish rates for natural gas produced

---

50. See Air Pollution Prevention and Control Act of 1977, 42 U.S.C. §§ 7401, 7421 (state and local authorities or advisory groups and federal agencies); Federal Coal Mine Health and Safety Act Amendments of 1977, 30 U.S.C. §§ 801, 812 (federal and state agencies and representatives of coal mine operators and miners).

51. Contract Work Hours and Safety Standard Act, 40 U.S.C. §333 (1970) (advisory committee of building trade employee representatives, contractors); Color Additive Amendments of 1960, 21 U.S.C. §376(b)(5)(D); Federal Coal Mine Health and Safety Act Amendments of 1977, 30 U.S.C. §§ 801, 812 (consult federal and state agencies and representatives of coal mine operators and miners).

52. Federal Coal Mine Health and Safety Act (HEW and Interior); Comprehensive Drug Abuse Prevention and Control Act (HEW and Department of Justice). See generally Hamilton, Procedures for the Adoption of Rules of General Applicability: The Need for Procedural Innovation in Administrative Rulemaking, 60 Calif. L. Rev. 1276 (1972).

in southern Louisiana, and the need for further conferences was acknowledged by industry and Commission staff representatives. However, without further notice or proceedings of any kind, the Commission subsequently issued uniform nation-wide rates for transportation of liquid and liquefiable hydrocarbons. Although the direct setting of rates for these products went far beyond prior practice, which merely limited the percentage of joint costs chargeable to natural gas, the Commission gave no reason for this change apart from the assertion that joint cost allocation was not a feasible means of protecting natural gas consumers from excessive rates.

The court first agreed with Mobil's contention that the FPC lacked statutory authority to set rates for liquid hydrocarbons. It then considered Mobil's contentions that the FPC was required to use trial-type on-the-record rulemaking procedures, and that the Commission's regulations were not supported by substantial evidence.

In addition to granting the FPC the authority to set "just and reasonable rates" for the transportation of natural gas in interstate commerce in §§ 4 and 5, the Natural Gas Act in §16 gives the FPC general authority to issue "such orders, rules, and regulations as it may find necessary or appropriate to carry out" the provisions of the Act. Section 21 of the Act provides that on judicial review of Commission decisions, "the finding of the Commission as to the facts, if supported by substantial evidence, shall be conclusive."]

Petitioner argues that the formal procedures outlined in sections 556 and 557 of Title 5 U.S.C. should have been followed in setting the disputed rates. These formal procedures by their terms, however, are only required when the substantive statute (in this case the Natural Gas Act) requires that rules be made "on the record after opportunity for an agency hearing." The Natural Gas Act does not provide on its face that rates will be made by an "on the record" proceeding. Taking the language of the APA and the Natural Gas Act together, but nothing else at this time, the strictures of sections 556 and 557 need not be followed here.

There is some danger in according too much weight to magic words such as "on the record." However, the Supreme Court's recent opinion in United States v. Florida East Coast Railway Co. emphasized the importance of this phrase and virtually established it as a touchstone test of when section 556 and section 557 proceedings are required. . . .

. . . The Natural Gas Act does not on its face require that rates be made "on the record" and we can find nothing in the Act's legislative history indicating that Congress felt that "on the record" rule-making, with all its procedural formalities, was required in this case. . . .

We conclude that the FPC need not employ the precise procedures set forth in sections 556 and 557 of the APA. It does not follow, however, that the Commission may proceed with only the guidance of the less rigorous standards of section 553.[53] The Commission's position assumes that there are only two per-

---

53. From the record it appears probable that the FPC did not even comply with the minimal requirements of section 553. Section 553 requires in part that notice shall be given

missible forms of procedures cognizable under the APA, that the two are mutually exclusive, and that their existence precludes the use of any other procedures that lie between them. This rigid interpretation of what is permitted and required under the APA is inaccurate, as it would not meet the multifarious situations arising before the numerous agencies charged with the administration of various and varied statutes.

Flexibility in fitting administrative procedures to particular functions is critically important in evaluating the APA and has been a dominant theme in a number of opinions by this court. No court, to our knowledge, has ever treated the explicit language of section 553 on the one hand and sections 556 and 557 on the other as expressing every type of procedure that might be called for in a particular situation.

[The court then referred to its previous decisions in American Airlines v. CAB, supra, p. 496; International Harvester Co. v. Ruckleshaus, discussed infra p. 509; and Chicago v. FPC, 458 F.2d 731 (D.C. Cir. 1971), cert. denied, 405 U.S. 1074 (1972), as authority for judicial creation of hybrid procedures.]

The APA may be viewed as providing the outer boundaries of administrative procedures. Congress has determined that the procedures outlined in section 553 will be the minimum protections upon which administrative action may be based, according to interested parties a simple notice and right to comment. At the opposite end of the spectrum lie the requirements of sections 556 and 557. Those may be viewed as representing the highest degree of administrative protection that Congress believed would be necessary to protect interested parties. There is no reason, however, to conclude that Congress in establishing these limits intended to preclude all the possible formulations that might lie in between the two extremes. . . .

. . . A final determination of what procedures are appropriate here must turn upon an analysis of the regulatory scheme envisioned by Congress in passing the Natural Gas Act and a determination of what is necessary to effectuate the policies of this regulatory statute. . . .

Any administrative proceeding designed to set rates for a large number of separate enterprises possesses elements of both a legislative policy determination and an adjudicative resolution of disputed facts. Although these distinct elements are intertwined and necessarily exist simultaneously in any rate-making, one may predominate over the other. Rate-making always involves factual predicates; yet the

---

of the "terms or substance of the proposed rule or a description of the subjects and issues involved." 5 U.S.C. §553(b)(3) (1970). In this case the parties were informed that the proceedings would be to consider the advisability of establishing a general policy of allocating costs to liquids and liquefiables. . . . The resulting rule established specific rates for these commodities. . . . Although there is certainly no requirement that the resulting rule conform precisely to that which is proposed, there is a serious question whether sufficient notice was given in this case.

Ed. note: For a representative decision invalidating regulations under §553 because of agency failure to give adequate notice of the rules eventually adopted, see American Iron and Steel Institute v. EPA, 568 F.2d 284 (1977).

facts relevant to rates in any given industry may be more or less well established. For example, if industry costs are well established, the rate-making process would consist primarily of policy judgments such as the fair rate of return or the desired level of safety; appropriate procedures for resolution of these policy disputes would not resemble adjudication. In contrast, if the rate of return policy was clear but the cost base uncertain, adjudication might be more appropriate. Congress could take into account the differences in these two type situations and require greater evidentiary support for factual findings in some instances than in others.

The degree of fact dispute resolution necessary in a particular proceeding is directly related to the degree of evidentiary support required by Congress in establishing a factual basis for a proposed rate. If a relatively high degree of evidentiary support is required in establishing a factual predicate, the rule-making procedures must be designed to create this. Thus, if we know the degree of evidentiary support required, this will indicate the type of procedures that Congress intended to be employed.

The Natural Gas Act explicitly states that factual determinations must be supported by "substantial evidence." Unlike many other forms of rule-making, rate-making necessarily rests upon findings of facts. The phrase "substantial evidence" is a term of art well recognized in administrative law. This requirement imposes a considerable burden on the agency and limits its discretion in arriving at a factual predicate. . . . It has also been established that in determining whether facts are supported by substantial evidence the entire record must be considered and not merely the evidence tending to support the finding.[54]

From this outline of the meaning of "substantial evidence," we can perceive the sort of procedures required. Clearly some evidence supporting the FPC's finding must be in the record. *More importantly for our purposes, the rule that the "whole record" be considered — both evidence for and against — means that the procedures must provide some mechanism for interested parties to introduce adverse evidence and criticize evidence introduced by others.* This process of introduction and criticism helps assure that the factual basis of the FPC rates will be accurate and provides the reviewing court with a record from which it can determine if the agency has properly exercised its discretion.

. . . Clearly the existence of the "substantial evidence" requirement in the Natural Gas Act demands that facts be determined and reviewed with a greater degree of certainty than is possible under the "informal" methods of section 553 of the APA. . . .

Our conclusion that the "substantial evidence" requirement necessitates some sort of adversary, adjudicative-type procedures is made more obviously necessary by considering the record in this case, such as it is. The FPC admittedly made findings of fact here regarding transportation costs and points to evidence which it claims supports the accuracy of these facts. It is clear, however, that none of the interested parties knew that this evidence — which was taken from a number of different sources — was to be the basis for the Commission's action. Consequently, no one was

54. Universal Camera Corp. v. NLRB, 340 U.S. 474 (1951).

able to introduce evidence in opposition, criticize the Commission's position, or point out flaws by questioning the validity of its sources. As the record stands, in reviewing the Commission's action we are unable to decide whether its factual determinations are supported by substantial evidence. Much of the evidence appears possibly suspect, we have no way of knowing from the record whether the figures are valid.[55] There is no evidence in the record except that which the Commission has chosen to include to support its position. . . .

Informal comments simply cannot create a record that satisfies the substantial evidence test. Even if controverting *information* is submitted in the form of comments by adverse parties, the procedure employed cannot be relied upon as adequate. A "whole record," as that phrase is used in this context, does not consist merely of the raw data introduced by the parties. It includes the process of testing and illumination ordinarily associated with adversary, adjudicative procedures. Without this critical element, informal comments, even by adverse parties, are two halves that do not make a whole. Thus, it is adversary procedural devices which permit testing and elucidation that raise information from the level of mere inconsistent data to evidence "substantial" enough to support rates.

[The court then asserted that its ruling was not inconsistent with the Supreme Court's *Florida East Coast* decision because §1(14)(a) of the Interstate Commerce Act merely provided that the ICC should give "consideration" to various specified factors in setting rates, and did not include the requirement in the Natural Gas Act that rates be supported by "substantial evidence."

The court also refused to follow Phillips Petroleum Co. v. FPC, 475 F.2d 842 (10th Cir. 1973), sustaining FPC use of notice and comment rulemaking procedures in establishing natural gas rates.]

The defect we find in the Commission's procedures here, and the resulting inadequacy of the evidence, could be remedied by according the procedure described under sections 556 and 557 of the APA, but such complete adjudicatory procedures are not required.

What is required are procedures which will adequately test the Commission's factual determinations and create a record that will allow a reviewing court to examine the agency's actions. The procedures required are related and proportionate to the test of evidentiary support which the agency's decision must ultimately withstand.

---

55. In establishing the rates under review the Commission used data relevant to only ten pipelines out of 116, without showing that these were typical or representative. It also appears from the record that this data was not matched as to test year, and yet the Commission gives equal weight to all the figures used without taking into account variances that might occur between years.

Mobil also contends that certain of the costs used by the Commission in formulating the rates had later been found to contain excessive amounts of depreciation expenses and that certain figures employed by the Commission have since been found to be overstatements of costs. Brief for Mobil Oil Co. at 30-31. Due to deficiencies in the record, however, we are unable to evaluate fully these contentions. This points up the basic inadequacy of the record before us and the procedures used in compiling it.

Compliance with this standard could conceivably be achieved in a number of ways.[56] There must, however, be some mechanism whereby adverse parties can test, criticize and illuminate the flaws in the evidentiary basis being advanced regarding a particular point. The traditional method of doing this is cross-examination, but the Commission may find it appropriate to limit or even eliminate altogether oral cross-examination and rely upon written questions and responses. In proceedings involving numerous parties, the Commission might find it expedient to screen the written interrogatories. . . . But whatever procedure is followed, it must assure that the Commission has a substantial evidentiary basis for its findings and it must provide the court with an adequate record on review. . . .

Notes and Questions on *Mobil Oil* and Judicial Construction of Statutes to Require Hybrid Procedures

1. Can *Mobil Oil* possibly be reconciled with *Florida East Coast?* While purporting to follow *Florida East Coast* in holding that FPC rulemaking is not "on the record after opportunity for an agency hearing" and is therefore not governed by §§ 556-557, *Mobil Oil* goes on to require the FPC to utilize the functional equivalent of §§ 556-557 and base its decision on a reviewable record. Should *Mobil Oil* have instead tested the limits of *Florida East Coast* by holding the FPC directly subject to §§ 556-557?

2. On the other hand, the *Florida East Coast* opinion itself recognizes the possibility that a particular statute might not trigger the formal rulemaking requirements of §§ 556-557, yet itself require procedures beyond the notice and comment requirements of §553. Once this possibility is admitted, the question comes down to the construction of particular statutes and the divination of congressional purpose with respect to hybrid procedures. *Mobil Oil* asserts that the statutory "substantial evidence" standard for judicial review of FPC orders is utterly inconsistent with notice and comment rulemaking and requires hybrid decisional procedures that will generate an evidentiary record for judicial review. Is the court's reasoning persuasive? Apparent anomalies in statutory provisions governing agency procedure and judicial review often occur because of last-minute compromise in conference or sheer inadvertence.[57]

56. It is not, of course, for this court to make rules governing the procedures to be employed in FPC rate-making. Our comments here are presented by way of illustration. Whatever innovations the FPC may attempt, we believe that sound administrative practice demands that a more accurate record of proceedings be kept than was done in this case. The minutes provided this court are at best an outline of what actually occurred. This flaw is totally unnecessary and could easily have been remedied by simply preparing a transcript of the proceedings.

57. For example, in enacting the Occupational Health and Safety Act, Congress provided for notice and comment rulemaking supplemented by informal legislative-type hearings but also provided for "substantial evidence" review. This structure was the result of a compromise in conference; the judicial review provision was drawn from the House bill, which had also provided for formal rulemaking, while the procedural provisions were drawn from the Senate version, which had been silent on the standard of review. See Note, Judicial Review Under the

3. What weight should the *Mobil Oil* court have given to the need for flexible and expeditious procedures in natural gas regulation? Does the decision largely undo the Commission's victory in FPC v. Texaco, Inc., supra p. 492? [58]

4. *Mobil Oil* had several precursors, and its basic approach has been accepted in a number of subsequent lower court decisions.[59] On the other hand, several lower court decisions have refused to follow the path taken in *Mobil Oil*, and have held that statutory references to a "record" or to a "substantial evidence" standard of review do not justify implication of hybrid rulemaking requirements.[60]

Occupational Safety and Health Act: The Substantial Evidence Test as Applied to Informal Rulemaking, 1974 Duke L.J. 459.

Judge McGowan has complained of the "additional burdens" on the judiciary "deriving from the illogic of legislative compromise," Industrial Union Department, AFL-CIO v. Hodgson, 499 F.2d 467, 469 (D.C. Cir. 1974), and Judge Friendly has remarked of congressional drafting that "One would almost think there had been a conscious effort never to use the same phraseology twice." Associated Indus. of New York, Inc. v. Department of Labor, 487 F.2d 342, 345 n.2 (2d Cir. 1973).

58. Should the court have simply set aside the FPC's action on the ground that the Federal Register notices of its proposed action was inadequate, or that it had not adequately explained its decision?

For evaluation of *Mobil Oil* and the issues there presented, see Dakin, Ratemaking as Rulemaking — The New Approach at the FPC: Ad Hoc Rulemaking in the Ratemaking Process, 1973 Duke L.J. 41; Fitzgerald, Mobil Oil Corp. v. Federal Power Commission and the Flexibility of the Administrative Procedure Act, 26 Ad. L. Rev. 287 (1974); Nathanson, Probing the Mind of the Administrator: Hearing Variations and Standards of Judicial Review under the Administrative Procedure Act and Other Federal Statutes, 75 Colum. L. Rev. 721, 734-740 (1975); Note, FPC Ratemaking: Judicial Control of Administrative Procedural Flexibility, 1974 Duke L.J. 326.

59. The ruling in *Mobil Oil* was prefigured in City of Chicago v. FPC, 458 F.2d 731 (D.C. Cir.), cert. denied, 405 U.S. 1074 (1972), where the court sustained an FPC rule based on procedures far more elaborate than bare notice and comment, and Walter Holm & Co. v. Hardin, 449 F.2d 1009 (D.C. Cir. 1971), which dealt with regulations issued by the the Secretary of Agriculture restricting the import of tomatoes from Mexico. The relevant statute provided for "notice and opportunity for hearing" and referred to agency findings "upon the evidence introduced at such hearing." The court, reflecting concern that the Secretary's action was the product of pressures from domestic producers, required opportunity for an "oral hearing" that might be "legislative in type," adding that "fairness may require an opportunity for cross-examination on the crucial issues." 449 F.2d at 1016. American Public Gas Assn. v. FPC, 498 F.2d 718 (D.C. Cir. 1974), expressed adherence to the *Mobil* principle but sustained FPC rulemaking procedures to establish terms and conditions for natural gas sales that included (a) specific notice of the information sought by the Commission, (b) exchange of written submission by all commentators, and (c) opportunity for a subsequent round of rebuttal submissions. The court found that litigants challenging these procedures had not demonstrated the existence of specific factual issues requiring cross-examination. See also Shell Oil Co. v. FPC, 520 F.2d 1061 (5th Cir. 1975). Cf. FTC v. Texaco, Inc., 555 F.2d 862, 932 (1977) (dissent) (finding insufficient adversariness to justify *Mobil Oil* procedures).

For discussion of recent cases requiring more complete notice and more detailed explanation by agencies in informal rulemaking, see K. Davis, Administrative Law of the Seventies 170-173 (1976). Judge Wright has suggested that these requirements could be developed into effective controls on informal rulemaking, obviating the need to impose procedural formalities such as cross-examination. See Wright, The Courts and the Rulemaking Process: The Limits of Judicial Review, 59 Cornell L. Rev. 375, 381-385 (1974).

60. Phillips Petroleum Co. v. FPC, 475 F.2d 842, 851-852 (10th Cir. 1973), cert. denied sub nom. Chevron Oil Co., Western Div. v. FPC, 414 U.S. 1146 (1974), held that FPC rulemaking with respect to natural gas regulation was governed by *Florida East Coast*, and that the "substantial evidence" standard of review in the Natural Gas Act did not require the FPC to

c. Judicial Development of Hybrid Procedures Not Based on Specific Statutory Provisions

The *Mobil Oil* approach relies upon provisions in specific statutes — such as the "substantial evidence" standard of review in the Natural Gas Act — as evincing a congressional intent to require hybrid rulemaking procedures. However, courts have also required hybrid procedures in cases where the APA requires only notice and comment rulemaking and the specific agency statute is devoid of language suggesting that additional formalities should be required.

"Paper hearing" procedures. This development has been accomplished in large part through decisions reviewing decisions by the federal Environmental Protection Agency, whose implementation of federal pollution control statutes involves major resource allocation decisions, and whose sloppy decisionmaking in the first few years after its creation in 1970 occasioned judicial concern.[61] Although the former provisions of EPA statutes, such as the Clean Air Act, 42 U.S.C. §1857, provided for EPA rulemaking without suggesting additional formalities, lower judicial courts have transformed traditional notice and comment practices into a "paper hearing" procedure in which all of the relevant evidence is reflected in documents submitted for the record by the agency or interested private persons and available to the courts on judicial review. Interestingly, the new revisions in the Clean Air Act seem to suggest additional formalities. 42 U.S.C. §7401 (1977).

The first step in this transformation was a judicial requirement that agencies engaged in informal rulemaking articulate the grounds for their decision in far greater detail than had been customary. This requirement, initially imposed in Kennecott Copper Corp. v. EPA, 462 F.2d 846 (D.C. Cir. 1972), was developed further in subsequent decisions reviewing a variety of informal EPA rulemaking decisions.[62]

These decisions not only required EPA to articulate in detail the grounds for its decisions, but also to respond in its decisions to criticisms and contrary evidence

---

go beyond notice and comment procedures. The Administrative Conference of the United States, in Recommendation 74-4(2), has recommended that the "substantial evidence" standard of review, without more, should not require the use of rulemaking procedures beyond notice and comment. See also Automotive Parts & Accessories Assn. v. Boyd, 407 F.2d 330 (D.C. Cir. 1968) (statutory provisions requiring filing in court of "the record of the proceedings upon which the Secretary based his order" does not require Transportation Secretary to go beyond notice and comment procedures in promulgating auto safety regulations); Bell Tel. Co. v. FCC, 503 F.2d 1250 (3d Cir. 1974) (FCC may utilize informal rulemaking to require ATT to furnish interconnection services to competitors; statutes required FCC to act "after opportunity for hearing" and based judicial review "on the record of the pleadings, evidence adduced, and the proceedings before the agency, when the agency has held a hearing"); Superior Oil Co. v. FERC, 563 F.2d 191, 201-202 (5th Cir. 1977).

61. E.g., South Terminal Corp. v. EPA, 504 F.2d 646, 662-667 (1st Cir. 1974); Portland Cement Assn. v. Ruckelshaus, 486 F.2d 375, 392-401 (D.C. Cir. 1973).

62. E.g., International Harvester Co. v. Ruckelshaus, 478 F.2d 615, 647-650 (D.C. Cir. 1973); South Terminal Corp. v. EPA, 504 F.2d 646, 655, 665-667 (1st Cir. 1974); Texas v. EPA, 499 F.2d 289, 296-297 (5th Cir. 1974); Portland Cement Assn. v. Ruckelshaus, 486 F.2d 375, 401-402 (D.C. Cir. 1973).

adduced in comments by those opposing EPA's proposed action. The requirement that EPA respond to criticisms has meant that the documentary evidence in written comments to EPA will be included in the materials that EPA must deal with in its decision and that a court will look to on review. In such circumstances, government lawyers eager to sustain EPA's action have not hesitated to include documents that they believed would support EPA's actions. Furthermore, internal agency documents that might undercut EPA's final decision can generally be obtained by opponents through resort to the pertinent provisions of the Freedom of Information Act, 5 U.S.C. §552, which is discussed in Chapter 10. As a result, a practice emerged under which a reviewing court will normally have before it a record consisting of all of the documentary materials relevant to the Agency's decision. In essence, what has emerged in procedural terms is a "paper hearing" that combines many of the advantages of a trial-type adversary process (excepting oral testimony and cross-examination) while avoiding undue delay and cost.[63] Similar "paper hearing" requirements have been imposed on other agencies as well.[64]

The courts responsible for developing "paper hearing" procedures in informal rulemaking have justified these requirements as necessary in order to provide an adequate evidentiary basis for meaningful judicial review of the merits of the agency's decision.

The development of a "paper hearing" procedure and the related requirement that the Agency explain in detail the bases for its decision have contributed to the improvement of EPA decisionmaking because the Agency must be prepared to expose the factual and methodological bases for its decision and face judicial review on a record that encompasses the contentions and evidence of the Agency and its opponents, including responses by the Agency to criticism of its decision. While the additional formalities may involve delays and added cost, some commentators have found a clear net gain in better Agency decisionmaking.[65]

Decisions requiring procedural formalities beyond "paper hearing." Occasional court decisions have gone beyond the requirements of detailed explanation and a "paper hearing" to require, on a largely ad hoc basic, that EPA grant a limited trial-type hearing on specified issues. For example, in International Harvester Co. v. Ruckelshaus, 478 F.2d 615 (D.C. Cir. 1973), the Court of Appeals for the District of Columbia Circuit set aside the EPA's refusal to grant an extension of the 1975 deadlines for achievement of certain automotive emission limitations, relying upon inadequacies in EPA's response to manufacturer criticisms of Agency meth-

---

63. See generally Pedersen, Formal Records and Informal Rulemaking, 85 Yale L.J. 38 (1975).

64. See Alaska Airlines, Inc. v. CAB, 545 F.2d 194 (D.C. Cir. 1976); Virgin Islands Hotel Assn. v. Virgin Islands Water & Power Authority, 476 F.2d 1263 (3d Cir. 1973), *cert. denied,* 414 U.S. 1067 (1973); Home Box Office, Inc. v. FCC, 567 F.2d 9 (D.C. Cir. 1977), *cert. denied,* 434 U.S. 829, *rehearing denied,* 434 U.S. 988.

65. See Pedersen, Formal Records and Informal Rulemaking, 85 Yale L.J. 38, 59-60 (1975); Stewart, The Development of Administrative and Quasi-Constitutional Law in Judicial Review of Environmental Decisionmaking: Lessons from the Clean Air Act, 62 Iowa L. Rev. 713, 731-732 & n.89.

odologies for handling relevant data. In remanding the case, the court indicated that limited cross-examination would be an appropriate means of dealing with directly disputed technical issues. Similarly, in Appalachian Power Co. v. Ruckelshaus, 477 F.2d 495 (4th Cir. 1973), the court stated that limited cross-examination should be afforded on certain types of technical and economic issues at some point before emission limitations in a state plan became effective.[66]

5. The Vermont Yankee Litigation

Natural Resources Defense Council v. Nuclear Regulatory Commn.

547 F.2d 633 (D.C. Cir. 1976)

[The Atomic Energy Commission, whose regulatory responsibilities were later transferred to the Nuclear Regulatory Commission, concluded that it should consider the environmental hazards associated with disposal and recycling of spent nuclear fuel in deciding whether to license additional nuclear generating plants. However, instead of dealing with such issues on a case-by-case basis in individual licensing proceedings, it instituted a generic rulemaking proceeding to specify the spent fuel hazards associated with a hypothetical "typical" plant. The results of the rulemaking would then be factored into adjudicatory decisions whether to license specific plants (decisions required by statute to be made through on-the-record adjudicatory hearings) without affording further proceedings on spent fuel hazards issues.

In the generic rulemaking interested persons were given notice, opportunity to submit written comments, and opportunity for oral argument before an AEC hearing panel. There were no relevant statutory provisions suggesting that anything other than §553 notice and comment procedures were required. Demands by environmental groups that they be afforded additional procedural rights, including the right to cross-examine AEC staff and probe the factual basis for staff documents and statements with respect to spent fuel disposal, were denied.

An important issue in the rulemaking proceedings was the disposal of spent fuel. There is at present no operational method for permanent disposal of nuclear waste. The most promising alternative is burial in stable geologic formations such as salt beds. However, efforts by the AEC to identify and operate such burial facilities have not yet succeeded, and there are unresolved scientific questions concerning the stability of such burial sites and the danger of leakage of radioactive

66. A review of the actual procedures utilized by the parties upon remand in *International Harvester* and similar decisions indicated that the industries challenging EPA's position did not, in the end, insist upon the use of trial-type procedures; technical issues were instead thrashed out through exchange of documents and informal meetings between technical experts. Williams, "Hybrid Rulemaking" Under the Administrative Procedure Act: A Legal and Empirical Analysis, 42 U. Chi. L. Rev. 401, 434-435 (1975). However, the success of these informal methods may in part have been attributable to the omnipresent possibility that either party could invoke trial-type procedures.

wastes. In the rulemaking proceedings Dr. Frank Pittman of the Commission staff presented a twenty page statement describing in general terms the problems in devising a secure method of storing radioactive wastes and the types of storage facilities (aboveground and underground) that might be developed. He provided some engineering details concerning a proposed aboveground storage facility. Two pages of his statement were devoted to the permanent storage problem, asserting that substantial progress on underground disposition of wastes was being made, and that the problem would probably be resolved in the relatively near future. The hearing panel asked a few general questions about the proposed surface storage facility. A staff background paper referred to technical publications on nuclear waste disposal issues. In their oral presentation, environmental groups strongly urged that current arrangements for nuclear waste disposal were inadequate. The Commission, relying heavily on Dr. Pittman's testimony, concluded that the environmental hazards associated with spent nuclear fuel were negligible, judging that "under normal conditions" no radioactivity would be released and that the possibility of a serious accident was "incredible." It incorporated this conclusion in a table specifying numerical values for various environmental hazards that would be posed by construction of an additional nuclear plant. The Commission then sustained the grant of an operating license to a nuclear generating plant located in Vermont (Vermont Yankee) on the basis of these conclusions without affording any hearing rights on the waste disposal issue in the Vermont Yankee licensing proceeding.

Environmental groups sought review of the license grant and of the rulemaking decision. In an opinion by Chief Judge Bazelon, the court of appeals reversed both decisions by the Commission. It found that the rulemaking proceeding was defective because the Commission had failed to expose and permit adequate adversary probing of waste disposal issues. Since the rulemaking proceeding was invalid, the license grant to Vermant Yankee, which was based on the rulemaking, was also held invalid. The essence of the court's ruling with respect to the rulemaking proceeding is contained in the following excerpt from its opinion:]

In substantial part, the materials uncritically relied on by the Commission in promulgating this rule consist of extremely vague assurances by agency personnel that problems as yet unsolved will be solved. That is an insufficient record to sustain a rule limiting consideration of the environmental effects of nuclear waste disposal to the numerical values [selected by the Commission]. To the extent that uncertainties necessarily underlie predictions of this importance on the frontiers of science and technology, there is a concomitant necessity to confront and explore fully the depth and consequences of such uncertainties. Not only were the generalities relied on in this case not subject to rigorous probing — in any form — but when apparently substantial criticisms were brought to the Commission's attention, it simply ignored them, or brushed them aside without answer. Without a thorough exploration of the problems involved in waste disposal, including past mistakes, and a forthright assessment of the uncertainties and differences in expert opinion, this type of agency action cannot pass muster as reasoned decisionmaking.

Many procedural devices for creating a genuine dialogue on these issues were available to the agency — including informal conferences between intervenors and staff, document discovery, interrogatories, technical advisory committees comprised of outside experts with differing perspectives, limited cross-examination, funding independent research by intervenors, detailed annotation of technical reports, surveys of existing literature, memoranda explaining methodology. We do not presume to intrude on the agency's province by dictating to it which, if any, of these devices it must adopt to flesh out the record. It may be that no combination of the procedures mentioned above will prove adequate, and the agency will be required to develop new procedures to accomplish the innovative task of implementing NEPA through rulemaking. On the other hand, the procedures the agency adopted in this case, if administered in a more sensitive, deliberate manner, might suffice. Whatever techniques the Commission adopts, before it promulgates a rule limiting further consideration of waste disposal and reprocessing issues, it must in one way or another generate a record in which the factual issues are fully developed. . . .

It has become a commonplace among proponents of nuclear power to lament public ignorance. The public — the "guinea pigs" who will bear the consequences of either resolution of the nuclear controversy — is apprehensive. But public concern will not be quieted by proceedings like the present. . . .

The Commission's action in cutting off consideration of waste disposal and reprocessing issues in licensing proceedings based on the cursory development of the facts which occurred in this proceeding was capricious and arbitrary. . . .

[Judge TAMM issued an opinion concurring in the result. He agreed that the record in the rulemaking proceedings did not provide adequate data or analysis to support the Commission's conclusion that spent fuel hazards were negligible, and concluded that the Commission's decision that such hazards were insignificant was therefore "arbitrary and capricious." However, he took issue with the majority opinion's emphasis on additional procedures:]

. . . [T]he inadequacy of the record demands that we remand this case to the Commission in order to ensure that it has taken a hard look at the waste storage issue. I cannot, however, without qualification, endorse the approach the majority has taken to reach this result or its suggested disposition on remand.

The majority appears to require the Commission to institute further procedures of a more adversarial nature than those customarily required for informal rulemaking by the Administrative Procedure Act, 5 U.S.C. §553 (1970). . . .[67] In my view, the deficiency is not with the *type of* proceeding below, but with the completeness of the record generated. More procedure will not, in this case, guarantee a better record, and a better record can be generated without reopening the oral proceeding at this time. . . .

---

67. . . . The "concise and general statement" required by section 553 must be sufficiently complete and detailed to enable the court to accomplish its reviewing function, assuring itself that the agency has engaged in reasoned decision-making, has given serious thought to alternative rulings, and has provided reasoned explanations for controversial normative and empirical determinations. In short, "the reviewing court must satisfy itself that the requisite dialogue occurred and that it was not a sham." Wright, The Courts and the Rulemaking Process: The Limits of Judicial Review, 59 Cornell L. Rev. 375, 381 (1974).

I am also troubled by two other aspects of the majority opinion. First, I am distressed because I believe the majority opinion fails to inform the Commission in precise terms what it must do in order to comply with the court's ad hoc standard of review. The majority sends the waste storage issue back to the Commission for a "thorough ventilation." The language, of course, means very little in procedural terms. In order to aid the Commission in filling in the gaps in the record, the majority enumerates a number of procedural alternatives in varying degrees of formality, some less intrusive into agency prerogatives than others. . . . Then, heeding the Supreme Court's admonition in FPC v. Transcontinental Gas Pipe Line Corp., 423 U.S. 326 (1976) (per curiam), that we may not, except in extraordinary circumstances, specify agency procedures on remand, the majority declines to give the Commission any direction as to which procedure or combination of them will suffice. . . . The result, I believe, is entirely predictable: the Commission may or may not adopt one of the majority's suggestions, but will in any case seek to comply by mechanically generating more "negative" information respecting current problems with disposal of high level radioactive wastes and then will "overcome" this information with citations to favorable studies and articles. Ultimately, of course, the Commission must decide which information to accept and which to reject, regardless of the type of procedure used. The majority opinion appears to recognize as much when it volunteers that, "On the other hand, the procedures the agency adopted in this case, if administered in a more sensitive, deliberate manner, might suffice." . . . This time, however, the decision whether licensing an additional reactor is worth the additional environment risk would be one of policy or risk assessment and, consequently, would be reviewable only according to the customary "arbitrary, capricious" standard. . . . I believe it almost inevitable that, after fully considering the problems and alternative methods of waste disposal and storage, the Commission will reach the same conclusion and therefore see little to be gained other than delay from imposing increased adversarial procedures in excess of those customarily required.

This brings me to my second, related concern with the majority's approach. I believe the majority's insistence upon increased adversariness and procedural rigidity, uneasily combined with its non-direction toward any specific procedures, continues a distressing trend toward over-formalization of the administrative decision-making process which ultimately will impair its utility. . . . The majority's reliance upon the so-called "hybrid rulemaking" cases for its conclusion that the procedures prescribed by section 553 are inadequate for resolution of the complex issues involved in this case and its insistence that the Commission adopt more formal adversary procedures are, I believe, misplaced. . . . Remanding an agency decision with instructions to initiate such procedures is an extraordinary judicial remedy which, I believe, should be reserved for extraordinary cases.

The appropriate remedy at this point is not to impose ad hoc procedural requirements in an attempt to raise the level of petitioners' participation, already adequate under section 553, but to remand for an explanation of the basis of Dr. Pittman's statements and staff conclusions with respect to the magnitude of spent fuel environmental hazards, i.e., for the documentation which the majority finds so conspicuously lacking.... If [the Commission cannot supply such documentation] then we will have no choice but to invalidate the Commission's rule under the "arbitrary, capricious" standard; if it can, we should defer to the administrative weighing of risks and benefits of additional reactors.

[Judge Tamm's concurrence provoked a separate opinion from Judge Bazelon for himself alone:]

Separate Statement of Chief Judge BAZELON:

I add a word of my own on some of the broader implications of Judge Tamm's concurrence.

I agree that courts should be reluctant to impose particular procedures on an agency.... But I reject the implication that any techniques beyond rudimentary notice and comment are needless "over-formulization" of informal rulemaking.... Unhappily, no such bright line can be drawn between rulemaking and adjudicatory proceedings.[68]

The purpose of rulemaking was to allow public input on policy, whereas adjudication was designed to resolve disputed facts.... However, in response to the "paralysis" of the administrative process in the last decade, rulemaking has been expanded into fact-intensive areas previously thought to require adjudicatory procedures. Administrative proceedings are now common which do not fit neatly into either the rulemaking or adjudicatory category. These new proceedings are "hybrids" in the sense that they involve issues of general applicability which can be treated efficiently only in generic proceedings, but nonetheless involve factual components of such relative importance that a greater assurance of accuracy is required than that which accompanies notice and comment procedures.

The need for reliable fact-finding does not necessarily imply transplanting trial-type procedures. Factual issues in hybrid proceedings tend to be complex scientific or technical ones involving mathematical or experimental data, or other "legislative facts" peculiarly inappropriate for trial-type procedures. Agencies should innovate procedural formats responsive to the new problems created by hybrid rulemaking. Some agencies (such as FDA and EPA) have already begun to do so.

Decisions in areas touching the environment or medicine affect the lives and health of all. These interests, like the First Amendment, have "always had a special claim to judicial protection." [69] Consequently, more precision may be required than

68. The concurrence relies on Wright, The Courts and the Rulemaking Process: The Limits of Judicial Review, 59 Cornell L. Rev. 375 (1974), which explicitly assumes an idealized model differentiating sharply between "policy type rules or standards, on the one hand, and proceedings designed to adjudicate particular cases on the other." Id. 386. This model posits that accurately determining facts is relatively unimportant in rulemaking because the "ultimate shape of the rule seldom 'follows from the facts.'" Id. 379 n.15. Based on this conceptual distinction drawn from Bi-Metallic Investment Co. v. State Bd. of Equalization, 239 U.S. 441 (1915), it is argued "An adjudication is fair to the individual only if the facts are accurately found.... [I]n the rulemaking context, fairness is not identified with accuracy, and procedures designed to maximize accuracy at the cost of all other values are simply inappropriate." Id. 379.

With all due respect, this assumes away the hybrid rulemaking problem which arises primarily when rulemaking procedures are used in contexts where accurate fact-finding *is* of high relative importance.

69. Environmental Defense Fund, Inc. v. Ruckelshaus, 439 F.2d 584, 598 (1971) (Bazelon, C.J.)....

the less rigorous development of scientific facts which may attend notice and comment procedures.

. . . With customary perspicacity, Judge Friendly has observed that often it does not really matter much whether a court says the record is remanded because the procedures used did not develop sufficient evidence, or because the procedures were inadequate.[70] *From the standpoint of the administrator,* the point is the same: the procedures prescribed by §553 will not automatically produce an adequate record. Thus, although Judge Tamm vehemently opposes the concept of procedural review of informal rulemaking, he agrees to send this case back for a fuller development of the facts *even though the dictates of §553 were followed.*

Of course, important differences remain *from the standpoint of a reviewing court.* I am convinced that in highly technical areas, where judges are institutionally incompetent to weigh evidence for themselves, a focus on agency procedures will prove less intrusive, and more likely to improve the quality of decisionmaking, than judges "steeping" themselves "in technical matters to determine whether the agency has exercised a reasoned discretion." See Ethyl Corp. v. EPA, 541 F.2d 1 (1976) (en banc) (Bazelon, C.J., concurring), *cert. denied,* 426 U.S. 941 (1976).

Vermont Yankee Nuclear Power Corp. v. Natural Resources Defense Council

435 U.S. 519 (1978)

Mr. Justice REHNQUIST delivered the opinion of the Court.

In 1946, Congress enacted the Administrative Procedure Act, which as we have noted elsewhere was not only "a new, basic and comprehensive regulation of procedures in many agencies," Wong Yang Sun v. McGrath, 339 U.S. 33 (1950), but was also a legislative enactment which settled "long-continued and hard-fought contentions, and enacts a formula upon which opposing social and political have come to rest." Id., at 40. Interpreting [§553] of the Act in United States v. Allegheny-Ludlum Steel Corp., 406 U.S. 742 (1972), and United States v. Florida East Coast Railroad Co., 410 U.S. 224 (1973), we held that generally speaking this section of the Act established the maximum procedural requirements which Congress was willing to have the courts impose upon agencies in conducting rulemaking procedures.[71] Agencies are free to grant additional procedural rights in the exercise of their discretion, but reviewing courts are generally not free to impose them if the agencies have not chosen to grant them. This is not to say necessarily that there are no circumstances which would ever justify a court in overturning agency action

70. . . . Friendly, Some Kind of Hearing, 123 U. Pa. L. Rev. 1267, 1313-1314 (1975). . . .

71. While there was division in this Court in United States v. Florida East Coast Railroad Co., supra, with respect to the constitutionality of such an interpretation in a case involving ratemaking, which Mr. Justice Douglas and Mr. Justice Stewart felt was "adjudicatory" within the terms of the Act, the cases in the Court of Appeals for the District of Columbia Circuit which we review here involve rulemaking procedures in their most pristine sense.

because of a failure to employ procedures beyond those required by the statute. But such circumstances, if they exist, are extremely rare.

Even apart from the Administrative Procedure Act this Court has for more than four decades emphasized that the formulation of procedures was basically to be left within the discretion of the agencies to which Congress had confided the responsibility for substantive judgments. In FCC v. Schreiber, 381 U.S. 279, 290 (1965), the Court explicated this principle, describing it as "an outgrowth of the congressional determination that administrative agencies and administrators will be familiar with the industries which they regulate and will be in a better position than federal courts or Congress itself to design procedural rules adapted to the peculiarities of the industry and the tasks of the agency involved." . . .

It is in the light of this background of statutory and decisional law that we granted certiorari to review two judgments of the Court of Appeals for the District of Columbia Circuit [Natural Resources Defense Council v. Nuclear Regulatory Commission, supra, and Aeschliman v. Nuclear Regulatory Commission, 547 F.2d 622 (D.C. Cir. 1976), a companion decision also written by Chief Judge Bazelon. Aeschliman invalidated the Commission's grant of a construction license for a nuclear plant in Midland, Michigan, in part, because the Commission had disposed of environmental hazards from the plant's spent fuel on the basis of the rulemaking proceeding found inadequate in NRDC] because of our concern that they had seriously misread or misapplied this statutory and decisional law cautioning reviewing courts against engrafting their own notions of proper procedures upon agencies entrusted with substantive functions by Congress. 429 U.S. 1090 (1977). We conclude that the Court of Appeals has done just that in these cases, and we therefore remand them to it for further proceedings. . . .

. . . But before determining whether the Court of Appeals reached a permissible result, we must determine exactly what result it did reach, and in this case that is no mean feat. Vermont Yankee argues that the court invalidated the rule because of the inadequacy of the procedures employed in the proceedings. . . . Respondent, NRDC, on the other hand, labeling petitioner's view of the decision a "straw man," argues to this Court that the court merely held that the record was inadequate to enable the reviewing court to determine whether the agency had fulfilled its statutory obligation . . .

After a thorough examination of the opinion itself, we conclude that while the matter is not entirely free from doubt, the majority of the Court of Appeals struck down the rule because of the perceived inadequacies of the procedures employed in the rulemaking proceedings. The court first determined the intervenors' primary argument to be "that the decision to preclude 'discovery or cross-examination' denied them a meaningful opportunity to participate in the proceedings as guaranteed by due process." . . . The court then went on to frame the issue for decision thusly: "Thus, we are called upon to decide whether the procedures provided by the agency were sufficient to ventilate the issues." . . . The court conceded that absent extraordinary circumstances it is improper for a reviewing court to prescribe the procedural format an agency must follow, but it likewise clearly thought it entirely appropriate to "scrutinize the record as a whole to insure that genuine opportunities to participate in a meaningful way were provided. . . ." . . . The court also refrained from actually ordering the agency to follow any specific procedure, . . . but there is little doubt in our minds that the ineluctable mandate of the court's decision is that the procedures afforded during the hearings were inadequate. . . .

In prior opinions we have intimated that even in a rulemaking proceeding when an agency is making a "quasi-judicial" determination by which a very small number of persons are " 'exceptionally affected, in each case upon individual grounds,' " in some circumstances additional procedures may be required in order to afford the aggrieved individuals due process. United States v. Florida East Coast Ry. Co., 410 U.S. at 242, 245, quoting from Bi-Metallic Investment Co. v. State Board of Equalization, 239 U.S. 441, 446 (1915). It might also be true, although we do not think the issue is presented in this case and accordingly do not decide it, that a totally unjustified departure from well settled agency procedures of long standing might require judicial correction.

But this much is absolutely clear. Absent constitutional constraints or extremely compelling circumstances "the administrative agencies 'should be free to fashion their own rules of procedure and to pursue method of inquiry capable of permitting them to discharge their multitudinous duties.' " Federal Communications Comm'n v. Schreiber, 381 U.S. 279, 290 (1965), quoting from Federal Communications Comm'n v. Pottsville Broadcasting Co., 309 U.S. 134, 143 (1940). [The Court referred to additional decisions, some antedating the APA, upholding agency procedural flexibility.]

Respondent NRDC argues that [§553] of the Administrative Procedure Act merely establishes lower procedural bounds and that a court may routinely require more than the minimum when an agency's proposed rule addresses complex or technical factual issues or "Issues of Great Public Import." [In rejecting this contention, the Court relied upon the legislative history of the APA.] The Senate Report explains what eventually became [§553(c)] thusly:

"This subsection states . . . the minimum requirements of public rule making procedure short of statutory hearing. Under it agencies might in addition confer with industry advisory committees, consult organizations, hold informal 'hearings,' and the like. Considerations of practicality, necessity, and public interest . . . will naturally govern the agency's determination of the extent to which public proceedings should go. Matters of great import, or those where the public submission of facts will be either useful to the agency or a protection to the public, should naturally be accorded more elaborate public procedures." S. Rep. No. 752, 79th Cong., 1st Sess., 14-15 (1945).

". . . The bill is an outline of minimum essential rights and procedures. . . . It affords private parties a means of knowing what their rights are and how they may protect them. . . .

". . . [The bill contains] the essentials of the different forms of administrative proceedings. . . ." H.R. Rep. No. 1980, 79th Cong., 2d Sess., 9, 16-17 (1946).

. . . [A]ll this leaves little doubt that Congress intended that the discretion of the *agencies* and not that of the courts be exercised in determining when extra procedural devices should be employed.

There are compelling reasons for construing [§553] in this manner. In the first place, if courts continually review agency proceedings to determine whether the agency employed procedures which were, in the court's opinion, perfectly tailored to reach what the court perceives to be the "best" or "correct" result, judicial review would be totally unpredictable. And the agencies, operating under this vague injunction to employ the "best" procedures and facing the threat of reversal if they did not, would undoubtedly adopt full adjudicatory procedures in every instance. Not only would this totally disrupt the statutory scheme, through which Congress enacted "a formula upon which opposing social and political forces have come to rest," Wong Yang Sun v. McGrath, supra, at 40, but all the inherent advantages of informal rulemaking would be totally lost.[72] . . .

Finally, and perhaps most importantly, this sort of review fundamentally misconceives the nature of the standard for judicial review of an agency rule. The court below uncritically assumed that additional procedures will automatically result in a more adequate record because it will give interested parties more of an opportunity to participate and contribute to the proceedings. But informal rulemaking need not be based solely on the transcript of a hearing held before an agency. Indeed, the agency need not even hold a formal hearing. See 5 U.S.C. §553(c) (1976 ed.) Thus, the adequacy of the "record" in this type of proceeding is not correlated directly to the type of procedural devices employed, but rather turns on whether the agency has followed the statutory mandate of the Administrative Procedure Act or other relevant statutes. If the agency is compelled to support the rule which it ultimately adopts with the type of record produced only after a full adjudicatory hearing, it simply will have no choice but to conduct a full adjudicatory hearing prior to promulgating every rule. In sum, this sort of unwarranted judicial examination of perceived procedural shortcomings of a rulemaking proceeding can do nothing but seriously interfere with that process prescribed by Congress. . . .

There remains, of course, the question of whether the challenged rule finds sufficient justification in the administrative proceedings that it should be upheld by the reviewing court. Judge Tamm, concurring in the result reached by the majority of the Court of Appeals, thought that it did not. There are also intimations in the majority opinion which suggest that the judges who joined it likewise may have thought the administrative proceedings an insufficient basis upon which to predicate the rule in question. We accordingly remand so that the Court of Appeals may review the rule as the Administrative Procedure Act provides. We have made it abundantly clear before that when there is a contemporaneous explanation of the agency decision, the validity of that action must "stand or fall on the propriety of that finding, judged, of course, by the appropriate standard of review. If that finding is not sustainable on the administrative record made, then the Comptroller's decision must be vacated and the matter remanded to him for further consideration." Camp v. Pitts, 411 U.S. 138, 143, (1973). See also SEC v. Chenery Corp., 318 U.S. 80 (1943). The court should engage in this kind of review and not stray beyond

---

72. See Wright, The Courts and the Rulemaking Process: The Limits of Judicial Review, 59 Cornell L. Rev. 375, 387-388 (1974).

the judicial province to explore the procedural format or to impose upon the agency its own notion of which procedures are "best" or most likely to further some vague, undefined public good.

[The Court also rejected additional rulings by the Court of Appeals in the *Aeschliman* case that the Commission had violated the National Environmental Policy Act by failing to consider conservation alternatives to the proposed nuclear plant, and had violated the Atomic Energy Act by failing to require greater detail in the report of its Advisory Committee on Reactor Safety on the proposed plant.]

. . . Nuclear energy may some day be a cheap, safe source of power or it may not. But Congress has made a choice to at least try nuclear energy, establishing a reasonable review process in which courts are to play only a limited role. The fundamental policy questions appropriately resolved in Congress and in the state legislatures are *not* subject to reexamination in the federal courts under the guise of judicial review of agency action. Time may prove wrong the decision to develop nuclear energy, but it is Congress or the States within their appropriate agencies which must eventually make that judgment. In the meantime courts should perform their appointed function. . . . It is to insure a fully informed and well-considered decision, not necessarily a decision the judges of the Court of Appeals or of this Court would have reached had they been members of the decisionmaking unit of the agency. Administrative decisions should be set aside in this context, as in every other, only for substantial procedural or substantive reasons as mandated by statute, . . . not simply because the court is unhappy with the result reached. . . .

Reversed and remanded.

Mr. Justice BLACKMUN and Mr. Justice POWELL took no part in the consideration or decision of these cases.

Notes and Questions on Vermont Yankee

1. The Supreme Court's *Vermont Yankee* opinion reads the APA to preclude, absent unspecified exceptional circumstances, judicial requirements that agencies utilize additional or hybrid procedures beyond those specified in the 1946 APA or other relevant statutes. Is this reading persuasive or wise? Should we rely entirely on Congress or agencies themselves to adopt procedural innovations to resolve the problems generated for reviewing courts by increased administrative use of rulemaking to devise and implement policy?

As previously noted, pp. 501-502 supra, Congress has in a number of recent statutes required specific agencies exercising particular regulatory functions to utilize hybrid procedures in rulemaking. A few agencies have, on their own initiative, adopted hybrid procedures of the "paper hearing" type, and the Administrative Conference of the United States has recommended wider agency adoption of such procedures.[73]

73. See U.S. Food and Drug Administration, Administrative Practices and Procedures, 40 Fed. Reg. 22950-23046 (1975) (amending various sections of Ch. I, 21 C.F.R.); Recommendation 76-3, 1976 Report of the Administrative Conference of the United States 43-47 (1977).

But would these initiatives have occurred in the absence of judicial prodding through decisions, such as *Mobil Oil* and *NRDC*, imposing judge-made hybrid procedural requirements? [74]

2. Does *Vermont Yankee* effectively overrule *Mobil Oil?*

3. While relying upon the assertedly preclusive intent of the APA, the Court's *Vermont Yankee* opinion raises two additional objections to judicial imposition of procedural requirements beyond those imposed by statutes: First, agencies will be uncertain as to what procedures reviewing courts may find necessary; as a defensive response to the uncertainty, they will adopt an elaborate panoply of formal procedures that will cripple the administrative process. Second, courts will manipulate procedural requirements in order to control, indirectly, policy decisions that should properly be made by agencies.[75] How weighty are these objections? Do they apply with equal force to *any* effort by courts to control agencies' exercise of discretion? Or does judicial imposition of procedural formalities beyond those required by statute involve special drawbacks not presented by other judicial techniques for controlling agency discretion?

4. The Supreme Court's *Vermont Yankee* opinion castigates the Court of Appeals majority for imposing procedures not required by statute. However, following the rationale expressed in Judge Tamm's concurring opinion, it acknowledges that courts may scrutinize the adequacy of the administrative "record" developed in notice and comment rulemaking, and may remand for further proceedings if the record is not adequate to permit a court to review and sustain the agency's decision on the merits.

Are these two aspects of the Court's decision consistent? The APA does not require agencies to create an evidentiary "record" in notice and comment rulemaking.[76] Nor does it authorize reviewing courts to remand for additional proceed-

---

74. For debate over the respective role of courts, agencies, and Congress in devising new procedures in response to changing patterns of administrative decisionmaking, compare Stewart, Vermont Yankee and the Evolution of Administrative Procedure, 91 Harv. L. Rev. 1805 (1978), with Byse, Vermont Yankee and the Evolution of Administrative Procedure: A Somewhat Different View, 91 Harv. L. Rev. 1823 (1978).

Should the APA be amended to require "hybrid" procedures in rulemaking? What should the content of those procedures be? Should they apply to all rulemaking other than "on the record" rulemaking subject to §§ 556-557 of the APA? The House Judiciary Committee has proposed an amendment to the APA, §553, providing for a documentary record in notice and comment rulemaking in terms similar to the "paper hearing" requirements developed by courts. See H.R. 12048, 94th Cong., 2d Sess. (1976), reprinted in H.R. Rep. No. 1014, 94th Cong., 2d Sess. 20-23 (1976).

75. For elaboration of this objection, see Breyer, Vermont Yankee and the Courts' Role in the Nuclear Power Controversy, 91 Harv. L. Rev. 1833 (1978). Professor Breyer argues that the Court of Appeals' effort in *Vermont Yankee* to impose stringent control over administrative licensing of nuclear plants will lead to increased reliance by the United States on construction of coal-fired plants to meet energy needs. He marshalls evidence for the proposition that coal is a more environmentally hazardous source of energy than nuclear material, and concludes that in any event the choice between the two sources should be made by administrators and Congress rather than the courts. A different view of the courts' role is presented in Stewart, Vermont Yankee and the Evolution of Administrative Procedure, 91 Harv. L. Rev. 1805 (1978).

76. As previously explained, pp. 478-479, the notice and comment provisions of §553 contemplate a "legislative" model of decision that does not involve creation of a "record" forming

ings when they judge the record inadequate even though an agency has fully complied with the procedural requirements of §553.[77] By endorsing a requirement of an "adequate record" in notice and comment rulemaking, has the Court violated its own ban on procedural innovation by courts? [78] Is an "adequate record" requirement subject to the very same objections which the Supreme Court levied on Judge Bazelon's approach: uncertainty in the content of the requirement and danger that it will be manipulated by reviewing courts in order to influence substantive policy outcomes? To what extent can the issue of the adequacy of the record be divorced from the procedures employed by agencies in making decisions? Will agencies continue to employ "paper hearing" or other "hybrid" procedures in order to avoid the danger of judicial remands based on the inadequacy of the rulemaking "record"?

5. What is the impact of *Vermont Yankee* on the debate between Judges Bazelon and Leventhal in *Ethyl*, pp. 304-306 supra, over the proper approach to judicial review of discretionary choices by agencies? Clearly the Supreme Court has rejected Judge Bazelon's emphasis on innovative procedural requirements as a means of controlling and improving such choices. Is *Vermont Yankee* equally fatal to Judge Leventhal's "hard look" approach? If courts are precluded from imposing procedures beyond those specified in §553, how can they determine whether agencies have taken a "hard look" at all relevant evidence and analysis? Is *Vermont Yankee* a signal for judicial retreat from efforts to review or control agency discretion?

6.   The Scope of Judicial Review of Agency Fact-Finding in Rulemaking

The increased use by agencies of rulemaking rather than formal adjudication in order to formulate and implement policy has given fresh importance to the appropriate scope of judicial review of agency fact-finding in rulemaking.

Where a relevant statute requires on the record rulemaking and triggers §§ 556-557, no special difficulties are presented because §§ 556-557 generate an evidentiary

---

a basis for review. The "substantial evidence" standard of review, which could serve as the basis of an "adequate record" requirement, is limited by §706(2)(E) to proceedings governed by §§ 556-557 or otherwise required by statute to be conducted on the record after opportunity for agency hearing, and therefore does not apply to notice and comment rulemaking.

In enacting the APA Congress apparently contemplated that facts needed to permit judicial review of the merits of notice and comment rulemaking or other informal agency decisions would be developed by reviewing courts themselves through a de novo evidentiary hearing. See Auerbach, Informal Rulemaking: A Proposed Relationship Between Administrative Procedures and Judicial Review, 72 Nw. U.L. Rev. 15, 25 & n.51 (1977), quoting from the legislative history of the APA:

"Congressman Walter, who guided passage of the APA on the floor of the House explained: 'where there is not statutory administrative hearing to which review is confined, the facts pertinent to any relevant question of law must of course be tried and determined de novo by the reviewing court.' Cong. Rec., May 24, 1946."

77. Recall that Chief Judge Bazelon criticizes Judge Tamm's position on this ground, see p. 516 supra.

78. The Supreme Court has also ruled that agencies, in order to facilitate judicial review of the merits, may be required to create an "adequate record" in informal adjudication, see pp. 524-530 infra, even though no such requirement is imposed by the APA.

record for review and APA §706(2)(E) directs the court to employ a "substantial evidence" standard of review. In theory, the scope of review is thus identical to that involved in judicial review of fact-finding in formal adjudication, although the greater role in many rulemaking proceedings of "legislative facts," specialized inferences, and policy judgments may in practice make for greater deference to agencies in rulemaking.

By contrast §706 does not specify what standard courts should use in reviewing fact-finding when an agency engages in notice and comment rulemaking. The draftsmen of the APA may have contemplated that reviewing courts would, in the absence of an agency record for review, themselves take evidence on the relevant factual issues; if so, the applicable scope of review could be §706(2)(F), directing courts to set aside agency action and findings "unwarranted by the facts to the extent that the facts are subject to trial de novo by the reviewing court." [79] But courts rejected this procedure as unduly cumbersome, and attempted to review informal rulemaking as best they could on the basis of the agency's explanations, the comments submitted by interested persons, and the briefs filed by the parties to the review proceedings. In order to provide a formula for judicial review of fact-finding in these circumstances, courts adopted the §706(2)(A) "arbitrary or capricious" standard, which, as we have seen in Chapter 4, is also utilized to review discretionary agency lawmaking.[80]

However labeled, the lack of an evidentiary record must necessarily attenuate judicial review of fact-finding in informal rulemaking, and the growing frustration of reviewing courts with such a situation goes far to explain the increased tendency to remand troublesome cases for fuller explanation.[81]

The development, by statute or judicial decision, of "paper hearing" or comparable hybrid rulemaking procedures creates further difficulty in defining the appropriate standard of review. Because such procedures tend to generate an evidentiary record of the basis for the agency's actions, it might be thought logical to employ a "substantial evidence" standard, but this would seem inconsistent with APA §706(2)(E), which restricts "substantial evidence" review to formal rulemaking governed by §§ 556-557.[82]

---

79. See Williams, "Hybrid Rulemaking" Under the Administrative Procedure Act: A Legal and Empirical Analysis, 42 U. Chi. L. Rev. 401, 417-424 (1975).

80. E.g., Automotive Parts & Accessories Assn. v. Boyd, 407 F.2d 330 (D.C. Cir. 1968); Boating Industry Assn. v. Boyd, 409 F.2d 408 (7th Cir. 1969).

81. See, e.g., Kennecott Copper v. EPA, p. 509 supra, at 336.

82. The choice of an appropriate standard is further clouded by Congress' practice of specifying a "substantial evidence" standard of review for informal, notice and comment rulemaking. See, e.g., the provisions of the Occupational Safety and Health Act, discussed p. 501 supra. Judicial efforts to reconcile these seemingly conflicting provisions include Industrial Union Dept., AFL-CIO v. Hodgson, 499 F.2d 467 (D.C. Cir. 1974); Associated Industries of New York, Inc. v. Department of Labor, 487 F.2d 342 (2d Cir. 1973); and Union Oil of California v. FPC, 542 F.2d 1036 (9th Cir. 1976). As illustrated by *Union Oil*, the prevailing judicial tendency is to regard the "substantial evidence" standard as evincing a congressional mood in favor of somewhat stricter review than customary under the traditionally utilized "arbitrary and capricious" test, and to rely upon the "substantial evidence" provision to demand a more complete documentary basis for judicial review than is customary in notice and comment rulemaking. But see Superior Oil Co. v. FERC, 563 F.2d 191 (5th Cir. 1977).

In instances where hybrid procedures generate an evidentiary record, some commentators have argued that either the "substantial evidence" or "arbitrary and capricious" standard of review can logically be applied, and that the "substantial evidence" standard is decisively more demanding.[83] Yet in the end one may be led to Judge Friendly's conclusion that the conceptual controversy between "arbitrary and capricious" and "substantial evidence" review of notice and comment or hybrid rulemaking is in large measure semantic.[84] The extent of judicial review of agency fact-finding in rulemaking is less likely to turn on the label attached to the standard of review than the extent and nature of the evidentiary materials generated, the judge's personal willingness to delve into complex factual issues, and her attitude toward the agency in question and the merits of its decision. Hybrid rulemaking procedures and insistence by reviewing courts of more complete records and explanations by agencies in rulemaking have added to the burdens of judicial review by generating massive, untidy records unillumined by cross-examination.[85] Recall the materials on the "hard look" doctrine, pp. 298-306 supra, discussing the limited capacity of courts to review complex technical issues. Ironically, insistence on more elaborate procedures or more complete records in rulemaking may ultimately serve to highlight the drawbacks of judicial review as a control on agency discretion.

Question: Does *Vermont Yankee* clarify the appropriate scope of judicial review of agency fact-finding in notice and comment rulemaking?

7. *Procedural Requirements and Judicial Review in Informal Adjudication*

(You should now review the decision in *Overton Park*, supra p. 276, with particular attention to the discussion of the procedural requirements which the agency must follow and the means by which the court may review informal adjudication.)

Section 554 of the APA (together with §§ 556-557), specifies trial-type procedures for "every case of adjudication required by statute to be determined on the record after opportunity for a hearing," but the APA contains no procedural requirements for informal adjudication where "on the record" hearings are not required by some other relevant statute.

Informal adjudication is a broad residual category including all agency actions that are not rulemaking and which are not required to be conducted through "on

83. See Verkuil, Judicial Review of Informal Rulemaking, 60 Va. L. Rev. 185 (1974); Wright, The Courts and the Rulemaking Process: The Limits of Judicial Review, 59 Cornell L. Rev. 375, 390-392 (1974); Note, Model Review of Informal Rulemaking: Recommendation 74-4 of the Administrative Conference of the United States, 1975 Duke L.J. 479. For additional discussion, see Note, Judicial Review of the Facts in Informal Rulemaking: A Proposed Standard, 84 Yale L.J. 1750 (1975).

84. Associated Industries of New York, Inc. v. Department of Labor, 487 F.2d 342, 349 (2d Cir. 1973).

85. Cf. Florida Peach Growers Assn. v. Department of Labor, 489 F.2d 120 (5th Cir. 1974); Ethyl Corp. v. EPA, 541 F.2d 1, 66-68 (D.C. Cir. 1976) (concurring opinion of Bazelon, J.), *cert. denied,* 426 U.S. 941 (1976).

the record" hearings. It has been estimated that 90 percent of the actions taken by government with respect to individuals consists of informal adjudication.[86]

Compared to the number of agency actions taken through informal adjudication, judicial review of such actions is relatively infrequent. Some agency decisions are of such slight consequence that it is not worth the cost to the complainant to seek review. Many cases of informal adjudication, such as bank licensing, involve the exercise of broad discretionary powers that until quite recently were thought to be beyond judicial review and even today are difficult to reverse in court. The absence of formal agency procedures, a record, and agency findings of fact and conclusions of law in informal adjudication makes it very difficult for a court to review the rationality of the agency's fact-finding, its conformance with law, and the reasonableness of its exercise of discretion.

One way to facilitate judicial review would be simply to insist on more formal decision-making.[87] This might be accomplished by expansive construction of §554 to extend the application of the trial-type procedural requirements in §§ 554 and 556-557. However, courts have often declined to find §554 applicable in the absence of statutory language indicating that decisions should be made on the basis of a formal evidentiary record after opportunity for an agency hearing.[88] If the require-

---

86. See Gardner, The Procedures by Which Informal Action Is Taken, 24 Ad. L. Rev. 155 (1972). There is an almost infinite diversity in informal adjudication; examples include the establishment of agricultural marketing quotas under the Agricultural Adjustment Act of 1938, the renewal of grain inspectors' licenses under the Grain Standards Act, issuance of permits to remove objects of antiquity under the Antiquity Act, grants and loans by the Bureau of Indian Affairs, outer continental shelf oil and gas leasing under the Outer Continental Shelf Lands Act, and meat and poultry inspections and plant quarantine certifications. The number of informal adjudicatory actions taken by an agency under a program may vary from infrequent Federal Maritime Commission subsidy contracts for ship construction to the annual processing of 113 million income tax returns or issuance of 310 million payments to social security beneficiaries. The dollar amounts may range from the few cents involved in a claim for overdue postage to several billion dollars in the development of new aircraft. See Gardner, id.; Verkuil, A Study of Informal Adjudication Procedures, 43 U. Chi. L. Rev. 739 (1976).

87. See P. Strauss, Rules, Adjudications, and Other Sources of Law in an Executive Department: Reflections on the Interior Department's Administration of the Mining Law, 74 Colum. L. Rev. 1231 (1974); H. Vickery, Judicial Review of Informal Agency Action: A Case Study of Shareholder Proposal No-Action Letters, 28 Hastings L.J. 307 (1976).

88. A more liberal construction of §554's applicability is reflected in a recent decision under the Bank Holding Company Act of 1956, 12 U.S.C. §1843 (1970). The Act provides that no bank holding company can acquire ownership or control of any nonbanking company unless the nonbanking company's activities are "so closely related to banking or managing or controlling banks as to be a proper incident thereto." 12 U.S.C. §1843(c)(8) (1970). The Act originally stated that the agency's decision be made "after due notice and hearing, and on the basis of the record made at such hearing, by order." 12 U.S.C. §1843(c)(8) (1956). In 1970 the latter section was amended to require only "opportunity for hearing" and to allow the agency to proceed either by order or by regulation. In Independent Bankers Assn. of Georgia v. Board of Governors of the Federal Reserve System, 516 F.2d 1206 (D.C. Cir. 1975), Judge Wilkey decided that where "the Board acts by order, as it must in judging the merit of individual applications where adjudicative facts are in dispute, it is required to accord a full hearing to interested parties who present a material factual contest to such applications," and ordered the Board to use formal adjudicatory procedures. Judge Wilkey distinguished Florida East Coast as concerning an essentially legislative determination, whereas here the Board's function was "quasi-judicial," and the relevant factual issues included the character of the holding company applicant and the economic effects of its proposal. But do these facts have any significance beyond establishing that

ments of §554 of the APA are not triggered by statutory language, they may still be made applicable by due process considerations. Wong Yang Sung v. McGrath, 339 U.S. 33 (1950), held that even though the relevant statute says nothing of a "hearing," due process required a trial-type hearing in deportation cases, that the statute should therefore be read to include an on-the-record hearing requirement in order to preserve its constitutionality, and that the requirements of §554 therefore apply. However, few instances of informal adjudication affect personal liberties as profoundly as did the deportation order in *Wong Yang Sung*.[89]

How are courts to review informal adjudication when neither relevant statutes, due process, nor the APA imposes any procedural requirements? There are two minimum requirements for judicial review. First, the court must in some manner be apprised of the agency's decision and the legal grounds to justify it. See SEC v. Chenery Corp., supra, pp. 334-351. Second, there must be some means for judicial evaluation of the relevant facts to ensure that the legal rationale for the agency's action has an adequate basis in fact. These requisites could be met if an agency prepared findings of fact and conclusions of law every time it engaged in informal adjudication, and if it simultaneously prepared a documentary record reflecting the factual bases for its decision. However, courts have been reluctant to require contemporaneous findings and conclusions, and even more reluctant to impose a documentary record procedure, fearing that such requirements would impair the speed, cheapness, and flexibility of informal adjudication.[90]

a. Administrative Findings and Conclusions

Overton Park refused to require contemporaneous findings and conclusions by the Secretary of Transportation in a highway routing case, perhaps because the Secretary's action was unambiguous and the legal grounds therefore could be

---

the Board's action consists of adjudication rather than rulemaking? Are they relevant in deciding whether the adjudication should be undertaken through trial-type procedures? More generally, does *Florida East Coast*, which narrowly construed the application of APA procedural formalities in rulemaking, indicate that courts should likewise narrowly construe the applicability of procedural formalities in adjudication? See pp. 736-737 infra, where this issue is discussed in the context of the separation of functions requirements of §554(d).

See generally Note, The Requirement of Formal Adjudication under Section 5 of the Administrative Procedure Act, 12 Harv. J. Legis. 194 (1975).

89. *Wong Yang Sung* is reproduced and discussed further at pp. 731-740 infra.

Even if due process does not dictate use of a trial-type hearing and therefore trigger the requirements of §554, might the Constitution compel lesser procedural protections, such as notice of the proposed action, an opportunity to comment, and an explanation of the agency's decision? Many informal adjudications concern the distribution of government benefits, grants, and other advantageous opportunities which until recently were thought not to be protected by due process. We consider in Chapter 7 the application of due process safeguards to the disbursement of government advantages, and the extent to which such safeguards should consist of trial-type hearings or some alternative form of proceeding. After reading *Wong Yang Sung* and those materials, you should consider what degree of due process procedural formality suffices to trigger the provisions of §§ 554-557.

90. See, e.g., California Legislative Council for Older Americans v. Weinberger, 375 F. Supp. 216 (S.D. Cal. 1974) (expressed fear of "bureaucratic delay").

readily inferred. Subsequently in Camp v. Pitts, 411 U.S. 138 (1973), the Supreme Court accepted as adequate a three-sentence finding by the Comptroller of the Currency denying a branch bank application which indicated that the denial had been based on a lack of need for additional banking services in the community. Lower courts have accepted contemporaneous statements by the Comptroller that he had "considered" the relevant statutory factors, or required no explanation at all when the grounds for his action were tolerably clear.[91] While this relaxed approach may enable reviewing courts to determine whether agencies have complied with relevant statutory directives, is it adequate for review of discretionary judgments? Can a court engage in a "hard look" at agency exercises of discretion without a rather extensive explanation by the agency of its choices? [92] Consider also that a practice of contemporaneous findings and conclusions might improve the quality of administrative decisions even if they are not later subject to judicial review.

In cases where an agency has refused to take enforcement action in behalf of the beneficiaries of a regulatory scheme, courts have been more insistent upon contemporaneous explanation by the agency of its decision.[93] Would it be unduly burdensome or productive of delay to require informal explanations in every case of informal adjudication? [94]

b. Developing an Evidentiary Record

A contemporaneous administrative record, composed of the principal documents considered in the course of decision, would go far toward resolving the

---

91. See First Bank & Trust Co. v. Smith, 545 F.2d 752 (1st Cir. 1976); First National Bank of Homstead v. Watson, 363 F. Supp. 466 (D.D.C. 1973).

92. See Scott, In Quest of Reason: The Licensing Decisions of the Federal Banking Agencies, 42 U. Chi. L. Rev. 235, 268 (1975), concluding that unless the Comptroller is required to offer a full explanation of his decision, courts are faced with the Hobson's choice of "pro forma endorsement" of the Comptroller's decision or "taking over policy judgments" that are properly the administrator's responsibility. For discussion and criticism of Professor Scott's analysis, see Murphy, What Reason for the Quest?: A Response to Professor Scott, 42 U. Chi. L. Rev. 299 (1975).

93. See Dunlop v. Bachowski, 421 U.S. 560 (1975) (refusal of Labor Dept. to institute formal proceedings against assertedly irregular union election). In Dunlop the Court based its requirement of findings and explanation on the particular statute in question, the Labor-Management Reporting and Disclosure Act. In a separate opinion dissenting in part, Justice Rehnquist argued that the requirement of an explanation should have been based on §555(e). How broad is the reach of §555(e)? For examples of its application, see Ross v. United States, 531 F.2d 839 (7th Cir. 1976) (denial of parole); Meadeville Master Antenna, Inc. v. FCC, 443 F.2d 282 (3d Cir. 1971) (denial of request for waiver of agency regulations).

94. Where agency findings and explanations are required and the agency has failed to satisfy that requirement, the normal course is to remand for further agency proceedings. However, in a few cases courts have permitted the agency to elucidate its action through briefs or other submissions in the course of judicial review. See California Legislative Council for Older Americans v. Weinberger, 375 F. Supp. 216 (S.D. Cal. 1974). Is this consistent with Chenery I and the disapproval in Overton Park of "post hoc rationalization"? On the other hand, might a requirement of remand in every case of inadequately explained informal adjudication be excessively burdensome and time consuming?

problem of judicial review of the factual basis for informal adjudicatory decisions.[95] Such a record would be analogous to "paper hearing" procedures in informal rule-making, see p. 509 supra. But courts have refused to impose such a requirement in informal adjudication. In the absence or inadequacy of contemporaneous records, there are three basic alternatives a reviewing court might use in order to determine the factual basis for the agency's action:

(1) The court could require the agency decisionmakers to state — through affidavits, deposition, or testimony in court — the factual grounds on which they relied in making their decision.

(2) The court could remand the entire proceeding to the agency for an assembly of the relevant evidence and a fresh determination.

(3) The court could hold an evidentiary hearing and itself amass the relevant evidence needed to determine whether the agency's fact-findings were reasonable.

Overton Park rejected the de novo hearing alternative, concluding that APA §706 reserved that procedure for cases where agency fact-finding capabilities were wholly inadequate, or where new factual issues are raised in judicial enforcement of agency sanctions. See p. 278 supra. While commentators have criticized this narrow view of the APA de novo hearing procedure,[96] it was reaffirmed in Camp v. Pitts, 411 U.S. 138 (1973), where the Supreme Court reversed a line of decisions in the Fourth Circuit requiring a judicial trial de novo when the Comptroller of the Currency had failed to develop an administrative record in branch banking decisions.[97] Even before Camp v. Pitts, many lower courts were reluctant to use de novo judicial hearings, stressing that this procedure deprived reviewing courts of agencies' specialized experience in fact-finding.[98]

Overton Park left to the discretion of the trial court the choice between the alternatives (1) requiring agency officials to elaborate upon their prior decision, and (2) remanding for creation of a complete administrative record and a fresh decision. However, the Court held that submission of affidavits by agency officials would not provide an adequate means, under alternative (1), of discovering the factual bases for the Secretary's prior decision, because such affidavits often consist of post hoc rationalization.

On remand, the district court in Overton Park decided to permit the use of pro-

95. Such a record might also compensate for the agency's failure to issue a contemporaneous explanation for its decision.

Even if this practice were followed, the administrative record offered by the agency might not adequately reflect the material actually considered in making the decision; where such danger is shown, courts have permitted discovery of the materials utilized by the agency in making its decision. E.g., Nuclear Data, Inc. v. AEC, 364 F. Supp. 423 (N.D. Ill. 1973).

96. See Nathanson, Probing the Mind of the Administrator: Hearing Variations and Standards of Judicial Review under the Administrative Procedure Act and Other Federal Statutes, 75 Colum. L. Rev. 721 (1975).

97. See, e.g., First National Bank of Smithfield, North Carolina v. Saxon, 352 F.2d 267 (4th Cir. 1965). Prior to this decision the Comptroller had not offered detailed explanations or an evidentiary record for his decisions for over a century. For review and analysis, see authorities cited at note 92, supra.

98. See, e.g., Secretary of Labor v. Farino, 490 F.2d 885 (7th Cir. 1973).

cedures discovery the Secretary and took testimony from his assistants in order to determine the factual basis for the Secretary's prior decision. See p. 281 supra. Despite its potential for harassment of agency officials, a number of other courts have also elected this alternative.[99] Other courts have refused to permit discovery or order testimony by agency officials absent a preliminary showing of bad faith, and have instead remanded for preparation by the agency of a more complete administrative record and reconsideration of the decision.[100]

In authorizing discovery or examination at trial of administrative officials regarding their decision making, *Overton Park* departed from the longstanding rule announced in United States v. Morgan, 313 U.S. 409 (1941). *Morgan* involved rate-setting by the Secretary of Agriculture. Although a decision and formal findings had been issued in the Secretary's name, litigants challenging the rate order alleged that the Secretary had not participated personally in the decision, in violation of statutory provisions, investing him with decisional responsibility, and sought discovery of the Secretary concerning the extent of his participation. Pointing out that it would be improper to examine a judge concerning his involvement in a judicial decision, the Court stated in broad terms that it is also improper to "probe the mental processes" of administrative decisionmakers. The apparent inconsistency between *Morgan* and *Overton Park* has since been explained by one court of appeals on the ground that in *Morgan* there was an administrative record and formal decision to serve as the basis for judicial review, whereas in *Overton Park* there were no such materials and the relevant facts had to be generated by the reviewing court.[101] If broadly adopted, this rationale would give administrators a strong incentive to prepare some form of decisional record and findings in order to avoid delay, harassment and potential embarrassment through discovery or examination at trial.

Questions

In Camp v. Pitts the Supreme Court endorsed the practice of remanding to the agency for development by it of a factual record, even though the APA does not require preparation of such a record in informal adjudication. Is this practice now barred by the Court's subsequent decision in *Vermont Yankee*?

Overton Park rejects the possibility of developing the relevant facts through litigation affidavits filed by the responsive agency officials inviting "post hoc rationalization." Do not the alternatives of post decision testimony or discovery, or remand

99. See, e.g., D.C. Federation of Civic Assns. v. Volpe, 434 F.2d 436 (D.C. Cir. 1970); D.C. Federation of Civic Assns. v. Volpe, 459 F.2d 1231 (D.C. Cir. 1972), *cert. denied*, 405 U.S. 1030 (1972); Businessmen Affected by the Second Year Action Plan v. District of Columbia, 442 F.2d 883 (D.C. Cir. 1971); GTE Sylvania Inc. v. Consumer Product Safety Comm., 404 F. Supp. 352 (D. Del. 1975); Nuclear Data Inc. v. AEC, 364 F. Supp. 423 (N.D. Ill. 1973).

100. E.g., South Terminal Corp. v. EPA, 504 F.2d 646 (1st Cir. 1974); Schicke v. United States, 346 F. Supp. 417 (D. Conn. 1972). The choice between remand and judicial discovery may depend in part on whether the reviewing court in the first instance is a district court, where discovery is readily available, or a court of appeals.

101. See National Nutritional Foods Ass'n. v. FDA, 491 F.2d 1141 (2d Cir. 1974). *National Nutritional Foods* and *Morgan* are considered at greater length in Chapter 8.

for further proceedings also invite "post hoc rationalization"? Should the Supreme Court have settled on one alternative or the other instead of leaving the choice to the district courts? [102]

What standard should the courts apply in reviewing agency fact-finding in informal adjudication: "Substantial evidence," "arbitrary and capricious," or some other standard? Should the scope of review depend upon which mechanism (remand, official testimony, etc.) is selected by reviewing courts for developing a record of the relevant evidence?

C. The Scope of the Right to Decision on the Record

1. The Need for Facts to be Found in the Record and the Official Notice Problem

One of the most basic principles of adversary jurisprudence is that the evidentiary facts upon which a decision rests must be found in an evidentiary record constituting the exclusive basis for decision. Without this rule, hearings could be rendered meaningless and judicial review might be totally frustrated. Section 7(d) of the APA, 5 U.S.C. §556(e), makes "[t]he transcript of testimony and exhibits, together with all papers and requests filed in the proceeding . . . the exclusive record for decision." This is the section (which applies to formal, on-the-record adjudication and rulemaking) that prevents agencies from relying on secret reports to decide cases or from questioning witnesses off the record.

Even in the court system, however, the requirement to spread all the relevant facts out upon the record is not taken literally. Through the device of judicial notice, courts have always dispensed with the necessity of proving those facts which are obvious and notorious.[103] Dean Wigmore contended that trial courts should assume all facts which are unlikely to be challenged, as well as those considered indisputable. This approach gives the trier of fact some flexibility in controlling the trial and avoids time-consuming proof of every proposition.[104] Another school of thought, led by Professor Morgan, seems less concerned with judicial administration and

---

102. Would consistent use of the remand alternative amount, in effect, to a requirement that agencies prepare a contemporaneous administrative record in every case? Might not a regular practice of discovery and testimony by agency officials have the same effect, given the desire of agency officials to avoid potentially embarrassing discovery and cross-examination? See D.C. Federation of Civic Assns. v. Volpe, 459 F.2d 1231 (D.C. Cir. 1972), cert. denied, 405 U.S. 1030 (1972). Does this suggest that it might be preferable for courts to require the preparation, in every informal adjudication, of an administrative record that discloses the factual bases of the decision adequately to permit judicial review of the merits?

103. See generally Note, Judicial Notice: Rule 201 of the Federal Rules of Evidence, 28 U. Fla. L. Rev. 723 (1976); Comment, The Presently Expanding Concept of Judicial Notice, 13 Vill. L. Rev. 528 (1968).

104. 9 Wigmore, Evidence §§ 2565-2583 (3d ed. 1940).

would limit the scope of judicial notice to matters which are indisputable.[105] Still a third position is that of Judge Weinstein. "Much more formality is required in jury trials — particularly in criminal trials — than in bench trials. In the former the Morgan approach should be applied with some precision. In the latter, the [Wigmore] view seems sound; . . ." [106] Rule 201 of the Federal Rules of Evidence defines a judicially noticed fact as one "not subject to reasonable dispute in that it is either (1) generally known within the territorial jurisdiction of the trial court or (2) capable of accurate and ready determination by resort to sources whose accuracy cannot reasonably be questioned."

A more difficult problem is raised when appellate courts resort to the use of extra-record facts. Such courts have lawmaking and policy-setting functions, particularly in the public law context, and may arguably resort to judicial notice of "legislative" facts in order to carry out these functions. When essentially private disputes are appealed, it can be argued that the appellate courts have a stronger duty to resolve the dispute based upon the record before them. But problems arise in a public law case when a litigant does not properly develop the record and prove some essential fact.[107]

In administrative decisionmaking, the hearing examiner and the agency heads (together with their staff) are familiar with technical issues and equipped to draw specialized inferences based on their experience. Should they have broader discretion to notice facts in the area of their expertise than a trial judge or appellate court? Professor Davis has long advocated broad latitude in the concept of official notice — the counterpart in administrative proceedings to the principle of judicial notice. He argues that the central purpose of the judicial process is the fair disposition of the controversy upon the record as made by the parties. Furthermore, requiring all of the factual bases for technical or policy judgments by agencies to be spread on the record would unduly hobble the administrative process.[108]

If the scope of official notice is to be broad, one must then inquire as to precisely what information may be noticed. What about previous decisions of the agency? What about the records in those cases and the facts proven therein? Must both parties have been involved in the previous case? One? What if neither party was involved? What about data concerning the financial condition of a regulated firm or industry or the scientific or technical state of the art in a given discipline?

105. E. Morgan, Basic Problems of Evidence 9 (1962); see McNaughton, Judicial Notice — Excerpts Relating to the Morgan-Wigmore Controversy, 14 Van. L. Rev. 779 (1961).

106. 1 J. Weinstein & M. Berger, Weinstein's Evidence 201-228 (1976); Fed. R. Evid. 201.

107. Should the court remand for further hearings, thereby consuming precious judicial resources, or should it utilize a relatively loose concept of judicial notice to decide the case? In Daniel v. Paul, 395 U.S. 298 (1969), a civil rights case turning upon the question of whether a segregated establishment served interstate travelers, the Supreme Court's finding of fact ("it would be unrealistic to assume that none of the 100,000 patrons actually served by the Club each season was an interstate traveler") was directly contrary to the findings of both lower courts. As Justice Black pointed out in dissent, "There is not a word of evidence that such an interstate traveler was ever there. . . ." 395 U.S. at 310.

108. K. Davis, Administrative Law Treatise §15.01 (1958).

If the agency notices any of this material, is it obligated to notify the parties and give them an adequate opportunity to respond? If we require agencies to follow strict adversary hearing standards, will they be tempted to rely on extra-record facts sub silentio and never notify anyone of such a reliance?

The APA provides a partial answer to the problem of official notice in "on the record" proceedings governed by 5 U.S.C. §556(e), which provides that "[w]hen an agency decision rests on official notice of a material fact not appearing in the evidence in the record, a party is entitled, on timely request, to an opportunity to show the contrary." Section 706 is also critical to an understanding of the APA approach: "In making the foregoing determinations, the court shall review the whole record or those parts of it cited by a party, and due account shall be taken of the rule of prejudicial error." So long as parties must be notified of agency reliance on facts officially noticed, one could argue that there is no reason to articulate limits on the doctrine. Professor Davis advocates as the proper test "whether or not the parties have adequate opportunity to meet those materials in the appropriate fashion, and that the determinations of what is the appropriate fashion depends upon whether the facts are adjudicative or legislative, upon the degree of certainty or doubt about the facts, and upon degree of importance of the facts to the particular controversy." [109] Does it follow that the APA permits an agency to officially notice its entire case, thereby shifting to the respondent the entire burden of coming forward with evidence? On the other hand, does APA §556(e) require an opportunity to rebut indisputable facts? If not, what is the hearing examiner to do when an argument arises as to whether a fact is indeed indisputable?

Perhaps a tripartite classification along the following lines would prove workable in practice and sufficiently responsive to the due process concerns of the parties:

(1) facts which an agency may officially notice and which are not subject to rebuttal;

(2) facts which an agency may officially notice and which are subject to rebuttal;

(3) facts which an agency must put into the record.

In thinking about this scheme, consider also the possible relevance of Professor Davis's distinction between "legislative" and "adjudicative" facts, p. 468 supra.

Three Supreme Court cases which follow — *Abilene & Southern, Ohio Bell Telephone*, and *Market Street Railway* — were all decided before the APA was enacted. The formalistic notions of due process — day in court, party control of the litigation, strict adherence to the rules of evidence, cross-examination of all

---

109. K. Davis, Administrative Law Treatise §15.12 (1958). Cf. K. Davis, Administrative Law of the Seventies §15 (1976). Most of the major federal agencies now have some provision concerning official notice in their rules of practice. The NLRB, for instance, merely copies the APA provision. 29 C.F.R. §101.10(b)(3) (1976). The FCC limits the scope of official notice to those matters that may be judicially noticed under the rules of evidence in matters not involving trial by jury in district courts. 47 C.F.R. §1.351 (1976). By way of contrast, the SEC declares that it may officially notice any material fact which might be noticed by a district court, any matter in the public records of the Commission, or any matter peculiarly within the knowledge of the SEC as an expert body. 17 C.F.R. §201.14(d) (1976).

witnesses, etc. — have had, and undoubtedly will continue to have, strong appeal for litigants and their attorneys. If any of these procedural safeguards are loosened in an agency proceeding, it may be difficult for a reviewing court to resist the losing litigant's claim of denial of due process. On the other hand, a purely functional approach to the hearing process would seek to ascertain whether the purposes of the hearing were satisfied. The basic aim of official notice is to dispense with adversary procedures of proof when they are not justified by the expense and delay involved and no party would be materially prejudiced by their elimination. But reviewing courts may be ill-equipped to apply a "functional" approach when an agency's exercise of official notice is strenuously challenged by private litigants. Consider these contrasting approaches in reviewing the decisions which follow.

United States v. Abilene & Southern Ry.

265 U.S. 274 (1924)

[This decision set aside an ICC order which granted a new division of joint rates on traffic interchanged between the Kansas City, Mexico and Orient Railway Company (Orient), which was then in receivership, and forty other railroads. Joint rates are single rates charged to a shipper when his goods must travel over more than one line; the interested carriers agree on the division of that rate, with the ICC retaining the statutory power to alter the division if it is found to be "unjust, unreasonable, inequitable or unduly preferential or prejudicial." The Orient's receiver offered evidence showing the failing financial posture of the Orient and stated that it would be unable to meet its expenses without a new division of rates. The trial examiner, acting pursuant to ICC rules, made use of the annual reports of the forty respondent railroads, and the ICC then made up a table comparing certain unit revenues, unit costs, and unit net returns of Orient and the other railroads. Among other matters, the figures showed that Orient had a net loss of 2.77 percent as against net profits ranging from 1.39 to 12.13 percent for the connecting lines, and were an important factor in the ICC's decision favoring Orient. The district court enjoined the ICC's order, concluding that it was based on a policy of shoring up financially weak carriers with the profits of prosperous lines, and that this policy was not authorized by the relevant statutes. The Supreme Court disagreed, finding that the Commission could allocate divisions in order to maintain a sound overall transportation system. However, the Court held that the ICC had failed to develop sufficient evidence of record to justify the particular divisions ordered, and that its decision must therefore be set aside. It also considered procedural objections:]

. . . The plaintiffs contend that the order is void because it rests upon evidence not legally before the Commission. It is conceded that the finding rests, in part, upon data taken from the annual reports filed with the Commission by the plaintiff carriers pursuant to law; that these reports were not formally put in evidence; that the parts containing the data relied upon were not put in evidence through excerpts; that attention was not otherwise specifically called to them; and that objection to the use of the reports, under these circumstances, was seasonably made by the carriers and was insisted upon. . . . The contention of the Commission is that, because its able examiner gave notice that "no doubt it will be necessary to refer to the annual reports of all these carriers," its Rules of Practice permitted matter in the reports to be used as freely as if the data had been formally introduced in evidence.

The mere admission by an administrative tribunal of matter which under the rules of evidence applicable to judicial proceedings would be deemed incompetent does not invalidate its order. . . . But a finding without evidence is beyond the power of the Commission. Papers in the Commission's files are not always evidence in a case. . . . Nothing can be treated as evidence which is not introduced as such. . . . The fact that the proceeding was technically an investigation instituted by the Commission would not relieve the Orient, if a party to it, from this requirement. Every proceeding is adversary, in substance, if it may result in an order in favor of one carrier as against another. Nor was the proceeding under review any the less an adversary one, because the primary purpose of the Commission was to protect the public interest through making possible the continued operation of the Orient system. The fact that it was on the Commission's own motion that use was made of the data in the annual reports is not of legal significance.

It is sought to justify the procedure followed by the clause in Rule XIII which declares that the "Commission will take notice of items in tariffs and annual or other periodical reports of carriers properly on file." But this clause does not mean that the Commission will take judicial notice of all the facts contained in such documents. Nor does it purport to relieve the Commission from introducing, by specific reference, such parts of the reports as it wishes to treat as evidence. It means that as to these items there is no occasion for the parties to serve copies. The objection to the use of the data contained in the annual reports is not lack of authenticity or untrustworthiness. It is that the carriers were left without notice of the evidence with which they were, in fact, confronted, as later disclosed by the finding made. The requirement that in an adversary proceeding specific reference be made, is essential to the preservation of the substantial rights of the parties.

Questions

1. Should litigants be permitted to challenge the factual accuracy of official reports submitted by them? Many courts have not permitted such challenge.[110] How likely is a litigant to succeed in attacking the accuracy of its own data? For what purposes other than challenging the accuracy of the underlying data might a litigant wish to be notified of the particular reports and records relied upon by an agency?

110. See Wisconsin v. FPC, 201 F.2d 183 (D.C. Cir. 1952), *cert. denied*, 345 U.S. 934 (1953); Riss & Co. v. United States, 117 F. Supp. 296 (W.D. Mo. 1952), *aff'd per curiam*, 346 U.S. 890 (1953).

2. How literally should we take Justice Brandeis' statement that: "Nothing can be treated as evidence which is not introduced as such"? The Commission might not be in a position to decide which of its official records were relevant until it is engaged in the process of decision, long after the hearing of evidence and submission of briefs. In such a case, why isn't it sufficient that the Commission specify in its decision the records relied upon, and provide the parties with the opportunity to petition for rehearing if they wish to challenge its use of such records? [111]

Ohio Bell Tel. Co. v. Public Utilities Commn.

301 U.S. 292 (1937)

[Employing traditional principles of utility ratesetting, the Commission held extensive hearings and accepted volumes of evidence bearing on the value of the Company's investment. After eight years, the Commission had enough evidence to enable it to fix the value of the Company's property as of the year 1925. It then adjusted the property value for each of the years 1926 to 1933 by taking official notice of price trends. On the basis of these calculations, it established the Company's return on investment for each year between 1925 and 1935 at levels requiring substantial refunds to customers. The price trends, which were not placed in the record and which the Company had no opportunity to rebut, were gleaned from examinations of (1) the tax values in communities where the Company had its largest real estate holdings, (2) price indexes in a construction industry magazine, and (3) the findings of an Illinois federal court in a case involving Western Electric, an affiliated corporation. There was no way for Ohio Bell to identify items (1) or (2) or learn their precise content. Mr. Justice CARDOZO delivered the opinion of the Court:]

... The fundamentals of a trial were denied to the appellant when rates previously collected were ordered to be refunded upon the strength of evidential facts not spread upon the record.

The Commission had given notice that the value of the property would be fixed as of a date certain. Evidence directed to the value at that time had been laid before the triers of the facts in thousands of printed pages. To make the picture more complete, evidence had been given as to the value at cost of additions and retirements. Without warning or even the hint of warning that the case would be considered or determined upon any other basis than the evidence submitted, the Commission cut down the values for the years after the date certain upon the strength of information secretly collected and never yet disclosed. The company protested. It asked disclosure of the documents indicative of price trends, and an opportunity to examine them, to analyze them, to explain and to rebut them. The response was a curt refusal. Upon the strength of these unknown documents

111. See P. Saldutti & Sons, Inc. v. United States, 210 F. Supp. 307 (D.N.J. 1962).

refunds have been ordered for sums mounting into millions, the Commission reporting its conclusion, but not the underlying proofs. The putative debtor does not know the proofs today. This is not the fair hearing essential to due process. It is condemnation without trial.

An attempt was made by the Commission and again by the state court to uphold this decision without evidence as an instance of judicial notice. . . . [T]o press the doctrine of judicial notice to the extent attempted in this case and to do that retroactively after the case had been submitted, would be to turn the doctrine into a pretext for dispensing with a trial.

What was done by the Commission is subject, however, to an objection even deeper. . . . There has been more than an expansion of the concept of notoriety beyond reasonable limits. From the standpoint of due process — the protection of the individual against arbitrary action — a deeper vice is this, that even now we do not know the particular or evidential facts of which the Commission took judicial notice and on which it rested its conclusion. Not only are the facts unknown; there is no way to find them out. When price lists or trade journals or even government reports are put in evidence upon a trial, the party against whom they are offered may see the evidence or hear it and parry its effect. Even if they are copied in the findings without preliminary proof, there is at least an opportunity in connection with a judicial review of the decision to challenge the deductions made from them. The opportunity is excluded here. The Commission, withholding from the record the evidential facts that it has gathered here and there, contents itself with saying that in gathering them it went to journals and tax lists, as if a judge were to tell us, "I looked at the statistics in the Library of Congress, and they teach me thus and so." This will never do if hearings and appeals are to be more than empty forms. . . .

. . . To put the problem more concretely: how was it possible for the appellate court to review the law and the facts and intelligently decide that the findings of the Commission were supported by the evidence when the evidence that it approved was unknown and unknowable? . . . What the Supreme Court of Ohio did was to take the word of the Commission as to the outcome of a secret investigation, and let it go at that. "A hearing is not judicial, at least in any adequate sense, unless the evidence can be known." . . .

Regulatory commissions have been invested with broad powers within the sphere of duty assigned to them by law. Even in quasi-judicial proceedings their informed and expert judgment exacts and receives a proper deference from courts when it has been reached with due submission to constitutional restraints. . . . Indeed, much that they do within the realm of administrative discretion is exempt from supervision if those restraints have been obeyed. All the more insistent is the need, when power has been bestowed so freely, that the "inexorable safeguard" . . . of a fair and open hearing be maintained in its integrity. . . . The right to such a hearing is one of "the rudiments of fair play" . . . assured to every litigant by the Fourteenth Amendment as a minimal requirement. . . . There can be no compromise on the footing of convenience or expediency, or because of a natural desire to be rid of harassing delay, when that minimal requirement has been neglected or ignored.

[The Court then considered the State's argument that the Commission's decision could be sustained on the basis of the Illinois Federal Court's findings concerning the historical trend of prices paid by Ohio Bell to Western Electric.]

... Even if we assume in favor of the state that the evidence, when in, could be considered as indicative of the trend of market values generally, the judgment is not helped. The Commission did not take the prices paid by appellant to the affiliated corporation as the only evidence of market trends, but merely as one factor along with many others. What weighting it gave them the record does not disclose, and the Commission denied the appellant an opportunity to inquire.[112]

Market Street Ry. v. Railroad Commn.

324 U.S. 548 (1945)

[The Market Street Railway Company operated a public transportation system in San Francisco. On its own motion the Railroad Commission began an inquiry into the Company's rates and reduced its fare from seven to six cents, finding that lowering fares would stimulate demand sufficiently to provide adequate revenues to cover its expense and a return on capital. (For a discussion of rate making, see Chapter 4, Section B, supra.) The California Supreme Court affirmed the Commission's order, and the Company appealed to the U.S. Supreme Court. Justice JACKSON, for a unanimous Court, rejected the Company's contentions that it had been denied procedural due process.]

It is ... contended that the order is invalid under the due process clause because it is unsupported by evidence and is based on the Commission's speculation

---

112. Ed. note: To what extent may an agency take official notice of evidence developed in facts found in other proceedings before the same agency?

In general, the courts have not hesitated to allow agencies to take official notice of the record in a previous case involving the same parties. For example, Paramount Cap Mfg. Co. v. NLRB, 260 F.2d 109 (8th Cir. 1958), the court held that it was proper for the NLRB to take official notice of agency records of prior interrelated litigation between the same parties in order to establish the existence of an unfair labor practice. The officially noticed facts were placed in the transcript, thereby providing both parties an adequate opportunity to rebut.

United States v. Pierce Auto Freight Lines, Inc., 327 U.S. 515 (1946), represents a slight extension of this proposition. In that case, the ICC had before it two separate applications for competing motor carrier service between San Francisco and Portland. The two applicants had previously rendered the service jointly, and each sought the exclusive right to operate on the route. Although each intervened in the other proceeding, the two hearings were not formally consolidated. The Commission nevertheless considered evidence from each record and treated the two records as one. In upholding the Commission's decision, the Court declared that "the mere fact that the determining body has looked beyond the record proper does not invalidate its action unless substantial prejudice is shown to result." 327 U.S. at 530. Perhaps the ICC could have disposed of the issue in a more efficient manner by consolidating the hearings, but it did allow each party to intervene in the other proceeding and protect its interests.

May an agency take official notice of evidence developed in prior proceedings in which the present respondent was not a party if the parties to the prior proceeding had a strong incentive to litigate thoroughly the identical facts that are in issue? See Safeway Stores, Inc. v. FTC, 366 F.2d 795 (9th Cir. 1966), cert. denied, 386 U.S. 932 (1967); Dayco Corp. v. FTC, 362 F.2d 180 (6th Cir. 1966), noted in 35 Geo. Wash. L. Rev. 840 (1967).

and conjecture. This charge relates particularly to those findings which predict the effect of a rate reduction in stimulating traffic.... Various considerations are advanced to show that the Commission's predictions were based on innocent analysis and were improbable.

... The complaint is that the Commission formed its own conclusions without the aid of expert opinions. It is contended that the Commission should draw conclusions from these facts only upon hearing testimony of experts as to the conclusions they would draw from the facts of record. Experts' judgments, however, would not bind the Commission. Their testimony would be in the nature of argument or opinion, and the weight to be given it would depend upon the Commission's estimate of the reasonableness of their conclusions and the force of their reasoning. There is nothing to indicate that any consideration which could be advanced by an expert has not been advanced by the Company in argument and fully weighed....

... We find no denial of due process in these circumstances from the fact that the Commission evaluated the Company's experience for itself without the aid of expert testimony.

It also is urged that the order is invalid under the due process clause because it is based on matters outside the record. The decision of the Commission stated that "In the eight months' period, January to August, inclusive, of 1943 the operating revenues of the company amounted to $5,689,775," and compared this with the operating revenues for the same period of 1942 and found an increase of 20 percent. On this basis it estimated the total for the full year of 1943 under the prevailing seven-cent fare. Challenged upon the ground that the operating revenues from January to August of 1943 were not in the record, the Commission admitted that these figures were taken from the appellant's monthly reports filed with the Commission. It contended that even if it was in error to refer to such reports, the error was harmless, since the record without the figures supported the reasonableness of the six-cent fare and it was therefore immaterial that the Commission used some additional figures. No contention is made here that the information was erroneous or was misunderstood by the Commission, and no contention is made that the Company could have disproved it or explained away its effect for the purpose for which the Commission used it. The most that can be said is that the Commission in making its predictive findings went outside of the record to verify its judgment by reference to actual traffic figures that became available only after the hearings closed. It does not appear that the Company was in any way prejudiced thereby, and it makes no showing that, if a rehearing were held to introduce its own reports, it would gain much by cross-examination, rebuttal, or impeachment of its own auditors or the reports they had filed. Due process, of course, requires that commissions proceed upon matters in evidence and that parties have opportunity to subject evidence to the test of cross-examination and rebuttal. But due process deals with matters of substance and is not to be trivialized by formal objections that have no substantial bearing on the ultimate rights of parties....

Questions: Can *Market Street Railway* be reconciled with *Ohio Bell* and *Abilene & Southern?* If not, which is the correct approach? [113]

2.   The Problem of Ex Parte Communications

We deal here with communications outside the record between agency decisionmakers and persons outside the agency. The problem of off-the record communications between agency decisionmakers and other personnel within the same agency is dealt with in Chapter 8.

a.   "On-the-Record" Proceedings

There are few judicial decisions dealing with the propriety of off-the-record communications (why is this so?). However, it has traditionally been understood that in adjudicatory or rulemaking proceedings required to be conducted "on the record" through trial-type hearing procedures like those specified in the APA, §§ 554, 556-557, it would be improper for an outside party to the proceedings to communicate evidence or argument off the record to agency decisionmakers during the course of the proceeding.

Congressional investigations into "influence peddling" during the late 1950s stimulated widespread public and professional concern over ex parte communications between federal regulators and private parties seeking favorable regulatory decisions. [114] In 1962 the Administrative Conference of the United States recom-

---

113. Cf. Baton Rouge Water Works Co. v. Louisiana Public Service Commn., 342 So. 2d 609 (La. Sup. Ct.), *cert. denied,* 434 U.S. 827 (1977).

Baton Rouge Water, a public utility, applied for higher water rates in order to secure a 13 percent return on equity. The Commission held hearings and the only evidence introduced was the testimony of the Company's expert witness, who testified to the appropriateness of a 13 percent return. The Commission authorized increased rates sufficient to yield a 10.5 percent return, the Company appealed, and the Louisiana trial court modified the order to allow the higher return. The Louisiana Supreme Court reversed, finding that the Commission's order was not arbitrary or capricious. The court was troubled, however, by the Commission's development of its justifications for a 10.5 percent return in its appellate brief rather than in the hearing record. However, the Louisiana Supreme Court concluded that the findings and reasons for the Commission's action were "necessarily implied by the record," and a remand to clear up the issue would have been only a "formality" and "little more than a gesture." A dissenter argued that the Company had proved the reasonableness of its request and that the Commission could not deny the request unless there was an evidentiary basis for its action.

See also McCarthy v. Industrial Commn., 194 Wis. 198, 215 N.W. 824 (1927).

114. See Investigation of Regulatory Commissions and Agencies, Hearings Before a Subcommittee of the House Commerce Committee, 85th Cong., 2d Sess. (1958). Concern by lawyers and administrators with the ex parte communication problem is reflected in the following: Peck, Regulation and Control of Ex Parte Communications with Administrative Agencies, 76 Harv. L. Rev. 233 (1962). See also Note, Ex Parte Contacts with the Federal Communications Commission, 73 Harv. L. Rev. 1178 (1960); Lovett, Ex Parte and the FCC: The New Regulations, 21 Fed. Com. B.J. 54 (1967); Colon, Court and the Commissioner: Ex Parte Contacts and the Sangamon Valley Case, 19 Fed. Com. B.J. 67 (1965); Ablard, Ex Parte Contacts with

mended that ex parte communications be banned in proceedings required to be held on the record.[115] Most of the major federal agencies have adopted these recommendations in whole or in large part.[116] In the post-Watergate era, Congress in 1976 enacted the Government in the Sunshine Act, the relevant provisions of which are contained in the APA in new sections 551(14) and 557(d), and in the fourth sentence of §556(d), which you should now carefully review. Note in particular that these provisions are limited to formal "on the record" proceedings governed by §§ 556-557.

The Sunshine Act leaves certain issues regarding ex parte communications unresolved. For example, the prohibitions of §557(d)(1) are directed at communications between agency decisionmakers and an "interested person," but the latter term is not defined. Is it limited to parties to the formal proceeding? Does it include any person, whether or not a party, who makes a communication arguably relevant to a proceeding? Or should the definition of "interested person" be located at some intermediate point between these extremes? [117] Consider also the timing of the Sunshine Act's prohibitions. Agency members must presumably be free to discuss informally with outsiders general issues of administrative policy that are not yet the subject of any proposed proceedings. Yet if the prohibition against ex parte communications did not become operative until after formal proceedings were commenced, there is a danger that the agency's ultimate position would already have been significantly influenced by off the record communications. How does the Sunshine Act resolve the timing problem?

The preceding questions reflect a basic difficulty in transferring ex parte communications principles developed in judicial proceedings to the context of a bureaucratic agency where formal proceedings are simply one element in a continuous, often informal, process of policy choice and implementation. This difficulty was nicely illustrated by the Civil Aeronautics Board in the early 1970s, when it adopted a policy of refusing to allow airlines to fly new routes — a policy known as the "route moratorium." This policy was implemented through delay or denial of individual carrier applications for new routes which were required by statute to be resolved through "on the record" proceedings. In commenting on the formula-

Federal Administrative Agencies, 47 A.B.A.J. 473 (1961); Ivins, Private Communications With Administrative Agencies Should Be Prohibited, 47 A.B.A.J. 278 (1961); McKay, An Administrative Code of Ethics, 47 A.B.A.J. 890 (1961); Stone, Ex Parte Communications: The Harris Bill, the CAB and the Dilemma of Where to Draw the Line, 13 Ad. L. Rev. 141 (1960-1961).

115. Recommendation No. 16, S. Doc. No. 24, 88th Cong., 1st Sess. 6 (1963).

116. See, e.g., 10 C.F.R. §§ 204.1-204.5 (1975) (FEA); 14 C.F.R. §§ 300-300.20 (1977) (CAB); 17 C.F.R. §§ 200.110-200.114 (1977) (SEC); 21 C.F.R. §10.55 (1977) (FDA); 29 C.F.R. §§ 102.126-102.133 (1977) (NLRB); 47 C.F.R. §§ 1.1201-1.1251 (1977) (FCC); 49 C.F.R. §1100.4(e) & Appendix C (1977) (ICC).

117. Note that the definition of "ex parte communication" in §551(14) excepts "status reports." Members of Congress often make inquiries, on behalf of constitutents or supporters, concerning the status of pending proceedings in which they are interested. These status requests have sometimes been regarded as an indirect means for influential legislators to signal the agency to decide in favor of the person on whose behalf the request is made, although the volume of such requests may considerably dilute the significance of any such "signal." Why shouldn't status requests be included in the record?

tion of this policy, the Senate Subcommittee on Administrative Practice and Procedure noted the following:[118]

> A further problem embedded in the Board's route moratorium procedures concerns the role of private off-the-record conversations between Board members and representatives of industry. Former Chairman Browne has stated that industry representatives came to see him frequently between 1969 and 1971. Their visits were often "courtesy calls," yet matters of substance were discussed. In particular, Mr. Browne would listen to industry complaints about overcapacity, low carrier profits, overly aggressive labor, and various other subjects of industry concern. And, as Board Member Minetti told the subcommittee, the larger carriers were urging the adoption of a route moratorium.
>
> An examination of the calendar and logs of members of the Civil Aeronautics Board for 1974 reveals that such private meetings are by no means uncommon. During that year there were 769 such meetings between Board members and members of the industry, as the following table reflects:

[TABLE 1]
Contacts by Members of the Civil Aeronautics Board with Industry Representatives
(Calendar Year 1974)

	Board Members					
	1	*2*	*3*	*4*	*5*	*Total*
January	30	13	22	13	13	91
February	31	10	5	14	4	64
March	16	9	12	11	1	49
April	34	4	14	7	4	63
May	32	7	19	18	3	79
June	40	9	6	16	6	77
July	21	7	21	6	5	60
August	46	5	18	5	0	74
September	32	7	10	10	3	62
October	23	10	16	14	1	64
November	10	8	12	13	1	44
December	14	3	13	12	0	42
Total	329	92	168	139	41	769

Source: This table was compiled by the Subcommittee on Administrative Practice and Procedure based upon information submitted by Board members for the calendar year 1974.

Large numbers of private meetings — while not necessarily improper on an individual basis — raise a problem of public confidence in the agency. Whether or not a Commission member can maintain perfect objectivity (and constant

---

118. Report of the Subcommittee on Adm. Prac. & Proc. on the Civil Aeronautics Board, 94th Cong., 1st Sess. (1975) at 91-93.

exposure to the industry viewpoint makes objectivity more difficult), the public
is uncertain whether, in fact, decisions of major importance have been made
on the merits for reasons set out in the public record. This concern is multiplied when private meetings with major members of the industry are followed by speeches that espouse that point of view into formal Board policy,
all without benefit of hearing or court review as occurred in the case of the
route moratorium.

The problem is difficult, however, for it seems unwise to forbid all meetings between members of the industry and the Board. To do so risks en-
closing Board members in an "ivory tower" from which the isolated Board
member may find it more difficult to obtain important, relevant information.
It is also probably desirable for Board members to meet major industry figures
personally, in order to have some idea what the people who run the airlines
are like.

Member West articulated this tension very well:

"I am aware that the appearance of a fair hearing and a fair opportunity
and fair treatment is oftentimes as important as the fact that you oftentimes
receive fair treatment, and I am not at all arguing that there is not a basis
for concern about kind of a persuasive influence.

"But I am a bit disturbed that there may be some rules that almost require you to live in a vacuum to prevent you from — now, I have been accused of not being an expert in this field, and I plead guilty, but I am not
sure how, if we are restricted to almost a vacuum-like atmosphere, that we
would be able to even determine what the questions are, let alone the solutions, and there is a problem in my own mind about how to conduct myself.

"I came from the bench in which the rules are more clearly defined.
In all fairness, you have to be, you understand what matters can be discussed
and under what circumstances, but here we are in a quasi-judicial situation,
and it is different, and I have not yet defined or determined the difference
that exists.

"In some respects, we are held to the same rigid standards that a court
is held, with regard to making decisions, and yet, we are determining policy
in which all sorts of inputs should be received before you can make very
much of a quality decision, and where I can obtain that is a bit of a problem
without some contact with the industry."

How satisfactorily does the Sunshine Act resolve this difficulty? What additional or alternative measures might be considered? What about requiring agency
members to keep a log, available to the public, recording the identity of all outsiders with whom the member has a communication relating to agency policies,
together with a brief description of the general subject matter of the communication?

b. Informal Agency Decisionmaking

The traditional understanding regarding ex parte communications sharply distinguished "on the record" proceedings, in which such communications were

banned, and informal proceedings, such as notice and comment rulemaking or informal adjudication, in which they were not.[119] The distinction was certainly logical; notice and comment rulemaking and other informal proceedings are not required to be decided on the basis of an exclusive "record" and leave the agency free to consult informally, in "legislative" fashion, with interested outsiders and sources of data.[120] In such informal processes of decision the very notion of an "on the record" communication is inappropriate. Recall also that the Sunshine Act's prohibitions against "ex parte communications" do not apply to notice and comment rulemaking or informal adjudication. However, this traditional distinction has been eroded by court decisions, the most notable of which follow.

Sangamon Valley Television Corp. v. United States

269 F.2d 221 (D.C. Cir. 1959)

EDGERTON, C.J.

[In 1958 a House investigation revealed that a private citizen, Harry Tenenbaum, and certain government officials, such as presidential assistant Sherman Adams, had exercised apparently improper influence upon various agencies.[121] Tenenbaum was the President of Signal Hill, which sought a VHF television license to serve St. Louis. He intervened in an effort to affect an FCC notice and comment rulemaking decision about whether to switch VHF Channel 2 from Springfield, Ill., to St. Louis and give Springfield two UHF channels instead. Signal Hill favored the switch as it knew it would get the license if Channel 2 were transferred to St. Louis. Sangamon, which wanted the VHF license for Springfield, opposed it.

Tenenbaum repeatedly spoke to FCC Commissioners in their offices about the need to switch Channel 2 to St. Louis; he entertained them in Springfield, and he sent them turkeys for Christmas. He also urged Congressmen and others to intervene at the Commission.]

While the proceeding involved here was pending before the Commission it gave notice to the parties, on October 12, 1956, that "Any interested person who is of the view that the proposals herein should not be adopted, or should not be adopted in the form set forth herein, may file with the Commission on or before November 15, 1956, written data, views, or arguments setting forth his comments. Comments in support of the proposals may also be filed on or before the same date. Comments or briefs in reply to such original comments as may be submitted should be filed within 15 days from the last day for filing said original comments

119. Compare S & E Contractors, Inc. v. United States, 433 F.2d 1373, 1379 (Ct. Cl. 1970), *rev'd on other grounds*, 406 U.S. 1 (1972), with Bethlehem Steel Corp. v. United States, 511 F.2d 529 (Ct. Cl), *cert. denied*, 423 U.S. 840 (1975).

120. See pp. 478-481, supra.

121. See Investigation of Regulatory Commissions and Agencies, Hearings before a Subcommittee of the House Commerce Committee, 85th Cong., 2d Sess. 3450-62, 3511-22 (1958) (testimony of Harry Tenenbaum).

or briefs. *No additional comments may be filed unless (1) specifically requested by the Commission or (2) good cause for filing such additional comments is established.* The Commission will consider all such additional comments submitted before taking further action in this matter, and if any comments appear to warrant the holding of a hearing, oral argument, or demonstration, notice of the time and place of such hearing, oral argument or demonstration will be given." (Emphasis added.)

Several parties filed comments. The Commission extended the time for filing reply comments until December 28, 1956. The parties, including intervenor Signal Hill Telecasting Corporation, filed timely reply comments.

On March 1, 1957, the Commission issued the order under review. It shifted VHF Channel 2 from Springfield to St. Louis, shifted UHF Channels 26 and 36 to Springfield, and modified Signal Hill's outstanding authorization for Channel 36 in St. Louis to permit temporary operation on Channel 2 subject to certain conditions.

Harry Tenenbaum, president of intervenor Signal Hill, admitted to the Legislative Oversight Committee that while the proceeding before the Commission was pending he spoke to its members individually "in privacy in their offices, not while they were sitting in a body as the Commission," of his desire to have Channel 2; "knowing, of course, or expecting, that if Channel 2 went to St. Louis [he] would have good opportunity to get it." He was "in all the Commissioners' offices" and went "from Commissioner to Commissioner." He "probably discussed" with every Commissioner his desire to have Channel 2. He testified that he had every Commissioner at one time or another as his luncheon guest, and that he gave turkeys to every Commissioner in 1955 and in 1956.

Finally, on February 20, 1957, seven weeks after the cut-off date, as extended, for filing comments and ten days before the Commission decided the case, Tenenbaum sent each Commissioner a letter in which he contended and tried to prove that "Channel 2, based in St. Louis, would reach 166,700 more homes in the state of Illinois than if it were based in Springfield, Illinois." [122] These letters did not go into the public record. The parties who were opposing the transfer of Channel 2 from Springfield to St. Louis could not question Tenenbaum's contention, since they did not know he was making it. Its importance was great and perhaps critical, for the principal contention of the opposing parties was that the transfer would deprive Illinois of the "fair, efficient, and equitable distribution of radio service" to which the Communications Act entitles each state and community.

Interested attempts "to influence any member of the Commission . . . except by the recognized and public processes" go "to the very core of the Commission's quasi-judicial powers. . . ." Massachusetts Bay Telecasters, Inc., v. Federal Communications Commission, 261 F.2d 55, 66, 67. That case involved licensing, not

---

122. On February 4, 1957, Gordon Sherman, President of WMAY-TV, Inc., sent the then Chairman of the Commission a telegram urging the Commission to keep Channel 2 in Springfield. Nelson Howard, Mayor of Springfield, "talked to a number of the Commissioners" in behalf of Springfield applicants.

rule-making. Ordinarily allocation of TV channels among communities is a matter of rule-making governed by [APA §553], rather than adjudication governed by §[554]. The Commission and the intervenor contend that because the proceeding now on review was "rule-making," ex parte attempts to influence the Commissioners did not invalidate it. The Department of Justice disagrees. On behalf of the United States, the Department urges that whatever the proceeding may be called it involved not only allocation of TV channels among communities but also resolution of conflicting private claims to a valuable privilege, and that basic fairness requires such a proceeding to be carried on in the open. We agree with the Department of Justice. Accordingly the private approaches to the member of the Commission vitiated its action and the proceeding must be reopened.

We agree also that the Commission proceedings must be reopened for another reason. Agency action that substantially and prejudicially violates the agency's rules cannot stand. At the time of this proceeding the Commission had no general regulations governing all rule-making, but when it proposed an allocation of TV channels to particular communities it was its usual practice, followed in this instance, to prescribe a cut-off date before which "Any interested person . . . may file with the Commission . . . written data, views, or arguments setting forth his comments" favoring or opposing the plan; a cut-off date for "comments or briefs in reply"; and that "No additional comments may be filed" without a request from the Commission or a showing of good cause. By plain implication, this rule forbade submitting material to the Commission's members after the time for filing it with the Commission had gone by. The rule cannot be interpreted to permit parties to make off the record contentions that it forbids them to make on the record.

[The court remanded the case to the FCC. After an investigation, the FCC concluded that ordinarily ex parte communications are proper in a rulemaking proceeding but where an individual has a strong self-interest such communications are improper. Eventually the whole case was begun again and in 1962 the Commission came to the same conclusion it had reached in 1957: it assigned Channel 2 to St. Louis.]

Home Box Office, Inc. v. FCC

567 F.2d 9 (D.C. Cir. 1977), cert. denied, 434 U.S. 829, rehearing denied, 434 U.S. 988 (1977)

Before WRIGHT and MacKINNON, Circuit Judges, and WEIGEL, District Judge.
[After notice and comment rulemaking proceedings the FCC adopted general regulations limiting the type of programming that could be offered by cable television services and subscription broadcast television stations, who sought judicial review of the Commission's actions. The Commission had specified a deadline for filing written comments on its proposed rules, and thereafter afforded oral argument to various industry and "public interest" representatives. The regulations adopted by the FCC made it difficult or impossible for "pay cable" companies to

originate certain popular sports events or certain feature films. The argument of the Commission and of traditional television broadcasters in support of the rules was that "pay cable" would "siphon" such popular programs from "free" TV and the viewer would end up paying directly for the same programs he now sees for "free." Whether such "siphoning" was actually likely to occur or whether the "antisiphoning rules" simply represented an effort by existing broadcasters to prevent potential pay cable competitors from getting started was hotly disputed before the Commission.

The court, in a per curiam opinion, held the FCC's rules invalid, for reasons related to the FCC's jurisdictional authority and to the First Amendment. It also dealt with the question of ex parte communications.]

It is apparently uncontested that a number of participants before the Commission sought out individual commissioners or Commission employees for the purpose of discussing ex parte and in confidence the merits of the rules under review here. In fact, the Commission itself solicited such communications in its notices of proposed rulemaking, and, without discussing the nature, substance, or importance of what was said, argues before us that we should simply ignore these communications because . . . Sangamon does not apply. In an attempt to clarify the facts this court sua sponte ordered the Commission to provide "a list of all of the ex parte presentations together with the details of each, made to it, or to any of its members or representatives, during the rulemaking proceedings." In response to this order the Commission filed a document over 60 pages long which revealed, albeit imprecisely,[123] widespread ex parte communications involving virtually every party before this court.[124] . . . It is important to note that many contacts occurred in the crucial period between the close of oral argument on October 25, 1974, and the adoption of the First Report and Order on March 20, 1975, when the rulemaking record should have been closed while the Commission was deciding what rules to promulgate. The information submitted to this court by the Commission indicates that during this period broadcast interests met some 18 times with Commission personnel, cable interests nine times, motion picture and sports interests five times each, and "public interest" intervenors not at all.

123. Because many Commission officials kept no accurate records on contacts, the list is incomplete and the dates of various contacts often uncertain or estimated.

124. Ex parte communications were also originated by many persons not party here, including members of Congress, members of the trade press, and representatives of various performing arts groups.

[A brief described some of these communications as follows:

"[Ex parte] presentations have, in fact, been made at crucial stages of the proceedings. Thus, in early 1974, then Chairman Burch sought to complete action in this proceeding. Because the Commission was 'leaning' in its deliberations towards relaxing the existing rules 'with "wildcard" rights for "block-buster" movies,' . . . American Broadcasting Company's representatives contacted 'key members of Congress,' who in turn successfully pressured the Commission not to take such action. Further, in the final crucial decisional period, the tentative course to be taken by the Commission would leak after each non-public meeting, and industry representatives would rush to make ex parte presentations to the Commissioners and staff. On March 10, 1975, the trade journals state that 'word of last week's changes . . . got out during the week, and both broadcast and cable lobbyists rushed to the Commission, unhappy with some facets' . . ."]

Although it is impossible to draw any firm conclusions about the effect of ex parte presentations upon the ultimate shape of the pay cable rules, the evidence is certainly consistent with often-voiced claims of undue industry influence over Commission proceedings, and we are particularly concerned that the final shaping of the rules we are reviewing here may have been by compromise among the contending industry forces, rather than by exercise of the independent discretion in the public interest the Communications Act vests in individual commissioners. . . . Our concern is heightened by the submission of the Commission's Broadcast Bureau to this court which states that in December 1974 broadcast representatives "described the kind of pay cable regulation that, in their view, broadcasters 'could live with.'". . . If actual positions were not revealed in public comments, as this statement would suggest, and, further, if the Commission relied on these apparently more candid private discussions in framing the final pay cable rules, then the elaborate public discussion in these dockets has been reduced to a sham.

Even the possibility that there is here one administrative record for the public and this court and another for the Commission and those "in the know" is intolerable. Whatever the law may have been in the past,[125] there can now be no doubt that implicit in the decision to treat the promulgation of rules as a "final" event in an ongoing process of administration is an assumption that an act of reasoned judgment has occurred, an assumption which further contemplates the existence of a body of material — documents, comments, transcripts, and statements in various forms declaring agency expertise or policy — with reference to which such judgment was exercised. Against this material, "the full administrative record that was before [an agency official] at the time he made his decision," Citizens to Preserve Overton Park, Inc. v. Volpe, . . . it is the obligation of this court to test the actions of the Commission for arbitrariness or inconsistency with delegated authority. See id. at 415-416. Yet here agency secrecy stands between us and fulfillment of our obligation. As a practical matter, Overton Park's mandate means that the public record must reflect what representations were made to an agency so that relevant information supporting or refuting those representations may be brought to the attention of the reviewing courts by persons participating in agency proceedings. This course is obviously foreclosed if communications are made to the agency in secret and

---

125. The legislative history of the Administrative Procedure Act has been read to imply that there is no such thing as an administrative record in informal rule making. See, e.g., U.S. Dept. of Justice, Attorney General's Manual on The Administrative Procedure Act 31 (1947) ("Section 4(b) does not require the formulation of rules upon the exclusive basis of any 'record' made in informal rule making proceedings"). Professor Nathanson has similarly concluded: "Section 553's notice-and-comment provisions were [originally] conceived of as instruments for the education of the administrator, especially on questions of policy; there is not the slightest indication that the purpose of the notice-and-comment proceedings was to develop a record by which a reviewing court could test the validity of the rule which the Administrator finally adopted. Apparently, an underlying assumption of the APA draftsmen was that any factual issues which became pertinent in a challenge to the validity of a Section 553 rule would be resolved in the first instance in judicial proceedings — either in enforcement proceedings or in suits to enjoin enforcement. . . ." Nathanson, Probing the Mind of the Administrator: Hearing Variations and Standards of Judicial Review Under the Administrative Procedure Act and Other Federal Statutes, 75 Colum. L. Rev. 721, 745-755 (1975). . . . See also Verkuil, Judicial Review of Informal Rule Making, 60 Va. L. Rev. 185, 202-205 (1974).

the agency itself does not disclose the information presented. Moreover, where, as here, an agency justifies its actions by reference only to information in the public file while failing to disclose the substance of other relevant information that has been presented to it, a reviewing court cannot presume that the agency has acted properly, Citizens to Preserve Overton Park, Inc. v. Volpe, 401 U.S. at 415, 419-420; see K. Davis, Administrative Law of the Seventies §11.00 at 317 (1976), but must treat the agency's justifications as a fictional account of the actual decision-making process and must perforce find its actions arbitrary. . . .

The failure of the public record in this proceeding to disclose all the information made available to the Commission is not the only inadequacy we find here. Even if the Commission had disclosed to this court the substance of what was said to it ex parte, it would still be difficult to judge the truth of what the Commission asserted it knew about the television industry because we would not have the benefit of an adversarial discussion among the parties. The importance of such discussion to the proper functioning of the agency decision-making and judicial review processes is evident in our cases. . . . We have insisted, for example, that information in agency files or consultants' reports which the agency has identified as relevant to the proceeding be disclosed to the parties for adversarial comment. Similarly, we have required agencies to set out their thinking in notices of proposed rulemaking. This requirement not only allows adversarial critique of the agency but is perhaps one of the few ways that the public may be apprised of what the agency thinks it knows in its capacity as a repository of expert opinion. From a functional standpoint, we see no difference between assertions of fact and expert opinion tendered by the public, as here, and that generated internally in an agency: each may be biased, inaccurate, or incomplete — failings which adversarial comment may illuminate. Indeed, the potential for bias in private preservations in rulemakings which resolve "conflicting private claims to a valuable privilege," Sangamon Valley Television Corp. v. United States, supra, 269 F.2d at 224, seems to us greater than in cases where we have reversed agencies for failure to disclose internal studies. We do not understand the rulemaking procedures adopted by the Commission to be inconsistent with these views since those procedures provide for a dialogue among interested parties through provisions for comment, reply-comment, and subsequent oral argument.[126] What we do find baffling is why the Commission, which ap-

126. The Commission's rules provide in relevant part:
"§1.415 Comments and replies.
"(a) After notice of proposed rule making is issued, the Commission will afford interested persons an opportunity to participate in the rule making proceeding through submission of written data, views, or arguments, with or without opportunity to present the same orally in any manner.
"(b) A reasonable time will be provided for submission of comments in support of or in opposition to proposed rules, and the time provided will be specified in the notice of proposed rule making.
"(c) A reasonable time will be provided for filing comments in reply to the original comments, and the time provided will be specified in the notice of proposed rule making.
"(d) No additional comments may be filed unless specifically requested or authorized by the Commission. . . ." 47 CFR §1.415 (1975).
Substantially similar rules were construed in Sangamon Valley Television Corp. v. United

parently recognizes that ready availability of private contacts saps the efficacy of the public proceedings, nonetheless continues the practice of allowing public and private comments to exist side by side.

Equally important is the inconsistency of secrecy with fundamental notions of fairness implicit in due process and with the ideal of reasoned decision-making on the merits which undergirds all of our administrative law. This inconsistency was recognized in *Sangamon,* and we would have thought that the principles announced there so clearly governed the instant proceeding that there could be no question of the impropriety of ex parte contacts here. Certainly any ambiguity in how *Sangamon* should be interpreted has been removed by recent congressional and presidential actions. In the Government in the Sunshine Act, for example, Congress has declared it to be "the policy of the United States that the public is entitled to the fullest practicable information regarding the decision-making process of the Federal Government," Pub. L. No. 94-409, §2, 90 Stat. 1241 (Sept. 13, 1976), and has taken steps to guard against ex parte contacts in formal agency proceedings. Perhaps more closely on point is Executive Order 11920, 12 Weekly Comp. of Presidential Documents 1040 (1976), which prohibits ex parte contacts with members of the White House staff by those seeking to influence allocation of international air routes during the time route certifications are before the President for his approval. The President's actions under Section 801 of the Federal Aviation Act are clearly not adjudicative, nor even quasi-judicial. Instead, the closest analogue is precisely that of *Sangamon:* informal official action allocating valuable privileges among competing private parties. Thus this is a time when all branches of government have taken steps "designed to better assure fairness and to avoid suspicions of impropriety," White House Fact Sheet on Executive Order 11920 (June 10, 1976), and consequently we have no hesitation in concluding with *Sangamon* that due process requires us to set aside the Commission's rules here.

States, . . . , 106 U.S. App. D.C. at 33-34, 269 F.2d at 224-225, to prohibit ex parte communications since such communications, as a practical matter, constituted additional comments for which no specific authority had been granted. See 47 C.F.R. §1.415(d) (1975). At the time of *Sangamon,* however, the Commissions' rules and practice required "a showing of good cause," 106 U.S. App. D.C. at 34, 269 F.2d at 225, for approval of a request to submit additional comments. In the absence of this language, and given the apparent long-standing Commission interpretation of its own rules to allow ex parte contacts, see Geller br. at 7, the inference that the Commission has violated its own rules is less easy to draw from the rather obvious inconsistency between the published rules' strict timetable for comment and the actual practice of allowing comment at any time. Nonetheless, the Commission's practice of announcing a relaxation in its comment and reply-comment rules through the cryptic phrase, "[i]n reaching a decision in this matter the Commission may take into account any other relevant information before it," 35 F.C.C.2d at 899, . . . is certainly inconsistent with the spirit of the policy disclosure requirements of the Freedom of Information Act, 5 U.S.C. §552(a)(2)(B) (1970), which seek to give the public an understanding of how an agency actually works. One not familiar with Commission practices would be hard put to understand that the foregoing phrase effectively repealed 47 C.F.R. §1.415(d), a fact corroborated by the complete absence of reported ex parte contracts from public interest intervenors other than amicus Geller, himself a former General Counsel of the Commission. In these circumstances, we do not think the Commission can be said to have specifically authorized additional comments as required by 47 C.F.R. §1.41[5(d)], cf. 5 U.S.C. §552(a)(2) (prohibiting agency reliance on undisclosed policy statements), and we, therefore, hold that the Commission violated its own rules.

From what has been said above, it should be clear that information gathered ex parte from the public which becomes relevant to a rulemaking will have to be disclosed at some time. On the other hand, we recognize that informal contacts between agencies and the public are the "bread and butter" of the process of administration and are completely appropriate so long as they do not frustrate judicial review or raise serious questions of fairness. Reconciliation of these considerations in a manner which will reduce procedural uncertainty leads us to conclude that communications which are received prior to issuance of a formal notice of rulemaking do not, in general, have to be put in a public file. Of course, if the information contained in such a communication forms the basis for agency action, then, under well-established principles, that information must be disclosed to the public in some form. Once a notice of proposed rulemaking has been issued, however, any agency official or employee who is or may reasonably be expected to be involved in the decisional process of the rulemaking proceeding [in the words of the Executive Order governing White House employees and international airline routes], should "refus[e] to discuss matters relating to the disposition of a [rulemaking proceeding] with any interested private party, or an attorney or agent for any such party, prior to the [agency's] decision..., Executive Order 11920, §4, supra, at 1041. If ex parte contacts nonetheless occur, we think that any written document or a summary of any oral communication must be placed in the public file established for each rulemaking docket immediately after the communication is received so that interested parties may comment thereon. Compare Executive Order 11920, §5, supra.

MacKinnon, Circuit Judge, concurring specially. Belatedly, I file the following special concurrence.... I agree that [the court's ruling that off the record communications are improper and should, if they occur, be placed in the public file] is the proper rule to apply in this case because the rulemaking undeniably involved competitive interests of great monetary value and conferred preferential advantages on vast segments of the broadcast industry to the detriment of other competing business interests. The rule as issued was in effect an adjudication of the respective rights of the parties vis-à-vis each other. And since that is the nature of the case and controversy that we are deciding and to which our opinion is limited, I would make it clear that that is all we are deciding. I would not make an excessively broad statement to include dictum that could be interpreted to cover the entire universe of informal rulemaking. There are so many situations where the application of such a broad rule would be inappropriate that we should not paint with such a broad brush.[127] ...

---

127. Professor Kenneth Culp Davis in his Administrative Law Treatise (1958) points out some of the advantages of informal rule making and its wide scope:

"§6.02. Written Presentations. Consultations, and Conferences.

"Informal written or oral consultation with affected parties or with advisory committees is the mainstay of rule making procedure. The principal requirement of the APA is 'opportunity to participate in the rule making through submission of written data, views, or arguments with or without opportunity to present the same orally in any manner.' ...

"The consultative process may take many forms. The administrator or staff member may talk over possible rules with selected parties, by telephone or in person, singly or in groups, by

Action for Children's Television v. FCC

564 F.2d 458 (D.C. Cir. 1977)

Before TAMM, MacKINNON and WILKEY, Circuit Judges.

TAMM, Circuit Judge:

[Action for Children's Television (ACT), a nonprofit "public interest" organization, petitioned the FCC to adopt regulations prohibiting commercials in or sponsorship of children's television programs and mandating a minimum amount of programming suitable for children of various age groups. The FCC instituted a notice and comment rulemaking proceeding on ACT's proposal; numerous written comments were received, most strongly supporting ACT's basic goals. The Commission also heard oral argument and panel discussions on the proposal.

In response to ACT's proposals, the broadcast industry took some initial steps toward self-regulation of children's program content and advertising. Following a private meeting between officials of the National Association of Broadcasters (NAB) and the Commission Chairman, the NAB amended its Television Code to limit the amount and content of advertising on children's programs. Thereafter the FCC issued a report in which it enunciated certain broad principles which it believed should govern advertising on children's programs but declined to adopt ACT's proposal or issue specific regulations on the ground that the broadcast industry was implementing these principles through self-regulation. The Commission stated that it would monitor the industry's efforts and take further steps if necessary.]

ACT claims at the outset that the manner in which the Commission concluded these rulemaking proceedings "epitomizes abuse of the administrative process" by its failure to solicit public comment on the industry proposals for self-regulation negotiated "behind the closed doors of Chairman Wiley's office in a private meeting with NAB officials ... [in which] the industry was clearly coerced into action under the threat of FCC regulation." Petitioner's Brief at 25. ACT contends that such action undermines the administrative process since it denies public participation at *every* stage of the regulatory process when issues of critical public importance are considered, frustrates effective judicial review, and renders the extensive comment-gathering stage "little more than a sop...." Id. at 26-28.

[The Court held that it would consider ACT's claim of improper ex parte

---

systematically and formally arranged conferences or interviews or in connection with fortuitous contacts occasioned by other business. To frame one set of rules the ICC once conducted 89 informal conferences attended by 1,740 individuals representing 1,286 carriers; to frame another set the Commission sent an interviewer through fifteen states to talk with representatives of motor carriers, members of state commissions, executives of insurance companies, and insurance agents and brokers, and then later conferences were held with committees representing the bus industry, the truck industry, and insurance associations. Sometimes consultation involves collaboration in planning and drafting, as when technical representatives of shipping companies cooperate with technicians of the Customs Bureau in preparing rules concerning construction of vessels....

"When parties are too numerous and individuals may not be representative, some organization often supplies what is needed. For instance, in the FCC 'regular contacts are maintained with well-established trade associations and some licensees and carriers....'"

contacts even though ACT had not raised it before the Commission. It also held that the possibility that the FCC might ultimately rely on industry self-regulation was clearly forseeable to ACT, and that the failure of the Federal Register notice of the rulemaking proceedings to mention that possibility did not violate 5 U.S.C. §553(b)(3), which requires that such notice describe "either the terms or substance of the proposed rule or a description of the subjects and issues involved."]

In addition to notice, an agency must permit meaningful public participation by giving "interested parties an opportunity to participate in the rulemaking through a submission of written data, views, arguments with or without opportunity for oral presentation." 5 U.S.C. §553(c) (Supp. V 1975). The procedures available to satisfy this requirement are correspondingly diverse, though less so than formerly. No hearing is usually required, and generally no procedural uniformity is imposed. 1 K. Davis, Administrative Law Treatise §6.01, at 360-61 (1958). The more limited procedural safeguards in informal rulemaking are justified by its more wide-ranging functional emphasis on questions of law, policy and legislatively conferred discretion rather than on the contested facts of an individual case. See 1 Davis, supra, at 413. The issues facing the Commission in the proceeding sub judice were clearly of a legislative nature, policy considerations predominated, and any rules ultimately adopted would have affected the television and advertising industries, and a significant proportion of television programming.

... The Commission substantially met [the requirements of §553] by permitting a lengthy period for the submission of written comments and by holding six days of informal panel discussions and formal oral arguments.... While the agency must consider, analyze and rely on these factual materials which are in the public domain, the agency may draw upon its own expertise in interpreting the facts or upon broader policy considerations not present in the record. We believe that the Commission operated within this framework in this case.[128]

... [T]he commission did explain the reason for its decision to rely for the time being on self-regulation rather than specific rules. This explanation is contained in the record now before us, and it furnishes a basis for effective judicial review.[129]

In holding that ACT's position was not prejudiced by the manner in which the commission pursued the temporary resolution of these proceedings, we wish to emphasize that we are not insensitive to ACT's disenchantment with what it considered to be the agency's undue deference to the interests of those it was created to regulate. Meaningful public participation is always to be encouraged.... Nevertheless, while it may have been impolitic for the Commission not to invite further comment on the NAB's proposals, especially in view of the fact that there

128. With this doubtlessly in mind, the FCC took care to point out in its Notice of Inquiry and Proposed Rule Making that it might "also take into account other relevant data before it, in addition to the specific data invited by this Notice." 28 F.C.C.2d at 372-373, ...
129. As a practical matter, of course, a reviewing court generally will have a less substantial record to review in cases of informal rulemaking than it will when faced with administrative action undertaken upon a formal hearing held pursuant to §§ 556 and 557. Consequently, a reviewing court must perforce rely even more on an agency's statement of reasons, if it is not effectively to abdicate its proper role in the administrative process....

was no necessity for deciding these difficult issues quickly, we still cannot say that the Commission abused its discretion in deciding not to. . . .[130]

In so concluding, we necessarily are confronted with the recent decision of this court in Home Box Office, Inc. v. FCC. . . . [Judge Tamm quotes portions of the last paragraph of the Court's *Home Box Office* opinion, p. 550, supra.]

For the reasons set forth below, we agree with Judge MacKinnon that the above-quoted rule should not apply — as the opinion clearly would have it — to every case of informal rulemaking. *Home Box Office*, supra (opinion concurring specially filed May 20, 1977). However, notwithstanding our views to the contrary, we hold only that *Home Box Office*'s broad proscription is not to be applied retroactively in the case sub judice inasmuch as it constitutes a clear departure from established law when applied to informal rulemaking proceedings. . . . See generally Linkletter v. Walker, 381 U.S. 618, 627-29. . . .

[The Court also distinguished *Home Box Office* and *Sangamon* on the ground that they involved "conflicting private claims to a valuable privilege," whereas the rulemaking proceedings here involved "the possible formulation of programming policy revisions of general applicability." It asserted that *Home Box Office*'s reliance on the Sunshine Act as support for its ruling was misplaced because the Act's prohibitions on ex parte communications are specifically limited to "on the record" proceedings governed by §§ 556-557 of the APA.]

On the other hand, though, we have Citizens to Preserve Overton Park, Inc. v. Volpe, 401 U.S. 402 (1971) — a somewhat Delphic opinion concerning informal administrative action rather than informal rulemaking — which we believe as a practical matter should not be read as mandating that the public record upon which our review is based reflect every informational input that may have entered into the decisionmaker's deliberative process. . . .

130. Petitioner also asserts that the FCC abused its authority by exploiting its sensitive relationship with broadcast licensees to coerce them into a measure of self-regulation, just as it had in the "family viewing hour" programming policy area. Petitioner's Brief at 26-27. In Writers Guild of America, West, Inc. v. FCC, 423 F. Supp. 1064 (C.D. Cal. 1976), a district court recently held that the adoption of the family viewing hour policy by the television networks and the NAB at the behest of the Commission violated the APA because the Commission ignored §553's requirement that interested persons have an opportunity to participate in the policy-making process, whether they be members of the public or representatives of the regulated industry. . . .

In the case sub judice, however, we have concluded that the FCC substantially complied with the procedural requirements of §553, and we do not consider that the meetings between the FCC's Chairman and NAB representatives compel a contrary conclusion. If we were to accept the proposition implicit in petitioner's argument — that the FCC may never resort to discussions with members of the industry in a general effort to have its regulatees conform to their public service obligations — the Commission would have little choice but to abandon any reasonable expectation of salutary self-regulation and to affirmatively regulate throughout the areas of children's programming and advertising. The problem, of course, is necessarily a matter of degree, and an agency may well be found to have abused its authority were it to employ overbearing "jawboning" or "arm-twisting" tactics. In the *Writers Guild* decision, the Commission was held to have overstepped its authority when the Commission Chairman threatened "regulatory actions up to and including the relicensing process . . . ," if broadcasters did not reduce substantially the amount of violent and "adult" material shown during evening hours. Id. at 1149. At least in the case now before us, however, we are satisfied that the Commission did not coerce the industry into accepting agency-decreed policies or standards negotiated at closed-door meetings. . . .

If we go as far as *Home Box Office* does in its ex parte ruling in ensuring a "whole record" for our review, why not go further to require the decisionmaker to summarize and make available for public comment every status inquiry from a Congressman or any germane material — say a newspaper editorial — that he or she reads or their evening-hour ruminations? See generally Davis, supra, §13.12 (Supp. 1970). In the end, why not administer a lie-detector test to ascertain whether the required summary is an accurate and complete one? The problem is obviously a matter of degree, and the appropriate line must be drawn somewhere. ... [W]e would draw that line at the point where the rulemaking proceedings involve "competing claims to a valuable privilege."

It is at that point where the potential for unfair advantage outweighs the practical burdens, which we imagine would not be insubstantial that [a rule prohibiting any off-the-record communications in informal rulemaking] would place upon administrators.

[The court held that the FCC's decision not to adopt regulations governing children's television advertising, and to instead rely upon industry self-regulation, was not an abuse of discretion.]

Questions

1. On what authority do the courts in *Sangamon* and *Home Box Office* prohibit agency reliance on off-the-record communications? Are the rulings based on due process? The APA? Have these decisions been effectively overruled by the subsequent decision of the Supreme Court in *Vermont Yankee*, supra p. 516? See United States Lines, Inc. v. FMC, 584 F.2d 519 (D.C. Cir. 1978).

2. Which is more persuasive, *Home Box Office* or *Action for Children's Television* (ACT)? ACT would limit the prohibition against ex parte communications in informal rulemaking to cases involving "competing private claims to a valuable privilege." Why? Can ACT be successfully distinguished from *Home Box Office* in terms of this standard? [131]

3. If *Home Box Office* is followed, should its requirements apply to all informal rulemaking? To informal adjudication? Suppose that in *Overton Park* the Secretary had, in the course of his deliberations, consulted informally with proponents of the park route without disclosing the substance of the communication to opponents? [132] Should the APA be amended in order to resolve these issues?

---

131. Judge MacKinnon also suggests in his *Home Box Office* concurrence that the standard should be whether the proceeding is "in effect an adjudication." (Justice Douglas's dissenting opinion in *Florida East Coast*, supra p. 486-488, suggests a similar test.) Is this test more appropriate or workable than the "competing claims" test?

How should a zoning variance be classified? In Jarrott v. Scrivener, 225 F. Supp. 827 (D.D.C. 1964), three members of the Board of Zoning Adjustment, two of whom were subordinate government employees, were secretly informed that highly placed persons in government wanted the Board to grant a foreign government's application for exception to erect an embassy building in a residential zone. The court held that a fair hearing had been denied, vacated the decision, and ordered a rehearing by a new board created for that purpose.

132. For discussion of *Overton Park*, see Auerbach, Informal Rulemaking: A Proposed Relationship Between Administrative Procedures and Judicial Review, 72 Nw. U.L. Rev. 15,

4. If *ACT* is followed, would the developing efforts of courts to monitor agency discretion exercised through rulemaking be largely destroyed? For example, how can a reviewing court determine whether an agency has taken a "hard look" at all relevant considerations if the agency is free to rely on materials and communications never disclosed to the court or to litigants challenging the agency's decision?

5. Should prohibitions against ex parte communications extend to communications between agency members and other officials of the federal government, such as members of Congress or the White House staff? Suppose, for example, that in *Sangamon* or *Home Box Office* the Commission Chairman, during or after the public comment period, had consulted, orally and off the record, with a White House aide about the disposition of the proceeding. Should the propriety of such communications turn on whether the agency in question is an "independent" one (such as the FCC) or is one of the traditional arms of the executive (such as the Interior Department)? What if the President himself initiated such consultations? The propriety of "off the record" White House intervention in informal rulemaking is a subject of current controversy (see p. 158, supra), but courts have not yet ruled on the legal issues presented.

6. Members of the FCC concede that all major rules governing CATV systems were worked out in part through negotiation with industry representatives at private meetings. When asked why these private meetings were necessary, they might respond as follows:

> Without privacy, negotiation will prove impossible, yet negotiation is important, particularly in the context of cable regulations, for several reasons. First, at issue are a set of rules that will allow a new set of competitors to enter the field and injure, or perhaps destroy, an existing major industry with billions of dollars of investment. We cannot determine, through studies of independent experts, the extent to which any given set of rules will hurt the

---

59 (1977). See also Recommendation 77-3 of the Administrative Conference of the United States, 1977 Report of the Administrative Conference 36 (1978), stating that a prohibition against all off-the-record communications in all informal rulemaking would be unwise; recommending that written communications addressed to the merits be placed in the public file; and further recommending that agencies "experiment in appropriate situations" . . . by including in the public file written summaries of oral communications.

Following the decisions in *Home Box Office* and Action for Children's Television v. FCC, the FTC amended its Rules of Practice to prohibit ex parte communications in all notice and comment rulemaking proceedings. (See 16 C.F.R. §§ 1.18(b)-1.18(c).) The new rules provide that, if an outsider does attempt to communicate with a Commissioner or a member of his or her personal staff after a rulemaking proceeding has begun, the communication will be placed in the public record but will be excluded from the Commissioners' consideration when they make their decision on the final rule. The rule excepts "status" inquiries and communications between the Commissioners and Commission employees, including the staff attorneys working on the proposed rules.

The Federal Trade Commission has adopted similar provisions for the conduct of trade regulation rule making. 16 C.F.R. §4.7. Commissioner Dole dissented, preferring a "less restrictive" alternative that would permit the Commission to consider written and oral communications not submitted as formal comments so long as such communications (or a written summary in the case of oral communications) were placed in the public record file.

broadcasters, for the studies conflict and information is imperfect. If the broadcasters agree or come close to agreeing that a given set of rules is acceptable, at least we know we are unlikely to destroy them, and if the cable owners agree, they must be getting something that will facilitate their entry.

Second, if we promulgate rules that are too threatening to the broadcasters, they will obtain legislation that will permanently block cable. Senator Blank, the chairman of the Communications Subcommittee, has phoned three of us several times and made it perfectly clear he does not want to see, as he puts it, the "industry destroyed." Unless we can negotiate a solution, informally, the industry will simply maintain total opposition and the Commission will retain very restrictive anticable rules.

Now, one might ask, why should the Commission listen to Senator Blank? Why should it not simply do what it thinks is right and let Congress, it it wishes, pass legislation nullifying the action? To take this attitude overlooks a sincere desire on the part of the Commissioners to achieve in the world a concrete result that they believe good for communications. It also overlooks the power of Senator Blank, who can not only seek legislation, but can also hold oversight hearings designed to embarrass us personally, cut our appropriation, or make certain we obtain no other job in the government ever. Moreover, if he is prevented from telling us his views by phone, he will do so in other ways. A negotiated solution satisfies him, the broadcasters, and the cable interests as well. It is most unlikely that any such solution here would injure the public.

Third, a negotiated solution will minimize the possibility of court challenge. We have worked on these rules for many years. To have a solution delayed for an additional four or five while a court reviews (and possibly remands) is undesirable.

Can it be possible that negotiated solutions are never permissible or desirable? They take place every day of the week within the legislature. Why then should the courts not allow agencies to use similar approaches — at least some of the time?

What do you think of this hypothetical argument?

7. The Federal Trade Commission has brought an action charging Happy Grocery Store with failing to mark prices individually upon each can of goods — which the FTC claims is "unfair" or "deceptive."

The Commission has also issued a press release stating that it is considering whether to institute rulemaking proceedings concerning the marking of price on food items in supermarkets. In particular, it is considering a rule requiring that each individual item be marked in "arabic numerals, regardless of whether it is marked in computer code or some other way."

The National Association of Grocery Retailers fears that such a rule would prevent the introduction of computer code pricing. Such pricing consists of bars marked on the food can by the manufacturer. A "reading machine" at the checkout counter automatically notes the price, thus saving time and eliminating mistakes. The store manager can tell the machine each day how to "translate" any given set of bars. Thus, he retains control of each pricing decision. Prices in arabic numerals would be noted on the shelf but not on the can, saving the labor costs involved in marking each can and recording the price of each item, at the checkout counter, by hand.

The President of the Association and several directors (none of whom is connected with Happy Grocery Store) seek a private meeting with the Chairman of the FTC and one or two other members, in order to make their views known "at the policymaking level." They are anxious to keep the meeting private in order to discuss what they believe to be the true basis of opposition to the "automated checkout" system — fear that the system will put some retail grocery employees out of work.

(a) At this point you, as counsel to the Association, are asked if the meeting should be held as planned. Should you join in it? What problems do you foresee? How would you overcome them?

(b) Assume you are FTC General Counsel advising the FTC Chairman. Should the Chairman hold such a meeting? If so, what conditions should he stipulate?

D. The Interaction Between Procedural Requirements and Regulatory Policies

1. *FDA Regulation of Drug Efficacy*

Note: The 1962 FDA Drug Efficacy Amendments and Their Implementation

The Food, Drug, and Cosmetic Act Amendments of 1962 were the first major revision of the FDA Act since 1938. During that quarter-century the prescription drug industry had expanded enormously, paralleling advances in medical research, to become a major industry, one whose products represent a crucial element of modern health care.

The 1962 Amendments evolved from two principal areas of concern: the industry as such, and its products. The basic bill originated in Senator Kefauver's Subcommittee on Antitrust and Monopoly of the Senate Judiciary Committee. It was an outgrowth of an investigation into four major industries — autos, steel, bread, and drugs — in which the Subcommittee found oligopoly and managed prices. The Subcommittee was also concerned by the critical bearing of drugs on the public welfare, the rigid limitation of consumer (patient) choice to the brand-name drug prescribed by the doctor (and brand-name reliance was a well-entrenched practice with doctors, supported by antisubstitution laws in 44 states which require the druggist to honor the brand-name choice), and the inelastic quality of consumer demand. The Subcommittee also stressed the inordinately large sums of money spent on advertising and promotion[133] and the high profit [134] level in the drug industry, despite the fact that only limited capital was required to establish a drug manufacturing facility of economic scale. All of these concerns made for a high level of public interest in the Subcommittee's investigations; the drug industry complained of political sensationalism.

The Subcommittee investigations disclosed that the means by which companies gain doctor acceptance include promotional brochures, free product samples, displays and hospitality at conventions, educational symposia and research grants, gifts of equipment to medical students and, most important, a corps of 15,000 to 20,000 hard-sell "detail men" who call on the doctors. An AMA study cited by Kefauver found that 65 percent of doctors listed these men as the "most effective" source of information on new drugs. Heavy advertising in the drug industry is also a crucial means of franchise-building. Heavy advertising and promotional efforts, when successful, render the brand-name product difficult to supplant, despite subsequent competitive improvements.

While Senator Kefauver was pursuing the industry from the perspective of economic regulation, HEW initiated a study of industry practices from the standpoint of the public health. In 1960, Arthur Fleming, Eisenhower's Secretary of HEW, asked the National Academy of Sciences–National Research Council to review the policy and proceedings of the FDA regarding new prescription drug processing and to present recommendations. Armed with these recommendations, which were subsequently incorporated in the 1962 Amendments, the new Secretary of HEW, Abraham Ribicoff, began work on an administration bill. By that time, however, Senator Kefauver had compiled twenty-one volumes of hearing and testimony on his own bill, and it was decided to put administration efforts into working with that bill, which was enacted in 1962.

The 1962 Amendments dealt with efficacy of drugs, factory inspection, quality control in manufacturing, and the role of advertising in drugs. The passage of the bill in its final form — and with no dissenting votes — is a tribute not so much to its unobjectionable quality (for it was fiercely contested by the Pharmaceutical Manufacturers Association and the American Medical Association), as to the thalidomide disaster, which developed during the final consideration of the bill, and which provided the crucial impetus for a strong bill.[135]

133. The Subcommittee found in 1958 that drug marketing expenses for 22 of the largest firms were 24.8 percent of sales, versus a much lower level for research — 6.5 percent.
134. The 1965 to mid-1969 range of quarterly post-tax earnings:

	On Sales	On Shareholders' Investment
All Mfgrs.	3.4-5.9%	6.8-14.7%
Drugs	9.1-11.7%	14.7-22.0%

135. The original 1938 Act also can be viewed as a response to tragedy involving the drug sulfanilamide which claimed over 100 lives before it was withdrawn from the market. Ironically, the thalidomide disaster was largely irrelevant to the issues involved in the 1962 Amendments. Thalidomide, which was widely used as a sedative in Europe and was subsequently found to produce serious fetal defects when ingested by pregnant women, had been barred by the FDA from widespread marketing in the United States. Moreover, thalidomide's side effects presented a problem of drug safety, whereas the 1962 Amendments were largely directed at problems of drug efficacy.

To understand the nature of the efficacy requirements of the 1962 Amendments, one must have some knowledge of the 1938 Act on which the Amendments are based. That Act set up the New Drug Application (NDA) procedure, the key to which was the designation of certain drugs as "new drugs." These were defined as drugs not generally recognized by experts as safe for use under the conditions prescribed, recommended, or suggested in their labeling, or as drugs which had become generally recognized as safe but which had not been used to a material extent or for a material time, or as drugs concerning which actual practice had shown bad effects. Such "new drugs" had to have an "effective" (not disapproved) NDA from the FDA. Such approval was required to be granted automatically 60 days after submission of the application unless the FDA issued formal disapproval.

The NDA procedure did not encompass all prescription drugs. Certain antibiotics and insulin drugs were exempted and were subjected instead to a "batch-certification system." Second, the NDA procedure made no provision for review of efficacy. Its concern was safety. An application on behalf of a totally innocuous, and equally useless, drug would theoretically be entitled to approval. FDA efforts to withdraw approved applications for ineffective drugs on the ground that such drugs endangered public health because they would be used in place of an efficacious drug were generally unsuccessful in the courts.[136]

Under the 1962 Amendments, applicants for New Drug Approval are now required to submit data showing efficacy as well as safety and the Secretary of HEW must disapprove any NDA if, after notice and opportunity for a hearing, he determines that the available data does not establish the safety of the drug, or that there is a lack of "substantial evidence" [137] that the drug will have the effect it purports or is represented to have under the conditions of use prescribed, recommended, or suggested in its labeling. Additionally, a positive stamp of approval, not just official inaction, is required to grant the NDA.

In addition, the Secretary is empowered to *withdraw* a previously approved new drug if he finds that experience has shown the drug to be unsafe; or if "new evidence" shows that the drug's safety is not established; or if "new information" discloses a lack of "substantial evidence" of the drug's efficacy. Such withdrawal is authorized only after "due notice and opportunity for hearing" to the applicant. However, if the Secretary finds "an imminent hazard to public health" he may *suspend* the drug's approval immediately (which has the effect of temporarily removing it from the market) pending notice and opportunity for hearing on the issue of permanent withdrawal.

As the legislative history makes clear, however, the Secretary's responsibility in all of the proceedings is limited to determining efficacy of the drug for the uses suggested in the drug's labeling. He was not empowered to determine whether a given drug is comparatively more or less effective than some other drug for a given

136. To the extent that a useless drug's labeling claimed efficacy, the FDA might bring an action to have the drug removed from the market as misbranded, but the FDA would have a substantial burden of proof to carry on the misbranding issue.

137. "Substantial evidence" is a statutorily defined term; see the excerpts from §505 of the Act quoted below.

therapeutic use; that determination the Congress intended to reserve to the prescribing physician.

The pertinent provisions of the amended Act which deal with new drugs and which are summarized above are contained in §505 of the Act, 21 U.S.C. §355:

Sec. 505 (a) No person shall introduce or deliver for introduction into interstate commerce any new drug, unless an approval of an application filed pursuant to subsection (b) is effective with respect to such drug. . . .

(d) If the Secretary finds, after due notice to the applicant in accordance with subsection (c) and giving him an opportunity for a hearing, in accordance with said subsection, that evaluated on the basis of the information submitted to him as part of the application and any other information before him with respect to such drug, there is a lack of substantial evidence that the drug will have the effect it purports or is represented to have under the conditions of use prescribed, recommended, or suggested in the proposed labeling thereof; . . . he shall issue an order refusing to approve the application. . . . As used in this subsection and subsection (e), the term "substantial evidence" means evidence consisting of adequate and well-controlled investigations, including clinical investigations, by experts qualified by scientific training and experience to evaluate the effectiveness of the drug involved, on the basis of which it could fairly and responsibly be concluded by such experts that the drug will have the effect it purports or is represented to have under the conditions of use prescribed, recommended, or suggested in the labeling or proposed labeling thereof.

(e) The Secretary shall, after due notice and opportunity for hearing to the applicant, withdraw approval of an application with respect to any drug under this section if the Secretary finds . . . (3) on the basis of new information before him with respect to such drug, evaluated together with the evidence available to him when the application was approved, that there is a lack of substantial evidence that the drug will have the effect it purports or is represented to have under the conditions of use prescribed, recommended, or suggested in the labeling thereof; . . . Provided, that if the Secretary (or in his absence the officer acting as Secretary) finds that there is an imminent hazard to the public health, he may suspend the approval of such application immediately, and give the applicant prompt notice of his action and afford the applicant the opportunity for an expedited hearing under this subsection; but the authority conferred by this proviso to suspend the approval of an application shall not be delegated. . . .

Antibiotic drugs, such as penicillin, tetracycline, etc. are dealt with in a separate provision, §507 of the Act, 21 U.S.C. §357. Antibiotics differ from other drugs in that they are inherently effective; antibiotics are scientifically defined as agents that destroy bacteria.[138] Accordingly, the provisions of §507 are apparently not directed to the effectiveness of any generic antibiotic, but to ensuring that particular batches of a product meet standards of identity for the generic antibiotic involved. These standards are to be established through regulations issued by the Secretary.

138. See the definition of "antibiotic drug" in §507(a) of the Act.

Section 507 of the Act, 21 U.S.C. §357, provides in relevant part:

> *Certification of Antibiotics.* (a) The Secretary of Health, Education, and Welfare, pursuant to regulations promulgated by him, shall provide for the certification of batches of drugs (except drugs for use in animals other than man) composed wholly or partly of any kind of penicillin, streptomycin, chlortetracycline, chloramphenicol, bacitracin, or any other antibiotic drug, or any derivative thereof. A batch of any such drug shall be certified if such drug has such characteristics of identity and such batch has such characteristics of strength, quality, and purity, as the Secretary prescribes in such regulations as necessary to adequately insure safety and efficacy of use, but shall not otherwise be certified.
>
> . . . For purposes of this section and of section 502(l), the term "antibiotic drug" means any drug intended for use by man containing any quantity of any chemical substance which is produced by a micro-organism and which has the capacity to inhibit or destroy micro-organisms in dilute solution (including the chemically synthesized equivalent of any such substance). . . .
>
> (f) Any interested person may file with the Secretary a petition proposing the issuance, amendment, or repeal of any regulation contemplated by this section. The petition shall set forth the proposal in general terms and shall state reasonable grounds therefor. The Secretary shall give public notice of the proposal and an opportunity for all interested persons to present their views thereon, orally or in writing, and as soon as practicable thereafter shall make public his action upon such proposal. At any time prior to the thirtieth day after such action is made public any interested person may file objections to such action, specifying with particularity the changes desired, stating reasonable grounds therefor, and requesting a public hearing upon such objections. The Secretary shall thereupon, after due notice, hold such public hearing. As soon as practicable after completion of the hearing, the Secretary shall by order make public his action on such objections. The Secretary shall base his order only on substantial evidence of record at the hearing and shall set forth as part of the order detailed findings of fact on which the order is based. The order shall be subject to the provisions of section 701 (f) and (g).[139]

Following the 1962 amendments, the FDA moved relatively promptly to implement the new efficacy requirements of §505 for new drug applications filed after the effective date of the amendments. However, difficulties were encountered in applying the new requirements to the thousands of "new drugs" whose NDAs had been approved during the 1938-1962 period, when the sole test had been safety. FDA initially took the position that there would be a two-year grace period during

---

139. Ed. note: Section 701(f), (g) provides for judicial review of an "order" of the FDA. Section 701(f) states that "The remedies provided for in this subsection shall be in addition and not in substitution for any other remedies provided by law." The reference to "safety and efficacy of use" in Section 507(a) was contained in the original version of the Section when it was added to the Act in 1945, and was not supplied by the 1962 Amendments.

None of the legislative history of the provisions in the 1962 amendments imposing new requirements as to efficacy for new drugs under Section 505 of the Act discussed the question whether those requirements would also be applicable to antibiotic drugs under Section 507.

which pre-1962 NDAs would not be subject to withdrawal on efficacy grounds unless the labeling of the product involved had been changed. In 1964, the FDA required all manufacturers to appraise their pre-1962 drugs in respect of any claims of efficacy in the labeling or promotional literature. At some points the FDA indicated that this requirement might also be applicable to antibiotic drug products. However, not much progress was made toward the review of outstanding NDAs, and in 1966 the FDA signed a contract with the National Academy of Sciences and the National Research Council (scientific research organizations chartered and funded by Congress) to undertake a full retrospective review — to include antibiotics and also insulin drugs (which are covered by still another provision, §506 of the Act) — of all pre-1962 prescription drug products and render advisory opinions as to their efficacy.

The NAS-NRC divided the task of evaluation among a number of panels composed of doctors and scientists whom it regarded as expert in the area. As required by FDA, manufacturers submitted data bearing on the efficacy of their products to these panels. Some 2800 products were evaluated by the panels, and the FDA initially sought on the basis of these evaluations to remove from the market as ineffective some 78 products.

The FDA's first such effort to remove from the market an established pre-1962 drug was directed at "Sanalba," a drug product manufactured by the Outom Company. Sanalba is a fixed combination drug composed of two antibiotics, tetracycline and novobiocin. Tetracycline is a comparatively broad-band antibiotic, i.e., it is effective in dealing with a relatively broad range of infectious bacteria. Novobiocin is a relatively narrow-band antibiotic which is, however, effective with a number of organisms for which tetracycline is not effective. Each dose of "Sanalba" contains a combination of 2 parts tetracycline and one part novobiocin (by weight). The labeling of the Sanalba product claims that the combination product is more effective than either ingredient alone.

Combination antibiotic drugs such as Sanalba are widely used by many practicing physicians to deal with infectious diseases that are not easily or quickly diagnosed. Because the combination antibiotic drug can deal with a broader range of possible infectious diseases than a single antibiotic, the use of a combination better assures effective treatment of infection without the necessity for expensive and time-consuming diagnosis. However, each antibiotic drug has side effects, ranging in severity from rash and discomfort to serious illness and death. A number of authorities in the FDA and leading medical schools oppose the use of fixed-combination antibiotic drugs as a lazy "shotgun" method of treatment that increases the likelihood of an adverse side affect because of the use of more than one antibiotic.[140] They contend that the best medical practice is to use a "rifle" method of treatment, diagnosing the precise infection involved and prescribing the one antibi-

---

140. Many authorities also assert that the questions of safety and efficacy can not be dissociated. Thus, most drugs are not absolutely "safe" because they have some side effects. The degree of side effects regarded as tolerable depends on the benefits which the drug's use may confer. Even a highly dangerous drug may be used if the patient would otherwise die and the drug has some possibility of effecting a cure. By the same token, it is contended, evaluation of efficacy can not be dissociated from the question of side effects.

otic that is most appropriate for treatment of that infection. Moreover, these authorities assert that even if the use of a combination antibiotic is sometimes desirable, the fixed combination offered by the manufacturer may not contain the most appropriate proportion of ingredients for the particular patient. However, the drug companies and many practicing physicians reply that, while theoretically superior, the "rifle" approach is simply not workable in practice in many areas. It may take 24 to 48 hours to diagnose precisely the nature of an infection; if the infection is serious, immediate treatment may be needed. Precise diagnosis may cost from $30 to $60 or more. Moreover, precise diagnosis and tailoring of dose or combination requires special equipment, technicians, and sophisticated medical judgment which may not be readily available in some areas of the nation.

Sanalba has been one of the most successful of the combination antibiotic drugs. It was first marketed in 1957 after the FDA issued regulations under §507 determining that the combination of teracycline-novobiocin was safe and effective and could be marketed. Although the regulation is general in terms, Outom is in fact the only manufacturer that produces a tetracycline-novobiocin combination. Since that time, over one billion doses of Sanalba have been prescribed, and the product has been regularly employed by over 23,000 practicing physicians. "Sanalba" is an Outom trademark which has been given heavy advertising and promotional support, and the price of the Sanalba product is much higher than the price of an equivalent generic tetracycline dose plus the price of an equivalent generic novobiocin dose. Sales of Sanalba have averaged more than $30 million per year in recent years. During all this time, batches of Sanalba have, in accordance with the requirements of §507, been continuously certified by the FDA as safe and effective prior to marketing.

On December 24, 1968 the Commissioner of Food and Drugs published a notice in the Federal Register stating that a drug efficacy panel of the National Academy of Science–National Research Counsel had evaluated Sanalba and found it "ineffective as a fixed combination." In other words, the panel had found that in any given therapeutic situation the combination product was no more effective than the use of the more appropriate of its two ingredients alone. The notice stated that the FDA "concurs that here is a lack of *substantial evidence* that each ingredient in [Sanalba] contributes to the claimed clinical effect" (emphasis supplied). The notice further stated that FDA intended to repeal the antibiotic regulations permitting the marketing of tetracycline-novobiocin combination. The notice solicited comments, to be filed within 30 days, on the proposed repeal.

Outom requested an extension of time for comments in order to assemble and present to FDA the data which it believed would establish the safety and efficacy of Sanalba. Outom claimed it had had no notice that the "substantial evidence" requirement in §505, dealing with "new drugs," [141] would be applicable to established antibiotic products, and that additional time was therefore necessary to assemble the material. The Commissioner of FDA acceded to this request.

In May, 1969, Congressman Fountain of the Subcommittee on Intergovern-

---

141. At this point you should reread the definition of "substantial evidence" in §505(d) quoted supra at p. 560.

mental Relations of the House Committee on Government Operations and Senator Nelson of the Subcommittee on Monopoly of the Senate Select Committee on Small Business, both of whom have been active critics of the pharmaceutical industry, expressed displeasure at the fact that Sanalba was still on the market, and held hearings in which they demanded that the Commissioner of Food and Drug explain his conduct. At these hearings, under sharp questioning from the respective congressmen, the Commissioner stated that there was "not any justification for a fixed combination" of the antibiotics in Sanalba and that it should be removed from the market. The Commissioner also stated that he concluded as early as March, 1969, that Outom did not possess "substantial evidence" of the efficacy of Sanalba.

On May 15, 1969, the same day that the House hearings were concluded, the FDA published in the Federal Register an order repealing the antibiotic regulations permitting the marketing of a tetracycline-novobiocin combination, effective in 30 days. The Commissioner stated that the data thus far submitted by Outom on an informal basis did not contain any "adequate and well-controlled studies" demonstrating the effectiveness of Sanalba, that Outom had therefore not discharged its burden of demonstrating that there was "substantial evidence" of efficacy for Sanalba, and therefore that Sanalba should be withdrawn from the market. The order further stated that any person adversely affected by the action could file within 30 days objections to the order stating reasonable grounds for and requesting a hearing on such objections. The order further stated that "a statement of reasonable grounds for a hearing must identify the claimed errors in the NAS-NRC evaluation and identify any adequate and well-controlled investigations on the basis of which it could reasonably be concluded that the combination drug would have the effectiveness claimed and would be safe for its intended uses."

Outom promptly filed objections to the FDA May 15 order and demanded a trial-type hearing. Outom claimed that a hearing was required so that (1) the FDA would be required to present the evidence supporting its conclusions as to the safety and efficacy of Sanalba and Outom would have an opportunity to rebut such evidence; (2) Outom would be able to ascertain the identity of the members of the NAS-NRC panel and cross-examine them as to the basis of their conclusions;[142] (3) Outom would be able to present its own evidence to support the safety and efficacy of Sanalba. Outom also submitted a number of affidavits from medical practitioners and educators asserting the efficacy of Sanalba, together with 54 published articles describing studies of Sanalba which, it contended, demonstrated the product's efficacy. It also moved to disqualify the Commissioner from making any further decisions in the case on the ground that his testimony before the congressional committee indicated that he had prejudged the matter.

After staying the effective date of the May 15 order so as to consider Outom's submission, on September 19, 1969, the Commissioner issued an order rejecting Outom's demand for a hearing. The Commissioner concluded that the hearing was not required because none of the evidence proffered by Outom met the required

---

142. The Commissioner had initially refused to give Outom a copy of the NAS-NRC report, and had continued to refuse to identify the members of the panel.

statutory standard of "substantial evidence," i.e., "adequate and well-controlled investigations, including clinical investigations on the basis of which it can fairly and responsibly be concluded by appropriately qualified experts" that the drugs in question will have the effectiveness they purport to possess. The Commissioner indicated that the standard type of "adequate and well-controlled study" is one in which the drug is tested against a control, normally a placebo, or inert substance, and neither the investigator nor the patient knows which substance is being administered. This type of study is often referred to as a "double blind" study. The Commissioner found that none of the medical articles cited by Outom consisted of "double blind" studies and none of them was otherwise adequately controlled. He found four of the studies to be "partially controlled" but they did not satisfy the statutory standard. The Commissioner added that "no amount of examination and cross-examination can change scientific study and the data reported into something they are not."

The Commissioner also denied Outom's motion to disqualify him, stating that in his testimony he had merely been responding to congressional requests for information, and also denied Outom's request that it be given additional time to develop the type of evidence required by the Commissioner. On this point, the Commissioner said that Outom should have known ever since 1962 that it would be required to present adequate evidence of Sanalba's efficacy. The Commissioner reaffirmed his May 15 order repealing the regulations under which Sanalba had been marketed.

On the same day as the above order was issued (September 19, 1969), the FDA also promulgated "general regulations" for the issuance, amendment, and repeal of antibiotic drug regulations. The regulations provide that in all cases the burden is on the manufacturer to demonstrate the efficacy of his products by "adequate and well-controlled studies," that a hearing for issuance or repeal of antibiotic regulations would not be provided unless evidence proffered by the manufacturer reveals a "genuine and substantial issue of fact" as to whether the required proof of efficacy was available, and particularized the characteristics of study which the Commissioner deemed to be "adequate" and "well-controlled." [143] The announcement of

143. These regulations, promulgated in 35 Fed. Reg. 7251 (1970) and codified in 21 C.F.R. §130 (1970), provided in part as follows:

"21 C.F.R. §130.12(a)(5)ii

"The following principles have been developed over a period of years and are recognized by the scientific community as the essentials of adequate and well-controlled clinical investigations. They provide the basis for the determination whether there is "substantial evidence" to support the claim of effectiveness for "new drugs" and antibiotic drugs.

"(a) The plan or protocol for the study and the report of the results of the effectiveness study must include the following:

"(1) A clear statement of the objectives of the study

"(2) A method of selection of the subjects that —

"(i) Provides adequate assurance that they are suitable for the purposes of the study, diagnostic criteria of the condition to be treated or diagnosed, confirmatory laboratory tests where appropriate, and, in the case of prophylactic agents, evidence of susceptibility and exposure to the condition against which prophylaxis is desired.

"(ii) Assigns the subjects to test groups in such a way as to minimize bias.

"(iii) Assures comparability in test and control groups of pertinent variables, such as age, sex, severity, or duration of disease, and use of drugs other than the test drug.

"(3) Explains the methods of observation and recording of results, including the variables the regulation referred to the decision in the Sanalba case as an illustration of the application of these principles. The regulations were stated to be "procedural and interpretative" and were made effective immediately.

Outom files a petition in the appropriate court of appeals to review the action of the Commissioner in finally repealing the antibotic regulations for tetracycline-novobiocin combinations, a repeal which effectively removes Sanalba from the market. In its petition for review, Outom emphasizes that this is a test case, and that the FDA should be carefully scrutinized because it will set a precedent for many other drugs. Outom makes the following specific contentions:

Questions

(1) Outom contends that even if the §505 definition of "substantial evidence" is applicable to an antibiotic drug, it is entitled under the Constitution, the APA, and the pertinent provisions of the Act, to a hearing on the questions of whether Sanalba is efficacious (including an opportunity to cross-examine members of the NAS-NRC panel) and whether its studies are "adequate and well controlled." The government contends that no hearing was required because the action of the Com-

---

measured, quantitation, assessment of any subjective response, and steps taken to minimize bias on the part of the subject and observer.

"(4) Provides a comparison of the results of treatment or diagnosis with a control in such a fashion as to permit quantitative evaluation. The precise nature of the control must be stated and an explanation given of the methods used to minimize bias on the part of the observers and the analysts of the data. Level and methods of "blinding," if used, are to be documented. . . .

"(c) Uncontrolled studies or partially controlled studies are not acceptable as the sole basis for the approval of claims of effectiveness. Such studies, carefully conducted and documented, may provide corroborative support of well-controlled studies regarding efficacy and may yield valuable data regarding safety of the test drug. Such studies will be considered on their merits in the light of the principles listed here, with the exception of the requirement for the comparison of the treated subjects with controls. Isolated case reports, random experience, and reports lacking the details which permit scientific evaluation will not be considered. . . .

"21 C.F.R. §130.14

"(a) The notice to the applicant of opportunity for a hearing on a proposal by the Commissioner to refuse to approve an application or to withdraw the approval of an application will specify the grounds upon which he proposes to issue his order. . . .

"(b) If the applicant elects to avail himself of the opportunity for a hearing, he is required to file a written appearance requesting the hearing within 30 days after the publication of the notice and giving the reason why the application should not be refused or should not be withdrawn, together with a well-organized and full factual analysis of the clinical and other investigational data he is prepared to prove in support of his opposition to the notice of opportunity for a hearing. A request for a hearing may not rest upon mere allegations or denials, but must set forth specific facts showing that there is a genuine and substantial issue of fact that requires a hearing. When it clearly appears from the data in the application and from the reasons and factual analysis in the request for the hearing that there is no genuine and substantial issue of fact which precludes the refusal to approve the application or the withdrawal of approval of the application, e.g., no adequate and well-controlled clinical investigations to support the claims of effectiveness have been identified, the Commissioner will enter an order on this data, making findings and conclusions on such data. If a hearing is requested and is justified . . . the issues will be defined, a hearing examiner will be named, and he shall issue a written notice of the time and place at which the hearing will commence. . . ."

missioner consisted of the repeal of regulations and was therefore "rulemaking" rather than "adjudication." Further, the government contends that no hearing was required because Outom had not met the threshold burden of proof as to the efficacy of its products and the adequacy of its studies. What result?

Outom contends that it would be unfairly retroactive and arbitrary to permit the Commissioner immediately to demand that an established product such as Sanalba meet his newly promulgated standard of "substantial evidence" when it takes at least two years with expert researchers to conduct such studies. Outom also states that most of the 3,800 pre-1962 drugs do not presently possess "substantial evidence" of efficacy as defined by the Administrator; that research personnel and facilities are not available to conduct "adequate and well-controlled studies" on all such drugs; and that the Administrator's enforcement of his new requirements is arbitrary in that the Administrator has stated that he will take no action against pre-1962 products that are classified as "effective" by NAS-NRC panels although data for such products do not satisfy the Administrator's definition of "adequate and well-controlled studies." What result? [144]

(2) Why did Congress attempt to deal with the problem of unsafe or ineffective drugs by requiring manufacturers to meet elaborate testing procedures mandated by FDA? Why wouldn't it be preferable simply to require manufacturers to disclose relevant information on their products' safety and efficacy to physicians and patients?

(3) What is the net social impact of FDA's tightened requirements as to proof of efficacy? Such requirements may retard or prevent the development of new drugs with significant new therapeutic benefits. Is the gain in assurance of efficacy offset by the loss of possible benefits? Some commentators have estimated that the average cost of development of a successful new chemical or biological entity for use in prescription drugs (including the apportioned cost of unsuccessful products) has increased from about $1 million in the 1950s to $10 or even $50 million today. During the same period the development of significant new products has slowed in many areas.[145] While many factors may account for these changes, the FDA's new requirements are regarded by commentators as significant. Based on these developments and other data, critics have argued that the net impact of strict FDA drug efficacy requirements on patient welfare has been negative because the gains from assured efficacy have been more than offset by the loss of therapeutic benefit from drugs whose marketing is delayed or prevented by expensive and time-consuming procedures for proof of efficacy. See S. Peltzman, Regulation of Phar-

---

144. See Weinberger v. Hynson, Wescott & Dunning, Inc., 412 U.S. 609 (1973); Weinberger v. Bentex Pharmaceuticals, Inc., 412 U.S. 645 (1973); Upjohn Co. v. Finch, 422 F.2d 944 (6th Cir. 1970); Pharmaceutical Manufacturers Assn. v. Richardson, 318 F. Supp 301 (1970). See also Ames & McCracken, Framing Regulatory Standards to Avoid Formal Adjudications: The FDA as a Case Study, 64 Cal. L. Rev. 14 (1976); Smithkline Corp. v. FDA, 43 P. & F. Ad. L. 2d 488 (D.C. Cir. 1978).

145. The need to meet these high research costs is one of the justifications advanced by the drug manufacturers for their pricing and marketing policies. Would research sponsored by the government be a better alternative? Should it be financed by a tax on prescriptions or from general reserves?

maceutical Innovation (1974); E. Lasagna, The Development and Regulation of New Medications, 200 Science 871 (1978). Even if this is true, does it follow that FDA should loosen drug efficacy requirements? Is there a difference between harm resulting from administration of an unsafe or ineffective drug and harm resulting from the fact that a potentially efficacious drug is not available?

(4) Does it make sense to insist that accepted and established pre-1962 drugs meet the same requirements as totally new drugs? Granted that some of the established products might be found to be "ineffective" under the well-controlled tests now required by the Commissioner, does it make sense to utilize a finite supply of research funds and researchers for this purpose rather than for developing new products? How did FDA attempt to resolve that problem? Is the solution disturbing from a lawyer's viewpoint?

(5) Isn't the heart of the fixed-combination drug problem a dispute over the proper medical practice, turning on questions of physicians' education and the economics and politics of health care delivery? Does it make sense to attempt to deal with these issues through restrictions on the choice of drugs available to the prescribing physician?

(6) Does the Sanalba case present ethical problems for the lawyer representing the drug manufacturer? Suppose the lawyer concludes that Outom has quite respectable legal claims to an agency hearing of some sort on its claims, but that its chances of ultimately prevailing on the merits are remote at best, and that there is some danger that continued marketing of the drug will result in side effects causing serious difficulties? [146] Is the situation distinguishable from a criminal case where a lawyer utilizes every possible procedural claim and delaying tactic to negotiate a lighter sentence for a client who is plainly guilty and potentially dangerous? More generally, are the ethical responsibilities of an administrative lawyer challenging government actions assertedly designed to protect large numbers of individuals different from the responsibilities of a lawyer in traditional civil or criminal litigation?

Does the Sanalba case present ethical problems for the lawyers representing FDA? If Sanalba was utterly lacking in efficacy and posed a danger of unwarranted side effects, why didn't FDA act immediately to remove the drug from the market as an "imminent hazard to health"?

2. CAB Regulation of Airline Rates

Prior to 1975, regulation of airlines by the Civil Aeronautics Board presented a classic case of a regulatory agency attempting to apply cost-of-service ratemaking methods to a structurally competitive industry. Those methods had long been

---

146. Suppose, for example, that the NAS-NRC panel reviewing Sanalba's efficacy had reported that novobiocin by itself should be utilized only in relatively rare cases of urinary tract infections because of its very narrow spectrum of efficacy, high incidence of dangerous or lethal side effects, and the ready development of strains resistant to it; and that accordingly, a combination drug product, widely dispensed, should certainly not contain novobiocin as an ingredient.

criticized by academic critics and others, who argued that they led to unnecessarily high fares. They pointed, for example, to the fact that fares on unregulated intrastate routes were about half as much as those on comparable regulated interstate routes. In 1974 and 1975, President Ford and Senator Kennedy became convinced that classic regulatory methods should be abandoned. Senator Kennedy's Subcommittee on Administrative Practice and Procedure examined the activities of the Board in detail; members of President Ford's administration argued for relaxation of regulatory restraints; and Senators Kennedy and Cannon introduced legislation that would achieve this result. President Carter, after taking office, supported "deregulation," and appointed a new Board chairman, Alfred Kahn, who took steps to carry it out. In October, 1978, a new act, effectively deregulating the industry, became law.

Despite the many recent changes, it is useful to study airline regulation as it existed before 1975. In doing so, one can identify a series of underlying institutional factors that brought about the charge of "regulatory failure," and draw conclusions that reach beyond airlines in their scope. Thus, we shall begin with regulation as it existed before the Kennedy hearings and conclude with a brief note describing the subsequent changes.

a.   The CAB Ratemaking Policies and Procedures before 1975

The Civil Aeronautics Board is an "independent" agency which is responsible for the promotion and regulation of the air transportation system of the United States in accordance with the Federal Aviation Act of 1958, 49 U.S.C. §§ 1301 et seq. The Board was first given independent status in 1940 with rulemaking, licensing, adjudicatory, and accident-investigating powers previously conferred on the Civil Aeronautics Authority and the Air Safety Board by the Civil Aeronautics Act of 1938.

Promotion of service and stability of the industry have been the dominant objectives of government economic regulation of commercial airlines. The two objectives, conceived to be complementary but potentially in conflict, are reflected in the Act's direction that the Board in discharging its duties consider "the public interest" and "the public convenience and necessity," statutorily defined as including, "among other things":

> (a) The encouragement and development of an air-transportation system properly adapted to the present and future needs of the foreign and domestic commerce of the United States, of the Postal Service, and of the national defense;
> (b) The regulation of air transportation in such manner as to recognize and preserve the inherent advantages of, assure the highest degree of safety in, and foster sound economic conditions in, such transportation, and to improve the relations between, and coordinate transportation by, air carriers;

(c) The promotion of adequate, economical, and efficient service by air carriers at reasonable charges, without unjust discriminations, undue preferences or advantages, or unfair or destructive competitive practices;

(d) Competition to the extent necessary to assure the sound development of an air-transportation system properly adapted to the needs of the foreign and domestic commerce of the United States, of the Postal Service, and of the national defense;

(e) The promotion of safety in air commerce; and

(f) The promotion, encouragement, and development of civil aeronautics.

With respect to domestic passenger traffic the Federal Aviation Act permits either air carriers or the CAB to set rates.[147] All rates established by carriers are required by statute to be filed with the CAB, and no change shall be made in any rate without notice to the CAB of the proposed change. The notice must be given 30 days in advance of the change, unless the Board consents to a shorter notice period. If the Board does not act, the tariffs take effect as "carrier-made rates." These rates are not subject to judicial review. Alternatively, the CAB may suspend proposed tariffs for up to 180 days and, following "notice and hearing," establish "Board-made" rates. Persons demonstrating "a substantial interest" in the outcome may seek judicial review. The substantive guidelines for ratemaking by the Board are set forth in §1002(e) of the Federal Aviation Act:

> In exercising and performing its powers and duties with respect to the determination of rates for the carriage of persons or property, the Board shall take into consideration, among other factors
>
> (1) The effect of such rates upon the movement of traffic;
> (2) The need in the public interest of adequate and efficient transportation of persons and property by air carriers at the lowest cost consistent with the furnishing of such service;
> (3) Such standards respecting the character and quality of service to be rendered by air carriers as may be prescribed by or pursuant to law;
> (4) The inherent advantages of transportation by aircraft; and
> (5) The need of each carrier for revenue sufficient to enable such carrier, under honest, economical, and efficient management, to provide adequate and efficient air carrier service.

Obviously, this set of guides offers no definite standards and some of the criteria are potentially conflicting. How high should rates be in view of the first and fifth of these guides — effect upon movement of traffic and "revenue sufficient . . . to provide adequate and efficient air carrier service"? Low rates will move traffic; high rates may possibly yield more net revenues. How should one determine the

147. Much of the background material herein has been derived from Redford, The Regulatory Process ch. 5 (1969).

"lowest cost consistent with the furnishing" of "adequate and efficient transportation"? What return to the airlines should be allowed as part of the "lowest cost"?

These difficulties have been exacerbated by the delays involved in fixing rates through a formal hearing; the CAB and carriers have assumed that the requirement in the Act for "notice and hearing" for Board-set rates mandates the use of trial-type hearings. These factors may explain why the CAB carried out only two formal investigations of domestic fares in its history. The first of these, the General Passenger Fare Investigation (GPFI), began in 1956 and concluded in 1960. Prior to 1956, fare increases were agreed upon by informal negotiation between the Board and airline representatives; the carriers then promulgated the agreed-upon rates, which were left undisturbed by the Board.[148] The second, the Domestic Passenger Fare Investigation (DPFI), began in 1969 and was concluded in 1974.

The GPFI and DPFI each began with proceedings before an Administrative Law Judge (formerly called a "hearing examiner"). After full hearings, which in the case of the DPFI involved nine separate sets of hearings on nine separate major issues, the ALJ reached a set of decisions. Each decision was then appealed to the Board.

In fact, in almost every case before the CAB, every significant conclusion of the examiner on important issues is challenged by the losing parties, and the appeal procedure to the Board covers every aspect of the case — legal, factual, and policy. The Board, in effect, tries the case all over again, frequently overturning the examiner's conclusions, which are certainly not considered binding and, on major issues, are not even treated as persuasive. There is often no mention of the examiner's decision or discussion of his specific mistakes or errors in the arguments to the Board. The appeal is treated by most parties as a new proceeding to be argued all over again. Cases are tried virtually de novo on the basis of briefs and oral arguments, to a body which will never really become familiar with the record.

If an administrative agency set clear policy, it would seldom be necessary to reverse an examiner on policy grounds. He would know the policy to be followed. Very often, however, policy is not enunciated on a general, formal basis by the agencies but is made rather on a case-by-case ad hoc basis, with the result that any resemblance between an examiner's recommended decision and the final decision of the Board in a significant case is almost coincidental.

Having taken over decision of a case, the members of the Board did the best they can, but there is no real chance for a review of the record. Cases are decided on the basis of an outline of the issues and a list of questions to be decided, prepared by the General Counsel's office and never seen by the parties. The members hear the oral argument — or read it if they are not present — and study the examiner's decision and the briefs to the Board, either personally or through their own personal assistant. The pressure of administrative matters, routine decisions, and other major cases effectively prevents any contact with the record. The thousands

148. A formal fare investigation had been initiated by the Board in 1952, but it was abandoned as the result of a compromise settlement in 1953.

of man-hours that went into the making of a record are thus virtually ignored at the crucial moment of final decision.

There could be one saving grace in all this. The Administrative Procedure Act provides that "[a]ll decisions ... shall include a statement of ... findings and conclusions, and the reasons or basis therefor, on all the material issues of fact, law or discretion presented on the record. ..." If this were done personally by the members of the agency who make the final decisions in adjudicating cases, the litigants and the public would know why the agency decided as it did, and at least one member would have to study the record personally in order to draft the opinion. This, of course, is the procedure followed in all our appellate courts.

Not so in most regulatory agencies. Decisions usually are written there by a staff of expert opinion-writers after the decision has been made — occasionally, even after it has been announced publicly. Any safeguard that the opinion requirement might provide is dissipated by the public announcement of a naked conclusion and the subsequent delegation of the opinion-writing job.

The GPFI was concluded without setting clear ratemaking guidelines. The Board determined, as a matter of policy, that carrier rates would be set at a level designed to earn the industry *taken as a whole* a reasonable profit. Thus, some individual carriers might earn more money and others less. But the Board concluded that the record, generated through lengthy trial-type procedures and dealing with a myriad of complex issues, was too "stale" to support any definitive decisions on rate policies. It instead granted short-term fare increase sought by the carriers. The rate-setting process after 1960 continued to be handled to a considerable extent through informal negotiation. The Board's second effort to develop precise ratesetting principles — the DPFI — was more successful. By 1974, the Board had concluded the detailed hearings on each of nine major DPFI issues; it had reached its decisions; and it had promulgated definite standards. Whether these standards represented desirable policy is another matter. They will be described below.

It proved even more difficult for the Board to develop a policy governing route awards. The Aviation Act required any airline wishing to fly interstate to secure Board approval. The Board was to grant approval to any carrier "fit, willing and able" to fly, provided the approval is consistent with "the public convenience and necessity." In applying this standard, the Board allowed virtually no new firms to enter the industry.[149] The ten major domestic trunk carriers[150] accounted for over ninety percent of all domestic interstate air travel in 1974. These ten were the lineal descendants of the sixteen firms in business in 1938 (the other six having been merged into the remaining firms). Between 1938 and 1974, the industry itself grew

149. The Board received 79 applications for routes from other than the ten major trunk carriers between 1950 and 1974. It granted none. See Civil Aeronautics Board Practices and Procedures, A Report of the Subcommittee on Administrative Practice and Procedure of the Senate Committee on the Judiciary, 94th Cong., 1st Sess. 6 (1975) (hereinafter referred to as the Kennedy Report).

150. United, TWA, American, Eastern, Delta, Continental, Northwest, Braniff, Texas International, and National. (Pan American flies international routes.) There are also local service carriers, such as Allegheny and North Central, commuter carriers, intrastate carriers, and supplemental (charter) carriers.

435 times in size, yet the market shares of the major competitors were quite similar to what they had been 36 years earlier.[151]

Most of the Board's route business consisted of applications by existing carriers to fly new routes. To succeed, an applicant would have to convince the Board on two points. First, it would have to show that the route needed a new competitor — that the existing service was insufficient. Second, it would have to show that it, rather than some other applicant, should be awarded the route. Hearings on the issues would take place before a hearing examiner, who would make a recommendation that could be appealed to the Board.

The route hearing was often complex, for if carrier A sought a route, for example, between Houston and San Diego, carriers B and C might decide they would also like the route, or at least prevent carrier A from obtaining it. Moreover, one or more carriers might apply for a different, but related, route, say Miami to San Diego with a stopover in Houston, that was inconsistent with an award of the original route to carrier A. Thus, route hearings tended to become elaborate proceedings, which often considered many related applications together. Making a set of awards was complicated by the further factor that each new route awarded, say to carrier A, affected the pattern of service it would offer over its entire route network and the carrier's overall profitability. It also affected the pattern of service and the profitability of its competitors.

The upshot was a pattern of awards described by outside critics as without standards.[152] The Board's own Bureau of Operating Rights, after studying the history of route awards, said that the Board may have followed standards in deciding *when* a particular route should be opened up to a new carrier, but its decisions in picking a particular applicant were "random." Moreover, beginning in 1970, the Board, fearful of too much competition, began to refuse to make new awards and refused even to set applications for hearing.[153]

As you read through the remainder of this section, you should ask yourself *why* the Board found it so difficult to develop general policy standards for awarding routes and setting rates. Did it overcome these problems as to rates by completing the DPFI? To what extent does the nature of the problem the Board faced (setting rates and awarding routes in a complex, competitively structured industry) lend itself to an adversary legalistic standard-setting process?

---

151. United, for example, accounted for about 20 percent of the market in 1938 and, after mergers, accounted for about 20 percent in 1974. See Kennedy Report at 6.

152. See, e.g., H. Friendly, The Federal Administrative Agencies 74-105 (1962).

153. The Board found it difficult to avoid hearings given a statutory requirement that all such applications be set for a speedy hearing. Yet it developed a system whereby it would hold all applications on its docket, granting hearings only if it approved a "motion for an expedited hearing." It would not grant such a motion unless it intended to grant an award. After three years, it would dismiss an unheard route application as "stale." Thus, World Airways did not receive a hearing on its application to fly between Los Angeles and New York at a fare of $79. The airlines did not appeal the lawfulness of this procedure to the courts, presumably because a favorable verdict would lead only to a hearing, with the Board still free to refuse to grant the route. This procedure is discussed and severely criticized in the Kennedy Report, supra n. 149, at 81-91.

The Kennedy Report [154]

94th Cong., 1st Sess. 104-113 (1975)

[This report examines both the substantive and procedural aspects of CAB ratemaking. After quoting the provisions of §1002(e) of the Act, set out at p. 570 supra, the report proceeds to discuss some of the problems in applying the statutory standards.]

It is nearly impossible to develop a coherent regulatory procedure that applies these general standards to the aviation industry because of four basic facts: (1) The industry is composed of different carriers, each with a different system, different costs and different revenues. (2) The industry is highly competitive and perfectly willing to substitute service for price competition. (3) The industry faces continuously changing cost and demand conditions. (4) In part, because of the first three facts, rate hearings involve many parties; they are complicated and lengthy.

During the 1960's the Board tried to deal with the first of the problems by stating that it would base its determination of a reasonable fare on average industry cost. Fares would allow the industry taken as a whole to recover its costs including a reasonable rate of return.

The third and fourth problems were less important then, for costs were falling, demand was rising, and there was, therefore, little pressure from the airlines to increase prices. In general, the companies did not ask for rate increases; the Board did not compel them to cut fares; price reductions took the form of discount plans. Thus in the 1960's regular fares stayed fairly constant, and fares considered as a whole fell less rapidly than did costs. . . . Since demand grew as well, industry profits in the mid-1960's were high; the airlines realized their three most profitable years out of the last 20. . . .

Toward the end of the sixties the major issues before the Board concerned price increases. The Board seemed to handle these matters "informally." Board members and representatives of the carriers would talk to each other either directly or by using members of the Board's staff as intermediaries to communicate views and positions between the Board and carrier representatives. Thus, one carrier representative testified that "there has been in the past a kind of informal communication between carriers and the Board's staff about what was going to be expected." And, one highly knowledgeable Washington lawyer added:

"It is true that carriers do try informally, and have for years, to get a sense of what the Board will approve. The problem is that if they don't they get suspensions and investigations rather than fare increases. . . . [I]f every carrier filed a different [fare] number independently, . . . the Board . . . would almost be forced to suspend all of them and investigate them. . . . [I]f they waited for the formal process to take effect where the Board initiates an investigation and suspends carrier tariffs and investigates then it would be 2 years before you got your fare increase, and you really would go down the drain."

154. Op. cit., supra n. 149.

He went on to say that:

"There was a practice that grew up at one time to which particular carriers would come in and have private meetings with the entire Board and would make a pitch. And, sometimes the ATA [Air Transport Association] came in and had its private meeting with the Board and made a pitch and discussed their problems and aspirations and so forth. And, it was a process that at least had a great potential for abuse because it was a total ex parte communication. Just because it was an elegantly produced one, it didn't prevent it being an opportunity for making comments on pending applications or pending positions on policy."

These informal procedures obviously allowed the Board to adjust its rate policy rapidly to changing economic conditions, but the price paid in terms of elementary procedural fairness was a high one. [During the 1970s, airline fares continued to rise at an accelerating pace until 1975.]

A. Kahn, The Economics of Regulation[155]

Vol. 2, pp. 209-220 (1966)

THE REGULATION OF NONPRICE COMPETITION: AIR TRANSPORT

[W]hen limitations are placed on price competition, but market conditions are such as to make continued interfirm rivalry likely, the consequence will be an accentuation of service competition. If the minimum rate regulation is effective, it will almost certainly hold price above the marginal costs of some producers, to which competition would otherwise drive it. . . . But if competition is sufficiently strong, potentially, to drive price down to that level, it will ordinarily be sufficiently strong to induce these suppliers, confronting a price above their marginal costs, to seek other, nonprice methods of producing additional sales. Specifically, they will be inclined to improve service in one way or another, until their marginal costs, inflated by the service improvements, are equated to price. . . .

If, therefore, regulatory commissions have the responsibility of keeping price rivalry from becoming destructive, they cannot escape the responsibility of deciding whether they ought to limit quality competition as well. As we have already pointed out in our discussion of the more traditional public utilities, in which the presumed danger is one of monopolistic exploitation, price regulation alone is meaningless except in terms of some specified unit and quality of service: a baker with a local monopoly can exploit his customers just as effectively by giving them only twelve rolls for some fixed price when in the presence of competition he would be likely to give them thirteen as by continuing to give them a baker's dozen but charging them 8½ percent more than the competitive price. Similarly when regulation is introduced to keep competition from driving a price *down*: it will be futile to affix a minimum price for a dozen rolls if bakers remain free to decide how many rolls constitute a dozen.

155. Professor Kahn was the Chairman of the Civil Aeronautics Board from 1977 to 1978.

Regulation has heretofore shirked this responsibility in trucking and the security brokerage business. . . . In air transportation, in contrast, the regulators have found it impossible to ignore, possibly because airline companies, catering much more than the others to the whims of the ultimate consumer, have competed much more intensely in this way. Partly for the same reason, the airline case is more difficult to judge than the others, because there would doubtless be a great deal of service rivalry even in the presence of much sharper price competition than now prevails. Nor is there any reason to doubt that this kind of competition is, within limits that are difficult to define, just as important a contributor to consumer welfare as price rivalry. . . .

Price competition is discouraged in this industry, first, by the oligopolistic character of airline markets, itself attributable partly to the restrictions on entry imposed by the Civil Aeronautics Board. The oligopolists in this industry show the familiar reluctance to engage in direct price rivalry. Possibly contributing to this same restraint is the fact that they have agreed to notify the Air Transport Association of all proposed rate changes at least 15 days before filing them with the CAB, which undoubtedly gives the other companies an opportunity to put pressure on any one of them proposing to reduce rates. Second, the CAB itself has tended quite consistently to discourage competitive rate reductions. In the international field, price competition has been even more effectively contained by the International Air Transport Association (IATA), which, backed by the authority of governments to deny or withdraw landing privileges to airlines that refuse to adhere to its rate schedules, has imposed a particularly high and noncompetitive schedule of rates on international traffic.

In part because the doors to price competition are closed, airline companies compete very strenuously among themselves in the quality of service they offer — most notably in adopting the most modern and attractive equipment and in the frequency with which they schedule flights, but also in providing comfort, attractive hostesses, in-flight entertainment, food and drink. Among these, the one most closely approaching destructiveness in character is scheduling. There is a general belief that the airline with the most flights between any two points is the one to which customers will turn first in making their reservations. The result, where competition is strong and particularly in markets where new entry threatens, is a cumulative tendency to excess capacity, with each company vying with the other by increasing the number of daily flights on its schedule. Ronald E. Miller attributes to this competitive overscheduling the major part of the blame for the excessive capacity in the industry, showing up in load factors (ratios of revenue passenger miles sold to total available seat miles in scheduled service) typically running below 60 percent.

This kind of competition, like persuasive advertising, is in considerable measure self-defeating. It may pay each individual company to advertise, whether aggressively or defensively — A having to advertise in order to keep from losing customers to B and B having to do the same for the same reason — but for all companies together the gain in revenue is probably typically less than the additional selling costs they have incurred. We shall have to take into account, before terminating this discussion, the fact that nonprice competition can mean an improvement in the quality of service; even persuasive advertising is not entirely unproductive, insofar as it provides some information and perhaps provides some assurance to customers of minimal standards of quality. The proliferation of scheduled flights, even more clearly, does mean greater convenience, offering the traveller a greater number of alternative times among which to choose in making any particular trip. But where the scheduling is purely duplicative and the traffic actually generated could be carried in fewer flights, the competition has produced only waste. . . .

[In addition, CAB] policies have encouraged irrational service inflation. This, as Caves points out, has been the consequence of Board decisions denying carriers with older and less attractive equipment permission to charge correspondingly lower fares: "the Board . . . forbids the carrier with older or inferior equipment to set a differential to protect its market position. These policies create an overwhelming incentive for carriers to acquire equipment as modern or as appealing as any used by their direct competitors. . . . The carrier suffering equipment inferiority has all major avenues to protecting its market position blocked except that one." . . . [Kahn suggests that CAB policies encouraging "service inflation" may be attributable to the Board's mandate to promote the growth of air travel.]

Rivalry in improving service can obviously be just as productive of benefit to the traveling public as in price. How, then, can an economist presume to judge that it has gone too far? He may not, directly. All he can do is ask whether the service improvements have been subjected to the test of a competitive market. That test requires that customers be provided with a sufficient variety of price-quality combinations — consistent with efficient production — so that each can register a free and tolerably well-informed monetary appraisal of the quality differentials that are offered. By this test product inflation could be said to have occurred only if quality competition had operated in such a way as to eliminate, or to fail to develop, lower quality-price combinations that consumers would willingly have purchased in quantities sufficient to cover the cost of providing them. The reason why it is questionable that the service improvements produced by competition in the airline industry have been worth the cost is that the restrictions on *price* competition have denied consumers the alternative of less sumptuous service at prices reflecting its lower cost. They have therefore not had the opportunity to determine whether the better quality is in their collective judgment worth the higher cost of providing it. . . .

The airline industry offers several evidences that price competition can, if it is given a chance, hold service inflation in check. Historically, passenger rates have been geared to first-class Pullman railroad fares, with a corresponding emphasis on luxurious service. "The first real break came when the irregular carriers introduced coach service at rates approximately 65 percent of standard trunk-line fares." These nonscheduled airlines were for the most part companies that had come into the business, by the hundreds, after World War II, generally carrying passengers or freight on an irregular basis, when demand justified it, at rates lower than those charged by the regularly certificated trunk-line carriers. For the first several years, coach service was offered only over high-density routes and during off-peak hours, with denser passenger seating than in first-class, and no meals were served. The enormous expansion of coach travel that followed, as the regular carriers introduced similar service of their own, clearly demonstrated that the majority of potential travelers preferred the lower price quality combination to the one that had previously been available to them. A similar illustration has been provided more recently by the popularity of the group charter flights, at rates substantially below those set by the IATA, and, later, the inclusive tour charters on scheduled North Atlantic flights. These, once again, were pioneered by the nonscheduled (later termed supplemental) air carriers and again subjected to various restrictions by the CAB and the IATA, in order to lessen their impact on the regular rate structures.

Another, even more striking illustration is provided by the extraordinary impact that essentially unregulated price competition has had on the price and volume of air traffic between Los Angeles and San Francisco, California. What made this possible was the fact that wholly intrastate air transport is free of CAB control and that the California Public Utilities Commission has no power to limit entry and has followed the practice, as far as rates are concerned, or approving virtually all changes. [Kahn summarizes evidence that competition from unregulated intrastate carriers resulted in 35-40 percent reductions in fares charged by all carriers between Los Angeles and San Francisco, and a large increase in passengers.]

[I]f price competition continues to be restrained, service should likewise be subjected to much more consistent and effective controls than have hitherto been imposed on it — thus providing another illustration of the necessity for the regulatory net to be spread wider . . .

The Kennedy Report [156]

94th Cong., 1st Sess. (1975)

THE BASIC ARGUMENT: SHOULD THERE BE MORE COMPETITION?

A. THE THEORY

The Board's critics claim that its reliance upon classical route-award and rate-making procedures has brought about fares that are far too high. The airline industry is potentially highly competitive, but the Board's system of regulation discourages the airlines from competing in price and virtually forecloses new firms from entering the industry. The result is high fares and security for existing firms. But the result does not mean high profits. Instead the airlines — prevented from competing in price — simply channel their competitive energies toward costlier service: more flights, more planes, more frills. Thus, the skies are filled with gourmet meals and Polynesian pubs; scheduled service is frequent. Yet planes fly across the continent more than half empty. And fares are "sky high."

The remedy is for the Board to allow both new and existing firms greater

---

156. Op. cit. supra n. 149, selection from the summary.

freedom to lower fares and greater freedom to obtain new routes. This freedom should lead the airlines to offer service in fuller planes at substantially lower prices, a form of service that most consumers desire.

Although a more competitive system with lower fares on fuller planes can be profitable, the process of introducing new firms or price competition may create added financial risk for some existing airlines in the short run. Yet short-term financial security for all individual carriers is currently being purchased at a fearsome price in excess fares — an excess used to support the purchase of more planes than are needed. This excess has been estimated at between $1 billion to $3.5 billion annually. It should be possible to introduce increased competition gradually without seriously jeopardizing the health of the industry thereby bringing air travel into the lives of millions of working people who now cannot afford it.

B. EMPIRICAL EVIDENCE

The strongest empirical confirmation of the critics' argument arises from comparing fares and service in California and Texas — where new firms and price competition have been allowed — with flights elsewhere in the Nation where competition is more restricted by the CAB. A traveler flying 456 miles from San Francisco to San Diego pays $27. On strictly comparable routes elsewhere in the country the traveler must pay at least 60 percent more. As of February 1, 1976, it costs $47 to fly 399 miles between Boston and Washington, D.C. A comparison of virtually any intrastate route (which the CAB does not regulate) with virtually any comparable interstate route (which the CAB does regulate) reveals similar fare differences.

Several major airlines argued that it was not CAB regulation but certain special circumstances that brought about such low fares within California and Texas. These included better weather, denser traffic, less congestion, the absence of interlining costs, the ability to operate turnaround service, and less need to support other routes in the system. The subcommittee examined each of these factors in detail and concluded that taken together, these factors account for less than half of the fare differences. Most of the difference arises from the fact that the intrastate carriers carry more passengers in their planes. The subcommittee also concluded that greater freedom to compete is probably responsible for these fuller planes and lower fares. New airlines willing and able to provide the public with fuller-plane, lower-fare service in California and Texas have been allowed to enter those markets, and the low-fare service they provide has led to greatly increased demand for air travel with a resulting increase in scheduled flights.

The California experience also suggests that a more competitive environment does increase business risks for individual carriers. But this added risk for individual firms does not seem to have seriously inconvenienced the public, for throughout this period continuity of low-fare service was maintained.

Further empirical evidence is contained in cost data submitted by Lockheed and Boeing, which show that it is economically and technically possible to provide California-type fuller plane, lower-fare service throughout the United States. With an all-coach seating configuration, for example, cross-country service could be provided in a B-747 flying on average from 50 percent to 70 percent full at fares that range from $75 to $95. The current (as of February 1, 1976) cross-country CAB-regulated fare is $175.

Similarly, "value of time" studies suggest that all except the highest paid executives would prefer lower fares even if they were accompanied by a significant reduction in the number of flights flown, which they would probably not be. Finally, studies of air service in Canada, commuter service, and Military Air Transport Service suggest that where competition has flourished, fares tend to be low; where there is strict price regulation, they are high.

C. COUNTER ARGUMENTS

The major arguments against allowing freer entry and greater price competition rest upon the fear of: (1) predatory pricing; (2) destructive competition; (3) monopolization; (4) reduced service to small communities; (5) destruction of the existing air service network; (6) reduced safety standards; and (7) greater financing difficulties. The subcommittee examined each of these claims.

In the subcommittee's view there is no substantial historical, empirical, or logical reason for believing that increased reliance upon competition would lead to predatory pricing, destructive competition, or risk of monopolization.

The small community and "network" argument have two separate forms. First, it is often claimed that fares on popular routes must be high to cover the cost of less popular service. Investigation of this claim suggests, however, that no significant amount of such "cross subsidy" takes place. The subcommittee has carefully examined empirical studies submitted by United Air Lines and the Air Transport Association. It concludes that a more competitive system, of the type recommended by this report, might lead the major trunk carriers to seek to discontinue service over routes that, at the very most, account for one-half of 1 percent of revenue passenger-miles now flown. Service over these routes even then would not terminate but, in all probability, would be supplied by commuter carriers. Even if contrary to the subcommittee's expectations, direct subsidy were needed, it could be supplied at a cost of several million dollars per year — a small price to pay for annual savings that could amount to more than a billion dollars.

Second, it is argued that increased competition will lead to fares that prevent the airlines from covering their overhead, forcing them to replace fewer planes and eventually to shrink their systems. Investigation of this claim suggests that though fares should fall as a result of fuller plane service and subsequent cost reduction, they will not fail to cover costs, for both new competitors and old ones will realize (as in all competitive industries) that failure to cover overhead means eventual bankruptcy. Of course, increased competition may lead to changes in the individual route maps of one or more existing carriers. But, it should not significantly alter the extent to which towns are served by the system *taken as a whole*. In fact, lower fares to and from major hubs should increase demand for air travel to and from smaller communities as well, with the probable result that service to those communities will increase, not diminish. In any event, the subcommittee projects that the gradual introduction of increased price competition and more liberalized entry will not diminish service to smaller towns, nor will it injure the nationwide service network.

The subcommittee is convinced that increased competition would not affect carrier safety. Safety is the primary responsibility not of the CAB, but of the Federal Aviation Administration. The FAA would continue to apply its rigid safety standards. The safety records of both the scheduled carriers, subject to full-fledged CAB rate and entry regulation, and the supplemental carriers, subject to less stringent rate and entry regulation, are excellent. As no change in safety regulation is proposed, those records should remain excellent.

The subcommittee does not believe that increased competition will raise any serious difficulty for the financing of new aircraft. It will, however, increase business risks for individual firms when compared with a more sheltered environment protected by the CAB, which has never allowed a major airline to go bankrupt. The subcommittee has sought to minimize these risks by recommending a gradual transition to a more competitive environment. This transition should also allow adequate time for any unforeseen adverse consequences to appear and to be dealt with.

In sum, the subcommittee believes that a gradual transition to a significantly more competitive industry environment will bring substantial benefit to the American traveler without jeopardizing the financial health of the aviation industry.

Try to understand how the Board arrived at the situation that the Subcommittee criticized. Did the Board make a mistake, or was the effort to regulate airlines misconceived from the beginning? Consider the following case discussing airline regulation prior to reform efforts.

Moss v. CAB

430 F.2d 891 (D.C. Cir. 1970)

J. Skelly WRIGHT, Circuit Judge:

This appeal presents the recurring question which has plagued public regulation of industry: whether the regulatory agency is unduly oriented toward the interests of the industry it is designed to regulate, rather than the public interest it is designed to protect. Petitioners, some 32 congressmen, alleged that the Civil Aeronautics Board, in considering the lawfulness of increases in domestic passenger fares filed by all the major air lines, excluded the public from ex parte meetings with representatives of the air line industry and then held a pro forma hearing limited to oral argument, as a result of which changes in the fare structure resulting in a six percent rise in domestic fares were unlawfully approved. The Board admits the ex parte meetings, denies that the hearing was pro forma, and admits that, without complying with the statutory procedural requirements and criteria for rate-making by the Board, it approved in advance the filing without suspension of air line tariffs providing for a six percent increase in air line revenues from passenger fares. We hold that the procedure used by the Board is contrary to the statutory rate-making plan in that it fences the public out of the rate-making process and tends to frustrate judicial review.

I

The statutory plan is relatively simple. Air line passenger rates can be made by the carrier or by the Board.... In determining and prescribing a rate the Board must take into consideration, among other factors, five statutory criteria.[157]

An air line carrier may change the existing rate by filing a new tariff with the Board indicating the new rate. Under the statute, on complaint or on its own initiative the Board, by giving the carrier a statement of its reasons, may suspend the new rate for a period not to exceed 180 days while conducting an investigation as to its lawfulness. After investigation and hearing, the Board may determine and prescribe the lawful rate, in accordance, of course, with the rate-making provisions of Sections 1002(d) and 1002(e) of the Federal Aviation Act.[158]

II

Petitioners had complained to the Board on prior occasions both about the Board's practice of holding ex parte, informal meetings with the carriers concerning their need for increased fares, and about the Board's lack of standards for testing the reasonableness of fares. In spite of these complaints, the informal sessions between carriers and Board members continued into the summer of 1969. In early August of 1969, following the lead of United Air Lines, the carriers filed increased passenger tariffs with the Board. While these proposed rate increases were pending before the Board, another ex parte meeting between the air line officials and members of the Board was scheduled for August 14, 1969. Petitioner Moss requested and was refused permission to attend this meeting. Following the ex parte meeting on August 14, the Board issued an order calling for oral argument on the advisability of exercising its power to investigate and suspend the new rates before they went into effect.... Petitioners, however, refused to participate in the oral argument on the ground that the Board's decision on the rate increases had already been made.

On September 12, 1969, eight days after the oral argument, the Board issued

157. Ed. note: The court quoted the relevant provisions of §1002(e) of the Federal Aviation Act, reproduced at p. 570 supra, specifying the criteria to be used by the Board when it "determines" rates.

158. Ed note: Section 1002(d) of the Act, 49 U.S.C. §1492(d), authorizes the Board to "determine" rates "after notice and hearing." This language has always been thought to require an "on the record" evidentiary hearing pursuant to APA §§ 556-557. Is this assumption still sound following *Florida East Coast?* Note that the judicial review provisions of the Act, §1006(e) (49 U.S.C. §1486(e)) require reviewing courts to use a "substantial evidence" standard for evaluating Board findings of fact.

its order. In that order the Board found that the proposed tariffs on file "may be unjust [or] unreasonable" and ordered the tariffs suspended and investigated, as it is authorized to do by Section 1002(g) of the Federal Aviation Act. Still purporting to act in accordance with its suspension authority, however, the Board went further. It found that the carriers had demonstrated a need for "some additional revenue" because of greatly increased costs, and decided that a limited fare increase was necessary in order to maintain the financial vitality of the carriers as a group. Accordingly, in the same order which suspended the rates proposed by the carriers, the Board outlined its own fare formula and announced its decision to "permit tariff filings implementing" that formula to be filed without suspension, thus assuring almost immediate effectiveness.

The carriers promptly withdrew their previous filings and filed for new increases based on the Board's model. Petitioners, in an application for reconsideration of the September 12 order, opposed the new filings and requested their suspension and investigation. On September 30, 1969, the application was denied and the fares based upon the Board formula were allowed to stand without suspension or investigation. The instant petition for review of both the September 12 and the September 30 orders followed.

III

The question presented by this appeal is whether the Board should have followed the procedures and standards established by Sections 1002(d) and 1002(e) of the Act before proposing the rate schedule it set forth in its September 12 order. Petitioners complain that the Board effectively "determined" rates, within the meaning of Sections 1002(d) and 1002(e), to be charged by the air carriers without proper notice and hearings as required by Section 1002(d) and without taking into account the rate-making factors enumerated in Section 1002(e). The Board admits that it would have been required to act in accordance with subsections (d) and (e) if its actions amounted to the making of rates. The Board, however, contends that it was not required to adhere to the standards of subsections (d) and (e) because, as the formal title of its September 12 order ("Order of Investigation and Suspension") indicates, it was not determining rates but only exercising its power under Section 1002(g) to suspend, pending a more complete investigation, the rates initially filed by the carriers in August.

... According to the Board, the detailed outline of the rate structure which it "proposed to accept" in its September 12 order was not an attempt to prescribe or determine rates for the future within the meaning of the statute, but merely served to explain to the carriers — as required by the statute — the Board's reasons for suspending the August filings. The Board points out that the carriers were not legally bound by the September 12 order of the Board to file a new tariff and list rates based on its formula. Therefore, the Board argues, even though the carriers did precisely what the Board indicated in its September 12 order should be done, the resulting rates are carrier-made rates for which the Board is not to be held accountable. ...

IV

After finding that the rates proposed by the carriers might be unjust or unreasonable and ordering an investigation, the Board went on in the September 12 order to point out that, because of the need for revenue which the carriers had shown, the Board would "be disposed to grant an increase computed in accordance with the criteria set out below." It then set forth a rate-making formula, variously described in the order as "the formula which we are proposing," the formula "we propose to accept, and the formula which "[w]e . . . adopt . . . for our model." The formula detailed by the Board, which is set out in the margin,[159] using coach fares as its base, attempts to cope with the increased per mile costs of short flights by establishing a fixed "terminal" charge ($9.00) for all markets, with an additional charge based on the airport-to-airport mileage. According to the formula, the per mile rate decreases in each successive 500-mile block. From this formula anyone could have filled in the figures and computed the acceptable coach fares.

The Board also "concluded" that it would be appropriate for all fares to be rounded off to the nearest whole dollar. It further "propose[d] that first class jet fares be set at 125 percent of the coach fare derived by the above formula." It "would accept night coach fares computed at 75 percent of the new coach fares." The order then listed each of the various promotional fares, such as Youth Fare and Discover America, and the discounts which "the Board would permit." [160]

---

159. The Board said:
"Turning now to the actual formula which we propose to accept, coach fares will form the core of the fare structure from which all other fares will be based. We believe that the revenue increase produced by the American formula is appropriate as discussed hereinafter, and therefore we adopt that formula for our model, to wit:
"Fixed charge for all markets: $9.00
              plus
A variable charge based on mileage and in accordance
with the following rates per mile for the applicable
portions of the total mileage:

Mileage Blocks	Rate Per Mile
0-500	6.0¢
501-1000	5.6¢
1001-1500	5.2¢
1501-2000	5.0¢
Over 2000	4.8¢"

160. "With respect to the various promotional fares, the Board would permit the following reduced discounts based on the coach fares derived from the above described formula:

Type of Fare	Percent Discount*
Discover America	20
Youth Standby	40
Youth Reservation	20
Family plan:	
Children 2-11	50
Children 12-21	33 1/3

" *With respect to the contention of Northwest Airlines that discounts on discounts should be eliminated, the Board would look with favor on tariff amend-

As a practical matter, the Board's order amounted to the prescription of rates because, as the Board admits, the pressures on the carriers to file rates conforming exactly with the Board's formula were great, if not actually irresistible. All the carriers had indicated an urgent need for an immediate increase in revenues; the Board had made it clear, by threatening to use its power to suspend proposed rates, that only rates conforming to its detailed model would be accepted and not suspended. . . .

. . . The Board . . . relies upon the fact that it never in so many words "ordered" the carriers to file the rates now being charged. According to the Board, as long as the Board only "suggests" and does not order the future rates, the rates remain carrier-made. In support of this proposition the Board cites a series of cases [involving the ICC]. . . . It has been held, for example, that the agency's refusal to suspend proposed rates does not constitute agency approval of those rates. To the extent that the ICC precedents are relevant to this case[161] we would agree with the Board that it takes more than a refusal to suspend profferred rates to transform them into agency-made rates.

We do not need to decide, however, in the context of this case the exact extent of agency participation which will make an agency responsible for the rates being charged by carriers. For the cases which the Board cites simply are not apposite. We are not dealing with rates filed by carriers which the Board has refused to suspend, or even with allowance of small percentage increases in revenue based on existing rates, but with a complete and innovative scheme for setting all passenger rates for the continental United States. . . .

If, as the Board argues, the rates resulting from this procedure are carrier-made, rather than agency-made, the public would not only be fenced out of its role in rate-making, but judicial review of the Board's actions would be severely limited. On appeal agency-made rates are tested against the Act's explicit rate-making procedures. Thus a court must decide whether, in determining rates, the Board has properly observed the statutory procedures and taken into account the factors which Congress has said should be considered when rates are made. If the statutory plan has been complied with, the court can then determine whether substantial evidence in the record supports the Board's rates. Here the Board has in effect determined rates and the record made in so doing is inadequate for judicial review. By contrast, if the tariffs filed pursuant to the Board's order of September 12 are not Board-determined rates, judicial review is practically nonexistent. Aggrieved parties can object to carrier-made rates and ask the Board to investigate them, but

---

ments that would eliminate these practices (such as children's 50 percent discount on Discover America excursion fares)."

Order, at 8.

161. While the rate-making provisions of the Federal Aviation Act and the Interstate Commerce Act are similar, the practice under them is not necessarily the same because, unlike the Interstate Commerce Act, the Federal Aviation Act has no provision for reparations. . . .

In the absence of such a retrospective remedy for reparations for air line passengers, the procedural safeguards provided in the Federal Aviation Act become the public's sole defense against unreasonable rates permitted by the Board.

the Board's refusal to investigate would be reviewable only for an abuse of discretion. And, of course, it would be very difficult indeed to apply this limited standard of review to a record made in large part behind closed doors.

Moreover, the Board's suspension authority, on which it relies for justification of its actions in this case, is totally insulated from judicial review. It is this power which the Board uses to work its will in rate-making rather than the judicially reviewable statutory rate-making plan designed by Congress to protect the public. In the absence of a compelling justification for the Board's admitted practice of making rates by use of its suspension power, we cannot help but conclude that the Board is only seeking to avoid the strict requirements of the rate-making portion of the statute and the resulting more stringent judicial review. No requirement of Board operation or policy of the Act seems to support the Board's blatant attempt to subvert the statute's scheme.

The Board has argued that to hold it accountable for these rates would "hobble the administrative process," seemingly because it feels that the procedures required by Sections 1002(d) and 1002(e) of the Act do not permit the Board to respond quickly enough to meet the immediate revenue needs of the carriers in times of rapidly rising costs.[162] While we recognize that under the statute the Board has an obligation to afford the carriers sufficient revenues, that obligation cannot become a carte blanche allowing the Board to deal only with the carriers and disregard the other factors, such as the traveling public's interest in the lowest possible fares and high standards of service, which are also enumerated in the Act as rate-making criteria.

Furthermore, we see no inconsistency between adhering to the statutory plan and awarding a speedy increase in carrier revenues. The statute does not require a complete, time-consuming, scholarly and theoretical review of *all* aspects of rate-making before the Board passes upon proposals which are submitted. The Board is expected to use its experience gleaned from ongoing studies and investigations in its day-to-day activities, and it can act with reasonable speed as long as it affords public notice, holds a proper hearing, and takes the statutory factors into account when it determines rates. In any case, ignoring the general public's interests in order to better serve the carriers is not the proper response to the difficulties supposedly created by an outdated or unwieldy statutory procedure. After all, there is more to rate-making than providing carriers with sufficient revenue to meet their obligations to their creditors and to their stockholders. . . .

Since the record shows, as the Board admits, that the public notice and hearing requirements of Section 1002(d) were not observed in issuing the order of September 12, that order is invalid and the tariffs filed by the carriers based thereon are unlawful. Under the circumstances, this case is remanded to the Board for further proceedings. . . .

162. At oral argument there was repeated reference to the incredible length of time (four and a half years) consumed by a recent general passenger fare rate investigation. Because the Board seems unable to complete such full investigations until years after successive rate increases have become necessary, the Board's reliance upon the new general rate investigation it has ordered as the proper solution to the problems raised by petitioners seems misplaced.

b. The Outcome of the DPFI

At the conclusion of the Domestic Passenger Fare Investigation in 1974, the CAB promulgated regulations specifying in considerable detail a new system for setting air fares. This system is described below.

The Kennedy Report [163]

94th Cong., 1st Sess. 109-112 (1975)

The Board's ratesetting rules and standards represent a serious effort to tailor classic ratemaking principles to the special needs of the aviation industry. Classic ratemaking is normally used to set the rates of a regulated monopolist, such as an electricity company. It seeks to set rates at a level where they will cover costs and attract investment sufficient to provide adequate services. In broad outline, classic ratemaking works as follows:

(1) The regulator takes a test year, say, 1974.

(2) The regulator adds the firm's operating costs, depreciation, and taxes for that year.

(3) The regulator adds to that sum a "reasonable profit." The reasonable profit is determined by multiplying a "reasonable rate of return" times a "rate base."

The total so far — the sum of operating expenses, depreciation, taxes, and a reasonable profit — equals the firm's "revenue requirement."

(4) The regulator sets prices so as to produce revenue for the firm equal to the firm's "revenue requirement."

(5) If the firm sells several different services, or serves different sorts of customers, the regulator may also determine the firm's "rate structure." That is to say, the regulator may set the precise proportions in which the company is to obtain its needed revenue from different classes of customers.

The Board's system, in a very rough way, follows the classic outline: The Board determines the carrier's "revenue requirement." It then sets rates at a level designed to yield that "revenue requirement." The Board, however, has made two very important modifications in the classic system. First, the Board sets rates on the basis of average industry costs. It determines a "revenue requirement" not for each individual carrier, but for the industry as a whole. Second, the Board now sets "load factor" (and other) standards prerequisite to applying the formula to an individual carrier. . . .

In a different part of the DPFI, the Board set rules governing the industry's rate structure — the level at which individual rates should be set in order to generate the industry's revenue requirement. The Board determined that equal fares would be charged for trips of equal mileage. Each fare would be calculated by setting a

163. Op. cit. n.149 supra.

fixed sum of $13.85 terminal charge and then adding to that figure a sum of a few cents per mile. The mileage charge for short trips is higher than for long trips, for, in the Board's view, shorter trips, in general, are more expensive per mile to fly. Thus, the mileage charge is 7.79 cents per mile for trips insofar as they are under 500 miles, 5.94 cents per mile for trips insofar as they are between 500 and 1,500 miles, and 5.71 cents per mile for trips insofar as they extend beyond 1,500 miles. In principle the sum of all fares calculated through the use of this formula should just equal the industry's revenue requirement calculated by means of steps 1-4 above.

The airlines submit cost figures to the Board every 3 months. Those figures provide information about costs, seats flown, and passengers carried for the preceding quarter. Every 3 months the Board, within a few weeks' time, uses those figures to calculate industry costs, revenues, and profits for the preceding year, which it then publishes. By making the calculations described in steps 1-5, the carriers, and the Board, can immediately determine whether a fare increase is called for. If so, carriers may immediately file for an increase, as they did in November 1974. Opponents of the increase may file arguments in response, but if the figures have been calculated properly, *there will not be much to argue about*. Thus, despite differences of opinion about a number of matters — such as whether discount fares were treated properly in the calculation — the Board allowed the carrier request for a fare increase in November 1974 to take effect *without a hearing*.

The net result was the creation of a system that improved prior practice in many ways and, from a purely administrative point of view, has much to recommend it. The DPFI formula determines, from the carriers' cost figures, submitted to the Board every 3 months, and from the use of mechanical formulas, just how much revenue the industry needs and what relation individual fares should bear to each other. They thus show automatically how individual fares can be adjusted to produce the needed revenue. Through the use of its tariff suspension power, the Board can make this system operate automatically. It stated: "*We will require* the carriers for the present to file *coach fares using the formula we have adopted*. Tariffs which change coach fares in individual markets and which are based on a formula which is farther from the cost curve — setting the proper relation between fares for routes of different mileage — at any distance will be rejected." Thus, the Board seemingly can set and adjust fares almost automatically without lengthy hearings on the one hand or ex parte, informal [contacts] on the other.

What then has gone wrong? Why has this remarkable system produced fares that are nearly twice as high as those in California or Texas for comparable routes? Why are fares 40 percent higher than cost estimates submitted by Lockheed and Boeing? Why are they double charter rates? Why, at a time of falling demand, have fares been increasing? . . . [T]he Board approved domestic fare increases totaling about 20 percent between December 1973 and November 1974. Most of the DPFI standards and practices have been in effect since the early seventies; and, as Ralph Nader pointed out, the CAB has "been on a binge of industrywide price increases" since that time.

Questions

1. What was the impact of *Moss*? Would it require on-the-record hearings even when the CAB uses the DPFI formula to determine the validity of particular fares?

2. Suppose consumer groups challenged the substantive validity of the DPFI formula and the CAB's rate regulation practices as contrary to the Civil Aeronautics Act. How likely would they be to succeed?

3. How sensible is the use of trial-type procedures in ratemaking? Recall the background of *Florida East Coast,* p. 458 supra, and the fate of the GPFI.[164]

4. The CAB holds a formal hearing to determine the proper coach fare between New York and Chicago. Five airlines fly this route: Red, White, Blue, Yellow, and Green.

Red, White and Blue — Group I airlines — claim the following costs of service for the route:

— Each airline has invested $75 million to buy three 747s, which will be devoted exclusively to the New York-Chicago route. Each airline has additional fixed investment of about $5 million.

— Each airline has "direct operating costs" — fuel, crew, depreciation — of about $20 million per year. Each airline's indirect operating costs — passenger service, terminal leases, etc. — amounts to another $20 million per year.

— These airlines assert that a coach fare of $120 will cover their costs and earn a 10 percent return on invested capital, assuming a 50 percent "load factor" (i.e., that their planes fly, on average, half full).

164. But consider also the following excerpts from Spritzer, Uses of the Summary Power to Suspend Rates, 120 U. Pa. L. Rev. 39, 95-96 (1971):

"It should be added that, in the view of some observers, cross-examination has only limited utility in the typical rate case. Most of the 'hard' evidence, they point out, is statistical and documentary, and its verification rarely depends upon the examination of witnesses. Moreover, the opinions expressed in the testimony are largely those of trained experts, persons not likely to be trapped by counsel or caught in '[s]elf-contradiction under cross-examination.' They may be more effectively answered, it is suggested, by the opinions of other experts.

"Yet, there are countervailing considerations. Cross-examination of an expert will sometimes prove revealing even if it does not show falsification or yield self-contradiction. Brice Clagett points out that '[a]n "expert" making "estimates" or "forecasts" necessarily makes certain assumptions, relies on certain data, and engages in certain intellectual processes which he regards as rational.' Why, he asks, 'is it *necessarily* not useful to require him to testify about these mattters, rather than allowing him to hide behind the anonymous expertise of an agency opinion writer?' Judge Harold Leventhal, writing in a case that involved an agency's disposition of difficult legal-economic issues, commented: 'Even though there may be no disputed "adjudicatory" facts, the application of the law to the underlying facts involves the kind of judgment that benefits from ventilation at a formal hearing.' A point often neglected is that the examination of expert witnesses on the stand may provide clarification, understanding, and insight not easily derived from a welter of canned testimony or from counsel's advocacy. As one experienced examiner has put it, 'An effective cross-examination can bring to life for the weary presiding examiner the nub of the controversy in a way that weeks and months of lonesome reading of the undiluted mass of written material could not possibly achieve.' "

Green and Yellow — Group II airlines — claim the following costs of service:

— Each airline has invested $10 million in DC-9s, which are devoted exclusively
  to the New York-Chicago route. Each has an additional fixed investment of
  $3 million.
— Each airline has direct operating costs of $21 million and indirect operating
  costs of another $21 million per year.
— These airlines assert that a fare of $110 will cover their costs and earn a 10
  percent return on invested capital, assuming a 50 percent load factor.

Should the Board choose a $110 fare or a $120 fare? What will be the consequences of one choice or another? Would a reviewing court set aside the Board's
choice of either fare?

5. Assume that the CAB, on January 1, 1972, set the New York-Chicago fare
at $120. The CAB also ordered each airline to submit to it semiannual reports of its
actual costs, its predicted costs for the next year, actual traffic, and predicted traffic.

(a) On February 1, 1973, Red, White, and Blue airlines simultaneously file
proposed tariffs to take effect March 1, 1973, with a New York-Chicago fare of
$130. Representatives of the airlines meet informally with the CAB Chairman
and members of the CAB Rate Bureau. The airlines argue that declining traffic,
and rising operating costs, as shown in their semiannual reports, require the rate
increase.

(b) On February 10, 1973, the Air Consumer's Union writes to the Chairman
requesting that the CAB hold a hearing as to whether it should suspend the new
proposed tariffs. The next day the Chairman replies that the Board will not do so
though it would be happy to receive any written submission from the Union.

(c) On February 18, 1973, the Board issues an order refusing to suspend the
tariffs.

(d) The Union seeks review in the Court of Appeals to set aside the Board's
order of February 18th, citing the *Moss* case. Should the court do so? If so, what
procedures must the Board follow?

c. Reform

After the Senate hearings in 1975, the Board began to relax its strict rate and
route standards. President Ford appointed a new Chairman, John Robson, more
favorably disposed toward competition. The Board set route cases for hearing and
gave the airlines greater freedom to adopt discount fares. President Carter also supported airline regulatory reform. He appointed as Board Chairman an economist,
Alfred Kahn (whose views you have read, p. 575 supra). The Board, under Chairman
Kahn, effectively abandoned the DPFI standards, and proposed to allow airlines
broad freedom to set rates (up to 10 percent above and 70 percent below DPFI
levels). It also abandoned a restrictive route award policy, effectively announcing
that it will award routes to any carrier "fit, willing and able" to fly.

The initial results of this change, as of 1978, are satisfactory. Airlines fares have fallen significantly. Yet, because of an unexpected (and possibly resulting) surge in demand, airplanes are flying so full that profits are higher than ever.

You should note that the Board has carried out this radical change in policy under the existing Aviation Act — the same Act used to justify its formerly restrictive behavior. Chairman Kahn's new policies have been, or will be, challenged in court as contrary to that statute's provisions. Would he win? Uncertainty on that score, as well as a desire to make permanent the changes that have taken place, led President Carter, Senator Kennedy, and Senator Cannon to work for passage of a new Aviation Act that makes clear the Board's authority to allow price competition and to open up routes freely to new competition.

In October, 1978, the Airline Deregulation Act of 1978 became law.[165] The new law provides nearly total deregulation. In doing so, it goes well beyond initial proposals of the Ford administration, the Carter administration, the Senate Aviation Subcommittee, and even those of Senator Kennedy. It substitutes almost total reliance upon the free market for the existing regulatory system. And it provides a rare instance in which months of Congressional debate and "compromise" in fact produced a "stronger" deregulatory bill than initial proposals.

The elements of a deregulatory policy essentially consist of freedom for the carriers to set rules, freedom of entry for any "fit" firm to provide whatever service it wishes, and use of the antitrust laws to prevent unfair practices. The essential elements of the new Act as it applies to the domestic industry are the following:

(a) *Principles*: The statements of principles that guide the Board when it sets route or rate policies have been changed. Rather than emphasizing stability and industry growth they now emphasize the primary importance of competition and freedom to offer different mixes of fares and services.

(b) *Entry*: These provisions are the key to the new law. They liberalize the entry requirements in several ways. First, they change the test for determining whether the Board shall grant authority to serve a route. Previously, a carrier had to show that it was "fit, willing and able" to fly and its service was "required by the public convenience and necessity." The new test substitutes for the words "required by" the words "consistent with." This change is not the small one that it may seem, for the Act also provides that the Board can deny entry to a "fit, willing and able carrier" only if it finds that the application is *not* "consistent with the public convenience and necessity" by a "preponderance of the evidence"; the burden of showing the inconsistency is on the opponents of entry. Moreover, the Board is allowed to use simplified procedures, and it must use speeded up time limits. The result, given the current Board, is that a rejection of an application for authority will be most unusual. There will be no retreat from this policy, for under the Act's "sunset" provisions, the "public, convenience and necessity" test *disappears entirely* from the statute at the end of 1981. Then any "fit, willing and able" carrier will be able to fly where it pleases. Indeed, the new statute also allows firms to abandon service virtually as they wish. It seeks to guarantee "essential air service"

165. Pub. L. No. 95-504, 92 Stat. 1705 (1978).

to smaller communities through a subsidy program, not by preventing abandonment. The Act contains additional provisions designed to facilitate new entry.

(c) *Rates:* The rate sections of the Act have been amended to allow carriers considerable flexibility in setting fares. The standards against which the reasonableness of rates is measured now will emphasize the importance of competition, and the "desirability of a variety of price and service options." Moreover, there is a "zone of flexibility" within which a carrier is free to set any price it wishes. The upper limit of that zone is 5 percent higher than the "standard industry fare level" — which is the fare in effect on July 1, 1977 *as adjusted for inflation.* This means considerable upward flexibility (but it does not apply in the case of a carrier that provides 70 percent or more of the service between two points). The carriers have still more flexibility in lowering fares, for each carrier may propose a fare up to 50 percent lower than the "standard industry fare level." In addition, the Board has the power to lower this lower bound still further by rule. (In fact, the Board has done so, setting a lower limit of 70 percent below the 1977 level.) Finally, all of the Board's powers over price will disappear on January 1, 1983.

(d) *Mergers and Antitrust:* The Board's powers to immunize mergers and agreements among carriers from antitrust attack have been significantly curtailed. Finally, the Act requires that any claim that a fare is too low be judged in accordance with ordinary antitrust "predatory" pricing standards — standards that will make it difficult to prevent fare cutting.

(e) *Sunset Provisions:* The Senate bill emerged from the House of Representative and the Senate/House Conference with Sunset provisions attached. These provisions state that at the end of 1981 the Board's authority to restrict entry will terminate. (All applications will be judged only under a "fit, willing and able" test.) At the beginning of 1983, the Board's authority to control rates ends, and its antitrust immunization authority is transferred to the Department of Justice. At the beginning of 1985 the Board will disappear. Its authority over international aviation will be transferred to the Department of Transportation and the Department of State. Its authority to administer a mail subsidy and determine air mail rates will be transferred to the Postal Service and its authority to provide a subsidy for air transportation to small communities will be transferred to the Department of Transportation. Thus, deregulation under the Act is nearly total for the domestic industry.

So far the airline case provides a good example of efforts to bring about one sort of regulatory reform: deregulation, or increased emphasis upon competition. The extent to which that example can or should be applied to other regulatory programs is hotly debated.

7

Due Process Hearing Rights and the Positive State

A. The Traditional Learning

Under the traditional model of administrative law, law was understood as a mechanism for preventing government officials from trespassing on private autonomy when such incursions have not been authorized by the legislature. The sphere of private autonomy protected against unauthorized intrusion was defined by the common law. Where a government official seizes a person's property to satisfy a tax claim, or imprisons him for failure to obey a government directive, the official has committed a common law tort that would be actionable unless his action had been authorized by the legislature. His actions would also constitute an intrusion on the person's interest in "property" or "liberty," which is traditionally protected by the due process clauses of the Fifth and Fourteenth Amendments.[1] In these circumstances, a trial-type hearing traditionally was required in order to establish the officer's authority to invade constitutionally recognized interests.

However, this traditional model affords no redress when a government official causes injury by withholding or terminating benefits not protected by the common law. If a private person fails to give me a gratuity, or refuses me employment, or denies me a supply contract, the common law ordinarily affords me no redress. Similarly, when a government official refuses me welfare benefits, or terminates my at-will employment, or declines to purchase my goods, that official has not infringed upon any of my common law-protected "liberty" or "property" interests, and accordingly need not show legislative warrant for his action. Even if he has assertedly transgressed legislative commands, it is *damnun absque injuria* as far as the traditional model is concerned. Because it is irrelevant whether the officer complied with applicable statutes, there is no occasion for a hearing to decide that question; nor

---

1. See Stewart, The Reformation of American Administrative Law, 88 Harv. L. Rev. 1667, 1717 n.235 (1975) (cases asserting congruence of interests protected by common law and interests protected by due process clause).

does due process require a hearing, because I have no protected "liberty" or "property" at stake.

This conceptual model, keyed to the protection of personal interests at common law, worked tolerably well up until the New Deal. The basic functions of government were comparatively limited, and primarily consisted of taxation and economic regulation enforced by sanctions that would invade common law-protected interests and would trigger the procedural protections of the traditional model (notable exceptions included military pensions and the allocation of the public lands). All of the decisions in Chapter 6 involved controls of this sort. However, the traditional model has serious defects in the context of the modern welfare and service state. Government today engages in a wide variety of activities that powerfully affect individual welfare. It disburses an array of disability, old age, unemployment, and other assistance payments and grants. Government is a major source of employment and supply contracts. It provides education at all levels. Through license schemes, it authorizes individuals and firms to engage in a variety of useful or profitable activities, such as driving automobiles or selling liquor. In short, government provides a wide variety of important advantageous opportunities.[2] Although deprivation of these advantages may have consequences to those affected equal to or greater than the exercise of traditional coercive sanctions, the common law would afford no redress for denial or withdrawal of such advantages by a private person, and therefore the traditional model of administrative law likewise provided no protection when the government refused or withdrew such advantages. Due process required no hearing, because such government action did not trench on common law-protected "liberty" or "property." This concept was encapsulated in the notion that licenses, grants, or government employment were "privileges," not procedurally protected "rights."

This chapter chronicles the gradual demise of the "right/privilege" distinction, and the expansion of due process procedural safeguards to include a variety of advantageous opportunities conferred by government. This "due process explosion" has also carried over into administrative "enclaves," such as hospitals, prisons, and the military, which traditionally were largely immune from judicial control. After examining applications of the earlier "right/privilege" doctrine, this chapter will examine, in turn, two aspects of the extension of due process safeguards: first, the expanding definition of interests entitled to due process protection; and second, judicial determination of what types of procedures are required by due process in a variety of circumstances. Recently, the Supreme Court has begun to restrict the expansion of due process protections, in part out of concern to avoid excessive burdens on the federal courts and intrusions upon the autonomy of state administrative practices. In reviewing this process of expansion and restriction, you should again consider what various purposes procedural safeguards might serve, and critically examine the doctrinal evolution in light of those purposes.

2. See Reich, The New Property, 73 Yale L.J. 733 (1964).

1. The Right/Privilege Distinction

This part illustrates traditional applications of the right/privilege notion in a number of subject areas. Subsequent Supreme Court decisions, such as Goldberg v. Kelly, 397 U.S. 254 (1970), have rejected or undermined the right/privilege distinction, but the earlier cases furnish essential background and arguably have some continuing vitality. This part seeks to convey the flavor of some of the decisions and the conceptual untidiness of many of the distinctions which they reflect. For additional discussion, see Van Alstyne, The Demise of the Right-Privilege Distinction in Constitutional Law, 81 Harv. L. Rev. 1439 (1968).

Licensing. Courts have long held that government may, at will, revoke licenses and other forms of official permission. As recently as 1969 the Iowa Supreme Court affirmed the state's power to revoke a liquor license without notice or hearing, relying on precedent which reasoned that:[3]

". . . [A] license to [sell liquor] is a privilege granted by the state and in no sense a property right. Such a license does not constitute a contract with the state. . . . When the licensee takes this privilege he does so subject to the provisions of the statutes under which it is granted; and if these statutes say or fairly imply that he is entitled to no notice or hearing before revocation, he cannot be heard to complain if he is given none."

However, this "privilege" rationale was not applied to all cases of licensing. In some instances, courts drew a distinction between activities (such as the sale of liquor) which the state could prohibit entirely, and those activities which it could only regulate. Where a state could prohibit absolutely, it was reasoned, the privilege of conducting such activities could be conditioned on whatever terms the state might please. But where the state could only regulate, and where it used a system of licensing to abet its regulatory ends, the citizen maintained a property or liberty interest and was entitled to due process protection. This distinction was used to require hearings prior to revocation of a license to drive a taxi, operate a school of

3. See Smith v. Iowa Liquor Control Commn. 169 N.W.2d 803 (Iowa, 1969), appeal dismissed, 400 U.S. 885 (1970), relying on Walker v. Clinton, 244 Iowa 1099, 1102, 59 N.W.2d 785, 787 (1953), citing State v. Dahnke, 244 Iowa 599, 603, 57 N.W.2d 553, 556 (1953). See also Darling Apartment Co. v. Springer, 25 D. Ch. 420, 22 A.2d 397, 401 (Del. 1941) (summary revocation of liquor license sustained because the "right of a licensee can rise no higher than the terms of the law under which the license is issued; and the licensee accepts the privilege subject to such conditions, including the cause and manner of revocation or suspension."); Lewis v. City of Grand Rapids, 356 F.2d 276 (6th Cir. 1966) (application for liquor license). Similar logic has been utilized to uphold summary revocation of licenses: to exhibit motion pictures, Thayer Amusement Corp. v. Moulton, 63 R.I. 182, 7 A.2d 682 (1939); to operate a motor vehicle, Nulter v. State Road Commission, 119 W. Va. 312, 193 S.E. 549 (1937); Lee v. State, 187 Kan. 566, 358 P.2d 765 (1961); to conduct a pocket billiards business, Commonwealth v. Kinsley, 133 Mass. 578 (1882); or to race horses, Fink v. Cole, 1 N.Y.2d 48, 150 N.Y.S.2d 175, 133 N.E.2d 691 (1956). To what extent might the denial of a hearing in these cases reflect a judgment that the licensing decision turns primarily on the character and reputation of the licensee, factors which might not be illumined through adversary trial-type processes?

cosmetology, or practice medicine.[4] The grounds of classification are often obscure; a Texas court found that a license to sell cigarettes was "somewhere in between" a "right" and a "privilege," and had difficulty determining whether it was more analogous to a liquor license ("privilege") or to a license to sell dental services ("property right"). The court finally concluded that a hearing was required.[5] Over the past two decades there has been a discernible trend in favor of shifting or ignoring the right/privilege distinction in order to expand the availability of procedural safeguards. See, in particular, the Hornsby v. Allen decision, p. 317, supra, in which a federal court found an applicant for a liquor license entitled to due process protection.[6]

Even before this recent trend, courts displayed a special solicitude in extending procedural safeguards to protect licensed professionals. As early as 1873, the Supreme Court held that a lawyer might not be disbarred without notice and opportunity for hearing, asserting that procedural safeguards are as necessary in proceedings "to deprive him of his right to practice his profession as when they are taken to reach his real or personal property." Ex parte Robinson, 86 U.S. 505 (1873). In Goldsmith v. Board of Tax Appeals, 270 U.S. 117 (1925), the Court read a hearing requirement into a federal statute governing the admission of a certified public accountant to the Board of Tax Appeals (now the Tax Court), while Willner v. Committee on Character and Fitness, 373 U.S. 96 (1963), required an evidentiary hearing when an applicant for admission to a state bar was denied admission because of alleged character deficiencies. The requirement of a hearing on applications for professional licensure has been extended to insurance brokers, beauticians, and pharmacists.[7] Do these decisions simply reflect judges' solicitude for lawyers and the extension of that solicitude to other professions? Or do they reflect a residue of substantive due process hostility to state regulation of private labor, coupled with a healthy suspicion that professional licensing is often used to restrict competition or practice various forms of discrimination? [8]

4. Hecht v. Monaghan, 307 N.Y. 461, 121 N.E.2d 421, 424 (1954); Gilchrist v. Bierring, 14 N.W.2d 724 (Iowa, 1944); Smith v. State Board of Medical Examiners, 140 Iowa 66, 117 N.W. 1116 (1908).

5. House of Tobacco, Inc. v. Calvert, 394 S.W.2d 654 (Tex. 1965). An activity may be labelled a "right" in one state and a "privilege" in another. Note, 44 Tex. L. Rev. 1360 (1966).

6. But see City Bank & Trust Co. v. Board of Bank Incorporation, 346 Mass. 29, 190 N.E.2d 107 (1963) (full evidentiary hearing not required on application to open branch bank); First National Bank of Abbeville v. Sehrt, 246 So. 2d 382 (La. App. 1971) (no hearing on existing bank's opposition to licensing of new competitor). The trend in favor of expanded due process protection is in part attributable to Professor Davis' sweeping indictment of the traditional distinction. See 1 K. Davis, Administrative Law, §§ 7.11-7.20 (1958). For discussion of the right to hearing in the context of license applications, see Byse, Opportunity to be Heard in License Issuance, 101 U. Pa. L. Rev. 57 (1952).

7. Koster v. Holz, 3 N.Y.2d 639, 148 N.E.2d 287 (1958); Tanner v. De Sapio, 2 Misc. 2d 130, 150 N.Y.S.2d 640 (Sup. Ct. 1956); Milligan v. Bd. of Registration in Pharmacy, 348 Mass. 491, 204 N.E.2d 504 (1965).

8. See M. Friedman, Capitalism and Freedom 149-159 (1962); Hetherington, State Economic Regulation and Substantive Due Process of Law, 53 Nw. U. L. Rev. 226 (1958); Kessel, The A.M.A. and the Supply of Physicians, 35 Law & Contemp. Prob. 267 (1970). See generally, Note, Due Process Limitations on Occupational Licensing, 59 Va. L. Rev. 1097 (1973).

Aliens. It has long been held that aliens may be excluded from the United States without notice or hearing. See The Chinese Exclusion Case (Chae Chan Ping v. United States), 130 U.S. 581 (1889). In United States ex rel. Knauff v. Shaughnessy, 338 U.S. 537 (1950), the Court upheld the exclusion, without hearing, of the alien wife of an American citizen who sought admission under the War Brides Act. Finding that Congress had authorized exclusion without hearing, the Court reasoned that "[a]dmission of aliens is a privilege granted by the sovereign United States Government . . . upon such terms as the United States shall prescribe," and that, accordingly, "(w)hatever the procedure authorized by Congress is, it is due process so far as an alien denied entry is concerned." [9] See also Shaughnessy v. United States ex rel. Mezei, 345 U.S. 206 (1953), sustaining the government's refusal to readmit an alien, resident in the United States for 25 years, who had sought readmission following a 19-month visit with relatives in Europe. Because of the refusal of any other nation to accept him, Mezei had been detained in limbo at Ellis Island for 23 months at the time of the Court's decision.

By contrast, an alien resident in the United States may not be deported without a hearing, at which the government must establish that the alien is subject to deportation under the relevant statutes and regulations. The Japanese Immigrant Case (Yamataya v. Fisher), 189 U.S. 86 (1903); Wong Yang Sung v. McGrath, 339 U.S. 33 (1950). This principle has been extended to the exclusion of an alien admitted to permanent residence who had shipped out of the country as a merchant seaman without going ashore abroad.[10] (Query: under the "privilege" rationale, why couldn't Congress admit an alien on the condition that he might be subject to deportation without hearing?)

Education. While not presenting procedural issues, Hamilton v. Regents of the University of California, 293 U.S. 245 (1934), illustrates the application of the right/privilege notion to public education. A college student was suspended for failure to attend a mandatory military training course because of religious scruples. While acknowledging that the student might have a constitutionally protected interest in avoiding mandatory military training, the Court ruled that the University might impose conditions on the "privilege" of attendance, and, since the student could refuse to attend, no deprivation of his liberty was involved. Steier v. New York State Education Commission, 271 F.2d 13 (2d Cir. 1959), ruled that due process did not require a hearing prior to expulsion of a student from Brooklyn College for public criticism of the college president, while Bluett v. University of

---

9. However, where a person seeking entry claimed to be a *citizen* entitled to entry as of right, a de novo judicial determination of the claim of citizenship was required in Ng Fung Ho v. White, p. 55, supra.

10. Kwong Har Chew v. Colding, 344 U.S. 590 (1953). However, the authority of the President to order the deportation, without hearing, of an alien during wartime was sustained in Ludecke v. Watkins, 335 U.S. 160 (1948). And in Jay v. Boyd, 351 U.S. 345 (1956), the Court held that an alien is not entitled to a hearing on the immigration authorities' refusal to exercise discretionary authority (conferred by statute) to suspend the deportation of an otherwise deportable alien meeting specified hardship, good character, and residence requirements, reasoning that the relief, like probation or suspension of a criminal sentence "comes as an act of grace" and "cannot be demanded as a right."

Illinois, 10 Ill. App. 2d 207, 134 N.E. 2d 635 (1956), followed many earlier cases in sustaining a college student's expulsion, without hearing, for alleged cheating.

However, the contemporary extension of due process safeguards to students was foreshadowed in Dixon v. Alabama State Board of Education, 294 F.2d 150 (5th Cir.), *cert. denied*, 368 U.S. 930 (1961), requiring that students at a state college be accorded rudimentary notice and hearing prior to expulsion for asserted misconduct (here, participation in sit-in demonstrations protesting lunch counter segregation). Stressing that education was a vital interest and that expulsion might so stigmatize the students in question that they could not obtain admission elsewhere, the majority of the court specifically rejected the state's argument that the student's admission had been contractually made subject to suspension without hearing, and concluded that even if higher education were a "privilege," it could not be conditioned on the students' waiver of rights to constitutional due process.[11] A dissenting judge protested the extension of "the injunctive power of federal courts to the problems of day to day dealings between school authorities and student discipline and morale."

Other subjects. Right/privilege thinking has been evident in many other areas where courts have traditionally refused to afford procedural rights or other legal protection to those denied advantageous opportunities by government, including public employment, draft exemptions, government contracts, parole, and government pensions.[12]

Bailey v. Richardson

182 F.2d 46 (D.C. Cir. 1950), aff'd by an equally divided Court, 341 U.S. 918 (1951)

PRETTYMAN, Circuit Judge.

This is a civil action brought in the United States District Court for the District of Columbia for a declaratory judgment and for an order directing plaintiff-appel-

11. In the rest of this chapter, you should consider the extent to which an exceptionally sympathetic fact situation (as in this case) has triggered major changes in due process doctrine.

For discussion of judicial treatment of students' claims to procedural rights in the 1950s and 1960s, see Wright, The Constitution on the Campus, 22 Vand. L. Rev. 1027 (1969); Van Alstyne, Procedural Due Process and State University Students, 10 U.C.L.A. L. Rev. 368 (1963).

12. See Laba v. Newark Board of Education, 23 N.J. 364, 129 A.2d 273 (1957) (public employment; hearing not required on discharge); Pickus v. Board of Education, 9 Ill. 2d 599, 138 N.E.2d 532 (1956) (same); United States v. Nugent, 346 U.S. 1 (1953) (confrontation and cross-examination by applicant of adverse witnesses not required in denial of conscientious objector exemption from draft); Hiatt v. Compagna, 178 F.2d 42 (5th Cir. 1949), aff'd, 340 U.S. 880 (1950) (hearing not required in revocation of parole); Hyser v. Reed, 318 F.2d 225 (D.C. Cir.), *cert. denied*, 375 U.S. 957 (1963) (same); Ex parte Anderson, 191 Or. 409, 229 P.2d 633 (1951) (same, discussing authorities); Perkins v. Lukens Steel Co., 310 U.S. 113 (1940) (no judicial review of government contractor's challenge to contract terms as contrary to statute); Reaves v. Ainsworth, 219 U.S. 296 (1911) (no judicial review of government rejection of pension claim).

lant's reinstatement in Government employ. [Plaintiff Bailey had been hired by the federal government in 1948, subject to removal within 18 months by the Civil Service Commission if investigation disclosed disqualification. The Commission's regulations listed as a disqualification:]

"(7) On all the evidence, reasonable grounds exist for belief that the person involved is disloyal to the Government of the United States."

On July 31, 1948, two months after her reinstatement, Miss Bailey received from the Regional Loyalty Board of the Commission a letter and an enclosed interrogatory. The letter said in part:

"During the course of an investigation of your suitability for appointment, information was received which the Commission believes you should be given an opportunity to clarify. Consequently, there [is] enclosed . . . an interrogatory to be answered by you under affirmation or oath. . . ."

The interrogatory said in part:

"As part of the process of determining your suitability for Federal Employment, an investigation of you has been conducted under the provisions of Executive Order 9835, which established the Federal Employees Loyalty Program. This investigation disclosed information which, it is believed, you should have an opportunity to explain or refute. . . .

"The Commission has received information to the effect that you are or have been a member of the Communist Party or the Communist Political Association; that you have attended meetings of the Communist Party, and have associated on numerous occasions with known Communist Party members.

"The Commission has received information to the effect that you are or have been a member of the American League for Peace and Democracy, an organization which has been declared by the Attorney General to come within the purview of Executive Order 9835.

"The Commission has received information to the effect that you are or have been a member of the Washington Committee for Democratic Action, an organization which has been declared by the Attorney General to come within the purview of Executive Order 9835.

"Are you now, or have ever been, a member of, or in any manner affiliated with, the Nazi or Fascist movements or with any organization or political party whose objective is now, or has ever been, the overthrow of the Constitutional Government of the United States?"

Miss Bailey answered the interrogatories directly and specifically, denying each item of information recited therein as having been received by the Commission, except that she admitted past membership for a short time in the American League for Peace and Democracy. She vigorously asserted her loyalty to the United States. She requested an administrative hearing. A hearing was held before the Regional Board. She appeared and testified and presented other witnesses and numerous affidavits. No person other than those presented by her testified. . . .

On the same day, a letter was sent by the Board to Miss Bailey, reading in part:

"As shown in the attached copy of a letter to your employing agency, it has been found that, on all the evidence, reasonable grounds exist for belief that you are disloyal to the Government of the United States.

"Your application for or eligibility from each of the examinations mentioned below has been cancelled and you have been barred from civil service examinations in the Federal service for a period of three years from October 29, 1948. When the period of debarment has expired the Commission will, upon request, consider the removal of the bar.

[The Commission's Loyalty Review Board then sustained the action of the Regional Board.]

CONFORMITY WITH EXECUTIVE ORDER

Appellant's first contention is that the procedure followed by the Loyalty Boards did not conform to the requirements of the Executive Order[13] which established them. That Order provided in part:

"The standard for the refusal of employment or the removal from employment in an executive department or agency on grounds relating to loyalty shall be that, on all the evidence, reasonable grounds exist for belief that the person involved is disloyal to the Government of the United States."

Appellant says that "evidence" does not include, in our jurisprudence, information secretly disclosed to a hearing tribunal. That is certainly true, but the question is whether the President used the term in its jurisprudential sense or whether he merely meant "information." We think he meant the latter. The Order, read as a whole, and particularly Part IV, conclusively and emphatically requires that the names of confidential informants be kept confidential. Moreover, the President, in a Memorandum published in the Federal Register of March 15, 1948, specifically and unequivocally directed that all reports, etc., relating to these cases be kept in strict confidence. "Evidence," as appellant defines the word, would require that informants appear, either in person or by affidavit, in the proceeding and upon the record. If the Loyalty Boards were violating the President's instructions in so crucial a part of a program so widely publicized, he would surely have known it and would have corrected the error. The procedure followed represented an administrative interpretation of an administrative order, and the courts follow such interpretations unless the error is clear.

[The court then held, following United States v. Lovett, 328 U.S. 303 (1946), that the Board's order banning Bailey from civil service employ for three years was "punishment" which, under the Sixth Amendment, could only be imposed through a criminal prosecution.

However, it also ruled that her dismissal from government service was not "punishment" and was accordingly not invalid under the Sixth Amendment.]

---

13. Exec. Order No. 9835, 5 U.S.C.A. §631 note, 12 Fed. Reg. 1935 (1947), 3 C.F.R. 132 (Supp. 1947).

FIFTH AMENDMENT

It is next said on behalf of appellant that the due process clause of the Fifth Amendment requires that she be afforded a hearing of the quasi-judicial type before being dismissed. The due process clause provides: "No person shall ... be deprived of life, liberty, or property, without the due process of law; ..." It has been held repeatedly and consistently that Government employ is not "property" and that in this particular it is not a contract. We are unable to perceive how it could be held to be "liberty." Certainly, it is not "life." So much that is clear would seem to dispose of the point. In terms the due process clause does not apply to the holding of a Government office.

Other considerations lead to the same conclusion. Never in our history has a Government administrative employee been entitled to a hearing of the quasi-judicial type upon his dismissal from Government service. That record of a hundred and sixty years of Government administration is the sort of history which speaks with great force. It is pertinent to repeat in this connection that the Lloyd-La Follette Act,[14] sponsored and enacted by advocates of a merit classified government service, expressly denies the right to such a hearing. Moreover, in the acute and sometimes bitter historic hundred-year contest over the wholesale summary dismissal of Government employees, there seems never to have been a claim that, absent congressional limitation, the President was without constitutional power to dismiss without notice, hearing or evidence; except for the question as to officials appointed with the advice and consent of the Senate. ...

Constitutionally, the criterion for retention or removal of subordinate employees is the confidence of superior executive officials. Confidence is not controllable by process. What may be required by acts of the Congress is another matter, but there is no requirement in the Constitution that the executive branch rely upon the services of persons in whom it lacks confidence. The opinions in the Myers case [272 U.S. 52 (1926)] supra, makes this proposition amply clear. ...

But it is said that the public does not distinguish, that she has been stigmatized and her chance of making a living seriously impaired. The position implicit in that assertion dissolves into two contentions. One is that even if executive authorities had power to dismiss Miss Bailey without a judicial hearing, they had no power to hurt her while doing so; that is, they had no power to call her disloyal even if they had power to dismiss her for that reason. But it has long been established that if the Government, in the exercise of a governmental power, injures an individual, that individual has no redress. ... And a person may be publicly stigmatized and ruined by utterances on the floor of Congress without any opportunity in any established forum to deny or to refute. These harsh rules, which run counter to every known precept of fairness to the private individual, have always been held necessary as a matter of public policy, public interest, and the unimpeded performance of the

14. Ed. Note: The Lloyd-La Follette Act, enacted in 1913 and codified in 5 U.S.C. §7501, does not provide for a trial-type hearing on dismissal of civil service employees. The Act's provisions are discussed in Arnett v. Kennedy, infra p. 629.

public business. On behalf of the individual, our sense of justice rebels, but the counterbalancing essentials of effective government lead us to assent without equivocation to the rules of immunity.

[The court also rejected Bailey's contention that her discharge was a sanction for her entertaining certain political views and therefore violated the First Amendment.]

EDGERTON, Circuit Judge (dissenting).

Without trial by jury, without evidence, and without even being allowed to confront her accusers or to know their identity, a citizen of the United States has been found disloyal to the government of the United States.

For her supposed disloyal thoughts she has been punished by dismissal from a wholly nonsensitive position in which her efficiency rating was high. The case received nation-wide publicity. Ostracism inevitably followed. A finding of disloyalty is closely akin to a finding of treason. The public hardly distinguishes between the two.

No charges were served on appellant. . . . The Federal Bureau of Investigation had reported that informants believed to be reliable had made general statements purporting to connect her with the Communist Party. These reports were not disclosed to the appellant and have not been disclosed in court. The informants were not identified to the appellant or even to the Board. Their statements were admittedly not made under oath. The appellant denied under oath any membership in and any relationship or sympathy with the Communist Party, any activities connected with it or with communism. . . .

Appellant had no power to subpoena witnesses. Though it takes courage to appear as a voluntary defense witness in a loyalty case, four appeared [for her]. The record consists entirely of evidence in her favor. Yet the Board purported to find "on all the evidence" that there were reasonable grounds for believing she was disloyal to the government of the United States. . . .

I. *Executive Order 9835 requires evidence and an opportunity for cross-examination.* . . .

II. *Dismissal for disloyalty is punishment and requires all the safeguards of a judicial trial.* Most dismissals, including among others dismissals for colorless or undisclosed reasons and dismissals for incompetence, are plainly not punitive. . . .

Punishment is infliction of harm, usually for wrong conduct but in appellant's case for wrong views. Dismissals to provide jobs for persons of certain affiliations, whatever else may be said of such dismissals, are not punitive. But dismissals for disloyal views are punitive.

. . . Appellant was dismissed from a nonsensitive position. She was a staff training officer in the United States Employment Service. In the case of such an officer, no way is apparent and none has been suggested in which "suspicion of disloyalty indicates a risk" to the security of the United States. *Appellant's dismissal for wrong thoughts has nothing to do with protecting the security of the United States.* . . .

Since dismissal from government service for disloyalty is punishment, due process of law requires that the accused employee be given all the safeguards of a judicial trial before it is imposed. . . .

Questions

1. In the celebrated case of McAuliffe v. City of New Bedford, 155 Mass. 216, 29 N.E. 517 (1892), Justice Holmes sustained the dismissal of a city policeman for engaging in political activities in violation of a city regulation with the curt observation that, "The petitioner may have a constitutional right to talk politics, but he has no constitutional right to be a policeman," and that, accordingly, he could not complain "as he takes the employment on the terms which are offered him." Is *Bailey* founded on this same conceptualism — here, that government employment may be conditioned on liability to discharge without a trial-type hearing? Or is the decision based upon the practical implications of recognizing government employment as a species of "liberty" or "property" protected by due process? If government employment were constitutionally protected, would a hearing be required for demotion? Transfer? Failure to hire? Failure to promote? Would the extension of hearing rights result in a contraction of the grounds for personnel decisions to those that could be established in a courtroom? Do civil service seniority rules and bureaucratic practices already make it too difficult to discharge incompetent government employees, a difficulty that would be exacerbated by the addition of trial-type hearing requirements and judicial review? [15] Is *Bailey* explained by the majority's fear of hard cases making bad law?

2. Note the majority's treatment of Ms. Bailey's claim to a hearing based on the injury to her reputation. Why shouldn't Ms. Bailey be entitled to a hearing to clear her name without being entitled to reinstatement? Could the stigma problem be avoided by making the sole ground of discharge "For the good of the Service"? [16]

2. Nonconstitutional Avenues to Procedural Protection

Greene v. McElroy

360 U.S. 474 (1959)

Mr. Chief Justice WARREN delivered the opinion of the Court.

[Greene had been given security clearances by Defense Department authorities on three occasions after World War II in connection with his responsibilities as

---

15. For current criticism of the civil service system as fostering inefficiency and sheltering incompetence, see Reed, Firing a Federal Employee, The Impossible Dream, Washington Monthly, July–Aug. 1977 at 14; Havemann, Can Carter Chop Through the Civil Service System? 1977 Natl. J. 616. But cf. Merrill, Procedures for Adverse Actions Against Federal Employees, 59 Va. L. Rev. 196 (1973).

16. See Jaffe & Nathanson, Administrative Law 839 (3d Ed. 1968).

For a relevant sampling of the extensive literature on government loyalty and security programs, see E. Bontecou, The Federal Loyalty-Security Program (1953); R. Brown, Loyalty and Security (1958); W. Gellhorn, Security, Loyalty, and Science (1950); Gardner, Bailey v. Richardson and the Constitution of the United States, 33 B.U. L. Rev. 176 (1953); Seasongood and Strecker, The Loyalty Review Board, 25 U. Cin. L. Rev. 1 (1956).

vice-president and general manager of a defense contractor. Beginning in 1951, Department officials initiated steps to revoke his security clearance on the grounds that between 1943 and 1947 he had associated with communists and visited officials of the Russian embassy. Greene appeared before several Department boards responsible for administration of security clearances for employees of defense contractors. He explained that the "suspect" persons with whom he had allegedly associated were friends of his then wife, whom he had since divorced, in part because of her communist sympathies. He explained his visits to foreign embassies as made in connection with efforts of his employer to sell its products abroad. He explicitly and fully denied communist sympathies and associations, and his testimony was corroborated in important respects by other witnesses, including officials of his employer and high ranking military officers with whom he had worked. The government presented no witnesses; in questioning Greene and witnesses appearing on his behalf, the departmental boards relied on confidential reports which they refused to disclose to Greene. Decisions by the departmental boards and the Secretary of the Navy ordered withdrawal of Greene's security clearance. As a result, he was discharged from his $18,000 per year position and forced to find employment as an architectural draftsman at a salary of $4,700 per year.]

Petitioner contends that the action of the Department of Defense in barring him from access to classified information on the basis of statements of confidential informants made to investigators was not authorized by either Congress or the President and has denied him "liberty" and "property" without "due process of law" in contravention of the Fifth Amendment. The alleged property is petitioner's employment; the alleged liberty is petitioner's freedom to practice his chosen profession. . . . [R]espondents contend that the admitted interferences which have occurred are indirect by-products of necessary governmental action to protect the integrity of secret information and hence are not unreasonable and do not constitute deprivations within the meaning of the Amendment. Alternatively, respondents urge that even if petitioner has been restrained in the enjoyment of constitutionally protected rights, he was accorded due process of law in that he was permitted to utilize those procedural safeguards consonant with an effective clearance program, in the administration of which the identity of informants and their statements are kept secret to insure an unimpaired flow to the Government of information concerning subversive conduct. But in view of our conclusion that this case should be decided on the narrower ground of "authorization," we find that we need not determine the answers to these questions.

[The Court then summarizes the various post-war Defense Department security clearance programs and procedures.]

All of these programs and procedures were established by directives issued by the Secretary of Defense or the Secretaries of the Army, Navy, and Air Force. None was the creature of statute or of an Executive Order issued by the President.

Respondents maintain that congressional authorization to the President to fashion a program which denies security clearance to persons on the basis of confidential information which the individuals have no opportunity to confront and test is unnecessary because the President has inherent authority to maintain military secrets inviolate. And respondents argue that if a statutory grant of power is necessary, such a grant can readily be *inferred* "as a necessarily implicit authority from the generalized provisions" of legislation dealing with armed services. But the question which must be decided in this case is not whether the President has inherent power to act or whether Congress has granted him such a power; rather, it is whether either the President or Congress exercised such a power and delegated to the Department of Defense the authority to fashion such a program.

Certain principles have remained relatively immutable in our jurisprudence. One of these is that where governmental action seriously injures an individual, and the reasonableness of the action depends on fact findings, the evidence used to prove the Government's case must be disclosed to the individual so that he has an opportunity to show that it is untrue. While this is important in the case of documentary evidence, it is even more important where the evidence consists of the testimony of individuals whose memory might be faulty or who, in fact, might be perjurers or persons motivated by malice, vindictiveness, intolerance, prejudice, or jealousy. We have formalized these protections in the requirements of confrontation and cross-examination. They have ancient roots.[17]

[The Court then reviewed various presidential directives to the Defense Department, general congressional statutes dealing with government secrets, and congressional appropriations for Defense Department programs as constituting authorization or at least ratification of the Department's security clearance program and procedures. However, the Court found that in no instance was there sufficiently explicit authorization of the procedures utilized in Greene's case.]

If acquiescence or implied ratification were enough to show delegation of authority to take actions within the area of questionable constitutionality, we might agree with respondents that delegation has been shown here. . . . We deal here with substantial restraints on employment opportunities of numerous persons imposed in a manner which is in conflict with our long-accepted notions of fair procedures. Before we are asked to judge whether, in the context of security clearance cases, a person may be deprived of the right to follow his chosen profession without full hearings where accusers may be confronted, it must be made clear that the President or Congress, within their respective constitutional powers, specifically has decided that the imposed procedures are necessary and warranted and has authorized their use. . . . Such decisions cannot be assumed by acquiescence or non-action. Kent v. Dulles, 357 U.S. 116. . . . They must be made explicitly not only to assure that individuals are not deprived of cherished rights under procedures not actually authorized . . . but also because explicit action, especially in areas of doubtful constitutionality, requires careful and purposeful consideration by those responsible for enacting and implementing our laws. Without explicit action by lawmakers, decisions of great constitutional import and effect would be relegated by default to

17. When Festus, more than two thousand years ago, reported to King Agrippa that Felix had given him a prisoner named Paul and that the priests and elders desired to have judgment against Paul, Festus is reported to have stated: "It is not the manner of the Romans to deliver any man to die, before that he which is accused have the accusers face to face, and have license to answer for himself concerning the crime laid against him." Acts 25:16.

administrators who, under our system of government, are not endowed with authority to decide them.

[The Court reversed the decision of the Court of Appeals sustaining the government's action.]

Mr. Justice Frankfurter, Mr. Justice Harlan and Mr. Justice Whittaker concur in the judgment on the ground that it has not been shown that either Congress or the President authorized the procedures whereby petitioner's security clearance was revoked, intimating no views as to the validity of those procedures. . . .

Mr. Justice CLARK, dissenting.

. . . Surely one does not have a constitutional right to have access to the Government's military secrets. . . . What for anyone else would be considered a privilege at best has for Greene been enshrouded in constitutional protection. This sleight of hand is too much for me.

[Justice Clark proceeded to argue with great vigor that (1) because Greene had no right to military secrets, the government need not afford him a hearing in terminating his security clearance, (2) that in any event Congress and the President had clearly authorized the Department's security clearance program and the procedures employed in it.]

Notes: Nonconstitutional Avenues to Procedural Protection

1. In *Greene* the Court held that the government could not take away a particular advantageous opportunity without a full trial-type hearing because neither Congress nor the President had specifically authorized such action. Where, earlier in these materials, have we seen this technique used? Why wasn't it used in Bailey v. Richardson?

2. During the 1950s the Court was assiduous in overturning employee discharges and revocations of security clearances without reaching the constitutional issues raised by plaintiffs. Cole v. Young, 351 U.S. 536 (1956), found insufficient Congressional authority for application of a loyalty program to a food and drug inspector in the FDA whose work was not closely related to national security. In Peters v. Hobby, 349 U.S. 331 (1955), the dismissal of a government employee as a security risk was set aside because the Court found no authority in applicable statutes or regulations for the Loyalty Review Board's sua sponte reversal of a judgment by a trial board favorable to the employee. In Service v. Dulles, 354 U.S. 363 (1957), and in Vitarelli v. Seaton, 359 U.S. 535 (1959), the Court found that employee discharges without hearings violated the relevant agencies' own procedural regulations despite quite plausible claims by the agencies that the regulations were inapplicable to dismissals because of suspected disloyalty or security risks.[18]

18. However, a lower federal court reached the constitutional issues in Parker v. Lester, 227 F.2d 708 (9th Cir. 1955), which invalidated denial, without any hearing, of security clearances for merchant seamen as a violation of due process. (The Solicitor General declined to seek certiorari). *Accord*, Homer v. Richmond, 292 F.2d 719 (D.C. Cir. 1961). By contrast, in Bland v. Connally, 293 F.2d 852 (D.C. Cir. 1961) and Davis v. Stahr, 293 F.2d 860 (D.C. Cir. 1961), the courts were able to find a want of statutory authority for discharge of inactive reservists because of subversive activities or derogatory remarks.

3. Nonconstitutional rulings have been used by lower courts to invalidate adverse governmental actions taken without opportunity for hearing in matters other than employment and security clearance.

For example, Garrott v. United States, 340 F.2d 615 (Ct. Cl. 1965), involved the withdrawal by the Civil Service Commission of a former government employee's retirement benefits pursuant to a statute prohibiting payment of benefits to former employees who had misrepresented facts relating to their Communist Party affiliations. Following *Greene*, the court found insufficient authority for the Commission to act without affording a full evidentiary hearing.

Gonzalez v. Freeman, 334 F.2d 570 (D.C. Cir. 1964), set aside the debarment, without hearing, of government contractors from participating in certain contracts with the Commodity Credit Corporation because of violation of applicable regulations. The Court held that the Department's debarment practices must be codified in regulations, and the failure to do so violated APA §552(a)(1)(B), requiring Federal Register publication of "statements of the general course and method by which its functions are channelled and determined, including the nature and requirements of all formal and informal procedures available." The Court observed that contractors were not apprised in advance of the grounds for debarment or the procedures utilized in determining misconduct. Emphasizing the serious impact of debarment on government contractors, the court concluded that a debarment could not be "left to administrative improvisation on a case-by-case basis." Cf. Morton v. Ruiz, supra, p. 415.

Cafeteria Workers v. McElroy

367 U.S. 886 (1961)

Mr. Justice STEWART delivered the opinion of the Court.

In 1956 the petitioner Rachel Brawner was a short-order cook at a cafeteria operated by her employer, M & M Restaurants, Inc., on the premises of the Naval Gun Factory in the city of Washington. She had worked there for more than six years, and from her employer's point of view her record was entirely satisfactory.

[The contract between the Gun Factory and M & M Restaurants required Restaurants' employees to meet naval security requirements. Mrs. Brawner's clearance to work at the base was revoked by Navy officials for failure to meet base security requirements. Her requests for a hearing or further explanation were denied.]

Since the day her identification badge was withdrawn Mrs. Brawner has not been permitted to enter the Gun Factory. M & M offered to employ her in another restaurant which the company operated in the suburban Washington area, but she refused on the ground that the location was inconvenient....

As the case comes here, two basic questions are presented. Was the commanding officer of the Gun Factory authorized to deny Rachel Brawner access to the installation in the way he did? If he was so authorized, did his action in excluding her operate to deprive her of any rights secured to her by the Constitution?...

I

... It cannot be doubted that both the legislative and executive branches are wholly legitimate potential sources of such explicit authority. The control of access to a military base is clearly within the constitutional powers granted to both Congress and the President. Article I, §8, of the Constitution gives Congress the power to "provide and maintain a navy"; to "make rules for the government and regulation of the land and naval forces"; to "exercise exclusive legislation . . . over all places purchased by the consent of the legislature of the state in which the same shall be, for the erection of forts, magazines, arsenals, dock-yards, and other needed buildings"; and to "make all laws which shall be necessary and proper for carrying into execution the foregoing powers. . . ." Broad power in this same area is also vested in the President by Article II, §2, which makes him the Commander in Chief of the Armed Forces.

Congress has provided that the Secretary of the Navy "shall administer the Department of the Navy" and shall have "custody and charge of all . . . property of the Department." 10 U.S.C. §5031(a) and (c). In administering his Department, the Secretary has been given statutory power to "prescribe regulations, not inconsistent with law, for the government of his department, . . . and the custody, use, and preservation of the . . . property appertaining to it." 5 U.S.C. §22. [The Court quoted general regulations giving commanding officers plenary authority over base questions.] The law explicitly requires that United States Navy Regulations shall be approved by the President, 10 U.S.C. §6011, and the pertinent regulations in effect when Rachel Brawner's identification badge was revoked had, in fact, been expressly approved by President Truman on August 9, 1948.

[The Court concluded that Congress and the President had sufficiently authorized the Navy's action in this case.]

II

The question remains whether Admiral Tyree's action in summarily denying Rachel Brawner access to the site of her former employment violated the requirements of the Due Process Clause of the Fifth Amendment. This question cannot be answered by easy assertion that, because she had no constitutional right to be there in the first place, she was not deprived of liberty or property by the Superintendent's action. "One may not have a constitutional right to go to Baghdad, but the Government may not prohibit one from going there unless by means consonant with due process of law." Homer v. Richmond, 110 U.S. App. D.C. 226, 229, 292 F.2d 719, 722. It is the petitioners' claim that due process in this case required that Rachel Brawner be advised of the specific grounds for her exclusion and be accorded a hearing at which she might refute them. We are satisfied, however, that under the circumstances of this case such a procedure was not constitutionally required.

The Fifth Amendment does not require a trial-type hearing in every conceivable case of government impairment of private interest. . . . The very nature of due process negates any concept of inflexible procedures universally applicable to every imaginable situation. . . . " '[D]ue process,' unlike some legal rules, is not a technical conception with a fixed content unrelated to time, place and circumstances." It is "compounded of history, reason, the past course of decisions. . . ." Joint Anti-Fascist Comm. v. McGrath, 341 U.S. 123, 162-163 (concurring opinion).

. . . [C]onsideration of what procedures due process may require under any given set of circumstances must begin with a determination of the precise nature of the government function involved as well as of the private interest that has been affected by governmental action. Where it has been possible to characterize that private interest (perhaps in oversimplification) as a mere privilege subject to the Executive's plenary power, it has traditionally been held that notice and hearing are not constitutionally required. . . .

What, then, was the private interest affected by Admiral Tyree's action in the present case? It most assuredly was not the right to follow a chosen trade or profession. . . . Rachel Brawner remained entirely free to obtain employment as a short-order cook or to get any other job, either with M & M or with any other employer. All that was denied her was the opportunity to work at one isolated and specific military installation.

Moreover, the governmental function operating here was not the power to regulate or license, as lawmaker, an entire trade or profession, or to control an entire branch of private business, but rather, as proprietor, to manage the internal operation of an important federal military establishment. . . . In that proprietary military capacity, the Federal Government, as has been pointed out, has traditionally exercised unfettered control.

. . . This case, like Perkins v. Lukens Steel Co., 310 U.S. 113, involves the Federal Government's dispatch of its own internal affairs. The Court has consistently recognized that an interest closely analogous to Rachel Brawner's, the interest of a government employee in retaining his job, can be summarily denied. It has become a settled principle that government employment, in the absence of legislation, can be revoked at the will of the appointing officer. . . . We may assume that Rachel Brawner could not constitutionally have been excluded from the Gun Factory if the announced grounds for her exclusion had been patently arbitrary or discriminatory — that she could not have been kept out because she was a Democrat or a Methodist. It does not follow, however, that she was entitled notice and a hearing when the reason advanced for her exclusion was, as here, entirely rational and in accord with the contract with M & M.

Finally, it is to be noted that this is not a case where government action has operated to bestow a badge of disloyalty or infamy, with an attendant foreclosure from other employment opportunity. . . . All this record shows is that, in the opinion of the security officer of the Gun Factory, concurred in by the Superintendent, Rachel Brawner failed to meet the particular security requirements of that specific military installation. There is nothing to indicate that this determination would in any way impair Rachel Brawner's employment opportunities anywhere else.[19] . . .

19. In oral argument government counsel emphatically represented that denial of access to the Gun Factory would not "by law or in fact" prevent Rachel Brawner from obtaining employment on any other federal property.

For all that appears, the Security Officer and the Superintendent may have simply thought that Rachel Brawner was garrulous, or careless with her identification badge.

For these reasons, we conclude that the Due Process Clause of the Fifth Amendment was not violated in this case.

Affirmed.

Mr. Justice BRENNAN, with whom the CHIEF JUSTICE, Mr. Justice BLACK and Mr. Justice DOUGLAS join, dissenting.

I have grave doubts whether the removal of petitioner's identification badge for "security reasons" without notice of charges or opportunity to refute them was authorized by statute or executive order. See Greene v. McElroy, 360 U.S. 474 (1959). But under compulsion of the Court's determination that there was authority, I pass to a consideration of the more important constitutional issue, whether petitioner has been deprived of liberty or property without due process of law in violation of the Fifth Amendment.

I read the Court's opinion to acknowledge that petitioner's status as an employee at the Gun Factory was an interest of sufficient definiteness to be protected by the Federal Constitution from some kinds of governmental injury.... In other words, if petitioner Brawner's badge had been lifted avowedly on grounds of her race, religion, or political opinions, the Court would concede that some constitutionally protected interest — whether "liberty" or "property" it is unnecessary to state — had been injured. But, as the Court says, there has been no such open discrimination here. The expressed ground of exclusion was the obscuring formulation that petitioner failed to meet the "security requirements" of the naval installation where she worked. I assume for present purposes that separation as a "security risk," if the charge is properly established, is not unconstitutional. But the Court goes beyond that. It holds that the mere assertion by government that exclusion is for a valid reason forecloses further inquiry. That is, unless the government official is foolish enough to admit what he is doing — and few will be so foolish after today's decision — he may employ "security requirements" as a blind behind which to dismiss at will for the most discriminatory of causes.

Such a result in effect nullifies the substantive right — not to be arbitrarily injured by Government — which the Court purports to recognize. What sort of right is it which enjoys absolutely no procedural protection? ... She may be the victim of the basest calumny, perhaps even the caprice of the government officials in whose power her status rested completely. In such a case, I cannot believe that she is not entitled to some procedures. "[T]he right to be heard before being condemned to suffer grievous loss of any kind, even though it may not involve the stigma and hardships of a criminal conviction, is a principle basic to our society." Joint Anti-Fascist Refugee Comm. v. McGrath, 341 U.S. 123, 168 (1951) (concurring opinion).... [T]he Court holds that petitioner has a right not to have her identification badge taken away for an "arbitrary" reason, but no right to be told in detail what the reason is, or to defend her own innocence, in order to show, perhaps, that the true reason for deprivation was one forbidden by the Constitution. That is an internal contradiction to which I cannot subscribe.

One further circumstance makes this particularly a case where procedural requirements of fairness are essential. Petitioner was not simply excluded from the base summarily, without a notice and chance to defend herself. She was excluded as a "security risk," that designation most odious in our times. . . . [The Court] ought not to affix a "badge of infamy" . . . to a person without some statement of charges, and some opportunity to speak in reply.

Questions

1. Why didn't the Court in *Cafeteria Workers* follow Greene v. McElroy, given the absence of any explicit authorization from Congress or the President for the denial of security clearance to civilian employees without explanation or opportunity for hearing? Is the Court more solicitous of corporate executives than short-order cooks?

2. Note that the Court adopts a "balancing" approach to due process. Does its approach repudiate the right/privilege distinction, or does it serve to preserve the distinction in a new guise? What are the ingredients in such a balancing process, and how are they to be weighed?

3. Why does the majority concede that Mrs. Brawner could not be discharged because of her race, religion, or political affiliation? If government employment, a security badge, or any other advantageous opportunity conferred by government is merely a "privilege," why may not it be denied or withdrawn on any ground whatsoever? Is the Court's concession compelled by its "balancing" test? What other justifications might there be for such a concession?

4. If the government may not deny employment, security clearance, or other benefits for certain reasons, then isn't Justice Brennan correct in concluding that administrators should provide an explanation for their action, which could be tested in an administrative hearing? Or is it sufficient that a person allegedly discriminated against could bring a lawsuit in court to protest the government's action and secure a judicial hearing on the reasons for it? Cf. Nickey v. Mississippi, 292 U.S. 393 (1934), sustaining the denial of an administrative hearing on a tax assessment because of the availability of de novo judicial review. See also the discussion of Southern Ry. v. Virginia, p. 468, supra. Even if there is no automatic right to an administrative hearing, should there not at least be a requirement that administrators provide a reason for their actions? [20]

Note: Pre-*Goldberg* Due Process Decisions by the Supreme Court

In the two decades prior to its 1970 decision in Goldberg v. Kelly, 397 U.S. 254 (requiring hearings prior to state termination of welfare payments to assertedly ineligible recipients), the Supreme Court issued a number of decisions imposing

---

20. See Rabin, Job Security and Due Process: Monitoring Administrative Discretion Through a Reasons Requirement, 44 U. Chi. L. Rev. 60 (1976).

constitutional restrictions on states' withdrawal or withholding of advantageous opportunities traditionally characterized as "privileges." For example, Wieman v. Updegraff, 344 U.S. 183 (1952), invalidated exclusion from employment in state colleges because of membership in specified "subversive" organizations, regardless of the member's knowledge of or commitment to the organization's goals. Slochower v. Board of Higher Education, 350 U.S. 551 (1956), prohibited summary dismissal of a state college professor for invocation of the privilege against self-incrimination in connection with testimony unrelated to his employment. Sherbert v. Verner, 374 U.S. 398 (1963) invalidated state denial of unemployment benefits because of the recipient's refusal, for religious reasons, to seek employment on a Saturday. But these and similar rulings involved an independent constitutional limitation on governmental action — First Amendment protections of speech and religious freedom, and the constitutional privilege against self-incrimination — rather than recognition of employment or other government benefits as "liberty" or "property" in themselves.[21]

B. The Evolution of the New Due Process: The Definition of Interests Entitled to Procedural Protection

In the remaining portions of this chapter, we examine the development of procedural due process protections following the Supreme Court's decision in Goldberg v. Kelly, 397 U.S. 254 (1970), which unambiguously extended constitutional safeguards to advantageous relations with government ("privileges"). In this section we examine, through a series of Supreme Court decisions, the expanding (and contracting) definition of the interests entitled to claim due process protection. In the two subsequent sections we review the determination by the federal courts of what types of procedural safeguards are required by due process in a variety of situations. Throughout the materials which follow you should again ask yourself what purposes are potentially served by procedural safeguards, and how emphasis on one purpose as opposed to another might influence the definition of protected interests or the choice among alternative procedural requirements.

21. A potential doctrinal breakthrough had been anticipated when the Supreme Court granted certiorari in Thorpe v. Housing Authority of Durham, 386 U.S. 670 (1967), in which a tenant in a federally assisted public housing project challenged termination of her lease without a hearing. However, the Supreme Court avoided the constitutional issue by remanding for reconsideration in light of a subsequent regulation of the Department of Housing and Urban Development prohibiting termination of a tenancy in federally assisted public housing projects without a statement of reasons and an opportunity for explanation or reply on the part of the tenant. On remand, the North Carolina Supreme Court adhered to its previous denial of relief, finding the HUD regulation to be entirely prospective in its application, but the Supreme Court subsequently reversed, holding that Ms. Thorpe was entitled to the benefit of the new regulation. 393 U.S. 268 (1969).

Goldberg v. Kelly

397 U.S. 254 (1970)

Mr. Justice BRENNAN delivered the opinion of the Court.

... This action was brought in the District Court for the Southern District of New York by residents of New York City receiving financial aid under the federally assisted program of Aid to Families with Dependent Children (AFDC) or under New York State's general Home Relief program. Their complaint alleged that the New York State and New York City officials administering these programs terminated, or were about to terminate, such aid without prior notice and hearing, thereby denying them due process of law. At the time the suits were filed there was no requirement of prior notice or hearing of any kind before termination of financial aid. However, the State and city adopted procedures for notice and hearing after the suits were brought, and the plaintiffs, appellees here, then challenged the constitutional adequacy of those procedures. . . .

[At the time of the Court's decision, state law provided for the following procedures for termination of assistance payments:] A caseworker who has doubts about the recipient's continued eligibility must first discuss them with the recipient. If the caseworker concludes that the recipient is no longer eligible, he recommends termination of aid to a unit supervisor. If the latter concurs, he sends the recipient a letter stating the reasons for proposing to terminate aid and notifying him that within seven days he may request that a higher official review the record, and may support the request with a written statement prepared personally or with the aid of an attorney or other person. If the reviewing official affirms the determination of ineligibility, aid is stopped immediately and the recipient is informed by letter of the reasons for the action. Appellees' challenge to this procedure emphasizes the absence of any provisions for the personal appearance of the recipient before the reviewing official, for oral presentation of evidence, and for confrontation and cross-examination of adverse witnesses. However, the letter does inform the recipient that he may request a post-termination "fair hearing." This is a proceeding before an independent state hearing officer at which the recipient may appear personally, offer oral evidence, confront and cross-examine the witnesses against him, and have a record made of the hearing. If the recipient prevails at the "fair hearing" he is paid all funds erroneously withheld. HEW Handbook, pt. IV, §§ 6200-6500; 18 NYCRR §§ 84.2-84.23. A recipient whose aid is not restored by a "fair hearing" decision may have judicial review. N.Y. Civil Practice Law and Rules, Art. 78 (1963). The recipient is so notified, 18 NYCRR §84.16.

I

The constitutional issue to be decided, therefore, is the narrow one whether the Due Process Clause requires that the recipient be afforded an evidentiary hearing *before* the termination of benefits. The District Court held that only a pre-termination evidentiary hearing would satisfy the constitutional command, and rejected the argument of the state and city officials that the combination of the post-termination "fair hearing" with the informal pre-termination review disposed of all due process claims. The court said: "While post-termination review is relevant, there is one overpowering fact which controls here. By hypothesis, a welfare recipient is destitute, without funds or assets. . . . Suffice it to say that to cut off a welfare recipient in the face of . . . 'brutal need' without a prior hearing of some sort is unconscionable, unless overwhelming considerations justify it." . . .

Appellant does not contend that procedural due process is not applicable to the termination of welfare benefits. Such benefits are a matter of statutory entitlement for persons qualified to receive them.[22] Their termination involves state action that adjudicates important rights. The constitutional challenge cannot be answered by an argument that public assistance benefits are "a 'privilege' and not a 'right.' ". . . Relevant constitutional restraints apply as much to the withdrawal of public assistance benefits as to disqualification for unemployment compensation, Sherbert v. Verner, 374 U.S. 398 (1963); or to denial of a tax exemption, Speiser v. Randall, 357 U.S. 513 (1958); or to discharge from public employment, Slochower v. Board of Higher Education, 350 U.S. 551 (1956).[23] The extent to which procedural due process must be afforded the recipient is influenced by the extent to which he may be "condemned to suffer grievous loss," Joint Anti-Fascist Refugee Committee v. McGrath, 341 U.S. 123, 168 (1951) (Frankfurter, J., concurring), and depends upon whether the recipient's interest in avoiding that loss outweighs the governmental interest in summary adjudication. Accordingly, as we said in Cafeteria & Restaurant Workers Union v. McElroy, 367 U.S. 886, 895 (1961), "consideration of what procedures due process may require under any given set of circumstances must begin with a determination of the precise nature of the government function involved as well as of the private interest that has been affected by governmental action." . . .

22. It may be realistic today to regard welfare entitlements as more like "property" than a "gratuity." Much of the existing wealth in this country takes the form of rights that do not fall within traditional common-law concepts of property. It has been aptly noted that:

> "[s]ociety today is built around entitlement. The automobile dealer has his franchise, the doctor and lawyer their professional licenses, the worker his union membership, contract, and pension rights, the executive his contract and stock options; all are devices to aid security and independence. Many of the most important of these entitlements now flow from government: subsidies to farmers and businessmen; routes for airlines and channels for television stations; long term contracts for defense, space, and education; social security pensions for individuals. Such sources of security, whether private or public, are no longer regarded as luxuries or gratuities; to the recipients they are essentials, fully deserved, and in no sense a form of charity. It is only the poor whose entitlements, although recognized by public policy, have not been effectively enforced."

Reich, Individual Rights and Social Welfare: The Emerging Local Issues, 74 Yale L.J. 1245, 1255 (1965). See also Reich, The New Property, 73 Yale L.J. 733 (1964).

23. See also Goldsmith v. United States Board of Tax Appeals, 270 U.S. 117 (1926) (right of a certified public accountant to practice before the Board of Tax Appeals); Hornsby v. Allen, 326 F.2d 605 (5th Cir. 1964) (right to obtain a retail liquor store license); Dixon v. Alabama State Board of Education, 294 F.2d 150 (C.A. 5th Cir.), cert. denied, 368 U.S. 930 (1961) (right to attend a public college).

It is true, of course, that some governmental benefits may be administratively terminated without affording the recipient a pre-termination evidentiary hearing.[24] But we agree with the District Court that when welfare is discontinued, only a pre-termination evidentiary hearing provides the recipient with procedural due process. Cf. Sniadach v. Family Finance Corp., 395 U.S. 337 (1969). For qualified recipients, welfare provides the means to obtain essential food, clothing, housing, and medical care. . . . Thus the crucial factor in this context — a factor not present in the case of the blacklisted government contractor, the discharged government employee, the taxpayer denied a tax exemption, or virtually anyone else whose governmental entitlements are ended — is that termination of aid pending resolution of a controversy over eligibility may deprive an *eligible* recipient of the very means by which to live while he waits. Since he lacks independent resources, his situation becomes immediately desperate. His need to concentrate upon finding the means for daily subsistence, in turn, adversely affects his ability to seek redress from the welfare bureaucracy.

Moreover, important governmental interests are promoted by affording recipients a pre-termination evidentiary hearing. From its founding the Nation's basic commitment has been to foster the dignity and well-being of all persons within its borders. We have come to recognize that forces not within the control of the poor contribute to their poverty. This perception, against the background of our traditions, has significantly influenced the development of the contemporary public assistance system. Welfare, by meeting the basic demands of subsistence, can help bring within the reach of the poor the same opportunities that are available to others to participate meaningfully in the life of the community. At the same time, welfare guards against the societal malaise that may flow from a widespread sense of unjustified frustration and insecurity. Public assistance, then, is not mere charity, but a means to "promote the general Welfare, and secure the Blessings of Liberty to ourselves and our Posterity." The same governmental interests that counsel the provision of welfare, counsel as well its uninterrupted provision to those eligible to receive it; pre-termination evidentiary hearings are indispensable to that end.

Appellant does not challenge the force of these considerations but argues that they are outweighed by countervailing governmental interests in conserving fiscal and administrative resources. These interests, the argument goes, justify the delay of any evidentiary hearing until after discontinuance of the grants. Summary adjudication protects the public fisc by stopping payments promptly upon discovery of reason to believe that a recipient is no longer eligible. Since most terminations are accepted without challenge, summary adjudication also conserves both the fisc

24. One Court of Appeals has stated: "In a wide variety of situations, it has long been recognized that where harm to the public is threatened, and the private interest infringed is reasonably deemed to be of less importance, an official body can take summary action pending a later hearing." R.A. Holman & Co. v. SEC, 299 F.2d 127, 131, *cert. denied*, 370 U.S. 911 (1962) (suspension of exemption from stock registration requirement). See also, for example, Ewing v. Mytinger & Casselberry, Inc., 339 U.S. 594 (1950) (seizure of mislabeled vitamin product); North American Cold Storage Co. v. Chicago, 211 U.S. 306 (1908) (seizure of food not fit for human use); Yakus v. United States, 321 U.S. 414 (1944) (adoption of wartime price regulations). . . .

and administrative time and energy by reducing the number of evidentiary hearings actually held.

We agree with the District Court, however, that these governmental interests are not overriding in the welfare context. The requirement of a prior hearing doubtless involves some greater expense, and the benefits paid to ineligible recipients pending decision at the hearing probably cannot be recouped, since these recipients are likely to be judgment-proof. But the State is not without weapons to minimize these increased costs. Much of the drain on fiscal and administrative resources can be reduced by developing procedures for prompt pre-termination hearings and by skillful use of personnel and facilities. Indeed, the very provision for a post-termination evidentiary hearing in New York's Home Relief program is itself cogent evidence that the State recognizes the primacy of the public interest in correct eligibility determinations and therefore in the provision of procedural safeguards. Thus, the interest of the eligible recipient in uninterrupted receipt of public assistance, coupled with the State's interest that his payments not be erroneously terminated, clearly outweighs the State's competing concern to prevent any increase in its fiscal and administrative burdens. . . .

II

We also agree with the District Court, however, that the pre-termination hearing need not take the form of a judicial or quasi-judicial trial. We bear in mind that the statutory "fair hearing" will provide the recipient with a full administrative review. Accordingly, the pre-termination hearing has one function only: to produce an initial determination of the validity of the welfare department's grounds for discontinuance of payments in order to protect a recipient against an erroneous termination of his benefits. Cf. Sniadach v. Family Finance Corp., 395 U.S. 337, 343 (1969) (Harlan J., concurring). Thus, a complete record and a comprehensive opinion, which would serve primarily to facilitate judicial review and to guide future decisions, need not be provided at the pre-termination stage. We recognize, too, that both welfare authorities and recipients have an interest in relatively speedy resolution of questions of eligibility, that they are used to dealing with one another informally, and that some welfare departments have very burdensome caseloads. These considerations justify the limitation of the pre-termination hearing to minimum procedural safeguards, adapted to the particular characteristics of welfare recipients, and to the limited nature of the controversies to be resolved. We wish to add that we, no less than the dissenters, recognize the importance of not imposing upon the States or the Federal Government in this developing field of law any procedural requirements beyond those demanded by rudimentary due process. . . . In the present context these principles require that a recipient have timely and adequate notice detailing the reasons for a proposed termination, and an effective opportunity to defend by confronting any adverse witnesses and by presenting his own arguments and evidence orally. These rights are important in cases such as those before us, where recipients have challenged proposed terminations as resting on incorrect or misleading factual premises or on misapplication of rules or policies to the facts of particular cases.[25]

[The Court found New York procedures for notifying recipients of proposed terminations to be adequate.]

The city's procedures presently do not permit recipients to appear personally with or without counsel before the official who finally determines continued eligibility. Thus a recipient is not permitted to present evidence to that official orally, or to confront or cross-examine adverse witnesses. These omissions are fatal to the constitutional adequacy of the procedures.

The opportunity to be heard must be tailored to the capacities and circumstances of those who are to be heard. It is not enough that a welfare recipient may present his position to the decision maker in writing or secondhand through his caseworker. Written submissions are an unrealistic option for most recipients, who lack the educational attainment necessary to write effectively and who cannot obtain professional assistance. . . .

In almost every setting where important decisions turn on questions of fact, due process requires an opportunity to confront and cross-examine adverse witnesses [citing Greene v. McElroy]. Welfare recipients must therefore be given an opportunity to confront and cross-examine the witnesses relied on by the department.

. . . We do not say that counsel must be provided at the pre-termination hearing, but only that the recipient must be allowed to retain an attorney if he so desires. Counsel can help delineate the issues, present the factual contentions in an orderly manner, conduct cross-examination, and generally safeguard the interests of the recipient. We do not anticipate that this assistance will unduly prolong or otherwise encumber the hearing. . . .

Finally, the decisionmaker's conclusion as to a recipient's eligibility must rest solely on the legal rules and evidence adduced at the hearing. Ohio Bell Tel. Co. v. PUC, 301 U.S. 292 (1937); United States v. Abilene & S. R. Co., 265 U.S. 274, 288-289 (1924). To demonstrate compliance with this elementary requirement, the decision maker should state the reasons for his determination and indicate the evidence he relied on, . . . though his statement need not amount to a full opinion or even formal findings of fact and conclusions of law. And, of course, an impartial decision maker is essential. . . . We agree with the District Court that prior involvement in some aspects of a case will not necessarily bar a welfare official from acting as a decision maker. He should not, however, have participated in making the determination under review.

Affirmed.

Mr. Justice BLACK, dissenting.

In the last half century the United States, along with many, perhaps most, other nations of the world, has moved far toward becoming a welfare state, that is,

25. This case presents no question requiring our determination whether due process requires only an opportunity for written submission, or an opportunity both for written submission and oral argument, where there are no factual issues in dispute or where the application of the rule of law is not intertwined with factual issues. . . .

a nation that for one reason or another taxes its most affluent people to help support, feed, clothe, and shelter its less fortunate citizens. The result is that today more than nine million men, women, and children in the United States receive some kind of state or federally financed public assistance in the form of allowances or gratuities, generally paid them periodically, usually by the week, month, or quarter. Since these gratuities are paid on the basis of need, the list of recipients is not static, and some people go off the lists and others are added from time to time. These ever-changing lists put a constant administrative burden on government and it certainly could not have reasonably anticipated that this burden would include the additional procedural expense imposed by the Court today. . . .

The more than a million names on the relief rolls in New York, and the more than nine million names on the rolls of all the 50 States were not put there at random. The names are there because state welfare officials believed that those people were eligible for assistance. Probably in the officials' haste to make out the lists many names were put there erroneously in order to alleviate immediate suffering, and undoubtedly some people are drawing relief who are not entitled under the law to do so. Doubtless some draw relief checks from time to time who know they are not eligible, either because they are not actually in need or for some other reason. Many of those who thus draw undeserved gratuities are without sufficient property to enable the government to collect back from them any money they wrongfully receive. But the Court today holds that it would violate the Due Process Clause of the Fourteenth Amendment to stop paying those people weekly or monthly allowances unless the government first affords them a full "evidentiary hearing" even though welfare officials are persuaded that the recipients are not rightfully entitled to receive a penny under the law. In other words, although some recipients might be on the lists for payment wholly because of deliberate fraud on their part, the Court holds that the government is helpless and must continue, until after an evidentiary hearing, to pay money that it does not owe, never has owed, and never could owe. I do not believe there is any provision in our Constitution that should thus paralyze the government's efforts to protect itself against making payments to people who are not entitled to them. . . .

I would have little, if any, objection to the majority's decision in this case if it were written as the report of the House Committee on Education and Labor, but as an opinion ostensibly resting on the language of the Constitution I find it woefully deficient. Once the verbiage is pared away it is obvious that this Court today adopts the views of the District Court "that to cut off a welfare recipient in the face of . . . 'brutal need' without a prior hearing of some sort is unconscionable," and therefore, says the Court, unconstitutional. The majority reaches this result by a process of weighing "the recipient's interest in avoiding" the termination of welfare benefits against "the governmental interest in summary adjudication." . . . Today's balancing act requires a "pre-termination evidentiary hearing," yet there is nothing that indicates what tomorrow's balance will be. Although the majority attempts to bolster its decision with limited quotations from prior cases, it is obvious that today's result does not depend on the language of the Constitution itself or the principles of other decisions, but solely on the collective judgment of the majority as to what would be a fair and humane procedure in this case.

This decision is thus only another variant of the view often expressed by some members of this Court that the Due Process Clause forbids any conduct that a majority of the Court believes "unfair," "indecent," or "shocking to their consciences." See, e.g., Rochin v. California, 342 U.S. 165, 172 (1952). Neither these words nor any like them appear anywhere in the Due Process Clause. If they did, they should leave the majority of Justices free to hold any conduct unconstitutional that they would conclude on their own to be unfair or shocking to them. Had the drafters of the Due Process Clause meant to leave judges such ambulatory power to declare laws unconstitutional, the chief value of a written constitution, as the Founders saw it, would have been lost. . . .

The Court apparently feels that this decision will benefit the poor and needy. In my judgment the eventual result will be just the opposite. While today's decision requires only an administrative, evidentiary hearing, the inevitable logic of the approach taken will lead to constitutionally imposed, time-consuming delays of a full adversary process of administrative and judicial review. In the next case the welfare recipients are bound to argue that cutting off benefits before judicial review of the agency's decision is also a denial of due process. Since, by hypothesis, termination of aid at that point may still "deprive an *eligible* recipient of the very means by which to live while he waits," . . . I would be surprised if the weighing process did not compel the conclusion that termination without full judicial review would be unconscionable. After all, at each step, as the majority seems to feel, the issue is only one of weighing the government's pocketbook against the actual survival of the recipient, and surely that balance must always tip in favor of the individual. Similarly today's decision requires only the opportunity to have the benefit of counsel at the administrative hearing, but it is difficult to believe that the same reasoning process would not require the appointment of counsel, for otherwise the right to counsel is a meaningless one since these people are too poor to hire their own advocates. Cf. Gideon v. Wainwright, 372 U.S. 335, 344 (1963). Thus the end result of today's decision may well be that the government, once it decides to give welfare benefits, cannot reverse that decision until the recipient has had the benefits of full administrative and judicial review, including, of course, the opportunity to present his case to this Court. Since this process will usually entail a delay of several years, the inevitable result of such a constitutionally imposed burden will be that the government will not put a claimant on the rolls initially until it has made an exhaustive investigation to determine his eligibility. While this Court will perhaps have insured that no needy person will be taken off the rolls without a full "due process" proceeding, it will also have insured that many will never get on the rolls, or at least that they will remain destitute during the lengthy proceedings followed to determine initial eligibility.

For the foregoing reasons I dissent from the Court's holding. The operation of a welfare state is a new experiment for our Nation. For this reason, among others, I feel that new experiments in carrying out a welfare program should not be frozen into our constitutional structure. They should be left, as are other legislative determinations, to the Congress and the legislatures that the people elect to make our laws.

[A companion case, Wheeler v. Montgomery, 397 U.S. 280 (1970), was briefly disposed on the basis of *Goldberg*. Chief Justice Burger and Justice Stewart filed dissenting opinions applicable both to *Goldberg* and *Wheeler*. The Chief Justice's dissent sounded themes similar to those voiced by Justice Black — the need for experimentation in welfare administration, and the danger of hasty judicial intervention. Justice Stewart, in a very brief opinion, stated that, "[a]lthough the question is for me a close one," he did not believe the state procedures at issue to violate due process, citing his opinion for the Court in *Cafeteria Workers*.]

Notes and Questions

1. On what basis does the Court decide that plaintiffs' interest in continued receipt of assistance payments is entitled to due process protection? Is it plaintiffs' "brutal need" that triggers constitutional safeguards? Or is it the fact that plaintiffs are entitled by statute to receive benefits if they meet statutory criteria of eligibility? Given that the State conceded the applicability of due process, did the Court even decide this question?

2. The statuory entitlement rationale was vigorously asserted by Charles Reich in his celebrated article, The New Property, 73 Yale L.J. 733 (1964), cited in footnote 22 (footnote 8 in the original) to the Court's opinion. Reich's basic argument is that in modern society much wealth consists of advantageous opportunities conferred by government. Reich further argues that where statutes provide that government benefits, such as assistance payments, shall be afforded to qualifying individuals, those individuals should be recognized as having a property right in such benefits, whose deprivation should be protected by procedural safeguards similar to those utilized to protect "old" property, such as land, from governmental deprivation. What difficulties might there be in extending procedural safeguards in this fashion? Should *substantive*, as well as procedural constitutional protection be extended to the "new property"? [26]

Board of Regents of State Colleges v. Roth

408 U.S. 564 (1972)

Mr. Justice STEWART delivered the opinion of the Court.

[David Roth was hired for a one year term as assistant professor at the Wisconsin State University, Oshkosh, from September 1968 through June 1969. At the

26. See Tushnet, The Newer Property: Suggestion for the Revival of Substantive Due Process, 1975 Sup. Ct. Rev. 261; Van Alstyne, Cracks in "The New Property": Adjudicative Due Process in the Administrative State, 62 Cornell L. Rev. 445 (1977) for two different views.

end of his term he was not rehired; no reason was given for the failure to rehire him. Under Wisconsin statutory law, a state university teacher acquires tenure only after four consecutive years of employment; the decision whether to rehire a one-year appointee is committed to the unfettered discretion of university officials. Roth brought suit against relevant university officials in federal district court under the 1871 Civil Rights Act, 42 U.S.C. §1983, contending that the failure to rehire him violated the Fourteenth Amendment. First, Roth asserted that the failure to rehire was retribution for his exercise of his free speech rights in issuing statements critical of the University administration. Second, he contended that in any event the University's failure to give him reasons or opportunity for hearing on the rehiring decision violated procedural due process. The District Court denied plaintiff's summary judgment on the free speech claim, finding disputed factual issues regarding the reasons for not rehiring Roth. However, the District Court granted summary judgment for Roth on the procedural due process issue. The Court of Appeals affirmed that judgment, and the Supreme Court granted certiorari. Since there had been no final resolution in the District Court on the free speech claim, it was not subject to appeal.]

I

The requirements of procedural due process apply only to the deprivation of interests encompassed by the Fourteenth Amendment's protection of liberty and property. When protected interests are implicated, the right to some kind of prior hearing is paramount. But the range of interests protected by procedural due process is not infinite.

The District Court decided that procedural due process guarantees apply in this case by assessing and balancing the weights of the particular interests involved. It concluded that the respondent's interest in re-employment at Wisconsin State University-Oshkosh outweighed the University's interest in denying him re-employment summarily. 310 F. Supp., at 977-979. Undeniably, the respondent's re-employment prospects were of major concern to him — concern that we surely cannot say was insignificant. And a weighing process has long been a part of any determination of the *form* of hearing required in particular situations by procedural due process. But, to determine whether due process requirements apply in the first place, we must look not to the "weight" but to the *nature* of the interest at stake. . . . We must look to see if the interest is within the Fourteenth Amendment's protection of liberty and property.

"Liberty" and "property" are broad and majestic terms. They are among the "[g]reat [constitutional] concepts . . . purposely left to gather meaning from experience. . . . [T]hey relate to the whole domain of social and economic fact, and the statesmen who founded this Nation knew too well that only a stagnant society remains unchanged." National Ins. Co. v. Tidewater Co., 337 U.S. 582, 646 (Frankfurter, J., dissenting). For that reason, the Court has fully and finally rejected the wooden distinction between "rights" and "privileges" that once seemed to govern the applicability of procedural due process rights.[27] The Court has also made clear that the property interests protected by procedural due process extend well beyond actual ownership of real estate, chattels, or money. By the same token, the Court has required due process protection for deprivations of liberty beyond the sort of formal constraints imposed by the criminal process.

Yet, while the Court has eschewed rigid or formalistic limitations on the protection of procedural due process, it has at the same time observed certain boundaries. For the words "liberty" and "property" in the Due Process Clause of the Fourteenth Amendment must be given some meaning.

II

"While this Court has not attempted to define with exactness the liberty ... guaranteed [by the Fourteenth Amendment], the term has received much consideration and some of the included things have been definitely stated. Without doubt, it denotes not merely freedom from bodily restraint but also the right of the individual to contract, to engage in any of the common occupations of life, to acquire useful knowledge, to marry, establish a home and bring up children, to worship God according to the dictates of his own conscience, and generally to enjoy those privileges long recognized ... as essential to the orderly pursuit of happiness by free men." Meyer v. Nebraska, 262 U.S. 390, 399. In a Constitution for a free people, there can be no doubt that the meaning of "liberty" must be broad indeed. . . .

There might be cases in which a State refused to re-employ a person under such circumstances that interests in liberty would be implicated. But this is not such a case.

The State, in declining to rehire the respondent, did not make any charge against him that might seriously damage his standing and associations in his community. . . . See Cafeteria Workers v. McElroy, 367 U.S. 886, 898. In such a case, due process would accord an opportunity to refute the charge before University officials. In the present case, however, there is no suggestion whatever that the respondent's "good name, reputation, honor, or integrity" is at stake.

Similarly, there is no suggestion that the State, in declining to re-employ the respondent, imposed on him a stigma or other disability that foreclosed his freedom to take advantage of other employment opportunities. . . .[28]

---

27. In a leading case decided many years ago, the Court of Appeals for the District of Columbia Circuit held that public employment in general was a "privilege," not a "right," and that procedural due process guarantees therefore were inapplicable. Bailey v. Richardson, 86 U.S. App. D.C. 248, 182 F.2d 46, aff'd by an equally divided Court, 341 U.S. 918. The basis of this holding has been thoroughly undermined in the ensuing years. . . .

28. The District Court made an *assumption* "that non-retention by one university or college creates concrete and practical difficulties for a professor in his subsequent academic career." 310 F. Supp., at 979. And the Court of Appeals based its affirmance of the summary judgment largely on the premise that "the substantial adverse effect non-retention is likely to have upon the career interests of an individual professor" amounts to a limitation on future employment opportunities sufficient to invoke procedural due process guarantees. 446 F.2d, at 809. But even

To be sure, the respondent has alleged that the nonrenewal of his contract was based on his exercise of his right to freedom of speech. But this allegation is not now before us. . . .[29]

Hence, on the record before us, all that clearly appears is that the respondent was not rehired for one year at one university. It stretches the concept too far to suggest that a person is deprived of "liberty" when he simply is not rehired in one job but remains as free as before to seek another. Cafeteria Workers v. McElroy, supra, at 895-896.

III

The Fourteenth Amendment's procedural protection of property is a safeguard of the security of interests that a person has already acquired in specific benefits. These interests — property interests — may take many forms.

Thus, the Court has held that a person receiving welfare benefits under statutory and administrative standards defining eligibility for them has an interest in continued receipt of those benefits that is safeguarded by procedural due process. Goldberg v. Kelly, 397 U.S. 254. . . .

. . . To have a property interest in a benefit, a person clearly must have more than an abstract need or desire for it. He must have more than a unilateral expectation of it. He must, instead, have a legitimate claim of entitlement to it. It is a purpose of the ancient institution of property to protect those claims upon which people rely in their daily lives, reliance that must not be arbitrarily undermined. It is a purpose of the constitutional right to a hearing to provide an opportunity for a person to vindicate those claims.

Property interests, of course, are not created by the Constitution. Rather, they are created and their dimensions are defined by existing rules or understandings that stem from an independent source such as state law — rules or understandings that secure certain benefits and that support claims of entitlement to those benefits. Thus, the welfare recipients in Goldberg v. Kelly, supra, had a claim of entitlement to welfare payments that was grounded in the statute defining eligibility for

---

assuming, arguendo, that such a "substantial adverse effect" under these circumstances would constitute a state-imposed restriction on liberty, the record contains no support for these assumptions. . . .

29. . . . The Court of Appeals, nonetheless, argued that opportunity for a hearing and a statement of reasons were required here "as a *prophylactic* against non-retention decisions improperly motivated by exercise of protected rights." 446 F.2d, at 810 (emphasis supplied). . . .

When a State would directly impinge upon interests in free speech or free press, this Court has on occasion held that opportunity for a fair adversary hearing must precede the action, whether or not the speech or press interest is clearly protected under substantive First Amendment standards. Thus, we have required fair notice and opportunity for an adversary hearing before an injunction is issued against the holding of rallies and public meetings. Carroll v. Princess Anne, 393 U.S. 175. . . .

In the respondent's case, however, the State has not directly impinged upon interests in free speech or free press in any way comparable to a seizure of books or an injunction against meetings. Whatever may be a teacher's rights of free speech, the interest in holding a teaching job at a state university, simpliciter, is not itself a free speech interest.

them. The recipients had not yet shown that they were, in fact, within the statutory terms of eligibility. But we held that they had a right to a hearing at which they might attempt to do so.

Just as the welfare recipients' "property" interest in welfare payments was created and defined by statutory terms, so the respondent's "property" interest in employment at Wisconsin State University-Oshkosh was created and defined by the terms of his appointment. Those terms secured his interest in employment up to June 30, 1969. But the important fact in this case is that they specifically provided that the respondent's employment was to terminate on June 30. They did not provide for contract renewal absent "sufficient cause." Indeed, they made no provision for renewal whatsoever.

Thus, the terms of the respondent's appointment secured absolutely no interest in re-employment for the next year. They supported absolutely no possible claim of entitlement to re-employment. Nor, significantly, was there any state statute or University rule of policy that secured his interest in re-employment or that created any legitimate claim to it.[30] In these circumstances, the respondent surely had an abstract concern in being rehired, but he did not have a *property* interest sufficient to require the University authorities to give him a hearing when they declined to renew his contract of employment.

IV

. . . We must conclude that the summary judgment for the respondent should not have been granted, since the respondent has not shown that he was deprived of liberty or property protected by the Fourteenth Amendment. The judgment of the Court of Appeals, accordingly, is reversed and the case is remanded for further proceedings consistent with this opinion.

It is so ordered.

[Mr. Justice POWELL took no part in the decision of this case. A dissenting opinion by Justice DOUGLAS is omitted.]

Mr. Justice MARSHALL, dissenting.

. . . In my view, every citizen who applies for a government job is entitled to it unless the government can establish some reason for denying the employment. This is the "property" right that I believe is protected by the Fourteenth Amendment and that cannot be denied "without due process of law." And it is also liberty — liberty to work — which is the "'very essence of the personal freedom and opportunity" secured by the Fourteenth Amendment. . . .

Employment is one of the greatest, if not the greatest, benefits that governments offer in modern-day life. When something as valuable as the opportunity to work is at stake, the government may not reward some citizens and not others without demonstrating that its actions are fair and equitable. And it is procedural

---

30. To be sure, the respondent does suggest that most teachers hired on a year-to-year basis by Wisconsin State University-Oshkosh are, in fact, rehired. But the District Court has not found that there is anything approaching a "common law" of re-employment, . . . so strong as to require University officials to give the respondent a statement of reasons and a hearing on their decision not to rehire him.

due process that is our fundamental guarantee of fairness, our protection against arbitrary, capricious, and unreasonable government action. . . .

It may be argued that to provide procedural due process to all public employees or prospective employees would place an intolerable burden on the machinery of government. Cf. Goldberg v. Kelly, supra. The short answer to that argument is that it is not burdensome to give reasons when reasons exist. . . .

It might also be argued that to require a hearing and a statement of reasons is to require a useless act, because a government bent on denying employment to one or more persons will do so regardless of the procedural hurdles that are placed in its path. Perhaps this is so, but a requirement of procedural regularity at least renders arbitrary action more difficult. Moreover, proper procedures will surely eliminate some of the arbitrariness that results, not from malice, but from innocent error. . . . When the government knows it may have to justify its decisions with sound reasons, its conduct is likely to be more cautious, careful, and correct. . . .

Perry v. Sindermann

408 U.S. 593 (1972)

[A companion case to Roth, Perry v. Sindermann involved a teacher who had been employed in the Texas state college system for ten years, most recently at Odessa Junior College, under a series of one-year contracts. The College had no tenure system. After embroilment in public controversy with the college's Board of Regents, the Board voted not to offer him a contract for the following year. No hearing or statement of reasons was provided. Sindermann brought suit in Federal District Court under 42 U.S.C. §1983, asserting that the Board's action was in retaliation for his exercise of First Amendment rights to free speech. The district court granted summary judgment for the Board; the Court of Appeals reversed and remanded for a trial on the merits. The Supreme Court affirmed in an opinion by Mr. Justice STEWART.

First, the Court held that if the Board's failure to renew Sindermann's contract was in retaliation for Sindermann's exercise of First Amendment rights, that action would be an unlawful infringement of constitutionally protected "liberty" regardless of the fact that Sindermann lacked tenure or a contractual right to renewal. The opinion asserted that "even though a person has no 'right' to a valuable government benefit and even though the government may deny him the benefit for any number of reasons, there are some reasons upon which the government may not rely. It may not deny a benefit to a person on a basis that infringes his constitutionally protected interests — especially, his interest in freedom of speech." Accordingly, Sindermann was entitled to an opportunity to prove his allegations that the failure to renew was based on his exercise of free speech.

Second, the Court considered Sindermann's claim that, despite the absence of a formal tenure system at the College, there was an informal system of tenure that gave him a "property" interest in continued employment protected by due process, quite apart from his free speech claim.]

... He claimed that he and others legitimately relied upon an unusual provision that had been in the college's official Faculty Guide for many years:

> "*Teacher Tenure*: Odessa College has no tenure system. The Administration of the College wishes the faculty member to feel that he has permanent tenure as long as his teaching services are satisfactory and as long as he displays a cooperative attitude toward his co-workers and his superiors, and as long as he is happy in his work."

Moreover, the respondent claimed legitimate reliance upon guidelines promulgated by the Coordinating Board of the Texas College and University System that provided that a person, like himself, who had been employed as a teacher in the state college and university system for seven years or more has some form of job tenure. Thus the respondent offered to prove that a teacher with his long period of service at this particular State College had no less a "property" interest in continued employment than a formally tenured teacher at other colleges, and had no less a procedural due process right to a statement of reasons and a hearing before college officials upon their decision not to retain him.

We have made clear in Roth ... that "property" interests subject to procedural due process protection are not limited by a few rigid, technical forms. Rather, "property" denotes a broad range of interests that are secured by "existing rules or understandings." ... A person's interest in a benefit is a "property" interest for due process purposes if there are such rules or mutually explicit understandings that support his claim of entitlement to the benefit and that he may invoke at a hearing.

A written contract with an explicit tenure provision clearly is evidence of a formal understanding that supports a teacher's claim of entitlement to continued employment unless sufficient "cause" is shown. Yet absence of such an explicit contractual provision may not always foreclose the possibility that a teacher has a "property" interest in re-employment. For example, the law of contracts in most, if not all, jurisdictions long has employed a process by which agreements, though not formalized in writing, may be "implied." ...

A teacher, like the respondent, who has held his position for a number of years, might be able to show from the circumstances of this service — and from other relevant facts — that he has a legitimate claim of entitlement to job tenure. Just as this Court has found there to be a "common law of a particular industry or of a particular plant" that may supplement a collective-bargaining agreement, United Steelworkers v. Warrior & Gulf Co., 363 U.S. 574, 579, so there may be an unwritten "common law" in a particular university that certain employees shall have the equivalent of tenure. . . .[31]

---

31. We do not now hold that the respondent has any such legitimate claim of entitlement to job tenure. For "[p]roperty interests ... are not created by the Constitution. Rather, they are created and their dimensions are defined by existing rules or understandings that stem from an independent source such as state law. ..." Board of Regents v. Roth, supra. ... If it is the law of Texas that a teacher in the respondent's position has no contractual or other claim to job tenure, the respondent's claim would be defeated.

In this case, the respondent has alleged the existence of rules and understandings, promulgated and fostered by state officials, that may justify his legitimate claim of entitlement to continued employment absent "sufficient cause." We disagree with the Court of Appeals insofar as it held that a mere subjective "expectancy" is protected by procedural due process, but we agree that the respondent must be given an opportunity to prove the legitimacy of his claim of such entitlement in light of "the policies and practices of the institution." 430 F.2d, at 943. Proof of such a property interest would not, of course, entitle him to reinstatement. But such proof would obligate college officials to grant a hearing at his request, where he could be informed of the grounds for his nonretention and challenge their sufficiency.

Therefore, while we do not wholly agree with the opinion of the Court of Appeals, its judgment remanding this case to the District Court is

Affirmed.

[Chief Justice Burger entered an opinion concurring in *Roth* and *Sindermann*, emphasizing that whatever "property" rights might entitle a state teacher to a hearing were created entirely by state law. Justice Brennan, joined by Justice Douglas, entered a brief opinion dissenting in part from the Court's opinions in *Roth* and *Sindermann*, indicating substantial agreement with the views expressed in *Roth* by Justice Marshall, who also dissented in part from the Court's *Sindermann* decision.]

Notes and Questions: *Roth* and *Sindermann*

1. Note that the Court breaks the due process determination into two steps: first, a threshold determination whether the interest in question is of a *type* that qualifies for due process protection as "liberty" or "property"; and, second, a determination of what process is due by weighing the interest in question against the countervailing interest of the government. Note also that Justice Stewart's opinion for the Court breaks down the threshold question of eligibility into two categories, "liberty" and "property." What justifications does the Court offer for this conceptual apparatus? Is it a sound one? Is it consistent with Justice Stewart's approach in *Cafeteria Workers*?

2. How is "liberty" defined by the Court? By Justice Marshall? Given the adverse effect on Roth's career and reputation of nonrenewal, why didn't the state's action constitute an infringement of "liberty"? If a sufficiently severe impact on career and reputation would infringe a liberty interest, how would the reviewing court determine whether or not such an infringement has taken place? Does it make any sense to have an elaborate trial on the extent to which nonrenewal would adversely affect the teacher's career? [32]

When a person enjoys a protected "liberty" interest in reputation or future employment opportunities, does it entail a substantive limitation on the power of

32. For discussion, see Note, The Due Process Rights of Public Employees, 50 N.Y.U. L. Rev. 310 (1975).

the government to infringe that liberty, or is the protection afforded only procedural? If it were established that Roth was an excellent teacher and scholar, and the decision not to renew his contract was unjustified, would the federal courts order the Board of Regents to renew his contract? If not, what relief would they give?

3. How is "property" defined by the Court? By Justice Marshall? How far does *Sindermann* go in recognizing expectations as giving rise to "property" entitled to due process protection? Suppose the Texas courts had ruled that practices and understandings identical to those relied upon by *Sindermann* imposed no constraints on the Board's discretion on whether or not to review a teaching contract. Would a federal court still be free to find that the practices and understandings created "property" for purposes of federal due process and that Sindermann should accordingly be given notice and opportunity for hearing?

4. Does it follow from *Roth* that a person has a "property" entitlement whenever she may bring a legal action to constrain official action? Did the plaintiffs in *Overton Park*, supra, p. 276, have a "property" entitlement because they had an enforceable right to control the Secretary of Transportation's decisions on highway location? Does it follow that the Secretary was constitutionally required to hold a trial-type hearing before making a route decision?

5. *Roth* seems to hold that a state may commit decisions on renewal of teaching contracts to the unfettered discretion of administrators, and that due process affords no protection to teachers in this situation. Does *Roth* overrule Hornsby v. Allen and Holmes v. New York Housing Authority, pp. 317-319, supra, or are these decisions distinguishable?

6. *Roth* and *Sindermann* indicate that a government employee who has no "property" right to renewal of his contract may nonetheless challenge a refusal to renew if the refusal is based upon constitutionally impermissible reasons, such as retaliation for the employee's exercise of free speech rights. Is this conclusion consistent with the basic logic of *Roth*? Does the employee have a "liberty" interest in voiding any impermissibly motivated government action adverse to his welfare? Why? Compare the *Cafeteria Workers* decision, supra. If so, why doesn't this "liberty" interest generate a pre-termination procedural entitlement? [33]

33. *Roth* and *Sindermann* follow the *Cafeteria Workers* majority in concluding that a claim that administrative action was impermissibly motivated or otherwise infringed substantive constitutional rights does not entitle the employee to an administrative hearing to test the claim; instead, he must press it in a subsequent federal court action.

What arguments are there for and against requiring the government to provide an administrative hearing on the employee's claim? Would the argument in favor of a prior hearing be any more persuasive if the employee made a strong prima facie showing of impermissible reasons, as opposed to a mere naked claim? See Justice Douglas' *Roth* dissent. See also, Van Alstyne, Cracks in "The New Property": Adjudicative Due Process in the Administrative State, 62 Cornell L. Rev. 445, 474-75 (1977).

What if government officials not only deny that their action was constitutionally impermissible in motive or effect, but also offer affirmative, alternative justifications, such as the employee's incompetence, for their action? Will the federal court try the issue of competence? Does the answer to this depend on whether or not the officials have afforded the employee a hearing on the issue of competence? If such a hearing is held, should the federal court determine the issue of competence de novo? Should it apply the substantial evidence standard of

Note: §1983 Litigation

The plaintiffs in *Roth* and *Sindermann* brought suit against the relevant state officials under the Civil Rights Act of 1871, now codified as 42 U.S.C. §1983. The Act provides for damage awards and equitable redress against persons who, "under color of" state law, deprive any person of "any rights, privileges, or immunities secured by the Constitution and laws" of the United States.[34] These "rights, privileges, and immunities," of course, include the hearing rights protected by the Fourteenth Amendment's due process clause. Jurisdiction for §1983 actions in the federal courts is provided, without regard to amount in controversy, by 28 U.S.C. §1343(3).[35]

Widespread invocation by litigants of §1983[36] has led to concern, particularly within the Supreme Court, that broad construction of §1983 itself and of the rights it protects would lead to significant intrusions by the federal judiciary on the autonomy of the states.[37] The exposure of state officials to damage awards for mistaken judgments about procedural rights makes decisional uncertainty in the applicability and content of due process safeguards particularly troubling.[38]

Arnett v. Kennedy

416 U.S. 134 (1974)

Mr. Justice REHNQUIST announced the judgment of the Court in an opinion in which The CHIEF JUSTICE and Mr. Justice STEWART join.

[Wayne Kennedy, a federal Civil Service employee in the Office of Economic Opportunity (OEO), was discharged by his superior, Wendell Verduin, on charges that Kennedy had falsely and recklessly accused Verduin with attempted bribery in connection with Verduin's official duties.

---

review? Some other standard? See Esteban v. Central Missouri State College, 415 F.2d 1077 (8th Cir. 1969), *cert. denied*, 398 U.S. 965 (1970). Compare the materials on "constitutional" and "jurisdictional" fact, supra pp. 44-57, 200-227.

34. Until recently, the principal exceptions were suits against municipalities, which were not considered to be "persons" within the meaning of §1983. Such suits had to be brought under 28 U.S.C. §1331, with the substantive cause of action being supplied by the Fourteenth Amendment itself. See Gentile v. Wallen, 562 F.2d 193, 195-96 (2d Cir. 1977). However, note that the Supreme Court recently partially overruled its previous ruling in Monroe v. Pape, 365 U.S. 167, 187-192 (1961), and held that municipalities *can* be sued as "persons" under §1983, Monnell v. Department of Social Services of N.Y., 436 U.S. 658 (1978).

35. Actions against *federal* officials for denial of hearing rights are generally grounded on 28 U.S.C. §1331 or on the mandamus provisions of 28 U.S.C. §1361. These and related jurisdictional issues are discussed at greater length in Chapter 9.

36. See generally Developments in the Law — Section 1983 and Federalism, 90 Harv. L. Rev. 1133 (1977).

37. See ibid. and Note, Reputation, Stigma and Section 1983: The Lessons of Paul v. Davis, 30 Stan. L. Rev. 191 (1977).

38. In some contexts, however, liability may be tempered by doctrines of official immunity, discussed in Chapter 9.

In accordance with the provisions of the Lloyd-La Follette Act, 5 U.S.C. §7501, and Civil Service Commission and OEO regulations, Kennedy was informed by Verduin of the charges and afforded an opportunity to respond to the charges orally and in writing, and to submit affidavits. Kennedy did not respond to the substance of the charges against him, but instead asserted that the charges were unlawful because he had a right to a pre-termination trial-type hearing before an impartial hearing officer before he could be removed from his employment, and because statements made by him were protected by the First Amendment. Verduin then notified Kennedy in writing of his removal from office, and of his right to appeal Verduin's decision either to the OEO or to the Civil Service Commission, and to obtain a trial-type hearing in the appeal procedures. A three-judge court granted summary judgment for Kennedy, holding that the procedures afforded were constitutionally inadequate, and that the Act and implementing regulations were unconstitutionally vague.]

The statutory provisions which the District Court held invalid are found in 5 U.S.C. §7501. Subsection (a) of that section provides that "[a]n individual in the competitive service may be removed or suspended without pay only for such cause as will promote the efficiency of the service."

Subsection (b) establishes the administrative procedures by which an employee's rights under subsection (a) are to be determined, providing:

> (b) An individual in the competitive service whose removal or suspension without pay is sought is entitled to reasons in writing and to —
> (1) notice of the action sought and of any charges preferred against him;
> (2) a copy of the charges;
> (3) a reasonable time for filing a written answer to the charges, with affidavits; and
> (4) a written decision on the answer at the earliest practicable date.
> Examination of witnesses, trial, or hearing is not required but may be provided in the discretion of the individual directing the removal or suspension without pay. Copies of the charges, the notice of hearing, the answer, the reasons for and the order of removal or suspension without pay, and also the reasons for reduction in grade or pay, shall be made a part of the records of the employing agency, and, on request, shall be furnished to the individual affected and to the Civil Service Commission. . . .

We must . . . decide whether these procedures established for the purpose of determining whether there is "cause" under the Lloyd-La Follette Act for the dismissal of a federal employee comport with procedural due process. . . .

For almost the first century of our national existence, federal employment was regarded as an item of patronage, which could be granted, withheld, or withdrawn for whatever reasons might appeal to the responsible executive hiring officer. Following the Civil War, grass-roots sentiment for "Civil Service reform" began to grow, and it was apparently brought to a head by the assassination of President James A. Garfield on July 2, 1881. . . .

[The Court details the development of federal civil service legislation, culminating in the enactment in 1913 of the Lloyd-La Follette Act, whose provisions are codified in 5 U.S.C. §7501, quoted previously.]

In Board of Regents v. Roth, we said:

> Property interests, of course, are not created by the Constitution. Rather, they are created and their dimensions are defined by existing rules or understandings that stem from an independent source such as state law — rules or understandings that secure certain benefits and that support claims of entitlement to those benefits. 408 U.S., at 577.

Here appellee did have a statutory expectancy that he not be removed other than for "such cause as will promote the efficiency of [the] service." But the very section of the statute which granted him that right, a right which had previously existed only by virtue of administrative regulation, expressly provided also for the procedure by which "cause" was to be determined, and expressly omitted the procedural guarantees which appellee insists are mandated by the Constitution. Only by bifurcating the very sentence of the Act of Congress which conferred upon appellee the right not to be removed save for cause could it be said that he had an expectancy of that substantive right without the procedural limitations which Congress attached to it. In the area of federal regulation of government employees, where in the absence of statutory limitation the governmental employer has had virtually uncontrolled latitude in decisions as to hiring and firing, Cafeteria Workers v. McElroy, 367 U.S. 886, 896-897 (1961), we do not believe that a statutory enactment such as the Lloyd-La Follette Act may be parsed as discretely as appellee urges. Congress was obviously intent on according a measure of statutory job security to governmental employees which they had not previously enjoyed, but was likewise intent on excluding more elaborate procedural requirements which it felt would make the operation of the new scheme unnecessarily burdensome in practice. Where the focus of legislation was thus strongly on the procedural mechanism for enforcing the substantive right which was simultaneously conferred, we decline to conclude that the substantive right may be viewed wholly apart from the procedure provided for its enforcement. The employee's statutorily defined right is not a guarantee against removal without cause in the abstract, but such a guarantee as enforced by the procedures which Congress has designated for the determination of cause.

The Court has previously viewed skeptically the action of a litigant in challenging the constitutionality of portions of a statute under which it has simultaneously claimed benefits. . . .

This doctrine has unquestionably been applied unevenly in the past, and observed as often as not in the breach. We believe that at the very least it gives added weight to our conclusion that where the grant of a substantive right is inextricably intertwined with the limitations on the procedures which are to be employed in determining that right, a litigant in the position of appellee must take the bitter with the sweet.

To conclude otherwise would require us to hold that although Congress chose to enact what was essentially a legislative compromise, and with unmistakable clarity granted governmental employees security against being dismissed without "cause," but refused to accord them a full adversary hearing for the determination of "cause," it was constitutionally disabled from making such a choice. . . .

Appellee also contends in this Court that because of the nature of the charges on which his dismissal was based, he was in effect accused of dishonesty, and that therefore a hearing was required before he could be deprived of this element of his "liberty" protected by the Fifth Amendment against deprivation without due process. . . . But that liberty is not offended by dismissal from employment itself, but instead by dismissal based upon an unsupported charge which could wrongfully injure the reputation of an employee. Since the purpose of the hearing in such a case is to provide the person "an opportunity to clear his name," a hearing afforded by administrative appeal procedures after the actual dismissal is a sufficient compliance with the requirements of the Due Process Clause. . . .

[The Court ruled that the post-termination hearing afforded Kennedy adequately protected his "liberty" interest in reputation by providing him an opportunity to rebut the charges upon which he was discharged.

The opinion also rejected Kennedy's contention that the statutory provisions authorizing discharge "for such cause as will promote the efficiency of the service" were unconstitutionally vague or overbroad, emphasizing the administrative regulations further defining the grounds for discharge and the stated willingness of officials to provide individual guidance with respect to their application.]

. . . Accordingly, we reverse the decision of the District Court on both grounds on which it granted summary judgment and remand for further proceedings not inconsistent with this opinion.

Reversed and remanded.

Mr. Justice POWELL, with whom Mr. Justice BLACKMUN joins, concurring in part and concurring in the result in part.

For the reasons stated by Mr. Justice Rehnquist, I agree that the provisions of 5 U.S.C. §7501(a) are neither unconstitutionally vague nor overbroad. I also agree that appellee's discharge did not contravene the Fifth Amendment guarantee of procedural due process. Because I reach that conclusion on the basis of different reasoning, I state my views separately.

I

. . . The Court's decisions in Board of Regents v. Roth, 408 U.S. 564 (1972), and Perry v. Sindermann, 408 U.S. 593 (1972), provide the proper framework for analysis of whether appellee's employment constituted a "property" interest under the Fifth Amendment. . . .

Application of these precedents to the instant case makes plain that appellee is entitled to invoke the constitutional guarantee of procedural due process. Appellee was a nonprobationary federal employee, and as such he could be discharged only for "cause." 5 U.S.C. §7501(a). The federal statute guaranteeing appellee continued employment absent "cause" for discharge conferred on him a legitimate claim of entitlement which constituted a "property" interest under the Fifth Amendment. Thus termination of his employment requires notice and a hearing.

The plurality opinion evidently reasons that the nature of appellee's interest in continued federal employment is necessarily defined and limited by the statutory procedures for discharge and that the constitutional guarantee of procedural due process accords to appellee no procedural protections against arbitrary or erroneous discharge other than those expressly provided in the statute. The plurality would thus conclude that the statute governing federal employment determines not only the nature of appellee's property interest, but also the extent of the procedural protections to which he may lay claim. It seems to me that this approach is incompatible with the principles laid down in *Roth* and *Sindermann*. Indeed, it would lead directly to the conclusion that whatever the nature of an individual's statutorily created property interest, deprivation of that interest could be accomplished without notice or a hearing at any time. This view misconceives the origin of the right to procedural due process. That right is conferred, not by legislative grace, but by constitutional guarantee. While the legislature may elect not to confer a property interest in federal employment, it may not constitutionally authorize the deprivation of such an interest, once conferred, without appropriate procedural safeguards. As our cases have consistently recognized, the adequacy of statutory procedures for deprivation of a statutorily created property interest must be analyzed in constitutional terms.

Having determined that the constitutional guarantee of procedural due process applies to appellee's discharge from public employment, the question arises whether an evidentiary hearing, including the right to present favorable witnesses and to confront and examine adverse witnesses, must be accorded *before* removal. The resolution of this issue depends on a balancing process in which the Government's interest in expeditious removal of an unsatisfactory employee is weighed against the interest of the affected employee in continued public employment. Goldberg v. Kelly, supra, at 263-266. . . .

In the present case, the Government's interest, and hence the public's interest, is the maintenance of employee efficiency and discipline. Such factors are essential if the Government is to perform its responsibilities effectively and economically. To this end, the Government, as an employer, must have wide discretion and control over the management of its personnel and internal affairs. This includes the prerogative to remove employees whose conduct hinders efficient operation and to do so with dispatch. Prolonged retention of a disruptive or otherwise unsatisfactory employee can adversely affect discipline and morale in the work place, foster disharmony, and ultimately impair the efficiency of an office or agency. Moreover, a requirement of a prior evidentiary hearing would impose additional administrative costs, create delay, and deter warranted discharges. Thus, the Government's interest in being able to act expeditiously to remove an unsatisfactory employee is substantial.

Appellee's countervailing interest is the continuation of his public employment pending an evidentiary hearing. Since appellee would be reinstated and awarded backpay if he prevails on the merits of his claim, appellee's actual injury would consist of a temporary interruption of his income during the interim. To be sure, even a temporary interruption of income could constitute a serious loss in many instances. But the possible deprivation is considerably less severe than that involved in *Goldberg*, for example, where termination of welfare benefits to the recipient would have occurred in the face of "brutal need." 397 U.S., at 261. Indeed, as the Court stated in that case, "the crucial factor in this context — *a factor not present in the cause of . . . the discharged government employee . . .* — is that termination of aid pending resolution of a controversy over eligibility may deprive an *eligible* recipient of *the very means by which to live while he waits.*" Id., at 264 (emphasis added). By contrast, a public employee may well have independent resources to overcome any temporary hardship, and he may be able to secure a job in the private sector. Alternatively, he will be eligible for welfare benefits. . . .

On balance, I would conclude that a prior evidentiary hearing is not required and that the present statute and regulations comport with due process by providing a reasonable accommodation of the competing interests.

[Mr. Justice WHITE filed an opinion concurring in part and dissenting in part. He joined Justice Rehnquist's opinion on the overbreadth issue. On the question of procedural due process, he concluded that a federal employee is entitled to a hearing on discharge for alleged misconduct, as opposed to "reasons of pure inefficiency," in which case "it would be at least arguable that a hearing would serve no useful purpose and that judgments [on efficiency] are best left to the discretion of administrative officials." Justice White further concluded that due process did not require a full trial-type hearing prior to discharge, and that the more informal pretermination procedures provided by Congress were generally adequate, at least where there was also opportunity for a full posttermination hearing. However, Justice White concluded that due process required an impartial pre-termination decisionmaker and that this requirement had been violated in Kennedy's case when he was discharged by the superior (Verduin) whom he had accused of crime, and who was therefore personally interested in the outcome.]

[A dissenting opinion by Justice DOUGLAS is omitted.]

Mr. Justice MARSHALL, with whom Mr. Justice DOUGLAS and Mr. Justice BRENNAN concur, dissenting.

I would affirm the judgment of the District Court, both in its holding that a tenured Government employee must be afforded an evidentiary hearing prior to a dismissal for cause and in its decision that 5 U.S.C. §7501 is unconstitutionally vague and overbroad as a regulation of employees' speech. . . .

We have already determined that a legitimate claim of entitlement to continued employment absent "sufficient cause" is a property interest requiring the protections of procedural due process. Thus, there can be little doubt that appellee's tenured Government employment, from which he could not legally be dismissed except for cause, must also be a "property" interest for the purposes of the Fifth Amendment. . . .

. . . Mr. Justice Rehnquist explains, however, that this claim is founded only in statute, and that the statute which guarantees tenure also provides that a hearing is not required before discharge. He concludes that "the property interest which appellee had in his employment was itself conditioned by the procedural limitations which had accompanied the grant of that interest," ... wryly observing that "a litigant in the position of appellee must take the bitter with the sweet," ante, at 154.

Courts once considered procedural due process protections inapplicable to welfare on much the same theory — that "in accepting charity, the appellant has consented to the provisions of the law under which charity is bestowed." Obviously, this Court rejected that reasoning in *Goldberg,* supra, where we held that conditions under which public assistance was afforded, which did not include a pretermination hearing, were violative of due process. . . .

Applying that analysis here requires us to find that although appellee's property interest arose from statute, the deprivation of his claim of entitlement to continued employment would have to meet minimum standards of procedural due process regardless of the discharge procedures provided by the statute. Accordingly, a majority of the Court rejects Mr. Justice Rehnquist's argument that because appellee's entitlement arose from statute, it could be conditioned on a statutory limitation of procedural due process protections, an approach which would render such protection inapplicable to the deprivation of any statutory benefit — any "privilege" extended by Government — where a statute prescribed a termination procedure, no matter how arbitrary or unfair. It would amount to nothing less than a return, albeit in somewhat different verbal garb, to the thoroughly discredited distinction between rights and privileges which once seemed to govern the applicability of procedural due process.

We have repeatedly observed that due process requires that a hearing be held "at a meaningful time and in a meaningful manner," ... but it remains for us to give content to that general principle in this case by balancing the Government's asserted interests against those of the discharged employee. Goldberg v. Kelly, 397 U.S., at 263; see Cafeteria Workers v. McElroy, 367 U.S. 886, 895 (1961). . . .

An exhaustive study by the United States Administrative Conference of the problem of agency dismissals led the author of the Conference's report to observe:

> "One cannot escape the conclusion, however, that the government employee who is removed from his job loses something of tremendous value that in a market of declining demand for skills may not be replaceable." [39]

And the report also observes:

> "[O]ne must acknowledge what seems to be an accepted, if regrettable, fact of life: Removal from government employment for cause carries a stigma that is probably impossible to outlive. Agency personnel officers are generally prepared to concede ... that it is difficult for the fired government worker to find employment in the private sector." . . .

---

39. Merrill, Report in Support of Recommendation 72-8, Procedures for Adverse Actions Against Federal Employees, in 2 Recommendations and Reports of the Administrative Conference of the United States 1007, 1015 (1972). . . .

Given the importance of the interest at stake, the discharged employee should be afforded an opportunity to test the strength of the evidence of his misconduct by confronting and cross-examining adverse witnesses and by presenting witnesses in his own behalf, whenever there are substantial disputes in testimonial evidence. . . .

It also seems clear that for the hearing to be meaningful, the hearing officer must be independent and unbiased and his decision be entitled to some weight.

[Justice Marshall then addressed the contention that affording the discharged employee a post-termination hearing satisfied due process. He noted that appeal procedures take several months, and in 25% of the cases result in a reversal of dismissal. He also noted that Kennedy had "been driven to the brink of financial ruin" after his dismissal.]

To argue that a dismissal from tenured Government employment is not a serious enough deprivation to require a prior hearing because the discharged employee may draw on the welfare system in the interim, is to exhibit a gross insensitivity to the plight of these employees. First, it assumes that the discharged employee will be eligible for welfare. Often welfare applicants must be all but stripped of their worldly goods before being admitted to the welfare roles, hence it is likely that the employee will suffer considerable hardship before becoming eligible. He may be required not only to exhaust his savings but also to convert many of his assets into cash for support before being able to fall back on public assistance. He may have to give up his home or cherished personal possessions in order to become eligible. . . .

The Government's asserted interests in not affording a predismissal hearing are twofold. First, appellants argue that the delay in holding the hearing makes the functioning of the agency more efficient. We rejected a similar rationale in *Goldberg*, 397 U.S., at 266. . . .

Moreover, the Government's interest in efficiency in this case is entirely unconvincing. The applicable statute does not prohibit prior hearings but rather makes them discretionary with the agency. Nine federal agencies, including the FCC, NLRB, HUD, HEW, the Department of Justice, and the Civil Service Commission itself, regularly accord evidentiary hearings prior to the dismissal of a tenured employee. The Administrative Conference of the United States, on the basis of its exhaustive study of federal agency proceedings for the dismissal of employees in the competitive service, strongly recommended that evidentiary hearings be held prior to discharge.

The Government also argues that if a supervisor were unable to effect an immediate removal of a troublesome employee from his agency, the discipline and efficiency of the whole office might be disrupted. Under the prevailing practice, an agency may not dismiss an employee until 30 days after he has received notice of the charges against him and has had an opportunity to reply. Thus, fellow workers and supervisors must now function with the threatened employee in their midst for at least a month, and there seems little reason why a hearing could not be held during that 30-day period. If the employee actually threatens to disrupt the operation of the office, he could be put on administrative leave or temporarily assigned to a less sensitive position pending his hearing, as currently provided for by regulation. 5 C.F.R. §752.202(d)....

Questions

Why do a majority of the Justices reject Justice Rehnquist's argument that if the legislature is free to grant or withhold a "property" entitlement as it pleases, it may condition those statutory entitlements it chooses to grant by specifying the procedural mechanisms by which the entitlement is granted. Is not his logic perfectly sound, and fully consistent with *Roth?* What reasons do Justice Powell and the dissenters give for rejecting his logic? [40]

Goss v. Lopez

419 U.S. 565 (1975)

Mr. Justice WHITE delivered the opinion of the Court.

This appeal by various administrators of the Columbus, Ohio, Public School System (CPSS) challenges the judgment of a three-judge federal court, declaring that appellees — various high school students in the CPSS — were denied due process of law contrary to the command of the Fourteenth Amendment in that they were temporarily suspended from their high schools without a hearing either prior to suspension or within a reasonable time thereafter, and enjoining the administrators to remove all references to such suspensions from the students' records.

Ohio law, Rev. Code Ann. §3313.64 (1972), provides for free education to all children between the ages of six and 21. Section 3313.66 of the Code empowers the principal of an Ohio public school to suspend a pupil for misconduct for up to 10 days or to expel him. In either case, he must notify the student's parents within 24 hours and state the reasons for his action. A pupil who is expelled, or his parents, may appeal the decision to the Board of Education and in connection therewith shall be permitted to be heard at the board meeting. The Board may reinstate the pupil following the hearing. No similar procedure is provided in §3313.66 or any other provision of state law for a suspended student.

---

40. Consider the argument advanced by Professor Tribe, Structural Due Process, 10 Harv. C.R.-C.L. L. Rev. 269, 280 (1975):

> It seems evident that a theory of "differential reliance" underlies the Court's distinction between the substantive content of an entitlement and the procedures provided for its protection in cases like *Arnett* ... : an employee ... seeking to avoid certain adverse consequences may justifiably rely, in shaping his primary conduct, on the statutes and contract provisions spelling out the events which trigger those consequences. But no parallel accommodation of behavior can realistically be expected to flow from the definition, in the same source of law, of truncated procedures for determining whether the triggering event has occurred.

Is Professor Tribe's "differential reliance" theory plausible? Should public employees be required to prove that they relied upon the substantive provision of a statute while disregarding the significance of its procedural provisions?

[The appellees were Senior High and Junior High School students suspended in connection with demonstrations and disorder in the CPSS. In some instances suspension was ordered immediately by school officials present at the disorders. No student was given a hearing.]

Here, on the basis of state law, appellees plainly had legitimate claims of entitlement to a public education. Ohio Rev. Code Ann. §§ 3313.48 and 3313.64 (1972 and Supp. 1973) direct local authorities to provide a free education to all residents between five and 21 years of age, and a compulsory-attendance law requires attendance for a school year of not less than 32 weeks. Ohio Rev. Code Ann. §3321.04 (1972). It is true that §3313.66 of the Code permits school principals to suspend students for up to 10 days; but suspensions may not be imposed without any grounds whatsoever. All of the schools had their own rules specifying the grounds for expulsion or suspension. Having chosen to extend the right to an education to people of appellees' class generally, Ohio may not withdraw that right on grounds of misconduct, absent fundamentally fair procedures to determine whether the misconduct has occurred. Arnett v. Kennedy, supra, at 164 (Powell, J., concurring), 171 (White, J., concurring and dissenting), 206 (Marshall, J., dissenting)....

The Due Process Clause also forbids arbitrary deprivations of liberty. "Where a person's good name, reputation, honor, or integrity is at stake because of what the government is doing to him," the minimal requirements of the Clause must be satisfied. Wisconsin v. Constantineau, 400 U.S. 433, 437 (1971); Board of Regents v. Roth supra, at 573. School authorities here suspended appellees from school for periods of up to 10 days based on charges of misconduct. If sustained and recorded, those charges could seriously damage the students' standing with their fellow pupils and their teachers as well as interfere with later opportunities for higher education and employment....

"Once it is determined that due process applies, the question remains what process is due." Morrissey v. Brewer, 408 U.S., at 481. We turn to that question....

Disciplinarians, although proceeding in utmost good faith, frequently act on the reports and advice of others; and the controlling facts and the nature of the conduct under challenge are often disputed. The risk of error is not at all trivial, and it should be guarded against if that may be done without prohibitive cost or interference with the educational process.

The difficulty is that our schools are vast and complex. Some modicum of discipline and order is essential if the educational function is to be performed.... The prospect of imposing elaborate hearing requirements in every suspension case is viewed with great concern....

We do not believe that school authorities must be totally free from notice and hearing requirements if their schools are to operate with acceptable efficiency. Students facing temporary suspension have interests qualifying for protection of the Due Process Clause, and due process requires, in connection with a suspension of 10 days or less, that the student be given oral or written notice of the charges against him and, if he denies them, an explanation of the evidence the authorities have and an opportunity to present his side of the story. The Clause requires at least these rudimentary precautions against unfair or mistaken findings of misconduct and arbitrary exclusion from school.[41]

... To impose in each [case of disciplinary suspension] even truncated trial-type procedures might well overwhelm administrative facilities in many places and, by diverting resources, cost more than it would save in educational effectiveness. Moreover, further formalizing the suspension process and escalating its formality and adversary nature may not only make it too costly as a regular disciplinary tool but also destroy its effectiveness as part of the teaching process.

On the other hand, requiring effective notice and informal hearing permitting the student to give his version of the events will provide a meaningful hedge against erroneous action. . . .

We should also make it clear that we have addressed ourselves solely to the short suspension, not exceeding 10 days. Longer suspensions or expulsions for the remainder of the school term, or permanently, may require more formal procedures. Nor do we put aside the possibility that in unusual situations, although involving only a short suspension, something more than the rudimentary procedures will be required.

[The judgment of the District Court was affirmed.]

Mr. Justice Powell, with whom The Chief Justice, Mr. Justice Blackmun, and Mr. Justice Rehnquist join, dissenting.

The Court today invalidates an Ohio statute that permits student suspensions from school without a hearing "for not more than ten days." The decision unnecessarily opens avenues for judicial intervention in the operation of our pubilc schools that may affect adversely the quality of education. The Court holds for the first time that the federal courts, rather than educational officials and state legislatures, have the authority to determine the rules applicable to routine classroom discipline of children and teenagers in the public schools. It justifies this unprecedented intrusion into the process of elementary and secondary education by identifying a new constitutional right: the right of a student not to be suspended for as much as a single day without notice and a due process hearing either before or promptly following the suspension.[42] . . .

---

41. Appellants point to the fact that some process is provided under Ohio law by way of judicial review. Ohio Rev. Code Ann. §2506.01 (Supp. 1973). Appellants do not cite any case in which this general administrative review statute has been used to appeal from a disciplinary decision by a school official. If it be assumed that it could be so used, it is for two reasons insufficient to save inadequate procedures at the school level. First, although new proof may be offered in a §2501.06 proceeding, Shaker Coventry Corp. v. Shaker Heights Planning Comm'n, 18 Ohio Op. 2d 272, 176 N.E.2d 332 (1961), the proceeding is not *de novo*. In re Locke, 33 Ohio App. 2d 177, 294 N.E.2d 230 (1972). Thus the decision by the school — even if made upon inadequate procedures — is entitled to weight in the court proceeding. Second, without a demonstration to the contrary, we must assume that delay will attend any §2501.06 proceeding, that the suspension will not be stayed pending hearing, and that the student meanwhile will irreparably lose his educational benefits.

42. The Court speaks of "exclusion from the educational process for more than a trivial period . . . ," ante, at 576, but its opinion makes clear that even one day's suspension invokes the constitutional procedure mandated today.

In identifying property interests subject to due process protections, the Court's past opinions make clear that these interests "are created and their *dimensions are defined* by existing rules or understandings that stem from an independent source such as state law." Board of Regents v. Roth, supra, at 577 (emphasis supplied). The Ohio statute that creates the right to a "free" education also explicitly authorizes a principal to suspend a student for as much as 10 days. Ohio Rev. Code Ann. §§ 3313.48, 3313.64, 3313.66 (1972 and Supp. 1973). Thus the very legislation which "defines" the "dimension" of the student's entitlement, while providing a right to education generally, does not establish this right free of discipline imposed in accord with Ohio law. Rather, the right is encompassed in the entire package of statutory provisions governing education in Ohio — of which the power to suspend is one.

The Court thus disregards the basic structure of Ohio law in posturing this case as if Ohio had conferred an unqualified right to education, thereby compelling the school authorities to conform to due process procedures in imposing the most routine discipline.[43]

But however one may define the entitlement to education provided by Ohio law, I would conclude that a deprivation of not more than 10 days' suspension from school, imposed as a routine disciplinary measure, does not assume constitutional dimensions....

The Court also relies on a perceived deprivation of "liberty" resulting from any suspension, arguing — again without factual support in the record pertaining to these appellees — that a suspension harms a student's reputation. In view of the Court's decision in Board of Regents v. Roth, supra, I would have thought that this argument was plainly untenable. Underscoring the need for "serious damage" to reputation, the *Roth* Court held that a nontenured teacher who is not rehired by a public university could not claim to suffer sufficient reputational injury to require constitutional protections. Surely a brief suspension is of less serious consequence to the reputation of a teenage student....

43. The Court apparently reads into Ohio law by implication a qualification that suspensions may be imposed only for "cause," thereby analogizing this case to the civil service laws considered in Arnett v. Kennedy, 416 U.S. 134 (1974). To be sure, one may assume that pupils are not suspended at the whim or caprice of the school official, and the statute does provide for notice of the suspension with the "reasons therefor." But the same statute draws a sharp distinction between suspension and the far more drastic sanction of expulsion. A hearing is required only for the latter. To follow the Court's analysis, one must conclude that the legislature nevertheless intended — without saying so — that suspension also is of such consequence that it may be imposed only for causes which can be justified at a hearing. The unsoundness of reading this sort of requirement into the statute is apparent from a comparison with *Arnett*. In that case, Congress *expressly* provided that nonprobationary federal employees should be discharged only for "cause." This requirement reflected congressional recognition of the seriousness of discharging such employees. There simply is no analogy between *termination* of nonprobationary employment of a civil service employee and the *suspension* of a public school pupil for not more than 10 days. Even if the Court is correct in implying some concept of justifiable cause in the Ohio procedure, it could hardly be stretched to the constitutional proportions found present in *Arnett*.

The State's generalized interest in maintaining an orderly school system is not incompatible with the individual interest of the student. Education in any meaningful sense includes the inculcation of an understanding in each pupil of the necessity of rules and obedience thereto. . . . When an immature student merits censure for his conduct, he is rendered a disservice if appropriate sanctions are not applied or if procedures for their application are so formalized as to invite a challenge to the teacher's authority — an invitation which rebellious or even merely spirited teenagers are likely to accept. . . .

It is common knowledge that maintaining order and reasonable decorum in school buildings and classrooms is a major educational problem, and one which has increased significantly in magnitude in recent years. Often the teacher, in protecting the rights of other children to an education (if not his or their safety), is compelled to rely on the power to suspend.

In assessing in constitutional terms the need to protect pupils from unfair minor discipline by school authorities, the Court ignores the commonality of interest of the State and pupils in the public school system. Rather, it thinks in traditional judicial terms of an adversary situation. To be sure, there will be the occasional pupil innocent of any rule infringement who is mistakenly suspended or whose infraction is too minor to justify suspension. But, while there is no evidence indicating the frequency of unjust suspensions, common sense suggests that they will not be numerous in relation to the total number, and that mistakes or injustices will usually be righted by informal means. . . .

No one can foresee the ultimate frontiers of the new "thicket" the Court now enters. Today's ruling appears to sweep within the protected interest in education a multitude of discretionary decisions in the educational process. Teachers and other school authorities are required to make many decisions that may have serious consequences for the pupil. They must decide, for example, how to grade the student's work, whether a student passes or fails a course, whether he is to be promoted, whether he is required to take certain subjects, whether he may be excluded from interscholastic athletics or other extracurricular activities, whether he may be removed from one school and sent to another, whether he may be bused long distances when available schools are nearby, and whether he should be placed in a "general," "vocational," or "college-preparatory" track.

In these and many similar situations claims of impairment of one's educational entitlement identical in principle to those before the Court today can be asserted with equal or greater justification. Likewise, in many of these situations, the pupil can advance the same types of speculative and subjective injury given critical weight in this case. . . .

If, as seems apparent, the Court will now require due process procedures whenever such routine school decisions are challenged, the impact upon public education will be serious indeed. The discretion and judgment of federal courts across the land often will be substituted for that of the 50 state legislatures, the 14,000 school board, and the 2,000,000 teachers who heretofore have been responsible for the administration of the American public school system. . . .

Questions

1. Is Justice Powell correct in asserting that the Court's decision logically requires that due process protection be extended to school decisions on grades, promotion, and "tracking"? Does the Ohio statute involved in *Goss* create a "property" interest in accurate academic evaluation? Is there a "liberty" interest in accurate academic evaluation? [44]

2. Does *Goss* require due process protections when administrators impose sanctions falling short of exclusion from school, such as disqualification from interscholastic athletic competition? [45]

3. Can Justice Powell's conclusion that no "property" is at stake in *Goss* be reconciled with his position in *Arnett*? Does his *Goss* dissent accept Justice Rehnquist's "bitter with the sweet" argument?

Bishop v. Wood

426 U.S. 341 (1976)

Mr. Justice STEVENS delivered the opinion of the Court.

Acting on the recommendation of the Chief of Police, the City Manager of Marion, North Carolina, terminated petitioner's employment as a policeman without affording him a hearing to determine the sufficiency of the cause for his discharge. Petitioner brought suit contending that since a city ordinance classified him as a "permanent employee," he had a constitutional right to a pretermination hearing. During pretrial discovery petitioner was advised that his dismissal was based on a failure to follow certain orders, poor attendance at police training classes, causing low morale, and conduct unsuited to an officer. Petitioner and several other police officers filed affidavits essentially denying the truth of these charges. The District Court granted defendants' motion for summary judgment. The Court of Appeals affirmed. . . .

The questions for us to decide are (1) whether petitioner's employment status was a property interest protected by the Due Process Clause of the Fourteenth Amendment, and (2) assuming that the explanation for his discharge was false, whether that false explanation deprived him of an interest in liberty protected by that clause.

---

44. For further discussion of these questions see pp. 702-708, infra.

45. See Hamilton v. Tennessee Secondary School Athletic Assn. 552 F.2d 681 (6th Cir. 1976) (no due process right to participate in high school interscholastic athletics); Colorado Seminary v. N.C.A.A., 570 F.2d 320 (10th Cir. 1978) (interest of the student athletes in participating in intercollegiate sports is not constitutionally protected). The latter case analogizes education to a bundle of sticks, and notes that withdrawal of a single stick doesn't necessarily deprive the student of his "bundle," i.e., his educational entitlement. How severe would a restriction on academic or extracurricular activities have to be before it constituted a "deprivation" of education? The issue is further discussed at p. 702, infra.

I

Petitioner was employed by the city of Marion as a probationary policeman on June 9, 1969. After six months he became a permanent employee. He was dismissed on March 31, 1972. He claims that he had either an express or an implied right to continued employment.

A city ordinance provides that a permanent employee may be discharged if he fails to perform work up to the standard of his classification, or if he is negligent, inefficient or unfit to perform his duties.[46] Petitioner first contends that even though the ordinance does not expressly so provide, it should be read to prohibit discharge for any other reason, and therefore to confer tenure on all permanent employees. In addition, he contends that his period of service, together with his "permanent" classification, gave him a sufficient expectancy of continued employment to constitute a protected property interest.

A property interest in employment can, of course, be created by ordinance, or by an implied contract. In either case, however, the sufficiency of the claim of entitlement must be decided by reference to state law. The North Carolina Supreme Court has held that an enforceable expectation of continued public employment in that State can exist only if the employer, by statute or contract, has actually granted some form of guarantee. Still v. Lance, 279 N.C. 25, 182 S.E.2d 403 (1971). Whether such a guarantee has been given can be determined only by an examination of the particular statute or ordinance in question.

On its face the ordinance on which petitioner relies may fairly be read as conferring such a guarantee. However, such a reading is not the only possible interpretation; the ordinance may also be construed as granting no right to continued employment but merely conditioning an employee's removal on compliance with certain specified procedures. We do not have any authoritative interpretation of this ordinance by a North Carolina state court. We do, however, have the opinion of the United States District Judge who, of course, sits in North Carolina and practiced law there for many years. Based on his understanding of state law, he concluded that petitioner "held his position at the will and pleasure of the city." This construction of North Carolina law was upheld by the Court of Appeals for the Fourth Circuit, albeit by an equally divided Court. In comparable circumstances, the Court has accepted the interpretation of state law in which the District Court and the Court of Appeals have concurred even if an examination of the state law issue without such guidance might have justified a different conclusion. . . .

In this case, as the District Court construed the ordinance, the City Manager's

46. Article II, §6, of the Personnel Ordinance of the city of Marion, reads as follows:
"*Dismissal.* A permanent employee whose work is not satisfactory over a period of time shall be notified in what way his work is deficient and what he must do if his work is to be satisfactory. If a permanent employee fails to perform work up to the standard of the classification held, or continues to be negligent, inefficient, or unfit to perform his duties, he may be dismissed by the City Manager. Any discharged employee shall be given written notice of his discharge setting forth the effective date and reasons for his discharge if he shall request such a notice."

determination of the adequacy of the grounds for discharge is not subject to judicial review; the employee is merely given certain procedural rights which the District Court found not to have been violated in this case.

Under that view of the law, petitioner's discharge did not deprive him of a property interest protected by the Fourteenth Amendment.

II

Petitioner's claim that he has been deprived of liberty has two components. He contends that the reasons given for his discharge are so serious as to constitute a stigma that may severely damage his reputation in the community; in addition, he claims that those reasons were false. . . .

In this case the asserted reasons for the City Manager's decision were communicated orally to the petitioner in private and also were stated in writing in answer to interrogatories after this litigation commenced. Since the former communication was not made public, it cannot properly form the basis for a claim that petitioner's interest in his "good name, reputation, honesty, or integrity" was thereby impaired. And since the latter communication was made in the course of judicial proceeding which did not commence until after petitioner had suffered the injury for which he seeks redress, it surely cannot provide retroactive support for his claim. A contrary evaluation of either explanation would penalize forthright and truthful communication between employer and employee in the former instance, and between litigants in the latter.

Petitioner argues, however, that the reasons given for his discharge were false. Even so, the reasons stated to him in private had no different impact on his reputation than if they had been true. . . .

A contrary evaluation of his contention would enable every discharged employee to assert a constitutional claim merely by alleging that his former supervisor made a mistake.

The federal court is not the appropriate forum in which to review the multitude of personnel decisions that are made daily by public agencies.[47] We must accept the harsh fact that numerous individual mistakes are inevitable in the day-to-day administration of our affairs. The United States Constitution cannot feasibly be construed to require federal judicial review for every such error. In the absence of

---

47. The cumulative impression created by the three dissenting opinions is that this holding represents a significant retreat from settled practice in the federal courts. The fact of the matter, however, is that the instances in which the federal judiciary has required a state agency to reinstate a discharged employee for failure to provide a pretermination hearing are extremely rare. The reason is clear. For unless we were to adopt Mr. Justice Brennan's remarkably innovative suggestion that we develop a federal common law of property rights, or his equally far reaching view that almost every discharge implicates a constitutionally protected liberty interest, the ultimate control of state personnel relationships is, and will remain, with the States; they may grant or withhold tenure at their unfettered discretion. In this case, whether we accept or reject the construction of the ordinance adopted by the two lower courts, the power to change or clarify that ordinance will remain in the hands of the City Council of the city of Marion.

any claim that the public employer was motivated by a desire to curtail or to penalize the exercise of an employee's constitutionally protected rights, we must presume that official action was regular and, if erroneous, can best be corrected in other ways. The Due Process Clause of the Fourteenth Amendment is not a guarantee against incorrect or ill-advised personnel decisions.

The judgment is affirmed.

Mr. Justice BRENNAN, with whom Mr. Justice MARSHALL concurs, dissenting.

Petitioner was discharged as a policeman on the grounds of insubordination, "causing low morale," and "conduct unsuited to an officer." ... It is difficult to imagine a greater "badge of infamy" that could be imposed on one following petitioner's calling; in a provision in which prospective employees are invariably investigated, petitioner's job prospects will be severely constricted by the governmental action in this case.

[The Justice argues that the Court's refusal to find a protected "liberty" interest is inconsistent with prior decisions.]

The Court purports to limit its holding to situations in which there is "no public disclosure of the reasons for the discharge," ... but in this case the stigmatizing reasons have been disclosed, and there is no reason to believe that respondents will not convey these actual reasons to petitioner's prospective employers. ...

I also fully concur in the dissenting opinions of Mr. Justice White and Mr. Justice Blackmun, which forcefully demonstrate the Court's error in holding that petitioner was not deprived of "property" without due process of law. I would only add that the strained reading of the local ordinance, which the Court deems to be "tenable," ... cannot be dispositive of the existence *vel non* of petitioner's "property" interest. There is certainly a federal dimension to the definition of "property" in the Federal Constitution; cases such as Board of Regents v. Roth, supra, held merely that "property" interests encompass those to which a person has "a legitimate claim of entitlement," Id., 408 U.S. at 577, 92 S. Ct. at 2709, and *can* arise from "existing rules or understandings" that derive from "an independent source *such as* state law." Ibid. (emphasis supplied). But certainly, at least before a state law is definitively construed as not securing a "property" interest, the relevant inquiry is whether it was objectively reasonable for the employee to believe he could rely on continued employment. Cf. ibid. ("It is a purpose of the ancient institution of property to protect those claims upon which people rely in their daily lives, reliance that must not be arbitrarily undetermined.").[48] At a minimum, this would require in this case an analysis of the common practices utilized and the expectations generated by respondents, and the manner in which the local ordinance would

---

48. By holding that States have "unfettered discretion" in defining "property" for purposes of the Due Process Clause of the Federal Constitution, the Court is, as my Brother White argues, effectively adopting the analysis rejected by a majority of the Court in Arnett v. Kennedy, 416 U.S. 134, 94 S. Ct. 1633, 40 L. Ed. 2d 15 (1974). More basically, the Court's approach is a resurrection of the discredited rights/privileges distinction, for a State may now avoid all due process safeguards attendant upon the loss of even the necessities of life, cf. Goldberg v. Kelly, 397 U.S. 254, 90 S. Ct. 1011, 25 L. Ed. 2d 287 (1970), merely by labelling them as not constituting "property."

reasonably be read by respondents' employees.[49] These disputed issues of fact are not meet for resolution, as they were, on summary judgment, and would thus at a minimum require a remand for further factual development in the district court. . . .

Mr. Justice WHITE, with whom Mr. Justice BRENNAN, Mr. Justice MARSHALL, and Mr. Justice BLACKMUN join, dissenting.

I dissent because the decision of the majority rests upon a proposition which was squarely addressed and in my view correctly rejected by six Members of this Court in Arnett v. Kennedy, 416 U.S. 134, 94 S. Ct. 1663, 40 L. Ed. 2d 15 (1974). . . . In the concluding paragraph of its discussion of petitioner's property interest, the majority holds that since neither the ordinance nor state law provides for a hearing, or any kind of review of the City Manager's dismissal decision, petitioner had no enforceable property interest in his job. The majority concludes:

> "In this case, as the District Court construed the ordinance, the City Manager's *determination of the adequacy of the grounds for discharge* is not subject to judicial review; the employee is merely given certain procedural rights which the District Court found not to have been violated in this case. The District Court's reading of the ordinance is tenable; . . ." (Emphasis added.)

The majority thus implicitly concedes that the ordinance supplies the "grounds" for discharge and that the City Manager must determine them to be "adequate" before he may fire an employee. The majority's holding that petitioner had no property interest in his job in spite of the unequivocal language in the city ordinance that he may be dismissed only for certain kinds of cause rests, then, on the fact that state law provides no *procedures* for assuring that the City Manager dismiss him only for cause. The right to his job apparently given by the first two sentences of the ordinance is thus redefined, according to the majority, by the procedures provided for in the third sentence and as redefined is infringed only if the procedures are not followed.

This is precisely the reasoning which was embraced by only three and expressly rejected by six Members of this Court in Arnett v. Kennedy, supra.

. . . The ordinance plainly grants petitioner a right to his job unless there is cause to fire him. Having granted him such a right it is the Federal Constitution, not state law, which determines the process to be applied in connection with any state decision to deprive him of it.

[Justice BLACKMUN's dissenting opinion, joined by Justice BRENNAN, asserted that Still v. Lance, 279 N.C. 254, 182 S.E.2d 403 (1971), relied upon by the majority,

49. For example, petitioner was hired for a "probationary" period of six months, after which he became a "permanent" employee. No reason appears on the record for this distinction, other than the logical assumption, confirmed by a reasonable reading of the local ordinance, that after completion of the former period, an employee may only be discharged for "cause." As to respondents' personnel practices, it is important to note that in a department which currently employs 17 persons, petitioner's was the only discharge, for cause or otherwise, during the period of over three years from the time of his hiring until the time of pretrial discovery.

did not support the reading of the Marion ordinance accepted by the majority because *Still* dealt with failure to renew the contract of a teacher hired from year to year, whereas Bishop enjoyed a form of tenure under which he could be discharged from his position as a "permanent" employee only for cause.]

Notes and Questions

1. *Bishop* clearly restricts the definition of "property" interests entitled to due process protection, but what logic does it adopt in doing so? Has a majority of the Court (including Justice Powell!) now adopted Justice Rehnquist's *Arnett* argument, permitting states (and, perhaps, Congress) discretion to qualify procedurally the substantive entitlements they create? Does *Bishop* encourage judges to artificially construe statutes or regulations in order to grant administrators discretion and eliminate a substantive entitlement that a more natural reading would have conferred? [50]

Doesn't either interpretation undercut expectation interests which might reasonably be generated in a case like *Bishop*, where the employee had successfully weathered a probationary period and enjoyed "permanent" status? [51]

---

50. The District court's opinion in *Bishop* can be read to reflect either of these two theories. The opinion antedated *Arnett*, and could be read as holding that while the ordinance conferred a right not to be discharged except for "cause," the ordinance procedurally qualified that right by providing that "cause" would be determined solely through the procedures specified in the ordinance. Alternatively, the District Court could be understood as reading the ordinance to grant only at-will employment, despite its distinction between provisional and permanent employees, following Still v. Lance, 279 N.C. 254, 182 S.E.2d 403 (1971). However, that decision involved a failure to review a one-year contract of employment, and was thus similar to the situation in *Roth*. Is *Still* plausible authority for reading an ordinance to permit dismissal at will of a "permanent" employee?

Bishop is discussed in Rabin, Job Security and Due Process: Monitoring Administrative Discretion Through a Reasons Requirement, 44 U. Chi. L. Rev. 60 (1976). Professor Rabin suggests that the reluctance of the Court to find an entitlement in *Bishop* and other cases is linked to the other prong of the *Roth* due process analysis — the "what-process-is-due" question. Rabin believes that the Court was reluctant to find an entitlement in state government employment because such an entitlement would almost inevitably trigger rather extensive procedural requirements that would impose excessive fetters and burdens on state employment decisions.

Is this view supportable in light of the Court's decision in Goss v. Lopez? The question of "minimum" due process rights is discussed infra at p. 675.

51. Reconsider Professor Tribe's analysis, note 40 supra. A number of subsequent lower court decisions have held that state statutes obviating tenure status override more informal understandings based on discharge only for cause. See Ryan v. Aurora City Bd. of Education, 540 F.2d 222 (6th Cir. 1976), *cert. denied*, 429 U.S. 1041 (1977), where a School Board regulation in a policy manual requiring reasons for non-renewal of teaching contracts was found to be inconsistent with state statutes. Teachers who were not renewed were held not to be entitled to any due process protection. The court asserted that a nontenured teacher has no "expectancy of continued employment, whatever may be the policies of the institution, where there exists a statutory tenure system" negating such expectancy. See also New Castle Gunning Bedford Educators' Ass'n v. Board of Ed., 421 F. Supp. 960 (D. Del. 1976) (provisions in statutory tenure system override master agreement between Board and teachers' association that teachers may be discharged only for cause).

Compare Soni v. Board of Trustees of the University of Tennessee, 513 F.2d 347 (6th Cir. 1975), a pre-*Bishop* decision holding that a professor who was an alien was entitled to due

2. Justice Brennan would apparently extend procedural due process safeguards to cases where it was "objectively reasonable" for an employee to conclude that she could be discharged only for "cause," regardless of state statutes or decisional law to the contrary. How would federal courts decide whether asserted expectation interests were "objectively reasonable"? What sort of evidence would be relevant? [52] Which side would bear the burden of uncertainty? What would be the impact of such an inquiry on collective bargaining arrangements between state employees and state governments?

Following Justice Brennan's approach, suppose that an employee were found to have an "objectively reasonable" expectation of tenure despite contrary state law, and was afforded a hearing at which the state failed to prove "cause" for discharge. Would the federal courts order the employee reinstated, despite state law to the contrary? If so, has not procedural due process been transformed into substantive due process? If not, what is the point of having a hearing?

Paul v. Davis

424 U.S. 693 (1976)

Mr. Justice REHNQUIST delivered the opinion of the Court.

[Davis, a Louisville newspaper reporter, had his photograph and name included in materials identifying "active shoplifters" that were prepared and circulated among local merchants by the chiefs of police of Louisville and Jefferson County, Kentucky.

---

process protection on discharge despite a state statute clearly precluding tenure for aliens, where the professor had received assurances of continued employment from university officials and had been allowed to participate in a retirement program generally restricted to tenured employees.

A post-*Bishop* decision, Megill v. Board of Regents of State of Florida, 541 F.2d 1073 (5th Cir. 1976) held that the existence of a statutory tenure system conferring no rights in plaintiff created a rebuttable presumption that no protected expectancy of permanence existed, but indicated that the presumption might be overcome by length of service.

How should federal judges construe state statutes relating to employment where there is no relevant state precedent? In Olshock v. Village of Skokie, 541 F.2d 1254 (7th Cir. 1976) and Jacobs v. Naues, 541 F.2d 222 (9th Cir. 1976), *cert. denied*, 429 U.S. 1094 (1977), statutory references to "cause" were held to create "property" rights to due process, while Barton v. City of Eustio, 415 F. Supp. 1355 (M.D. Fla. 1976), entertained a presumption of entitlement where no state decisional law clearly precludes it. Compare the effort in *Bishop* to distinguish *Arnett*. Is the Court suggesting that federal judges should be less willing to find a "cause" requirement in a state statute than in an equivalent federal statute?

52. Would it be "objectively reasonable" for an employee to rely on the following statute as guaranteeing that he or she would only be discharged for "cause"?

> The board . . . may refuse to renew the contract of any probationary teacher . . . for any cause it deems sufficient; provided, however, that the cause may not be arbitrary, capricious, discriminatory or for personal or political reasons. N.C. Gen. Stat. Section 115-142(m)(2).

The Fourth Circuit, in Sigmon v. Poe, 528 F.2d 311 (1975), decided that no entitlement was created by the statute, following the construction given it by the state courts in Taylor v. Crisp, 286 N.C. 488, 212 S.E.2d 381, 386 (1975).

Davis had been arrested for shoplifting but the charge had not been tried at the time the materials were circulated; the charge was subsequently dismissed.

Davis brought an action under 42 U.S.C. §1983 in the District Court, alleging violation of his constitutional rights and alleging, inter alia, that the defamation seriously impaired his future employment opportunities. Although the District Court dismissed for failure to state a claim, the Court of Appeals reversed on the authority of Wisconsin v. Constantineau, 400 U.S. 433 (1971). *Constantineau* held that it was a violation of due process for a police chief (acting pursuant to a Wisconsin statute designed to deal with habitual drunkards) to post, without prior hearing, a notice in all retail liquor outlets in town that sales or gifts to Norma Constantineau were forbidden for one year. The Court stated that " 'posting' . . . is such a stigma or badge of disgrace that procedural due process requires notice and an opportunity to be heard."

The Court first rejected the broad contention that the Fourteenth Amendment provides redress against torts committed by state officials. It then dealt with the narrower claim that it protects individuals' interest in reputation against defamation by state officials.]

. . . While we have in a number of our prior cases pointed out the frequently drastic effect of the "stigma" which may result from defamation by the government in a variety of contexts, this line of cases does not establish the proposition that reputation alone, apart from some more tangible interests such as employment, is either "liberty" or "property" by itself sufficient to invoke the procedural protection of the Due Process Clause. . . .

In United States v. Lovett, 328 U.S. 303, 66 S. Ct. 1073, 90 L. Ed. 1252 (1946), the Court held that an Act of Congress which specifically forbade payment of any salary or compensation to three named government agency employees was an unconstitutional bill of attainder. The three employees had been proscribed because the House of Representatives Subcommittee found them guilty of "subversive activity," and therefore unfit for government service. The Court, while recognizing that the underlying charges upon which Congress' action was premised "stigmatized [the employees'] reputation and seriously impaired their chance to earn a living," id., at 314 . . . also made it clear that "what is involved here is Congressional proscription of [these employees], prohibiting their ever holding a government job." Ibid.

[The Court discussed additional post-*Lovett* cases.]

Two things appear from the line of cases beginning with *Lovett*. The Court has recognized the serious damage that could be inflicted by branding a government employee as "disloyal," and thereby stigmatizing his good name. But the Court has never held that the mere defamation of an individual, whether by branding him disloyal or otherwise, was sufficient to invoke the guarantees of procedural due process absent an accompanying loss of government employment. . . .

It was against this backdrop that the Court in 1971 decided *Constantineau*. There the Court held that a Wisconsin statute authorizing the practice of "posting" was unconstitutional because it failed to provide procedural safeguards of notice and an opportunity to be heard, prior to an individual's being "posted." Under the statute "posting" consisted of forbidding in writing the sale or delivery of alcoholic beverages to certain persons who were determined to have become hazards to themselves, to their family, or to the community by reason of their "excessive drinking." The statute also made it a misdemeanor to sell or give liquor to any person so posted. See 400 U.S., at 434 n.2. . . .

There is undoubtedly language in *Constantineau*, which is sufficiently ambiguous to justify the reliance upon it by the Court of Appeals:

> "Yet certainly where the State attaches 'a badge of infamy' to the citizen due process comes into play. . . .
> "Where a person's good name, reputation, honor, or integrity is at stake *because of what the government is doing to him*, notice and an opportunity to be heard are essential." 400 U.S. 433, 437, . . . (emphasis supplied)

We think that the italicized language in the last sentence quoted, "because of what the government is doing to him," referred to the fact that the governmental action taken in that case deprived the individual of a right previously held under state law — the right to purchase or obtain liquor in common with the rest of the citizenry. "Posting," therefore, significantly altered his status as a matter of state law, and it was that alteration of legal status which, combined with the injury resulting from the defamation, justified the invocation of procedural safeguards. The "stigma" resulting from the defamatory character of the posting was doubtless an important factor in evaluating the extent of harm worked by that act, but we do not think that such defamation, standing alone, deprived Constantineau of any "liberty" protected by the procedural guarantees of the Fourteenth Amendment. . . .

[The Court asserted that *Roth* had entertained the possibility that injury to reputation might give rise to constitutional protection only in a factual context where there was also a failure to rehire. In *Goss*, it pointed out, the stigma of suspension was imposed in connection with denial of a statutory entitlement to attend school.]

In each of these cases, as a result of the state action complained of, a right or status previously recognized by state law was distinctly altered or extinguished. It was this alteration, officially removing the interest from the recognition and protection previously afforded by the State, which we found sufficient to invoke the procedural guarantees contained in the Due Process Clause of the Fourteenth Amendment. But the interest in reputation alone which respondent seeks to vindicate in this action in federal court is quite different from the "liberty" or "property" recognized in those decisions. Kentucky law does not extend to respondent any legal guarantee of present enjoyment of reputation which has been altered as a result of petitioners' actions. Rather his interest in reputation is simply one of a number which the State may protect against injury by virtue of its tort law, providing a forum for vindication of those interests by means of damages actions. And any harm or injury to that interest, even where as here inflicted by an officer of the State, does not result in a deprivation of any "liberty" or "property" recognized by state or federal law, nor has it worked any change of respondent's status as theretofore recognized under the State's laws. For these reasons we hold that the interest in reputation asserted in this case is neither "liberty" nor "property" guaranteed against state deprivation without due process of law.....

Mr. Justice Stevens took no part in the consideration or decision of this case.

Mr. Justice BRENNAN, with whom Mr. Justice MARSHALL concurs and Mr. Justice WHITE concurs in part, dissenting.

I dissent. The Court today holds that police officials, acting in their official capacities as law enforcers, may on their own initiative and without trial constitutionally condemn innocent individuals as criminals and thereby brand them with one of the most stigmatizing and debilitating labels in our society. If there are no constitutional restraints on such oppressive behavior, the safeguards constitutionally accorded an accused in a criminal trial are rendered a sham, and no individual can feel secure that he will not be arbitrarily signaled out for similar ex parte punishment by those primarily charged with fair enforcement of the law. The Court accomplishes this result by excluding a person's interest in his good name and reputation from all constitutional protection, regardless of the character of or necessity for the Government's actions. The result, which is demonstrably inconsistent with our prior case law and unduly restrictive in its construction of our precious Bill of Rights, is one in which I cannot concur.

[The Justice then contends that the Court's ruling is inconsistent with the logic of *Cafeteria Workers, Roth, Goss* and *Constantineau.*]

... Our precedents clearly mandate that a person's interest in his good name and reputation is cognizable as a "liberty" interest within the meaning of the Due Process Clause, and the Court has simply failed to distinguish those precedents in any rational manner in holding that no invasion of a "liberty" interest was effected in the official stigmatizing of respondent as a criminal without any "process" whatsoever.

Questions

1. *Paul* apparently creates a "defamation plus" test for deprivation of liberty. Thus, defamation alone is not an invasion of Fourteenth Amendment liberty, but defamation coupled with some additional deprivation may trigger due process protection. What sort of additional deprivation is required? Must the additional deprivation itself constitute an infringement of an independent "liberty" or "property" interest or will any additional deprivation satisfy *Paul's* "defamation plus" test? [53]

53. Compare Colaizzi v. Walker, 542 F.2d 969 (7th Cir. 1976), *cert. denied*, 430 U.S. 960 (1977) (termination of employment plus defamatory press release stating reasons for termination held to be a deprivation of liberty requiring due process protection, even though plaintiff had no property interest in his employment) with Mitchell v. King, 537 F.2d 385, 390 (10th Cir. 1976) (interpreting *Paul* as holding that reputation is not protected at all by the Due Process Clause; plaintiff was not deprived of liberty by being defamed in the course of being terminated from government employment where there was no property interest). See also Moore v. Otero, 557 F.2d 435 (5th Cir. 1977) (defamation plus demotion from police corporal to patrolman not a deprivation of liberty); Sullivan v. Brown, 544 F.2d 279 (6th Cir. 1976) (defamation plus transfer of tenured school teacher from one school to another, with no reduction in compensation, not

2. What affirmative justification does the Court offer for its "defamation plus" test? Is the test in any event a sound one? [54]

3. In *Paul* the Court suggests that the defamation in question might be actionable as a tort under state law. If so, why doesn't state law thereby create a "property" entitlement subject to due process safeguards? Does the availability of a tort action provide sufficient due process protection of that entitlement, if it exists? [55]

4. Codd v. Velger, 429 U.S. 624 (1977) further restricted the availability of §1983 actions to plaintiffs alleging deprivation of reputation. Velger, who had been dismissed from his position as a patrolman in the New York City Police Department, brought suit in the Southern District of New York, alleging that his termination had deprived him of a property interest in his job without due process of law. The district court ruled that Velger was a probationary employee and therefore had not been deprived of property. Velger then amended his complaint to allege that he had been deprived of liberty by virtue of the fact that the police department had placed in his personnel file certain stigmatizing information — that he "had been dismissed because while still a trainee he had put a revolver to his head in an apparent suicide attempt" — which had subsequently been released to the Penn Central Railroad, for whom Velger had gone to work after his termination from the police department. As a result, he was dismissed by Penn Central. (Velger had signed a form which authorized the department to release information from his personnel file to Penn Central.)

The District Court rejected Velger's contention that he had been deprived of a liberty interest. The Second Circuit reversed, and the Supreme Court, in a per curiam opinion, reversed the Second Circuit. The Court said:

> Assuming all of the other elements necessary to make out a claim of stigmatization under *Roth* and *Bishop*, the remedy mandated by the Due Process Clause of the Fourteenth Amendment is "an opportunity to refute the charge." 408 U.S., at 573, 92 S. Ct., at 2707. "The purpose of such

---

a deprivation of liberty). See generally Note, Reputation, Stigma, and Section 1983: The Lessons of Paul v. Davis, 30 Stan. L. Rev. 191, 221 n.169 (1977).

How close a connection between the defamation and the additional deprivation must there be in order to satisfy the "defamation plus" test? Compare Owen v. City of Independence, 560 F.2d 925 (8th Cir. 1977) (city councilman released results of investigation indicating misconduct by police chief one day before chief's discharge by city manager; "liberty" interest found) with Gentile v. Wallen, 562 F.2d 193 (2d Cir. 1977) (post-discharge statement by officials to state unemployment compensation authorities that plaintiff had been discharged for misconduct; no "liberty" interest found).

If a plaintiff who meets the "defamation plus" test prevails in a §1983 damage action, what should the measure of damages be? Should it be limited to injury to reputation? Should recovery be limited to the additional deprivation — such as discharge from employment — constituting the "plus"? Or should plaintiff be entitled to recover both for injury to reputation and for the additional deprivation? See Cox v. Northern Virginia Transportation Comm'n, 551 F.2d 555 (4th Cir. 1976) (limiting damages to discharge from employment and denying recovery for injury to reputation).

54. For a description of the aftermath of *Paul* by the plaintiff in that case, see 6 Juris Doctor 31 (July/August 1976).

55. Compare Ingraham v. Wright, infra p. 676.

notice and hearing is to provide the person an opportunity to clear his name," id., n.12. But if the hearing mandated by the Due Process Clause is to serve any useful purpose, there must be some factual dispute between an employer and a discharged employee which has some significant bearing on the employee's reputation. Nowhere in his pleadings or elsewhere has respondent affirmatively asserted that the report of the apparent suicide attempt was substantially false. Neither the District Court nor the Court of Appeals made any such finding. When we consider the nature of the interest sought to be protected, we believe the absence of any such allegation or finding is fatal to respondent's claim under the Due Process Clause that he should have been given a hearing.

. . . Since the District Court found that respondent had no Fourteenth Amendment property interest in continued employment, the adequacy or even the existence of reasons for failing to rehire him presents no federal constitutional question. Only if the employer creates and disseminates a false and defamatory impression about the employee in connection with his termination is such a hearing required. *Roth*, supra; *Bishop*, supra.

Our decision here rests upon no overly technical application of the rules of pleading. Even conceding that the respondent's termination occurred solely because of the report of an apparent suicide attempt, a proposition which is certainly not crystal clear on this record, respondent has at no stage of this litigation affirmatively stated that the "attempt" did not take place as reported. The furthest he has gone is a suggestion by his counsel that "[i]t might have been all a mistake, [i]t could also have been a little horseplay." This is not enough to raise an issue about the substantial accuracy of the report.

Brennan, Marshall, Stewart, and Stevens, J.J., dissented. Justice Blackmun filed a concurring opinion, emphasizing that "in this case there is no suggestion that the information in the file, if true, was not information of a kind that appropriately might be disclosed to prospective employers. We therefore are not presented with a question as to the limits, if any, on the disclosure of prejudicial, but irrelevant, accurate information."

Meachum v. Fano

427 U.S. 215 (1976)

Mr. Justice WHITE delivered the opinion of the Court.

[Plaintiffs, Fano and others, prisoners in Massachusetts state prisons, were transferred from a medium-security prison to a maximum-security prison following a hearing on their responsibility for incidents of arson at the former institution. While they were permitted to testify at the hearings and submit supporting evidence, they were not permitted to confront and cross-examine adverse witnesses, including Meachum, the prison superintendent. Plaintiffs brought a §1983 action challenging the transfer without hearing and prevailed in the courts below. The Court of Appeals had relied heavily on the Supreme Court's earlier decision in Wolff

v. McDonnell, 418 U.S. 539 (1974), holding that prison authorities could not, without affording notice and opportunity for hearing, deprive a prisoner, on grounds of misconduct, of "good time" credit to which he would otherwise be entitled and which would reduce the length of his sentence.]

The initial inquiry is whether the transfer of respondents from Norfolk to Walpole and Bridgewater infringed or implicated a "liberty" interest of respondents within the meaning of the Due Process Clause. Contrary to the Court of Appeals, we hold that it did not. We reject at the outset the notion that *any* grievous loss visited upon a person by the State is sufficient to invoke the procedural protections of the Due Process Clause. [Citing *Roth*] We there held that the determining factor is the nature of the interest involved rather than its weight. . . .

Similarly, we cannot agree that *any* change in the conditions of confinement having a substantial adverse impact on the prisoner involved is sufficient to invoke the protections of the Due Process Clause. The Due Process Clause by its own force forbids the State from convicting any person of crime and depriving him of his liberty without complying fully with the requirements of the Clause. But given a valid conviction, the criminal defendant has been constitutionally deprived of his liberty to the extent that the State may confine him and to subject him to the rules of its prison system so long as the conditions of confinement do not otherwise violate the Constitution. The Constitution does not require that the State have more than one prison for convicted felons; nor does it guarantee that the convicted prisoner will be placed in any particular prison, if, as is likely, the State has more than one correctional institution. The initial decision to assign the convict to a particular institution is not subject to audit under the Due Process Clause, although the degree of confinement in one prison may be quite different from that in another. The conviction has sufficiently extinguished the defendant's liberty interest to empower the State to confine him in *any* of its prisons.

. . . Confinement in any of the State's institutions is within the normal limits or range of custody which the conviction has authorized the State to impose. That life in one prison is much more disagreeable than in another does not in itself signify that a Fourteenth Amendment liberty interest is implicated when a prisoner is transferred to the institution with the more severe rules. . . .

Wolff v. McDonnell, on which the Court of Appeals heavily relied, is not to the contrary. Under that case, the Due Process Clause entitles a state prisoner to certain procedural protections when he is deprived of good-time credits because of serious misconduct. But the liberty interest there identified did not originate in the Constitution, which "itself does not guarantee good-time credit for satisfactory behavior while in prison." 418 U.S., at 557, 94 S. Ct., at 2975. The State itself, not the Constitution, had "not only provided a statutory right to good time but also specifies that it is to be forfeited only for serious misbehavior." Ibid. . . .

The liberty interest protected in *Wolff* had its roots in state law, and the minimum procedures appropriated under the circumstances were held required by the Due Process Clause "to insure that the state-created right is not arbitrarily abrogated." Id., at 557, 94 S. Ct., at 2975. This is consistent with our approach in other due process cases. [Citing *Goss, Roth, Sindermann,* and *Goldberg*]

Here, Massachusetts law conferred no right on the prisoner to remain in the prison to which he was initially assigned, defeasible only upon proof of specific acts of misconduct. Insofar as we are advised, transfers between Massachusetts prisons are not conditioned upon the occurrence of specified events. On the contrary, transfer in a wide variety of circumstances is vested in prison officials. The predicate for invoking the protection of the Fourteenth Amendment as construed and applied in Wolff v. McDonnell is totally nonexistent in this case.

Even if Massachusetts has not represented that transfers will occur only on the occurrence of certain events, it is argued that charges of serious misbehavior, as in this case, often initiate and heavily influence the transfer decision and that because allegations of misconduct may be erroneous, hearings should be held before transfer to a more confining institution is to be suffered by the prisoner. . . .

But, as we have said, Massachusetts prison officials have the discretion to transfer prisoners for any number of reasons. Their discretion is not limited to instances of serious misconduct. As we understand it no legal interest or right of these respondents under Massachusetts law would have been violated by their transfer whether or not their misconduct had been proved in accordance with procedures that might be required by the Due Process Clause in other circumstances. Whatever expectation the prisoner may have in remaining at a particular prison so long as he behaves himself, it is too ephemeral and insubstantial to trigger procedural due process protections as long as prison officials have discretion to transfer him for whatever reason or for no reason at all.

Holding that arrangements like this are within reach of the procedural protections of the Due Process Clause would place the Clause astride the day-to-day functioning of state prisons and involve the judiciary in issues and discretionary decisions that are not the business of federal judges. We decline to so interpret and apply the Due Process Clause. The federal courts do not sit to supervise state prisons, the administration of which is of acute interest to the States. . . .

Reversed.

Mr. Justice Stevens, with whom Mr. Justice Brennan and Mr. Justice Marshall join, dissenting.

The Court's rationale is more disturbing than its narrow holding. If the Court had merely held that the transfer of a prisoner from one penal institution to another does not cause a sufficiently grievous loss to amount to a deprivation of liberty within the meaning of the Due Process Clause of the Fourteenth Amendment, I would disagree with the conclusion but not with the constitutional analysis. The Court's holding today, however, appears to rest on a conception of "liberty" which I consider fundamentally incorrect.

The Court indicates that a "liberty interest" may have either of two sources. According to the Court, a liberty interest may "originate in the Constitution," . . . or it may have "its roots in state law." . . . Apart from those two possible origins, the Court is unable to find that a person has a constitutionally protected interest in liberty.

If a man were a creature of the state, the analysis would be correct. But neither the Bill of Rights nor the laws of sovereign States create the liberty which the Due

Process Clause protects. The relevant constitutional provisions are limitations on the power of the sovereign to infringe on the liberty of the citizen. The relevant state laws either create property rights, or they curtail the freedom of the citizen who must live in an ordered society. Of course, law is essential to the exercise and enjoyment of individual liberty in a complex society. But it is not the source of liberty, and surely not the exclusive source.

I had thought it self-evident that all men were endowed by their Creator with liberty as one of the cardinal unalienable rights. It is that basic freedom which the Due Process Clause protects, rather than the particular rights or privileges conferred by specific laws or regulations.

A correct description of the source of the liberty protected by the Constitution does not, of course, decide this case. For, by hypothesis, we are dealing with persons who may be deprived of their liberty because they have been convicted of criminal conduct after a fair trial. We should therefore first ask whether the deprivation of liberty which follows conviction is total or partial....

[The Court has held that the liberty of a parolee] "is valuable and must be seen as within the protection of the Fourteenth Amendment. Its termination calls for some orderly process, however informal." Morrissey v. Brewer, 408 U.S. 471, 482, 92 S.Ct. 2593, 2601, 33 L.Ed.2d 484.... It demeans the holding in Morrissey — more importantly it demeans the concept of liberty — to ascribe to that holding nothing more than a protection of an interest that the State has created through its own prison regulations. For if the inmate's protected liberty interests are no greater than the State chooses to allow, he is really little more than the slave described in the 19th century cases. I think it clear that even the inmate retains an unalienable interest in liberty — at the very minimum the right to be treated with dignity — which the Constitution may never ignore.

...I agree with the Court of Appeals that the transfer involved in this case was sufficiently serious to invoke the protection of the Constitution.

I respectfully dissent.

Notes and Questions: *Meachum*

1. *Meachum* rationalizes the prior decision in *Wolff* as if it were a "property" case. Although *Wolff* spoke of denial of good time credits for misconduct as an infringement of "liberty," *Meachum* explains the decision as involving asserted denial of an entitlement created by state law.[56]

Does it follow that "liberty" no longer exists as an independent source of due process protection? Or does "liberty" consist of those substantive constraints on official conduct imposed by the federal Constitution, while "property" includes all constraints imposed by statute or state law? Suppose an inmate challenges a de-

56. See also Franklin v. Fortner, 541 F.2d 494 (5th Cir. 1976) (no due process protection for prison transfers where transfers committed to discretion of prison authorities under state law); Cooper v. Riddle, 540 F.2d 731 (4th Cir. 1976) (same).

But cf. Holmes v. Board of Parole, 541 F.2d 1243 (7th Cir. 1976) (prisoner entitled to due process protection on reclassification where reclassification likely to prejudice grant of parole).

cision, without hearing, by state prison officials to place him in solitary confinement, on the ground that his alleged misconduct did not occur and that solitary confinement would constitute cruel and unusual punishment in violation of the Eighth Amendment. If state law vests total discretion in prison authorities to order solitary confinement, would the inmate nevertheless have a "liberty" interest protected by due process?

2. How would Justice Stevens define "liberty"? Following his analysis, suppose that a hearing were held in *Meachum* and it was determined that the transferred prisoners had not engaged in misconduct. Would the federal courts require that the transfer be rescinded? If so, would procedural due process be transformed into substantive due process? If not, what is the point of the hearing? Compare Justice Stevens' expansive view of "liberty" in *Meachum* with the expansive definition of "property" embraced by Justice Brennan in *Bishop,* and the broad view of both "liberty" and "property" expressed by Justice Marshall in *Roth* and *Sindermann.*

Notes and Questions: The Definition of Interests Protected by Due Process

1. What factors — aside from the changing composition of the Court — explain the contraction in the definitions of "liberty" and "property" advanced by the Court in recent decisions? Is it a fear that imposing increased procedural requirements on agencies will interfere with the effective discharge of their basic missions? Review Justice Black's dissent in *Goldberg.* Certainly the factor mentioned by Justice Rehnquist in *Paul* — the fear of "federalization" of state tort law via 42 U.S.C. §1983 — is significant.[57] To what extent are these federalization concerns compounded by the fear that constitutional review by federal judges of state agency procedures will inevitably slide into review of their substantive policies as well?

57. See Note, Reputation, Stigma and Section 1983; The Lessons of Paul v. Davis, 30 Stan. L. Rev. 191, 199, 207 (1977):

> [In construing section 1983, the Court] has repeatedly voiced concern for state autonomy, and this concern has apparently led it to construe narrowly the Constitutional rights protected by section 1983. Construing the constitutional rights narrowly in the section 1983 context raises doubts about the proper construction of those rights when state autonomy is irrelevant: when the rights are asserted against the federal government . . .
>
> By attempting to forestall development of a general federal tort law through a restrictive interpretation of the Due Process Clause, the Court failed to deal with the true cause of its concern: section 1983 itself.

Cf. Brennan, State Constitutions and the Protection of Individual Rights, 90 Harv. L. Rev. 489, 503 (1977), wherein Justice Brennan suggests that state courts should act to ameliorate the impact of decisions such as *Meachum:*

> [T]he very premise of the cases that foreclose federal remedies constitutes a clear call to the state courts to step into the breach. . . . With federal scrutiny diminished, state courts must respond by increasing their own.
>
> Moreover, it is not only state-granted rights that state courts can safeguard. If the Supreme Court insists on limiting the content of due process to the rights created by state law, state courts can breathe new life into the federal due process clause by interpreting their common law, statutes and constitutions to guarantee a "property" and "liberty" that even the federal courts must protect.

Professor Davis explains the Court's recent decisions as an attempted antidote to "overreaction" and excessive procedural zeal by the lower federal courts, citing decisions such as Muscare v. Quinn, 520 F.2d 1212 (7th Cir. 1975) (hearing required on suspension of fireman because his goatee violated departmental hair regulations); Greenhill v. Bailey, 519 F.2d 5 (8th Cir. 1975) (informal hearing required on suspension, because of poor academic performance, of medical student who ranked near bottom of class and had failed two courses); Fox v. Morton, 505 F.2d 254 (9th Cir. 1974) (evidentiary hearing on nonrenewal of work/assistance program for Indians because of insufficient funds). See K. Davis, Administrative Law of the Seventies 272-276 (1976).

2. Does the doctrinal evolution from *Goldberg* through the most recent cases show that *Roth*'s two-stage analysis and its property/liberty division of protected interests is unsound? Should the Court have adhered to the open-ended balancing test utilized in *Cafeteria Workers*? Are there any other alternatives? Evaluate the following suggestions by two critics of the Court's recent decisions:

> a.   [I]s it plausible to treat freedom from arbitrary adjudicative procedures as a substantive element of one's liberty as well — a freedom whose abridgement government must sustain the burden of justifying, even as it must do when it seeks to subordinate other freedoms, such as those of speech and privacy? I believe that it is plausible to so regard the matter, and that the ideas of liberty and substantive due process may easily accommodate a view that government may not adjudicate the claims of individuals by unreliable means.
>
> Nor does the idea of a liberty-immunity from unwarranted procedural grossness lack ... flexibility. ... [T]he processing of a social security application will always require different procedural protections than will a criminal trial. It is perfectly familiar learning that when due process applies, its particular dimensions are nevertheless the function of many contextual considerations.[58]

> b. The major alternative to *Meachum*'s entitlement view reflected in recent prison discipline cases may be called an impact view of due process. Unlike the *Meachum* view, impact analysis does not presume that any single variable is absolutely essential before due process becomes operative. Rather, it considers all of the adverse impacts or effects of a state disciplinary action on an inmate. The key principle animating the impact view is that if "grievous" harm would ensue from a disciplinary deprivation, then procedural protections under the Fourteenth Amendment are warranted. The operation of this principle requires a practical assessment of the desirability of procedural safeguards in each individual case. It differs from a narrow entitlement analysis in that it does not require the existence of an independently grounded legal rule under which a claim of right may be advanced.[59]

58. Van Alstyne, Cracks in "The New Property": Adjudicative Due Process in the Administrative State, 62 Cornell L. Rev. 445, 487-489 (1977). The idea that procedural rights exist as independent entitlements which need not be justified by the extent to which they protect other entitlements will be discussed infra at p. 673.

59. Note, Two Views of a Prisoner's Right to Due Process: Meachum v. Fano, 12 Harv. C.R.-C.L. L. Rev. 405, 421 (1977).

Note that both these passages suggest that the Court, in effect, recognizes *all* interests (or at least all interests passing a threshold level of "weight" or grievousness of harm) as protected against the state by the Due Process clause. The question of what process is due for any particular interest would be resolved by a balancing test. These approaches would represent a return to an earlier, more encompassing view of due process expressed in decisions such as Meyer v. Nebraska.[60] (Note that such a view could invite a potentially freewheeling extension of procedural due process to substantive due process.) The adoption in *Roth* of an "entitlement" definition of protected interest marks the decisive shift from this earlier view. Why did the Court in *Roth* make this shift? [61]

3. Professor Van Alstyne summarizes the post-*Goldberg* trends in terms of the following Mick Jagger Lyric:

> You Can't Always Get What You W*ant*
> You Can't Always Get What You W*ant*
> You Can't Always Get What You W*ant*
> But if you try sometime,
> . . . you just might find you get what you *need!* [62]

Is this assessment accurate? Was *Goldberg* a sui generis case explicable solely in terms of the special situation of terminated welfare beneficiaries?

4. Under California's Automobile Franchise Act, retail auto dealers located within 10 miles of a proposed new dealership may protest its establishment before a state New Motor Vehicle Board, which may, after hearing, prohibit the new dealership if it finds that there is "good cause" so to do. An auto manufacturer proposing to establish a protested new dealership is precluded from so doing pending completion of the administrative proceedings, thus enabling existing dealers to foreclose competition for a period of time simply by filing a protest. Does this procedure deprive manufacturers wishing to establish new dealerships of "liberty" or "property"? See New Motor Vehicle Bd. v. Orrin W. Fox Co., 99 S. Ct. 403 (1978).

5. Do recent Supreme Court decision such as *Bishop*, *Paul* and *Meachum* mean that Bailey v. Richardson is still (or again) good law?

60. 262 U.S. 390 (1923), quoted in *Roth*, p. 622, supra.

61. The intellectual roots of *Roth*'s entitlement approach might be found in Charles Reich's landmark article The New Property, 73 Yale L.J. 733 (1964), arguing that "new property" such as welfare entitlements be given the same type of procedural protections as traditional property interests. Although Reich's purpose was to expand procedural protections, his approach, ironically, represents the analytic foundation of the Court's current restriction of due process safeguards.

Monaghan, Of "Liberty" and "Property," 62 Cornell L. Rev. 405 (1977) analyzes the concept of liberty put forward in recent Supreme Court decisions in terms of the historical development of the concept. Recent "liberty" cases are critiqued in The Supreme Court, 1975 Term, 90 Harv. L. Rev. 56, 86-104 (1976), and in Note, Democratic Due Process: Administrative Procedure after Bishop v. Wood, 1977 Duke L. Rev. 453.

62. M. Jagger and K. Richard, You Can't Always Get What You Want (© 1969, Abkco. Music, Inc.), quoted in Van Alstyne, Cracks in "The New Property": Adjudicative Due Process in the Administrative State, 62 Cornell L. Rev. 445, 470 (1977).

6. Under Georgia law, the Georgia Department of Human Resources has the responsibility of finding adoptive parents for infants in state custody. In a lengthy process, potential adoptive families, including not only parents but also grand-parents, uncles, aunts, and cousins, are exhaustively evaluated for suitability. The goal of this process, according to the Department of Human Resources' Adoption Services Manual, is to "seek . . . parents who are emotionally and physically capable of assuming the responsibility of parenthood and who are flexible enough to accept [adopted children] for their intrinsic worth."

While this selection process is going on, children are, if possible, placed in foster homes. Under the statutory scheme, foster homes are considered temporary way-stations on the way to permanent adoption.

In December, 1973, Department officials assumed custody of a one-month old child named Timmy who had been left with an elderly neighbor by his mother before taking a trip to California with a friend. After two weeks, the neighbor, unable to continue to care for the child, had called the Department. Two weeks later, Timmy was placed for temporary care in the home of a Mr. and Mrs. Drum-mond while the Department conducted a search for adoptive parents. After a year, no adoptive parents had been found, but the Drummonds had become sufficiently attached to Timmy to request permission to adopt him themselves. Although the Drummonds had been rated as excellent foster parents, the Department con-sidered it unwise to allow their relationship with Timmy to ripen into a permanent adoptive one, and decided to reassume custody of Timmy. The reason for this decision seems to have been the fact that Timmy was a "mixed race" child, while the Drummonds were white. The agency believed that adoptions by parents of the same race of the child were more likely to be successful than were interracial adoptions. (Although Timmy's mother was white and his father black, his char-acteristics were found by the agency to be more closely "black" than "white.") The Drummonds were not present during the sessions at which this decision was reached. The Adoption services manual, mentioned above, asserts that "[a] perma-nent home or plan is the right of every child."

a. What claims for deprivation of procedural due process might be asserted in a §1983 suit against Department officials on behalf of Timmy's mother? Mr. and Mrs. Drummond? Timmy himself? How should the court dispose of the respective claims? [63]

b. How would the Drummonds' due process claims be affected, if at all, if the Department had taken Timmy from the Drummonds' custody in order to place him with specific foster or adoptive parents whom it considered to be better quali-fied?

63. See Drummond v. Fulton County Dept. of Family and Children's Services, 563 F.2d 1200 (5th Cir. 1977), *cert. denied*, 437 U.S. 910 (1978); Duchesne v. Sugarman, 566 F.2d 817 (2d Cir. 1977).

In thinking about the issues presented, consider the Supreme Court's decision in Smith v. Organization of Foster Families for Equality and Reform [OFFER], 431 U.S. 816 (1977). In OFFER, plaintiff foster parents brought suit to prevent the transfer of their foster child back to his natural parents. The Court failed to decide whether a protected interest existed, ruling that even if an entitlement existed, the plaintiffs received all the process they were due. Justice Stevens, concurring, asserted that the Court should have reached the protected interest question, and decided it against the plaintiffs.

C.   Determining What Process Is Due

Recall that *Roth* and subsequent decisions divide issues of procedural due process into a two-step inquiry. First, what interests are entitled to due process protection? Second, what procedures must be afforded to protected interests? In this section we examine the latter question. These materials should give you a sense of the perplexities encountered in extending notions of procedural due process developed in the context of coercive regulation of private economic activity to the variegated activities of the modern welfare state. It should also lead you critically to consider what purposes are or should be served by procedural formalities in this context, and to reexamine the wisdom of *Roth*'s two-step division of due process issues into an "entitlement" threshold and a "what process is due" balancing approach.

Judges characteristically approach the question of how much process is due in terms of the extent to which an administrative proceeding must adopt the panoply of procedural formalities that are found in court trials. Judge Friendly, in his very useful article, "Some Kind of Hearing," 123 U. Pa. L. Rev. 1267 (1975),[64] lists many of the ingredients of judicial due process:

(1) An unbiased tribunal.

(2) Notice of the proposed action and the grounds asserted for it.

(3) Opportunity to present reasons why the proposed action should not be taken.

(4) The right to present evidence, including the right to call witnesses.

(5) The right to know opposing evidence.

(6) The right to cross-examine adverse witnesses.

(7) Decision based exclusively on the evidence presented.

(8) Right to counsel.

(9) Requirement that the tribunal prepare a record of the evidence presented.

(10) Requirement that the tribunal prepare written findings of fact and reasons for its decision.

How should courts decide which of these measures are required by due process in a given instance of administrative decision? Does it depend on the severity of the deprivation imposed by the government? If so, how should severity be measured? Should it be assessed case-by-case, or by broad categories? Should it depend upon the extent of the affected individual's expectation interests? On whether benefits regularly granted in the past are terminated or a new claim for benefits denied? What interests of the government are relevant? The expense of added formalities? The delay which they may involve? Their impact on substantive policies? The possibility that adversary procedures may generate adversary relations that make effective and cooperative governance impossible? What of the interests of third persons,

---

64. The title is a somewhat jocular quotation of Justice White's generalization that "some kind of hearing is required at some time before a person is finally deprived of his property interests." Wolff v. McDonnell, 418 U.S. 539, 557-58 (1974).

such as other beneficiaries who may have benefits reduced if scarce funds are expended for procedural formalities? Consider also the nature of the issues involved. Are procedural formalities required when the central facts are not disputed, and only questions of policy are at issue? Should the extent of hearing rights afforded depend on whether the relevant evidence consists of witness' testimony, or documentary records?

How should these various factors be weighed in deciding what process is due? Judge Friendly's article fails to provide a comprehensive system for deciding given cases, although he advances some shrewd and useful suggestions, including the principle of functional substitution: satisfaction of one basic requirement (such as impartial decisionmaker), may advance due process objectives as much as several alternative requirements (such as requiring a formal hearing, record, and findings when the decisionmaker is not impartial). It also seems fair to say that no consistent framework for deciding what process is due has emerged from the decisional law, although you will wish to draw your own conclusions from the cases which are discussed below. Is it indeed possible to develop a consistent set of procedural guidelines under an interest-balancing approach to due process, or must decisions necessarily be ad hoc and considerably subjective? [65]

Goldberg v. Kelly

397 U.S. 254 (1970)

(Reread this opinion, reproduced at pp. 613-620, supra.)

Notes and Questions

1. The Court in *Goldberg* stated that the pre-termination hearing it required "need not take the form of a judicial or quasi-judicial hearing." But reread the opinion and consider whether "a judicial or quasi-judicial hearing" isn't exactly what the Court ordered. The following are the *pre-termination* safeguards required by *Goldberg*:

— an impartial decisionmaker;
— right to present argument orally;
— right to present evidence orally;
— right to confront and cross-examine adverse witnesses;
— right to be accompanied by counsel;
— decision based solely on the evidence adduced at the hearing;
— statement by the decisionmaker of the reasons for decision and of the hearing evidence relied upon.

65. For discussion, see Note, Specifying the Procedures Required by Due Process: Toward Limits on the Use of Interest Balancing, 88 Harv. L. Rev. 1510 (1975).

In addition, *Goldberg* required adequate notice to the claimant of the proposed action and the grounds for it, but found that this requirement had been satisfied.

Is this not an extraordinary set of measures to impose upon a state agency (the New York City Human Resources Administration) which processes over 2,000 contested cases monthly? What justifies such an imposition? Is it:

— the circumstance that claimants have a well-defined statutory entitlement to benefits if in fact they meet eligibility requirements?
— the claimants' "brutal need"?
— the susceptibility of the state agency in question to insistent political pressures to trim the welfare rolls?
— the likely presence of factual issues most appropriately resolved by oral, trial-type hearing procedures?

In *Goldberg's* application of a balancing approach, the private interest side of the balance is fairly clear here as in other contexts: the individual has a strong interest in not having welfare payments cut off unjustifiably. But the treatment of the government's interest is more complex. The government concededly has an interest in conserving its fiscal resources, and this interest counterbalances the individual interest in not having payments cut off. But *Goldberg* emphasizes that the government also has an interest in preventing the "social malaise" which would result from unjustified terminations. 397 U.S., at 265. This governmental interest would seem to tip the balance in the direction of more procedural safeguards.[66]

Is this a valid way of implementing the what-process-is-due balancing test? Since the legislature did not impose additional procedural safeguards initially, isn't it fair to presume that the asserted governmental "interest" really doesn't exist? Is it reasonable to impute to the government an "interest" it denies having? [67]

2. *Goldberg* did not require the agency to provide free appointed counsel for welfare termination proceedings. Will the other safeguards mandated by the Court, such as the right to confront and cross-examine, be of any value without appointed counsel? It has been estimated that only about 2 percent of welfare recipients participating in termination hearings are actually represented by counsel. Davis,

66. Similar points are made by the Court in Morrissey v. Brewer, 408 U.S. 471, 484 (1972) (society has interest in preventing unjustified revocation of parole) and in Memphis Light, Gas, and Water Div. v. Craft, 436 U.S. 1 (1978) (municipal utility has interest in maintaining public confidence by not terminating utility services unjustifiably).

67. Might *Goldberg's* technique of attributing to the government an interest that it denies having also be applied to the definition of the private interest at stake? Could it be argued in school discipline cases that the student has a long-range interest in submitting to punishment and thereby improving his or her character? Consider in this respect discussions of *Goss* suggesting that the imposition of procedural safeguards in the context of educational discipline is inappropriate, since the relationship between teacher and student is "nonadversary," and the school system and its representatives really have the best interests of the student at heart. Thus, Justice Powell, dissenting in *Goss*, notes: "[T]he Court ignores the commonality of interests of the State and pupils in the public school system. . . ." 419 U.S., at 593. See Note, Procedural Due Process in Public Schools, 1976 Wisc. L. Rev. 934, 951-53.

Administrative Law of the Seventies 262 (1976). According to one student of the welfare process, "It is all too clear that without adequate representation the best fair hearing system becomes useless." D. Baum, The Welfare Family and Mass Administrative Justice 70 (1974). Assuming that Baum is correct, what should the courts do?

The issue of counsel raises a more general question: Are trial-type adversary safeguards an appropriate response to the problems of "mass justice" in a bureaucracy? In answering this question, consider the following excerpt from D. Baum, Mass Administrative Justice: AFDC Fair Hearings (1973):

> At the problem's root are the difficulties raised by a high volume of cases and quality and quantity of staff. Centralization with a pyramid structure for review will backlog work. Decentralization, even with a mobile review staff, makes it hard for orders and policies to be passed down, received, understood, and acted upon. Moreover, there is the added difficulty of institutional motivation. To some extent the incentives operating upon a welfare agency are not geared to maximizing recipient benefits. Often they are geared, even as official policy, toward effecting welfare savings, sometimes articulated as "taking the cheaters off of the rolls." In such a setting one can safely say that there may be absolute disincentives operating on eligibility technicians, income maintenance specialists, and their supervisors to give an overly high priority in providing recipients advance notice of benefit reduction or termination. . . .
>
> Reflect for a moment on certain statistics: New York City either terminates or reduces the benefits of 40,000 welfare applicants each month. It sends advance notice concerning such action to only about 12,000 applicants. It receives a total of about 2,000 requests for fair hearings each month. None could dispute the large number of fair hearing requests. By the same token, none could dispute the low percentage of fair hearings relative either to the total number of benefit decreases (five percent) or notices of intent to decrease (less than twenty percent). . . .
>
> In New York City fair hearings are held at the massive World Trade Center. The are conducted by a relatively highly paid group of lawyers ($17,000 a year) who docket the cases and notify the City and the claimant. The hearings are scheduled at half hour intervals, but rarely does the examiner meet the schedule. Usually all hearings docketed for 2 p.m. are carried over to the next day. The result tends to bring a police court kind of environment; there is a rushed sense that pervades the hearings. Claimants certainly are not made to feel that an informal process has been designed for a full, relaxed opportunity to present their case. Nor is the City pleased. It is pressured to prepare its case on short notice. Then it is faced with delay and lost manpower simply waiting to be heard.
>
> At the hearing itself the examiner takes notes. These together with a proposed decision are sent to a fair hearing unit within the state welfare department. There the decision is reviewed and often rewritten to comport with one of numerous forms developed by the state. . . .
>
> The decision itself is to be rendered within sixty days following request for a fair hearing. Based upon the sheer volume of litigation it is not surpris-

ing that decision time is lagging somewhat behind that sixty-day deadline. In the interim, of course, the city must continue to pay benefits. . . .

[G]ross data has been compiled on varying aspects of the fair hearing [process]. The National Center for Social Statistics report for January–June 1970 was the first government effort to publish statistical information on hearings in public assistance since 1954. During that six-month period (with California not reporting) there was a national total of 19,400 requests for fair hearings. This figure more than doubled for the reporting period January–June 1971. There was a total of 46,500 requests for fair hearings received. Three states — California, New York, and Texas — accounted for slightly more than half (53.5 percent) of all hearing requests filed by applicants and recipients.

Fair hearings, it is recalled, presently cover all categorical aid programs and medical assistance. AFDC accounted for the largest number of requests for hearings. . . . The requests for hearings did not always result in fair hearings taking place. Twelve states, including California and New York, reported that *more than one-half* of their hearing requests were disposed of without a formal hearing. The nature of that disposition generally, and by a considerable margin, was not in favor of the claimant. Indeed, where the matter was disposed of without hearing, the largest category was that of "request withdrawn," though this did not always mean a decision against the claimant. Where the matter went to hearing the claimant generally, and by a considerable margin, lost. The hearing decision ratio on a national basis for the reporting period January–June 1971 was about 3-to-1 against the claimant.[68]

Is a different (and lower) standard of due process inevitable in the case of "new property"? How would you answer the following question from Jones, The Rule of Law and the Welfare State, 58 Colum. L. Rev. 143, 155-156 (1958)?

Mass-produced goods rarely have the quality of goods made in far smaller quantity by traditional hand craftsmanship; an analogous problem challenges the welfare state. In an era when rights are mass produced, can the quality of their protection against arbitrary official action be as high as the quality of the protection afforded in the past to traditional legal rights less numerous and less widely dispersed among the members of society?

3. *Goldberg* posits more accurate fact-finding and law application as an important due process goal. Drawing on studies by Baum and others, Mashaw, The Management Side of Due Process: Accuracy, Fairness and Timeliness in Adjudication of Social Welfare Claims, 59 Cornell L. Rev. 772 (1974), argues that there is little evidence that court decisions imposing procedural formalities have led to

68. See also D. Baum, The Welfare Family and Mass Administrative Justice (1974); Champagne & Danube, An Empirical Analysis of Decisions of Administrative Law Judges in the Social Security Disability Program, 64 Geo. L.J. 43 (1975); Dixon, The Welfare State and Mass Justice: A Warning from the Social Security Disability Program, 1972 Duke L.J. 681.

markedly more accurate decisions in the context of "mass justice" welfare bureaucracies. Mashaw asserts that procedural rulings have little impact because of bureaucratic imperatives requiring speedy and inexpensive determination of the thousands of cases that must be processed, and the fact that most claimants are too poor, too ill-informed, or too vulnerable to informal imposition of sanctions by caseworkers and other administrators to use effectively the procedural rights which they theoretically possess. Mashaw suggests the use of alternative measures to promote more accurate decisions, including the routinization of key decisions with specific decision rules, retrospective audits to monitor decisional accuracy, comprehensive statistical data to identify and correct deviations from established decisional norms, and the use of appropriate incentives for accurate decisions.[69]

Would Mashaw's alternatives be appropriate if the aims of due process included not only accuracy, but other objectives, such as ensuring those affected by agency decisions an opportunity to influence discretionary policy choices? Might *other* types of alternatives to adversary formalities be appropriate in securing these other objectives? Consider, in this respect, the use of grievance mechanisms, ombudsmen or mediation techniques, or political representation of those affected by the decision in the decision-making structure. A still different approach to controlling bureaucratic decision is followed in Britain, which makes extensive use of tribunals composed of laymen to review welfare eligibility decisions as a way of counterbalancing bureaucratic bias or insensitivity, and relies far less on procedural formalities.[70]

Should courts accept or encourage adoption of Mashaw's "management" techniques or other alternatives to procedural formalities in satisfaction of due process requirements? How would courts evaluate such alternatives? If courts had been readier to accept and encourage the use of such alternatives in the past, would the Supreme Court today be so concerned about limiting the class of interests protected by due process?

4. The possibility of devising alternatives to trial-type formalities in the context of "mass justice" bureaucracies raises the question of the respective roles of the court and agency in devising procedures or institutional arrangements to satisfy due process. In *Goldberg* the Court laid down a fairly specific set of procedural safeguards to be implemented by the agency. An alternative approach might have been for the Court to indicate in very general terms what factors were to be weighed, and then to have invited the agency on remand to come up with acceptable procedures or practices, which would be subject to subsequent review for adequacy by the courts. What advantages and drawbacks do you see in this latter approach? [71]

69. For example, HEW has penalized, through reduced grants, federally-funded state welfare agencies that are found to have an excessively high number of ineligible recipients on their rolls, but no similar penalty is imposed in the case of *failure to include eligible* recipients *on* the rolls, resulting in a net bias in favor of denying eligibility.

70. For discussion, see B. Schwartz & H. Wade, Legal Control of Government 304-314 (1972).

71. Might the Court's *Vermont Yankee* decision, p. 516, supra, point to judicial recognition of a greater role for agencies in devising procedures to satisfy due process?

Mathews v. Eldridge

424 U.S. 319 (1976)

Mr. Justice POWELL delivered the opinion of the Court.

The issue in this case is whether the Due Process Clause of the Fifth Amendment requires that prior to the termination of Social Security disability benefit payments the recipient be afforded an opportunity for an evidentiary hearing. . . .

Cash benefits are provided to workers during periods in which they are completely disabled under the disability insurance benefits program created by the 1956 amendments to Title II of the Social Security Act. 70 Stat. 815, 42 U.S.C. §423.[72] Respondent Eldridge was first awarded benefits in June 1968. [In May, 1972, the Social Security Administrator determined that he was no longer eligible to receive disability benefits.]

Instead of requesting reconsideration Eldridge commenced this action challenging the constitutional validity of the administrative procedures established by the Secretary of Health, Education, and Welfare for assessing whether there exists a continuing disability. . . .

The District Court concluded that the administrative procedures pursuant to which the Secretary had terminated Eldridge's benefits abridged his right to procedural due process. . . . [The Court of Appeals affirmed.]

[The Secretary had conceded that Social Security disability benefits were statutory entitlements representing "property" protected by due process. The Court then considered what process was due.]

In recent years this Court increasingly has had occasion to consider the extent to which due process requires an evidentiary hearing prior to the deprivation of some type of property interest even if such a hearing is provided thereafter. In only one case, Goldberg v. Kelly, 397 U.S. 254, 266-271 (1970), has the Court held that a hearing closely approximating a judicial trial is necessary. . . .

[Justice Powell contrasts *Goldberg* with other Supreme Court decisions, including Cafeteria and Restaurant Workers v. McElroy and Arnett v. Kennedy, requiring less or nothing in the way of pre-termination proceedings.]

[O]ur prior decisions indicate that identification of the specific dictates of due process generally requires consideration of three distinct factors: first, the private interest that will be affected by the official action; second, the risk of an erroneous deprivation of such interest through the procedures used, and the probable value,

---

72. The program is financed by revenues derived from employee and employer payroll taxes. 26 U.S.C. §§ 3101(a), 3111(a); 42 U.S.C. §401(b). It provides monthly benefits to disabled persons who have worked sufficiently long to have an insured status, id., §423(c)(1)(A), and who have had substantial work experience in a specified interval directly preceding the onset of disability. Id., §423(c)(1)(B). Benefits also are provided to the worker's dependents under specified circumstances. Id., §§ 402(b)-(d). When the recipient reaches age 65 his disability benefits are automatically converted to retirement benefits. Id., §§ 416(2)(D), 423(a)(1). In fiscal 1974 approximately 3,700,000 persons received assistance under the program. Social Security Administration, The Year in Review 21 (1974).

if any, of additional or substitute procedural safeguards; and finally, the government's interest, including the function involved and the fiscal and administrative burdens that the additional or substitute procedural requirement would entail.

We turn first to a description of the procedures for the termination of Social Security disability benefits, and thereafter consider the factors bearing upon the constitutional adequacy of these procedures.

The disability insurance program is administered jointly by state and federal agencies. . . . The principal reasons for benefits terminations are that the worker is no longer disabled or has returned to work. . . .

The continuing eligibility investigation is made by a state agency acting through a "team" consisting of a physician and a nonmedical person trained in disability evaluation. The agency periodically communicates with the disabled worker, usually by mail — in which case he is sent a detailed questionnaire — or by telephone, and requests information concerning his present condition, including current medical restrictions and sources of treatment, and any additional information that he considers relevant to his continued entitlement to benefits. . . .

Information regarding the recipient's current condition is also obtained from his sources of medical treatment. . . . If there is a conflict between the information provided by the beneficiary and that obtained from medical sources such as his physician, or between two sources of treatment, the agency may arrange for an examination by an independent consulting physician. . . . Whenever the agency's tentative assessment of the beneficiary's condition differs from his own assessment, the beneficiary is informed that benefits may be terminated, provided a summary of the evidence upon which the proposed determination to terminate is based, and afforded an opportunity to review the medical reports and other evidence in his case file. He also may respond in writing and submit additional evidence. . . .

The state agency then makes its final determination, which is reviewed by an examiner in the SSA Bureau of Disability Insurance. . . . If, as is usually the case, the SSA accepts the agency determination it notifies the recipient in writing, informing him of the reasons for the decision, and of his right to seek *de novo* reconsideration by the state agency. . . . Upon acceptance by the SSA, benefits are terminated effective two months after the month in which medical recovery is found to have occurred. . . .

If the recipient seeks reconsideration by the state agency and the determination is adverse, the SSA reviews the reconsideration determination and notifies the recipient of the decision. He then has a right to an evidentiary hearing before an SSA administrative law judge. . . . The hearing is nonadversary, and the SSA is not represented by counsel. As at all prior and subsequent stages of the administrative process, however, the claimant may be represented by counsel or other spokesmen. . . . If this hearing results in an adverse decision, the claimant is entitled to request discretionary review by the SSA Appeals Council, . . and finally may obtain judicial review. . . .

Should it be determined at any point after termination of benefits, that the claimant's disability extended beyond the date of cessation initially established, the worker is entitled to retroactive payments. . . .

If, on the other hand, a beneficiary receives any payments to which he is later determined not to be entitled, the statute authorizes the Secretary to attempt to recoup these funds in specific circumstances.

Despite the elaborate character of the administrative procedures provided by the Secretary, the courts below held them to be constitutionally inadequate, concluding that due process requires an evidentiary hearing prior to termination. In light of the private and governmental interests at stake here and the nature of the existing procedures, we think this was error.

Since a recipient whose benefits are terminated is awarded full retroactive relief if he ultimately prevails, his sole interest is in the uninterrupted receipt of this source of income pending final administrative decision on his claim. . . .

Eligibility for disability benefits, [in contrast to the benefits at issue in *Goldberg*] is not based upon financial need. Indeed, it is wholly unrelated to the worker's income or support from many other sources. . . .

In view of the torpidity of this administrative review process . . . and the typically modest resources of the family unit of the physically disabled worker, the hardship imposed upon the erroneously terminated disability recipient may be significant. Still, the disabled worker's need is likely to be less than that of a welfare recipient. . . . In view of [other] potential sources of temporary income, there is less reason here than in *Goldberg* to depart from the ordinary principle, established by our decisions, that something less than an evidentiary hearing is sufficient prior to adverse administrative action.

An additional factor to be considered here is the fairness and reliability of the existing pretermination procedures, and the probable value, if any, of additional procedural safeguards. Central to the evaluation of any administrative process is the nature of the relevant inquiry. . . . In order to remain eligible for benefits, . . . a medical assessment of the worker's physical or mental condition is required. This is a more sharply focused and easily documented decision than the typical determination of welfare entitlement. . . .

By contrast, [t]he decision whether to discontinue disability benefits will turn, in most cases, upon "routine, standard, and unbiased medical reports by physician specialists," Richardson v. Perales, 402 U.S., at 404, concerning a subject whom they have personally examined. . . .

To be sure, credibility and veracity may be a factor in the ultimate disability assessment in some cases. But procedural due process rules are shaped by the risk of error inherent in the truthfinding process as applied to the generality of cases, not the rare exceptions. The potential value of an evidentiary hearing, or even oral presentation to the decisionmaker, is substantially less in this context than in *Goldberg*.

The decision in *Goldberg* also was based on the Court's conclusion that written submissions were an inadequate substitute for oral presentation because they did not provide an effective means for the recipient to communicate his case to the decisionmaker. . . .

[Here] the information critical to the entitlement decision usually is derived from medical sources, such as the treating physician. Such sources are likely to be able to communicate more effectively through written documents than are welfare recipients or the lay witnesses supporting their cause. The conclusions of physicians often are supported by X-rays and the results of clinical or laboratory tests, information typically more amenable to written than to oral presentation. . . .

A further safeguard against mistake is the policy of allowing the disability recipient or his representative full access to all information relied upon by the state agency. . . .

Despite these carefully structured procedures, *amici* point to the significant reversal rate for appealed cases as clear evidence that the current process is inadequate. Depending upon the base selected and the line of analysis followed, the relevant reversal rates urged by the contending parties vary from a high of 58.6% for appealed reconsideration decisions to an overall reversal rate of only 3.3%.[73] Bare statistics rarely provide a satisfactory measure of the fairness of a decision-making process. Their adequacy is specially suspect here since the administrative review system is operated on an open-file basis. A recipient may always submit new evidence, and such submissions may result in additional medical examinations. Such fresh examinations are held in approximately 30% to 40% of the appealed cases, either at the reconsideration or evidentiary hearing stage of the administrative process. . . . In this context, the value of reversal rate statistics as one means of evaluating the adequacy of the pretermination process is diminished. Thus, although we view such information as relevant, it is certainly not controlling in this case.

In striking the appropriate due process balance the final factor to be assessed is the public interest. This includes the administrative burden and other societal costs that would be associated with requiring, as a matter of constitutional right, an evidentiary hearing upon demand in all cases prior to the termination of disability benefits. The most visible burden would be the incremental cost resulting from the increased number of hearings and the expense of providing benefits to ineligible recipients, pending decision. No one can predict the extent of the increase, but the fact that full benefits would continue until after such hearings would assure the exhaustion in most cases of this attractive option. Nor would the theoretical right of the Secretary to recover undeserved benefits result, as a practical matter, in any substantial offset to the added outlay of public funds. The parties submit widely varying estimates of the probable additional financial cost. We only need say that experience with the constitutionalizing of government procedures suggests that the ultimate additional cost in terms of money and administrative burden would not be insubstantial.

73. By focusing solely on the reversal rate for appealed reconsideration determinations *amici* overstate the relevant reversal rate. As we indicated last term in Fusari v. Steinberg, 419 U.S. 379, 383 n.6 (1975), in order fully to access the reliability and fairness of a system of procedure, one must also consider the overall rate of error for all denials of benefits. Here that overall rate is 12.2% Moreover, about 75% of these reversals occur at the reconsideration stage of the administrative process. Since the median period between a request for reconsideration review and decision is only two months, . . . the deprivation is significantly less than that concomitant in the lengthier delay before an evidentiary hearing. Netting out these reconsideration reversals, the overall reversal rate falls to 3.3%. . . .

Financial cost alone is not a controlling weight in determining whether due process requires a particular procedural safeguard prior to some administrative decision. But the Government's interest, and hence that of the pubilc, in conserving scarce fiscal and administrative resources, is a factor that must be weighed. At some point the benefit of an additional safeguard to the individual affected by the administrative action and to society in terms of increased assurance that the action is just, may be outweighed by the cost. Significantly, the cost of protecting those whom the preliminary administrative process has identified as likely to be found undeserving may in the end come out of the pockets of the deserving since resources available for any particular program of social welfare are not unlimited.

But more is implicated in cases of this type than ad hoc weighing of fiscal and administrative burdens against the interests of a particular category of claimants. The ultimate balance involves a determination as to when, under our constitutional system, judicial-type procedures must be imposed upon administrative action to assure fairness. We reiterate the wise admonishment of Mr. Justice Frankfurter that differences in the origin and function of administrative agencies "preclude wholesale transplantation of the rules of procedure, trial, and review which have evolved from the history and experience of the courts." FCC v. Pottsville Broadcasting Co., 309 U.S. 134, 143 (1940). The judicial model of an evidentiary hearing is neither a required, nor even the most effective, method of decision-making in all circumstances....

We conclude that an evidentiary hearing is not required prior to the termination of disability benefits and that the present administrative procedures fully comport with due process.

The judgment of the Court of Appeals is *Reversed*.

Mr. Justice STEVENS took no part in the consideration or decision of this case.

Mr. Justice BRENNAN, with whom Mr. Justice MARSHALL concurs, dissenting.

For the reasons stated in my dissenting opinion in Richardson v. Wright, 405 208, 212 (1972), I agree with the District Court and the Court of Appeals that, prior to termination of benefits, Eldridge must be afforded an evidentiary hearing of the type required for welfare beneficiaries under Title IV of the Social Security Act, 42 U.S.C. §601 et seq. See Goldberg v. Kelly, 397 U.S. 254 (1970).

[Justice Brennan argued, largely on the basis of Goldberg v. Kelly and other precedent, that a trial-type hearing must be afforded prior to termination of benefits.] I would add that the Court's consideration that a discontinuance of disability benefits may cause the recipient to suffer only a limited deprivation is no argument. It is speculative. Moreover, the very legislative determination to provide disability benefits, without any prerequisite determination of need in fact, presumes a need by the recipient which is not this Court's to denigrate. Indeed, in the present case, it is indicated that because disability benefits were terminated there was a foreclosure upon the Eldridge home and the family's furniture was repossessed, forcing Eldridge, his wife and children to sleep in one bed. Tr. of Oral Arg., at 39, 47-48. Finally, it is also no argument that a worker, who has been placed in the untenable position of having been denied disability benefits, may still seek other forms of public assistance.

Notes and Questions

1. Justice Powell assumes that the sole function of due process procedural requirements is to promote accurate decisionmaking. Does he adduce any justifications for this premise? Is it compelled by *Roth*?

2. The opinion suggests a calculus under which additional procedural safeguards are warranted so long as:

increased accuracy from additional procedures	×	interest of claimant	>	increased burden on government

a. Is the sort of "interest balancing" represented by this calculus an intellectually coherent or operationally feasible enterprise? How can courts identify and compare, in any consistent fashion, the "weight" of an individual's "property" or liberty interest in relation to general societal interests in sound and efficient administration? Should courts reject "balancing" and require a standardized "package" of due process rights irrespective of the particular "liberty" or "property" interest at stake? [74]

b. Assuming that "interest balancing" is feasible, was the Court's application of its balancing calculus in Mathews v. Eldridge satisfactory? It is strongly criticized by Professor Mashaw,[75] who asserts that the Court's analysis of the competing private and public interest at stake is "subjective and impressionistic," noting that the Court failed to resolve or require the development of data on the total value of terminated disability claims; the mean and median values of individual claims; the comparative distribution of neediness among disability and welfare claimants; and the costs to the government of additional procedural formalities. Mashaw argues that most disputed cases do not turn on technical "medical" questions but on broader and more elusive "disability" issues that include the functional impact of a given medical condition on a claimant's ability to work in a variety of vocational settings, and "the interaction of claimant's age, education, and prior work experience with his functional limitations and his response to them, and the effect of this combination of factors on his capacity for work available in the national economy." The notion of "accuracy" in resolving such issues is, he asserts, inappropriate because they rest on competing considerations of policy and a judgment assessment of "the whole person" that would be facilitated by a personal hearing.[76]

74. See Note, Specifying the Procedures Required by Due Process: Toward Limits on the Use of Interest Balancing, 88 Harv. L. Rev. 1510 (1975).
75. Mashaw, The Supreme Court's Due Process Calculus for Administrative Adjudication in Mathews v. Eldridge: Three Factors in Search of a Theory of Value, 44 U. Chi. L. Rev. 28 (1976).
76. In support of his view that "accuracy" is a questionable basis for assessing disability claim procedures, Mashaw points to a General Accounting Office (GAO) study that indicates the difficulties in ensuring consistency in deciding such claims. GAO collected the files of

c. Should the courts' specification of what process is due be performed on a "wholesale" basis for large categories of disputes, or on a "retail" basis taking into account the particular characteristics of each case? Mathews v. Eldridge seems to embrace the "wholesale" approach.[77] Compare with this the approach taken by the Court in Gagnon v. Scarpelli, 411 U.S. 778, 790 (1972), which stated that the question of whether appointed counsel should be required in probation revocation hearings should be decided on a case-by-case basis, primarily by state officials.

d. Does traditional due process doctrine governing "old property" permit the sort of utilitarian balancing embraced by Justice Powell? Does the amount of due process enjoyed by a taxpayer of a regulated firm depend on the dollar amount at stake? Is there a "double standard" in due process — one for "old property" and one for "new property"?

3. What goals or purposes other than accuracy should appropriately be considered in determining what process is due? Some commentators have contrasted the "instrumental" analysis of formal procedures as a means to securing given outcomes, with intrinsic "process" values that serve expressive functions.[78] For example, the approach taken in Mathews v. Eldridge is "instrumental" because procedures are viewed purely as a means for securing accuracy in dispensing statutory entitlements. Another conceivable instrumental goal of due process procedural requirements would be to secure adoption of disability policies more favorable to claimants by increasing their ability to impose costly delays on the agency and thus increasing their bargaining leverage. By contrast, under a "process" approach, affording a disability claimant an oral hearing would be justified on the ground that it affirms her worth and dignity as an individual by enabling her to participate in government decisions seriously affecting her welfare.[79] Alternatively, procedural formalities can be evaluated in terms of how well they satisfy and affirm traditional

---

221 disability claims that had been decided by a state agency, and transmitted them to ten other state agencies and to federal social security officials to determine how they would decide the same cases. In only 32% of the cases was there complete agreement on the disposition of the claim. In only about two-thirds of the cases did a majority of the state agencies agree on the disposition of the claim, and in 95% of these cases the majority states disagreed on the rationale for deciding the claim. The federal officials agreed with the majority of the states' disposition in less than half of these cases. Id. at 45.

Does Mashaw's analysis of the issues involved in disability decisions undercut his earlier espousal, p. 666, supra, of "management techniques" as an alternative to trial type procedural formalities in "mass justice" bureaucracies?

77. "[P]rocedural due process rules are shaped by the risk of error inherent in the truth-finding process as *applied to the generality of cases, not the rare exceptions*," 424 U.S. 319, at 344 (1976) (emphasis added).

78. See L. Tribe, American Constitutional Law 502-503, 554 (1978); Michelman, Formal and Associational Aims in Procedural Due Process, in Nomos: Due Process 126 (1977) (J. Pennock and J. Chapman, eds.). See also Subrin and Dykstra, Notice and the Right to be Heard: The Significance of Old Friends, 9 Harv. C.R.-C.L. L. Rev. 449, 454-57 (1974); Summers, Evaluating and Improving Legal Processes — A Plea for "Process Values," 60 Cornell L. Rev. 1 (1974). For a useful discussion of the instrumental view of due process as securing entitlements, see Note, Two Views of A Prisoner's Right to Due Process: Meachum v. Fano, 12 Harv. C.R.-C.L. L. Rev. 405, 411-14 (1977).

79. See Michelman, id.; Tribe, Structural Due Process, 10 Harv. C.R.-C.L. L. Rev. 269 (1975).

community standards of fair play.[80] Should courts take these other goals and values into account in determining what process is due? [81]

4. Unlike most of the preceding cases in this chapter, Mathews v. Eldridge involves the administration of a federal, rather than a state, program. Does this (or should it) make any difference in the due process review of the program by the federal courts? [82] Consider in this respect Richardson v. Perales, 402 U.S. 389 (1971),

---

80. Thibaut, Walker, LaTour, and Houlden, Procedural Justice as Fairness, 26 Stan. L. Rev. 1271 (1974), reports the results of an experiment which seems to demonstrate that people strongly prefer adversarial procedures to procedures which provide them with less participation in the adjudicative process. Should such perceptions matter in assessing what process is due? Consider the following frequently quoted statement from Justice Frankfurter's concurrence in Joint Anti-Fascist Refugee Committee v. McGrath:

> No better instrument has been devised for arriving at the truth than to give a person in jeopardy of serious loss notice of the case against him and an opportunity to meet it. Nor has a better way been found for generating *the feeling, so important to a popular government that justice has been done.* 341 U.S. 123, 171-72 (1951) (FRANKFURTER, J., concurring) (emphasis added).

See also Cramton, A Comment on Trial-Type Hearings in Nuclear Plant Siting, 58 Va. L. Rev. 585, 591-93 (1972).

81. In footnote 25 of its *Goldberg* opinion, p. 617, supra (footnote 15 in the original), the Court reserved the question "whether due process requires only an opportunity for written submission, or an opportunity both for written submission and oral argument, where there are no factual issues in dispute or where the application of the rule of law is not intertwined with factual issues." How should this question be resolved? Does its resolution depend on what purpose or purposes due process should serve?

California regulations permitted the reduction or termination of welfare benefits prior to a full hearing whenever the appropriate state official decided that the recipient's appeal only raised issues of "general policy" and no issues of fact or judgment about the individual's case. In Yee-Litt v. Richardson, 353 F. Supp. 996 (N.D. Cal. 1973) the majority of a three-judge district court concluded that the policy-fact distinction was unclear and unmanageable and produced too many erroneous decisions. The dissenting judge disputed the majority's conclusion that the policy-fact distinction resulted in an unacceptable number of mistakes. He pointed out that according to the plaintiff's affidavits, on which the majority had in part relied, out of the thousands of hearing requests filed in a month, only five cases were shown to involve error in administering the policy-fact distinction. The Supreme Court affirmed without decision sub nom Carlson v. Yee-Litt, 412 U.S. 924 (1973). In Viverito v. Smith, 421 F. Supp. 1305 (S.D.N.Y. 1976), welfare recipients challenged state regulations similar to those in *Yee-Litt* which required a pre-termination hearing "except in a case in which the department has determined . . . that the issue is one of state policy (including law and departmental regulation)." The court held that the state's method of applying the regulation was not "well-calculated to deny pre-termination hearings only to persons raising questions of policy alone," and raised substantial questions whether the "fact/policy" distinction is "inherently unworkable." Consequently, the court preliminarily enjoined state and city welfare officials from applying the "policy exemption." Compare Mothers' and Children's Rights Organization v. Sterrett, 467 F.2d 797 (7th Cir. 1972) in which the court held that if a case presented purely questions of law, an evidentiary hearing prior to termination or reduction was unnecessary, but the recipient should nevertheless have an opportunity to present oral argument. The court insisted on an opportunity for a recipient to present an oral argument in part because the recipient might be able to successfully challenge the factual premises of the agency's policy decision.

82. "When dealing with federal law, the Court has the power to construe a statute (or regulations promulgated pursuant to it), and in the process of so doing, it may impose additional procedural requirements on sub-constitutional grounds, purely as a matter of statutory construction. This is roughly analogous to the supervisory function performed by the Court in the area of federal criminal and civil procedure. Furthermore, considerations of federalism, as distinct from simple deference to the democratic choice of the legislature, are not present in a case such as *Eldridge*." Note, Democratic Due Process: Administrative Procedure after Bishop v. Wood, 1977 Duke L. Rev. 435, 467 n.83.

which was relied upon in Mathews v. Eldridge, p. 669, supra, and discussed in Chapter 4, p. 194, supra. *Perales* validated procedures utilized in the resolution of disputed claims in the federal Social Security program in which a hearing examiner is supposed to wear "three hats" by presenting the government's case, representing the claimant (who is normally not represented by counsel), then adjudicating the claim.[83] *Perales* also sustained the termination of Social Security disability payments on the basis of written reports by medical consultants retained by the government which were relied upon by the hearing examiner to reject otherwise uncontradicted testimony by Perales and his physician concerning his disability.[84]

5. Can *Perales* be reconciled with *Goldberg?* Is it significant that *Goldberg* involved a local agency (the New York City Human Resources Administration) that is subject to strong political pressures to reduce the welfare rolls and has a reputation for inefficiency, whereas *Perales* (and *Eldridge*) involved a federal agency (the Social Security Administration) that enjoys greater political independence and a reputation for competence? Or is the denial of full adversary hearing rights in *Perales* explained (as the Court in *Perales* suggested) by the greater inherent reliability of medical diagnoses as opposed to assessments of welfare eligibility? Or does the explanation lie in the circumstance that *Perales* involved disability insurance, while *Goldberg* involved welfare (AFDC) payments?

Goss v. Lopez

419 U.S. 565 (1975)

(Review this case, supra at 637.)

Notes and Questions

1. The safeguards required by *Goss* have been described as "skeletal due process." Where an entitlement exists, should courts ever impose a level of procedural protection *less* than that imposed in *Goss?* Should there be a "threshold" minimum for procedural rights that apply whenever an entitlement exists? [85] What should the contents of such a minimum be?

83. Professor Schwartz says: "With all its faults, however, the inquisitorial type of procedure developed in SSA hearings may represent a practical method of dealing with many of the problems met with in agencies dispensing mass justice. The great need is to deal efficiently and fairly with hordes of cases rather than to preserve all the accoutrements of the courtroom. Particularly in a case where a claimant is not represented by counsel, the active development of the case on both sides by an independent judge may actually be fairer to the claimant than the more traditional adversary procedure. In addition, the elimination of the adversary element makes for greater efficiency; nothing delays the administrative process more than the 'trial by battle' permitted in the more formal type of hearing." Schwartz, Administrative Law 254 (1976).

84. The Court emphasized the similarity among the government doctors' independent diagnosis of Perales' condition (based on a review of his medical file) as evidence of their reliability, and also relied on the circumstance that Perales (who was represented by counsel) possessed but did not exercise the right under departmental regulations to subpoena the government doctors. See p. 194, supra.

85. See Rabin, Job Security and Due Process: Monitoring Administrative Discretion Through a Reasons Requirement, 44 U. Chi. L. Rev. 60 (1976). Professor Rabin believes that

2. What is the purpose of the hearing mandated by *Goss?* To ensure accurate fact finding? To promote a dialogue between students and administrators? [86] To advance the interests of blacks and other minorities within a bureaucracy often perceived by them as insensitive and unsympathetic? [87] To what extent will the procedure mandated in *Goss* be successful in securing these various objectives? [88]

Ingraham v. Wright

430 U.S. 651 (1977)

Mr. Justice POWELL delivered the opinion of the Court.

[Plaintiffs had been paddled by public school officials for alleged disciplinary

---

"minimal" due process should consist of a right to a reasoned explanation. Compare Davis, Administrative Law of the Seventies 267-68 (1976):

> Where interests are small, perhaps the Court should reject the balancing approach and should consider something along this line: In absence of an emergency requiring summary action, when adjudicative facts are in dispute, a party with an interest that is more than de minimis should have a due process right, before governmental action is taken against his interest, to notice of the alleged facts against him and a chance to respond orally to the officer having the power to make or to recommend the initial decision, and the balancing approach should be limited to problems of whether or not to allow confrontation, cross-examination, or testimony of witnesses.

See also Geneva Towers Tenants Organization v. Federated Mortgage Investors, 504 F.2d 483 (9th Cir. 1974), in which tenants in housing projects financed by the federal government under §221(d)(3) of the Housing Act of 1961, 12 U.S.C. 1715*l*(d)(3) sought "recission of rent increases granted their landlords by the Federal Housing Administration (FHA) and an injunction compelling the federal defendants to grant the tenants a full and fair hearing prior to the implementation of the rent increases," 504 F.2d, at 485. The court found that the Housing Act created an entitlement, and affirmed a decree of the district court imposing upon the FHA the following procedural requirements:

> (1) Notice to the tenants of the landlord's application for a rent increase
> (2) Opportunity for the tenants to make written objections
> (3) A statement of FHA's reasons for approving the rent increase.

Judge Hufstedler, dissenting, did not believe that the Housing Act created an entitlement:

> Even if I agreed with my brothers that the tenants had an entitlement, I could not join the majority opinion because, in the guise of granting due process, it eviscerates the due process protections that it purports to grant. The great procedural protections of due process are reduced by the majority to little more than a right to send and receive mail. Procedural due process is flexible, but it is not flaccid. At the barest of minimums, due process requires not only adequate prior notice but also a meaningful evidentiary hearing with a right to personal appearance and a right to call and to examine witnesses as well as to present documentary evidence.

86. See Kirp, Proceduralism and Bureaucracy: Due Process in the School Setting, 28 Stan. L. Rev. 141 (1976); Tribe, Structural Due Process, 10 Harv. C.R.-C.L. L. Rev. 269 (1975).

87. See note 3, supra, p. 673.

88. Consider the following: "Given a choice between supporting the teachers or the students, most school officials have no difficulty recognizing their natural allies. Among the school administrators we interviewed, one told us candidly he would never support a student in a dispute with a teacher but would only try to convey an impression of fairness 'to prevent parents from getting involved.'" Haney & Zimbardo, It's Tough to Tell a High School from a Prison, Psychology Today 26 (June, 1975), quoted in Wilkinson, Goss v. Lopez: The Supreme Court as School Superintendent, 1975 Supreme Court Review 25, 42 n.100. However, Professor Wilkinson takes a more optimistic view of school administrators' motivations and of the impact of hearing requirements. See id., at 70.

violations while junior high school students in Dade County, Florida, without notice or opportunity for a prior hearing on the disciplinary charges. They brought a class action suit against school officials in federal court under 42 U.S.C. §1983, asserting that the paddling constituted cruel and unusual punishment in violation of the Eighth Amendment, and that the failure to afford a hearing prior to paddling violated due process.

The Supreme Court found no violation of the Eighth Amendment. However, the Court found that the actions by state officials in physically restraining students and administering corporal punishment for asserted misconduct invaded "liberty" interests protected by due process. It then considered what process was due in the circumstances, invoking the three-part balancing calculus formulated in Mathews v. Eldridge.]

1

. . . The concept that reasonable corporal punishment in school is justifiable continues to be recognized in the laws of most States. . . . It represents "the balance struck by this country," between the child's interest in personal security and the traditional view that some limited corporal punishment may be necessary in the course of a child's education. Under that longstanding accommodation of interests, there can be no deprivation of substantive rights as long as disciplinary corporal punishment is within the limits of the common law privilege.

This is not to say the child's interest in procedural safeguards is unsubstantial. . . . In any deliberate infliction of corporal punishment on a child who is restrained for that purpose, there is some risk that the intrusion on the child's liberty will be unjustified and therefore unlawful. In these circumstances the child has a strong interest in procedural safeguards that minimize the risk of wrongful punishment and provide for the resolution of disputed questions of justification.

We turn now to a consideration of the safeguards that are available under applicable Florida law.

2

Florida has continued to recognize, and indeed has strengthened by statute, the common law right of a child not to be subjected to excessive corporal punishment in school. Under Florida law the teacher and principal of the school decide in the first instance whether corporal punishment is reasonably necessary under the circumstances in order to discipline a child who has misbehaved. But they must exercise prudence and restraint. For Florida has preserved the traditional judicial proceedings for determining whether the punishment was justified. If the punishment inflicted is later found to have been excessive — not reasonably believed at the time to be necessary for the child's discipline or training — the school authorities inflicting it may be held liable in damages to the child and, if malice is shown, they may be subject to criminal penalties.[89]

89. [The Court cited relevant Florida civil and criminal statutes.] Both the District Court, . . . and the Court of Appeals, . . . expressed the view that the common law tort remedy was available to the petitioners in this case. . . .

Although students have testified in this case to specific instances of abuse, there is every reason to believe that such mistreatment is an aberration. The uncontradicted evidence suggests that corporal punishment in the Dade County schools was "[w]ith the exception of a few cases, . . . unremarkable in physical severity." . . . Moreover, because paddlings are usually inflicted in response to conduct directly observed by teachers in their presence, the risk that a child will be paddled without cause is typically insignificant. . . .

In those cases where severe punishment is contemplated, the available civil and criminal sanctions for abuse — considered in light of the openness of the school environment — afford significant protection against unjustified corporal punishment. . . . Teachers and school authorities are unlikely to inflict corporal punishment unnecessarily or excessively when a possible consequence of doing so is the institution of civil or criminal proceedings against them.

3

But even if the need for advance procedural safeguards were clear, the question would remain whether the incremental benefit could justify the cost. Acceptance of petitioners' claims would work a transformation in the law governing corporal punishment in Florida and most other states. Given the impracticability of formulating a rule of procedural due process that varies with the severity of the particular imposition,[90] the prior hearing petitioners seek would have to precede *any* paddling, however moderate or trivial.

Such a universal constitutional requirement would significantly burden the use of corporal punishment as a disciplinary measure. Hearings — even informal hearings — require time, personnel, and a diversion of attention from normal school pursuits. School authorities may well choose to abandon corporal punishment rather than incur the burdens of complying with the procedural requirements. Teachers, properly concerned with maintaining authority in the classroom, may well prefer to rely on other disciplinary measures — which they may view as less effective — rather than confront the possible disruption that prior notice and a hearing may entail. Paradoxically, such an alteration of disciplinary policy is most likely to occur in the ordinary case where the contemplated punishment is well within the common law privilege.[91]

Elimination or curtailment of corporal punishment would be welcomed by many as a societal advance. But when such a policy choice may result from this Court's determination of an asserted right to due process, rather than from the normal

90. "[P]rocedural due process rules are shaped by the risk of error inherent in the truth-finding process as applied to the generality of cases, not the rare exceptions. . . ." Mathews v. Eldridge, 424 U.S., at 344. . . .

91. The effect of interposing prior procedural safeguards may well be to make the punishment more severe by increasing the anxiety of the child. For this reason, the school authorities in Dade County found it desirable that the punishment be inflicted as soon as possible after the infraction. . . .

processes of community debate and legislative action, the societal costs cannot be dismissed as insubstantial. We are reviewing here a legislative judgment, rooted in history and reaffirmed in the laws of many States, that corporal punishment serves important educational interests. . . .

"At some point the benefit of an additional safeguard to the individual affected . . . and to society in terms of increased assurance that the action is just, may be outweighed by the cost." Mathews v. Eldridge, 424 U.S., at 348. . . . We think that point has been reached in this case. We conclude that the Due Process Clause does not require notice and a hearing prior to the imposition of corporal punishment in the public schools, as that practice is authorized and limited by the common law.

Mr. Justice WHITE, with whom Mr. Justice BRENNAN, Mr. Justice MARSHALL, and Mr. Justice STEVENS join, dissenting.

The Court now holds that [the] "rudimentary precautions against unfair or mistaken findings of misconduct," [imposed in Goss] are not required if the student is punished with "appreciable physical pain" rather than with a suspension, even though both punishments deprive the student of a constitutionally protected interest. Although the respondent school authorities provide absolutely no process to the student before the punishment is finally inflicted, the majority concludes that the student is nonetheless given due process because he can later sue the teacher and recover damages if the punishment was "excessive."

This tort action is utterly inadequate to protect against erroneous infliction of punishment for two reasons. First, under Florida law, a student punished for an act he did not commit cannot recover damages for a teacher "proceeding in utmost good faith . . . on the reports and advice of others" . . . ; the student has no remedy at all for punishment imposed on the basis of mistaken facts, at least as long as the punishment was reasonable from the point of view of the disciplinarian, uninformed by any prior hearing. The "traditional common law remedies" on which the majority relies . . . thus do nothing to protect the student from the danger that concerned the Court in Goss — the risk of reasonable, good faith mistake in the school disciplinary process.

Second, and more important, even if the student could sue for good faith error in the infliction of punishment, the lawsuit occurs after the punishment has been finally imposed. The infliction of physical pain is final and irreparable; it cannot be undone in a subsequent proceeding.

The majority's conclusion that a damage remedy for excessive corporal punishment affords adequate process rests on the novel theory that the State may punish an individual without giving him any opportunity to present his side of the story, as long as he can later recover damages from a state official if he is innocent. The logic of this theory would permit a State that punished speeding with a one-day jail sentence to make a driver serve his sentence first without a trial and then sue to recover damages for wrongful imprisonment. Similarly, the State could finally take away a prisoner's good time credits for alleged disciplinary infractions and require him to bring a damage suit after he was eventually released. There is no authority for this theory, nor does the majority purport to find any, in the procedural due process decisions of this Court. . . .

The majority emphasizes, as did the dissenters in *Goss*, that even the "rudimentary precautions" required by that decision would impose some burden on the school disciplinary process. But those costs are no greater if the student is paddled rather than suspended; the risk of error in the punishment is no smaller . . . The disciplinarian need only take a few minutes to give the student "notice of the charges against him and, if he denies them, an explanation of the evidence the authorities have and an opportunity to present his side of the story." [Quoting *Goss*.]

[Justice Stevens also entered a separate dissenting opinion, acknowledging that in some cases a post-deprivation hearing might satisfy due process, particularly where the controversy involved property interest whose deprivation could more readily be redressed by damage awards. As support for this view, he cited Ewing v. Mytinger & Casselberry, 339 U.S. 594 (1950) and Phillips v. Commissioner, 283 U.S. 589 (1931), described at pp. 476-477, supra. He also suggested that the result in Paul v. Davis, supra p. 648, might be justified by the availability of a state tort remedy for official defamation. However, he concluded that in the present case post-discipline remedies had not been shown to afford an adequate safeguard against or redress for unjustified corporal punishment.]

Notes and Questions

1. Compare Memphis Light, Gas, and Water Division v. Craft, 436 U.S. 1 (1978). In *Craft* the plaintiffs, whose electricity service had been terminated for nonpayment of a disputed bill, brought suit under 42 U.S.C. §1983 against officers and employees of the municipal utility[92] responsible for the termination. After ruling that under Tennessee law there exists an entitlement to uninterrupted service where a customer has refused to pay a bill which is the object of a bona fide dispute between the utility and the customer, and that this entitlement represents a "property" interest protected by due process, the Court went on to consider what process was due. It concluded that the administrative procedures afforded by the utility for resolving disputes prior to service termination were inadequate, and that this deficiency was not cured by the potential availability under state law of direct judicial remedies for improper termination of service:

> Petitioners contend that the available common-law remedies of a pretermination injunction, a post-termination suit for damages, and post-payment action for a refund are sufficient to cure any perceived inadequacy in MLG&W's procedures. Ordinarily, due process of law requires an opportunity

92. Since Memphis Light was a government-owned utility, this case did not present the question whether actions taken by a public utility which is not owned by the government but which enjoys a governmentally-conferred monopoly and obligation of service in a given area are "state action" for the purposes of the Fourteenth Amendment. See Note, Fourteenth Amendment Due Process in Terminations of Utility Services, 86 Harv. L. Rev. 1477 (1973); Jackson v. Metropolitan Edison Co., 419 U.S. 345 (1974); Taylor v. Con. Ed. of NY, Inc., 552 F.2d 39 (2d Cir.), *cert. denied*, 434 U.S. 845 (1977).

for "some kind of hearing" prior to the deprivation of a significant property interest.... On occasion, this Court has recognized that where the potential length or severity of the deprivation does not indicate a likelihood of serious loss and where the procedures underlying the decision to act are sufficiently reliable to minimize the risk of erroneous determination, government may act without providing additional "advance procedural safeguards," Ingraham v. Wright, 430 U.S. 651, 680 (1977)....

The factors that have justified exceptions to the requirement of some prior process are not present here. Although utility service may be restored ultimately, the cessation of essential services for any appreciable time works a uniquely final deprivation.... Moreover, the probability of error in utility cut-off decisions is not so insubstantial as to warrant dispensing with all process prior to termination.

The injunction remedy referred to by petitioner would not be an adequate substitute for a pre-termination review of the disputed bill with a designated employee. Many of the Court's decisions in this area have required additional procedures to further due process, notwithstanding the apparent availability of injunctive relief or recovery provisions. It was thought that such remedies were likely to be too bounded by procedural constraints and too susceptible to delay to provide an effective safeguard against an erroneous deprivation. These considerations are applicable in the utility termination context.

Judicial remedies are particularly unsuited to the resolution of factual disputes typically involving sums of money too small to justify engaging counsel or bringing a lawsuit. An action in equity to halt an improper termination, because it is less likely to be pursued and less likely to be effective, even if pursued, will not provide the same assurance of accurate decisionmaking as would an adequate administrative procedure. In these circumstances, an informal administrative remedy, along the lines suggested above, constitutes the process that is "due."

[Justice Stevens filed a dissenting opinion joined by Chief Justice Burger and Justice Rehnquist. The majority responded to one of the dissent's arguments as follows:]

... The dissent intimates that due process was satisfied in this case because "a customer can always avoid termination by the simple expedient of paying the disputed bill and claiming a refund...." This point ignores the predicament confronting many individuals who lack the means to pay additional, unanticipated utility expenses.

2. Compare *Ingraham* and *Memphis Light* with earlier decisions evaluating the need for pre-deprivation administrative proceedings in light of potential state law court remedies. See, e.g., North American Cold Storage Co. v. Chicago, supra p. 472; Southern Ry. v. Virginia, supra p. 468. Are those decisions still good law?

What sort of data would a court require in order to determine whether post-deprivation court remedies would either provide adequate deterrence against administrative infringements of constitutionally protected "liberty" or "property" interests or adequate compensation for those infringements that did occur? By what evaluative criteria would "adequacy" be judged? In recognizing post-deprivation court remedies as a possible alternative to pre-deprivation administrative remedies, does *Ingraham* introduce unmanageable complexity into the "what process is due" calculation?

3. Contrast with *Ingraham* the Court's recognition of post-deprivation administrative remedies as a factor to be weighed in assessing the constitutional adequacy of pre-deprivation administrative procedures. Consider, for example, the respective significance accorded in Goldberg v. Kelly, supra pp. 613-620, and Mathews v. Eldridge, supra pp. 667-671, to the availability of a post-deprivation trial-type administrative hearing and retroactive payment of improperly terminated benefits. See also Dixon v. Love, 431 U.S. 105 (1977), sustaining summary revocation of an Illinois truck driver's license on the basis of administrative records showing that the driver's license had been suspended on three separate occasions within 10 years and an administrative regulation authorizing license revocation in such circumstances. A full trial-type administrative hearing was available after revocation became effective; the Court found this to be adequate protection in view of the circumstances that the deprivation was less severe than *Goldberg*; that the revocation decision was relatively automatic in character and the likelihood of administrative error in determining whether the requisite number of suspensions had occurred was low; and that Illinois had a strong interest in removing unsafe or irresponsible drivers from its highways immediately.[93]

The Court's opinion seems to rule out "process" or "dignity" values as a factor in determining what process is due. Noting that the licensee had not disputed the existence of valid suspensions justifying revocation of his license, it found that "he is really asserting the right to appear in person only to argue that the Secretary should show leniency." The Court concluded that:

> Such an appearance might make the licensee feel that he has received more personal attention, but it would not serve to protect any substantive rights. We conclude that requiring additional procedures would be unlikely to have significant value in reducing the number of erroneous deprivations.

---

93. Compare Bell v. Burson, 402 U.S. 535 (1971), invalidating as contrary to due process a Georgia statute providing for automatic revocation of the registration and driver's license of an uninsured motorist involved in an accident, regardless of his fault or responsibility for the accident, unless the motorist presented a release from liability plus proof of future financial responsibility, or presented security for the amount of damages claimed by other parties to the accident. Plaintiff had unsuccessfully sought a hearing on his claims that he had not been at fault and that continued use of his car was essential to his work as a minister. The Court held that he was entitled to a hearing on the question of his likely liability in damages for the amounts claimed by the other party to the accident. Query: Isn't the Court's procedural ruling based on a substantive determination that it is impossible for Georgia to exclude consideration of fault or likely liability from the revocation decision? Does the decision show how procedural due process can evolve into substantive due process?

Hahn v. Gottlieb

430 F.2d 1243 (1st Cir. 1970)

COFFIN, Circuit Judge.

I. STATUTORY SCHEME

[Plaintiffs, tenants in a privately owned low- and middle-income housing project subsidized by the federal government under §221(d)(3) of the National Housing Act, protested a $28 per month rent increase which the owners proposed to impose on each apartment in the project, and sought an oral evidentiary hearing before local officials of the Federal Housing Administration (FHA) which was required to approve the increase. The FHA denied a hearing and approved the increase. The plaintiffs brought suit in federal district court, asserting a constitutional right to the requested hearing and seeking judicial review of the merits; the district court denied all relief.]

... The general goal of national housing policy is to provide "a decent home and a suitable living environment for every American family." 12 U.S.C. §§ 1441, 1441a. Section 221(d)(3) seeks to implement this goal by assisting "private industry in providing housing for low and moderate income families and displaced families." 12 U.S.C. §1715l(a). This assistance to the private sector takes two forms. First, the FHA provides insurance on long-term mortgage loans covering up to 90 percent of the project's cost, thus encouraging private investment in projects which would otherwise be too risky. Second, eligible borrowers can obtain below-market interest rates on FHA-insured loans, thus reducing the rentals necessary to service the landlord's debt obligation. 12 U.S.C. §1715l(d)(5).

To administer this two-pronged program, the statute confers broad discretion to the Secretary of HUD. The Secretary is authorized to approve mortgagors and to supervise their operations "under a regulatory agreement or otherwise, as to rents, charges, and methods of operation, in such form and in such manner as in the opinion of the Secretary will effectuate the purposes of this section." 12 U.S.C. §1715l(d)(3)....

Implementing these broad grants of authority, the Secretary has promulgated regulations concerning priorities and income limits for occupancy in §221(d)(3) projects. 24 C.F.R. §221.537. The Secretary also regulates the landlord's return on his investment by strictly supervising accounting practices, 24 C.F.R. §221.531(b), and, in the case of limited distribution mortgagors like defendants Gottlieb and Druker, by setting a six percent ceiling on return. 24 C.F.R. §221.532(a). Applications for rent increases must be submitted to the FHA, which takes into account the rental income necessary to maintain a project's economic soundness and "to provide a reasonable return on the investment consistent with providing reasonable rentals to the tenants." 24 C.F.R. §221.531(c). FHA's agreement with the landlord in this case further provides that rental increases will be approved if necessary to compensate for increases in expense "over which the owners have no effective control."

These regulations illustrate that the success of a §221(d)(3) project requires a flexible exercise of administrative discretion. . . . Of course, the need for administrative flexibility does not of itself preclude an agency hearing or judicial review, but we must take care lest we kill the goose in our solicitude for the eggs.

II. RIGHT TO A HEARING

. . . Broadly speaking, resolution of this claim requires us to balance the interests of the government in the procedure adopted against the citizen's interest in greater safeguards. Goldberg v. Kelly. . . .

In this case, as we have seen, the primary role of the government is that of insurer for private investors. The government attempts to regulate its contractual relations with mortgagors in order to advance public welfare, but its freedom to pursue social goals is limited by the need to avoid excessive losses. While the government may have less freedom as an insurer than it does as an employer, compare Cafeteria & Restaurant Workers Union v. McElroy, . . . the government needs considerable procedural flexibility in either case.

The private interest affected, on the other hand, is the interest of low and middle income families in housing they can afford. The government has not, however, undertaken to provide this assistance directly under the §221(d)(3) program. Instead, the government provides a limited subsidy to private landlords, who then enter an ordinary lease arrangement with eligible tenants. Plaintiffs are not legally "entitled" to low rents in the same sense that the welfare recipient in Goldberg v. Kelly, supra, was entitled to basic sustenance under a system of categorical assistance. . . . Moreover, the tenant's interest is not directly jeopardized each time the FHA approves a rent increase. The increase may be small, and rent supplement programs are available to those in greatest need. Thus the government action in this case poses a less serious threat to the private interest involved than the termination of welfare benefits in Goldberg v. Kelly, supra. . . .

The proceeding in which plaintiffs seek to assert their interest is basically an informal rate-making process. The landlord who seeks a rent increase submits documentation to the FHA, showing his expenses, return on investment, and the like. The FHA staff then examines his proposal in the light of the terms of the regulatory agreement, the broad criteria of the regulations, and current economic conditions. Plaintiffs seek to encumber these negotiations with a formal hearing, the right to cross-examine adverse witnesses, and an impartial decision-maker, who must state the reasons for his decision and the evidence on which he relies. These procedural safeguards are characteristic of adjudicatory proceedings, where the outcome turns on accurate resolution of specific factual disputes. . . . Such safeguards are not, however, essential in "legislative" proceedings, such as rate-making, where decision depends on broad familiarity with economic conditions. . . . As Professor Davis has pointed out, when decision turns on "legislative" rather than "adjudicative" facts, a formal adversary hearing may contribute little or nothing to the agency's understanding of the issues. 1 K. Davis, Administrative Law §7.02 at 413 (1958).

The distinction between "legislative" and "adjudicative" facts is particularly apt in this case, where it is the tenants rather than the landlord who seek a hearing. The tenants are unlikely to have special familiarity with their landlord's financial condition, the intricacies of project management, or the state of the economy in the surrounding area. Hopefully, the FHA can check the accuracy of the landlord's documentation without their assistance. They may be aware of construction defects in their own living areas, but if, contrary to §1715*l*(d)(2), a building has been approved which does not conform to applicable standards, there would seem to be limited utility in rehearsing old mistakes each time a rental increase is sought. Of course, tenants' complaints about maintenance and living conditions ought to be heard, but such grievances can be dealt with without requiring a trial-type hearing with each rent increase. Indeed, an effective grievance system should be operable at all times, not merely when the landlord seeks to raise his rents. Thus the elaborate procedural safeguards which plaintiffs demand are unlikely to elicit essential information in the general run of cases.

These procedures would, however, place a significant burden on the relationship between the landlord and the FHA. At present, applications for rent increases are merely one aspect of an on-going relationship between insured and insurer. Plaintiffs would turn these applications into occasions for full-scale review of the relationship, as their conduct in the hearing they have already received illustrates. Such reconsideration may delay economically necessary rent increases and discourage private investors from entering the §221(d)(3) program at all. Equally important, the project in question contains some 500 tenants, each of whom has the same interest in low-rent housing. As Justice Holmes pointed out in Bi-Metallic Investment Co. v. State Bd. of Equalization, 239 U.S. 441 . . . (1915): "Where a rule of conduct applies to more than a few people it is impracticable that every one should have a direct voice in its adoption. The Constitution does not require all public acts to be done in a town meeting or an assembly of the whole." Accord, Bowles v. Willingham, 321 U.S. 503, 519, 64 S. Ct. 641, 649, 88 L. Ed. 892 (1944).

Applying the constitutionally relevant test, therefore, it seems to us that the government interest in a summary procedure for approving rent increases outweighs the tenants' interest in greater procedural safeguards. The procedures demanded by plaintiffs would place substantial additional burden on the insurer-insured relationship without necessarily improving the fundamental fairness of the proceedings. We therefore hold that tenants in housing financed under §221(d)(3) of the National Housing Act are not constitutionally entitled to an administrative hearing on their landlord's proposals for increased rents.

[Portions of Part III of the Court's opinion, ruling against the availability of federal review of the substantive merits of FHA's approval of the rent increase, are omitted here but will be considered in Chapter 9.]

Our decision will not, we hope, discourage efforts to develop effective procedures for the airing of tenant grievances. See, e.g., Symposium, Citizen Participation — Challenge to HUD, 2 Urban Lawyer 1, 39 (1970). We have considerable sympathy for the plight of those who must submit to the fiat of a large and sometimes insensitive bureaucracy. We realize that agencies ostensibly dedicated to the public welfare can sometimes become preoccupied with the needs of their immediate clients, thus promoting what one cynic has described as "socialism for the rich and free enterprise for the poor." And we suspect that, the larger the bureaucracy, the more need there is for instituting procedures of communication and participation for those it is intended to serve — as a means of making better decisions in a more tranquil atmosphere. At the same time, we must also recognize that the achievement of a fair and effective housing program is inescapably in legislative and administrative hands. Accommodating procedures for tenant participation to the needs of effective housing management is, we think, primarily a task for Congress and the FHA, not the courts.

Affirmed.

Questions

1. Why isn't the short answer to plaintiffs' hearing claim that the government's action consists of rulemaking, and that there is no constitutional right to a hearing in rulemaking? Recall the *Florida East Coast* decision, supra p. 481. Is the traditional rule that there is no due process right to procedural safeguards in rulemaking consistent with *Roth, Eldridge,* and the other decisions considered in this chapter? [94]

2. How persuasive do you find the court's use of the legislative/adjudicative fact distinction to deny a hearing? Is the distinction relevant and useful in determining how much process is due "new property"?

3. Doesn't the court's opinion in *Hahn* rest ultimately on a judgment that hearing rights might jeopardize the success of the program in question? Might not the same concern justify denial of hearing rights in school discipline, prison administration, and many other contexts?

4. Note the conclusion of Judge Coffin's opinion, expressing the hope that some workable procedures can be found to permit expression of tenant views. Is that simply wishful thinking? Will agencies have any incentives to devise such procedures unless courts hold that they are constitutionally required? Consider the recent wave of "rent strikes" in public housing projects. Should courts hold that some procedures for expression of tenant views are constitutionally required, but permit the agency to devise appropriate procedures — perhaps nonjudicial in character — in the first instance?

---

94. See generally Sinaiko, Due Process Rights of Participation in Administrative Rulemaking, 63 Cal. L. Rev. 886 (1975). Cf. Tribe, American Constitutional Law 503-504 (1978), arguing that whether one accepts an "instrumental" or an "intrinsic" view of the purposes of due process, the case for additional safeguards becomes greater the more "government acts in a way that singles out identifiable individuals."

Note that APA §553 notice and comment procedures are not required in *Hahn* because of the 553(a) exemption for matters relating to government loans, grants, or benefits.

Review Questions

1. Section 2057 of the Ames Traffic Code authorizes the State Police to tow any vehicles illegally parked on state roads. Owners of towed vehicles can reclaim their cars by (1) paying the traffic ticket plus towing and storage charges, or (2) requesting a hearing at which the question of whether the car was in fact illegally parked will be litigated. Because of the congested dockets of the administrative agency which has been authorized by statute to conduct such hearings, several months typically pass between the times the hearings are requested and the times they are held. If the owner of the car chooses to pay the money and retrieve his or her car immediately, and if he or she requests a subsequent hearing at which it is established that the car was not in fact illegally parked, then the money is returned.

On April 23, Dr. Leslie Smith's car was towed while parked in front of a fire hydrant. Instead of either requesting a hearing or ransoming her car, Dr. Smith filed a suit against the Ames State Police in federal District Court under 42 U.S.C. §1983, alleging that when her car was towed, she was making an emergency medical call. Ames Traffic Code section 2133 exempts from all parking regulations doctors making such calls. Dr. Smith claimed that the towing of the car deprived her of life, liberty, and property without due process of law. She also claimed that the loss of her car has impaired her ability to make housecalls and has thereby resulted in losses to her of some $750 in professional fees. What due process claims might she assert in a §1983 lawsuit, and how should they be decided? [95]

2. Robert Sherrill, who has been the Washington correspondent for *The Nation* for many years and who has at all relevant times had credentials for the House and Senate press galleries, applied for and was denied a White House press pass. The denial resulted solely from the determination of the Secret Service, after investigating Mr. Sherrill, that he not be issued the pass. A memorandum from the Secret Service to then White House Press Secretary Moyers requested that the background information obtained about Mr. Sherrill upon which this determination was based "not be disclosed to Mr. Sherrill or his employer."

Although there exist no written procedures pertaining to the issuance of press passes for the White House, it was established in the District Court that these passes are routinely obtained in the following manner. A journalist submits a request for a pass to the White House Press Office. After determining that the applicant has obtained a pass for the House and Senate press galleries, resides in the Washington, D.C. area, and needs to report from the White House on a regular basis (the latter usually being verified by an editor of the publication for which the applicant is a correspondent), the Press Office forwards the application to the Secret Service for a security check, including a background FBI investigation. Whether a pass is then issued depends solely on the recommendation of the Secret Service. There exist no published or internal regulations stating the criteria upon which a White

---

95. What damages might she collect? Ignore any issues of official immunity which might be involved. For related cases, see Stypmann v. City and County of San Francisco, 557 F.2d 1338 (9th Cir. 1977); Carey v. Piphus, 435 U.S. 247 (1978).

House press pass security clearance is based. When Mr. Sherrill asked why he had been rejected, Secret Service personnel replied that "We can't tell you the reasons."

What relief, if any, may Mr. Sherrill obtain through litigation challenging denial of a White House press pass? [98]

D.   Due Process in Particular Contexts

This section briefly reviews Supreme Court and lower federal court due process decisions in the areas of public assistance, housing, public employment, education, and prisons.[97] In reviewing these materials, you should keep the following questions in mind:

— To what extent are discrepancies between decisions in different subject areas explicable in terms of various "inarticulate factors"; in particular, sympathy or lack of sympathy with the substantive purposes of particular agencies and programs?

— Have the lower courts achieved consistent results in applying recent Supreme Court decisions? In what areas is clarification from the Court most needed?

— Has the threshold test of *Roth,* as elaborated in subsequent Supreme Court decisions, and the balancing test of Mathews v. Eldridge provided a manageable, consistent framework for due process litigation? Is it possible, either in theory or in practice, to separate the determination of what interests are protected by due process from the determination of what process is due?

96. See Sherrill v. Knight, 569 F.2d 124 (D.C. Cir. 1977).

97. Also note that the Court has decided at least four major cases in the last decade dealing with the applicability of due process safeguards to prejudgment attachment, garnishment, replevin, and detinue — devices primarily invoked by creditors who are contemplating legal action against defaulting debtors and who wish to seize or immobilize some of the debtor's property pending a final judgment in such an action. These decisions will not be discussed in detail here since they deal with controls on judicial rather than administrative action (although there are many instructive parallels between the two, and although it is possible to view the court system [with its attendant bureaucracy of clerks, sheriffs, and marshalls] as an administrative agency). The decisions include Sniadach v. Family Finance Corporation, 395 U.S. 337 (1969) (invalidating a state statute allowing prejudgment garnishment of debtors' wages without a prior hearing); Fuentes v. Shevin, 407 U.S. 67 (1972) (invalidating a state statute permitting prejudgment replevin of goods in which the creditor had retained a security interest); Mitchell v. W. T. Grant Co., 416 U.S. 600 (1974) (upholding validity of Louisiana statute authorizing prejudgment seizure of goods by a secured creditor where the statute called for immediate post-seizure hearing plus other safeguards designed to minimize risk of erroneous seizure); and North Georgia Finishing, Inc. v. Di-Chem, Inc., 419 U.S. 601 (1975) (invalidating a garnishment statute which failed to provide the *Mitchell* safeguards). The Court has consistently recognized the interest of the debtor in retaining possession of funds or goods as "property" for purposes of the due process clause. On the question of what process is due, however, the opinions have vacillated considerably, reflecting in part the circumstances that the four opinions straddled a major change in the composition of the Court, a fact noted with some irritation by Justice Stewart in his dissenting opinion in *Mitchell,* 416 U.S., at 635 and n.8.

— To what extent are courts faced, in various areas, with a tension between procedural justice in individual cases and other, broader policy concerns? [98]
— In what contexts do courts feel that procedures such as cross-examination or oral presentation of evidence are or are not needed? Why?
— Have lower court decisions justified the Supreme Court's fear that if due process rights are interpreted too broadly, local law will be "federalized," particularly via §1983 actions? Is such federalization undesirable?
— Have the lower courts shown any signs of adopting a "process" or "dignitary" view of due process?

1. Public Assistance Payments

(Review Goldberg v. Kelly, supra, p. 613; Mathews v. Eldridge, supra, p. 667; and discussions appended thereto).

a. Post-*Goldberg* Decisions

Following *Goldberg*, the lower courts were soon faced with a variety of public assistance cases brought by recipient-plaintiffs whose need was seemingly not quite so pressing as that of the AFDC (Aid for Dependent Children) claimants in *Goldberg*.

98. Consider the following excerpt from Stewart, The Reformation of American Administrative Law, 88 Harv. L. Rev. 1667, 1721-22 (1975):

In bipolar controversies, it is still possible to conceive of administrative law as mediating claims of private autonomy and governmental authority. While traditional notions of autonomy would not encompass a person's demands for assistance payments or for continued employment from the government, proponents of the "due process revolution" have assumed that the transition from the right to be let alone to the right to maintain certain basic advantageous relations with government can be accomplished without undue strain on the logic or operation of the traditional model [of administrative law]. The objective is still the maintenance of some sphere of private advantage by prohibiting unauthorized governmental conduct. The mechanics of forbidding a government official from withdrawing an entitlement seem little different in form from forbidding the imposition of an unauthorized tax, since the controversy is on-off in form, and seems to fit within the familiar paradigm of adjudication.

Such appearances may, however, be misleading, particularly when the procedural protections afforded concern, as they frequently do, governmental advantages that are limited in comparison to the demand for them — public housing, government employment, educational scholarships. For in such cases distributional decisions lurk right under the surface of formally bipolar procedural issues. If trial-type procedural requirements make it difficult to evict existing tenants in public housing, or terminate assistance payments to present recipients, it may be more difficult for new applicants to obtain such benefits. Moreover, the right to invoke procedural protections will give recipients of governmental benefits a degree of bargaining leverage over decisions of agency policy, a consideration which suggests that the extension of due process safeguards to termination of welfare assistance payments, or prison disciplines, or suspensions from school of student demonstrators, may be grounded as much in a perceived need to impose a counterweight to bias in administrative policies as in concern to promote more accurate fact finding in individual cases.

For example, does *Goldberg* require a hearing where benefits are reduced rather than terminated, or where requested increases are not granted? Hunt v. Edmunds, 328 F. Supp. 468 (D. Minn. 1971), concluded that reduction of AFDC benefits without notice and hearing did violate due process, relying on (a) a "brutal need" on the part of the plaintiff, and (b) the fact that "the decision turns on the resolution of an issue on which the recipient himself may have something to add in an evidentiary way." Failure to grant requested AFDC increases was subjected to a hearing requirement in Banner v. Smolenski, 315 F. Supp. 1076 (D. Mass. 1970). (However, *Banner* refused to require the agency to give the plaintiff access to his case record in preparation for the denial hearing.) [99]

Some courts declined to extend the *Goldberg* requirement of prior oral hearings to cases that involved retirement, disability, or unemployment payments, as opposed to the welfare assistance payments at issue in *Goldberg, Hunt,* and *Banner,* reasoning that "brutal need" was not present.[100] But other courts did not agree, although there was often a wide disparity of views as to what procedures were required for particular programs.[101]

b. Lower Court Decisions Since Mathews v. Eldridge

To what extent has Mathews v. Eldridge resolved the uncertainties generated by *Goldberg?*

The lower courts have displayed considerable variation in applying the calculus utilized by Justice Powell in *Eldridge;* the critical variable appears to be the assessment of the claimant's interest or need. In Mattern v. Mathews, 427 F. Supp. 1318

99. Professor Schwartz notes, "It is difficult to justify the termination-reduction distinc-tinction logically," but cautions that "[t]o hold that Goldberg v. Kelly applies to all the welfare cases alluded to by Chief Justice Burger (i.e., reductions, denial of increases, and requests for special assistance) may, however, lead to ludicrous consequences." B. Schwartz, Administrative Law 241 (1976). Some of the ludicrous consequences are described in id., at 242.

100. See, e.g., Anderson v. Finch, 322 F. Supp. 195 (N.D. Ohio, 1971) (no pre-termination hearing required with respect to social security survivor's benefits). This distinction was later embraced in Mathews v. Eldridge, supra, p. 669.

101. Two district court cases required pre-termination *Goldberg* hearings prior to termina-tion of unemployment benefits. Java v. California Department of Human Resources Develop-ment, 317 F. Supp. 875 (N.D. Cal. 1970), and Crow v. California Department of Human Resources Development, 325 F. Supp. 1314 (N.D. Cal. 1970). The Supreme Court affirmed *Java,* 402 U.S. 121 (1971), but did so on statutory grounds and declined to reach the con-stitutional issue. *Crow,* however, was reversed by the Ninth Circuit, 490 F.2d 580 (1973), which upheld the customary procedures, which involved an informal pre-termination hearing and no cross-examination. The court noted that *Crow* was not a grievous loss case, as *Goldberg* was. Formal pre-termination hearings were required in Wheeler v. State of Vermont, 335 F. Supp. 856 (D. Vt. 1971) and Pregent v. New Hampshire Department of Employment Security, 361 F. Supp. 782 (D.N.H. 1973), *vacated and remanded on question of mootness,* 417 U.S. 903 (1974). Less formal pre-termination procedures (consisting primarily of informal consultations) far less rigorous than those required in *Goldberg* were sustained against constitutional challenge in Stone v. Philbrook, 528 F.2d 1084 (2d Cir. 1975); and in Torres v. New York State De-partment of Labor, 333 F. Supp. 341 (S.D.N.Y. 1971), *aff'd. mem.* 405 U.S. 949 (1972). A three judge district court held that Connecticut procedures for the termination of unemploy-ment benefits "were constitutionally defective in failing to provide a pre-termination hearing satisfying the standards of Goldberg v. Kelly . . .", Fusari v. Steinberg, 364 F. Supp. 922 (D. Conn. 1973); the Supreme Court subsequently vacated the decision and remanded for reconsid-eration in light of "intervening changes in Connecticut law." 419 U.S. 379 (1975).

(E.D. Penn 1977), following a remand by the Supreme Court for reconsideration in the light of Mathews v. Eldridge, the district court reversed a previous decision and held that a *Goldberg* hearing was not required prior to administrative recoupment of alleged overpayments of Social Security disability benefits by deducting the overpayments from continuing payments concededly due. The court held that the potential deprivation to the claimant was less than in *Eldridge*, and that the issues involved were more sharply focused and more easily documented. It also asserted that *Goldberg* was now limited to cases concerning the "margin of subsistence." But the Court of Appeal reversed, finding that the *Eldridge* balancing test required a hearing prior to recoupment where claimants requested waiver of recoupment on grounds of hardship. Mattern v. Mathews, 582 F.2d 248 (3rd Cir. 1978). Also relying on *Eldridge*, Graves v. Meystrik, 425 F. Supp. 40 (E.D. Mo.), *aff'd* 431 U.S. 910 (1977), approved existing procedures which provided for hearings after termination of unemployment compensation benefits. The court noted that such benefits were not based on need, that there was a predetermination interview, and that the reversal rate and delay on appeal was less than in *Eldridge*.[102]

But other courts have not read *Eldridge* as authority for limiting *Goldberg* to its facts. Elliott v. Weinberger, 371 F. Supp. 960 (E.D. Hawaii 1974), like Mattern v. Mathews, supra, dealt with the recoupment of social security disability benefits determined to have been overpaid to the beneficiary. The district court held that *Goldberg* applied and that an oral hearing was required prior to recoupment. The Ninth Circuit decided the case on appeal, 564 F.2d 1219 (1977), after *Eldridge* had been decided by the Supreme Court. Applying the Mathews v. Eldridge balancing test, the Court of Appeals found the following: (a) "[T]he strength of the interest of the plaintiffs in the present case lies somewhere between *Eldridge* and *Goldberg*." (b) The value of additional procedures depends upon whether the beneficiary is seeking reconsideration or waiver of the recoupment decision. A reconsideration addresses itself to the factual basis of the recoupment; i.e., the question of whether an overpayment actually occurred. The court found that reconsiderations generally involved arithmetic and documentary questions which generally did not require oral submission of evidence. Waiver is statutorily authorized where the recipient of the overpayment is "without fault" and if recoupment "would defeat the purpose of [the disability payments program] or would be against equity and good conscience." The court concluded that these determinations required an individualized assessment that would be promoted by an oral hearing. (c) The government's administrative and financial interest in denying an oral hearing is not compelling. Applying (a), (b), and (c), the court concluded that claimants requesting a reconsideration were not entitled to a prior oral hearing, but waiver claimants were.[103]

102. See also McGrath v. Weinberger, 541 F.2d 249 (10th Cir. 1976), *cert. denied*, 430 U.S. 933 (1977), which dealt with the SSA procedures whereby a beneficiary may be determined to be incapable of managing his assets and a "representative payee" appointed. Applying the Mathews v. Eldridge balance, the court held that no prior hearing was required.
103. At the hearing, the waiver claimant would be entitled to the right to present his or her case orally and to submit evidence, the right to cross examine, the right to be represented by counsel, the right to an impartial hearing officer, the right to a statement of reasons, and the right to receive adequate notice of the recoupment and of the beneficiary's procedural rights and options.

In other contexts as well, many courts have found ways to distinguish *Eldridge*. Himmler v. Weinberger, 422 F. Supp. 196 (E.D. Mich. 1976), found that the needs of an indigent Medicare benefits claimant were more like those of the claimants in *Goldberg* than in *Eldridge*. The court held that where the claimant's physician and a review committee had certified that the claimant's in-patient treatment was medically necessary, an oral hearing must be held before a decision is made not to pay for the treatment. In Johnson v. Matthews, 539 F.2d 1111 (8th Cir. 1976), the court held that notice and an evidentiary hearing was required before the termination of Supplemental Security Income benefits (SSI). The court noted that SSI benefits were cited by the Supreme Court in Eldridge as an alternative source of governmental assistance, and concluded that the private interest "approaches if not equals, the interest found in *Goldberg*." Further, the recipient was given no opportunity to submit information to the decisionmaker before termination, as in *Eldridge*. *Accord*, Tatum v. Mathews, 541 F.2d 161 (6th Cir. 1976).

In Basel v. Knebel, 551 F.2d 395 (D.C. Cir. 1977), the Court of Appeals reversed the decision of the district court approving agency regulations for the termination of food stamp benefits and remanded the case for reconsideration in light of *Eldridge*. The trial court had concluded that the plaintiff was not in "brutal need," based apparently on its sole finding that the average food stamp recipient's bonus is only $17.45 per month. The Court of Appeals stated that consideration of *Eldridge*'s three factors required a much broader factual inquiry than that made by the district court,[104] pointed out that food stamp program was based on need, and that in *Eldridge* the Supreme Court had mentioned food stamps as an alternative source of government aid.

Questions:

Do these decisions indicate that *Eldridge* has not greatly restrained lower court efforts to deal with perceived inadequacies in governmental assistance programs by imposing procedural formalities? Do they suggest that the lower federal courts are concerned about objectives other than accuracy?

2. Public Housing

a. Nonrenewal of Leases

In most public housing projects funded under the National Housing Act, leases range from periods of between a month and a year, and either party could elect not to renew. Contemporaneous with *Goldberg* are decisions that public

---

104. In assessing the adequacy of existing procedures, federal courts have been forced to immerse themselves in the details of bureaucratic administration. See, e.g., Perez v. Lavine, 412 F. Supp. 1340 (S.D.N.Y. 1976) (methods for distributing claim forms); Barrett v. Roberts, 551 F.2d 662 (5th Cir. 1977) (cost of modifying computer programs for payment procedures).

housing authorities may not refuse to renew a tenant's lease without a *Goldberg*-type prior hearing.[105] These decisions were challenged following the Supreme Court's decision in *Roth*, on the ground that since there was generally no requirement in applicable statutes and regulations that leases be renewed, tenants had no constitutionally protected "property" interest in continued tenancy. However, lower courts continued to require hearings prior to nonrenewal, on the ground that the purposes of the National Housing Act in providing decent housing, together with the customary administrative practice in renewing almost all leases, conferred upon tenants a constitutionally-protected "property" interest in continued occupancy until the housing administration established "good cause" for nonrenewal.[106]

Questions:

Is this rationale consistent with Bishop v. Wood and other more recent Supreme Court decisions?

Given that there are generally long waiting lines of qualified persons seeking admission to limited public housing facilities, is there less justification for procedural formalities in tenancy nonrenewals than in *Goldberg*? Is there a danger that limiting nonrenewal to "cause" provable at a hearing will interfere with the legitimate interests of most existing tenants by unduly limiting officials' ability to exclude disruptive tenants?

b. Applications for Tenancy

Courts have divided on whether an evidentiary hearing is required on initial applications for public housing tenancy.[107]

c. Rent Increases in Federally Subsidized Housing

Review Hahn v. Gottlieb, pp. 683-686, supra. In addition to the subsidy program involved in *Hahn*, which was established under §221 of the National Housing Act, there are numerous other programs of direct or indirect federal assistance for

105. Escalera v. New York Housing Authority, 425 F.2d 853 (2d Cir.), *cert. denied,* 400 U.S. 853 (1970); Caulder v. Durham Housing Authority, 433 F.2d 998 (4th Cir.), *cert. denied,* 401 U.S. 1003 (1971).

106. Joy v. Daniels, 479 F.2d 1236 (4th Cir. 1973); Lopez v. Henry Phipps Plaza South, Inc., 498 F.2d 937 (2d Cir. 1974). See also Anderson v. Denny, 365 F. Supp. 1254 (W.D. Va. 1973); Green v. Copperstone Limited Partnership, 28 Md. App. 498, 346 A.2d 686 (1975).

107. Davis v. Toledo Metropolitan Housing Authority, 311 F. Supp. 795 (N.D. Ohio 1970), and Neddo v. Housing Authority of City of Milwaukee, 335 F. Supp. 1397 (E.D. Wisc. 1971) believed that *Goldberg* compelled an evidentiary hearing before applications could be denied. But in Sumter v. White Plains Housing Authority, 29 N.Y.2d 420, 278 N.E.2d 892, *cert. denied,* 406 U.S. 928 (1972), the court rejected an applicant's claim to an evidentiary hearing, holding sufficient a statutorily-required personal interview at which the applicant was informed of the reason for the denial. Which is the better view?

specified categories of eligible tenants.[108] Particularly where the subsidy is indirect, as in *Hahn*, difficult problems regarding the availability of due process procedural rights are presented.

In Langevin v. Chenango Court, Inc., 447 F.2d 296 (2d Cir. 1971) (a section 221 case), Judge Friendly's opinion for the court reached the same result as in *Hahn* on similar facts. Unlike the court in *Hahn*, Judge Friendly believed that the facts in issue were primarily "adjudicative," but agreed that hearing rights might jeopardize the success of the BMIR (Below Mortgage Interest Rate) program.[109] Judge Friendly also stressed that the government "did not itself increase the rents, but simply allowed the landlord to institute an increase upon termination of existing tenancies." He held that the due process clause did not forbid Congress from placing the rent increase decision with the landlords, subject to discretionary review by FHA pursuant to its regulatory agreement with them, rather than requiring the government to make rent decisions, an alternative which would trigger hearing rights. Other §221 cases have reached the same result.[110]

Two circuits have held that tenants are entitled to participate in the decision to raise rents of subsidized housing. The Court of Appeals for the District of Columbia found that the purposes of federally-assisted housing implied a statutorily-based interest on the part of tenants in avoiding rent increases, and that because of this "entitlement" to low cost housing, the tenants of public housing, Thompson v. Washington, 497 F.2d 626 (D.C. Cir. 1973) and the tenants of subsidized housing, Marshall v. Lynn, 497 F.2d 643 (D.C. Cir. 1973), *cert. denied*, 419 U.S. 970 (1974), had a right to be heard before the implementation of rent increases. How-

---

108. For example, §220 of the National Housing Act, 12 U.S.C. §1715k, aims at aiding in "the elimination of slums and blighted conditions and the prevention of deterioration of residential property by supplementing the insurance of mortgages...." 12 U.S.C. §1715k(a). Section 236, 12 U.S.C. §1715z-1, authorizes the Secretary of Housing and Urban Development "to make, and to contract to make, periodic interest reduction payments on behalf of the owner of a rental housing project designed for occupancy by lower income families, which shall be accomplished through payments to mortgagees holding mortgages meeting the special requirements specified in this section." A number of other statutory provisions also exist arguably creating due process entitlements for tenants with respect to rent increases. See, e.g., 42 U.S.C. §1486, which provides for grants designed to offset the cost of low rent housing for farm laborers; this section was held to create a due process entitlement in Ponce v. Housing Authority of the County of Tulare, 389 F. Supp. 635 (E.D. Cal. 1975). See also the low rent public housing program established under the U.S. Housing Act of 1937, 42 U.S.C. §1401 et seq., as amended, described in Thompson v. Washington, 497 F.2d 626 (D.C. Cir. 1973).

In evaluating the cases, it is important to keep in mind the particular statutory provision with which each case deals and the legislative purpose underlying that provision. See, e.g., Tenants' Council of Tiber Island-Carrollsburg Square v. Lynn, 497 F.2d 648, 651-52 (D.C. Cir. 1973), *cert. denied*, 419 U.S. 970 (1974); Ellis v. HUD, 551 F.2d 13 (3d Cir. 1977).

109. The court was no doubt influenced by the fact that Chenango Court, the owner of the project seeking a rent increase, had lost $122,000 and never paid any dividends.

110. People's Right Organization v. Bethlehem Assn., 356 F. Supp. 407 (E.D. Pa.), *aff'd mem.* 487 F.2d 1395 (3d Cir. 1973); Harlib v. Lynn, 511 F.2d 51 (7th Cir. 1975); Fenner v. Bruce Manor, Inc., 409 F. Supp. 1332 (D.Md. 1976); Rodriguez v. Towers Apartments, Inc., 416 F. Supp. 304 (D. Puerto Rico 1976). In Grace Towers Tenants Assn. v. Grace Housing Development Fund Co., Inc., 538 F.2d 491 (2d Cir. 1976), the Court of Appeals held that *Roth* and *Sindermann* did not alter its conclusions in *Langevin* since the Housing Act did not confer on tenants of public housing a legitimate claim of entitlement to the continuation of the existing rent level.

ever, the court rejected oral evidentiary hearings, and held that tenants were instead entitled to notice of the proposed rent increase, an opportunity to make written objections, and a statement by FHA of reasons for its decision.[111] The Ninth Circuit Court of Appeals in Geneva Towers v. Federated Mortgage, Inc., 504 F.2d 483 (1974) (decided after *Roth*) held that tenants of housing subsidized under §221(d)(3) possessed a "property" interest as a result of their statutorily created expectation that they would continue to receive the benefits of low cost housing. Unlike Judge Coffin in *Hahn*, the court believed that the tenants were in a good position to provide pertinent information and further, that affording the tenants a right to participation "generat[es] the feeling, that justice is being done." The court ordered the same procedures as did the D.C. Court of Appeals in Thompson v. Marshall. Judge Hufstedler dissented with respect to the procedures afforded, finding them inadequate, and charging that the court's decision "eviscerates the due process protections that it purports to grant" by reducing them "to little more than the right to send and receive mail." 504 F.2d, at 498.[112]

The ultimate difference between the courts that grant and those that deny procedural rights to tenants with respect to rent increases in subsidized housing seems to turn on the relative emphasis given to long-run fiscal and management problems and to the immediate interests of tenants.

Question:

Are those decisions which find that tenants have a constitutionally protected "entitlement" in avoiding rent increases consistent with *Roth* and *Bishop*? [113]

111. These procedures were subsequently embodied in HUD regulations and made applicable to most of the subsidized housing programs. 24 C.F.R. §401.

112. See also Burr v. New Rochelle Municipal Housing Authority, 479 F.2d 1165 (2nd Cir. 1973).

Two district court decisions required that tenants in federally-subsidized projects be afforded hearing rights before HUD exercises its statutory right to override local rent control regulations precluding or limiting rent increases in such projects. 515 Associates v. City of Newark, 424 F. Supp. 984 (D.N.J. 1977); Argo v. Hills, 425 F. Supp. 151 (E.D.N.Y. 1977), aff'd mem. 578 F.2d 1366 (2nd Cir. 1978). Both courts emphasized the positive action involved in HUD's preemption. Tenants were entitled to a notice, a reasonable opportunity to inspect the materials sent to HUD by their landlord, a reasonable opportunity to send written comments to HUD and a written statement by HUD explaining its decision. See generally, Note, HUD Preemption of Local Rent Control Ordinances — Tenants Entitled to Due Process Rights, 30 Rutgers L. Rev. 1025 (1977).

On whether tenants of housing subsidized under §236 of the National Housing Act (authorizing direct payment by the federal government of mortgage subsidies to mortgagees) have a due process right to be heard prior to HUD authorization of rent increases, see Paulsen v. Coachlight Apartments Co., 507 F.2d 401 (6th Cir. 1974) (no); Bloodworth v. Oxford Village Townhouses, Inc., 377 F. Supp. 709 (N.D. Ga. 1974) (yes); Fenner v. Bruce Manor, 409 F. Supp. 1332 (D. Md. 1976) (no) (deals with both §221 and §236 housing); Dew v. McLendon Gardens Associates, 394 F. Supp. 1223 (N.D. Ga. 1975) (yes).

113. For perceptive discussion of this and related issues, see Michelman, Formal and Associational Aims in Procedural Due Process, in J. Pennock & J. Chapman, eds., Nomos: Due Process 126 (1977), arguing that lower court judges in housing cases are prone to find "fake entitlements," by reading into statutes rights that cannot fairly be found there, in order to

3. Public Employment

(Review the decisions in Board of Regents v. Roth, Perry v. Sindermann, Arnett v. Kennedy, Bishop v. Wood, and Codd v. Velger, supra, pp. 620, 625, 629, 642, and 652, respectively.)

a. Determination of Protected "Property" Interests

Supreme Court decisions have created continuing confusion in the lower courts in determining when a person who has separated from public employ has the right to claim due process procedural safeguards.

Courts have found an absence of protected "property" interests where a "probationary" teacher's contract was not renewed, even though the applicable state statute required that reasons for nonrenewal be given, Schirck v. Thomas, 486 F.2d 691 (7th Cir. 1973); where a nontenured teacher's year-to-year contract was not renewed after five previous renewals, Ryan v. Aurora City Board of Education, 540 F.2d 222 (6th Cir. 1976), cert. denied, 429 U.S. 1041 (1977); and where a non-tenured teacher's contract was not renewed under a system providing for automatic renewal absent affirmative action by the school administration.[114]

However, where a system differentiates between probationary and nonprobationary employees and a nonprobationary employee is discharged, courts have found a protected property interest when the discharge is required under state law to be

---

provide a basis for affording procedural rights designed to secure aims — such a participation and representation — other than accuracy in the application of statutes.

Consider also Judge Hufstedler's dissent in Geneva Towers. Is it preferable to define narrowly the interest protected by due process in order to avoid undue dilution of traditional notions of what process is due? See the discussion following the Goss case, supra p. 675.

See generally, Comment, Due Process Protection Under the Entitlement Doctrine for Tenants of Federally Supported Housing, 63 Geo. L.J. 1301 (1975); Annot., Tenants' Rights, Under Due Process Clause of Federal Constitution, to Notice and Hearing Prior to Imposition of Higher Rents or Additional Service Charges for Government-Owned or Government-Subsidized Housing, 28 A.L.R. Fed. 739.

114. See Schirck v. Thomas, 486 F.2d 691 (7th Cir. 1973); Ryan v. Aurora City Bd. of Educ., 540 F.2d 222 (6th Cir. 1976). In Prince v. Bridges, 537 F.2d 1269 (4th Cir. 1976), procedural rights were denied plaintiff, an employee of a local welfare department in apparently "permanent" status, who was discharged without explanation. She appealed, under the state's "merit system plan" to the Merit System Council, which recommended her reinstatement, but her superior declined to follow this recommendation, which under state law was purely advisory. The court, following Justice Rehnquist's opinion in Arnett and the Court's opinion in Bishop v. Wood, believed that the extent of the plaintiff's rights to continued employment under the "merit" system was defined by the procedures afforded under state law, and since these were fully satisfied, plaintiff had no further entitlements warranting additional due process protection.

With respect to the Perry v. Sindermann argument for a property interest arising by virtue of a "de facto" tenure system, see Willens v. University of Massachusetts, 570 F.2d 403 (1st Cir. 1978), holding that the possibility of such a system was precluded by the University's highly structured system of de jure tenure.

for "cause," and in some instances have inferred a requirement of "cause" even though it is not explicit in the state statute.[115]

Courts have rather uniformly held that, absent explicit protection in state law, there is no constitutionally protected "property" interest in a particular position or circumstances of employment, and have declined to provide due process protection for changes in employment conditions falling short of employment termination.[116]

Questions:

It is a fair generalization to say that courts are considerably more reluctant to find a protected property "entitlement" in the case of public employment than in the case of public housing. What explains this difference? Is it that we view public housing as provided for the sake of the tenants, where the purpose of public employment is less to provide employment than to secure useful services for the benefit of the public? [117]

b. Determination of Protected "Liberty" Interests

Recall that *Roth* acknowledged the possibility that the grounds or circumstances of severance from public employment might so jeopardize future employment opportunities as to effect a deprivation of constitutionally-protected "liberty" interests.[118] Little agreement has emerged in the lower courts in deciding when discharge is so stigmatizing as to cause an impairment of "liberty" triggering due process protections.[119]

---

115. See Indiana State Employees Ass'n, Inc. v. Boehning, 511 F.2d 834 (7th Cir.), *vacated on other grounds*, 423 U.S. 6 (1975); Eley v. Morris, 390 F. Supp. 913 (N.D. Ga. 1975); Young v. Hutchins, 383 F. Supp. 1167 (M.D. Fla. 1974).

116. See Confederation of Police v. City of Chicago, 547 F.2d 375 (7th Cir. 1977) (transfer to lower paying or more onerous positions); Sullivan v. Brown, 544 F.2d 279 (6th Cir. 1976) (teacher reprimand and transfer to another school); Coe v. Bogart, 519 F.2d 10 (6th Cir. 1975) (demotion from principal to teacher or subordinate administrator).

117. For discussion, see Michelman, supra, note 113.

118. However, recall also that Paul v. Davis, supra, p. 648, clouded the issue of due process protection against government injury to reputation by insisting that some injury in addition to defamation was required to create a protected "liberty" interest. See also Codd v. Velger, supra, p. 652, holding that "liberty" is not infringed unless the person defamed challenges the truth of the defamation.

119. Courts have held that terminations based upon the following charges do not amount to a deprivation of liberty: "malfeasance," Adams v. Walker, 492 F.2d 1003 (7th Cir. 1974); "noncooperation," Irby v. McGow, 380 F. Supp. 1024 (S.D. Ala. 1974); "display of an anti-establishment obsession," Lipp v. Bd. of Education, 470 F.2d 802 (7th Cir. 1972); failure to meet a particular job's requirements, Russell v. Hodges, 470 F.2d 312 (2d Cir. 1972); or failure to cooperate with fellow workers, Schirck v. Thomas 486 F.2d 691 (7th Cir. 1973). The following charges have been found to impair "liberty" interests: alleged racism, Wellner v. Minnesota State Junior College Board, 487 F.2d 153 (8th Cir. 1973); excessive prescription of drugs, Surarez v. Waver, 484 F.2d 678 (7th Cir. 1973); dishonesty and lack of integrity, McNeill v. Butz, 480 F.2d 314 (4th Cir. 1973), Hostrop v. Bd. of Jr. College Dist. No. 515,

A number of pre-*Bishop* decisions found an impairment of "liberty" where the grounds for discharge were stigmatizing even though they had not been published to third parties, reasoning that the charges would probably become known to outsiders.[120] After *Bishop*, one court has held that no "liberty" interest was invaded when the reasons for discharge were not published until a hearing requested by plaintiff. Cato v. Collins, 539 F.2d 656 (8th Cir. 1976). But in Churchwell v. United States, 545 F.2d 59 (8th Cir. 1976), a pre-termination hearing, based on deprivation of "liberty," was required when, after termination of employment, petitioner's former employer (the Public Health Service) released to a prospective employer derogatory information concerning the grounds for petitioner's discharge.

Questions:

Can *Cato* and *Churchwell* be reconciled? If not, which is correct?

c. What Process Is Due

After *Arnett*, the lower courts have uniformly held that a post-termination hearing can satisfy due process. However, in Boehning v. Indiana State Employees Ass'n, 423 U.S. 6, 7-8n. (1975), in a footnote to a per curiam decision, the Supreme Court stated that a tenured employee's right to a pre-removal hearing "has been determined by this Court only in the context of a statute providing notice and opportunity to respond in writing *before* removal coupled with a full hearing after removal." Are pre-termination notice and opportunity to respond necessary to legitimize a system that affords a post-termination oral evidentiary hearing? The lower courts have been divided on the question.[121] In some contexts courts have not required an oral evidentiary hearing at any stage.[122] Compare American Federation of Gov't Employees, Local 1858 v. Callaway, 398 F. Supp. 176 (N.D. Ala. 1975),

---

471 F.2d 488 (7th Cir. 1972) *cert. denied*, 411 U.S. 967 (1973); alleged mental instability, Stewart v. Pearce, 484 F.2d 1031 (9th Cir. 1973); unwillingness to carry out institutional policies, Wilderman v. Nelson, 467 F.2d 1173 (8th Cir. 1972); moral turpitude, Abeyta v. Town of Taos, 499 F.2d 323 (10th Cir. 1974); and distribution, by "sexpot" teacher, of "obscene" classroom materials, McGhee v. Draper, 564 F.2d 902 (10th Cir. 1977).

120. See, e.g., McNeill v. Butz, 480 F.2d 314 (4th Cir. 1973); Rew v. Ward, 402 F. Supp. 331 (D.N.M. 1975).

121. Yes: Eley v. Morris, 390 F. Supp. 913 (N.D. Ga. 1975); Young v. Hutchins, 383 F. Supp. 1167 (M.D. Fla. 1974); Kennedy v. Robb, 547 F.2d 408 (8th Cir. 1976), *cert. denied*, 431 U.S. 959 (1977). No: Jacobs v. Kune, 541 F.2d 222 (9th Cir. 1976), *cert. denied*, 429 U.S. 1094 (1977) (post-termination hearing only is permitted so long as full back pay is awarded if the employee prevails); Magri v. Giarrusso, 379 F. Supp. 353 (E.D. La. 1974) (special fact situation in which the plaintiff was clearly forewarned of the consequences if his behavior persisted).

122. In Rew v. Ward, 402 F. Supp. 331 (D.N.M. 1975), notice of the discharge and the basis for the action, and an opportunity to respond in writing sufficed for the discharge of an airman, considering the nature of the military interest. Stretten v. Wadsworth Veteran's Hospital, 537 F.2d 361 (9th Cir. 1976), held that similar procedures were sufficient to protect a medical intern dismissed from a residency program.

where civil service employees of the Defense Department were granted a preliminary injunction that precluded the Army from awarding a private contract which would result in a reduction in force, since the reduction would frustrate the Civil Service hearing rights and procedures to which the employees were entitled under federal law.[123]

Should an employee have the right to be represented by appointed legal counsel? [124] The right of cross-examination? [125]

Must the decisionmaker be impartial? This question has often occurred in connection with school boards, where members had prior contact with the employee or had actually ordered or approved the employee's dismissal. Most courts have held that prior involvement of this sort is not automatically disqualifying, and have insisted on proof of "actual bias." [126] The Supreme Court has also held that a school board's prior embroilment in collective bargaining with a teacher's union did not disqualify the Board in dismissing teachers for striking in violation of state law.[127]

Underlying these various decisions[128] are fundamental questions concerning the degree and form of job security that government employees should enjoy. Professor Merrill believes that the present federal Civil Service system does not provide sufficient safeguards against injustice, and that "removal from government employ for cause carries a stigma that it is probably impossible to outlive," since the charges typically reflect adversely on the employee's character and integrity. Merrill would require that an oral evidentiary hearing be conducted before adverse action is taken, in part to alleviate the economic pressures that induce many employees to acquiesce in actions based only on allegations.[129]

Professor Frug, on the other hand, believes that "the civil service system is a basic cause of the peculiar inability of the government to improve its [inadequate] standard of performance," since "employees [covered by Civil Service protections] are rarely discharged from government for inadequately doing their jobs." He believes that present procedural protections seriously restrict the government's ability to enforce an effective standard of job performance. Since the "key to fairness in the determination of competence ... is not the resolution of purely factual issues

---

123. In American Federation of Govt. Emp., Local 1850 v. Hoffman, 427 F. Supp. 1048 (N.D. Ala. 1976), the injunction granted in *Callaway* was dissolved on the grounds, inter alia, that the contracts were committed to agency discretion beyond judicial review, that the contracts benefited the Army rather than the plaintiffs, and that plaintiffs failed to show any protectable interest in employment.

124. Downing v. LeBritton, 550 F.2d 689 (1st Cir. 1977), held no, even though the employee being discharged was mentally retarded.

125. McNeill v. Butz, 480 F.2d 314 (4th Cir. 1973), required cross-examination of adverse witnesses when the case turned on factual determinations and the evidence consisted primarily of individual testimony, but the decision seems exceptional. McGhee v. Draper, 564 F.2d 902 (10th Cir. 1977), found confrontation and cross-examination to be required when a teacher was accused of distributing "obscene" books to students and acting as a "sexpot."

126. Cato v. Collins, 539 F.2d 656 (8th Cir. 1976); Chamberlain v. Wichita Falls Independent School District, 539 F.2d 566 (5th Cir. 1976).

127. Hortonville Joint School Dist. No. 1 v. Hortonville Educ. Assn., 426 U.S. 482 (1976).

128. For discussion of the cases in greater detail, see Lowy, Constitutional Limits on the Dismissal of Public Employees, 43 Brooklyn L. Rev. 1 (1976).

129. Merrill, Procedures for Adverse Actions Against Federal Employees, 59 Va. L. Rev. 196 (1973).

but the process used by a supervisor in evaluating competence," he disapproves of the judicialization of the employment process. Instead, he would seek to improve communication between employee and supervisor, so that the employee would receive notice and an opportunity to perform as expected and a chance to participate in forming these expectations. If, after having an opportunity to perform adequately, the employee was still unsatisfactory, Frug would have another supervisor inside the agency inquire into the work situation, but would give the employee no opportunity to litigate administratively or judicially whether the discharge was "correct." He believes that the role of the courts should be to review the fairness of the evaluation process. In this respect, his proposal bears similarities to Professor Mashaw's advocacy of "management" alternatives to judicial procedures.[130]

How do you think the interest of the government in obtaining effective performance by its employees and the interest of the employee in securing fair treatment should be resolved? Can the issue of procedural rights be separated from issues concerning the collective bargaining rights of government employees? Do you agree with Frug that fairness can be insured without an inquiry into the facts by an outsider? [131] Is the adjudicative process proposed by Merrill an efficient and effective means of ferreting out employees who are inadequate rather than those who have, say, stolen government supplies?

Professor Rabin suggests that the proper balance between the interests of the government and those of the employee might be struck by requiring the government to provide a reasoned explanation as to the basis of its action against the employee, but not formal hearing procedures. He believes that a reasons requirement would foster among officials a heightened sense of accountability and an added incentive to investigate thoroughly and check dubious motives. To add teeth to the requirement, Rabin would allow judicial review, but in order to forestall pressures for the use of formal procedures to develop the underlying facts, he would confine judicial review to an examination of the reasons stated to determine whether the statement, without more, shows that the decision is so irrational as to be arbitrary and capricious.[132] Would a reasons requirement be an adequate substitute for an evidentiary hearing in ensuring accurate decision-making? Given the current trend in judicial review of informal adjudication under the arbitrary and capricious standard, see pp. 524-530, supra, might not a reasons requirement expand into an evidentiary proceeding after all?

130. Frug, Does the Constitution Prevent the Discharge of Civil Service Employees? 124 U. Pa. L. Rev. 942 (1976).
131. Consider that in 1971, it was estimated that in the federal government 15,700 adverse actions were initiated, of which about one-quarter were contested. Merrill, supra note 129, at 198. Yet out of over two million civilian federal employees, between 1972 and 1974 only 300 to 500 individuals annually were discharged for inefficiency. Frug, ibid. at 945 n.13. See also Reed, Firing a Federal Employee, The Impossible Dream, The Washington Monthly, July-August 1977, p. 15, arguing that the very low rate of discharge for inefficiency among federal employees is not a reflection of such employees' outstanding competence but the burdensome and time-consuming procedures that must be followed in order to discharge an incompetent employee.
132. Rabin, Job Security and Due Process: Monitoring Administrative Discretion Through a Reasons Requirement, 44 U. Chi. L. Rev. 60 (1976).

4. *Education*

[Review Goss v. Lopez and Ingraham v. Wright, pp. 637-641 and 676-680, supra.]

a. Expulsion, Suspension, and Other Forms of Discipline

Most of the due process decisions in the field of public education have arisen in the context of expulsions and suspensions. In the several years preceding *Goss*, courts uniformly held that students had a constitutionally protected interest in education that would be infringed by expulsion, and most required an evidentiary hearing. The decisions regularly quoted Brown v. Board of Education, 347 U.S. 483, 493 (1954), to the effect that: "[T]hese days, it is doubtful that any child may reasonably be expected to succeed in life if he is denied the opportunity of an education." However, there was less agreement with respect to suspensions, particularly in identifying the dividing line between short suspensions and longer ones requiring more in the way of procedural safeguards. In the case of short suspensions — often identified as those lasting from 5 to 10 days' duration — at most, informal consultation with the student was required.[133] Where the suspension was deemed more serious, courts often required notice of the action and the basis for it: knowledge of adverse witnesses and evidence, an opportunity to present the student's case, retained legal counsel if the student wished, and an unbiased decisionmaker (with impartiality criteria similar to those applied in cases of dismissal of government employees — prior contact with the student did not disqualify a decisionmaker without positive evidence of bias). Some split developed on the extent to which a student could confront adverse witnesses.[134]

Since *Goss*, rather full trial-type safeguards continued to be required in expulsion cases, but there are suggestions that courts are now granting less in the way of procedural rights in the case of more serious suspensions than was customary before *Goss*. For example, in Alex v. Allen, 409 F. Supp. 379 (W.D. Pa. 1976), the court cited *Goss* for the propositions that the rights of students to fair procedures are limited, and that federal courts must rely on the discretion and good judgment of school officials. Therefore, even though a student was being suspended for thirty days, he had no right to a full-fledged oral evidentiary hearing procedure, and the combination of the functions of judge and prosecutor in the School Board's attorney did not offend the student's rights. In Garshman v. Penn State Univ., 395 F. Supp. 912 (M.D. Pa. 1975), involving a medical student accused of cheating on an

---

133. See Vail v. Bd. of Education of Portsmouth School District, 354 F. Supp. 592 (D.N.H. 1973); Linwood v. Bd. of Education, City of Peoria, 463 F.2d 763 (7th Cir.), *cert. denied*, 409 U.S. 1027 (1972); Black Students of North Fort Myers Jr.-Sr. High School v. Williams, 470 F.2d 957 (5th Cir. 1972).

134. Compare Graham v. Knutzen, 351 F. Supp. 642 (D. Neb. 1972) (no cross-examination; fear of retaliation) with DeJesus v. Penberthy, 344 F. Supp. 70 (D. Conn. 1972) (cross-examination required). Many of the suspension decisions are collected in *Goss*, 419 U.S., at 576-578, n.8.

exam, the court declined to enjoin a disciplinary hearing where he had a right to help from a professor or friend but was denied the right to be represented by retained counsel. The court distinguished *Goldberg* on the ground that the threatened loss was less severe than termination of welfare benefits, and that the student, "unlike the vast majority of welfare recipients, has the ability to understand his rights and express himself." 395 F. Supp., at 921.

What of other forms of discipline? Ingraham v. Wright, supra, p. 676, found that a prior administrative hearing was not required in the case of corporal punishment because the availability of state court tort and other remedies for unjustified infliction of punishment constituted sufficient due process. But what of suspension from interscholastic athletics competition or from extracurricular activities? [135] Should a student be entitled to an oral hearing in disciplinary cases even when no facts are in dispute? [136]

b. Procedural Rights with Respect to Other Interests in Education

Expulsion or suspension terminates the student's relationship with an educational institution, and paddling is clearly punishment. Suppose, however, the student remains in a school but challenges the terms or content of the education provided by objecting to being placed in a vocational, as opposed to college-preparatory, education "track," or to being assigned to a particular school, or to not being promoted because of inadequate academic performance? Assuming that the relevant state statutes and regulations give educational authorities considerable discretion with respect to such matters, is there a protected "property" or "liberty" interest involved on the part of the student? If so, what process is due? These issues have

135. Hamilton v. Tennessee Secondary Athletic Association, 552 F.2d 681 (6th Cir. 1976), decided that there is no due process right to participate in high school interscholastic athletics, and therefore that no hearing need be afforded in barring such participation as a disciplinary sanction. Accord, Colorado Seminary v. NCAA, 570 F.2d 320 (10th Cir. 1978). But in Warren v. National Association of Secondary School Principals, 375 F. Supp. 1043 (N.D. Texas 1974), the court set aside the expulsion by school officials of a student from a National Honor Society for drinking six ounces of beer, finding that ejection impaired plaintiff's liberty interest because it was entered in his permanent school records, and that the tribunal was biased because one of the officials claimed to have witnessed the alleged incident.

For general discussion of procedural rights in disciplinary cases, see W. Buss, Procedural Due Process for School Discipline: Probing the Constitutional Outline, 119 U. Pa. L. Rev. 545 (1971).

136. In Black Coalition v. Portland School District, No. 1, 484 F.2d 1040 (9th Cir. 1973), the court held that the procedures used to expel students did not satisfy due process, but since the plaintiff had admitted all the essential facts which it was the purpose of a due process hearing to establish, he was entitled to no relief. Accord, Smith v. Webb, 420 F. Supp. 600 (E.D. Pa. 1976) (expulsion, but plaintiff had had a juvenile court hearing on the facts); Fenton v. Stear, 423 F. Supp. 767 (W.D. Pa. 1976) (in-school suspension). But in Strickland v. Inlow, 519 F.2d 744 (8th Cir. 1975), the court held that an opportunity to be heard is no less important where there is no serious factual dispute because "[t]hings are not always as they seem to be, and the student will at least have an opportunity to characterize his conduct" and put it in context, citing Goss v. Lopez. Accord, Betts v. Bd. of Education of City of Chicago, 466 F.2d 629 (7th Cir. 1972).

posed considerable difficulty for the lower courts, in part because of the lack of relevant guidance from the Supreme Court prior to its decision in Board of Curators of University of Missouri v. Horowitz, 435 U.S. 78 (1978) (discussed below), and in part because of the entanglement of procedural questions with intractable issues of substantive educational policy.[137] The notion of a "right to education" is deeply rooted in the national self-image, but its contours remain undefined, and there has also been a strong tradition of deference to local school authorities in devising educational policy within the constraints of locally determined school budgets.

Board of Curators of University of Missouri v. Horowitz

435 U.S. 78 (1978)

Mr. Justice REHNQUIST delivered the opinion of the Court.

[Horowitz, a student at the University of Missouri-Kansas City Medical School, was dismissed from the school because of her inadequate performance in the clinical segment of the curriculum. Faculty members found that her "performance was below that of her peers in all clinical patient-oriented settings," that she was erratic in her attendance at clinical sessions, and that she showed a serious disregard for personal cleanliness and hygiene. Practicing physicians in the area also reported adversely on her clinical performance with them. Her performance was evaluated by a faculty-student Council on Evaluation and a faculty Coordinating Committee, both of which recommended that she be dismissed for inadequate academic performance. The School's Dean approved this recommendation, and the University's Provost for Health Services sustained her dismissal after reviewing her file. Horowitz was not afforded an opportunity to participate in the deliberations of the Council or the Committee, nor was she afforded a trial-type evidentiary hearing. However, she was informed by the Dean, both orally and in writing, of the deficiencies in her performance, given an opportunity to improve her performance, and also given the opportunity to present her views in meetings with the Dean and other school officials. She brought suit against school officials under 42 U.S.C. §1983, asserting that she had been deprived of a constitutionally protected "liberty" interest without due process. (She did not assert deprivation of a "property" interest.) The District Court found that the procedures afforded were adequate, but the Court of Appeals reversed, asserting that Horowitz had been stigmatized in a manner that severely damaged her chances of assuming a medical career. Justice Rehnquist's opinion initially raises the question whether, in view of Bishop v. Wood, supra p. 642, Horowitz was deprived of a "liberty" interest in being dismissed from school where the grounds for dismissal were communicated to her but were made public. Justice Rehnquist noted:]

137. See generally, Comment, Procedural Due Process in Public Schools: The "Thicket" of Goss v. Lopez, 1976 Wisc. L. Rev. 934.

We need not decide, however, whether respondent's dismissal deprived her of a liberty interest in pursuing a medical career. Nor need we decide whether respondent's dismissal infringed any other interest constitutionally protected against deprivation without procedural due process. Assuming the existence of a liberty or property interest, respondent has been awarded at least as much due process as the Fourteenth Amendment requires. The School fully informed respondent of the faculty's dissatisfaction with her clinical progress and the danger that this posed to timely graduation and continued enrollment. The ultimate decision to dismiss respondent was careful and deliberate. These procedures were sufficient under the Due Process Clause of the Fourteenth Amendment.... [W]e have frequently emphasized that "[t]he very nature of due process negates any concept of inflexible procedures universally applicable to every imaginable situation." Cafeteria Workers v. McElroy, 367 U.S. 886, 895.... The need for flexibility is well illustrated by the significant difference between the failure of a student to meet academic standards and the violation by a student of valid rules of conduct. This difference calls for far less stringent procedural requirements in the case of an academic dismissal.[138]

...A school is an academic institution, not a courtroom or administrative hearing room.... [D]isciplinary reasons have a sufficient resemblance to traditional judicial and administrative factfinding to call for a "hearing" before the relevant school authority....

Academic evaluations of a student, in contrast to disciplinary determinations, bear little resemblance to the judicial and administrative fact-finding proceedings to which we have traditionally attached a full hearing requirement. In Goss, the school's decision to suspend the students rested on factual conclusions that the individual students had participated in demonstrations that had disrupted classes, attacked a police officer, or caused physical damage to school property. The requirement of a hearing, where the student could present his side of the factual issue, could under such circumstances "provide a meaningful hedge against erroneous action."... The decision to dismiss respondent, by comparison, rested on the academic judgment of school officials that she did not have the necessary clinical ability to perform adequately as a medical doctor and was making insufficient progress toward that goal. Such a judgment is by its nature more subjective and evaluative than the typical factual questions presented in the average disciplinary decision. Like the decision of an individual professor as to the proper grade for a student in his course, the determination whether to dismiss a student for academic reasons requires an expert evaluation of cumulative information and is not readily adapted to the procedural tools of judicial or administrative decisionmaking.

138. We fully recognize that the deprivation to which respondent was subjected — dismissal from a graduate medical school — was more severe than the 10-day suspension to which the high school students were subjected in Goss.... But the severity of the deprivation is only one of several factors that must be weighed in deciding the exact due process owed. Ibid. We conclude that considering all relevant factors, including the evaluative nature of the inquiry and the significant and historically supported interest of the school in preserving its present framework for academic evaluations, a hearing is not required by the Due Process Clause of the Fourteenth Amendment.

Under such circumstances, we decline to ignore the historic judgment of educators and thereby formalize the academic dismissal process by requiring a hearing. The educational process is not by nature adversarial; instead, it centers around a continuing relationship between faculty and students, "one in which the teacher must occupy many roles — educator, adviser, friend, and, at times, parent-substitute." Goss v. Lopez, 419 U.S. 565, 594, 95 S. Ct. 729, 746, 42 L. Ed. 2d 725 (1975) (Powell, J., dissenting).... We decline to further enlarge the judicial presence in the academic community and thereby risk deterioration of many beneficial aspects of the faculty-student relationship. We recognize, as did the Massachusetts Supreme Judicial Court over 60 years ago, that a hearing may be "useless or even harmful in finding out the truth as to scholarship." Barnard v. Inhabitants of Shelburne [216 Mass. 19, 23; 102 N.E. 1095, 1097 (1913)].

"Judicial interposition in the operation of the public school system of the Nation raises problems requiring care and restraint.... By and large, public education in our Nation is committed to the control of state and local authorities." Epperson v. Arkansas, 393 U.S. 97, 104,... (1968). We see no reason to intrude on that historic control in this case.[139] ...

[Justice POWELL, concurring in the Court's opinion and judgment, expressed his view that Horowitz had been "dismissed solely on academic grounds" rather than "for unsatisfactory personal conduct."

Justice WHITE, Justice MARSHALL, and Justice BLACKMUN (joined by Justice BRENNAN) each entered separate opinions concurring in the result on the ground that the procedures afforded Horowitz were fully adequate to satisfy due process, assuming a constitutionally protected interest. However, each expressed disagreement with portions of the Court's opinion indicating that no hearing procedures of any kind are required in cases of "academic" as opposed to "'disciplinary" dismissals. In addition, Justice MARSHALL challenged the Court's application of the academic/disciplinary distinction to the case at bar. He suggested that dismissal of Horowitz on the basis (in part) of her personal hygiene, lack of punctuality, and other personal characteristics in the context of clinical practice was closer to punishment for misconduct of the sort involved in Goss than to traditional academic evaluations based on written exercises, and that procedures at least as extensive as those imposed in Goss were therefore consitutionally required.]

Questions

1. Did Ms. Horowitz have a constitutionally protected "liberty" or "property" interest?

139. Respondent contends in passing that she was not dismissed because of "clinical incompetence," an academic inquiry, but for disciplinary reasons similar to those involved in Goss. Thus, as in Goss, a hearing must be conducted. In this regard, respondent notes that the school warned her that significant improvement was needed not only in the area of clinical performance but also in her personal hygiene and in keeping to her clinical schedules. The record, however, leaves no doubt that respondent was dismissed for pure academic reasons, a fact assumed without discussion by the lower courts. Personal hygiene and timeliness may be as important as factors in a school's determination of whether a student will make a good medical doctor as the student's ability to take a case history or diagnose an illness.

2. Assuming the existence of a constitutionally protected interest, would a public school student dismissed for failing grades be entitled to a hearing if he claimed that clerical errors had occurred in calculating the grades?

3. A law student in a clinical course in a state law school is given a failing grade because of "unethical behavior in dealing with a client." Is she entitled to any procedural rights if she disputes the evaluation? Does the answer turn on whether or not the evaluation appears on her official transcript? On whether or not her failing grade causes her to be dismissed for unsatisfactory academic performance?

4. Is an unsuccessful applicant for admission to a state professional school constitutionally entitled to a statement of reasons or any other procedural rights with respect to the grounds for denial of admission? [140] Is the decision in Regents of University of California v. Bakke, 438 U.S. —, 98 S. Ct. 2733 (1978) (prohibiting racial quotas in state professional school admissions programs) relevant in answering this question?

What are the implications of Horowitz for the "tracking" of students into different academic programs (e.g., vocational, college preparatory, "general") or the assignment of children with learning disabilities into special schools or programs? The tracking system in the District of Columbia public schools was invalidated in Hobson v. Hansen,[141] but the decision was placed on racial discrimination and equal protection grounds. Pennsylvania's practices in dealing with children with learning disabilities — assignment to special schools or programs or outright exclusion from school if the child is judged "uneducable" — were challenged as violative of equal protection and due process in Pennsylvania Ass'n for Retarded Children v. Pennsylvania, 334 F. Supp. 1257 (E.D. Pa. 1971). The "special education" provided for such children was grossly inadequate, and the children were assigned to "special education" schools or programs without much in the way of notice and hearing. Under a consent agreement, children were to have a hearing right on initial assignment or any program change, and on re-evaluations to be performed every two years. Parents could examine relevant documents and summon and question school officials. A similar set of procedures was mandated in Mills v. Bd. of Education of District of Columbia, 348 F. Supp. 866 (D.D.C. 1972), which not only found that due process required hearings on school decisions classifying and assigning students with learning disabilities, but also found (based on Brown v. Board of Education) that children with learning disabilities had a constitutional right to educational programs appropriate to their needs and abilities.[142]

140. Grove v. Ohio State Univ., College of Veterinary Medicine, 424 F. Supp. 377 (S.D. Ohio 1976), decided that a three-time frustrated applicant to the veterinary program had a liberty interest infringed upon by his rejections, since the court held that they constituted an effective denial of an opportunity to participate in his chosen profession. The court required that reasons for rejection have a rational connection with the profession, and sustained Ohio State's admission procedures only after a thorough scrutiny.

141. 269 F. Supp. 401 (D.D.C. 1967), aff'd with directions sub nom. Smuck v. Hobson, 408 F.2d 175 (D.C. Cir. 1969) (en banc), appeal dismissed, 393 U.S. 801 (1970).

142. An empirical study of the subsequent administration of special education programs found that the Pennsylvania experience was more satisfactory than that in the District of Colum-

Question

Raphael Claret is a 14-year old student in a junior high school in Los Angeles. After a period of more than a year of behavioral difficulties, Claret was suspended from school by the principal and the case was referred to the District Superintendent. The Superintendent notified Claret's parents, asking them to appear at a "guidance conference." The parents consulted an attorney, who requested permission to appear at the conference. The attorney submitted to the Board a request that at the conference, Claret be allowed: "(1) the right to counsel, (2) the right to confront and cross examine, (3) written findings, (4) a written record, (5) an impartial decisionmaker." When this request was denied, the present federal court action was commenced to enjoin the Superintendent and the Board of Education from proceeding with the hearing or taking any action in the case.

Under state law, persons between the ages of seven and sixteen are required to attend school. A student may, however, be suspended for being "insubordinate or disorderly" as well as on other grounds. Such a suspension may be a "principal suspension" (for not more than 5 days) or an "administrative suspension" which remains in effect pending a further decision by the District Superintendent. The latter suspension was imposed in Claret's case, and pursuant to the Board's procedural regulations, the parents were notified of a Guidance Conference and invited to attend along with the child. The regulations provide that the parents may bring an interpreter if they do not speak English, but may not bring an attorney. (Mr. and Mrs. Claret did not speak English.) The conference is attended by the principal, the school guidance counselor, the District Superintendent, and a "school-court coordinator," who takes notes of the conference. (No statements made at the conference, however, are admissible in any subsequent Family Court or criminal proceeding.)

At this conference, the school personnel discuss the case and then the parents and the child are asked what they think should be done. Sometimes, a social worker

---

bia because there was a well-organized parents' organization in Pennsylvania and the program was administered under the direction of court-appointed special masters. Parents represented by counsel were more likely to obtain the result they wished. Teachers were often upset by the adversary character of the hearings, and in some instances stopped referring children for special education programs in order to avoid such hearings. The hearings cost the State an average of $500 each — about half the average annual cost of educating a child in Pennsylvania. The hearing procedure was better suited for dealing with cases where exclusion was recommended than with decisions concerning in which special education program a child should be placed, raising difficult issues of educational policy. In the District of Columbia, most hearings were run by psychologists or special educators, and were conducted like informal conferences. Parents were less satisfied that the interests of their children were receiving adequate individual attention. See Kirp, Buss, and Kuriloff, Legal Reform of Special Education: Empirical Studies and Procedural Proposals, 62 Calif. L. Rev. 40 (1974). See also Kirp, Schools as Sorters: The Constitutional and Policy Implications of Student Classification, 121 U. Pa. L. Rev. 705 (1973); Dimond, The Constitutional Right to Education: The Quiet Revolution, 24 Hastings L. J. 1087 (1973); Shea, An Educational Perspective of the Legality of Intelligence Testing and Ability Grouping, 6 J. Law & Educ. 137 (1977); Sorgen, Testing and Tracking in Public Schools, 24 Hastings L. J. 1129 (1973).

who knows the family may also take part. The following actions can be taken as a result of this conference.

(a) The suspended child may be reinstated in the same school.

(b) The suspended child may be transferred to another school of the same level.

(c) The suspended child may be transferred to a special day school for maladjusted children (the "600" schools), provided that the parents consent. It sometimes takes up to six months or more to be admitted to such a school. If the parents refuse to consent, they may be prosecuted for dereliction of parental duties and for violation of the compulsory education laws, and the child may be placed in a special school (or in some institution if appropriate) by the Family Court. The full panoply of procedural rights are available to both the parents and the child in the Family Court. (California State Education Law §3214 provides: "After reasonable notice to [the child and his parents] ... and an opportunity for them to be heard, [the child may be ordered] ... to attend a special day school....")

(d) The case may be referred to the Bureau of Child Guidance (BCG) or other agency for study and recommendation. The BCG may recommend to the Superintendent that the child be sent to a school with a special program, that he be sent to a "600" day school or "residential institution," or that he be temporarily or permanently "exempted" from school for medical or other reasons. Once again, the child cannot be sent to a "600" day school or residential institution without the parents' consent, except on petition to the Family Court.

Should the injunction sought by the Clarets be granted? If so, on what conditions should the guidance conference be permitted to proceed?

5. Prison Administration

During the past decade, prison disturbances throughout the nation have served to focus public attention on conditions of confinement within penal institutions. Until the late 1960s, the federal courts were reluctant to review and closely scrutinize the administration of correctional institutions. This restraint was rooted both in the deference the courts believed that they owed to the special experience and responsibility which prison officials have in the difficult area of prison administration, and in judicial reluctance to undertake the burden of continuing supervision of prison practices. By the early 1970s, the lower federal courts had begun to assume a major, albeit ambivalent, role in attempting to abolish some of the perceived abuses of the correctional system. The Civil Rights Act of 1871, 42 U.S.C. §1983, revivified in the prison context by the 1961 Supreme Court decision in Monroe v. Pape, 365 U.S. 167 (1961), has provided the vehicle for numerous prisoners rights suits by state court prisoners which allege violations of First, Eighth, and Fourteenth Amendment rights. In 1974, 18% of all civil cases filed in United

States District Courts concerned inmates, of which 31% involved §1983 suits. This latter figure amounted to a 2,338% increase over comparable 1966 figures.[143]

Early prison decisions utilized a "grievous loss" approach in determining the the applicability of due process.[144] This approach persisted even after *Roth*,[145] until it was definitively rejected in Meachum v. Fano, 427 U.S. 215 (1976), supra, p. 653, applying a narrow "entitlement" test to the threshold definition of protected interests.[146]

Application of the Mathews v. Eldridge balancing test to prison cases requires consideration of a number of special government interests, including the necessity for maintaining discipline in the unruly, often overcrowded, and potentially explosive prison context. There seems to be a growing consensus that the courts are ill-equipped to deal with problems of prison administration. The Supreme Court, which at first followed the lead of the lower federal courts, has recently begun to restrict the scope of constitutional protection afforded inmates and their access to federal court. However, the sanctions imposed on prisoners are often severe, and there is a real danger of arbitrary exercise of power by prison officials and of mistaken or maliciously motivated informants.[147]

a. Disciplinary Proceedings

Prisons typically have formal disciplinary proceedings to punish infractions of prison rules. Sanctions range from serious losses, such as solitary confinement or loss of "good time" credits entitling an inmate to early release from prison, to milder measures, such as assignment to less desirable prison work, loss of visitor privileges, or issuance of a reprimand. Any action taken will be entered in the inmate's file and may adversely affect his chances for parole. Disciplinary proceedings may not be easily distinguished from administrative measures utilized by

143. Prison Grievance Procedures, Special Report: National Association of Attorneys General Committee on the Office of the Attorney General, July 1976, p.3; Note, A Review of Prisoners' Rights Litigation Under 42 U.S.C. §1983, 11 U. Rich. L. Rev. 803 (1977).

In suits by federal prisoners, usually brought under 28 U.S.C. §1331 (general federal question jurisdiction), the question may arise whether procedures in prison administration are governed by the APA. Clardy v. Levi, 545 F.2d 1241 (9th Cir. 1976) held that prisons were *not* agencies within the APA. This decision is criticized in Davis, Administrative Law of the Seventies 92-93 (1978 Pocket Part).

144. See, e.g., Morrissey v. Brewer, 408 U.S. 471, 481-482 (1972).

145. E.g., U.S. ex rel. Miller v. Twomey, 479 F.2d 701, 717 (7th Cir. 1973); Berch v. Stahl, 373 F. Supp. 412, 422 (W.D.N.C. 1974).

146. See Walker v. Hughes, 558 F.2d 1247 (6th Cir. 1977) (discussion of the "grievous loss" and "entitlement" views). Some critics of the *Meachum* decision have suggested that the "grievous loss" analysis should be revived in prison cases. See Comment, Two Views of a Prisoner's Right to Due Process: Meachum v. Fano, 12 Harv. C.R.-C.L. L. Rev. 405 (1977).

147. See Note, Procedural Due Process in Parole Release Proceedings — Existing Rules, Recent Court Decisions, and Experience in the Prison, 60 Minn. L. Rev. 341, 364-68 (1976). For more general discussion, see H. Hoffman, Prisoners' Rights: Treatment of Prisoners and Post-Conviction Remedies (1976); H. Kerper & J. Kerper, Legal Rights of the Convicted (1974); L. Ohlin, ed., Prisoners in America (1973).

officials to maintain order. Different areas of the prison may vary in security and control measures with "problem" prisoners assigned to high security areas where freedom of movement and privileges are restricted. Prisoners may also be re-assigned to higher-security prisons. Intra-prison or inter-prison transfers are often effectuated through informal procedures that are not typed as "disciplinary," al-though such transfers may be utilized by officials, and are often viewed by prison-ers, as a form of sanction for alleged misconduct. Guards exercise a substantial amount of discretionary control over prisoner activities, and this discretion can also be utilized as a form of sanction-imposition.

Virtually anything an inmate does in the institution may be defined as a dis-ciplinary infraction. Speaking back to a correctional officer in a hostile tone may be regarded as insolence and thus punishable.

Disciplinary proceedings have traditionally been dispositional in character. If the inmate disputes a charge, the factual issues in most cases turn on questions of credibility between inmates and guards. Since the disciplinary board normally consists of prison officials, there are powerful bureaucratic incentives to accept the guard's version. Courts originally refused to review the adequacy of the procedures utilized in such proceedings.[148]

However, lower federal court decisions in the early 1970s began to extend due process protection in cases resulting in serious sanctions.[149] But courts often dis-agreed about what process was due. The District Court and Second Circuit deci-sions in Sostre v. Rockefeller[150] exemplify this split in opinion. The District Court responded to the segregation of an inmate in a form of solitary confinement for over one year by imposing full trial-type protections, including written notice of the charges, a recorded hearing before a disinterested official, representation by retained counsel or appointed counsel-substitute, direct and cross-examination of witnesses and a decision supported by written rationale. The Court of Appeals limited the procedural safeguards required, ruling only that the inmate should be able to con-front his accuser, should be informed of the evidence against him, and should be given a reasonable opportunity to explain his actions.

The lower courts which did intervene in the disciplinary process immediately incurred the burden of supervising the implementation of their orders. For exam-ple, Judge Pettine of the United States District Court for Rhode Island approved a consent decree giving inmates procedural rights in disciplinary cases consisting of notice of charges, representation by an institutional counselor, an opportunity to present evidence (though not necessarily the opportunity to call or cross-examine witnesses), and an administrative review procedure.[151] Thereafter Judge Pettine was

148. See, e.g., William v. Steele, 194 F.2d 32 (8th Cir. 1952); United States ex rel. Atterbury v. Ragen, 237 F.2d 953 (7th Cir. 1956); Graham v. Willingham, 384 F.2d 367 (10th Cir. 1967).
149. See, e.g., Nolan v. Scafati, 430 F.2d 548 (1st Cir. 1970); Landman v. Royster, 333 F. Supp. 621 (E.D. Va. 1971); cases collected in King v. Higgins, 370 F. Supp. 1023 (D. Mass. 1974).
150. 312 F. Supp. 863 (S.D.N.Y. 1970) *modified sub nom.* Sostre v. McGinnis, 442 F.2d 178 (2d Cir. 1971), *cert. denied,* 405 US. 978 (1972).
151. Morris v. Travisono, 310 F. Supp. 857 (D.R.I. 1970).

required to set aside the second and fourth Friday of each month to hear inmate complaints. It is not clear what was achieved by these judicial efforts. A study by the Harvard Center for Criminal Justice found that implementation of the decree's procedural safeguards was often slipshod or nonexistent; that prison staff, which had not been involved in formulating the decree, resented the court's intrusion; and that prisoners continued to be found guilty as charged in all but a handful of cases. However, there was some evidence indicating that punishments were lightened, and that prisoners viewed the court's intervention favorably because it forced officials to acknowledge that prisoners had rights.[152] Excerpts are printed at pp. 718-724, infra.

The Supreme Court considered the issue of procedural rights in prison discipline in Wolff v. McDonnell, 418 U.S. 539 (1974), finding Nebraska's procedures for imposing a loss of good time credit to be inadequate. Using the two-step *Roth* analysis, the Court found a protected "liberty" interest in the loss of good time credits where the state had statutorily created a system of good time credits leading to early release from prison, and had also authorized deprivation of credits as sanction for major misconduct.

In considering what process was due, the Court concluded that procedural safeguards in prison discipline did not have to be as stringent as those previously imposed for parole revocation in Morrissey v. Brewer.[153] It ruled that inmates in disciplinary proceedings have a right to written notice of the claimed violation at least twenty-four hours before the hearing. After the hearing the inmates are entitled to receive a written statement of the disciplinary board's findings of fact and the evidentiary basis of and reasons for the disciplinary action taken. The Court also ruled that an impartial hearing board was required, although the standard of impartiality did not exclude a board composed entirely of prison personnel. The majority held that representation by counsel or counsel-substitute was necessary only when the inmate is illiterate or the case is complex. The Court granted the right to call witnesses and to prepare and present documentary evidence unless prison authorities find that its exercise would jeopardize institutional safety or rehabilitative goals. Finally, the Court found no right to confront or cross-examine adverse witnesses because of the potential for escalating hostility and retaliation that such confrontation provides.

Wolff left open important issues, including its applicability to disciplinary sanctions other than loss of good time credits, and the precise extent of certain procedural safeguards, such as right to counsel. Lower federal courts consistently found that the *Wolff* safeguards applied where the sanction imposed was solitary confinement.[154] Moreover, the procedural rights granted in *Wolff* were interpreted expansively. Palmigiano v. Baxter, 487 F.2d 1280 (1st Cir. 1973), *on remand*, 418

152. See Harvard Center for Criminal Justice, Judicial Intervention in Prison Discipline, 63 J. Crim. L.C. & P.S. 200 (1972). Subsequent Rhode Island developments are discussed in Prison Reform: The Judicial Process, 23 BNA Crim. Law Rep. No. 17 (Supp. Aug. 2, 1978).

153. See infra, p. 716.

154. See Gates v. Collier, 501 F.2d 1291 (5th Cir. 1974); Willis v. Ciccone, 506 F.2d 1011 (8th Cir. 1974).

U.S. 908 (1974), modified, 510 F.2d 534 (1974), ruled that a prisoner had a right to remain silent in disciplinary proceedings where the misconduct charged might also give rise to a criminal prosecution; that the disciplinary authorities might not draw inferences adverse to the prisoner by reason of his silence; and that he was entitled to the presence of retained counsel at the hearing. In Clutchette v. Procunier, 497 F.2d 809 (9th Cir. 1974), modified, 510 F.2d 613 (1975), the court held that an inmate must be provided with counsel or a counsel-substitute whenever discipline imposed is "serious," such as prolonged solitary confinement; and that denial of confrontation or cross-examination must be justified by written explanation. *Clutchette* also ruled that notice and opportunity to respond must be afforded even where a temporary suspension of privileges is imposed.

The Supreme Court consolidated and reversed *Clutchette* and *Palmigiano*, ruling that inmates have no automatic right to counsel in serious disciplinary proceedings and that prison authorities were free to draw adverse inferences from silence, regardless of the possibility of criminal prosecution charges, because the disciplinary proceeding was similar to a civil action or administrative proceeding. The Court also ruled that *Clutchette*'s requirement of written reasons for the denial of confrontation and cross examination was inconsistent with *Wolff*'s emphasis on administrative discretion. Baxter v. Palmigiano, 425 U.S. 308, 324 (1976).

In reviewing the *Clutchette* decision, the Supreme Court explicitly left open the question whether any due process safeguards apply to lesser deprivations, such as loss of privileges. When a new assignment within a prison or an inter-institutional transfer is induced by a disciplinary violation and causes a loss of privileges or significant change in the conditions of custody, the administrative decision may have the purpose and effect of discipline. In recognition of this equivalence, some earlier lower federal court decisions had found that classification or transfer involves "grievous loss" triggering due process safeguards.[155] This development was, however, repudiated in Meachum v. Fano, supra, p. 653, which you should now review. *Meachum* casts serious doubt on the availability of procedural safeguards in cases other than those where a system of avowed sanctions is utilized to penalize infractions of disciplinary sanctions.[156]

The logic of the *Meachum* decision cuts back on the definition of constitutionally protected interests in a manner consistent with the general shift to a positivist

---

155. See Morris v. Travisono, 310 F. Supp. 857 (D.R.I. 1970); Newkirk v. Butler, 499 F.2d 1214 (2d Cir. 1974), *vac. for mootness,* 422 U.S. 395 (1975).

156. A number of circuit court opinions have dealt with internal classification of certain prisoners as "special offenders" in the federal prisons. The Seventh Circuit found that procedural due process did apply to special offender classification in Holmes v. Board of Parole, 541 F.2d 1243 (7th Cir. 1976). *Holmes* was overruled by the same circuit in Solomon v. Benson, 563 F.2d 339 (7th Cir. 1977), a result which the Circuit felt was compelled by the Supreme Court's intervening decision in Moody v. Daggett, 429 U.S. 78 (1976). But the applicability of due process to special offender classifications was upheld in Polizzi v. Sigler, 564 F.2d 792 (8th Cir. 1977). The court in *Polizzi* distinguished *Meachum* partially on the basis that "[t]he unique constraints imposed on 'special offenders' distinguish this classification system from interprison transfers that are, in the words of the Supreme Court in *Meachum,* 'within the normal limits or range of custody which the conviction has authorized the State to impose.'" 564 F.2d, at 797.

theory of protected entitlements in contemporary due process doctrine. As a consequence, state prison rules, as embodied in a statute or in departmental regulations, have attained a position of crucial importance. Any inmate challenging an institutional practice must point to an expectation created by these rules that such practices are prohibited by state law.[157] In light of *Meachum*, Massachusetts and other states are amending their statutes and regulations to reduce reliance on specific standards and formal procedures for controlling inmates and increasing the discretion of administrative officials. In many quarters it is believed that such discretion, exercised in swift and decisive fashion, is the only feasible means of dealing with prison disorders. Efforts to provide prisoners a substantial measure of procedural safeguards are not completely moribund.[158] But the entitlement approach to classifying the interests protected by due process, together with renewed judicial deference to prison officials in determining what process is due, has resulted in a substantial dimunition of the federal judicial role in prison discipline and administration.[159]

Questions

Section 10 of the disciplinary regulations issued by the Rhode Island Department of Corrections pursuant to statutory authority specifies some 25 disciplinary offenses, including disobeying an order of a staff member, "willful refusal to perform work," "tampering with windows or locks," "setting fires," "engaging in unauthorized sexual acts with others," and so forth. Section 10.25 prohibits "any conduct which disrupts or interferes with the security or orderly functioning of the institution." Section 11 of the regulations specifies the sanctions that may be imposed for violations: loss of good time credits, solitary confinement, loss of visiting privileges, extra work assignments, or reprimand.

William Wayward, let us hypothesize, is an inmate at the Rhode Island Correctional Institute for Men. About half the inmates at the Institute (not including Wayward) engaged in a work strike to protest poor food and inadequate medical services. Wayward and two other nonstriking inmates were selected by the strikers to present a formal list of grievances to the warden and seek to negotiate a settlement. The warden agreed to delay any action to terminate the strike for 24 hours in order to receive and consider the list of grievances. Wayward and his colleagues

157. For example, in Four Unnamed Plaintiffs v. Hall, 424 F. Supp. 357 (D. Mass. 1976), the District Court had ordered that inmates transferred to an isolation unit "with severe deprivations accompanying it" without any notice of the charges, be given rudimentary protections. The court interpreted the state classification regulations as giving rise to the expectation that an inmate will not be moved from general population to isolation units absent particular conditions and specific procedures. The Court of Appeals disagreed with its interpretation of the regulations (which it found granted wide discretion to prison officials) and upheld the summary transfer. 550 F.2d 1291 (1st Cir. 1977).

158. See ABA Criminal Justice Section 1, Tentative Draft, Criminal Justice Section Project on Standards Relating to the Legal Status of Prisoners, 14 Am. Crim. L. Rev. 377 (1977).

159. See generally, Note, Two Views of a Prisoner's Right to Due Process: Meachum v. Fano, 12 Harv. C.R.-C.L. L. Rev. 405 (1977).

report to the Warden that they are unable to agree on a list of grievances. After once extending the 24 hour deadline, the warden is convinced that Wayward is deliberately stalling. The warden disbands the Wayward group and takes action to break the strike.

The next day the warden initiates a disciplinary proceeding against Wayward, charging that his actions during the strike violated §10.25, before a board consisting of two guards and one social worker, all of whom are employed by the Institute. The warden testifies that Wayward was deliberately stalling in order to prolong the strike. Wayward, who is ably represented by a law student, is allowed to question the warden and testify himself, but is not permitted to call witnesses. The board finds Wayward guilty as charged and sentences him to 45 days in solitary confinement. The same day, the warden issues an order that after Wayward's sentence is served, he will not be allowed to return to the minimum security portion of the Institute where he was formerly assigned, but will be transferred to cellblock 7, a maximum security wing with close and continued surveillance and tightly restricted privileges.

Wayward brings a §1983 action in the United States District Court for the District of Rhode Island, seeking to enjoin his confinement to solitary and his transfer to cellblock 7. What result?

b. Grievance Mechanisms

Many institutional problems relating to prison administration and conditions seemingly do not rise to the level of constitutional importance and do not lend themselves to judicial resolution. Chief Justice Burger noted with dismay a prisoner who engaged the attention of "one district court judge twice, three circuit judges on appeal, and six others in a secondary sense — to say nothing of lawyers, court clerks, bailiffs, court reporters, and all the rest" [160] — in an attempt to recover seven packs of cigarettes allegedly taken improperly by a guard. Federal courts have generally refused to respond to complaints of this sort either by requiring procedural hearings or by limiting the substantive discretion of state prison officials.[161] To combat the inherent problems of supervision, enforcement, and triviality of many §1983 suits dealing with work rules, medical services, physical facilities, visitor and other privileges, unjustified treatment by guards, and other complaints concerning conditions of confinement, the federal judiciary has increasingly advocated the use of alternative, administrative mechanisms to resolve internal prison disputes.

160. Warren Burger, Report on the Federal Judicial Branch — 1973, American Bar Association Journal, Vol. 59 (October, 1973), at 1128-1129. The case referred to is Russell v. Bodner, 478 F.2d 1399 (3rd Cir. 1973).

161. Some of the reasons for this reluctance were recently voiced by Judge Kaufman: "A judge is far removed from the atmosphere of the maximum security prison and his sole personal contact with the hard tensions of the prison comes in the form of avid, though able, adversarial debate within the secure walls of a courthouse. He simply does not have the precise sense for the nuances or even the sweat of prison life." Kaufman, Prison: The Judge's Dilemma, 41 Fordham L. Rev. 495, 510 (1973).

Although grievance mechanisms in prisons are not constitutionally mandated, they are becoming extensively used. In a 1973 national survey covering 209 adult correctional facilities, containing over two-thirds of all males held in state institutions and nearly all state-held women, 77% of the responding prisons reported having a formal grievance procedure, 31% reported an ombudsman program, and 56% had inmate councils.[162] Such grievance mechanisms also contribute to the penological objectives of prison administrators.

One commonly recognized correctional goal is that of rehabilitation. Some riots occur because inmates believe they have no other method of gaining public attention to their conditions. Having complaints reach decision-making sources through established channels, which ensure that valid grievances will be considered, may lessen inmate tensions.

Institutional order, inmate safety, and general security are the overriding operational concerns of prison administrators. A grievance mechanism can be utilized for more effective institutional control due to the increased information flow accruing to officials. Potential problems and "trouble spots" can be identified at an early stage. Lastly, federal court suits, however futile, challenging prison practices might decline if fair, accessible alternative methods of dispute resolution were available. Although exhaustion of administrative remedies has not been required before an inmate may file a §1983 suit, courts have been willing to defer if a "speedy, sufficient, and readily available" remedy exists.[163]

Legislation has been introduced in Congress (H.R. 9400, 94th Cong.) which would provide federal encouragement of alternative dispute settlement mechanisms by providing for certification by the Attorney General of state prison grievance mechanisms meeting federal standards for staff and inmate participation in design and operation of the system; deadlines for processing grievances; and outside review of the disposition of grievances by a reviewing body independent of prison authorities.[164] In order to provide some incentive to state officials to qualify for certifica-

162. Virginia A. McArthur, Inmate Grievance Mechanisms: A Survey of 209 American Prisons, Federal Probation, Vol. 38, No. 4, December, 1974, p.41.

163. Morgan v. LaVallee, 526 F.2d 221 (2nd Cir. 1975).

164. The several factors listed in the bill to be included in the minimum standards are borrowed directly from the grievance mechanism model designed by the Center for Correctional Justice in Washington, D.C. J. Michael Keating, Jr., et. al., Grievance Mechanisms in Correctional Institutions, National Institute of Law Enforcement and Criminal Justice (September 1975). The requirement of inmate and line staff participation in the design, implementation, and operation of the system is essential so that those who know the institution best will have been involved in tailoring a system well adapted to the particular mechanism and will have a vested interest in seeing that system work. Line staff will be less resistant to a mechanism they helped implement.

The last requirement is perhaps the most difficult to implement for it requires outside, independent review at some stage of the procedure. The objective, neutral perspective of an individual or group not affiliated with the institution lends credibility to the mechanism and imposes the necessity of acting reasonably upon lower levels of the procedure. Review by persons responsible to the corrections department will hardly win the confidence of inmates and outside critics in the review process. The review need not be binding to be effective; to be credible, it need only be fair and independent, with correctional officials demonstrating good faith in their acceptance or rejection of decisions by written explanations. On the other hand, fear that independent review will lead to excessive outside interference in prison administration may be un-tion, the bill would authorize federal courts to require, in the case of certified grievance systems, that inmate plaintiffs in §1983 suits first exhaust their administrative remedies within such systems.

Questions:

Does the abrupt pattern of judicial intervention and retreat in prison discipline and classification result from judicial preoccupation with adversary trial-type procedures? Might more solid and lasting progress have been made if courts had acknowledged the merit of alternatives to adversary hearings? How would courts evaluate such alternatives? Compare the discussion of Mashaw's proposals, supra, p. 666.

c. Probation and Parole

In Morrissey v. Brewer, 408 U.S. 471 (1972), the Supreme Court extended due process protection to parolees facing revocation of their parole:

> [T]he liberty of a parolee, although indeterminate, includes many of the core values of unqualified liberty and its termination inflicts a "grievous loss" on the parolee and often on others. It is hardly useful any longer to try to deal with this problem in terms of whether the parolee's liberty is a "right" or a "privilege." By whatever name, the liberty is valuable and must be seen as within the protection of the Fourteenth Amendment. Its termination calls for some orderly process, however informal.[165]

Two hearings were mandated by the Court, a preliminary probable cause hearing "conducted at or reasonably near the place of the alleged parole violation or arrest," 408 U.S. at 485, and a subsequent, more formal, hearing leading "to a final evaluation of any contested revelant facts and consideration of whether the facts as determined warrant revocation." 408 U.S., at 488.[166] *Morrissey* reserved the question

---

warranted because experience indicates that most grievances are resolved before the stage of outside review is reached — statistics for the California Youth Authority experiment with outside advisory arbitration show that under one percent of the 7000 grievances were appealed to outside review. Nonetheless, grievance mechanisms and other "reform" measures may be bitterly opposed by these prisoners who enjoy a dominant position in the existing informal power structure of prisons. See Note, Bargaining in Correctional Institutions: Restructuring the Relation Between the Inmate and the Prison Authority, 81 Yale L.J. 726 (1972).

165. Id. at 482. Query: Is the Court's liberty rationale still valid after Meachum v. Fano, supra p. 653? Under what circumstances might a parollee have a "property" interest in not having parole revoked?

166. At the preliminary hearing, the parolee is entitled to (a) a decisionmaker not directly involved in the case, (b) notice of the hearing, and (c) an opportunity to offer evidence on his own behalf. Confrontation of adverse witnesses may be allowed on a limited and discretionary

whether a parolee was entitled to retained or appointed counsel at either hearing. In Gagnon v. Scarpelli, 411 U.S. 778 (1973), the Court extended the *Morrissey* requirement of preliminary and final hearings to the revocation of probation. A flexible, case-by-case approach was adopted to determine whether an indigent probationer or parolee had a due process right to appointed counsel.

Do procedural due process safeguards apply to an initial decision granting or denying parole, as opposed to the revocation of parole? Some courts have reasoned that due process requirements only attach when a plaintiff is being deprived of a right he or she *currently* enjoys; this approach would mean that due process protection would apply to the revocation but not the grant of parole.[167] The Circuits are divided on the question whether failure to grant parole is subject to due process safeguards, and the Supreme Court has not yet resolved the conflict.[168]

Questions:

Can the notion that due process safeguards apply only to deprivations of rights currently enjoyed be reconciled with an "entitlement" definition of protected interests? Under what circumstances might a person have a "liberty" or "property" interest in revocation of parole or probation but not in the initial grant?

E. The Effects of "Due Process"

The following excerpts from the Journal of Criminal Law, Criminology and Police Science provide an interesting example of the practical outcome of applying "due process" requirements to an area where they had previously been absent.

---

basis. The hearing officer is required to make a summary, or digest, of the hearing. At the revocation hearing, required procedures include: (a) written notice of the claimed violations of parole; (b) disclosure to the parolee of evidence against him; (c) opportunity to be heard in person and to present witnesses and documentary evidence; (d) the right to confront and cross-examine adverse witnesses (unless the hearing officer specifically finds good cause for not allowing confrontation); (e) a "neutral and detached" hearing body such as a traditional parole board, members of which need not be judicial officers or lawyers; and (f) a written statement by the factfinders as to the evidence relied on and reasons for revoking parole. Id. at 486-489.

167. See Comment, Entitlement, Enjoyment, and Due Process of the Law, 1974 Duke L. J. 89, 101-102, 111-114 (1974); Note, Procedural Due Process in Parole Release Proceedings — Existing Rules, Recent Court Decisions, and Experience in the Prison, 60 Minn. L. Rev. 341, 345-48 (1976); Scarpa v. Board of Parole, 477 F.2d 278, 282 (5th Cir. 1973), *vacated and remanded for reconsideration of mootness*, 414 U.S. 809 (1973).

168. Compare Craft v. Texas Board of Pardons and Paroles, 550 F.2d 1054 (5th Cir.), *cert. denied*, 434 U.S. 926 (1977) with Williams v. Ward, 556 F.2d 1143 (2d Cir.), *cert. dismissed*, 434 U.S. 944 (1977). For discussion, see Note, The Applicability of Due Process and State Freedom of Information Acts to Parole Release Hearings, 27 Syracuse L. Rev. 1011 (1976).

Judicial Intervention in Prison Discipline
Harvard Center for Criminal Justice

63 J. Crim. L.C. & P.S. 200 (1972)

In recent years there has been growing attention to the question of prisoners' rights and to problems relating to discretion in prison administration. The catastrophe at Attica greatly increased the concern over conditions and inadequacies in our nation's correctional institutions.

One crucial aspect of correctional problems — inmate discipline — was faced in a consent decree issued on March 11, 1970, by Federal Judge Raymond J. Pettine. In Morris v. Travisono [310 F. Supp. 857 (D.R.I. 1970)], Judge Pettine established comprehensive procedural regulations for the handling of disciplinary matters in the Rhode Island Adult Correctional Institution (ACI). A short time after the entry of that decree, the Center for Criminal Justice at Harvard Law School agreed to study the impact of the *Morris* decision within the prison. This article documents and analyzes the results of that study....

III. FINDINGS — THE PROCEDURAL MODEL

Judge Pettine's consent decree was aimed at insuring fairness in the prison's disciplinary proceedings by establishing a variety of procedural safeguards.... In this section, we shall examine the *Morris* order's major procedural provisions and, with respect to each of them, consider the following questions:

1. What was the situation at the ACI with regard to the particular problem prior to the entry of the order?
2. What were the explicit provisions of the order which were designed to meet the particular problem area?
3. What effect did the pertinent provision of the order have? To what extent was the provision implemented?
4. Could the specific provision have been improved to better meet this problem area?
5. What alternative means are available to deal with the problem?

A. NOTICE OF THE CHARGES

For the initiation of the disciplinary proceedings, the order requires that an inmate violation report be completed which details the alleged violation, and that both oral and written notice be given to the inmate of the disciplinary infraction with which he is charged. Notice is required, apparently not only to establish the precise nature of the offense and to inform the inmate fully of the charges, but also to give him an opportunity to prepare a defense.

These notice provisions met with substantial compliance. The violation report form serves as the foundation for the entire proceeding and was almost always filled out. In the vast majority of cases, oral notice was given the inmate when he was booked. Written notice consisted of a copy of the violation report form, and, when given, was presented to the inmate by the classification counselor, usually on the day following the booking.

The notice, especially the description of the alleged violation, was generally very cursory. The charge was stated, but the circumstances surrounding the incident were rarely given. Names were often misspelled, the writing sometimes illegible, and the continuation of a single incident was often written up on two or three separate forms as distinct charges with the times of infractions only minutes apart. Any or all of these factors could contribute to the inmate's confusion about the charges against him. . . .

B. PREHEARING DETENTION

One of the primary objectives of the new regulations was to limit detention prior to a Disciplinary Board hearing to exceptional cases only, with such detention conducted in a "non-punitive" manner. However, the lack of clarity in defining an "exceptional" case fostered abuse of that basic objective. . . .

In addition to the "immediate threat" and "serious wrong doing" requirements, unlike the situation in "lock-ups," a written record of the reassignment must be forwarded to the Warden and the Deputy Warden for approval or disapproval. Furthermore, such reassignments are to be reviewed at the next sitting of the Classification Board, which is to take place not longer than one week from the date of the reassignment. No such review is required for regular lock-ups. Therefore, although it appears that "lock-up pending a disciplinary board hearing" and "temporary reassignments" under the emergency provisions of the rules result in the same segregation (i.e., confinement to cell) and treatment of the inmate . . . lock-up can be effected without meeting the emergency requirements of immediate threat to the safety or security of the ACI and without the subsequent review necessary for temporary reassignment.

This confusion in the regulations may account in part for the fact that, contrary to the apparent intention of the consent decree, the incidence of prehearing detentions after the entry of the decree remained about the same as it had been before. Perhaps another reason is that such detention may really be necessary in many cases. While the regulation's standards were somewhat unclear, it is apparent that the main purpose of prehearing detention is to segregate the inmate from the rest of the population when it appears that the alleged violation makes him a threat to himself, to others, or to the security of the institution. In the context of a prison setting, with its close quarters and substantial numbers of people with previous histories of violence, it is very possible that almost any irregular incident can be seen as a likely threat and a potential spark to serious disturbances. Certainly, the prediction of future trouble, even in the relatively immediate future, is highly speculative, but overprediction in the prison setting, and therefore overdetention, might be more justified than on the outside because of the potentially volatile nature of penal institutions. . . .

C. SUPERIOR OFFICER'S INVESTIGATION

The superior officer's investigation is another important aspect of the decree; the Disciplinary Board relies heavily on it in its consideration of the case. Our study revealed that the superior officer's investigation was in most cases quite summary and the reports often very inadequate. In many incidents there were no witnesses, but even in those in which there were, rarely was anyone except the charging officer and the inmate interviewed. In most cases, the summary of the investigation amounted to one sentence stating either whether the inmate admitted the offense or whether the superior officer thought the inmate was guilty. In addition, the superior officer frequently gave his opinion (usually negative) of the inmate's attitude, and, in a few cases, he gave his view of the proper sentence. The superior officer's report seldom shed any light on the facts of the incident itself or the circumstances surrounding it. The inadequacy of the reports is probably due to a number of reasons: a lack of training regarding the significance of these investigations, a resistance to additional paper work, and, perhaps most important, a feeling that there is no need for more, since the Board has generally found these quite summary reports sufficient for its purposes. The cursory nature of the superior officer's investigation is a corollary to the subsequent de-emphasis of the fact-finding process by the Disciplinary Board.

D. REPRESENTATION

The *Morris* decree mandated classification counselors as the representatives of the inmate at the Disciplinary Board hearing. The decree makes the counselor responsible for transmitting the written notice of the charges and hearing to the inmate, for informing the inmate of his right to have a counselor assist him at the hearing, and for assisting the inmate on appeal if he is dissatisfied with the Board's decision.

The experience at the ACI in making the correctional staff responsible for serving as inmates' advocates in disciplinary proceedings is instructive. At the hearings themselves, classification counselors generally seemed to play an extremely limited role. This might be due to the fact that the defense was usually an outright denial, and the result often rested on the question of credibility, the officer's against the inmate's. Usually though, the counselors were reluctant to become ardent advocates for inmates in the disciplinary hearings. Our staff interviews indicated that the reason for this reluctance was the conflict they felt between their role as advocate for the inmates and their role as a member of the prison staff:

> There's a basic conflict — we are caught between the inmate and the rest of the staff. If we win a case for him, the staff resents it; if we lose, he resents us.

> There is also a problem in that the counselor is resented by the staff when an inmate he represented at a disciplinary board hearing is found not guilty.

Classification Counselors are confused as to how they should act. They are required to be something between a lawyer and a social worker.

At the same time, almost all the inmates in the interview sample said they were dissatisfied with the counselor's representation at the hearing.

An alternative to using correctional staff for representational purposes might be to use outside counsel, but this, also, presents a number of problems. Outsiders, especially those assuming an adversary role, are often viewed with hostility and suspicion by the staff. Their "interference" in prison affairs is resented, and they are seen as a threat by the staff, who fear any undermining of their authority and the possibility of civil liability suits against them. These fears might lead the staff to bypass the formal disciplinary process, where they would be subjected to counsel's investigation and interrogation, either by disciplining the inmates informally or by ignoring infractions of the prison rules. Outside counsel is also resisted because of a fear that Board proceedings will be transformed into criminal trials. A number of staff members felt that the decree already went too far in that respect:

The fallacy is in instituting court procedures in the ACI hearings. We are not a court. . . . There are too many confusing technicalities in the order.

The entire order is wrong as to discipline. The system should not be so formal. The average inmate is glad to get his court appearance over. He can then relax and do his time. However, with the new system, it is like he is always going back to court. The average inmate doesn't want to bother with such a formal system.

Moreover, if retained counsel were permitted, equal protection problems would be raised regarding indigent inmates who could not afford such counsel. Finally, given the institutional de-emphasis on the entire fact-finding process, legal representation at Board hearings may not in fact be necessary in all disciplinary cases. To provide for such legal representation in particular cases would be tantamount to refocusing the disciplinary inquiry.

E.   DISCIPLINARY HEARING — THE DISCIPLINARY BOARD

1.   COMPOSITION OF THE BOARD

The *Morris* decree required that the Disciplinary Boards in both the maximum and medium-minimum security institutions have three members, consisting of the Deputy Warden of the particular facility and two members "selected from the custody and treatment departments." This provision was interpreted as requiring one member from custody and one from treatment, and these requirements were almost always met.

The compositional provision of the decree was subjected to substantial criticism by both staff and inmates. The staff problem of having to use classification counselors (who were also supposed to represent inmates) on the Board to meet the treatment member requirement, has already been discussed. On the other hand, the inmates simply felt that the Board was unfairly constituted. In citing the composition of the Board as the most unfair aspect of the disciplinary process at the ACI, the inmates characterized the board as a "kangaroo court" and a "biased board" which did not "know how to be fair." They alleged that the Board members held "grudges" and showed favoritism, and they particularly criticized the presence of guards on the Board as well as the absence of blacks, in alleging racial prejudice.

The impartiality of the Disciplinary Board may be impeded by several factors. In a small, closed institution like the ACI, staff members are familiar with many of the inmates and usually bring to the Board hearings a great deal of personal knowledge about a particular inmate and sometimes bias, either favorable or unfavorable, toward him. The result often is that the disciplinary decision is made on the basis of the personal and usually unarticulated feelings of a staff member, rather than on the facts presented at the hearing.

Board members may not act impartially because they feel that their duty is to support the staff in all cases. As one Board member put it, "The philosophy in the past has been always back up your officers, whether they are right or wrong." Such a view is particularly harmful to the integrity of the disciplinary process, when, as in most contested hearings, the evidence consists mainly of conflicting testimony by the prisoner and a staff member.

Another factor which may affect the disposition of the case is the inmate's behavior before the Board. An inmate who is "defiant" or had a "hard attitude" or insists on his "rights" is unlikely to win the sympathy of the Board.

These factors affecting the Board's decisions — personal knowledge of, and sometimes bias toward, the inmate defendant, tendency to support staff, and reaction to inmate attitude before the Board — combine to make the prison disciplinary process something less than a hearing before impartial arbiters based only upon evidence and argument in open court....

2. JURISDICTION OF THE BOARD

While the *Morris* decree did not specifically resolve the question of what particular patterns of behavior could be subject to prison discipline, our study revealed that inmates were disciplined for a broad range of actions, suggesting the many purposes for which a prison disciplinary system is used. These purposes include the promotion of staff status and respect, the maintenance of control, order and security, deterrence, punishment, and at least theoretically, rehabilitation. Obviously this multiplicity of purpose may create conflicting pressures in particular situations, pressures which may require different procedures than those used in traditional due process proceedings.

3. HEARING PROCEDURES

The *Morris* decree established the following procedures for conducting the hearing: reading to the inmate the charges and the record of the surrounding circumstances; admission or denial of the charges by the inmate; interrogation of the inmate by the Board; and presentation of evidence by the inmate.

In most of the cases observed by our researchers there was considerable discussion of the case preceding the inmate's entry into the hearing room. Following the inmate's arrival, standard procedure was to tell the inmate the charge and to ask him whether he admitted or denied the allegations. If he admitted them, the charge would be read in full and frequently the sentence would then be imposed. If he denied the charge, the charging officer would be called into the room to re-read the charge to the inmate. There was seldom any detailed questioning of the officer about the facts of the case or the circumstances surrounding it. The inmate was given an opportunity to tell his version of the incident. While there is no explicit provision in the decree authorizing the inmate to call witnesses, on a number of occasions inmates made such a request and were denied, although one case was observed in which a witness was permitted. Generally the classification counselor rendered limited assistance. After this usually brief presentation of the evidence, the inmate would be sent out of the room and disposition would be discussed, with the chairman's recommendation most often the controlling opinion. The inmate would then be called back into the room and told of the Board's decision and the disposition.

In sum, the disciplinary hearings were very cursory affairs. The changing [sic] and investigative reports upon which the Board relied almost exclusively presented the circumstances surrounding the alleged infraction inadequately. Furthermore, although only in a minority of the monitored cases did the inmate deny the charges, when there were such denials the fact-finding inquiry was minimal. Even when conflicting factual testimony was presented, no attempt was made to probe more deeply or to reconcile the contradictions. Perhaps this resulted primarily from fear of calling into question the charging officer's credibility, a fear which colors the entire disciplinary process. If an inmate were found not guilty in the face of an officer's assertion of the inmate's guilt, the officer might well take such a finding as an attack on his truthfulness. Rather than so insult the charging officer, a prison official with whom each member of the Disciplinary Board must work and live, the presumption of credibility is strongly biased against the inmate or inmate witness in any contested case.

The real function of the Board is dispositional in nature. Even in contested cases, with the presumption of credibility so heavily weighted against the inmate, the Board's fact-finding role is subordinated to its dispositional function. If the predominant purpose of the Disciplinary Board were to evaluate an inmate's general progress in the institution rather than to find facts regarding a particular alleged offense, errors in fact-finding might be tolerated. However, where the disposition is keyed directly to the charged misconduct, as is ostensibly the case at the ACI, fact-finding is critical. Indeed, to minimize fact-finding would tend to reduce inmate morale and confidence in the integrity of the disciplinary process.

4. DISPOSITION

a. *Procedure.* As has already been noted, after the evidence is presented at the hearing, the inmate leaves the room while the Board discusses its decision and the appropriate disposition. The regulations dictate that the Board's decision be based upon "substantial evidence." While this requirement might be thought to be useful in assuring at least a minimum of testimony that the alleged infraction actually occurred, in practice there is almost always such evidence because the officer's testimony usually states sufficient facts to constitute a prima facie case of inmate violation. . . .

b. *Types of Dispositions.* A broad range of dispositions is used by the Disciplinary Boards at the ACI. . . .The punishments generally thought to be most severe, i.e., segregation and the loss of good time, comprised only 19% and 7% respectively of the dispositions after the decree. Before the decree 30% of the dispositions involved segregation and 15% loss of good time. At the same time, the "lighter" dispositions, such as reprimands, suspensions, and probations increased, as did the percentage of charges dropped and findings of not guilty. . . . This change, however, does not necessarily reflect the impact of the decree. . . .

Following Morris v. Travisono Judge Pettine was bombarded by cases challenging conditions of confinement and inmate transfer practices. The procedures decreed in *Morris* were suspended in 1973 following an inmate riot. In response to the riot and the subsequent murder of a prison guard, state officials expelled from the ACI an Inmate Legal Assistance Project run by two attorneys to assist inmates in exercising their *Morris* rights.

Subsequently Judge Pettine, frustrated that "[a]ll the litigation seems to have produced only hollow victories," imposed specific requirements for operation of the ACI, including revised classification procedures; deadlines for rehabilitating physical facilities to meet specified minimum standards; and a deadline for shutdown of the ACI's maximum security section. He also appointed a special master to administer the decree and threatened state officials with contempt sanctions. State officials are making efforts to comply, but the ultimate effects of Judge Pettine's more recent intervention remains unclear.[169]

Question

How, if at all, does this study affect your judgment about the wisdom of, the justification for, or the constitutional validity of the due process decisions that you have read in this chapter?

---

169. See Prison Reform: The Judicial Process, 23 BNA Crim. Law Rep. No. 17 (Supp. Aug. 2, 1978).

Organizing and Managing a Bureaucratic Agency: The FTC and Its Reform

A. Introduction

1. Overview of Chapter Eight

This chapter focuses on the structure and performance of the Federal Trade Commission during the late 1960s and early 1970s, a period when intense criticism sparked major internal reforms. This chapter deals with agency staff, agency structure, and the marshalling of agency resources to achieve a concrete regulatory objective. First, it will analyze several problems related to the characteristic structure of the independent agency, focusing upon the tensions that result from the fact that agencies often perform prosecutorial, adjudicatory, legislative, and managerial functions — all under one roof.

Second, the chapter presents excerpts from several important critical surveys of the FTC's performance, and describes the subsequent efforts of Chairman Caspar Weinberger to overcome the agency's problems. The method he used — reorganizing personnel and restructuring the agency — is often advocated as a cure-all for agency failures. A brief exploration of the claimed relationship between agency structure and performance will help you to evaluate the potential fruitfulness of this approach to reform.

Third, the chapter will examine the internal effort at revitalizing the FTC undertaken by Robert Pitofsky, head of its Consumer Protection Bureau. Pitofsky sought to use the bureaucratic tools that the agency provided to achieve a specific substantive goal — improved regulation of advertising. In examining his efforts, the substance of advertising regulation will be explored: it offers an excellent example of the methods used and the difficulties faced by the government when it seeks to regulate the flow of information without violating the First Amendment. In addition, the ways in which an agency's ability to accomplish its mission successfully is constrained by its staff, structure, and the political environment in which it works will begin to become apparent.

2. The Federal Trade Commission

[The Federal Trade Commission] is a new device in administrative machinery, introduced by Congress in the year 1914, in the hope thereby of remedying conditions in business which a great majority of the American people regarded as menacing the general welfare, and which for more than a generation they had vainly attempted to remedy by the ordinary processes of law. FTC v. Gratz, 253 U.S. 421, 432 (1920) (Brandeis, J., dissenting).

The Federal Trade Commission was born in a spirit of reform in 1914. The Commission has summarized its structure and powers as follows:

The Federal Trade Commission

1978/79 United States Government Manual 545-552 (1978)

The basic objective of the Federal Trade Commission is the maintenance of strongly competitive enterprise as the keystone of the American economic system. Although the duties of the Commission are many and varied under law, the foundation of public policy underlying all these duties is essentially the same: to prevent the free enterprise system from being stifled, substantially lessened or fettered by monopoly or restraints on trade, or corrupted by unfair or deceptive trade practices.

In brief, the Commission is charged with keeping competition both free and fair. This basic purpose finds its primary expression in the Federal Trade Commission Act, cited below, and the Clayton Act (38 Stat. 730; 15 U.S.C. 12), both passed in 1914 and both successively amended in the years that have followed.[1] The Federal Trade Commission Act lays down a general prohibition against the use in commerce of "unfair methods of competition" and "unfair or deceptive acts or practices." The Clayton Act outlaws specific practices recognized as instruments of monopoly. As an administrative agency, acting quasi-judicially and quasi-legislatively, the Com-

---

1. Ed. note: "The Federal Trade Commission was organized as an independent administrative agency in 1951, pursuant to the Federal Trade Commission Act of 1914 (38 Stat. 717; 15 U.S.C. 41-51). Related duties subsequently were delegated to the Commission by the Wheeler-Lea Act, the Trans-Alaska Pipeline Authorization Act, the Clayton Act, the Export Trade Act, the Wool Products Labeling Act, the Fur Products Labeling Act, the Textile Fiber Products Identification Act, the Fair Packaging and Labeling Act, the Lanham Trade-Mark Act of 1946, the Truth in Lending Act, the Fair Credit Reporting Act, the Robinson-Patman Act, the Hobby Protection Act, and the Magnuson-Moss Warranty-Federal Trade Commission Improvement Act." 1978/79 U.S. Govt. Manual (1978), at 546.

mission was established to deal with trade practices on a continuing and corrective basis. It has no authority to punish; its function is to "prevent," through cease-and-desist orders and other means, those practices condemned by the law of Federal trade regulation; however, court ordered civil penalties up to $10,000 may be obtained for each violation of a Commission order. . . .

The Commission's law enforcement work falls into two general categories: actions to foster law observance voluntarily; and formal litigation leading to mandatory orders against offenders.

For the most part, law observance is obtained through voluntary and cooperative action by way of staff level advice, which is not binding on the Commission, advisory opinions by the Commission, trade regulation rules, and through issuance of guides delineating legal requirements as to particular business practices.

The formal litigative proceedings are similar to those used in courts. Cases are instituted by issuance of a complaint charging a person, partnership, or corporation — the respondent — with violation of one or more of the statutes administered by the Commission. Cases may be settled by consent orders or occasionally through informal administrative correction of minor violations. If the charges are not contested, or if in a contested case and after hearing the charges are found to be true, an order to cease and desist is issued requiring discontinuance of the unlawful practices. . . .

Cases before the Commission may originate through complaint by a consumer or a competitor; the Congress or from Federal, State, or municipal agencies. Also, the Commission itself may initiate an investigation to determine possible violation of the laws administered by it. No formality is required in submitting a complaint. A letter giving the facts in detail is sufficient, but it should be accompanied by all evidence in possession of the complaining party in support of the charges made. It is the policy of the Commission not to disclose the identity of any complainant, except as required by law.

Upon receipt of a complaint, various criteria are applied in determining whether the particular matter should be docketed for investigation. Within the limits of its resources, investigations are initiated which are considered to best support the Commission's goals of maintaining competition and protecting consumers.

On completion of an investigation, there may be a staff recommendation for: informal settlement of the case; issuance of a formal complaint; or closing the matter.

If the Commission decides to issue a complaint the respondent is served with a copy of the complaint and proposed order. Prior to the hearings, respondent and Commission counsel may negotiate a cease-and-desist order to which the respondent agrees to consent. If such a consent order is worked out, the respondent does not admit any violation of the law but agrees to discontinue the challenged practice.

If an agreement containing a consent order is not entered into, litigation usually ensues.

The case is heard by an administrative law judge who, after taking testimony at public hearings, issues an initial decision. This becomes the decision of the Commission at the end of 30 days unless the respondent or the counsel supporting the complaint appeals the decision to the Commission, or the Commission by order stays the effective date or places the case on its own docket for review. In the Commission's decision on such appeal or review, [if the initial decision was against the respondent and] is sustained, or modified, a cease-and-desist order is issued.

. . . [T]he order to cease and desist, or to take other corrective action such as affirmative disclosure, divestiture or restitution, becomes final 60 days after the date of service upon the respondent, unless within that period the respondent petitions an appropriate United States court of appeals to review the order. In case of review, the order of the Commission becomes final after affirmance by the court of appeals or by the Supreme Court of the United States, if taken to that court on certiorari. Violations of an order to cease and desist after it becomes final subjects the offender to suit by the Government in a United States district court for the recovery of a civil penalty of not more than $10,000 for each violation and, where the violation continues, each day of its continuance is a separate violation. . . .

In carrying out the statutory directive to "prevent" the use in commerce of unfair practices, the Commission makes extensive use of voluntary and cooperative procedures. Through these procedures business and industry may obtain authoritative guidance and a substantial measure of certainty as to what they may do under the laws administered by the Commission.

Notes

Examine the organizational table of the FTC on page 729. Note first that it is headed by a body of five commissioners. Each is appointed for a term of seven years by the President, with the advice and consent of the Senate. The terms are staggered such that no more than one expires in any given year. Not more than three of the five commissioners may be members of the same political party. Before 1950, the Commission elected its Chairman. Now the President appoints the Chairman, who makes staff appointments with the full Commission's approval.[2]

The chief staff members include the General Counsel, who represents the FTC in court, advises the Commission on questions of law and policy, works with state and local officials, and coordinates all liaison activities with Congress. He is also responsible for preparing advisory opinions for companies and individuals who want to check the legality of proposed actions.

The Executive Director is the chief operating officer and exercises administrative supervision over all FTC offices, bureaus, and staff members. Under him are three major bureaus. The Bureau of Competition enforces the basic antitrust law, primarily the FTCA and the Clayton Act. The Bureau of Consumer Protection investigates and litigates matters involving unfair or deceptive acts or practices, as well as some product safety. Finally, the Bureau of Economics advises the Commission on the economic aspects of its activities and assists the other two Bureaus in their investigations and trial work.

2. 15 U.S.C. §41 sets forth the basic procedure for appointment of Federal Trade Commissioners.

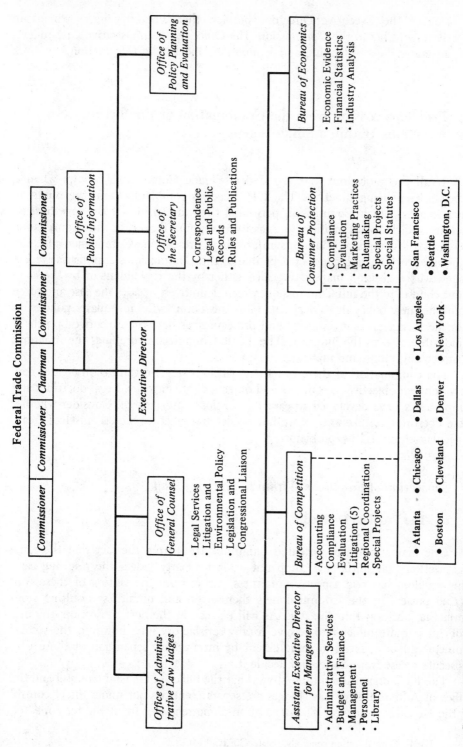

Federal Trade Commission

Commissioner	Commissioner	Chairman	Commissioner	Commissioner

Office of
Public Information

Office of
Policy Planning
and Evaluation

Executive Director

Office of
the Secretary
· Correspondence
· Legal and Public
  Records
· Rules and Publications

Bureau of Economics
· Economic Evidence
· Financial Statistics
· Industry Analysis

Office of Adminis-
trative Law Judges

Office of
General Counsel
· Legal Services
· Litigation and
  Environmental Policy
· Legislation and
  Congressional Liaison

Bureau of
Consumer Protection
· Compliance
· Evaluation
· Marketing Practices
· Rulemaking
· Special Projects
· Special Statutes

· San Francisco
· Seattle
· Washington, D.C.

· Los Angeles
· New York

Assistant Executive Director
for Management
· Administrative Services
· Budget and Finance
· Management
· Personnel
· Library

Bureau of Competition
· Accounting
· Compliance
· Evaluation
· Litigation (5)
· Regional Coordination
· Special Projects

· Dallas
· Denver

· Atlanta
· Boston

· Chicago
· Cleveland

Source: 1977/1978 United States Government Manual

Outside the Executive Director's purview there are four offices which are directly responsible to the Commission: the Offices of Administrative Law Judges, the Secretary, Policy Planning and Evaluation, and Public Information.[3]

B. Problems Arising from the Combination of Conflicting Functions Within a Single Agency

Recall the procedure that the Federal Trade Commission follows when it exercises its policing function. The FTC receives complaints from the public or other sources, which Commission personnel then investigate. If the investigation discloses sufficient information to constitute a prima facie case, the Commission itself issues a complaint. Commission attorneys present the Commission's case in an adjudicatory hearing conducted by one of the Commission's administrative law judges, whose decision may be appealed either by the respondent or by the complaint counsel to the full Commission, which definitively decides the case and often establishes new policy in its decision. Thus the Commission formulates policies, as does the Congress. It investigates and prosecutes, as does the executive branch. It adjudicates, as does the judiciary. The Trade Commission combines the functions of prosecutor, judge, and manager.

The combination of these functions within a single organization creates conflicts between objectives of fairness and objectives of efficiency. Legal doctrines and compromises have developed to ease the tensions thus created. Consider whether these doctrines are likely to create fair results and whether they themselves create particular administrative problems.

1. Separation of Functions Within the Agency Staff

a. The Problem Defined

One major source of potential unfairness arises from the fact that the same organization that initiates a complaint against a party judges the resulting case. This problem has two aspects: unfairness arising from the vesting of these conflicting powers in the Commissioners themselves, and unfairness resulting from conflicting duties within the staff. As will be seen in the next subsection, the first problem is quite difficult to resolve in any satisfactory way; however, the second problem can be relieved to some extent by intra-agency separation of those who prosecute a case from those who decide it.

The FTC organization table shows that the Office of General Counsel and the Office of Administrative Law Judges are separate entities not under direct control of the Executive Director. This separation alone relieves part of the tension. Yet,

3. For FTC organization generally, see 16 C.F.R. 0.1-0.18.

prosecutions within the Commission are handled by Bureau lawyers (the General Counsel's office primarily represents the FTC in the courts); and the prosecutors and judges are still responsible to the Commission. Might this not compromise the independence of one or another of these groups? Moreover, the agency staff might view itself as a group, thus generating loyalties and esprit de corps which transcend the barriers on an organizational chart. Can "isolated" parts of an organization hope to function neutrally when their members ride the same bus to work, work in adjoining offices, share coffee breaks and lunches, and move in the same social circles? Do these criticisms also apply to judges and members of the local bar?

Plans to separate functions at both Commission and staff levels have been proposed. In 1937, for example, a blue-ribbon panel recommended to the President that each of the independent commissions should be replaced by a truly independent "judicial" section and an Executive-controlled "administrative" section.[4] Proponents soon found that it was difficult or impossible to separate the adjudicatory functions from related responsibilities, and the plan foundered.[5] Another possible response to the problem is that adopted by the NLRB —near total separation of the General Counsel (who issues complaints) from the rest of the agency. The NLRB is the only agency which has adopted this organizational structure.[6]

The uneasy compromise which carried the day politically is that embodied in the Administrative Procedure Act, which attempts to make hearing examiners (now known as "administrative law judges") independent within the agency. The history behind this development and the competing policy justifications for this separation of functions are developed more fully by Mr. Justice Jackson in Wong Yang Sung v. McGrath.

Wong Yang Sung v. McGrath

339 U.S. 33 (1950)

Mr. Justice JACKSON delivered the opinion of the Court.

This habeas corpus proceeding involves a single ultimate question — whether administrative hearings in deportation cases must conform to requirements of the Administrative Procedure Act. . . .

4. Report of the President's Committee on Administrative Management 40-42, 223 (1937). The second Hoover Commission Report in 1955 made a somewhat similar proposal. See Commission on Organization of the Executive Branch of the Government, Legal Services and Procedure 87-88 (1955).

5. Note that while total separation of "judicial" and "executive" activity may be impossible, concentration of the power to issue complaints in an "independent" office within the agency is relatively easy. This practice is fairly common within federal agencies; in fact, the FTC has been criticized because its organization is still structured so as to allow the Commissioners themselves to issue complaints. See Report of the ABA Commission to Study the Federal Trade Commission 82-84 (1969).

6. See Klaus, The Taft-Hartley Experiment in Separation of NLRB Functions, 11 Ind. & Lab. Rel. Rev. 371 (1958). The "experiment" did not work out very well. Ms. Klaus relates in harrowing terms the constant sniping between the General Counsel and the Board, which has occasionally broken out into open warfare. Repeated legislative attempts to reform the agency into a more conventional structure have come to naught.

Wong Yang Sung, native and citizen of China, was arrested by immigration officials on a charge of being unlawfully in the United States through having overstayed shore leave.... A hearing was held before an immigrant inspector who recommended deportation. The Acting Commissioner approved; and the Board of Immigration Appeals affirmed.

Wong Yang Sung then sought release from custody by habeas corpus proceedings in District Court for the District of Columbia, upon the sole ground that the administrative hearing was not conducted in conformity with [the separation of functions requirements of] §§ 5 and 11 of the Administrative Procedure Act.[7] The Government admitted noncompliance, but asserted that the Act did not apply....

I

...Multiplication of federal administrative agencies and expansion of their functions to include adjudications which have serious impact on private rights has been one of the dramatic legal developments of the past half-century. Partly from restriction by statute, partly from judicial self-restraint, and partly by necessity — from the nature of their multitudinous and semilegislative or executive tasks — the decisions of administrative tribunals were accorded considerable finality, and especially with respect to fact finding. The conviction developed, particularly within the legal profession, that this power was not sufficiently safeguarded and sometimes was put to arbitrary and biased use....

[The Court then traced the history of efforts to reform administrative agency procedures from 1929, when Senator Norris proposed an "administrative court," through the 1937 and 1939 Presidential studies and Congressional hearings.]

The McCarran-Sumners bill, which evolved into the present Act, was introduced in 1945. Its consideration and hearing, especially of agency interests, was painstaking. All administrative agencies were invited to submit their views in writing. A tentative revised bill was then prepared and interested parties again were invited to submit criticisms. The Attorney General named representatives of the Department of Justice to canvass the agencies and report their criticisms, and submitted a favorable report on the bill as finally revised. It passed both Houses without opposition and was signed by President Truman June 11, 1946.

The Act thus represents a long period of study and strife; it settles long-continued and hard-fought contentions, and enacts a formula upon which opposing social and political forces have come to rest. It contains many compromises and generalities and, no doubt, some ambiguities. Experience may reveal defects. But it would be a disservice to our form of government and to the administrative process itself if the courts should fail, so far as the terms of the Act warrant, to give effect to its remedial purposes where the evils it was aimed at appear.

II

Of the several administrative evils sought to be cured or minimized, [the most relevant is] ... the purpose to curtail and change the practice of embodying in one

7. Ed. note: The student should refer to the appendix and examine the statute.

person or agency the duties of prosecutor and judge. The President's Committee on Administrative Management voiced in 1937 the theme which, with variations in language, was reiterated throughout the legislative history of the Act. . . . [It] said:

> . . . the independent commission is obliged to carry on judicial functions under conditions which threaten the impartial performance of that judicial work. The discretionary work of the administrator is merged with that of the judge. Pressures and influences properly enough directed toward officers responsible for formulating and administering policy constitute an unwholesome atmosphere in which to adjudicate private rights. But the mixed duties of the commissions render escape from these subversive influences impossible.
>
> Furthermore, the same men are obliged to serve both as prosecutors and as judges. This not only undermines judicial fairness; it weakens public confidence in that fairness. Commission decisions affecting private rights and conduct lie under the suspicion of being rationalizations of the preliminary findings which the commission, in the role of prosecutor, presented to itself. [Administrative Management in the Government of the United States, Report of the President's Committee on Administrative Management, 36-37 (1937)]

. . . Another study was made by a distinguished committee named by the Secretary of Labor, whose jurisdiction at the time included the Immigration and Naturalization Service. . . . [Focusing directly upon the immigration inspector who presides at the hearing and also introduces evidence, the committee wrote:]

> A genuinely impartial hearing, conducted with critical detachment, is psychologically improbable if not impossible, when the presiding officer has at once the responsibility of appraising the strength of the case and of seeking to make it as strong as possible. Nor is complete divorce between investigation and hearing possible so long as the presiding inspector has the duty himself of assembling and presenting the results of the investigation. . . . [The Secretary of Labor's Committee on Administrative Procedure, The Immigration and Naturalization Service, 81-82 (mimeo. 1940)]

And the Attorney General's Committee on Administrative Procedure, which divided as to the appropriate remedy, was unanimous that this evil existed. Its Final Report said:

> These types of commingling of functions of investigation or advocacy with the function of deciding are thus plainly undesirable. But they are also avoidable and should be avoided by appropriate internal division of labor. For the disqualifications produced by investigation or advocacy are personal psychological ones which result from engaging in those types of activity; and the problem is simply one of isolating those who engage in the activity. Creation of independent hearing commissioners insulated from all phases of a case other than hearing and deciding will, the Committee believes, go far toward solving this problem at the level of the initial hearing provided the proper safeguards are established to assure the insulation. . . . [Rep. Atty. Gen. Comm. Ad. Proc. 56 (1941), S. Doc. No. 8, 77th Cong., 1st Sess. 56 (1941)]

The Act before us adopts in general this recommended form of remedial action. A minority of the Committee had, furthermore, urged an even more thoroughgoing separation and supported it with a cogent report. Id. at 203 et seq.

Such were the evils found by disinterested and competent students. Such were the facts before Congress which gave impetus to the demand for the reform which this Act was intended to accomplish. It is the plain duty of the courts, regardless of their views of the wisdom or policy of the Act, to construe this remedial legislation to eliminate, so far as its text permits, the practices it condemns.

III

Turning now to the case before us, we find the administrative hearing a perfect exemplification of the practices so unanimously condemned.

This hearing, which followed the uniform practice of the Immigration Service, was before an immigrant inspector, who, for purposes of the hearing, is called the "presiding inspector." Except with consent of the alien, the presiding inspector may not be the one who investigated the case. . . . But the inspector's duties include investigation of like cases; and while he is today hearing cases investigated by a colleague, tomorrow his investigation of a case may be heard before the inspector whose case he passes on today. An "examining inspector" may be designated to conduct the prosecution, . . . but none was in this case; and, in any event, the examining inspector also has the same mixed prosecutive and hearing functions. The presiding inspector, when no examining inspector is present, is required to "conduct the interrogation of the alien and the witnesses in behalf of the Government and shall cross-examine the alien's witnesses and present such evidence as is necessary to support the charges in the warrant of arrest." . . . It may even become his duty to lodge an additional charge against the alien and proceed to hear his own accusation in like manner. . . . Then, as soon as practicable, he is to prepare a summary of the evidence, proposed findings of fact, conclusions of law, and a proposed order. A copy is furnished the alien or his counsel, who may file exceptions and brief, . . . whereupon the whole is forwarded to the Commissioner.

The Administrative Procedure Act did not go so far as to require a complete separation of investigating and prosecuting functions from adjudicating functions. But that the safeguards it did set up were intended to ameliorate the evils from the commingling of functions as exemplified here is beyond doubt. And this commingling, if objectionable anywhere, would seem to be particularly so in the deportation proceeding, where we frequently meet with a voteless class of litigants who not only lack the influence of citizens, but who are strangers to the laws and customs in which they find themselves involved and who often do not even understand the tongue in which they are accused. Nothing in the nature of the parties or proceedings suggests that we should strain to exempt deportation proceedings from reforms in administrative procedure applicable generally to federal agencies.

. . . We come, then, to examination of the text of the Act to determine whether the Government is right in its contentions: first, that the general scope of §5 of the Act does not cover deportation proceedings; and, second, that even if it does, the proceedings are excluded from the requirements of the Act by virtue of §7.

IV

The Administrative Procedure Act, §5, establishes a number of formal requirements to be applicable "In every case of adjudication required by statute to be determined on the record after opportunity for an agency hearing." The argument here depends upon the words "adjudication required by statute." The Government contends that there is no express requirement for any hearing or adjudication in the statute authorizing deportation, and that this omission shields these proceedings from the impact of §5. . . .

Both parties invoke many citations to legislative history as to the meaning given to these key words by the framers, advocates or opponents of the Administrative Procedure Act. Because §5 in the original bill applied to hearings required "by law," because it was suggested by the Attorney General that it should be changed to "required by statute," the Government argues that the section is intended to apply only when explicit statutory words granting a right to adjudication can be pointed out. Petitioner on the other hand cites references which would indicate that the limitation to statutory hearing was merely to avoid creating by inference a new right to hearings where no right existed otherwise. We do not know. The legislative history is more conflicting than the text is ambiguous.

But the difficulty with any argument premised on the proposition that the deportation statute does not require a hearing is that, without such hearing, there would be no constitutional authority for deportation. The constitutional requirement of procedural due process of law derives from the same source as Congress' power to legislate and, where applicable, permeates every valid enactment of that body. It was under compulsion of the Constitution that this Court long ago held that an antecedent deportation statute must provide a hearing at least for aliens who had not entered clandestinely. . . .

We think that the limitation to hearings "required by statute" in §5 of the Administrative Procedure Act exempts from that section's application only those hearings which administrative agencies may hold by regulation, rule, custom, or special dispensation; not those held by compulsion. We do not think the limiting words render the Administrative Procedure Act inapplicable to hearings, the requirement for which has been read into a statute by the Court in order to save the statute from invalidity. They exempt hearings of less than statutory authority, not those of more than statutory authority. We would hardly attribute to Congress a purpose to be less scrupulous about the fairness of a hearing necessitated by the Constitution than one granted by it as a matter of expediency. . . .

V

The remaining question is whether the exception of §7(a) of the Administrative Procedure Act exempts deportation hearings held before immigrant inspectors. It provides:

Sec. 7. In hearings which section 4 or 5 requires to be conducted pursuant to this section —

(a) Presiding Officers. — There shall preside at the taking of evidence (1) the agency, (2) one or more members of the body which comprises the agency, or (3) one or more examiners appointed as provided in this Act; but nothing in this Act shall be deemed to supersede the conduct of specified classes of proceedings in whole or part by or before boards or other officers specially provided for by or designated pursuant to statute. . . . [60 Stat. 237, 241, 5 U.S.C. §1006]

The Government argues that immigrant inspectors are "specially provided for by or designated pursuant to" §16 of the Immigration Act, which, in pertinent part, reads:

. . . The inspection . . . of aliens, including those seeking admission or readmission to or the privilege of passing through or residing in the United States, and the examination of aliens arrested within the United States under this Act, shall be conducted by immigrant inspectors. . . . [8 U.S.C. §152]

Certainly nothing here specifically provides that immigrant inspectors shall conduct deportation hearings or be designated to do so. . . . [T]hat Congress by grant of these powers has specially constituted them or provided for their designation as hearing officers in deportation proceedings does not appear.

Section 7(a) qualifies as presiding officers at hearings the agency and one or more of the members of the body comprising the agency, and it also leaves untouched any others whose responsibilities and duties as hearing officers are established by other statutory provisions. But if hearings are to be had before employees whose responsibility and authority derives from a lesser source, they must be examiners whose independence and tenure are so guarded by the Act as to give the assurances of neutrality which Congress thought would guarantee the impartiality of the administrative process.

We find no basis in the purposes, history or text of this Act for judicially declaring an exemption in favor of deportation proceedings from the procedural safeguards enacted for general application to administrative agencies. We hold that deportation proceedings must conform to the requirements of the Administrative Procedure Act if resulting orders are to have validity. Since the proceeding in the case before us did not comply with these requirements, we sustain the writ of habeas corpus and direct release of the prisoner.

Reversed.

[Mr. Justice REED dissented on the ground that §7(a) of the APA exempts from its provisions all hearings at which Congress specifically provided that persons other than hearing examiners should preside. He believed that §16 of the Immigration Act specifically provided that "inspectors" should preside at deportation hearings.]

Note: Separation of Functions in the APA

The basic separation of functions provision of the Administrative Procedure Act is contained in §554(d). To determine when that section applies, however, one must trace through the following labyrinth:

(1) Section 554(d) applies to adjudications when an "employee who presides at the reception of evidence pursuant to section 556 ... shall make the recommended decision or initial decision required by section 557."

(2) Section 557 states that a hearing examiner makes an "initial" or "recommended" decision; and section 556(a) provides that he (or a commissioner) shall preside in cases that "section 553 or 554" require "to be conducted in accordance with" section 556 *unless* some statute specifically states that someone else shall preside.

(3) Sections 553(c) and 554(a) require that section 556 procedures be used when a statute (or, under *Wong Yang Sung,* the Constitution) requires that the rule or order be made "on the record after opportunity for agency hearing."

Thus §554(d) normally applies to adjudications when a hearing examiner presides at a hearing which the underlying substantive statute requires to be held "on the record." (Note that it does not apply to "on the record" rulemaking.)

Section 554(d) requires that:

(1) The hearing examiner may not "consult a person or party on a fact in issue, unless on notice and opportunity for all parties to participate";

(2) The hearing examiner cannot be subject to the direction of an agency employee involved in investigative or prosecuting functions;

(3) No agency employee who investigates or prosecutes a case may, in that case "or a factually related case, participate or advise in the decision, recommended decision or agency review pursuant to section 557 ... except as witness or counsel...."

But the constraints of §554(d) do not apply "in determining applications for initial licenses; ... to proceedings involving ... rates, facilities or practices of public utilities or carriers; or ... to the agency or a member ... of the body comprising the agency."

At this point, you should look at the full language of these sections contained in the appendix. In addition, examine APA §11, which reinforces the independence of the hearing examiner.[8]

Questions

Consider the following complaint in an actual FTC case:

Forever Young, Inc.

Paragraph Two: Respondents advertise, offer for sale and sell to the general public a medical process called the Forever Young treatment, which is a chemical peeling of the skin on the face and neck for cosmetic purposes. The treatment involves the application of a chemical solution which peels off the outer layers of the skin, producing an alteration in skin appearance as the skin heals. The purported purpose of this treatment is to remove manifestations of aging such as wrinkles, lines, folds, spots, and undesirable features such as blemishes, large pores,

8. See 5 U.S.C. §§ 554, 3105, 7521, 5362, 3344, 1305.

and acne marks, in order to make a person appear younger or more attractive. Forever Young, Inc. grants licenses for the purpose of selling the treatment. According to available information there are presently licensees in Hawaii, California, Washington, Colorado, Virginia and Oregon. . . .

Paragraph Six: The Nature of the Treatment. Respondents represent the treatment, without any further description, as a technique of facial regeneration which does not involve surgery or abrasions, implying by this and other representations that the treatment is merely a cosmetic process. In fact, the treatment involves application of an abrasive chemical solution (containing phenol, also known as carbolic acid) to the skin, causing a second-degree burn which peels off the outer layers of the skin and produces a change in skin appearance solely by the body's own wound-healing process. The treatment is known as chemosurgery and is a serious medical procedure.

Paragraph Seven: Pain. Respondents advertise the treatment without mentioning the subject of pain or discomfort. One of their brochures represents that the client should not have any pain during the recuperation period and another represents that clients can read, sew, or write letters during that time. In fact, the pain associated with the process can be so severe that respondents' patients are always sedated or anesthetized during the application of acid and may require medication for days, weeks, or months afterward to reduce pain and other discomforts, such as itching and burning. During the treatment, many patients experience such discomforts as the eyes swelling shut and difficulties breathing, and swallowing.

Paragraph Eight: Safety: Systematic Dangers. Respondents represent that the treatment is safe. In fact, the process had, in addition to the pain described above, a number of inherent dangers to the entire body, which respondents do not disclose, including but not limited to:

1. Systematic toxic reaction (poisoning). The chemical used in the Forever Young treatment, phenol, is toxic to kidneys, liver, and other organs of the body when present in sufficient quantities. Phenol can be absorbed through the skin during the treatment in quantities sufficient to cause serious and even fatal illness in some people. One patient died during the Forever Young treatment from this cause. Persons with kidney infections are particularly susceptible to adverse phenol reaction. Yet, Forever Young does perform the treatment on persons with kidney infections. Furthermore, Forever Young does not provide the personnel, facilities, equipment or techniques adequate to prevent or minimize the effects of a systematic toxic reaction.

————————————

Assume that this case is now before the hearing examiner.

(1)(a) If the FTC general counsel has not participated in the case so far, can the hearing examiner ask him his opinion as to whether the claim that there is no surgery or abrasion is unlawfully deceptive

(b) If the FTC's staff medical expert has not participated in the case, can the examiner ask him whether Forever Young's treatment is toxic?

(c) Could the examiner consult, on this same question, a member of the Commission's scientific staff who testified before the examiner on this question?

(d) May the examiner consult with the staff attorney who prepared the case on questions of either fact or law?

(2) Would it make any difference if, on appeal of the examiner's decision, one of the Commissioners wished to do the consulting described above?

b. The Aftermath of *Wong Yang Sung*

Congress responded to *Wong Yang Sung* by attaching a rider to the Supplemental Appropriations Act of 1951 which explicitly exempted deportation and exclusion hearings from APA requirements. This provision was repealed one year later by the Immigration and Nationality Act, which detailed the procedural requirements for deportation hearings.[9] The "special inquiry officer" can still take the dual role of prosecutor and hearing officer, though he may not hear cases that he has specifically investigated. The special inquiry officer is still subject to supervision and control by the Attorney General and District Directors of the INS. The Supreme Court upheld these procedures as constitutional,[10] thus suggesting that *Wong Yang Sung* decided as a matter of statutory interpretation, not constitutional law, that APA §5 was meant to apply to hearings required by the Constitution.[11]

The "separation of functions" provisions of the APA apply only when an adjudication is required by statute (or, given *Wong Yang Sung*, by the Constitution) to be determined on the record after opportunity for an agency hearing. Recall that United States v. Florida East Coast Ry Co., supra at 481, involved statutory interpretation to determine if a "hearing . . . on the record" was required for rulemaking. The Court refused to find such a requirement unless the specific words "hearing" and "on the record" appeared in the statute. When the defendant in an adjudication has complained of the lack of an independent hearing examiner, however, the Supreme Court in the past has seemed more willing to infer a statutory requirement of an on-the-record proceeding, even without those magic words. Thus in Riss & Co. v. United States, 96 F. Supp. 452 (W.D. Mo.), *rev'd per curiam* 341 U.S. 907 (1951), the Court apparently found that the statute which authorized the ICC to issue "certificates of convenience and necessity" to motor carriers required a hearing on the record, even though the statute never mentions either

---

9. 8 U.S.C. §1252(b).

10. Marcello v. Bond, 349 U.S. 302 (1955). Later cases extended the narrow *Marcello* holding that the immigration judge in the initial deportation hearing is exempt from the separation of functions requirements of the APA; for instance, Giambanco v. Immigration and Naturalization Service, 531 F.2d 141 (3d Cir. 1976) extended the exemption to deportation suspension hearings, and Cisternas-Estay v. Immigration and Naturalization Service, 531 F.2d 155 (3d Cir.), *cert. denied* 429 U.S. 853 (1976) further extended the exemption to review proceedings before the Board of Immigration Appeals. Nevertheless, the courts in both of these cases were sharply divided over the proper interpretation of the scanty legislative history, leading one commentator to conclude that the decisions "[s]eem to have a greater effect in stirring up the question of applicability of the APA than in settling the question." K. Davis, Administrative Law of the Seventies §13.06 (1978 Supp.).

11. This view is given further support by Wah v. Shaughnessy, 190 F.2d 488 (2d Cir. 1951), which concerned *exclusion* of an alien, an area where the Constitution did not require a hearing.

"hearings" or "record." The Court applied a similar analysis to a statute which allowed the Postal Service to issue mail fraud orders "upon evidence satisfactory to the postal service." [12]

A further question arises if one remembers that the Constitution may require hearings of varying degrees of formality depending on the circumstances. Does *Wong Yang Sung* require an APA-type hearing whenever due process analysis requires a hearing of any sort whatsoever? Although the case has never been overruled, the courts have been understandably reluctant to extend the holding to the entire spectrum of administrative activity.[13] And, some commentators feel that *Wong Yang Sung* today has little precedential value.[14] Is it possible that *Wong Yang Sung*, which involves deportation, is sui generis? Are there many other administrative actions which entrench so drastically upon an individual's liberty?

c. The Independence of the Hearing Examiner

Enactment of the Administrative Procedure Act began a period which has seen the steady increase of the independence, stature, and authority of the hearing examiner. The APA provided that hearing officers were to have no assigned tasks "inconsistent with their duties and responsibilities as hearing examiners" and were in no circumstances to be subject to supervision or direction by anyone "engaged in the performance of investigative or prosecuting functions for an agency." [15] They could not be removed by the agency employing them, but only by the Civil Service Commission, and then only after notice and a hearing.[16] Their pay was to be set by the Civil Service Commission "independently of agency recommendations or ratings," thereby insulating them from agency reprisals for decisions which displeased

12. See Cates v. Haderlein, 189 F.2d 369 (7th Cir.), *rev'd per curiam*, 342 U.S. 804 (1951). First Amendment considerations may be at work here. See Kirby v. Shaw, 358 F.2d 446, 448 (9th Cir. 1966); Door v. Donaldson, 195 F.2d 764 (D.C. Cir. 1952). Note that even when the statute in question requires that an adjudicatory-style hearing take place on the record, §554(d) may apply only to a late stage in the proceeding. Earlier stages may be viewed as "informal" or preliminary. Thus, in International Tel. & Tel. Corp., Communications Equipment & Systems Div. v. Local 134, Internat'l Brotherhood of Electrical Workers, 419 U.S. 428 (1975), the Court held that a §10(k) NLRA proceeding was a "preliminary administrative determination," and did not have the requisite finality for §554(d) to be required.

13. See Note, The Requirement of Formal Adjudication under Section 5 of the Administration Procedure Act, 12 Harv. J. Legis. 194 (1975).

14. "Despite the authority of the Wong case, the tendency of the lower federal courts to give a literal interpretation to the words 'required by statute' continues to be strong and persistent. A large proportion of the decisions seem to violate the holding of the Wong case. Numerous other cases hold that §5 of the APA does not apply to administrative action which neither a statute nor due process requires to be determined on the record after opportunity for agency hearing." 2 Davis, Administrative Law Treatise §13.08 (1958).

15. 5 U.S.C. §554(d)(2).

16. 5 U.S.C. §7521. An interesting Civil Service Commission decision defining the outer limits of the hearing examiner's operational independence from his agency is Karl Stecher, 11 Ad. Law. 2d 868 (1961). In general, "[h]earing examiners are subject to supervision and direction in matters of administration and management not directly involving the actual performance of hearing examiner functions." Ibid., at 875. General provisions on procedures for removal of hearing examiners are detailed in 5 C.F.R. §930.221-§930.234.

the agency heads.[17] The officer who presided over a hearing was expected to render an initial decision which would bind the agency and the parties unless review proceedings were commenced in a timely manner.[18]

The initial attempts of the Civil Service Commission to select and retain able hearing examiners was somewhat less than successful; in fact, one commentator called it a "fiasco." [19] The Commission revised its approach and issued regulations which provided for different grade classifications of hearing examiners within any given agency; opportunities for promotion from one grade to another depended upon recommendation of the agency; likewise, case assignments were made according to grade ("in rotation to cases of the level of difficulty and importance that are normally assigned to positions of the salary grade they hold") and tenure for the purposes of layoffs during slack periods was determined under conditions similar to those governing other federal employees. In Ramspeck v. Federal Trial Examiners Conference, 345 U.S. 128 (1953), the Court sustained these regulations, over the dissent of Justices Black, Frankfurter and Douglas, who felt that the regulations gave the agency too much power over the examiners and hence tended to destroy their independence. The Civil Service Commission has since amended its regulations to classify hearing examiners in each agency at the same grade, except for the Chief in each agency's cadre.[20]

The debate on the independence of these officials has not abated. There have been periodic suggestions that the present system of keeping a permanent staff of hearing examiners affiliated with each agency be abolished, and that a common pool of examiners for *all* federal agencies be created, with a Director of Federal Administrative Procedure to rotate the examiners among the agencies.[21] These proposals have withered on the vine, but in 1972 the Civil Service Commission changed the title of "hearing examiner" to "administrative law judge," as a method of enhancing their prestige.[22] Critics of this action have argued that the prestige of the federal judiciary might be eroded if the government confers the title of "judge" on too many non-Article III judges;[23] however, few argue that these officials should be less independent.

17. 5 U.S.C. §5362. General provisions on the appointment and pay of hearing examiners are in 5 C.F.R. §930.201-§930.215.
18. 5 U.S.C. §557(b).
19. Fuchs, The Hearing Examiner Fiasco Under the Administrative Procedure Act, 63 Harv. L. Rev. 737 (1950). See also Note, The Status of the Trial Examiner in Administrative Agencies, 66 Harv. L. Rev. 1065 (1953). The initial Civil Service rules for management of hearing examiners can be found in 5 C.F.R. §34.1 et seq. (1949).
20. See Dullea, Development of the Personnel Program for Administrative Law Judges, 25 Ad. L. Rev. 41 (1973).
21. See Report of the Attorney General's Committee on Administrative Procedure 46 (1941); A. Scalia, The Hearing Examiner Loan Program, 1971 Duke L. J. 319, 360-366 (1971).
22. 37 Fed. Reg. 16787 (1972). See Cramton, A Title Change for Federal Hearings Examiners? "A Rose by Any Other Name...," 40 Geo. Wash. L. Rev. 918 (1972).
23. To "deflate" this criticism, the Civil Service Commission has also specified that "Each agency ... may not use the word 'judge' as the title or part of the title for any other position for any purpose." 5 C.F.R. §930. 203a (1977).
The status of the hearing examiner has also been enhanced in more tangible ways. For instance, while salaries of some examiners were about one-third as large as those of district judges in the 1950s, the maximum ALJ salary as of 1976 was $37,800, compared with $42,000 for district judges. See K. Davis, Administrative Law of the Seventies §10.05 (1976).

Finally there is still some disagreement over the extent to which other government officials performing similar functions should be classified as administrative law judges. The controversy primarily revolves around the hearing officers in the Department of Health, Education and Welfare, who decide claims to Social Security disability benefits. Ironically, present administrative law judges oppose expanding their ranks for reasons similar to those advanced by those opposing the elevation of "hearing examiners" to "administrative law judges." [24]

2. Combination of Functions and Bias at the Commission Level

The combination of several functions potentially biases the judgment of the commission itself. But unlike conflicts within the agency staff, there is no easy way to divide functions structurally among commissioners. The problem can be broken down into several parts.

a. Combining Prosecuting and Judging

First consider the fact that most commissions both issue the complaint which initiates the hearing process and decide the resulting case on appeal.[25] Former Trade Commissioner Philip Elman has argued that the combination of these two functions biases Commissioners against defendants on appeal because a high dismissal rate on appeal would tend to cast doubt on the Commissioner's judgment in having authorized the complaint, would rebuff the staff upon which the Commission depends, and would tend to encourage disregard of the statute the Commission is pledged to enforce.[26]

Withrow v. Larkin

421 U.S. 35 (1975)

Mr. Justice WHITE delivered the opinion of the Court.

The statutes of the State of Wisconsin forbid the practice of medicine without a license from an Examining Board composed of practicing physicians. The statutes

24. See, e.g., Note, Social Security Hearings for the Disabled — Who Decides: Trial Examiners or Administrative Law Judges, 69 Nw. U. L. Rev. 915 (1975).

For an excellent general appraisal of the status of the hearing examiner, see B. Segal, The Administrative Law Judge, 62 A.B.A.J. 1424 (1976). Copious statutory, administrative, and critical documentation can be found in J. Macy, The APA and the Hearing Examiner: Products of a Viable Political Society, 27 Fed. B. J. 351 (1967). Arguments for greater individual responsibility at all levels within the agencies can be found in J. Zwerdling, Reflections on the Role of an Administrative Law Judge, 25 Ad. L. Rev. 9 (1973).

25. All five Federal Trade Commissioners spend time reviewing complaints themselves and have been criticized for not delegating this function. See Note, The Federal Trade Commission and Reform of the Administrative Process, 62 Colum. L. Rev. 671 (1962).

26. P. Elman, Administrative Reform of the Federal Trade Commission, 59 Geo. L. J. 777, 810 (1971).

also define and forbid various acts of professional misconduct. . . . To enforce these provisions, the Examining Board is empowered . . . to warn and reprimand, temporarily to suspend the license, and "to institute criminal action or action to revoke license when it finds probable cause therefor under criminal or revocation statute. . . ."

[Larkin practiced medicine in Wisconsin. The Board investigated his abortion practices. It first held an "investigative hearing" at which Larkin was present but was not allowed to cross-examine witnesses. It then sent him notice that it would hold a "contested hearing" to determine whether he had practiced under another name, split fees, or allowed unlicensed doctors to perform abortions.

Larkin obtained a federal court injunction against this further "contested hearing" on the ground that it was unfair and unconstitutional to have the investigator make the final decision.

After the court enjoined the "contested hearing," the Board held another "investigative hearing." It determined that there was probable cause to believe Larkin had engaged in unprofessional conduct, and it certified his case to the local district attorney for prosecution.

The Board here appeals from the lower federal court's decision to enjoin the "contested hearing" — a decision which it based on the unfairness of taking from a doctor "his liberty or property absent the intervention of an independent, neutral and detached decision maker."]

III

The District Court framed the constitutional issue, which it addressed as being whether "for the board temporarily to suspend Dr. Larkin's license at its own contested hearing on charges evolving from its own investigation would constitute a denial to him of his rights to procedural due process." 368 F. Supp. at 797.[27] The question was initially answered affirmatively, and in its amended judgment the court asserted that there was a high probability that appellee would prevail on the question. Its opinion stated that the "state medical examining board [did] not qualify as [an independent] decisionmaker [and could not] properly rule with regard to the merits of the same charges it investigated and, as in this case, presented to the district attorney." Id., at 798. We disagree. On the present record, it is quite unlikely that appellee would ultimately prevail on the merits of the due process issue presented to the District Court, and it was an abuse of discretion to issue the preliminary injunction.

Concededly, a "fair trial in a fair tribunal is a basic requirement of due process." In re Murchinson, 349 U.S. 133, 136 (1955). This applies to administrative agencies which adjudicate as well as to courts. Gibson v. Berryhill, 411 U.S. 564, 579 (1973). Not only is a biased decisionmaker constitutionally unacceptable but

---

27. After the District Court made its decision, the Board altered its procedures. It now assigns each new case to one of the members for investigation, and the remainder of the Board has no contact with the investigative process. . . . That change, designed to accommodate the Board's procedures to the District Court's decision, does not affect this case.

"our system of law has always endeavored to prevent even the probability of unfairness." In re Murchison, [349 U.S. 133, 136 (1955)] at 136; . . .In pursuit of this end, various situations have been identified in which experience teaches that the probability of actual bias on the part of the judge or decisionmaker is too high to be constitutionally tolerable. Among these cases are those in which the adjudicator has a pecuniary interest in the outcome and in which he has been the target of personal abuse or criticism from the party before him.

The contention that the combination of investigative and adjudicative functions necessarily creates an unconstitutional risk or bias in administrative adjudication has a much more difficult burden of persuasion to carry. It must overcome a presumption of honesty and integrity in those serving as adjudicators; and it must convince that, under a realistic appraisal of psychological tendencies and human weaknesses, conferring investigative and adjudicative powers on the same individuals poses such a risk of actual bias or prejudgment that the practice must be forbidden if the guarantee of due process is to be adequately implemented. . . .

That is not to say that there is nothing to the argument that those who have investigative should not then adjudicate. The issue is substantial, it is not new, and legislators and others concerned with the operations of administrative agencies have given much attention to whether and to what extent distinctive administrative functions should be performed by the same persons. No single answer has been reached. Indeed, the growth, variety, and complexity of the administrative processes have made any one solution highly unlikely. Within the Federal Government itself, Congress has addressed the issue in several different ways, providing for varying degrees of separation from complete separation of functions to virtually none at all. For the generality of agencies, Congress has been content with §5 of the Administrative Procedure Act, 5 U.S.C. §554(d), which provides that no employee engaged in investigating or prosecuting may also participate or advise in the adjudicating function but which also expressly exempts from this prohibition "the agency or a member or members of the body comprising the agency."

It is not surprising, therefore, to find that "[t]he case law, both federal and state, generally rejects the idea that the combination [of] judging [and] investigating functions is a denial of due process. . . ." 2 K. Davis Administrative Law Treatise §13.02, p. 175 (1958). Similarly, our cases, although they reflect the substance of the problem, offer no support for the bald proposition applied in this case by the District Court that agency members who participate in an investigation are disqualified from adjudicating. The incredible variety of administrative mechanisms in this country will not yield to any single organizing principle.

Appellee relies heavily on In re Murchison, . . . in which a state judge, empowered under state law to sit as a "one-man grand jury" and to compel witnesses to testify before him in secret about possible crimes, charged two such witnesses with criminal contempt, one for perjury and the other for refusing to answer certain questions, and then himself tried and convicted them. This Court found the procedure to be a denial of due process of law not only because the judge in effect became part of the prosecution and assumed an adversary position, but also because as a judge, passing on guilt or innocence, he very likely relied on "his own personal knowledge and impression of what had occurred in the grand jury room," an impression that "could not be tested by adequate cross-examination." 349 U.S., at 138. . . .

. . . [T]here [is nothing] in this case that comes within the strictures of *Murchison.* When the Board instituted its investigative procedures, it stated only that it would investigate whether proscribed conduct had occurred. Later in noticing the adversary hearing, it asserted only that it would determine if violations had been committed which would warrant suspension of appellee's license. Without doubt, the Board then anticipated that the proceeding would eventuate in an adjudication of the issue; but there was no more evidence of bias or risk of bias or prejudgment than inhered in the very fact that the Board had investigated and would now adjudicate. Of course, we should be alert to the possibilities of bias that may lurk in the way particular procedures actually work in practice. The processes utilized by the Board, however, do not in themselves contain an unacceptable risk of bias. The investigative proceeding had been closed to the public, but appellee and his counsel were permitted to be present throughout; counsel actually attended the hearings and knew the facts presented to the Board. [Larkin was also given a chance to appear after the "investigative" hearing and explain the evidence.] No specific foundation has been presented for suspecting that the Board had been prejudiced by its investigation or would be disabled from hearing and deciding on the basis of the evidence to be presented at the contested hearing. The mere exposure to evidence presented in nonadversary investigative procedures is insufficient in itself to impugn the fairness of the Board members at a later adversary hearing. Without a showing to the contrary, state administrators "are assumed to be men of conscience and intellectual discipline, capable of judging a particular controversy fairly on the basis of its own circumstances." United States v. Morgan, 313 U.S. 409, 421 (1941).

We are of the view, therefore, that the District Court was in error when it entered the restraining order against the Board's contested hearing and when it granted the preliminary injunction based on the untenable view that it would be unconstitutional for the Board to suspend appellee's license "at its own contested hearing on charges evolving from its own investigation. . . ." The contested hearing should have been permitted to proceed.

IV

Nor do we think the situation substantially different because the Board, when it was prevented from going forward with the contested hearing, proceeded to make and issue formal findings of fact and conclusions of law asserting that there was probable cause to believe that appellee had engaged in various acts prohibited by the Wisconsin statutes. . . .

Judges repeatedly issue arrest warrants on the basis that there is probable cause to believe that a crime has been committed and that the person named in the warrant has committed it. Judges also preside at preliminary hearings where they must decide whether the evidence is sufficient to hold a defendant for trial. Neither of these pretrial involvements has been thought to raise any constitutional barrier against the judge's presiding over the criminal trial and, if the trial is without a jury, against making the necessary determination of guilt or innocence. Nor has it been thought that a judge is disqualified from presiding over injunction proceedings because he has initially assessed the facts in issuing or denying a temporary restraining order or a preliminary injunction. It is also very typical for the members of administrative agencies to receive the results of investigations, to approve the filing of charges or formal complaints instituting enforcement proceedings, and then to participate in the ensuing hearings. This mode of procedure does not violate ... due process of law. We should also remember that it is not contrary to due process to allow judges and administrators who have had their initial decisions reversed on appeal to confront and decide the same questions a second time around. . . .

Here, the Board stayed within the accepted bounds of due process. Having investigated, it issued findings and conclusions asserting the commission of certain acts and ultimately concluding that there was probable cause to believe that appellee had violated the statutes.

The risk of bias or prejudgment in this sequence of functions has not been considered to be intolerably high or to raise a sufficiently great possibiilty that the adjudicators would be so psychologically wedded to their complaints that they would consciously or unconsciously avoid the appearance of having erred or changed position. Indeed, just as there is no logical inconsistency between a finding of probable cause and an acquittal in a criminal proceeding, there is no incompatibility between the agency filing a complaint based on probable cause and a subsequent decision, when all the evidence is in, that there has been no violation of the statute. Here, if the Board now proceeded after an adversary hearing to determine that appellee's license to practice should not be temporarily suspended, it would not implicitly be admitting error in its prior finding or probable cause. Its position most probably would merely reflect the benefit of a more complete view of the evidence afforded by an adversary hearing. . . .

That the combination of investigative and adjudicative functions does not, without more, constitute a due process violation, does not, of course, preclude a court from determining from the special facts and circumstances present in the case before it that the risk of unfairness is intolerably high. . . . The judgment of the District Court is reversed and the case is remanded to that court for further proceedings consistent with this opinion.[28]

Note: Empirical Testing of Agency Bias

Professor Richard Posner has tried to investigate empirically the claims of Commissioner Elman and others to the effect that combining prosecution and judging in the Commissioners tends to produce unfairness.[29] He compared the FTC, which has never delegated its authority over the issuance of complaints, with

---

28. See also F. Davis, Case Commentary: Withrow v. Larkin and the "Separation of Functions" Concept in State Administrative Proceedings, 27 Ad. L. Rev. 407 (1975).

29. R. Posner, The Behavior of Administrative Agencies, 1 J. Legal Stud. 305, 328 (1972).

the National Labor Relations Board which has done so. Prior to 1942, all NLRB complaints required Board approval. Between 1942 and 1947, regional directors had primary responsibility for their issuance. Since 1947, the Board's General Counsel — appointed by the President, not the NLRB — makes the decision to issue a complaint independently.

After seeking to measure possible differences in dismissal rates in a variety of ways, Posner found little evidence to support the hypothesis that the combination of functions within an agency leads to agency reluctance to dismiss complaints. His findings were based on statistical comparisons such as the following:

Dismissal Rate — Significant Dismissals Only

Agency	Period	Total Contested Cases	Significant Dismissals	Significant Total Dismissals Only	% Dismissed	% Dismissed in Entirety
NLRB	1938	33	15	5	.45	.15
	1941	18	4	1	.22	.06
	1943	26	14	6	.54	.23
	1945	16	5	4	.31	.25
	1946	27	11	6	.41	.22
	1947	20	10	5	.50	.25
	Total	140	59	27	.42	.19
FTC	1938	60	12	7	.20	.12
	1941	61	17	17	.28	.28
	1943	32	8	7	.25	.22
	1945	43	11	9	.26	.21
	1946-47	70	18	15	.26	.21
	Total	266	66	55	.25	.21
NLRB	1949	38	26	11	.68	.29
	1950	52	15	9	.29	.17
	1951	57	26	9	.46	.16
	1956	57	30	9	.53	.16
	1960	105	48	22	.46	.21
	1965	103	21	12	.20	.12
	1969	70	29	16	.41	.23
	Total	482	195	88	.40	.18
FTC	1949-50	53	11	9	.21	.17
	1951-52	62	15	12	.24	.19
	1955-56	36	10	7	.28	.19
	1959-60	58	21	7	.36	.12
	1965	34	12	10	.35	.29
	Total	243	69	45	.28	.19

On the other hand, how readily can one dismiss the first hand impressions of those who, like Commissioner Elman, have served on the Federal Trade Commission themselves?

Questions

(a) Does *Withrow* make it plain that *Wong Yang Sung* does not rest on constitutional grounds? *Withrow* suggests, however, that certain "special facts and circumstances" might tip the constitutional balance. What sort of facts might these be?

(b) What safeguards in this area are adequate? How should the FTC decide when to issue a complaint?

b.   Combining Policymaking and Adjudicating

FEDERAL TRADE COMMISSION v. CEMENT INSTITUTE, 333 U.S. 683 (1948)

[The Commission charged producers of Portland cement, including Marquette Company, with violating Section 5 of the Federal Trade Commission Act by using a "multiple basing point" pricing system. After all testimony had been taken, Marquette moved that the Commissioners disqualify themselves on the grounds of bias and prejudgment, in light of the fact that the Commission had previously issued a series of reports condemning the use of multiple basing point pricing systems, particularly in the steel industry, and suggesting that cement was like steel. The Commission denied the motion for disqualification; the court of appeals sustained this denial even after assuming that the Commission had formed an opinion as to the illegality of the pricing system in the cement industry. The court (relying heavily upon the "rule of necessity," which will be discussed below) pointed out that the FTC was "the only tribunal clothed with the power and charged with the responsibility of protecting the public against unfair methods of competition and price discrimination."

In affirming, the Supreme Court said:]

In the first place, the fact that the Commission had entertained such views as the result of its prior ex parte investigations did not necessarily mean that the minds of its members were irrevocably closed on the subject of the respondents' basing point practices. Here, in contrast to the Commission's investigations, members of the cement industry were legally authorized participants in the hearings. They produced evidence — volumes of it. They were free to point out to the Commission by testimony, by cross-examination of witnesses, and by arguments, conditions of the trade practices under attack which they thought kept these practices within the range of legally permissible business activities.

Moreover, Marquette's position, if sustained, would to a large extent defeat the congressional purposes which prompted passage of the Trade Commission Act.

Had the entire membership of the Commission disqualified in the proceedings against these respondents, this complaint could not have been acted upon by the Commission or by any other government agency. Congress has provided for no such contingency. It has not directed that the Commission disqualify itself under any circumstances, has not provided for substitute commissioners should any of its members disqualify, and has not authorized any other government agency to hold hearings, make findings, and issue cease and desist orders in proceedings against unfair trade practices. Yet if Marquette is right, the Commission, by making studies and filing reports in obedience to congressional command, completely immunized the practices investigated, even though they are "unfair," from any cease and desist order by the Commission or any other governmental agency.

There is no warrant in the Act for reaching a conclusion which would thus frustrate its purposes.[30]

AMERICAN CYANAMID CO. v. FEDERAL TRADE COMMISSION, 363 F.2d 757 (6th Cir. 1966)

[As Chief Counsel of a Senate subcommittee, Paul Rand Dixon helped conduct a broad-ranging investigation into drug industry pricing of broad spectrum antibiotics, including tetracycline, and into the patent office's issuance of the tetracycline patent. Mr. Dixon was in charge of the selection of documents; he conducted examination of witnesses, and he worked on the subcommittee report on its investigation. The Cyanamid case, which began in 1958, included allegations of collusion in tetracycline pricing and possibly unlawful conduct by the firm in obtaining its patent. The hearing examiner found for the drug companies on all issues. When complaint counsel appealed, the companies moved that Dixon, then Chairman of the FTC, disqualify himself. He refused. The Commission found against the company. (Chairman Dixon's vote was not critical.) The Sixth Circuit, on appeal, held that Dixon's participation in the hearing "amounted . . . to a denial of due process which invalidated the order under review. . . . It is fundamental that both unfairness and the appearance of unfairness should be avoided. Wherever there may be reasonable suspicion of unfairness, it is best to disqualify." 363 F.2d at 767. The court remanded the case for a de novo consideration of the record without the participation of Chairman Dixon.[31]]

30. 333 U.S. at 701-702. See also Kennecott Copper Corporation v. FTC, 467 F.2d 67, 79-80 (10th Cir. 1972), cert. den., 416 U.S. 909 (1974). Compare All-State Industries of North Carolina, Inc. v. FTC, 423 F.2d 423 (4th Cir. 1970). Prior to the start of unfair trade practice proceedings against All-State, the chairman of the FTC had written a Senate subcommittee "decrying the prevalence of practices in national trade paralleling those of All-State." This was held to be insufficient cause for disqualification: "The Commission was performing its overriding duty under the Act — to investigate appearances and apprehensions of activities hurtful to the economy of the country. It was incumbent upon this body to speak out, as it did, upon commercial behavior thought to be of overtopping importance because of its apparently deceiving character and potential expansion." 423 F.2d at 424.

31. On remand, the FTC again found against the company. The FTC was finally vindicated in Charles Pfizer & Co. v. FTC, 401 F.2d 574 (6th Cir. 1968), cert. den., 394 U.S. 920 (1969) — 11 years after the complaint was first filed.

TEXACO, INC. v. FEDERAL TRADE COMMISSION, 336 F.2d 754 (D.C. Cir. 1964), *vacated and remanded on other grounds*, 381 U.S. 739 (1965)

[In 1956, after a four-year investigation, the FTC issued a complaint against Texaco and B.F. Goodrich charging that the companies had entered into an unlawful contract where Texaco agreed to have its dealers sell only Goodrich tires. The Commission remanded the case to the hearing examiner on March 9, 1961, and 12 days later Paul Rand Dixon became Chairman of the FTC. In July 1961, Dixon made a speech before the National Congress of Petroleum Retailers in which he said:]

We at the Commission are well aware of the practices which plague you and we have challenged their legality in many important cases.

You know the practices — price fixing, price discrimination, and overriding commission on TBA [Tires, Batteries, and Accessories].

You know the companies — Atlantic, Texas, Pure, Shell, Sun, Standard of Indiana, American, Goodyear, Goodrich, and Firestone. . . .

Some of these cases are still pending before the Commission; some have been decided by the Commission and are in the courts on appeal. You may be sure that the Commission will continue and, to the extent that increased funds and efficiency permit, will increase its efforts to promote fair competition in your industry. [336 F.2d at 759.]

[The companies then moved that the Commission disqualify Dixon, but the motion was denied. Dixon declined to withdraw. The FTC entered a cease and desist order, but was reversed on appeal. The D.C. Circuit concluded that "a disinterested reader of Chairman Dixon's speech could hardly fail to conclude that he had in some measure decided in advance that Texaco had violated the Act." Id., at 760. Dixon's participation amounted to a denial of due process, and the court also found that the charges were not supported by substantial evidence, remanding with instructions to dismiss the complaint.] [32]

CINDERELLA CAREER AND FINISHING SCHOOLS, INC. v. FEDERAL TRADE COMMISSION, 425 F.2d 583 (D.C. Cir. 1970)

[The FTC brought a complaint against the Cinderella School, alleging that Cinderella had made false claims that its graduates would be able to successfully compete in beauty contests and get better jobs. The hearing examiner dismissed all 13 of the Commission's charges. On appeal to the Commission, six charges were reinstated and Cinderella was ordered to cease and desist its false advertising. Cinderella appealed. The Court held that the FTC had erred in overturning the decision of its hearing examiner without adequate reason. It added the following:]

32. After a trip to the Supreme Court and another round of FTC hearings (without Mr. Dixon), a cease and desist order against Texaco was eventually issued, and upheld in FTC v. Texaco, Inc., 393 U.S. 223 (1968). The FTC had filed its initial complaint in 1956, "after an investigation which began at least as early as 1952. . . ." 336 F.2d at 756. Thus the lag between investigation and final judgment here was 16 years.

An additional ground which requires remand of these proceedings — and which would have required reversal even in the absence of the above-described procedural irregularities — is participation in the proceedings by the then Chairman of the Federal Trade Commission, Paul Rand Dixon.

Notice that the hearing examiner's dismissal of all charges would be appealed was filed by the Commission staff on February 1, 1968 (Brief for Petitioners at 18). On March 12, 1968, this court's decision was handed down in a prior appeal arising from this same complaint, in which we upheld the Commission's issuance of press releases which called attention to the pending proceedings. Then, on March 15, 1968, while the appeal from the examiner's decision was pending before him, Chairman Dixon made a speech before the Government Relations Workshop of the National Newspaper Association in which he stated:

> What kind of vigor can a reputable newspaper exhibit? . . . How about ethics on the business side of running a paper? What standards are maintained on advertising acceptance? . . . What about carrying ads that offer college educations in five weeks, . . . or becoming an airline's hostess by attending a charm school? . . . Granted that newspapers are not in the advertising policing business, their advertising managers are savvy enough to smell deception when the odor is strong enough. And it is in the public interest, as well as their own, that their sensory organs become more discriminating. The Federal Trade Commission, even where it has jurisdiction, could not protect the public as quickly.

We indicated in our earlier opinion in this case that "there is in fact and law authority in the Commission, acting in the public interest, to alert the public to *suspected violations* of the law by *factual press releases* whenever the Commission shall have reason to believe that a respondent is engaged in activities made unlawful by the Act. . . ." . . . This does not give individual Commissioners license to prejudge cases or to make speeches which give the appearance that the case has been prejudged. Conduct such as this may have the effect of entrenching a Commissioner in a position which he has publicly stated, making it difficult, if not impossible, for him to reach a different conclusion in the event he deems it necessary to do so after consideration of the record. . . .

As we noted in our earlier opinion, Congress has specifically vested the administrative agencies both with the "power to act in an accusatory capacity" and with the "responsibility of ultimately determining the merits of the charges so presented." . . .

Chairman Dixon, sensitive to theory but insensitive to reality, made the following statement in declining to recuse himself from this case after petitioners requested that he withdraw:

> As . . . I have stated . . . this principle "is not a rigid command of the law, compelling disqualification for trifling causes, but a consideration addressed to the discretion and sound judgment of the administrator himself in determining whether, irrespective of the law's requirements, he should disqualify himself."

... We find it hard to believe that former Chairman Dixon is so indifferent to the dictates of the Courts of Appeals that he has chosen once again to put his personal determination of what the law requires ahead of what the courts have time and again told him the law requires. If this is a question of "discretion and judgment," Commissioner Dixon has exercised questionable discretion and very poor judgment indeed, in directing his shafts and squibs at a case awaiting his official action. We can use his own words in telling Commissioner Dixon that he has acted "irrespective of the law's requirement"; we will spell out for him once again, avoiding tired cliché and weary generalization, in no uncertain terms, exactly what those requirements are, in the fervent hope that this will be the last time we have to travel this wearisome road.

The test for disqualification has been succinctly stated as being whether "a disinterested observer may conclude that [the agency] has in some measure adjudged the facts as well as the law of a particular case in advance of hearing it." Gilligan, Will & Co. v. SEC, 267 F.2d 461, 469 (2d Cir.), *cert. denied*, 361 U.S. 896, 80 S. Ct. 200, 4 L. Ed. 2d 152 (1959).

That test was cited with approval by this court in Texaco, Inc. v. FTC....

After our decision in *Texaco* the United States Court of Appeals for the Sixth Circuit was required to reverse a decision of the FTC because Charman Dixon refused to recuse himself from the case *even though he had served as Chief Counsel and Staff Director* to the Senate Subcommittee which made the initial investigation into the production and sale of the "wonder drug" tetracycline.... It is appalling to witness such insensitivity to the requirements of due process; it is even more remarkable to find ourselves once again confronted with a situation in which Mr. Dixon, pouncing on the most convenient victim, has determined either to distort the holdings in the cited cases beyond all reasonable interpretation or to ignore them altogether. We are constrained to this harshness of language because of Mr. Dixon's flagrant disregard of prior decisions.

The rationale for remanding the case despite the fact that former Chairman Dixon's vote was not necessary for a majority is well established: Litigants are entitled to an impartial tribunal whether it consists of one man or twenty and there is no way which we know of whereby the influence of one upon the others can be quantitatively measured. Berkshire Employees Ass'n of Berkshire Knitting Mills v. NLRB, 121 F.2d 235, 239 (2d Cir. 1941)....

Vacated and remanded.[33]

Questions

(a) Can the opinions in the cases in this subsection be reconciled?

(b) Pillsbury, the nation's largest flour company, acquired two small regional

---

33. Ed. note: On remand, the FTC went through another round of hearings and entered a cease and desist order, In re School Services, Inc., 79 F.T.C. 543 (1971). Reviewing courts tread a fine line in analyzing extramural statements by adjudicatory officials. Compare Kennecott Copper Corporation v. FTC, 467 F.2d 67, 79-80 (10th Cir. 1972), *cert. den.* 416 U.S. 909 (1974), which carefully distinguished statements about the merits of a pending case from statements about the allegations of the complaint.

flour companies. In June 1963 the FTC issued a complaint, charging a violation of Clayton Act §7. The hearing examiner dismissed the complaint a year later. FTC counsel appealed to the Commission, arguing that an acquisition of this sort was per se illegal. The Commission reversed the dismissal, but held that no "per se" doctrine applied under §7.

Soon afterwards, the antitrust subcommittees of both Houses of Congress held hearings and called the Chairman of the FTC as a witness. Angry senators and representatives questioned the Commission's ruling and expressed their opinions that Congress intended the per se doctrine to apply in just such cases. The questions were so specifically related to the *Pillsbury* case that the FTC Chairman announced that he would have to disqualify himself from the pending case. Although two other commissioners were present at various stages of the hearings, they did not testify.

After two more years of hearings, the examiner found no "substantial lessening of competition" and again dismissed the complaint. On appeal the Commission again reversed, finding substantial evidence to support the charges, but again it refused to apply a "per se" doctrine to §7 acquisition cases. The Commission vote was 3-1. The Chairman did not participate. The two remaining commissioners who had been exposed to the Congressional hearings voted in the majority.

On judicial review, what result? [34]

(c) Recall the drug regulation problem at p. 557 supra. On judicial review Outom seeks to set aside FDA's Sept. 19, 1969 repeal of the regulations permitting Sanalba to be marketed, on the ground that the FDA Commissioner's appearance at Congressional hearings in May, 1969 disclosed bias on his part and exposed him to improper Congressional pressure. What result?

(d) Besides conflicts arising from the combination of adjudication with prosecuting or policymaking, what about conflicts arising from a combination of adjudication with investigation?

Pangburn was the pilot of a commercial plane which crashed while landing at La Guardia Airport. As required by law, the Civil Aeronautics Board began an investigation into the crash. Soon thereafter, independent proceedings were launched by the CAB to suspend Pangburn's pilot's license. Pangburn asked the CAB to refrain from issuing its accident investigation report until after the suspension proceedings were resolved; however, the CAB released its report, which fixed "pilot error" as the cause of the crash, two days before the hearing examiner in the suspension case decided against Pangburn. Pangburn's appeal to the CAB was denied.

On appeal, what result? [35]

(e) Note the procedure by which the issue of bias is raised. The Administrative Procedure Act, §556(b), states that "A presiding or participating employee may at any time disqualify himself. On the filing in good faith of a timely and

---

34. See Pillsbury Co. v. FTC, 354 F.2d 952 (5th Cir. 1966). After remand, the FTC entered a final order of dismissal, explaining that the case was then 14 years old and it was impossible to fashion an effective remedy. Pillsbury Mills, Inc., 69 F.T.C. 482 (1966). See Recent Decisions, 52 Va. L. Rev. 946-954 (1966). Compare American Pub. Gas. Assn. v. FPC, 567 F.2d 1016 (D.C. Cir. 1977).

35. See Pangburn v. CAB, 311 F.2d 349 (1st Cir. 1962).

sufficient affidavit of personal bias or other disqualification of a presiding or participating employee, the agency shall determine the matters as a part of the record and decision in the case."

Does this apply to members of the agency itself? What standard is to be used for determining what is "sufficient"?

Can a member of an agency be disqualified by the other members? The answer is unclear, but see Berkshire Employees Ass'n. v. NLRB, 121 F.2d 235 (3d Cir. 1941).

c. Other Forms of Bias

Gibson v. Berryhill

411 U.S. 564 (1973)

Mr. Justice WHITE delivered the opinion of the Court.

Prior to 1965, the laws of Alabama relating to the practice of optometry permitted any person, including a business firm or corporation, to maintain a department in which "eyes are examined or glasses fitted," provided that such department was in the charge of a duly licensed optometrist.... In 1965, [the section conferring this permission] was repealed in its entirety by the Alabama Legislature, and [the law] was amended so as to eliminate any direct reference to optical departments maintained by corporations or other business establishments under the direction of employee optometrists.

Soon after these statutory changes, the Alabama Optometric Association, a professional organization whose membership is limited to independent practitioners of optometry *not* employed by others, filed charges [with the Alabama Optometry Board against salaried optometrists at Lee Optical Co., alleging unprofessional conduct. The Association charged the named individuals with aiding and abetting a corporation in the illegal practice of optometry].

Two days after these charges were filed by the Association in October 1965, the Board filed a suit of its own in state court against Lee Optical, seeking to enjoin the company from engaging in the "unlawful practice of optometry." The Board's complaint also named 13 optometrists employed by Lee Optical as parties defendant....[36]

... Those individuals countered on May 14, 1971, by filing a complaint in the United States District Court naming as defendants the Board of Optometry and its individual members, as well as the Alabama Optometric Association and other individuals. [They sought an injunction against the Board's hearing the Association charges] on the grounds that the statutory scheme regulating the practice of optom-

---

36. Ed. note: The state court dismissed the charges against the individuals, but held the company guilty of illegally practicing optometry. The state Supreme Court later reversed, holding that the Alabama law still allowed a corporate business to practice optometry. See Lee Optical Co. of Alabama v. State Bd. of Optometry, 288 Ala. 338, 261 So. 2d 17 (1972).

etry in Alabama was unconstitutional . . . The thrust of the complaint was that the Board was biased and could not provide the plaintiffs with a fair and impartial hearing in conformity with due process of law.

A three-judge court . . . entered judgment for plaintiffs. . . .

. . . For the District Court, the inquiry was not whether the Board members were "actually biased but whether, in the natural course of events, there is an indication of a possible temptation to an average man sitting as a judge to try the case with bias for or against any issue presented to him." 331 F. Supp., at 125. Such a possibility of bias was found to arise in the present case from a number of factors. First, was the fact that the Board, which acts as both prosecutor and judge in de-licensing proceedings, had previously brought suit against the plaintiffs on virtu-ally identical charges in the state courts. This the District Court took to indicate that members of the Board might have "preconceived opinions" with regard to the cases pending before them. Second, the court found as a fact that Lee Optical Co. did a large business in Alabama, and that if it were forced to suspend operations the individual members of the Board, along with other private practitioners of optometry, would fall heir to this business. Thus, a serious question of a personal financial stake in the matter in controversy was raised. Finally, the District Court appeared to regard the Board as a suspect adjudicative body in the cases then pending before it, because only members of the Alabama Optometric Association could be members of the Board, and because the Association excluded from mem-bership optometrists such as the plaintiffs who were employed by other persons or entities. The result was that 92 of the 192 practicing optometrists in Alabama were denied participation in the governance of their own profession.

The court's ultimate conclusion was "that to require the Plaintiffs to resort to the protection offered by state law in these cases would effectively deprive them of their property, that is, their right to practice their professions, without due process of law and that irreparable injury would follow in the normal course of events." 331 F. Supp., at 126. . . .

[The Court first considered the procedural question of whether the federal district court could enjoin a state proceeding. It held that in the circumstances here present it could do so.]

III

It is appropriate, therefore, that we consider the District Court's conclusions that the State Board of Optometry was so biased by prejudgment and pecuniary interest that it could not constitutionally conduct hearings looking toward the revocation of appellees' licenses to practice optometry. We affirm the District Court in this respect.

The District Court thought the Board to be impermissibly biased for two reasons. First, the Board had filed a complaint in state court alleging that appellees had aided and abetted Lee Optical Co. in the unlawful practice of optometry and also that they had engaged in other forms of "unprofessional conduct" which, if proved, would justify revocation of their licenses. These charges were substantially similar to those pending against appellees before the Board and concerning which the Board had noticed hearings following its successful prosecution of Lee Optical in the state trial court.

Secondly, the District Court determined that the aim of the Board was to revoke the licenses of all optometrists in the State who were employed by business corporations such as Lee Optical, and that these optometrists accounted for nearly half of all the optometrists practicing in Alabama. Because the Board of Optometry was composed solely of optometrists in private practice for their own account, the District Court concluded that success in the Board's efforts would possibly redound to the personal benefit of members of the Board, sufficiently so that in the opinion of the District Court the Board was constitutionally disqualified from hearing the charges filed against the appellees.

The District Court apparently considered either source of possible bias — prejudgment of the facts or personal interest — sufficient to disqualify the members of the Board. Arguably, the District Court was right on both scores, but we need reach, and we affirm, only the latter ground of possible personal interest.

It is sufficiently clear from our cases that those with substantial pecuniary interest in legal proceedings should not adjudicate these disputes. Tumey v. Ohio, 273 U.S. 510 (1927). And Ward v. Village of Monroeville, 409 U.S. 57 (1972), indicates that the financial stake need not be as direct or positive as it appeared to be in Tumey.[37] It has also come to be the prevailing view that "[m]ost of the law concerning disqualification because of interest applies with equal force to . . . administrative adjudicators." K. Davis, Administrative Law Text §12.04, p. 250 (1972), and cases cited. The District Court proceeded on this basis and, applying the standards taken from our cases, concluded that the pecuniary interest of the members of the Board of Optometry had sufficient substance to disqualify them, given the context in which this case arose. As remote as we are from the local realities underlying this case and it being very likely that the District Court has a firmer grasp of the facts and of their significance to the issues presented, we have no good reason on this record to overturn its conclusion and we affirm it.[38]

Note: Judicial Disqualification

Consider the following standards for judicial disqualification, 28 U.S.C. §455 as amended Dec. 5, 1974, Pub. L. 93-512 §1, 88 Stat. 1609:

(a) Any justice, judge, magistrate, or referee in bankruptcy of the United States shall disqualify himself in any proceeding in which his impartiality might reasonably be questioned.

37. Ed. note: Tumey v. Ohio struck down a criminal conviction before a township judge who received his personal salary from the fines he levied on persons convicted in his court. Ward v. Village of Monroeville extended this principle to trials before the mayor of a village which received half of its revenues from fines levied in the mayor's court.
38. Ed. note: The Supreme Court remanded the case to the District Court to reconsider the meaning of the Alabama statute in the light of an intervening state court decision interpreting it.

(b) He shall also disqualify himself in the following circumstances:

(1) Where he has a personal bias or prejudice concerning a party, or personal knowledge of disputed evidentiary facts concerning the proceedings. . . .

(4) . . . [when he] . . . has a financial interest in the subject matter in controversy . . . or any other interest that could be substantially affected by the outcome of the proceeding. . . .

(e) No justice . . . shall accept from the parties to the proceeding a waiver of any ground for disqualification enumerated in subsection (b). Where the ground for disqualification arises only under subsection (a), waiver may be accepted provided it is preceded by a full disclosure on the record of the basis for disqualification.

District court proceedings are governed by 28 U.S.C. §144:

Whenever a party to any proceeding in a district court makes and files a timely and sufficient affidavit that the judge before whom the matter is pending has a personal bias or prejudice either against him or in favor of any adverse party, such judge shall proceed no further therein, but another judge shall be assigned to hear such proceeding.

The American Bar Association Code of Judicial Conduct, adopted in 1972, provides in Canon 3-C that:

A judge should disqualify himself in a proceeding in which his impartiality might reasonably be questioned. . . .

How do these standards differ? How do they compare with the standards for administrative disqualification? [39]

d. The "Rule of Necessity"

At common law, the judge was disqualified from participating in any case in which he had a direct pecuniary interest. But the common law courts very early adopted, assimilated, and applied a rule with an opposite effect — "the rule of necessity." It was realistically recognized that the concepts of disqualification and necessity are inseparable, for the object of disqualification is to ensure that, where possible, a judge is disinterested in the matters at issue; its object is not to preclude access to a judicial forum, or to bar judicial determination of the legal issues raised. Where the policy of disqualification conflicts with a litigant's rights to obtain a

39. See Memorandum of Mr. Justice Rehnquist, Laird v. Tatum, 409 U.S. 824 (1972); Note, Disqualification of Judges and Justices in the Federal Courts, 86 Harv. L. Rev. 736 (1973); J. Frank, Commentary on Disqualification of Judges — Canon 3-C, 1972 Utah L. Rev. 377 (1972).

judicial remedy, it has been generally conceded that the former must yield to the latter, trusting the conscience of the court to achieve a just result.

The English courts have traced the history of the "rule of necessity" back to 1430 and the Yearbooks.[40] Parliament in 1743 provided that tax paying justices of the peace could sit in local government cases, avoiding any need for them to disqualify themselves as tax payers:

> Thus grew the modern rule of "necessity," that judges should not decline to sit where no substitute was readily available. As Pollock later expressed it, "the settled rule of law is that, although a judge had better not, if it can be avoided, take part in a decision of a case in which he has any personal interest, yet he not only may, but must do so if the case can not be heard otherwise." And this remains the American practice.[41]

The "rule of necessity" has allowed judges to sit on matters involving judicial salaries.[42] In fact, it led Chancellor Kent to decide a case in which his brother was a party. And it applies with equal force to administrative as well as to judicial tribunals.

An example of how the rule operates is provided by United States v. Corrigan, 401 F. Supp. 795 (D. Wyo. 1975). Corrigan asked for disqualification on the ground that the judge was a defendant in a different suit that Corrigan had filed against nearly every federal judge in the country. The court held that the judge need not disqualify himself. The court stated:

> Another statute, 28 U.S.C. §455, provides that a judge shall disqualify himself in any case in which he has a substantial interest or his impartiality might be questioned. Ordinarily when a judge is named as a defendant in a suit brought by a defendant before him in trial, such judge should automatically disqualify himself.
>
> However, necessity may obviate this rule when virtually no judge would be available to hear the suit because all federal judges are co-defendants. . . . In this situation, if we were to disqualify ourself from hearing the matter on the ground urged by defendant, there would be few, if any, federal judges who could hear the trial and none in this circuit. Thus, we conclude that the necessity for the case to be heard by a federal judge militates strongly against disqualification of this judge. [401 F. Supp. at 798]

40. Dimes v. Grand Junction Canal Co., 10 Eng. Rep. 301, 313 (1852). See generally Lederman, The Independence of the Judiciary, 34 Can. B. Rev. 769, 797 (1956).

41. J. Frank, Disqualification of Judges, 56 Yale L. J. 605, 611 (1947). See Brinkley v. Hassig, 83 F.2d 351, 357 (10th Cir. 1936).

42. See, e.g., Evans v. Gore, 253 U.S. 245 (1920). The most recent major court elaboration on the rule of necessity, along with extensive citations, was in Atkins v. United States, 556 F.2d 1028 (Ct. Cl. 1977), cert. den., 434 U.S. 1009 (1978). One hundred forty federal circuit court and district court judges unsuccessfully sued for additional pay. Their theory was that Article III, Section 1 of the Constitution ("The Judges, both of the supreme and inferior Courts, shall . . . receive for their Services, a Compensation, which shall not be diminished during their Continuance in Office"), was violated when inflation reduced the real value of their salaries by one-third over a six-year period.

Questions

(1) The laws of a certain state provide that in any proceeding before the Department of Medical Practice to revoke a doctor's license to practice medicine, the matter shall be referred to a medical committee for hearing and recommendation. A revocation proceeding was initiated against Dr. Walter Evans on the ground that he had made false claims as to the therapeutic value of a treatment for cancer known as the "Koch" treatment.

For thirty years prior to this proceeding, the American Medical Association had denounced the Koch treatment as valueless. The Journal of the American Medical Association had published over twenty articles condemning it, and the AMA had joined in efforts to revoke the licenses of all doctors who used it. All five of the doctors who were regular members of the medical committee were members and officers of the AMA. One of the five was a cancer specialist who had published several articles saying that the only known methods of fighting most forms of cancer are radium, cobalt treatments, X-rays, and surgery.

Dr. Evans' counsel filed a request with the medical committee and the Department that the committee be disqualified for bias and that a new ad hoc committee be named of doctors who were not members of the AMA and who had not prejudged the issues. This request was denied, the hearing was held, and the committee's recommendation that Evans' license be revoked was adopted by the Director on behalf of the Department.

Should a court on judicial review sustain Dr. Evan's contention that he is entitled to a new hearing because of the bias of the medical committee?

(2) In 1968, the Doubloon Company applied to the City Council of the City of Oxbridge for a zoning variance to permit the construction of two parking lots adjacent to a three-story department store that it was then building. The City Council approved the variance but the resolution of approval specified that "nothing shall prevent the City Council, in its discretion, from revoking or modifying this resolution, or the variance herein provided for, after regular public hearings in regard thereto."

The lots in question were then paved and used for parking, and shortly thereafter the granting of such variances became a lively political issue in Oxbridge. At the next City Council election, held in 1970, three of the seven members elected stated in the campaign that if elected they would take necessary steps to have the variances revoked. After the election, a public hearing was held on the proposed revocation of the Doubloon variance. A number of witnesses, including Doubloon's president, appeared and were questioned. The variance was revoked, 4-3. Three of those who voted for revocation were the three who had campaigned on a revocation platform.

Doubloon brings a declaratory judgment action in state court against the City of Oxbridge and the City Council to have the revocation of the variance declared invalid on the ground of bias. What result? [43]

43. On the question of bias, see generally Comment, Prejudice and Administrative Process, 59 Nw. U. L. Rev. 216 (1964). Note, Disqualification of Administrative Officials for Bias, 13 Vand. L. Rev. 712 (1960).

3. Who Decides?

As in most large federal agencies, one of the major problems facing Federal Trade commissioners is finding the time to decide the numerous cases that reach them while also deciding major issues of policy and administering a large agency. Heads of major agencies rely heavily upon staff assistance in deciding a case. A commissioner is most unlikely to read the record or even the briefs personally. Staff members will probably digest the briefs for him and prepare a memorandum noting the main points of the arguments. After reaching a decision, the commissioner will probably not even write his own opinion. That function will be given to a special opinion writing section in the General Counsel's Office.

The problem of how a busy administrative official finds time to decide a highly complex adjudication arose in the following case (the first of four Supreme Court opinions in a lengthy and intricate litigation).

Morgan v. United States [Morgan I]

298 U.S. 468 (1936)

Mr. Chief Justice HUGHES delivered the opinion of the Court.

These are fifty suits, consolidated for the purpose of trial, to restrain the enforcement of an order of the Secretary of Agriculture, fixing the maximum rates to be charged by market agencies for buying and selling livestock at the Kansas City Stock Yards....

[The statute which authorizes the Secretary of Agriculture to fix the rates provides in part: "Whenever after full hearing ... the Secretary is of the opinion that any rate ... of a stockyard owner ... is or will be unjust, unreasonable or discriminatory, the Secretary — (a.) May determine and prescribe what will be the just and reasonable rate...."]

[Plaintiffs alleged in part] [t]hat the Secretary, without warrant of law delegated to Acting Secretaries the determination of issues with respect to the reasonableness of the rates involved.... That the Secretary at the time he signed the order in question had not personally heard or read any of the evidence presented at any hearing in connection with the proceeding and had not heard or considered oral arguments relating thereto or briefs submitted on behalf of the plaintiffs, but that the sole information of the Secretary with respect to the proceeding was derived from consultation with employees in the Department of Agriculture out of the presence of the plaintiffs or any of their representatives.

[The District Court in which the action was brought struck out these allegations on the ground that they could not state a claim upon which relief could be granted. Plaintiffs appealed the dismissal of the claim.]

Certain facts appear of record. The testimony was taken before an examiner. ... Oral argument upon the evidence was had before the Acting Secretary of Agriculture. Subsequently, a brief was filed on plaintiff's behalf. Thereafter, reciting "careful consideration of the entire record in this proceeding," findings of fact and conclusions, and an order prescribing rates, were signed by the Secretary of Agriculture. . . .

Second — The outstanding allegation, which the District Court struck out, is that the Secretary made the rate order without having heard or read any of the evidence, and without having heard the oral arguments or having read or considered the briefs which the plaintiffs submitted. That the only information which the Secretary had as to the proceeding was what he derived from consultation with employees of the Department.

. . . [T]he fundamental question [should not] be confused with one of mere delegation of authority. The Government urges that the Acting Secretary who heard the oral argument was in fact the Assistant Secretary of Agriculture. . . . If the Secretary had assigned to the Assistant Secretary the duty of holding the hearing, and the Assistant Secretary accordingly had received the evidence taken by the examiner, had heard argument thereon and had then found the essential facts and made the order upon his findings, we should have had simply the question of delegation. But while the Assistant Secretary heard argument he did not make the decision. The Secretary who, according to the allegation, had neither heard nor read evidence or argument, undertook to make the findings and fix the rates. The Assistant Secretary, who had heard, assumed no responsibility for the findings or order, and the Secretary, who had not heard, did assume that responsibility.[44]

Third — What is the essential quality of the proceeding under review, and what is the nature of the hearing which the statute prescribes?

The proceeding is not one of ordinary administration, conformable to the standards governing duties of a purely executive character. . . . Congress has required the Secretary to determine, as a condition of his action, that the existing rates are or will be "unjust, unreasonable, or discriminatory." If and when he so finds he may "determine and proscribe" what shall be the just and reasonable rate, or the maximum or minimum rate, thereafter to be charged. That duty is widely different from ordinary executive action. It is a duty which carries with it fundamental procedural requirements. There must be a full hearing. There must be evidence adequate to support pertinent and necessary findings of fact. . . .

A proceeding of this sort requiring the taking and weighing of evidence, determinations of fact based upon the consideration of the evidence, and the making of an order supported by such findings, has a quality resembling that of a judicial proceeding. Hence it is frequently described as a proceeding of a quasi-judicial character. The requirement of a "full hearing" has obvious reference to the tradition of judicial proceedings in which evidence is received and weighed by the trier of the facts. The "hearing" is designed to afford the safeguard that the one who decides shall be bound in good conscience to consider the evidence, to be guided by that alone, and to reach his conclusion uninfluenced by extraneous considerations which in other fields might have play in determining purely executive action. The "hearing" is the hearing of evidence and argument. If the one who determines the facts

---

44. Ed. note: The power of an official to "subdelegate" his powers to another official when not explicitly given the right to do so by the legislature is analyzed in 1 Davis, Administrative Law §9.01 et. seq. (1958); see also Note, Subdelegation by Federal Administrative Agencies, 12 Stan. L. Rev. 808 (1960).

which underlie the order has not considered evidence or argument, it is manifest that the hearing has not been given.

There is thus no basis for the contention that the authority conferred by §310 of the Packers and Stockyards Act is given to the Department of Agriculture, as a department in the administrative sense, so that one official may examine evidence, and another official who has not considered the evidence may make the findings and order. In such a view, it would be possible, for example, for one official to hear the evidence and argument and arrive at certain conclusions of fact, and another official who had not heard or considered either evidence or argument to overrule those conclusions and for reasons of policy to announce entirely different ones. It is no answer to say that the question for the court is whether the evidence supports the findings and the findings support the order. For the weight ascribed by the law to the findings — their conclusiveness when made within the sphere of the authority conferred — rests upon the assumption that the officer who makes the findings has addressed himself to the evidence and upon that evidence has conscientiously reached the conclusions which he deems it to justify. That duty cannot be performed by one who has not considered evidence or argument. It is not an impersonal obligation. It is a duty akin to that of a judge. The one who decides must hear.

This necessary rule does not preclude practicable administrative procedure in obtaining the aid of assistants in the department. Assistants may prosecute inquiries. Evidence may be taken by an examiner. Evidence thus taken may be sifted and analyzed by competent subordinates. Argument may be oral or written. The requirements are not technical. But there must be a hearing in a substantial sense. And to give the substance of a hearing, which is for the purpose of making determinations upon evidence, the officer who makes the determinations must consider and appraise the evidence which justifies them. That duty undoubtedly may be an onerous one, but the performance of it in a substantial manner is inseparable from the exercise of the important authority conferred. . . .

Our conclusion is that the District Court erred in striking out the allegations of Paragraph IV of the bill of complaint with respect to the Secretary's action. The defendants should be required to answer these allegations and the question whether plaintiffs had a proper hearing should be determined.

The decree is reversed and the cause is remanded for further proceedings in conformity with this opinion.

Reversed.

Note: The Ash Council Report

The Ash Council [45] made several specific recommendations designed to free the Commissioner's time for policy making:

> If administrative agencies, and particularly regulatory commissions, are to discharge their legislative implementation responsibilities, they should rely

---

45. The President's Advisory Council on Executive Organization, A New Regulatory Framework; Report on Selected Independent Regulatory Agencies 49-50 (1971).

less on the case-by-case approach to policy formulation and move increasingly in the direction of rulemaking, especially informal rulemaking, and other expeditious procedures. The disadvantages of the prevailing individual case approach are apparent.

First, commissioners tend to view themselves as judges atop an administrative-judicial hierarchy, with principal responsibility to hear appeals from initial or recommended decisions of hearing examiners acting as finders of fact. They do not, however, accord the usual degree of appellate deference to findings and determinations of the trier of fact and indeed cannot so long as case-by-case review is the predominant vehicle for establishing agency policy.

Second, this preoccupation with quasi-judicial activities has diverted attention and resources away from the more important responsibility of comprehensive and anticipatory policymaking. To the extent that policy is formulated in an adversary context, commissions must fit their policy declarations within the limiting confines of an adversary record. This approach is a barrier to anticipating problems that should be addressed informally without need for, and long before, the culmination of protracted proceedings.

Third, overjudicialization of the agency review process has a generally debilitating effect on the administrative mechanism. Proceedings before hearing examiners have become more complex as the scope of issues which must be considered has broadened. Rarely is it possible for a hearing examiner to try more than one or two cases simultaneously. Most agencies have three or four examiners for each commissioner and it is becoming commonplace for most decisions to be the subject of administrative appeal.

Consequently, a commission may have before it for resolution at any one time a dozen or more complex proceedings, each the subject of protracted hearings. Obviously, it cannot be expected that every commissioner, indeed that any commissioner, will be able to undertake an independent and full review of the more extensive records. Nor should they in view of the delays that would result. To meet this dilemma, most commissions have established special opinion-writing sections comprised of middle-level staff who review the record and write a draft of the "commission opinion." To a great extent, they define the limits of the commission's sensitivity and its ability to exercise judgment in many cases. Former CAB Member Louis Hector, commenting on this procedure, has noted that: "In the CAB and other regulatory agencies, the members of the agency merely vote on the outcome of a case and the opinion justifying the outcome is written by a professional staff. Members of these opinion-writing staffs explain that they consciously avoid statements of general principle as much as possible in the opinions they write, because they must be able to write an opinion justifying an opposite conclusion the next day, and hence must not be hampered by prior statements of general principles."

As a result, the review function shifts from the commission to a staff group. This in turn relegates the hearing examiner to a subordinate role, which can have detrimental consequences. Hearing examiners may become demoralized and view their function as one of limited utility — an attitude that can encourage appeals, including a multiplicity of interlocutory appeals, which serve to further prevent a commission from directing attention to more important, comprehensive policysetting.

If these serious deficiencies are to be overcome, it will be necessary to place a greater share of the responsibility for individual case determinations on the hearing examiners, leaving the administrator relatively free to concentrate on more appropriate means of formulating broad policy.

We propose that instead of engaging in the systematic review of initial decisions, administrators review, on their own motion, selected cases primarily for consistency with agency policy.

Note: Probing the Mental Processes of the Decisionmaker

Morgan I, above, is noteworthy not only because of its resounding statement that "the one who decides must hear," but because it seemed to allow the lower courts carte blanche in probing the mental processes of the decisionmaker when evaluating challenged administrative action. Notice that the second holding does not inevitably follow the first: it is possible that a plaintiff who claims that an administrator did not adequately study the evidence may be held to have a perfectly good cause of action, while at the same time, the reviewing court will not allow the plaintiff to gather the evidence he needs to prove his claim by interrogating the decisionmaker. There are good reasons why such a doctrine might be adopted: just as with the doctrine of immunity from personal liability for government officials for acts done in good faith in the course of official duties,[46] the "no probing of the decision process" rule would allow officials to perform their duties without fear of harassment from lawsuits and unseemly probing of their mental operations, thus encouraging efficient administration of the laws. Such a doctrine would then leave the primary checks on undesirable decision processes to the political branches of the government.

In any case, the sweeping *Morgan I* holding was short-lived. Subsequent opinions in the *Morgan* litigation itself limited the scope of the initial holding.

After *Morgan I*, the Supreme Court remanded the case to the District Court, which then took evidence on the question of whether the Secretary in fact had "decided" the controversy — issuing the rate order — without having heard or read the evidence or considered the arguments submitted. The Secretary and his associates answered interrogatories and testified that: (1) the examiner compiled a record consisting of about 10,000 transcript pages of oral testimony and 1,000 pages of statistics exhibits; (2) the Acting Secretary (Mr. Tugwell) held an oral hearing where the argument was general and sketchy; (3) the Government did not prepare a brief for, or formulate issues prior to, the oral hearing; the appellants (the market agencies) submitted roughly the same briefs that they had submitted to the examiner; the examiner had prepared no report; (4) after the oral hearing, the Bureau staff prepared 180 complex proposed findings, which it did not show to the appellants (the market agencies), but which it did send to the Secretary (no longer Mr. Tugwell); (5) the Secretary did not hear the oral argument before Mr. Tugwell, but he dipped into the record which was placed upon his desk, he read the briefs of the market agencies, he read the transcript of the oral argument, and he had several

---

46. See Chapter 9.

conferences with the Bureau staff and Department lawyers to discuss the proposed findings. With a few changes, he adopted the proposed findings of the Bureau. He stated that he had considered the evidence and the order represented his own independent conclusion based on Bureau findings; it represented his "own independent reaction to the findings of the men in the Bureau of Animal Industry." The District Court sustained the Secretary's rate order, holding that the hearing was adequate.

On appeal, in Morgan v. United States, 304 U.S. 1 (1938) (*Morgan II*), the Supreme Court again reversed the District Court. Chief Justice Hughes first limited the broad latitude that *Morgan I* apparently gave the lower courts to probe the mind of the administrator. He summarized the testimony of the Secretary as set out above and stated:

> In the light of this testimony there is no evidence to discuss the extent to which the Secretary examined the evidence and we agree with the Government's contention that it was not the function of the court to probe the mental processes of the Secretary in reaching his conclusions if he gave the hearing which the law required. The Secretary read the summary presented by appellants' briefs and he conferred with subordinates who had sifted and analyzed the evidence. We assume that the Secretary sufficiently understood its purport. . . .

The Court went on to hold, however, that the hearing was nonetheless inadequate, for the market agencies had not had a "reasonable opportunity" to be "fairly advised of what the Government proposed and to be heard upon" the Government's proposals before the Government issues its "final command." The Chief Justice wrote that the "right to a hearing embraces not only the right to present evidence but also a reasonable opportunity to know the claims of the opposing party and to meet them." Since there had been no specific complaint at the time the proceeding was begun, since there was no tentative report of the hearing examiner, and since the market agencies were not shown the Bureau's proposed findings, they did not know precisely what claims they had to meet. "The requirements of fairness are not exhausted in the taking or consideration of evidence but extend to the concluding parts of the procedure as well. . . ." 304 U.S. 1, 20 (1938) (this portion of *Morgan II* raises an issue considered at pp. 539-557 supra).

Upon remand of *Morgan II*, the district court had to decide what to do with funds that the plaintiff Morgan had paid into court — money equal to the difference between the pre-existing rates and the new, lower rates in the order that the agencies were protesting. The district court decided that, since the rate order was invalid under *Morgan II*, the funds should be returned to Morgan. The Supreme Court reversed the district court (for the third time). It held in United States v. Morgan, 307 U.S. 183 (1939) (*Morgan III*), that the District Court should have impounded the funds, holding them until a new rate was completed. The Court noted that the Secretary could order reparations for past years. When the Secretary had made his decision on these matters, the district court could dispose of the funds in an appropriate way.

After remand of *Morgan II* the Secretary and the market agencies agreed upon a higher rate schedule that would take effect on September 1, 1937. The Secretary thereafter made a new decision that the period 1933-37 (the period for which the funds were impounded) would be governed by precisely the same rate schedule that he had originally promulgated (and which the Supreme Court had set aside in *Morgan II*). The district court refused to apply the Secretary's decision to the impounded funds because the decision was based upon the test years of 1929, 1930, and 1931, yet costs had gone up between 1933 and 1937. On appeal, in United States v. Morgan, 313 U.S. 409 (1941) (*Morgan IV*), the Supreme Court reversed the district court for the fourth time. Justice Frankfurter wrote that the Secretary, in his new order, had heard and considered the relevant arguments. Market conditions were unstable; the proper rate was difficult to determine. "It is not for us to try to penetrate the precise course of the Secretary's reasoning. Our duty is at an end when we find, as we do find, that the Secretary was responsibly conscious of conditions at the market during the years following 1933, that he duly weighed them, and nevertheless concluded that rates similar to those in the 1933 order were proper." Id. at 420.

Justice Frankfurter then turned to the question of probing the mind of the administrator. He wrote:

> ... Over the Government's objections the district court authorized the market agencies to take the deposition of the Secretary. [Note that this took place after remand of *Morgan III* and concerned the Secretary's decision about the impounded money. This is *not* the decision discussed in *Morgan I* and *Morgan II*.] The Secretary thereupon appeared in person at the trial. He was questioned at length regarding the process by which he reached the conclusions of his order, including the manner and extent of his study of the record and his consultation with subordinates. His testimony shows that he dealt with the enormous record in a manner not unlike the practice of judges in similar situations, and that he held various conferences with the examiner who heard the evidence. Much was made of his disregard of a memorandum from one of his officials who, on reading the proposed order, urged considerations favorable to the market agencies. But the [gist] of the business is that the Secretary should never have been subjected to this examination. The proceeding before the Secretary "has adequately [resembled] that of a judicial proceeding." Morgan v. United States, 289 U.S. 468, 480. Such an examination of a judge would be destructive of judicial responsibility. We have explicitly held in this very litigation that "it was not the function of the court to probe the mental processes of the Secretary." 304 U.S. 1, 18. Just as a judge cannot be subjected to such a scrutiny, compare Foyerweather v. Rilch, 195 U.S. 276, 306, 307, so the integrity of the administrative process must be equally respected. ... It will bear repeating that although the administrative process has had a different development and pursues somewhat different ways from those of courts, they are to be deemed collaborative instrumentalities of justice and the appropriate independence of each should be respected by the other. ... [Id. at 421-422.]

The following case summarizes the current state of the law:

National Nutritional Foods Association v. FDA

491 F.2d 1141 (2d Cir. 1974)

[The Food and Drug Administration issued a notice of proposed revision of regulations on food labelling. The statute required their adoption after rulemaking hearings "on the record." The end-product of the subsequent twelve-year cycle of rulemaking proceedings was a record consisting of over 32,000 pages of testimony and thousands of pages of exhibits. Based on this material, the FDA drew up and published a set of "tentative final orders." By the time the period for public comment ended, formal exceptions to the proposed rules spread over 1,000 pages; there were over 20,000 additional letters. Meanwhile, the Commissioner of the FDA, who had overseen this entire proceeding, resigned, and Alexander Schmidt was appointed new chief of the FDA four months later. Within twelve days, he signed fourteen final regulations, thirteen proposed regulations, and six miscellaneous notices. On the thirteenth day after he took office, he signed the rules in question. Plaintiffs petitioned for review of these regulations, contending that it was impossible for Commissioner Schmidt to have reviewed the objections prior to promulgating the rules. The instant opinion derives from the petitioner's motion to depose Commissioner Schmidt and to instigate other discovery devices.]

FRIENDLY, Circuit Judge: . . .

Conceding that it is not the function of this court "to probe the mental processes" of the Commissioner, Morgan v. United States, 304 U.S. 1, 18, 58 S. Ct. 773, 82 L. Ed. 1129 (1938) (Morgan II), petitioners insist they are entitled to probe whether he exercised his own mental processes at all. More particularly, they claim they are entitled to do this in a situation where two unusual and indisputable facts, namely, the short time between Commissioner Schmidt's assumption of office and his signing of the regulations here at issue, and the large number of other rules promulgated by him in the interval, create more than ordinary basis for doubt as to the extent of his personal reading and consideration.

It is plain enough that if this motion had come before us in the period between the first Morgan case, Morgan v. United States, 298 U.S. 468, 481, 56 S. Ct. 906, 912, 80 L. Ed. 1288 (1936), holding that in administrative proceedings "The one who decides must hear" and that a court seized of a review proceeding must inquire whether he had, and the fourth and last appearance of the Morgan case in the Supreme Court, United States v. Morgan, 313 U.S. 409, 61 S. Ct. 999, 85 L. Ed. 1429 (1941), we would have been obliged to grant it. But the life of this aspect of Morgan I was extremely brief. In Morgan IV Mr. Justice Frankfurter, writing for a Court unanimous on this point, took back most or all of what the first decision had given, 313 U.S. at 421-422, 61 S. Ct. 999. Morgan IV dealt with a proceeding wherein the Secretary of Agriculture had fixed rates for the Kansas City stockyards that would govern distribution of funds impounded during the long pendency of the litigation. Upon a challenge to the extent of the Secretary's participation in the making of these rates similar to that which had been made in Morgan I, the district court had taken his testimony as the Court had directed in Morgan I. After strongly suggesting that it would reject on the merits a challenge with respect to the degree of the Secretary's personal consideration, the Court went on to hold: "But the short of the business is that the Secretary should never have been subjected to this examination." 313 U.S. at 422, 61 S. Ct. at 1004. Professor Kenneth Culp Davis has correctly characterized this, 2 Administrative Law Treatise §11.05, at 59 (1958), as a return to the law declared in De Cambra v. Rogers, 189 U.S. 119, 122, 23 S. Ct. 519, 521, 47 L. Ed. 734 (1903):

> It is hardly necessary to say that when a decision has been made by the Secretary of the Interior, courts will not entertain an inquiry as to the extent of his investigation and knowledge of the points decided, or as to the methods by which he reached his determination.

Subsequent Supreme Court decisions have not detracted from the force of Morgan IV.... [Petitioners rely on] a portion of Mr. Justice Marshall's opinion in Citizens to Preserve Overton Park, Inc. v. Volpe, 401 U.S. 402, 420, 91 S. Ct. 814, 825, 28 L. Ed. 2d 136 (1971), stating that on remand the district court "may require the administrative officials who participated in the decision to give testimony explaining their action." But Overton Park was a case where the Secretary of Transportation had made no formal findings; the taking of testimony, suggested as being within the range of proper action for the district court on remand, was for the purpose of ascertaining why the highway construction had been authorized, a function performed by the extensive preambles to the regulations here at issue. The Court reaffirmed Morgan IV, saying that where findings accompany the decision, "there must be a strong showing of bad faith or improper behavior" before testimony with regard to reasons can be taken. Id. Indeed, the opinion went on to say that testimony might not be required even in Overton Park if the Secretary could prepare post hoc findings sufficient to withstand scrutiny. Id. at 420-421, 91 S. Ct. 814. Nothing in the opinion suggests that the Court intended to allow inquiry into the relative participation of the Secretary and his subordinates. Similarly, strong preliminary showings of bad faith have been required in the court of appeals cases cited by petitioners before the taking of testimony has been permitted with regard to internal agency deliberations. See, e.g., Singer Sewing Machine Co. v. NLRB, 329 F.2d 200, 206-208 (4th Cir. 1964).

The facts of this case do not constitute nearly the showing of bad faith necessary to justify further inquiry; indeed they vividly illustrate the necessity of adhering to the presumption of regularity with respect to the participation of the officer authorized to sign administrative orders, especially in the context of the promulgation of legislative rules as distinguished from adjudication.... It would suffice under the circumstances that Commissioner Schmidt considered [staff-written] summaries of the objections and of the answers contained in the elaborate preambles and conferred with his staff about them. There is no reason why he could not have done this even in the limited time available....

The motion to take the testimony of the Commissioner and to have other discovery . . . is denied.[47]

Questions

(1) Assume that the Federal Trade Commission is considering the following plan to lighten the adjudicatory burden upon the Commissioners: cases would be categorized as either "major" or "minor," according to the importance of the policy issues they contain. In minor cases, the record from the initial hearing along with briefs and other submissions would be summarized by a member of the opinion writing section. That summary, together with a recommended decision, would be forwarded to the Commissioners but not made public. There would be no oral argument. Commissioners would of course remain free to read the briefs or record if they so desired. The relevant statute says that "the Commission" shall decide if the Act has been violated.

Is this proposed change lawful?

(2) Were you shocked to learn that most Commissioner's opinions are written by an opinion writing section of the staff? What problems do you see in such a practice? What do you think of the following suggestion: "If it were known that agency members were going to have to produce opinions, it is very likely that a higher quality of agency member would result." [48] Should Commissioners be assigned law clerks to assist them in a way similar to traditional judicial practice? [49]

---

47. Ed. note: Compare Cinderella Schools v. FTC, discussed supra, p. 750, where the court set aside the FTC's order partly because the FTC did not give adequate consideration to the record. No "probing of mental processes" was necessary, because the FTC's own opinion said "[I]n view of our decision to independently analyze — and without assistance from consumers or other witnesses — the challenged advertisements and their impact . . . it becomes unnecessary to review the testimony of these expert and consumer witnesses." This was held to be a denial of due process. 425 F.2d at 585, 586.

See also Montrose Chemical Corp. of California v. Train, 491 F.2d 63 (D.C. Cir. 1974), which held that an action under the Freedom of Information Act to obtain internal agency memoranda concerning an agency proceeding in which the plaintiff was interested would fail if the memoranda fell within the category of "probes into the mental process of decisionmakers."

See also N. Nathanson, Probing the Mind of the Administrator, 75 Colum. L. Rev. 721 (1975). See generally, Gifford, The Morgan Cases: A Retrospective View, 30 Ad. L. Rev. 237 (1978). For a strong rejection of probing mental processes, see Nat'l Nutritional Foods Ass'n v. Weinberger, 376 F. Supp. 142 (S.D.N.Y. 1974), rev'd 512 F.2d 688 (2d Cir.), cert. den. sub nom. Nat'l Nutritional Foods Ass'n v. Mathews, 423 U.S. 827 (1975). Such probing is also disfavored due to the "post hoc rationalization" nature of the evidence presented. GTE Sylvania, Inc. v. Consumer Prod. Safety Comm'n, 404 F. Supp. 352, 368-369 n.70 (D. Del. 1975).

48. H. Westwood, The Davis Treatise: Meaning to the Practitioner, 43 Minn. L. Rev. 607, 617 (1959).

49. The problem of the institutional decision is a much-debated one. For an empirical study, see D. Wellborn, Assigning Responsibility for Regulatory Decisions to Individual Commissioners: The Case of the ICC, 18 Ad. L. Rev. 13 (1966). See also, L. Hector, Government by Anonymity: Who Writes our Regulatory Opinions? 45 A.B.A.J. 1260 (1959); C. Peck, Regulation and Control of Ex Parte Communications with Administrative Agencies, 76 Harv. L. Rev. 233 (1962).

C.   The Reorganization of the Federal Trade Commission

This section will consider the serious criticisms made of the Federal Trade Commission during the 1960s. Next, it will examine the efforts of a new chairman to answer the critics through reorganizations of staff and agency structure.

1.   The Criticisms

The two most important written critiques of the Commission's work are those published in 1969 by the American Bar Association and by Ralph Nader. Their criticisms should be compared with the critiques contained in Chapter 3.

Report of the American Bar Association Commission to Study the FTC

1-3, 32-37 (1969) [50]

I.   SUMMARY

The Federal Trade Commission, an independent regulatory agency established in 1914, is assigned the responsibility of administering a wide variety of antitrust and trade regulation laws. Over the past 50 years, a succession of independent scholars and other analysts have consistently found the FTC wanting in the performance of its duties by reason of inadequate planning, failure to establish priorities, excessive preoccupation with trivial matters, undue delay, and unnecessary secrecy. . . .

The FTC of the 1960s is probably superior to most of its predecessors, but continues to fail in many respects. Through lack of effective direction the FTC has failed to establish goals and priorities, to provide necessary guidance to its staff, and to manage the flow of its work in an efficient and expeditious manner.

All available statistical measures of FTC activity show a downward trend in virtually all categories of its activities in the face of a rising budget and increased staff. Moreover, present enforcement activity rests heavily on a voluntary compliance program devoid of effective surveillance or sanctions. It thus appears that both the volume and the force of FTC law enforcement have declined during this decade.

We believe that the FTC has mismanaged its own resources. Through an inadequate system of recruitment and promotion, it has acquired and elevated to important positions a number of staff members of insufficient competence. The

---

50. The ABA Commission was appointed at the request of President Nixon to evaluate the FTC's enforcement efforts.

failure of the FTC to establish and adhere to a system of priorities has caused a misallocation of funds and personnel to trivial matters rather than to matters of pressing public concern.

The primary responsibility for these failures must rest with the leadership of the Commission. . . .

Turning to specific areas of FTC efforts, we find, first, that in the field of consumer protection, the agency has been preoccupied with technical labeling and advertising practices of the most inconsequential sort. . . .

At the same time, the FTC has exercised little leadership in the prevention of retail marketing frauds. . . .

In the antitrust field, we believe that the FTC can perform valuable service in bringing the administrative process to bear on difficult and complex problems. We therefore propose that the concurrent jurisdiction of the FTC and the Department of Justice in antitrust enforcement be retained. We urge, however, that the present allocation of enforcement resources be reexamined and realigned in a manner more nearly consistent with the objectives of antitrust policy.

The work of the FTC's Bureau of Economics has been of substantial value. We think, however, that its public acceptance would be improved by a structural division into two separate units — one to provide support to the enforcement work of the FTC, and the other to engage in fundamental economic research.

Finally, we believe that several serious and pervasive deficiencies at the FTC must be acknowledged and corrected.

. . . [It is] imperative that the FTC embark on a program to establish goals, priorities, and effective planning controls. . . .

E. CONCLUSIONS. . . .

Additional aspects of recent FTC performance are also disturbing; underallocation of resources for consumer protection, for anti-merger enforcement, monitoring of false advertising, and for compliance programs, have sapped the FTC's effectiveness. . . . [R]esources are meanwhile being wasted in other areas, such as overenforcement of labeling and disclosure requirements on textiles and furs, and promulgation and enforcement of guides and rules relating to trivial advertising and labeling problems. . . .

Often the agency has seemed more concerned with protecting competitors of an enterprise practicing deception rather than consumers. . . .

We conclude also that the FTC's enforcement program, which depends heavily on voluntary compliance by businessmen, with no effective check on that compliance, is unlikely adequately to protect the public interest. . . .

We have found further that problems of delay have been significant. . . .

. . . When actual performance is measured against the potential which the FTC continues to possess, that agency's performance must be regarded as a failure on many counts. . . .

If the proposals in this report are ever to be implemented, and if the FTC is to fulfill the role we believe it can play, it must have the continuous vigorous sup-

port of the President and Congress. The first important manifestation of that support should be the appointment of a Commission Chairman with executive ability,
knowledge of the tasks Congress has entrusted to the agency, and sufficient
strength and independence to resist pressures from Congress, the Executive Branch,
or the business community that tend to cripple effective performance by the FTC.
Because an urgent responsibility facing the new Chairman will be to unify the
agency, we believe that it is important to appoint to this position someone not
previously affiliated with it. . . .

The Nader Report [51]

We propose to analyze the real problem of the Federal agency — not through
the cloak and dagger of abstraction — but openly, frankly, and systematically. The
real problem of the FTC — and indeed of any faltering agency — can usually be
traced to people. Misguided leadership is the malignant cancer that has already
assumed control of the Commission, that has been silently destroying it, and that
has spread its contagion on the growing crisis of the American consumer.

We propose to consider the nature and makeup of the FTC, who controls it,
how and why, and for what purposes. We shall review partisan political activity and
relations — or arrangements — with Congress. Then we shall take a look at the
Commission's collective background, its treatment of minorities, its hiring practices,
and occupational biases.

PARTISAN POLITICS

The official image of the Federal Trade Commission is, as it should be, a nonpolitical agency that regulates interstate commerce against anticompetitive and
unfair practices in the public interest. . . .

Yet in the case of the present regime at the FTC, the Hatch Act and the Civil
Service Law are treated as mere rhetoric. Most attorneys at the FTC are labeled as
either Democrat or Republican, and their party affiliation has a definite bearing on
the positions they are offered. All staff attorneys at the FTC from bureau chief to
executive director hold their positions on appointment from Chairman Dixon who,
in effect, may replace them whenever he desires and reduce them from a supergrade
to a GS-15. Ideally, the Chairman rotates the FTC staff to place the best men at
the top of each operating bureau. When Mr. Dixon became Chairman in 1960, it
seems that the "best men" were all Democrats. Any Republican in a high position
was offered the choice of becoming a trial lawyer at the bottom of the organization
chart or resigning.

As a result, fourteen highly experienced career men left the Commission almost
immediately. In its November 20, 1961, issue, Advertising Age called partisan

51. E. Cox, R. Fellmeth & J. Schultz, The Consumer and the Federal Trade Commission
129-159 (1969) [reprinted in 115 Cong. Rec. 1539 (1969)].

politics the major reason for a shake-up at the FTC. As a result, the magazine said, the quality of key personnel had deteriorated. In time most of the Republicans found it hard to swallow their pride and left. A few able ones, such as the former Assistant Executive Director, Basil Mezines, and John Walker, an attorney, have stuck it out. Throughout this time, however, being "out" has grown increasingly uncomfortable. . . .

Besides permitting his staff to violate the spirit and the letter of the Civil Service Law in promotion and hiring, Chairman Dixon himself has violated the Hatch Act. Highly reliable sources at the FTC revealed that until recently Mr. Dixon was notorious for dunning the agency's personnel as far down as the GS-14 level for political contributions. This group includes approximately one-quarter of the more than 300 lawyers working in the central office in Washington. . . . Members of the staff have testified to receiving solicitation cards from the Democratic National Committee with a code number in the corner which everyone involved knew would indicate to Chairman Dixon who gave and who did not. This method was not well received by those who were being coerced into giving against their will. Eventually, the threat of action by the Justice Department under the Hatch Act forced Chairman Dixon to give up open political exploitation of his employees. He now uses more discreet methods. For example, he personally asks his subordinates to buy $100-a-plate tickets to Democratic fund-raising dinners. Thus Chairman Dixon persists in playing partisan politics, while neglecting his responsibilities as a public servant.

FRIENDS ON CAPITOL HILL

Even more destructive to the sense of purpose and nonpolitical ideal of the Commission are the Congressional politics that permeate it. Congressional pressures have made nonsense of priorities for action which related only in theory to the importance of the social issue involved.

According to Joseph W. Shea, Secretary of the FTC, any letter the Commission gets from a Congressman's office is specially marked with an "expedite" sticker. The sticker gives the letter high priority, assuring the Congressman of an answer within five days.

All matters that Congressmen deem important are handled by telephone or in person. These cordial personal contacts are constant. They are also more than casual. One lawyer in the Bureau of Deceptive Practices commented candidly, "Everyone who wants to go anywhere at the FTC has a political connection." He then unblushingly named a Congressman who was his own sponsor.

The personal influence of Congressmen begins at the top. Chairman Dixon was appointed by President Kennedy under heavy pressure from the late Senator Estes Kefauver of Tennessee. The runner-up for the chairmanship, A. Everette MacIntyre, was sponsored by Representative Wright Patman of Texas. He was given the next available Commissioner's post as a consolation prize. Casual scrutiny of the FTC reveals a number of other political sponsors. One day we were fortunate enough to find William Jibb, director of the FTC's Office of Information, at his desk. (According to reporters who deal with the Office of Information regularly, Mr. Jibb is rarely there. We also found this to be true. Wilbur Weaver, Mr. Jibb's assistant, seems to be able to run the office quite well apparently without aid from Mr. Jibb.) Mr. Jibb insisted on telling us that he had been an old college friend and political aide of Senator G. Smathers of Florida.

Other members of the Commission's staff are less talkative about their political connections, which are nonetheless well known — Joseph Shea's for example. Mr. Shea comes from Boston, and his official title, stated in his bibliography, is "Secretary and Congressional Liaison Officer." The Commission telephone book and budget control reports list him simply as "Secretary." His bibliography also notes "came to Washington, D.C., April 19, 1931, under sponsorship of Speaker John W. McCormack as a clerk at $1,000 per annum and attended evening law school." Around the Federal Trade Commission he is known "to be like a son" to the Speaker of the House....

... The 1965 Civil Service Commission study of FTC management practices seemed disturbed by this fact and the very high supergrade to GS-16 with a salary of $24,875 that Mr. Shea held. Their report stated:

> The Secretary's position was placed in grade GS-16 upon the statements of the Chairman regarding the personal contributions the Secretary has made to the Commission through his highly successful personal contacts outside the Commission. Personal contributions of this nature do not permit their delegation to subordinates in the principal's absence. The other responsibilities of the Secretary — i.e., the preparation of the Minutes and maintaining the official records of the Commission — were not factors influencing the classification of this position. (p. 48)

Other officers in high position at the FTC have political contacts or relations similar to Mr. Shea's....

Perhaps the Congressman with the most influence in the decisions of the FTC is Representative Joe Evins — of Tennessee — who is also Chairman of the House Appropriations Subcommittee, which approves the FTC's budget. One staff member of the FTC stated the rule: "Ambitious staff attorneys at the FTC who are from Tennessee have to know Joe Evins." For example, when a political friend, Judge Castro C. Geer, wanted to work near his home town in Tennessee, the FTC obligingly set up an office in Oak Ridge, although it does not have any office in, for instance, Detroit or Philadelphia. Although the FTC never announced the opening of its new office, Representative Evins did make an announcement which, together with a picture of Judge Geer, appeared on the front page of The Chattanooga Times.

Bill Weaver of the FTC Office of Information discovered the new branch of the FTC only from casual conversation with people in the supply room who were shipping office equipment to Oak Ridge. Even two of the Commissioners were unaware of the Oak Ridge Branch until informed by sources outside the Commission. In addition, Judge Geer is the only FTC field operative anywhere in the country not listed under the Bureau of Field Operations, but directly responsible to the Bureau of Deceptive Practices, which is directed by Chairman Dixon's close friend, Frank Hale. In a telephone interview Mr. Hale could not say precisely what kind of work occupied Judge Geer, adding parenthetically "but I understand there's a good deal of work down there." A telephone interview with the judge himself proceeded as follows:

Interviewer: What date was the Oak Ridge Office opened?

Judge Geer: You will have to get that information from the central office.

Interviewer: What type of work primarily occupies you?

Judge Geer: You will have to get that information from the central office.

Interviewer: You mean to say that they know more about your work in Washington than you do in Oak Ridge?

Judge Geer: Well, they have the first hand information there.
         (*pause*)

Interviewer: Is it an FTC policy to release all information only through the central office?

Judge Geer: (pause) I don't know if it is or not.

Interviewer: On what grounds, then, do you refuse to give even the most innocuous information?

Judge Geer: You will have to get that information from the central office.

Since the Office of Information did not know about the Oak Ridge office, we talked directly to the Executive Director, John Wheelock. He went into a long explanation of why the Oak Ridge office was attached to the Atlanta field office instead of the Cleveland office ("Very few attorneys like to serve in Cleveland because of this weather"). Even this explanation, as subsequent investigation showed, was false. Judge Geer continues to collect his salary of $17,500. . . .

[The Nader group then explored the backgrounds of the top personnel of the FTC. They noted that Chairman Dixon was from Tennessee and that an unusually large number of the hierarchy came from small towns in the South. Included in this class were the Executive Director, the assistant to the Chairman, five of the six bureau chiefs, the General Counsel, and the Director of the Office of Hearing Examiners. In the Kansas City and San Francisco Field Offices, where the regional directors were originally from Georgia and Virginia, the Nader Group found a "reverse carpetbagger" effect. It implied that this "clubhouse ambience" was responsible for the Commission's failure to investigate "discrimination by deception" and "the exploitation of the ghetto poor."]

In "The Dim Light of Paul Rand Dixon," an article that appeared in The Washingtonian, October, 1968, Milton Viorst concludes:

Paul Rand Dixon's chief failure . . . seems to be that he's been with the Federal Trade Commission for too long. Dixon is so accustomed to doing what he's always done that he finds it difficult to conceive of doing anything very different. . . .

He simply lacks the clarity of conception necessary to give the FTC broad new objectives, as well as the tenacity of spirit needed to build a staff equal to achieving them. . . .

Some of the men in the General Counsel's Office are desperately in need of face-saving. One of these is Charles Grandey. When two members of our task force went to interview Mr. Grandey in his office, they found him fast asleep on a couch with the sports section of The Washington Post covering his head. They woke him up, and he walked to his desk, where he propped his chin up with his hands on top of a pile of books. Asked what his work entailed, Mr. Grandey gave a very vague reply. Further inquiries with other FTC attorneys established that he really did very little, his chief occupation being to abstract cases pertinent to the Commission's work. His yearly salary is $22,695. He is officially listed in the Commission telephone book as Assistant General Counsel for Voluntary Compliance, along with the other assistant general counsels who head divisions. He is also listed on organization charts, in the same manner, but in the confidential budget-control reports, he is simply placed along with the assistants to the General Counsel. And just exactly what the Division of Voluntary Compliance does is a mystery not solved even by the FTC's Justification of Estimates of Appropriations for Fiscal Year for 1968 and 1969, which are presented to Congress. In these tomes the Division of Voluntary Compliance mysteriously disappears and remains unjustified. . . .

According to the myth about hiring that the Federal Trade Commission encourages, it seeks out the best young attorneys and offers them appointments. Our confidential interviews told a different story. Young attorneys are accepted for various reasons. Some on the merits of their case — grades, extracurricular activities, and Law School Admission Test scores; but many more are accepted because the interviewers "liked" them, or because of old school ties, regional background, or a political endorsement. . . .

The myth of a hunt for the best available legal talent has been dispelled by Chairman Dixon, who has been quoted as saying: "Given a choice between a really bright man, and one who is merely good, take the good man. He'll stay longer."

Chairman Dixon's well-known prejudice against "Ivy League Lawyers" is deeply rooted in Southern populist tradition, which is the background of the Commission's ruling clique. As a result, graduates of prestigious law schools such as Harvard and Pennsylvania, which have very capable antitrust departments, have a poor chance of joining the FTC, compared with graduates of law schools like Kentucky and Tennessee. . . .

Within four years 80 percent of the new lawyers leave the FTC. Their reasons vary from a chance at a better paying job to complete detestation for the agency. We interviewed five young attorneys who had left or were about to leave. We spoke briefly with a sixth, but he subsequently balked at a full interview, fearing recriminations in the form of bad recommendations from the FTC. He, too, was in the process of leaving. All of these attorneys were unanimous in the opinion that the FTC was a discouraging place for a young attorney. Most had stayed for as long as they did only to finish their "graduate-on-the-job training" in antitrust law and to qualify for good recommendations.

One lawyer who had been at the FTC in the late 1950s and early 1960s stated that the aggressive trial approach of Chairman Earl Kintner was ideal for young lawyers who wanted to take responsibility. He calculated that he had tried nineteen cases in his first two-and-a-half years because his boss liked nothing better than to shift his workload on to willing young attorneys. After those exciting first years, however, things slowed down under the Dixon regime and its voluntary-compliance approach. . . .

An old hand at the Federal Trade Commission stated that there were two kinds of people among the lawyers that decided to make a career of the FTC;

1. the intelligent, idealistic public servants who desire a certain degree of security, and

2. the not-so-smart lawyers who need the security of the FTC.

Most of the career men at the FTC fall into the second category. . . .

In the last analysis, the major problem at the FTC is motivational. The men who lead the Commission desire only to do the work they have always done in a manner that recalls Samuel Beckett's existential tragedy *Waiting for Godot*. In the meantime, the young attorneys at the bottom languish for want of direction and remind themselves they are there for only a short while to receive a practical legal education.

2. Efforts to Reform the FTC through Personnel Changes and Structural Reorganization

The Nader Report, followed nine months later by the ABA Report, created a sensation. The press editorialized, the public was outraged, and Congressmen pressed for action.[52] In October 1969, President Nixon nominated Caspar Weinberger, formerly California state director of finance, to replace Paul Rand Dixon as chairman of the FTC. Weinberger took office in January 1970 but had served only six months when the President moved him to the Office of Management and Budget. His successor was Miles Kirkpatrick, who had chaired the ABA committee investigating the FTC. Kirkpatrick was therefore intimately familiar with the problems of the Commission and vigorously pursued the reforms initiated by his predecessor. Those reforms were initially of an administrative or bureaucratic nature. Weinberger sought to reorganize the FTC and to fire incompetent personnel.

a. Can The Chairman Fire Personnel?

One of the most pressing problems which faced Weinberger and Kirkpatrick was reforming the lethargic legal staff of the FTC. The instinctive managerial response is to fire incompetent attorneys — if their work is not worth their salaries, let them find jobs elsewhere. But first the Chairman must determine whether he has the legal power to do so. He must then develop a practical plan for eliminating deadwood selectively, rather than firing employees indiscriminately.

52. See e.g., NY Times, Sept. 26, 1969, at 1, col. 1; Newsweek, Sept. 29, 1969, at 85.

Chairman Weinberger asked for a memo from his staff about his legal authority to dismiss. He might have received a memo like the following:

Since FTC personnel are appointed and not elected, every employee is by definition in the "civil service." [53]

The Civil Service Commission administers the "competitive service," which consists of all civil service positions other than those excepted by statute,[54] or by the President.[55] The Civil Service Commission has been authorized by Executive Order to except positions whenever it determines that appointments through competitive examinations are not practical (Schedule A), or when such positions are of a confidential or policy-determining character (listed under "Schedule C").[56] Attorneys are listed in Schedule A and thus excepted.[57] Several positions in the FTC are listed in Schedule C, including two secretaries to the Chairman, the Director of Public Information, and one secretary to the Director of Public Information.[58]

Persons "in the competitive service may be removed or suspended without pay only for such cause as will promote the efficiency of the service." [59] Specific procedural safeguards protect the employee against adverse actions, which include removal, suspension for more than 30 days, furlough without pay, or reduction in rank or pay. The removal procedure includes service of notice and a copy of the charges, a reasonable time in which to reply, and the receipt of a written decision on the reply.[60] The Civil Service rules also guarantee the employee the opportunity for a full hearing before the Appeals Authority of the Commission though a suspension may take effect before this appeal is heard.[61]

53. 5 U.S.C. §2101(1) (1978).
54. 5 C.F.R. §213.3102(d) (1977).
55. 5 C.F.R. §213.3334 (1977).
56. 15 U.S.C. §42 (1978).
57. 5 C.F.R. §213.3102(d) (1977). Section 2 of the FTC Act also excepts "the secretary, a clerk to each Commissioner, the attorneys, and such special experts and examiners as the Commission may from time to time find necessary for the conduct of its work," 15 U.S.C. §42.
58. 5 C.F.R. §213.3334 (1977).
59. 5 U.S.C. §7501. Among the "causes" which have been held to promote the efficiency of the service are: absence without leave, disobedience, insubordination, misrepresentation, untrustworthiness, inefficiency, and incompetence. See, e.g., 5 C.F.R. §731.202(b) (1977). The courts generally defer to the agency as the judge of what constitutes "cause," and the substantial evidence rule is not applicable to adverse agency action, although there must be some evidence tending to substantiate the "cause" for removal. Judicial review has been principally concerned with whether an agency's action was arbitrary or capricious. But see Comment, The Scope of Judicial Review of a Civil Service Determination, 19 Am. U. L. Rev. 520 (1970). See also Johnson & Stoll, Judicial Review of Federal Employee Dismissals and Other Adverse Actions, 57 Cornell L. Rev. 178 (1972). A new employee is on probation for one year and is not considered to be part of the competitive service for that time period. See Johnson, Probationary Government Employees and the Dilemma of Arbitrary Dismissals, 44 U. Cin. L. Rev. 698 (1975).
60. 5 U.S.C. §7501(b).
61. 5 C.F.R. §§752, 771, 772 (1977), contain the standards and procedures for all disciplinary actions against civil service employees. The Commission is required to render "substantial compliance" with its own rules. Seebach v. Cullen, 338 F.2d 663, 664 (9th Cir. 1964). Some commentators have argued that the Civil Service system is unwieldy and a basic cause of government's inability to improve its standard of performance. See, e.g., Frug, Does the Constitution Prevent the Discharge of Civil Service Employees?, 124 U. Pa. L. Rev. 942 (1976); Reed, Firing a Federal Employee: The Impossible Dream, 9 The Washington Monthly 14 (July/August 1977).

"Excepted personnel" — on Schedule A and C — have no statutory retention rights, nor do the Civil Service statutes grant them any of the procedural safeguards afforded employees in the competitive service. There is, however, one important exception: "Preference eligible" employees — veterans — are guaranteed the full protection of civil service rules and regulations, *no matter what schedule they are on.*[62]

With the aid of these general rules, FTC personnel can be categorized as follows: First, the personnel in the competitive service (who are therefore entitled to formal hearing procedures before adverse action can be taken) include all veterans and all economists and accountants, the Comptroller, the Director of the Office of Administration, the Director of Personnel, the Management Office, and the nonprofessional staff. The following have no retention rights unless they are veterans: noncareer executives[63] (including the heads of the major administrative units) and personnel holding appointments excepted by Schedule A or C (thus including all staff lawyers.)[64]

The Chairman of the FTC has considerable power over the hiring and dismissal of Commission personnel. Reorganization Plan No. 8 of 1950 transferred to the Chairman the powers of "appointment and supervision of personnel employed under the Commission." This authority was qualified in three respects, however. First, the Chairman is governed by the general rules and policies of the Commission and its decisions. Second, the appointment of the heads of major administrative units are subject to the approval of the full Commission.[65] Third, personnel in the personal office of the other Commissioners are not subject to the plan.[66]

62. 5 U.S.C. §§ 7512, 7701, 5 U.S.C. §§ 2108, 7511.

63. Individuals appointed to noncareer executive assignments can be dismissed only if a majority of Commissioners agree. They are persons who:
  (a) are deeply involved in the advocacy of Administration programs and support of their controversial aspects;
  (b) participate significantly in the determination of major political policies of the Administration; or
  (c) serve principally as personal assistant to or advisor of a Presidential appointee or other key political figure. 5 C.F.R. §9.20 (1977).

64. In 1947, attorneys were reclassified from the competitive service to the excepted service. Any attorney whose appointment dates from before 1947 is still theoretically in the "competitive service" and thus is entitled to the same procedural safeguards as those in the competitive service. Roth v. Brownell, 215 F.2d 500 (D.C. Cir.), *cert. denied*, 348 U.S. 863 (1954). The fact that an attorney holds a supergrade position (but is not a head of a major administrative unit) does not change his excepted status. Appointments to supergrade positions (GS-16 and above) must be approved by the Civil Service Commission. If the FTC dismisses the person in the supergrade position, there is no assurance that the Commission will authorize a supergrade for the replacement.

65. On January 31, 1969, a majority of the Commission decided, over the Chairman's objection, to increase from 11 to 63 the number of positions which should be regarded as "heads of major administrative units." Upon solicitation of his views, the Chairman of the Civil Service Commission stated that, in his opinion, the term "major administrative unit," as used in the 1950 Reorganization Plan, applied to individuals with a grade of GS-16 or above in certain positions. Only 11 positions were so categorized. See Elman, Administrative Reform of the Federal Trade Commission, 59 Geo. L.J. 777, 857-858 (1971).

66. Reorg. Plan No. 8 of 1950, 3 C.F.R. 1005 (1949-1953 Compilation), reprinted in 15 U.S.C. §41 (1970), and in 64 Stat. 1264 (1950).

The Civil Service Reform Act of 1978, Pub. L. No. 95-454, (1978), has made a number of changes in the existing law with respect to the firing of federal employees. The Act contains the following new provisions: (1) The evidentiary burden an agency must satisfy when it fires an employee for incompetence is changed from a preponderance of evidence test to one of substantial evidence. (2) The parties are provided with the option of waiving the appeal in favor of arbitration. (3) Appeals are no longer permitted in cases involving changes in titles or duties not involving a reduction in grade or pay. (4) Reasonable attorney fees are available to employees successful on appeal.

Other changes in the existing law should also be noted. (1) A new Senior Executive Service (SES) is created to deal with problems of staffing and managing senior executive positions in government. Supervisors of these top level civil servants have considerable flexibility in adjusting their pay and in moving them from place to place within the agency. (2) A merit pay system for middle level civil servants allows their supervisors considerable flexibility in using monetary incentives. (3) The Civil Service Commission is abolished; and in its place two agencies are created: The Office of Personnel Management, charged with personnel management, agency advisory functions, and conducting research in public management, and the Merit System Protection Board, charged with insuring adherence to merit system principles and laws. (4) Responsibility for Federal labor-management activities and procedures, presently divided between the Assistant Secretary of Labor for Management Relations and the part-time Federal Labor Relations Council, is consolidated in an independent Federal Labor Relations Authority. In addition, provisions of the federal labor relations program which has operated under Executive Orders since 1962 have been modified and cast into law. (5) Through the Merit Systems Protection Board, whistle blowers — federal employees who make lawful disclosures of illegal or improper government activities — are accorded greater protection against retaliatory actions. (6) Agencies are required to establish performance appraisal systems by October, 1981, when the existing government-wide evaluation system will be abolished.

Questions

(a) Recall the earlier material on Presidential control of administrative agency personnel, especially the *Myers* and *Humphrey's Executor* cases. Do the civil service rules seem to strike an appropriate balance between the need for political control and the desirability of protecting individuals from arbitrary governmental action?

(b) Assuming that Weinberger and Kirkpatrick feel the need to remove some of the FTC personnel, particularly the attorneys, what specific steps should they take to achieve their objectives? Specifically, how should they determine which attorneys are "incompetent"? Can the Chairman fire them? What other avenues are open to Weinberger to get rid of incompetent personnel? Will it be difficult to fire the lawyers? [67]

67. Could a nonveteran female attorney claim a denial of equal protection on the grounds that opportunities for women to attain veteran's status are so substantially limited as to be

b. Structural Reorganization

In the past 30 years the FTC has been studied and investigated perhaps more than any other federal agency. Almost invariably, the studies devote significant attention to the internal organization of the FTC. Specifically, the debate has revolved around whether the Commission should be organized along functional (investigation, litigation, etc.) or along programmatic (antitrust, deceptive practices, etc.) lines. In the late 1940s the Commission was organized functionally, an arrangement which the First Hoover Report criticized, recommending a programmatic organization.[68] The FTC reorganized as suggested, but in 1954 the Heller Report recommended a reversion to the former practice.[69] The Commission dutifully reorganized. In his famous 1960 report James Landis recommended a return to programmatic structure, stating that the functional system "resulted in a fractionalization of the handling of cases before the Commission and has proved to be a failure." [70] In 1964 another extensive study of the FTC resulted in a recommendation that it "experiment with the organization of its work along major-commodity group lines." Under this model the Commission would eradicate restraints of trade and deceptive practices in the markets for particular commodities.[71] Chairman Dixon implemented the Landis proposal but rejected the later suggestions. Neither the Nader nor the ABA reports focused closely on the question of structural reorganization.

Nonetheless, suggestions to reorganize both internal and external agency structure constitute a common type of agency reform proposal. Thus, it may prove helpful to consider the relevance of structure to the problems of agency failure.

(1) Structural Reorganization at the FTC

When Caspar Weinberger became FTC Chairman, he immediately began reorganizing the Commission. In the excerpts from his internal memorandum outlining the reorganization, he supports his plan with a number of arguments. How persuasive are they? What difference does it make how the FTC is organized? What benefits are to be gained from a reorganization? Does a reorganization help to solve any of the problems facing the FTC described earlier?

---

discriminatory? Cf. Anthony v. Massachusetts, 415 F. Supp. 485 (D. Mass. 1976) *vacated and remanded to state supreme court sub nom.* Massachusetts v. Feeney, 434 U.S. 884 (1977); Comment, Veterans' Public Employment Preference as Sex Discrimination: Anthony v. Massachusetts and Branch v. DuBois, 90 Harv. L. Rev. 805 (1977).

68. U.S. Commission on Organization of the Executive Branch of the Government, Task Force Report on Regulatory Commissions, Appendix N (1949).

69. Federal Trade Commission Management Survey Report of Robert Heller & Associates, Inc. (1954).

70. Senate Committee on the Judiciary, 86th Cong., 2d Sess., Report on Regulatory Agencies to the President-Elect 48-50 (committee print, 1960). (The Landis Report.)

71. Auerbach, The Federal Trade Commission: Internal Organization and Procedure, 48 Minn. L. Rev. 383, 386-417, 514-515 (1964).

Weinberger Memorandum

May 7, 1970

TO: The Commission   DATE: May 7, 1970

FROM: Caspar W. Weinberger, Chairman

SUBJECT: Proposed Internal Reorganization of the Federal Trade Commission

This memorandum sets forth a proposal for an internal reorganization of the Federal Trade Commission. The reorganization plan conceives of the Commission continuing its basic reorganization of 1961, in which the two key operating Bureaus, Deceptive Practices and Restraint of Trade, divided the work of the Commission according to statutory responsibilities as distinguished from function (as in the predecessor Bureaus of Investigation and Litigation). This plan proposes that we recognize that the work of the Commission is now essentially divided into two main areas:

I — Antitrust and restraint of trade matters; and

II — Consumer Protection (broadly defined)

Under this concept some existing Bureaus, such as the Bureaus of Industry Guidance, and Textiles and Furs, would have their functions allocated to the two main operating Bureaus, with some of the present administrative and management duties of the various bureaus given to an overall managerial office.

I. The Need for Reorganization

After observing and studying our procedures and various reports, I have concluded that reorganization would contribute substantially to the solution of the following problems which the Bureau of the Budget, and others, suggest need prompt action:

A. Redefinition and strengthening of position of Executive Director, with proper staffing;

B. Need for systematic program review and planning with emphasis on initiation of programs rather than sole reliance on suggestion from the Bureaus, or mail complaints from individuals and others;

C. Isolation of Bureau of Textiles and Furs from other Commission activities and consequent lack of need to compete for resources with other Bureaus;

D. Low output of Bureau of Industry Guidance;

E. Low morale in field offices, and question as to need for administrative review of their work by the Bureau of Field Operations headquarters' staff.

In addition, other specific criticisms were aimed at the Bureaus of Restraint of Trade and Deceptive Practices by the Budget study. (Pg. 14, 15)

Those with broad experience within the Commission have arrived at conclusions similar to the management team's. On January 24, 1969, Commissioner Nicholson was directed by the Commission to inquire into policy planning and to make specific recommendations as to how the Commission should plan policy. His memorandum obviously served as one of the bases for our recent decision to revitalize the Program Review Office. I do not propose to review his findings and recommendations in depth, but some of them are relevant to my present suggestions. Perhaps his most significant finding is that the *staff* — not the outside bar, or Congress, or the press — "shares in the view that the Commission does not act with any clearly and previously formulated purpose or objective." This should give us all pause: If this is true (or even if the staff thinks this is true) then the Commission is not fulfilling its function. Major decisions are not being made by us but by the staff.

Another undesirable situation is created by lack of central control and policy planning. If the staff believes that its activities are not subject to central control and evaluation, a perfect opportunity is given them to delay or disregard vexing problems. This is especially true at the Division levels. Instead of allocating their staff in accordance with Commission-imposed criteria, the Division Chiefs have, I suspect, called their own tune for a number of years. The result has been excessive paperwork at the intra-Division level, but little real communication with the Commission.

We have already made a solid contribution toward strengthening the morale of personnel in our field offices by granting them authority to contribute more meaningfully to the Commission's activities. The following proposals suggest that the other problem areas can be solved to some extent by reorganization — but only to some extent. It is my feeling that Commissioner Dixon vastly improved the organization of the Commission in 1961, and I would like to build on his basic plan. I am also well aware of the force of the many arguments against extensive reorganization, and this plan has been developed with these admonitions in mind. You will find that the major features of this plan are: (1) recognition of the two major programs of the Commission; and (2) maximum flexibility for the staff leaders of these two programs to deal with their assignments. For example, there would be full authority in the Director of the Antitrust Bureau to assign each of his professional staff to one or more different tasks. The lack of rigid definition of functions *within* the Bureau will have to be counterbalanced by more knowledgeable and detailed leadership by each Director, but this is the purpose of the plan — to require the Director to engage in, to know about and perhaps even be expert in the day-to-day activities of his Bureau. . . .

Proposed Minute

In re: Internal Reorganization of the Commission

Chairman Weinberger by memorandum of May 7, 1970, recommended that the Commission adopt his proposed plan for internal reorganization.

After consideration, on motion of Chairman Weinberger, the Commission adopted the internal reorganization plan and directed the Office of Administration, the Office of General Counsel and the Rule Committee to take all necessary steps to have the plan in operation by July 1, 1970.

Specifically, the Commission directed these administrative components, using

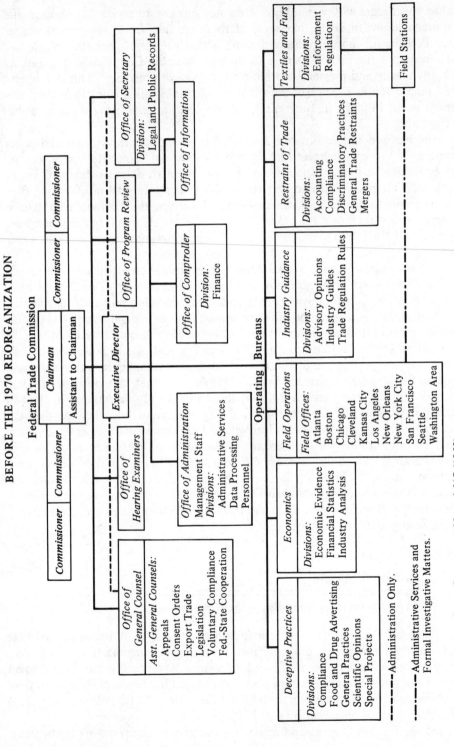

BEFORE THE 1970 REORGANIZATION

Federal Trade Commission

Commissioner | Commissioner | Chairman | Commissioner | Commissioner

Assistant to Chairman

Office of General Counsel
Asst. General Counsels:
Appeals
Consent Orders
Export Trade
Legislation
Voluntary Compliance
Fed.-State Cooperation

Office of Hearing Examiners

Executive Director

Office of Program Review

Office of Secretary
Division:
Legal and Public Records

Office of Information

Office of Administration
Management Staff
Divisions:
Administrative Services
Data Processing
Personnel

Office of Comptroller
Division:
Finance

Operating Bureaus

Deceptive Practices
Divisions:
Compliance
Food and Drug Advertising
General Practices
Scientific Opinions
Special Projects

Economics
Divisions:
Economic Evidence
Financial Statistics
Industry Analysis

Field Operations
Field Offices:
Atlanta
Boston
Chicago
Cleveland
Kansas City
Los Angeles
New Orleans
New York City
San Francisco
Seattle
Washington Area

Industry Guidance
Divisions:
Advisory Opinions
Industry Guides
Trade Regulation Rules

Restraint of Trade
Divisions:
Accounting
Compliance
Discriminatory Practices
General Trade Restraints
Mergers

Textiles and Furs
Divisions:
Enforcement
Regulation

Field Stations

------ Administration Only.

—·—·— Administrative Services and
Formal Investigative Matters.

Source: 1969 United States Government Manual 617 (1969)

the Chairman's memorandum as a guide, to prepare all papers needed to accomplish the following:

1. Create two new positions, Economic Adviser and Office of Congressional Relations, outline their duties and place both positions under the Chairman's office.

2. Create two new positions, Deputy Executive Director for Management, and Deputy Executive Director for Operations, and place under the Executive Director.

3. Abolish the Office of Administration and Office of Comptroller and transfer their functions to the Deputy Executive for Management.

4. Place the Office of Public Information under the Chairman's office.

5. Abolish the Bureau of Field Operations and transfer responsibility for major decisions in administration in the field offices to the Deputy Executive Director for Management. Minor administrative matters may be referred directly to the office concerned. The Deputy Executive Director for Operations will resolve operational problems of the field offices to the extent that they cannot be resolved by the Bureau Directors to whom the field offices will report on operational matters. Outline the duties of the Deputy Executive Directors for Management and Operations.

6. Outline the new duties of the Executive Director, specifically those relating to administration of the field offices through the Deputy Executive Directors for Operations and Management and the Bureau Directors.

7. Establish the two new sections in the Office of the Secretary and outline their duties. These offices will be:

    a. The Rules and Publications Section;

    b. The Mail Correspondence Section.

8. Abolish Divisions within the Office of the General Counsel and create a new position of Assistant General Counsel for the Advisory Opinions. The positions of Assistant General Counsel for Litigation, Legal Services and Legislation and Federal-State Cooperation will be retained. Outline the duties of the General Counsel and his Assistants.

9. Abolish the Bureau of Textiles and Furs and transfer its functions to the Consumer Protection Bureau.

10. Abolish the Bureau of Industry Guidance and transfer its Guides and Rules functions to the two operating Bureaus; Antitrust and Consumer Protection, as appropriate. The duties of rendering Advisory Opinions will be transferred to the Office of the General Counsel.

11. Change the name of the Bureau of Restraint of Trade to the Antitrust Bureau.

12. Abolish the positions of Division Chief and Assistant Director in the Bureau of Restraint of Trade.

13. Create the new position of Assistant Director in the Antitrust Bureau for each of the following areas of endeavor and outline their duties, as well as those of the Director of the Antitrust Bureau:

    a. Assistant Director for Evaluations;

    b. Assistant Director for Industry Guidance;

    c. Assistant Director for Compliance;

    d. Assistant Director for Small Business;

    e. Assistant Director for Accounting;

    f. Assistant Director for General Litigation;

    g. Assistant Director for Special Projects.

14. Change the name of the Bureau of Deceptive Practices to Consumer Protection Bureau.

15. Abolish the positions of Division Chief and Assistant Director in the Bureau of Deceptive Practices.

16. Create the new position of Assistant Director in the Consumer Bureau for each of the following areas of endeavor and outline their duties, as well as those of the Director of the Consumer Protection Bureau:

    a. Assistant Director for Evaluations;

    b. Assistant Director for Industry Guidance;

    c. Assistant Director for Compliance;

    d. Assistant Director for Textiles and Furs;

    e. Assistant Director for Food and Drug;

    f. Assistant Director for Scientific Opinions;

    g. Assistant Director for Litigation;

    h. Assistant Director for Special Projects;

    i. Assistant Director for Education.

Questions

1. What was the theory behind Weinberger's reorganization plan?

2. How successful would you expect that plan to be? Why?

(2)   Restructuring Agencies: In General

Chairman Weinberger's reorganization reflects a variant on the "structural" approach to regulatory reform by attempting greater centralization of decision-making authority. He has many distinguished predecessors in this tradition; for instance, Dean Landis advocated giving more power to the Chairman. More recently, serious "structural" reformers have advocated abolishing most multimember Commissions entirely, placing all power in a single head, and making that head directly responsible to the President. The reasons for favoring the change from multimember commission to single administrator are set forth in the following statement from the Ash Council Report:

The Ash Council Report

The President's Advisory Council on Executive Organization, A New Regulatory Framework: Report on Selected Independent Regulatory Agencies 34-44 (1971)

The disabilities of the collegial form and the attendant advantages of the single administrator form are best reflected in an examination of four aspects of

AFTER THE 1970 REORGANIZATION

Federal Trade Commission

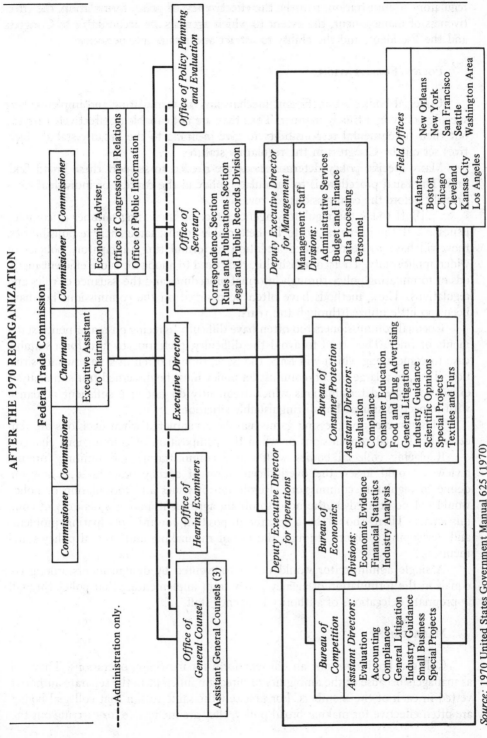

- - - - Administration only.

Source: 1970 United States Government Manual 625 (1970)

regulatory administration; namely, the effectiveness of policy formulation, the effectiveness of management, the extent to which agencies are accountable to Congress and the President, and the ability to attract and retain able personnel.

POLICY FORMULATION

Collegial bodies are inefficient mechanisms for formulating and implementing specific policy in a timely manner. Thus they are not capable of effectively carrying out their fundamental responsibility to give meaning to the broadly stated objectives set out by Congress in the regulatory statutes. . . .

Many specific policy determinations are needed to support these broad findings. The usual procedure is to formulate policy in the context of individual cases brought before the commissions for review. . . .

. . . [But] today the regulatory agencies face an increasing number of complex issues. . . . If the agencies are to be better able to discharge their responsibilities, they will have to devote added attention to formulating anticipatory policies of wider applicability. To accomplish this, they need to adopt the more efficient methods of formulating policy through informal procedures and the issuance of rules and regulations. These methods have often been urged on the commissions but have been too little utilized through the years.

Coequal commissioners too often have difficulty agreeing on major policy statements or rules. They tend to avoid the difficulty, preferring to wait for a suitable case to come along which will force the issue, though often in a narrow fact situation. Thus, to a large extent, commission policy must be discerned from an analysis of ad hoc case determinations which frequently do not give sufficient guidance with respect to similar but distinguishable situations.

This unnecessary guessing game may be accentuated when decisions are rendered by divided commissions or when the composition of commissions changes.

Replacing collegial bodies with single administrators and limiting internal review . . . would lessen the overjudicialization of agency procedures . . . now endemic to regulatory commissions. Resolution of issues and formulation of policy would not be delayed by the need to obtain agreement among a majority of commissioners. There should be a greater disposition toward anticipating problems and developing solutions through the use of rulemaking and normal policy statements. . . .

A single administrator would not be prevented by disagreements among coequals in the formulation of agency policy from implementing that policy through appropriate delegations of authority to agency staff. . . .

MANAGEMENT

Collegial bodies are not an efficient form for managing operations. They fail as managers because of the ambiguity of direction inherent in the separate authority vested in each of the members. For precisely the same reason that collegial bodies are often effective for making broad policy, they are ineffective for carrying out the management of that policy. Extensive deliberation, multiple and conflicting values, and disparate views, necessary to developing broad policy, are the very factors which create inefficiency when trying to implement policy through the management of resources in day-to-day operations. . . .

. . . [The First Hoover Commission] restated what is now almost a management axiom: "Administration by a plural executive is universally regarded as inefficient." The Hoover Commission's task force report, issued in the same year, concurred that: "it is very difficult for five or more Commissioners to direct the work of the bureaus, or for the bureau chief to report to five or more masters."

We believe the inefficiency of collegial bodies as managers is an outgrowth of two characteristics inherent in the collegial form. The first is court-like behavior, leading to an overjudicialization of agency process; the second, an absence of authoritative and adaptable management, able on its own to exercise each management function in such a way as to carry out broad policy. Agencies lack such management precisely because they determine and administer policy through the same medium, the case.

Ineffectiveness manifests itself in four key areas of management, in that:

— Collegial bodies fail to coordinate regulatory policy with other executive agencies. As a result, they may develop policies inconsistent with those of other agencies or with broad governmental economic thrusts.
— The processes of collegial administration are unnecessarily protracted, creating backlogs and concentrating on details often at the expense of expeditious action and administrative flexibility. Such processes also prevent collegial bodies from adapting to ongoing changes in the economics, structure, and technology of the regulated industries. . . .

COORDINATION

. . . [C]oordination is impeded, if not frustrated, by the requirement that a majority position be reached before a commission can participate on a cooperative basis with another agency. The traditional reluctance of one agency to concede jurisdiction to another is exacerbated when negotiations with another agency must be approved, as now, by a multimember commission.

Consequently, most efforts at policy coordination take place as a result of statutory requirements for consultation or in the context of formal proceedings with other agencies appearing as parties to the proceeding. . . .

A single agency head, unhampered by the necessity of achieving agreement among a majority of commissioners, could respond to coordination needs in a timely and effective way. He could speak more authoritatively for the agency and better adjust his position as conditions required.

ADAPTABLE ADMINISTRATION

One of the most pervasive characteristics of the regulatory commissions is their lack of adaptability. . . . This is largely due to the fact that collegial administration, relying on compromise and case-by-case policy formulation, tends toward continuity rather than adaptability of policy. While important, stability should be balanced with adaptability to permit agency policy to reflect those changes in industry which materially affect the provision of public services and the strength of the regulated industry.

A single administrator would more likely to be receptive to changes made necessary by changes in technology, economic circumstances, or industry structure. Unlike a commission chairman, he would not have to garner a majority in order to act. . . .

The delays and the resulting case backlogs which characterize most of the commissions are also an outgrowth of administration by case. . . . Moreover, the emphasis on cases limits the extent to which agencies may use informed procedures in consulting with industry and consumer representatives to resolve difficulties in advance.

A single administrator, comparatively unhindered by direct involvement in the cases pending before agency examiners, could develop more efficient procedures for handling complaints, cases, and the like. He could also adopt innovations for constructive consultation with the public and the regulated industry.

LEGALISTIC ENVIRONMENT

The legalistic environment resulting from commission predisposition to case-by-case analysis contributes to a passive, overly judicial approach in regulation. . . . Commissions generally view themselves as panels of judges emphasizing procedural niceties rather than the determination of broad policy. Agency staff has frequently become occupied with legalistic solutions to problems, to the exclusion or de-emphasis of other valuable input from economists, engineers, environmentalists, and persons trained in related disciplines.

A single administrator, with a limited time for reviewing only selected cases primarily to assure consistency with agency policy . . . , could effectively change the legalistic milieu that pervades regulation today. He would, as a consequence, have more time to direct attention to setting priorities, formulating anticipatory policies, and addressing the many and varied socioeconomic factors affecting regulation.

RESOURCE ALLOCATIONS

Multiheaded management may also result in a misallocation of agency resources. . . . While a commission chairman may have theoretical authority to direct staff activities, as a practical matter the staff will be inclined to respond to all commissioners. . . .

Moreover, as noted, many agency activities are most efficiently carried out in a less formal environment than that which surrounds commission case determinations. . . .

Relieved of the weight of case-by-case administration, a single administrator may give attention to the appropriate allocation of agency resources, building where necessary the staff and the competence to perform a broader and less restrictive range of functions. . . .

ACCOUNTABILITY

Independent regulatory agencies headed by collegial bodies do not and probably cannot provide for the political accountability required to insure public responsibility. . . .

Accountability is an essential element of democratic government. The Congress and the President are accountable to the people for the performance of government. In turn, agencies of government headed by appointed officials should be responsive and responsible to the Congress, to the Executive, and through them, ultimately to the public.

The overseeing of economic regulation by responsible public officials, necessary to assure effective discharge of agency responsibilities, cannot exist if the decision-makers are immune from public concerns as expressed through their elected representatives. A serious flaw of the collegial structure is an inability to fix responsibility due to the inherent diffusion of authority among relatively anonymous coequal members. In addition, appointment for fixed terms gives commissioners a degree of independence that may serve to protect them from improper influence but was not intended to allow them to become unresponsive. . . .

. . . [I]t is not surprising that the agencies receive inadequate attention. Legislative and budget proposals seldom evoke active support outside the agencies and their problems receive relatively low priority.

Replacing the commissions with single administrators would provide the opportunity for accountability and support which does not now exist. A single administrator, serving at the pleasure of the President and personally answerable to the Congress, could not avoid public exposure and would be more responsive for that reason. Because his performance would directly reflect on the executive branch, the President would be more inclined to attempt to remedy agency shortcomings whether due to a lack of legislative authority, ineffective administration, or inadequate funding. Congress, too, could look to an identifiable person to whom it could delegate responsibilities and direct its oversight inquiries. . . .

A single administrator might well be more immune from [improper influences] on his decisions than would a member of a collegial body. Individual responsibility and public exposure would afford him a broad and varied constituency which should serve as a protective shield against special interest pressures. Since he alone would be responsible for balancing all interests, the opposing tensions might well cancel one another out. . . .

ATTRACTING AND RETAINING ABLE PERSONNEL

Good organization does not automatically produce good results. Good men are also required. It is equally true that the effectiveness of able administrators can be seriously impeded by inadequate organizational structure. We believe that the talents of many good appointees have been wasted in the past due to the inherent limitations of the collegial form. Indeed, talented executives have been deterred from accepting appointments to commissions because of these structural deficiencies. . . .

The services of a talented administrator are difficult to secure when he will have to share authority with others. The opportunity to serve as sole administrator of the regulatory agency would magnify the challenge which collegial administration subordinates. At the same time, the single administrator structure would tend to insure appointments based on merit rather than weighted by considerations of balance, whether industry, political, or geographic. If a President has only one position to fill as the head of a regulatory agency, the appointment will receive more careful consideration since the administrator will be responsible for all operation of the agency and his performance will reflect more directly on the President. Moreover, it would clearly be easier to find one highly qualified executive than it is to find five, seven or eleven for a single agency. . . .

ALTERNATIVES CONSIDERED

In arriving at our recommendation for a single administrator, we' considered and rejected several alternative structural reforms.

Among the alternatives considered were:

(i) Reduction of the number of commissioners on each commission. — Simply reducing the number of members of a collegial body would result in some improvement in agency performance. . . . We rejected the alternative because it clearly would not go far enough. The basic defects we found are inherent in the collegial form itself, not in the number of Commissioners.

(ii) Statutory placement of all administrative functions in the chairman and limiting other commissioners to reviewing cases. — There have been attempts, as discussed previously, to effect this type of solution through various reorganization plans and proposals. They have failed to achieve their intended purpose because as a practical matter the functions are inseparable. In view of the need for agreement from his fellow commissioners on policy matter, there appears to be no satisfactory way to give the chairman undiluted authority to manage the agency.

(iii) Statutory placement of all administrative and case review functions in the chairman and limiting other commissioners to policy formulation. — This type of structure would reserve to the agency executive and the collegial body those functions for which each is best suited. We believe, however, that overall management of operations, review of cases, and policy formulation are so interrelated that separating them would project an artificial cleavage which could result in conflict between administrator and board. This conflict cannot be resolved without placing responsibility for review of agency performance in the hands of the board. Although the board would be more remote than it now is, the arrangement would preserve much of the ambiguous responsibility of the existing commissions and vitiate accountability for that reason.

(iv) Creation of a commission on commissions to oversee selection of appointees. — This alternative assumes that the major cause of ineffective regulation lies in the quality of commissioners. While we have found that the attraction and retention of highly qualified personnel poses a significant problem for the regulatory agencies, the inability of commissions to perform satisfactorily results more from their organizational structure than from defects in the recruitment process. Even if the best qualified person filled each position, the collegial structure would impede effective performance.

(v) Establishment of a commission to resolve cases involving overlapping jurisdiction or conflicting policies among commissions. — This alternative would be an attempt to overcome the problem of lack of coordination among agencies carrying out related activities. But the creation of another layer of regulation would raise more problems than it solves in further fragmenting accountability and responsibility for regulatory performance. If it is unclear now who is responsible for decisions, it would be even less clear with the creation of such a commission. . . .

CONCLUSION

Frustration surrounds the appointment of commissioners who cannot, because of organization barriers, exert needed leadership. Regulation by committee has proved both ineffective and unresponsive. Limitations of the collegial form have impeded the modernization of procedures to keep pace with changes in the regulated industries, trends in the economy, and the needs of the public. Eliminating the commission form is not, of course, a guarantee of improvement. There can be no assurance that a single administrator may not be short-sighted or that he will not consistently wait for controversies to develop before deciding policy. The form itself will not automatically produce an effective leader, but it does afford the opportunity for leadership.

The single administrator would be more visible to all concerned and therefore more easily held accountable for agency performance.

The burden of responsibility would be shouldered by one identifiable person. Agency policy and direction would more likely conform to the interests of the public, Congress and the executive branch, and would result in a more expeditious and fair response to the regulated industries.

Note

Compare the following statement by former FTC Commissioner Philip Elman. After producing a set of criticisms similar to those contained in the ABA and Nader Reports and showing statistically that by any measure the FTC accomplished far less in 1968 than in 1960, Commissioner Elman concluded as follows:

> Reversal of this tradition [of no work and no accomplishment] will not be easy. A useful first step would be for the members of the Commission to share responsibility for the appointment of key staff members. Under Reorganization Plan No. 8 of 1950, administrative responsibility for day-to-day

operations of the Commission was to be vested in the Chairman, thus freeing the members of the agency to perform their policymaking functions and to deal with the substantive problems of regulation. In the conduct of the Commission's day-to-day operations, the Chairman was to be bound by the general policies established by the Commission and by its regulatory decisions, findings, and determinations. More important for present purposes, the heads of major administrative units could be appointed only with the approval of the Commission. The purpose of this provision, which applies to several of the independent regulatory agencies, was obviously to prevent the agencies from being staffed by cronies, incompetents, or political hacks.

At the Federal Trade Commission, the reorganization plan has been implemented to the extent that it centralizes certain powers in the Chairman. The other members of the Commission have not been permitted to exercise the reciprocal powers, or checks and balances, vested in them under the reorganization plan. Specifically, although the Commission's approval is required for the appointment of heads of major administrative units, the Commission has in fact been asked to approve only the appointment of the Directors of the operating Bureaus, the Executive Director, Program Review Officer, Secretary, General Counsel, and Chief Hearing Examiner. It has never been asked to approve the appointment of the Directors of the Offices of Administration and Information, the Comptroller, Assistant Bureau Directors, Division Chiefs, Attorneys-in-Charge of field offices and a number of other key officials. More than a matter of principle is at stake. An unusually large number of retirements during February 1969 created several vacancies in important staff positions. Reorganization of some offices thus became possible without removing, shifting or demoting incumbents. In addition, these vacancies provided a unique opportunity to begin to make over the Commission's leadership by appointing progressive, dynamic, and forward-looking persons to infuse a new sense of direction and purpose. The Chairman thwarted the Commission's efforts to participate in this renovation process by making interim "acting" appointments. Whatever may be the merits of any individual appointee, the members of the Commission other than the Chairman cannot be blamed if, in view of the circumstances, they do not vest their full confidence in persons appointed without their consultation, advice or consent.[72]

Questions

(a) Who is right, Commissioner Elman or the Ash Report?

(b) In light of Elman's criticisms did Weinberger do just the wrong thing? Is it possible that both are right? How?

(c) Consider the diagnosis of the FTC's problems contained in Chairman Weinberger's memo. To what extent do you think agency structure — including "combination of function" problems — is responsible for them? To what extent do you think the reorganization will cure them? What is his theory of reorganization? How successful do you think it will be?

72. P. Elman, Administrative Reform of the Federal Trade Commission. 59 Geo. L.J. 777, 857-858 (1971).

D. Revitalizing the FTC: The Regulation of False Advertising

This section explores the FTC's efforts to reassert itself by launching an aggressive enforcement campaign against false or misleading advertising. Consider how an agency manager, seeking to achieve a given result, might look not only to his staff and such traditional legal tools as laws, regulations, cases, and precedents, but also to less formal techniques of coercion and persuasion; for instance, the agency's ability to use the press and its power to affect the political branches of government. The following materials examine in some detail the manner in which the Commission sought to marshal all of these forces in its effort to obtain a concrete result and how that effort in turn enhanced the Commission's power to achieve other results.

In addition, this section explores one form of economic regulation of speech — the regulation of advertising. It describes the problems thought to call for regulation and the relevant legal doctrines available to the Commission: traditional false advertising litigation, corrective advertising, substantiation requirements, and counter-advertising. Consideration of counter-advertising leads naturally to a discussion both of FCC regulation of television content, and of the constitutional doctrine that governs the regulation of "commercial speech."

In reading these materials, evaluate the success of the FTC's program, in terms of both rejuvenating the agency's regulatory authority and achieving a socially beneficial result. You may remain somewhat skeptical about how much the quality of advertising has improved since the FTC's campaign. If you conclude that the efforts have not been successful, consider why not. What light does your answer shed on the causes of agency failure and the potential for reform?

1. Pitofsky's Choices

The ABA Report attacked every facet of the FTC's program against marketing fraud and consumer deception. Noting an increasing public concern with consumer problems, the Report charged that the Commission's efforts in this area were inadequate:

> [T]he FTC has fallen far short of what it could have done. It has failed to instill a sense of mission in its own personnel or in the states and municipalities which are so badly in need of the information and expertise which should be at the FTC's disposal. Its efforts have been piecemeal, and have lacked the study and planning which are essential to identify the most pressing problems faced by consumers, and to create a unified approach toward their solution. Often the agency has seemed more concerned with protecting competitors of an enterprise practicing deception rather than consumers.

As counsel to the Bar Association Committee, Robert Pitofsky helped write this broad-based criticism. A year later, in the fall of 1971, when Caspar Weinberger left the FTC for the Office of Management and Budget, Miles Kirkpatrick became Chairman of the FTC and asked Pitofsky to leave an NYU professorship to become the head of the Bureau of Consumer Protection at the FTC. Though his academic specialty was antitrust law, Pitofsky sensed that the consumer job held great potential for securing effective reform; public and Congressional support seemed secure, and the statutory base was adequate, unlike the situation in the antitrust field.

The public was watching to see whether reform would emerge. Pitofsky's task was to revitalize the newly-organized bureau despite a challenging set of obstacles:

— he had a very small staff — perhaps ten competent attorneys and one highly-regarded assistant bureau chief;
— consumer problems were numerous;
— neither voluntary compliance agreements nor cease and desist orders, the Commission's traditional remedies against offenders, seemed to deter misconduct;
— the Commission had no evaluative systems — it had no way of determining what impact its orders against a particular company had on future operations within that company or, more significantly, within other companies in the same industry.

Pitofsky had earlier criticized the Commission for failing to set adequate priorities in the consumer area. After a few months on the job, he had made minor adjustments. He then had to face a major question of strategy: Where should he concentrate his resources? Pitofsky considered, as candidates for special attention, each of the following problems:

— advertising;
— fur and textile labeling;
— truth in lending;
— creditors' remedies (e.g., the fairness of "holder in due course" doctrine; "sewer service");
— product safety;
— warranties;
— ghetto fraud.

Questions

(1) How would you decide which of these problems Pitofsky should make the focus of the FTC's consumer protection activities?
  (a) What are his major goals in choosing an area of concentration?
  (b) What are the resources at his disposal?
  (c) Suppose he asks you for an intuitive reaction to each topic. Would you have selected advertising? How do you feel about each of the other proposed areas?
(2) Pitofsky chose "advertising" as his major field of endeavor.
  (a) Why did he choose advertising?
  (b) What should be the goals of his advertising enforcement program?

2. Should Advertising Be Regulated?

Pitofsky sought to "revitalize" the Commission by launching a conspicuously visible and novel attack on an important, specific set of problems in the advertising area. Before evaluating his approach, it is necessary to become familiar with the aspects of advertising which have prompted the call for government intervention.

a. Does Advertising "Manufacture" Wants?

Some critics of advertising argue that advertising leads people to buy what they do not really want or need, such as hula-hoops or electric toothbrushes, with the result that too little is spent to satisfy important public needs, such as education.

Professor John Kenneth Galbraith states that:

> ... [P]roduction, not only passively through emulation, but actively through advertising and related activities, creates the wants it seeks to satisfy. ...
>
> ... The fact that wants can be synthesized by advertising, catalyzed by salesmanship, and shaped by the discreet manipulations of the persuaders shows that they are not very urgent. A man who is hungry need never be told of his need for food. If he is inspired by his appetite, he is immune to the influence of Messrs. Batten, Barton, Durston & Osborn. The latter are effective only with those who are so far removed from physical want that they do not already know what they want. In this state alone, men are open to persuasion.

Professor Galbraith argues that "public" needs far more urgently warrant satisfaction.[73]

Professor George Stigler replies as follows:

> "Galbraith is of course aware that the naked parading of a Harvard professor's tastes would not seem very persuasive to the American public (although the dislike of plebeian luxury is not restricted to Harvard professors)... [So, he argues that] we neglect public needs for private waste because private desires are synthesized and artificially stimulated by massive, skillful advertising.... On the other hand, the public wants, the wants for public provision of services, are not synthesized or created artificially.
>
> I find this a most unconvincing and peculiar distinction. On the one hand I would have thought that all private and public wants or if you wish, tastes, were at all times synthesized — that a man is not born in to the world with a particular set of literary and gastronomic tastes. In good part our tastes have been a traditional cultural heritage, developing largely by imitation of the upper classes by the lower classes. Perhaps the most striking phenomenon of modern times in this respect is that the formation of tastes instead of

73. J. Galbraith, The Affluent Society 150-152 (2d ed. 1969).

being traditional and in a certain sense dictatorial (one is born into a stable society and abides by it) has become competitive. Anyone in our society who sees prospects for gain can attempt to change tastes in any direction. And advertising is no monolithic force: indeed much advertising takes the form of cancelling itself out: the automobile manufacturers attempting to get people to buy automobiles, the steamship or airplane people wishing that they would travel instead by their media, the banks meanwhile urging people to do neither but to put their money in a savings account.

On the other hand, the implicit assumption that public wants are not advertised seems to me especially anomalous. In the year 1960 at a very modest estimate at least $200 million of radio and television time was devoted to creating dissatisfaction with the provision of public services in the United States. And indeed the public sector has the valuable boon that its advertising is deemed to be news, and hence escapes both the costs and measurement of other forms of advertising. . . .[74]

b. Is There Too Much Irrational Puffery?

Some advertising is undoubtedly desirable, for it informs the consumer about prices and a product's characteristics, and improves competition by helping consumers make informed, rational choices. On the other hand, critics claim that much advertising seeks only to build irrational preferences in the consumer's mind; for example, by associating soap with wedding bells, or a cigarette with cowboys. Such advertising is wasteful or worse. Also, in judging the value of advertising as a whole, one should consider how rarely one sees sober, truthful information about price and quality and how often one sees irrational preference building.[75]

Yet advertising's defenders may ask, why is catering to these "irrational preferences" so undesirable? Buyers are not idiots. If a young woman buys Lux soap because it carries an association of marriage, it must reflect the fact that the soap gives her a certain amount of pleasure for that reason. What harm is done? Cigarettes may be a special case. But the person who pays much more for an advertised toothpaste because of its advertised associations probably realizes he is paying for those associations as well. After all, most supermarkets carry house brands at lower prices. In any event, who is to say to what extent the "image" is, or is not, a desired part of the product? Why should we have to eat Wheaties without breakfasting like champions?[76]

c. Does Advertising Spread "Commercial Values"?

Some critics of advertising are concerned about the values that much advertising communicates — particularly to children. Mary Gardener Jones, a former

74. G. Stigler, "Private Vice and Public Virtue," 4 J. Law & Econ. 1, 5-6 (1961).
75. See K. Boulding, Economic Analysis 672 (3d ed. 1955).
76. See W. Taplin, Advertising: A New Approach 51-52 (1963).

Federal Trade Commissioner, has argued: "Central to the message of the TV commercial is the premise that it is the acquisition of *things* which will gratify our basic and inner needs and aspirations.... A second inescapable premise of these ads is that we are all externally motivated, wanting to emulate our neighbors or popular successful individuals.... [T]he TV commercial also presents a very special and limited view of American society.... [It] mirrors a specific aspect of American culture — typically that of the white suburban middle-income, middle class family." [77]

d. Is Advertising Economically Wasteful?

The economic effects of advertising are much debated. Some critics have argued that advertising simply wastes resources. Advertising costs about $30 billion per year or roughly 2% of gross national product. On the other hand defenders have argued that advertising not only disseminates information but also lowers costs by expanding production output.[78]

e. Is Advertising Anticompetitive?

Consider the following assessments of the effects of advertising:

The question remains, Does heavy advertising lead to sustained supra-normal profits — a prime manifestation of monopoly power? If entry into advertising-prone industries is easy, the profits gained through image differentiation should be eroded away as newcomers are drawn by the profit lure to play the same game. High advertising may also contribute to the breakdown of oligopolistic pricing discipline by increasing the dimensionality of sellers' rivalry, with a consequent negative impact on earnings. On the other hand, if firms by advertising heavily can erect barriers to new entry, they may be able persistently to earn monopoly returns. Each of these influences undoubtedly operates to some degree. Which is dominant?

Casual observation suggests that successful product differentiation through advertising is an important source of exceptionally high industrial profits. Prominent among the most profitable firms on Fortune's annual list of the 500 largest U.S. industrial corporations have been Avon Products, Alberto-Culver, Gillette, American Home Products and Bristol-Myers, which owe their success in large measure to massive advertising. All earned after-tax returns on stockholders' equity exceeding 20 percent between 1964 and 1966.

For a more general perspective, the definitive work is a statistical study by Comanor and Wilson. Using multiple regression techniques, they analyzed the

---

77. M. Jones, The Cultural and Social Impact of Advertising on American Society, 1970 Law & Social Order 379, 383-385 (1970).

78. See generally J. Bockman, Advertising and Competition (1967); J. Galbraith, The New Industrial State 205 passim (1967).

effect of advertising expenditures on the average 1954-1957 after-tax return on stockholders' equity in 41 three-digit consumer goods industry groups, taking into account also the influence of market concentration, production scale economies, the absolute amount of capital required to enter the industry, and the rate of growth of demand. They discovered a positive and statistically significant relationship between the ratio of advertising to sales and profit returns, other things being held equal. Industries with high advertising outlays were found to command profits roughly 50 percent higher on the average (i.e., 12 percent as opposed to 8 percent) than industries spending modest amounts on advertising, *ceteris paribus*. Their results provide strong support for a conclusion that intensive image differentiation through advertising is an important source of monopoly profits, allowing its practitioners to hold prices above costs without encouraging the competition of new entrants. Scherer, Industrial Market Structure and Economic Performance [343-344 (1970)].

———————

Defenders of advertising have replied as follows:

It is widely believed that advertising can reduce competition by the creation of brand loyalty for the advertised brands. This proposition is testable by comparing the brand-share stability of two classes of products, one which is more advertised and the other which is little advertised. The brand shares in the heavily advertised product class should be more stable over time than brand shares in the little-advertised product group. I tested this proposition by comparing the share stability of a group of toiletries and cosmetics, a heavily advertised product class, with a group of food items, a much less advertised product.

Contrary to hypothesis, brand-share stability is *lower* for the more advertised than for the less advertised group. The life-span of a brand in the cosmetic-toiletry category is shorter than for a product in the foods category. The explanation is clear. The high level advertising results from the high frequency of introduction of new products in the cosmetic class. Far from creating brand *loyalty*, the high advertising outlays are the result of brand *disloyalty*. Consumers become dissatisfied with the existing brands of cosmetics, toiletries, and toothpaste and are constantly ready to test the promise of new varieties — promises hardly capable of fulfillment.

Similar reasoning explains the large sums spent in promoting drugs. There is frequent introduction of new drugs. To gain acceptance for these new products, the drug companies spend large sums on detail men and advertising. If the drug companies spent smaller sums in accelerating the acceptance of new products, they would obtain a lower rate of return and would also spend less on research and development.

The conclusion is that some of the large advertising outlays are explained by the rapid rate of introduction of new products. It also appears that advertising by itself seems incapable of maintaining consumer acceptance of a product that is found to be unsatisfactory. . . .

Closer study of the relations between advertising and competition is possible. One measure of competition in an industry, widely accepted by economists, is the concentration of sales among the four leading firms in the industry. The larger the share of the total going to the four leading firms, the less the competition. If advertising reduces competition, then there ought to be high levels of advertising in those industries in which the leading firms have a large share of total sales and low levels of advertising in industries where the leading firms have small shares. This seems to be true in some industries, for instance, soaps, cigarettes, and breakfast cereals, but it is false in other industries, drugs, and cosmetics. The best way to test the proposition is to examine the data for all consumer-product industries. Such an examination shows a negligible positive association between advertising intensity and concentration. In other words, the exceptions to the hypothesis nearly outweigh the conforming cases. Changes in concentration and advertising intensity ought to move in the same direction according to the hypothesis that advertising lessens competition. The data for the period 1947-57 show, if anything, the opposite relation — an inverse association between changes in advertising intensity and changes in concentration. . . .

Although a continuously high rate of profit year after year is a symptom of monopoly, occasional high profits are not, even if these may result from a successful advertising campaign. Some highly advertised consumer products strike the public fancy and yield a handsome return, and this can also happen to unadvertised goods for much the same reasons. Examples of the latter abound — best sellers, hula hoops, *Gone With the Wind,* and miniskirts. Neither Xerox nor IBM owes its profits to advertising. Conspicuous examples of success due to advertising are offset by the more numerous and unpublicized failures (the Edsel?). The result is an average rate of return.

Despite these facts there are some who believe that advertising is an unusually powerful money-maker. The case for a tax on advertising had better rest on firmer grounds than the contention that advertising lessens competition, as evidenced by the high profits that advertising can generate — a position defended by Assistant Attorney General Donald Turner. [Telser, Some Aspects of the Economics of Advertising, 41 J. Bus., 166, 169-170 (1960)].

f. Is "Deceptive" Advertising Worth Regulating?

Consider the following advertisement — the subject of lengthy FTC litigation:

Video	*Audio*
Ted Mack behind Desk, no unit in view	TED MACK: Well now, has the weather been like this in your part of the country? Snowy? blustery, cold?
Film Clip of Winter Scene	*Sound:* Wind Howling
Cut back to Mack	As a result, have you been suffering from the flu, a cold or sore throat?

Video	*Audio*
Dolly back to reveal unit	Remember, the combination of a winter illness and iron-poor blood can drag you down. And I'd like to point out, if you have been taking vitamins
Dolly in to lose unit	and *still* feel tired, remember *vitamins alone* can't build-up iron-poor blood.
Hold up bottle of GERITOL TABLETS	But GERITOL can! Because just 2 GERITOL tablets
Picks up bottle of GERITOL LIQUID in right hand. Points to it	or 2 tablespoons of GERITOL liquid
Dissolve bottom super: Card #8-548R3 "7 vitamins +" (pull +)	contain 7 vitamins *plus*
Undercut bottom super: Card #G-164R3 Twice the iron in a pound of calves' liver	*twice* the iron in a pound of calves' liver.
Lose Super	In only *one* day GERITOL-iron is in your bloodstream carrying *strength* and *energy* to *every* part of your body. Check with your doctor. And if you've been feeling wornout because of iron-poor blood
Cut to product display	take GERITOL *every day.*
Bottom pull reveals #G-131 "Feel stronger fast"	You'll *feel stronger fast* in just 7 days or your money back from the GERITOL folks.[79]

The evidence before the FTC showed that the vast majority of persons who suffer from tiredness or a "run-down" feeling do not have any deficiency of iron. Geritol will not help them. In fact, those few persons who are tired because of iron deficiency may not be helped either, for the deficiency is likely to be caused by a disease that Geritol cannot cure. There is no reason to believe that Geritol helps cure colds or flu or hastens convalescence. The FTC found that the Geritol ad was misleading.

Misleading ads such as this one clearly seem undesirable. But some have argued that the FTC should not try to stop them:

Posner, The Federal Trade Commission

37 U. Chi. L. Rev. 47, 61-64 (1969)

... A ... fundamental question, although one rarely put because most people consider the answer self-evident is whether there should be a government agency that proceeds against sellers who try to mislead consumers.

79. J. B. Williams Company, 68 F.T.C. 491, 493-494 (1965).

Even in the absence of legal remedies of any kind, it is unlikely that deceptive selling would be rampant. The principal preventives against deception have always been nonlegal. There is first of all the incentive of the consumer to exercise reasonable care and common sense in purchasing and to learn from any unhappy experiences. Second, there is competition. A seller has a strong incentive not to antagonize customers lest he lose their patronage to his competitors. This factor alone should make fraud rare among sellers who depend heavily on repeated sales of the same items to the same consumers (such as grocery stores) or who would find it costly to liquidate their business on short notice as a result of having forfeited consumer good will by dealing unfairly (such as department stores and most manufacturers). Correlatively, competitors of deceptive sellers have an incentive to give consumers prompt and accurate information in order to correct any misrepresentation that might cause a substantial diversion of sales.

In the political arena we posit a marketplace of ideas in which good ideas can be expected to prevail in open competition with bad, and one can take the same approach to advertising. Individuals know more about household products than they do about political questions, so if we trust them to evaluate competing and often fraudulent claims by political candidates . . . [we should also trust them to evaluate product claims].

An inadequate understanding of the competitive process is also evident in the prevalent view that "one false advertisement is likely to breed others in response" rather than to invite refutation. There will almost always be some sellers who have more to gain from exposing than from joining in a deceptive practice. Thus, producers of genuine cowhide and distributors holding stock of the product would hardly be in a position to join with sellers of a cheap substitute who were trying to pass it off as the genuine article; to protect their business they must expose the fraud. Beyond that, some sellers will want to expose competitors' misrepresentations in order to establish a superior reputation for honesty and reliability. And competitive disparagement — blatant in face-to-face selling, subtle but not less effective in television and other advertising — is in fact quite common. It is an important function of trade associations.

Competitors are not the only source of product information to the consumer in a free market. It is relatively rare for a consumer to deal with only one firm, one source of information, in making a purchase. Consumers consult physicians, appraisers, securities brokers, home improvement contractors, newspaper and magazine columnists, interior decorators, travel agents, and a host of others whose business it is to advise consumers on choosing among competing products and whose livelihood depends to no small extent on the honesty and accuracy of their advice. An important example is the department store, which "may be viewed as an institution which searches for the superior qualities of goods and guarantees that they are good quality." These "information brokers" do not exist primarily to prevent deception, but they have that effect. They provide at least a partial answer to the problem, to be discussed below, of the misrepresentation that is not challenged by a competing seller because there is no competing seller who would not be equally discredited by the truth.

While market processes should provide broadly adequate protection against the deception of consumers, they will not provide complete protection. Since the provision of information is not costless, there will be cases where the amount of sales affected by the deceptive practice is so small that it does not pay competitors or information brokers to supply correct information. These are doubtful cases for any form of corrective action, public or private, not only because any corrective action will involve some direct costs and the benefits will be slight, but also because efforts to protect a few particularly gullible or vulnerable people may result in the denial of useful information to the many or the imposition of unwanted information on them.

Questions

(1) Is the Geritol commercial "deceptive"? How should such advertisements be controlled? If civil penalties prove inadequate, would you recommend criminal penalties?

(2) Reconsider Pitofsky's objectives. What exactly is it about advertising, or about advertisements, that he hopes to eliminate? Why is government action desirable?

(3) Restate Pitofsky's substantive goals.

3. Summary of the FTC's Legal Power to Regulate False Advertising

Before Pitofsky commits himself to an all-out enforcement campaign against misleading advertising, he should assess the weapons at his disposal. In the materials which immediately follow, the substantive and procedural details of the relevant law are set forth. (We draw heavily upon the excellent description of the law in this area in Robinson and Gellhorn, The Administrative Process ch. 4 (1974).) In reading these materials, keep in mind the general question: Should the "new FTC" have committed itself so heavily to advertising enforcement?

a. The Substantive Law

The FTC's power to regulate false or deceptive advertising arises from §5(a)(1) of the Federal Trade Commission Act, which provides that "[u]nfair methods of competition in commerce, and unfair or deceptive acts or practices in commerce, are hereby declared unlawful." Section 5(a)(6) further provides that the FTC "is hereby empowered and directed to prevent persons . . . from using" such unfair methods of competition and unfair or deceptive acts or practices. Whenever the Commission "shall have reason to believe" that anyone is engaging in such acts and "if it shall appear to the Commission that a proceeding by it in respect thereof would be to the interest of the public," the FTC "shall issue a complaint" and after an adjudicative hearing determine whether an order should be entered requiring the charged party "to cease and desist from using" such unlawful practices.[80]

80. Federal Trade Commission Act, 38 Stat. 719 (1914), now codified with minor changes in wording in 15 U.S.C. §45(a),(b) (1978).

Charles of the Ritz Distributors Corp. v. FTC

143 F.2d 676 (2d Cir. 1944)

CLARK, Circuit Judge.

This is a petition to set aside a cease and desist order issued by the Federal Trade Commission. . . . During the years from 1934 until December, 1939, . . . petitioner's Rejuvenescence Cream enjoyed a vast popularity. . . . [A]dvertisements typically . . . stated that the preparation brings to the user's "skin quickly the clear radiance . . . the petal-like quality and texture of youth," that it *"restores natural moisture* necessary for a live, healthy skin," with the result that "Your face need know no *drought years,"* and that it gives to the skin "a bloom which is wonderfully rejuvenating," and is "constantly active in keeping your skin clear, radiant, and young looking." (Emphasis in the original.)

After a hearing, the Commission found that such advertising falsely represented that Rejuvenescence Cream will rejuvenate and restore youth or the appearance of youth to the skin, regardless of the condition of the skin or the age of the user. . . . [S]ince there is no treatment known to medical science by which changes in the condition of the skin of an individual can be prevented or by which an aged skin can be rejuvenated or restored to a youthful condition, [it] ordered petitioner to cease and desist disseminating in commerce any advertisement of Charles of the Ritz Rejuvenescence Cream: "(a) In which the word 'Rejuvenescence' . . . is used. . . ."

. . . [Petitioner denies] that by use of the trademark "Rejuvenescence" it has represented that its preparation will rejuvenate and restore the appearance of youth to the skin. . . . But the dictionaries treat "rejuvenescence" as a common word with a plain meaning of "a renewing of youth" or the perhaps more usual "rejuvenation." . . . In the light of this plain meaning, petitioner's contention can hardly be sustained that "rejuvenescence" is a nondeceptive "boastful and fanciful word," utilized solely for its attractiveness as a trade-mark. . . .

There is no merit to petitioner's argument that, since no straight-thinking person could believe that its cream would actually rejuvenate, there could be no deception. Such a view results from a grave misconception of the purposes of the Federal Trade Commission Act. The law was not "made for the protection of experts, but for the public — that vast multitude which includes the ignorant, the unthinking and the credulous," . . . and the "fact that a false statement may be obviously false to those who are trained and experienced does not change its character, nor take away its power to deceive others less experienced." . . . The important criterion is the net impression which the advertisement is likely to make upon the general populace. . . . And, while the wise and the worldly may well realize the falsity of any representations that the present product can roll back the years, there remains "that vast multitude" of others who, like Ponce de Leon, still seek a perpetual fountain of youth. As the Commission's expert further testified, the average woman, conditioned by talk in magazines and over the radio of "vitamins, hormones, and God knows what," might take "rejuvenescence" to mean that this "is one of the modern miracles" and is "something which would actually cause her youth to be restored." It is for this reason that the Commission may "insist upon the most literal truthfulness" in advertisements . . . and should have the discretion, undisturbed by the courts, to insist if it chooses "upon a form of advertising clear enough so that, in the words of the prophet Isaiah, 'wayfaring men, though fools, shall not err therein.'" . . .

That the Commission did not produce consumers to testify to their deception does not make the order improper, since actual deception of the public need not be shown in Federal Trade Commission proceedings . . . [a]nd, as we have seen, the facts here more than warrant a conclusion of such capacity. Likewise it is not material that there was no consumer testimony as to the meaning of petitioner's representations. The testimony of the dermatologist, a person whose occupation took him among the buyers of Rejuvenescence Cream, is a qualified source of information "as to the buyers' understanding of the words they hear and use." . . .

The order is affirmed and an enforcement decree will be entered.

b. Elements of an FTC False Advertising Case

Robinson and Gellhorn summarize the elements of an FTC false advertising case as follows:[81]

There are two "jurisdictional" requirements: The advertisement must be "in commerce"[82] and the FTC intervention must be "in the interest of the public." The latter requirement does not seriously hinder the FTC as it means only that the FTC cannot intervene in purely private disputes.[83]

There are four substantive requirements: First, who is the advertisement likely to deceive? Its capacity to deceive will be judged in terms of the audience at which it is aimed. It must not mislead the average reader in the audience it can be expected to reach.[84]

Second, what did the advertisement promise? As Charles of the Ritz suggests, the ad is viewed as a whole and judged by the general impression it creates. When ads are ambiguous or convey hosts of ambiguous, subtle implications, the FTC will use its "expertise" to help determine what the audience is likely to take an ad to mean. This expertise may rest in turn upon dictionary definitions, testimony of experts, or consumer surveys. The courts give the Commission wide latitude in determining the meaning of an advertisement.[85]

---

81. E. Gellhorn & G. Robinson, The Administrative Process, 427-429 (1974); See generally, Millstein, The Federal Trade Commission and False Advertising, 64 Colum. L. Rev. 439 (1964); Weston, Deceptive Advertising and the Federal Trade Commission; Decline of Caveat Emptor, 24 Fed. B.J. 548 (1964).

82. 15 U.S.C. §45(a),(b) (1978). See FTC v. Bante Bros., Inc., 312 U.S. 349 (1941).

83. See FTC v. Klesner, 280 U.S. 19 (1929), but cf. Exposition Press, Inc. v. FTC, 295 F.2d 869, 875 (2d Cir. 1961) (Friendly, J., dissenting).

84. See, e.g., Heinz v. Kirchner, 63 F.T.C. 1282 (1963), aff'd, 337 F.2d 751 (9th Cir. 1964).

85. J. B. Williams Co. v. FTC, 381 F.2d 884 (6th Cir. 1967).

Third, is the ad's claim true? "Truth," under the statute, is an issue of fact which must be "supported by evidence." [86] The FTC has often been quite rigorous in enforcing a standard close to literal truth. (Though "literal truth" is not sufficient to save an ad with misleading implications.) "Puffing" raises a host of difficult questions. Subjective evaluations (such as an "easy diet," or "brightens the smile") are allowed unless they can be "objectively" disproved, although the line between subjective and objective cannot easily be drawn.[87]

Fourth, is the claim material? Is it capable of affecting consumers purchasing decisions? Unless consumers' buying preferences are likely to be distorted by the claim, there is no basis for FTC action.[88]

c. Enforcement Procedures

In the typical case, the FTC staff will decide to examine a particular practice after a complaint from a consumer or a competitor. The formality of the investigation varies; but it may involve taking testimony under oath before a staff attorney or requesting documents and reports under §§ 6 and 9 of the FTC Act. Under §10, investigatory powers are enforceable by court order, violations of which are punishable as contempt, or by judicially imposed penal sanctions.

During this investigatory stage, parties can negotiate settlements with the FTC. If this is not done, and if the staff believes it has sufficient facts to warrant initiating formal preceedings, it will seek Commission approval of a complaint.[89] This complaint is a public document and is announced with a press release by the Commission, and then referred to an administrative law judge for hearing.[90] The ALJ prepares an initial decision, which either party may appeal to the Commission. Unless the initial decision is appealed or the Commission takes the case on its own motion, the initial decision becomes the FTC's final order.

The Commission hears appeals in a way analogous to appellate court review of lower court decisions, but it need *not* apply a limited standard of review, and

---

86. 15 U.S.C. §45(c) (1978). Carter Prods. v. FTC, 268 F.2d 461, 491-497 (9th Cir. 1959) interpreted "supported by evidence" to mean "supported by substantial evidence as a whole."

87. See Sewall v. FTC, 240 F.2d 228 (9th Cir. 1956), *rev'd per curiam*, 253 U.S. 969 (1957).

88. See, e.g., FTC v. Colgate-Palmolive Company, 380 U.S. 374 (1965), and L. Elrod, The Federal Trade Commission: Deceptive Advertising and the Colgate-Palmolive Company, 12 Washburn L.J. 133 (1973). This case involved the question whether consumer preferences in shaving cream were likely to be altered by a television commercial which purported to show that a particular brand of shaving cream would aid in shaving sandpaper.

89. Prior to 1975, the FTC used a two-step procedure. It first issued a "proposed," or Part II, complaint, gave the respondent an opportunity to settle, and then issued an "adjudicative," or Part III, complaint if no settlement was forthcoming. The Commission abolished this procedure in 1975, evidently concluding that it encouraged unnecessary delay in administrative proceedings. 40 Fed. Reg. 15235 (1975). FTC procedures for investigation, informal enforcement, and implementing consent orders are codified in 16 C.F.R. §§ 2.1-2.35.

90. Rules of practice for FTC adjudications are codified in 16 C.F.R. §§ 3.1-3.72. See generally, 15 U.S.C. §45(b) (1978).

has a substantial measure of power to redecide the controversy de novo.[91] If the FTC determines that a violation has occurred, it will issue a cease and desist order. The respondent may seek review in one of the federal court of appeals. Once affirmed by the courts, the order takes effect. Failure to obey an effective order subjects the offender to fines up to $10,000 per violation (with each day considered a separate violation).[92] The fines may be recovered in civil suits commenced in a district court by the FTC (prior to 1973 the Attorney General had this enforcement responsibility). The FTC is empowered to bypass this procedural machinery and seek a preliminary injunction from a district court where an injunction halting false or deceptive advertising "would be in the interest of the public." 15 U.S.C. §53(a).

4. Selecting a False Advertising Case

Once Pitofsky made the strategic decision to make the campaign against misleading advertising the primary effort of the FTC, he faced a serious tactical problem in allocating his scarce litigative resources. Should he try to maximize his chances of winning his cases by concentrating on small firms that make outrageously deceptive statements? Or should he issue complaints against major advertisers whose ads are only arguably misleading? If pursuing the advertising giants means the commitment of a substantial portion of his resources for several years with an attendant low probability of victory, is the effort worthwhile? Consider the following case before answering these questions.

In re Coca-Cola Company

83 F.T.C. 746 (1973)

By DENNISON, Commissioner.

. . . The ultimate questions before the Commission on this appeal are factual ones, involving the determination, first, of whether or not certain representations were made in the advertising of Hi-C, and, second, whether any representations found to have been made had the tendency or capacity to deceive. . . .

Appeal from the dismissal of the complaint [by an Administrative Law Judge] has been taken with respect to four . . . allegations of false and misleading advertising. . . . [T]he complaint allege[d] that Hi-C advertisements represent that: . . .

---

91. APA §557(b). See also the *Universal Camera* litigation, discussed in Chapter 4 supra.

92. For a discussion of civil penalties and the FTC, see United States v. J. B. Williams Co., Inc., 498 F.2d 414, 424 (2d Cir. 1974), Comment, United States v. J. B. Williams Co., 88 Harv. L. Rev. 1035 (1975). See also Note, Administrative Civil Money Penalties and the Right to Jury Trial, 33 Wash. & Lee L. Rev. 719 (1976); Franklin, Deceptive Advertising, FTC Fact Finding and the Seventh Amendment, 43 Fordham L. Rev. 606 (1975).

c. Said drink is the beverage that is "The Sensible Drink," nutritionally and economically, as a source of vitamin C.

d. Said drink is made with fresh fruit and has a high fruit content comparable to fresh fruits and fruit juices.

e. Said drink is unqualifiedly good for children and children can drink as much of it as they like without adverse health or nutritional implications.

f. Said drink is particularly high in vitamin C content even as compared to other beverages widely known as high in vitamin C content, specifically fruit juices.

... [The complaint alleged that these four representations were false and misleading. In fact, the advertisements themselves used, in a variety of contexts, words like the following:] "the sensible drink," "made with fresh fruit," children "can drink as much ... as they like," and "high in Vitamin C." ...

Reviewing first the four express representations, we find that the administrative law judge's rulings [that they were true were] amply supported in the record.

Thus, for example, in relation to the claim that Hi-C is "the sensible drink" as a source of vitamin C, the testimony of five nutritionists supports the conclusion that Hi-C is "an excellent source" of vitamin C, judged in terms of its nutritional, and minimal caloric, content. A six ounce serving of Hi-C would provide 110 percent of the Recommended Dietary Allowance for vitamin C for children, while making only a "marginally significant" contribution to the Recommended Dietary Allowance for calories for a six year old child. ...

The express claims "made from fresh fruit" and "made with real fruit" appear in several of the Hi-C advertisements. They are challenged by complaint counsel as communicating the misrepresentation that Hi-C is made with fresh fruit, in the specific sense that unprocessed fruit was used in the manufacturing process. We endorse the initial decision's findings that consumers would not be reasonably likely to take this meaning from these words. The claims are true in the sense that the fruit components of the product are made from fresh fruit rather than from artificial or synthetic ingredients, and consumers are likely to so interpret the representation, based upon their understanding of canned, unrefrigerated fruit drinks.

Similarly, we find no merit in the allegations concerning the explicit claim that children "can drink as much as they like," appearing in two newspaper advertisements and, in a different phrasing, in the 60 second version of one television commercial. These words have been challenged throughout this proceeding as contributing to a misrepresentation that Hi-C can be consumed by children in unlimited quantities, to the exclusion of other foods, without adverse health or nutritional implications. We do not see that meaning as reasonably to be derived from these advertisements.

We turn now to the fourth express claim found in the advertisements and specifically challenged in the complaint: that Hi-C is "high in Vitamin C." ... Using the Recommended Dietary Allowance for vitamin C as a frame of reference, these witnesses established Hi-C as "high" in vitamin C in relation to human nutritional needs. Their judgment was based upon the fact that a single six ounce serving of Hi-C contains 44 milligrams of vitamin C, compared to the Recommended

Dietary Allowance of 40 milligrams for the primary consumers of the product, children between the ages of two and twelve.

The initial decision determined the validity of the "high in Vitamin C" claim "in relation to human nutritional needs." The Commission agrees with the reasonableness of this criterion. . . .

Having determined that no misrepresentations were contained in the challenged express claims made in Hi-C's advertising, the Commission recognizes the far more vital task now before it; an analysis of the representations that reasonably may have been implied or suggested by these advertisements.

A common and critical thread running throughout the allegations of the complaint and the conduct of the hearings centered on the contention that these advertisements in some way compared Hi-C to citrus juices in general, and to orange juice in particular.

. . . [T]he complaint alleges that Hi-C cannot "accurately be termed the "Sensible Drink" because "Orange is more sensible. . . ." [sic]

. . . [E]ven though Hi-C was shown to be more economical as a source of Vitamin C than . . . other citrus juices, and other forms of orange juice, complaint counsel have urged that Hi-C is not "the sensible drink" as a source of vitamin C because frozen concentrated orange juice, accounting for some 69 percent of orange juice consumption, provides the Recommended Dietary Allowance for vitamin C at slightly less cost than does Hi-C. . . . [2.44¢ per 40 mg. of vitamin C compared with 3.82¢ for Hi-C, 4.06¢ for canned orange juice, and 6.25¢ for fresh orange juice.]

The alleged deception envisioned in the claim that Hi-C is "high" in vitamin C is premised directly upon the communication of a comparison of the product's vitamin C content to a selected standard: orange juice. . . . Primary reliance placed by complaint counsel upon the indication in [a] survey of consumer attitudes that some 85 percent of consumers canvassed by telephone in June of 1971 named orange juice when asked to identify the one beverage which they believed best fit the phrase "highest in Vitamin C."

Further portions of the same survey, introduced by respondents, indicate that only 1.8 percent of those same consumers named fruit drinks as "highest in Vitamin C." Equally dramatic differences in consumer attitudes toward orange juice and fruit drinks are reflected in responses concerning the beverage seen to be "best for breakfast" and the "most natural drink." . . .

. . . [Even if] a majority of the people surveyed would have named orange juice [as] "high in Vitamin C" . . . [that is no] reason to infer that Hi-C's representation of high vitamin C content would convey to consumers a claim of comparability or equivalence to orange juice. . . . [O]range juice has not preempted the right to make a representation of high vitamin C content.

. . . [C]omplaint counsel introduced portions of periodic consumer research surveys conducted by Audits and Surveys, Inc., for the Coca-Cola Company. . . . Out of over 13,000 questionnaires, completed from January 1, 1969, through March 30, 1971, including responses from 6,386 fruit drink users and 1,469 recallers of Hi-C advertising, only one individual stated that he got the impression of a comparison to orange juice from Hi-C advertisements. We note also that a total of only 31 individuals were recorded as having recalled a comparison to any beverage suggested in Hi-C advertising; of these, 18 saw the implied comparison as involving soft drinks. These results lend support to the contention that Hi-C advertising did not suggest comparisons to any beverages, let alone to orange juice. . . .

Complaint counsel [also argued that Hi-C contains] . . . fewer essential nutrients [than orange juice, and] Hi-C is therefore less "sensible" drink than orange juice. . . .

[W]e are persuaded that all testimony concerning the relative nutritional composition of Hi-C and orange juice is relevant to this case only insofar as we are able to find a comparison to orange juice, a claim of nutritional equivalence, in the advertising.

. . . [T]he Commission has reviewed carefully the Hi-C advertisements involved in this litigation. To interpret fully the possible implied or suggested meanings conveyed, we have considered each Hi-C advertisement in its entirety.

In reviewing Hi-C's advertising, we have looked at the nutritionally oriented claims singly and in the context of the prominent representations, as well as overall mood and ambience, conveying messages of appealing taste, enjoyment, fun, refreshment, convenience, and variety of flavors. Thus, for example, in light of the comparisons alleged to have been made to orange juice, we note the absence in Hi-C advertising of breakfast scenes so generally associated with the consumption of orange juice.

Having completed a review of the advertisements challenged in this case, the Commission finds that the advertising representations made in behalf of Hi-C are not reasonably likely to have communicated the comparisons and claims of equivalence to citrus juices, and to orange juice, so critical to the allegations advanced by complaint counsel. . . .

We find that the false and misleading representations alleged to have been made in Hi-C's advertising are not reasonably likely to have been conveyed to consumers. . . .

The decision of the administrative law judge is therefore affirmed, and the complaint dismissed.

[Commissioner JONES dissented.]

Notes and Questions

During World War II the government began a program to combat such diseases as iron deficiency anemia, beri beri, riboflavinosis, and pellagra through the enrichment of white bread with iron and three B vitamins. The program has been credited as a substantial contributing factor in the virtual disappearance of these diseases in the United States.

Wonder Bread is an enriched white bread that conforms to FDA standards. It has always been heavily advertised, particularly on television. From 1950 to 1964 millions of American children (and their parents) were constantly told that "Wonder Bread Helps Build Strong Bodies 12 Ways." This campaign generally emphasized the nutritional value of the product. From 1964 to 1970 Wonder Bread was stamped on the public consciousness through the "Wonder Years" ad campaign, which was then followed by the "How Big" campaign.

In 1971, the FTC filed a complaint against the makers of Wonder Bread, ITT Continental Baking Co. The Administrative Law Judge dismissed the complaint. The Bureau of Consumer Protection appealed to the Commission:

The complaint alleged that the respondents falsely represented that:

"Wonder Bread is an outstanding source of nutrients, distinct from other enriched breads;

"Consuming said Wonder Bread in the customary manner that bread is used in the diet will provide a child age one to twelve with all nutrients, in recommended quantities, that are essential to healthy growth and development;

"Parents can rely on Wonder Bread to provide their children with all nutrients that are essential to healthy growth and development;

"The optimum contribution a parent can make to his child's nutrition during the formative years of growth is to assure that the child consumes Wonder Bread regularly;

"The protein supplied by said Wonder Bread is complete protein of high nutritional quality necessary to assure maximum growth and development."

[T]he complaint challenged certain of respondent's advertisements as both deceptive and unfair insofar as they tend to exploit the aspirations of children for rapid and healthy growth and development by falsely portraying, directly or by implication, said Wonder Bread as an extraordinary food for producing dramatic growth in children.

[T]he complaint challenged certain of respondent's advertisements as both deceptive and unfair insofar as they tend to exploit the emotional concern of parents for the healthy physical and mental growth and development of their children by falsely portraying Wonder Bread as a necessary food for their children to grow and develop to the fullest extent during the pre-adolescent years. . . .

Respondents stipulated that their television advertisements were primarily directed at two groups: mothers, between the ages of 18 and 49, and children between the ages of 1 and 12. . . .

Respondents' 60-second commercial entitled "Cardboard House" is typical of the ads appearing in respondents' Wonder Years campaign. It depicts several children playing in a cardboard house. The commercial opens with the announcer stating: "These are the 'Wonder Years,' the formative years one through twelve when your child develops in many ways, actually grows to 90% of her adult height."

Then the audio portion continues: "How can you help? By serving nutritious Wonder Enriched Bread. Wonder helps build strong bodies in 12 ways. Carefully enriched with foods for body and mind, Wonder Bread tastes so good, and it is so good for growing child, for active adult."

While the announcer is talking, the T.V. screen shows a child eating Wonder Bread and then growing from a very young child to a twelve-year-old.

Respondents' "How Big" campaign, . . . introduced to . . . replace the

Wonder Years campaign, [placed] greater emphasis on the theme "How Big.". . .

Respondents' "How Big" campaign also included television advertisements which appeared on two children's programs, Captain Kangaroo and Bozo Circus:

Captain Kangaroo: Mr. Moose, I have an interesting question for you. If you could be as big as you wanted to be . . . how big would you want to be?

Mr. Moose: Gee . . . as big . . . as big . . . I know. As big as a tree. Then I could see *everything* around me for miles and miles.

Captain Kangaroo: Wouldn't that be fun, Mr. Moose?

Mr. Moose: Yes. Do you think eating Wonder Bread would get me that big?

Captain Kangaroo: Well . . . not *quite* as big as a tree . . . but Wonder does help boys and girls grow up big and strong, and give them energy for work and play. Each slice of Wonder is baked with vitamins and other good things that help you grow.

Mr. Moose: And Wonder tastes so good, too.

Captain Kangaroo: It does indeed — it's so light and tender and white, baked soft just the way you like it best. Great for lunchtime sandwiches . . . and anytime snacks. You'll want to enjoy Wonder Enriched Bread soon. Mother, please look for the red, yellow, and blue balloons printed on every wrapper. Remember, Wonder helps build strong trees — uh, bodies 12 ways.

Should the Commission reverse the Administrative Law Judge's dismissal? [93]

5. The Problem of Remedy

a. The Traditional Remedies

The remedies available to the FTC in a false advertising case depend upon whether the Commission has proceeded through rulemaking or through adjudication.[94] Until 1974 the FTC's power to proceed through rulemaking was unclear. But now it is provided by statute.[95] If the FTC chooses rulemaking, once the rule is enacted, the FTC can proceed directly in court against violators. The statute provides that a court can grant relief which "include[s], but [is] not limited to rescission or reformation of contracts, the refund of money or return of property, the payment of damages, and public notification respecting the rule violation or the unfair or

---

93. See In re ITT Continental Baking Co., 83 F.T.C. 865 (1973).

94. Any lingering doubts about the FTC's power to promulgate substantive regulations have been erased by National Petroleum Refiners Assn. v. FTC, 482 F.2d 672 (D.C. Cir. 1973), *cert. denied,* 415 U.S. 951 (1974) (see Chapter 5), and by the subsequent enactment of the Magnuson-Moss Warranty — Federal Trade Commission Improvement Act, 88 Stat. 2183 (1975), 15 U.S.C. §§ 2301 et seq. (1975).

95. See note 94.

deceptive act or practice, as the case may be; except that nothing in this subsection is intended to authorize the imposition of any exemplary or punitive damages." 15 U.S.C. §57b(b).

If the FTC proceeds through adjudication and finds that the respondent has advertised falsely, the Commission will issue a cease and desist order.[96] It is the responsibility of the FTC to monitor compliance with these orders and to prosecute violations which subject the violator to a fine of up to $10,000 per day. One court has recently inferred from the FTC Act a private cause of action for consumers to enforce cease and desist orders.[97] In adjudication the respondent is permitted one unpenalized illegal practice the first time an order issues; the next time he is punished for violating it.[98]

The FTC normally seeks to draft broad orders,[99] since the broader the order, the easier it will be to bring subsequent penalty proceedings against future violations that resemble present conduct.[100] Another reason is that the Commission wishes to deter defendants from searching for alternative ways to advertise the same message. Of course, general constraints of due process limit the FTC's power to enforce excessively vague or imprecise orders.[101] The Commission may proceed against the advertising agency as well as the advertiser.[102]

b. Corrective Advertising

Pitofsky's campaign against misleading advertising tested the bounds of the Commission's remedial discretion: Does the FTC have the power to exact a penalty in its order? Can it order an advertiser to confess its sins publicly in future advertising?

96. 15 U.S.C. §45(b). For an exhaustive commentary, see Kauper, Cease and Desist: The History, Effect, and Scope of Clayton Act Orders of the Federal Trade Commission, 66 Mich. L. Rev. 1095 (1968).

97. Guernsey v. Rich Plan of the Midwest, 408 F. Supp. 582 (N.D. Ind. 1976); see Naclerio, The Federal District Court as a Small Claims Tribunal: An Argument Against the Holding in Guernsey v. Rich Plan, 5 Hofstra L. Rev. 345 (1977); also noted in 11 Ga. L. Rev. 220 (1976); 20 St. Louis U. L.J. 679 (1976); 38 U. Pitt. L. Rev. 113 (1976); 29 Vand. L. Rev. 1077 (1976).

98. Before 1938, the FTC Act provided that when a person has failed to obey a cease and desist order, the Commission had to apply to a court of appeals "for enforcement of its order." Only a violation of the court order would be treated as contempt. Thus a defendant had two free bites at the apple.

The NLRB still follows a related procedure. It must transform its order into a judicial order by appealing to a court for enforcement. It does not require a second violation, however, to obtain the judicial decree.

99. See, e.g., FTC v. Mandel Bros., 359 U.S. 385 (1959); FTC v. Ruberoid Co., 343 U.S. 470, 473 (1952).

100. Cf. J. B. Williams Co. [1968-70 Transfer Binder] Trade Reg. Rep. (CCH) ¶118,821.

101. See FTC v. Henry Brock & Co., 368 U.S. 360, 368 (1962).

102. See Jacob Siegel Co. v. FTC, 327 U.S. 608 (1946); Coro, Inc. v. FTC, 338 F.2d 149, 153-154 (1st Cir. 1964), cert. denied, 380 U.S. 954 (1965) (FTC need only show violation is "a sufficient reason on which to hang an order.") But see FTC v. Gratz, 253 U.S. 421 (1920); Chrysler Corp. v. FTC, 561 F.2d 357 (D.C. Cir. 1977); Colgate-Palmolive Co. v. FTC, 326 F.2d 517, 523-524 (1st Cir. 1963), rev'd 380 U.S. 374, 382, n.8 (1965); McLaughlin & White, Advertising Agencies: Their Legal Liability Under the FTC Act, 17 Kan. L. Rev. 587 (1969).

Most "cease and desist" orders are phrased negatively, but occasionally the FTC has required the defendant affirmatively to disclose a particular fact when failure to do so would mislead the audience.[103] In Alberty v. FTC, 182 F.2d 36, (D.C. Cir. 1950), *cert. denied*, 340 U.S. 818 (1950), the D.C. Circuit held that the FTC went too far in requiring an iron vitamin supplement manufacturer to disclose that most fatigue is not due to iron deficiency. Since the advertiser claimed only to cure iron deficiency, it was unreasonable for the Commission to require him to state what his product would not do. But in J.B. Williams Co. v. FTC, 381 F.2d 884 (1967), the court held that the FTC could force the makers of Geritol — another iron supplement — to disclose that most people who are tired do not suffer from iron deficiency. The makers of Geritol, unlike the defendant in *Alberty*, had suggested in its ads that Geritol would cure most tiredness; hence the omission would be misleading.

It was a small step for the FTC to move from the remedy used in *J. B. Williams Co.* to out-and-out "corrective advertising" — advertising which would tell the public that the company had violated the law and which would correct the previously given impression. SOUP, a "public interest intervenor," first suggested the use of a corrective advertisement in the case of Campbell Soup Company, 77 F.T.C. 664 (1970). (Campbell had put clear marbles in its advertised soup to make the vegetables rise to the surface where they could be photographed). In that case, the Commission decided that corrective advertising was unnecessary, but it subsequently approved complaints which sought a corrective advertising remedy,[104] and began to require corrective advertising in negotiated consent decrees.[105]

In re Firestone Tire & Rubber Co.

81 F.T.C. 398 (1972), aff'd. sub nom. *Firestone Tire & Rubber Co. v. FTC, 481 F.2d 246*, cert. denied, *414 U.S. 1112 (1973)*

By Commissioner JONES:
[The hearing examiner found that Firestone made misleading safety claims and wrongly implied it had adequate scientific tests to back up its claims. The Commission affirmed.]

Intervenor SOUP [Students Opposing Unfair Practices, a nonprofit organization of law students] contends that a mere prohibitory order requiring Firestone not to repeat its deceptive advertising claims in the future will not constitute adequate relief for the deceptions; . . . [Firestone should be] required to publicize the

103. See, e.g., Aronberg v. FTC, 132 F.2d 165 (7th Cir. 1942).
104. See, e.g., In re Coca-Cola Co., 83 F.T.C. 764 (1973) ("Hi-C"), In re Standard Oil Co. of California, 84 F.T.C. 1401 (1974) (Chevron F-310 gasoline).
105. See, e.g., In re Sugar Inform. 'ion, Inc., 81 F.T.C. 711 (1972). See generally Cornfeld, A New Approach to an Old Enemy: Corrective Advertising and the Federal Trade Commission, 61 Iowa L. Rev. 693 (1976); Note, "Corrective Advertising" Orders of the Federal Trade Commission, 85 Harv. L. Rev. 477 (1971).

fact that it had in the past made false claims about the performance and efficacy of its tires. . . . [T]here are residual effects . . . in consumer's minds which will not be eradicated by a mere prohibition on the making of these misrepresentations in the future. SOUP also argued that Firestone is still deriving sales benefits from the deceptive ads. . . .

Respondent and ANA [Association of National Advertisers, Inc.] [argue] . . . that the Commission's power extends only to terminating past illegal conduct and insuring that similar violations do not recur in the future. They assert that orders must be prospective in nature and that the order sought by SOUP seeking to dissipate the effects of respondent's past utterances is retrospective and, therefore, beyond the scope of the Commission's authority. Both ANA and respondent see the corrective order as a punitive measure and ANA argues further that it would have a chilling effect on respondent's advertising in violation of the First Amendment. We disagree.

The courts have repeatedly recognized that to deal with the ever expanding scope of unfair and deceptive practices, the Commission must be permitted wide latitude in fashioning effective relief. . . .

. . . As the Ninth Circuit stated in Carter Products, Inc. v. FTC, 268 F.2d 461, 490 (9th Cir. 1959):

"Shaping a remedy is essentially an administrative function. Congress has entrusted the Commission with the responsibility of selecting *the means* of achieving a statutory policy — the relation of remedy to policy is peculiarly a matter for administrative competence." . . .

Respondent and ANA argue, however, that the Commission is not permitted to impose orders which are solely punitive in nature, with the only purpose and effort being to impose penalties on wrongdoers for past actions. While their statement of the law is accurate, its application to the proposed order provision in the instant case is misplaced.

The fact that the remedy may be deemed by the court to have severe consequences to the respondent does not in itself render the order punitive if the order is also deemed a "needed public precaution." . . . Nor does the fact that the party's *past* conduct is taken into account in fashioning a remedy render the order retroactive or punitive in nature. . . .

. . . In our view . . . such an order is quite obviously not retrospective if its purpose and effect is to terminate *continuing* injury to the public. This continuing injury may be in the form of lingering effects which a misrepresentation may have on consumers' minds or in the form of a lessening of competitive vigor in the marketplace due to the deceptive practices. Under such circumstances, the appropriate relief is that which will terminate the continuing injury to the public. . . .

Thus we conclude that an order requiring corrective advertising is well within the arsenal of relief provisions which the Commission may draw upon in fashioning effective remedial measures to bring about termination of the acts or practices found to have been unfair or deceptive. If such relief is warranted to prevent continuing injury to the public, it is neither punitive nor retrospective.

Finally, ANA argues that in addition to the Commission's lack of authority to issue corrective advertising orders, such orders would be unlawful for the reason that they would conflict with the First Amendment guarantee of free speech. ANA argues that the remedy is so harsh that it will have a "chilling effect" upon respondent's freedom to advertise truthfully. . . .

. . . ANA's contentions are at variance with existing case law where issues of the First Amendment's relationship to advertising have been involved. The regulation of false commercial advertising has been repeatedly upheld as constitutional. . . . Furthermore, in Valentine v. Chrestensen, 316 U.S. 52, 54 (1942), the Supreme Court expressly held that the First Amendment does not protect "purely commercial advertising." [106] . . .

ANA contends, however, that the argument that the First Amendment does not protect false advertising is not at issue here because the chilling effect of corrective advertising would curtail truthful as well as false claims. This argument proceeds essentially on the premise — which we have found inapplicable to the advertisement here in question — that the First Amendment guarantees apply to commercial speech. Moreover, the argument fails even if viewed on the basis of its own factual premises. The order here is designed to cure the effects of unfair and deceptive advertising. ANA argues that it is so difficult to determine whether a claim is accurate that advertisers will shy away from making any factual claims at all for fear of prosecution by the Commission. . . . How an advertiser reacts to a particular order provision is clearly within his province. But his dire predictions that it will lead him to discontinue advertising or to eliminate factual claims from his advertisement is hardly a basis on which we could justify ordering a particular relief measure which in our judgment was less effective than another. . . .

Accordingly, we find no merit in ANA's contention. . . .

We turn now to the question of whether a corrective advertising order is warranted on the basis of the record in this case. Commissioners Kirkpatrick, Dixon, MacIntyre and Dennison do not believe that the order in this case should contain a corrective advertising provision. Accordingly SOUP's request for such a provision is rejected. . . .

Notes and Questions

How effective a remedy "corrective advertising" will prove is unclear. In 1971, ITT entered into a consent decree under which it agreed to correct the false impression given in previous ads that eating Profile Bread would help the consumer lose weight. The "corrective ad" pointed out that ounce for ounce, Profile has as many calories as other breads. The speaker added that each slice contains fewer calories than the average bread because Profile is sliced thinner. The corrective ad did not seem to hurt Profile's sales. See In re ITT Continental Baking Company, 79 F.T.C. 248 (1971).

106. Ed. note: The Supreme Court has recently modified and perhaps overruled this case. See pp. 838-841 infra.

Are you convinced by the arguments of Commissioner Jones in *Firestone*? Are there any economic justifications for corrective advertising? What is your best guess as to the likely impact of corrective advertising? When should the FTC seek corrective advertising?

Note: The *Listerine* Case

In 1975 the Commission finally found a case where it felt justified in ordering corrective advertising. In In re Warner-Lambert Company, 86 F.T.C. 1398 (1975), the Commission ordered the respondent to include the following statement prominently displayed in all advertising: "Contrary to prior advertising, Listerine will not help prevent colds or sore throats or lessen their severity." The duty to disclose this fact was to continue until the company expended on Listerine advertising an amount equal to the company's average annual advertising expenditure for the period April 1962 to March 1972. On appeal, the D.C. Circuit affirmed but held that the company did not have to include the words "[c]ontrary to prior advertising," as a preamble to its required advertisements. The Court stated that this preamble was not necessary: "It can serve only two purposes: either to attract attention that a correction follows or to humiliate the advertiser. The Commission claims only the first purpose for it, and this we think is obviated by the other terms of the order. The second purpose, if it were intended, might be called for in an egregious case of deliberate deception, but this is not one. While we do not decide whether petitioner proffered its cold claims in good faith or bad, the record compiled could support a finding of good faith. On these facts, the confessional preamble to the disclosure is not warranted." [107]

6. *Publicity as an Enforcement Weapon*

To some extent, the deterrent effect of bringing a case, and of corrective advertising, rests upon the bad publicity it creates for the defendant company. Should publicity, then, be viewed directly as an enforcement tool?

Professor Ernest Gellhorn has described the controversy surrounding the Trade Commission's publicity practices as follows:

> Early critics of the Commission challenged, on statutory and constitutional grounds, its right to make complaints public and to hold public adjudicatory hearings. These challenges were easily repulsed, and in light of the Freedom of Information Act they now have a quaint ring. The more serious challenge has been to the Commission's practice, adopted in 1918, of issuing

107. Warner-Lambert Co. v. FTC, 562 F.2d 749, 763 (D.C. Cir. 1977), *cert. denied*, 435 U.S. 950 (1978). See generally Pitofsky, Beyond Nader: Consumer Protection and the Regulation of Advertising, 90 Harv. L. Rev. 661, 699-701 (1977); Cornfeld, A New Approach to an Old Remedy: Corrective Advertising and the Federal Trade Commission, 61 Iowa L. Rev. 693 (1976); Thain, Corrective Advertising: Theory and Cases, 19 N.Y.L.F. 1 (1973).

a press release immediately upon filing a complaint, copies of which are presently mailed to over 1,000 publications and to approximately 20,000 subscribers on the FTC's general distribution list. Because FTC investigations of individual firms are made public only if they lead to the filing of a complaint, press releases accompanying such complaints make up nearly all the agency's adverse publicity.

[Prior to 1975] the FTC rules provide[d] for the filing of two types of complaints: one for use in consent procedures, the other for use in adjudicative procedures. The former, governed by Part II of the FTC's rules, are known as "Part II" or "proposed" complaints. They are only tentatively approved by the Commission; before a matter in which such a complaint has been filed is assigned to an administrative law judge for hearing, the respondent is given an opportunity for extra-adjudicative settlement, usually by negotiation of a consent order. Part II complaints are not only public documents, they are also regularly accompanied by Commission-approved press releases. If a proposed complaint does not produce a negotiated settlement, the matter in which it was filed is returned to the Commission for approval and issuance of an "adjudicative," or "Part III," complaint. Unless the matter in which it is filed has for some reason escaped the Part II procedure and its attendant publicity, a Part III complaint is not accompanied by a press release. Thus, whenever it first becomes a matter of public information, every FTC complaint is deliberately publicized through a press release. In particularly significant cases, the Commission will hold a press conference as well.

According to the FTC, routine use of press releases and frequent use of background briefings, ensure accurate, fair news coverage. . . .[108]

FTC v. Cinderella Career and Finishing School, Inc.

404 F.2d 1308 (D.C. Cir. 1968)

TAMM, Circuit Judge:

This case presents, precisely and concisely, the question whether the Federal Trade Commission is authorized to issue a factual news release concerning pending adjudicatory proceedings before it.

Appellee corporations operate and grant franchises for the operation of schools offering various courses in modeling, fashion merchandising, charm, and self-improvement. . . .

Following an investigation, the appellant Federal Trade Commission, on February 13, 1967, issued a complaint . . . against appellees. . . .

This complaint was mailed to appellees on February 17, 1967. On February 20, 1967, appellees, "mindful and aware of the FTC's practice of issuing news releases and the adverse effects resulting therefrom," petitioned the Commission to defer the issuance of any news release with respect to this proceeding, . . . until

---

108. Gellhorn, "Adverse Publicity by Administrative Agencies," 86 Harv. L. Rev. 1380, 1388-90 (1973). [The two-part complaint procedure was changed in 1975. See note *supra*.]

after a final adjudication was had in the proceeding. On March 1, 1967, the Commission notified appellees that their petition had been denied. . . .

[T]he appellees . . . sought a restraining order against the issuance of the news release. . . . [They lost this action; the release was issued, and appellees then sought an injunction against further releases.]

. . . [T]he preliminary injunction requested by appellees was granted. . . .

We have no doubt that a press release of the kind herein involved results in a substantial tarnishing of the name, reputation, and status of the named respondent throughout the related business community as well as in the minds of some portion of the general public. Three hundred eighty-eight volumes ago, it was observed that "[w]here much has been said, something will be believed. . . ." We are confronted, then, not with the question of whether the appellees have suffered actual damage but whether the action of the Commission is so authorized or permitted in law as to place the appellees in the position of suffering *damnum absque injuria.* . . .

We [note first that the Commission's complaint automatically becomes] . . . a matter of public record. . . . [Moreover], court decisions hold "[t]he purpose of the Federal Trade Commission Act is to protect the public, not to punish a wrongdoer, . . . and it is in the public interest to stop a deception at its incipiency." . . .

In defining the Commission's authority and responsibility in protecting the public interest, Congress specifically authorized the Commission "[t]o make public from time to time such portions of the information obtained by it hereunder . . . as it shall deem expedient in the public interest. . . ." 15 U.S.C. §46(f) (1964).

Since the Commission is charged by the broad delegation of power to it to eliminate unfair or deceptive business practices in the public interest, and since it is specifically authorized to make public information acquired by it, we conclude that there is in fact and law authority in the Commission, acting in the public interest, to alert the public to suspected violations of the law by factual press releases whenever the Commission shall have reason to believe that a respondent is engaged in activities made unlawful by the Act which have resulted in the initiation of action by the Commission. The press releases predicated upon official action of the Commission constitute a warning or caution to the public, the welfare of which the Commission is in these matters charged. We note that there is no contention in this case that the allegations in the Commission's complaint were knowingly false. . . .

. . . The second paragraph of the press release issued by the Commission on March 3, 1967 describing the complaint filed against appellees stated:

(Note — A complaint is issued whenever the Commission has found "reason to believe" that the law has been violated and that a proceeding is in the public interest. It is emphasized that the issuance of a complaint simply marks the initiation of a formal proceeding in which the charges in the complaint will be ruled upon after a hearing and on the record. The issuance of a complaint does not indicate or reflect any adjudication of the matters charged.)

The quoted caution was well intended and is commendable. We have no doubt, however, that its practical value in minimizing the derogatory inferences upon the respondents' integrity was at best minimal, "for many will read the charge who may never see the answer...." Respublica v. Oswald, 1 U.S. (1 Dall.) 319, 324, 1 L. Ed. 155 (1788). We agree with the learned and experienced trial judge that "[i]n the event the final adjudication in Docket No. 8729 were to be in Plaintiffs' [appellees] favor, Plaintiffs would not be able to repair or remedy the damage suffered by them through the issuance and distribution of these news releases." Unfortunate though this result may be, we are convinced that this damage does not constitute a transgression of the appellee's legal rights. In appraising a somewhat similar situation, involving another government agency, we held that "[i]n the discharge by Congress of a dominant trust for the benefit of the public, the possibility of incidental loss to the individual is sometimes unavoidable." American Sumatra Tobacco Corporation v. SEC, 71 App. D.C. 259, 262-63, 110 F.2d 117, 120-21 (1940).

The action of the District Court in denying the Commission's motion to dismiss is reversed, and the case is remanded to that court with instructions to dismiss appellees' complaint.

Reversed.

Note: The Perils of Publicity

Gellhorn, Adverse Publicity by Administrative Agencies

86 Harv. L. Rev. 1380, 1408-1410 (1973)

The FDA is one of the few agencies granted specific statutory authority to issue adverse publicity. Without recourse to this power it is doubtful whether the agency could perform the functions expected of it today. Nevertheless, the FDA's use of adverse publicity in the recall program has been highly controversial.

The controversy can be traced to the 1959 cranberry episode, a public announcement which was in effect an involuntary recall. In the cranberry episode, the FDA issued a national public warning for the first time, with consequences so devastating to the industry that henceforth the mere threat of a public announcement functioned to help enforce a voluntary recall procedure. On November 9, 1959, a day still known as "Black Monday" in the industry, Secretary of Health, Education, and Welfare Arthur Flemming held a news conference at which he urged the public not to buy cranberries grown in Washington and Oregon, saying they might be contaminated with a chemical weed killer, aminotriazole, that had been found to cause cancer in laboratory rats. Although the Secretary admitted he had no information suggesting that cranberries from other states were dangerous, he would not say they were safe. Answering a reporter's question, the Secretary stated he would not be eating cranberries that Thanksgiving. Not surprisingly, most of the nation followed suit. Since cranberries are purchased primarily for the holiday season, virtually the entire crop remained unsold, even though 99 percent of it was subsequently "cleared" and marketed as government "approved."

In retrospect, the Secretary's action seems, at best, questionable. Given a sufficient dosage of aminotriazole, laboratory rats had indeed contracted cancer of the thyroid. But as the scientist who carried out the experiments noted, it would have taken years for a consumer to ingest enough contaminated cranberries to reproduce the laboratory results. Moreover, even if the situation required a wholesale removal of the product, the issuance of a public warning, particularly one accompanied by such inflammatory statements, may not have been justified. The industry was cooperating and, to the extent that its self-policing program was deficient, seizures or injunctions would have been preferable remedies. Nor did the Secretary's action take account of the cost to the industry of the unsold crop.

With the aid of enormous political pressure, the cranberry growers quickly convinced Congress that they were entitled to assistance and compensation. Congress first provided emergency loans; later it indemnified the growers at market prices, at a cost of approximately $9 million. It was, by any standard, an expensive news conference.

Question

Pitofsky receives the following memorandum from a staff member:

Volvo motors has been running ads which show a Swedish family in their kitchen. The father is seated at the table with a pencil in his hand going over his accounts. The mother is putting away the groceries.

An announcer states:

"The cost of living in Sweden is as high as it is in the United States. But the average income is lower. So when it comes to buying things, the Swedes are inclined to be exceedingly practical.

"Especially when it comes to something as expensive as a car.

"A 40% down payment is required.

"A car has to be economical. Gasoline is $0.80 a gallon."

The father and mother begin to look at the brochure. The announcer says:

"This family could buy an inexpensive import. But their car has to hold up through many long, cold, Swedish winters. They couldn't afford to buy a new car every couple of years. So, like most Swedes, they'll spend a little more and get the car that will live up to these demands.

"Volvo. We build them the way we build them, because we have to."

The ad suggests that Volvo is more economical and lasts longer than other cars. In fact, Volvo has done no comparative testing that would show either.

I recommend that we make Volvo a test case to forbid an advertiser from implying that his brand is better without comparative testing. We may lose before the Commission, but Volvo may well settle first and give us a precedent. Volvo probably can't afford the adverse publicity that a case will bring. If Volvo settles, so will others, for we'll have our precedent, and the others will fear the publicity as well.

Should Pitofsky bring this case?

7. Advertising Substantiation

Pitofsky sought to develop another legal weapon for possible use in his campaign — a weapon which he called "ad substantiation." The "substantiation" program was to have two parts. First, the Commission would be asked to hold it unlawful for a firm to make scientific claims about a product without adequate testing. Second, the Commission would seek information about those tests and would *itself* make that information public. Thus, the Commission would become a centralized source of accurate, important product information, which would help consumers make more intelligent buying decisions.[109]

a. The Need for Back-up Testing

In re Pfizer, Inc.

81 F.T.C. 23 (1972)

By KIRKPATRICK, Commissioner: . . .
. . . The complaint cited the following radio and television advertising for Un-Burn as typical and representative:

New Un-Burn actually anesthetizes *nerves* in sensitive sunburned skin.
    Un-Burn relieves pain *fast*. . . .
    . . . I'm a blonde . . . and I know what it means to have sensitive skin. Why I'm half afraid of moon burn! That's why I'm mad about Un-Burn. It stops sunburn pain in . . . less time than it takes me to slip out of my bikini. That's awfully nice to know when you're the sensitive type. . . .

The complaint alleges that the foregoing advertising claims were not substantiated by Pfizer by "adequate and well-controlled scientific studies or tests prior to the making of such statements."

    [Complaint counsel alleged that] Pfizer's advertising constituted a *deceptive practice* in representing to consumers that "each of the statements respecting the pain-relieving properties of the said product has been substantiated by respondent by adequate and well-controlled scientific studies or tests prior to the making of such statements."

109. See generally, Note, The FTC Ad Substantiation Program, 61 Geo. L.J. 1427 (1973).

... In response, respondent argues that the total setting of the ad, the frivolous nature of the dialogue, the use of a bikinied model, and the general "aura of sexiness" prevent the ad, taken as a whole, from carrying the scientific overtones argued by complaint counsel.

The Commission does not believe that an implied representation [of the sort complaint counsel suggests] can reasonably be found in respondent's advertising.

[Complaint counsel *also* charges that it is an *unfair* practice to advertise in this manner without adequate and well-controlled scientific studies or tests.]

... The recent *S & H* case sets forth a succinct confirmation of the Commission's jurisdiction over unfair practices:

> [T]he Federal Trade Commission does not arrogate excessive power to itself if, in measuring a practice against the elusive, but congressionally mandated standard of fairness, it, like a court of equity, considers public values beyond simply those enshrined in the letter or encompassed in the spirit of the antitrust laws.[110]

In footnoting this statement, the court said:

> The Commission has described the factors it considers in determining whether a practice which is neither in violation of the antitrust laws nor deceptive is nonetheless unfair:
> (1) whether the practices, without necessarily having been previously considered unlawful, offends [sic] public policy as it has been established by statutes, the common law, ... or otherwise — whether, in other words, it is within at least the penumbra of some common law, statutory, or other established concept of unfairness; (2) whether it is immoral, unethical, oppressive or unscrupulous; (3) whether it causes substantial injury to consumers (or competitors or other businessmen). ...

... [W]ith the development and proliferation of highly complex and technical products, there is often no practical way for consumers to ascertain the truthfulness of affirmative product claims prior to buying and using the product. ... The consumer simply cannot make the necessary tests or investigations to determine whether the direct and affirmative claims made for a product are true.

Given the imbalance of knowledge and resources between a business enterprise and each of its customers, economically it is more rational, and imposes far less cost on society, to require a manufacturer to confirm his affirmative product claims rather than impose a burden upon each individual consumer to test, investigate, or experiment for himself. The manufacturer has the ability, the knowhow, the equipment, the time and the resources to undertake such information by testing or otherwise — the consumer usually does not.

110. FTC v. Sperry & Hutchinson, 932 F.2d 146 (5th Cir. 1970), *rev'd.*, 405 U.S. 233 (1973).

...[T]he Commission is of the view that it is an unfair practice in violation of the Federal Trade Commission Act to make an affirmative product claim without a reasonable basis for making that claim....

...A consumer should not be compelled to enter into an economic gamble to determine whether a product will or will not perform as represented. The economic gamble involved in a consumer's reliance upon affirmative product claims is created by the vendors' activities, and cannot be easily avoided by consumers. Taking a different and analytical perspective and weighing the minimal cost and burden on vendors by requiring that there be a reasonable basis for affirmative product claims, against economic losses to consumers which can fairly be ascribed to advertising claims lacking such reasonable basis (losses which are, in a practical sense, unavoidable for the consumer), it is likewise clear that economic fairness requires that this obligation be imposed on vendors....

The question of what constitutes a reasonable basis is essentially a factual issue which will be affected by the interplay of overlapping considerations such as (1) the type and specificity of the claim made — e.g., safety, efficiency, dietary, health, medical; (2) the type of product — e.g., food, drug, potentially hazardous consumer product, other consumer products; (3) the possible consequences of a false claim — e.g., personal injury, property damage; (4) the degree of reliance by consumers on the claims; (5) the type, and accessibility, of evidence adequate to form a reasonable basis for making the particular claims. More specifically, there may be some types of claims for some types of products for which the only reasonable basis, in fairness and in the expectations of consumers, would be a valid scientific or medical basis. The precise formulation of the "reasonable basis" standard, however, is an issue to be determined at this time on a case-by-case basis. This standard is determined by the circumstances at the time the claim was made, and further depends on both those facts known to the advertiser, and those which a reasonable prudent advertiser should have discovered. Such facts should be possessed *before* the claim is made....

Complaint counsel argue that the only reasonable basis for making efficacy and performance claims for a drug such as Un-Burn would be adequate and well-controlled scientific studies or tests conducted prior to the marketing of the product....

...[If a test alone is to support the ad's claim, it] should be an adequate and well-controlled scientific test. Such a test should be conducted on human beings, not on animals. A pre-existing test protocol is usually essential to an adequate test. The record also indicated the strong desirability of double-blind scientific tests.... [Although Pfizer conducted such a test *after* marketing Un-Burn,] tests must have been conducted prior to, and actually relied upon in connection with, the marketing of the product in question....

It is thus clear that the tests conducted by Pfizer did not provide a reasonable basis for the making of these performance claims.... [However,] complaint counsel have not demonstrated that the only reasonable basis for these affirmative product claims would be adequate and well-controlled scientific studies or tests....

The record evidence is sufficient to demonstrate to the Commission that medical literature might, in some instances, be sufficient basis for making affirmative product claims. . . .

Closely allied with medical literature as a reasonable basis, would be the general state of medical knowledge at the time the claims were made, regardless of how that knowledge is ascertained. . . . Thus, the examiner found that:

> Recognized medical literature and the medical practice of dermatologists for between 50 and 70 years regarded the active ingredients in Un-Burn as efficacious for the relief of sunburn pain.

Persuasive in this regard is the fact that the NAS-NRC panels utilized by the Food and Drug Administration were permitted to recognize as probative reports on studies contained in the medical and scientific literature. . . .

[The basis for Pfizer's statement basically consisted of a review of the medical literature, statements by Pfizer's scientists that the active ingredient, benzocaine, was a well known local anesthetic, and tests on guinea pigs which showed that nothing in the formula stopped benzocaine from working. The Commission held that complaint counsel had not proved this basis *un*reasonable]. . . .

. . . In future cases, we would be interested in both the qualifications of the medical and scientific advisors, and some showing that their judgments were rendered on an informed and unbiased basis. Also properly considered here would be the issue of whether reliance upon medical literature and clinical evidence as to the separate ingredients in Un-Burn is appropriate, or whether additional consideration must be given to the combination [and to varying conditions of use.]. . .

Evidently respondent made no written report setting forth the actions which were taken to support the existence of a reasonable basis for its advertising claims. Such a report, if made in good faith prior to marketing, if reasonable in scope and approach, and if reasonably clear as to the evidentiary basis for the specific claims in question (be they scientific tests, specified medical references, or specific clinical evidence), would certainly have, in itself, gone a considerable distance in demonstrating the existence of a reasonable basis for their affirmative product claims.

Having reviewed the record, initial decision, briefs and argument in this proceeding, the Commission has determined that the hearing examiner's dismissal of the complaint should be affirmed. . . .

The significance of this particular case lies, therefore, [in the decision that] the failure to possess a reasonable basis for affirmative product claims constitutes an unfair practice in violation of the Federal Trade Commission Act.

b. Providing the Public with Substantiating Information

The next step in the FTC's "ad substantiation" program was to collect the substantiating information held by the companies. Its collection served two purposes. First, it would help the FTC decide whether to bring a case based on *Pfizer*. Second, the information could be made public, helping to inform consumers about the true worth of a product. The program's goal in large part was to give the consumer *more* information as well as to police the accuracy of what the companies chose to advertise.

(1) The FTC's Statutory Authority

The Commission's information gathering powers are granted by Federal Trade Commission Act §§ 6, 9, and 10:[111]

§6. The commission shall also have power —

(a) To gather and compile information concerning, and to investigate from time to time the organization, business, conduct, practices, and management of any persons . . . engaged in or whose business affects commerce. . . .

(b) To require, by general or special order, persons, . . . to file with the commission in such form as the commission may prescribe annual or special, . . . reports or answers in writing to specific questions . . . as to the organization, business, conduct, practices, management, and relation to other [businesses]. . . .

§9. [T]he commission . . . shall at all reasonable times have access to, for the purpose of examination, and the right to copy any documentary evidence of any person . . . being investigated and shall have power to require by subpoena the attendance and testimony of witnesses and the production of all such documentary evidence relating to any matter under investigation. . . .

§10. Any person who shall neglect or refuse to attend and testify, or to answer any lawful inquiry, or to produce documentary evidence . . . in obedience to the lawful requirement of the commission, shall be guilty of an offense and upon conviction shall be punished by a fine [$1,000 to $5,000] or by imprisonment [up to one year] or by both. . . .

If any corporation required [by this Act] to file any annual or special report shall fail so to do and such failure shall continue for thirty days after notice of such default, the corporation shall forfeit to the United States the sum of $100 for each and every day of the continuance of such failure.

(2) The FTC's Substantiation Order

Resolution Requiring Submission of Special Reports Relating to Advertising Claims and Disclosure Thereof By the Commission in Connection with a Public Investigation

36 Fed. Reg. 12,058 (1971)

. . . The claims made in advertising consumer products often lead the consuming public to believe that such claims are substantiated by adequate and well-controlled scientific tests, studies, and other fully-documented proof.

111. 15 U.S.C. §§ 46, 49, 50 (1978).

If the public and the Commission knew whether substantiation actually exists and the adequacy of substantiation, they would be aided in evaluating competing claims for products, and in distinguishing between the seller who is advertising truthfully and one who is unfairly treating both consumers and competitors by representing, directly or by implication, that it has proof when in fact there is none or the proof is inadequate.... [The Commission] ... *resolves* that advertisers shall be required, on demand by the Commission, to submit with respect to any advertisement such tests, studies or other data (including testimonials or endorsements) as they had in their possession prior to the time claims were made which purport to substantiate any claims, statements or representations made in the advertisement regarding the safety, performance, efficacy, quality, or comparative price of the product advertised.

The claims, statements or representations subject to the above requirement will be identified in orders to file special reports which will be issued to such advertisers as may be selected from time to time by the Commission. If the advertiser had no data to substantiate these claims before they were made, he shall notify the Commission of this fact before the return date of the Order to File Special Reports.

The Commission will compel the production of said tests, studies or other data (including testimonials or endorsements) in the exercise of the powers vested in it by Sections 6, 9 and 10 of the Federal Trade Commission Act (15 U.S.C. 46, 49 and 50), and with the aid of any and all powers conferred upon it by law and any and all compulsory processes available to it....

... Except for trade secrets, customer lists, or other financial information which may be privileged or confidential, pursuant to Section 6(f) of the Federal Trade Commission Act, the material obtained by the Commission pursuant to this resolution will be made available to the public under such terms and conditions as the Commission may from time to time determine. In addition, the Commission may release summaries, reports, indices, or such other publications which will inform the public about material delivered or not delivered to it hereunder.

In deciding to make this material available to the public, and to publish summary reports, the Commission is persuaded by the following policy considerations:

1. Public disclosure can assist consumers in making a rational choice among competing claims which purport to be based on objective evidence and in evaluating the weight to be accorded to such claims.

2. The public's need for this information is not being met voluntarily by advertisers.

3. Public disclosure can enhance competition by encouraging competitors to challenge advertising claims which have no basis in fact.

4. The knowledge that documentation or the lack thereof will be made public will encourage advertisers to have on hand adequate substantiation before claims are made.

5. The Commission has limited resources for detecting claims which are not substantiated by adequate proof. By making documentation submitted in response

to this resolution available to the public, the Commission can be alerted by consumers, businessmen, and public interest groups to possible violations of Section 5 of the Federal Trade Commission Act.

(3) *Constitutional Limitations on the Agency's Authority to Compel the Production of Information*

The agency must obtain information to do its work, whether it writes standards, allocates licenses, or enforces orders. Lack of information often is at the heart of the administrator's problems; and the agency's power to obtain information is the subject of much litigation.

In exercising its broad statutory powers, the FTC, like other agencies, is subject to constraints stemming both from the APA's requirement of "reasonableness" and the constitutional constraints contained in the Fourth Amendment.

FTC v. American Tobacco Co.

264 U.S. 298 (1924)

[The Supreme Court held unlawful FTC demands for all letters, telegrams, reports, contracts, and other documents, sent or received from customers, salesmen, trade associations, and others during 1921. Although the FTC was legitimately investigating resale price maintenance, its demand was too broad.]

[Mr. Justice HOLMES wrote for the Court that the demand exceeded the Commission's statutory authority:] . . . .

The mere facts of carrying on a commerce not confined within state lines and of being organized as a corporation do not make men's affairs public. . . . Anyone who respects the spirit as well as the letter of the Fourth Amendment would be loath to believe that Congress intended to authorize one of its subordinate agencies to sweep all our traditions into the fire . . . and to direct fishing expeditions into private papers on the possibility that they may disclose evidence of crime. We do not discuss the question whether it could do so if it tried, as nothing short of the most explicit language would induce us to attribute to Congress that intent. The interruption of business, the possible revelation of trade secrets, and the expense that compliance with the Commission's wholesale demand would cause are the least considerations. It is contrary to the first principles of justice to allow a search through all the respondents' records, relevant or irrelevant, in the hope that something will turn up. . . .

The right of access given by the statute is to documentary evidence — not to all documents, but to such documents as are evidence. The analogies of law do not allow the party wanting evidence to call for all documents in order to see if they do not contain it. Some ground must be shown for supposing that the documents called for do contain it. . . . Some evidence of the materiality of the papers demanded must be produced. Hale v. Henkel, 201 U.S. 43, 77. . . .

We have considered this case on the general claim of authority put forward by the Commission. The argument for the Government attaches some force to the investigations and proceedings upon which the Commission had entered. The investigations and complaints seem to have been only on hearsay or suspicion — but, even if they were induced by substantial evidence under oath, the rudimentary principles of justice that we have laid down would apply. We cannot attribute to Congress an intent to defy the Fourth Amendment or even to come so near to doing so as to raise a serious question of constitutional law.

Oklahoma Press Publishing Co. v. Walling

327 U.S. 186 (1946)

[The administrator of the Fair Labor Standards Act was allowed to subpoena information without a prior complaint or charge of violation. Justice RUTLEDGE's majority opinion said in part:]

Without attempt to summarize or accurately distinguish all of the cases, the fair distillation, in so far as they apply merely to the production of corporate records and papers in response to a subpoena of order authorized by law and safeguarded by judicial sanction,[112] seems to be that the Fifth Amendment affords no protection by virtue of the self-incrimination provision, whether for the corporation or for its officers;[113] and the Fourth, if applicable,[114] at the most guards against abuse only by way of too much indefiniteness or breadth in the things required to be "particularly described," if also the inquiry is one the demanding agency is authorized by law to make and the materials specified are relevant. The gist of the protection is in the requirement, expressed in terms, that the disclosure sought shall not be unreasonable.

As this has taken form in the decisions, the following specific results have been worked out. It is not necessary, as in the case of a warrant, that a specific charge or complaint of violation of law be pending or that the order be made pursuant to one. It is enough that the investigation be for a lawfully authorized purpose, within the power of Congress to command.[115] This has been ruled most often perhaps in relation to grand jury investigations, but also frequently in respect to general or statistical investigations authorized by Congress. The requirement of "probable cause, supported by oath or affirmation," literally applicable in the case of a warrant, is satisfied in that of an order for production by the court's determina-

---

112. Ed. note: Note that enforcement of an administrative subpoena is usually a two-step affair. The agency first issues the subpoena demanding information. If it meets resistance, it then asks a court to enforce it. (But see 15 U.S.C. §60 which provides criminal penalties for failure to answer a "lawful inquiry" of the FTC. This provision has rarely been used.)

113. Ed. note: Hale v. Henkel, 201 U.S. 43 (1906).

114. Ed. note: The Fourth Amendment was held applicable to corporations in Silverthorn Lumber Co. v. United States, 251 U.S. 385 (1920). See also Hale v. Henkel, 201 U.S. 43 (1906); ICC v. Brimson, 154 U.S. 447 (1894).

115. Ed. note: See Endicott Johnson Corp. v. Perkins, 317 U.S. 501 (1943).

tion that the investigation is authorized by Congress, is for a purpose Congress can order, and the documents sought are relevant to the inquiry. Beyond this the requirement of reasonableness, including particularity in "describing the place to be searched, and the persons or things to be seized," also literally applicable to warrants, comes down to specification of the documents to be produced adequate, but not excessive, for the purposes of the relevant inquiry. Necessarily, as has been said, this cannot be reduced to formula; for relevancy and adequacy or excess in the breadth of the subpoena are matters variable in relation to the nature, purposes and scope of the inquiry. . . .

United States v. Morton Salt Co.

338 U.S. 632 (1950)

Mr. Justice JACKSON delivered the opinion of the Court:

[The FTC brought an action against Morton Salt, ordering it to desist from certain pricing practices. The Court of Appeals affirmed the FTC order and demanded compliance. The FTC then, on its own, demanded that Morton send it a series of special reports that would demonstrate compliance. Morton argued that the FTC lacked power to compel the reports. The District Court agreed, and refused to enforce the FTC demands.]

The respondents' case and the decision below are rested heavily on this argument that the Commission is invading the province of the judiciary. . . .

If the Commission had petitioned the court itself to order additional reports of compliance, it could properly have been required to present some evidence of probable violation to overcome the "presumption of legality," of innocence, and of obedience to the law which respondents here urge. Courts hesitate to alter or supplement their decrees except the need be proved as well as asserted. Evidence the Commission did not have; it had at most a suspicion, or let us say a curiosity as to whether respondents' reported information in business methods was an abiding one.

Must the decree, after a single report of compliance, rest upon respondents' honor unless evidence of a violation fortuitously comes to the Commission? May not the Commission, in view of its residual duty of enforcement, affirmatively satisfy itself that the decree is being observed? Whether this usurps the courts' own function is, we think, answered by consideration of the fundamental relationship between the courts and administrative bodies.

The Trade Commission Act is one of several in which Congress, to make its policy effective, has relied upon the initiative of administrative officials and the flexibility of the administrative process. Its agencies are provided with staffs to institute proceedings and to follow up decrees and police their obedience. While that process at times is adversary, it also at times is inquisitorial. These agencies are expected to ascertain when and against whom proceedings should be set in motion and to take the lead in following through to effective results. . . .

The court in this case advisedly left it to the Commission to receive the report of compliance and to institute any contempt proceedings. This was in harmony with our system. When the process of adjudication is complete, all judgments are handed over to the litigant or executive officers, such as the sheriff or marshal, to execute.

. . . The respondents argue that since the Commission made no charge of violation either of the decree or the statute, it is engaged in a mere "fishing expedition" to see if it can turn up evidence of guilt. We will assume for the argument that this is so. Courts have disapproved the employment of the judicial process in such an enterprise. Federal judicial power itself extends only to adjudication of cases and controversies and it is natural that its investigative powers should be jealously confined to these ends. . . .

We must not disguise the fact that sometimes, especially early in the history of the federal administrative tribunal, the courts were persuaded to engraft judicial limitations upon the administrative process. The courts could not go fishing, and so it followed neither could anyone else. Administrative investigations fell before the colorful and nostalgic slogan "no fishing expeditions." It must not be forgotten that the administrative process and its agencies are relative newcomers in the field of law and that it has taken and will continue to take experience and trial and error to fit this process into our system of judicature. More recent views have been more tolerant of it than those which underlay many older decisions.

. . . [An agency] has a power of inquisition, if one chooses to call it that, which is not derived from the judicial function. It is more analogous to the Grand Jury, which does not depend on a case or controversy for power to get evidence but can investigate merely on suspicion that the law is being violated, or even just because it wants assurance that it is not. When investigative and accusatory duties are delegated by statute to an administrative body, it, too, may take steps to inform itself as to whether there is probable violation of the law. . . .

[The court added that FTC Act §6, authorizing a demand for "special reports," gave the Commission authority to demand this as part of compliance to an otherwise valid order.] Speaking of . . . this section, the [House Report said that the Commission] may also require such special reports as it may deem advisable. By this means, if the ordinary data furnished by a corporation in its annual report does not adequately disclose its organization, financial condition, business practices, or relation to other corporations, there can be obtained by a special report such additional information as the Commission may deem necessary. . . . The special report was used to enable the Commission to elicit any information beyond the ordinary data of a routine annual report. . . .

The Commission's order is criticized upon grounds that the order transgresses the Fourth Amendment's proscription of unreasonable searches and seizures and the Fifth Amendment's due process of law clause.

It is unnecessary here to examine the question of whether a corporation is entitled to the protection of the Fourth Amendment. . . . Although the "right to be let alone — the most comprehensive of rights and the right most valued by civilized men," Brandeis, J., dissenting in Olmstead v. United States, 277 U.S. 438,

478, is not confined literally to searches and seizures as such, but extends as well to the orderly taking under compulsion of process, Boyd v. United States, 116 U.S. 616, Hale v. Henkel, 201 U.S. 43, 70, neither incorporated nor unincorporated associations can plead an unqualified right to conduct their affairs in secret.

While they may and should have protection from unlawful demands made in the name of public investigation, cf. Federal Trade Comm'n v. American Tobacco Co., 264 U.S. 298, corporations can claim no equality with individuals in the enjoyment of a right to privacy. Cf. United States v. White, supra. They are endowed with public attributes. They have a collective impact upon society, from which they derive the privilege of acting as artificial entities. The Federal Government allows them the privilege of engaging in interstate commerce. Favors from government often carry with them an enhanced measure of regulation. Even if one were to regard the request for information in this case as caused by nothing more than official curiosity, nevertheless law-enforcing agencies have a legitimate right to satisfy themselves that corporate behavior is consistent with the law and the public interest.

Of course a governmental investigation into corporate matters may be of such a sweeping nature and so unrelated to the matter properly under inquiry as to exceed the investigatory power. Federal Trade Comm'n v. American Tobacco Co., supra. But it is sufficient if the inquiry is within the authority of the agency, the demand is not too indefinite and the information sought is reasonably relevant. "The gist of the protection is in the requirement, expressed in terms, that the disclosure sought shall not be unreasonable." Oklahoma Press Publishing Co. v. Walling, 327 U.S. 186, 208. Nothing on the face of the Commission's order transgressed these bounds. . . .

Notes

(a) Does the *Pfizer* decision along with the FTC's demand for substantiating information bring the FTC within the purview of those cases allowing the government to require individuals to keep certain records and then produce them? In Shapiro v. United States, 335 U.S. 1 (1948), for example, the Court held that the government could, consistent with the Fifth Amendment, require an individual to keep records of sales and then inspect those records to see whether price control laws were violated. More recently, the Court has upheld the constitutionality of the 1970 Bank Security Act, which requires banks to keep records of many financial transactions (e.g. all checks over $100) and to disclose certain domestic and foreign transactions to the government.[116]

(b) The FTC has the power to inspect records at firms' offices. Such inspections are subject to the Fourth Amendment, but the amendment imposes less

116. The Court noted the limited nature of a corporation's Fourth Amendment rights, and it left open the possibility that in a proper case, affected individuals could contest certain report requirements (as might the banks) were those requirements to become unreasonable. California Bankers Ass'n v. Shultz, 416 U.S. 21 (1974).

severe restrictions upon administrative bodies than upon police departments and other criminal investigators. At one time, a health inspector did not need a warrant to enter a house provided his behavior was "reasonable." [117] But more recently the Supreme Court held that some form of warrant for fire, health, and safety inspections, is necessary.[118] In such cases, "probable cause" is satisfied "if reasonable legislative or administrative standards for conducting an area inspection are satisfied." [119] The Court has allowed warrantless searches of firms in the "pervasively regulated" firearms industry to determine compliance with the Gun Control Act.[120]

The Fourth Amendment questions raised here are related to, and form a small portion of general "search and seizure" doctrine.[121]

(c) You should keep in mind the fact that a defendant may successfully object to an FTC demand for the production of documents or information on grounds other than the Fourth Amendment. A request that is unduly burdensome or unreasonably broad would constitute an abuse of the Commission's discretion.[122] A request must be reasonably related to the Commission's statutorily defined objectives.[123] Requests are also subject to such traditional common law constraints as that of attorney-client privilege,[124] and to such statutory constraints as 15 U.S.C. §46(f), which allows the FTC "to make public from time to time such portions of the information obtained by it hereunder, except trade secrets and names of customers, as it shall deem expedient in the public interest. . . ."

Questions

(a) The following is an actual information demand made by the FTC, pursuant to its ad substantiation program and July 7 order. The Commission ordered Warner-Lambert to file a special report in respect to the following ad:

> *Little sister:*   A pimple, huh?
> *Brother:*   Don't bug me. I've got a date.
> *Little sister:*   What are you washing with?
> *Brother:*   Listerex Acne Scrub — It's from the Listerine people so you know it's gonna work. And it kills germs.
> *Sister:*   What's in this?
> *Brother:*   Cleansing grains that scrub away dirt and excess oil.
> *Sister:*   How's it feel?

117. Frank v. Maryland, 359 U.S. 360 (1959).
118. Camara v. Municipal Court, 387 U.S. 523 (1967); See v. City of Seattle, 387 U.S. 541 (1967); Marshall v. Barlow's, Inc., 436 U.S. 307 (1978).
119. Camara v. Municipal Court, 387 U.S. 523, 538 (1967).
120. United States v. Biswell, 406 U.S. 311 (1972). See also Colonnade Catering Corp. v. United States, 397 U.S. 72 (1970) (refusal to admit federal liquor inspectors unlawful).
121. On the subject of the FTC's authority to obtain information, see generally, Mueller, Access to Corporate Papers under the FTC Act, 11 U. Kan. L. Rev. 77 (1962).
122. See, e.g., Genuine Parts Co. v. FTC, 445 F.2d 1382 (5th Cir. 1971).
123. See, e.g., FTC v. Crafts, 244 F.2d 882 (7th Cir.), rev'd, 355 U.S. 9 (1957).
124. See In re Viviano Macaroni Co. 69 F.T.C. 1104, 1107 (1966), aff'd, 411 F.2d 255 (1969).

Brother: Like it's working, OK.
Sister: Does she use Listerex too?
Brother: (Pushing her head down) Would you get out of here!
ANNCR (VO):   Wash with Listerex everyday — a better way to help fight acne problems from the Listerine people.

The Special Report is to contain the following information:

All documentation and other substantiation for the claims that Listerex Acne Scrub:

(1) has been proven to be an effective treatment for the acne, pimples, or oily complexions of any potential user;

(2) contains cleansing grains which scrub away dirt and excess oil;

(3) is more effective than all other acne treatments and cleansers;
     including, but not limited to:

A. a full explanation of the meaning of the following words and terms as used in the advertisements, including an indication of the source of the definition where appropriate:

   (1) "acne"
   (2) "pimples"
   (3) "excess oil"
   (4) "cleansing grains"

B. if the determination that Listerex (i) is an effective treatment for acne, pimples, and oily complexions and (ii) that it is more effective than all other acne treatments and cleansers involved surveys, tests or experimental methodology, submit the following documentation including, but not limited to:

   (1) a complete explanation of the survey and experimental methodology used in the study;

   (2) a complete description of the subjects, their number, their age, their sex and geographic place of residence, how recruited and under what conditions, and the generalizability of the sample;

   (3) a complete description of the experience and training of all experimenters, interviewers, and other personnel dealing with subjects or processing the data; or if the study was undertaken by an independent research organization, the name(s) address(es), and professional qualifications of the party or parties who conducted the study;

   (4) a list of all other products or brands tested with Listerex, including the size and description of package or container. If an experimental design was used, indications whether labels and other identifying characteristics were removed from test products;

   (5) disclosure of whether the interviewer (or experimenter) and the experimenter) and the respondents (or subjects) were aware of the fact that the client in the study was Listerex;

   (6) disclosure of all statistical designs and techniques of statistical inference used in testing hypotheses, including statistical assumptions necessary for tests of significance and the level of confidence (alpha risk) considered to be acceptable;

   (7) submission of sufficient data to allow one to replicate the study to test the reliability of the results and;

(8) submission of all data necessary to check the appropriateness of the statistical inference made using similar or more appropriate statistical tools;

(9) submission of copies of all questionnaires, tests, scales and other materials read, shown, or presented to subject.

C. a complete list of all the ingredients in Listerex Acne Scrub, the quantity of each ingredient as a percentage of the total volume of the product, and a full explanation of the function of each ingredient;

D. a complete list of ingredients which are medically proven to be effective in the treatment of skin problems commonly known as, acne, pimples, oily skin, indicating the source(s) of the data specifically; a complete explanation, including documentation, of the kinds of complexion problems for which Listerex has been proven to be an effective treatment including, but not limited to:

(1) a complete explanation of all known factors which cause or contribute to the presence of acne, pimples, oily skin, including but not limited to a complete discussion of the relationship between each of the following conditions and the complexion problems to which they contribute, adding all additional factors contributing to complexion problems of which you are aware:

a. adolescent oily skin
b. unfavorable environmental conditions
c. unhygenic conditions
d. occupational exposures
e. use of various types of drugs
f. hormonal factors
g. diet
h. bacteria;

(2) a full explanation, including documentation, of the degree of effectiveness of Listerex in the treatment of the above listed (and unlisted) causes or contributors (cited in paragraph (1) above) to acne, pimples, oily skin and the treatment of each of these conditions once it is present;

(3) a full explanation, including documentation, of the degree of effectiveness of Listerex in the treatment of acne problems having each of the following medically identified degrees of severity:

a. acne pustulosa
b. acne indurata
c. acne vulgaris
d. acne of the face with predominance
e. deep seated infiltrations
f. abscesses
g. cysts
h. acne corporis

including an indication of the percentage of the population suffering from each. With citation of the source(s) of the data;

F. a full explanation of the short and long term effects of the regular use of antibacterial agents on the skin.

Warner-Lambert was also ordered to provide "a complete summary of all the documentation and substantiation submitted in such language as to enable an ordinary consumer to understand it."

Suppose that Warner-Lambert had felt this request was unreasonable and did not wish to comply. What objections could it have made?

(b) Consider the effects of ad substantiation programs:[125]

In *Pfizer,* the Commission claimed that as an economic matter, consumer gains from the program will outweigh verification and administrative costs. The Warner-Lambert example suggests those costs may be substantial. Do you think the Commission is right?

Will the program involve technical personnel (and lawyers) within the corporation's ad creation process? Would such involvement in itself tend to make advertisements more factual?

Or is the program likely to lead to less factual advertisements and greater reliance on irrational appeal?

Does it place an undue burden on the free flow of commercial information?

Pitofsky has described the aims of ad substantiation in part as follows:

> ... [S]ince market incentives are sometimes inadequate to ensure the availability of important product information, and since it is virtually impossible to redress consumer injuries after the fact, a consumer-oriented program would emphasize required disclosure of accurate and important product information that consumers could then use to protect their interests. ... [It] would deemphasize enforcement which tends to diminish the availability of useful information ... or which involves disputes over information that ... is at some remove from the concerns of most consumers. ...[126]

Do you believe the program is likely to satisfy this objective? What are the obstacles in its path?

8. Counter-Advertising

In January of 1972, Pitofsky sought to use another weapon in his campaign to provide more complete and more accurate product information to the consumer. The FTC sent a memorandum to the Federal Communications Commission asking that agency to require television stations to allow "counter-advertising." This "counter-advertising" would consist of answers to claims by advertisers presented by those who disagreed with them. The stations would have to allow access

---

125. The FTC has also included ad substantiation provisions in consent decrees. See, e.g., Fedders Corp., 85 F.T.C. 38 (1975); In re Standard Oil of Calif., 84 F.T.C. 1401, 1489-1493 (1974).

126. Pitofsky, Beyond Nader: Consumer Protection and the Regulation of Advertising, 90 Harv. L. Rev. 661, 674-675 (1977).

to those willing to pay for "counter-ads" and also to set aside a limited amount of free airtime for those who could not afford to pay.[127]

Consideration of Pitofsky's proposal will allow us to explore some of the First Amendment doctrines related to government regulation of commercial speech generally, and the content of television advertising specifically. After briefly setting forth some of these doctrines, the subsection will turn to the specific counter-advertising proposal made by Pitofsky, which should lead you to consider how constitutional, statutory, and administrative factors interact as regulators try to formulate policy.

a. The Constitutionality of Regulating Commercial Speech

Virginia State Board of Pharmacy v. Virginia Citizens Consumer Council, Inc.

425 U.S. 748 (1976)

Mr. Justice BLACKMUN delivered the opinion of the Court.

[Appellants challenged the constitutionality of a Virginia statute that prohibited pharmacists from advertising the prices of prescription drugs. A three-judge District Court held the statute unconstitutional.]

The appellants contend that the advertisement of prescription drug prices is outside the protection of the First Amendment because it is "commercial speech." There can be no question that in past decisions the Court has given some indication that commercial speech is unprotected. In Valentine v. Chrestensen, [316 U.S. 52 (1942)], ... the Court upheld a New York statute that prohibited the distribution of any "handbill, circular ... or other advertising matter whatsoever in or upon any street." The Court concluded that, although the First Amendment would forbid the banning of all communication by handbill in the public thoroughfares, it imposed "no such restraint on government as respects purely commercial advertising." 316 U.S., at 54. ...

Last Term, in Bigelow v. Virginia, 421 U.S. 809 (1975), the notion of unprotected "commercial speech" all but passed from the scene. We reversed a conviction for violation of a Virginia statute that made the circulation of any publication to encourage or promote the processing of an abortion in Virginia a misdemeanor. The defendant had published in his newspaper the availability of abortions in New York. ... We rejected the contention that the publication was unprotected because it was commercial. *Chrestensen's* continued validity was questioned, and its holding was described as "distinctly a limited one" that merely upheld "a reasonable regulation of the manner in which commercial advertising could be distributed." 421 U.S., at 819. ...

---

127. See generally, Collins, Counter-advertising in the Broadcast Media: Bringing the Administrative Process to Bear upon a Theoretical Imperative, 15 Wm. & Mary L. Rev. 799 (1974).

Here, . . . the question whether there is a First Amendment exception for "commercial speech" is squarely before us. Our pharmacist does not wish to editorialize on any subject, cultural, philosophical, or political. He does not wish to report any particularly newsworthy fact, or to make generalized observations even about commercial matters. The "idea" he wishes to communicate is simply this: "I will sell you the X prescription drug at the Y price." Our question, then, is whether this communication is wholly outside the protection of the First Amendment. . . .

We begin with several propositions that already are settled or beyond serious dispute. It is clear, for example, that speech does not lose its First Amendment protection because money is spent to project it, as in a paid advertisement of one form or another. . . . Speech likewise is protected even though it is carried in a form that is "sold" for profit, . . . and even though it may involve a solicitation to purchase or otherwise pay or contribute money. . . .

If there is a kind of commercial speech that lacks all First Amendment protection, therefore, it must be distinguished by its content. Yet the speech whose content deprives it of protection cannot simply be speech on a commercial subject. No one would contend that our pharmacist may be prevented from being heard on the subject of whether, in general, pharmaceutical prices should be regulated, or their advertisement forbidden. Nor can it be dispositive that a commercial advertisement is noneditorial, and merely reports a fact. Purely factual matter of public interest may claim protection. . . .

Our question is whether speech which does "no more than propose a commercial transaction," Pittsburgh Press Co. v. Human Relations Comm'n, 413 U.S. at 385, is so removed from any "exposition of ideas," Chaplinsky v. New Hampshire, 315 U.S. 568, 572 (1942), and from "truth, science, morality, and arts in general, in its diffusion of liberal sentiments on the administration of Government," Roth v. United States, 354 U.S. 476, 484 (1957), that it lacks all protection. Our answer is that it is not.

Focusing first on the individual parties to the transaction that is proposed in the commercial advertisement, we may assume that the advertiser's interest is a purely economic one. That hardly disqualifies him from protection under the First Amendment. The interests of the contestants in a labor dispute are primarily economic, but it has long been settled that both the employee and the employer are protected by the First Amendment when they express themselves on the merits of the dispute in order to influence its outcome. . . .

As to the particular consumer's interest in the free flow of commercial information, that interest may be as keen, if not keener by far, than his interest in the day's most urgent political debate. Appellees' case in this respect is a convincing one. Those whom the suppression of prescription drug price information hits the hardest are the poor, the sick, and particularly the aged. . . .

Generalizing, society also may have a strong interest in the free flow of commercial information. Even an individual advertisement, though entirely "commercial," may be of general public interest. . . .

Moreover, there is another consideration that suggests that no line between publicly "interesting" or "important" commercial advertising and the opposite kind could ever be drawn. Advertising, however tasteless and excessive it sometimes may seem, is nonetheless dissemination of information as to who is producing and selling what product, for what reason, and at what price. So long as we preserve a predominantly free enterprise economy, the allocation of our resources in large measure will be made through numerous private economic decisions. It is a matter of public interest that those decisions, in the aggregate, be intelligent and well informed. To this end, the free flow of commercial information is indispensable. . . . And if it is indispensable to the proper allocation of resources in a free enterprise system, it is also indispensable to the formation of intelligent opinions as to how that system ought to be regulated or altered. Therefore, even if the First Amendment were thought to be primarily an instrument to enlighten public decisionmaking in a democracy, we could not say that the free flow of information does not serve that goal.

[The Court then considered the justifications offered by the State for its price-advertising ban: price advertising would encourage price competition, erode pharmacists' profits and destroy the pharmacist-customer relationship. Pharmacists would become less professional, less likely to know the needs of their clients, with resulting risks to health. The Court held that however desirable the ends, they could not be pursued by suppressing information.]

. . . It is precisely this kind of choice, between the dangers of suppressing information, and the dangers of its misuse if it is freely available, that the First Amendment makes for us. Virginia is free to require whatever professional standards it wishes of its pharmacists; it may subsidize them or protect them from competition in other ways. Cf. Parker v. Brown, 317 U.S. 341 (1943). But it may not do so by keeping the public in ignorance of the entirely lawful terms that competing pharmactists are offering. In this sense, the justifications Virginia has offered for suppressing the flow of prescription drug price information, far from persuading us that the flow is not protected by the First Amendment, have reinforced our view that it is. We so hold.

In concluding that commercial speech, like other varieties, is protected, we of course do not hold that it can never be regulated in any way. Some forms of commercial speech regulation are surely permissible. We mention a few only to make clear that they are not before us and therefore are not foreclosed by this case.

There is no claim, for example, that the prohibition on prescription drug price advertising is a mere time, place, and manner restriction. We have often approved restrictions of that kind provided that they are justified without reference to the content of the regulated speech, that they serve a significant governmental interest, and that in so doing they leave open ample alternative channels for communication of the information. . . .

Nor is there any claim that prescription drug price advertisements are forbidden because they are false or misleading in any way. Untruthful speech, commercial or otherwise, has never been protected for its own sake. . . . Obviously, much commercial speech is not provably false, or even wholly false, but only deceptive or misleading. We foresee no obstacle to a State's dealing effectively with this problem.[128] The First Amendment, as we construe it today, does not prohibit the State from insuring that the stream of commercial information flow cleanly as well as freely. . . . See, for example, Va. Code Ann. §18.2-216 (1975).

Also, there is no claim that the transactions proposed in the forbidden advertisements are themselves illegal in any way. . . . Cf. Pittsburgh Press Co. v. Human Relations Comm'n, 413 U.S. 376 (1973); United States v. Hunter, 459 F.2d 205 (CA4), *cert. denied*, 409 U.S. 934 (1972).

Finally, the special problems of the electronic broadcast media are likewise not in this case. Cf. Capitol Broadcasting Co. v. Mitchell, 333 F. Supp. 582 (D.C. 1971), *aff'd sub nom.* Capitol Broadcasting Co. v. Acting Attorney General, 405 U.S. 1000 (1972).

What is at issue is whether a State may completely suppress the dissemination of concededly truthful information about entirely lawful activity, fearful of that information's effect upon its disseminators and its recepients. Reserving other questions,[129] we conclude that the answer to this one is in the negative.

The judgment of the District Court is affirmed.

It is so ordered.[130]

128. In concluding that commercial speech enjoys First Amendment protection, we have not held that it is wholly undifferentiable from other forms. There are commonsense differences between speech that does "no more than propose a commercial transaction," . . . and other varieties. Even if the differences do not justify the conclusion that commercial speech is valueless, and thus subject to complete suppression by the State, they nonetheless suggest that a different degree of protection is necessary to insure that the flow of truthful and legitimate commercial information is unimpaired. The truth of commercial speech, for example, may be more easily verifiable by its disseminator than, let us say, news reporting or political commentary, in that ordinarily the advertiser seeks to disseminate information about a specific product or service that he himself provides and presumably knows more about than anyone else. Also, commercial speech may be more durable than other kinds. Since advertising is the sine qua non of commercial profits, there is little likelihood of its being chilled by proper regulation and foregone entirely.

Attributes such as these, the greater objectivity and hardiness of commercial speech, may make it less necessary to tolerate inaccurate statements for fear of silencing the speaker. . . . Compare New York Times Co. v. Sullivan, 376 U.S. 254 (1964), with Dun & Bradstreet, Inc. v. Grove, 404 U.S. 898 (1971). They may also make it appropriate to require that a commercial message appear in such a form, or include such additional information, warnings, and disclaimers, as are necessary to prevent its being deceptive. Compare Miami Herald Publishing Co. v. Tornillo, 418 U.S. 241 (1974), with Banzhaf v. FCC, 132 U.S. App. D.C. 14, 405 F.2d 1082 (1968), *cert. denied sub nom.* Tobacco Institute, Inc. v. FCC, 396 U.S. 842 (1969). Cf. United States v. 95 Barrels of Vinegar, 265 U.S. 438, 443 (1924) ("It is not difficulft to choose statements, designs and devices which will not deceive"). They may also make inapplicable the prohibition against prior restraints. . . .

129. We stress that we have considered in this case the regulation of commercial advertising by pharmacists. Although we express no opinion as to other professions, the distinctions, historical and functional, between professions may require consideration of quite different factors. Physicians and lawyers, for example, do not dispense standardized products; they render professional services of almost infinite variety and nature, with the consequent enhanced possibility for confusion and deception if they were to undertake certain kinds of advertising.

130. Ed. note: *Virginia State Board* effected somewhat of a revolution in the field of "commercial speech," and its implications have not been fully digested. See Note, First Amendment Protection for Commercial Advertising: The New Constitutional Doctrine, 44 U. Chi. L. Rev. 205 (1976); Bayus, The Constitutional Status of Commercial Expression, 3 Hastings Con. L.Q. 761 (1976).

Questions

(a) What is the effect of *Virginia State Board* on the ordinary false advertising case? The "corrective advertising" remedy? The "ad substantiation" program?

(b) Will the courts themselves determine whether an instance of speech is commercial and thus subject to regulation or will they defer to the agency's view? How dead is the *Ben Avon* doctrine? See Chapter 4, supra.

b. The Fairness Doctrine

The regulation of the content of television advertising requires some consideration of the possibly special First Amendment relationship to the electronic media. The relationship arises out of the "fairness doctrine," which places upon the broadcaster the obligation to broadcast all sides of controversial issues. This doctrine is broader, and more general, than the specific "equal time" requirement that the Federal Communications Act, 47 U.S.C. §315, imposes in respect to candidates for political office. Pitofsky was asking the FCC to apply the "fairness doctrine" to television advertising.

Red Lion Broadcasting Co. v. Federal Trade Commission

395 U.S. 367 (1969)

Mr. Justice WHITE delivered the opinion of the Court. . . .

[The FCC's fairness doctrine requires "that discussion of public issues be presented on broadcast stations, and that each side of those issues must be given fair coverage. . . . This must be done at the broadcaster's own expense if sponsorship is unavailable." The FCC set forth regulations under this doctrine specifying when, and how, a station should allow an individual to reply to a personal attack. It also required a Pennsylvania radio station to allow an author to respond to an attack by a radio commentator. The Court sustained the regulations, the order, and the doctrine itself.]

The statutory authority of the FCC to promulgate these regulations derives from the mandate to the "Commission from time to time, as public convenience, interest, or necessity requires" to promulgate "such rules and regulations and prescribe such restrictions and conditions . . . as may be necessary to carry out the provisions of this chapter. . . ." 47 U.S.C. §303 and §303(r). . . .

. . . [W]e cannot say that when a station publishes personal attacks or endorses political candidates, it is a misconstruction of the public interest standard to require the station to offer time for a response rather than to leave the response entirely within the control of the station which has attacked either the candidacies or the men who wish to reply in their own defense When a broadcaster grants time to a political candidate, Congress itself requires that equal time be offered to his opponents. It would exceed our competence to hold that the Commission is unauthorized by the statute to employ a similar device where personal attacks or political editorials are broadcast by a radio or television station.

... [Thus] we think the fairness doctrine and its component personal attack and political editorializing regulations are a legitimate exercise of congressionally delegated authority....

The broadcasters challenge the fairness doctrine and its specific manifestations in the personal attack and political editorial rules on conventional First Amendment grounds, alleging that the rules abridge their freedom of speech and press. Their contention is that the First Amendment protects their desire to use their allotted frequencies continuously to broadcast whatever they choose, and to exclude whomever they choose from ever using that frequency. No man may be prevented from saying or publishing what he thinks, or from refusing in his speech or other utterances to give equal weight to the views of his opponents. This right, they say, applies equally to broadcasters.

Although broadcasting is clearly a medium affected by a First Amendment interest, ... differences in the characteristics of new media justify differences in the First Amendment standards applied to them....

Just as the Government may limit the use of sound-amplifying equipment potentially so noisy that it drowns out civilized private speech, so may the Government limit the use of broadcast equipment. The right of free speech of a broadcaster, the user of a sound truck, or any other individual does not embrace a right to snuff out the free speech of others....

... [O]nly a tiny fraction of those with resources and intelligence can hope to communicate by radio at the same time if an intelligible communication is to be had, even if the entire radio spectrum is utilized in the present state of commercially acceptable technology.

... [B]ecause the frequencies reserved for public broadcasting were limited in number, it was essential for the Government to tell some applicants that they could not broadcast at all because there was room for only a few.

Where there are substantially more individuals who want to broadcast than there are frequencies to allocate, it is idle to posit an unabridgeable First Amendment right to broadcast comparable to the right of every individual to speak, write, or publish. If 100 persons want broadcast licenses but there are only 10 frequencies to allocate, all of them may have the same "right" to a license; but if there is to be any effective communication by radio, only a few can be licensed and the rest must be barred from the airwaves. It would be strange if the First Amendment, aimed at protecting and furthering communications, prevented the Government from making radio communication possible by requiring licenses to broadcast and by limiting the number of licenses so as not to overcrowd the spectrum.

... There is nothing in the First Amendment which prevents the Government from requiring a licensee to share his frequency with others and to conduct himself as a proxy or fiduciary with obligations to present those views and voices which are representative of his community and which would otherwise, by necessity, be barred from the airwaves.

This is not to say that the First Amendment is irrelevant to public broadcasting. On the contrary, it has a major role to play as the Congress itself recognized in §326, which forbids FCC interference with "the right of free speech by means of radio communication." ... It is the right of the viewers and listeners, not the right of the broadcasters, which is paramount.... It is the purpose of the First Amendment to preserve an uninhibited marketplace of ideas in which truth will ultimately prevail, rather than to countenance monopolization of that market, whether it be by the Government itself or a private licensee....

[Were these rules unconstitutional], station owners and a few networks would have unfettered power to make time available only to the highest bidders, to communicate only their own views on public issues, people and candidates, and to permit on the air only those with whom they agreed. There is no sanctuary in the First Amendment for unlimited private censorship operating in a medium not open to all. "Freedom of the press from governmental interference under the First Amendment does not sanction repression of that freedom by private interests." ...

It is strenuously argued, however, that if political editorials or personal attacks will trigger an obligation in broadcasters to afford the opportunity for expression to speakers who need not pay for time and whose views are unpalatable to the licensees, then broadcasters will [reduce] their coverage of controversial public issues....

... [But this] possibility is at best speculative... [And] the Commission... [can require licensees] to present representative community views on controversial issues.... Congress need not stand idly by and permit those with licenses to ignore the problems which beset the people or to exclude from the airwaves anything but their own views of fundamental questions....

We need not and do not now ratify every past and future decision by the FCC with regard to programming. There is no question here of the Commission's refusal to permit the broadcaster to carry a particular program or to publish his own views; of a discriminatory refusal to require the licensee to broadcast certain views which have been denied access to the airwaves; of government censorship of a particular program contrary to §326; or of the official government view dominating public broadcasting. Such questions would raise more serious First Amendment issues. But we do hold that the Congress and the Commission do not violate the First Amendment when they require a radio or television station to give reply time to answer personal attacks and political editorials.

It is argued that even if at one time the lack of available frequencies for all who wished to use them justified the Government's choice of those who would best serve the public interest by acting as proxy for those who would present differing views, or by giving the latter access directly to broadcast facilities, this condition no longer prevails so that continuing control is not justified. To this there are several answers.

Scarcity is not entirely a thing of the past....

Even where there are gaps in spectrum utilization, the fact remains that existing broadcasters have often attained their present position because of their initial government selection in competition with others before new technological advances opened new opportunities for further uses. Long experience in broadcasting, confirmed habits of listeners and viewers, network affiliation, and other advantages in program procurement give existing broadcasters a substantial advantage over new entrants, even where new entry is technologically possible. These advantages are the fruit of a preferred position conferred by the Government. Some present possibility for new entry by competing stations is not enough, in itself, to render unconstitutional the Government's effort to assure that a broadcaster's programming ranges widely enough to serve the public interest.

In view of the scarcity of broadcast frequencies, the Government's role in allocating those frequencies and the legitimate claims of those unable without governmental assistance to gain access to those frequencies for expression of their views, we hold the regulations and ruling at issue here are both authorized by statute and constitutional. . . .

Miami Herald Publishing Co. v. Tornillo

418 U.S. 241 (1974)

Mr. Chief Justice BURGER delivered the opinion of the Court. [The decision was unanimous, with Justices BRENNNAN and WHITE filing concurring opinions. Justice REHNQUIST joined in BRENNAN's concurrence.]

The issue in this case is whether a state statute granting a political candidate a right to equal space to reply to criticism and attacks on his record by a newspaper violates the guarantees of a free press.

In the fall of 1972, appellee . . . was a candidate for the Florida House of Representatives. . . . [A]ppellant printed editorials critical of appellee's candidacy. . . . [Appellee demanded an opportunity to reply under] Florida Statute §104.38 (1973), . . . which provides that if a candidate for nomination or election is assailed regarding his personal character or official record by any newspaper, the candidate has the right to demand that the newspaper print, free of cost to the candidate, any reply the candidate may make to the newspaper's charges. . . .

Appellant contends the statute is void on its face because it purports to regulate the content of a newspaper in violation of the First Amendment. . . .

The appellee and supporting advocates of an enforceable right of access to the press vigorously argue that government has an obligation to ensure that a wide variety of views reach the public. . . . [A]t the time the First Amendment to the Constitution was ratified in 1791 as part of our Bill of Rights the press was broadly representative of the people it was serving. . . . Entry into publishing was inexpensive; pamphlets and books provided meaningful alternatives to the organized press. . . . A true marketplace of ideas existed in which there was relatively easy access to the channels of communication.

. . . [T]oday, however, [n]ewspapers have become big business and there are far fewer of them to serve a largely literate population. Chains of newspapers, national newspapers, national wire and news services, and one-newspaper towns,[131] are

131. "Nearly half of U.S. daily newspapers, representing some three-fifths of daily and Sunday circulation, are owned by newspaper groups and chains, including diversified business

the dominant features of a press that has become noncompetitive and enormously powerful and influential in its capacity to manipulate popular opinion and change the course of events. Major metropolitan newspapers have collaborated to establish news services national in scope. Such national news organizations provide syndicated "interpretive reporting" as well as syndicated features and commentary, all of which can serve as part of the new school of "advocacy journalism." . . .

The obvious solution, which was available to dissidents at an earlier time when entry into publishing was relatively inexpensive, today would be to have additional newspapers. But the same economic factors which have caused the disappearance of vast numbers of metropolitan newspapers, have made entry into the marketplace of ideas served by the print media almost impossible. It is urged that the claim of newspapers to be "surrogates for the public" carries with it a concomitant fiduciary obligation to account for that stewardship. From this premise it is reasoned that the only effective way to insure fairness and accuracy and to provide for some accountability is for government to take affirmative action. The First Amendment interest of the public in being informed is said to be in peril because the "marketplace of ideas" is today a monopoly controlled by the owners of the market.

. . . [This Court has held that] "Freedom of the press from governmental interference under the First Amendment does not sanction repression of that freedom by private interests." [Associated Press v. United States, 326 U.S. 1, 20 (1945)].

However much validity may be found in these arguments, at each point the implementation of a remedy such as an enforceable right of access necessarily calls for some mechanism, either governmental or consensual. If it is governmental coercion, this at once brings about a confrontation with the express provisions of the First Amendment and the judicial gloss on the Amendment developed over the years.

. . . [T]he Court has expressed sensitivity as to whether a restriction or requirement constituted the compulsion exerted by government on a newspaper to print that which it would not otherwise print. The clear implication has been that any such compulsion to publish that which " 'reason' tells them should not be published" is unconstitutional. A responsible press is an undoubtedly desirable goal, but press responsibility is not mandated by the Constitution and like many other virtues it cannot be legislated.

Appellee's argument that the Florida statute does not amount to a restriction of appellant's right to speak because "the statute in question here has not prevented the *Miami Herald* from saying anything it wished" begs the core question. Compelling editors or publishers to publish that which " 'reason' tells them should not be published" is what is at issue in this case. . . . The Florida statute exacts a penalty on the basis of the content of a newspaper. The first phase of the penalty . . . is exacted in terms of the cost in printing and composing time and materials and in taking up

conglomerates. One-newspaper towns have become the rule, with effective competition operating in only 4 percent of our large cities." Background paper by Alfred Balk in Twentieth Century Fund Task Force Report for a National News Council, A Free and Responsive Press 18 (1973). Footnote 13, 418 U.S. at 249.

space that could be devoted to other material the newspaper may have preferred to print. . . .

Faced with the penalties that would accrue to any newspaper that published news or commentary arguably within the reach of the right of-access statute, editors might well conclude that the safe course is to avoid controversy. . . .

Even if a newspaper would face no additional costs to comply with a compulsory access law and would not be forced to forego publication of news or opinion by the inclusion of a reply, the Florida statute fails to clear the barriers of the First Amendment because of its intrusion into the function of editors. A newspaper is more than a passive receptacle or conduit for news, comment, and advertising.[132] The choice of material to go into a newspaper, and the decisions made as to limitations on the size and content of the paper, and treatment of public issues and public officials — whether fair or unfair — constitute the exercise of editorial control and judgment. It has yet to be demonstrated how governmental regulation of this crucial process can be exercised consistent with First Amendment guarantees of a free press as they have evolved to this time. Accordingly, the [Florida statute is held unconstitutional.]

Questions

The Court in *Tornillo* did not mention *Red Lion*. Can the two cases be distinguished? [133]

c. The Fairness Doctrine and Advertising

Columbia Broadcasting Systems, Inc. v. Democratic National Committee

412 U.S. 94 (1973)

Mr. Chief Justice BURGER delivered the opinion of the Court.

[The Democratic National Committee (DNC) and the Business Executives Movement for Vietnam Peace (BEM) asked the FCC to require a television station to accept paid political advertising, including advertisements attacking the war in Vietnam. The Commission held that as long as the stations presented full and fair coverage of the questions involved, they did not have to accept the ads. The Court

132. "[L]iberty of the press is in peril as soon as the government tries to compel what is to go into a newspaper. A journal does not merely paint observed facts the way a cow is photographed through a plateglass window. As soon as the facts are set in their context, you have interpretation and you have selection, and editorial selection opens the way to editorial suppression. Then how can the state force abstention from discrimination in the news without dictating selection?" 2 Z. Chafee, Government and Mass Communications 633 (1947).

133. See Note, Reconciling *Red Lion* and *Tornillo*: A Consistent Theory of Media Regulation, 28 Stan. L. Rev. 563 (1976).

of Appeals reversed the Commission on the ground that the broadcaster's policy of refusing editorial advertising violated the First Amendment. A divided Supreme Court reversed the Court of Appeals. Three members (Burger, Stewart, Rehnquist) held that the First Amendment did not apply to broadcasters because their action, in refusing advertisement, was not "governmental action." Five members (Burger, White, Blackmun, Powell, and Rehnquist) held that even if "governmental action" is involved, the First Amendment does not require the broadcasters to accept the ads. Justice Douglas concurred, arguing that the First Amendment treats broadcasters and newspapers alike. Justices Brennan and Marshall dissented. Chief Justice Burger wrote, for the Court, that the Commission acted reasonably when it decided in its discretion not to require stations to accept political advertising:]

The Commission was justified in concluding that the public interest in providing access to the marketplace of "ideas and experiences" would scarcely be served by [requiring the acceptance of advertising — a system that would be] . . . heavily weighted in favor of the financially affluent, or those with access to wealth. . . .

[Even if advertising time were allocated on a first-come, first-served basis,] the views of the affluent could well prevail over those of others, since they would have it within their power to purchase time more frequently. Moreover, . . . the time allotted for editorial advertising could be monopolized by those of one political persuasion. . . .

If the Fairness Doctrine were applied to editorial advertising, . . . [there could] be a further erosion of the journalistic discretion of broadcasters in the coverage of public issues, and a transfer of control over the treatment of public issues from the licensees who are accountable for broadcast performance to private individuals who are not . . . [for a] broadcaster would be largely precluded from rejecting editorial advertisements that dealt with matters trivial or insignificant or already fairly covered by the broadcaster. . . .

Nor can we accept the Court of Appeals' view that every potential speaker is "the best judge" of what the listening public ought to hear or indeed the best judge of the merits of his or her views. All journalistic tradition and experience is to the contrary. For better or worse, editing is what editors are for; and editing is selection and choice of material. That editors — newspaper or broadcast — can and do abuse this power is beyond doubt, but that is no reason to deny the discretion Congress provided. Calculated risks of abuse are taken in order to preserve higher values. . . .

To agree that debate on public issues should be "robust, and wide-open" does not mean that we should exchange "public trustee" broadcasting, with all its limitations, for a system of self-appointed editorial commentators. . . .

[The Court of Appeals would give political advertisers a "right of access" defined by "reasonable regulations" designed to prevent domination by a few groups or a few viewpoints, to allocate time fairly and to prevent financial injury to broadcasters. This approach overlooks a] . . . problem of critical importance to broadcast regulation and the First Amendment — the risk of an enlargement of Government control over the content of broadcast discussion of public issues. . . . This risk is inherent in the Court of Appeals' remand requiring regulations and procedures to sort out requests to be heard — a process involving the very editing that licensees now perform as to regular programming. . . .

Under a constitutionally commanded and Government-supervised right-of-access system urged by respondents and mandated by the Court of Appeals, the Commission would be required to oversee far more of the day-to-day operations of broadcasters' conduct, deciding such questions as whether a particular individual or group has had sufficient opportunity to present its viewpoint and whether a particular viewpoint has already been sufficiently aired. Regimenting broadcasters is too radical a therapy for the ailment respondents complain of.

Under the Fairness Doctrine the Commission's responsibility is to judge whether a licensee's overall performance indicates a sustained good-faith effort to meet the public interest in being fully and fairly informed. The Commission's responsibilities under a right-of-access system would tend to draw it into a continuing case-by-case determination of who should be heard and when. Indeed, the likelihood of Government involvement is so great that it has been suggested that the accepted constitutional principles against control of speech content would need to be relaxed with respect to editorial advertisements. To sacrifice First Amendment protections for so speculative a gain is not warranted, and it was well within the Commission's discretion to construe the Act so as to avoid such a result. . . .

Reversed.

Banzhaf v. FCC

405 F.2d 1082 (D.C. Cir. 1968), cert. den. sub nom. *Tobacco Institute v. FCC, 396 U.S. 842 (1969)*

BAZELON, Chief Judge:
In these appeals we affirm a ruling of the Federal Communications Commission requiring radio and television stations which carry cigarette advertising to devote a significant amount of broadcast time to presenting the case against cigarette smoking. . . .

[The Commission, at the request of John Banzhaf,] directed stations which carry cigarette commercials to provide "a significant amount of [free] time for the other viewpoint. . . ." And by way of illustration it suggested they might discharge their responsibilities by presenting "each week . . . a number of the public-service announcements of the American Cancer Society or HEW in this field."

. . . The Commission . . . in a lengthy . . . opinion . . . did make clear that cigarette advertising in general, not any particular commercials, necessarily conveys the controversial view that smoking is a good thing. [T]he Commission stressed again that its ruling was "limited to this product — cigarettes." . . .

Subsequently, . . . the Commission ruled that stations which carry cigarette advertising are under no obligation to provide the cigarette companies free time in which to respond to broadcast claims that smoking endangers health. . . .

II. The Commission Under the Public Interest Standard of the Communication Act

A. The Commission's Authority Over Broadcast Content in General

[The court first noted, citing National Broadcasting Co. v. United States, 319 U.S. 190 (1943), that the Commission has some power to regulate program content.] [N]either courts nor Commission have thought it had to make its decisions among competing applicants blindfolded to the content of their programs. Both the old Radio Commission and the FCC have likewise refused to renew licenses on the basis of past programming not in the public interest, and this court affirmed such a refusal as long ago as 1931. If agency power to designate programming "not in the public interest" is a slippery slope, the Commission and the courts started down it too long ago to go back to the top now unless Congress or the Constitution sends them. But Congress has apparently specifically endorsed this understanding of the public interest.[134] And whatever the limits imposed by the First Amendment, we do not think it requires eradicating every trace of a programming component from the public interest standard. . . .

[I]n applying the public interest standard to programming, the Commission walks a tightrope between saying too much and saying too little. In most areas it has resolved this dilemma by imposing only general affirmative duties — e.g., to strike a balance between the various interests of the community, or to provide a reasonable amount of time for the presentation of programs devoted to the discussion of public issues. The licensee has broad discretion in giving specific content to these duties, and on application for renewal of a license it is understood the Commission will focus on his overall performance and good faith rather than on specific errors it may find him to have made. In practice, the Commission rarely denies licenses for breaches of these duties. Given its long-established authority to consider program content, this general approach probably minimizes the dangers of censorship or pervasive supervision.

In other areas, however, the Commission has on occasion imposed more specific duties or found specific programs or advertisements to be contrary to the public interest. Such rulings must be closely scrutinized lest they carry the Commission too far in the direction of the forbidden censorship. But particularity is not in itself a vice; indeed, in some circumstances it may serve to limit an otherwise impermissibly broad intrusion upon a licensee's individual responsibility for programming. . . .

The danger cigarettes may pose to health is, among others, a danger to life itself. . . . Moreover, the danger, though not established beyond all doubt, is documented by a compelling cumulation of statistical evidence. . . .

In these circumstances, the Commission could reasonably determine that news broadcasts, private and governmental educational programs, the information pro-

---

134. Ed. note: Justice Bazelon points to the "equal time for candidates to public office" statute, 47 U.S.C. §315, passed in 1964, as evidence of congressional acquiescence to the FCC's program content regulation.

vided by other media, and the prescribed warnings on each cigarette pack, inadequately inform the public of the extent to which its life and health are most probably in jeopardy. . . .

Thus, as a public health measure addressed to a unique danger authenticated by official and congressional action, the cigarette ruling is not invalid on account of its unusual particularity. It is in fact the product singled out for special treatment which justifies the action taken. In view of the potentially grave consequences of a decision to continue — or above all to start — smoking, we think it was not an abuse of discretion for the Commission to attempt to insure not only that the negative view be heard, but that it be heard repeatedly. . . .

III. THE FIRST AMENDMENT

Intervenors NBC, et al. argue cogently that the public interest standard cannot constitutionally now include any component of program content. They say the First Amendment obviously would not tolerate administrative supervision of the material published by the newspaper press. The radio press was initially treated differently only because (1) peculiar technical factors require a policeman to prevent interference between different stations, and (2) the then available broadcasting channels were so limited in number that the Commission could hardly ignore all considerations of the nature and quality of programming in choosing among applicants. The first reason does not justify the supervision of content, they say, and the second, if ever sufficient, is an anachronism now that the available channels often outnumber the applicants and the broadcasting stations serving most areas far outnumber the newspapers. Accordingly, in their view the First Amendment now limits the Commission's licensing discretion to technological considerations; the content of broadcasting, like that of the publishing press, must be left entirely to the licensees and ultimately to the market. . . .

. . . Unlike broadcasting, the written press includes a rich variety of outlets for expression and persuasion, including journals, pamphlets, leaflets, and circular letters, which are available to those without technical skills or deep pockets. Moreover, the broadcasting medium may be different in kind from publishing in a way which has particular relevance to the case at hand. Written messages are not communicated unless they are read, and reading requires an affirmative act. Broadcast messages, in contrast, are "in the air." In an age of omnipresent radio, there scarcely breathes a citizen who does not know some part of a leading cigarette jingle by heart. Similarly, an ordinary habitual television watcher can avoid these commercials only by frequently leaving the room, changing the channel, or doing some other such affirmative act. It is difficult to calculate the subliminal impact of this pervasive propaganda, which may be heard even if not listened to, but it may reasonably be thought greater than the impact of the written word. . . .

These considerations are at least sufficient to convince us that . . . the proper approach to the difficult First Amendment issues . . . is to consider them . . . on a case-by-case basis. . . . And whatever the constitutional infirmities of other regulations of programming, we are satisfied that the cigarette ruling does not abridge the

First Amendment freedoms of speech or press. We reach this conclusion in the light of the following considerations:

(1) The cigarette ruling does not ban any speech. . . .

(2) The speech which might conceivably be "chilled" by this ruling barely qualifies as constitutionally protected "speech." . . . It is rather a form of merchandising subject to limitation for public purposes like other business practices. . . . [E]ven if cigarette commercials are protected speech, we think they are at best a negligible "part of any exposition of ideas, and are of . . . slight social value as a step to truth. . . ."

(3) In any event, the danger that even this marginal "speech" will be significantly chilled as a result of the ruling is probably itself marginal. . . . [T]he cigarette manufacturers' interest in selling their product guarantees a continued resourceful effort to reach the public. . . .

(4) Even if some valued speech is inhibited by the ruling, the First Amendment gain is greater than the loss. A primary First Amendment policy has been to foster the widest possible debate and dissemination of information on matters of public importance. . . .

. . . If the fairness doctrine cannot withstand First Amendment scrutiny, the reason is that to insure a balanced presentation of controversial issues may be to insure no presentation, or no vigorous presentation, at all. But where, as here, one party to a debate has a financial clout and a compelling economic interest in the presentation of one side unmatched by its opponent, and where the public stake in the argument is no less than life itself — we think the purpose of rugged debate is served, not hindered, by an attempt to redress the balance.

(5) Finally, not only does the cigarette ruling not repress any information, it serves affirmatively to provide information. . . . We do not think the principle of free speech stands as a barrier to required broadcasting of facts and information vital to an informed decision to smoke or not to smoke.

Affirmed.

Notes: After *Banzhaf*

The FCC hesitated to take advantage of the judicial support provided by the 1968 *Banzhaf* decision. In 1970 it rejected the claim that advertisements for large cars and leaded gasoline presented only one side of the air pollution issue; it allowed the broadcasters to refuse time for counter-ads. The D.C. Circuit reversed the Commission: "When there is undisputed evidence, as there is here, that the hazards to health implicit in air pollution are enlarged and aggravated by such products, then the parallel with cigarette advertising is exact and the relevance of *Banzhaf* inescapable." Friends of the Earth v. FCC, 449 F.2d 1164, 1169 (1971).

The *Friends of the Earth* court, in overriding the Commission's judgment went beyond *Banzhaf* which simply supported that judgment. Still, the Commission reacted cautiously. On remand, the FCC construed *Friends of the Earth* narrowly, holding that NBC could satisfy its fairness obligation through overall program balance, without running spot announcements.[135] The case was settled in 1973 when NBC agreed to participate in a New York City air pollution publicity campaign.[136] At the same time, the Commission held that Chevron's F-310 gasoline commercials fell outside the fairness doctrine, for the ads "made no attempt to glorify conduct or products which endangered public health or contributed to pollution." This time the court upheld the Commission.[137]

The FCC also considered the application of the fairness doctrine to product commercials, that deal more explicitly with public issues. In *National Broadcasting Company*,[138] two environmental groups filed a complaint alleging that Esso commercials showing oil development in Alaska implicitly suggested that Alaskan oil was needed and that its production would not injure the environment. The Commission found that the issues had a "cognizable bearing" on the Alaskan pipeline controversy, but that NBC had presented balancing viewpoints in its general programming. The Commission avoided the question of whether military recruitment commercials required "counterads" by holding that they raised only such "noncontroversial" issues as whether the United States should maintain armed forces.[139] Finally, the FCC reviewed Georgia Power Co.'s ads relating to whether it was entitled to the rate increase it had recently requested. The Commission ruled that the ads "clearly" presented only one side of a controversial issue.[140]

d. Pitofsky's Request for Counterads

(1) The Proposal

In 1971 the Federal Communications Commission began rulemaking hearings aimed at defining the contours of the fairness doctrine. One portion of those hearings concerned the application of the doctrine to television advertising.[141] The Federal Trade Commission submittted a memorandum in support of a set of rules that would explicitly provide for counteradvertising in the following areas:

(a) Product claims that explicitly raise controversial issues of current public importance, such as pollution, nutrition, and automobile safety;

(b) Advertising themes that implicitly raise controversial issues of current public importance, such as ads that encourage poor nutritional habits,

135. 33 F.C.C.2d 648 (1972).
136. 39 F.C.C.2d 564 (1973).
137. Neckritz v. FCC, 502 F.2d 411, 418 (D.C. Cir. 1974).
138. 30 F.C.C.2d 643 (1971).
139. See Green v. FCC, 447 F.2d 323 (D.C. Cir. 1971); San Francisco Women for Peace, 24 F.C.C.2d 156 (1970); Neckritz, 24 F.C.C.2d 175 (1970).
140. Media Access Project, 44 F.C.C.2d 755 (1973).
141. "The Handling of Public Issues under the Fairness Doctrine and the Public Interest Standards of the Communication Act Part III: Access to the Broadcast Media as a Result of Carriage of Product Commercials," 30 F.C.C.2d 26 (1971). For a catalogue of the literature spawned by the entire set of hearings, see Lange, The Role of the Access Doctrine in the Regulation of the Mass Media: A Critical Review and Assessment, 52 N.C.L. Rev. 1, 2 n.5 (1973).

contribute to pollution, or encourage the use of drugs to solve personal problems;

(c) Advertising that rests upon scientific premises currently subject to controversy within the scientific community, such as ads for drugs to cure the common cold or ads stressing the nutritional value of "enriched" foods; counter-advertising, setting forth the controversy, would be more effective than "ad substantiation";

(d) Advertising that is silent about a product's negative characteristics, such as ads that claim a small car is more economical but that do not reveal that it is less safe; ads claiming that life insurance is a wise investment could be balanced by others claiming it is foolish; ads claiming a food is superior could be balanced by others claiming it is not.

The FTC advocated an access policy that would require: (1) limits upon access rights within each category; (2) prohibiting replies to particular, individual ads; (3) reserving blocks of time for "counterads," which could be shorter than initial ads.

The FTC asked the FCC (1) to impose an obligation on licensees to follow these principles; (2) to require access to anyone wishing to advertise at regular rates; (3) to require licensees to set aside a block of time for free counterads. Licensees would have considerable discretion in implementing this program.[142]

Questions

The National Association of Broadcasters has submitted a statement in opposition to the FTC request.

(a) What arguments would you make for the NAB?

(b) The NAB notes that complaints about "fairness doctrine" violations filed with the FCC have increased from 1,632 in 1964 to 41,861 in 1976.[143] What is the relevance of this fact for the FTC proposal?

(c) What other administrative problems do you foresee in the FTC proposal?

(d) Does the proposal raise constitutional problems?

(e) What alternative methods are available to the FCC to obtain fairness in advertising? Is the general fairness doctrine adequate? Should the FCC devote more resources to checking station compliance with it?

(f) The Public Interest Advocates have petitioned the FCC to require a Maine television station to present counter-ads to snowmobile commercials. PIA argues that the commercials raise environmental issues of great public importance, particularly since the Maine legislature is currently considering bills that would ban snowmobiles.[144]

142. See Statement of the Federal Trade Commission, FCC Docket No. 19260 (1971), reprinted in Scanlon, The FTC, the FCC, and the "Counter-Ad" Controversy, 5 Antitrust Law & Econ. Rev. 43, 46-58 (1971).

143. Simmons, The Problem of "Issue" in the Administration of the Fairness Doctrine, 65 Calif. L. Rev. 546, 548 n.8 (1977).

144. See Public Interest Research Group v. FCC. 522 F.2d 1060 (1st Cir. 1975), cert. den., 424 U.S. 965 (1976), noted in 25 Emory L.J. 479 (1976).

PIA asks the FCC to adopt a rule that would require that particular station and any other station showing snowmobile ads to show counterads in a ratio of 30 seconds of counter-ad to every five minutes of snowmobile commercial. Alternatively, PIA requests that stations be required to sell time for counter-ads at "non-discriminatory rates." What results?

(2) The FCC's Decision

The FCC issued its Fairness Report in 1974. The Commission reiterated its basic position that the fairness doctrine established "an affirmative responsibility on the part of broadcast licensees to provide a reasonable amount of time for the presentation over their facilities of program devoted to the discussion and consideration of public issues. . . ." But the primary responsibility for adherence to the fairness doctrine belongs to the individual licensee. The FCC will review licensee judgments "only to determine their reasonableness and good faith under the particular facts and circumstances presented."

The standards which the Commision developed for the application of the fairness doctrine are highly general. Licensees must provide adequate time for the discussion of public issues and a reasonable opportunity for opposing viewpoints on a "controversial issue of public importance." The fairness doctrine would apply to "editorial advertising," such as an advertisement advocating a constitutional amendment to ban abortions. However, advertisements for commercial products or services would be generally considered outside the scope of the fairness doctrine. "[W]e do not believe that the usual product commercial can realistically be said to inform the public on any side of a controversial issue of public importance." Specifically addressing the FTC proposal, the FCC rejected it in toto. The FCC referred to *Banzhaf* as a "serious departure from the doctrine's central purpose . . . to facilitate 'the development of an informed public opinion.' . . . While such an approach may have represented good policy from the standpoint of public health, the precedent is not at all in keeping with the basic purposes of the fairness doctrine." [145]

9. Other Approaches to Advertising Regulation

Consider the following three excerpts, one from an economist, one from the former head of the Antitrust Division of the Justice Department, and one from a former FTC Commissioner:

(1) . . . The really difficult problem is the omission or concealment of relevant information, such as that though it tastes good it will kill you several years before your time, or that it makes no noise because it is designed to use

---

145. Fairness Report, 48 F.C.C.2d 1, 39 Fed. Reg. 26,372 (1974). See generally, Simmons, op. cit. note 143; Simmons, Commercial Advertising and the Fairness Doctrine: The New FCC Policy in Perspective, 75 Colum. L. Rev. 1083 (1975).

considerably more electricity and wears out faster than rival models. Problems of this sort have become especially acute in modern times, in consequence of advancing medical knowledge and the increasing technical complexity of consumer goods, especially those containing machinery, which make it difficult for the consumer even to know what characteristics of a product are important to his welfare. But governmental control or censorship of advertising does not seem likely to be very effective in overcoming this type of deception, because the government cannot readily force advertisers to advertise the defects of their products, and forbidding one type of appeal may simply cause it to be replaced by another of an equally undesirable sort. In the United States, for example, the prohibition of cigarette advertising stressing cancer-risk-reducing qualities has simply led cigarette advertisers to adopt campaigns that insidiously encourage youngsters to smoke. Moreover, government intervention in advertising aimed at preventing misleading appeals ought in fairness to apply also the alternative of personal selling, and this seems an impossible undertaking.[146]

(2) As Professor Johnson and others have suggested, I believe the most promising approach is to introduce new sources of consumer information. It is the extent of uncertainty about the relative merits of competing products which contributes to the large effect of advertising, and this suggests that Government policies be directed toward neutral vehicles of information which tend to deal directly with the uncertainty. We all know that such consumer research organizations as Consumer Reports tend to promote informed consumer judgment, and we can reasonably surmise that reports of that kind, if generally circulated, would significantly limit the ability of advertising to enhance degrees of monopoly power, to say nothing of enabling consumers to spend their dollars more fruitfully. A similar service exists for physicians in the form of the Medical Letter, which is published by a group of physicians, and designed to supply technical information about the therapeutic value of new drugs. In both of these areas, a major difficult is that these publications are produced by non-profit organizations and that they frequently face difficulties in obtaining the funds required for adequate testing and evaluation. One prospective solution would be governmental efforts in this direction, either direct governmental evaluation and publication, or financial support for private organizations of this type. In the case of drugs, for example, there is much to be said for providing government funds to the organization which publishes the Medical Letter so that its publications may be supplied free to all doctors. In addition, the letter could be expanded to insure that doctors receive their first information about a new drug from this source rather than from the lips of a detail man.[147]

(3) One of these alternative approaches seems particularly promising to me, the idea of requiring certain deception-prone industries to affirmatively disclose the major performance characteristics of their products on a systematic,

146. H. Johnson, The Canadian Quandary 283-284.
147. D. F. Turner, Speech before the Federal Bar Ass'n, June 2, 1966.

routine basis. A hypothetical situation will illustrate the principle here. Assume that the widget industry is a large one that sells a highly-advertised, big-ticket product and that, within the industry, different sellers offer a physically identical product at prices that vary by as much as, say, 50% between the "best buy" and the "worst" one. Since consumers do not willingly pay a 50% premium for a product that is physically identical to the lower-priced competing products unless they have been led to believe that it is superior to those other products — that is, unless they have been deceived — it follows that the consumers who are buying this higher-priced product are lacking in certain material facts needed to make a sensible purchase decision here.

An FTC task force of staff attorneys and economists has made a preliminary study[148] of the alternative courses of action we might take in this area. The substance of this report is that the Commission may have been focusing the bulk of its resources on a wrong approach to the problem of deceptive advertising over the years. This staff study suggests that, rather than suing the firms in the major deception-prone industries and ordering them to "cease and desist" making particular false claims, the Commission should adopt the alternative approach of (a) finding out what it is consumers would need to know about these important products in order to make a sensible purchase decision there and (b) requiring each seller in those industries to affirmatively disclose, in his ads and on the product itself, those specific material facts found to be necessary for such sensible buying. Once the consumer has been told just how well the product actually performs in all of the important dimensions, any false claims the seller might thereafter feel the urge to make for it would allegedly be like so much rainwater running off the duck's back.

While the staff seems confident that we have the legal authority to make such disclosures of material facts mandatory,[149] if necessary, it is difficult to believe that any responsible company of the size talked about in this report would actually decline to make these disclosures on a voluntary basis if encouraged to do so by the Commission. The honest seller should have no objection to disclosing how well his product performs in comparison with his competitor's product. Phrased another way, the fellow who drags his feet too long in a cooperative effort of this kind would be telling us something just by his foot-dragging. If a cattleman refuses to let you look too closely at his registration papers, he's not the sort of fellow you should buy a used bull from.[150]

---

148. See Preliminary Staff Study (Precis): Self-Regulation, Product Standardization, Certification, and Seals of Approval, FTC Staff Report (April 20, 1972).

149. This staff report concludes that "there is no inherent legal right for a seller of a product to withhold information about this product that, if known, would affect the consumer's decision to buy that product versus some other seller's product. Put another way, we take as established for the purposes of this analysis that the Federal Trade Commission, acting under the authority of Section 5 of its organic statute, can declare such withholding unlawful and require the disclosure of that information." Ibid., at 31-32.

150. Address by FTC Commissioner Mayo J. Thompson before the American Advertising Federation, Oct. 27, 1973, reprinted in M. Thompson, Advertising and the FTC: The Role of Information in a Free-Enterprise Economy, 6 Antitrust Law & Econ. Rev. 73, 79-81 (1973).

Questions: The Regulation of False Advertising

(a) What do you think of these proposals? How would you go about implementing them?

(b) What is your overall evaluation of the likely effect of the advertising enforcement program of the "new FTC"?

(c) Reconsider the goals of the program. Which is it likely to achieve? What effect will it have on the others?

(d) What are the major obstacles in the program's path?

(e) Reconsider Pitofsky's personal goals. Should he have decided to focus on advertising?

(f) Reconsider Kirkpatrick's goals for the Commission. To what extent will the advertising program help to revitalize the FTC?

9

The Availability and Timing of Judicial Review

Assume that your client wishes to challenge an action of an agency or government official in a court of law. He wishes to argue that the agency is acting unlawfully. How does he get into court? Where does he find a court with jurisdiction? Is the agency action complained of "reviewable"? Does he have "standing"? Is the action "ripe" for review? Has he properly "exhausted his administrative remedies"?

This section will deal with these questions, exploring the major doctrines of administrative law that govern whether and when a court can consider whether an agency action is unlawful.

A. Jurisdiction and the Forms of Action

The first step in going to court is to find the court's jurisdictional authority to consider your claim. This subject, which is usually covered in courses on procedure or federal courts, will be discussed here only briefly.

1. History[1]

Historically, a plaintiff seeking judicial review of an agency action had to find a basis for the court's jurisdiction based upon its power to grant relief. Aside from the court's tort, property, and criminal law jurisdiction, plaintiffs could assert jurisdiction by asking it to issue one of the "great writs."

Professor Jaffe finds the origins of modern judicial review in *Dr. Bonham's Case*.[2] Bonham, a seventeenth century English doctor, was fined and imprisoned by

1. This section draws heavily from (and often paraphrases) Jaffe & Henderson, Judicial Review and the Rule of Law: Historical Origins, 72 Law Q. Rev. 345 (1956). See also, Jaffe, The Right to Judicial Review, 71 Harv. L. Rev. 401 (1958).
2. 8 Co. Rep. 107 (C.P. 1610).

the Board of Censors for practicing medicine in London without a license from the College of Physicians. He brought an action of false imprisonment. Lord Coke asserted the court's power to review the findings of the Board. He held that the Board's power to fine doctors for practicing without a license was void because the Board kept half the fine — it was judging where it had self-interest. Such a procedure was "against common right and reason, repugnant or impossible to be performed; the common law will control it, and adjudge such act to be void. . . ." He added that the Board could imprison for malpractice but Dr. Bonham would be allowed to show the court that he was not "inexpert" (he was a Cambridge graduate), for otherwise he would have no remedy since the Board "are not made judges."

Dr. Bonham's Case illustrates one method a plaintiff still might have of obtaining court review of the legality of an agency action. He might seek review of an agency action in a common law suit for damages or tort. (Obviously, to succeed, he must show a common law tort has been committed.[3]) A court might also review the lawfulness of an agency action in a criminal proceeding (as when a draftee, refusing conscription, claims he was unlawfully classified I-A) or on a writ of habeas corpus.

The action of an agency or government official, however, might injure private persons without technically causing a tort or imprisonment. After *Dr. Bonham's Case* English law saw use of the "great writs" to provide a method for court review of unlawful administrative behavior. The two most important of the writs were certiorari and mandamus.

a.   Certiorari[4]

The writ of certiorari first appears in cases about 1275-1280.[5] Before Coke's time it was not used for purposes of review, but rather primarily to obtain a record (or a case) from one court for use in another. For example:

> . . . to remove a case to the King's Bench before trial or judgment where the King's interest was involved or perhaps occasionally to test the lower court's jurisdiction; to obtain a record from one court for use in a suit in another, as in debt on a record; to obtain execution against property of the defendant situated in another county; to obtain information from non-judicial officials for use in a lawsuit: — whether a certain manor is of the ancient demesne or not; whether there has been issued to a defendant a royal protection, etc. . . . [T]he procedure was [also] used principally for change of venue, on account of the defendant's influence or for some similar reason.

---

3. He may also have to show that the government officer who committed it does not enjoy some special privilege or immunity. See pp. 878-891, infra.
4. Quotations are from Jaffe & Henderson, op. cit. note 1.
5. Prior to Bridlington v. Abbot of Citeaux in 1 Sayles, Select Cases in the King's Bench, Selden Society, vol. 55, at 50 (1279), cited in Jaffe & Henderson, op. cit.

After *Dr. Bonham's Case*, however, judges began to use the writ of certiorari to review decisions of the Sewer Commissions. The Sewer Commissions, which originated in the thirteenth century, were charged with seeing that dikes were built, that fens and marshes were drained, that "vagrant waters" were controlled, and that benefited landlords paid for these works. Originally, they were viewed as "a judicial body" authorized to apply the laws of landowner liability. But by the late fifteenth century they acquired both legislative and judicial functions, making "ordinances and statutes for the safety of the said seacoasts and neighboring parts," as well as collecting money from landlords for the building and repairing of dikes, ditches, and walls.

By the mid-fifteenth century, the sewer commissioners, who included many large landowners, began to undertake huge public works projects.

[They] began to think of draining the fens and thus recovering for agriculture large tracts of land. The most dramatic of these projects was the Great Level, the fen country around Cambridge and Ely. The Privy Council from 1600-1637 took an interest in the project. The Council supported the large owners, chief of whom was the Earl of Bedford, who in return for generous grants of the reclaimed lands organised the project. The fens were the basis of a peculiar economy. They yielded fodder, reeds for thatch, fish and fowl, livelihood and sport. A long struggle ensued . . . [and, according to one early "environmentalist" the songbirds did complain]:

"Behold the great design, which they do not determine,
Will make our bodies pine, a prey to crows and vermin:
For they do mean all fens to drain, and waters overmaster,
All will be dry, and we must die, lest Essex calves want pasture."

Bedford had to be assured that the commissioners would assist him "to suppress riots, insolencies and disturbances."

No custom or law of England made clear who was to pay for these projects. The Commissioners exercised discretion, and in 1599 the courts began to review the lawfulness of their decisions.[6] In 1616 the King's Council and Bacon, the Attorney General, passed an order which prohibited the judiciary from interfering with the Commissioners; the King's Council and its special "prerogative courts" would do that work instead. But in 1641 the prerogative courts were abolished. Then, starting in 1643,[7] the judges of the King's Bench used the writ of certiorari to review the sewer commissioners' decisions. After 1647 the writ was used to review orders of sessions;[8] in 1673, to review orders of a mayor taxing foreign merchants;[9]

6. In *Rooke's Case*, 5 Co. Rep. 99b (C.P. 1599), the court held that the Commission erred in limiting assessments for river bank repair to property located on the river. The action was one in replevin — for return of property seized by the Commissioners.
7. Commins v. Massam, March 196, as quoted in Jaffe & Henderson, 72 Law Q. Rev. at 355-356 (1956).
8. Anonymous (1647) Style 14.
9. 2 Lev. 86; 3 Keb. 154; (1673) Freeman 99.

and by 1700, to review the fining (by the censors of the College of Physicians) of Dr. Groenvelt for "administering insalubres pillulas et noxia medicamenta." Groenvelt v. Burwell (1700) 1 Ld. Raym. 454, 1 Salk. 144. Lord Chief Justice Holt wrote that Groenvelt had a remedy in certiorari:

> That a certiorari lies, for no court can be intended exempt from the superintendency of the king in this court of B. R. (Banco Regis). It is a consequence of every inferior jurisdiction of record that their proceedings be removable into this court, to inspect the record and see whether they keep themselves within the limits of their jurisdictions. . . .

In the same year in R. v. Glamorganshire a writ of certiorari was issued to the justices of peace concerning a levy to repair Cardiffe bridge. ". . . [T]his court will examine the proceedings of all jurisdictions erected by act of Parliament." In another report of the case Holt says "wherever any new jurisdiction is erected, be it by private or public act of Parliament, they are subject to the inspections of this court by writ of error, or by certiorari and mandamus." [10]

When Lord Holt says "jurisdiction," he is not thinking of courts alone, for the word "retained a good deal of the breadth which it had in the Middle Ages. . . .[I]n Holt's view all agencies empowered to affect property rights are 'courts.' It is immaterial that the statute does not give authority to the court to issue certiorari; it is 'by the *common law* that this court will examine if other courts exceed their jurisdictions.' " [11] And, the notion of "exceeding jurisdiction" came close to what we mean by "abuse of discretion." [12]

In nineteenth century America, judges used certiorari to review administrative action, in the absence of statutes providing for review. The reviewing court would call upon the agency to "certify" the record involved. And in accord with the practice of the King's Bench, certiorari was not available if the agency action challenged by the litigant had not been exclusively on the basis of a record. (This limitation is conventionally expressed through the rule that only "quasi-judicial" and not "legislative" action is reviewable on certiorari.)

Congress has never bestowed upon the federal district courts the power to issue writs of certiorari, and, since the end of the nineteenth century, certiorari has not been used in the federal courts to obtain review of administrative action. In Degge v. Hitchcock, 229 U.S. 162 (1913), the Supreme Court held that certiorari ran only "from court to court," not from court to agency. Certiorari is still extensively used in the state courts; each jurisdiction subjects its use to myriad statutory and judge-made limitations.[13]

10. 1 Salk. 146. It was also argued in this case that the writ did not go to the Justices of the Peace in Wales, but Holt replied that the writ went to "any jurisdiction."

11. Jaffe, The Right to Judicial Review, 71 Harv. L. Rev. 401, 415, 417 (1958).

12. "We puzzle foreigners by our lax use of the word 'jurisdiction.' . . . Whatever the justice has had to do has become the exercise of a jurisdiction; whether he was refusing a licence or sentencing a thief, this was an exercise of jurisdiction, an application of the law to a particular case." Maitland, "The Shallows and Silences of Real Life," in 1 The Collected Papers 467, 478 (1911).

13. See 2 F. Cooper, State Administrative Law 644 (1965).

b. Mandamus

Mandamus issues to compel an officer to perform a duty that the law requires.
Jaffe and Henderson write:

[The origin of mandamus] is something of a mystery. For about ten years
before *James Bagg's Case* [(1615) 11 Co. Rep. 94] the Court of King's
Bench had been granting judgments by which plaintiffs who had been unjustly removed from municipal office were restored to it, but the origin of
this rather surprising activity is not at all clear. From this meagre beginning
Coke conceived the notion of a sweeping jurisdiction over all errors judicial
and extra-judicial[;] James Bagg, a chief Burgess of Plymouth, was removed by
his fellow burgesses. The King's Bench ordered them to show cause for the
removal. Their return to the writ told of a devilishly persistent campaign by
Bagg to impair the authority of a whole succession of Lord Mayors by a calculated plan of vilification and expression of obscene contempt. . . . Coke adjudged the return insufficient and ordered Bagg reinstated. Bagg's conduct,
however reprehensible, did not warrant the loss of his "freehold" of office.
[He then made the] following massive assertion of jurisdiction:
  "And in this case it was resolved, that to this Court of King's Bench belongs authority, not only to correct errors in judicial proceedings, but other
errors and misdemeanors extra-judicial, tending to the breach of peace, or
oppression of subjects, or to the raising of faction, controversy, debate or any
manner of misgovernment; so that no wrong or injury, neither private nor
public, can be done, but that it shall be here reformed or punished by due
course of law." [(1615) 11 Co. Rep. 98]
  This asserted jurisdiction bears, perhaps, some resemblance to the jurisdiction of the Council and the prerogative courts. Coke's opinion in *Bagg's
Case* may have been part of his war on the prerogative — its date was 1615 —
and to this end he may have been staking a claim by the common law courts
to the jurisdiction of the Star Chamber or even of the Council itself.
  In spite of Lord Coke's sweeping language, seventeenth-century lawyers
were very cautious in extending the doctrine of *Bagg's Case* beyond its narrow-
est holding. For fifty years after that case much energy of counsel was spent on
a search for authority for it, (which was on the whole fruitless). Almost all
the cases in this period deal with restoration to office. Very gradually the new
remedy was extended to other fact situations; it issued in 1649 to the prerogative courts, requiring them to grant administration of a descendant's estate
according to statute [Luskins v. Carver (1649) Style 7]; in 1661 to a town
officer who had been removed, commanding him to deliver the records of his
office to his successor [Case of the Sheriff of Nottingham (1661)]; in 1672
to the Mayor's Court of London, requiring it to give judgment for the relator
when a verdict had gone in his favour [Amherst's Case (1672)]; in 1699 to
certain justices of the peace, to require them to make a rate for the poor
[Anon. (1699)].
  A series of cases in the years 1700-1740 developed the principle that mandamus would not lie where the respondent's function was "judicial" but only
where it was "ministerial." . . . Lord Mansfield characterised mandamus with
something of Coke's sweep and flourish. "It was introduced," he said, "to

prevent disorder from failure of justice and defect of the police. Therefore, it ought to be used for all occasions where the law has established no specific remedy, and where in justice and good government there ought to be one." [In R. v. Barker (1762)].

. . . Mandamus has, however, developed along more modest lines. Nevertheless, . . . throughout the eighteenth century the older tradition prevailed that administration under law was subject to control by the High Court. It is clear that many of the acts and proceedings of the Justices of the Peace were not "judicial," yet all of them were subject to review on certiorari and mandamus.[14]

Unlike certiorari, the mandamus power has been granted to the federal district courts by statute; it is therefore currently used to check administrative unlawfulness, although its function in the federal system has been superseded in good measure by the general remedy of injunction.[15] Prior to the statute's enactment, the Supreme Court had held that federal courts did *not* possess the mandamus power,[16] except for the District of Columbia courts, which had inherited the common law powers of their Maryland predecessors.[17] Then, in 1962, Congress enacted §1361, which provided that all the federal "district courts shall have original jurisdiction of any action in the nature of mandamus to compel an officer or employee of the United States or agency thereof to perform a duty owed to the plaintiff." [18]

In principle, both mandatory injunctions and mandamus are available to compel "ministerial" acts — where "the duty . . . is so plainly prescribed as to keep from doubt," but not to compel acts which involve "the character of judgment or discretion." [19] This distinction has spawned a host of conflicting and confusing interpretations of the terms "ministerial" and "discretionary," and has sometimes led judges to withhold relief where the action is related to discretionary authority even though the plaintiff claims that the official has exceeded the lawful scope of his discretion.[20] Some leading commentators[21] on the subject have urged the abolition of the distinction, or, at least, a return to the principles enunciated by Chief Justice Taft, who wrote: "Mandamus issues to compel an officer to perform a purely ministerial duty. It cannot be used to compel or control a duty in the discharge of which by law he is given discretion. The duty may be discretionary within limits. He cannot transgress those limits, and if he does so, he may be controlled by injunction or

14. Jaffe & Henderson, op. cit. note 1, 359-361.

15. Mandatory injunctions, however, are sometimes treated as writs of mandamus and hedged with the same restrictions. See Miguel v. McCarl, 291 U.S. 442 (1934), Panama Canal Co. v. Grace Line, Inc.; 356 U.S. 309, 318 (1958).

16. M'Intire v. Woods, 11 U.S. (7 Cranch) 504 (1813).

17. Kendall v. United States ex rel. Stokes, 37 U.S. (12 Pet.) 524 (1838).

18. 28 U.S.C. §1361.

19. Wilbur v. United States, 281 U.S. 206 (1930).

20. See generally, W. Gellhorn and C. Byse, Administrative Law, Cases and Comments at 151-153 (6th ed. 1974); L. Jaffe, Judicial Control of Administrative Action 192-193 (1965); Note, Mandamus in Administrative Actions: Current Approaches, 1973 Duke L. J. 207.

21. Gellhorn & Byse, id. at 152.

mandamus to keep within them." [22] So viewed, mandamus would allow a court to grant affirmative injunctive relief to check an administrative abuse of discretion.

There are other technical limitations upon the use of mandamus. For example, the issuance of mandamus is controlled by equitable principles. Thus a court "may refuse to enforce or protect legal rights, the exercise of which may be prejudicial to the public interest." [23] Furthermore, mandamus will not lie if the relief requested is negative rather than affirmative.[24] Despite these limitations and the confusion surrounding the ministerial/discretionary distinction, mandamus is a useful remedy and federal jurisdiction is sometimes predicated upon the explicit grant of mandamus authority.[25]

The states provide mandamus as a method for review of administrative actions but its use is the subject of "baffling procedural technicalities. . . . Years of historical development, in each state, have accumulated intricate age-encrusted filigrees which vary from state to state." [26]

c. Other Writs

Other historically based writs include the following: *Prohibition* is used to prevent a "judicial" or "quasi-judicial" body from exercising jurisdiction. Its purpose is to avoid an unnecessary hearing, yet it is not issued if review at a later stage would be adequate. *Quo warranto* is used to test an office holder's right to his office. *Habeas corpus* is used to test the lawfulness of confinement. The first two of these are used in state, but rarely in federal, proceedings. The last is, of course, well known and used particularly in federal administrative proceedings involving deportation and other immigration matters.[27]

2. *Present Practice*[28]

With the exception of habeas corpus, the common law writs are not often used today to obtain review of federal [29] administrative actions. In fact, APA §703 makes clear that a claim need not take the form of such a writ.[30] Rather, plaintiffs typically

---

22. Work v. United States ex rel. Rives, 267 U.S. 175, 177 (1925).
23. United States ex rel. Greathouse v. Dern, 289 U.S. 352, 360 (1933).
24. Aguayo v. Richardson, 473 F.2d 1090 (2d Cir. 1973).
25. 28 U.S.C. §1361. See, e.g., Frost v. Weinberger, 515 F.2d 57 (2d Cir. 1975).
26. 2 F. Cooper, State Administrative Law 653-654 (1965).
27. See generally Jaffe, Judicial Control of Administrative Action 192-193 (1965) and sources cited; Gellhorn & Byse, op. cit. note 20, 165-167.
28. For an extensive discussion of the system of judicial remedies, see Jaffe, Judicial Control of Administrative Action, 152-196 (1965).
29. The traditional writs, however, often provide a basis for reviewing actions of state administrative bodies. It is best to consult a treatise on this topic, such as 2 Cooper, State Administrative Law (1965).
30. See Appendix, p. 1087.

base their claims on a specific statute that provides for review of an agency's decision; or, more generally, they plead that they have been (or will be) injured by an unlawful action of an official or agency and seek an injunction, a declaration of illegality, or damages. As Lord Denning observed, "Just as the pick and shovel is no longer suitable for the winning of coal, so also the procedure of mandamus, certiorari, and actions on the case are not suitable for the winning of freedom. . . . They must be replaced by . . . declarations, injunctions and actions for negligence." [31] Some of the general limitations on the use of such actions will be explored in later sections of this chapter. Here we shall focus on the first step for bringing any action in a federal court — finding a statute that provides the court with subject matter jurisdiction.[32]

a. Specific Statutory Review

Judicial review is sometimes mandated by a statutory provision that specifically provides how action of the particular agency is to be reviewed in court. Statutes may prescribe review either by an appellate court or by a district court.[33] Most commonly, specific statuory provisions provide that a party can petition the federal court of appeals to have an order set aside; the appeals court forum is appropriate when there is no need to take further evidence and review may proceed on the record made before the agency. Thus the Communications Act, for example, provides for review of an FCC order in the Court of Appeals for the District of Columbia, provided that a notice of appeal is filed within 30 days.[34] However, if the record reviewed is inadequate and if there is "a genuine issue of material fact" on which an agency hearing was not required, the court of appeals in some instances is authorized by statute to transfer the case to the district court.[35]

Less commonly, specific statutes provide for review of certain agency action in the district courts,[36] where it is easier to develop a record. Moreover, as we shall see below, statutes of general jurisdiction grant that jurisdiction to district courts. Thus, a plaintiff bringing a single case with several different issues may find that statutes

31. Quoted in B. Schwartz & H. W. R. Wade, Legal Control of Government: Administrative Law in Britain and the United States 222 (1972).
32. APA §703 makes clear that plaintiff's action can take the form of a special statutory review proceeding, an application for a traditional writ, or an action for declaratory judgment or injunction. But any such action must be brought "in a court of competent jurisdiction."
33. This and the next paragraph draw heavily upon Bator, Mishkin, Shapiro & Wechsler, Hart & Wechsler's The Federal Courts and the Federal System 1332-1333 (2d ed. 1973). See also Friendly, Federal Jurisdiction: A General View 34-35 (1973); Currie & Goodman, Judicial Review of Federal Administrative Action: Quest for an Optimum Forum, 75 Colum. L. Rev. 1 (1975).
34. 48 Stat. 1093, 47 U.S.C. §402. See also 44 Stat. 449, 455, 29 U.S.C. §160(L) (NLRB); see also 61 Stat. 149, 29 U.S.C. §160(1), 48 Stat. 80, 15 U.S.C. §77i (SEC).
35. See 80 Stat. 621 as amended, 28 U.S.C. §§ 2341-2351; 8 U.S.C. §1105a(b) (deportation); 42 U.S.C. §2239(b) (Nuclear Regulatory Commission). See note 47, p. 500, supra.
36. See, e.g., 49 Stat. 760, 7 U.S.C. §608(c)(15); 7 U.S.C. §1508(c) (Sec'y of Agriculture); 53 Stat. 1360, 1370, 42 U.S.C. §405(g) (old age benefits); 44 Stat. 1424, 1456, 33 U.S.C. §921(d) (harbor worker compensation).

provide for jurisdiction over some aspects of his case in the district court and over others in the court of appeals. In such circumstances, a single court might take jurisdiction over the whole case on a theory akin to pendent jurisdiction.[37]

b. Review under Statutes of General Jurisdiction

If no specific statutory review is provided, a plaintiff may seek review under more general principles of administrative law — principles that allow him to prevent unlawful governmental action or to obtain redress when he has been injured. If he seeks review under such general principles, he still must find a statute that provides a federal court with jurisdiction to hear his claim. His most obvious choice is to proceed under 28 U.S.C. §1331, which grants the district courts jurisdiction over any civil case that "arises under the Constitution, laws, or treaties of the United States." Other statutes are also available, which may provide jurisdiction, a more specific basis for review, or both. For example, he can bring a civil rights action against state officials under 42 U.S.C. §1983; file for habeas corpus under 28 U.S.C. §§ 2241-2255 or mandamus under 28 U.S.C. §1361; bring a tort suit against the government under 28 U.S.C. §1346(b); or proceed under statutes such as 28 U.S.C. §1336, which grants jurisdiction in cases involving the regulation of commerce and restraints of trade; or 28 U.S.C. §1339, which grants jurisdiction over actions relating to the postal service, or under other statutes which grant specialized jurisdiction. Despite the existence of many different jurisdictional statutes, note that, when seeking the most commonly desired forms of relief — an injunction and a declaratory judgement — a plaintiff can almost always find jurisdiction under the general federal question provision (28 U.S.C. §1331). When seeking damages for injuries, a plaintiff may bring a tort suit against the officers who injured him, based on federal question or diversity jurisdiction, or he may sue the government directly, in which case he can find jurisdiction in the Federal Torts Claims Act, 28 U.S.C. §1346(b).

(1) Section 1331 and the $10,000 Limitations

Until recently, plaintiffs seeking to assert jurisdiction under §1331 were faced with the requirement that "the matter in controversy [exceed] the sum or value of $10,000." Plaintiffs were sometimes unable to meet this requirement, particularly when they alleged a deprivation of a constitutional right,[38] for it might be hard to

---

37. For discussion of the issues involved, see Note, Jurisdiction to Review Federal Administrative Action: District Court or Court of Appeals, 88 Harv. L. Rev. 980 (1975). See also Currie & Goodman, Judicial Review of Federal Administrative Action: Quest for the Optimum Forum, 75 Colum. L. Rev. 1 (1975).

38. See Lynch v. Household Finance Corp., 405 U.S. 538 (1972); Wright, Miller & Cooper, 13 Federal Practice and Procedure §3561 (1975).

show that a right to a hearing, for example, was worth $10,000.[39] Thus plaintiffs sought jurisdiction under other statutes and sometimes were forced to argue that the Administrative Procedure Act, in providing that administrative actions were reviewable, itself bestowed jurisdiction on the district courts to review them.[40]

The scope of §1331 was broadened significantly in 1976 when the $10,000 requirement was eliminated in any civil "action brought against the United States, any agency thereof, or any officer or employee thereof in his official capacity." [41] This amendment makes §1331 available as a source of jurisdiction for almost any suit challenging federal agency action. And, as the following case shows, it was a factor in the Supreme Court's determination of whether the APA itself bestowed jurisdiction — an issue more of theoretical interest than practical significance.

Califano v. Sanders

430 U.S. 99 (1977)

Mr. Justice BRENNAN delivered the opinion of the Court.

The questions for decision are (1) whether §10 of the Administrative Procedure Act, 5 U.S.C. §§ 701-706 is an independent grant to district courts of subject-matter jurisdiction to review a decision of the Secretary of Health, Education, and Welfare not to reopen a previously adjudicated claim for social security benefits and (2) if not, whether §205(g) of the Social Security Act[42] authorizes judicial review of the Secretary's decision.

I

Title II of the Social Security Act provides disability benefits for a claimant who demonstrates that he suffers a physical or mental disability within the meaning of the Act. . . . §205(g) of the Act, . . . authorizes federal judicial review of "any final decision of the Secretary made after a hearing to which [the claimant] was a party. . . ."

. . . By regulation, however, the administrative scheme provides for additional consideration of the claim. This is in the form of regulations for reopening of the agency determination within specified time limits. . . . [T]he regulations permit reopening "[a]t any time" for the purpose of correcting clerical errors or errors on the face of relevant evidence. . . .

---

39. See, generally, e.g., Note, A Federal Question Question: Does Priceless Mean Worthless? 14 St. Louis U. L.J. 268 (1969).

40. See, e.g., L. Jaffe, Judicial Control of Administrative Action 165 (1965).

41. 90 Stat. 2721 (1976).

42. Section 205(g) of the Social Security Act, . . . 42 U.S.C. §405(g), provides in part:

"Any individual, after any final decision of the Secretary made after a hearing to which he was a party, irrespective of the amount in controversy, may obtain a review of such decision by a civil action commenced within sixty days after the mailing to him of notice of such decision or within such further time as the Secretary may allow. . . ."

On January 30, 1964, respondent filed his initial claim with the agency for disability payments. . . .

. . . The claim proceeded through the several steps of the administrative procedures. An Administrative Law Judge found that respondent was ineligible for benefits on the ground that he had not demonstrated a relevant disability of sufficient severity. The Appeals Council, in June 1976, sustained this decision, and respondent did not pursue judicial review of the Secretary's final decision under §205(g).

Almost seven years later, on March 5, 1973, respondent filed a second claim alleging the same bases for eligibility. His claim was again processed through administrative channels under the Secretary's regulations. The Administrative Law Judge viewed the new application as barred by res judicata, . . . but also treated the application as requiring the determination "whether the claimant is entitled to have his prior application reopened. . . ." App. 33-34. Concluding that respondent's evidence was "merely rep[e]titio[u]s and cumulative," id., at 35, and finding no errors on the face of the evidence, ibid., the Administrative Law Judge denied reopening and dismissed the claim.

Respondent thereupon filed this action in the District Court for the Northern District of Indiana, challenging the Secretary's decision not to reopen, and resting jurisdiction on §205(g), 42 U.S.C. §405(g). The District Court dismissed the complaint on the ground stated in its unpublished memorandum that "this court is without jurisdiction to consider the subject matter of this suit." . . . The Court of Appeals for the Seventh Circuit reversed. Sanders v. Weinberger, 522 F.2d 1167 (1975). The Court of Appeals agreed that jurisdiction to review a refusal to reopen a claim proceeding on the ground of abuse of discretion was not authorized by the Social Security Act. Id., at 1169. The court held, however, that §205(h)[43] did not limit judicial review to those methods "expressly authorize[d]" by the Social Security Act itself. Therefore, the Court of Appeals concluded that §10 of the Administrative Procedure Act (APA), which "contains an independent grant of subject-matter jurisdiction, without regard to the amount in controversy," afforded the District Court jurisdiction of respondent's complaint. Ibid. We granted certiorari sub nom. Mathews v. Sanders, 426 U.S. 905 (1976). We reverse.

II

A

The Court of Appeals acknowledged that its construction of §10 of the APA as an independent grant of subject-matter jurisdiction is contrary to the conclusion

---

43. Section 205(h) of the Social Security Act, 42 U.S.C. §405(h), provides:

"The findings and decisions of the Secretary after a hearing shall be binding upon all individuals who were parties to such hearing. No findings of fact or decision of the Secretary shall be reviewed by any person, tribunal, or governmental agency except as herein provided. No action against the United States, the Secretary, or any officer or employee thereof shall be brought under section 41 of Title 28 to recover on any claim arising under this subchapter [i.e., no 'federal question' jurisdiction]."

reached by several other Courts of Appeals.... This conflict is understandable. None of the statutory sections codified in §10 is phrased like the usual grant of jurisdiction to proceed in the federal courts. On the other hand, the statute undoubtedly evinces Congress' intention and understanding that judicial review should be widely available to challenge the actions of federal administrative officials. Consequently, courts and commentators[44] have sharply divided over whether the statute should be read to provide a distinct basis of jurisdiction for the review of agency actions. Three decisions of this Court arguably have assumed, with little discussion, that the APA is an independent grant of subject-matter jurisdiction. See Citizens to Preserve Overton Park v. Volpe, 401 U.S. 402, 410 (1971); Abbott Laboratories v. Gardner, 387 U.S. 136, 141 (1967); Rusk v. Cort, 369 U.S. 367, 372 (1962). However, an Act of Congress enacted since our grant of certiorari in this case now persuades us that the better view is that the APA is not to be interpreted as an implied grant of subject-matter jurisdiction to review agency actions.

On October 21, 1976, Congress enacted Pub. L. 94-574, 90 Stat. 2721, which amends 28 U.S.C. §1331(a) to eliminate the requirement of a specified amount in controversy as a prerequisite to the maintenance of "any [§1331] action brought against the United States, any agency thereof, or any officer or 'employee thereof in his official capacity." The obvious effect of this modification, subject only to preclusion-of-review statutes created or retained by Congress, is to confer jurisdiction on federal courts to review agency action, regardless of whether the APA of its own force may serve as a jurisdictional predicate. We conclude that this amendment now largely undercuts the rationale for interpreting the APA as an independent jurisdictional provision....

[T]he argument in favor of APA jurisdiction rests exclusively on the broad policy consideration that, given the shortcomings of federal mandamus jurisdiction, such a construction is warranted by the rational policy of affording federal judicial review of actions by federal officials acting pursuant to federal law, notwithstanding the absence of the requisite jurisdictional amount.... We do not find this argument to be compelling in light of Congress' apparent intention by the 1976 amendment to restructure afresh the scope of federal-question jurisdiction.

In amending §1331, Congress obviously has expressly acted to fill the jurisdictional void created by the pre-existing amount-in-controversy requirement. This new jurisdictional grant was qualified, however, by the retention of §205(h) as preclusive of actions such as this that arise under the Social Security Act. Read together, the expansion of §1331, coupled with the retention of §205(h), apparently expresses Congress' view of the desired contours of federal-question jurisdiction over agency action. A broad reading of the APA in this instance would serve no

44. Compare, e.g., Byse & Fiocca, Section 1361 of the Mandamus and Venue Act of 1962 and "Nonstatutory" Judicial Review of Federal Administrative Action, 81 Harv. L. Rev. 308 (1967); Davis, Administrative Law Treatise §23.02 (Supp. 1976); and Jaffe, Judicial Control of Administrative Action 165 (1965) (all advocating APA jurisdiction); with Cramton, Nonstatutory Review of Federal Administrative Action: The Need for Statutory Reform of Sovereign Immunity, Subject Matter Jurisdiction, and Parties Defendant, 68 Mich. L. Rev. 389 (1970); and Wright, Miller & Cooper, Federal Practice and Procedure: Jurisdiction §3568 (1975) (rejecting APA jurisdiction).

purpose other than to modify Congress' new jurisdictional enactment by overriding its decision to limit §1331 through the preservation of §205(h)....

We thus conclude that the APA does not afford an implied grant of subject-matter jurisdiction permitting federal judicial review of agency action....

Reversed.

(2) Sovereign Immunity

Until recently, a plaintiff seeking an injunction predicated on court review of an agency action had to consider whether his suit was barred by the doctrine of sovereign immunity. That doctrine holds that the United States cannot be sued without its consent.[45] Congress has, of course, consented to many suits, as in the Tucker Act of 1877 allowing suits for breach of contract,[46] and the Federal Torts Claims Act of 1946.[47] Moreover, in most contexts a plaintiff can avoid the doctrine of sovereign immunity by suing an officer or employee of the United States instead of the "United States" itself, and by alleging that the officer was acting contrary to the Constitution or statute.[48] Nonetheless, statutes granting consent have often been interpreted strictly.[49] Suits against officers and employees — particularly those seeking to control the disposition of government property — are sometimes dismissed on the ground that they are in reality suits against the United States[50] or that the United States is an indispensable party.[51] The rules governing when the doctrine of sovereign immunity bars a suit, particularly a suit seeking an injunction, are complex, confusing, and far from consistent.[52] They will not be described here for, in our view, the subject is better treated in a course on the federal courts.[53]

45. See, e.g., Holmes, J., in Kawananakoa v. Polyblank, 205 U.S. 349, 353 (1907); Scholder v. United States, 428 F.2d 1123 (9th Cir. 1970).

46. The Tucker Act broadened the jurisdiction of the Court of Claims to include all claims for money damages "founded upon the Constitution ... or any law ... except for pensions, or upon any regulation ... or upon any contract, express or implied, with the Government ... or for damages ... in cases not sounding in tort, in respect of which claims the party would be entitled to redress against the United States... if the United States were suable." 24 Stat. 505 (1877). These provisions as amended are now contained in 28 U.S.C. §1346 (district courts) and 28 U.S.C. §1491 (Court of Claims).

47. See 28 U.S.C. §1346(b). This act will be discussed briefly at pp. 873-878, infra.

48. See, e.g., United States v. Lee, 106 U.S. 196 (1882).

49. See, e.g., United States v. Sherwood, 312 U.S. 584, 590 (1941). But see, e.g., United States v. Muniz, 374 U.S. 150 (1963).

50. See, e.g., Larson v. Domestic & Foreign Commerce Corp., 337 U.S. 682 (1949). An official cannot raise a defense of sovereign immunity to a claim that he is acting outside his statutory authority or unconstitutionally; cf. Ex Parte Young, 209 U.S. 123, 160 (1908), but he can raise such a defense to certain other claims of unlawfulness (e.g., a suit based on tort or property law and seeking specific performance).

51. See, e.g., Mine Safety Appliances Co. v. Forrestal, 326 U.S. 371 (1945).

52. See, e.g., Report of the Committee on Judicial Review of the Administrative Conference of the United States, 1 Recommendations and Reports of the Administrative Conference 191, 194 (1969); S. Rep. No. 94-996, 94th Cong. 2d Sess. at 7 (1976) (testimony of Prof. Roger Cramton).

53. See, for example, the comprehensive discussion of the subject in Bator, Mishkin, Shapiro & Wechsler, Hart & Wechsler's The Federal Courts and the Federal System 1339-1377 (2d ed. 1973).

In any event, the problem of sovereign immunity has been reduced significantly for those seeking review of agency action by an amendment to APA §702 adopted in 1976. That amendment provides:[54]

An action in a court of the United States seeking relief other than money damages and stating a claim that an agency or an officer or employee thereof acted or failed to act in an official capacity or under color of legal authority shall not be dismissed nor relief therein be denied on the ground that it is against the United States or that the United States is an indispensable party. The United States may be named as a defendant in any such action, and a judgment or decree may be entered against the United States: Provided, that any mandatory or injunctive decree shall specify the Federal officer or officers (by name or by title), and their successors in office, personally responsible for compliance. Nothing herein (1) affects other limitations on judicial review of the power or the duty of the court to dismiss any action or deny relief on any other appropriate legal or equitable ground; or (2) confers authority to grant relief if any other statute that grants consent to suit expressly or impliedly forbids the relief which is sought.

Note that this statute does *not* apply to actions for money damages, where the rules of sovereign immunity still apply, nor does it remove or affect any other doctrines that may limit review. Yet, in suits seeking an injunction or declaratory relief, sovereign immunity should no longer constitute a problem.

(3)   Venue and Service of Process

Before 1962, venue and service of process provisions required many plaintiffs seeking judicial review of government actions to file suit in Washington, D.C. — a forum that many potential plaintiffs found inconvenient and expensive. In 1962, Congress liberalized these requirements, enacting the provisions now embodied in 28 U.S.C. §1391(e). Now, unless some other statute specifically provides to the contrary,[55] when one sues an officer or employee of the United States,[56] an agency, or the United States itself, venue is proper "in any judicial district in which (1) a defendant in the action resides, or (2) the cause of action arose, or (3) any real property involved in the action is situated, or (4) the plaintiff resides if no real property is involved in the action." Moreover, §1391(e) provides that service of process is governed by the Federal Rules of Civil Procedure, except that "the de-

---

54. 90 Stat. 2721 (1976). At the same time Congress amended APA §703 to avoid the dismissal of a suit because the plaintiff made a technical mistake in naming the party defendant. The amendment states: "If no special statutory review proceeding is applicable, the action for judicial review may be brought against the United States, the agency by its official title, or the appropriate officer." 90 Stat. 2721 (1976).

55. Statutes containing specific venue provisions include 7 U.S.C. §608(c)(15) (Sec'y of Agriculture); 15 U.S.C. §45(c) (Federal Trade Commission); 42 U.S.C. §405(g)(HEW); 49 U.S.C. §1486(b)(CAB).

56. Acting in his official capacity.

livery of the summons and complaint to the officer or agency . . . may be made by certified mail beyond the territorial limits of the district in which the action is brought." Thus, venue and service requirements do not often inhibit the bringing of a suit challenging agency action.[57]

(4) Tort Actions as a Method of Review·

Tort actions have long been used as a means to obtain judicial review of the illegality of actions by the government or its officers. The injured plaintiff typically has a choice of suing the government directly (usually on a theory of respondeat superior) or suing the employees who caused the harm. Either choice presents problems.

(a) A *suit against the government.* A suit against the United States is barred by the doctrine of sovereign immunity unless the United States has consented to be sued. The 1976 amendments to the Judicial Code, which effectively abolished that defense in suits seeking injunctions, retained the defense in actions for money damages. Thus, one can sue the United States for tort damages only if a statute specifically consents to the suit.

Since 1946, the United States has consented to many tort claims through the Federal Tort Claims Act.[58] That act, however, constitutes a waiver of immunity that is limited. Its key provision waives sovereign immunity by granting jurisdiction to the district courts:

> The district courts . . . shall have exclusive jurisdiction of civil actions on claims against the states, for money damages . . . for injury or loss of property, or personal injury or death caused by the negligent or wrongful act or omission of any employee of the Government while acting within the scope of his . . . employment, under circumstances where the United States, if a private person, would be liable to the claimant. . . . [28 U.S.C. §1346(b)]

This grant of jurisdiction has numerous exceptions which are contained in 28 U.S.C. §2680. Immunity is not waived where certain specific agencies[59] or

---

57. A 1976 amendment makes it clear that a plaintiff can join private parties to his suit against the government, but if he does so, he must comply with whatever venue requirements would apply to a suit against the private party were the government defendants not involved. 90 Stat. 2721 (1976), 28 U.S.C. §1391. The Supreme Court has recently granted certiorari to decide whether 28 U.S.C. §1391(e) does, or constitutionally may, grant district courts nationwide jurisdiction over officers sued in their individual capacity. Colby v. Driver, 47 U.S.L.W. 3472 (1979).

58. 60 Stat. 842 (1946), now codified in 28 U.S.C. §1346(a) (jurisdiction), §1402(b) (venue), §§ 1504 and 2110 (Court of Claims review), §2401 (limitation period), §2402 (no jury trial), §2411 (interest), §2412 (costs), §§ 2671-2680 (procedure and exceptions).

59. The Act does not apply to claims for damages "caused by the fiscal operations of the treasury" (i), or by activities of the military in wartime (j), the Tennessee Valley Authority (l), the Panama Canal Company (m), or certain federal banks (n).

certain specific programs[60] are involved, or if the tort occurs in a foreign country.[61] Moreover, an action of assault, battery, false imprisonment, false arrest, malicious prosecution or abuse of process can be brought only if *a law enforcement officer* allegedly committed the tort.[62] Further, no action can be brought for "libel, slander, misrepresentation, deceit, or interference with contract rights." [63] The most complex exception however is that contained in §2680(a), which provides that the waiver of sovereign immunity does *not* apply to "[a]ny claim based upon an act or omission of an employee of the Government, exercising due care, in the execution of a statute or regulation, whether or not such statute or regulation be valid, or based upon the exercise or performance or the failure to exercise or perform a discretionary function or duty on the part of a federal agency or an employee of the Government, whether or not the discretion involved be abused."

Dalehite v. United States

346 U.S. 15 (1953)

Mr. Justice REED delivered the opinion of the Court:

[This case arose out of a disastrous explosion of fertilizer on board ship in the Texas City harbor — an explosion which killed 560 people, injured 3,000 and leveled a portion of the city. The fertilizer was being shipped abroad pursuant to a government program. It was manufactured and packaged under a "Plan" drafted by the office of the Field Director of Ammunition Plants in 1946. Plaintiffs charged that it was negligent to use an explosive in fertilizer, that the fertilizer was manufactured in a negligent manner, that it was packaged and shipped negligently, that there should have been warning labels, and that there should have been closer supervision of the loading of the fertilizer on board ship. The District Court found negligence in the manufacture and packaging of the fertilizer. The Court of Appeals reversed its finding of liability.]

Turning to the interpretation of the [Torts Claims] Act, our reasoning as to its applicability to this disaster starts from the accepted jurisprudential principle that no action lies against the United States unless the legislature has authorized it. . . . This statute is another example of the progressive relaxation by legislative enactments of the rigor of the immunity rule. . . . In interpreting the exceptions to the generality of the grant, courts include only those circumstances which are within the words and reasons of the exception. . . .

---

60. The Act does not apply to damages arising out of most postal activities (b), tax or customs activities (c), quarantines (f), regulation of the monetary system (i), or activities under the Trading with the Enemy Act (e).

61. 28 U.S.C. §2680(k).

62. Prior to 1974 the Act excepted these torts completely. In 1974 an amendment was enacted waiving sovereign immunity as to these torts "with regard to acts or omissions of investigative or law enforcement officers." 88 Stat. 50 (1974).

63. 28 U.S.C. §2670(h).

So, our decisions have interpreted the Act to require clear relinquishment of sovereign immunity to give jurisdiction for tort actions. Where jurisdiction was clear, though, we have allowed recovery despite arguable procedural objections.

One only need read §2680 in its entirety to conclude that Congress exercised care to protect the Government from claims, however negligently caused, that affected the governmental functions. . . . [The Act] excepts acts of discretion in the performance of governmental functions or duty "whether or not the discretion involved be abused." . . . The "discretion" protected by the section is not that of the judge — a power to decide within the limits of positive rules of law subject to judicial review. It is the discretion of the executive or the administrator to act according to one's judgment of the best course, a concept of substantial historical ancestry in American law. . . .

It is unnecessary to define, apart from this case, precisely where discretion ends. It is enough to hold, as we do, that the "discretionary function or duty" that cannot form a basis for suit under the Tort Claims Act includes more than the initiation of programs and activities. It also includes determinations made by executives or administrators in establishing plans, specifications or schedules of operations. Where there is room for policy judgment and decision there is discretion. It necessarily follows that acts of subordinates in carrying out the operations of government in accordance with official directions cannot be actionable. If it were not so, the protection of §2680(a) would fail at the time it would be needed, that is, when a subordinate performs or fails to perform a causal step, each action or non-action being directed by the superior, exercising, perhaps abusing, discretion.

. . . That the cabinet-level decision to institute the fertilizer export program was a discretionary act is not seriously disputed. Nor do we think there is any doubt that the need for further experimentation with FGAN [the fertilizer] to determine the possibility of its explosion, under conditions likely to be encountered in shipping, and its combustibility was a matter to be determined by the discretion of those in charge of the production. Obviously, having manufactured and shipped the commodity FGAN for more than three years without even minor accidents, the need for further experimentation was a matter of discretion. . . .

[Justice REED then describes how each element of the manufacturing process followed specifications laid down in the Plan, which was adopted as an exercise of discretion.]

In short, the alleged "negligence" does not subject the Government to liability. The decisions held culpable were all responsibly made at a planning rather than operational level and involved considerations more or less important to the practicability of the Government's fertilizer program. [The decision of the Court of Appeals was sustained.]

Mr. Justice JACKSON, joined by Mr. Justice BLACK and Mr. Justice FRANKFURTER, dissenting.

. . . The Government insists that each act or omission upon which the charge of negligence is predicated — the decisions as to discontinuing the investigation of hazards, bagging at high temperature, use of paper-bagging material, absence of labeling and warning — involved a conscious weighing of expediency against caution and was therefore within the immunity for discretionary acts provided by the Tort Claims Act. It further argues, by way of showing that by such a construction the reservation would not completely swallow the waiver of immunity, that such discretionary decisions are to be distinguished from those made by a truck driver as to the speed at which he will travel so as to keep the latter within the realm of liability.

We do not predicate liability on any decision taken at "Cabinet level" or on any other high-altitude thinking. Of course, it is not a tort for government to govern, and the decision to aid foreign agriculture by making and delivering fertilizer is no actionable wrong. Nor do we find any indication that in these deliberations any decision was made to take a calculated risk of doing what was done, in the way it was done, on the chance that what did happen might not happen. Therefore, we are not deterred by fear that governmental liability in this case would make the discretion of executives and administrators timid and restrained. However, if decisions are being made at Cabinet levels as to the temperature of bagging explosive fertilizers, whether paper is suitable for bagging hot fertilizer, and how the bags should be labeled, perhaps an increased sense of caution and responsibility even at that height would be wholesome. The common sense of this matter is that a policy adopted in the exercise of an immune discretion was carried out carelessly by those in charge of detail. We cannot agree that all the way down the line there is immunity for every balancing of care against cost, of safety against production, of warning against silence. . . .

The Government also relies on the body of law developed in the field of municipal liability for torts which deal with discretionary, as opposed to ministerial, acts. Whatever the substantiality of this dichotomy, the cases which have interpreted it are in hopeless confusion; some have used "discretionary" and "ministerial" interchangeably with "proprietary" and "governmental," while others have rather uncritically borrowed the same terminology from the law of mandamus. But even cases cited by the Government hold that, although the municipality may not be held for its decision to undertake a project, it is liable for negligent execution or upkeep.

We think that the statutory language, the reliable legislative history, and the common-sense basis of the rule regarding municipalities, all point to a useful and proper distinction preserved by the statute other than that urged by the Government. When an official exerts governmental authority in a manner which legally binds one or many, he is acting in a way in which no private person could. Such activities do and are designed to affect, often deleteriously, the affairs of individuals, but courts have long recognized the public policy that such official shall be controlled solely by the statutory or administrative mandate and not by the added threat of private damage suits. For example, the Attorney General will not be liable for false arrest in circumstances where a private person performing the same act would be liable, and such cases could be multiplied. The official's act might inflict just as great an injury and might be just as wrong as that of the private person, but the official is not answerable. The exception clause of the Tort Claims

Act protects the public treasury where the common law would protect the purse of the acting public official.

But many acts of government officials deal only with the housekeeping side of federal activities. The Government, as landowner, as manufacturer, as shipper, as warehouseman, as shipowner and operator, is carrying on activities indistinguishable from those performed by private persons. In this area, there is no good reason to stretch the legislative text to immunize the Government or its officers from responsibility for their acts, if done without appropriate care for the safety of others. Many official decisions even in this area may involve a nice balancing of various considerations, but this is the same kind of balancing which citizens do at their peril and we think it is not within the exception of the statute.

The Government's negligence here was not in policy decisions of a regulatory or governmental nature, but involved actions akin to those of a private manufacturer, contractor, or shipper. Reading the discretionary exception as we do, in a way both workable and faithful to legislative intent, we would hold that the Government was liable under these circumstances. Surely a statute so long debated was meant to embrace more than traffic accidents. If not, the ancient and discredited doctrine that "The King can do no wrong" has not been uprooted; it has merely been amended to read, "The King can do only little wrongs."

Notes and Questions

The Supreme Court has vacillated between broad and narrow interpretations of the Tort Claims Act's exceptions. In Rayonier, Inc. v. United States, 352 U.S. 315 (1957), for example, the Court allowed a claim charging the Forest Service with negligence in fighting fires; though in *Dalehite* (in a portion of the opinion not reproduced here) the Court refused to allow a rather similar claim against Coast Guard firefighters. Moreover, lower courts have tended to interpret the "discretion" exception more narrowly to allow recovery based on acts of lower echelon officials.[64]

Do you believe that *Dalehite* was correctly decided? How would you decide the following cases:

(1) Plaintiff claims that its ship ran aground because the Coast Guard negligently maintained a beacon light. The Government argues that maintaining a lighthouse is a peculiarly governmental function and hence the government could not be liable "as if a private person." [65]

(2) The plaintiff was injured by a mentally ill patient whom, he alleges, government doctors negligently released from confinement.[66]

(3) Plaintiff suffered damage to his North Carolina property from sonic booms caused by military aircraft. He sues the United States, arguing that North

---

64. See, e.g., Duncan v. United States, 355 F. Supp. 1167 (D.D.C. 1973); Griffin v. United States, 351 F. Supp. 10 (E.D. Pa. 1972).
65. See Indian Towing Co. v. United States, 350 U.S. 61 (1955).
66. See Fahey v. United States, 153 F.2d 878 (S.D.N.Y. 1957).

Carolina tort law allows recovery based on principles of strict liability in such circumstances.[67]

The potential for unfair results implicit in the Tort Claims Act's exceptions is mitigated by the fact that administrators have authority to settle claims informally,[68] and Congress often enacts private bills granting compensation. The most striking movement towards allowing recovery, however, has taken place among the states. Since the early 1960s many of the states have partially or completely abolished the doctrine of sovereign immunity in tort cases, often by judicial decision. The leading case is Muskopf v. Corning Hospital District, 55 Cal. 2d 211, 359 P.2d 457 (1961), in which the California Supreme Court disavowed the doctrine of immunity from tort liability, describing it as an "anachronism" which "must be discarded."

(b) *Tort suits against government officers.* A plaintiff barred by sovereign immunity from suing the government for damages might consider suing its officers or employees instead. Under traditional common law principles, those employees would have been exposed to liability to the same extent as their counterparts in the private sector, if not more so. Indeed, in a famous tort action to recover damages for a horse that a health inspector had destroyed, Justice Holmes held that the inspector was liable unless the horse was *actually* diseased. The health inspector's reasonable belief that the horse was sick was no defense if erroneous, for the statute allowed him to destroy only horses that were *actually* sick, not those he believed so to be.[69]

This tough line of authority was not applied, however, to judges, who enjoyed an absolute immunity from tort actions unless there was "clear absence of all jurisdiction over the subject-matter." Bradley v. Fisher, 80 U.S. (13 Wall.) 335 (1871).[70] This immunity was needed, according to the Supreme Court, for the judge must be "free to act upon his own convictions, without apprehension of personal consequences to himself." [71] This principle was gradually extended to provide immunity to certain executive branch officials, such as the Postmaster General,[72] the Secretary of the Interior,[73] and the Attorney General: thus, in

67. See Laird v. Nelms, 406 U.S. 797 (1972).

68. See 80 Stat. 306, 308 (1966), 28 U.S.C. §§ 2672, 2675. The agency may have to pay for settled claims out of its own budget however, while a litigated judgment may be paid from a separate appropriation.

69. Miller v. Horton, 152 Mass. 540, 26 N.E. 100 (1891). For a more recent case with this point of view, see Belt v. Rither, 385 Mich. 402, 189 N.W.2d 221 (1971).

70. Nor was it applied to legislators, see U.S. Constitution Art. I, sec. 6; Doe v. McMillan, 412 U.S. 306 (1973).

71. See the discussion of the basis for immunity in Jennings, Tort Liability of Administrative Officers, 21 Minn. L. Rev. 263, 271-272 (1937).

72. Kendall v. Stokes, 44 U.S. (3 How.) 87 (1845). The Court held that the Postmaster General could not be sued for wrongful failure to allow plaintiff's claim for money damages even if he had acted out of malice. The Court stated that a "public officer is not liable to an action if he falls into error in a case where the act to be done is not merely a ministerial one but is one in relation to which it is his duty to exercise judgment and discretion; even though an individual may suffer by his mistake." 44 U.S. at 98.

73. Glass v. Ickes, 117 F.2d 273 (D.C. Cir. 1940), *cert. denied,* 311 U.S. 718 (1941).

Gregoire v. Biddle, 177 F.2d 579 (2d Cir. 1949), the Second Circuit considered a suit for damages against the Attorney General and other officials based on plaintiff's claim that the defendant had wrongly detained him as an enemy alien on the pretext that he was German, despite a judicial finding that he was French. The Court of Appeals, in an opinion written by Judge Learned Hand, held that officers of the Department of Justice, in the performance of duties imposed by law, enjoy the same absolute privilege as do judges. The court found that the public interest requires that these officers should speak and act freely and fearlessly in the discharge of their important functions:

> It does indeed go without saying that an official, who is in fact guilty of using his powers to vent his spleen upon others, or for any other personal motive not connected with the public good, should not escape liability for the injuries he may so cause; and, if it were possible in practice to confine such complaints to the guilty, it would be monstrous to deny recovery. The justification for doing so is that it is impossible to know whether the claim is well founded until the case has been tried, and that to submit all officials, the innocent as well as the guilty, to the burden of a trial and to the inevitable danger of its outcome, would dampen the ardor of all but the most resolute, or the most irresponsible, in the unflinching discharge of their duties. Again and again the public interest calls for action which may turn out to be founded on a mistake, in the face of which an official may later find himself hard put to it to satisfy a jury of his good faith. There must indeed be means of punishing public officers who have been truant to their duties; but that is quite another matter from exposing such as have been honestly mistaken to suit by anyone who has suffered from their errors. As is so often the case, the answer must be found in a balance between the evils inevitable in either alternative. In this instance it has been thought in the end better to leave unredressed the wrongs done by dishonest officers than to subject those who try to do their duty to the constant dread of retaliation. Judged as res nova, we should not hesitate to follow the path laid down in the books.
>
> The decisions have, indeed, always imposed as a limitation upon the immunity that the official's act must have been within the scope of his powers; and it can be argued that official powers, since they exist only for the public good, never cover occasions where the public good is not their aim, and hence that to exercise a power dishonestly is necessarily to overstep its bounds. A moment's reflection shows, however, that that cannot be the meaning of the limitation without defeating the whole doctrine. What is meant by saying that the officer must be acting within his power cannot be more than that the occasion must be such as would have justified the act, if he had been using his power for any of the purposes on whose account it was vested in him. For the foregoing reasons it was proper to dismiss the first count.[74]

The principle enunciated by Judge Hand in *Gregoire* was adopted and extended by four Justices of the Supreme Court in the following 1959 case.

74. Gregoire v. Biddle, 177 F.2d 579, 581 (2d Cir. 1949).

Barr v. Matteo

360 U.S. 564 (1959)

[Matteo and Madigan were two officials in the Office of Housing Expediter, an agency about to go out of business. After discovering about $2.6 million in a "terminal leave" fund, which might have been unavailable the following year, they devised a plan to discharge employees, pay them accrued annual leave from the fund, and rehire them as temporary employees until the agency's authority either was renewed or actually expired. After this plan took effect, it was attacked in the Senate as a "raid on the treasury." By that time, Barr was in charge of the office. Although the plan was held lawful by the courts, Barr suspended Matteo and Madigan and issued a press release denouncing them. Matteo and Madigan then sued Barr for defamation, alleging malice. The jury found against Barr. The Court of Appeals rejected Barr's claim of absolute privilege, but held that he had a qualified privilege, which could be defeated by showing he had acted maliciously or without reasonable grounds for believing in the truth of his press release.]

Mr. Justice HARLAN announced the judgment of the Court, and delivered an opinion, in which Mr. Justice FRANKFURTER, Mr. Justice CLARK, and Mr. Justice WHITTAKER join.

We are called upon in this case to weigh in a particular context two considerations of high importance which now and again come into sharp conflict — on the one hand, the protection of the individual citizen against pecuniary damage caused by oppressive or malicious action on the part of officials of the Federal Government; and on the other, the protection of the public interest by shielding responsible governmental officers against the harassment and inevitable hazards of vindictive or ill-founded damage suits brought on account of action taken in the exercise of their official responsibilities.... The law of privilege as a defense by officers of government to civil damage suits for defamation and kindred torts has in large part been of judicial making, although the Constitution itself gives an absolute privilege to members of both Houses of Congress in respect to any speech, debate, vote, report, or action done in session. This Court early held that judges of courts of superior or general authority are absolutely privileged as respects civil suits to recover for actions taken by them in the exercise of their judicial functions, irrespective of the motives with which those acts are alleged to have been performed, Bradley v. Fisher, 13 Wall. 335, and that a like immunity extends to other officers of government whose duties are related to the judicial process. Yaselli v. Goff, 12 F.2d 396, *aff'd per curiam*, 275 U.S. 503, involving a Special Assistant to the Attorney General. Nor has the privilege been confined to officers of the legislative and judicial branches of the Government and executive officers of the kind involved in *Yaselli*. In Spalding v. Vilas, 161 U.S. 483, petitioner brought suit against the Postmaster General, alleging that the latter had maliciously circulated widely among postmasters, past and present, information which he knew to be false and which was intended to deceive the postmasters to the detriment of the plaintiff. This Court sustained a plea by the Postmaster General of absolute privilege, stating that (498-499): "... if [the head of the Executive Department] acts, having authority, his conduct cannot be made the foundation of a suit against him personally for damages." The reasons for the recognition of the privilege have been often stated. It has been thought important that officials of government should be free to exercise their duties unembarrassed by the fear of damage suits in respect of acts done in the course of those duties — suits which would consume time and energies which would otherwise be devoted to governmental service and the threat of which might appreciably inhibit the fearless, vigorous, and effective administration of policies of government. . . .

[Justice HARLAN then quoted from Gregoire v. Biddle, supra.]

We do not think that the principle announced in *Vilas* can properly be restricted to executive officers of cabinet rank, and in fact it never has been so restricted by the lower federal courts. The privilege is not a badge or emolument of exalted office, but an expression of a policy designed to aid in the effective functioning of government. The complexities and magnitude of governmental activity have become so great that there must of necessity be a delegation and redelegation of authority as to many functions, and we cannot say that these functions become less important simply because they are exercised by officers of lower rank in the executive hierarchy.

To be sure, the occasions upon which the acts of the head of an executive department will be protected by the privilege are doubtless far broader than in the case of an officer with less sweeping functions. But that is because the higher the post, the broader the range of responsibilities and duties, and the wider the scope of discretion, it entails. It is not the title of his office but the duties with which the particular officer sought to be made to respond in damages is entrusted — the relation of the act complained of to "matters committed by law to his control or supervision," Spalding v. Vilas, supra, at 498 — which must provide the guide in delineating the scope of the rule which clothes the official acts of the executive officer with immunity from civil defamation suits.

Judged by these standards, we hold that petitioner's plea of absolute privilege in defense of the alleged libel published at his direction must be sustained. . . . [Justice HARLAN went on to state that, although the question was close,] the action here taken was within the outer perimeter of petitioner's line of duty. . . . [This fact] is enough to render the privilege applicable, despite the allegations of malice in the complaint, for as this Court has said of legislative privilege:

> The claim of an unworthy purpose does not destroy the privilege. Legisla-
> tors are immune from deterrents to the uninhibited discharge of their legisla-
> tive duty, not for their private indulgence but for the public good. One must
> not expect uncommon courage even in legislators. The privilege would be of
> little value if they could be subjected to the cost and inconvenience and dis-
> tractions of a trial upon a conclusion of the pleader, or to the hazard of a
> judgment against them based upon a jury's speculation as to motives. Tenney
> v. Brandhove, 341 U.S. 367, 377.

We are told that we should forbear from sanctioning any such rule of absolute privilege lest it open the door to wholesale oppression and abuses on the part of

unscrupulous government officials. It is perhaps enough to say that fears of this sort
have not been realized within the wide area of government where a judicially formulated absolute privilege of broad scope has long existed. . . .

Reversed.

[Mr. Justice BLACK concurred separately. Chief Justice WARREN, and Justices
STEWART, DOUGLAS and BRENNAN dissented. Justice BRENNAN, dissenting, stated, in
part:]

. . . In my view, only a qualified privilege is necessary here. . . . It would protect
the government officer unless it appeared on trial that his communication was (a)
defamatory, (b) untrue, and (c) "malicious." . . .

[Justice BRENNAN went on to ask:] . . . To what extent does fear of litigation
actually inhibit the conduct of officers in carrying out the public business? To what
extent should it? Where does healthy administrative frankness and boldness shade
into bureaucratic tyranny? To what extent is supervision by an administrator's
superiors effective in assuring that there will be little abuse of a freedom from suit?
To what extent can the referral of constituent complaints by Congressmen to the
executive agencies . . . take the place of actions in the courts of law in securing the
injured citizen redress? Can it be assumed . . . that an absolute privilege . . . will not
be subject to severe abuse? Does recent history afford instructive parallels? . . . If the
fears expressed materialized and great inconvenience to the workings of the Government arose out of allowing [a more limited claim of privilege], . . . Congress might
well be disposed to intervene. . . . Pursuant to an act of Congress, the inconvenience
to the . . . defendants in these suits has been alleviated through the participation of
the Department of Justice. . . . Congress might be disposed to intervene further and
pay the judgments rendered against executive officers, or provide for a Tort Claims
Act amendment to encompass such actions, eliminating the officer as a formal party.

Notes

As *Barr* indicates, both state[75] and federal [76] courts had extended the principle
of immunity well beyond judges to cover most executive officials whose actions
involved significant discretion. After *Barr*, the extension of immunity continued.[77]
Suits were dismissed, for example, alleging that Justice Department officials had
wrongly had plaintiffs detained and beaten;[78] that an army doctor had negligently
left surgical sutures in a patient's kidney;[79] even that a paving maintenance supervisor had negligently allowed an asphalt spreader to run over plaintiff's leg.[80] In each
instance the courts found the official's position sufficiently important and the acts

75. See, e.g., McGuire v. Amyx, 317 Mo. 1061, 297 S.W. 968 (1927). See generally
3 Davis, Administrative Law Treatise §26.04 (1958).
76. See, e.g., Jones v. Kennedy, 121 F.2d 40 (D.C. Cir. 1941). See generally 3 Davis,
Administrative Law Treatise §26.04 (1958); Parker, The King Does No Wrong — Liability
for Maladministration, 5 Vand. L. Rev. 167, 174-176 (1952).
77. See, e.g., Howard v. Lyons, 360 U.S. 593 (1959); Heine v. Raus, 339 F.2d 785 (4th
Cir. 1968); Poss v. Lieberman, 299 F.2d 358 (2d Cir.), cert. denied, 370 U.S. 944 (1962).
78. Norton v. McShane, 332 F.2d 855 (5th Cir. 1964), cert. denied, 380 U.S. 981 (1965).
79. Bailey v. Van Buskirk, 345 F.2d 298 (9th Cir. 1965), cert. denied, 383 U.S. 948
(1966).
80. Garner v. Rathburn, 346 F.2d 55 (10th Cir. 1965).

sufficiently related to their duties to warrant application of an absolute privilege in their favor.[81]

At the same time, however, a contrary line of authority was developing in the civil rights area in decisions subjecting state government officials to liability when they infringed on a plaintiff's constitutional rights. The Civil Rights Act of 1871, 42, U.S.C. §1983, provides that "Every person who, under color of any [state law, regulation, or custom] ... subjects ... any ... person ... to the deprivation of any rights, privileges, or immunities secured by the Constitution and laws, shall be liable ... in an action at law ... or other proper proceeding for redress." In Monroe v. Pape, 365 U.S. 167 (1961), the Supreme Court held that plaintiffs could recover damages under the act against policemen who broke into their homes without a warrant, used physical violence against them, and illegally detained them. This case spawned a host of civil rights actions against city and state officials in federal courts.[82] In Pierson v. Ray, 386 U.S. 547 (1967), the Court narrowed the scope of this liability, holding that the traditional absolute immunity of judicial officials applied even in suits under the Civil Rights Act.[83] The Court reaffirmed, however, that police officers enjoyed a far more limited defense: "if the jury found that the officers reasonably believed in good faith that the arrest was constitutional, then a verdict for the officers would follow even though the arrest was in fact unconstitutional." [84]

While the Civil Rights Act provided a tort cause of action *against* state officials, in Bivens v. Six Unknown Named Agents of the Federal Bureau of Narcotics, 403 U.S. 388 (1971), the Supreme Court held that a tort action for injuries caused by violations of the Fourth Amendment by federal officials could be inferred from the amendment itself. It remanded the case to the Court of Appeals to determine whether the federal narcotics officers nonetheless were immune in light of their government position. The Court of Appeals held they were not, stating that federal police officers should enjoy no more than the qualified immunity granted to state police officers under *Pierson*. 456 F.2d 1339, 1347 (2d Cir. 1972).

The Supreme Court recently reviewed the issue of an official's immunity in the following case:

Butz v. Economou

===

434 U.S. 994 (1978)

[Economou, a commodity futures dealer, was charged by Department of Agriculture officials with willfully violating Department financial requirements. He was

81. See generally Gellhorn & Byse, Administrative Law, Cases and Comments, 335-362 (6th ed. 1974); and the collection of cases in 3 Davis, Administrative Law Treatise §§ 26.01, 26.04, 26.05 (1970 Supp.).

82. See, e.g., Egan v. City of Aurora, 365 U.S. 514 (1961), Scheuer v. Rhodes, 416 U.S. 232 (1974).

83. The Act had also been read to preserve the immunity traditionally enjoyed by legislative officials. Tenney v. Brandhove, 341 U.S. 367 (1951). See generally, Note, Limiting the Section 1983 Action in the Wake of Monroe v. Pape, 82 Harv. L. Rev. 1486 (1969).

84. 386 U.S. at 557.

found guilty by the Department's hearing examiner and judicial officer, but this determination was reversed on appeal to the Second Circuit. In the meantime, Economou sued the Secretary of Agriculture, the hearing examiner, the judicial officer, and others for damages. He alleged, among other things, that the Department had proceeded against him because he had publicly criticized it — thus violating his freedom of expression — and it had used unfair procedures, thus depriving him of due process of law.]

    Mr. Justice WHITE delivered the opinion of the Court.

    This case concerns the personal immunity of federal officials in the Executive Branch from claims for damages arising from their violations of citizens' constitutional rights. Respondent filed suit against a number of officials in the Department of Agriculture claiming that they had instituted an investigation and an administrative proceeding against him in retaliation for his criticism of that agency. The District Court dismissed the action on the ground that the individual defendants, as federal officials, were entitled to absolute immunity for all discretionary acts within the scope of their authority. The Court of Appeals reversed, holding that the defendants were entitled only to the qualified immunity available to their counterparts in state government. 535 F.2d 688. . . .

II

    The single submission by the United States on behalf of petitioners is that all of the federal officials sued in this case are absolutely immune from any liability for damages even if in the course of enforcing the relevant statutes they infringed respondent's constitutional rights and even if the violation was knowing and deliberate. Although the position is earnestly and ably presented by the United States, we are quite sure that it is unsound and consequently reject it.

    . . . The Government places principal reliance on Barr v. Matteo, 360 U.S. 564 (1959). . . .

    Barr does not control this case. . . .

    Barr did not . . . purport to depart from the general rule, which long prevailed, that a federal official may not with impunity ignore the limitations which the controlling law has placed on his powers. . . .

    In Spalding v. Vilas, 161 U.S. 483 (1896), on which the Government relies, the principal issue was whether the malicious motive of an officer would render him liable in damages for injury inflicted by his official act that otherwise was within the scope of his authority. The Postmaster General was sued for circulating among the postmasters a notice that assertedly injured the reputation of the plaintiff and interfered with his contractual relationships. The Court first inquired as to the Postmaster's authority to issue the notice. . . . Because the Postmaster in issuing the circular in question "did not exceed his authority, nor pass the line of his dut[ies]," id., at 499, it was irrelevant that he might have acted maliciously.

    Spalding made clear that a malicious intent will not subject a public officer to liability for performing his authorized duties as to which he would otherwise not be subject to damages liability. . . . It did not purport to immunize officials who ignore limitations on their authority imposed by law.... If any inference is to be drawn from *Spalding* in any of these respects, it is that the official would not be excused from liability if he failed to observe obvious statutory or constitutional limitations on his powers or if his conduct was a manifestly erroneous application of the statute.

Insofar as cases in this Court dealing with the immunity or privilege of federal officers are concerned, this is where the matter stood until Barr v. Matteo, 360 U.S. 564 (1959). There, as we have set out above, immunity was granted even though the publication contained a factual error, which was not the case in *Spalding*. The plurality opinion and judgment in *Barr* also appears — although without any discussion of the matter — to have extended absolute immunity to an officer who was authorized to issue press releases, who was assumed to know that the press release he issued was false and who therefore was deliberately misusing his authority. Accepting this extension of immunity with respect to state tort claims, however, we are confident that *Barr* did not purport to protect an official who has not only committed a wrong under local law, but has also violated those fundamental principles of fairness embodied in the Constitution. Whatever level of protection from state interference is appropriate for federal officials executing their duties under federal law, it cannot be doubted that these officials, even when acting pursuant to congressional authorization, are subject to the restraints imposed by the Federal Constitution....

III

... In Scheuer v. Rhodes, [416 U.S. 232 (1974)], the issue was whether "higher officers of the executive branch" of state governments were immune from liability under §1983 for violations of constitutionally protected rights. 416 U.S., at 246. There, the governor of a State, the senior and subordinate officers of the state national guard, and a state university president had been sued on the allegation that they had suppressed a civil disturbance in an unconstitutional manner. We explained that the doctrine of official immunity from §1983 liability, although not constitutionally grounded and essentially a matter of statutory construction, was based on two mutually dependent rationales: "(1) the injustice, particularly in the absence of bad faith, of subjecting to liability an officer who is required, by the legal obligation of his position, to exercise discretion; (2) the danger that the threat of such liability would deter his willingness to execute his office with the decisiveness and the judgment required by the public good." Id., at 240. The opinion also recognized that executive branch officers must often act swiftly and on the basis of factual information supplied by others, constraints which become even more acute in the "atmosphere of confusion, ambiguity and swiftly moving events" created by a civil disturbance. 416 U.S., at 246-247. Although quoting at length from Barr v. Matteo, supra, we did not believe that there was a need for absolute immunity from §1983 liability for these high-ranking state officials. Rather the considerations discussed above indicated that:

in varying scope, a qualified immunity is available to officers of the executive branch of government, the variation being dependent upon the scope of discretion and responsibilities of the office . . . and all the circumstances, coupled with good-faith belief, that affords a basis for qualified immunity of executive officers for acts performed in the course of official conduct. 416 U.S., at 247-248.

Subsequent decisions have applied the *Scheuer* standard in other contexts. . . .

We agree with the perception of these courts that, in the absence of congressional direction to the contrary, there is no basis for according to federal officials a higher degree of immunity from liability when sued for a constitutional infringement as authorized by *Bivens* than is accorded state officials when sued for the identical violation under §1983. . . . Surely, *federal* officials should enjoy no greater zone of protection when they violate *federal* constitutional rules than do *state* officers. . . .

IV

As we have said, the decision in *Bivens*, supra, established that a citizen suffering a compensable injury to a constitutionally protected interest could invoke the general federal question jurisdiction of the district courts to obtain an award of monetary damages against the responsible federal official. As Mr. Justice Harlan, concurring, pointed out, the action for damages recognized in *Bivens* could be a vital means of providing redress for persons whose constitutional rights have been violated. The barrier of sovereign immunity is frequently impenetrable. Injunctive or declaratory relief is useless to a person who has already been injured. "For people in Bivens' shoes, it is damages or nothing." 403 U.S., at 410. . . .

This is not to say that considerations of public policy fail to support a limited immunity for federal executive officials. We consider here, as we did in *Scheuer*, the need to protect officials who are required to exercise their discretion and the related public interest in encouraging the vigorous exercise of official authority. Yet *Scheuer* and other cases have recognized that it is not unfair to hold liable the official who knows or should know he is acting outside the law, and that insisting on an awareness of clearly established constitutional limits will not unduly interfere with the exercise of official judgment. We therefore hold that, in a suit for damages arising from unconstitutional action, federal executive officials exercising discretion are entitled only to the qualified immunity specified in *Scheuer*, subject to those exceptional situations where it is demonstrated that absolute immunity is essential for the conduct of the public business. . . . Federal officials will not be liable for mere mistakes in judgment, whether the mistake is one of fact or one of law. . . . The principle should prove as workable in suits against federal officials as it has in the context of suits against state officials. Insubstantial lawsuits can be quickly terminated by federal courts alert to the possibilities of artful pleading. Unless the complaint states a compensable claim for relief under the Federal Constitution, it should not survive a motion to dismiss. Moreover, the Court recognized in *Scheuer* that damage suits concerning constitutional violations need not proceed to trial, but can be terminated on a properly supported motion for summary judgment based on the defense of immunity.... [A]nd firm application of the Federal Rules of Civil Procedure will ensure that federal officials are not harassed by frivolous lawsuits.

V

Although a qualified immunity from damages liability should be the general rule for executive officials charged with constitutional violations, our decisions recognize that there are some officials whose special functions require a full exemption from liability.

[The Court has granted such a full exemption to judges, Bradley v. Fisher, 80 U.S. (13 Wall.) 335 (1872), federal prosecutors, Yaselli v. Goff, 275 U.S. 503 (1927), and state prosecutors, Imbler v. Pachtman, 424 U.S. 409 (1976).]

The cluster of immunities protecting the various participants in judge-supervised trials stems from the characteristics of the judicial process rather than its location. As the *Bradley* Court suggested, 80 U.S. (13 Wall.), at 348-349, controversies sufficiently intense to erupt in litigation are not easily capped by a judicial decree. The loser in one forum will frequently seek another, charging the participants in the first with unconstitutional animus. See Pierson v. Ray, supra, at 554. Absolute immunity is thus necessary to assure that judges, advocates, and witnesses can perform their respective functions without harassment or intimidation.

At the same time, the safeguards built into the judicial process tend to reduce the need for private damage actions as a means of controlling unconstitutional conduct. The insulation of the judge from political influence, the importance of precedent in resolving controversies, the adversary nature of the process, and the correctability of error on appeal are just a few of the many checks on malicious action by judges. Advocates are restrained not only by their professional obligations, but by the knowledge that their assertions will be contested by their adversaries in open court. Jurors are carefully screened to remove all possibility of bias. Witnesses are, of course, subject to the rigors of cross-examination and the penalty of perjury. Because these features of the judicial process tend to enhance the reliability of information and the impartiality of the decisionmaking process, there is a less pressing need for individual suits to correct constitutional error.

We think that adjudication within a federal administrative agency shares enough of the characteristics of the judicial process that those who participate in such adjudication should also be immune from suits for damages. These conflicts which federal hearing examiners seek to resolve are every bit as fractious as those which come to court.... Moreover, federal administrative law requires that agency adjudication contain many of the same safeguards as are available in the judicial process.... We therefore hold that persons subject to these restraints and performing adjudicatory functions within a federal agency are entitled to absolute immunity from damages liability for their judicial acts. Those who complain of error in such proceedings must seek agency or judicial review.

We also believe that agency officials performing certain functions analogous to those of a prosecutor should be able to claim absolute immunity with respect to such acts. The decision to initiate administrative proceedings against an individual or corporation is very much like the prosecutor's decision to initiate or move forward with a criminal prosecution. . . .

The discretion which executive officials exercise with respect to the initiation of administrative proceedings might be distorted if their immunity from damages arising from that decision was less than complete. . . .

We believe that agency officials must make the decision to move forward with an administrative proceeding free from intimidation or harassment. Because the legal remedies already available to the defendant in such a proceeding provide sufficient checks on agency zeal, we hold that those officials who are responsible for the decision to initiate or continue a proceeding subject to agency adjudication are entitled to absolute immunity from damages liability for their parts in that decision.

We turn finally to the role of an agency attorney in conducting a trial and presenting evidence on the record to the trier of fact. We can see no substantial difference between the function of the agency attorney in presenting evidence in an agency hearing and the function of the prosecutor who brings evidence before a court. . . . If agency attorneys were held personally liable in damages as guarantors of the quality of their evidence, they might hesitate to bring forward some witnesses or documents. . . . Administrative agencies can act in the public interest only if they can adjudicate on the basis of a complete record. We therefore hold that an agency attorney who arranges for the presentation of evidence on the record in the course of an adjudication is absolutely immune from suits based on the introduction of such evidence. . . .

[The case is remanded to the Court of Appeals] with instructions to remand the case to the District Court for further proceedings consistent with this opinion.

Mr. Justice REHNQUIST, with whom THE CHIEF JUSTICE, Mr. Justice STEWART, and Mr. Justice STEVENS join, concurring in part and dissenting in part. . . .

. . . [It is illogical and impractical to distinguish between] constitutional and common law claims for purposes of immunity. . . . [I]f we allow a mere allegation of unconstitutionality, obviously unproven at the time made, to require a Cabinet-level official, charged with the enforcement of the responsibilities to which the complaint pertains, to lay aside his duties and defend such an action on the merits, the defense of official immunity will have been abolished in fact if not in form. The ease with which a constitutional claim may be pleaded in a case such as this, where a violation of statutory or judicial limits on agency action may be readily converted by any legal neophyte into a claim of denial of procedural due process under the Fifth Amendment, will assure that. The fact that the claim fails when put to trial will not prevent the consumption of time, effort, and money on the part of the defendant official in defending his actions on the merits. The result can only be damage to the "interests of the people," *Spalding*, 161 U.S., at 498, which "requires that due protection be accorded to [cabinet officials] in respect to their official acts."

It likewise cannot seriously be argued that an official will be less deterred by the threat of liability for unconstitutional conduct than for activities which might constitute a common-law tort. The fear that inhibits is that of a long, involved lawsuit and a significant money judgment, not the fear of liability for a certain type of claim. Thus, even viewing the question functionally — indeed, *especially* viewing the question functionally — the basis for a distinction between constitutional and common-law torts in this context is open to serious question. Even the logical justification for raising such a novel distinction is far from clear. That the Framers thought some rights sufficiently susceptible of legislative derogation that they should be enshrined in the Constitution does not necessarily indicate that the Framers likewise intended to establish an immutable hierarchy of rights in terms of their importance to individuals. The most heinous common-law tort surely cannot be less important to, or have less of an impact on, the aggrieved individual than a mere technical violation of a constitutional proscription.

... The Court ... suggests in sweeping terms that the cause of action recognized in *Bivens* would be " 'drained of meaning' if federal officials were entitled to absolute immunity for their constitutional transgressions." ... But *Bivens* is a slender reed on which to rely when abrogating official immunity for Cabinet-level officials. In the first place, those officials most susceptible to claims under *Bivens* [police officers] have historically been given only a qualified immunity. . . . In any event, it certainly does not follow that a grant of absolute immunity to the Secretary and Assistant Secretary of Agriculture requires a like grant to federal law enforcement officials. But even more importantly, on the federal side, when Congress thinks redress for grievances is appropriate, it can and generally does waive sovereign immunity, allowing an action directly against the United States. This allows redress for deprivations of rights, while at the same [time] limiting the outside influences which might inhibit an official in the free and considered exercise of his official powers. It likewise allows discipline of officials to take place largely within the confines of the normal governmental process. . . . [And] Congress has expressly waived sovereign immunity for this type of suit. . . .

My biggest concern, however, is not with the illogic or impracticality of today's decision, but rather with the potential for disruption of government that it invites. The steady increase in litigation, much of it directed against governmental officials and virtually all of which could be framed in constitutional terms, cannot escape the notice of even the most casual observer. From 1961 to 1977, the number of cases brought in the federal courts under civil rights statutes increased from 296 to 13,113. See 1977 Annual Report of the Director of the Administrative Office of the United States Courts, Table 11; 1976 id., Table 17. It simply defies logic and common experience to suggest that officials will not have this in the back of their minds when considering what official course to pursue. It likewise strains credulity to suggest that this threat will only inhibit officials from taking action which they should not take in any event. It is the cases in which the grounds for action are doubtful, or in which the actor is timid, which will be affected by today's decision. . . .

Notes

While *Economou* was being argued before the Supreme Court, the D.C. Court of Appeals decided Expeditions Unlimited, Inc. v. Smithsonian Institution, 566 F.2d 289 (D.C. Cir. 1977). The plaintiff, Expeditions Unlimited, brought a libel action against Clifford Evans, the chairman of the Anthropology Department at

the Smithsonian Institution's Museum of Natural History. It was based on a letter
that Evans wrote criticizing plaintiff's abilities in the field of underwater archeolog-
ical exploration. The court held that Evans enjoyed "absolute immunity," not
simply a "qualified privilege."

Judge Leventhal wrote:

> The federal common law rule of absolute immunity of officials sued for
> defamation furthers the goals of effective administration of government in the
> public interest.[85] A qualified immunity would be dependent upon a myriad of
> factors and a particularistic assessment of the facts of each case,[86] leaving an
> official at hazard to anticipate whether or not he is protected. "An absolute
> immunity defeats a suit at the outset, so long as the official's actions were
> within the scope of the immunity. The fate of an official with qualified im-
> munity depends upon circumstances and motivations of his actions, as estab-
> lished by the evidence at trial." Imbler v. Pachtman, 424 U.S. 409, 419
> n.13. . . . Even the need to find the time and money for a defense,[87] would
> have a chilling, if not paralyzing, effect on an official's willingness to speak out,
> in the exercise of his discretion, to further the public interest. . . .

Judge Leventhal added that the §1983 decisions do not overrule *Barr*.

> They rather establish the rule for cases where fundamental, constitutional
> rights are involved, and declare that ordinary rules of official immunity must
> yield when the executive is charged with exercising his special power as a
> government official in a way prohibited by the Constitution. . . .
> The defamation action in the case at bar involves damage to business
> reputation — an interest of no greater weight than the interest in personal
> reputation involved in *Barr*. While damage to reputation is not inconsequen-
> tial, and can, under some circumstances, qualify for procedural protection
> under the due process clause, it is not as basic to a free society as the Fourth
> Amendment right to be free from arbitrary searches and seizure . . . , a right so
> precious that a remedy in damages has been inferred from the Constitution
> itself. [Citing *Bivens*.]

85. The need to determine whether an official is acting within the outer perimeter of
his duties will not defeat the purpose of absolute immunity. For example, on the facts of this
case, the determination of whether Evans was acting within the scope of his employment may
be made on the basis of affidavits from his superiors elucidating his duties and the procedures
usually followed in answering queries from foreign governments. This type of limited inquiry
may typically be dealt with on a motion for summary judgment. Even at trial the issue is for
the court. The official knows the scope of his discretion. The possibility of such an inquiry
is unlikely to deter any official in the vigorous pursuit of his responsibilities.

86. In Scheuer v. Rhodes, 416 U.S. 232, 94 S. Ct. 1683, 40 L. Ed. 2d 90 (1974), which
held that *state* executive officers sued under 42 U.S.C. §1983 were only entitled to a qualified
immunity, the Supreme Court explained that the limited privilege was dependent upon "the
existence of reasonable grounds for belief formed at the time and in light of all the circumstances, coupled with good faith belief. . . ." 416 U.S. at 247-248, 94 S. Ct. at 1692.

87. Although government counsel now often defend even personal actions against federal
officers arising out of their official duties, they are not required to do so. See, e.g., 28 U.S.C.
§517 (1970): "The Solicitor General, or any officer of the Department of Justice, may be sent
by the . . . United States to attend to the interests of the United States in a suit pending in a
court of the United States, or in a court of a State, or to attend to the interest of the United
States."

Judge Leventhal noted that even under §1983, officials exercising judicial or quasi-judicial power[88] and those in the legislative branch[89] enjoy absolute immunity. The Court then remanded for "limited inquiry" whether Evans' letter "was within the outer perimeter of his duties."

Questions

(1) Is *Expeditions Unlimited* consistent with *Economou*? Is it true that even a "legal neophyte" can convert an ordinary tort claim into a constitutionally based claim, thereby changing an "absolute immunity" into a "qualified privilege"? Or, is it still open to the courts to prevent this development through the use of principled distinctions?

(2) What sense does it make to abolish sovereign immunity as a defense in actions seeking injunctions (see pp. 871-872 supra) while maintaining it, at least to a limited extent, in actions against the government for tort damages? Would its elimination in the latter area allow the development of a more rational structure of rules governing damages suits against the government and its officers? [90]

(3) Put yourself in the position of the plaintiffs in these cases and assume your claims are well founded. Which solution to your problems is to be preferred: (a) no recovery, (b) recovery from the responsible officers but not from the United States; (c) recovery from the United States but not from the responsible officers; (d) recovery from either the United States or the officers; (e) relief by private act of Congress; (f) or self-help? [91]

(4) To what extent might post-decision damage actions serve as a functional substitute for requirements that administrators conduct a hearing before deciding a claim or taking other action? Reconsider Ingraham v. Wright, pp. 676-680, supra.

B. Reviewability

Even if an individual has a claim and there is jurisdiction under appropriate statutes, the courts may still decline to review the agency's action. How is that possible?

1. The Presumption of Reviewability

Despite the facility with which the English courts used the prerogative writs to review and to correct improper agency action, the American courts in the nine-

88. See, e.g., Imbler v. Pachtman, 424 U.S. 409 (1976).
89. See, e.g., Doe v. McMillan, 412 U.S. 306 (1973).
90. See Jaffe, Judicial Control of Administrative Action 235 et. seq. (1965).
91. This question is proposed by Bator, Mishkin, Shapiro & Wechsler, Hart and Wechsler's The Federal Courts and the Federal System 1410 (2d ed. 1973).

teenth century took a much narrower view of their power to correct erroneous administrative action. One student of the subject described the basis for review as follows:

> Prior to 1887 the fields of federal administration where review proceedings might have been desirable were few, — mainly customs and internal revenue, the regulation of immigration and navigation, and proprietary functions of the Government such as those relating to public lands, patents, postal service, and pensions and other claims. Congress had no considered policy of court review of administrative action and these fields, with few exceptions, were open only to whatever relief common law and equitable remedies afforded.
>
> Among the remedies at law was an action for damages, for money had and received, or for recovery of property. Practically these were of little importance outside of revenue matters. Moreover, review of administrative orders by certiorari was apparently never attempted during this period. In 1913 when the attempt was first made certiorari was held by the Supreme Court to be unavailable for such purposes. [Degge v. Hitchcock, 229 U.S. 162 (1913)].
>
> The Judiciary Act of 1789 gave the federal courts authority to issue "writs not specially provided for by statute, which may be necessary for the exercise of their respective jurisdictions and agreeable to the principles and usages of law." Among such writs was that of mandamus. This authority, however, was inapplicable to review of administrative orders for it was held to permit use of the writs only as an auxiliary to some suit over which the court had present or prospective jurisdiction original or appellate. The jurisdiction must already exist and could not be conferred by the writ.
>
> Mandamus was, however, available in the courts of the District of Columbia, within whose jurisdiction could be found most of the principal officers of the Government. Also the equitable remedy of injunction was available in all the federal courts including those of the District of Columbia. In most situations these two remedies afforded the only means for judicial consideration of administrative orders but their value was slight. Mandamus would not lie to review an exercise of judgment or discretion by an administrative officer or agency not to perform a function similar to that of a writ of error. Thus it would not lie to correct errors made by administrative officers or agencies in construing the law, much less to correct discretionary action of the type now dealt with as arbitrary or as being without substantial evidence to support it. The desire to avoid possibility of conflict between the courts and executive officers ran strong.
>
> When the remedy of injunction was first employed to review administrative action the Supreme Court held that the doctrine of non-reviewability of administrative discretion was as applicable to the writ of injunction as to the writ of mandamus. [Litchfield v. Richards, 5 U.S. (9 Wall.) 575 (1870)] [92]

An excellent example of the narrow approach towards reviewability is provided by Decatur v. Paulding, 39 U.S. (14 Pet.) 497 (U.S. 1840) — a case in which the widow of the famous naval hero sought a writ of mandamus to compel the Secretary

92. Lee, The Origins of Judicial Control of Federal Executive Action, 36 Geo. L.J. 287, 295-296 (1948).

of the Navy to pay her two pensions — one under a general pension law and the other under a special act of Congress passed for her alone. The Court held the Secretary's decision was "discretionary," not "ministerial," because he had to decide (1) whether to reverse a predecessor's decision on the subject, (2) how half pay should be calculated, and (3) whether there was enough money in the pension fund to satisfy all claims. The Court's attitude is well expressed in its statement that the "interference of the courts with the performance of the ordinary duties of the executive departments of the government, would be productive of nothing but mischief." 14 Pet. at 516.

However, the availability of relief was not always as narrow as *Decatur* and the article excerpt might suggest. Injunctive relief was often available to control administrative action in excess of "jurisdiction," and the concept of "jurisdiction" was often flexible.[93] Over time, a more expansive attitude toward the availability and scope of review began to permeate the courts, as the following case suggests.

American School of Magnetic Healing v. McAnnulty

187 U.S. 94 (1902)

Mr. Justice PECKHAM ... delivered the opinion of the court.

[Plaintiff ran a mail order business based in Nevada. It taught how to use "the faculty of the brain and mind," to cure sickness. It received about 3,000 letters per day containing payments which averaged $1600 per day. The Postmaster General, after a hearing, ordered the Post Office not to deliver plaintiff's mail, but to return it (and all checks) to senders and to mark it "fraudulent" under a statute giving the Postmaster General authority to do this "upon evidence satisfactory to him that any person is engaged in any fraudulent ... scheme for the distribution of money." 28 Stat. 963, 964.]

[T]he questions arising in the case will be limited, (1) to the inquiry as to whether the action of the Postmaster General under the circumstances set forth in the complainants' bill is justified by the statutes; and (2) if not, whether the complainants have any remedy in the courts.

First. As the case arises on demurrer, ... [i]t is, therefore, admitted that the business of the complainants is founded "almost exclusively on the physical and practical proposition that the mind of the human race is largely responsible for its ills, ... and that the human race does possess the innate power, through proper exercise of the faculty of the brain and mind, to largely control and remedy the ills that humanity is heir to." ...

There can be no doubt that the influence of the mind upon the physical condition of the body is very powerful. ... How far these claims are borne out by actual experience may be matter of opinion. Just exactly to what extent the mental condition affects the body, no one can accurately and definitely say. ...

93. See J. Dickinson, Administrative Justice and the Supremacy of Law in the United States 41-49 (1927).

... [T]he claim of complainants ... cannot be proved as a fact to be a fraud ... nor can it properly be said that those who assume to heal bodily ills or infirmities by a resort to this method of cure are guilty of obtaining money under false pretenses, such as are intended in the statutes, which evidently do not assume to deal with mere matters of opinion upon subjects which are not capable of proof as to their falsity.

Unless ... the question may be reduced to one of fact as distinguished from mere opinion, we think these statutes cannot be invoked for the purpose of stopping the delivery of mail matter. ...

That the complainants had a hearing before the Postmaster General ... cannot affect the case, [for we proceed on demurrer on the basis of undisputed facts]. ... From these admitted facts it is obvious that complainants in conducting their business, so far as this record shows, do not violate the laws of Congress. The statutes do not as matter of law cover the facts herein.

Second. Conceding ... the conclusive character of the determination by the Postmaster General of any material and relevant question still of fact ... the question remains as to the power of the court to grant relief where the Postmaster General ... has ordered the detention of mail matter when the statutes have not granted him power so to order. Has Congress entrusted the administration of these statutes wholly to the discretion of the Postmaster General, [so] that his determination is conclusive ... ?

That the conduct of the Post Office is a part of the administrative department of the government is entirely true, but that does not necessarily and always oust the courts of jurisdiction to grant relief to a party aggrieved by any action ... of that department which is unauthorized by statute. ... [I]n case an official violates the law ... the courts generally have jurisdiction to grant relief. ...

The facts, which are here admitted of record, show that the case is not one which by any construction of those facts is covered or provided for by the statutes under which the Postmaster General has assumed to act, and his determination that those admitted facts do authorize his action is a clear mistake of law, ... and the courts, therefore, must have power in a proper proceeding to grant relief. Otherwise, the individual is left to the absolutely uncontrolled and arbitrary action of a public and administrative officer, whose action is unauthorized by any law and is in violation of the rights of the individual. Where the action of such an officer is thus unauthorized he thereby violates the property rights of the person whose letters are withheld.

In our view of these statutes the complainants had the legal right under the general acts of Congress relating to the mails to have their letters delivered at the post office as directed. They had violated no law which Congress passed, and their letters contained checks, drafts, money orders and money itself, all of which were their property as soon as they were deposited in the various post offices for transmission by mail. They allege, and it is not difficult to see that the allegation is true, that, if such action be persisted in, these complainants will be entirely cut off from all mail facilities, and their business will necessarily be greatly injured if not wholly destroyed, such business being, so far as the laws of Congress are concerned, legitimate and lawful. In other words, irreparable injury will be done to these complainants by the mistaken act of the Postmaster General in directing the defendant to retain and refuse to deliver letters addressed to them. The Postmaster General's order being the result of a mistaken view of the law could not operate as a defence to this action on the part of the defendant, though it might justify his obedience thereto until some action of the court. In such a case, as the one before us, there is no adequate remedy at law, the injunction to prohibit the further withholding of the mail from complainants being the only remedy at all adequate to the full relief to which the complainants are entitled. . . .

Judgment reversed.

Notes

In *American School of Magnetic Healing*, the Court proved willing to review a determination of an administrator in an action that essentially seeks an injunction. Contrast that attitude with the Supreme Court's views in the much later case of Perkins v. Lukens Steel Co., 310 U.S. 113 (1940): seven steel producers sought an injunction and a declaratory judgment effectively setting aside action by the Secretary of Labor affecting the minimum wage to be paid their employees. A statute required the companies to pay those who worked on filling their government contracts the prevailing minimum wage in the "locality" where they did the work. The Secretary promptly divided the whole country into six "localities." The companies protested and the Court of Appeals agreed that the Secretary misinterpreted the word "locality." The Supreme Court reversed on the ground that the Secretary's action neither "invaded or threatened" any of the companies' "legal rights." In adding that the government as a purchaser, "enjoys the unrestricted power" to fix contract terms, does the Court imply that a plaintiff must assert a common-law, or a specifically granted statutory, cause of action? In any event the Court quotes *Decatur's* language about too much judicial interference causing "mischief" and adds that its decision rests "upon reasons deeply rooted in the constitutional divisions of authority in our system of government and the impropriety of judicial interpretations of law at the instance of those who show no more than a mere possible injury to the public." 310 U.S. at 132.

Although *Perkins* is the later case, it is the attitude expressed in *McAnnulty* that has prevailed. Professor Jaffe has argued that the courts now grant a "presumption" of reviewability — a presumption that has been codified in the Administrative Procedure Act's §10(a), which states that a "person suffering legal wrong because of agency action, or adversely affected or aggrieved by agency action within the meaning of a relevant statute *is entitled to judicial review thereof*." [94] Indeed in Abbott Laboratories v. Gardner, 387 U.S. 136, 140-141 (1967), the Supreme Court wrote:

> [A] survey of our cases shows that judicial review of a final agency action by an aggrieved person will not be cut off unless there is a persuasive reason to believe that such was the purpose of Congress. . . . [T]he Administrative Proce-

---

94. 5 U.S.C. §702 (Emphasis added). See Jaffe, Judicial Control of Administrative Action 336-359 (1959).

dure Act, which embodies the basic presumption of judicial review to one "suffering legal wrong because of agency action, or adversely affected or aggrieved
by agency action within the meaning of a relevant statute," 5 U.S.C. §702, so
long as no statute precludes such relief or the action is not one committed by
law to agency discretion, 5 U.S.C. §701(a). The Administrative Procedure Act
provides specifically not only for review of "[a]gency action made reviewable
by statute" but also for review of "final agency action for which there is no
other adequate remedy in a court," 5 U.S.C. §704. The legislative material
elucidating that seminal act manifests a congressional intention that it cover
a broad spectrum of administrative actions, and this Court has echoed that
theme by noting that the Administrative Procedure Act's "generous review
provisions" must be given a "hospitable" interpretation. . . .

As *Abbott Laboratories* notes, however, the general rule — reviewability —
has two exemptions which are codified in the APA: the APA's review provisions
do *not* apply "to the extent that (1) statutes preclude judicial review, or (2) agency
action is committed to agency discretion by law." 5 U.S.C. §701.

We shall now turn to those two exceptions. In considering whether they
will deprive your client of judicial review, it will help to keep the following point
in mind: You are seeking review of an order or an action or an inaction of an
agency, which you allege is unlawful. But whether you obtain review depends very
much upon *what type of claim* you are making. What is the *basis* of your allegation of unlawfulness? That is to say, are you claiming that the agency (1) made
an erroneous finding of fact; (2) wrongly applied or violated its own rules and
regulations; (3) wrongly applied the statute to a particular set of facts; (4) wrongly
interpreted the statute itself; (5) acted unconstitutionally? The *sort* of claim you
are making will have much to do with whether the court reviews your case. Court
review of an action does not exist "in the air"; rather, court review consists of
passing upon the merits of a specific claim that relates to an agency's action.

2. Preclusion by Statute

APA §701(a)(1) states that the APA's judicial review provisions do not apply
"to the extent that . . . statutes preclude review. . . ." As this language suggests,
judicial review may be unavailable because some statute, other than the APA,
provides that review is not to be had. In interpreting language in statutes that seek
to limit review, however, courts start with a "presumption of reviewability," [95]
which means that they will interpret such statutes narrowly.[96] Thus, courts frequently interpret language that, on its face, seems to preclude review not to do so.[97]
As we shall see, the factors considered in regard to the question of commitment to
agency discretion under §701(a)(2) also play an important role in interpreting
these statutes.

95. See also Barlow v. Collins, 397 U.S. 159, 166 (1970).
96. See Abbott Laboratories v. Gardner, 387 U.S. 136, 140 (1967).
97. See L. Jaffe, Judicial Control of Administrative Action 336 (1965).

a. Legislative Silence

Legislative silence about the availability of review is normally not construed to show an intent to preclude review.[98] As Professor Jaffe has pointed out, judicial review "is a basic right; it is a traditional power and the intention to exclude it must be made specifically manifest." [99] Occasionally, however, courts have read a statute to preclude review though it says nothing specifically about the matter. Consider the following case.

Switchmen's Union v. National Mediation Board

320 U.S. 297 (1943)

Mr. Justice DOUGLAS delivered the opinion of the Court.

This is an action by the petitioners, the Switchmen's Union of North America and some of its members against the National Mediation Board, its members, the Brotherhood of Railroad Trainmen, and the New York Central Railroad Company and the Michigan Central Railroad Company. [The Switchmen and the Brotherhood had disagreed about how yardmen should be classified for purposes of voting in a union election.]

... The Brotherhood sought to be the representatives for all the yardmen of the rail lines operated by the New York Central system. The Switchmen contended that yardmen of certain designated parts of the system should be permitted to vote for separate representatives instead of being compelled to take part in a system-wide election.

[The Board was asked to decide the dispute under §2, Ninth of the Railway Labor Act.[100]] The Board designated all yardmen of the carriers as participants in the election. The election was held and the Brotherhood was chosen as the representative. Upon the certification of the result to the carriers, petitioners sought to have the determination by the Board cancelled. This suit for cancellation was brought in the District Court. That court upheld the decision of the Board.... The Circuit Court of Appeals affirmed by a divided vote. The case is here on a petition for a writ of certiorari....

We do not reach the merits of the controversy. For we are of the opinion that

98. See, e.g., Kingsbrook Jewish Medical Center v. Richardson, 486 F.2d 663 (2d Cir. 1973). See generally, Note, Reviewability of Administrative Action: The Elusive Search for a Pragmatic Standard, 1974 Duke L. J. 382, 383-388.

99. L. Jaffe, op. cit. note 97, at 346.

100. Section 2, Ninth provides: "If any dispute shall arise among a carrier's employees as to who are the representatives of such employees designated and authorized in accordance with the requirements of this Act, it shall be the duty of the Mediation Board, upon request of either party to the dispute, to investigate such dispute and to certify to both parties, in writing, within thirty days after the receipt of the invocation of its services, the name or names of the individuals or organizations that have been designated and authorized to represent the employees involved in the dispute, and certify the same to the carrier. Upon receipt of such certification the carrier shall treat with the representative so certified as the representative of the craft or class for the purposes of this Act."

the District Court did not have the power to review the action of the National Mediation Board in issuing the certificate.

... Generalizations as to when judicial review of administrative action may not be obtained are of course hazardous. Where Congress has not expressly authorized judicial review, the type of problem involved and the history of the statute in question become highly relevant in determining whether judicial review may be nonetheless supplied. ... [T]he emergence of railway labor problems from the field of conciliation and mediation into that of legally enforceable rights has been quite recent. Until the 1926 Act the legal sanctions of the various acts had been few. The emphasis of the legislation were publicity and public opinion. Since 1926 there has been an increasing number of legally enforceable commands incorporated into the Act. And Congress has utilized administrative machinery more freely in the settlement of disputes. But large areas of the first still remain in the realm of conciliation, mediation, and arbitration. On only a few phases of this controversial subject has Congress utilized administrative or judicial machinery and invoked the compulsions of the law. ...

In that connection the history of §2, Ninth is highly relevant. It was introduced into the Act in 1934 as a device to strengthen and make more effective the processes of collective bargaining. ... It was aimed not only at company unions which had long plagued labor relations but also at numerous jurisdictional disputes between unions. Commissioner Eastman, draftsman of the 1934 amendments, explained the bill at the Congressional hearings. He stated that whether one organization or another was the proper representative of a particular group of employees was "one of the most controversial questions in connection with labor organization matters." ... He stated that it was very important "to provide a neutral tribunal which can make the decision and get the matter settled." But the problem was deemed to be so "highly controversial" that it was thought that the prestige of the Mediation Board might be adversely affected by the rulings which it would have to make in these jurisdictional disputes. ... Accordingly §2, Ninth was drafted so as to give the Mediation Board the power to "appoint a committee of three neutral persons who after hearing shall within ten days designate the employees who may participate in the election." That was added so that the Board's "own usefulness of settling disputes that might arise thereafter might not be impaired." ... Where Congress took such great pains to protect the Mediation Board in its handling of an explosive problem, we cannot help but believe that if Congress had desired to implicate the federal judiciary and to place on the federal courts the burden of having the final say on any aspect of the problem, it would have made its desire plain.

... While the Mediation Board is given specified powers in the conduct of elections, there is no requirement as to hearings. And there is no express grant of subpoena power. The Mediation Board makes no "order." And its only ultimate finding of fact is the certificate. ... The function of the Board under §2, Ninth is more the function of a referee. To this decision of the referee Congress has added a command enforcible by judicial decree. But the "command" is that "of the statute, not of the Board."

. . . [T]he intent seems plain — the dispute was to reach its last terminal point when the administrative finding was made. There was to be no dragging out of the controversy into other tribunals of law.

That conclusion is reinforced by the highly selective manner in which Congress has provided for judicial review of administrative orders or determinations under the Act. There is no general provision for such review. But Congress has expressly provided for it in two instances. Thus Congress gave the National Railroad Adjustment Board jurisdiction over disputes growing out of "grievances or out of the interpretation or application of agreements concerning rates of pay, rules, or working conditions." §3, First(i). The various divisions of the Adjustment Board have authority to make awards. §3, First(k)-(o). And suits based on those awards may be brought in the federal district courts. §3, First(p). In such suits "the findings and order of the division of the Adjustment Board shall be prima facie evidence of the facts therein stated." The other instance in the Act where Congress provided for judicial review is under §9 [§9 allows the award of an arbitration panel to be "impeached" in court under certain circumstances]. . . . When Congress in §3 and in §9 provided for judicial review of two types of orders or awards and in §2 of the same Act omitted any such provision as respects a third type, it drew a plain line of distinction. And the inference is strong from the history of the Act that that distinction was not inadvertent. The language of the Act read in light of that history supports the view that Congress gave administrative action under §2, Ninth a finality which it denied administrative action under the other sections of the Act.

. . . What is open when a court of equity is asked for its affirmative help by granting a decree for the enforcement of a certificate of the Mediation Board under §2, Ninth raises questions not now before us. . . .

Reversed.

[Justices REED, ROBERTS, and JACKSON dissented. They pointed out that the Board had accepted the Brotherhood's position because it believed that the statute gave it "no discretion to split a single carrier" when determining voting eligibility. The Switchmen claimed that the statute did give the Board discretion. Thus the Switchmen sought to raise on review a pure question of law. "Nothing to which our attention has been called appears in the legislative history indicating a determination of Congress to exclude the courts from their customary power to interpret the laws of the nation in cases or controversies arising from administrative violations of statutory standards." 320 U.S. at 318]

_____

As Professor Jaffe has pointed out, the *Switchmen's Union* case "has borne little fruit" — even in the labor area.[101] In Leedom v. Kyne, 358 U.S. 184 (1958), the Court considered a challenge to an NLRB certification of a bargaining unit. Language in the National Labor Relations Act strongly suggested that there was to be no direct review of a certification decision; the courts were to wait until a

101. L. Jaffe, Judicial Control of Administrative Action 354 (1965).

later "refusal to bargain" with the certified union.[102] The Supreme Court held, however, that the decision was reviewable because the NLRB had made an egregious mistake; its certification of the union was "contrary to a specific prohibition in the Act." [103]

In other areas, it is difficult to find cases in which a statute, silent on the subject, is interpreted to preclude review. However, they may exist. In Consumer Fed. of America v. FTC, 515 F.2d 367 (D.C. Cir. 1975), the court held that FTC cease and desist orders could be reviewed only at the behest of those subject to them. It wrote that, despite *Abbott Laboratories*, "the prohibition need not be express. Legislative intent to prohibit review may be shown by legislative history." 515 F.2d at 370.

b. Narrow Construction of Preclusive Language

The more common situation is for the courts to read language that apparently precludes review so that it does not do so:

Harmon v. Brucker

355 U.S. 579 (1958)

Per Curiam.

The Secretary of the Army, . . . discharged petitioners from the Army and issued to each of them a discharge certificate in form other than "honorable." In so doing, he took into account preinduction activities of petitioners rather than basing his action exclusively upon the record of their military service. After having exhausted available administrative remedies, petitioners separately brought these proceedings in the District Court seeking judgments declaring those determinations and actions of the Secretary to be void as in excess of his powers under the circumstances, and directing him to issue "honorable" discharge certificates to them. Being of the view that it was without jurisdiction to consider the actions, the District Court dismissed them, and the Court of Appeals affirmed. . . .

The respective contentions made here may be summarized as follows:

(1) Petitioners contend (a) that the Secretary acted in excess of his powers, because the statutes referred to did not authorize . . . consideration of petitioners' preinduction activities in determining the type of discharges to be issued to them upon separation from the Army, and (b) that the action of respondent . . . deprived petitioners of due process under the Fifth Amendment, and of a judicial trial under the Sixth Amendment, of the Constitution.

(2) Respondent contends (a) that by 10 U.S.C. §652a, Congress required that, upon separation from the Army, a former soldier be given "a certificate of

---

102. See American Federation of Labor v. NLRB, 308 U.S. 401 (1940).
103. But cf. Boire v. Greyhound Corp., 376 U.S. 473 (1964).

discharge, . . . in the manner prescribed by the Secretary of the Department of the Army . . . " ; (b) that, inasmuch as all certificates of discharge are not required to be "honorable" ones, he was authorized to, and did, prescribe various types of discharge certificates running the gamut from the accolade of "Honorable discharge" to the odious "Dishonorable discharge"; (c) that by 38 U.S.C. §693h, Congress directed the establishment of an Army Review Board with power to review, upon its own motion or that of the former soldier, the type of discharge issued, and "to change, correct, or modify any discharge or dismissal, and to issue a new discharge in accord with the facts presented to the board," and prescribed that "the findings thereof [shall] be final subject only to review by the Secretary of the Army"; (d) that the findings of the Board, made under those procedures so afforded to and availed of by petitioners, were *final* subject only to review by the Secretary of the Army; and (e) that, therefore, such administrative procedure is exclusive and the courts are without jurisdiction to review those findings.

In keeping with our duty to avoid deciding constitutional questions presented unless essential to proper disposition of a case, we look first to petitioners' nonconstitutional claim that respondent acted in excess of powers granted him by Congress. Generally, judicial relief is available to one who has been injured by an act of a government official which is in excess of his express or implied powers. American School of Magnetic Healing v. McAnnulty, 187 U.S. 94, 108. . . .

The District Court had not only jurisdiction to determine its jurisdiction but also power to construe the statutes involved to determine whether the respondent did exceed his powers. If he did so, his actions would not constitute exercises of his administrative discretion, and, in such circumstances as those before us, judicial relief from this illegality would be available. . . .

This brings us to the merits. The Solicitor General conceded that if the District Court had jurisdiction to review respondent's determinations as to the discharges he issued these petitioners and if petitioners had standing to bring these suits, the action of respondent is not sustainable. On the basis of that concession and our consideration of the law and this record we conclude that the actions of the Secretary of the Army cannot be sustained in law. By §652a, which provides that no person be discharged from military service "without a certificate of discharge," Congress granted to the Secretary of the Army authority to issue discharges. By §693h it provided for review by the Army Review Board of the exercise of such authority. Surely these two provisions must be given an harmonious reading to the end that the basis on which the Secretary's action is reviewed is coterminous with the basis on which he is allowed to act. Section 693h expressly requires that the findings of the Army Review Board "shall be based upon all available records of the [Army] relating to the person requesting such review. . . ." We think the word "records," as used in the statute, means *records of military service*, and that the statute, properly construed, means that the type of discharge to be issued is to be determined solely by the soldier's military record in the Army. . . .

The judgments of the Court of Appeals are reversed and the cases are remanded to the District Court for the relief to which petitioners are entitled in the light of this opinion.

Reversed.

Mr. Justice CLARK, dissenting.

... Throughout our history the function of granting discharge certificates has been entrusted by the Congress to the President and, through him, to the respective Secretaries of the Armed Forces. At no time until today have the courts interfered in the exercise of this military function. The lack of any judicial review is evidenced by the fact that for over 70 years Congress itself reviewed military discharges and frequently enacted private bills directing the appropriate Secretary to correct the type of discharge certificate given. By legislation in 1944 and 1946, Congress authorized creation of administrative boards to which it transferred the review of military discharges in an effort to conserve its own time. That legislation makes no provision for judicial review; on the contrary, the 1944 Act expressly states that the findings of the Army Discharge Review Board shall be "final subject only to review by the Secretary of [the Army]," and the 1946 Act, as amended in 1951, expressly provides that the determination of the Board to Correct Military Records shall be "final and conclusive on all officers of the Government except when procured by means of fraud." When this legislative expression of finality is viewed in context with the uninterrupted history of congressional review, culminated by Congress' transfer of the review function to administrative bodies, it cannot be said, in the absence of specific legislative grant, that Congress intended to permit judicial review. The Court avoids these considerations by positing jurisdiction to review simply on its determination that the Secretary's action exceeded his statutory authority.

In reaching this exceptional position the Court construes §693h of the 1944 Act, supra, which provides that review of discharges shall be based on "all available records" of the department involved, to include not "all available records" of the Army concerning petitioners, but merely those "*solely* [concerned with] the soldier's military record in the Army." (Emphasis added.) This limitation of the clear meaning of the words used by the Congress — so that "all" is deemed to mean "some" — is lacking of any justification.[104]

c. Finality Provisions

The courts' tendency to interpret statutes that apparently preclude review or otherwise restrict its availability to allow review nonetheless is well illustrated in immigration cases. Consider Shaughnessy v. Pedreiro, 349 U.S. 48 (1955). Predreiro was ordered deported by the Attorney General. The 1952 Immigrations Act made the Attorney General's decisions "final." The Supreme Court had held that the word "final" in the prior 1917 Immigration Act meant that review was

---

104. Ed. note: See Lunding, Judicial Review of Military Administrative Discharges, 83 Yale L.J. 33 (1973).

available through habeas corpus and not otherwise.[105] Despite the earlier decision, the Court here held that the word "final" in the 1952 Act referred "to finality in administrative procedure" not to "cutting off the right of judicial review in whole or in part," for Congress would not have required "a person ordered deported to go to jail in order to obtain review by a court." [106] Thus, review in an action for declaratory and injunctive relief was proper.

When matters less important than citizenship are at stake, the courts have interpreted "finality" clauses less favorably to plaintiffs.[107] But Congress still has had to make its intent to preclude review very specific to be effective. In the Veterans Benefits Act, for example, Congress wrote that "the decisions of the Administrator on any question of law or fact concerning a claim for benefits or payments under any law administered by the Veterans Administration shall be final and conclusive and no other official or any court of the United States shall have power or jurisdiction to review any such decision." 72 Stat. 1115 (1958).

This section was read to preclude review[108] until the D.C. Circuit held that since the statute used the words "claim for benefits," it did not apply to administrative action *terminating benefits*.[109] Congress responded by amending the statute to read: "[T]he decisions of the Administrator on any question of law or fact under any law administered by the Veterans Administration providing benefits for veterans and their dependants or survivors shall be final and conclusive and no other official or any court shall have power or jurisdiction to review any such decision by an action in the nature of mandamus or otherwise." 38 U.S.C. §211(a) (1970).

What could be more clear? [110] Yet, consider the next case.

105. Heikkila v. Barber, 345 U.S. 229 (1953).

106. 349 U.S. at 51. See also Rusk v. Cort, 369 U.S. 367 (1962), in which the Court allowed an American nonresident, who had been refused a passport on the ground that he had lost his citizenship by avoiding the draft, to obtain review in a declaratory judgment action, despite a statute that apparently required such persons to travel to the United States and obtain a ruling about citizenship from the Attorney General. The statute provided that, "a final determination by the Attorney General" of inadmissibility "shall be subject to review by any court of competent jurisdiction in habeas corpus proceedings and not otherwise." 8 U.S.C. §1503(c). This language, according to the Court, was not meant to preclude review of the question of citizenship in a declaratory judgment action. For a further interesting discussion of the review of immigration and citizenship questions, see Note, Deportation and Exclusion: A Continuing Dialogue Between Congress and the Courts, 71 Yale L. J. 760 (1962). See also Foti v. Immigration Service, 375 U.S. 217 (1963).

107. See Note, Judicial Review of Federal Administrative Decisions Concerning Gratuities, 49 Va. L. Rev. 313 (1963).

108. See Barefield v. Byrd, 320 F.2d 455 (5th Cir. 1963); Davis, Veterans Benefits, Judicial Review, and the Constitutional Problems of "Positive" Government, 39 Ind. L. J. 183 (1964).

109. See, e.g., Tracy v. Gleason, 379 F.2d 469 (D.C. Cir. 1967).

110. De Rodulfa v. United States, 461 F.2d 1240 (D.C. Cir.) *cert. denied*, 409 U.S. 949 (1972) (no review of the Administrator's award of counsel fees). Compare a Circuit Court of Appeals decision to review the lawfulness of a compensation award despite language in the relevant statute making the decision reviewed "final and conclusive for all purposes notwithstanding any other provisions of law to the contrary and not subject to review." Ralpho v. Bell, 569 F.2d 607 (D.C. Cir. 1977).

Johnson v. Robison

415 U.S. 361 (1974)

Mr. Justice BRENNAN delivered the opinion of the Court:

[Plaintiff, a conscientious objector who served required alternative civilian service, applied for Veterans Benefits and was turned down by the Administrator, for the statute provided benefits only for veterans of military service. The Administrator rejected plaintiff's claim that as so interpreted, the statute was unconstitutional. The Court first decided that the decision of the Administrator denying benefits was reviewable.]

... We consider first appellant's contention that section 211(a) bars federal courts from deciding the constitutionality of veterans' benefits legislation. Such a construction would, of course, raise serious questions concerning the constitutionality of §211(a)[111] and in such case "it is a cardinal principle that this Court will first ascertain whether a construction of the statute is fairly possible by which the [constitutional] question[s] may be avoided." ...

Plainly, no explicit provision of §211(a) bars judicial consideration of appellee's constitutional claims. That section provides that "the *decisions* of the Administrator on any question of law or fact *under* any law administered by the Veterans' Administration providing benefits for veterans ... shall be final and conclusive and no ... court of the United States shall have power or jurisdiction to review any such decision. ..." (Emphasis added.) The prohibitions would appear to be aimed at review only of those decisions of law or fact that arise in the *administration* by the Veterans' Administration of a *statute* providing benefits for veterans. A decision of law or fact "under" a statute is made by the Administrator in the interpretation or application of a particular provision of the statute to a particular set of facts. Appellee's constitutional challenge is not to any such decision of the *Administrator*, but rather to a decision of *Congress* to create a statutory class entitled to benefits that does not include I-O conscientious objectors who performed alternative civilian service. Thus, as the District Court stated: "The questions of law presented in these proceedings arise under the Constitution, not under the statute whose validity is challenged." ...

Nor does the legislative history accompanying the 1970 amendment of §11(a) demonstrate a congressional intention to bar judicial review even of constitutional questions. No-review clauses similar to §211(a) have been a part of veterans' benefits legislation since 1933. While the legislative history accompanying these precursor no-review clauses is almost nonexistent, the Administrator, in a letter written in 1952 in connection with a revision of the clause under consideration by the Subcommittee of the House Committee on Veterans' Affairs, comprehensively

---

111. Compare Ex parte McCardle, 7 Wall. 506 (1869); Sheldon v. Sill, 8 How. 441 (1850), with Martin v. Hunter's Lessee, 1 Wheat. 304 (1816); St. Joseph Stock Yards Co. v. United States, 298 U.S. 38, 84 (1936) (Brandeis, J., concurring). See Hart, The Power of Congress to Limit the Jurisdiction of Federal Courts: An Exercise in Dialectic, 66 Harv. L. Rev. 1362 (1953).

explained the policies necessitating the no-review clause and identified two primary purposes: (1) to insure the veterans' benefits claims will not burden the courts and the Veterans' Administration with expensive and time-consuming litigation, and (2) to insure that the technical and complex determinations and applications of Veterans' Administration policy connected with veterans' benefits decisions will be adequately and uniformly made.

The legislative history of the 1970 amendment indicates nothing more than a congressional intent to preserve these two primary purposes. Before amendment, the no-review clause made final "the decisions of the Administrator on any question of law or fact *concerning a claim for benefits or payments under* [certain] law[s] administered by the Veterans' Administration" (emphasis added).... In a series of decisions ... the Court of Appeals for the District of Columbia Circuit interpreted the term "claim" as a limitation upon the reach of §211(a), and as a consequence held that judicial review of actions by the Administrator *subsequent* to an original grant of benefits was not barred.

Congress perceived this judicial interpretation as a threat to the dual purposes of the no-review clause. First, the interpretation would lead to an inevitable increase in litigation with consequent burdens upon the courts and the Veterans' Administration....

Second, Congress was concerned that the judicial interpretation of §211(a) would involve the courts in day-to-day determination and interpretation of Veterans' Administration policy....

Thus, the 1970 amendment was enacted to overrule the interpretation of the Court of Appeals for the District of Columbia Circuit, and thereby restore vitality to the two primary purposes to be served by the no-review clause. Nothing whatever in the legislative history of the 1970 amendment, or predecessor no-review clauses, suggests any congressional intent to preclude judicial cognizance of constitutional challenges to veterans' benefits legislation. Such challenges obviously do not contravene the purposes of the no-review clause, for they cannot be expected to burden the courts by their volume, nor do they involve technical considerations of Veterans' Administration policy. We therefore conclude, in agreement with the District Court, that a construction of §211(a) that does not extend the prohibitions of that section to actions challenging the constitutionality of laws providing benefits for veterans is not only "fairly possible" but is the most reasonable construction, for neither the text nor the scant legislative history of §211(a) provides the "clear and convincing" evidence of congressional intent required by this Court before a statute will be construed to restrict access to judicial review. See Abbott Laboratories v. Gardner, 387 U.S. 136, 141 (1967).

3. "Committed to Agency Discretion"

a. APA §10e (5 U.S.C. 706) states that a reviewing court "shall ... hold unlawful and set aside agency action ... found to be ... an abuse of discretion...." But §10(a)(2), 5 U.S.C. §701(a)(2), says that the whole chapter, including 10(a), does *not* apply to "agency action . . . committed to agency discretion by law." Does this exception mean that there is a class of matters as to which an agency *can* abuse its discretion, and that there is no redress available in a court of law, even though there is no statute precluding review?

Raoul Berger argues that §701(a)(2) excepts from the review provisions only *lawful* exercise of discretion. Any *abuse* of discretion would be reviewable unless a statute precludes review.[112] One might need such a section in the APA to remind courts that agencies enjoy very broad discretionary authority — authority that can extend into the area of "lawmaking" itself. Without the section, courts might too often set aside agency actions that, for example, might involve decisions of law, even though the action represents a lawful exercise of agency discretion. At this point, review the materials on "question of law" at pp. 227-258, supra, to remind yourself how potentially broad is the realm in which the agency can exercise discretion free of court interference. In the Berger view, then, in the absence of a *statute* precluding review, whenever an agency exceeds these bounds, or balances factors unreasonably in a given case, a court should stand ready to intervene.

Professor Jaffe comes close to supporting the Berger view when he argues that the discretionary powers granted agencies always have limits, and a court should stand ready to intervene when those limits are overstepped. He writes, "A power may appear to be granted in absolute terms and [its] . . . character . . . [or] statutory history . . . may support the apparent implication. . . . But such an interpretation of a statute should be tolerated only on a very strong showing. This is not to be taken as a plea for judicial interference with discretion; the argument is rather that the presence of discretion should not bar a court from considering a claim of illegal or arbitrary use of discretion. . . . The upshot is that there are few discretions, however broad, substantially affecting the person or property of an individual which cannot at some point come under judicial surveillance." [113]

Note, however, that Professor Jaffe apparently accepts the *occasional* case where the courts will not review discretion for illegality or "abuse." [114] Professor Davis points to the existence of such cases as evidence for a different interpretation of §701(a)(2). He argues that it means what it says, namely, that an agency might in some instances *abuse* its discretion, yet court review would be precluded. He states, "the presumption of reviewability can be overcome by showing (a) intent of Congress to cut off review, (b) inappropriateness of the subject matter for judicial consideration *or* (c) some other reason that a court deems sufficient for unreviewability." [115] The courts determine whether a claim falls within (b) or (c)

---

112. Berger, Administrative Arbitrariness and Judicial Review, 65 Colum. L. Rev. 55 (1965).

113. See Jaffe, Judicial Control of Administrative Action 359, 375 (1965).

114. See Littell v. Morton, 445 F.2d 1207 (4th Cir. 1971); Scanwell Laboratories, Inc. v. Schaffer, 424 F.2d 859, 874 (2d Cir. 1970); Wong Wing Hang v. Immigration and Naturalization Service, 360 F.2d 715, 718 (2d Cir. 1966). All have explicitly adopted Professor Jaffe's point of view that discretion is almost always subject to review for abuse or illegality.

115. Davis, Administrative Law of the Seventies 634-635 (1976). Insofar as *Abbott Laboratories* implies the contrary, says Professor Davis, it is inconsistent with the holdings in other Supreme Court cases both before and after that case.

"on practical grounds in particular cases." [116] Professor Davis supports his "strong" interpretation of §701(a)(2) with reference to particular cases,[117] at least some of which Berger might argue were incorrectly decided.[118]

Consider the following case, cited by Professor Davis as support for his position. How much support does it give him? Would the Court have reached the same result in the absence of §701(a)(2)?

Panama Canal Co. v. Grace Line, Inc.

356 U.S. 309 (1958)

Mr. Justice DOUGLAS delivered the opinion of the Court.

[American shipping companies using the canal sued the Panama Canal Co., a government agency, to set new tolls and for a refund of past overcharges. The applicable statute provided that "tolls shall be prescribed at ... rates calculated to cover, as nearly as practicable, all costs of maintaining and operating the Panama Canal, together with the facilities and appurtenances related thereto, including interest and depreciation, and an appropriate share of the net costs of operation of the ... Canal Zone Government." In determining the "appropriate share" the company is to give "substantial weight" to the ratio of canal tolls to its income from various other sources. The Comptroller General (an investigatory agency responsible to Congress), in reviewing the tolls, reported to Congress that the tolls were too high because the company allocated too much of the cost of the Canal Zone Government to tolls and too little to auxiliary or supporting activities. The shippers then sued, and the Court of Appeals found in their favor. The Supreme Court reversed.]

Section 10 of the Administrative Procedure Act ... excludes from the categories of cases subject to judicial review "agency action" that is "by law committed to agency discretion." We think the initiation of a proceeding for readjustment of the tolls of the Panama Canal is a matter that Congress has left to the discretion of the Panama Canal Co. Petitioner is, as we have seen, an agent or spokesman of the President in these matters. It is "authorized" to prescribe tolls and to change them. . . . But the exercise of that authority is far more than the performance of a ministerial act. As we have seen, the present conflict rages over questions that at heart involve problems of statutory construction and cost accounting: whether an operating deficit in the auxiliary or supporting activities is a legitimate cost in maintaining and operating the Canal for purpose of the toll formula. These are matters on which experts may disagree; they involve nice issues of judgment and

116. 4 K. Davis, Administrative Law Treatise 80-81 (1958).
117. See, e.g., Ferry v. Udall, 336 F.2d 706, 712 (9th Cir. 1964), *cert. denied* 381 U.S. 904 (1965), explicitly adopting the Davis view.
118. For further development of the Davis/Berger debate, see Davis' reply in the 1965 Pocket Part of his treatise at §28.16, then a series of replies, final words, rejoinders, and postscripts, all collected at 114 U. Pa. L. Rev. 783 et seq. (1966), and finally Berger, Administrative Arbitrariness: A Synthesis, 78 Yale L. J. 965 (1969).

choice, ... which require the exercise of informed discretion.... The case is, therefore, quite unlike the situation where a statute creates a duty to act and an equity court is asked to compel the agency to take the prescribed action.

... We put the matter that way since the relief sought in this action is to compel petitioner to fix new tolls. The principle at stake is no different than if mandamus were sought — a remedy long restricted, Marbury v. Madison, 1 Cranch 137, 166; Decatur v. Paulding, 14 Pet. 497, 514-517, in the main, to situations where ministerial duties of a nondiscretionary nature are involved. Where the matter is peradventure clear, where the agency is clearly derelict in failing to act, where the inaction or action turns on a mistake of law, then judicial relief is often available. ... But where the duty to act turns on matters of doubtful or highly debatable inference from large or loose statutory terms, the very construction of the statute is a distinct and profound exercise of discretion.... We then must infer that the decision to act or not to act is left to the expertise of the agency burdened with the responsibility for decision.

We think this case is in that area. The petitioner, as agent of the President, is given questions of judgment requiring close analysis and nice choices. Petitioner is not only agent for the President but a creature of Congress. It is on close terms with its committees, reporting to the Congress, airing its problems before them, looking to Congress for guidance and direction. It is at least arguable that Congress to date has sided with petitioner and against the Comptroller General in construing §§ 411 and 412 of the Code. For Congress, fully advised of the Comptroller General's views in his Report for 1954, approved the budgets for the Panama Canal Co. for 1956, 1957, and 1958, based on petitioner's interpretation of the statute and its methods of accounting and cost allocation, 69 Stat. 235-237, 70 Stat. 322-324, 71 Stat. 78. That does not necessarily mean that the construction of the Act, pressed on us and on Congress by petitioner, is the correct one. It does, however, indicate that the question is so wide open and at large as to be left at this stage to agency discretion. The matter should be far less cloudy, much more clear for courts to intrude.

Reversed.[119]

---

b. There are other areas in which courts have decided *not* to review because of the subject matter at issue or the impact of review on the conduct of government business. The decisions do not all fit comfortably within the "committed to agency discretion" rationale. Yet as a practical matter, they make up the content of that doctrine.

(1) In Chicago & Southern Air Lines v. Waterman Steamship Corp., 333 U.S. 103 (1948), Waterman sought judicial review of a CAB order awarding a certificate for an overseas air route to a competitor. The Board order, since it involved overseas routes, had the specific approval of the President (as required by Civil Aviation Act §801, 49 U.S.C. 601.) The Board argued that its order was incomplete

119. Cf. Schilling v. Rogers, 363 U.S. 666 (1960).

and hence not ripe for review prior to presidential review, while afterwards it was, as a Presidential action, immune from judicial review. The Supreme Court (dividing 5-4) agreed. The Court wrote, in part:

> While the changes made at direction of the President may be identified, the reasons therefor are not disclosed beyond the statement that "because of certain factors relating to our broad national welfare and other matters for which the Chief Executive has special responsibility, he has reached conclusions which require" changes in the Board's opinion.
>
> The court below considered, and we think quite rightly, that it could not review such provisions of the order as resulted from Presidential direction. The President, both as Commander-in-Chief and as the Nation's organ for foreign affairs, has available intelligence services whose reports are not and ought not to be published to the world. It would be intolerable that courts, without the relevant information, should review and perhaps nullify actions of the Executive taken on information properly held secret. Nor can courts sit *in camera* in order to be taken into executive confidences. But even if courts could require full disclosure, the very nature of executive decisions as to foreign policy is political, not judicial. Such decisions are wholly confided by our Constitution to the political departments of the government, Executive and Legislative. They are delicate, complex, and involve large elements of prophecy. They are and should be undertaken only by those directly responsible to the people whose welfare they advance or imperil. They are decisions of a kind for which the Judiciary has neither aptitude, facilities nor responsibility and which has long been held to belong in the domain of political power not subject to judicial intrusion or inquiry. . . .
>
> . . . We therefore agree that whatever of this order emanates from the President is not susceptible of review by the Judicial Department.

The Court also rejected the possibility that the courts should review the validity of the Board's order before it had been approved or modified by the President. The judgment was reversed.[120]

United States ex rel. Schonbrun v. Commanding Officer

403 F.2d 371 (2d Cir. 1968), cert. denied, 394 U.S. 929 (1969)

FRIENDLY, Circuit Judge:

Stephen Schonbrun, a member of the Army Reserves, has sought a writ of habeas corpus releasing him from an order to report for active duty. Schonbrun enlisted in the reserves on July 28, 1963, and is now a member of the 203d Transportation Company. The unit was activated on May 13, 1968. Anticipating this, in late April he wrote two letters to his Commanding Officer seeking exemption from active duty pursuant to Army Regulations because of extreme personal and

---

120. *Waterman* was recently followed in Braniff Airways v. CAB, 581 F.2d 846 (D.C. Cir. 1978).

community hardship. As to "extreme personal hardship," he submitted that his wife was suffering from a psychiatric disorder, that his presence in the household materially aided her and tended to promote her recovery, and that his departure would have a serious and immediate deteriorating effect. Two psychiatrists and a psychologist attested the seriousness of her ailment; one of the psychiatrists and the psychologist confirmed the likelihood that Schonbrun's departure would have a harmful effect. Further confirmation was afforded by a letter from the Rabbi of the Schonbruns' synagogue and by a Lutheran pastor. The case for "extreme community hardship" was that Schonbrun had been teaching a class of 10 severely disturbed boys in a Special Service School located in a poverty area in Queens, with great success. His value there was attested by the Principal of the school, the Assistant Principal, and the Social Studies Chairman.

On May 6 Schonbrun was given a 30-day extension and was told to contact Fort Wadsworth for further instructions before this expired. While not officially notified, he learned that his application had been denied. He claims that was without assignment of reasons, although Army Regulations 601-25,[121] 3-14, require that when the area commander denies the request, he must "notify the member of such denial and the reason therefor, together with his right to appeal such decision."

[The court considered whether, in light of special statutes governing review of armed forced actions, habeas corpus or mandamus was the appropriate method to challenge the action. It concluded that, whatever the proper route,] . . . the necessity for expedition in the military's administration of personnel admittedly subject

---

121. The applicable provisions of Army Regulation 601-25 are:

[b(3)] . . . Delay or exemption of all Ready reservists, other than those described in (1) and (2) above, is authorized in accordance with either of the following criteria:

(a) In exceptional cases when the involuntary order to active duty will result in an extreme personal or community hardship (para. 1-12); . . .

1-12. Criteria for hardship conditions.

a. Extreme personal hardship.

(1) Illness of a member of immediate family. When, in the opinion of the attending physician, the illness of the member is such that —

(a) Fatality appears to be imminent; or

(b) Presence of the reservist is an important factor in the recovery of the patient and his immediate departure would have a serious effect upon the patient. . . .

b. Extreme community hardship. In general, this requirement will be met only when all of the following conditions are determined to exist:

(1) The service performed by the reservist is essential to the maintenance of health, safety, or welfare of his community.

(2) The service cannot be performed by other persons residing in the area concerned.

(3) The reservist cannot be replaced in the community by another person who can perform such services. . . .

3-11. Action on requests for delay or exemptions. . . .

(c) Requests for delay or exemption submitted on the basis of extreme personal or community hardship —

(1) May be considered when the extreme personal or community hardship condition occurs not more than 6 months prior to receipt of alert or active duty orders.

(2) May not be considered when such hardship condition existed at the time applicant submitted DA Form 1140-1 (Army Reserve Status Verification Questionnaire) as prescribed in AR 140-25, whichever is the more recent, and applicant failed to request transfer from the Ready Reserve by reason of hardship.

to its jurisdiction raises a serious question whether the courts should apply this principle with respect to a call-up order, and if that be the correct result in mandamus, the result should not be different even if habeas or an injunction are also available remedies.

The very purpose of a "ready reserve" is that the reserve shall be ready. Under the regulations, delay or exemption from active duty in hardship cases is authorized but not required. The hardship must be "extreme," and while the regulations wisely give more specific content to this criterion, a good deal is necessarily left to the judgment of the commanding officer. In contrast to the yea or nay character of entitlement to the conscientious objection exemption, administration of the hardship exemption necessarily involves a balancing of the individual's claims against the nation's needs, and the balance may differ from time to time and from place to place in a manner beyond the competence of a court to decide. While no one could reasonably assert that the country would perish if Schonbrun did not serve with his company, delay in the call-up of a reservist, even during the period necessary for judicial consideration of his claim to discretionary exemption, inevitably means either a gap in the unit or the call of another reservist who otherwise might not have been reached. Although Schonbrun's case is appealing ... the courts must have regard to the flood of unmeritorious applications that might be loosed by such interference with the military's exercise of discretion and the effect of the delays caused by these in the efficient administration of personnel who have voluntarily become part of the armed forces. We conclude that this is a subject on which civil review of discretionary action by the military should be declined — and this irrespective of the rubric under which the action is brought.[122] While the Army's alleged violation of its own regulations, in failing to give notice of denial of his initial request and the reasons for it, might stand differently, Schonbrun was not prejudiced thereby.

Affirmed.[123]

122. The extent to which the Administrative Procedure Act applies to actions of the military is far from clear. Section 4, which governs rulemaking, excludes "any military naval or foreign affairs function of the United States," and §5, which deals with adjudication, exempts "the conduct of military, naval, or foreign affairs functions." However, the breadth of the definition of "agency" in §2(a) indicates that the "agency action" of which §10 speaks embraces far more than adjudication and rulemaking. "Agency" appears to include the military, except "courts martial and military commissions," "military or naval authority exercised in the field in time of war in occupied territory," and the Selective Service System. Thus the callup of reservists would seem to be subject to the provision of §10 except so far as "statutes preclude judicial review" or "agency action is by law committed to agency discretion," judicial review shall be afforded to "any person suffering legal wrong because of any agency action within the meaning of any relevant statute." Our holding here that the correctness of a discretionary refusal to grant the hardship exemption is not subject to review by the courts necessarily represents a determination that such a refusal "is by law committed to agency discretion" so far as to render inapplicable the provisions of §10(e). See 4 Davis, Administrative Law Treatise §28-16, especially pp. 81-82 (1958).

123. For a similar case, see Curran v. Laird, 420 F.2d 122 (D.C. Cir. 1969), in which a maritime union claimed that the President abused his discretion in refusing to use "reserve" ships to transport cargo to Vietnam. The Cargo Preference Law required that "available American ships" must be used before foreign vessels. But the government replied, ships placed in the National Defense Reserve (created by the Merchant Ship Sales Act) are not "available." Judge

Hahn v. Gottlieb

430 F.2d 1243 (1st Cir. 1970)

[The facts and earlier part of the opinion are printed at pp. 683-686 supra. Essentially, plaintiffs claimed that the FHA abused its discretion in approving rent increases made by landlords owning FHA financed housing:]

COFFIN, Circuit Judge. . . .

III. JUDICIAL REVIEW

This brings us to plaintiffs' second major claim, that they are entitled to judicial review of FHA decisions to grant a rent increase. Since the National Housing Act does not explicitly bar resort to the courts, we address ourselves to the alternate exception to judicial review, recognized in section 10 of the Administrative Procedure Act: whether "agency action is committed to agency discretion by law". 5 U.S.C. §701(a)(2). In approaching this question, we recognize a strong presumption in favor of review, which is overcome only by "clear and convincing evidence" that Congress intended to cut off review above the agency level. . . . Such evidence may, however, be drawn not only from explicit language, but also from a statute's purpose and design. . . . In the absence of a clear declaration of Congressional intent, three factors seem to us determinative: first, the appropriateness of the issues raised for review by the courts; second, the need for judicial supervision to safeguard the interests of the plaintiffs; and third, the impact of review on the effectiveness of the agency in carrying out its assigned role. . . .

Looking first to the appropriateness of judicial review, we note that courts are ill-equipped to superintend economic and managerial decisions of the kind involved here. . . . A partial list of the issues raised by plaintiffs either in the FHA hearing or in the court below includes: whether the landlord's increased operating costs were attributable to poor design and construction defects; whether and to what extent costs attributable to such defects should be absorbed by the landlord or passed on to the tenants; whether estimates of the vacancy rate, of commercial occupancy, and of managerial expenses were reasonable; and whether the FHA had properly determined the investment base for computing a reasonable return. Our only guides in answering such questions are the sometimes conflicting statutory goals of increased low-rent housing through private investment and the extremely

---

Leventhal wrote that the courts would not review the President's discretion as to when ships would be placed in the "reserve" or as to how they would be used once there: "That the matter before us for consideration lies in the special zones of the exception, rather than the ordinary area of judicial reviewability, is established by several cardinal aspects of the issues. The case involves decisions relating to the conduct of national defense; the President has a key role; the national interest contemplates and requires flexibility in management of defense resources; and the particular issues call for determinations that lie outside sound judicial domain in terms of aptitude, facilities, and responsibility." But cf. Feliciano v. Laird, 426 F.2d 424 (2d Cir. 1970).

broad regulatory criteria of maintaining "the economic soundness of the project" while insuring "a reasonable return on the investment consistent with providing reasonable rentals to tenants." 24 C.F.R. §221.531(c). Under these circumstances, we willingly confess our incapacity to contribute intelligently to the general course of decisions on rents and charges. . . .

The second consideration, the need for judicial intervention to protect plaintiffs' interest in low-rent housing, is by no means insubstantial. Plaintiffs' choices are limited; their bargaining power generally not strong. But, as we have already noted, plaintiffs' interests are not threatened by every rent increase, and other forms of relief, such as rent supplements, are available. We must, in addition, take into account the kind of program which Congress has erected to meet plaintiffs' needs. The National Housing Act does not provide categorical assistance to those in need of housing, nor does it erect detailed statutory safeguards to protect their interests, such as those provided for persons displaced by urban renewal. . . . Instead Congress has attempted to meet plaintiffs' needs indirectly, by stimulating private investors to supply low-rent housing. Rents in such housing are to be regulated, but only "in such manner as in the opinion of the Secretary will effectuate the purposes of this section." 12 U.S.C. §1715l(d)(3). Given this mechanism, we think plaintiffs' long-run interest may not be well served by a judicially-imposed system of review of all rent increases. Delay, the frictions engendered by the process of litigation, and the possibility — seldom discussed — of landlord appeals from FHA decisions in favor of tenants may lead to higher rentals and ultimately to less participation by private investors.

Turning finally to the impact of review on agency effectiveness, we think that resort to the courts might have a serious adverse impact on the performance of the FHA. Close judicial scrutiny inevitably leads to more formalized decision-making. This result may be tolerable and even desirable in some cases. However, FHA consideration of rent increases can recur as often as leases expire over the life of a forty-year mortgage. To impose the formalities which attend review on all these essentially managerial decisions seems to us inconsistent with the constant Congressional urgings to simplify procedures and expedite work. . . .

Equally important, such review would discourage the increased involvement of the private sector which is the goal of §221(d)(3). . . . Were judicial review added to the already onerous burdens which the landlord assumes when he contracts with the FHA, the net effect would be to discourage private investment.

In sum, it seems to us that the inappropriateness of judicial review, its minimal utility in safeguarding plaintiff's rights, and its adverse impact on agency operations all provide "clear and convincing evidence" that Congress did not intend courts to supervise FHA rent decisions. We therefore hold that the approval of rents and charges is a "matter committed to agency discretion by law," and thus not subject to judicial review. In so holding, we do not reach the question whether courts may intervene in those rare cases where the FHA has ignored a plain statutory duty, exceeded its jurisdiction, or committed constitutional error. The present case, which at best concerns a failure to give proper weight to all the relevant considerations, plainly falls within the area committed to agency discretion. . . .

Langevin v. Chenango Court, Inc.

447 F.2d 296 (2d Cir. 1971)

FRIENDLY, Chief Judge:

[The facts were similar to Hahn v. Gottlieb. Plaintiffs claimed that the FHA abused its discretion in approving increases in their rent. Judge Friendly disagreed with *Hahn's* conclusion that the matter of rent increases was not appropriate for judicial review and was committed to agency discretion.]

While this [*Hahn* opinion] may find some support in the inscrutable opinion in Panama Canal Co. v. Grace Line, Inc., 356 U.S. 309, we fail to see why a court is any worse equipped to pass on the reasonableness of a rent increase approval than it is to consider . . . an order granting or refusing an increase in liability insurance premiums, or, for that matter, orders made in the administration of local rent control programs. This is especially true when rent increases are limited by the regulatory agreement to those "necessary to compensate for any net increase, occurring since the last approved rent schedule, in taxes . . . and operating and maintenance expenses over which owners have no effective control." Assessing the reasonableness of an increase which is to be governed by such a standard does not seem beyond judicial competence.

Nevertheless, we reach the same conclusion of nonreviewability as the First Circuit, on the basis [that Congress intended to make it nonreviewable.] Assuming as we do that the FHA's approval constitutes "agency action" within the broad definition of 5 U.S.C. §551(13), it would be most unusual for Congress to subject to judicial review discretionary action by an agency in administering a contract which Congress authorized it to make. Other factors tending in the direction of nonreviewability are the managerial nature of the responsibilities confided to the FHA, . . . the need for expedition to achieve the Congressional objective, which we have already discussed, and the quanity of appeals that would result if FHA authorizations to increase rents were held reviewable. . . . Like the First Circuit, "we do not reach the question whether courts may intervene in those rare cases where the FHA has ignored a plain statutory duty, exceeded its jurisdiction, or committed constitutional error," 430 F.2d at 1251, including cases where it is alleged that the agency decision clearly "rested on an impermissible basis such as an invidious discrimination against a particular race or group." . . . We hold only that a mere claim of error, even of gross error, is not enough to escape the second exception in 5 U.S.C. §701(a). And, whatever bounds the due process clause may set upon nonreviewability of agency action, see 4 Davis, Administrative Law Treatise §§ 28.18 and 28.19; Jaffe, Judicial Control of Administrative Action 381-89 (1965), no case goes to the extent of holding that due process mandates judicial review of an order approving — on the basis of an ex parte submission of facts — a rent increase to a landlord who has benefited from a federal aid program. As already indicated, our decision leaves room for court review of questions as to agency jurisdiction and compliance with constitutional and statutory demands. See Crowell v. Benson, 285 U.S. 22, 54.

(2) Would the courts review, even in a clear-cut case of abuse, an exercise of presidential discretion in, for example, awarding a medal, granting a pardon, recalling an ambassador, or appointing a cabinet officer? [124]

(3) Prosecutorial discretion to initiate administrative, civil, or criminal enforcement proceedings, particularly decisions not to prosecute, is ordinarily shielded from review — even for alleged abuse.[125] Yet, recently the courts have begun to review exercises of prosecutorial discretion in the administrative and civil context under an "arbitrary or capricious" standard. In Dunlop v. Bachowski, 421 U.S. 560 (1975), the Supreme Court held that this type of review was available and required the Secretary of Labor to produce a statement of his rationale for failing to proceed against alleged violators of the Labor-Management Reporting and Disclosure Act.[126]

c. It would be wrong to conclude that in certain sensitive areas — foreign affairs or national defense, for example — government actions are *immune* from review. The reviewability of decisions in those areas is more likely to depend on various factors,[127] including the importance of the plaintiff's claim, the ease with which the court can determine the issue, the extent to which the process of court review will itself interfere with the ongoing work of the agency, and perhaps on other considerations as well.[128] In *Overton Park* the Supreme Court stated that the §701(a)(2) exception for action's "committed to agency discretion" is a narrow one "applicable to those rare instances where 'statutes are drawn in such terms that in a given case there is no law to apply.' " [129] This language, although opaque, suggests that the agency action is immune when there exists no legal standard against which its lawfulness can be judged.[130]

In practice, in deciding whether to review, courts take a variety of factors into account, balancing individual, agency, and judicial interests. As the opinions in *Hahn* and *Langevin* suggest, they take into account such factors as the nature and importance of the interests of the parties, the complexity of the issues, and the obviousness of the violations of law.[131] At this point, it will prove helpful to review

124. Cf. Orloff v. Willoughby, 345 U.S. 83 (1953).

125. Cf. e.g., Linda R. S. v. Richard D., 410 U.S. 614 (1973). Professor Davis argued strongly that exercises of prosecutorial discretion ought to be reviewable. Davis, Discretionary Justice (1966); Davis, Administrative Law of the Seventies 605-630 (1976).

126. See also Nader v. Saxbe, 497 F.2d 676 (D.C. Cir. 1974); Note, Reviewability of Prosecutorial Discretion: Failure to Prosecute, 75 Colum. L. Rev. 130 (1975).

127. For instances in which the courts have granted review, see e.g., Harmon v. Brucker, 355 U.S. 579 (1958) (review of Army Secretary's less than honorable discharge of plaintiffs based on preinduction activities); Berdo v. Immigration and Naturalization Service, 432 F.2d 824 (6th Cir. 1970) (setting aside deportation order after reversing INS findings that plaintiff was a communist).

128. The effect of these considerations will become apparent when we consider how the courts interpret congressional statutes that appear to foreclose review, for the same considerations play a role in determining the applicability of both exceptions in 701(a). See pp. 896-905, supra.

129. 401 U.S. at 410.

130. For a trenchant criticism of this opinion, see Davis, Administrative Law of the Seventies 637-641 (1976).

131. Professor Saferstein lists the following factors as among those the courts will consider: (1) broad agency discretion, (2) expertise and experience needed to understand the relevant area, (3) managerial nature of the agency, (4) impropriety of judicial intervention,

the factors determining the scope of agency discretion considered in the sections on review of fact and review of law, Chapter 4, since these factors are obviously related to those used to determine the scope of the "committed to agency discretion" exception.[132]

Questions

Do you believe that the court in *Hahn* or in *Langevin* would have refused to review the lawfulness (i.e. the reasonableness) of the rent increases if the court's jurisdiction had been invoked by the defendants in order to enforce the increase? Suppose the landlords had sought judicial help in collecting rent or evicting the tenants for nonpayment. Would the courts have enforced the rent increase order without inquiring into the lawfulness of the rent it contained? Certainly Crowell v. Benson, which Judge Friendly cited, suggests not. (Marbury v. Madison does too, doesn't it?) But would that review of lawfulness have included a review of the reasonableness of the rent? One cannot easily invoke a court's jurisdiction to enforce an order and at the same time argue that the court is precluded from reviewing the legality of the order to be enforced. On this interesting subject, you should read Professor Hart's famous dialogue in Bator, Mishkin, Shapiro & Wechsler, Hart & Wechsler's The Federal Courts and the Federal System 330, 338-344 (2d ed. 1973).

4. The Constitutionality of Preclusion of Review

The Court in *Robinson* stated that its finding of reviewability helped to avoid a constitutional question. That question is whether, or when, Congress can constitutionally curtail a right to judicial review. The question was discussed in Crowell v. Benson, supra, in which Justice Brandeis suggested that "under certain circumstances, the constitutional requirement of due process is a requirement of judicial process." When does "due process" include judicial review? Or, put another way, to what extent can Congress constitutionally preclude judicial review of a decision of a government official? This question is considered at length in Bator, Mishkin, Shapiro & Wechsler, Hart & Wechsler's The Federal Courts and the Federal System 330-375 (2d ed. 1973). We refer you to that discussion. The subject is a difficult and intricate one, which we shall only summarize briefly here.[133]

---

(5) need for informal decisionmaking, (6) inability of the court to insure a later correct agency decision, (7) need for expeditious operation of the agency program, (8) number of potentially appealable actions, (9) existence of other ways to deal with abuse of discretion. H. Saferstein, Nonreviewability: A Functional Analysis of "Committed to Agency Discretion," 82 Harv. L. Rev. 367 (1968).

132. Judge Coffin's opinion in Hahn v. Gottlieb also relies on these factors, 430 F.2d at 1250: "We suppose that there would rarely be a rent increase which some tenant would not challenge in court if he could."

133. See Jaffe, Judicial Control of Administrative Action 376 (1965).

The problem arises out of Article III, Section 1, of the Constitution, which states that the "judicial power of the United States, shall be vested in one Supreme Court, and in such inferior courts as the Congress may from time to time ordain and establish." This section suggests that Congress *may*, but need not, establish lower federal courts. The Supreme Court in Sheldon v. Sill, 49 U.S. (8 How.) 441 (1850), accepted this view and went on to hold that Congress can restrict the jurisdiction of the lower federal courts; it need not grant them full power to hear all federal question cases, "diversity cases," or other sorts of cases that Article III lists as within the scope of the federal judicial power. This view was consistent with the position of those who saw Article III as a Madisonian compromise between those who wanted a strong centralizing federal judicial system and those who feared such a system would strip the state courts of their general jurisdiction, which included jurisdiction over federal questions. Under that compromise Congress would decide the extent to which lower federal courts were needed.[134]

Although Article III may give Congress power to limit the jurisdiction of the federal courts, one might ask whether the exercise of that power could, in a given instance, violate the Due Process Clause. Might it, in depriving a litigant of judicial review, ever deprive him of his life, liberty, or property without due process of law?

This question is the subject of Professor Hart's famous dialogue on the power of Congress to limit the jurisdiction of the federal courts.[135] It is a most important discussion for our purposes; it focuses on an act of Congress that would foreclose the federal courts from hearing a claim that the government has denied a litigant an important constitutional right — a claim, for example, that it has deprived him of free speech or his liberty. Professor Hart concludes that as long as *some* judicial forum — state or federal — is available to test the legality of the claim, Congress can constitutionally foreclose access to other forums. If, for example, all federal courts were denied jurisdiction to hear a particular claim (say, that a litigant was denied free speech), that litigant might raise the claim in a state court, and review of that decision could eventually be sought in the Supreme Court. Under these circumstances, the Act of Congress limiting or foreclosing access to the federal courts would be constitutional. So also may Congress impose reasonable restrictions on the right to review within the federal court system. For example, it may ordinarily direct that review be brought in a specified forum, that a petition to review be filed within 30 days after the challenged agency decision, and so forth.[136]

But suppose that Congress were to enact a statute precluding all review of a

---

134. For a contrary view, that Congress was obliged to endow the lower federal courts with the full scope of Article III's powers, see Martin v. Hunter's Lessee, 1 Wheat. 304 (1816) (Story, J.); Eisenberg, Congressional Authority to Restrict Lower Federal Court Jurisdiction, 83 Yale L. J. 498 (1974).

135. Bator, Mishkin, Shapiro & Wechsler, op. cit. note 91, at 330.

136. In Yakus v. United States, 321 U.S. 414 (1944), for example, the court held that Congress could constitutionally prohibit courts in a criminal prosecution brought under the price control act from considering arguments that the act or regulations issued under it were unconstitutional. However, provision was made for opportunity to raise constitutional issues by judicial challenge to regulations or rent orders, in a Temporary Emergency Court of Appeals prior to prosecution.

particular claim that a federal action was unlawful or unconstitutional. The constitutionality of such an act might depend upon several factors, such as the importance of the underlying right of which the litigant was arguably deprived, the ability of the litigant to obtain some kind of review in some other forum, and the extent to which the courts are already involved in the litigant's case.

We have seen this last mentioned factor at work in Crowell v. Benson, supra. In that case, a litigant invoked the court's jurisdiction to obtain a court order transferring to him property (money) belonging to his employer. Under those circumstances, both the Court and Justice Brandeis indicated that some review of all the legal merits of the claim was constitutionally compelled by due process (and, the Court added, by Article III as well). But, would the Court or Justice Brandeis have reached the same conclusion had the case involved a government benefit rather that a coercive order against an individual's property? Consider, in this respect, the relevance of the decisions in Chapter 7 with respect to due process hearing rights. If a person is entitled to some form of administrative hearing where "liberty" or "property" is at stake, should he not also be entitled to judicial review, not only to ensure agency conformance with due process requirements, but also to determine whether the agency had statutory authority to deprive that person of "liberty" or "property" in the given circumstances?

The courts have not dealt explicitly with the doctrine of a constitutional right to judicial review, nor have they defined its contours. They approached the question tangentially, however, in a series of selective service cases involving the issue of *when* review must take place. In Falbo v. United States, 320 U.S. 549 (1944), the Supreme Court held that a person drafted by his selective service board could not raise questions concerning the legality of his draft classification until *after* he was inducted; he could raise such issues only as a defense in a criminal trial (for refusing induction) or in a habeas corpus proceeding (after induction). In Wolff v. Selective Service Local Board No. 16, 372 F.2d 817 (2d Cir. 1967), however, the Court of Appeals enjoined a draft board from inducting plaintiffs. The court accepted plaintiffs' argument that the board was retaliating against plaintiffs' anti-war demonstration; hence the induction violated First Amendment rights, and for that reason a pre-induction injunction was proper. Congress responded to *Wolff* by enacting a statute explicitly depriving the courts of power to review "the classification or processing of any registrant . . . except as a defense to a criminal prosecution" after induction.[137] 50 U.S.C. App. §460(b)(3). The Supreme Court, interpreting that statute in Oestereich v. Selective Service System Local Board No. 11, 393 U.S. 233 (1968), held that it did *not* prevent a court from issuing a pre-induction injunction barring the board from drafting a divinity student who had protested against the war. The Court argued that another part of the statute specifically exempts full-time ministry students from the draft; since the exemption is "plain and unequivocal," and since the board's action was clearly wrong, "pre-induction judicial review is not precluded . . ." by the statute. 393 U.S. at 238, 239.

---

137. This statute was not intended to deprive those drafted of the right to seek habeus corpus.

Justice Harlan, concurring, wrote that a failure to interpret the statute to allow him review would deprive petitioner of his liberty "without the prior opportunity to present to any competent forum — agency or court — his substantial claim. . . . Such an interpretation [of the statute] . . . would raise serious constitutional problems." 393 U.S. at 243. Justice Harlan then wrote the following footnote: "It is doubtful whether a person may be deprived of his personal liberty without the prior opportunity to be heard by some tribunal competent fully to adjudicate his claims. . . . [citing, among other cases, Londoner v. Denver, 210 U.S. 373, 385 (1908), with "But cf." citations to North American Cold Storage Co. v. Chicago, 211 U.S. 306 (1908), and Bowles v. Willingham, 321 U.S. 503, 520 (1944).]" He asserted that the validity of summary administrative deprivation of liberty without a full hearing may turn on the availability of a prompt subsequent hearing, "something, not made meaningful available to petitioner here, either by the option of defending a criminal prosecution for refusing to report for induction . . . or by filing a petition for a writ of habeas corpus after induction. . . . [If petitioner's argument that the board is punishing him by drafting him is correct,] then postponement of a hearing until after induction is tantamount to permitting the imposition of summary punishment, followed by loss of liberty, without possibility of bail, until [habeas corpus can be secured]." Justice Stewart, responding to Justice Harlan, pointed out that persons arrested for criminal offenses are frequently deprived of their liberty prior to a full hearing. 393 U.S. at 250, n.10.

The reach of *Oestereich* was limited by Clark v. Gabriel, 393 U.S. 256 (1968), which held that pre-induction review was not proper where plaintiffs' claims to deferment raised issues which were not plain and unequivocal. A majority of the Court held that there was no constitutional objection to this interpretation of the statute. A few weeks after deciding *Clark*, the Court applied it to reject a request for pre-induction review of plaintiffs' attack on student deferments based on equal protection grounds. Again, presumably, the Constitution raised no obstacle to postponing review of this constitutional question until after induction.[138]

Questions

a. Did the governing statute in *McAnnulty* provide for judicial review? If not, what is the basis for court review of the Postmaster General's action?

b. Why did the *Switchmen* Court refuse to review the National Mediation Board's decision? Suppose that the Railroad had sided with the Switchmen instead of with the Board and the Brotherhood, and suppose it had refused to bargain with the Brotherhood. Suppose further that the Brotherhood had brought an action in equity asking for enforcement of the Board's certificate. Would the Court, before issuing the order, have examined the lawfulness of the Board's order?

138. See also Breen v. Selective Service System Local Board No. 16, 396 U.S. 460 (1970) (following *Oestereich* to allow preinduction review); Fein v. Selective Service System Local Board No. 7, 405 U.S. 365 (1972) (following *Gabriel* to deny preinduction review). See generally, Donahue, The Supreme Court v. Section 10(b)(3) of the Selective Service Act: A Study in Ducking Constitutional Issues, 17 U.C.L.A. L. Rev. 908 (1970).

c. Examine the two exceptions written into APA §701. Is the exception for "agency action committed to agency discretion by law" in fact an exception? Why does it not just mean that agency action that is lawful (because it does not abuse agency discretion) will not be set aside by a court?

d. Do *Goldberg, Roth* and other due process hearing cases imply that judicial review is sometimes required by due process? If so, under what circumstances is review constitutionally mandated and what is the required scope of review?

e. John Smith was a conscientious objector during the Vietnam war. He spent two years of alternate service in a public hospital, after which he enrolled as a student at State University. In July 1974 he read that the federal courts had interpreted the relevant statutes to require that veterans' educational benefits must be made available to conscientious objectors as well as to armed forces veterans. He telephoned the Veterans' Administration in Washington and asked how to apply for benefits for the following school year. He was told, by a Mr. Jones, that he could apply by letter, which should reach the VA on or before August 31. As he hung up the phone he thought he heard a voice say, "That'll teach the little pacifist fink," but he thought no more of it until his application for benefits was returned with a form which stated that all applications had to reach the VA by July 31.

Smith appealed to the VA for reconsideration, but he was told that no late application would be considered regardless of the reason for delay. Smith now wishes to ask for court review of this decision. The relevant statute states, "All decisions made by the Veterans Administration as to the awarding of veterans benefits or any related benefit or as to any question of fact or law related to any such benefit are final and no such decision nor any related question, whether of fact or of law, shall be reviewed in any way in any court."

What arguments for review might Smith make?

f. Since the beginning of the Republic, statutory provisions in the military draft have existed recognizing the special status of conscientious objectors. Despite this consistent policy, there has never been any statutory protection afforded those who become conscientious objectors after entering the armed services. In 1962, however, the Secretary of Defense issued a directive that "bona fide conscientious objection by persons who are members of the Armed Forces will be recognized to the extent practicable and equitable." Pursuant to this directive, each of the services has promulgated regulations applicable to such persons.

The relevant provisions of the Department of Defense Directive and the Navy Department's regulations may be briefly summarized.[139] A member of the service who seeks discharge on the ground that he has become a conscientious objector since he entered the service must file a discharge request containing substantial personal information and, if possible, supporting statements from others. The applicant is then to be interviewed by his commanding officer, who forwards a recommendation to the Chief of Naval Personnel. The Chief of Naval Personnel is required to refer each application to the head of the Selective Service System for an "advisory opinion," and to give the opinion great weight. The regulations do not

139. These regulations are roughly, but not precisely, equivalent to those in effect in 1970.

provide for any opportunity to be heard other than in the application and in the interview with the commanding officer. It is further provided by the directive and in the regulations that "[d]etermination of a request for discharge is committed to the discretion of the department, and such determination shall be final and binding and not subject to further review in any tribunal with respect to the administrative separation of its members."

Henry Emerson, then a 17-year-old high school student, enlisted in the Naval Reserve in 1966 and has been a participating member of the active reserves ever since. He was not called for active duty. In June, 1970, he became a member of a pacifist organization and in December, 1970, he submitted a request for discharge on the ground of conscientious objection. After the prescribed interview, the commanding officer concluded that Emerson was sincere in his convictions and recommended discharge. The case was then forwarded to the head of the Selective Service System for an advisory opinion, and the opinion given, without further explanation was that: "Based on the information in his file, it is my opinion that Henry Emerson would not be classified as a conscientious objector if he were being considered for induction at this time."

Emerson's request was denied without explanation, and he was ordered to continue attending drills in accordance with his reserve obligation. When he refused, he was ordered to report for active duty on December 1, 1971. Emerson has just filed, in the federal district court of his residence, a petition for a writ of habeas corpus on the ground that the denial of his conscientious objector status was "without basis in fact," and that the decision violated his rights under the First and Fifth Amendments. The Government has moved to dismiss the writ on the ground that the decision of the Navy is not subject to judicial review.

How should the Court rule on the motion? Should the disposition of the motion turn on whether there is merit to Emerson's claim of a *constitutional* right to be discharged?

C. Standing to Secure Judicial Review

1. Introductory Note

In addition to establishing that administrative action is reviewable, a litigant challenging such action must also satisfy requirements of standing that limit the class of persons entitled to secure judicial review. As developed below, American administrative law has traditionally restricted the right of judicial review to persons who can show particularized injury recognized by law as entitled to protection.[140]

---

140. While reviewability and standing are logically distinct requirements, standing limitations may sometimes be so restrictive in impact as to disqualify all would-be litigants, thus immunizing from judicial review otherwise reviewable agency action. See, e.g., Perkins v. Lukens Steel Co., 310 U.S. 113, 125 (1940).

Specific agency statutes sometimes spell out who is entitled to seek review. For example, the Federal Communications Act, §402(b)(1), 47 U.S.C. §402(b)(1) (1970), provides for review by disappointed applicants for a license. Very frequently, however, specific agency statutes provide generally for review without identifying who is entitled to review. When a litigant seeks "non-statutory" review under the federal district courts' general jurisdiction there is likewise no statutory specification of standing. In these contexts, standing law is judge-made. The Administrative Procedure Act, §702, attempted to codify federal judge-made standing rules by providing for judicial review for a "person suffering legal wrong because of agency action, or adversely affected or aggrieved within the meaning of a relevant statute." However, as demonstrated in the materials that follow, the federal courts have not read the APA as a static codification of standing law as of 1946; on the contrary, they have displayed considerable freedom in modifying judicially-formulated standing doctrines in accordance with current perceptions and needs.

During the development of the traditional model of administrative law at the end of the nineteenth century, standing was ordinarily limited to persons who, due to government action, had suffered specific injury of a type that would be protected at common law if the perpetrator had been a private person. For example, if a government official committed what would otherwise be a common-law tort, by seizing a person's property to satisfy a tax claim or arresting a person for violation of a cease and desist order, the person could seek judicial review to test the statutory authority of the official to impose such an injury. If, however, a government official simply declined to pay a person a welfare benefit or afford her an educational scholarship, no interest protected at common law would be infringed, and she would accordingly lack standing to secure judicial review of the official's conduct even if it were in flagrant violation of relevant statutes. This limitation of the right to judicial review to instances where common law interests are invaded parallels the "right/privilege" limitation of traditional due process hearing rights, both of which find roots in the use in English law of common law tort actions to control official conduct.[141] They also reflect a particular version of contractarian political theory, in which the government is viewed as an artificial person, subject to the same limitations and enjoying the same liberties as any other person under the common law. If government invaded an individual's common-law protected interest, it might defend on the ground that the plaintiff consented to the invasion through legislation enacted by a representative assembly. On this view, judicial review becomes the occasion for testing the validity of this justification for what otherwise would be a common law wrong.[142]

141. For a discussion of the right/privilege limitation in the due process context, see pp. 595-603, supra. Some of the common law prerogative writs also required plaintiff to establish particular forms of specific injury, although in other instances prerogative writs might be invoked by any private citizen in order to facilitate control by the king's judges of unlawful behavior by subordinate officials. See L. Jaffe, Judicial Control of Administrative Action 462-475 (1965). See generally, J. Vining, Logical Identity (1978).

142. See Stewart, The Reformation of American Administrative Law, 88 Harv. L. Rev. 1667, 1723-1725 (1975). See also J. Vining, op. cit. note 141.

As developed below, standing has been expanded by extending the right of judicial review to interests recognized and protected by the statute which the agency is charged with violating; this expansion is consistent with a contractarian theory.

With the rise of the modern welfare state, this model of administrative law has increasingly proven both theoretically and functionally inadequate. Limiting standing to common-law protected interests would effectively immunize from judicial review many activities of modern government; in particular, the disposition of advantageous opportunities such as assistance payments, housing, government employment, and the like. In addition, the growing sense of agency "failure" has led to a perceived need for judicial protection of the supposed beneficiaries of traditional regulatory activities, such as airline passengers or television viewers, or of other interests (such as those of environmental groups) indirectly affected by agency decisions such as highway routings. But, unlike regulated firms subject to coercive sanctions, such persons are normally not affected by regulatory activities in ways that would give rise to standing under the traditional model.

In response to the perceived inadequacies of traditional standing doctrines both with respect to administrative regulation of business conduct and the activities of the modern welfare state, the last several decades have witnessed a considerable liberalization of judge-made standing rules. However, the federal courts have declined to embrace the "public action," in which any citizen (or, in some contexts, any taxpayer) is recognized as having a sufficient stake in maintaining the rule of law to bring suit challenging assertedly unlawful official action.[143] Federal courts still insist that the plaintiff establish that he has suffered some specific, tangible injury as a direct result of government conduct in order to secure judicial review of its legality. This requirement tends to ensure that courts decide legal issues in the context of a sharply defined factual situation at the instance of a litigant with an immediate stake in the outcome. A traditional justification for this requirement is that only plaintiffs with a concrete personal stake will litigate a case with sufficient adversary vigor; this justification has been criticized on the ground that *any* plaintiff willing to undertake the travail and expense of litigation is likely to litigate vigorously. Another justification for the requirement rests on democratic political theory: courts should not undertake to resolve general issues of policy that are better dealt with through the political branches, and should only intervene to protect discrete individual interests.[144] Do these considerations indeed justify federal refusal to entertain "public actions"? Is a requirement of specific injury required by Article III of the Constitution, which limits federal courts' jurisdiction to "cases or controversies"? If a requirement of specific injury is constitutionally required or otherwise desirable, how should it be defined in the context of the modern regulatory and

143. For explication and advocacy of the "public action," see L. Jaffe, Judicial Control of Administrative Action 459-500 (1965); Jaffe, The Citizen as Litigant in Public Actions: The Non-Hohfeldian or Ideological Plaintiff, 116 U. Pa. L. Rev. 1033 (1968).

As Professor Jaffe points out, the "public action" is recognized (in certain contexts) in England and in many states. The acceptance of the "public action" in the states may in part reflect the status of the state courts as heirs to the prerogative authority of the English judges (including the authority to check unlawful conduct by inferior officials), and in part the greater concern at the state level with governmental corruption and the corresponding reliance on citizen suits as an antidote.

The closest approximation to acceptance by the Supreme Court of the public action is Flast v. Cohen, 392 U.S. 83 (1968), upholding the standing of federal taxpayers to challenge the constitutionality of federal expenditures as violative of the Establishment Clause.

144. See Note, Congressional Access to the Federal Courts, 90 Harv. L. Rev. 1632 (1977).

welfare state? These questions should be the focus of your inquiry in examining the materials which follow.

2. The Federal Law of Standing Prior to Data Processing

Alabama Power Co. v. Ickes
===

302 U.S. 464 (1938)

Mr. Justice SUTHERLAND delivered the opinion of the Court. . . .

[Petitioner Alabama Power Co., a privately owned electric power company, brought suit challenging grants by the Federal Energy Administrator of financial aid to municipal electric power companies as part of a federal public works program. Alabama Power contended that it would be competitively injured as a result of the grants, and asserted that the grants violated the Constitution and relevant federal statutes.]

Unless a different conclusion is required from the mere fact that petitioner will sustain financial loss by reason of the unlawful competition which will result from the use by the municipalities of the proposed loans and grants, it is clear that petitioner has no such interest and will sustain no such legal injury as enables it to maintain the present suits. Petitioner alleges that it is a taxpayer; but the interest of a taxpayer in the moneys of the federal treasury furnishes no basis for an appeal to the preventive powers of a court of equity. Massachusetts v. Mellon, 262 U.S. 447, 486 et seq. The principle established by the case just cited is that the courts have no power to consider in isolation and annul an act of Congress on the ground that it is unconstitutional; but may consider that question "only when the justification for some direct injury suffered or threatened, presenting a justiciable issue, is made to rest upon such an act." The term "direct injury" is there used in its legal sense, as meaning a wrong which directly results in the violation of a legal right. "An injury, legally speaking, consists of a wrong done to a person, or, in other words, a violation of his right. It is an ancient maxim, that a damage to one, without an injury in this sense, (damnum absque injuria), does not lay the foundation of an action; because, if the act complained of does not violate any of his legal rights, it is obvious, that he has no cause to complain. . . . Want of right and want of remedy are justly said to be reciprocal. Where therefore there has been a violation of a right, the person injured is entitled to an action." Parker v. Griswold, 17 Conn. 288, 302-303. The converse is equally true, that where, although there is damage, there is no violation of a right no action can be maintained.

The only pertinent inquiry, then, is what enforceable legal right of petitioner do the alleged wrongful agreements invade or threaten? If conspiracy or fraud or malice or coercion were involved a different case would be presented, but in their absence, plainly enough, the *mere* consummation of the loans and grants will not constitute an actionable wrong. Nor will the subsequent application by the municipalities of the moneys derived therefrom give rise to an actionable wrong, since such application, being lawful, will invade no legal right of petitioner. The claim that petitioner will be injured, perhaps ruined, by the competition of the municipalities brought about by the use of the moneys, therefore, presents a clear case of damnum absque injuria. Stated in other words, these municipalities have the right under state law to engage in the business in competition with petitioner, since it has been given no exclusive franchise. If its business be curtailed or destroyed by the operations of the municipalities, it will be by lawful competition from which no legal wrong results. . . .

John Doe, let us suppose, is engaged in operating a grocery store. Richard Roe, desiring to open a rival and competing establishment, seeks a loan from a manufacturing concern which, under its charter, is without authority to make the loan. The loan, if made, will be *ultra vires*. The state or a stockholder of the corporation, perhaps a creditor in some circumstances, may, upon that ground, enjoin the loan. But may it be enjoined at the suit of John Doe, a stranger to the corporation, because the lawful use of the money will prove injurious to him and this result is foreseen and expected both by the lender and the borrower, Richard Roe? Certainly not, unless we are prepared to lay down the general rule that A, who will suffer damage from the lawful act of B, and who plainly will have no case against B, may nevertheless invoke judicial aid to restrain a third party, acting without authority, from furnishing means which will enable B to do what the law permits him to do. Such a rule would be opposed to sound reason, as we have already tried to show, and cannot be accepted.

[Mr. Justice BLACK concurred in the result.]

Notes and Questions

See also Perkins v. Lukens Steel Co., 310 U.S. 113 (1940), mentioned at p. 895, supra. The Davis-Bacon Act requires government suppliers to pay their employees wages not less than those prevailing in the "locality" of employment. The Secretary of Labor, who was authorized to define geographic localities for purposes of this provision, divided the entire nation into six "localities." The Act does not provide specifically for judicial review of the Secretary's determinations. A number of suppliers obtained an injunction in federal district court against operation of the minimum-wage requirements, contending that the Secretary's definition of "localities" was unduly broad and was contrary to the Act. The Supreme Court held that the suppliers' actions should have been dismissed because the suppliers had not shown "an invasion of recognized legal rights" of their own, "as distinguished from the public's interest in the administration of the law." The Court reasoned that: "Like private individuals and businesses, the Government enjoys the unrestricted power . . . to determine those with whom it will deal, and to fix the terms and conditions upon which it will make needed purchases." The Court also asserted that the Davis-Bacon Act "was not intended to be a bestowal of litigable rights upon those desirous of selling to the government. . . ."

In view of *Alabama Power* and *Lukens Steel*, should Decatur v. Paulding, p. 892 supra, be understood as a standing decision? *Switchmen's Union*? What was the basis for plaintiff's standing in *American School of Magnetic Healing?*

The Chicago Junction Case

264 U.S. 258 (1924)

[As part of a larger scheme to regulate competition in the railroad industry, the Transportation Act of 1920 amended the Interstate Commerce Act to require ICC approval of railroad consolidations upon a determination that such consolidations were in the "public interest." Section 3(3) provided that carriers shall afford "reasonable, proper and equal facilities for the interchange of traffic." The ICC approved the New York Central's acquisition of two terminal railways in Chicago engaged in switching through traffic from one carrier to another. Six carriers who were competitors of the Central sought judicial review of the Commission's action, claiming that the acquisition would enable the Central to obtain a disproportionate share of through traffic. The Act provided for judicial review of ICC orders by a three-judge district court without specifying who was entitled to seek judicial review. The Supreme Court, in an opinion by Mr. Justice Brandeis, reversed the district court's dismissal of the competitors' action.]

[BRANDEIS, J.]

The defendants contend that the plaintiffs have not the legal interest necessary to entitle them to challenge the order. That they have in fact a vital interest is admitted. They are the competitors of the New York Central. Practically all the tonnage originated at or destined to points on these terminal railroads is competitive, in that the same can be hauled either over the lines of the New York Central or over those of the plaintiffs. Prior to the date of the order, and while the terminal railroads were uncontrolled by any trunk line carrier, they were all served impartially and without discrimination; and they competed for the traffic on equal terms. The order substitutes for neutral control of the terminal railroads, monopoly of control in the New York Central; and, in so doing, necessarily gives to it substantial advantage over all its competitors and subjects the latter to serious disadvantage and prejudice. The main purpose of the acquisition by the New York Central was to secure a larger share of the Chicago business. By means of the preferential position incident to the control of these terminal railroads, it planned to obtain traffic theretofore enjoyed by its competitors. Because such was the purpose of the New York Central control, and would necessarily be its effect, these plaintiffs intervened before the Commission. That their apprehensions were well founded is shown by the results. The plaintiffs are no longer permitted to compete with the New York Central on equal terms. A large volume of traffic has been diverted from their lines to those of the New York Central. The diversion of traffic has already subjected the plaintiffs to irreparable injury. The loss sustained exceeds $10,000,000. Continued control by the New York Central will subject them to an annual loss in net earnings of approximately that amount....

This loss is not the incident of more effective competition.... It is injury inflicted by denying to the plaintiffs equality of treatment. To such treatment carriers are, under the Interstate Commerce Act, as fully entitled as any shipper. Pennsylvania Co. v. United States, 236 U.S. 351. It is true that, before Transportation Act, 1920, the Interstate Commerce Act would not have prohibited the owners of the terminal railroads from selling them to the New York Central. Nor would it have prohibited the latter company from making the purchase. . . . [T]he purchase might have enabled the New York Central to exclude all other carriers from use of the terminals. . . . But Transportation Act, 1920, . . . made provision for securing joint use of terminals; and it prohibited any acquisition of a railroad by a carrier, unless authorized by the Commission. By reason of this legislation, the plaintiffs, being competitors of the New York Central and users of the terminal railroads theretofore neutral, have a special interest in the proposal to transfer the control to that company. . . .

Mr. Justice SUTHERLAND dissenting. [Justices MCREYNOLDS and SANFORD concurred in this dissent.]

I think the injuries alleged to have been sustained by complainants are not such as to afford the basis for a legal remedy. Complainants are interested only in the sense that the acquisition of the rights here in question by their competitor will enable the latter to absorb a larger share of the business. That is not enough to constitute a remediable interest.

Before Transportation Act, 1920, the New York Central would have been free to acquire these terminals without the consent of the Commission. If it had done so, its gain of business with the resulting loss to complainants would have been the same; but it would be inadmissible to assert that complainants might have maintained a suit to annul or enjoin the acquisition on the ground of that injury. "The effort of a carrier to obtain more business . . . proceeds from the motive of self-interest which is recognized as legitimate." United States v. Illinois Central R. R. Co., 263 U.S. 515, 523.

It is claimed, however, that Transportation Act, 1920, so alters the rule as to give a right of action to complainants where none existed before. I am unable to perceive any sound basis for the conclusion. That act, so far as this question is concerned, requires the carrier, as a prerequisite to an acquisition of the charter here under consideration, to secure the authorization of the Commission, which that body may grant if "it will be in the public interest." The mere effect of such acquisition upon the business of competing lines is no more to be considered since the Act of 1920 than it was prior to the passage thereof. It is the public, not private, interest which is to be considered.

The complainants have no standing to vindicate the rights of the public, but only to protect and enforce their own rights. . . . The right of the complainants to sue, therefore, cannot rest upon the alleged violation of a public interest, but must rest upon some distinct grievance of their own. Loss of business, or of opportunities to get business, attributable to the activity or increase of facilities on the part of the competitor is not enough. Transportation Act, 1920, lays down no new or additional rule by which the question, What constitutes a legal or equitable right, interference with which may give rise to an action? may be tested. . . .

Questions

(1) Can *Chicago Junction* be reconciled with *Alabama Power* and *Perkins?*

(2) What question divides Justice Brandeis and Justice Sutherland in *Chicago Junction?* How would you go about deciding that question?

(3) Standing is ordinarily thought of as a threshold determination that can be resolved before the court reaches the merits. Does *Chicago Junction* destroy this understanding by making plaintiff's standing depend on whether plaintiff has a "legal right" that has been invaded, and equating the question of plaintiff's "legal right" with its ability to prevail on the merits? Is a test based on the existence of a "legally protected interest" ultimately circular, since a court cannot determine whether an interest is legally protected until it reaches the merits of a controversy, which it cannot do until it resolves the standing issue?

FCC v. Sanders Brothers Radio Station

309 U.S. 470 (1940)

[Sanders Brothers intervened in a proceeding before the FCC on the application by the Telegraph Herald, a newspaper located in Dubuque, Iowa, for a license to establish a radio station in that city. The station would compete in the same service area as Sanders Brothers' station; Sanders Brothers contended that there was insufficient advertising revenue in the area to sustain two stations, and that competition between the two stations might drive both of them into bankruptcy, depriving the local public of radio service. The Commission granted the license sought by the Telegraph Herald. Sanders Brothers sought judicial review of the Commission's action, relying upon §402(b) of the Federal Communications Act, which provides for review of FCC actions by the District of Columbia Circuit Court of Appeals at the behest of a license applicant or "by any other person aggrieved or whose interests are adversely affected by any decision of the Commission granting or refusing [a license application]." The Court of Appeals ruled the FCC had erred in failing to make adequate findings on the extent of adverse financial impact on Sanders Brothers resulting from the license grant, and set aside the FCC's action. Following the Supreme Court's grant of certiorari, the government reiterated its claim that Sanders Brothers lacked standing to secure judicial review of the FCC's actions.]

[ROBERTS, J.]

First. We hold that resulting economic injury to a rival station is not, in and of itself, and apart from considerations of public convenience, interest, or necessity, an element the petitioner must weigh, and as to which it must make findings, in passing on an application for a broadcasting license.

Section 307(a) of the Communications Act directs that "the Commission, if public convenience, interest, or necessity will be served thereby, subject to the limitations of this Act, shall grant to any applicant therefore a station license provided for by this Act." ... The Act contains no express command that in passing upon an application the Commission must consider the effect of competition with an existing station. Whether the Commission should consider the subject must depend upon the purpose of the Act and the specific provisions intended to effectuate that purpose.

The genesis of the Communications Act and the necessity for the adoption of some such regulatory measure is a matter of history. The number of available radio frequencies is limited. The attempt by a broadcaster to use a given frequency in disregard of its prior use by others, thus creating confusion and interference, deprives the public of the full benefit of radio audition. Unless Congress has exercised its power over interstate commerce to bring about allocation of available frequencies and to regulate the employment of transmission equipment the result would have been an impairment of the effective use of these facilities by anyone. The fundamental purpose of Congress in respect of broadcasting was the allocation and regulation of the use of radio frequencies by prohibiting such use except under license.

In contradistinction to communication by telephone and telegraph, which the Communications Act recognizes as a common carrier activity and regulates accordingly in analogy to the regulation of rail and other carriers by the Interstate Commerce Commission, the Act recognizes that broadcasters are not common carriers and are not to be dealt with as such. Thus the Act recognizes that the field of broadcasting is one of free competition. The sections dealing with broadcasting demonstrate that Congress has not, in its regulatory scheme, abandoned the principle of free competition, as it has done in the case of railroads,[145] in respect of which regulation involves the suppression of wasteful practices due to competition, the regulation of rates and charges, and other measures which are unnecessary if free competition is to be permitted.

An important element of public interest and convenience affecting the issue of a license is the ability of the licensee to render the best practicable service to the community reached by its broadcasts. That such ability may be assured the Act contemplates inquiry by the Commission, inter alia, into an applicant's financial qualifications to operate the proposed station.[146]

The policy of the Act is clear that no person is to have anything in the nature of a property right as a result of the granting of a license. Licenses are limited to a maximum of three years' duration, may be revoked, and need not be renewed. Thus the channels presently occupied remain free for a new assignment to another licensee in the interest of the listening public.

Plainly it is not the purpose of the Act to protect a licensee against competition but to protect the public. Congress intended to leave competition in the business of broadcasting where it found it, to permit a licensee who was not interfering electrically with other broadcasters to survive or succumb according to his ability to make his programs attractive to the public.

This is not to say that the question of competition between a proposed station and one operating under an existing license is to be entirely disregarded by the Commission, and, indeed, the Commission's practice shows that it does not disregard that question. It may have a vital and important bearing upon the ability of

145. Compare Texas & Pacific Ry. v. Gulf, C. & S.F. Ry. Co., 270 U.S. 266, 277; Chicago Junction Case, 264 U.S. 258.
146. See §308(b), 47 U.S.C. §308(b).

the applicant adequately to serve his public; it may indicate that both stations — the existing and the proposed — will go under, with the result that a portion of the listening public will be left without adequate service; it may indicate that, by a division of the field, both stations will be compelled to render inadequate service. These matters, however, are distinct from the consideration that, if a license be granted, competition between the licensee and any other existing station may cause economic loss to the latter. If such economic loss were a valid reason for refusing a license this would mean that the Commission's function is to grant a monopoly in the field of broadcasting, a result which the Act itself expressly negatives, which Congress would not have contemplated without granting the Commission powers of control over the rates, programs, and other activities of the business of broadcasting.

We conclude that economic injury to an existing station is not a separate and independent element to be taken into consideration by the Commission in determining whether it shall grant or withhold a license.

Second. It does not follow that, because the licensee of a station cannot resist the grant of a license to another, on the ground that the resulting competition may work economic injury to him, he has no standing to appeal from an order of the Commission granting the application.

Section 402(b) of the Act provides for an appeal to the Court of Appeals of the District of Columbia (1) by an applicant for a license or permit, or (2) "by any other person aggrieved or whose interests are adversely affected by any decision of the Commission granting or refusing any such application."

The petitioner insists that as economic injury to the respondent was not a proper issue before the Commission it is impossible that §402(b) was intended to give the respondent standing to appeal, since absence of right implies absence of remedy. This view would deprive subsection (2) of any substantial effect.

Congress had some purpose in enacting §402(b)(2). It may have been of opinion that one likely to be financially injured by the issue of a license would be the only person having a sufficient interest to bring to the attention of the appellate court errors of law in the action of the Commission in granting the license. It is within the power of Congress to confer such standing to prosecute an appeal.

We hold, therefore, that the respondent had the requisite standing to appeal and to raise, in the court below, any relevant question of law in respect of the order of the Commission.

[On the merits, the Court concluded that the Commission had made adequate findings on the financial impact of the license grant as it affected service to the public, and reversed the judgment of the Court of Appeals.]

Notes and Questions

1. Can *Sanders Bros.* be reconciled with *Alabama Power* and *Chicago Junction*?

2. If Sanders Brothers is not granted standing to protect its own economic interests, precisely whose interests is it supposed to be representing as a surrogate? Does this arrangement threaten conflicts of interest?

Compare the reasoning in *Sanders Bros.* with that in Associated Industries v. Ickes, 134 F.2d 694 (2d Cir.), *vacated on suggestion of mootness*, 320 U.S. 707 (1943), sustaining the standing of a trade association representing major energy consumers to seek judicial review of a government decision increasing the price of coal. The relevant statute provided for judicial review by persons "aggrieved" by orders issued in proceedings to which they were a party. Associated Industries had been a party in the administrative proceedings leading to the coal order, but the government contended that Associated Industries had no "legal right" to a particular price for coal and that it was therefore not "aggrieved" within the meaning of the statute. The court held, however, that the term "aggrieved" was equivalent to the "adversely affected or aggrieved" language in the Communications Act relied upon in *Sanders Bros.*; and that Associated Industries was sufficiently adversely affected (and therefore "aggrieved") by the coal price increase to enjoy statutory standing to represent the interests of the "public" in the guise of a "private attorney general."

Note: The Effect of the APA on Standing

The APA §702, affords standing for a "person suffering legal wrong . . . or adversely affected or aggrieved by agency action within the meaning of a relevant statute." This provision is best understood as codifying the various bases for standing developed in previous judicial decisions. The term "legal wrong" encompasses injuries to interests of plaintiff protected either by common law or statute, while the phrase "adversely affected or aggrieved within the meaning of a relevant statute" encompasses cases like *Sanders Bros.* and *Associated Industries*, where a specific agency statute granted standing to parties "adversely affected or aggrieved," even though their injury was not otherwise legally protected.[147]

3. *The* Data Processing *Test*

Association of Data Processing Service Organizations v. Camp

397 U.S. 150 (1970)

Mr. Justice DOUGLAS delivered the opinion of the Court.

Petitioners sell data processing services to businesses generally. In this suit they

147. See Stewart, The Reformation of American Administrative Law, 88 Harv. L. Rev. 1667 (1975).

Professor Davis has long contended that the APA should be construed to extend standing to any person suffering "injury in fact" as a result of agency action, on the supposition that such persons are "adversely affected" within the meaning of §702. 3 K. Davis, Administrative Law Treatise 291 (1958). However, this construction ignores the qualifying phrase "within the meaning of a relevant statute," and would also render superfluous §702's reference to "legal wrong" and "aggrieved." Moreover, such a construction would have worked a dramatic liberalization of standing in the law as of 1946. There is no evidence that Congress contemplated such a change, or that it intended anything more than a codification of preexisting judge-made standing law.

seek to challenge a ruling by respondent Comptroller of the Currency that, as an incident to their banking services, national banks, including respondent American National Bank & Trust Company, may make data processing services available to other banks and to bank customers. The District Court dismissed the complaint for lack of standing of petitioners to bring the suit. 279 F. Supp. 675. The Court of Appeals affirmed. 406 F.2d 837. . . .

Generalizations about standing to sue are largely worthless as such. One generalization is, however, necessary and that is that the question of standing in the federal courts is to be considered in the framework of Article III which restricts judicial power to "cases" and "controversies." As we recently stated in Flast v. Cohen, 392 U.S. 83, 101, "[I]n terms of Article III limitations on federal court jurisdiction, the question of standing is related only to whether the dispute sought to be adjudicated will be presented in an adversary context and in a form historically viewed as capable of juicial resolution." *Flast* was a *taxpayer's* suit. The present is a *competitor's* suit. And while the two have the same Article III starting point, they do not necessarily track one another.

The first question is whether the plaintiff alleges that challenged action has caused him injury in fact, economic or otherwise. There can be no doubt but that petitioners have satisfied this test. The petitioners not only allege that competition by national banks in the business of providing data processing services might entail some future loss of profits for the petitioners, they also allege that respondent American National Bank & Trust Company was performing or preparing to perform such services for two customers for whom petitioner Data Systems, Inc., had previously agreed or negotiated to perform such services. . . .

The Court of Appeals viewed the matter differently, stating:

> [A] plaintiff may challenge alleged illegal competition when as complainant it pursues (1) a legal interest by reason of public charter or contract, . . . (2) a legal interest by reason of statutory protection, . . . or (3) a "public interest" in which Congress has recognized the need for review of administrative action and plaintiff is significantly involved to have standing to represent the public. . . . 406 F.2d, at 842-843.[148] . . .

The "legal interest" test goes to the merits. The question of standing is different. It concerns, apart from the "case" or "controversy" test, the question whether the interest sought to be protected by the complainant is arguably within the zone of interests to be protected or regulated by the statute or constitutional guarantee in question. Thus the Administrative Procedure Act grants standing to a person

---

148. The first two tests applied by the Court of Appeals required a showing of a "legal interest." But the existence or nonexistence of a "legal interest" is a matter quite distinct from the problem of standing. The third test mentioned by the Court of Appeals, which rests on an explicit provision in a regulatory statute conferring standing and is commonly referred to in terms of allowing suits by "private attorneys general," is inapplicable to the present case. See FCC v. Sanders Bros. Radio Station, 309 U.S. 470; Associated Industries v. Ickes, 134 F.2d 694, vacated on suggestion of mootness, 320 U.S. 707.

"aggrieved by agency action within the meaning of a relevant statute." 5 U.S.C. §702 (1964 ed., Supp. IV). That interest, at times, may reflect "aesthetic, conservational, and recreational" as well as economic values. Scenic Hudson Preservation Conf. v. FPC, 354 F.2d 608, 616; Office of Communication of United Church of Christ v. FCC, 123 U.S. App. D.C. 328, 334-340, 359 F.2d 994, 1000-1006. . . .

We mention these noneconomic values to emphasize that standing may stem from them as well as from the economic injury on which petitioners rely here. Certainly he who is "likely to be financially" injured, FCC v. Sanders Bros. Radio Station, 309 U.S. 470, 477, may be a reliable private attorney general to litigate the issues of the public interest in the present case.

Apart from Article III jurisdictional questions, problems of standing, as resolved by this Court for its own governance, have involved a "rule of self-restraint." Barrows v. Jackson, 346 U.S. 249, 255. Congress can, of course, resolve the question one way or another, save as the requirements of Article III dictate otherwise. Muskrat v. United States, 219 U.S. 346.

Where statutes are concerned, the trend is toward enlargement of the class of people who may protest administrative action. The whole drive for enlarging the category of aggrieved "persons" is symptomatic of that trend. In a closely analogous case we held that an existing entrepreneur had standing to challenge the legality of the entrance of a newcomer into the business, because the established business was allegedly protected by a valid city ordinance that protected it from unlawful competition. Chicago v. Atchison, T. & S. F. R. Co., 357 U.S. 77, 83-84. In that tradition was Hardin v. Kentucky Utilities Co., 390 U.S. 1, which involved a section of the TVA Act designed primarily to protect, through area limitations, private utilities against TVA competition. We held that no explicit statutory provision was necessary to confer standing, since the private utility suit was within the class of persons that the statutory provision was designed to protect.

It is argued that the *Chicago* case and the *Hardin* case are relevant here because of §4 of the Bank Service Corporation Act of 1962, 76 Stat. 1132, 12 U.S.C. §1864, which provides: "No bank service corporation may engage in any activity other than the performance of bank services for banks."

The Court of Appeals for the First Circuit held in Arnold Tours, Inc. v. Camp, 408 F.2d 1147, 1153, that by reason of §4 a data processing company has standing to contest the legality of a national bank performing data processing services for other banks and bank customers:

> Section 4 had a broader purpose than regulating only the service corporations. It was also a response to the fears expressed by a few senators, that without such a prohibition, the bill would have enabled "banks to engage in a non-banking activity," S. Rep. No. 2195, [87th Cong., 2d Sess., 7-12] (Supplemental views of Senators Proxmire, Douglas, and Neuberger), and thus constitute "a serious exception to the accepted public policy which strictly limits banks to banking." (Supplemental views of Senators Muskie and Clark). We think Congress has provided the sufficient statutory aid to standing even though the competition may not be the precise kind Congress legislated against.

We do not put the issue in those words, for they implicate the merits. We do think, however, that §4 arguably brings a competitor within the zone of interests protected by it. . . .

[The Court rejected the claim that judicial review of the Comptroller's action was precluded.]

Whether anything in the Bank Service Corporation Act or the National Bank Act[149] gives petitioners a "legal interest" that protects them against violations of those Acts, and whether the actions of respondents did in fact violate either of those Acts, are questions which go to the merits and remain to be decided below.

We hold that petitioners have standing to sue and that the case should be remanded for a hearing on the merits.

Notes

In a companion case, Barlow v. Collins, 397 U.S. 159 (1970), Justice Douglas used the principles developed in *Data Processing* to sustain the standing of tenant farmers to challenge regulations issued by the Secretary of Labor under the upland cotton programs of the Food and Agriculture Act of 1965, providing for advance payment of federal crop subsidies to farmers. The challenged regulation, which regulated the disposition of such advance payments, permitted their assignment to secure payment of cash rents. The tenant farmers complained that this regulation would permit their landlords to exercise their superior bargaining power to demand, as a condition of lease, assignment of the federal payments to cover rent due. Deprived of the liquidity afforded by government payments, the tenant farmers would also allegedly become dependent on their landlords for advances, at assertedly exhorbitant prices, of materials and food during the growing season. The Court held that these allegations demonstrated "injury in fact," and held further that the tenants were "arguably within the zone" of interests protected by the Food and Agriculture Act of 1965, which provides in general terms, without specific reference to the disposition of advance payments, that the Secretary should "provide adequate safeguards to protect the interests of tenants. . . ."

Mr. Justice Brennan, joined by Mr. Justice White, filed an opinion in *Data Processing* and *Barlow* concurring in the result but dissenting from the Court's reasoning. He argued that the Court's dual test for standing confused three distinct issues: standing, reviewability, and the merits.

The requirement of standing was equated by Justice Brennan with the "case or controversy" requirement of Article III that plaintiff have "such a personal stake in the outcome of a controversy as to assure that concrete adverseness which sharpens the presentation of issues upon which the court so largely depends for

149. Ed. Note: Petitioners had also claimed that the Comptroller's ruling violated the National Bank Act, Rev. Stat. §5136, 12 U.S.C. §24 Seventh, which provides that national banks have power to exercise "all such incidental powers as shall be necessary to carry on the business of banking." The Court indicated that this Act also conferred standing on petitioners, who claimed that the Act did not authorize banks to offer data processing services to the public.

illumination of difficult . . . questions." Justice Brennan concluded that this requirement is met when plaintiff alleges that the challenged government action "has caused him injury in fact, economic or otherwise," regardless of whether his interest is protected by the common law or a relevant statute. This standing was equated with a *constitutional* requirement of "injury in fact."

The second issue, argued Justice Brennan, is reviewability, which involves not only the issue whether the agency's action is *generally* subject to review, but also whether Congress intended to preclude review by a given class of persons of which plaintiff is a member. The third issue concerns the merits — whether the specific interest asserted by plaintiff is legally protected by the relevant statute, and whether the challenged agency action invaded that protected interest. Justice Brennan feared that the majority's "arguably within the zone" test confused standing and the merits, and would lead to poorly reasoned and erroneous decisions by the lower federal courts.

Questions

1. What justifications does Justice Douglas offer for construing the APA to afford standing to any litigant that can allege "injury in fact" and is "arguably within the zone of interests to be protected or regulated by the statute or constitutional guarantee in question"? How does one determine whether a litigant is "arguably within the zone"? Note that the Court of Appeals had based its decision on the well-established preexisting law. Why did the Supreme Court believe it is necessary to modify the prior law?

2. Justice Brennan is correct, is he not, in asserting that when a plaintiff bases standing on an interest protected by statute, the question whether plaintiff's interest is legally protected is the same as the question whether plaintiff has a claim on the merits? What purpose is served by introducing the notion whether plaintiff is "arguably within the zone" of protected interests? Note Justice Douglas' suggestion that the "arguably within the zone" test enables the court to dispose of the threshold question of standing while postponing a ruling on the merits. But why shouldn't the court, if it conveniently can, dispose at the outset of the question whether plaintiff's interest is or is not protected by statute? For example, why shouldn't the Court now decide whether the National Banking Act protects bank competitors from competition? It may be that the Court would prefer to defer a definitive ruling on this purely legal issue until development of the relevant facts at trial. But in some cases it would be possible to resolve this legal issue at the outset, averting wasted proceedings thereafter.

3. Were the restrictions of the National Banking Act and the Bank Service Corporation Act designed to protect nonbanking enterprises from competition by banks? If not, whose interests were they designed to protect? Even if the statutes were not intended to protect data processers, might they still be afforded standing on grounds similar to those in *Sanders Bros.*?

4. Evaluate Justice Brennan's concern that the majority's "arguably within

the zone" test will confuse analysis and lead to erroneous results in the context of two related cases:

In Arnold Tours v. Camp, 400 U.S. 45 (1970), independent travel agencies challenged a ruling by the Comptroller that national banks might provide travel services. The lower courts had dismissed for want of standing. The Supreme Court reversed summarily, stating that "Here, as in *Data Processing*, we are concerned with §4 of the Bank Service Corporation Act, ... When national banks begin to provide travel services for their customers, they compete with travel agents no less than they compete with data processors when they provide data processing services to their customers." [150]

Investment Company Institute v. Camp, 401 U.S. 617 (1971), involved a challenge by investment companies to regulations issued by the Comptroller authorizing national banks to operate joint investment funds. The Court asserted that *Data Processing* established plaintiffs' standing. On the merits, it concluded that Congress in the Glass-Steagall Act of 1933 had prohibited national banks from operating such funds. The Court did not convincingly refute Justice Harlan's contention, in dissent, that there was no evidence that Congress had intended to protect bank competitors. Chief Justice Burger took no part in the decision; sitting in the Court of Appeals' decision of the same case, he had expressed views similar to those of Justice Harlan, but ultimately concluded in favor of standing because there would otherwise be no litigant who could effectively challenge the Comptroller's ruling. 420 F.2d 83, 101-108 (D.C. Cir. 1969).[151]

5. Does it follow that "injury in fact" should be the sole test for standing?

Flast v. Cohen

392 U.S. 83 (1968)

[Plaintiffs were taxpayers who claimed that federal expenditures to finance instruction and the purchase of educational materials for use in religious schools violated the First Amendment's Establishment Clause. The Court held that plaintiffs had standing to sue as taxpayers. The Court, in an opinion by Chief Justice WARREN, stated:]

Whether such individuals have standing to maintain that form of action turns on whether they can demonstrate the necessary stake as taxpayers in the outcome of the litigation to satisfy Article III requirements.

The nexus demanded of federal taxpayers has two aspects to it. First, the

---

150. On remand, the Court of Appeals ruled that the "incidental powers" provision of the National Bank Act did not authorize operation of a travel agency by a national bank, and affirmed a judgment for plaintiffs. 472 F.2d 427 (1st Cir. 1972). The court never squarely addressed the question whether the Act was designed to protect competitors.

151. See generally, Albert, Standing to Challenge Administrative Action: An Inadequate Surrogate for Claim for Relief, 83 Yale L. J. 425 (1974).

taxpayer must establish a logical link between that status and the type of legislative enactment attacked. Thus, a taxpayer will be a proper party to allege the unconstitutionality only of exercises of congressional power under the taxing and spending clause of Art. I, §8, of the Constitution. It will not be sufficient to allege an incidental expenditure of tax funds in the administration of an essentially regulatory statute. . . . Secondly, the taxpayer must establish a nexus between that status and the precise nature of the constitutional infringement alleged. Under this requirement, the taxpayer must show that the challenged enactment exceeds specific constitutional limitations imposed upon the exercise of the congressional taxing and spending power and not simply that the enactment is generally beyond the powers delegated to Congress by Art. I, §8. . . .

The taxpayer-appellants in this case have satisfied both nexuses to support their claim of standing under the test we announced today. . . .

[The Court distinguished Frothingham v. Mellon, 262 U.S. 447 (1923), which denied standing to a federal taxpayer challenging federal expenditures for infant care as exceeding Congress' constitutional authority to levy taxes and spend monies for the "General Welfare" and invading powers reserved to the States by the Tenth Amendment, on the ground that the plaintiff had failed to establish the necessary nexus between taxpayer status and the constitutional violations asserted.

In dissent, Justice Harlan contended that the interest of taxpayers in preventing unconstitutional expenditures of government funds was no different than that of citizens generally. A given taxpayer could hardly establish that her tax liability would be different but for the challenged expenditure, and no taxpayer had any special lien or interest, different from that of citizens generally, on the use of tax monies once paid into the Treasury. Justice Harlan stated that Article III did not necessarily preclude federal courts from entertaining "public" actions by taxpayers or citizens to redress generalized grievances. However, if the courts regularly entertained such suits, there "is every reason to fear" that the judiciary would take over the resolution of matters better left to the political branches. Accordingly, the Court ought ordinarily to impose prudential limitations on standing to foreclose "public actions" like Flast's. However, Justice Harlan indicated, if Congress enacted a statute specifically authorizing a "public action," the courts might entertain it because the statute would represent a judgment by the political branches that exercise of jurisdiction by the courts would not disrupt the allocation of authority among the three branches.]

Questions

1. How does the standing test enunciated in *Flast* differ, if at all, from that announced in *Data Processing*?

2. Should the test for standing to challenge statutes or other governmental action as unconstitutional be the same as the test for standing to challenge administrative action as contrary to statute?

4. *The Decisional Law Since* Data Processing

Sierra Club v. Morton
---
405 U.S. 727 (1972)

Mr. Justice STEWART delivered the opinion of the Court.

I

The Mineral King Valley is an area of great natural beauty nestled in the Sierra Nevada Mountains in Tulare County, California, adjacent to Sequoia National Park. It has been part of the Sequoia National Forest since 1926, and is designated as a national game refuge by special Act of Congress. Though once the site of extensive mining activity, Mineral King is now used almost exclusively for recreational purposes. Its relative inaccessibility and lack of development have limited the number of visitors each year, and at the same time have preserved the valley's quality as a quasi-wilderness area largely uncluttered by the products of civilization.

[The United States Forest Service, which is entrusted with the maintenance and administration of national forests, invited bids from private developers for the construction and operation of a ski resort in Mineral King that would also serve as a summer recreation area, and selected a proposal of Walt Disney Enterprises, Inc.]

The final Disney plan, approved by the Forest Service in January 1969, outlines a $35 million complex of motels, restaurants, swimming pools, parking lots, and other structures designed to accommodate 14,000 visitors daily. This complex is to be constructed on 80 acres of the valley floor under a 30-year use permit from the Forest Service. Other facilities, including ski lifts, ski trails, a cog-assisted railway, and utility installations, are to be constructed on the mountain slopes and in other parts of the valley under a revocable special-use permit. To provide access to the resort, the State of California proposes to construct a highway 20 miles in length. A section of this road would traverse Sequoia National Park, as would a proposed high-voltage power line needed to provide electricity for the resort. Both the highway and the power line require the approval of the Department of the Interior, which is entrusted with the preservation and maintenance of the national parks.

Representatives of the Sierra Club, who favor maintaining Mineral King largely in its present state, followed the progress of recreational planning for the valley with close attention and increasing dismay. They unsuccessfully sought a public hearing on the proposed development in 1965, and in subsequent correspondence with officials of the Forest Service and the Department of the Interior, they expressed the Club's objections to Disney's plan as a whole and to particular features included in it. In June 1969 the Club filed the present suit in the United States District Court for the Northern District of California, seeking a declaratory judgment that various aspects of the proposed development contravene federal laws and regulations governing the preservation of national parks, forests, and game refuges,[152] and also seeking preliminary and permanent injunctions restraining the federal officials involved from granting their approval or issuing permits in connection with the Mineral King project. The petitioner Sierra Club sued as a membership corporation with "a special interest in the conservation and the sound maintenance of the national parks, game refuges and forests of the country," and invoked the judicial-review provisions of the Administrative Procedure Act, 5 U.S.C. §701 et seq.

[The District Court granted a preliminary injunction. The Court of Appeals reversed, finding that Sierra Club lacked standing to sue and also that it had failed to show sufficient irreparable injury or likelihood of success on the merits to justify injunctive relief.]

II

The first question presented is whether the Sierra Club has alleged facts that entitle it to obtain judicial review of the challenged action.

[Sierra Club based its standing on §702 of the APA. The Supreme Court restated the "injury in fact" and "zone of interests" tests of Data Processing, and stated that: "In deciding this case we do not reach any questions concerning the meaning of the 'zone of interests' test or its possible application to the facts here presented."]

. . . [N]either Data Processing nor Barlow addressed itself to the question, which has arisen with increasing frequency in federal courts in recent years, as to what must be alleged by persons who claim injury of a noneconomic nature to interests that are widely shared. That question is presented in this case.

III

The injury alleged by the Sierra Club will be incurred entirely by reason of the change in the uses to which Mineral King will be put, and the attendant change in the aesthetics and ecology of the area. Thus, in referring to the road to be built through Sequoia National Park, the complaint alleged that the development "would destroy or otherwise adversely affect the scenery, natural and historic objects and

152. As analyzed by the District Court, the complaint alleged violations of law falling into four categories. First, it claims that the special-use permit for construction of the resort exceeded the maximum acreage limitation placed upon such permits by 16 U.S.C. §497, and that issuance of a "revocable" use permit was beyond the authority of the Forest Service. Second, it challenged the proposed permit for the highway through Sequoia National Park on the grounds that the highway would not serve any of the purposes of the park, in alleged violation of 16 U.S.C. §1, and that it would destroy timber and other natural resources protected by 16 U.S.C. §§ 41 and 43. Third, it claims that the Forest Service and the Department of the Interior had violated their own regulations by failing to hold adequate public hearings on the proposed project. Finally, the complaint asserted that 16 U.S.C. §45c requires specific congressional authorization of a permit for construction of a power transmission line within the limits of a national park.

wildlife of the park and would impair the enjoyment of the park for future generations." We do not question that this type of harm may amount to an "injury in
fact" sufficient to lay the basis for standing under §[702] of the APA. Aesthetic and
environmental well-being, like economic well-being, are important ingredients of
the quality of life in our society, and the fact that particular environmental interests are shared by the many rather than the few does not make them less deserving
of legal protection through the judicial process. But the "injury in fact" test requires more than an injury to a cognizable interest. It requires that the party seeking review be himself among the injured.

The impact of the proposed changes in the environment of Mineral King will
not fall indiscriminately upon every citizen. The alleged injury will be felt directly
only by those who use Mineral King and Sequoia National Park, and for whom the
aesthetic and recreational values of the area will be lessened by the highway and
ski resort. The Sierra Club failed to allege that it or its members would be affected
in any of their activities or pastimes by the Disney development. Nowhere in the
pleadings or affidavits did the Club state that its members use Mineral King for any
purpose, much less that they use it in any way that would be significantly affected
by the proposed actions of the respondents.[153]

[The Court then discussed its decision in *Sanders Bros.*, which it distinguished
from the instant case on the grounds that the competitor there had alleged economic injury from the license grant and that its standing to represent the public
interest had been explicitly granted by a congressional statute.]

The trend of cases arising under the APA and other statutes authorizing judicial review of federal agency action has been toward recognizing that injuries
other than economic harm are sufficient to bring a person within the meaning of
the statutory language, and toward discarding the notion that an injury that is
widely shared is ipso facto not an injury sufficient to provide the basis for judicial
review. We noted this development with approval in *Data Processing*, 397 U.S.,
at 154, in saying that the interest alleged to have been injured "may reflect 'aes-

153. The only reference in the pleadings to the Sierra Club's interest in the dispute is
contained in paragraph 3 of the complaint, which reads in its entirety as follows:
"Plaintiff Sierra Club is a non-profit corporation organized and operating under the laws
of the State of California, with its principal place of business in San Francisco, California since
1892. Membership of the club is approximately 78,000 nationally, with approximately 27,000
members residing in the San Francisco Bay Area. For many years the Sierra Club by its activities
and conduct has exhibited a special interest in the conservation and the sound maintenance of
the national parks, game refuges and forests of the country, regularly serving as a responsible
representative of persons similarly interested. One of the principal purposes of the Sierra Club
is to protect and conserve the national resources of the Sierra Nevada Mountains. Its interests
would be vitally affected by the acts hereinafter described and would be aggrieved by those
acts of the defendants as hereinafter more fully appears."
In an amici curiae brief filed in this Court by the Wilderness Society and others, it is
asserted that the Sierra Club has conducted regular camping trips into the Mineral King area,
and that various members of the Club have used and continue to use the area for recreational
purposes. These allegations were not contained in the pleadings, nor were they brought to the
attention of the Court of Appeals. Moreover, the Sierra Club in its reply brief specifically declines to rely on its individualized interest, as a basis for standing. . . . Our decision does not,
of course, bar the Sierra Club from seeking in the District Court to amend its complaint by a
motion under Rule 15, Federal Rules of Civil Procedure.

thetic, conservational, and recreational' as well as economic values." But broadening the categories of injury that may be alleged in support of standing is a different matter from abandoning the requirement that the party seeking review must himself have suffered an injury.

Some courts have indicated a willingness to take this latter step by conferring standing upon organizations that have demonstrated "an organizational interest in the problem" of environmental or consumer protection. Environmental Defense Fund v. Hardin, 138 U.S. App. D.C. 391, 395, 428 F.2d 1093, 1097. It is clear that an organization whose members are injured may represent those members in a proceeding for judicial review. See, e.g., NAACP v. Button, 371 U.S. 415, 428. But a mere "interest in a problem," no matter how longstanding the interest and no matter how qualified the organization is in evaluating the problem, is not sufficient by itself to render the organization "adversely affected" or "aggrieved" within the meaning of the APA. The Sierra Club is a large and long-established organization, with a historic commitment to the cause of protecting our Nation's natural heritage from man's depredations. But if a "special interest" in this subject were enough to entitle the Sierra Club to commence this litigation, there would appear to be no objective basis upon which to disallow a suit by any other bona fide "special interest" organization, however small or short-lived. And if any group with a bona fide "special interest" could initiate such litigation, it is difficult to perceive why any individual citizen with the same bona fide special interest would not also be entitled to do so.

The requirement that a party seeking review must allege facts showing that he is himself adversely affected does not insulate executive action from judicial review, nor does it prevent any public interests from being protected through the judicial process.[154] It does serve as at least a rough attempt to put the decision as to whether review will be sought in the hands of those who have a direct stake in the outcome. That goal would be undermined were we to construe the APA to authorize judicial review at the behest of organizations or individuals who seek to do no more than vindicate their own value preferences through the judicial process.[155] The principle that the Sierra Club would have us establish in this case would do just that.

---

154. In its reply brief, after noting the fact that it might have chosen to assert individualized injury to itself or to its members as a basis for standing, the Sierra Club states:

> The Government seeks to create a "heads I win, tails you lose" situation in which either the courthouse door is barred for lack of assertion of a private, unique injury or a preliminary injunction is denied on the ground that the litigant has advanced private injury which does not warrant an injunction adverse to a competing public interest. Counsel have shaped their case to avoid this trap.

The short answer to this contention is that the "trap" does not exist. The test of injury in fact goes only to the question of standing to obtain judicial review. Once this standing is established, the party may assert the interests of the general public in support of his claims for equitable relief.

155. Every schoolboy may be familiar with Alexis de Tocqueville's famous observation, written in the 1830s, that "[s]carcely any political question arises in the United States that is not resolved, sooner or later, into a judicial question." 1 Democracy in America 280 (1945). Less familiar, however, is De Tocqueville's further observation that judicial review is effective

As we conclude that the Court of Appeals was correct in its holding that the Sierra Club lacked standing to maintain this action, we do not reach any other questions presented in the petition, and we intimate no view on the merits of the complaint. The judgment is

Affirmed.

Mr. Justice POWELL and Mr. Justice REHNQUIST took no part in the consideration or decision of this case.

Mr. Justice DOUGLAS, dissenting.

I share the views of my Brother BLACKMUN and would reverse the judgment below.

The critical question of "standing" would be simplified and also put neatly in focus if we fashioned a federal rule that allowed environmental issues to be litigated before federal agencies or federal courts in the name of the inanimate object about to be despoiled, defaced, or invaded by roads and bulldozers and where injury is the subject of public outrage. Contemporary public concern for protecting nature's ecological equilibrium should lead to the conferral of standing upon environmental objects to sue for their own preservation. See Stone, Should Trees Have Standing? — Toward Legal Rights for Natural Objects, 45 S. Cal. L. Rev. 450 (1972). This suit would therefore be more properly labeled as Mineral King v. Morton.

[Justice DOUGLAS would grant standing to hikers, fishermen, zoologists, or others with a "meaningful relation" to a natural object to seek judicial review on its behalf.]

[T]he pressures on agencies for favorable action one way or the other are enormous. The suggestion that Congress can stop action which is undesirable is true in theory; yet even Congress is too remote to give meaningful direction and its machinery is too ponderous to use very often. The federal agencies of which I speak are not venal or corrupt. But they are notoriously under the control of powerful interests who manipulate them through advisory committees, or friendly working relations, or who have that natural affinity with the agency which in time develops between the regulator and the regulated. . . .

The Forest Service — one of the federal agencies behind the scheme to despoil Mineral King — has been notorious for its alignment with lumber companies, although its mandate from Congress directs it to consider the various aspects of multiple use in its supervision of the national forests. . . .

The voice of the inanimate object, therefore, should not be stilled. That does not mean that the judiciary takes over the managerial functions from the federal agency. It merely means that before these priceless bits of Americana (such as a

---

largely because it is not available simply at the behest of a partisan faction, but is exercised only to remedy a particular, concrete injury.

"It will be seen, also, that by leaving it to private interest to censure the law, and by intimately uniting the trial of the law with the trial of an individual, legislation is protected from wanton assaults and from the daily aggressions of party spirit. The errors of the legislator are exposed only to meet a real want; and it is always a positive and appreciable fact that must serve as the basis of a prosecution." Id., at 102.

valley, an alpine meadow, a river, or a lake) are forever lost or are so transformed as to be reduced to the eventual rubble of our urban environment, the voice of the existing beneficiaries of these environmental wonders should be heard. . . .

Ecology reflects the land ethic; and Aldo Leopold wrote in A Sand County Almanac 204 (1949), "The land ethic simply enlarges the boundaries of the community to include soils, waters, plants, and animals, or collectively, the land."

That, as I see it, is the issue of "standing" in the present case and controversy.

Mr. Justice BLACKMUN, dissenting.

The Court's opinion is a practical one espousing and adhering to traditional notions of standing as somewhat modernized by Data Processing Service v. Camp, 397 U.S. 150 (1970); Barlow v. Collins, 397 U.S. 159 (1970); and Flast v. Cohen, 392 U.S. 83 (1968). If this were an ordinary case, I would join the opinion and the Court's judgment and be quite content.

But this is not ordinary, run-of-the-mill litigation. The case poses — if only we choose to acknowledge and reach them — significant aspects of a wide, growing, and disturbing problem, that is, the Nation's and the world's deteriorating environment with its resulting ecological disturbances. Must our law be so rigid and our procedural concepts so inflexible that we render ourselves helpless when the existing methods and the traditional concepts do not quite fit and do not prove to be entirely adequate for new issues?

The ultimate result of the Court's decision today, I fear, and sadly so, is that the 35.3-million-dollar complex, over 10 times greater than the Forest Service's suggested minimum, will now hastily proceed to completion; that serious opposition to it will recede in discouragement; and that Mineral King, the "area of great natural beauty nestled in the Sierra Nevada Mountains," to use the Court's words, will become defaced, at least in part, and, like so many other areas, will cease to be "uncluttered by the products of civilization."

I believe this will come about because: (1) The District Court, although it accepted standing for the Sierra Club and granted preliminary injunctive relief, was reversed by the Court of Appeals, and this Court now upholds that reversal. (2) With the reversal, interim relief by the District Court is now out of the question and a permanent injunction becomes most unlikely. (3) The Sierra Club may not choose to amend its complaint or, if it does desire to do so, may not, at this late date, be granted permission. (4) The ever-present pressure to get the project under way will mount. (5) Once under way, any prospect of bringing it to a halt will grow dim. Reasons, most of them economic, for not stopping the project will have a tendency to multiply. And the irreparable harm will be largely inflicted in the earlier stages of construction and development.

Rather than pursue the course the Court has chosen to take by its affirmance of the judgment of the Court of Appeals, I would adopt one of two alternatives:

1. I would reverse that judgment and, instead, approve the judgment of the District Court which recognized standing in the Sierra Club and granted preliminary relief. I would be willing to do this on condition that the Sierra Club forthwith amend its complaint to meet the specifications the Court prescribes for standing. . . .

2. Alternatively, I would permit an imaginative expansion of our traditional concepts of standing in order to enable an organization such as the Sierra Club, possessed, as it is, of pertinent, bona fide, and well-recognized attributes and purposes in the area of environment, to litigate environmental issues. This incursion upon tradition need not be very extensive. Certainly, it should be no cause for alarm. It is no more progressive than was the decision in *Data Processing* itself. It need only recognize the interest of one who has a provable, sincere, dedicated, and established status. We need not fear that Pandora's box will be opened or that there will be no limit to the number of those who desire to participate in environmental litigation. The courts will exercise appropriate restraints just as they have exercised them in the past. . . .

. . . [A]ny resident of the Mineral King area — the real "user" — is an unlikely adversary for this Disney-governmental project. He naturally will be inclined to regard the situation as one that should benefit him economically. His fishing or camping or guiding or handyman or general outdoor prowess perhaps will find an early and ready market among the visitors. But that glow of anticipation will be short-lived at best. If he is a true lover of the wilderness — as is likely, or he would not be near Mineral King in the first place — it will not be long before he yearns for the good old days when masses of people — that 14,000 influx per day — and their thus far uncontrollable waste were unknown to Mineral King.

Do we need any further indication and proof that all this means that the area will no longer be one "of great natural beauty" and one "uncluttered by the products of civilization?" Are we to be rendered helpless to consider and evaluate allegations and challenges of this kind because of procedural limitations rooted in traditional concepts of standing? I suspect that this may be the result of today's holding. . . .

The Court chooses to conclude its opinion with a footnote reference to De Tocqueville. In this environmental context I personally prefer the older and particularly pertinent observation and warning of John Donne.[156]

Questions

1. Why did the lawyers for *Sierra Club* decline to allege that members of the Club used the Mineral King Valley? It is clear, is it not, that if they had so alleged, the Supreme Court would have upheld Sierra Club's standing? Does the Court's rationale place excessive weight on this pleading issue?

2. Precisely why should "injury in fact" be a prerequisite for standing? Why shouldn't a person or organization with a demonstrated and sincere interest in an issue be afforded standing, so long as the case is vigorously litigated?

---

156. "No man is an Iland, intire of itselfe; every man is a peece of the Continent, a part of the maine; if a Clod bee washed away by the Sea, Europe is the lesse, as well as if a Promontorie were, as well as if a Mannor of thy friends or of thine owne were; any man's death diminishes me, because I am involved in Mankinde; And therefore never send to know for whom the bell tolls; it tolls for thee." Devotions XVII.

In his dissenting opinion in *Data Processing* and *Barlow,* Justice Brennan, relying upon Flast v. Cohen, indicates that "injury in fact" is constitutionally required by the "case or controversy" provision of Article III. Is this sound? Even if "injury in fact" is required for standing when a litigant challenges a statute as contrary to the Constitution, does it follow that the same requirement applies when administrative action is challenged as contrary to statute? Does *Sierra Club* hold that "injury in fact" is constitutionally required in this context?

3. Why shouldn't the Sierra Club be afforded standing to act as a "private attorney general" or surrogate plaintiff under the rationale established in *Sanders Bros.* and *Associated Industries?*

United States v. SCRAP

412 U.S. 669 (1973)

[Plaintiffs, Students Challenging Regulatory Agency Procedures (SCRAP), Environmental Defense Fund, National Parks and Conservation Association, and Izaak Walton League, and other environmental groups, brought suit in the United States District Court for the District of Columbia challenging the Interstate Commerce Commission's action in permitting the nation's railroads to institute a 2.5 percent across-the-board increase in railroad freight rates. The Commission had declined to exercise its statutory authority to suspend the proposed increase for a full seven months pending an ICC investigation of their legality. Plaintiffs contended that the ICC should not have decided against suspension without first filing an Environmental Impact Statement (EIS) concerning its action, as assertedly required by the National Environmental Policy Act (NEPA). Plaintiffs' theory was that recycled goods generally incur greater transportation charges (from a recycling facility to the consumer and back to the recycling facility) than disposable goods (which are transported from extraction and processing locations to the consumer and then discarded), that any general increase in freight rates would therefore make recycled goods more expensive relative to disposable items, thus discouraging recycling, promoting additional virgin source extraction, and creating additional solid waste. The ICC rejected plaintiffs' theory, found that the increase would not have significant environmental consequences, and refused to prepare an EIS before permitting the rate increases to go into effect.

A three-judge District Court sustained plaintiffs' contentions, rejected claims by the ICC and a group of railroads which had intervened that plaintiffs lacked standing to bring the suit, and enjoined implementation of the rate increase pending ICC preparation of an EIS. The ICC and the railroads appealed to the Supreme Court, which sustained the plaintiffs' standing to bring the litigation but held, in accordance with prior decisions, that the ICC's refusal to exercise its suspensory power was not subject to judicial review, and that the enactment of NEPA had not altered this principle. The Court accordingly dissolved the District

Court's injunction. Only certain portions of Justice STEWART's opinion for the Supreme Court dealing with standing are reproduced here.]

SCRAP stated in its amended complaint that it was "an unincorporated association formed by five law students . . . in September, 1971. Its primary purpose is to enhance the quality of the human environment for its members, and for all citizens. . . ." To establish standing to bring this suit, SCRAP . . . claimed that each of its members "suffered economic, recreational and aesthetic harm directly as a result of the adverse environmental impact of the railroad freight structure [as modified by the proposed rate increase and the ICC's refusal to suspend it]." Specifically, SCRAP alleged that each of its members was caused to pay more for finished products, that each of its members "[u]ses the forests, rivers, streams, mountains, and other natural resources surrounding the Washington Metropolitan area and at his legal residence, for camping, hiking, fishing, sightseeing, and other recreational [and] aesthetic purposes," and that these uses have been adversely affected by the increased freight rates, that each of its members breathes the air within the Washington metropolitan area and the area of his legal residence and that this air has suffered increased pollution caused by the modified rate structure, and that each member has been forced to pay increased taxes because of the sums which must be expended to dispose of otherwise reusable waste materials.

[The Court found that the allegations of the other environmental plaintiffs with respect to standing were similar to those of SCRAP. As in *Sierra Club*, the SCRAP plaintiffs based their standing to sue on the APA, 5 U.S.C. §702.]

In *Sierra Club*, [we stressed] the importance of demonstrating that the party seeking review be himself among the injured, for it is this requirement that gives a litigant a direct stake in the controversy and prevents the judicial process from becoming no more than a vehicle for the vindication of the value interests of concerned bystanders. No such specific injury was alleged in *Sierra Club*. . . . Here, by contrast, the appellees claimed that the specific and allegedly illegal action of the Commission would directly harm them in their use of the natural resources of the Washington Metropolitan Area.

Unlike the specific and geographically limited federal action of which the petitioner complained in *Sierra Club*, the challenged agency action in this case is applicable to substantially all of the Nation's railroads, and thus allegedly has an adverse environmental impact on all the natural resources of the country. Rather than a limited group of persons who used a picturesque valley in California, all persons who utilize the scenic resources of the country, and indeed all who breathe its air, could claim harm similar to that alleged by the environmental groups here. But we have already made it clear that standing is not to be denied simply because many people suffer the same injury. . . . To deny standing to persons who are in fact injured simply because many others are also injured, would mean that the most injurious and widespread Government actions could be questioned by nobody. We cannot accept that conclusion.

But the injury alleged here is also very different from that at issue in *Sierra Club* because here the alleged injury to the environment is far less direct and perceptible. . . . The railroads protest that the appellees could never prove that a general increase in rates would have [the environmental effects asserted by plaintiffs], and they contend that these allegations were a ploy to avoid the need to show some injury in fact.

Of course, pleadings must be something more than an ingenious academic exercise in the conceivable. A plaintiff must allege that he has been or will in fact be perceptibly harmed by the challenged agency action, not that he can imagine circumstances in which he could be affected by the agency's action. And it is equally clear that the allegations must be true and capable of proof at trial. But we deal here simply with the pleadings in which the appellees alleged a specific and perceptible harm that distinguished them from other citizens who had not used the natural resources that were claimed to be affected.[157] If, as the railroads now assert, these allegations were in fact untrue, then the appellants should have moved for summary judgment on the standing issue and demonstrated to the District Court that the allegations were sham and raised no genuine issue of fact. We cannot say on these pleadings that the appellees could not prove their allegations which, if proved, would place them squarely among those persons injured in fact by the Commission's action, and entitled under the clear import of *Sierra Club* to seek review. The District Court was correct in denying the appellants' motion to dismiss the complaint for failure to allege sufficient standing to bring this lawsuit.

[Justice WHITE, joined by Chief Justice BURGER and Justice RHENQUIST, dissented from the court's disposition of the standing question on the ground that the injuries alleged were too "remote, speculative and insubstantial in fact." Justice POWELL did not participate in the decision.]

Questions

1. Is *SCRAP* consistent with *Sierra Club*? What possible justification is there for denying standing to an established and well-organized California-based environmental group seeking to challenge a particular development in California,

---

157. The Government urges us to limit standing to those who have been "significantly" affected by agency action. But, even if we could begin to define what such a test would mean, we think it fundamentally misconceived. "Injury in fact" reflects the statutory requirement that a person be "adversely affected" or "aggrieved," and it serves to distinguish a person with a direct stake in the outcome of a litigation — even though small — from a person with a mere interest in the problem. We have allowed important interests to be vindicated by plaintiffs with no more at stake in the outcome of an action than a fraction of a vote, see Baker v. Carr, 369 U.S. 186; a $5 fine and costs, see McGowan v. Maryland, 366 U.S. 420; and a $1.50 poll tax, Harper v. Virginia Bd. of Elections, 383 U.S. 663. While these cases were not dealing specifically with §10 of the APA, we see no reason to adopt a more restrictive interpretation of "adversely affected" or "aggrieved." As Professor Davis has put it, "The basic idea that comes out in numerous cases is that an identifiable trifle is enough for standing to fight out a question of principle; the trifle is the basis for standing and the principle supplies the motivation." Davis, Standing: Taxpayers and Others, 35 U. Chi. L. Rev. 601, 613. See also K. Davis, Administrative Law Treatise §§ 22.09-5, 22.09-6 (Supp. 1970). Cf. Scott, Standing in the Supreme Court: A Functional Analysis, 86 Harv. L. Rev. 645 (1973), which distinguishes "access standing," which focuses on the nature and extent of harm to the plaintiff as a means of rationing scarce judicial resources, from "decision standing," which stresses the allocation of policymaking responsibility among the branches of government.

while granting standing to an ad hoc group of law students to challenge a nation-wide rate increase?

2. What purpose is served by conducting a threshold hearing, directed at the question of standing, on whether the ICC's rate increase will generate more litter in Washington, D.C., parks where plaintiffs are likely to view such litter? Does this prospect support Justice Brennan's criticisms of *Data Processing*?

Note: Subsequent Supreme Court Standing Decisions

In Schlesinger v. Reservists Committee to Stop the War, 418 U.S. 208 (1974), plaintiffs, consisting of an association of present and former members of the Armed Forces Reserve opposing United States involvement in Vietnam, and five members of the association, who were also taxpayers and citizens, brought suit against the Secretary of Defense, challenging Reserve membership by members of Congress as violating Article I, §6, clause 2, of the Constitution, prohibiting members of Congress from holding "any office under the United States." The Supreme Court dismissed for want of standing, concluding that standing could not be based on plaintiffs' status as taxpayers because there was no "logical nexus" between such status and the claim asserted. Plaintiffs were also denied standing to sue in their capacity as citizens because any injury that might result from the asserted consti-tutional violation was one suffered by all citizens generally, and did not represent the sort of tangible, individual injury involved in *Data Processing* and SCRAP. (Would a reservist alleging that he had been sent to Vietnam as a result of legisla-tion in which Reserve members of Congress had supplied the decisive votes have standing?)

In United States v. Richardson, 418 U.S. 166 (1974), a taxpayer's challenge to the Central Intelligence Agency Act, permitting the CIA to account to Con-gress for its expenditures "solely on the certificate of the Director," as violative of Art I, §9, clause 7, of the Constitution, which requires a regular statement and account of public funds, was also dismissed for lack of standing. The Court rea-soned that there was no "logical nexus" between plaintiff's taxpayer status and the claim asserted, and that insofar as plaintiff claimed that the failure to account deprived him in his capacity as citizen and voter to scrutinize legislative and execu-tive action and take appropriate action, the grievance was a generalized one shared by the citizenry at large, and afforded no basis for standing.

Justice Powell, concurring in *Richardson*, stressed that "relaxation of standing requirements" would result in "expansion of judicial power" that would displace political processes for the resolution of "generalized grievances" and that unless the Court imposed prudential limitations on standing, the constitutional scheme of balanced and separated powers would be upset.

Warth v. Selden, 422 U.S. 490 (1975), and Village of Arlington Heights v. Metropolitan Housing Development Corp., 429 U.S. 252 (1977), both involved challenges to local zoning ordinances as violative of the Fourteenth Amendment and provisions of the Civil Rights Acts on the ground that they effectively ex-cluded persons of low and moderate income. The Court denied standing in *Warth* because the plaintiffs or plaintiff-intervenors (taxpayers and low-income residents of other municipalities in the area; a nonprofit association to expand housing opportunities; a local builders' association; and a county housing council) had failed to allege or show any specific harm to them as a direct result of the ordinances; for example, the low-income residents of other municipalities had not contracted for or actively sought housing in the defendant municipality, and the builders' association had not established that any of its members had lost a specific item of business because of the zoning. But *Arlington Heights* sustained the standing of a nonprofit developer and an individual because the developer had contracted to develop a parcel within the defendant municipality to provide low and moderate-income housing, while the individual, a black who worked in the municipality but lived elsewhere, had demonstrated a substantial interest in the housing opportunity that could probably be created if the zoning ordinance prohibiting the development were invalidated.

Simon v. Eastern Kentucky Welfare Rights Organization

426 U.S. 26 (1976)

Mr. Justice POWELL delivered the opinion of the Court.

[Plaintiffs, several indigents and organizations representing indigents, challenged a Revenue Ruling issued by the Internal Revenue Service modifying the responsibilities of non-profit hospitals qualifying under §501(c)(3) of the Internal Revenue Code as "charitable" organizations, contributions to which are tax-deductible. A 1956 IRS Ruling, No. 56-185, required that such a hospital must accept some patients in need of hospital services who cannot pay for them, and must do so "to the extent of its financial ability."

In 1969, the IRS issued Revenue Ruling 69-545, describing two hospitals, identified as "A" and "B." The ruling stated that Hospital A, which operated an emergency room open to all but otherwise accepted only paying customers, qualified as a §501(c)(3) charitable organization, even though it did not accept indigents "to the extent of its financial ability."

Each of the individual plaintiffs alleged specific incidents of deprivation, because of their indigency, of medical services by hospitals determined by the IRS to be §501(c)(3) charities. They further alleged that the defendants (the Secretary of the Treasury and the IRS Commissioner), were "encouraging" such hospitals to deny services to indigents through the 1969 revenue ruling. They asserted that the ruling was contrary to the Code, claiming that "charitable" in §501(c)(3) means "relief of the poor." They also asserted that as poor persons they were intended beneficiaries of this provision. Finally, they contended that the IRS' failure to afford notice and opportunity for comment in the 1969 ruling violated the APA, §553 because the ruling did not fall within the §553 exception for "interpretive" rulemaking.]

In this Court petitioners have argued that a policy of the IRS to tax or not to tax certain individuals or organizations, whether embodied in a Revenue Ruling or otherwise developed, cannot be challenged by third parties whose own tax liabilities are not affected. Their theory is that the entire history of this country's revenue system, including but not limited to the evolution of the Internal Revenue Code, manifests a consistent congressional intent to vest exclusive authority for the administration of the tax laws in the Secretary and his duly authorized delegates, subject to oversight by the appropriate committees of Congress itself....

In addition, petitioners analogize the discretion vested in the IRS with respect to administration of the tax laws to the discretion of a public prosecutor as to when and whom to prosecute. They thus invoke the settled doctrine that the exercise of prosecutorial discretion cannot be challenged by one who is himself neither prosecuted nor threatened with prosecution. See Linda R. S. v. Richard D., 410 U.S. 614, 619 (1973).[158]

... We do not reach either the question of whether a third party ever may challenge IRS treatment of another, or the question of whether there is a statutory or immunity bar to this suit. We conclude that the District Court should have granted petitioners' motion to dismiss on the ground that respondents' complaint failed to establish their standing to sue.

No principle is more fundamental to the judiciary's proper role in our system of government than the constitutional limitation of federal-court jurisdiction to actual cases or controversies. See Flast v. Cohen, 392 U.S. 83, 95, 88 S. Ct. 1942, 1950, 20 L. Ed. 2d 947, 958 (1968). The concept of standing is part of this limitation.

... The necessity that the plaintiff who seeks to invoke judicial power stand to profit in some personal interest remains an Art. III requirement. A federal court cannot ignore this requirement without overstepping its assigned role in our system of adjudicating only actual cases and controversies.[159]

... The standing question in this suit therefore turns upon whether any individual respondent has established an actual injury, or whether the respondent organizations have established actual injury to any of their indigent members.

The obvious interest of all respondents, to which they claim actual injury, is that of access to hospital services.... We ... assume, for purpose of analysis, that some members have been denied service. But injury at the hands of a hospital is insufficient by itself to establish a case or controversy in the context of this suit, for no hospital is a defendant. The only defendants are officials of the Department of the Treasury, and the only claims of illegal action respondents desire the courts

---

158. Ed. note: This decision is described at p. 326 n.9, supra.

159. The *Data Processing* decision established a second, nonconstitutional standing requirement that the interest of the plaintiff, regardless of its nature in the absolute, at least be "arguably within the zone of interests to be protected or regulated" by the statutory framework within which his claim arises. See 397 U.S., at 153, 90 S. Ct. at 830, 25 L. Ed. 2d, at 188. As noted earlier, respondents in this case claim that they, and of course their particular interests involved in this suit, are the intended beneficiaries of the charitable organization provisions of the Code. In view of our disposition of this case, we need not consider this "zone of interests" test.

to adjudicate are charged to those officials. "Although the law of standing has been greatly changed in [recent] years, we have steadfastly adhered to the requirement that, at least in the absence of a statute expressly conferring standing, federal plaintiffs must allege some threatened or actual injury resulting from the putatively illegal action before a federal court may assume jurisdiction." Linda R. S. v. Richard D., 410 U.S., at 617, 93 S. Ct., at 1148, 35 L. Ed. 2d, at 540.[160] In other words, the "case or controversy" limitation of Art. III still requires that a federal court act only to redress injury that fairly can be traced to the challenged action of the defendant, and not injury that results from the independent action of some third party not before the court.

The complaint here alleged only that petitioners, by the adoption of Revenue Ruling 69-545, had "encouraged" hospitals to deny services to indigents.... It is purely speculative whether the denials of service specified in the complaint fairly can be traced to petitioners' "encouragement" or instead result from decisions made by the hospitals without regard to the tax implications.

It is equally speculative whether the desired exercise of the court's remedial powers in this suit would result in the availability to respondents of such services.... The Solicitor General states in his brief that, nationwide, private philanthropy accounts for only 4% of private hospital revenues....

Prior decisions of this Court establish that unadorned speculation will not suffice to invoke the federal judicial power.

[In a footnote, the court also discussed the relevance of SCRAP:

"The courts below erroneously believed that United States v. SCRAP, 412 U.S. 669, 93 S. Ct. 2405, 37 L. Ed. 2d 254 (1973), supported respondents' standing. In SCRAP, although the injury was indirect and 'the Court was asked to follow [an] attenuated line of causation,' id., at 688, 93 S. Ct., at 2416, 37 L. Ed. 2d, at 270, the complaint nevertheless 'alleged a specific and perceptible harm' flowing from the agency action. Id., at 689, 93 S. Ct., at 2416, 37 L. Ed. 2d, at 270. Such a complaint withstood a motion to dismiss, although it might not have survived challenge on a motion for summary judgment. Id., at 689 and n. 15. But in this case the complaint is insufficient even to survive a motion to dismiss, for it fails to allege an injury that fairly can be traced to petitioners' challenged action. See supra, at 40-43. Nor did the affidavits before the District Court at the summary judgment stage supply the missing link.

"... In the instant case respondent's injuries might have occurred even in the absence of the IRS Ruling that they challenge; whether the injuries fairly can be traced to that Ruling depends upon unalleged and unknown facts about the relevant hospitals."]

160. The reference in Linda R. S. to a "statute expressly conferring standing" was in recognition of Congress' power to create new interests the invasion of which will confer standing. See 410 U.S., at 617 n.3; Trafficante v. Metropolitan Life Ins. Co., 409 U.S. 205 (1972). When Congress has so acted, the requirements of Art. III remain: "[T]he plaintiff still must allege a distinct and palpable injury to himself, even if it is an injury shared by a large class of other possible litigants." Warth v. Seldin, supra, at 501. See also United States v. SCRAP, 412 U.S. 669 (1973); cf. Sierra Club v. Morton, 405 U.S. at 732 n.3.

...A federal court, properly cognizant of the Art. III limitation upon its jurisdiction, must require more than respondents have shown before proceeding to the merits.

Accordingly, the judgment of the Court of Appeals is vacated and the cause is remanded to the District Court with instructions to dismiss the complaint.

It is so ordered.

Mr. Justice STEVENS took no part in the consideration or decision of these cases.

Mr. Justice STEWART, concurring.

I join the opinion of the Court holding that the plaintiffs in this case did not have standing to sue. I add only that I cannot now imagine a case, at least outside the First Amendment area, where a person whose own tax liability was not affected ever could have standing to litigate the federal tax liability of someone else.

Mr. Justice BRENNAN, with whom Mr. Justice MARSHALL joins, concurring in the judgment.

[Because the Revenue Ruling in issue applied by its terms only to a hypothetical hospital "A" of specified size and operating characteristics, Justice Brennan concluded that the plaintiffs had failed to establish a sufficient nexus between the Ruling and the potential denial of services to plaintiffs by the particular hospitals which they sought to utilize.]

The Court ... however ... assumes that the governmental action complained of *is* encouraging the hospitals affecting respondents to provide fewer medical services to indigents.... This is done in order to make the gratuitous and erroneous point that respondents, as a prerequisite to pursuing any legal claims regarding the Revenue Ruling, must allege and later prove that the hospitals affecting respondents "are dependent upon" their tax-exempt status ... would not in the absence of the Ruling's assumed "encouragement" "elect to forego favorable tax treatment," and that the absence of the allegedly illegal inducement would "result in the availability to respondents of such services." ...[161]

... The wrong of which respondents complain is that the disputed Ruling gives erroneous economic signals to nonprofit hospitals whose subsequent responses affect respondents; they claim the IRS is offering the economic inducement of tax-exempt status to such hospitals under terms illegal under the Internal Revenue Code. Respondents' claim is not, and by its very nature could not be, that they have been and will be illegally denied the provision of indigent medical services by the hospitals. Rather, if respondents have a claim cognizable under the law, it is that the Internal Revenue Code requires the government to offer economic inducements

161. Moreover, by requiring that this "line of causation," ante, at 45, n.25, be precisely and intricately elaborated in the complaint, the Court continues its recent policy of "reverting to the form of fact pleading long abjured in the federal courts." Warth v. Seldin, 422 U.S. 490, 528[, 95 S. Ct. 2197, 2220, 45 L. Ed. 2d 343, 372] (Brennan, J., dissenting). One waits in vain for an explanation for this selectively imposed pleading requirement; a requirement so at odds with our usual view that under the Federal Rules of Civil Procedure "a complaint should not be dismissed for failure to state a claim unless it appears beyond doubt that the plaintiff can prove no set of facts in support of his claim which would entitle him to relief." Conley v. Gibson, 355 U.S. 41, 45-46[, 78 S. Ct. 99, 102, 2 L. Ed. 2d 80, 84] (1957).

to the relevant hospitals only under conditions which are likely to benefit respondents. The relevant injury in light of this claim is, then, injury to this beneficial interest — as respondents alleged, injury to their "opportunity and ability" to receive medical services. Respondents sufficiently alleged this injury and if, as the Court so readily assumes, they had made a showing sufficient to create an issue of material fact that the government was injuring this interest, they would continue to possess standing to press the claim on the merits.

Second, the Court's treatment of the injury-in-fact requirement directly conflicts with past decisions. . . .

[Justice BRENNAN argued that the injury alleged by plaintiffs — the unlawful withdrawal by the IRS of inducements for charitable hospital care — would, assuming a sufficient link between the Revenue Ruling and the hospitals serving plaintiffs, satisfy the requirement of "injury-in-fact" because it would give them a personal stake in the outcome distinct from the interests of citizens generally.][162]

Of course the most disturbing aspect of today's opinion is the Court's insistence on resting its decision regarding standing squarely on the irreducible Art. III minimum of injury in fact, thereby effectively placing its holding beyond congressional power to rectify. Thus, any time Congress chooses to legislate in favor of certain interests by setting up a scheme of incentives for third parties, judicial review of administrative action that allegedly frustrates the congressionally intended objective will be denied, because any complainant will be required to make an almost impossible showing. Clearly the Legislative Branch of the Government cannot supply injured individuals with the means to make the factual showing in a specific context that the Court today requires. More specific indications of a congressional desire to confer standing upon such individuals would be germane, not to the Art. III injury-in-fact requirement, but only to the Court's "zone of interests" test for standing, that branch of standing lore which the Court assiduously avoids reaching. . . .

Questions

1. Was plaintiffs' failure in *Simon* due to insufficient specificity in pleading? Suppose plaintiffs had alleged that, immediately following the Revenue Ruling, the boards of trustees of the hospitals at which they sought care had, in reliance on the ruling, voted to reverse previous policies of providing care for indigents in order to qualify §501(c)(3) status?

---

162. It clearly cannot be determinative for purposes of constitutionally required standing that there is only a probabilistic connection between the immediate interest, to which injury is alleged, and some more ultimate injury to the complaining party. United States v. SCRAP, 442 U.S., at 689, n.14, [93 S. Ct. at 2417, 37 L. Ed. 2d, at 270,] specifically rejected the argument that for standing purposes "significant" injury must be alleged. Rather, the Court held that Art. III policies were adequately fulfilled even though the ultimate injury is very small indeed. Ibid. Clearly there is no difference for purposes of Art. III standing — personal interest sufficient for concrete adverseness — between a small but certain injury and a harm of a larger magnitude discounted by some probability of its nonoccurrence. If the probability of the more ultimate harm is so small as to make the claim clearly frivolous, "the plaintiff can be hastened from the court by summary judgment." . . .

2. Does *Simon* enlarge or change the two-part standing test announced in *Data Processing*? Does it overrule *SCRAP*? Or does it represent a special rule for tax cases? What would be the implications for tax policy if beneficiaries of tax provisions whose own tax liability is not at stake had standing to secure review of IRS administration of such provisions?[163] Would General Motors (or any other plaintiff) have standing to challenge governmental regulations relating to mineral depletion allowances as unduly liberal and contrary to the Internal Revenue Code?

3. Does *Simon* say that a congressional statute specifically granting standing to the plaintiffs in that case would be unconstitutional? Compare the "citizen suit" provisions of §304 of the Federal Clean Air Act, authorizing "any person" to bring suit against the Administrator of the federal Environmental Protection Agency to compel him to carry our mandatory duties imposed by the Act. Is this provision constitutional? [164]

---

163. Does *Simon* overrule Green v. Kennedy, 309 F. Supp. 1127 (D.D.C. 1970), *later decision reported sub nom.* Green v. Connally, 330 F. Supp. 1150 (D.D.C. 1971), *aff'd sub nom.* Colt v. Green, 404 U.S. 997 (1971), which held that minority children might challenge the constitutionality of tax deductions for segregated private schools on the ground that it "encouraged" the maintenance of such schools and deprived plaintiffs of the benefits of integrated public education?

Cf. Tax Analysts & Advocates v. Simon, 390 F. Supp. 927 (D.D.C. 1975), *appeal dismissed,* 512 F.2d 992 (D.C. Cir. 1975), denying standing to plaintiffs, taxpayers and the owner of an interest in a domestic oil well, who challenged as contrary to the Code revenue rulings providing favorable tax treatment for domestic corporations producing oil abroad. The district court found a lack of injury in fact and also that plaintiffs were clearly outside the relevant statutory zone of interests.

164. For scholarly commentary supporting the constitutionality of the "public action," see Berger, Standing to Sue in Public Action: Is It a Constitutional Requirement? 78 Yale L. J. 816 (1969); Jaffe, The Citizen as Litigant in Public Actions: The Non-Hohfeldian or Ideological Plaintiff, 116 U. Pa. L. Rev. 1033 (1968). See also Justice Harlan's dissenting opinion in Flast v. Cohen, supra, p. 936.

Trafficante v. Metropolitan Life Ins. Co., 409 U.S. 205 (1972), held that black and white tenants had standing to challenge alleged racial discrimination by their landlord as violative of the 1968 Civil Rights Act 42 U.S.C. §3610, affording standing to "persons aggrieved." Justice White, in a concurring opinion, seemed to suggest, absent this statutory grant of standing, that there would have been no Article III case or controversy. In Linda R. S. v. Richard D., 410 U.S. 614 (1973), Justice Marshall, for the Court, stated that, consistent with Article III, "Congress may enact statutes creating legal rights, the invasion of which creates standing, even though no inquiry would exist without the statute." On the other hand, in Schlesinger v. Reservists' Comm. to Stop the War, 418 U.S. 208 (1974), Chief Justice Burger stated, for the Court, that despite the existence of a statute creating a legal right, Article III would still require that the plaintiff allege "a specific invasion of the right suffered by him." And in Warth v. Seldin, 422 U.S. 490, 501 (1973), it was held Congress may grant an express right of action to persons who otherwise would be barred by *prudential* standing rules. Of course, Article III's requirement remains: the plaintiff still must meet the case or controversy requirement.

If an individual cannot sue, to what extent would the state of which he is a citizen sue on his behalf, parens patriae? Under the classical rule of Massachusetts v. Mellon, the state could not sue. However, this doctrine has been eroded by recent decisions allowing states and state authorities to challenge administrative action as contrary to federal law, Washington Utilities & Transportation Commission v. FCC, 513 F.2d 1142 (9th Cir. 1975); Guam v. Federal Maritime Commission, 329 F.2d 251 (D.C. Cir. 1964); Florida v. Weinberger, 492 F.2d 488 (5th Cir. 1974). But see Pennsylvania v. Kleppe, 533 F.2d 668 (D.C. Cir. 1976), *cert. denied,* 97 S. Ct. 485 (1976) (denying standing).

4. A rejected applicant for admission to a public professional school challenges as unconstitutional the use by the school of quotas or more flexible preferences favoring applicants who are members of racial minorities. In order to establish standing, must plaintiff prove that he would have been admitted but for the challenged practice? [165] If so, might schools adopt informal admission systems that would make such proof impossible?

Duke Power Co. v. Carolina Environmental Study Group

98 S. Ct. 2620 (1978)

[Duke Power Co. and the Nuclear Regulatory Commission (NRC) were sued by environmental organizations and their members, who lived in areas where Duke proposed to construct nuclear power plants. Plaintiffs attacked the constitutionality of the Price-Anderson Act, 42 U.S.C. §2210 et seq., which provides a government insurance scheme of indemnity for losses suffered by the public as a result of nuclear power accidents. The statute, which is administered by the NRC, limits liability to a maximum of $560 million for any single accident. Plaintiffs contended that this limitation violated equal protection and due process by restricting their common-law remedies, thus "taking" their "property," and shifting the risks of nuclear power generation from electricity consumers, utility shareholders, and utility suppliers to nearby residents. They alleged that, but for the limitation of liability, the plant would not be built by Duke. The District Court upheld plaintiffs' standing and ruled in their favor on the merits. Defendants pursued a direct appeal to the Supreme Court.

The District Court had held four days of hearings on the standing issue. The Supreme Court, in an opinion by Chief Justice Burger, summarized prior decisions, such as *Warth* and *Simon* as requiring a "distinct and palpable injury" to plaintiff and a "fairly traceable causal connection" between that injury and defendants' conduct.]

We turn first to consider the kinds of injuries the District Court found the appellees suffered. It discerned two categories of effects which resulted from the operation of nuclear power plants in potentially dangerous proximity to appellees' living and working environment. The immediate effects included: (a) the production of small quantities of nonnatural radiation which would invade the air and water; (b) a "sharp increase" in the temperature of two lakes presently used for recreational purposes resulting from the use of the lake waters to produce steam and to cool the reactor; (c) interference with the normal use of the waters of the Catawba River; (d) threatened reduction in property values of land neighboring the power plants; (e) "objectively reasonable" present fear and apprehension re-

---

165. See Regents of University of California v. Bakke, 438 U.S. —, 98 S. Ct. 2733, 2743 n.14 (1978) (opinion of Powell, J.).

garding the "effect of the increased radioactivity in the air, land and water upon [appellees] and their property, and the genetic effects upon their descendants"; and (f) the continual threat of "an accident resulting in uncontrolled release of large or even small quantities of radioactive material" with no assurance of adequate compensation for the resultant damage. . . .

For purposes of the present inquiry, we need not determine whether all the putative injuries identified by the District Court, particularly those based on the possibility of a nuclear accident and the present apprehension generated by this future uncertainty, are sufficiently concrete to satisfy constitutional requirements. . . . Certainly the environmental and aesthetic consequences of the thermal pollution of the two lakes in the vicinity of the disputed power plants is the type of harmful effect which has been deemed adequate in prior cases to satisfy the "injury in fact" standard. See United States v. SCRAP, supra. Cf. Sierra Club v. Morton. . . . And the emission of nonnatural radiation into appellees' environment would also seem a direct and present injury. . . .

The more difficult step in the standing inquiry is establishing that these injuries "fairly can be traced to the challenged action of the defendant," Simon v. Eastern Kentucky Welfare Rights Org., 426 U.S. 26, 41, . . . or put otherwise, that the exercise of the Court's remedial powers would redress the claimed injuries. Id., at 43, . . . The District Court discerned a "but for" causal connection between the Price-Anderson Act, which appellees challenged as unconstitutional, "and the construction of the nuclear plants which the [appellees] view as a threat to them." 431 F. Supp. 219. Particularizing that causal link to the facts of the instant case, the District Court concluded that "there is a substantial likelihood that Duke would not be able to complete the construction and maintain the operation of the McGuire and Catawba Nuclear Plants but for the protection provided by the Price-Anderson Act." Id., at 220.

These findings, which, if accepted, would likely satisfy the second prong of the constitutional test for standing as elaborated in *Simon*, are challenged on two grounds.

[The Court rejected contentions (a) that the evidence failed to support the District Court's factual findings; and (b) that plaintiffs must establish that, in the absence of the Price-Anderson Act and private development of nuclear power, the government would not itself have developed nuclear power, creating the same risks of which plaintiffs now complain.]

The District Court's finding of a "substantial likelihood" that the McGuire and Catawba Nuclear Plants would be neither completed nor operated absent the Price-Anderson Act rested in major part on the testimony of corporate officials before the Joint Committee on Atomic Energy (JCAE) in 1956-1957 when the Price-Anderson Act was first considered and again in 1975 when a second renewal was discussed. During the 1956-1957 hearings, industry spokesmen for the utilities and the producers of the various competent parts of the power plants expressed a categorical unwillingness to participate in the development of nuclear power absent guarantees of a limitation on their liability. 431 F. Supp. 215. . . . By 1975, the tenor of the testimony had changed only slightly. While large utilities and producers were somewhat more equivocal about whether a failure to renew Price-Anderson would entail their leaving the industry, the smaller producers of component parts and architects and engineers — all of whom are essential to the building of the reactors and generating plants — considered renewal of the Act as the critical variable in determining their continued involvement with nuclear power. 431 F. Supp. 216-217....

Nor was the testimony at the hearing in this case, evaluation of which is the primary responsibility of the trial judge, at odds with the impression drawn from the legislative history. The testimony of Vice President Lee of Duke Power simply echoed the views presented by Duke and others to Congress in 1975, that is, although some of the utilities themselves might be confident enough with respect to safety factors to proceed with nuclear power absent a liability limitation, the suppliers of critical parts and the utility shareholders could reasonably be expected to take a more cautious view....

It is further contended that in addition to proof of injury and of a causal link between such injury and the challenged conduct, appellees must demonstrate a connection between the injuries they claim and the constitutional rights being asserted. This nexus requirement is said to find its origin in Flast v. Cohen, 392 U.S. 83, 88 S. Ct. 1942, 20 L. Ed. 2d 947 (1968), where the general question of taxpayer standing was considered.

> The nexus demanded of federal taxpayers has two aspects to it. First, the taxpayers must establish a logical link between that status and the type of legislative enactment attacked.... Secondly, the taxpayer must establish a nexus between that status and the precise nature of the constitutional infringement alleged. Id., at 102, 88 S. Ct. at 1954.

See also United States v. Richardson, 418 U.S. 166, 174-175 ... (1974). Since the environmental and health injuries claimed by appellees are not directly related to the constitutional attack on the Price-Anderson Act, such injuries, the argument continues, cannot supply a predicate for standing.[166] We decline to accept this argument.

The major difficulty with the argument is that it implicitly assumes that the nexus requirement formulated in the context of taxpayers' suits has general applicability in suits of all other types brought in the federal courts. No cases have been cited outside the context of taxpayer suits where we have demanded this type of subject matter nexus between the right asserted and the injury alleged and we are aware of none....

We ... cannot accept the contention that, outside the context of taxpayers' suits, a litigant must demonstrate anything more than injury in fact and a substan-

---

166. The only injury that would possess the required subject matter nexus to the due process challenge is the injury that would result from a nuclear accident causing damages in excess of the liability limitation provisions of the Price-Anderson Act.

tial likelihood that the judicial relief requested will prevent or redress the claimed injury to satisfy the "case and controversy" requirement of Art. III.

[The Court acknowledged that in cases such as *Warth* and *Reservists* it had recognized prudential limitations on standing where the harm asserted amounted only to a generalized grievance shared by a large number of citizens in a substantially equal measure or where the harm accrues primarily to third parties. It asserted that such prudential limitations on standing should not apply to the instant case because the harm complained of accrued primarily to persons such as plaintiffs, in a direct and concrete manner.

The Court then proceeded to rule against plaintiffs on the merits of their constitutional claims, concluding that the indemnity provisions of the Price-Anderson Act constituted a reasonable substitute for common law tort claims.

Justice REHNQUIST entered an opinion, joined by Justice STEVENS, concurring in the judgment on the ground that the district court lacked subject-matter jurisdiction over the controversy. The opinion argues that plaintiffs' claims against Duke are based essentially on state tort law, and the circumstance that Duke might in defense assert federal law, including the Price-Anderson Act, does not satisfy the requirement in 28 U.S.C. §1331 (establishing general federal question jurisdiction) that the claim "arise under" federal law. The Justice also found no basis for a federal question claim against NRC, since there was no allegation that NRC had done anything unconstitutional; plaintiffs' fire was directed at the limitation of liability, which was imposed by Congress and plays no operational role in the NRC's administration of statutes relating to nuclear power.]

Mr. Justice STEVENS, concurring in the judgment.

The string of contingencies that supposedly holds this case together is too delicate for me. We are told that but for the Price-Anderson Act there would be no financing of nuclear power plants, no development of those plants by private parties, and hence no present injury to persons such as appellees; we are then asked to remedy an alleged due process violation that may possibly occur at some uncertain time in the future, and may possibly injure the appellees in a way that has no significant connection with any present injury. It is remarkable that such a series of speculations is considered sufficient either to make this case ripe for decision or to establish appellees' standing; it is even more remarkable that this occurs in a case which as Mr. Justice Rehnquist demonstrates, there is no federal jurisdiction in the first place.

The Court's opinion will serve the national interest in removing doubts concerning the constitutionality of the Price-Anderson Act. I cannot, therefore, criticize the statemanship of the Court's decision to provide the country with an advisory opinion on an important subject. Nevertheless, my view of the proper function of this Court, or of any other federal court, in the structure of our government is more limited. We are not statesmen; we are judges. When it is necessary to resolve a constitutional issue in the adjudication of an actual case or controversy, it is our duty to do so. But whenever we are persuaded by reasons of expediency to engage in the business of giving legal advice, we chip away a part of the foundation of our independence and our strength.

Questions

1. Is *Duke Power* consistent with *Simon*? With *Alabama Power*?

2. Does *Duke Power* eliminate the "zone of interests" test for standing? Does it adopt a standing for *constitutional* challenges that is less restrictive than that governing statutory challenge to administrative action?

3. Reconsider, in light of *Duke Power*, Justice Brennan's claim in his *Simon* dissent that "injury in fact" has become "a catchall for an inarticulated discretion" on the part of the Court. Is, as Justice Brennan there claims, the law of standing in a state of hopeless confusion that invites ad hoc manipulation of doctrine? [167] If so, where did the Court take a wrong turn in the development of standing doctrine? How should the law be restructured?

4. The Federal Housing Act, 42 U.S.C. §§ 1441-1490C, originally enacted in 1949 and frequently amended, gives the Secretary of Housing and Urban Development authority to make capital grants to local public agencies for urban renewal projects. Many limitations and conditions are placed on the making of such grants, including the following (42 U.S.C. §1456(g)):

> No provision permitting the new construction of hotels or other housing for transient use in the re-development of any urban renewal area under this Act shall be included in the urban renewal plan unless the community in which the project is located, under regulations prescribed by the Secretary, has caused to be made a competent independent analysis of the local supply of transient housing and as a result thereof has determined that there exists in the area a need for additional units of such housing.

The Act contains no provisions for judicial review.

Among the projects formulated under this Act was one for Utica, New York. The plan drawn up by the local public agencies and approved by the Secretary for the award of a grant, included in the project area a new hotel for transients. The owners of the Hotel Utica, a large hotel in the city located near the project area, have brought an action in a federal court against the Secretary of HUD, the regional administrator of HUD, and certain local officials, to enjoin the use of any local or federal funds for the erection of hotels or other transient housing in the project area. The owners allege (i) that they would suffer severe economic loss from the erection of transient housing, (ii) that the competent, independent study required by law has not been made, and (iii) that there is already a substantial surplus of transient housing in the Utica metropolitan area.

Defendants have moved to dismiss on the grounds that plaintiffs lack standing to maintain the action and that judicial review of the plan on the basis alleged may not be had. What result?

---

167. See also Tushnet, The New Law of Standing: A Plea for Abandonment, 62 Cornell L. Rev. 663 (1977).

D.   The Timing of Judicial Review

1.   *Ripeness*

Columbia Broadcasting System, Inc. v. United States

316 U.S. 407 (1942)

[CBS's radio network comprised 123 stations, seven of which were owned by CBS and one of which was leased by it. The remaining 115 affiliated stations had entered into contracts with CBS, usually for five year periods, under which the stations agreed to broadcast on demand from CBS specified numbers of hours of network programming weekly. Stations affiliated with CBS agreed not to broadcast the programs of any other network.

The Federal Communications Commission is given statutory authority to issue and renew broadcast licenses for individual stations but has no statutory authority to regulate networks as such. In 1941, the Commission promulgated "Chain Broadcasting Regulations," which provided for nonrenewal or cancellation of the license of any station having network affiliation contracts which prohibited a local station from carrying programs of another network or required stations to carry network programs except under narrowly specified conditions. Many of the provisions in the existing contracts between CBS and its affiliates were proscribed by the Regulations. In a report issued simultaneously with the Regulations, the Commission argued that they were necessary in order to enhance competition in the broadcast industry.

CBS sought immediate judicial review of the Regulations pursuant to §402(a) of the Federal Communications Act and the Urgent Deficiencies Act (since repealed), which authorized three-judge district courts to entertain suits "to enforce, enjoin, set aside, annul, or suspend any order of the Commission," except FCC orders granting or denying applications for licenses or for their renewal or modification, review of which is vested by §402(b) of the Act in the Court of Appeals for the D.C. Circuit.]

Mr. Chief Justice STONE delivered the opinion of the Court.

. . . [CBS] allege[d] that since the stations fear the loss of their licenses, as a result of the regulations, they will not negotiate for or renew affiliation contracts containing such provisions. And because they fear the loss of their licenses, the stations have threatened to cancel and repudiate their affiliation contracts, and many have notified appellant that they will not be bound by their contracts after the regulations become effective. As a consequence, appellant's ability to conduct its business and maintain its public broadcasting service is seriously impaired and the regulations will make the operation of appellant's business more costly, reduce its earnings and render its property and business less valuable.

[The day after the suit was filed, the FCC issued a supplemental "Minute" stating that stations, in a renewal proceeding, might contest the validity of the Regulations without fear of nonrenewal if they agreed to comply with the Regulations in the future if they were held valid. CBS then submitted an affidavit asserting, despite the "Minute," that stations had continued to threaten cancellation or non-renewal of their contracts; it submitted additional affidavits to that effect by five affiliated stations.

The three-judge district court dismissed the suit for want of jurisdiction. The Supreme Court reversed, holding that the issuance of the Regulations constituted a reviewable "order" within the meaning of §402(a) of the Communications Act and the Urgent Deficiencies Act, and that the complaint demonstrated equitable grounds for immediate review. Enforcement of the regulations had been stayed pending the resolution of the litigation.]

The regulations here prescribe rules which govern the contractual relationships between the stations and the networks. If the applicant for a license has entered into an affiliation contract, the regulations require the Commission to reject his application. If a licensee renews his contract, the regulations . . . authorize the Commission to cancel his license. . . . The regulations are not any the less reviewable because their promulgation did not operate of their own force to deny or cancel a license. It is enough that failure to comply with them penalizes licensees, and appellant, with whom they contract. If an administrative order has that effect it is reviewable and it does not cease to be so merely because it is not certain whether the Commission will institute proceedings to enforce the penalty incurred under its regulations for noncompliance. . . .

Most rules of conduct having the force of law are not self-executing but require judicial or administrative action to impose their sanctions with respect to particular individuals. Unlike an administrative order or a court judgment adjudicating the rights of individuals, which is binding only on the parties to the particular proceeding, a valid exercise of the rule-making power is addressed to and sets a standard of conduct for all to whom its terms apply. It operates as such in advance of the imposition of sanctions upon any particular individual. It is common experience that men conform their conduct to regulations by governmental authority so as to avoid the unpleasant legal consequences which failure to conform entails. And in this case it is alleged without contradiction that numerous affiliated stations have conformed to the regulations to avoid loss of their licenses with consequent injury to appellant.

Such regulations have the force of law before their sanctions are invoked as well as after. When, as here, they are promulgated by order of the Commission and the expected conformity to them causes injury cognizable by a court of equity, they are appropriately the subject of attack under the provisions of §402(a) and the Urgent Deficiencies Act. [citing cases] . . .

Of course, the Commission was at liberty to follow a wholly different procedure. Instead of proclaiming general regulations applicable to all licenses, in advance of any specific contest over a license, it might have awaited such a contest to declare that the policy which these regulations embody represents its concept of the public interest. As a matter of sound administrative practice, both the rule-making proceeding and the specific license proceeding undoubtedly have much to commend them. But they are by no means the same, nor do they necessarily give rise to the same kind of judicial review. Having adopted this order under its rule-making power, the Commission cannot insist that the appellant be relegated to that judicial review which would be exclusive if the rule-making power had never been exercised and consequently had never subjected appellant to the threatened irreparable injury.

[The Court rejected the view that the proper remedy for CBS was by way of an injunctive action in a single-judge district court, under general federal question jurisdiction, because the statutory review proceeding in §402(a) did not apply to the issuance of an injunction.]

The Commission argues that, since its Report characterized the regulations as announcements of policy, the order promulgating them is no more subject to review than a press release similarly announcing its policy. Undoubtedly, regulations adopted in the exercise of the administrative rule-making power, like laws enacted by legislatures, embody announcements of policy. But they may be something more. When, as here, the regulations are avowedly adopted in the exercise of that power, couched in terms of command and accompanied by an announcement of the Commission that the policy is one "which we will follow in exercising our licensing power," they must be taken by those entitled to rely upon them as what they purport to be — an exercise of the delegated legislative power — which, until amended, are controlling alike upon the Commission and all others whose rights may be affected by the Commission's execution of them. The Commission's contention that the regulations are no more reviewable than a press release is hardly reconcilable with its own recognition that the regulations afford legal basis for cancellation of the license of a station if it renews its contract with appellant....

... [T]he allegations of the complaint and ... the effect of the Commission's order if those allegations are sustained upon the trial, [are] enough to establish the threat of irreparable injury to appellant's business and to show also that the injury can not be avoided, as the Commission suggests, by appellant's intervention in proceedings upon applications for renewal of licenses by its affiliates or in proceedings to cancel their licenses, if and when such proceedings are instituted....

Nor does the Commission's minute, filed after the present suit was brought, afford an adequate basis for requiring appellant to seek relief by intervention in a proceeding on application for a license reviewable under §402(b).... Without full exploration of the subject, such as can be had only at the trial, we cannot say that the minute will afford a sufficient inducement to persuade the affiliated stations to cease cancellations and assume the initiative in litigating the validity of the regulations and of the contracts which they undertake to condemn. The affidavit filed in the court below on the application for a stay is to the contrary....

Reversed.

Mr. Justice BLACK took no part in the consideration or decision of this case.

Mr. Justice FRANKFURTER, dissenting:

[Justice Frankfurter noted that §402(a) of the Communications Act and The Urgent Deficiencies Act (which also governed review of certain ICC actions) authorized three-judge court review of an agency "order," and argued that the FCC's issuance of Chain Broadcast Regulations did not constitute a reviewable "order" under precedent discussing the meaning of that term in the context of review of ICC actions.]

In promulgating these regulations the Communications Commission merely announced its conception of one aspect of the public interest, namely, the relationship of certain provisions in network-affiliation contracts to the obligation of a station licensee to render the most effective service to the listening public. The regulations themselves determine no rights. They alter the status of neither the networks nor licensees. As such they require nobody —neither the networks, the licensees, nor the Commission — to do anything. They are merely an announcement to the public of what the Commission intends to do in passing upon future applications for station licenses. No action of the stations or the networks can violate the regulations, for there is nothing the regulations require them to do or refrain from doing.

Announcements of general policies intended to be followed by administrative agencies customarily take any one of various forms. Sometimes they are noted in the agency's annual report to Congress, sometimes in a public announcement or press release, and sometimes, as was the case here, they are published as "rules" or "regulations." See Final Report of the Attorney General's Committee on Administrative Procedure (1941), pp. 26-27. But whatever form such announcements may take, their nature and effect is the same. . . .

The regulations do not . . . commit the Commission to any definitive course of action in passing upon applications for licenses. Consistently with the regulations. . . . the Commission is free to dilute them with amendments and exceptions. The construction of the regulations and their application to particular situations is still in the hands of the Commission. Administrative adjudication is still open. Before its completion it is not ripe for judicial review. . . .

This leaves only the suggestion that since the action taken by the Commission, although not the completion of its adjudicatory process, nevertheless drastically affects substantial business interests, it is proper for the courts to intercede at this stage. . . . As a practical matter, the impact upon the business operations of the network and their affiliated stations would probably be as disturbing as if the policies formulated in the regulations had been expressed through a press release. . . . But assume that the greater formality given to the announcement of the Commission's statement of policy through the regulations intensified the practical business consequences. Congress has not conferred upon the district courts jurisdiction over "practical business consequences." They can review action of administrative agencies only when there is an "order," and when Congress in §402(a) made only an "order" of the Communications Commission reviewable, it incorporated the settled doctrine established by an unbroken series of decisions in this Court that the courts could review only a final determination by an agency whereby its administrative process has been concluded. . . .

. . . While formally we may appear to be dealing with technicalities, behind these considerations lie deep issues of policy in the division of authority as between administrative agencies and courts in carrying out the constitutional will of Congress. . . .

. . . If threatened damage through general pronouncement of policy for future administrative action, even if cast in the formal language of a regulation, is to give rise to equitable review, . . . the same basis of irreparable harm which is here equated to jurisdiction will bear rich litigious fruit in the case of "regulations" issued by the Securities and Exchange Commission which are damaging in their immediate repercussions to stock exchange and holding companies, or regulations announced by the Treasury for the guidance of taxpayers but which adversely affect business interests, or regulations by the Federal Power Commission, etc. . . .

We need go no farther than this litigation to perceive the unfortunate effects of premature judicial review. The chain broadcasting regulations were issued on May 2, 1941, more than a year ago. They were adopted by the Commission as a consequence of its finding, after an investigation lasting more than three years, that certain features of network-affiliation contracts prevented licensees from effectively discharging their obligation to render the fullest service to the listening public. The policy formulated by the Commission may or may not be wise — that is not our concern. But we cannot blink the fact that this litigation has for more than a year prevented the Commission from testing by experience the practical wisdom of a policy found by it to be required by the public interest. The commencement of a proceeding under §402(b) [of the Communications Act, authorizing review by the District of Columbia Circuit Court of Appeals of FCC orders granting or denying license applications] would not have presented the jurisdictional problems present in this proceeding. Surely those desirous of a speedy adjudication of the issue of the validity of the regulations were aware that the commencement of a proceeding under §402(a) would not produce a prompt adjudication on the merits, but that it would instead result in postponing for a considerable period the effective date of the regulations, with all the contingent advantages afforded by such postponement.

Hardship there may well come through action of an administrative agency. But to slide from recognition of a hardship to assertion of jurisdiction is once more to assume that only the courts are the guardians of the rights and liberties of the people. . . .

Mr. Justice REED and Mr. Justice DOUGLAS join in this dissent.

Notes and Questions

1. What is the basis of CBS's standing to bring suit?

2. Does Justice Frankfurter adduce any concrete reasons for refusing to hear CBS's contentions at this time? What will be the consequences of such a refusal for CBS and the Commission? Are his objections to the Court's ruling more academic than realistic?

3. For additional decisions relaxing preexisting notions of finality and ripeness in judicial review — in which review was generally available only when enforcement action was being undertaken or was imminent — see the following:

United States v. Storer Broadcasting Co., 351 U.S. 192 (1956), permitted Storer, which already owned five television stations, to obtain review, under the Federal Communications Act, of regulations issued by the FCC limiting the total number of stations any person might own to five. The majority cited CBS and reasoned that the regulations "now operate to control the business affairs" of Storer, that they interfered with Storer's ability to plan future business policy (Storer was planning to ask FCC approval to acquire a sixth station), and exposed Storer to the risk of a license forfeiture if its stocks were bought up by a person controlling another station.

Frozen Foods Express v. United States, 351 U.S. 40 (1956), held to be a reviewable order a 71-page ICC report setting forth the Commission's very narrow interpretations of a statutory provision exempting the carriage of "agricultural commodities (not including manufactured products thereof)" from the general requirements of ICC licensure for interstate transport. The application of the exemption with respect to dozens of partially processed commodities (e.g., frozen chickens) had long been disputed. Reviewability was found on the ground that carriers who disagreed with the Commission's narrow construction of the exemption were subject to cease-and-desist orders and possible criminal penalties if they continued to carry, without an ICC permit, products which the Commission had ruled not exempt. Justice Harlan, dissenting, pointed out that the ICC had stated that it would not regard its report as binding in the decision of particular cases.

Query: Is either *Storer* or *Frozen Foods* compelled by *CBS*? [168]

4. Did the enactment of the APA extend or otherwise clarify the principles governing the timing of judicial review? Consider carefully the provisions of 5 U.S.C. §704.

Abbott Laboratories v. Gardner

387 U.S. 136 (1967)

[As part of the 1962 Amendments to the Food, Drug and Cosmetic Act (see pp. 557-566, supra) Congress, in §502(e)(1)(B) of the Act, required prescription drug manufacturers to print on labels, advertising, and other printed materials the "established name" of a drug "prominently and in type at least half as large as that used thereon for the proprietary name or designation for such drug." The "proprietary" name was the trademarked or brand name established by a particular manufacturer for a given drug, while the "established" name was a generic name (designated by the FDA) for all drugs of the same chemical composition, regardless of the various brand names under which they were sold. The purpose of this requirement was to encourage price competition among manufacturers in marketing chemically identical generic drugs by alerting physicians, patients, and pharmacists to the identity,

---

168. For a more restrictive approach to pre-enforcement review, see International Longshoremen's & Warehousemen's Union v. Boyd, 347 U.S. 222 (1954), declining to entertain a challenge by a union and several of its members who travelled to Alaska every summer for employment to an announced policy of the Seattle District Director of Immigration and Naturalization to treat aliens returning from Alaskan summer employment as if they were aliens entering the United States for the first time. Justice Frankfurter, for the Court, warned that a legal ruling "in advance of . . . immediate adverse effect in the context of a concrete case involves too remote and abstract an inquiry for the proper exercise of the judicial function." 347 U.S. at 224.

and by discouraging manufacturers from advertising to promote a brand name for a drug.

Pursuant to his statutory authority to issue regulations for the "efficient enforcement" of the Act, the Commissioner of Food and Drug, following notice and opportunity for comment, issued regulations requiring the established name of a drug must "accompany each appearance" of the drug's proprietary name in all labels, enclosures, advertising, and promotional literature for the drug.

The Pharmaceutical Manufacturers' Association and 37 of its members brought an injunction action in district court asserting that the regulation's requirement that the established name of the drug accompany the proprietary name *every time* the latter is used exceeded the authority granted to the FDA by the 1962 amendments.

The District Court ruled for plaintiffs on the merits. On appeal, the Third Circuit Court of Appeals reversed on jurisdictional grounds, holding that the Food, Drug and Cosmetic Act precluded court review of the regulations prior to their enforcement against a given manufacturer, and that no justiciable "case or controversy" was presented.]

Mr. Justice HARLAN delivered the opinion of the Court: . . .

The first question we consider is whether Congress by The Federal Food, Drug and Cosmetic Act intended to forbid pre-enforcement review of this sort of regulation promulgated by the Commissioner. The question is phrased in terms of "prohibition" rather than "authorization" because a survey of our cases shows that judicial review of a final agency action by an aggrieved person will not be cut off unless there is persuasive reason to believe that such was the purpose of Congress. . . . The Administrative Procedure Act provides specifically not only for review of "[a]gency action made reviewable by statute" but also for review of "final agency action for which there is no other adequate remedy in a court," 5 U.S.C. §704. The legislative material elucidating that seminal act manifests a congressional intention that it cover a broad spectrum of administrative actions.[169] . . . [O]nly upon a showing of "clear and convincing evidence" of a contrary legislative intent should the courts restrict access to judicial review. See also Jaffe, Judicial Control of Administrative Action 336-359 (1965).

Given this standard, we are wholly unpersuaded that the statutory scheme in the food and drug area excludes this type of action. The Government relies on no explicit statutory authority for its argument that pre-enforcement review is unavailable, but insists instead that because the statute includes a specific procedure for such review of certain enumerated kinds of regulations,[170] not encompassing those of the kind involved here, other types were necessarily meant to be excluded from

---

169. See H. R. Rep. No. 1980, 79th Cong., 2d Sess., 41 (1946): "To preclude judicial review under this bill a statute, if not specific in withholding such review, must upon its face give clear and convincing evidence of an intent to withhold it. The mere failure to provide specially by statute for judicial review is certainly no evidence of intent to withhold review." See also S. Rep. No. 752, 79th Cong., 1st Sess., 26 (1945).

170. Section 701(e) [of the Food, Drug and Cosmetic Act] provides a procedure for the issuance of regulations under certain specifically enumerated statutory sections. Section 701(f) establishes a procedure for direct review by a court of appeals of a regulation promulgated under §701(e).

any pre-enforcement review. The issue, however, is not so readily resolved; we must go further and inquire whether in the context of the entire legislative scheme the existence of that circumscribed remedy evinces a congressional purpose to bar agency action not within its purview from judicial review. As a leading authority in this field has noted, "The mere fact that some acts are made reviewable should not suffice to support an implication of exclusion as to others. The right to review is too important to be excluded on such slender and indeterminate evidence of legislative intent." Jaffe, supra, at 357.

[The Court then reviewed in detail the structure and legislative history of the Act.]

We conclude that nothing in the Food, Drug and Cosmetic Act itself precludes this action. . . .

A further inquiry must, however, be made. The injunctive and declaratory judgment remedies are discretionary, and courts traditionally have been reluctant to apply them to administrative determinations unless these arise in the context of a controversy "ripe" for judicial resolution. Without undertaking to survey the intricacies of the ripeness doctrine it is fair to say that its basic rationale is to prevent the courts, through avoidance of premature adjudication, from entangling themselves in abstract disagreements over administrative policies, and also to protect the agencies from judicial interference until an administrative decision has been formalized and its effects felt in a concrete way by the challenging parties. The problem is best seen in a twofold aspect requiring us to evaluate both the fitness of the issues for judicial decision and the hardship to the parties of withholding court consideration.

As to the former factor, we believe the issues presented are appropriate for judicial resolution at this time. First, all parties agree that the issue tendered is a purely legal one: whether the statute was properly construed by the Commissioner to require the established name of the drug to be used *every time* the proprietary name is employed. Both sides moved for summary judgment in the District Court, and no claim is made here that further administrative proceedings are contemplated. It is suggested that the justification for this rule might vary with different circumstances, and that the expertise of the Commissioner is relevant to passing upon the validity of the regulation. This of course is true, but the suggestion overlooks the fact that both sides have approached this case as one purely of congressional intent, and that the Government made no effort to justify the regulation in factual terms.

Second, the regulations in issue we find to be "final agency action" within the meaning of §10 of the Administrative Procedure Act, 5 U.S.C. §704, as construed in judicial decisions. An "agency action" includes any "rule," defined by the Act as "an agency statement of general or particular applicability and future effect designed to implement, interpret, or prescribe law or policy," §§ 2(c), 2(g), 5 U.S.C. §§ 551(4), 551(13). The cases dealing with judicial review of administrative actions have interpreted the "finality" element in a pragmatic way.

[The Court cited *CBS, Frozen Food Express*, and *Storer Broadcasting*.]

The Government argues, however, that the present case can be distinguished from cases like *Frozen Food Express* on the ground that in those instances the agency involved could implement its policy directly, while here the Attorney General must authorize criminal and seizure actions for violations of the statute. In the context of this case, we do not find this argument persuasive. These regulations are not meant to advise the Attorney General, but purport to be directly authorized by the statute. Thus, if within the Commissioner's authority, they have the status of law and violations of them carry heavy criminal and civil sanctions. Also, there is no representation that the Attorney General and the Commissioner disagree in this area; the Justice Department is defending this very suit. It would be adherence to a mere technicality to give any credence to this contention.

This is also a case in which the impact of the regulations upon the petitioners is sufficiently direct and immediate as to render the issue appropriate for judicial review at this stage. These regulations purport to give an authoritative interpretation of a statutory provision that has a direct effect on the day-to-day business of all prescription drug companies; its promulgation puts petitioners in a dilemma that it was the very purpose of the Declaratory Judgment Act to ameliorate.[171] As the District Court found on the basis of uncontested allegations, "Either they must comply with the every time requirement and incur the costs of changing over their promotional material and labeling or they must follow their present course and risk prosecution." 228 F. Supp. 855, 861. The regulations are clear-cut, and were made effective immediately upon publication; as noted earlier the agency's counsel represented to the District Court that immediate compliance with their terms was expected. If petitioners wish to comply they must change all their labels, advertisements, and promotional materials; they must destroy stocks of printed matter; and they must invest heavily in new printing type and new supplies. The alternative to compliance — continued use of material which they believe in good faith meets the statutory requirements, but which clearly does not meet the regulation of the Commissioner — may be even more costly. That course would risk serious criminal and civil penalties for the unlawful distribution of "misbranded" drugs.[172]

It is relevant at this juncture to recognize that petitioners deal in a sensitive industry, in which public confidence in their drug products is especially important. To require them to challenge these regulations only as a defense to an action brought by the Government might harm them severely and unnecessarily. Where the legal issue presented is fit for judicial resolution, and where a regulation requires an immediate and significant change in the plaintiffs' conduct of their affairs with serious penalties attached to noncompliance, access to the courts under the Administrative Procedure Act and the Declaratory Judgment Act must be permitted, absent a statutory bar or some other unusual circumstance, neither of which appears here. . . .

Finally, the Government urges that to permit resort to the courts in this type of case may delay or impede effective enforcement of the Act. We fully recognize

171. See S. Rep. No. 1005, 73d Cong., 2d Sess., 2-3 (1934); Borchard, Challenging "Penal" Statutes by Declaratory Action, 52 Yale L. J. 445, 454 (1943).

172. Section 502(e)(1)(B) declares a drug not complying with this labeling requirement to be "misbranded." Section 301, 21 U.S.C. §331, designates as "prohibited acts" the misbranding of drugs in interstate commerce. Such prohibited acts are subject to injunction, §302, 21 U.S.C. §332, criminal penalties, §303, 21 U.S.C. §333, and seizure, §304(a), 21 U.S.C. §334(a).

the important public interest served by assuring prompt and unimpeded administration of the Pure Food, Drug and Cosmetic Act, but we do not find the Government's argument convincing. First, in this particular case, a pre-enforcement challenge by nearly all prescription drug manufacturers is calculated to speed enforcement. If the Government prevails, a large part of the industry is bound by the decree; if the Government loses, it can more quickly revise its regulation.

The Government contends, however, that if the Court allows this consolidated suit, then nothing will prevent a multiplicity of suits in various jurisdictions challenging other regulations. The short answer to this contention is that the courts are well equipped to deal with such eventualities. . . .

[The opinion noted the power of federal courts to transfer venue in order to consolidate related litigation, or to enjoin multiple or harassing lawsuits.]

In addition to all these safeguards against what the Government fears, it is important to note that the institution of this type of action does not by itself stay the effectiveness of the challenged regulation. There is nothing in the record to indicate that petitioners have sought to stay enforcement of the "every time" regulation pending judicial review. See 5 U.S.C. §705. If the agency believes that a suit of this type will significantly impede enforcement or will harm the public interest, it need not postpone enforcement of the regulation and may oppose any motion for a judicial stay on the part of those challenging the regulation. Ibid. It is scarcely to be doubted that a court would refuse to postpone the effective date of an agency action if the Government could show, as it made no effort to do here, that delay would be detrimental to the public health or safety. . . .

[The Court remanded the case to the Court of Appeals for decision by that court on the merits of the controversy.]

Reversed and remanded.

Mr. Justice BRENNAN took no part in the consideration or decision of this case.

[Decided the same day as *Abbott Laboratories* were Toilet Goods Ass'n, Inc. v. Gardner, 387 U.S. 158 (1967), and Gardner v. Toilet Goods Ass'n, Inc., 387 U.S. 167 (1967), both of which arose out of a pre-enforcement District Court action by a cosmetic manufacturers' trade association and its members, seeking declaratory and injunctive relief against various regulations issued by FDA under the 1960 Color Additives Amendments to the Food, Drug and Cosmetic Act, expanding FDA's authority to regulate color additives. The District Court held that it had jurisdiction to hear the controversy.

The Second Circuit reversed the District Court's jurisdictional ruling with respect to one regulation (the access regulation) which provided that if a manufacturer refused to permit duly authorized FDA employees "free access" to all "manufacturing facilities, processes, and formulae" involved in the manufacture of color additives, the FDA would suspend batch certification service of additives (a prerequisite to their subsequent marketing) until access was permitted.

In Toilet Goods Ass'n v. Gardner the Supreme Court, in an opinion by Justice HARLAN, agreed with the Court of Appeals that the validity of this regulation was not ripe for review. The regulation, it conceded, represented the FDA's "considered and formalized determination" and also presented a pure issue of law under the statute, which specifically grants FDA inspection authority for prescription drugs but not color additives. The Court (over the dissent of Justice Douglas) nonetheless concluded that the issues were not ripe for review:]

... The regulation serves notice only that the Commissioner *may* under certain circumstances order inspection of certain facilities and data, and that further certification of additives *may* be refused to those who decline to permit a duly authorized inspection until they have complied in that regard. At this juncture we have no idea whether or when such an inspection will be ordered and what reasons the Commissioner will give to justify his order.... [The issue of the regulations' validity] will depend not merely on an inquiry into statutory purpose, but concurrently on an understanding of what types of enforcement problems are encountered by the FDA, the need for various sorts of supervision in order to effectuate the goals of the Act, and the safeguards devised to protect legitimate trade secrets (see 21 CFR §130.14(c)). We believe that judicial appraisal of these factors is likely to stand on a much surer footing in the context of a specific application of this regulation than could be the case in the framework of the generalized challenge made here....

... Moreover, no irremediable adverse consequences flow from requiring a later challenge to this regulation by a manufacturer who refuses to allow this type of inspection. Unlike the other regulations challenged in this action, in which seizure of goods, heavy fines, adverse publicity for distributing "adulterated" goods, and possible criminal liability might penalize failure to comply, ... a refusal to admit an inspector here would at most lead only to a suspension of certification services to the particular party, a determination that can then be promptly challenged through an administrative procedure, which in turn is reviewable by a court. Such review will provide an adequate forum for testing the regulation in a concrete situation.

[The companion case, Gardner v. Toilet Goods Ass'n, Inc., reviewed the Second Circuit's affirmance of the District Court's ruling that it had jurisdiction to review a number of other FDA color additive regulations (the definitional regulations), amplifying the statutory definition of color additives to include diluents, including certain cosmetics, within the scope of color additives, and narrowly construing the statutory exemption for hair dyes. The Supreme Court affirmed this aspect of the Court of Appeals' ruling, concluding that the regulations' reviewability was established by *Abbott Laboratories*.

The effect of the regulations in question was to expand the FDA's preexisting definition of color additives. Under the Act, manufacture and distribution of color additives is prohibited and subject to criminal sanctions unless the color additive is approved by FDA as safe, and particular batches of the additive have been certified by FDA. The Court reasoned that the regulations represented the FDA's considered view; that their validity involved a pure question of statutory construction that could be resolved now; and that issuance of the regulations placed the manufacturers in the dilemma of acquiescing in the regulations and complying, at substantial expense, with FDA clearance procedures, or defying the regulations at the risk of incurring serious sanctions.

Justice BRENNAN took no part in either of the *Toilets Goods* cases.

Justice FORTAS, joined by Chief Justice WARREN and Justice CLARK, issued an opinion concurring in Toilet Goods Ass'n, Inc., v. Gardner (the access regulations) and dissenting in Gardner v. Toilet Goods Ass'n, Inc. (the definitional regulations) and *Abbott Laboratories.*]

With all respect, I submit that established principles of jurisprudence, solidly rooted in the constitutional structure of our Government, require that the courts should not intervene in the administrative process at this stage, under these facts and in this gross, shotgun fashion. . . .

The Court, by today's decisions, . . . has opened Pandora's box. Federal injunctions will now threaten programs of vast importance to the public welfare. The Court's holding here strikes at programs for the public health. The dangerous precedent goes even further. It is cold comfort — it is little more than delusion — to read in the Court's opinion that "It is scarcely to be doubted that a court would refuse to postpone the effective date of an agency action if the Government could show . . . that delay would be detrimental to the public health or safety." Experience dictates, on the contrary, that it can hardly be hoped that some federal judge somewhere will not be moved as the Court is here, by the cries of anguish and distress of those regulated, to grant a disruptive injunction. . . .

. . . I believe that [the Court's] approach improperly and unwisely gives individual federal district judges a roving commission to halt the regulatory process, and to do so on the basis of abstractions and generalities instead of concrete fact situations, and that it impermissibly broadens the license of the courts to intervene in administrative action by means of a threshold suit for injunction rather than by the method provided by statute.

[Justice Fortas argued that the review provisions of the Act, which provided specifically for the pre-enforcement review of certain FDA regulations, but not those involved here, should be read to preclude judicial review of the regulations involved here except in the context of an enforcement proceeding against a given firm.]

In evaluating the destructive force and effect of the Court's action in these cases, it is necessary to realize that it is arming each of the federal district judges in this Nation with power to enjoin enforcement of regulations and actions under the federal law designed to protect the people of this Nation against dangerous drugs and cosmetics. Restraining orders and temporary injunctions will suspend application of these public safety laws pending years of litigation — a time schedule which these cases illustrate.[173] They are disruptive enough, regardless of the ultimate outcome. The Court's validation of this shotgun attack upon this vital law and its administration is not confined to these suits, these regulations, or these plaintiffs — or even this statute. It is a general hunting license; and I respectfully submit, a license for mischief because it authorizes aggression which is richly re-

---

173. The "every time" regulation was published about four years ago, on June 20, 1963, 28 Fed. Reg. 6375. As a result of litigation begun in September of 1963, it has not yet been put into force. The "definition" regulations and the "access" regulation with respect to color additives were published on June 22, 1963, 28 Fed. Reg. 6439, 6446. Litigation was begun in November of 1963, and the regulations are not yet operative.

warded by delay in the subjection of private interests to programs which Congress believes to be required in the public interest. . . .

[Justice Fortas then argued that even if pre-enforcement review is not precluded by the Food, Drug and Cosmetic Act, the controversies in question were not "ripe" for review at the present time.]

. . . Where personal status or liberties are involved, the courts may well insist upon a considerable ease of challenging administrative orders or regulations. . . . But in situations where a regulatory scheme designed to protect the public is involved, this Court has held that postponement of the opportunity to obtain judicial relief in the interest of avoiding disruption of the regulatory plan is entirely justifiable. Ewing v. Mytinger & Casselbery, 339 U.S. 594 (1950). . . .[174]

[Justice Fortas then discussed CBS, Frozen Food Express and Storer Broadcasting.]

Considering the impact of these three cases on the problem of "ripeness" in the instant cases, I first note that each of these three cases is, in effect, two-dimensional. The meaning, effect, and impact of the accused rule or decision are clear, simple, and obvious. None is part of the warp and woof of an elaborate administrative pattern, intimately woven into the congressional design. None of them is apt to take different shape or to be modified by practical administrative action. None of them is subject to the give-and take of the administrative process as it works, for example, in the realities of the complex world of food, drug, and cosmetic regulation. None of them is subject to exception upon application.

[Justice Fortas then argued that the same considerations which led the Court to refuse pre-enforcement review of the color additive inspection access regulations also dictated postponing decision on the validity of the various regulations expanding the prior definition of "color additives" until they had been applied to a concrete factual situation in the context of an enforcement proceeding.

With respect to the "every time" regulations in Abbott Laboratories, Justice Fortas denied that the asserted hardship faced by the manufacturers in choosing whether to comply with the regulations or subject themselves to enforcement liabilities was sufficient ground for affording preenforcement review.]

I submit that a much stronger showing is necessary than the expense and trouble of compliance and the risk of defiance. Actually, if the Court refused to permit this shotgun assault, experience and reasonably sophisticated common sense show that there would be orderly compliance without the disaster so dramatically predicted by the industry, reasonable adjustments by the agency in real hardship cases, and where extreme intransigence involving substantial violations occurred, enforcement actions in which legality of the regulation would be tested in specific, concrete situations. . . .

Mr. Justice CLARK, dissenting.

I join My Brother Fortas' dissent. As he points out the regulations here merely require common honesty and fair dealing in the sale of drugs. The pharmaceutical companies, contrary to the public interest, have through their high-sounding trade-

---

174. Ed. note: See the description of Mytinger & Casselberry at p. 477, supra.

marks of long-established medicines deceitfully and exorbitantly extorted high prices therefor from the sick and infirm. Indeed, I was so gouged myself just recently when I purchased some ordinary eyewash drops and later learned that I paid 10 times the price the drops should have cost. Likewise, a year or so ago I purchased a brand name drug for the treatment of labyrinthitis at a cost of some $12, which later I learned to buy by its established name for about $1.

The Court says that its action in so sabotaging the public interest is required "because the laboratories will have to change" all their labels, advertisements, and promotional materials . . . destroy stocks of printed matter; and they must invest heavily in new printing type and new supplies. I submit that this is a lame excuse for permitting the continuance of such a dishonest practice. Rather than crying over the plight that the laboratories have brought on themselves the Court should think more of the poor ailing folks who suffer under the practice. I dare say that the practice has prevented millions from obtaining needed drugs because of the price. The labels involved here misled the public by passing off ordinary medicines as fancy cures. The Commissioner was right in directing that the practice be stopped.

I hope that the Congress will not delay in amending the Act to close this judicial exition that the Court has unwisely opened up for the pharmaceutical companies.

Notes and Questions

1. Note that *Abbott Laboratories* affirms a presumption of review despite selective review provisions in the Food, Drug and Cosmetic Act (see footnote 170) that authorized preenforcement review of certain FDA regulations, but not these in issue in *Abbott*. Does *Abbott* effectively overrule *Switchmen's Union*?

2. Is Justice Harlan correct in arguing (p. 967) that *Abbott Laboratories* follows a fortiori from *CBS* and *Storer*? From *Frozen Food Express*? Are the Court's rulings in *Abbott Laboratories* and Gardner v. Toilet Goods Ass'n (definitional regulations) consistent with its rationale in Toilet Goods Ass'n v. Gardner (access regulations)?

3. Justices Fortas and Clark are evidently concerned about the substantive impact of the Court's procedural ruling. What is that impact likely to be? Isn't Justice Fortas arguing, in effect, that it is proper and legitimate to permit agencies to threaten regulated firms with enforcement of illegal regulations in order to coerce settlements more favorable to the agency?

4. As might be expected, the ripeness principles enunciated in *Abbott Laboratories* have made routine pre-enforcement review of agency regulations.[175] It is

175. See, e.g,, Citizens Communications Center v. FCC, 447 F.2d 1201 (D.C. Cir. 1971), reproduced at p. 388 supra. Current decisions as well as historical background are catalogued in Fuchs, Prerequisites to Judicial Review of Administrative Agency Action, 51 Indiana L. Rev. 817, 819-859 (1976). For a comprehensive analysis strongly defending the result in *Abbott Laboratories* and liberal availability of pre-enforcement review, see Vining, Direct Review and the Doctrine of Ripeness in Administrative Law, 69 Mich. L. Rev. 1445 (1971).

against the background of *Abbott Laboratories* and the accompanying expansion of pre-enforcement review that you can now more fully appreciate why so much judicial attention has been directed during the past 10 years to the problems of judicial review of rulemaking in instances where regulations have not yet been applied in a particular adjudication.[176]

Note: Statutory vs. "Nonstatutory" Review of Regulations Prior to Their Application

There are two basic jurisdictional alternatives in securing judicial review of regulations before their application. A specific statute providing for review of specified agency action — such as an agency "order" — may be construed to encompass the issuance of regulations. This was the approach taken in *CBS*. (Note that *CBS* was a pre-APA decision, but even today the word "order" in a specific review statute may be construed to apply to the promulgation of regulations, even though such promulgation would not constitute an "order" under the APA, which limits the term to dispositions of adjudication, 5 U.S.C. §551(6)).

If the relevant specific review statute cannot be construed to include the issuance of regulations, "nonstatutory" review may be sought under the federal district courts' general jurisdiction. This was the course approved in *Abbott Laboratories*, which rejected the government's claim that such review was impliedly precluded.

These alternatives are reflected in 5 U.S.C. §703. The choice between them is significant because the forum will normally be different. Most specific statutory review provisions provide for review in a Court of Appeals, whereas "nonstatutory" review must be sought in a District Court. Suppose it is unclear whether a specific statutory provision, calling for court of appeals review of certain agency actions, applies to the issuance of regulations. Should the statute be construed to permit review in the Court of Appeals, or should the plaintiff be remitted to "nonstatutory" review in a District Court? What are the considerations that bear on such a decision? [177]

National Automatic Laundry and Cleaning Council v. Shultz

443 F.2d 689 (D.C. Cir. 1971)

LEVENTHAL, Circuit Judge:
[Counsel for the National Automatic Laundry and Cleaning Council (NALCC), a trade association for the coin-operated laundry and dry cleaning industry,

176. See pp. 478-481, supra (procedures in rulemaking); pp. 522-524, supra (scope of review of fact-finding in notice and comment rulemaking); pp. 227-239, supra (scope of review of legal issues in rulemaking).

177. For general discussion of these and related issues, see Currie and Goodman, Judicial Review of Federal Administrative Action: Quest for the Optimum Forum, 75 Colum L. Rev. 1 (1975); Note, Jurisdiction to Review Federal Administrative Action: District Court or Court of Appeals, 88 Harv. L. Rev. 980 (1975).

Suppose a statute specifies review in a Court of Appeals within 30 days after the agency's action. Is district court review by a declaratory or injunctive action filed after the 30th day barred?

wrote the Federal Wage and Hour Administration concerning the applicability to coin-operated laundry employees of the maximum hour and minimum wage provisions of the Fair Labor Standards Act. The question of coverage was posed in the context of three representative factual situations specified in the letter. In a reply letter, the Administrator stated his view that in each situation the employees would be covered by the Act, which would require the employers to pay a specified minimum wage, and time-and-a-half for overtime, or face awards for back pay, attorneys' fees, and (potentially) civil or criminal sanctions. NALCC brought an action against the Secretary of Labor in District Court, contending that the Administration's interpretation was erroneous, and seeking declaratory and injunctive relief. The District Court dismissed for want of jurisdiction. The Court of Appeals reversed on the jurisdictional issue, but ruled in favor of the government on the merits. An excerpt from the court's opinion summarizing its discussion of the jurisdictional issue follows:]

... The ultimate question is whether the problems generated by pre-enforcement review are of such a nature that, taken together, they outweigh the hardship and interest of plaintiff's members and establish that judicial review of the interpretative ruling should be deferred. To some extent a balancing is involved....

Plainly there is a need for advisory interpretations by agency officials. The overwhelming bulk of these are not given by the agency head, and are not within the scope of our ruling announced today. When a general, interpretative ruling signed by the head of an agency has been crystallized following reflective examination in the course of the agency's interpretative process, and is accordingly entitled to deference not only as a matter of fact from staff and citizenry expected to conform but also as a matter of law from a court reviewing the question, there coexist both multiple signposts of authoritative determination, finality and ripeness, and a concomitant indication that the resultant pointing toward prompt judicial review will benefit the total administrative process by resolving uncertainties without intolerable burden or disruption. In the last analysis the Administrator will have latitude to restrict the rulings he signs. There is warrant, then, for discerning at least a limited presumption of pre-enforcement judicial review in the case of authoritative interpretative rulings.

There is the possibility that judicial review at too early a stage removes the process of agency refinement, including give-and-take with the regulated interests, that is an important part of the life of the agency process. The considerations developed in the dissent of Justice Fortas in *Abbott Laboratories* describe realities of the administrative process that must be taken into account.

They can be taken into account under our decision. As we have indicated, an affidavit by the agency head — not a mere argument by its court counsel — that a matter is still under meaningful refinement and development, will likely provide the element of tentativeness and reconsideration that should negative finality, or in any event ripeness....

The overruling of threshold objections does not necessarily portend the propriety of a court ruling on the merits. A declaratory judgment, like other forms of equitable relief, is granted only as a matter of judicial discretion, exercised in the public interest.... Public Affairs Associates v. Rickover, 369 U.S. 111 (1962);

9. The Availability and Timing of Judicial Review

Lampkin v. Connors, 123 U.S. App. D.C. 371, 360 F.2d 505 (1966). In *Rickover*, the Court exercised its discretion and remanded for amplification of the record, saying, "These are delicate problems. . . . Adjudication of such problems, certainly by way of resort to a discretionary declaratory judgment, should rest on an adequate and full-bodied record. The record before us is woefully lacking in these requirements." 369 U.S. at 113. But that kind of discretion is more soundly exercised after the court has probed the merits, and not by way of a threshold consideration.

[Judge Leventhal then acknowledged the government's potential interest in avoiding multiple pre-enforcement litigation and in binding all members of a regulated industry to the outcome of a pre-enforcement challenge. He suggested that these interests could be satisfied by insisting on maintenance of a pre-enforcement challenge as a class action, an alternative that probably would be feasible where the challenge was brought by a trade association.]

In the course of time other problems of administration or litigation may emerge. We anticipate that they can be managed by reference to doctrines that govern the conduct of litigation, or the scope of relief granted. We find no threshold obstacle that requires dismissal of the action before us merely because it seeks judicial review of the "agency action" of interpretation prior to the institution of an agency action for enforcement.

Notes and Questions

1. What is left of traditional principles of ripeness after *NALCC*? Recall that in *CBS*, p. 963, supra, Justice Frankfurter in dissent had jocularly argued that the Chain Broadcasting Regulations had no greater legal effect than an FCC press release, and that since a press release certaintly would not be judicially reviewable, neither were the regulations. Is it clear today that a press release would not be judicially reviewable? [178]

178. See A. E. Staley Mfg. Co. v. United States, 310 F. Supp. 485 (D. Minn. 1970). Compare Independent Broker-Dealers' Trade Ass'n v. SEC, 442 F.2d 132 (D.C. Cir.), *cert. denied*, 404 U.S. 828 (1971), sustaining the general equity jurisdiction of a federal district court to review a written request from the SEC to the New York Stock Exchange asking for a particular change of Exchange rules. The Exchange, with the subsequent acquiescence of the Commission, adopted a modified version of the requested change, which assertedly worked injury to plaintiffs. The Securities Exchange Act authorized the SEC to require, after notice and hearing, modifications in exchange rules if SEC requests for such changes were not heeded.

As Judge Leventhal points out in *NALCC*, a ruling that an issue is ripe for review does not necessarily establish that a litigant in a district court action will be entitled to relief if she prevails on the merits, because a court may still refuse to exercise its equitable discretion to award declaratory or injunctive relief. See, e.g., A. O. Smith v. FTC, 530 F.2d 515 (3d Cir. 1976), sustaining the District Court's ruling that a challenge by business firms to the breadth of the FTC's "line of business" requirements for reporting corporate data was ripe for review, but overturning the District Court's grant of a preliminary injunction against the requirements on the ground that the firms had not shown either that the expenses of compliance or the civil fines to which they would be subjected if they chose not to comply were so grave as to constitute "irreparable injury" warranting relief. Is the issue of irreparable injury distinct from the issue of ripeness?

2. While *NALCC's* "functional" approach has been emulated by other courts in finding assertedly nonfinal agency action ripe for review, see Continental Airlines v. CAB, 522 F.2d 107 (D.C. Cir. 1975), ripeness limitations on reviewability still exist. For example, in New York Stock Exchange v. Bloom, 562 F.2d 736 (D.C. Cir. 1977), an informal opinion letter signed by the Comptroller General, which stated that proposed investment services by a national bank would not violate relevant statutes, was held not ripe for review at the behest of the New York Stock Exchange, seeking to protect its member firms from bank competition. *NALCC* was distinguished on the ground that the Comptroller had explicitly reserved the possibility of a change of views if further facts were presented. Moreover, unlike the plaintiffs in *Abbott Laboratories* and *NALCC*, the Stock Exchange was not put to the Hobson's choice of complying with an assertedly illegal agency policy or defying it and running the risk of serious sanctions. Also, the Stock Exchange could protect its interests by a private suit against the banks to enjoin their competition as illegal.

Are *Bloom* and *NALCC* fairly distinguishable?

3. Why should an agency be able to escape judicial review of its legal position by the refusal of the agency head to sign a formal letter of advice or clarification? Given bureaucratic realities, won't the staff's formally-expressed position have nearly as much impact on private conduct as that of an agency head? See Kixmiller v. SEC, 492 F.2d 641 (D.C. Cir. 1974), utilizing the distinction between advice from staff and advice from agency heads to deny review of staff advice.

4. Review the *Duke Power* decision, pp. 955-958, supra. Were plaintiffs' claims ripe? Should the test of ripeness be different in constitutional adjudication than in action challenging administrative action as violative of statute? Is ripeness a constitutional "case or controversy" requirement, or merely a prudential doctrine? [179]

2. *Exhaustion*

Myers v. Bethlehem Shipbuilding Corp.

303 U.S. 41 (1938)

Mr. Justice BRANDEIS delivered the opinion of the Court.

The question for decision is whether a federal district court has equity jurisdiction to enjoin the National Labor Relations Board from holding a hearing upon a complaint filed by it against an employer alleged to be engaged in unfair labor practices prohibited by National Labor Relations Act, July 5, 1935, c.372, 49 Stat. 449. . . .

---

179. Compare Rizzo v. Goode, 423 U.S. 362 (1976), O'Shea v. Littleton, 414 U.S. 488 (1974), Clark v. Valco, 559 F.2d 642 (D.C. Cir.), *aff'd mem. sub nom.* Clark v. Kimmett, 431 U.S. 950 (1977), and Laird v. Tatum, 408 U.S. 1 (1972), with Buckley v. Valeo, 424 U.S. 1, 113-118 (1976) and Regional Rail Reorganization Act Cases, 419 U.S. 102 (1974).

The declared purpose of the National Labor Relations Act is to diminish the causes of labor disputes burdening and obstructing interstate and foreign commerce; and its provisions are applicable only to such commerce. . . .

[On April 13, 1936, The Board filed an administrative complaint against Bethlehem Shipbuilding, asserting that it was engaging in unfair labor practices at its Fore River Plant in Quincy, Mass., and that the plant was engaged in interstate commerce. The Board notified Bethlehem of the time and date of an administrative hearing at which Bethlehem could introduce evidence and argument in opposition to the complaint's allegations. On the day of the scheduled hearing Bethlehem filed a bill in equity in the United States District Court for Massachusetts to enjoin the Board proceedings, asserting that it had not committed any unfair labor practice, that its plant was not engaged in interstate commerce, and that the Board had no jurisdiction to proceed. The District Court granted a temporary restraining order and, subsequently, a preliminary injunction against the proceedings. The latter was affirmed by the Court of Appeals.]

We are of the opinion that the District Court was without power to enjoin the Board from holding the hearings.

First. There is no claim by the Corporation that the statutory provisions and the rules of procedure prescribed for such hearings are illegal; or that the Corporation was not accorded ample opportunity to answer the complaint of the Board; or that opportunity to introduce evidence of the allegations made will be denied. The claim is that the provisions of the Act are not applicable to the Corporation's business at the Fore River Plant, because the operations conducted there are not carried on, and the products manufactured are not sold, in interstate or foreign commerce, that, therefore, the Corporation's relations with its employees at the plant cannot burden or interfere with such commerce; that hearings would, at best, be futile; and that the holding of them would result in irreparable damage to the Corporation, not only by reason of their direct cost and the loss of time of its officials and employees, but also because the hearings would cause serious impairment of the good will and harmonious relations existing between the Corporation and its employees, and thus seriously impair the efficiency of its operations.

Second. The District Court is without jurisdiction to enjoin hearings because the power "to prevent any person from engaging in any unfair practice affecting commerce," has been vested by Congress in the Board and the Circuit Court of Appeals, and Congress has declared: "This power shall be exclusive, and shall not be affected by any other means of adjustment or prevention that has been or may be established by agreement, code, law, or otherwise." The grant of that exclusive power is constitutional, because the Act provided for appropriate procedure before the Board and in the review by the Circuit Court of Appeals an adequate opportunity to secure judicial protection against possible illegal action on the part of the Board. No power to enforce an order is conferred upon the Board. To secure enforcement, the Board must apply to a Circuit Court of Appeals for its affirmance. And until the Board's order has been affirmed by the appropriate Circuit Court of Appeals, no penalty accrues for disobeying it. The independent right to apply to a Circuit Court of Appeals to have an order set aside is conferred upon any party aggrieved by the proceeding before the Board....

It is true that the Board has jurisdiction only if the complaint concerns interstate or foreign commerce. Unless the Board finds that it does, the complaint must be dismissed. And if it finds that interstate or foreign commerce is involved, but the Circuit Court of Appeals concludes that such finding was without adequate evidence to support it, or otherwise contrary to law, the Board's petition to enforce it will be dismissed, or the employer's petition to have it set aside will be granted. Since the procedure before the Board is appropriate and the judicial review so provided is adequate, Congress had power to vest exclusive jurisdiction in the Board and the Circuit Court of Appeals....

Third. The Corporation contends that, since it denies that interstate or foreign commerce is involved and claims that a hearing would subject it to irreparable damage, rights guaranteed by the Federal Constitution will be denied unless it be held that the District Court has jurisdiction to enjoin the holding of a hearing by the Board. So to hold would, as the Government insists, in effect substitute the District Court for the Board as the tribunal to hear and determine what Congress declared the Board exclusively should hear and determine in the first instance. The contention is at war with the long settled rule of judicial administration that no one is entitled to judicial relief for a supposed or threatened injury until the prescribed administrative remedy has been exhausted. That rule has been repeatedly acted on in cases where, as here, the contention is made that the administrative body lacked power over the subject matter.

Obviously, the rule requiring exhaustion of the administrative remedy cannot be circumvented by asserting that the charge on which the complaint rests is groundless and that the mere holding of the prescribed administrative hearing would result in irreparable damage. Lawsuits also often prove to have been groundless; but no way has been discovered of relieving a defendant from the necessity of a trial to establish the fact....

Notes and Questions: *Bethlehem Shipbuilding* and Different Versions of the Exhaustion Requirement

1. The second reason given by Justice Brandeis for precluding judicial review of the Labor Board's proceeding until it is complete is that the National Labor Relations Act vests exclusive jurisdiction in the Courts of Appeals to review Board decisions, and that a "nonstatutory" District Court action to enjoin NLRB proceedings is thereby precluded by statute. In light of *Abbott Laboratories* and other more recent cases establishing a strong presumption in favor of review, is this part of the *Bethlehem* opinion still good law? Has this aspect of *Bethlehem* been overruled by enactment of APA §703, which provides for review in "the special statutory review proceeding relevant to the subject matter in a court specified by statute, or, in the absence or inadequacy thereof, any applicable form of legal action, including actions for declaratory judgments or writs of prohibitory or mandatory injunction,"

and further provides, in §704, for review of "[a]gency action made reviewable by statute and final agency action for which there is no other adequate remedy in a court. . ."?[180] Recall, however, that the reach of these provisions is limited by §701(a), which excepts situations where "statutes preclude judicial review."

2. Apart from the argument of statutory preclusion, what other reasons does Justice Brandeis present for denying judicial review prior to completion of the agency's proceedings? How persuasive do you find them, assuming that Bethlehem's claim of lack of jurisdiction is a strong one and that the administrative proceedings will be protracted and expensive?

3. The requirement that administrative proceedings be completed before judicial review is sought in some respects resembles the general requirement in federal courts that a District Court proceeding go to final judgment before review by the Court of Appeals may be heard. Are the arguments for a requirement of finality before review in administrative proceedings stronger or weaker than in the context of court trials?[181]

4. Is the requirement of exhaustion different from the requirement of ripeness? If so, what is the difference?

5. The circumstances in which the requirement of exhaustion may be enforced can be divided into three basic categories, with two subdivisions within each of the last two categories:

(a) A litigant seeks judicial review of a claim before agency proceedings have been completed and without having presented the claim to the agency. This was the situation in *Bethlehem*, and presents the most powerful case for requiring exhaustion.

(b) A litigant seeks judicial review, before completion of agency proceedings, of a claim which has been presented to the agency and initially rejected by it, but:

   (i) there are unexhausted procedures for reconsideration or appellate view within the agency of the rejected claim; or

---

180. Consider also the last sentence in §704, which provides that a petition for reconsideration, internal agency appeal, or the like is not a prerequisite to judicial review unless statutes otherwise require or agency rules provide that agency action is not final and effective until such further agency proceedings have been completed. For discussion, see K. Davis, Administrative Law of the Seventies §20.08 (1976); United States v. Consolidated Mine Smelting Co., 455 F.2d 432 (9th Cir. 1971).

181. As pointed out by Judge Friendly in PepsiCo, Inc. v. FTC, 472 F.2d 179 (2d Cir. 1972), *cert. denied*, 414 U.S. 876 (1973), and exemplified in cases discussed later in this section, in most instances where a litigant is required to "exhaust" administrative remedies, the litigant has already done so by presenting her claim to the agency and having it rejected. The real issue is whether interlocutory judicial review of particular agency rulings should be granted, or whether the litigant should be compelled to await the final outcome of the administrative process.

In civil litigation in the federal courts, an exception to the basic rule of finality is provided by 28 U.S.C. §1291(b), specifying a procedure for interlocutory appellate review. Should there be a similar provision in the APA to permit interlocutory court review of administrative rulings? You should consider the extent to which judge-made exceptions to the exhaustion requirement, discussed subsequently in this section, constitute the functional equivalent of such a provision.

    (ii) the litigant has other claims pending before the agency upon which he might prevail, making moot the claim he now seeks to raise before the court.

(c) After administrative proceedings have been completed, a litigant seeks to raise before a reviewing court:

    (i) a claim that he never raised before the agency; or

    (ii) a claim that was raised before the agency and initially rejected by it, but as to which there were available reconsideration or appeal procedures within the agency which the litigant failed to exhaust.

In which of the subcategories — (b)(i), (b)(ii), (c)(i), (c)(ii) — is the exhaustion requirement most appropriate? In which is it least appropriate? Does the ranking depend on the type of claim involved?

In the note immediately following we examine the decisional law dealing with category (b), where a litigant seeks review, prior to completion of the administrative process, of a claim that has, at least initially, been rejected by the agency. Thereafter we consider decisions in category (c), where the administrative proceedings have terminated and the litigant seeks court review of a claim that was either not presented or was not fully pursued before the agency.

Note: The Exhaustion Requirement and Interlocutory Review

    The *Bethlehem* decision illustrates the traditional insistence by federal courts that administrative procedures be completed prior to judicial review.[182] By contrast, some state courts have taken a decidedly pragmatic approach. See, in particular, the opinions of Chief Justice Vanderbilt of the New Jersey Supreme Court in Ward v. Keenan, 3 N.J. 298, 70 A.2d 77 (1949), and Nolan v. Fitzpatrick, 9 N.J. 477, 89 A.2d 13 (1952), arguing that a sweeping requirement of finality often leads to wasteful drawn-out administrative proceedings that must later be set aside; that undue interference with administrative procedures can be avoided by judges with the common sense to distinguish potentially meritorious threshold claims from those intended solely to delay or harass; and that the exhaustion requirement is often unduly burdensome and otherwise unfair to persons in the toils of the administrative process.[183] The two cited decisions recognized an exception to the exhaustion requirement where the person seeking interlocutory judicial review made a persuasive claim that the administrative tribunal lacked jurisdiction or that the charge presented was without merit, and the reviewing court could resolve the claim without extensive factual inquiry.

182. For analysis of some of the traditional learning, which shows that the rigorous statement of the exhaustion principle in *Bethlehem Shipbuilding* was not always followed, see Berger, Exhaustion of Administrative Remedies, 48 Yale L. J. 980 (1939); K. Davis, Administrative Law Treatise §20 (1958).

183. Could undue delay in the administrative process lead courts to "compel agency action unlawfully withheld or unreasonably delayed," as authorized by APA §706(1)? For a rare example of a court decision invoking this provision to mandate agency expedition, see Deering Milliken, Inc. v. Johnston, 295 F.2d 856 (4th Cir. 1961).

Over the years the federal courts have also evolved exceptions to the finality aspect of the exhaustion requirement, but in most instances this has been a case-by-case process and the exceptions have not been elaborated in general doctrinal rules. Professor Davis asserts that the federal decisions are often inconsistent and "uninspiring," because "[p]robably no judge at any level has put his mind to the problem of working out a rational overall system." [184] The materials below indicate the flavor of the federal law, and should encourage inquiry into whether sound general principles can or should be developed.[185]

Agency "Jurisdiction." Although *Bethlehem* refused to entertain a threshold challenge to the agency's jurisdiction, the Supreme Court entertained such a claim in Allen v. Grand Central Aircraft Co., 347 U.S. 353 (1954), where it was asserted that the President lacked statutory authority to create a National Enforcement Commission with power to disallow employer income tax deductions for wages paid in excess of regulatory wage ceilings. The Supreme Court, without specifically discussing exhaustion doctrine, determined to settle this basic issue regarding the validity of the new agency's very existence without requiring completion of the administrative proceedings. More recently, Judge Friendly, in a characteristically illuminating opinion discussing the relevance of APA §§ 703 and 704, accepted "for the sake of argument" that immediate judicial review would be allowed if an agency "refuses to dismiss a proceeding that is plainly beyond its jurisdiction as a matter of law," but went on to find that the case at hand did not meet that criterion. PepsiCo, Inc. v. FTC, 472 F.2d 179 (2d Cir. 1972), *cert. denied*, 414 U.S. 876 (1973).[186]

Claimed Defects in Agency Procedures. In *PepsiCo*, Judge Friendly also suggested that the exhaustion doctrine should not apply when the agency proceeding is "being conducted in a manner that cannot result in a valid order." This suggestion is borne out by federal decisions dispensing with exhaustion when plaintiff makes a strong claim that the procedures she would otherwise be required to exhaust fall short of statutory or constitutional right. A relatively early example is Yanish v. Wixon, 81 F. Supp. 499 (N.D. Cal. 1948), *aff'd on the issue of jurisdiction*, 181 F.2d 292 (9th Cir. 1950), in which the court heard an interlocutory challenge to an alien deportation hearing claiming failure to utilize APA procedures for formal adjudication. Immediate judicial review has also been allowed when the person subject to termination of benefits in employment asserts that due process

---

184. K. Davis, Administrative Law of the Seventies 449 (1976).

185. For an exhaustive collection of cases and extensive discussion of exhaustion, see Fuchs, Prerequisite to Judicial Review of Administrative Agency Actions, 51 Ind. L. J. 817, 859-911 (1976).

186. For additional authority that immediate judicial review is available when the agency has plainly exceeded its statutory or constitutional authority, see Skinner and Eddy Corp. v. United States, 249 U.S. 557, 562-563 (1919).

On the traditional view, an agency is without authority to hold statutory provisions unconstitutional; if so, one should not require, as a prerequisite to judical review, final agency determination of a claim that its enabling statute is unconstitutional because the agency is without authority to entertain the claim. For discussion and criticism of the traditional view, see Note, The Authority of Administrative Agencies to Consider the Constitutionality of Statutes, 90 Harv. L. Rev. 1682 (1977).

requires a pre-termination hearing. See, e.g., Goldberg v. Kelly, p. 613, supra;[187] In Mathews v. Eldridge, 424 U.S. 319 (1976), p. 667, supra, the Court entertained a challenge to the agency procedures as unconstitutional, even though other, non-constitutional claims had not been exhausted.[188]

On the other hand, the Supreme Court in Allen v. Grand Central Aircraft, supra, declined to rule on the company's due process and Seventh Amendment jury trial right objections to the procedures utilized by the National Enforcement Commission, requiring that the objections first be presented in administrative proceedings. Other decisions refusing to entertain substantial procedural claims prior to final agency decision include Beard v. Stahr, 370 U.S. 41 (1962) (failure of Army Board of Inquiry to permit cross-examination of adverse witnesses in connection with recommendation to Secretary of Army that an officer be discharged as homosexual); Wallace v. Lynn, 507 F.2d 1186 (D.C. Cir. 1974) (asserted agency failure to follow its own regulations).[189]

Should the application of the exhaustion requirement with respect to procedural claims turn on whether the asserted defect is constitutional or not? On the strength of the claim? On the likelihood that it might be corrected by the agency in the midst of its proceedings?

Administrative Impasse and Delay. In Order of Railway Conducters v. Swan, 329 U.S. 520 (1947), the Court decided that yard-masters were not "yard service employees" within the meaning of a railway management-union contract even though the interpretation of such contracts was remitted by statute to the National Railroad Adjustment Board in the first instance and the Board had not yet decided

---

187. Note that *Goldberg* was a suit against state officials under the Civil Rights Act, alleging deprivation of federal constitutional rights. Exhaustion of state administrative remedies is generally not required for such claims, whether they are procedural or not.

Note that requiring a litigant to exhaust administrative procedures might moot her claims of procedural defect if she prevailed on the courts in the administrative proceedings. What other considerations might justify relaxation of finality with respect to procedural claims? The practical unlikelihood, in cases where appellate remedies within the agency remain unexhausted, that the agency will invalidate its own procedures? See American Federation of Government Employees v. Acree, 475 F.2d 1289 (D.C. Cir. 1973); Finnerty v. Cowen, 508 F.2d 979, 982-983 (2d Cir. 1974). The circumstances that courts tend to regard procedural issues as issues of "pure law," as to which agency "expertise" and fact finding capability is largely irrelevant? See Hormel v. Helvering, 312 U.S. 552 (1941); American Nursing Home Ass'n v. Cost of Living Council, 497 F.2d 909 (Temp. Emerg. Ct. App. 1974).

188. The Court also relied on the principle that an exhaustion defense to judicial review is waived by an agency unless timely asserted, following Weinberger v. Salfi, 422 U.S. 749 (1975).

189. In Amos Treat & Sons v. SEC, 306 F.2d 260 (D.C. Cir. 1962), immediate review was permitted of a claim by respondent in a disciplinary proceeding that an SEC commissioner should be disqualified from participating because of his prior involvement, as SEC staff member, in the issues. But SEC v. R. A. Holman & Co., 323 F.2d 284 (D.C. Cir.), *cert. denied,* 375 U.S. 943 (1963) refused to hear a similar claim prior to completion of the administrative proceedings where (unlike *Amos Treat*) the facts relating to the prior involvement in the case as staff members of commissioners was disputed by the SEC, the court voicing fear that judicial pursuit of the claim in the midst of an agency proceeding "could lead to a breakdown in the administrative process which has long been criticized for its slow pace." 323 F.2d at 287. See also Smith v. Illinois Bell Tel. Co., 270 U.S. 587 (1926), where exhaustion was not required when the relevant agency had lain "dormant" for two years; Walker v. Southern Ry. Co., 385 U.S. 196 (1966) (administrative delay of up to 10 years).

the issue. The Board's failure to decide the issue resulted from a jurisdictional deadlock between two divisions of the Board (each of which was composed of equal numbers of management and union representatives) as to which had jurisdiction of the dispute. The Court asserted that it was "dealing with jurisdictional frustration on an administrative level." In a separate opinion, Justice Frankfurter suggested that if "thus far deadlock has resulted, it does not follow that it will continue, if the Court keeps hands off." [190]

Federalism Issues. In Public Utilities Commission of Ohio v. United Fuel Gas Co., 317 U.S. 456 (1943), the Court sustained a district court order, issued in the midst of proceedings before the Ohio Commission, enjoining the Commission from requiring production of records by an interstate natural gas transmission enterprise which the Court found to be within the exclusive jurisdiction of the Federal Power Commission. Illinois Commerce Commission v. Thanson, 318 U.S. 675 (1943) is similar.

In a considerable number of decisions, the Supreme Court has ruled that state administrative proceedings need not be exhausted when federal court plaintiffs assert a deprivation by state officials of federal rights protected by the Civil Rights Act of 1871, 42 U.S.C. §1983. Examples include assertions of racial discrimination and denials of due process.[191] On the other hand, in Penn v. Schlesinger, 497 F.2d 970 (5th Cir. 1974) (en banc), the court held that exhaustion *was* required in a suit, based on 42 U.S.C. §1981, alleging unconstitutional discrimination by various *federal* officials. The majority stressed that the Civil Service Commission, pursuant to federal order, had issued "comprehensive regulations that are particularly well calculated to ensure ready reception and prompt and fair disposition of discrimination claims" such as those presented by plaintiffs.

Do these decisions reflect unjustified suspicion of the fairness and adequacy of state administrative and judicial remedies?

Note: Waiver of Claims Not Raised or Exhausted Before Administrative Tribunals

Where judicial review is sought of final administrative decisions, courts have almost invariably refused to hear claims that were not presented to the agency when there was opportunity to do so.[192] This rule is designed to vindicate the principle of exhaustion, and the related *Chenery* principle, see pp. 334-347, supra, that a re-

---

190. See generally, Goldman, Administrative Delay and Judicial Relief, 66 Mich. L. Rev. 1423 (1968). An alternative solution to the problem of delay is for the court to order prompt completion of the administrative proceedings. See note 183, supra.

191. See, e.g., McNeese v. Bd. of Ed., 373 U.S. 668 (1963); Wilwording v. Swenson, 404 U.S. 249 (1971). For discussion, see K. Davis, Administrative Law of the Seventies §20.01-1 (1976) (strongly criticizing what Davis perceives as a flat and unexplained Supreme Court bar on federal court exhaustion requirements in such cases); Comment, Exhaustion in Section 1983 Cases, 41 U. Chi. L. Rev. 537 (1974); Note, Developments in the Law, Section 1983 and Federalism, 90 Harv. L. Rev. 1133, 1264-1274 (1977).

192. See, e.g., United States v. L.A. Tucker Truck Lines, 344 U.S. 33 (1952); Bank of St. Charles v. Bd. of Governors, Fed. Reserve Sys., 509 F.2d 1004 (8th Cir. 1975).

viewing court will not undertake to decide in the first instance an issue that is an agency's initial responsibility.

However, federal courts have occasionally refused to enforce the principle of waiver.

McKart v. United States

395 U.S. 185 (1969)

Mr. Justice MARSHALL delivered the opinion of the Court.

[Petitioner was convicted for wilfully failing to report for induction into the armed forces. He had originally been classified 4-A by his local draft board, exempt from induction because he was the sole surviving son in a family whose head had been killed in World War II. However, when petitioner's mother died, the local board, after consulting with the State Director, reclassified him 1-A on the theory that the family unit had ceased to exist and that the statutory exemption for sole surviving sons therefore no longer applied. The petitioner failed to avail himself of the opportunity, provided by Selective Service regulations, to appear before the local board to contest reclassification and to appeal the reclassification through the Selective Service system. He also failed to report for induction when ordered so to do.

The Court first concluded, in a review of the relevant statute and its legislative history, that petitioner was entitled to a sole surviving son exemption even after his mother's death, and that the local board had therefore erred in reclassifying him as eligible for induction.

The Court then considered the government's claim that petitioner was precluded from raising the defense of erroneous classification in his criminal prosecution because he had failed to exhaust administrative remedies on the reclassification issue.]

Perhaps the most common application of the exhaustion doctrine is in cases where the relevant statute provides that certain administrative procedures shall be exclusive. See Myers v. Bethlehem Shipbuilding Corp., 303 U.S. 41 (1938) (National Labor Relations Act). The reasons for making such procedures exclusive, and for the judicial application of the exhaustion doctrine in cases where the statutory requirement of exclusivity is not so explicit, are not difficult to understand. A primary purpose is, of course, the avoidance of premature interruption of the administrative process. The agency, like a trial court, is created for the purpose of applying a statute in the first instance. Accordingly, it is normally desirable to let the agency develop the necessary factual background upon which decisions should be based. And since agency decisions are frequently of a discretionary nature and frequently require expertise, the agency should be given the first chance to exercise that discretion or to apply that expertise. And of course it is generally more efficient for the administrative process to go forward without interruption than it is to permit the parties to seek aid from the courts at various intermediate stages. The very same reasons lie behind judicial rules sharply limiting interlocutory appeals.

Closely related to the above reasons is a notion peculiar to administrative law. The administrative agency is created as a separate entity and invested with certain powers and duties. The courts ordinarily should not interfere with an agency until it has completed its action, or else has clearly exceeded its jurisdiction. As Professor Jaffe puts it, "[t]he exhaustion doctrine is, therefore, an expression of executive and administrative autonomy." [193] This reason is particularly pertinent where the function of the agency and the particular decision sought to be reviewed involve exercise of discretionary powers granted the agency by Congress, or require application of special expertise.

Some of these reasons apply equally to cases like the present one, where the administrative process is at an end and a party seeks judicial review of a decision that was not appealed through the administrative process. Particularly, judicial review may be hindered by the failure of the litigant to allow the agency to make a factual record, or to exercise its discretion or apply its expertise. In addition, other justifications for requiring exhaustion in cases of this sort have nothing to do with the dangers of interruption of the administrative process. Certain very practical notions of judicial efficiency come into play as well. A complaining party may be successful in vindicating his rights in the administrative process. If he is required to pursue his administrative remedies, the courts may never have to intervene. And notions of administrative autonomy require that the agency be given a chance to discover and correct its own errors. Finally, it is possible that frequent and deliberate flouting of administrative processes could weaken the effectiveness of an agency by encouraging people to ignore its procedures.

... [I]t is well to remember that use of the exhaustion doctrine in criminal cases can be exceedingly harsh. The defendant is often stripped of his only defense; he must go to jail without having any judicial review of an assertedly invalid order. This deprivation of judicial review occurs not when the affected person is affirmatively asking for assistance from the courts but when the Government is attempting to impose criminal sanctions on him. Such a result should not be tolerated unless the interests underlying the exhaustion rule clearly outweigh the severe burden imposed upon the registrant if he is denied judicial review. The statute as it stood when petitioner was reclassified said nothing which would require registrants to raise all their claims before the appeal boards. We must ask, then, whether there is in this case a governmental interest compelling enough to outweigh the severe burden placed on petitioner. Even if there is no such compelling interest when petitioner's case is viewed in isolation, we must also ask whether allowing all similarly situated registrants to bypass administrative appeal procedures would seriously impair the Selective Service System's ability to perform its functions.

The question of whether petitioner is entitled to exemption as a sole-surviving son is, as we have seen, solely one of statutory interpretation. The resolution of that issue does not require any particular expertise on the part of the appeal board; the proper interpretation is certainly not a matter of discretion. In this sense, the issue is different from many Selective Service classification questions which do in-

193. L. Jaffe, Judicial Control of Administrative Action 425 (1965).

volve expertise or the exercise of discretion, both by the local boards and the appeal boards.[194] Petitioner's failure to take his claim through all administrative appeals only deprived the Selective Service System of the opportunity of having its appellate boards resolve a question of statutory interpretation. Since judicial review would not be significantly aided by an additional administrative decision of this sort, we cannot see any compelling reason why petitioner's failure to appeal should bar his only defense to a criminal prosecution. . . .

We are thus left with the Government's argument that failure to require exhaustion in the present case will induce registrants to bypass available administrative remedies. The Government fears an increase in litigation and a consequent danger of thwarting the primary function of the Selective Service System, the rapid mobilization of manpower. . . .

We do not, however, take such a dire view of the likely consequences of today's decision. At the outset, we doubt whether many registrants will be foolhardy enough to deny the Selective Service System the opportunity to correct its own errors by taking their chances with a criminal prosecution and a possibility of five years in jail. The very presence of the criminal sanction is sufficient to ensure that the great majority of registrants will exhaust all administrative remedies before deciding whether or not to continue the challenge to their classifications. And, today's holding does not apply to every registrant who fails to take advantage of the administrative remedies provided by the Selective Service System. For, as we have said, many classifications require exercise of discretion or application of expertise; in these cases; it may be proper to require a registrant to carry his case through the administrative process before he comes into court. . . .

We hold that petitioner's failure to appeal his classification and failure to report for his preinduction physical do not bar a challenge to the validity of his classification as a defense to his criminal prosecution for refusal to submit to induction. We also hold that petitioner was entitled to exemption from military service as a sole surviving son. Accordingly, we reverse the judgment of the court below and remand the case for entry of a judgment of acquittal.

It is so ordered.

[Justice WHITE entered an opinion concurring in the result. He disagreed with the Court's conclusion that exhaustion should not be required because the case turned on an issue of statutory construction, asserting that the courts frequently defer to agencies' interpretation of statutes and that reviewing courts should have the benefit of such interpretations. However, he believed that the essentials of the exhaustion requirement had been satisfied because petitioner had presented his claim for exemption to the local board, and the local board had consulted with higher authorities within the Selective Service System before rejecting it.]

---

194. Conscientious objector claims, Military Selective Service Act of 1967, §6(j), 81 Stat. 104, 50 U.S.C. App. §456(j) (1964 ed., Supp. III), or deferments for those engaged in activities deemed "necessary to the maintenance of the national health, safety, or interest," id., §6(h)(2), 81 Stat. 102, 50 U.S.C. App. §456(h)(2) (1964 ed., Supp. III), would appear to be examples of questions requiring the application of expertise or the exercise of discretion.

Note

Contrast *McKart* with McGee v. United States, 402 U.S. 479 (1971), in which a registrant, convicted for failure to report for induction, had failed to exhaust administrative remedies on claims of exemption as a conscientious objector and theology student. The Court ruled that there were "factual issues which should have been fully pursued before and resolved by the agency. Decision of the registrant's claim to exemption was said to depend on "the application of expertise by administrative bodies in resolving underlying issues of fact," subject to quite limited judicial review. In these circumstances, exhaustion should be required in order to permit the agency "to make a factual record, or to exercise its discretion or apply its expertise. . . ." [195]

Other factors considered in waiver rulings are whether the opportunity to present an issue to the agency was well-established, or whether a litigant was discouraged or misled by agency officials with respect to invocation of such opportunities. Should exhaustion requirements be relaxed in favor of "preferred" interests? In Sierra Club v. ICC, 8 E.L.R. 20265 (D.C. Cir. 1978), the court of appeals refused to apply exhaustion requirements to bar claims, raised for the first time on judicial review, that an ICC Environmental Impact Statement was inadequate, finding that the "marginal protection to the integrity of the administrative process" afforded by requiring exhaustion was outweighed by the public interest in assuring that administrative agencies give adequate consideration to environmental concerns.

Ordinarily, a litigant is not precluded from asserting the invalidity of agency *regulations* when they are sought to be enforced against her in an administrative proceeding, even though there was opportunity to obtain judicial review of such regulations' validity prior to their attempted enforcement.[196] However, statutes have in some instances required pre-enforcement challenge to agency regulations, and precluded use of objections to the regulations' validity as a defense to subsequent enforcement proceedings. The validity of such provisions has been sustained over due process objections. The most famous ruling is Yakus v. United States, 321 U.S. 414 (1944), holding that Congress might validly bar challenge to the validity of price control regulations in criminal prosecution for their violation and instead require that they be challenged shortly after their promulgation.[197]

Questions

1. Section 14(a) of the Securities Exchange Act of 1934 makes unlawful any proxy solicitation which is "in contravention of such rules and regulations as the

195. Are due process problems raised by barring the assertion of a defense to a criminal prosecution unless defendant has earlier raised the defense in an administrative proceeding? Cf. Yakus v. United States 321, U.S. 414 (1944).

196. Query: Should this general rule be modified in light of the expanded availability of pre-enforcement review resulting from decisions such as Abbott Laboratories v. Gardner, p. 965, supra?

197. See also Bowles v. Willingham, 321 U.S. 503 (1944); United States v. Ruzicka, 329 U.S. 287 (1956); Currie & Goodman, Judicial Review of Federal Administrative Actions: Quest for the Optimum Forum, 75 Colum. L. Rev. 1 (1975).

[Securities and Exchange] Commission may prescribe as necessary or appropriate in the public interest or for the protection of investors." To implement this provision, the Commission has promulgated Regulations 14A (17 C.F.R. 240.14a-1 et seq.). Rule 14a-8, 17 C.F.R. 240.14a-8, governs proposals by shareholders; in general, it requires corporations to include shareholder proposals in its proxy solicitation materials. Subsection (c) thereof permits the company to omit certain shareholder proposals, including those submitted "primarily for the purpose of promoting general economic, political, racial, religious, social or similar causes" (Rule 14a-8(c)(2)) and those involving "a matter relating to the conduct of the ordinary business operations of the issuer" (Rule 14a-8(c)(5)). If the company "asserts that a proposal . . . may properly be omitted," it must so notify the shareholder and file with the Commission the proposal and a statement of reasons for its conclusion.

Early in 1971, the Medical Committee for Human Rights, a shareholder in Victor Chemical Company, requested Victor to submit to its shareholders, in its proxy solicitation material for the 1971 annual meeting, a resolution requesting that the company's charter be amended to prohibit the company from manufacturing napalm. Victor decided to omit the proposal, giving the Committee two reasons for its decision — (1) the Committee's primary purpose in submitting the proposal was to promote a general political, social, or similar cause, and (2) the proposal related to the conduct of ordinary business operations. The Committee protested Victor's decision to the company and the Commission, and requested review of Victor's decision by the Commission staff and oral argument before the Commission if the staff should agree with Victor. Victor then filed with the Commission the Committee's proposal and the company's reason for deciding to omit it from the proxy solicitation materials.

On February 18, the Commission's Division of Corporate Finance advised Victor and the Committee that it objected to the omission of the proposal from Victor's proxy material. Victor asked the Commission to review this determination, and, on March 24, the Secretary of the Commission wrote Victor a letter stating that the Commission agreed with its Corporate Finance Division that omission of the proposal was not consistent with Regulation 14A. No reasons for the conclusion were given by either the Division or the Commission itself. (The Commission reviews about 5300 proxy statements each year, most of them in the spring months.) There are no administrative processes for the issuance of orders enforcing the requirements of §14(a) and the regulations under it. If the offending company is listed on an exchange (as Victor is), the Commission may institute administrative proceedings of a disciplinary nature for an unlawful omission from a proxy solicitation, and may even use a violation of §14(a) as a basis for delisting the security. And it may ask the Attorney General to institute a criminal prosecution against a willful violation. Finally, it may in its discretion (under §21(e) of the Securities Exchange Act) bring a federal court action to enjoin the company from engaging in a violation of §14(a). As of this date, no such action has been brought, and the Commission has not indicated whether it intends to bring one. Victor is required by the rules of the Stock Exchange of which it is a member to send out a proxy solicitation in advance of its annual meeting, but it is not required so to do by any state or federal law.

Victor has filed a petition in the Court of Appeals for the District of Columbia seeking judicial review of the Commission's action. It alleges that it has been aggrieved by the Commission's action because it cannot send out a proxy statement omitting the proposal without risking severe administrative or criminal sanctions. It further alleges that it must print the statements promptly if they are to be distributed in time for its annual meeting this summer. Finally, it alleges that the Commission's action was erroneous as a matter of law, and should be set aside, because the proposal was covered by the exemptions in Rule 14a-8(c)(2) and (5).

Section 25(a) of the Securities Exchange Act provides that "any person aggrieved by an order issued by the Commission in a proceeding under this Act to which such person is a party may obtain a review of such order in the ... United States Court of Appeals for the District of Columbia."

The Commission has moved to dismiss the petition for review for lack of jurisdiction. In its petition the Commission argues that the action taken on March 24 was not an "order" within the meaning of §24(a). Rather it was merely informal advice to Victor that formal proceedings may follow if the proposal of the Medical Committee is not included in the proxy solicitation material.

A. What result?

B. Suppose that the Commission had concluded that omission of the proposal was consistent with the Commission's regulations and the Medical Committee seeks review. What result?

(N.B. — the courts have implied a private right of action on behalf of a shareholder whose proposal is improperly omitted by management — thus Medical Committee could always bring its own suit against Victor.)

2. The Federal Trade Commission Act authorizes the FTC to institute administrative proceedings and eventually issue cease and desist orders against firms engaged in "unfair or deceptive acts or practices." By unanimous vote of its five commissioners, the FTC institutes such a proceeding against television networks and advertisers, arguing that their advertising practices with respect to children's television programs are deceptive and unfair. The case is referred to one of the Commission's administrative law judges for a hearing. The respondent networks and advertisers file a motion with the Commission to disqualify the Commission chairman on grounds of prejudgment; they attach to the complaint numerous public statements by the chairman which, they assert, demonstrate disqualifying bias and prejudgment. They also allege that the chairman caused the Commission to institute the proceedings against them, and request that they be discontinued. The Commission (with the chairman participating) unanimously denies the motion. The respondents promptly institute suit against the Commission and the individual commissioners, repeating their allegations and requesting disqualification of the chairman and dismissal of the administrative proceedings against them.

The Federal Trade Commission Act provides that any person subject to an FTC cease and desist order "may obtain a review of such order" by filing a petition for review in an appropriate Court of Appeals within 60 days after the service of such order.

The defendants (the Commission and the commissioners) move to dismiss the suit instituted by the networks and advertisers asserting that their claims are not subject to review at this time, and that the district court lacks jurisdiction over them. What result?

3. *Judicial Stay of Administrative Action Pending Review or Grants of Interim Relief*

Courts generally have authority to stay administrative action until judicial review of that action has been completed. Both 28 U.S.C. §2349 and 5 U.S.C. §705 of the Administrative Procedure Act itself, so provide. In any case, in Scripps-Howard Radio, Inc. v. FCC, 316 U.S. 4 (1942), Justice Frankfurter strongly implied that the power to issue such stays was inherent in the federal courts, independent of statutory authorization. The traditional considerations to be weighed in granting a stay were articulated in the oft-cited decision of Virginia Petroleum Jobbers' Ass'n v. FPC, 259 F.2d 921, 925 (1958):

> (1) Has the petitioner made a strong showing that he is likely to prevail on the merits of his appeal? (2) Has the petitioner shown that without such relief he will be irreparably injured? (3) Would the issuance of a stay substantially harm other parties interested in the proceedings? (4) Where lies the public interest?"

However, the scope of the power of the federal courts to issue stays has recently been thrown into doubt by the Court's decision in Sampson v. Murray, 415 U.S. 61 (1974). Respondent, who had been discharged from probationary government employment, contended that the administrative procedures afforded her were inadequate because the discharge was based in part on her previous government employment, and therefore procedures more elaborate than those normally afforded probationary employees applied. After her request for additional procedures was denied, she filed an administrative appeal to the Civil Service Commission; if successful on appeal, she would be entitled to full back pay, but not *necessarily* to reinstatement. While the appeal was pending, she successfully sought an order from the District Court enjoining her discharge until the administrative appeal was exhausted. The Court of Appeals affirmed, pointing out that the Civil Service Commission had no authority to order a stay of discharge pending administrative appeals, and finding that the interim injury to respondent's reputation and loss of earnings constituted irreparable injury. The Supreme Court reversed, noting that the statutes governing the Civil Service system did not explicitly authorize judicial relief of the sort afforded by the courts below; that, unlike *Scripps-Howard*, administrative proceedings had not yet been completed; that the relief afforded was the equivalent of a total victory for respondent; and that the government should enjoy broad latitude in personnel matters. The Court concluded that these considerations did not altogether deprive the District Court of inherent authority to issue stays of administrative action pending judicial review, but they did require that such authority be exercised only to prevent serious irreparable injury. It found injury to reputation from discharge and interim loss of earnings to fall far short of the necessary showing of irreparable injury. Justices Douglas, Brennan and Marshall dissented.

Compare the "irreparable injury" issue in *Murray* with the comparable issue in the context of pre-discharge hearing rights in Arnett v. Kennedy, p. 629, supra. Consider also *Murray*'s reliance in part on the circumstance that the discharged employee had not yet exhausted her administrative remedies. Does this whipsaw litigants between the exhaustion requirement and *Murray*'s reluctance for courts to grant relief during the pendency of administrative proceedings that might vindicate the litigant?

Courts occasionally confront a situation the converse of *Murray*, in which an agency asks a court to grant interim relief in favor of the agency pending completion of agency proceedings. Agencies sometimes obtain interim relief through self-help.[198] In other instances, statutes authorize agencies (such as the Labor Board) to apply to courts for interim relief. In the absence of such enabling statutes, however, courts have often held that they are without jurisdiction to grant relief. But in FTC v. Dean Foods Co., 384 U.S. 597 (1966), the Court held that the Courts of Appeals have jurisdiction to enjoin a merger pending the resolution of a suit filed by the FTC.[199]

E. Primary Jurisdiction

1. Introduction

The cases based upon the doctrine of primary jurisdiction are typically complex and often confusing. The subject will be treated here only briefly.[200]

Under the doctrine of primary jurisdiction a party is likely to have begun an action in court, possibly seeking relief against another private party; however, the court will withhold relief because the case involves an issue that might be decided by an administrative agency. It is desirable, in the court's view, that the agency decide that issue before the court reaches its own decision. Thus the court may hold

---

198. See, e.g., North Am. Cold Storage Co. v. Chicago, p. 472, supra; Ewing v. Mytinger & Casselberry, p. 477, supra. However, as the materials in Chapter 7 illustrate, due process may require that an administrative hearing be afforded before action is taken. In other instances statutes may provide for prompt judicial review of summary administrative action; the statute involved in *Ewing* so provided. Also, summary action may be subject to later review in a tort suit against the responsible officials.

199. See generally, Jaffe & Nathanson, Administrative Law 890-893 (1976).

200. For a more elaborate view, see L. Jaffe, Judicial Control of Administrative Action, Ch. 4 (1965); K. Davis, Administrative Law Treatise, Ch. 19 (1958); and P. Areeda & D. Turner, Antitrust Law 134-178 (1978).

the case on its docket and refer the party to the agency. Sometimes the court will add that once the agency reaches its decision, the matter is at an end; it will not hold the case on its docket. In this case the agency has not only "primary," but also "exclusive," jurisdiction.

The notion of "primary jurisdiction" is sometimes traced to Texas & Pacific R.R. Co. v. Abilene Cotton Oil Co., 204 U.S. 426 (1907). The statutory scheme involved there was unusual. Before the Interstate Commerce Act, a shipper who believed that a railroad had overcharged him could sue in court for the difference between the charge and a "reasonable rate." The Interstate Commerce Act, however, gave the ICC the power to hear a shipper's claim that a particular rate was unreasonable, and to order reparations for an overcharge. The Act prohibited not only unreasonably high rates but also unreasonable discrimination among shippers. See pp. 445-456, supra. Section 22 of the Act stated that "nothing in this Act . . . shall in any way abridge or alter the remedies now existing at common law or by statute but the provisions of this Act are in addition to such remedies."

A cotton oil company sued the railroad, in a district court, for an overcharge. The Supreme Court held, despite the language of Section 22, that the Interstate Commerce Act required a shipper to bring his claim for an overcharge before the ICC as an initial matter. Any other result, in the Court's view, could lead to a hodgepodge of railroad rates contrary to the expressed intent of the Act. Mr. Justice White wrote that "if, without previous action by the Commission, power might be exerted by courts and juries generally to determine the reasonableness of an established rate, it would follow that unless all courts reached an identical conclusion a uniform standard of rates in the future would be impossible, as the standard would fluctuate and vary, depending upon the divergent conclusions reached as to the reasonableness by the various courts called upon to consider the subject as an original question. Indeed, the recognition of such a right is wholly inconsistent with the administrative power conferred upon the Commission and with the duty, which the statute casts upon that body, of seeing to it that the statutory requirement as to the uniformity and equality of rates is observed. Equally obvious is it that the existence of such a power in the courts, independent of prior action by the Commission, would lead to favoritism, to the enforcement of one rate in one jurisdiction and a different one in another, would destroy the prohibition against preferences and discrimination, and afford, moreover, a ready means by which, through collusive proceedings, the wrongs which the statute was intended to remedy could be successfully inflicted." 204 U.S. at 440-441.

As to Section 22, the Court wrote, "This clause, however, cannot be construed as continuing in shippers a common law right, the continued existence of which would be absolutely inconsistent with the provisions of the act. In other words, the act cannot be held to destroy itself." 204 U.S. at 446.

The Court's opinion suggests that the Act simply abolished a preexisting common law remedy and created a new one, which the Commission was to enforce (despite the statutory disclaimer). But, whether the ICC's jurisdiction was in fact "exclusive" is not clear, since the statute required a shipper, who had been awarded reparations by the ICC, to sue in district court to collect the reparations from the railroad. Thus, as a practical matter, the opinion requires the shipper to go *first* to the ICC to obtain an opinion about a rate's reasonableness and *then* to go to the district court (if necessary) to collect an overcharge. Insofar as the later court action takes the form of ordinary review of an agency decision, one might say the Commission had "exclusive" jurisdiction. Insofar as the later action was de novo, the effect of the *Abilene* decision was to give the courts the benefit of the agency's views concerning an issue that the courts might later decide. Then one might call the ICC's jurisdiction "primary" but not "exclusive."

In a later case, Great Northern Ry. Co. v. Merchants Elevator Co., 259 U.S. 285 (1922), a shipper sued to recover a small overcharge. The railroad claimed the charge was proper under its tariffs. The issue turned on the construction of the tariffs. Justice Brandeis, for the Court, wrote that "the task to be performed is to determine the meaning of words of the tariff which were used in their ordinary sense, and to apply that meaning to the undisputed facts." 259 U.S. at 294. Hence, the shipper need not go to the Commission for relief but can apply directly to the courts. "Preliminary resort to the Commission is necessary where the inquiry is essentially one of fact and of discretion in technical matters and uniformity can be secured only if its determination is left to the Commission. Moreover, that determination is reached ordinarily upon voluminous and conflicting evidence, for the adequate appreciation of which acquaintance of many intricate facts of transportation is indispensable; and such acquaintance is commonly to be found only in a body of experts." 259 U.S. at 291.

2.   *The Classic Doctrine*

United States v. Western Pacific R.R.

352 U.S. 59 (1956)

[The government shipped napalm bombs on the Western Pacific Railroad. It was charged the high tariff rate applicable to "incendiary bombs." The government stated, since the bombs contained no "burster charge" or fuse, that they could not explode. Hence the lower tariff rate for "gasoline in steel drums" should apply. The government refused to pay the high rate; the railroad sued in the Court of Claims. The Court of Claims itself construed the tariffs and held that the high tariff for "incendiary bombs" applied. The court also rejected the government's claim that the ICC should (as a matter of primary jurisdiction) pass upon whether the tariff was "reasonable."]

Mr. Justice HARLAN delivered the opinion of the Court:

We are met at the outset with the question of whether the Court of Claims properly applied the doctrine of primary jurisdiction in this case; that is, whether it correctly allocated the issues in the suit between the jurisdiction of the Interstate Commerce Commission and that of the court. In the view of the court below, the case presented two entirely separate questions. One was the question of the construction of the tariff — whether Item 1820 [governing "incendiary bombs"] was applicable to these shipments. The second was the question of the reasonableness of that tariff, if so applied. The Court of Claims assumed . . . that the first of these — whether the "1820" rate applied — was a matter simply of tariff construction and thus properly within the initial cognizance of the court. The second — the reasonableness of the tariff as applied to these shipments — it seemed to regard as being within the initial competence of the Interstate Commerce Commission. Before this Court neither side has questioned the validity of the lower court's views in these respects. Nevertheless, because we regard the maintenance of a proper relationship between the courts and the Commission in matters affecting transportation policy to be of continuing public concern, we have been constrained to inquire into this aspect of the decision. We have concluded that in the circumstances here presented the question of tariff construction, as well as that of the reasonableness of the tariff as applied, was within the exclusive primary jurisdiction of the Interstate Commerce Commission.

The doctrine of primary jurisdiction, like the rule requiring exhaustion of administrative remedies, is concerned with promoting proper relationships between the courts and administrative agencies charged with particular regulatory duties. "Exhaustion" applies where a claim is cognizable in the first instance by an administrative agency alone; judicial interference is withheld until the administrative process has run its course. "Primary jurisdiction," on the other hand, applies where a claim is originally cognizable in the courts, and comes into play whenever enforcement of the claim requires the resolution of issues which, under a regulatory scheme, have been placed within the special competence of an administrative body; in such a case the judicial process is suspended pending referral of such issues to the administrative body for its views. . . .

No fixed formula exists for applying the doctrine of primary jurisdiction. In every case the question is whether the reasons for the existence of the doctrine are present and whether the purposes it serves will be aided by its application in the particular litigation. These reasons and purposes have often been given expression by this Court. In the earlier cases emphasis was laid on the desirable uniformity which would obtain if initially a specialized agency passed on certain types of administrative questions. See Texas & Pacific R. Co. v. Abilene Cotton Oil Co., 204 U.S. 426. More recently the expert and specialized knowledge of the agencies involved has been particularly stressed. See Far East Conference v. United States, 342 U.S. 570. The two factors are part of the same principles,

> now firmly established, that in cases raising issues of fact not within the conventional experience of judges or cases requiring the exercise of administrative discretion, agencies created by Congress for regulating the subject matter should not be passed over. This is so even though the facts after they have been appraised by specialized competence serve as a premise for legal consequences to be judicially defined. Uniformity and consistency in the regulation of business entrusted to a particular agency are secured, and the limited functions of review by the judiciary are more rationally exercised, by preliminary resort for ascertaining and interpreting the circumstances underlying legal is-

sues to agencies that are better equipped than courts by specialization, by insight gained through experience, and by more flexible procedure. Id., at 574-575.

The doctrine of primary jurisdiction thus does "more than prescribe the mere procedural time table of the lawsuit. It is a doctrine allocating the law-making power over certain aspects" of commercial relations. "It transfers from court to agency the power to determine" some of the incidents of such relations.

Thus the first question presented is whether effectuation of the statutory purposes of the Interstate Commerce Act requires that the Interstate Commerce Commission should first pass on the construction of the tariff in dispute here; this, in turn, depends on whether the question raises issue of transportation policy which ought to be considered by the Commission in the interests of a uniform and expert administration of the regulatory scheme laid by that Act. . . .

[The Court went on to hold that to decide whether the term "incendiary bomb" applied to these shipments was a complex matter, requiring considerable expertise. Does the higher rate reflect only the risk of an explosion or are there other commercial factors at work? Moreover, one cannot readily separate the question of the tariff's construction from its reasonableness. Both call for the Commission's expertise.]

. . . We say merely that where, as here, the problem of cost allocation is relevant, and where therefore the questions of construction and reasonableness are so intertwined that the same factors are determinative on both issues, then it is the Commission which must first pass on them.[201]

[Reversed and remanded.]

Note

In the preceding cases, agency action may completely dispose of the entire controversy. Often, however, agency action may dispose of, or help to clarify, only one issue in a complex case. In such a case, a district court might hold the case on its docket until after the agency has acted. Consider the following example:

In General American Tank Car Corp. v. El Dorado Terminal Co., 308 U.S. 422 (1940), a shipper of coconut oil leased railroad cars from a private leasing company, filled them with oil, and gave them to the railroad to transport. The oil company paid the railroad the ordinary coconut oil rate, but, because the oil company supplied its own cars, the railroad set aside 1.5 cents per mile for return to the company. The railroad paid this sum (1.5 cents per mile), not to the oil company directly, but to the leasing company that rented its cars to the oil company.[202] The leasing company was supposed to deduct the 1.5 cents per mile from the rental fee that the oil company owed it. This amount turned out to be greater

---

201. The Court went on to hold that the Commission was not barred from deciding these matters by the statute of limitations.

202. The railroad did this because the leasing company's marks were on the cars; and its tariff provided it would give the 1.5 cents to the person whose marks were on the cars.

than the rental fee. The leasing company refused to give the extra sum to the oil company on the ground that doing so would effectively make the oil company's shipping charge lower than its competitors', thus constituting an illegal transportation rebate. The oil company sued for the sum in an ordinary contract action in district court. The ICC filed an amicus brief arguing for primary jurisdiction and maintaining, in any event, that the payment would constitute an illegal rebate. The Supreme Court wrote:

> The action was an ordinary one . . . on a written contract. The court had jurisdiction of the subject matter and of the parties. But it appeared here . . . that the question of the reasonableness and legality of the practices of the parties was subjected by the Interstate Commerce Act to the administrative authority of the Interstate Commerce Commission. The policy of the Act is that reasonable allowances and practices . . . are to be fixed and settled after full investigation by the Commission, and that there is remitted to the courts only the function of enforcing claims arising out of the failure to comply with the Commission's lawful orders.
>
> When it appeared in the course of the litigation that an administrative problem, committed to the Commission, was involved, the court should have stayed its hand pending the Commission's determination of the lawfulness and reasonableness of the practices under the terms of the Act. There should not be a dismissal, but, . . . the cause should be held pending the conclusion of an appropriate administrative proceeding. Thus any defenses the petitioner may have will be saved to it. . . . [308 U.S. at 432-433]

Nader v. Allegheny Airlines

426 U.S. 290 (1976)

[Ralph Nader held a confirmed reservation on Allegheny's Washington/Hartford 10:15 a.m. flight. He was "bumped" because Allegheny had sold more confirmed reservations than there were seats on the plane. In fact, Allegheny deliberately and secretly overbooked the flight (as do all airlines on many flights) because it knew from statistical studies that some confirmed passengers would not show up. The practice of "deliberate overbooking" tends to prevent airplanes from leaving with empty seats; on the other hand, it can severely inconvenience the passengers who are bumped. These latter, under CAB rule, receive "denied boarding compensation" equal roughly to the price of their ticket.

Nader refused the offer of denied boarding compensation and sued in federal district court for compensatory and punitive damages. His case rested in part on a common law claim of fraudulent misrepresentation. He argued that he should, at least, have been told by the airline about its overbooking practice so that he could plan accordingly.]

Mr. Justice POWELL delivered the opinion of the Court.

The only issue before us concerns the Court of Appeals' disposition on the merits of petitioner's claim of fraudulent misrepresentation. . . . [Section 411 of the Civil Aeronautics Act provides that the Board may "determine whether any air carrier . . . is engaged in unfair or deceptive practices" and, if so, issue a "cease and desist" order. The Court of Appeals] held that a determination by the Board that a practice is not deceptive within the meaning of §411 would, as a matter of law, preclude a common-law tort action seeking damages for injuries caused by that practice. Therefore, the court held that the Board must be allowed to determine in the first instance whether the challenged practice (in this case, the alleged failure to disclose the practice of overbooking) falls within the ambit of §411. The court took judicial notice that a rulemaking proceeding concerning possible changes in reservation practices in response to the 1973-1974 fuel crisis was already underway and that a challenge to the carriers' overbooking practices had been raised by an intervenor in that proceeding. The District Court was instructed to stay further action on petitioner's misrepresentation claim pending the outcome of the rule-making proceeding. The Court of Appeals characterized its holding as "but another application of the principles of primary jurisdiction, a doctrine whose purpose is the coordination of the workings of agency and court." . . .

The question before us, then, is whether the Board must be given an opportunity to determine whether respondent's alleged failure to disclose its practice of deliberate overbooking is a deceptive practice under §411 before petitioner's common-law action is allowed to proceed. The decision of the Court of Appeals requires the District Court to stay the action brought by petitioner in order to give the Board an opportunity to resolve the question. If the Board were to find that there had been no violation of §411, respondent would be immunized from common-law liability.

Section 1106 of the Act, 49 U.S.C. §1506, provides that "[n]othing contained in this chapter shall in any way abridge or alter the remedies now existing at common law or by statute, but the provisions of this chapter are in addition to such remedies." The Court of Appeals found that "although the saving clause of §1106 purports to speak in absolute terms it cannot be read so literally." 167 U.S. App. D.C., at 367, 512 F.2d, at 544. In reaching this conclusion, it relied on Texas & Pacific R. Co. v. Abilene Cotton Oil Co., 204 U.S. 426 (1907).

In this case, unlike *Abilene*, we are not faced with an irreconcilable conflict between the statutory scheme and the persistence of common-law remedies. In *Abilene* the carrier, if subject to both agency and court sanctions, would be put in an untenable position when agency and court disagreed on the reasonableness of a rate. The carrier could not abide by the rate filed with the Commission, as required by statute, and also comply with a court's determination that the rate was excessive. The conflict between the court's common-law authority and the agency's ratemaking power was direct and unambiguous. The court in the present case, in contrast, is not called upon to substitute its judgment for the agency's on the reasonableness of a rate — or, indeed, on the reasonableness of any carrier practice. There is no Board requirement that air carriers engage in overbooking or that they fail to disclose that they do so. And any impact on rates that may result from the imposition of tort liability or from practices adopted by a carrier to avoid such liability would be merely incidental. Under the circumstances, the common-law action and the statute are not "absolutely inconsistent" and may coexist, as contemplated by §1106.

... The Court of Appeals ... also held ... that the Board has the power in a §411 proceeding to approve practices that might otherwise be considered deceptive and thus to immunize carriers from common-law liability. . . .

We cannot agree. No power to immunize can be derived from the language of §411. And where Congress has sought to confer such power it has done so expressly, as in §414 of the Act, 49 U.S.C. §1384, which relieves those affected by certain designated orders (not including orders issued under §411) "from the operations of the 'antitrust laws.' " . . . Section 411, in contrast, is purely restrictive. It contemplates the elimination of "unfair or deceptive practices" that impair the public interest. Its role had been described in American Airlines, Inc. v. North American Airlines, Inc., supra, at 85:

> "Unfair or deceptive practices or unfair methods of competition," as used in §411, are broader concepts than the common-law idea of unfair competition. . . . The section is concerned not with punishment of wrongdoing or protection of injured competitors, but rather with protection of the public interest.

As such, §411 provides an injunctive remedy for vindication of the public interest to supplement the compensatory common-law remedies for private parties preserved by §1106. . . .

Section 411 is both broader and narrower than the remedies available at common law. A cease-and-desist order may issue under §411 merely on the Board's conclusion, after an investigation determined to be in the public interest, that a carrier is engaged in an "unfair or deceptive practice." No findings that the practice was intentionally deceptive or fraudulent or that it in fact has caused injury to an individual are necessary. . . . On the other hand, a Board decision that a cease-and-desist order is inappropriate does not represent approval of the practice under investigation. It may merely represent the Board's conclusion that the serious prohibitory sanction of a cease-and-desist order is inappropriate, that a more flexible approach is necessary. A wrong may be of the sort that calls for compensation to an injured individual without requiring the extreme remedy of a cease-and-desist order. . . .

In sum, §411 confers upon the Board a new and powerful weapon against unfair and deceptive practices that injure the public. But it does not represent the only, or best, response to all challenged carrier actions that result in private wrongs.

... Even when common-law rights and remedies survive and the agency in question lacks the power to confer immunity from common-law liability, it may be appropriate to refer specific issues to an agency for initial determination where that procedure would secure "[u]niformity and consistency in the regulation of business entrusted to a particular agency" or where "the limited functions of review by the judiciary [would be] more rationally exercised, by preliminary resort for ascertaining and interpreting the circumstances underlying legal issues to agencies that are better equipped than courts by specialization, by insight gained through experience, and by more flexible procedure." Far East Conference v. United States, 342 U.S., at 574-575. . . .

The doctrine has been applied, for example, when an action otherwise within the jurisdiction of the court raises a question of the validity of a rate or practice included in a tariff filed with an agency, . . . particularly when the issue involves technical questions of fact uniquely within the expertise and experience of an agency — such as matters turning on an assessment of industry conditions. . . . In this case, however, considerations of uniformity in regulation and of technical expertise do not call for prior reference to the Board.

Petitioner seeks damages for respondent's failure to disclose its overbooking practices. He makes no challenge to any provision in the tariff, and indeed there is no tariff provision or Board regulation applicable to disclosure practices. . . .

Referral of the misrepresentation issue to the Board cannot be justified by the interest in informing the court's ultimate decision with "the expert and specialized knowledge" . . . of the Board. The action brought by petitioner does not turn on a determination of the reasonableness of a challenged practice — a determination that could be facilitated by an informed evaluation of the economics or technology of the regulated industry. The standards to be applied in an action for fraudulent misrepresentation are within the conventional competence of the courts, and the judgment of a technically expert body is not likely to be helpful in the application of these standards to the facts of this case.

We are particularly aware that, even where the wrong sought to be redressed is not misrepresentation but bumping itself, which has been the subject of Board consideration and for which compensation is provided in carrier tariffs, the Board has contemplated that there may be individual adjudications by courts in common-law suits brought at the option of the passenger. The present regulations dealing with the problems of overbooking [provide] . . . that the bumped passenger will have a choice between accepting denied boarding compensation as "liquidated damages for all damages incurred . . . as a result of the carrier's failure to provide the passenger with confirmed reserved space," or pursuing his or her common-law remedies. . . .

We conclude that petitioner's tort action should not be stayed pending reference to the Board and accordingly the decision of the Court of Appeals on this issue is reversed. The Court of Appeals did not address the question whether petitioner had introduced sufficient evidence to sustain his claim. We remand the case for consideration of that question and for further proceedings consistent with this opinion.

It is so ordered.

Mr. Justice WHITE, concurring.

I join the Court's opinion with these additional words. . . . [T]here is not present here the additional consideration that a §411 proceeding would be helpful in resolving, or affecting in some manner, the state-law claim for compensatory and punitive damages. Cf. Ricci v. Chicago Mercantile Exchange, 409 U.S. 289 (1973); Chicago Mercantile Exchange v. Deaktor, 414 U.S. 113 (1973). I seriously doubt that any pending or future §411 case would reveal anything relevant to this case about the Board's view of the propriety of overbooking and of overselling that is not already apparent from prior proceedings concerning those subjects.

Questions

a. The following situation occurs from time to time throughout the law: rights and duties of large numbers of people are created by a statute or a common law system, which we shall call General Scheme A. Congress then enacts a new statute, say Regulatory Statute B, which governs a smaller group of people. Congress might state in Statute B that a portion of A does not apply to the smaller group. Congress may have provided a roughly equivalent substitute for A in B, but it need not have done so; Congress may have said *expressly* that A does not apply, but it also may say it only through *implication.* Suppose that Congress, in enacting B, provides such an exemption from A, and suppose further that B is enforced by an agency, not a court. Then, if a plaintiff sues in court under A, but asserts a cause of action that falls within the exemption provided by B, it is hardly surprising that the court will dismiss the action, for statute A simply does not apply. Thus, if Congress implies in the Civil Aviation Act that the antitrust laws do not apply to certain airline practices, a court will dismiss an antitrust case attacking them. Similarly, if the Aviation Act supercedes state tort law, a state court will dismiss a tort claim. In either case, the Act might give plaintiffs a related cause of action before the agency itself.

(1) Does this describe *Abilene? Western Pacific? American Tank Car?*

(2) The above description may account for "exclusive jurisdiction," but it certainly does not account for the whole of the doctrine of primary jurisdiction. Of what else does that doctrine consist?

b. In *American Tank Car* the ICC submitted an amicus brief to the court setting forth its position. Why then was there any need to refer the case to the agency? Indeed, given the power of the courts to request amicus briefs and the agency's ability to supply them on matters it deems important, what need is there for the doctrine of primary jurisdiction?

3. Primary Jurisdiction and Antitrust

Many cases in which the courts discuss primary jurisdiction concern the relation between the antitrust laws and a regulatory statute. Focusing upon the issues that arise in those cases will help you understand the topic in other areas as well. We present these issues through excerpts from two cases and an analytic note that follows. We suggest you read these cases and the note together.

Far East Conference v. United States

342 U.S. 570 (1952)

[The Sherman Act makes unlawful agreements among competitors that unreasonably restrain trade. The Justice Department can bring a suit in a district court to enjoin any such agreement, and any private person injured by such an agreement can sue for treble damages.

The Shipping Act requires ocean shipping lines to file agreements concerning rates with the Federal Maritime Commission. To fail to file any such agreement violates that Act and the offender can be punished by fines and subjected to cease and desist orders. The Commission's approval of any such agreement exempts the agreement from the Sherman Act and all other antitrust laws.

The Far East Conference was an association of steamship companies. It filed a rate agreement which the Commission approved. Later, the Conference established a "dual-rate" system under which shipper who used *only* conference ships would receive a lower rate than shippers who also used ships of the Conference's competitors. This "dual-rate" system agreement was *not* filed with the Commission.

The United States sued the Conference under the Sherman Act, claiming that the "dual-rate" agreement was an unreasonable restraint of trade, and seeking an injunction. The defendants moved that the court dismiss the case, requiring plaintiff to resort to the Commission (then called the Federal Maritime Board) which, they argued, had primary jurisdiction. The Board intervened on the side of defendants on this point. The district court denied the motion and the Supreme Court agreed to review this denial.]

Mr. Justice FRANKFURTER delivered the opinion of the Court.

At the threshold we must decide whether, in a suit brought by the United States to enjoin a dual-rate system enforced in concert by steamship carriers engaged in foreign trade, a District Court can pass on the merits of the complaint before the Federal Maritime Board has passed upon the question. We see no reason to depart from United States Navigation Co. v. Cunard Steamship Co., 284 U.S. 474. That case answers our problem. There a competing carrier invoked the Antitrust Acts for an injunction against a combination of carriers in the North Atlantic trade which were alleged to operate a dual-rate system similar to that here involved. The plaintiff had not previously challenged the offending practice before the United States Shipping Board, the predecessor in authority of the present Maritine Board. This Court sustained the two lower courts, ... dismissing the bill because initial consideration by the Shipping Board of the circumstances in controversy had not been sought. After a detailed analysis of the provisions of the Shipping Act and their relation to the construction theretofore given to the Interstate Commerce Act, this was the conclusion:

> The [Shipping] act is restrictive in its operation upon some of the activities of common carriers by water, and permissive in respect of others. Their business involves questions of an exceptional character, the solution of which may call for the exercise of a high degree of expert and technical

knowledge. Whether a given agreement among such carriers should be held to contravene the act may depend upon a consideration of economic relations, of facts peculiar to the business or its history, of competitive conditions in respect of the shipping of foreign countries, and of other relevant circumstances, generally unfamiliar to a judicial tribunal, but well understood by an administrative body especially trained and experienced in the intricate and technical facts and usages of the shipping trade; and with which that body, consequently, is better able to deal. . . .

A comparison of the enumeration of wrongs charged in the bill with the provisions of the sections of the Shipping Act above outlined conclusively shows, without going into detail, that the allegations either constitute direct and basic charges of violations of these provisions or are so interrelated with such charges as to be in effect a component part of them; and the remedy is that afforded by the Shipping Act, which to that extent supersedes the antitrust laws. . . . The matter, therefore, is within the exclusive preliminary jurisdiction of the Shipping Board. . . .

The Court thus applied a principle, now firmly established, that in cases raising issues of fact not within the conventional experience of judges or cases requiring the exercise of administrative discretion, agencies created by Congress for regulating the subject matter should not be passed over. This is so even though the facts after they have been appraised by specialized competence serve as a premise for legal consequences to be judicially defined. Uniformity and consistency in the regulation of business entrusted to a particular agency are secured, and the limited functions of review by the judiciary are more rationally exercised, by preliminary resort for ascertaining and interpreting the circumstances underlying legal issues to agencies that are better equipped than courts by specialization, by insight gained through experience, and by more flexible procedure.

The sole distinction between the *Cunard* case and this is that there a private shipper invoked the Antitrust Acts and here it is the Government. This difference does not touch the factors that determined the *Cunard* case. The same considerations of administrative expertise apply, whoever initiates the action. The same Antitrust Laws and the same Shipping Act apply to the same dual-rate system. To the same extent they define the appropriate orbits of action as between court and Maritime Board. . . .

Having concluded that initial submission to the Federal Maritime Board is required, we may either order the case retained on the District Court docket pending the Board's action, . . . or order dismissal of the proceeding brought in the District Court. As distinguished from the situation presented by the first *El Dorado* case, . . . which was a contract action raising only incidentally a question proper for initial administrative decision, the present case involves questions within the general scope of the Maritime Board's jurisdiction. . . . An order of the Board will be subject to review by a United States Court of Appeals, with opportunity for further review in this Court on writ of certiorari. . . . If the Board's order is favorable to the United States, it can be enforced by process of the District Court on the Attorney General's application. . . . We believe that no purpose will here be served to hold the present action in abeyance in the District Court while the proceeding before the Board and subsequent judicial review or enforcement of its order are being pursued. A similar suit is easily initiated later, if appropriate. Business-like procedure counsels that the Government's complaint should now be dismissed, as was the complaint in United States Navigation Co. v. Cunard Steamship Co., supra.

The judgment of the District Court must be

Reversed.

Mr. Justice DOUGLAS, with whom Mr. Justice BLACK concurs, dissenting.

The Shipping Act would have to be amended for me to reach the result of the majority. The Conference agreement, approved by the Board in 1922, provides for the adoption by the Conference of a tariff of rates and charges. It states that there shall be no unjust discrimination against shippers and no rebates paid to them. There is no provision in the agreement for dual rates — no arrangement for allowing one rate to shippers who give all their business to the members and for retaliations against nonsubscribing shippers by exacting from them a higher rate. Nevertheless petitioners have prescribed this dual rate system for the purpose of barring from the outbound Far East trade steamship lines that are not members of the combination. At least these are the facts if we are to believe the allegations of the complaint, as we must on the motion to dismiss.

If the Board had expressly approved the dual rate system, and the dual rate system did not violate the Shipping Act, then there would be immunity from the Sherman Act, since §15 of the Shipping Act, 39 Stat. 733, as amended, 46 U.S.C. §814, gives the Board authority to approve agreements fixing or regulating rates, in effect makes "lawful" the rates so approved, and exempts from the Sherman Act every "lawful" agreement concerning them. But that exemption from the Sherman Act can be acquired only in the manner prescribed by §15. Here no effort was made to obtain it. Hence the petitioners are at large, subject to all of the restraints of the Sherman Act.

Why should the Department of Justice be remitted to the Board for its remedy? The Board has no authority to enforce the Sherman Act. If the rates were filed, of course the Board would have exclusive jurisdiction to pass on them. . . .

The jurisdiction of the Department of Justice must commence at this point, unless we are to amend the Act by granting an anti-trust exemption to rate fixing not only when the rates are filed by the companies and approved by the Board but also when they are not filed at all or are rates which, if filed, could not be approved. I would read the Act as written and require the steamship companies to obtain the anti-trust exemption in the precise way Congress has provided.

Note

In Carnation Co. v. Pacific Westbound Conference, 383 U.S. 213 (1966), a shipper charged that two shipping cartels had raised their rates pursuant to an unfiled, unapproved agreement. The Supreme Court held that the Shipping Act did *not* immunize unfiled, unapproved agreements from the antitrust laws. Thus shipping lines that joined in any such agreement would be subject to the sanctions provided in both the antitrust laws and the Shipping Act. The Court distinguished *Far East Conference* on the ground that the plaintiff there had asked for an injunction — a remedy that might interfere with the Commission's prospective power to approve the agreements — while here plaintiff seeks only damages relating to past, unapproved conduct. Are you convinced by this distinction? Did *Carnation* overrule *Far East Conference*? If so, in what respect?

Ricci v. Chicago Mercantile Exchange

409 U.S. 289 (1973)

[Ricci, a dealer in commodity futures, brought an antitrust action against the Siegel Trading Co. and the Chicago Mercantile Exchange. He alleged that they conspired to deprive him of a seat on the exchange when Siegel, which had loaned him the money to buy the seat, transferred it to another person over Ricci's objection. The Court of Appeals stayed proceedings in the District Court on grounds of primary jurisdiction: The Commodities Exchange Act requires "contract markets," such as the Chicago Mercantile Exchange, to file rules and regulations governing "trading requirements" (such as membership rules) with the Secretary of Agriculture, who may disapprove them. Moreover, any interested person can petition the Commodities Exchange Commission to require the Exchange to enforce its rules. Thus, the court reasoned, Ricci should first be required to go before these agencies to see whether the conduct that he challenged violated Exchange rules.]

Mr. Justice WHITE delivered the opinion of the Court.

The problem to which the Court of Appeals addressed itself is recurring. It arises when conduct seemingly within the reach of the antitrust laws is also at least arguably protected or prohibited by another regulatory statute enacted by Congress. Often, but not always, the other regime includes an administrative agency with authority to enforce the major provision of the statute in accordance with that statute's distinctive standards, which may or may not include concern for competitive considerations. . . . [W]e agree with the Court of Appeals that, given administrative authority to examine the Ricci-Exchange dispute in the light of the regulatory scheme and Exchange rules, the antitrust action should be stayed until the administrative officials have had opportunity to act. This judgment rests on three related premises: (1) that it will be essential for the antitrust court to determine whether the Commodity Exchange Act or any of its provisions are "incompatible with the maintenance of an antitrust action," id., at 358; (2) that some facets of the dispute between Ricci and the Exchange are within the statutory jurisdiction of the Commodity Exchange Commission; and (3) that adjudication of that dispute by the Commission promises to be of material aid in resolving the immunity question.[203]

203. Thus our judgment is not that Congress intended the Commodity Exchange Act to be the exclusive instrument for the governance of the Exchange and its members. . . . Nor do we

As to the first premise, the argument that the Commodity Exchange Act to some extent limits the applicability of the antitrust laws, and may limit them in this case, is plainly substantial. Repeal of the antitrust laws is not to be lightly assumed.... But here the express will of Congress is that to deal in commodity futures one must either be, or deal through, a member of a board of trade having specified qualifications and carrying official designation as a contract market. The Act clearly contemplates a membership organization and hence the existence of criteria for the acquisition, transfer, and loss of membership. The Chicago Mercantile Exchange has such membership rules, and it had the statutory duty to enforce them to the extent that they constituted or were related to "trading requirements," 7 U.S.C. §7a(8). If the transfer of Ricci's membership was pursuant to a valid rule, the immediate question for the antitrust court is whether the rule itself and Ricci's exclusion under it are insulated from antitrust attack. The question has substance, for the Commodity Exchange Act, like the Securities Exchange Act, contemplates that the Exchange and its members will "engage in restraints of trade which might well be unreasonable absent sanction" by the Act.... On the other hand, if, as Ricci alleges, loss of his membership was contrary to Exchange rules, the antitrust action should very likely take its normal course, absent more convincing indications of congressional intent than are present here that the jurisdictional and remedial powers of the Commission are exclusive.

The question whether this membership dispute is within the jurisdiction of the Commodity Exchange Commission, the second premise for our judgment, was answered in the affirmative by the Court of Appeals. Because trading in futures may be done only by or through members, the membership rules of the Exchange were held to relate to "trading requirements" and were thus among those rules which the Exchange could not ignore without violating the Act and bringing itself within the jurisdiction of the Commission to adjudicate and remedy any violation "of the provisions of this chapter or any of the rules, regulations, or orders of the Secretary ... or the commission thereunder...." 7 U.S.C. §§ 8(a) and 13a. We need not finally decide the jurisdictional issue for present purposes, but there is sufficient statutory support for administrative authority in this area that the agency should at least be requested to institute proceedings.[204]

---

find that Congress intended the Act to confer general antitrust immunity on the Exchange and its members with respect to that area of conduct within the adjudicative or rule-making authority of the Commission or the Secretary. The Act contains no categorical exemption of this kind; indeed, it confers no express exemption at all, not even with respect to conduct that is directed or authorized by the Commission or the Secretary. Moreover, the area of administrative authority does not appear to be particularly focused on competitive considerations; there is no express provision in the Act directing administrative officials to consider the policies of the antitrust laws in carrying out their duties and there is no other indication that Congress intended the adjudicative authority given the Commission and the Secretary to be a complete substitute for judicial enforcement of the antitrust laws.

204. Mr. Justice Marshall's dissent complains that jurisdiction of the Commodity Exchange Commission is not clear, that the Commission need not institute proceedings, that the complainant must intervene to become a party, and that agency remedies are discretionary. But proceeding by complaint and intervention is not an unusual system for invoking administrative action. And surely if administrative proceedings are sought in vain, there would be no further problem for the antitrust court....

We also think it very likely that a prior agency adjudication of this dispute will be a material aid in ultimately deciding whether the Commodity Exchange Act forecloses this antitrust suit, a matter that seems to depend in the first instance on whether the transfer of Ricci's membership was in violation of the Act for failure to follow Exchange rules. That issue in turn appears to pose issues of fact and questions about the scope, meaning, and significance of Exchange membership rules. These are matters that should be dealt with in the first instance by those especially familiar with the customs and practices of the industry and of the unique marketplace involved in this case. . . . They are matters typically lying at the heart of an administrative agency's task and here they appear to be matters that Congress has placed within the jurisdiction of the Commodity Exchange Commission. We should recognize "that the courts, while retaining the final authority to expound the statute, should avail themselves of the aid implicit in the agency's superiority in gathering the relevant facts and in marshaling them into a meaningful pattern." . . . The adjudication of the Commission, if it is forthcoming, will be subject to judicial review and would obviate any necessity for the antitrust court to relitigate the issues actually disposed of by the agency decision. . . . Of course, the question of immunity, as such, will not be before the agency; but if Ricci's complaint is sustained, the immunity issue will dissolve, whereas if it is rejected and the conduct of the Exchange warranted by a valid membership rule, the court will be in a much better position to determine whether the antitrust action should go forward. Affording the opportunity for administrative action will "prepare the way, if the litigation should take its ultimate course, for a more informed and precise determination by the Court of the scope and meaning of the statute as applied to [these] particular circumstances." Ibid. . . .

Mr. Justice DOUGLAS, dissenting.

While I concur in my Brother MARSHALL's dissent, I wish to add that even if the Commodity Exchange Commission were empowered to make a determination regarding the relief sought by petitioner, it would appear to be an anomaly to direct the plaintiff in a civil action to a federal supervising agency for a determination as to whether the regulations which it is charged to enforce have been violated, when the agency has, by its inaction, already shown every indication of sanctioning the alleged violation. By remanding, we are requiring the petitioner to seek from the regulators an admission of their failure to regulate (or negligence in regulating). . . .

. . . The road this litigant is now required to travel to obtain justice is equally long and expensive and available only to those with long purses, even though he is remitted only to a federal regulatory agency.

Mr. Justice MARSHALL, with whom Mr. Justice DOUGLAS, Mr. Justice STEWART, and Mr. Justice POWELL join, dissenting. . . .

[Mr. Justice Marshall first argued that although the Commission and the Secretary may have the power to examine the Exchange's practices, they may decide not to exercise it. Or, if they so do, they need not allow Ricci to appear as a party before them. He next argued that approval of the Exchange's action, or a determination that it was consistent with approved Exchange rules, would not necessarily immunize it from antitrust attack. Neither the Commission nor the

Secretary need take antitrust considerations into account. Hence,] . . . if the Secretary were to refuse to invalidate the rules involved in this action, his decision would only mean that those rules were not prohibited by any specific provision of the Commodity Exchange Act. . . .

I do not meant to suggest that the Commission's consideration of this case is certain to prove totally useless when the District Court ultimately resumes its deliberations. Should the Secretary invalidate the rules that the Commission relies on, for example, his action would materially aid petitioner, although his claim would still not be conclusively established since the Exchange's actions might be justified by a legitimate regulatory purpose, even though the rule relied upon violated a provision of the Act. Similarly, the Commission may make findings of fact or statements as to the law within areas of its expertise which the court might find helpful.

But I had not thought that petitioner need meet the burden of showing that resort to administrative remedies would be totally useless before securing adjudication from a court. Indeed, in virtually every suit involving a regulated industry, there is something of value that an administrative agency might contribute if given the opportunity. But we have never suggested that such suits must therefore invariably be postponed while the agency is consulted.

It has been argued that the doctrine of primary jurisdiction involves a mere postponement, rather than relinquishment of judicial jurisdiction. See, e.g., 3 K. Davis, Administrative Law Treatise 3-4 (1958). However, that observation should not be taken to mean that invocation of the doctrine therefore imposes no costs. On the contrary, in these days of crowded dockets and long court delays, the doctrine frequently prolongs and complicates litigation. More fundamentally, invocation of the doctrine derogates from the principle that except in extraordinary situations, every citizen is entitled to call upon the judiciary for expeditious vindication of his legal claims of right. . . . This principle is especially worthy of protection in the antitrust field where it is unmistakably clear that Congress has given courts, rather than agencies, the primary duty to act. . . .

. . . Where the plaintiff has no means of invoking agency jurisdiction, where the agency rules do not guarantee the plaintiff a means of participation in the administrative proceedings, and where the likelihood of a meaningful agency input into the judicial process is remote, I would strike a balance in favor of immediate court action. Since the majority's scale is apparently differently calibrated, I must respectfully dissent.

Notes and Questions: Primary Jurisdiction in Antitrust Cases

The antitrust cases, and perhaps other primary jurisdiction cases, become easier to understand if one distinguishes two questions. First, a court might ask: Is the particular conduct that plaintiff here attacks under the antitrust laws in fact immune from attack because a regulatory statute exempts it from the antitrust laws? If the court answers this first question — the "immunity question" — affirmatively, it must dismiss the case, for plaintiff has no cause of action. Second, a judge might decide that the conduct is *not* immune from antitrust attack but go on to ask: "Should I refer this case to the agency to answer a regulatory question, the answer to which will help decide the antitrust question?" This second question — the "referral question" — suggests that the court will retain the case on its docket pending agency action.

The "immunity question" is often difficult to answer because immunity need not be granted expressly in the regulatory statute, and because there are permutations among many possible circumstances in which immunity might be implied. Regulatory states typically provide that agencies may, or must, forbid certain types of conduct; other types of conduct may, or must, be submitted to the agency for approval. Antitrust immunity may attach to some, or to all, approved conduct, to some, or to all, unapproved conduct; in principle, it could even attach to disapproved conduct of the sort that might have been approved but was not. Whether, and to what extent, immunity will be implied depends upon the nature of the specific regulatory scheme involved. Thus, in Gordon v. New York Stock Exchange, 422 U.S. 659 (1975), the Supreme Court considered a challenge to agreements among securities dealers fixing commission rates. In the absence of a regulatory statute, these agreements would constitute unlawful price fixing. Yet, because the securities laws gave the SEC the power to supervise Exchange rules fixing reasonable rates, the Court held that this type of conduct was immune from the antitrust laws. (The Commission had tolerated fixed rates for many years, but then began to eliminate fixed rates and to insist upon rate competition.) The Court found antitrust immunity despite statutory silence on the question, for, in its view, such immunity was necessary to make the Securities Act work. Moreover, in United States v. National Ass'n of Securities Dealers, 422 U.S. 694 (1975), the Court held that certain price-maintenance practices in the sale of mutual funds were immune from antitrust scrutiny because the SEC had the *power* to forbid or to modify them even though the SEC had never actually considered the merits of those practices in any proceeding.

When the Court has considered television regulation or gas pipeline regulation, however, it has reached a different result. Thus, in United States, v. RCA, 358 U.S. 334 (1959), the Court held that FCC approval of the transfer of a television license from Westinghouse to NBC did not preclude a later antitrust suit attacking the transaction. And, in California v. FPC, 369 U.S. 482 (1962), the Court held that the FPC's approval of a pipeline merger did not immunize it from the antitrust laws.

When the Court has considered the Shipping Act, it has recognized that filed agreements approved by the Maritime Commission are specifically granted antitrust immunity by statute. After skirting the issue in *Far East Conference*, the Court held, in Carnation Co. v. Pacific Westbound Conference, 383 U.S. 213 (1966), that unfiled, unapproved agreements affecting rates were not immune from antitrust attack. In considering the Aviation Act, the courts have held that certain conduct, at the core of the Act's regulatory concern, is immune from antitrust attack although the regulator has not yet approved it.[205] Other conduct, less

---

205. See Hughes Tool Co. v. TWA, 409 U.S. 363 (1973) as discussed in Areeda & Turner, op. cit. note 200, at 166.

central to the regulatory objective, was not immune when not specifically approved.[206]

The point here is not to evaluate whether, or when, or to what extent, conduct should be given antitrust immunity. Rather, it is to point out, first, that the scope of immunity may differ depending on the regulatory system and conduct at issue, and, second, that the existence and scope of the immunity raises a question of law — a question of statutory interpretation — that must be answered by a court.

Now consider typical circumstances under which an antitrust court might wish to refer a question to an agency on the ground that an agency decision will help the court make a later legal determination. First, a court may already have decided that conduct approved under a regulatory statute is immune from the antitrust laws, but unapproved conduct is not immune. The court may then be faced with an antitrust attack upon conduct that arguably fits within a broadly phrased, prior agency approval. It might then wish to refer, to the agency, the question of whether the specific conduct in question has, in fact, been approved [207] by falling within the scope of the general prior approval.

Second, the conduct at issue might be subject to the antitrust laws, yet also arguably unlawful under the regulatory statute. In such a case referral to the agency may serve to enlighten the court because an exploration of the merits of the case under the regulatory statute will help the court later to determine whether the conduct was "reasonable" for purposes of the antitrust statute; "reasonableness" is often a defense to an antitrust claim.[208]

Third, a court might face an antitrust attack on conduct also subject to attack before an agency when the court has not yet decided the scope of antitrust immunity. The court might then refer the parties to the agency in the hope that the agency proceeding will somehow enlighten the court about the proper scope of antitrust immunity. Is this not the situation in *Ricci*? If it is, one might ask precisely how the agency decision is supposed to enlighten the court. Could the agency not express its views on the proper scope of antitrust immunity equally well by filing an amicus brief with the court? Alternatively, does *Ricci* represent an effort by the Court to avoid deciding a difficult legal question: namely, the scope of antitrust immunity as it concerns agency-approved conduct? Does the Court hope that it can make this question "go away" by insisting that the parties first refer the conduct to the agency? If so, one might ask why the courts should seek to avoid deciding the difficult legal question of immunity. After all, it is a statutory, not a constitutional, question. Surely litigants should not be forced to extend lengthy, expensive proceedings simply because the legal question is "difficult." Are there any other reasons why the *Ricci* Court should have referred the question to the agency?

Fourth (though this is not strictly speaking a matter of "referral"), courts have sometimes considered antitrust actions seeking an injunction against un-

206. See Foremost Int'l Tours v. Qantas Airways Ltd., 525 F.2d 281 (9th Cir. 1975).
207. See, e.g., Carnation Co. v. Pacific Westbound Conf., 383 U.S. 213 (1966).
208. Cf. Carter v. AT&T Co., 365 F.2d 486 (5th Cir. 1966), *cert. denied*, 385 U.S. 1008 (1967).

approved conduct in circumstances where approved, but not unapproved, conduct would be immune. In such circumstances, the court might hesitate to issue an injunction, even if the conduct before it is unlawful, for fear that the injunction might interfere with a later agency decision to approve the conduct.[209] Was this the situation in *Far East Conference?* The court in that case refused to listen to a request for an injunction, but in the similar *Carnation* case, the court agreed to hear an antitrust claim for damages. Should the court have refused to hear the injunction request? Why could it not have issued an injunction that did not interfere with the commission's work — an injunction, for example, that would expire if the commission approved the agreement? [210]

In reviewing these and other cases, consider whether primary jurisdiction is as necessary to the proper functioning of the administrative process as the courts have indicated. Could not many of the problems, thought to call for its exercise, be resolved through the use of an amicus brief? What are the advantages and disadvantages of increased reliance upon amicus briefs compared with referral of the case to the agency? Might the diminished use of primary jurisdiction lead to plaintiff's forum-shopping? Might it lead to the institution of spurious antitrust claims in an effort to interfere with agency action? Can the courts adequately deal with this latter problem through the increased use of their power to grant defendants summary judgment in antitrust cases?

As of 1950, the Civil Aeronautics Act provided the following (as paraphrased):

(a) Every air carrier shall file tariffs showing all rates. . . . and to the extent required by regulations of the Board, all classifications, rules, regulations, practices, and services in connection with such air transportation. . . . The Board is empowered to reject any tariff so filed that is not consistent with its regulations or this Act. Any rejected tariff shall be void.

(b) No air carrier shall charge a different rate than, or receive different compensation from, the amounts stated in its filed tariffs.

(c) It shall be the duty of every air carrier to provide safe and adequate service . . . and to establish just and reasonable rules, regulations and practices.

(d) The Board may investigate any rate, rule, regulation, or practice of every air carrier to determine whether that rate or practice is reasonable upon its own motion or upon complaint by any person. The Board must investigate any such complaint if there are reasonable grounds for such an investigation.

(e) If after notice and hearing the Board concludes that a rate, rule, regulation or practice of any air carrier is unjust or unreasonable or unjustly discriminatory or unduly preferential, it can set it aside and prescribe a lawful rate, rule, regulation, or practice.

Board rules require that carriers file tariffs containing "all terms which affect rates, fares, or charges; all provisions governing all carrier services; all other provisions

------

209. Cf. Pan American World Airways v. United States, 371 U.S. 296 (1963).
210. These and other cases are discussed in greater detail in P. Areeda & D. Turner, op. cit. note 200, at 134-178 (1978).

which in any way increase or decrease the value of services rendered." Once the carrier has filed tariffs, it must abide by their terms.

Several airlines, including Blue Airlines, filed tariffs containing the following provisions:

> *Tariff 1 x:* "The carrier shall not be liable for death or personal injury of any passenger unless the carrier is notified in writing of the death or injury by the claimant within sixty days of the occurrence of the death or injury."
>
> *Tariff 1 y:* "The liability of the carrier for the loss of, damage to, or delay in the delivering of baggage shall be limited to $100 for each fare-paying passenger unless the passenger has, at the time of tending the baggage, declared a higher value and paid an additional 10 cents for every additional $100 of evaluation."

Neither of these tariff provisions ever has been challenged before the Board, and the Board has never passed on their validity.

On October 12, 1953, a Blue Airlines plane crashed, killing several passengers and injuring others. In late 1954, Smith and several other injured passengers filed a tort claim for damages against Blue, asserting negligence. Smith asked for $100,000 damages for personal injury and $10,000 for loss of his luggage, which contained valuable and rare literary manuscripts and expensive clothes.

Blue, in defense, noted that Smith did not notify the airline of his injury or loss until nine months after the accident. Blue pointed to the tariff provisions printed above, and moved that the court dismiss both claims on grounds of primary jurisdiction.

What arguments might be made by Blue and by Smith? How should the court decide the motion? [211]

---

211. Cf. H. Hart & A. Sacks, Materials on the Legal Process 265-289 (tentative ed. 1958). See also Note, Air-Carrier Tariff Provisions Limiting Liability for Negligence, 70 Harv. L. Rev. 1282 (1957) and cases cited therein.

10

"Public Interest" Administrative Law: Representation and Disclosure

At this point you should briefly review the materials on agency "failure" in Chapter 3, and consider the ways in which courts have attempted to meet charges of agency "failure." Recalling that the traditional model of administrative law is geared to confining agencies within statutory directives, and that it is the breadth of these directives that creates the problem of discretion, review the courts' efforts to go beyond the strict logic of the traditional model to control discretion directly (see especially Chapter 5) or indirectly through procedural requirements (Chapters 6 and 7). Consider also the expansion of reviewability and standing, and the relaxation of ripeness requirements, discussed in Chapter 9.

In the first part of this chapter, we suggest that many of these and other recent developments examined in this book can be understood as an effort by the judiciary to advance or protect unorganized "public interests" — interests shared by large numbers of individuals (such as consumers, racial minorities, persons concerned with environmental quality) who are not well enough organized to pool their mutual stake in agency policies and participate effectively in the administrative process on a par with business firms, labor unions, and other organized economic interests. During the past 15 years, a great variety of "public interest" advocate groups — primarily nonprofit organizations, such as the Environmental Defense Fund, National Welfare Rights Organization, Ralph Nader's Public Citizen Litigation Group, Children's Defense Fund — have been formed to represent these unorganized "public interests." [1] Public interest lawyers have spearheaded the expansion of broadened rights to participation in the administrative process and efforts to change agency policies to advance the interests of their constituencies. For a comprehensive analysis and survey of public interest litigation, see B. Weisbrod, Public Interest Law (1978).

---

1. Long-established "public interest" litigating groups include the American Civil Liberties Union and the NAACP. See Rabin, Lawyers for Social Change: Perspectives on Public Interest Law, 28 Stan. L. Rev. 207 (1976).

Under the traditional model of administrative law, rights to an agency hearing and judicial review were normally limited to those directly subject to administrative controls, exactions, or sanctions — regulated firms, taxpayers, and the like. The first part of this chapter examines the expansion of rights to participation and review to include public interest groups and other firms or organizations, which have an indirect but important stake in agency policies. This expansion, to a considerable degree, has transformed the traditional model of administrative law (the basic purpose of which was to limit the coercive power of government officials) into an interest representation model of administrative law (the basic purpose of which is to ensure the equitable exercise of discretionary policy-making power by administrators).[2] We will examine the steps in this transformation together with some of the implications of an interest-representation model of administrative law.

The second part of this chapter deals with congressional responses to the problem of agency "failure." We examine two statutes — the Freedom of Information Act and The Government in the Sunshine Act — which mandate public disclosure of federal agency documents and open meetings by multimember federal agencies.

A. The Judicial Development of an Interest Representation Model of Administrative Law

1. The Rationale of Expanded Standing to Seek Judicial Review

Although the Supreme Court's decision in *Data Processing* and subsequent cases, pp. 931-959, supra, substantially liberalized traditional standing rules, the Court's opinions contain little or no discussion of the reasons for these changes in the law. What justifications underlie the expansion of standing? Consider the following lower court decisions, which antedate *Data Processing*.

Office of Communication of the United Church of Christ v. FCC (Church of Christ I)

359 F.2d 994 (D.C. Cir. 1966)

BURGER, Circuit Judge:

This is an appeal from a decision of the Federal Communications Commission granting to the Intervenor a one-year renewal of its license to operate television station WLBT in Jackson, Mississippi. Appellants filed with the Commission a timely petition to intervene to present evidence and arguments opposing the renewal application. The Commission dismissed Appellants' petition and, without a

---

2. See generally, Stewart, The Reformation of American Administrative Law, 88 Harv. L. Rev. 1669 (1975).

hearing, took the unusual step of granting a restricted and conditional renewal of the license. Instead of granting the usual three-year renewal, it limited the license to one year from June 1, 1965, and imposed what it characterizes here as "strict conditions" on WLBT's operations in that one-year probationary period.

The questions presented are (a) whether Appellants, or any of them, have standing before the Federal Communications Commission as parties in interest under Section 309(d) of the Federal Communications Act to contest the renewal of a broadcast license; and (b) whether the Commission was required by Section 309(e) to conduct an evidentiary hearing on the claims of the Appellants prior to acting on renewal of the license.

Because the question whether representatives of the listening public have standing to intervene in a license renewal proceeding is one of first impression, we have given particularly close attention to the background of these issues and to the Commission's reasons for denying standing to Appellants.

BACKGROUND

The complaints against Intervenor embrace charges of discrimination on racial and religious grounds and of excessive commercials. As the Commission's order indicates, the first complaints go back to 1955 when it was claimed that WLBT had deliberately cut off a network program about race relations problems on which the General Counsel of the NAACP was appearing and had flashed on the viewers' screens a "Sorry, Cable Trouble" sign. In 1957 another complaint was made to the Commission that WLBT had presented a program urging the maintenance of racial segregation and had refused requests for time to present the opposing viewpoint. Since then numerous other complaints have been made.

When WLBT sought a renewal of its license in 1958, the Commission at first deferred action because of complaints of this character but eventually granted the usual three-year renewal because it found that, while there had been failures to comply with the Fairness Doctrine, the failures were isolated instances of improper behavior and did not warrant denial of WLBT's renewal application.

Shortly after the outbreak of prolonged civil disturbances centering in large part around the University of Mississippi in September 1962, the Commission again received complaints that various Mississippi radio and television stations, including WLBT, had presented programs concerning racial integration in which only one viewpoint was aired. In 1963 the Commission investigated and requested the stations to submit detailed factual reports on their programs dealing with racial issues. On March 3, 1964, while the Commission was considering WLBT's responses, WLBT filed the license renewal application presently under review.

To block license renewal, Appellants filed a petition in the Commission urging denial of WLBT's application and asking to intervene in their own behalf and as representatives of "all other television viewers in the State of Mississippi." The petition stated that the Office of Communication of the United Church of Christ is an instrumentality of the United Church of Christ, a national denomination with substantial membership within WLBT's prime service area. It listed Appellants

Henry and Smith as individual residents of Mississippi, and asserted that both owned television sets and that one lived within the prime service area of WLBT; both are described as leaders in Mississippi civic and civil rights groups. Dr. Henry is president of the Mississippi NAACP; both have been politically active. Each has had a number of controversies with WLBT over allotment of time to present views in opposition to those expressed by WLBT editorials and programs. Appellant United Church of Christ at Tougaloo is a congregation of the United Church of Christ within WLBT's area.

The petition claimed that WLBT failed to serve the general public because it provided a disproportionate amount of commercials and entertainment and did not give a fair and balanced presentation of controversial issues, especially those concerning Negroes, who comprise almost forty-five percent of the total population within its prime service area; it also claimed discrimination against local activities of the Catholic Church. . . .

The Commission denied the petition to intervene on the ground that standing is predicated upon the invasion of a legally protected interest or an injury which is direct and substantial and that "petitioners . . . can assert no greater interest or claim of injury than members of the general public." . . .

Upon considering Petitioners' claims and WLBT's answers to them on this basis, the Commission concluded that

> serious issues are presented whether the licensee's operations have fully met
> the public interest standard. Indeed, it is a close question whether to designate
> for hearing these applications for renewal of license.

Nevertheless, the Commission conducted no hearing but granted a license renewal, asserting a belief that renewal would be in the public interest since broadcast stations were in a position to make worthwhile contributions to the resolution of pressing racial problems, this contribution was "needed immediately" in the Jackson area, and WLBT, if operated properly, could make such a contribution. Indeed the renewal period was explicitly made a test of WLBT's qualifications in this respect.

> We are granting a renewal of license, so that the licensee can demonstrate
> and carry out its stated willingness to serve fully and fairly the needs and in-
> terests of its entire area — so that it can, in short, meet and resolve the
> questions raised.

The one-year renewal was on conditions which plainly put WLBT on notice that the renewal was in the nature of a probationary grant. . . .

Appellants contend that, against the background of complaints since 1955 and the Commission's conclusion that WLBT was in fact guilty of "discriminatory programming," the Commission could not properly renew the license even for one year without a hearing to resolve factual issues raised by their petition and vitally important to the public. . . .

STANDING OF APPELLANTS[3]

The Commission's denial of standing to Appellants was based on the theory that, absent a potential direct, substantial injury or adverse effect from the administrative action under consideration, a petitioner has no standing before the Commission and that the only types of effects sufficient to support standing are economic injury and electrical interference. It asserted its traditional position that members of the listening public do not suffer any injury peculiar to them and that allowing them standing would pose great administrative burdens.

Up to this time, the courts have granted standing to intervene only to those alleging electrical interference, NBC v. FCC (KOA), 76 U.S. App. D.C. 238, 132 F.2d 545 (1942), aff'd, 319 U.S. 239... (1943), or alleging some economic injury, e.g., FCC v. Sanders Bros. Radio Station, 309 U.S. 470, 60 S. Ct. 693, 84 L. Ed. 869 (1940). It is interesting to note, however, that the Commission's traditionally narrow view of standing initially led it to deny standing to the very categories it now asserts are the only ones entitled thereto. In *Sanders* the Commission argued that economic injury was not a basis for standing, and in *KOA* that electrical interference was insufficient. This history indicates that neither administrative nor judicial concepts of standing have been static....

It is important to remember that the cases allowing standing to those falling within either of the two established categories have emphasized that standing is accorded to persons not for the protection of their private interest but only to vindicate the public interest.

> The Communications Act of 1934 did not create new private rights. The purpose of the Act was to protect the public interest in communications. By §402(b)(2), Congress gave the right of appeal to persons "aggrieved or whose interests are adversely affected" by Commission action.... But *these private litigants have standing only as representatives of the public interest*. Federal Communications Commission v. Sanders Radio Station, 309 U.S. 470, 477, 642, 60 S. Ct. 693, 698, 84 L. Ed. 869, 1037. Associated Industries of New York State, Inc. v. Ickes, 134 F.2d 694, 703 (2d Cir. 1943), vacated as moot, 320 U.S. 707, 64 S. Ct. 74, 88 L. Ed. 414 (1943), quoting Scripps-Howard Radio, Inc. v. FCC, 316 U.S. 4, 14, 62 S. Ct. 875, 86 L. Ed. 1229 (1942).

On the other hand, some Congressional reports have expressed apprehensions, possibly representing the views of both administrative agencies and broadcasters, that standing should not be accorded lightly so as to make possible intervention into proceedings "by a host of parties who have no legitimate interest but solely

---

3. All parties seem to consider that the same standards are applicable to determining standing before the Commission and standing to appeal a Commission order to this court. See Philco Corp. v. FCC, 103 U.S. App. D.C. 278, 257 F.2d 656 (1958), *cert. denied*, 358 U.S. 946, 79 S. Ct. 350, 3 L. Ed. 2d 352 (1959); Metropolitan Television Co. v. FCC, 95 U.S. App. D.C. 326, 221 F.2d 879 (1955). We have, therefore, used the cases dealing with standing in the two tribunals interchangeably.

with the purpose of delaying license grants which properly should be made." But the recurring theme in the legislative reports is not so much fear of a plethora of parties in interest as apprehenson that standing might be abused by persons with no *legitimate* interest in the proceedings but with a desire only to delay the granting of a license for some private selfish reason. The Congressional Committee which voiced the apprehension of a "host of parties" seemingly was willing to allow standing to anyone who could show economic injury or electrical interference. Yet these criteria are no guarantee of the legitimacy of the claim sought to be advanced, for, as another Congressional Committee later lamented, "In many of these cases the protests are based on grounds which have little or no relationship to the public interest." . . .

The Commission's rigid adherence to a requirement of direct economic injury in the commercial sense operates to give standing to an electronics manufacturer who competes with the owner of a radio-television station only in the sale of appliances, while it denies standing to spokesmen for the listeners, who are most directly concerned with and intimately affected by the performance of a licensee. Since the concept of standing is a practical and functional one designed to insure that only those with a genuine and legitimate interest can participate in a proceeding, we can see no reason to exclude those with such an obvious and acute concern as the listening audience. This much seems essential to insure that the holders of broadcasting licenses be responsive to the needs of the audience, without which the broadcaster could not exist. . . .

Nor does the fact that the Commission itself is directed by Congress to protect the public interest constitute adequate reason to preclude the listening public from assisting in that task. Cf. UAW v. Scofield, 382 U.S. 205, 86 S. Ct. 335, 15 L. Ed. 2d 304 (1965). The Commission of course represents and indeed is the prime arbiter of the public interest, but its duties and jurisdiction are vast, and it acknowledges that it cannot begin to monitor or oversee the performance of every one of thousands of licensees. Moreover, the Commission has always viewed its regulatory duties as guided if not limited by our national tradition that public response is the most reliable test of ideas and performance in broadcasting as in most areas of life. . . . Taking advantage of this "'active interest in the . . . quality" of broadcasting rather than depending on governmental initiative is also desirable in that it tends to cast governmental power, at least in the first instance, in the more detached role of arbiter rather than accuser.

The theory that the Commission can always effectively represent the listener interests in a renewal proceeding without the aid and participation of legitimate listener representatives fulfilling the role of private attorneys general is one of those assumptions we collectively try to work with so long as they are reasonably adequate. When it becomes clear, as it does to us now, that it is no longer a valid assumption which stands up under the realities of actual experience, neither we nor the Commission can continue to rely on it. The gradual expansion and evolution of concepts of standing in administrative law attests that experience rather than logic or fixed rules has been accepted as the guide. . . .

We cannot believe that the Congressional mandate of public participation which the Commission says it seeks to fulfill was meant to be limited to writing letters to the Commission, to inspection of records, to the Commission's grace in considering listener claims, or to mere non-participating appearance at hearings. We cannot fail to note that the long history of complaints against WLBT beginning in 1955 had left the Commission virtually unmoved in the subsequent renewal proceedings, and it seems not unlikely that the 1964 renewal application might well have been routinely granted except for the determined and sustained efforts of Appellants at no small expense to themselves. Such beneficial contribution as these Appellants, or some of them, can make must not be left to the grace of the Commission.

Public participation is especially important in a renewal proceeding, since the public will have been exposed for at least three years to the licensee's performance, as cannot be the case when the Commission considers an initial grant, unless the applicant has a prior record as a licensee. In a renewal proceeding, furthermore, public spokesmen, such as Appellants here, may be the only objectors. In a community served by only one outlet, the public interest focus is perhaps sharper and the need for airing complaints often greater than where, for example, several channels exist. Yet if there is only one outlet, there are no rivals at hand to assert the public interest, and reliance on opposing applicants to challenge the existing licensee for the channel would be fortuitous at best. Even when there are multiple competing stations in a locality, various factors may operate to inhibit the other broadcasters from opposing a renewal application. An imperfect rival may be thought a desirable rival, or there may be a "gentleman's agreement" of deference to a fellow broadcaster in the hope he will reciprocate on a propitious occasion.

Thus we are brought around by analogy to the Supreme Court's reasoning in *Sanders*; unless the listeners — the broadcast consumers — can be heard, there may be no one to bring programming deficiencies or offensive overcommercialization to the attention of the Commission in an effective manner. By process of elimination those "consumers" willing to shoulder the burdensome and costly processes of intervention in a Commission proceeding are likely to be the only ones "having a sufficient interest" to challenge renewal application. The late Edmond Cahn addressed himself to this problem in its broadest aspects when he said, "Some consumers need bread; others need Shakespeare; others need their rightful place in the national society — what they all need is processors of law who will consider the people's needs more significant than administrative convenience." Law in the Consumer Perspective, 112 U. Pa. L. Rev. 1, 13, (1963).

Unless the Commission is to be given staff and resources to perform the enormously complex and prohibitively expensive task of maintaining constant surveillance over every licensee, some mechanism must be developed so that the *legitimate* interests of listeners can be made a part of the record which the Commission evaluates. An initial applicant frequently floods the Commission with testimonials from a host of representative community groups as to the relative merit of their champion, and the Commission places considerable reliance on these vouchers; on a renewal application the "campaign pledges" of applicants must be open to comparison with "performance in office" aided by a limited number of responsible representatives of the listening public when such representatives seek participation. . . . In order to safeguard the public interest in broadcasting, therefore, we hold that some "audience participation" must be allowed in license renewal proceedings. We recognize this will create problems for the Commission but it does not necessarily follow that "hosts" of protestors must be granted standing to challenge a renewal application or that the Commission need allow the administrative processes to be obstructed or overwhelmed by captious or purely obstructive protests. . . .

The Commission should be accorded broad discretion in establishing and applying rules for such public participation, including rules for determining which community representatives are to be allowed to participate and how many are reasonably required to give the Commission the assistance it needs in vindicating the public interest. The usefulness of any particular petitioner for intervention must be judged in relation to other petitioners and the nature of the claims it asserts as basis for standing. Moreover it is no novelty in the administrative process to require consolidation of petitions and briefs to avoid multiplicity of parties and duplication of effort.

The fears of regulatory agencies that their processes will be inundated by expansion of standing criteria are rarely borne out. Always a restraining factor is the expense of participation in the administrative process, an economic reality which will operate to limit the number of those who will seek participation; legal and related expenses of administrative proceedings are such that even those with large economic interests find the costs burdensome. Moreover, the listening public seeking intervention in a license renewal proceeding cannot attract lawyers to represent their cause by the prospect of lucrative contingent fees, as can be done, for example, in rate cases. . . .

HEARING

We hold further that in the circumstances shown by this record an evidentiary hearing was required in order to resolve the public interest issue. Under Section 309(e) the Commission must set a renewal application for hearing where "a substantial and material question of fact is presented *or* the Commission for any reason is unable to make the finding" that the public interest, convenience, and necessity will be served by the license renewal. (Emphasis supplied.)

The Commission argues in this Court that it accepted all Appellants' allegations of WLBT's misconduct and that for this reason no hearing was necessary. . . .

Assuming *arguendo* that the Commission's acceptance of Appellants' allegations would satisfy one ground for dispensing with a hearing, i.e., absence of a question of fact, Section 309(e) also commands that in order to avoid a hearing the Commission must make an affirmative finding that renewal will serve the public interest. Yet the only finding on this crucial factor is a qualified statement that the public interest would be served, provided WLBT thereafter complied strictly with the specified conditions. Not surprisingly, having asserted that it accepted Petitioners' allegations, the Commission thus considered itself unable to make a categorical determination that on WLBT's record of performance it was an appropriate entity to receive the license. It found only that *if* WLBT changed its ways, something which the Commission did not and, of course, could not guarantee, the licensing would be proper. The statutory public interest finding cannot be inferred from a statement of the obvious truth that a properly operated station will serve the public interest.

We view as particularly significant the Commission's summary:

> We are granting a renewal of license, so that the licensee can demonstrate and carry out its stated willingness to serve fully and fairly the needs and interests of its entire area — so that it can, in short, meet and resolve the questions raised.

The only "stated willingness to serve fully and fairly" which we can glean from the record is WLBT's protestation that it had always fully performed its public obligations. As we read it the Commission's statement is a strained and strange substitute for a public interest finding.

We recognize that the Commission was confronted with a difficult problem and difficult choices, but it would perhaps not go too far to say it elected to post the Wolf to guard the Sheep in the hope that the Wolf would mend his ways because some protection was needed at once and none but the Wolf was handy. This is not a case, however, where the Wolf had either promised or demonstrated any capacity and willingness to change, for WLBT had stoutly denied Appellants' charges of programming misconduct and violations. In these circumstances a pious hope on the Commission's part for better things from WLBT is not a substitute for evidence and findings. . . .

Even if the embodiment of the Commission's hope be conceded *arguendo* to be a finding, there was not sufficient evidence in the record to justify a "policy determination" that the need for a properly run station in Jackson was so pressing as to justify the risk that WLBT might well continue with an inadequate performance. The issues which should have been considered could be resolved only in an evidentiary hearing in which all aspects of its qualifications and performance could be explored.

[The court remanded for further proceedings.]

Scenic Hudson Preservation Conf. v. FPC (Scenic Hudson I)

354 F.2d 608 (2d Cir. 1965), **cert. denied,**
384 U.S. 941 (1966)

[Briefly review the excerpts from this opinion at pp. 293-298, supra. The following excerpt deals with plaintiffs' standing to sue.]

Respondent argues that "petitioners do not have standing to obtain review" because they "make no claim of any personal economic injury resulting from the Commission's action."

Section 313(b) of the Federal Power Act, 16 U.S.C. §825*l*(b), reads:

> (b) Any party to a proceeding under this chapter aggrieved by an order issued by the Commission in such proceeding may obtain a review of such order in the United States Court of Appeals for any circuit wherein the licensee or public utility to which the order relates is located. . . .

The Commission takes a narrow view of the meaning of "aggrieved party" under the Act. The Supreme Court has observed that the law of standing is a "complicated specialty of federal jurisdiction, the solution of whose problems is in any event more or less determined by the specific circumstances of individual situations. . . ." United States ex rel. Chapman v. Federal Power Comm., 345 U.S. 153, 156 . . . (1953). Although a "case" or "controversy" which is otherwise lacking cannot be created by statute, a statute may create new interests or rights and thus give standing to one who would otherwise be barred by the lack of a "case" or "controversy." The "case" or "controversy" requirement of Article III, §2 of the Constitution does not require that an "aggrieved" or "adversely affected" party have a personal economic interest.. . .

[Citations, including FCC v. Sanders Bros. Radio Station, 309 U.S. 470.]
. . . The Federal Power Act seeks to protect non-economic as well as economic interests. . . .

In order to insure that the Federal Power Commission will adequately protect the public interest in the aesthetic, conservational, and recreational aspects of power development, those who by their activities and conduct have exhibited a special interest in such areas, must be held to be included in the class of "aggrieved" parties under §313(b). We hold that the Federal Power Act gives petitioners a legal right to protect their special interests. . . .

Moreover, petitioners have sufficient economic interest to establish their standing. The New York-New Jersey Trail Conference, one of the two conservation groups that organized Scenic Hudson, has some seventeen miles of trailways in the area of Storm King Mountain. Portions of these trails would be inundated by the construction of the project's reservoir. . . .

We see no justification for the Commission's fear that our determination will encourage "literally thousands" to intervene and seek review in future proceedings. We rejected a similar contention in Associated Industries, Inc. v. Ickes, 134 F.2d 694, 707 (2d Cir.), vacated as moot, 320 U.S. 707, 64 S. Ct. 74 (1943), noting that "no such horrendous possibilities" exist. Our experience with public actions confirms the view that the expense and vexation of legal proceedings is not lightly undertaken.

In any case, the Federal Power Act creates no absolute right of intervention; §308(a), 16 U.S.C. §825g(a), reads:

> In any proceeding before it, the Commission, in accordance with such rules and regulations as it may prescribe, may admit as a party any interested State, State commission, municipality, or any representative of interested consumers

or security holders, or any competitor of a party to such proceeding, or any other person whose participation in the proceeding may be in the public interest.

Since the right to seek review under §313(a) and (b) is limited to a "party" to the Commission proceeding, the Commission has ample authority reasonably to limit those eligible to intervene or to seek review. See Alston Coal Co. v. Federal Power Comm., 137 F.2d 740, 742 (10th Cir. 1943). Representation of common interests by an organization such as Scenic Hudson serves to limit the number of those who might otherwise apply for intervention and serves to expedite the administrative process. . . .

Questions

1. On what rationale do *Church of Christ* and *Scenic Hudson* grant standing to the plaintiffs in question to secure judicial review? Is this rationale consistent with the Supreme Court's subsequent decision in *Sierra Club*, supra p. 938? Even if it is not, would plaintiffs in *Church of Christ* and *Scenic Hudson* still be entitled to standing under the Supreme Court's more recent standing decisions?

2. Do the Supreme Court's standing decisions since *Data Processing* impose, in practice, any real limits on the standing of public interest litigating groups to obtain judicial review of federal regulatory agencies' decisions? If not, why shouldn't standing requirements be abolished in this context? Consider that even though public interest groups may eventually be able to surmount standing hurdles, their interposition by government defendants will serve to delay and complicate litigation, draining the limited financial resources of such organizations (particularly if a threshold evidentiary hearing on the existence of "injury in fact" is required). In dealing with this question, consider that liberalized standing rules may inure as much or more to the benefit of business firms (see, e.g., *Data Processing*) as to public interest groups.

3. On what grounds do the courts in *Church of Christ* and *Scenic Hudson* reject government arguments that loosening of standing requirements will bring a flood of litigation? Is it not odd to justify the expansion of standing rights to include television viewers, environmentalists, and other beneficiaries of regulatory schemes on the ground that in most instances such beneficiaries will not have the funds actually to undertake litigation and exercise their rights?

4. On what grounds does *Church of Christ* order the FCC to conduct an evidentiary hearing in which viewer representatives may participate? Are there any important disputed facts which a hearing would serve to resolve? If the Commission's explanation for its decision is inadequate why doesn't the court follow *Chenery* in remanding for a fuller (or different) explanation? If the court believes that renewal of WLBT's license is unwarranted on any grounds, why doesn't it so hold?

5. Review the materials on radio and television license renewals, see pp. 359-398, supra. To what extent does affording viewing groups the right to petition for denial

of a station's license and participate in renewal hearings promise to help solve the Commission's renewals problem? To what extent might it exacerbate the problem?

2. Rights of Intervention and Participation in Agency Proceedings

Should the right to participate in formal agency proceedings be co-equal with the right to seek judicial review of the resulting agency decision? When the test for standing was narrower than it now is, many commentators adhered to the view that the right to participate in formal agency proceedings should be broader than standing. Only persons with a legally protected interest could seek judicial review, and, it might well be, only such persons could demand that a hearing or other formal proceeding be held by the agency before a sanction could be visited on that person (consider the traditional limitation of a due process hearing rights to persons with a common law protected interest). But once a hearing or the formal proceeding had been initiated by the agency, so the argument ran, it would be desirable in many cases to have other affected interests participate in the agency process of decision so that the agency could consider all of the factors involved in the eventual decision. This view implied a logical division of function between court and agency. The function of the agency was to assess what decision was in the public interest after a process of consultation with all affected interests, while the function of the court was to protect the legal rights of those interests directly subject to agency sanctions; and many agencies in their practice explicitly followed this pattern by granting the right to intervene in agency hearings to persons other than those directly subject to sanctions. For example, the Federal Power Commission, in proceedings to license new pipelines, would grant intervention to competitors, such as coal interests, affected labor unions, municipalities who were seeking gas pipeline service, railroads whose carriage of coal would be affected, and so forth. At times the liberal grant of intervention was required by the governing statute; in other instances it was adopted as a matter of agency practice. *Scenic Hudson* is a good example of an agency prepared to grant intervention with a liberal hand while still seeking to narrow the class of those entitled to seek judicial review. On the other hand, not all agencies followed a liberal policy on intervention, as the *Church of Christ* decision suggests. Why would agencies be unwilling to grant intervention to a range of affected interests other than those directly subject to sanctions?

By contrast, some commentators, most notably Professor Jaffe, Judicial Control of Administrative Action 524-526 (1965), argued that standing should be granted more generously than intervention in agency proceedings. Professor Jaffe's argument is that intervention at the agency level will add to complexity, cost and delay in the agency proceedings. On the other hand, to permit additional persons to seek judicial review will not greatly add to delay or expense. Indeed, Professor Jaffe would go so far as to grant standing to any person, where there has been clearly illegal agency action, and, he asserts that it is in the public interest for the court to invalidate the agency action. This is the so-called "public action." To what extent do *Data Pro-*

cessing and subsequent Supreme Court decisions accept or reject the "public action" theory?

If there is a manifest public interest in enforcing the statutory command, and if the command is clear, perhaps there is a good deal of merit in Professor Jaffe's suggestion. But suppose that we no longer believe in the existence of an objective "public interest" but only that there are a variety of competing private interests that must somehow be reconciled? And suppose the statutory command is not at all clear? Might not a sensible solution be for all such interests to participate in the formulation of agency policy so that the eventual decision will reflect an appropriate consideration of each?

The latter rationale seems to underlie the relation between standing and intervention today. Standing to challenge regulatory and other administrative decisions has been broadly expanded. Except in relatively unusual contexts where standing tests present a real obstacle to judicial review, the possibility of granting intervention rights more generously than standing has largely been eliminated. In many cases, the decisive question today is whether intervention rights should be withheld from some interests that would have standing to seek judicial review. The dominant tendency today has been to grant the right to intervene when there is a right to seek judicial review, as illustrated by the decision in *Church of Christ*. Some of the reasons for granting the right to intervene whenever there is a right to seek judicial review are suggested by the following decision.

The National Welfare Rights Organization v. Finch

429 F.2d 725 (D.C. Cir. 1970)

Before BAZELON, Chief Judge, and WRIGHT and McGOWAN, Circuit Judges.
J. Skelly WRIGHT, Circuit Judge:
In November 1969 the Department of Health, Education and Welfare announced that in December 1969 and January 1970 hearings would be held to determine whether the welfare laws of the states of Nevada and Connecticut respectively were in conformity with certain federal standards in the Social Security Act so that those states might continue to receive payments of federal aid for their state welfare assistance programs. Plaintiff-appellants, a national voluntary association of welfare recipients, state affiliate organizations in Nevada and Connecticut, and welfare recipients individually and in behalf of all welfare recipients and needy children requested that they be permitted to participate as parties in the hearings. When the request was refused, appellants sought injunctive relief in the District Court. . . .

The Social Security Act of 1935 established several grant-in-aid programs whereby any state at its option might apply for federal funds to allocate to its welfare assistance programs for certain statutorily specified categories of needy individuals and families. At present in order to participate in these programs, the state must submit the plans for its program in any of the categories to the Secretary of Health, Education and Welfare. The Secretary's duty is to measure the plan against standards which Congress has designated for each program. If the state plan meets the designated requirements, the Secretary "shall approve" it.

Existing approved plans continue to bear the Secretary's scrutiny. He may discontinue payments if he finds that the plans, as written or as applied, no longer conform to federal standards. An administrative review procedure for testing continued conformity of an approved plan is provided. Before funds may be cut off the Secretary must "give reasonable notice and opportunity for hearing" to the state agency administering the plan. The Secretary has implemented this requirement in the Act by a regulation favoring informal negotiations between state officials and HEW representatives as an initial step toward conformity, with subsequent resort to formal hearings if resolution is not reached by informal means. Any state which objects to a determination of the Secretary arising out of negotiations or a hearing may seek review of that determination in the United States Court of Appeals for the circuit in which the state is located.

[HEW asserted that the AFDC programs of Nevada and Connecticut failed in certain respects to comply with the Social Security Act and HEW regulations. When informal negotiations failed to produce changes in either states' program, the Secretary of HEW notified the states that hearings would be held on the matter. Plaintiff welfare rights organizations sought to intervene in these proceedings; their request for intervention was denied by the Secretary.]

Appellees read the Social Security Act to provide that the Department of Health, Education and Welfare and the state shall be the exclusive participants in the prehearing negotiations and the formal conformity hearings. Appellees contend that congressional silence on participation by any other interest groups or individuals is clear evidence of Congress' determination not to confer any role in the administration of state conformity on other groups or individuals. Thus Congress has entrusted exclusive responsibility for surveillance of state plans to the Secretary. In this submission, they rely on the statutory scheme which speaks only of the functions of the Secretary and the rights of the state to a hearing and judicial review.

An extension of this argument is that the decisions relied upon by appellants, e.g., Office of Communication of United Church of Christ v. FCC, 123 U.S. App. D.C. 328, 359 F.2d 994 (1966), involved applications for intervention before agencies governed by specific statutes conferring standing on collateral "parties in interest" and Congress has passed no such explicit statute here. . . .

That congressional silence on specific grants of standing does not require the inference which appellees would draw is suggested by the emerging principles in the area of standing to seek judicial review of administrative action. Although by no means concomitant, "[t]he problem of right to intervene in administrative proceedings is closely related to and in some measure governed by the elaborate body of law concerning standing to challenge and to enforce administrative action." Cases concerning the question of standing before one or the other tribunal have been used interchangeably in resolving questions of standing to intervene. [Citing

Church of Christ.] Except for the adjustments necessary for assuring the manage-ability of administrative proceedings, the criteria for standing for review of agency action appear to assimilate the criteria for standing to intervene. Neither the administrative nor the judicial concepts of standing have remained static. In both the trend has been away from the closed concept of legally protected interests as the basis of standing to criteria such as "economic injury" of a competitor or "electrical interference" or "representation of the public interest by persons aggrieved-in-fact." . . .

[The court found that NWRO had standing to secure judicial review of HEW's determinations as to whether state programs met federal standards, reject-ing the government's contention that because the relevant statute specifically pro-vided for judicial review by the states, that standing for other litigants was implicitly precluded. While conceding that a statute might impliedly restrict standing, it found no "clear and convincing evidence" that Congress intended to deny review "to the primary beneficiaries under the statute."]

The right of judicial review cannot be taken as fully realized, however, if appellants are excluded from participating in the proceeding to be reviewed. Such was the basis of Judge Lumbard's opinion for the court in American Communica-tions Association v. United States, 298 F.2d 648, 650-651 (2d Cir. 1962).

> Although this is not a case . . . where any potentially aggrieved person must in fairness be permitted to intervene at the hearing stage because only "parties" can seek judicial review, a similar principle applies to the present situation. In *National Coal* [Ass'n v. FPC, 89 U.S. App. D.C. 135, 191 F.2d 462 (1951)] intervention was necessary to secure the right to review; here *intervention is necessary in order to make the right to review effective.* [Peti-tioning for the taking of new evidence by the Commission] is not an effective substitute for the right to adduce evidence, to cross examine witnesses, and to present arguments at the initial hearing. . . . (emphasis added)

Judge Lumbard's view was foreshadowed as long ago as 1935 when Associate Justice Groner in a dissent likened a decision denying prejudicial review participa-tion to "locking the stable door after the horse is gone." Sykes v. Jenny Wren Co., 64 App. D.C. 379, 78 F.2d 729, *cert. denied,* 296 U.S. 624, 56 S. Ct. 147, 80 L. Ed. 443 (1935). . . .

Similarly, without participation in the administrative hearing, issues which appellants here might wish to raise about the character of the state's plans may have been foreclosed as a topic for review. Moreover, under 42 U.S.C. §1316(a)(4) the Secretary's finding of fact if supported by substantial evidence will be conclu-sive, both with respect to the content of the state's plans and with respect to the character of the state's administrative machinery and behavior. This limited review underscores the need for appellants' participation in the administrative hearing as a party.

Nor should it be thought that this right to judicial review is completed by the court's authority to remand "the case to the Secretary to take further evidence." The thrust of Judge Lumbard's opinion in *American Communications* suggests the contrary, that is, that such reconsideration is not an adequate substitute for full participation in the initial agency hearing and that a procedure which encourages remand hearings can be wasteful and obstructive in addition to not advancing the public interest. We agree.

Besides functioning as a means of perfecting the right to review, intervention will serve to foster an important legislative goal. The Social Security Act of 1935 was expressly enacted "to provide for the general welfare." . . . As intervenors in conformity hearings appellants may serve the public interest in the maintenance of an efficient state-federal cooperative welfare system. Appellants' role would be analogous to that of persons accorded standing, not for the protection of their own private interests, but because they are especially well suited to represent an element of the public interest. Thus they serve as "private attorneys general." . . .

It is true that increased participation through intervention creates problems for both the tribunal and other parties; multiple and extended cross-examination may be deleterious to the administrative process. Agencies may fear that "their processes will be inundated by expansion of standing criteria." Certainly keeping conformity hearings manageable may be a legitimate interest, but as this court set out in Virginia Petroleum Jobbers Ass'n v. FPC, 105 U.S. App. D.C. 172, 176 n.1, 265 F.2d 364, 367 n.1 (1959):

> . . . Efficient and expeditious hearings should be achieved, not by exclud-
> ing parties who have a right to participate, but by controlling the proceeding
> so that all participants are required to adhere to the issues and to refrain
> from introducing cumulative or irrelevant evidence.

The threat of hundreds of intervenors in conformity hearings is more apparent than real. The expense of participation, particularly for welfare beneficiaries, is a factor limiting participation; legal and related expenses can be burdensome. Moreover, as *Scenic Hudson* established for the FPC, agencies have some discretion in limiting intervention. . . .

In finding that appellants may intervene in a conformity hearing called by the Secretary under 42 U.S.C. §604(a). . . .[4] [w]e do not hold that this intervenor status creates in appellants a right to participate in any way in the Secretary's informal efforts, before or after the calling of a hearing, to bring a state into conformity. . . .

———————————

Also reread those portions of *Church of Christ*, supra, which relate to the rights of viewer representatives to participate in agency hearings.

Notes and Questions

1. Under the *NWRO* approach — which has not been restricted in any basic, overall manner in subsequent decisions — a quite large variety of firms, organiza-

———————————

4. . . . Reliance for proper control of the hearings and the orderly compilation of the hear-ing record must, of course, be on the hearing examiner. He is fully authorized to be the arbiter of the relevance of proffered testimony and of the proper scope of cross-examination, and to insist that all parties address themselves to the business at hand with dignity and dispatch.

tions, governmental bodies and individuals would have the right to participate in trial-type agency adjudications, including the right to present witnesses, to cross-examine, and so forth. Even taking due account of the funding limitations of many would-be intervenors, increased participation rights threaten to make administrative proceedings excessively complex, protracted, and costly. Consider, for example, the *Scenic Hudson* litigation, pp. 293-303, supra. What steps may agencies take to minimize these adverse "side effects"? Consider carefully the suggestions advanced by the courts in *NWRO* and *Church of Christ*.[5]

To what extent will these measures be effective in reducing delay and complexity? To the extent that they *are* effective, will they undermine the basic reasons for expanding participation rights? Many public interest litigants oppose measures to "streamline" the administrative process by requiring parties to specify disputed issues in advance and provide threshold evidentiary justification for hearing a given issue; imposing tight timetables; restricting cross-examination, and the like. These measures, they contend, tend to penalize public interest groups that lack funds and other resources to thoroughly investigate the issues in advance, prepare a well-supported presentation, and mount a small army of lawyers and experts to litigate the issues at a smooth and speedy clip. Given limited resources, public interest groups must depend upon cross-examination of agency and evidentiary witnesses to explore and identify issues and develop relevant evidence. To what extent should courts undercut requirements of efficient litigation management because of the special problems faced by many public interest litigants? Recall that in *Scenic Hudson I*, p. 293, supra, the court required the FTC to reopen the case to consider evidence submitted by a public interest group long after the hearings before the trial examiner had closed, and after the Commission had heard oral argument. But in Business and Professional People for the Public Interest v. AEC, 502 F.2d 424 (D.C. Cir. 1974), the court sustained the Commission's denial of intervention to a public interest group that had failed to comply with a Commission rule requiring intervenors to file "a supporting affidavit identifying the specific aspect ... of the proceeding as to which he wishes to intervene and setting forth with particularity both the facts pertaining to his interest and the basis for his contentions. . . ."

2. The shift by agencies from adjudication to rulemaking was, at least in part, a response to the rise of public interest litigation and the implications of decisions such as *NWRO* and *Church of Christ*. For example, the Atomic Energy Commission began to treat nuclear safety issues through "generic" rulemaking in large part because decisions on such issues plant-by-plant through adjudicatory procedures with environmental intervenors led to long delays in licensing proceedings.[6] But the use

---

5. For further discussion, consult Gellhorn, Public Participation in Administrative Proceedings, 81 Yale L. J. 359 (1972); Cramton, A Comment on Trial-Type Hearings in Nuclear Power Plant Siting, 58 Va. L. Rev. 585 (1972).

Consider also the efforts by regulatory agencies, such as the FDA, to limit the hearing rights of regulated firms. See pp. 557-568, supra. Might these same techniques be applied to "public interest" and other intervenors? For a comparative analysis of intervention issues in administrative and other contexts, see Shapiro, Some Thoughts on Intervention Before Courts, Agencies, and Arbitrators, 81 Harv. L. Rev. 721 (1968).

6. See generally, Note, The Use of Generic Rulemaking to Resolve Environmental Issues in Nuclear Power Plant Licensing, 61 Va. L. Rev. 869 (1975).

of notice-and-comment rulemaking sharply reduces the participation rights enjoyed by public interest groups critical of agency performance and undermines the goals of decisions like *Scenic Hudson*, *Church of Christ*, and *NWRO*. Given these effects, should courts review an agency's choice between rulemaking and adjudication, see pp. 403-420, supra, more closely and carefully?

The development by the courts of hybrid procedures, see pp. 499-516, supra, can be viewed, at least in part, as a judicial countermove designed to provide more substantial participation rights for public interest groups in notice-and-comment rulemaking.[7] This countermove was in turn checked by the Supreme Court's condemnation of hybrid rulemaking requirements in *Vermont Yankee*, supra, pp. 516-520, where environmental groups sought increased procedural rights as part of an effort to block nuclear power development.[8] Should *Vermont Yankee* be read as a sign of developing judicial counter reaction against public interest advocacy, now that some of the costs associated with such advocacy are becoming more apparent?

3.   Initiation of Agency Enforcement and Review of Agency Inaction

The right of public interest groups, representing the beneficiaries of regulatory or public assistance systems, to intervene in ongoing agency proceedings to enforce standards, would be of little moment if the responsible agency simply failed to take enforcement action or, reached informal compromises with those subject to regulation or control. On the other hand, judicial review of agency failure to initiate enforcement would be inconsistent with traditions of deference to prosecutorial discretion, see pp. 325-326, supra. Dictation by private parties, or by reviewing courts, of priorities in the deployment of administrative resources could contradict many of the reasons for establishing agencies in the first place. Consider the following decision.

Environmental Defense Fund, Inc. v. Ruckelshaus

439 F.2d 584 (D.C. Cir. 1971)

Before BAZELON, Chief Judge, and ROBINSON and ROBB, Circuit Judges.
BAZELON, Chief Judge:
This is a petition for review of an order of the Secretary of Agriculture,[9] refusing to suspend the federal registration of the pesticide DDT or to commence

7. Recall, however, that many decisions creating "hybrid rulemaking" requirements were in cases brought by industry challenging agency regulation.
8. One of the lawyers for one of the environmental litigants in *Vermont Yankee*, who argued part of the case in the Supreme Court, had a well publicized reputation as an abrasive litigant determined to utilize fully any available procedural mechanisms to block or delay nuclear power development. See Emshwiller, Nuclear Nemesis: Using the Law's Delay, Myron Cherry Attacks Atomic Power Projects, Wall St. Journal, March 10, 1978, p. 1. col. 1.
9. The functions of the Secretary of Agriculture under the relevant statute have been transferred to the Administrator of the new Environmental Protection Agency. Reorg. Plan No. 3 of 1970, §2(8)(i), U.S. Code Cong. & Ad. News. p. 2996, 2998, 91st Cong., 2d Sess. (1970). Accordingly, the Administrator has been substituted for the Secretary as a party to this litigation. 5 U.S.C. §907(c) (Supp. V, 1970).

the formal administrative procedures that could terminate that registration. We conclude that the order was based on an incorrect interpretation of the controlling statute, and accordingly remand the case for further proceedings.

I

At the outset, we reject respondents' contention that this court lacks jurisdiction to entertain the petition. The Federal Insecticide, Fungicide, and Rodenticide Act (FIFRA) provides that for certain purposes pesticides must be registered with the Secretary of Agriculture, and that in order to be registered a pesticide must conform to the statutory standards for product safety. When it appears that a registered pesticide fails to conform to these standards, its registration is subject to cancellation in accordance with procedures prescribed by statute. In the ordinary case, the administrative process begins when the Secretary issues a notice of cancellation to the registrant. The matter may then be referred, at the request of the registrant, to a scientific advisory committee, and to a public hearing, before the Secretary issues the order that effectively cancels or continues the registration. Instead of issuing a notice of cancellation, the Secretary may alternatively initiate the process by summarily suspending a registration, when "necessary to prevent imminent hazard to the public." In that case, the registrant is similarly entitled to call for a scientific advisory committee and a public hearing, though the hearing is to be expedited. The suspension order thus operates to afford interim relief during the course of the lengthy administrative proceedings. Certain orders of the Secretary relating to suspension or cancellation are reviewable in this court at the instance of any person who will be adversely affected.

Petitioners here are organizations engaged in activities relating to environmental protection. On October 31, 1969, they submitted a petition to the Secretary requesting him to issue notices of cancellation with respect to all registrations of pesticides containing DDT, and further, to suspend those registrations pending the conclusion of the administrative proceedings. They submitted extensive scientific documentation in support of their petition. The Secretary initially issued notices of cancellation with respect to some uses of DDT, and published in the Federal Register a notice announcing his intention to issue cancellation notices with respect to all other DDT uses that are not essential for the protection of human health; he invited comments on that proposal. No action was taken on the request for summary suspension.

On May 28, 1970, this court concluded that the Secretary's silence on the request for suspension was equivalent to a denial of that request, and that the denial was reviewable as a final order, because of its immediate impact on the parties.[10]

---

10. EDF v. Hardin, 138 U.S. App. D.C. at 396-397, 428 F.2d at 1098-1099. The test of finality for purposes of review is not whether the order is the last administrative order contemplated by the statutory scheme, but rather whether it imposes an obligation or denies a right with consequences sufficient to warrant review.

. . .[T]he denial of a suspension order must be reviewable as a final order where, as here, the moving papers before the court support the allegation that the denial subjects the public to an imminent hazard, and that any injury is irreparable.

The court remanded the case to the Secretary for a fresh determination on the question of suspension and for a statement of the reasons for his decision. With respect to the request for cancellation notices, we similarly remanded for a decision on the record or for a statement of reasons for deferring the decision, but we reserved judgment on the question whether there was presently a decision ripe for review in this court. We rejected the suggestion that petitioners lack standing to seek review of the action of the Secretary, and that the decisions with respect to suspension and cancellation are committed by law to the unreviewable discretion of the Secretary.[11] No new arguments have been presented that cast doubt on the correctness of those conclusions, and we reaffirm them today.

[The court, in parts II and III of its opinion, reconsidered its previous ruling that the Secretary's failure to initiate cancellation and suspension proceedings was ripe for review in light of the subsequent decision in Nor-Am Agricultural Products, Inc. v. Hardin, 435 F.2d 117 (7th Cir. 1970). The court reaffirmed that a formal decision by the Secretary refusing to initiate cancellation proceedings or order interim suspension would be a final "order" reviewable by the Court of Appeals under FIFRA's judicial review provisions, at least where environmental groups made a substantial showing that continued use of the pesticide could result in serious injury to the environment or humans. It argued that an order *initiating* cancellation proceedings would not ordinarily be reviewable because a manufacturer would have full opportunity to present its claim to the agency and reviewing court before decisive actions were taken against it. Finally, the court stated that an order initiating *suspension* might be immediately reviewable at the behest of a manufacturer because the harm caused by suspension could not be fully redressed by an eventual victory in the associated cancellation proceedings.]

III

... If the Secretary had simply refused to issue the requested notices of cancellation, we would have no difficulty concluding that his order was a final order, ripe for review in this court in accordance with the FIFRA. Here, however, the Secretary has taken the position that investigations are still in progress, that final determinations have not yet been made concerning the uses for which cancellation notices have not yet issued. Therefore, with respect to the cancellation notices, we treat the petition as a request for relief in the nature of mandamus, to compel the Secretary to issue notices as required by statute.

The FIFRA gives this court jurisdiction to review any order granting or denying the cancellation of a pesticide registration. The Secretary could defeat that jurisdiction, however, by delaying his determination indefinitely. Petitioners contend that the Secretary's own findings with respect to DDT compel him to issue cancellation notices, and hence that his action is "unlawfully withheld or unreason-

11. Ed. note: The court so concluded, despite the fact that the statute provides that the Secretary "may" institute cancellation or suspension proceedings if it appears that the pesticide does not comply with FIFRA's standards.

ably delayed" within the meaning of the Administrative Procedure Act. In order to protect our appellate jurisdiction, this court has jurisdiction to entertain a request for relief in the form of an order directing the Secretary to act in accordance with the FIFRA.

The relevant question, therefore, is whether the FIFRA requires the Secretary to issue cancellation notices in the circumstances of this case. The statute provides that "[t]he Secretary, in accordance with the procedures specified herein, may suspend or cancel the registration of an economic poison whenever it does not appear that the article or its labeling or other material required to be submitted complies with the provisions of sections 135-135k of this title." That language vests discretion in the Secretary to determine whether an article is in compliance with the act, and to decide what action should be taken with respect to a nonconforming article. Nevertheless, his decisions are reviewable for abuse of discretion. For guidance in defining the limits of his discretion, we must turn to the legislative history and to the statutory scheme as a whole. [The court discussed the legislative history of FIFRA.]

Not only the legislative history, but also the statutory scheme itself points to the conclusion that the FIFRA requires the Secretary to issue notices and thereby initiate the administrative process whenever there is a substantial question about the safety of a registered pesticide. For when Congress creates a procedure that gives the public a role in deciding important questions of public policy, that procedure may not lightly be sidestepped by administrators. The cancellation decision does not turn on a scientific assessment of hazard alone. The statute leaves room to balance the benefits of a pesticide against its risks. The process is a delicate one, in which greater weight should be accorded the value of a pesticide for the control of disease, and less weight should be accorded its value for the protection of a commercial crop. The statutory scheme contemplates that these questions will be explored in the full light of a public hearing and not resolved behind the closed doors of the Secretary. There may well be countervailing factors that would justify an administrative decision, after committee consideration and a public hearing, to continue a registration despite a substantial degree of risk, but those factors cannot justify a refusal to issue the notices that trigger the administrative process.

In this case the Secretary has made a number of findings with respect to DDT. On the basis of the available scientific evidence he has concluded that (1) DDT in large doses has produced cancer in test animals and various injuries in man, but in small doses its effect on man is unknown; (2) DDT is toxic to certain birds, bees, and fish, but there is no evidence of harm to the vast majority of species of nontarget organisms; (3) DDT has important beneficial uses in connection with disease control and protection of various crops. These and other findings led the Secretary to conclude "[t]hat the use of DDT should continue to be reduced in an orderly, practicable manner which will not deprive mankind of uses which are essential to the public health and welfare. To this end there should be continuation of the comprehensive study of essentiality of particular uses and evaluations of potential substitutes."

There is no reason, however, for that study to be conducted outside the procedures provided by statute. The Secretary may, of course, conduct a reasonable preliminary investigation before taking action under the statute. Indeed, the statute expressly authorizes him to consult a scientific advisory committee, apart from the committee that may be appointed after the issuance of a cancellation notice. But when, as in this case, he reaches the conclusion that there is a substantial question about the safety of a registered item, he is obliged to initiate the statutory procedure that results in referring the matter first to a scientific advisory committee and then to a public hearing. We recognize, of course, that one important function of that procedure is to afford the registrant an opportunity to challenge the initial decision of the Secretary. But the hearing, in particular, serves other functions as well. Public hearings bring the public into the decision-making process, and create a record that facilitates judicial review. If hearings are held only after the Secretary is convinced beyond a doubt that cancellation is necessary, then they will be held too seldom and too late in the process to serve either of those functions effectively.

The Secretary's statement in this case makes it plain that he found a substantial question concerning the safety of DDT, which in his view warranted further study. Since we have concluded that that is the standard for the issuance of cancellation notices under the FIFRA, the case must be remanded to the Secretary with instructions to issue notices with respect to the remaining uses of DDT, and thereby commence the administrative process.

IV

While the Secretary recognized a substantial question concerning the safety of DDT, he concluded that the evidence did not warrant summary suspension of its registration for any purpose. That conclusion reflects both a factual determination and the application of a legal standard. Suspension is designed to protect the public from an "imminent hazard" during the course of further administrative proceedings. In order to decide whether it is warranted in a particular case, the Secretary must first determine what harm, if any, is likely to flow from the use of the product in question during the course of administrative proceedings. He must consider both the magnitude of the anticipated harm, and the likelihood that it will occur. Then, on the basis of that factual determination, he must decide whether the anticipated harm amounts to an "imminent hazard to the public."

Petitioners do not challenge the Secretary's determination of the kinds of harm that may be associated with DDT. They argue that his estimate of the probability that harm will occur is too low, in light of the available reports of scientific studies. They also argue that he has set the standard of proof too high, in light of the clear legislative purpose. On the first point, we think it appropriate in the circumstances of this case to defer to the administrative judgment. We have neither an evidentiary record, nor the scientific expertise, that would permit us to review the Secretary's findings with respect to the probability of harm. We have found no error of law that infects the Secretary's inferences from the scientific data. And we have recognized that it is particularly appropriate to defer to administrative findings of fact in reviewing a decision on a question of interim relief.

The second part of the petitioners' challenge, however, is entirely appropriate for judicial consideration at this time. The formulation of standards for suspension is entrusted to the Secretary in the first instance, but the court has an obligation to ensure that the administrative standards conform to the legislative purpose, and that they are uniformly applied in individual cases.

The statute provides for suspension in order "to prevent an imminent hazard to the public." Congress clearly intended to protect the public from some risks by summary administrative action pending further proceedings. The administrator's problem is to determine which risks fall in that class. The Secretary has made no attempt to deal with that problem, either by issuing regulations relating to suspension, or by explaining his decision in this case. If regulations of general applicability were formulated, it would of course be possible to explain individual decisions by reference to the appropriate regulation. It may well be, however, that standards for suspension can best be developed piecemeal, as the Secretary evaluates the hazards presented by particular products. Even so, he has an obligation to articulate the criteria that he develops in making each individual decision. We cannot assume, in the absence of adequate explanation, that proper standards are implicit in every exercise of administrative discretion.

Since the Secretary has not yet provided an adequate explanation for his decision to deny interim relief in this case, it will be necessary to remand the case once more, for a fresh determination on that issue. On remand, the Secretary should consider whether the information presently available to him calls for suspension of any registrations of products containing DDT, identifying the factors relevant to that determination, and relating the evidence to those factors in a statement of the reasons for his decision.

In the course of this and subsequent litigation, the Secretary has identified some of the factors he deems relevant to the question of suspension, and resolved some questions of statutory interpretation. He has concluded that the most important element of an "imminent hazard to the public" is a serious threat to public health, that a hazard may be "imminent" even if its impact will not be apparent for many years, and that the "public" protected by the suspension provision includes fish and wildlife. These interpretations all seem consistent with the statutory language and purpose. An important beginning has been made, and the task of formulating standards must not be abandoned now.

We stand on the threshold of a new era in the history of the long and fruitful collaboration of administrative agencies and reviewing courts. For many years, courts have treated administrative policy decisions with great deference, confining judicial attention primarily to matters of procedure. On matters of substance, the courts regularly upheld agency action, with a nod in the direction of the "substantial evidence" test, and a bow to the mysteries of administrative expertise. Courts occasionally asserted, but less often exercised, the power to set aside agency action on the ground that an impermissible factor had entered into the decision, or a crucial factor had not been considered. Gradually, however, that power has come into more frequent use, and with it, the requirement that administrators articulate the factors on which they base their decisions.

Strict adherence to that requirement is especially important now that the character of administrative litigation is changing. As a result of expanding doctrines of standing and reviewability, and new statutory causes of action, courts are increasingly asked to review administrative action that touches on fundamental personal interests in life, health, and liberty. These interests have always had a special claim to judicial protection, in comparison with the economic interests at stake in a ratemaking or licensing proceeding.

To protect these interests from administrative arbitrariness, it is necessary, but not sufficient, to insist on strict judicial scrutiny of administrative action. For judicial review alone can correct only the most egregious abuses. Judicial review must operate to ensure that the administrative process itself will confine and control the exercise of discretion.[12] Courts should require administrative officers to articulate the standards and principles that govern their discretionary decisions in as much detail as possible. Rules and regulations should be freely formulated by administrators, and revised when necessary. Discretionary decisions should more often be supported with findings of fact and reasoned opinions.[13] When administrators provide a framework for principled decision-making, the result will be to diminish the importance of judicial review by enhancing the integrity of the administrative process, and to improve the quality of judicial review in those cases where judicial review is sought.

Remanded for further proceedings consistent with this opinion.

ROBB, Circuit Judge (dissenting):

In my view the majority opinion substitutes the judgment of this court for the judgment of the Secretary in a matter committed to his discretion by law. This action is taken without the benefit of any administrative hearing in which the validity of the petitioner's forebodings and the soundness of the Secretary's discretionary action might be tested. In effect, the court is undertaking to manage the Department of Agriculture. Finding nothing in the statutes that gives us such authority I respectfully dissent.

Notes and Questions

1. Review Moss v. CAB, p. 581, supra.

Consider also the decision in Medical Committee for Human Rights v. SEC, 432 F.2d 659 (D.C. Cir. 1970), *vacated as moot*, 404 U.S. 403 (1972). The facts of *Medical Committee* are those set forth in version B of the Question at p. 988, supra. The Committee owned shares of stock in a corporation (Dow Chemical Co.) that was engaged in the manufacture of napalm; the Committee sought to require

---

12. For a thoughtful discussion of this problem, see K. Davis, Discretionary Justice (1969). This court has often commented on the importance of providing a structure for the exercise of administrative discretion, in the course of reviewing administrative decisions regarding the disposition of the mentally ill.

13. Professor Davis suggests that such a requirement would be a suitable replacement for the old nondelegation doctrine, which purports to require legislators to set meaningful standards when they delegate discretionary powers to administrators. Davis, op. cit. at 57-59.

management to include in management's proxy materials the Committee's proposed resolution that Dow cease to manufacture napalm except under adequate assurances that it would not be used against humans. Given the costs of soliciting proxies and the fact that most shareholders give proxies, inclusion in management proxy materials is the only practical way that a small shareholder can present a proposal for vote by other shareholders. SEC proxy regulations required management to include shareholder proposals in management proxy materials, but the regulations contained exceptions for, among other matters, proposals "relating to the ordinary business operations" of the corporation or proposals submitted "primarily for the purpose of providing general economic, political, racial, religious, social or similar causes." Dow management contended that the Committee proposal fell within each of these exceptions, and refused to include it in management proxy materials. After inquiries from the Committee and Dow, the Secretary of the SEC wrote a "no action" letter to Dow stating that it was the Commission's view that the proposal fell within the exceptions and was not required by SEC regulations to be included in management proxy materials, and that therefore the Commission, as presently advised, intended to take no legal action against Dow if it failed to include the proposal. The Committee sought judicial review of the SEC's position in the Court of Appeals pursuant to a provision in the Securities Exchange Act for judicial review by that court of an "order" issued by the Commission.

The court rejected the government's contentions that the decision whether to initiate an enforcement proceeding was a matter committed to the discretion of the SEC and that judicial review was therefore precluded by the APA, §701(a)(2). While acknowledging that the agency enjoyed some such discretion, the court emphasized published criticism of the SEC's administration of its proxy rules and the Committee's claim that the SEC's failure to require Dow to include its proposal was contrary to Congress' intent to strengthen the position of shareholders in corporate governance. The court also rejected the government's claim that the controversy was not ripe for review. It found that the issue presented was purely one of law (the interpretation of the Commission's proxy regulations); that the denial of relief by the Commission was effectively final so far as the Committee was concerned; and that the Secretary's letter, issued at the Commission's directive after its decision of the issue on the basis of written presentations by Dow and the Committee, had sufficient indicia of considered formality to warrant review. The court discounted the fact that the Committee could bring a private action against Dow for violation of the SEC's proxy regulations, noting that in any such litigation it would have "lost the potential benefit of the Commission's resources and expertise as an ally" and would have the burden of overcoming the Commission's determination that its regulations had not been violated. The court noted that the Commission had been established in part for the very purpose of acting to protect small investors whose individual stake was too small to warrant private litigation. The court also discounted SEC claims that judicial review of "no action" letters would require the Commission to adopt more formal procedures for dealing with proxy matters and burden its willingness and ability to give informal advice.

The court also concluded that the SEC's letter was reviewable as an "order" under the statutory review provision in the Exchange Act, rejecting the government argument that the letter was not an "order" and therefore was only subject to review, if at all, in a district court under the general federal question jurisdiction. The Court emphasized that facts were not in dispute and that review by a court of appeals in the first instance would speed ultimate resolution of the controversy.

On the merits, the Court found that the Commission had not adequately justified or explained its conclusion that the Committee proposal fell within the exceptions relied upon, and remanded for reconsideration by the Commission.

2. Note how *EDF, Moss* and *Medical Committee* deal with doctrines of ripeness and reviewability in order to secure effective judicial control over agency inaction or agency predilections for informal accommodations that do not trigger formal hearing procedures in which public interest representatives could participate as of right. These decisions and those surveyed earlier in this chapter illustrate the interplay between technical doctrines like reviewability, standing, and ripeness, and the effective balance of forces in administrative decision making.

3. Isn't Judge Robb correct in asserting that the *EDF* majority is "undertaking to manage" the relevant agency? Might not the same be said of the court in *Medical Committee*? Agency resources are typically inadequate to discharge all of the responsibilities with which the agency is charged. Are judicial review and more formalized agency decision-making procedures the appropriate response to limited agency resources and flagging agency zeal? How successful are such measures likely to be in curing agency "failure"? [14] Consider also that while more formal procedures and judicial review may offer advantages for public interest advocacy organizations, they also draw heavily on such organizations' limited resources. But what alternatives are realistically available? DDT was eventually taken off the market for most uses, over the strong protest of not only the manufacturers of DDT but of agricultural interests and their congressional representatives. Would such action have ever been taken without the *EDF* decision? Note that responsibility for regulating pesticides was transferred from the Agriculture Department to the Environmental Protection Agency in the midst of the *EDF* litigation. Does this transfer suggest that more vigorous enforcement action would have occurred even in the absence of a lawsuit? Consider that most of the EPA personnel responsible for regulating pesticides were also transferred from the Agriculture Department.

4. Suppose that in *Medical Committee* the Commission's letter had noted that it agreed with the Committee that Dow had violated SEC proxy regulations by refusing to include the Committee's proposal in management proxy materials, but that its resources were too limited and other responsibilities too pressing to enable it to take enforcement action against Dow. Would judicial review of the SEC's position be available to the Committee? If so, what would be the standard of review, and what relief could the court provide?

5. Courts have continued to review, at the behest of plaintiffs representing the

---

14. Why did the court in *Citizens Communication Center II*, p. 394 supra, refuse to require the Commission to initiate proceedings to deal with the court's previous suggestion for changing the standards in television license renewals?

beneficiaries of administrative schemes, administrators' exercise of enforcement discretion. See, e.g., Dunlop v. Bachowski, 421 U.S. 560 (1975). (But note that the statute involved in *Bachowski* expressly precluded private actions to enforce its requirements, whereas the *Medical Committee* plaintiffs could have brought a private action against Dow for violation of the SEC's proxy regulations.) What techniques should courts utilize in reviewing the exercise of such discretion? Consider in particular the approach suggested by Judge Bazelon in *EDF* with respect to the suspension question. Can the multiple factors appropriately considered in the allocation of enforcement resources be reduced to consistent, articulated rules and principles? See also K. Davis, Discretionary Justice (1969), and the discussion at pp. 325-326, supra. What standard of review should the court utilize?

In a substantial number of recent decisions, courts have found that the relevant statute mandates the agency's initiation of enforcement actions whenever a beneficiary of the regulatory scheme makes a substantial showing that the statute is violated. See, e.g., *EDF* (ruling on the cancellation issue); Adams v. Richardson, 480 F.2d 1159 (D.C. Cir. 1973); Rockbridge v. Lincoln, 449 F.2d 567 (9th Cir. 1971). Is it ever appropriate to permit agency enforcement actions to be dictated by private litigants in this fashion?

6. The FTC issues a complaint and then enters into a settlement agreement with the respondent. May consumer representatives (a) intervene in the settlement negotiations, or (b) obtain judicial review of the settlement's adequacy? What if a consent settlement is negotiated before any complaint is filed? See Action on Safety and Health v. FTC, 498 F.2d 757 (D.C. Cir. 1974); Note, Intervention in Government Enforcement Actions, 89 Harv. L. Rev. 1174 (1976).

Note: Private Rights of Action to Enforce Regulatory Statutes

In a number of recent regulatory statutes, Congress has responded to the problem of agency "underenforcement" through "citizen suit" provisions permitting "any person" to initiate enforcement of administrative controls where the responsible agency fails so to do. See, e.g., §304 of the Clean Air Act, 42 U.S.C. §7604.[15]

Responding (in many instances) to a similar perception of inadequate agency enforcement, federal courts have implied private rights of action for enforcement through injunctive relief or damages of federal regulatory statutes. See, e.g., J.I. Case Co. v. Borak, 377 U.S. 426 (1964); Allen v. State Board of Elections, 393 U.S. 544 (1969). Implied private rights of action are a major element in the enforcement of SEC regulations, particularly 10b-5. In recent years the Supreme Court has been less hospitable in implying private rights of action. For example, it has limited the class of plaintiffs with standing to initiate such actions. See, e.g., Piper v. Chris-Craft Industries, 430 U.S. 1 (1977); Cort v. Ash, 422 U.S. 66 (1975). These deci-

---

15. Section 304 also authorizes "any person" to file suit challenging a failure by the Administrator of the Environmental Protection Agency to discharge statutory duties that are "not discretionary." Do such provisions raise constitutional problems with respect to standing? See p. 954, supra.

sions seem to reflect a developing judicial concern with the burdens that such actions impose on courts, and with the perception that private litigation, particularly when driven by the prospect of large damage awards, is often not the most efficient or equitable mechanism for enforcement of regulatory controls.

Should courts ever imply private rights of action when Congress has failed to provide for them explicitly? Why isn't judicial review of agency failure to initiate enforcement an adequate safeguard? On the other hand, if private rights of action exist, should a court ever review the agency's exercise of its prosecutorial discretion, since a disappointed beneficiary of the regulatory program can always initiate her own enforcement suit? See *Medical Committee,* supra.

Note that creation of private rights of action would ordinarily require courts to decide all issues of statutory interpretation presented in such suits. But if some enforcement suits continue to be brought by the agency, the agency will be deciding these same issues, and in such cases a reviewing court would often defer to the agency's ruling even though the court might decide the issue the other way as an initial matter. Thus a dual enforcement structure raises a serious possibility of persistent inconsistency in the interpretation of the same regulatory statute. Should courts therefore refuse to recognize private rights of action? What is the bearing of primary jurisdiction doctrine[16] on these questions?

4. Judicial Review Under an Interest Representation Model

Reread *Scenic Hudson II,* pp. 299-303, supra. Consider also the following decision.

Office of Communication of United Church of Christ v. FCC (Church of Christ II)

425 F.2d 543 (D.C. Cir. 1969)

[After remand from *Church of Christ I,* p. 1014 supra, the FCC awarded a three year license renewal to WLBT after an evidentiary hearing in which the viewer representatives, who had sought review in *Church of Christ I,* were permitted to participate. The court, in an opinion by Judge BURGER, recounted the history of the proceedings, emphasizing that the Commission had originally found WLBT's performance so defective that it had awarded an exceptional probationary renewal for one year only. The court further emphasized that this one-year extension had been set aside in *Church of Christ I.*]

When the matter was again before the Commission on our remand, therefore, it was in a posture that the licensee had yet to demonstrate that it was in the public interest for the license to be renewed. This was a less favorable posture for the li-

16. See pp. 992-1012, supra.

censee than would have been the case absent the "probationary license" grant. This is important, but its significance seems to have eluded the hearing Examiner and the Commission as well; we emphasize this now to remove any lingering doubts as to our evaluation of a "probationary" grant — a grant which by its nature assumes that the renewal-licensee has been unable to persuade the Commission that it is presently in the public interest to grant a three-year renewal. That the Examiner failed to grasp this fact is reflected throughout his report and noticeably in his statement that

> the evidentiary hearing ... presented [Appellants] ample and sufficient opportunity to come forward and *sustain their serious allegations* that they had made against the applicant. They have woefully failed to do so. . . .

Lamar Life Broadcasting Co., 14 F.C.C. 2d 495, 549 (1967) (emphasis added).

Since the Commission itself had previously found that some of these "serious allegations" were sufficient to withhold the grant of the traditional three-year license, the Examiner's approach, and its subsequent adoption by the Commission, signifies an attitude considerably at odds with the Commission's earlier action in refusing a three-year license. The Examiner seems to have regarded Appellants as "plaintiffs" and the licensee as "defendant," with burdens of proof allocated accordingly. This tack ... was a grave misreading of our holding on this question. We did not intend that intervenors representing a public interest be treated as interlopers. Rather, if analogues can be useful, a "Public Intervenor" who is seeking no license or private right is, in this context, more nearly like a complaining witness who presents evidence to police or a prosecutor whose duty it is to conduct an affirmative and objective investigation of all the facts and to pursue his prosecutorial or regulatory function if there is probable cause to believe a violation has occurred.

This was all the more true here because prior to the efforts of the actively participating intervenors, the Commission itself had long since found the licensee wanting. It was not the correct role of the Examiner or the Commission to sit back and simply provide a forum for the intervenors; the Commission's duties did not end by allowing Appellants to intervene; its duties began at that stage.

A curious neutrality-in-favor-of-the-licensee seems to have guided the Examiner in his conduct of the evidentiary hearing. . . .

[The court here quotes excerpts from the record before the hearing examiner which, it finds, reflects disregard of the intervenors' evidence and charges and a failure to follow through their implications.]

[T]he Examiner's erroneous concept of the burden of proof [as being on intervenors] shows a failure to grasp the distinction between "allegations" and testimonial evidence, and prevented the development of a satisfactory record. . . .

We need not continue recitals from the record or examples of similar situations which shed light on the nature of the hearings; in our view the entire hearing was permeated by similar treatment of the efforts of the intervenors, and the pervasive impatience — if not hostility — of the Examiner is a constant factor which made fair and impartial consideration impossible. The Commission and the Examiners have an affirmative duty to assist in the development of a meaningful record which can serve as the basis for the evaluation of the licensee's performance of his duty to serve the public interest. The Public Intervenors, who were performing a public service under a mandate of this court, were entitled to a more hospitable reception in the performance of that function. As we view the record the Examiner tended to impede the exploration of the very issues which we would reasonably expect the Commission itself would have initiated; an ally was regarded as an opponent. . . .

The record now before us leaves us with a profound concern over the entire handling of this case following the remand to the Commission. The impatience with the Public Intervenors, the hostility toward their efforts to satisfy a surprisingly strict standard of proof, plain errors in rulings and findings lead us, albeit reluctantly, to the conclusion that it will serve no useful purpose to ask the Commission to reconsider the Examiner's actions and its own Decision and Order under a correct allocation of the burden of proof. The administrative conduct reflected in this record is beyond repair.

The Commission itself, with more specific documentation of the licensee's shortcomings than it had in 1965 has now found virtues in the licensee which it was unable to perceive in 1965 and now finds the grant of a full three-year license to be in the public interest.

We are compelled to hold, on the whole record, that the Commission's conclusion is not supported by substantial evidence. For this reason the grant of a license must be vacated forthwith and the Commission is directed to invite applications to be filed for the license. We do refrain, however, from holding that the licensee be declared disqualified from filing a new application; the conduct of the hearing was not primarily the licensee's responsibility, although as the applicant it had the burden of proof. Moreover, the Commission necessarily did not address itself to the precise question of WLBT's qualification to be an applicant in the new proceeding now ordered, and we hesitate to pass on this subject not considered by the Commission. . . .

Reversed and remanded for further proceedings in accordance with this opinion.

[On rehearing en banc, the Court of Appeals unanimously rejected the Commission's contention that the court lacked power to order the grant of the license revoked, that this power resided only in the Commission, and that the court was limited to remanding the case to the Commission.]

Notes and Questions

The interest representation model attempts to promote the equitable exercise of agency discretion by assuring interested groups and parties the right to participate in formal agency decision making. It acknowledges the "legislative" character of agency choice, and attempts to develop formal, legalistic modes of representation as a surrogate for the political mechanisms of representation applicable to legislatures. In so doing, the interest representative model tends to highlight the multiple trade offs among values and interests that are at the heart of many administrative decisions. See, e.g., the *Scenic Hudson* litigation.

What approach should courts take in reviewing the balance struck by an agency in a given case?

1. Courts might simply proceed by assuming that formal procedures and broadened participation rights alone will ensure agency decisions more responsive to a broader range of affected interests. Such an assumption might reflect the view that although bureaucratic agencies can not be expected on their own to pay much heed to loosely organized interests, administrators will respond when representatives of those interests submit pertinent information and argument. Alternatively, one might believe that agencies will accommodate public interest groups because such groups can otherwise threaten to exercise their right to trigger formal proceedings which will impose costly delays on the agency. On this view, broadened participation rights are justified because they give strategic "bargaining chips" to "under-represented" public interest groups.

Will broadened participation rights override the basic, systemic reasons for asserted agency "failure"? For example, would they lead the FCC to downgrade the continued financial health of the broadcast industry as a basic priority? Moreover, the "bargaining chips" theory assumes that agencies are incapable of taking counter-measures to undercut the strategic advantages gained by public interest groups. To what extent has the agencies' shift to rulemaking undermined the premises behind the notion that procedures will, by themselves, assure "better" or "fairer" outcomes?

2. Courts could attempt to review whether agencies gave "adequate consideration" to the various interests at stake, and whether they took a "hard look" at the evidence and argument advanced by their representatives. See *Scenic Hudson I* and the accompanying discussion, pp. 293-299, supra. But consider whether this approach ultimately dissolves into "pure proceduralism" of the sort summarized in paragraph 1 (longer proceedings, more complete records, more elaborate opinions, etc.), or into substitution by courts of their judgment for that of the agency as to how the balance between competing considerations should be struck. See *Scenic Hudson II* and accompanying discussion, pp. 299-303, supra.

3. Reviewing courts could seek to tip the balance between competing interests by reference to controlling statutory directives or underlying statutory purposes. Cf. *Overton Park*, pp. 276-282, supra. But consider that the interest-representation model may tend to transform each controversy — for example, *Scenic Hudson* — into a highly crystallized and particularistic configuration of multipolar interests, making each controversy unique and less tractable to resolution by reference to generally applicable statutory directives. Consider also that the legislature's inability or unwillingness to strike a decisive balance among competing interests is a prime reason for legislative delegations to agencies in the first place.

4. The reviewing court might invalidate the agency's resolution as "arbitrary and capricious." This, in essence, was the response of the court in *Church of Christ II*. (Was the court's action consistent with *Chenery I*, p. 334, supra?) But how often will courts be justified in taking this step, and willing so to do? Consider that the interest-representative model will tend to accentuate the "legislative" or "political" character of the tradeoffs confronting the agency and the reviewing court. Under what circumstances (if any) would courts be justified in intervening, without any persuasive warrant in relevant statutes, and requiring that the agency give

greater weight to some interests at the expense of others? Consider Judge Bazelon's assertion in EDF v. Ruckleshaus, pp. 1030-1036, supra, that certain "fundamental personal interests" have a "special claim to judicial protection" in comparison with "economic interests." Would you agree? Is the "special protection" to which such interests are entitled defined solely in procedural terms, or is it "substantive" as well?

5. Are there any other alternatives that a reviewing court might consider?

5. Funding Interest Representation

To what extent will loosely organized "public interests" be able to exercise broadened rights to participate in agency decisions and obtain judicial review? The very factors that make it difficult for interest groups (such as consumers) to organize in the first place — the large numbers of individuals involved, the small stake of any one individual in a given administrative decision, and the absence of compulsory mechanisms of representation — make it difficult to develop the financial resources needed to fund protracted and costly administrative litigation.[17] Some membership "public interest" groups, such as Ralph Nader's Public Citizen, the ACLU, and the Sierra Club, have managed to raise appreciable sums through membership contributions. Foundations have played a major role in funding public interest advocates. But the funding available is quite modest in relation to the resources deployed by other administrative litigants, such as business firms.[18] Should changes be made in legal rules or governmental policies in order to provide greater funding for public interest advocacy? Consider the following decisions.

Wilderness Society v. Morton

495 F.2d 1026 (D.C. Cir. 1974) (en banc)

J. Skelly WRIGHT, Circuit Judge:

Appellants Wilderness Society, Environmental Defense Fund, Inc. and Friends of the Earth request an award of expenses and attorneys' fees related to the litigation they successfully prosecuted to bar construction of the trans-Alaska

---

17. A member of an unorganized interest (such as air travelers) may often be unwilling to contribute voluntarily to the costs of a litigation effort (such as opposing a proposed air fare increase before the CAB) because she will benefit from a victory even if she contributes nothing. But if all individuals reason in the same way, the effort will not be undertaken. This is the so-called "free rider" effect. Conceivably a contract might be negotiated under which each individual might agree to contribute if all the others did. But negotiation and enforcement of such a contract would itself be quite costly, again posing the "free rider" problem. Furthermore, these problems could not readily be solved by government intervention to require compulsory contributions; given the unorganized character of consumer or environmental interests, it is not feasible to require the equivalent of a union dues check-off. See generally M. Olson, The Logic of Collective Action (1965).

18. See generally, Council for Public Interest Law, Balancing the Scales of Justice: Financing Public Interest Law in America (1976); B. Weisbrod, Public Interest Law 42-79 (1978).

pipeline. See Wilderness Society v. Morton, 156 U.S. App. D.C. 121, 479 F.2d 842, *cert. denied*, 411 U.S. 917 . . . (1973). . . .

[In that decision the Court of Appeals sustained plaintiffs' claim that the Interior Department's authorization of proposed construction of the pipeline would contravene provisions in the 1920 Mineral Leasing Act limiting right-of-ways across public lands for private pipelines to a 50-foot width, and did not reach plaintiffs' alternative claim that the Environmental Impact Statement prepared by Interior on the project was inadequate. Following the decision, Congress enacted a statute, Public Law 93-153, 93d Cong., 1st Sess. (1973), specifically authorizing construction of the pipeline with certain conditions, including provision for a carrier-financed liability fund for damage caused by the pipeline. The statute directed that construction should go forward "without further action under the National Environmental Policy Act" and excluded all judicial review of the pipeline authorization except the constitutionality of Congress' action in excluding other review; the statute provided that such litigation should be decided by a United States District Court without any appellate review.]

. . . [W]e hold that an award of attorneys' fees is appropriate and remand the case to the District Court to determine the fees.

I

There have always existed equitable exceptions to the traditional America rule barring recovery of attorneys' fees by a successful litigant. In cases in which a party has acted in bad faith, assessment of fees properly serves to punish that party's obdurate behavior. See Hall v. Cole, 412 U.S. 1, 5 . . . (1973). Another exception includes cases in which the plaintiff's suit confers a benefit on the members of an ascertainable class and in which an award of fees will serve to spread the costs of litigation among its beneficiaries. See Mills v. Electric Auto-Lite Co., 396 U.S. 375 . . . (1970).

Neither of these historic exceptions is applicable here. Appellees' legal position as to the meaning of the Mineral Leasing Act and relevant administrative regulations, though ultimately rejected by the court, was manifestly reasonable and assumed in good faith, particularly in view of the long administrative practice supporting it. See Wilderness Society v. Morton, supra, 156 U.S. App. D.C. at 143-149, 479 F.2d at 864-870. And although the "common benefit" exception has been given expanded scope in recent cases, compare Hall v. Cole, supra, with Sprague v. Ticonic National Bank, 307 U.S. 161 . . . (1939), we would have to stretch it totally outside its basic rationale to apply it here. As is discussed more fully below, this litigation may well have provided substantial benefits to particular individuals and, indeed, to every citizen's interest in the proper functioning of our system of government. But imposing attorneys' fees on Alyeska will not operate to spread the costs of litigation proportionately among these beneficiaries, the key requirement of the "common benefit" theory. . . .

The Supreme Court has recently indicated, however, that the equitable power of federal courts to award attorney's fees when the interests of justice so require is not a narrow power confined to rigid sets of cases. Rather, it " 'is part of the original authority of the chancellor to do equity in a particular situation' " Hall v. Cole, supra, 412 U.S. at 5 . . . , quoting Sprague v. Ticonic National Bank, supra, 307 U.S. at 166 . . . , and should be used whenever " 'overriding considerations indicate the need for such a recovery.' " Id., quoting Mills v. Electric Auto-Lite Co., supra, 396 U.S. at 391-392. . . .

Recognizing their broad equitable power, some courts have concluded that the interests of justice require fee shifting in a third class of cases where the plaintiff acted as a " 'private attorney general,' vindicating a policy that Congress considered of the highest priority." . . .

We find persuasive the arguments advanced by these courts in adopting a private attorney general exception to the traditional American rule.

> The violation of an important public policy may involve little by way of actual damages, so far as a single individual is concerned, or little in comparison with the cost of vindication. . . . If a defendant may feel that the cost of litigation, and, particularly, that the financial circumstances of an injured party may mean that the chances of suit being brought, or continued in the face of opposition, will be small, there will be little brake upon deliberate wrongdoing. In such instances public policy may suggest an award of costs that will remove the burden from the shoulders of the plaintiff seeking to vindicate the public right. . . ."

Knight v. Auciello, . . . 453 F.2d at 853. In much litigation, whether or not formally designated as a class action, a party sues not only to vindicate his own interests, which often are minor, but to enjoin injuries to a broad class — injuries which may be quite extensive when viewed collectively. See, e.g., Sierra Club v. Morton, 405 U.S. 727, 736-738 & 739 n.15. . . ; United States v. Students Challenging Regulatory Agency Procedures, 412 U.S. 669 . . . (1973). In such cases, "[i]f successful plaintiffs were routinely forced to bear their own attorneys' fees, few aggrieved parties would be in a position to advance the public interest by invoking the injunctive powers of the federal courts." Newman v. Piggie Park Enterprises, Inc., . . . 390 U.S. at 402. . . . When violation of a congressional enactment has caused little injury to any one individual, but great harm to important public interests when viewed from the perspective of the broad class intended to be protected by that statute, not to award counsel fees can seriously frustrate the purposes of Congress. See Hall v. Cole, supra, 412 U.S. at 13-14. . . . Where the law relies on private suits to effectuate congressional policy in favor of broad public interests, attorneys' fees are often necessary to ensure that private litigants will initiate such suits . . . . Substantial benefits to the general public should not depend upon the financial status of the individual volunteering to serve as plaintiff or upon the charity of public-minded lawyers. . . .

II

The chief rationale behind the American rule is the notion that parties might be unjustly discouraged from instituting or defending actions to vindicate their rights if the penalty for losing in court included the fees of their opponent's counsel. See Fleischmann Distilling Corp. v. Maier Brewing Co., 386 U.S. 714, 718 . . . (1967); McCormick, Counsel Fees and Other Expenses of Litigation as an Element of Damages, 15 Minn. L. Rev. 619, 639-642 (1931). The possibility of unjust deterrence of litigation is most often stated from the plaintiff's point of view. An individual with a relatively small damage claim, for example, could easily be discouraged from pressing that claim in court, no matter how meritorious he in good faith believed it to be, if losing the lawsuit meant paying the defendant's attorney's fees which might approach or even exceed the value of his claim. . . . But see Ehrenzweig, Reimbursement of Counsel Fees and the Great Society, 54 Calif. L. Rev. 792 (1966). Of course, the argument has equal merit from the defendant's point of view. A defendant faced with a relatively small claim might well be induced to capitulate to the plaintiff's demands, even though he legitimately felt he had a good defense, if losing the case in court would mean paying the plaintiff's attorney's fees. See McCormick, supra, 15 Minn. L. Rev. at 641. Simply stated, then, imposition of attorneys' fees on the losing party is thought to raise the stakes of litigation and thereby to discourage individuals from submitting their rights to judicial determination.

Whatever force this argument concededly has in the great run of civil litigation, we think it plainly inapposite to the circumstances of the present case. As Alyeska has so often brought to our attention, the value of its investment at stake in this litigation was over a billion dollars. Each week's delay in constructing the pipeline imposed an additional $3.5 million in costs. Any award of fees in this case, though conceivably large in absolute sense, will be paltry in comparison with the interest Alyeska had in defending this appeal. Where the interest at stake is many times greater than the expected cost of one's opponent's attorney's fees, any possibility of deterrence is surely remote if not nonexistent. . . .[19]

Looking at this case from appellants' point of view, the unavailability of attorneys' fees might significantly deter them from having brought this meritorious litigation. In prosecuting this case, appellants undertook litigation of monumental proportions. According to their bill of costs, the matters appealed consumed over 4,500 hours of lawyers' time, all in addition to the efforts before the District Court in 1970 when this action was commenced and preliminary injunctive relief obtained. See Wilderness Society v. Hickel, D.D.C., 325 F. Supp. 422 (1970). This burden was assumed not in the hope of obtaining a monetary award, nor to protect an interest peculiar to appellants and their members, but rather to vindicate important statutory rights of all citizens whose interest might be affected by construction of the pipeline.

Whether we consider the Mineral Leasing Act and administrative regulation issues upon which the court rested its opinion declaring the pipeline unlawful, or the National Environmental Policy Act (NEPA) issues which the court left un-

19. Had appellees been the prevailing parties and sought attorneys' fees from appellants, the possibility of deterrence would be significant and the rationale of the American rule would therefore bar recovery of fees. In this sense there is an admitted lack of reciprocity in granting attorneys' fees under a private attorney general theory.

decided, appellants succeeded in their role as private attorneys general protecting vital statutory interests.

It is argued that the width limitation in Section 28 of the Mineral Leasing Act of 1920 does not amount to a congressional policy of preeminent importance. But the dispute in this case was more than a debate over interpretation of that Act. Appellees' primary argument was that, whatever the width restrictions in the Act originally meant, a settled administrative practice to evade those restrictions took precedence. In the final analysis, this case involved the duty of the Executive Branch to observe the restrictions imposed by the Legislative, see Freeman v. Ryan, 133 U.S. App. D.C. 1, 3, 408 F.2d 1204, 1206 (1968), and the primary responsibility of the Congress under the Constitution to regulate the use of public lands. Wilderness Society v. Morton, supra, 156 U.S. App. D.C. at 170-172, 479 F.2d at 891-893.

The proper functioning of our system of government under the Constitution is, of course, important to every American, and in this sense appellants' suit had great therapeutic value. . . . But requiring the Congress to revise the Mineral Leasing Act rather than permitting continued evasion of its clear, though anachronistic, restrictions has had other more concrete and equally important benefits. As a result of this suit, Congress has amended the Mineral Leasing Act to remove the restrictions of the 1920 statute and permit construction of the trans-Alaska pipeline. Public Law 93-153, 93rd Cong., 1st Sess. (November 16, 1973). The statute imposes several important new requirements designed to protect the public interest. Rather than continue the prior practice of permitting free use of Government land, the new statute requires the issuing agency to receive the "fair market value" of the right-of-way and empowers the agency to assess against the right-of-way recipient all reasonable administrative costs of processing an application and monitoring the right of way. Pub. L. 93-153, §101 (amending Mineral Leasing Act of 1920, §28(l)). The statute contains special provisions making the operator of the pipeline strictly liable for damages resulting from use of the right-of-way, id., §204. The same section of the new statute requires the operator to maintain a $100,000,000 liability fund to satisfy the claims, id., §204(c)(5). Forcing Alyeska to go to Congress to amend the 1920 Act certainly was not a sterile exercise in legal technicalities devoid of public significance.

The equities in favor of awarding fees for appellants' efforts on NEPA issues are just as compelling.[20] Elaborate specific procedures are provided under the 1973

20. The environmental benefit from this litigation is generously recognized by the Honorable Russell E. Train, then chairman of the President's Council on Environmental Quality and now Administrator of the Environmental Protection Agency, before the Joint Judicial Conference of the Eighth and Tenth Circuits on June 29, 1973:

"The Alaska Pipeline may not have been a tidy example of the judicial process, but it has been an excellent example where NEPA and the courts have forced the reconciliation of environmental concerns with sound engineering practices on a major energy project. The President has now called for construction of the pipeline at the earliest possible date, and the Administration has introduced legislation which would remove the present right-of-way restrictions and is urging swift action on the bill.

"To some any delay in the completion of the pipeline is unreasonable. In reality, though, much of the delay has been beneficial. The problems of constructing a hot oil pipeline across permafrost are very real. The problems of constructing a pipeline across one of the most seismically active and remote areas of the world are likewise very real. These and other significant amendments to ensure protection of environmental interests. Id. §101 (amending Mineral Leasing Act of 1920, §28(h)(1) & (2)). One need not have the hindsight of history to know that the commitment to improving and protecting our natural environment is one of the most vital of current national policies. NEPA is only one part of a vast legislative effort toward that end, but it is among the most important because of its broad scope. . . . And effective pursuit of congressional policy under NEPA, as with much legislation in the environmental area, depends on the diligence of private attorneys general and their willingness to bring suit to further broad public interests.

Nor do we think it of controlling importance that this court did not actually decide the NEPA issues and that Congress has subsequently decided in the pipeline legislation that the impact statement prepared by the Department of the Interior shall be deemed sufficient under NEPA. See Pub. L. 93-153, supra, §203(d). The advancement of important legislative policy justifying an award of attorneys' fees can be accomplished even where the plaintiff does not obtain the ultimate relief sought by the filing and prosecution of his suit. . . . When litigation serves as a catalyst to effect change and thereby achieves a valuable public service, an award of fees may be appropriate even though the suit never proceeds to a successful conclusion on the merits. . . .

Although Congress has now given the go-ahead to the pipeline on the basis of the impact statement prepared by the Department, this appeal helped focus attention in Congress on the major issue raised — the relative merits of a trans-Canadian versus a trans-Alaskan route. See, e.g., 119 Con. Rec. S12795-S12803 (daily ed., July 9, 1973). See also Title III of Pub. L. 93-153, supra. We take the action of Congress approving the impact statement, not as a total rejection of the arguments made on appeal, but rather as a recognition that appellants had raised a very substantial question which the courts were likely to require considerable time to resolve and that, time being of the essence in providing for delivery of North Slope oil, a congressional resolution was required.

We also deem it significant that the Mineral Leasing Act issues on which appellants clearly prevailed were somewhat interrelated with the NEPA issues. . . .

In sum, the equities of this particular case support an award of attorneys' fees to the successful plaintiffs-appellants. Acting as private attorneys general, not only have they ensured the proper functioning of our system of government, but they have advanced and protected in a very concrete manner substantial public interests . . . .

---

problems were simply not adequately faced in the initial proposal presented to the Department of the Interior in 1969.

"If the pipeline had been constructed using the original design specifications, it would very likely have resulted in not only very serious environmental but also serious operations problems. Indeed, the physical integrity of the pipeline itself was very much at stake.

"Thus, the case of the Alaska pipeline has not been simply one of aesthetics, or of concern over wildlife and wilderness disturbance, or worries over water pollution, important as all of these are. It was clearly an example where sound environmental analysis was essential to sound engineering and siting.

"In all honesty, the process has been one of learning for both industry and government."

III

Even if fees are to be awarded under a private attorney general theory, a question is posed as to whether Alyeska should bear them. Technically it is the Interior Department, on Alyeska's application, which violated the Mineral Leasing Act by granting rights-of-way in excess of the Act's width restrictions, and it is the Interior Department's failure to comply with NEPA which was challenged on appeal. Under 28 U.S.C. §2412, however, no attorneys' fees can be imposed against the United States. Alyeska argues that it is inappropriate to circumvent the statute by taxing it for a dereliction not its own.

Fee shifting under the private attorney general theory, however, is not intended to punish law violators, but rather to ensure that those who have acted to protect the public interest will not be forced to shoulder the entire cost of litigation. Cf. Hall v. Cole, supra 412 U.S. at 14, 93 S. Ct. 1943. After successfully persuading the Interior Department to grant the rights-of-way, Alyeska intervened in this litigation to protect its massive interests. Since Alyeska unquestionably was a major and real party at interest in this case, actively participating in the litigation along with the Government, we think it fair that it should bear part of the attorneys' fees. . . . In recognition of the Government's role in the case, on the other hand, Alyeska should have to bear only half of the total fees. The other half is properly allocated to the Government and, because of the statutory bar, must be assumed by appellants. In this manner the equitable principle that appellees bear their fair share of this litigation's full cost and the congressional policy that the United States not be taxable for fees can be accommodated. . . . .

MacKinnon, Circuit Judge, dissenting:

The majority opinion orders that Alyeska, a private party, pay one-half on appellants' attorneys' fees. The other half, presumably the obligation of the Government, will not be paid because the Government cannot be assessed for costs in such cases. In awarding attorneys' fees against Alyeska the majority is promoting a continuance of some of the same errors that were contained in their initial opinion and which were in effect overridden by Congress in the enactment of the Alaska Pipeline bill.

The majority say they —

> take the action of Congress approving the impact statement, not as a total
> rejection of the arguments made on appeal, but rather as a recognition that
> appellants had raised a very substantial question which the courts were likely
> to require considerable time to resolve and that, time being of the essence in
> providing for delivery of North Slope oil, a congressional resolution was re-
> quired. . . .

To my view it is perfectly obvious that Congress' action in approving the Impact Statement by a rarely used legislative finding amounted to "a total rejection of the arguments made on appeal," because Congress would not deprive a court (this court) of its basic jurisdiction unless it felt that the court had misused its power in the past and could not, at least with respect to this case, be relied on in the future. Certainly the need for expedition was not the principal motive; if that were the case, Congress could simply have required a speedy decision by this court in the statute. Also, the issues dealt with in the Impact Statement were too important in the national scheme not to be properly resolved in a project of this tremendous magnitude. So Congress approved the Impact Statement, where this court had refused to even consider it, by declaring that the Alaska Pipeline should be constructed as described in the Final Environmental Impact Statement of the Department of Interior . . . without further action under the National Environmental Policy Act of 1969. . . . Indeed, Congress went further and deprived this court of its normal right to judicially review decisions of the U.S. District Court under the Alaska Pipe Line bill by providing in effect that this court should not have jurisdiction of any claim challenging "the actions of the Federal officers concerning the issuance of the necessary rights-of-way [etc.] claims alleging the invalidity of [§203(d)] . . . and [even] claims alleging [the denial of] . . . rights under the Constitution. . . ." Certainly such drastic, unheard of and almost unprecedented action cannot be explained away on such self-serving grounds as the majority sets forth, supra. To my mind, the action by Congress is a plain indication that it considered the prior refusal of this court to perform its constitutional duty as an indication that it should not be expected properly to perform its duty with respect to this matter in the future.

Then to add insult to injury, the majority attempts to compensate attorneys for their work on the NEPA issue, the main objective of which sought to protect the *American* environment by compelling construction of the pipeline through Canada, a foreign country. The majority of this court did not consider the NEPA issue; instead it left it as a factor to be decided in the future, with the delay necessarily attendant to such deferred consideration. Congress, however, considered and found the NEPA Impact Statement to be adequate. So the efforts of appellants' attorneys with respect to NEPA drew a complete blank. Under such circumstances, it is unreasonable by any fair standard to compensate them for that phase of the case. . . .

For this reason I would refuse to compensate appellants' attorneys for any work they did on the NEPA issue — the main thrust of which would have made us further dependent upon another foreign nation, albeit our good neighbor, the Queen of the Snows to the north, for resources vital to our well-being as an independent nation. When we subsidize lawyers to bring such suits against our national interests we promote our own destruction. That we should not do.

In addition to recovery on the basis of an issue never decided by this court, appellants' victory here is premised on the narrow statutory interpretation issue on which they actually prevailed on the merits. This is a slender reed on which to rest recovery, however, for the width limitation surely was not the motivating force behind appellants' decision to institute legal action. Nonetheless, the majority seizes it with alacrity and raises it to such cosmic proportions that the issue becomes no less than "[t]he proper functioning of our system of government under the Constitution." This attenuated approach is demonstrably flawed when applied to Alyeska.

Assuming arguendo that forcing the Government to channel its actions within the law could be a valid basis for requiring the Government itself to reimburse appellants' attorney fees, the argument fails as applied to Alyeska. The majority, which discourses freely and at great length on how appellants' have benefited the public weal, apparently feels constrained to limit to three sentences its argument that makes Alyeska, a private party, liable for governmental actions. . . . Brevity is not always to be desired — especially on the pivotal issue of whether Alyeska should be held answerable for what the majority apparently perceives to be the sins of the Government. Perhaps this brevity, so admirable in other contexts, is attributable to an inability to marshal cogent arguments to support the proposition advanced; more likely, however, such brevity is required to mask sub silentio the major premise of the opinion. That is, oil companies are prosperous, appellants are poor, and therefore oil companies should finance both sides of this litigation. Thus the essence of the majority's argument is contained in the phrase "we think it fair"; the fact that the State of Alaska, also a party defendant and otherwise indistinguishable from Alyeska, escapes liability is an anomaly that also supports this reading of the majority opinion. . . .

Differing perceptions of justice and the public interest are understandable and to be expected, but a judiciary that in large measure depends for its influence on continued public confidence should, at a minimum, set forth in a frank and candid exposition the true bases of its decisions. Only in this manner can they fairly be judged.

For the reasons stated above I dissent from the payment of any fees to appellants.

WILKEY, Circuit Judge, joined by MacKINNON and ROBB, Circuit Judges, dissenting.

We respectfully dissent. It is difficult to see that either of these plaintiffs "acted as a 'private attorney general,' vindicating a policy that Congress considered of the highest priority." Judging from Congress' most recent action, these plaintiffs have been frustrating the policy Congress considers highly desirable and of the utmost urgency.

Nor do we agree that "this litigation may well have provided substantial benefits to particular individuals." Aside from the numerous lawyers involved, we are at a loss to know who those "particular individuals" enjoying "substantial benefits" might be. It is hard to visualize the average American in this winter of 1973-74, turning down his thermostat and with a careful eye on his auto fuel gauge, feeling that warm flow of gratitude to those public-spirited plaintiffs in the Alaska Pipeline case.

While no one questions the sincere motives of these "public interest" plaintiffs, it is not enough for a plaintiff to have a sincere feeling of self-righteous correctness in bringing litigation. There is the matter of good judgment in assaying just where the public interest lies. Did the plaintiffs exercise good judgment here in bringing suit to block the Alaska Pipeline? In retrospect, we submit they did not. . . .

. . . We are not impressed by the suggestion that the plaintiffs would not have sued, absent the prospect of legal fees to be paid by the defendants or the intervenors. At oral arguments it was conceded that all counsel for the plaintiffs were salaried employees of the complaining organizations. This litigation must have been within the scope of the employment of these lawyers; indeed, the prosecution of litigation of this sort was one of the objects and purposes for which the plaintiff organizations were charted and existed. We think it unrealistic to say that no suit would have been brought if the plaintiffs had not been able to count on the payment by others of the salaries of their staff attorneys. The plaintiffs were equipped and prepared to act, and no added financial encouragement was necessary.

With regard to other attorneys and potential plaintiffs, not so securely situated, the hope of attorneys' fees spawned by this ill-advised decision may be just the stimulus needed to launch them in the direction of the courthouse, embarrassed by any humility as to their knowledge of where the "public interest" lies. The flood of "public interest" litigation, particularly in the environmental field, is given a new impetus by the majority decision. . . .

For mark this: no longer is it necessary for such plaintiffs to prevail on the legal theory of their case, nor to confer a discernible undisputed public benefit; it now suffices only to gain the sympathy of the court ultimately passing on legal fees for the substantive merits of plaintiffs' case, and lo, plaintiffs can fail to prevail legally and dislocate the economy in trying, but can be awarded a consolation prize of attorneys' fees — in this case greater than plaintiffs would otherwise have paid. . . . We can think of no greater encouragement to ill-founded litigation.

Alyeska Pipeline Service Company v. Wilderness Society

421 U.S. 240 (1975)

[In this decision, the Court, in an opinion by Mr. Justice WHITE, reversed the decision in Wilderness Society v. Morton. In doing so, the Court placed great weight on an 1853 federal statute defining those expenses that might be taxed by the court against the losing party in favor of the prevailing party. The statute, 10 Stat. 161, which did not include attorneys' fees as taxable costs or expenses, has been codified in part in 28 U.S.C. §§ 1920, 1923(a). These the Court read as expressing a general congressional policy against the award of attorneys' fees. The Court then sought to deal with the judicially created exceptions to the "American rule" that attorneys' fees are not an item in taxable costs and expenses:]

To be sure, the . . . statutes have been construed to allow, in limited circumstances, a reasonable attorneys' fee to the prevailing party in excess of the small sums permitted by §1923. In Trustees v. Greenough, 105 U.S. 527 (1882), the 1853 Act was read as not interfering with the historic power of equity to permit the trustee of a fund or property, or a party preserving or recovering a fund for the benefit of others in addition to himself, to recover his costs, including his attorneys' fees, from the fund or property itself or directly from the other parties enjoying the benefit. That rule has been consistently followed. . . . Also, a court may assess attorneys' fees for the "willful disobedience of a court order ... as part of the fine to be levied on the defendant ..." or when the losing party has "acted in bad faith, vexatiously, wantonly, or for oppressive reasons. . . ." These exceptions are unquestionably assertions of inherent power in the courts to allow attorneys' fees in particular situations, unless forbidden by Congress, but none of the exceptions is involved here. The Court of Appeals expressly disclaimed reliance on any of them. . . .

Congress has not repudiated the judicially fashioned exceptions to the general rule against allowing substantial attorney fees; but neither has it retracted, repealed or modified the limitations on taxable fees contained in the 1853 statute and its successors. Nor has it extended any roving authority to the Judiciary to allow counsel fees as costs or otherwise whenever the courts might deem them warranted. What Congress has done, however, while fully recognizing and accepting the general rule, is itself to make specific and explicit provisions for the allowance of attorneys' fees under selected statutes granting or protecting various federal rights. These statutory allowances are now available in a variety of circumstances, but they also differ considerably among themselves. Under the antitrust laws, for instance, allowance of attorneys' fees to a plaintiff awarded treble damages is mandatory. In patent litigation, in contrast, "[t]he court in *exceptional* cases *may* award reasonable attorney fees to the prevailing party." 35 U.S.C. §285 [emphasis added]. Under Title II of the Civil Rights Act of 1964, 42 U.S.C. §2000a-3(b), the prevailing party is entitled to an attorney's fee, at the discretion of the court, but we have held that Congress intended that the award should be made to the successful plaintiff absent exceptional circumstances. Newman v. Piggie Park Enterprises, Inc., 390 U.S. 400, 402 (1968). See also Northcross v. Board of Education of the Memphis City Schools, 412 U.S. 427 (1973). Under this scheme of things, it is apparent that the circumstances under which attorneys' fees are to be awarded and the range of discretion of the courts in making those awards are matters for Congress to determine.

It is true that under some, if not most, of the statutes providing for the allowance of reasonable fees, Congress has opted to rely heavily on private enforcement to implement public policy and to allow counsel fees so as to encourage private litigation. Fee-shifting in connection with treble damage awards under the antitrust laws is a prime example; ... and we have noted that Title II of the Civil Rights Act of 1964 was intended "not simply to penalize litigants who deliberately advance arguments they know to be untenable but, more broadly, to encourage individuals injured by racial discrimination to seek judicial relief under Title II." *Newman,* supra, at 402 ... (footnote omitted). But congressional utilization of the private attorney general concept can in no sense be construed as a grant of authority to the Judiciary to jettison the traditional rule against nonstatutory allowances to the prevailing party and to award attorneys' fees whenever the courts deem the public policy furthered by a particular statute important enough to warrant the award.

Congress itself presumably has the power and judgment to pick and choose among its statutes and to allow attorneys' fees under some but not others. But it would be difficult, indeed, for the courts without legislative guidance to consider some statutes important and others unimportant and to allow attorneys' fees only in connection with the former. If the statutory limitation of right-of-way widths involved in this case is a matter of the gravest importance, it would appear that a wide range of statutes would arguably satisfy the criterion of public importance and justify an award of attorneys' fees to the private litigant. And, if any statutory policy is deemed so important that its enforcement must be encouraged by awards of attorneys' fees, how could a court deny attorneys' fees to private litigants in actions under 42 U.S.C. §1983 seeking to vindicate *constitutional* rights? Moreover, should courts, if they were to embark on the course urged by respondents, opt for awards to the prevailing party, whether plaintiff or defendant, or only to the prevailing plaintiff? Should awards be discretionary or mandatory? Would there be a presumption operating for or against them in the ordinary case? . . .

As exemplified by this case itself, it is also evident that the rationale application of the private-attorney-general rule would immediately collide with the express provision of 28 U.S.C. §2412. Except as otherwise provided by statute, that section permits costs to be taxed against the United States, "but not including the fees and expenses of attorneys," in any civil action brought by or against the United States or any agency or official of the United States acting in an official capacity. If, as respondents argue, one of the main functions of a private attorney general is to call public officials to account and to insist that they enforce the law, it would follow in such cases that attorneys' fees should be awarded against the Government or the officials themselves. Indeed, that very claim was asserted in this case. But §2412 on its face, and in light of its legislative history, generally bars such awards, which, if allowable at all, must be expressly provided for by statute, as, for example, under Title II of the Civil Rights Act of 1964, 42 U.S.C. §2000a-3(b).

We need labor the matter no further. It appears to us that the rule suggested here and adopted by the Court of Appeals would make major inroads on a policy matter that Congress has reserved for itself. Since the approach taken by Congress to this issue has been to carve out specific exceptions to a general rule that federal courts cannot award attorneys' fees beyond the limits of 28 U.S.C. §1923, those courts are not free to fashion drastic new rules with respect to the allowance of attorneys' fees to the prevailing party in federal litigation or to pick and choose among plaintiffs and the statutes under which they sue and to award fees in some cases but not in others, depending upon the courts' assessment of the importance of the public policies involved in particular cases. Nor should the federal courts purport to adopt on their own initiative a rule awarding attorneys' fees based on the private attorney general approach when such judicial rule will operate only against private parties and not against the Government.

We do not purport to assess the merits or demerits of the "American rule" with respect to the allowance of attorneys' fees. It has been criticized in recent years, and courts have been urged to find exceptions to it. It is also apparent from our national experience that the encouragement of private action to implement public policy has been viewed as desireable in a variety of circumstances. But the rule followed in our courts with respect to attorneys' fees has survived. It is deeply rooted in our history and in congressional policy; and it is not for us to invade the legislature's province by redistributing litigation costs in the manner suggested by respondents and followed by the Court of Appeals.

The decision below must therefore be reversed.

[Mr. Justice Douglas and Mr. Justice Powell took no part in the consideration or decision of the case. Mr. Justice Brennan dissented on the basis of Judge Wright's decision for the Court of Appeals. Mr. Justice Marshall also dissented, arguing that the beneficiaries of plaintiffs' efforts were the general public and that imposing a fee award upon Alyeska would ultimately serve to impose the fee burden on the public.]

Notes and Questions

1. What limits, if any, are there in the "private attorney general" rationale for award of attorneys' fees? Is it enough that plaintiff represents a broad class that would assertedly be benefited by litigation? Would reimbursement be limited to cases based on "important" statutory policies? If so, how would "importance" be defined? Does plaintiff have to win in order to secure a fee award? What sorts of litigants would be entitled to fee awards in litigation against the federal government? A nonprofit organization, such as Pacific Legal Foundation, representing business interests? A union? A state or local government? A small business firm?

2. Is it ever appropriate to use the "private attorney general" rationale to award fees against a private party to the litigation because the government is statutorily immune?

3. As noted in the Supreme Court's decision, attorney fee awards are occasionally authorized in specific statutes. For example, following *Alyeska*, Congress amended 42 U.S.C. §1988 to authorize fee awards in suits brought against state officials or authorities under provisions of the Civil Rights Acts, 42 U.S.C. §1981-1983, 1985-1986. During the 1970s, Congress has frequently included attorney fee provisions in newly enacted regulatory statues. These provisions — which are designed to encourage "citizen suits" to enforce regulatory controls against private firms where the agency fails so to do, and to challenge the agency's failure to discharge its statutory mandate — generally authorize an award of fees against the government as well as other parties. See e.g., Clean Air Act sections 304(d), 307(f), 42 U.S.C. §§ 7604(d), 7607(f). These statutes usually fail to provide specific criteria for courts to decide when fees should be awarded or what the amount of fees should be. For example, §304(d) of the Clean Air Act authorizes fee awards "to any party whenever the court determines such an award is appropriate." [21] Should more specific criteria be provided?

Senator Kennedy has proposed legislation, S.2715, 94th Cong. (1975), that would authorize fee awards against the federal government in all litigation involving it if: (1) the court (or the agency, after suit is filed) affords the litigant the relief sought in substantial measure; (2) the court determines that the litigation

---

21. Does this provision authorize a fee award against a plaintiff? In what circumstances would such an award be appropriate?

"served an important public purpose"; and (3) the economic interest of the litigant (or of most of its members, if the litigant is a group or organization) is small in comparison to the costs of the litigation, or the litigant demonstrates that he does not have sufficient resources to participate in the absence of a fee award.

The legislation was reintroduced in the 95th Congress, however, and was not passed (S.240, 95th Cong. (1975)).

In response to the practices of some district judges in awarding fees to public interest lawyers at lower than commercial private practice rates, the statute would require all awards to be based on prevailing market rates.

Does this proposed legislation provide justifiable and workable criteria for fee awards? [22]

4. Provisions for award of attorneys' fees and court litigation expenses apply only to the stage of judicial review of administrative action. But the expenses of participating in a complex and protracted administrative proceeding can exceed by many times the costs of court review. Even in the case of notice and comment rulemaking, the costs of effective participation can be high if there are large amounts of technical material that must be mastered by lawyers and expert advisers. What arrangements, if any, should be made for advancing or reimbursing such expenses out of government funds or otherwise?

There are a few instances where specific statutes authorize agencies to reimburse litigants for the expenses of participating in administrative proceedings before the agency. For example, the FTC is authorized to reimburse the expenses of participants in certain FTC rulemaking proceedings where the participant could not otherwise afford to participate,[23] and represents an interest "which would not otherwise be adequately represented" and whose representation "is necessary for a fair determination of the rulemaking proceeding taken as a whole." Other federal agencies have recently explored whether their general statutory mandates give them implicit authority to spend agency funds to support intervenors, although the Second Circuit has recently adopted a restricted approach and rejected a claim of such implied authority when made by a litigant seeking reimbursement.[24]

Should there be broader authorization for awards by agencies to participants in agency proceedings? What criteria for awards is appropriate? Should they be different than those for the award of attorneys' fees and litigation expenses at the judicial review stage? What problems are created by letting the agency decide which participants should receive awards? Might public interest groups in time

---

22. See Public Participation in Federal Agency Proceedings, S.2715, Hearings Before the Administrative Practice and Procedures Subcomm. of the Senate Judiciary Comm., 94th Cong., 2d Sess. (1976).

23. See 5 U.S.C. §18(h)(i). Would this exclude a national public interest consumer group with a $1 million operating budget?

24. See Greene County Planning Bd. v. FPC, 559 F.2d 1227 (2d Cir. 1977) (*en banc*), *cert. denied*, 434 U.S. 1086 (1978).

The legislation proposed by Senator Kennedy to authorize attorney fee awards generally in litigation against the federal government, S.2715, would also provide general authorization for agency award of participation expense. See note 22, supra. See generally Note, Federal Agency Assistance to Impecunious Intervenors, 88 Harv. L. Rev. 1815 (1975).

be "co-opted" by the hand that feeds them? What should be the scope of judicial review (if any) of agency decision on awards of participation expenses?

A "public interest" intervenor in a licensing or enforcement proceeding negotiates a settlement with the applicant or respondent. May the settlement provide for payment of the intervenor's attorney fees and expenses by the applicant or respondent? Would such a practice encourage interventions for "hold up" purposes? What is the responsibility of the agency or reviewing court in policing such settlements? See Office of Communications of United Church of Christ v. FCC, 465 F.2d 519 (D.C. Cir. 1972).

6. Concluding Notes and Questions: The Interest Representative Model of Administrative Law

(1) Is "interest representation" a viable concept for administrative law? Is it feasible to provide a surrogate for political processes through formal adversary procedures and judicial review?

Quite apart from some of the other problems we have surveyed, how do we ensure that public interest advocates are faithfully representing the constituencies for which they claim to speak? To what extent would these problems be resolved or exacerbated by creation of government advocate agencies, such as the proposed Consumer Protection Agency (see p. 162, supra), to represent special constituencies?

(2) Will the funds ever be made available to provide representation for organized "public" interests on a par with that now enjoyed by business firms and the federal government itself? If so, will the burden of litigation and adversary procedures grow intolerable? If not, the interest representative model will not be fully implemented and may serve a function that is in large part cosmetic.

(3) If we wish to redirect administrative decisionmaking along "interest representation" lines, why not restructure the administrative process in explicitly political terms? For example, why not have Congress provide for popular election of agency heads? [25] Would such an arrangement be constitutional? Cf. Humphrey's Executor v. United States, p. 88, supra.

Alternatively, major regulatory agencies might be headed by collegial bodies whose membership would be selected or elected by specified private interest groups — trade associations, labor unions, consumer organizations, environmental groups, etc.[26] Would such an arrangement be constitutional? Consider the Schechter decision, p. 63, supra.

(4) Is interest representation in any event an appropriate ideal for administrative decision? Do we always want administrative policies to represent a compromise among the various interests affected by them? Might an interest representative model exacerbate rather than remedy agency "failure"?

---

25. Many states during the late 19th Century provided for popular election of regulatory commissioners. See Stewart, The Reformation of American Administrative Law, 88 Harv. L. Rev. 1667, 1793 (1975).

    26. See Id. at 1793-1797.

B. Public Disclosure of Agency Information and Decisionmaking

In this section we examine two recent statutes which reflect an approach to control of agency discretion quite different from the interest representation model examined in the previous section. The Freedom of Information Act mandates (with specified exemptions) disclosure, upon request by "any person," by federal agencies, of any document in their possession. The Government in the Sunshine Act requires that all meetings (subject to specified exceptions) of certain multimember federal agencies be open to the public. The theory of both statutes seems to be that public disclosure will improve agency decisionmaking and check the influence of well organized interests that are adept at informal lobbying. Alternatively, they may reflect the view that in a democratic political system, public disclosure is a virtue in itself, quite apart from its impact on substantive policy outcomes. In reviewing the materials which follow, you will want to assess these objectives and the success of the two statutes in meeting them. Consider that there are legitimate and often powerful governmental and private interests in confidentiality, and that disclosure requirements are often invoked for commercial or litigation purposes. Consider also the role of the courts, which are given a key role by the statutes in reviewing agencies' failure to disclose documents or open meetings to the public. Does it differ from that exercised by courts in reviewing administrative agencies in more traditional contexts?

1. The Freedom of Information Act

The Freedom of Information Act (FOIA), which requires federal agencies to make available to the public any written information in their possession unless specifically exempted, is a revision of the original (1946) §3 of the Administrative Procedure Act, the first general statutory provision for disclosure of executive branch records. Because the original §3 contained many provisions which hindered its effectiveness as a disclosure statute, a series of legislative attempts were made to close the loopholes, culminating in the passage of the Freedom of Information Act in 1966, codified in portions of §552 of the APA. The Act requires federal agencies, upon application, to make available to "any person" any written information in their possession unless the information is within one of nine exemptions from compelled disclosure. Applicants for information are entitled to have their complaint heard de novo by a federal district court, and "the burden is on the agency to sustain its action." Noncompliance with court orders is punishable as contempt. The FOIA was broadly conceived as a means of reducing governmental secrecy by making public disclosure the general rule rather than the exception. Although thousands of persons successfully utilized the FOIA to obtain information during the first years of its operation, a number of commentators and legislators voiced disappointment with the functioning of the Act, identifying the following general problems in the administration of the Act:

Excessive bureaucratic delays in responding to requests for documents (a combination of bureaucratic delays and urgent news deadlines led to little utilization of the law by the news media); excessive fees that were charged for searching and copying documents; agency requirements that requesters identify with precision the documents requested (in circumstances where requesters typically had little or no knowledge as to what documents the agency possessed); and the cost and delay of lawsuits (usually successful) to force agency disclosure. In sum, although much improvement was found in the dissemination of information compared with the pre-FOIA situation, the efficient operation of the FOIA was "hindered by years of foot-dragging by the Federal bureaucracy." [27]

To remedy these shortcomings, amendments to the FOIA were passed over President Ford's veto in 1974. The amended Act provides for the indexing of certain documents, sets administrative time limits within which an agency must respond to requests for information, and subjects government officials who act arbitrarily or capriciously in withholding information to disciplinary proceedings conducted by the Civil Service Commission. In addition, the amendments: permit in camera judicial inspection of classified documents at the discretion of the district court; require that the government serve an answer to a complaint within thirty days, rather than the usual 60 days allowed the government (unless the court otherwise directs for good cause shown); require annual agency reports to Congress; revise the wording of two exemptions; and permit the awarding of attorneys' fees to plaintiffs who are forced to litigate to secure documents and who substantially prevail in the court suit. Uniform agency fees for search and duplication, limited to direct costs, were also established. The fees may be waived or reduced if "furnishing the information can be considered as primarily benefiting the general public."

Although the avowed purpose of the FOIA is to promote public oversight of the conduct of government, requesters have sought to force disclosure of agency documents for a great variety of purposes. Substantial FOIA litigation has been brought by "public interest" groups to expose the workings of government or scrutinize the implementation and enforcement of statutes. The press and media have also utilized the FOIA. But the FOIA is more frequently used to obtain information which an agency has required third parties to file with it. In most such instances, the requesting party is a business firm seeking to discover a rival's trade secrets or other competitively sensitive information. In some cases, however, "public interest" groups have sought to force disclosure of product safety and performance information filed by manufacturers.

---

27. House Comm. on Government Operations, Administration of the Freedom of Information Act, H.R. Rep. No. 1419, 92d Cong., 2d Sess. 8 (1972) (hereinafter cited as House Report). See also Katz, The Games Bureaucrats Play: Hide and Seek Under the Freedom of Information Act, 48 Tex. L. Rev. 1261 (1970); Nader, Freedom From Information: The Act and the Agencies, 5 Harv. C.R.-C.L. L. Rev. 1 (1970); Note, The Freedom of Information Act: A Seven-Year Assessment, 74 Colum. L. Rev. 895, 957 (1974) ("That the Act is a substantial improvement over section 3 of the APA is undeniable. Less clear but equally certain is that the present [unamended] statute cannot attain the lofty ideals that mesmerized its drafters."); Note, The Freedom of Information Act: A Critical Review, 38 Geo. Wash. L. Rev. 150 (1969).

FOIA requests are also utilized as a litigation tool. Discovery may be used to acquire evidence for use in agency adjudication, or in judicial review of informal rulemaking. Or the documents requested may be utilized in litigation with third parties. Discovery is sometimes sought to ascertain "secret law" — the informal practices which an agency utilizes, for example in settling disputed tax claims.[28] In 1972, a House Report estimated that FOIA requests by corporations and private law firms were three times the total requests from news media, public-owned interest organizations, and researchers.[29]

To what extent should the courts, in construing the various provisions of the Act, consider the purposes for which the information is sought?

a. The Exemptions from Disclosure

At this point, you should review the nine exemptions from disclosure, set forth in 5 U.S.C. §552(b).

(1) The National Security Exemption

The present version of the first exemption reflects 1974 amendments responding to the Supreme Court's decision in EPA v. Mink, 410 U.S. 73 (1973), which involved an attempt to compel disclosure of classified executive documents pertaining to the environmental effects of a scheduled underground nuclear test. Prior to the 1974 amendments, Exemption One applied to matters "specifically required by Executive order to be kept secret in the interest of the national defense or foreign policy." The Supreme Court held that the statute did not authorize courts to reexamine the justification for executive classification of a document as secret for purposes of national security; the executive's classification must be accepted at face value. It also reversed the District Court for ordering in camera inspection of agency documents to determine whether disclosure of unclassified portions was feasible. The 1974 amendments specifically authorize in camera review of requested documents in all FOIA cases at the discretion of the district court. See §552(a)-(4)(B). The amendments also redrafted Exemption One to restrict executive discretion to classify documents as secret by requiring that the executive develop criteria for classification and that the documents sought to be withheld in fact be properly classified in accordance with such criteria. In theory, the new provisions would permit de novo court review of national security classification by the executive; this feature of the 1974 Amendments was the focus of President Ford's veto

---

28. Litigation reflecting these and other uses of the FOIA is summarized in a useful handbook, ACLU Foundation Project on National Security and Civil Liberties, Litigation Under the Amended Federal Freedom of Information Act (C. Marwick, ed.; 4th ed. 1978).

29. H.R. Rep. No. 1419, 92d Cong. 2d Sess. (1972).

message to Congress.[30] In practice, however, courts may be reluctant to inspect classified documents in camera or to second-guess executive decisions in national security classification.[31]

The scope of Exemption One may be importantly affected by Executive Order 12065, issued by President Carter in 1978, which imposes new limitations, procedures, and criteria designed to curtail the classification of documents as secret or confidential where such classification is not warranted by considerations of national security. Section 3-303 provides a balancing test for declassification of classified documents with national security significance where the "need to protect such information may be outweighed by the public interest in disclosure of the information." Responsible officials are directed to determine "whether the public interest in disclosure outweighs the damage to national security that might reasonably be expected from disclosure." Are these provisions judicially enforceable?

(2) The Internal Personnel Rules and Practices Exemption

Section 552(b)(2) exempts from disclosure documents which are "related solely to the international personnel rules and practices of an agency." A number of commentators have suggested that this exemption is unnecessary and out of keeping with the full-disclosure philosophy of the Act.[32] The House and Senate reports on the FOIA reports appear to vary considerably on the scope of Exemption Two. The Senate report suggests a narrow interpretation, with the exemption permitting the nondisclosure of such information as parking regulations, lunch schedules, and sick-leave policies; the House report would extend the internal per-

---

30. Vetoing H.R. 12471, To Amend Freedom of Information Act, A Message from the President of the United States, H. Doc. 383, 93d Cong., 2d Sess. (1974). Ford's veto message also objected to the rewriting of section seven (the investigatory law enforcement file provision) and to the "unrealistic" time limits for administrative responses to requests for information.

The veto message also suggested that the 1974 FOIA amendments may be unconstitutional. The legislation extends judicial power to the inspection of even the most highly secret documents and this extension is likely to some day clash with an assertion of executive privilege.

31. See, e.g., Epstein v. Resor, 421 F.2d 930 (9th Cir.), cert. den., 398 U.S. 965 (1970) ("[W]hat is desirable in the interest of national defense and foreign policy is not the sort of question that courts are designed to deal with."); Wolfe v. Froehlke, 358 F. Supp. 1318 (D.D.C. 1973), aff'd, 510 F.2d 654 (D.C. Cir. 1974); Weissman v. CIA, 565 F.2d 692 (D.C. Cir. 1977).

For discussion of the appropriate judicial role with respect to classified documents, see Note, In Camera Inspections Under the Freedom of Information Act, 41 U. Chi. L. Rev. 557 (1974); Note, The Freedom of Information Act: A Seven-Year Assessment, 74 Colum. L. Rev. 895, 933-936 (1974); Developments in the Law, The National Security Interest and Civil Liberties, 85 Harv. L. Rev. 1130, 1221-1228 (1974).

32. Davis, The Information Act: A Preliminary Analysis, 34 U. Chi. L. Rev. 761, 786 (1967); Note, The Freedom of Information Act: A Seven-Year Assessment, 74 Colum. L. Rev. 895, 956-957 (1974) ("An apparently insoluble puzzle is why exemption 2 exists at all."). But see Note, The 1966 Freedom of Information Act, 44 U. Wash. L. Rev. 641, 664 n.103 (1969) (The public has "no interest in most records used for internal housekeeping, and requests for such records would probably be motivated by a desire to harass rather than by genuine interest.").

sonnel rules and practices exemption to permit nondisclosure of operating rules, guidelines and manuals of procedures.[33]

Two primary purposes might arguably underlie Exemption Two: the protection of employee personal privacy (although this matter is specifically addressed in Exemption Six) and the protection of agencies from harassment. Although its language could be interpreted in an extremely broad fashion, the usefulness of Exemption Two to agencies as a means of withholding information from the public has been substantially limited by the Supreme Court in the following case.

Dept. of the Air Force v. Rose

425 U.S. 352 (1976)

BRENNAN, J., delivered the opinion of the Court:

Respondents, student editors or former student editors of the New York University Law Review researching disciplinary systems and procedures at the military service academies for an article for the Law Review, were denied access by petitioners to case summaries of honor and ethics hearings, with personal references or other identifying information deleted, maintained in the United States Air Force Academy's Honor and Ethics Code reading files.... Thereupon respondents brought this action under the Freedom of Information Act ... in the District Court for the Southern District of New York.... The district court granted petitioner Agency's motion for summary judgment [finding that the requested documents came within Exemption Two. However, the District Court rejected the Academy's reliance on Exemption Six, §552(b)(6), for "personnel and medical files and similar files the disclosure of which would constitute a clearly unwarranted invasion of personal privacy." The Court of Appeals reversed the District Court's ruling on Exemption Two. With respect to Exemption Six, it found that the Academy had not established a blanket right to exemption, but that the privacy concerns implicated were potentially substantial; accordingly, it directed the Academy to submit the case summaries to the District Court for in camera inspection, and suggested that the Academy cooperate with the judge in redacting (editing) the summaries to protect privacy values. The Court of Appeals indicated that the District Court might ultimately decide not to require any disclosure if important privacy values could be protected by redacting.

The Court summarized disciplinary procedures for enforcement of the Academy's Honor Code, which are supervised by an Honor Committee. Upon completion of disciplinary hearings a] case summary consisting of a brief statement, usually only one page, of the significant facts is prepared by the Committee.... [C]opies of the summaries are posted on 40 squadron bulletin boards throughout the Academy, and distributed among Academy faculty and administration officials. Cadets

---

33. S. Rep. No. 813, 89th Cong., 1st Sess. at 8 (1965); H.R. Rep. No. 1497, 88th Cong., 2d Sess. at 10 (1966).

are instructed not to read the summaries, unless they have a need, beyond mere curiosity, to know their contents, and the [Committee's] Reading Files are covered with a notice that they are "for official use only." Case summaries for not guilty and discretion cases are circulated with names deleted; in guilty cases, the guilty cadet's name is not deleted from the summary, but posting on the bulletin boards is deferred until after the guilty cadet has left the Academy.

. . . The implication for the general public of the Academy's administration of discipline is obvious, particularly so in light of the unique role of the military. What we have said of the military in other contexts has equal application here: it "constitutes a specialized community governed by a separate discipline from that of the civilian," in which the internal law of command and obedience invests the military officer with "a particular position of responsibility." Within this discipline, the accuracy and effect of a superior's command depends critically upon the specific and customary reliability of subordinates, just as the instinctive obedience of subordinates depends upon the unquestioned specific and customary reliability of the superior. The importance of these considerations to the maintenance of a force able and ready to fight effectively renders them undeniably significant to the public role of the military. Moreover, the same essential integrity is critical to the military's relationship with its civilian direction. Since the purpose of the Honor and Ethics Code administered and enforced at the Air Force Academy is to ingrain reflexes basic to these responsibilities in future Air Force officers, and to select out those candidates apparently unlikely to serve these standards, it follows that the nature of this instruction — and its adequacy or inadequacy — is significantly related to the substantive public role of the Air Force and its Academy.

. . . Exemption 2 is not applicable to matters subject to such a genuine and significant public interest. The exemption was not designed to authorize withholding of all matters except otherwise secret law bearing directly on the propriety of actions of members of the public. Rather, the general thrust of the exemption is simply to relieve agencies of the burden of assembling and maintaining for public inspection matters in which the public could not reasonably be expected to have an interest. The case summaries plainly do not fit that description. They are not matters with merely internal significance. They do not concern only routine matters. Their disclosure entails no particular administrative burden. [The Court concluded that the case summaries, edited to preserve anonymity, did not fall within Exemption Two.]

Additional questions are involved in the determination whether Exemption 6 exempts the case summaries from mandatory disclosure as "personnel and medical files and similar files the disclosure of which would constitute a clearly unwarranted invasion of personal privacy." [The Court rejected the Academy's arguments that the case summaries were "personnel files," and that all "personnel files" were automatically exempt because the "unwarranted invasion of privacy" requirement applies only to "similar files."]

[Respondents'] request for access to summaries "with personal references or other identifying information deleted," respected the confidentiality interests embodied in Exemption 6. As the Court of Appeals recognized, however, what constitutes identifying information regarding a subject cadet must be weighed not only from the viewpoint of the public, but also from the vantage of those who would have been familiar, as fellow cadets or Academy staff, with other aspects of his career at the Academy. Despite the summaries' distribution within the Academy, many of this group with earlier access to summaries may never have identified a particular cadet, or may have wholly forgotten his encounter with Academy discipline. And the risk to the privacy interests of a former cadet, particularly one who has remained in the military, posed by his identification by otherwise unknowing former colleagues or instructors cannot be rejected as trivial. We nevertheless conclude that consideration of the policies underlying the Freedom of Information Act, to open public business to public view when no "clearly unwarranted" invasion of privacy will result, requires affirmance of the holding of the Court of Appeals. . . . [The in camera procedure ordered by the Court of Appeals] will further the statutory goal of Exemption Six: a workable compromise between individual rights "and the preservation of public rights to Government information."

To be sure, redaction cannot eliminate all risks of identifiability, as any human approximation risks some degree of imperfection, and the consequences of exposure of identity can admittedly be severe. But redaction is a familiar technique in other contexts and exemptions to disclosure under the Act were intended to be practical workable concepts. Moreover, we repeat, Exemption 6 does not protect against disclosure every incidental invasion of privacy — only such disclosures as constitute "clearly unwarranted" invasions of personal privacy.

Affirmed.

Mr. Justice STEVENS took no part in the consideration or decision of this case.

Mr. Chief Justice BURGER, dissenting.

The Court correctly notes that Congress, in enacting Exemption 6, intended to strike "a proper balance between the protection of the individual's right of privacy and the preservation of the public's right to Government information by excluding those kinds of files the disclosure of which might harm the individual." H. R. Rep. No. 1497, at 11. Having acknowledged the necessity of such a balance, however, the Court, in my view, blandly ignores and thereby frustrates the congressional intent by refusing to weigh, realistically, the grave consequences implicit in release of this particular information, in any form, against the relatively inconsequential claim of "need" for the material alleged in the complaint.

The opinions of this Court have long recognized the opprobrium which both the civilian and the military segments of our society attribute to allegations of dishonor among commissioned officers of our Armed Forces. . . . The absence of the broken sword, the torn epaulets and the *Rogue's March* from our military ritual does not lessen the indelibility of the stigma.

Admittedly, the Court requires that, before release, these documents be subject to in camera inspection with power of excising parts. But, as the Court admits, any such attempt to "sanitize" these summaries would still leave the very distinct possibility that the individual would still be identifiable and thereby injured. In light of Congress' recent manifest concern in the Privacy Act of 1974, it is indeed difficult to attribute to Congress a willingness to subject an individual citizen to the risk of possible severe damage to his reputation simply to permit law students to invade individual privacy to prepare a law journal article. . . . [The Chief Justice quoted a passage from the Senate Report on the FOIA equating "clearly unwarranted invasion of individual privacy" with "protecting an individual's private affairs from unnecessary public scrutiny."]

Moreover, excision would not only be ineffectual in accomplishing the legislative intent of protecting an individual's affairs from unnecessary public scrutiny, but it would place an intolerable burden upon a district court which, in my view, Congress never intended to inflict. Although the 1974 amendments to the Freedom of Information Act request that "[a]ny reasonably segregable portion of a record . . . ," 5 U.S.C. §552(b), otherwise exempt, be provided, there is nothing in the legislative history of the original Act or its amendments which would require a district court to construct, in effect, a new document. Yet, the excision process mandated here could only require such a sweeping reconstruction of the material that the end product would constitute an entirely new document. No provision of the Freedom of Information Act contemplates a federal district judge acting as a "re-write editor" of the original material.

If the Court's holding is indeed a fair reflection of congressional intent, we are confronted with a "split-personality" legislative reaction, by the conflict between a seeming passion for privacy and a comparable passion for needless invasions of privacy.

Accordingly, I would reverse the judgment of the Court of Appeals.

[The dissenting opinions of Justice BLACKMUN and Justice REHNQUIST are omitted.]

(3)   The Exemption for Documents Governed by Statutes Which Specifically Direct Nondisclosure

As originally enacted in 1966, Exemption Three simply stated that nondisclosure is permissible if the matter is "specifically exempted from disclosure by statute." The primary question concerning Exemption Three was whether the language of the exemption authorized nondisclosure when a statute granted discretionary power to an agency to determine whether disclosure is in the public interest and the agency decided not to disclose. Courts of Appeals had gone both ways on the issue until the Supreme Court spoke on the matter in 1975. In FAA Administration v. Robertson, 422 U.S. 255 (1975), the Court held that the FOIA authorizes nondisclosure where a statute grants an agency discretionary power not to disclose. Congress in 1976 legislatively overruled Robertson, adopting the present language of Exemption Three, 5 U.S.C. §552(b)(3).[34] As a result of the 1976 amendment, carried as a rider to the Sunshine Act, the focus of Exemption Three has been significantly narrowed. See American Jewish Congress v. Kreps, 574 F.2d

_____

34. Pub. L. 94-409, 90 Stat. 1247 (1976). See generally, Note, Effect of the 1976 Amendment to Exemption Three of the Freedom of Information Act, 76 Colum. L. Rev. 1029 (1976).

624 (D.C. Cir. 1978). It is possible that Congress will find it necessary to specifically redraft other statutes if it is desired to preserve certain types of data from disclosure.

(4) The Private Business Information Exemption

Exemption Four of the Act, 5 U.S.C. §552(b)(4), provides that "trade secrets or commercial and financial information obtained from a person and privileged or confidential need not be disclosed to the public." [35] The Exemption reflects the fact that the primary purpose of the FOIA is citizen scrutiny of the federal government rather than to open private businesses to public scrutiny.

Documents containing information that represents a common-law "trade secret" are automatically exempted from disclosure. Otherwise they must (a) contain "commercial or financial information," (b) obtained from a "person," (c) which is "confidential or privileged." National Parks and Conservation Ass'n v. Morton, 498 F.2d 765, 770 (D.C. Cir. 1974) held that information is "confidential" and thus within Exemption Four if its disclosure would be likely to "cause substantial harm to the competitive position" of the person who submitted it, or if disclosure is likely to "impair the Government's ability to obtain necessary information in the future." Commentators critical of National Parks have argued, relying on the legislative history, that the exemption should be limited to information "which would not be released to the public by the person from whom it was obtained," [36] and that competitive harm is otherwise irrelevant. If "competitive harm" is relevant, what showing of competitive harm is necessary to block disclosure? [37] Alternatively, what must be shown to establish an exemption based on the chilling effect that disclosure would have on the government's ability to obtain information? Is it sufficient that the government pledged confidentiality when it elicited the information in question? [38] That the government has legal authority to compel disclosure of such information?

35. See generally, Drachsler, The Freedom of Information Act and the "Right" of Non-Disclosure, 28 Ad. L. Rev. 1 (1976); Kuersteiner & Herbach, Freedom of Information Act: An Examination of the Commercial or Financial Exemption, 16 Santa Clara L. Rev. 193 (1976); Note, Public Disclosure of Confidential Business Information Under the Freedom of Information Act: Toward a More Objective Standard, 60 Cornell L. Rev. 109 (1974); Comment, 88 Harv. L. Rev. 470 (1974).

36. S. Rep. No. 813, 89th Cong., 1st Sess. 9 (1965). See, e.g., Patten & Weinstein, Disclosure of Business Secrets Under the Freedom of Information Act: Suggested Limitations, 29 Ad. L. Rev. 193, 196 (1977) ("[I]t is probably accurate to say that Congress did not have anything like the National Parks test for confidentiality in mind...."). But cf., Project, Government Information and the Rights of Citizens, 73 Mich. L. Rev. 971, 1061-1069 (1975) (suggesting that the National Parks test is a major advance). A majority of commentators have argued that the exemption is too narrow, with some taking the position than any information elicited under a promise of confidentiality should not have to be divulged. See, e.g., Davis, The Information Act: A Preliminary Analysis, 34 U. Chi. L. Rev. 761, 787-788 (1967).

37. See the decision in National Parks after remand, 547 F.2d 673 (D.C. Cir. 1976).

38. See Ackerley v. Ley, 420 F.2d 1336, 1339-1340 n.3 (D.C. Cir. 1969).

The phrase "obtained from a person" is generally said to limit the availability of the exemption to information obtained from persons outside the government.[39] Litigation and administrative problems encountered by businesses which seek to prevent agency disclosure of information which they submitted to the agency — the so-called "Reverse FOIA" problem — will be discussed below.

(5) The Exemption for Agency Memoranda

Exemption Five, 5 U.S.C. §552(b)(5) was intended to incorporate the common law privilege of the government from discovery in litigation.[40] Thus pre-FOIA cases dealing with traditional concepts of privilege are relevant to the scope of this exemption. The purpose of Exemption Five is to preserve free and frank discussions within government, which would be hindered if each opinion and recommendation during the deliberative process could be obtained by the public. The contours of Exemption Five are discussed in the following decision.

Mead Data Central, Inc. v. Dept. of the Air Force

566 F.2d 242 (D.C. Cir. 1977)

TAMM, Circuit Judge:
In early 1975, Mead Data filed a FOIA request with the Air Force seeking disclosure of several categories of documents dealing generally with the Department's "Project FLITE [an acronym for Federal Legal Information Through Electronics]," a computerized legal research system. [As part of its planning for FLITE, the Air Force proposed to use the West Publishing Company's "key number" system, and entered into negotiations with West for that purpose. Various copyright issues were raised by these negotiations and by FLITE in general. Mead offers a computerized case indexing system in competition with another such system offered by West.] The Air Force agreed to disclose some of the requested documents, but [refused to disclose seven documents, which it claimed to be subject to Exemption Five.] The Air Force characterized three of these seven documents as legal opinions of Air Force attorneys advising their client as to applicable law and recommending courses of action with respect to Project FLITE. The other four were described as internal memoranda prepared by Air Force employees, which reflect the course of negotiations between the Air Force and West Publishing Co. for a licensing agreement to use the copyrighted West key number system and offer recommendations

---

39. Grumman Aircraft Engineer. Corp. v. Renegotiation Board, 425 F.2d 578, 582 (D.C. Cir. 1970); Consumers Union v. VA, 301 F. Supp. 796 (S.D.N.Y. 1969), *appeal dismissed*, 436 F.2d 1363 (2d Cir. 1971).

40. Exemption Five provides that agencies may withhold "inter-agency or intra-agency memorandums or letters which would not be available by law to a party other than an agency in litigation with the agency." See generally, Note, The Freedom of Information Act and the Exemption for Intra-Agency Memoranda, 86 Harv. L. Rev. 1047 (1973).

as to negotiating positions. The Air Force claimed that the legal opinions fell within the attorney-client privilege incorporated into Exemption Five of the FOIA, and that the internal memoranda were also covered by that exemption because their disclosure would adversely affect the decisional process within the Air Force by inhibiting the expression of candid opinions. . . .

The dispute between the parties in this case over whether the information sought by Mead Data is within Exemption Five of the FOIA centers basically around the question of how that information ought to be characterized. Mead Data contends that the information is purely factual and that consequently its disclosure would not adversely affect the Air Force's deliberative process. . . .

Where there is such a factual dispute over the nature of the information sought in a FOIA suit, the lack of access of the party seeking disclosure undercuts the traditional adversarial theory of judicial dispute resolution. Vaughn v. Rosen (*Vaughn I*), 484 F.2d 820, 824-825 (D.C. Cir. 1973), *cert. denied*, 415 U.S. 977 (1974). Although in camera inspection of the disputed documents may compensate somewhat for this deficiency, it is a far from perfect substitute. Moreover, as this court held in *Vaughn I*, supra at 825, the burden which the FOIA specifically places on the Government to show that the information withheld is exempt from disclosure cannot be satisfied by the sweeping and conclusory citation of an exemption plus submission of disputed material for in camera inspection. Id. at 825-826. Thus, we require that when an agency seeks to withhold information it must provide a relatively detailed justification, specifically identifying the reasons why a particular exemption is relevant and correlating those claims with the particular part of a withheld document to which they apply. . . .

Considering the elaborated description and justification provided by the Air Force's affidavits, we agree with the district court that the withheld documents were described in sufficient detail to allow Mead Data to argue effectively against the Department's exemption claims. In this respect, the present case is far different from the situation which sparked the remand in *Vaughn I* — broad, sweeping, generalized claims under several exemptions covering voluminous information running many hundreds of pages. . . . We agree that the attorney-client privilege has a proper role to play in Exemption Five cases. The policy objective of that privilege is certainly consistent with the policy objective of the exemption. Exemption Five is intended to protect the quality of agency decision-making by preventing the disclosure requirement of the FOIA from cutting off the flow of information to agency decision-makers. Certainly this covers professional advice on legal questions which bears on those decisions. The opinion of even the finest attorney, however, is no better than the information which his client provides. In order to ensure that a client receives the best possible legal advice, based on a full and frank discussion with his attorney, the attorney-client privilege assures him that confidential communications to his attorney will not be disclosed without his consent. We see no reason why this same protection should not be extended to an agency's communications with its attorneys under Exemption Five. . . . [However, the court noted that, in the Federal courts, the privilege for attorney-client communications was limited to those based on information disclosed by the client to the attorney in confidence. With respect to two out of the three withheld documents for which an attorney-client privilege was claimed, the court found no showing that they had been based on such information. The third document was based on the course of the negotiations between the Air Force and West — the information in it was held not to support a privilege between the Air Force and its legal officers because the information was also known to West.] On remand, the court should order disclosure of these documents unless the Air Force demonstrates either that the attorney-client privilege does apply to these documents because the information on which they are based was supplied by the Air Force with the expectation of secrecy and was not known by or disclosed to any third party, or that they fall within Exemption Five for some other reason. . . .

It generally has been accepted that Exemption Five incorporates the governmental privilege, developed in discovery cases, to protect documents containing advisory opinions and recommendations or reflecting deliberations comprising the process by which government policy is formulated. Under this facet of Exemption Five, the courts have required disclosure of essentially factual material but allowed agencies to withhold documents which reveal their deliberative or policy-making processes.

Congress adopted Exemption Five in recognition of the merits of arguments from the executive branch that the quality of administrative decision-making would be seriously undermined if agencies were forced to "operate in a fishbowl" because the full and frank exchange of ideas on legal or policy matters would be impossible. A decision that certain information falls within Exemption Five should therefore rest fundamentally on the conclusion that, unless protected from public disclosure, information of that type would not flow freely within the agency.

Many Exemption Five disputes may be able to be decided by application of the simple test that factual material must be disclosed but advisory material, containing opinions and recommendations, may be withheld. The test offers a quick, clear, and predictable rule of decision, but courts must be careful not to become victims of their own semantics. Exemption Five is intended to protect the deliberative process of government and not just deliberative material. Montrose Chemical Corp. v. Train, 491 F.2d 63, 68-71 (D.C. Cir. 1974). Perhaps in the great majority of cases that purpose is well served by focusing on the nature of the information sought. In some circumstances, however, the disclosure of even purely factual material may so expose the deliberative process within an agency that it must be deemed exempted by §552(b)(5). . . .

. . . Predecisional materials are not exempt merely because they are predecisional; they must also be a part of the deliberative process within a government agency. Vaughn v. Rosen (Vaughn II), 523 F.2d 1136, 1144 (D.C. Cir. 1975). The documents in this case which would reveal the Air Force's internal self-evaluation of its contract negotiations, including discussion of the merits of past efforts, alternatives currently available, and recommendations as to future strategy, fall clearly within this test. Information about the "deliberative" or negotiating process outside an agency, between itself and an outside party, does not. Moreover, neither of the policy objectives which Exemption Five is designed to serve — avoiding premature disclosure of agency decisions and encouraging the free exchange of ideas among administrative personnel — is relevant to a claim of secrecy for a proceeding between an agency and an outside party. All of the information as to what the Air Force offered West Publishing, initially and in response to West's counteroffers, has already been fully disclosed to at least one party outside the Department — West itself — and the Department has no control over further disclosure.

Perhaps it could be shown that the threat of disclosure of negotiation proceedings would so inhibit private parties from dealing with the Government that agencies must be permitted to withhold such information in order to preserve their ability to effectively arrange for contractual agreements. . . . Arguments that the disclosure mandated by the FOIA would seriously hamper the performance of an agency's other duties have not fared well in the courts, however. An agency cannot meet its statutory burden of justification by conclusory allegations of possible harm. It must show by specific and detailed proof that disclosure would defeat, rather than further, the purposes of the FOIA. [The court concluded that two of the remaining four documents withheld reflected internal negotiation strategy discussion within the Air Force and were exempt, while at least one of the remaining documents merely recounted the progress of negotiations with West, and was, on the showing thus far made, not exempt. However, the court concluded that the entire matter should be remanded because the Air Force had failed to establish that the materials deserving confidential treatment could not be edited out of the documents.]

The district court's judgment that Exemption Five of the FOIA permits the Air Force to withhold all of the material in the seven documents at issue in this case rests on an impermissibly broad interpretation of the attorney-client privilege and the deliberative process privilege. We therefore remand the case for further proceedings. . . .

McGOWAN, Circuit Judge, dissenting:

First, with respect to the attorney-client privilege, I have grave doubts about some of the assumptions which seem to form the foundation of the majority's position. The majority apparently believes that, because West was privy to the course of contract negotiations between itself and the Air Force, the attorney-client privilege cannot apply to legal opinions rendered by Air Force legal officers to the service's contracting and other supervisory personnel. . . .

Adoption of this position would go a long way toward eliminating the attorney-client privilege altogether. In the vast majority of cases, attorney-client discussions concern the client's dealing or relationship with one or more third parties. The mere fact that those third parties are aware of the factual details of their interaction with the client cannot automatically defeat a claim of confidentiality asserted in connection with the client's recounting of that interaction to his attorney. If it could, legal opinions based in part on a client's version of prior negotiations with third parties would always be outside the scope of the privilege.

I think the majority errs in assigning such crucial importance to West's knowledge in this case. The key point is not whether West is familiar with the course of negotiations between the parties, but whether the Air Force's communication with its legal counsel was confidential, i.e., whether the Air Force legitimately expected that its summary of past events to its counsel would remain undisclosed. I do not see why it should not have had that expectation. There is no indication that West or any other third person was privy to the communications between the Air Force and its attorneys. There is no indication that the Air Force publicized, intended to publicize, or expected its attorneys to publicize the substance of those communications to anyone outside the service. That West was aware of some of the facts reported to the Air Force lawyers seems to be largely irrelevant.

Secondly, I think the majority has taken an unnecessarily restrictive view of what constitutes the deliberative process. The opinion states that documents revealing "internal self-evaluation" of contract negotiations would be comprehended within the deliberative process privilege, but information about the actual progress of negotiations with a third party would not. This distinction seems to be untenable. Even a bare recitation of the offers and counter-offers between West and the Air Force cannot help but reflect internal agency decisions and negotiation strategy. Offers made in the course of contract negotiations do not inevitably represent final agency decisions, simply by virtue of the fact that such offers were made to private parties during the bargaining process. The preferable view, I think, is that final action occurs only when the agency definitively determines whether or not to enter into a contract. It is entirely possible, for example, that a particular contract offer was made to West in the full expectation that it would in all likelihood be refused, but would nevertheless lay the groundwork for a later, and substantially altered, proposal.

[See also Mead Data Central Inc. v. Dept. of Air Force, 575 F.2d 932 (D.C. Cir. 1978), upholding the Air Force's invocation of Exemption Five in denying related requests by Mead for Air Force memoranda evaluating Mead's proposal to the Air Force.]

(6) The Personal Privacy Exemption

Under the personal privacy exemption, the public's right to government information must be weighed against the individual's right to privacy. See Department of Air Force v. Rose, supra, discussing this exemption. The Privacy Act of 1974 may have altered the manner in which agencies should apply FOIA Exemption Six, which protects "personnel and medical files and similar files the disclosure of which would constitute a clearly unwarranted invasion of personal privacy." [41] Unlike the FOIA exemption, the Privacy Act prohibits the disclosure of any kind of retrievable information (retrieved by use of the subject's name or number) about an individual. Although the Privacy Act's prohibitives contain a specific exemption for disclosures

---

41. The Privacy Act, 88 Stat. 1897, codified at 5 U.S.C. §552a, permits individuals on whom files are kept by federal agencies to participate in the use, review, and disposal of their files. See generally, Hanus & Relyea, Policy Assessment of the Privacy Act of 1974, 25 Am. U. L. Rev. 555 (1976); Note, Privacy Act of 1974: An Overview, 1976 Duke L. J. 301.

Exemption Six is discussed in Comment, Freedom of Information Act: Personal Information Exempted from Disclosure, 16 B.C. Ind. & Com. L. Rev. 240 (1975); Note, Release of Private Information Under Open Records Laws, 55 Tex. L. Rev. 911 (1977).

mandated by FOIA, and was supposed to have no effect on the FOIA, in practice its impact may prove to be substantial:[42]

> The FOIA privacy exemption is not easy to apply since the standards under it are not concrete nor fully predictable. Before the Privacy Act was enacted an agency would have probably released most requested files and thus minimized the risks. Today, an agency knows that if the file is held to be exempt from FOIA mandatory disclosure, its release might violate the Privacy Act.
>
> Agencies are now faced with a dilemma. If they refuse to disclose the material they risk being sued by the party who requested the file under the FOIA. Under the FOIA the court may award to a successful plaintiff his costs and attorney's fees. If on the other hand, agencies release material, they risk being sued under the Privacy Act by the person who is the subject of the file. In that case, the plaintiff might win by showing that the file was exempt from disclosure under the FOIA. A successful Privacy Act plaintiff can collect not only his costs and attorney's fees but also actual damage sustained because of the disclosure. Thus agencies open themselves to possible liability for damages either by honoring, or refusing to honor, an FOIA request.
>
> Given this situation, agencies would probably choose not to disclose voluntarily under the FOIA in any close case. . . . Even if the agency is of the opinion that the file probably is not exempt from the FOIA, it might still routinely refuse to disclose voluntarily whenever there is any doubt. Such a policy would mean larger numbers of FOIA suits, but it would avoid the risk of the occasional surprising — and expensive — loss of a Privacy Act suit. This problem is simply further indication that the clash between the concerns embodied in the Privacy Act and the open government concerns of the Freedom of Information Act are unlikely to be easily harmonized.

(7) The Investigatory Records Exemption

The initial version of the seventh exemption to the Freedom of Information Act permitted nondisclosure of "investigatory files compiled for law enforcement purposes except to the extent available by law to a party other than an agency." Exemption Seven's broad interpretation by agencies and courts soon brought calls for its revision.[43] Congress rewrote and narrowed the investigatory records exemption in 1974. As amended, Exemption Seven, §552(b)(7), permits information to be withheld if its disclosure would interfere with enforcement proceedings, deprive a person of a fair trial, create an unwarranted invasion of personal privacy, disclose the identity of a confidential source, disclose investigative techniques and procedures, endanger the life or safety of law enforcement personnel, or interfere with enforcement proceeding. Because the consequences of an erroneous decision not to withhold in an Exemption Seven case could be extremely serious, courts are likely

42. Comment, The Freedom of Information Act's Privacy Exemption and the Privacy Act of 1974, 11 Harv. C.R.-C.L. L. Rev. 596, 626 (1976).
43. See, e.g., Nader, Freedom from Information: The Act and the Agencies, 5 Harv. C.R.-C.L. L. Rev. 1, 5-7 (1970).

to continue to display reluctance to overturn an agency decision not to disclose, despite the greater specificity of the amended exemption. See NLRB v. Robbins Tire & Rubber Co., 98 S. Ct. 2311 (1978), relying on Exemption Seven to deny respondents, in an unfair labor practice proceeding, discovery of witness statements taken by Board staff; the Court expressed fear that such discovery would lead to intimidation of employee witnesses by employers. Despite such decisions, there are indications that the FBI has systematically destroyed files potentially valuable for law-enforcement purposes in order to avoid FOIA-Privacy Act requests and litigation. See FBI Agents Rap Policy of Burning Files, Link It to Public-Access Acts, Wall St. J., Sept. 27, 1978, p. 1, col. 1.

(8) The Financial Institution and Geological Exploration Exemptions

Section 552(b)(8) permits nondisclosure of reports prepared by federal agencies, such as the Federal Reserve Board or Federal House Loan Banks Board, about the operations of banks and financial institutions. The purpose of the exemption is to "insure the stability of our financial institutions," [44] although it has been suggested that the amendment is superfluous because Exemption Four (confidential commercial and financial information) would appear adequate to cover banking reports.

Exemption Nine, §552(b)(9), is perhaps the least explained of the exemptions. It exempts "geological and geophysical information and data, including maps concerning wells...," although again the confidential commercial information protection of Exemption Four probably would have sufficed to protect this type of valuable information.

Notes and Questions: FOIA Procedures and Policies

FOIA litigation is a voluminous and fast-growing branch of federal administrative law. These materials can only serve to provide an overview and raise some basic questions. As we have noted, the FOIA can be viewed as a mechanism for correcting agency "failure" by providing broader public knowledge and scrutiny of administrative practices and providing another court-enforced procedural mechanism for citizen involvement in government. But, as the foregoing materials illustrate, the FOIA is invoked for other motives and purposes as well. Moreover, unrestrained disclosure can damage important governmental and societal interests. But in many respects the FOIA fails to provide ascertainable directives for resolving these considerations. As with many other statutes, the FOIA creates a problem of discretion.

---

44. S. Rep. 813, 89th Cong., 1st Sess. 10 (1965). Professor Davis, after quoting the language of the Senate Report, stated: "We must be careful or the facts about our financial institutions might become known! We want the public to know the truth about almost all our institutions, but not about our financial institutions! ... The law is clear, but I still wish the lobbyists for the banking agencies had been less effective." Davis, The Information Act: A Preliminary Analysis, 34 U. Chi. L. Rev. 761, 801 (1967).

Should the courts deal with this problem of discretion, in the FOIA context, in the same way as they have in other administrative law contexts?

1. In most other administrative law contexts, a court will normally attach a presumption of correctness to an agency decision that it is called upon to review. The agency has been given initial responsibility to implement a given statute, and normally has specialized experience that the court cannot match. The court's role is ordinarily a "backstopping" one: making sure that the agency has stayed within its statutory authority and exercised its discretion in a considered fashion. But the FOIA is a statute reflecting distrust and suspicion of agencies who will, for bureaucratic reasons, tend to resist disclosure unless forced to by the courts.[45] Thus if the agencies' discretion to withhold disclosure is to be effectively constrained, courts must take the lead role in exercising discretion to resolve the FOIA's ambiguities. This reversal of the normal court/agency role is confirmed by the unusual de novo standard of judicial review specified in the Act.

But in many respects, the courts are ill equipped to discharge the role implied by the FOIA. In the first place, it is obviously difficult for a court to review agency claims to exemption without examining the documents in question. But since disclosure to the requester for purposes of litigation would often hand him a victory, such examination must proceed in camera. Although the FOIA authorizes this procedure and it is now a common practice, in camera inspections pose serious problems, as noted in *Mead Data*. The requester is fenced out, and the District Court is deprived of the benefits of the full adversary process. Thorough in camera review places heavy burdens on judges ill equipped by tradition, professional orientation, and institutional capacity to assume an inquisitorial role. On appeal, an appellate court must either defer almost completely to the district judge or itself utilize uncongenial in camera procedures.[46] Judge Gesell argued eloquently in Military Audit Project v. Bush, 418 F. Supp. 876, 878-879 (D.D.C. 1976), that the in camera procedure authorized by the 1974 Amendments regularizes an ex parte decisionmaking process that is wholly inconsistent with our jurisprudential traditions. (Yet he later reluctantly concluded in the same case that in camera inspection was the only means of determining the agency's compliance with FOIA, see id. at 880.)

Second, even if the documents are available to the court, it is often ill equipped to assess the justifications for exemption asserted by the agency. Does national security justify secret classification of given documents? Will public disclosure seriously hamper the government's ability to acquire given types of information from private firms? The resolution of such questions is one of the basic reasons why agencies are established in the first place. There is a danger that courts will either defer unduly to agencies or impose essentially subjective or arbitrary curbs on agency withholding of documents.

45. In this respect the FOIA resembles the National Environmental Policy Act, see Stewart and Krier, Environmental Law and Policy Ch. 8 (2d ed. 1978), and efforts by courts, examined earlier in this chapter, to protect "underrepresented" interests.

46. See Note, In Camera Inspections Under the Freedom of Information Act, 41 U. Chi. L. Rev. 557 (1974).

In order to avoid these ultimate difficulties, reviewing courts in FOIA cases have, as in other administrative contexts, sought to develop procedural requirements to control agency decisions. For example, in Vaughn v. Rosen, 484 F.2d 820 (D.C. Cir. 1973), *cert. denied,* 415 U.S. 977 (1974), the court required the agency (which had resisted disclosure with sweeping claims of exemption): to prepare an index of the documents covered by the request; to set forth detailed justifications for its claims of exemption; to cross-index documents and justifications; and also to explain why it was not feasible to separate out and disclose information in the requested documents that did not fall within the exemptions. These requirements are now routinely imposed by federal reviewing courts. However, it and similar procedural requirements can only go part way toward resolving the problems which the FOIA poses for reviewing courts. See Ray v. Turner, 587 F.2d 1187 (D.C. Cir. 1978), strictly enforcing *Vaughn* requirements and rejecting the District Court's presumption against in camera review in national security.

2. Does all of this suggest that courts should not be given the "front-line" role in enforcing the FOIA? What alternatives are there? Might the Justice Department, which must defend FOIA suits on behalf of a withholding agency, play a role? On May 5, 1978, the Attorney General wrote a letter to all federal agency heads, noting the substantial burdens of FOIA litigation (six hundred cases then pending in federal courts) and stating that the Justice Department, in the future, would defend such suits only "when disclosure is demonstrably harmful," even though the documents requested come within one of the statutory exemptions.[47]

3. To what extent is the interest of the particular plaintiff seeking disclosure relevant to a court's decision whether agency nondisclosure is justified? This issue can be posed as a question of standing: what interest in the information must a requester show in order to seek review of nondisclosure? Must she show "injury in fact" of the sort required in Simon v. Eastern Kentucky Welfare Rights Org., supra, p. 949? Does the mere fact that the requested information has not been disclosed suffice to establish "injury in fact"? Most courts have apparently so assumed, and the government has not pressed the question.

Plaintiffs' interest is also arguably relevant in the court's ultimate decision on the merits. Should the strength or weakness of plaintiff's need for the requested information tip a close case one way or the other? Chief Justice Burger, dissenting in *Rose,* p. 1065, supra, would apparently grant an exemption in part because of the assertedly slight interest of New York law review editors in Air Force Academy disciplinary records. Should the Court in *Mead* have "tilted" against disclosure because the plaintiff sought the information for commercial purposes? Is it consistent with the Act's basic purposes to give weight (one way or another) to the interests or the need of the person making the request?

4. Section 552(a)(6)(A) contains extremely stringent time limits within which the agency is directed to process requests for information. What if the agency fails to meet these deadlines because of a backlog of requests and an inadequate budget?

---

47. The letter is reproduced in Litigation Under the Amended Federal Freedom of Information Act, supra note 28, at App., 94.

For example, in Open America v. Watergate Special Prosecution Force, 547 F.2d 605 (D.C. Cir. 1976), the FBI was unable to process a request in timely fashion because it had a backlog of 5,137 FOIA requests. It had assigned 200 FBI agents and supporting staff to FOIA tasks and was presently working on 1,084 of the requests.[48] Can a requester jump to the head of the administrative queue by filing a lawsuit? What remedy can the courts provide if agencies regularly fail to meet FOIA deadlines because of backlogs? Can they order that all requests not processed by the deadlines must be granted?

b. Reverse-FOIA Litigation

The prevalence of requests by competitors (and, on occasion, by "public interest" groups) for information submitted to agencies by business firms has given rise to reverse-FOIA suits in which a plaintiff seeks to enjoin agency disclosure to third-person requesters of information which the plaintiff was requested or compelled to disclose to an agency. Congress did not legislate an affirmative right of action to protect confidential submissions to an agency, but courts have nonetheless recognized such a right. Just as the perceived evils of government secrecy gave rise to the FOIA, so, by a process of counter-reactions, the FOIA has spawned "reverse-FOIA" law. Although most of the reverse-FOIA litigation to date has involved threatened agency disclosure of material which a business considers to be within the FOIA's exemption for trade secrets and confidential commercial or trade information, reverse-FOIA suits can be filed to prevent disclosure of information under other exemptions, such as Exemption Six relating to personal privacy.[49]

Reverse FOIA litigation presents distinctive threshold and procedural issues, such as the showing a submitter of information must make to establish standing and the jurisdictional bases for such suits.[50] A more basic set of problems concerns the logical relation between Reverse FOIA suits and the structure of FOIA:

— What if the requested documents do not fall within any FOIA exemption and thus the agency would ordinarily be required to disclose? Does a court enjoy

---

48. The total number of FOIA requests filed annually has been estimated at 150,000. See Weaver, U.S. Information Act: Difficulties Despite Successes, N.Y. Times, Aug. 8, 1977, p. 1, col. 1.

49. See generally, Clement, The Rights of Submitters to Prevent Agency Disclosure of Confidential Business Information: The Reverse Freedom of Information Act Lawsuit, 55 Tex. L. Rev. 587 (1977); Patten & Weinstein, Disclosure of Business Secrets Under the Freedom of Information Act: Suggested Limitations, 29 Ad. L. Rev. 193 (1977); Note, Protection from Government Disclosure — the Reverse FOIA Suit, 1976 Duke L.J. 330.

50. The most commonly asserted basis for jurisdiction is 28 U.S.C. §1331(a). Can you think of others? Submitters are likely to "shop" for a convenient forum. If a request is made for information submitted be several firms, this may result in multiple lawsuits. What of the requester? Must he be joined in the reverse FOIA suit as an indispensable party under Rule 19, F.R.C.P.? May the requester bring litigation — perhaps in another form — to compel disclosure after a reverse FOIA suit has been filed? Is there a case or controversy given that the agency is willing to disclose the information? See Exxon Corp. v. FTC, 436 F. Supp. 1012, 1016-1017 (D. Del. 1977).

equitable discretion to refuse an injunction requiring disclosure by the agency? Does a court enjoy equitable power to prevent an agency from disclosing the material? [51]

— Suppose that the requested material *does* fall within a FOIA exemption, but the agency decides to disclose it anyway. On the face of it, nothing in the FOIA precludes such disclosure, because the exemptions are merely exceptions to the FOIA requirement of mandatory disclosure, and do not compel confidentiality. May a court nonetheless enjoin such disclosure at the behest of a submitter claiming that it will cause serious injury?

— If courts do have the power (from what source?) to enjoin disclosure in the latter context, in which circumstances should they do so? Should they automatically enjoin disclosure whenever the material falls within an FOIA exemption? [52] Should the court balance, de novo, the interests in disclosure and in confidentiality? Should it defer to the agency's resolution of the competing interests and, if so, what should the extent of that deference be? [53] Is the "arbitrary and capricious" standard of review appropriate? Must the agency show that disclosure is authorized by its enabling statute, or at least that disclosure would advance its program goals?

These issues have left the lower federal courts divided in many respects; the Supreme Court has granted certiorari in an effort to resolve the confusion.[54]

Other reverse-FOIA issues which remain unresolved are whether the submitter has a due process right to notice and an opportunity to be heard before information is disclosed to a third party and whether a submitter has any grounds for resisting an agency's demand for information that may later be disclosed to competitors. If an agency does not notify the submitter that someone is requesting information submitted by him, he will probably not have a chance to present his case to the agency or seek a reverse-FOIA injunction. It has been suggested that a major reason that there have not been more reverse-FOIA suits is the present general lack of any

51. Most circuits have concluded that courts have no equitable discretion to refuse enforcement of the FOIA's mandatory disclosure requirements; a fortiori, they do not enjoy power to block agency disclosure of documents required to be disclosed. See, e.g., Charles River Park "A," Inc. v. HUD, 519 F.2d 935 (D.C. Cir. 1975).

52. This approach was endorsed in Westinghouse Elec. Corp. v. Schlesinger, 542 F.2d 1190 (4th Cir. 1976), *cert. denied*, 431 U.S. 924 (1977), but has not been followed elsewhere.

53. For contrasting views on these matters, see Chrysler Corp. v. Schlesinger, 565 F.2d 1172 (3d Cir. 1977), *cert. granted*, 98 S. Ct. 1466 (1978); Pennzoil Co. v. FTC, 534 F.2d 627 (5th Cir. 1976); Sears, Roebuck & Co. v. GSA, 553 F.2d 1378 (D.C. Cir.), *cert. denied*, 434 U.S. 826 (1977). The issues are further complicated by the uncertain relevance of 18 U.S.C. §1905, a criminal statute prohibiting federal officials from disclosing, "in any manner or to any extent not authorized by law," information acquired in an official capacity relating to trade secrets, confidential statistical and financial data, etc., of "any person." The scope of this prohibition is a subject of continuing debate; too few prosecutions have been brought to afford the courts much opportunity to clarify the law.

54. Many of the principal decisions among the lower courts are traced in Chrysler Corp. v. Schlesinger, 565 F.2d 1172 (3d Cir. 1977). The Supreme Court has granted certiorari in *Schlesinger*, 98 S. Ct. 1466 (1978).

requirement for agencies to notify submitters of requests for information.[55] Does due process require such notice? [56]

2. The Government in the Sunshine Law

a. Introduction

Requirements that administrative agencies deliberate in public were first developed at the state level. By 1962, 26 states had passed laws requiring open meetings by administrative boards, commissions, and similar bodies, and presently every state and the District of Columbia has an open meeting law or constitutional provision.[57]

In 1976 an overwhelming majority of Congress passed the Government in the Sunshine Act, whose open-meeting provisions are codified in 5 U.S.C. §552b.[58] For the first time, meetings of multi-member federal agencies[59] must be open to the public. "Meeting" is defined by the Act to include the deliberations of at least a quorum of members where the deliberations determine or result in the conduct of agency business — indicating that some degree of formality is required before a gathering is considered to be a meeting. The Act requires that every part of every meeting must be open to the public unless it falls within one of ten specific exemptions.

No meeting may be closed unless a majority of the membership votes to take that action. At least one week in advance, the members must identify the proposed agenda and compare it with the Act's ten provisions exempting described meeting subjects from the open meeting requirement. The chief legal officer of the agency must prepare and file a statement certifying and giving reasons why the meeting may be closed. A copy of each vote on closing a meeting must be made available to the public in order to inform the public as to the voting record of agency members on open meetings. The agency must announce the time and a place of a closed

---

55. See Patten & Weinstein, supra note 29, at 204.
56. Cf. GTE Sylvania, Inc. v. Consumer Product Safety Commn., 443 F. Supp. 1152, 1156-1157 (D. Del. 1977).
57. Florida's open meeting statute has been expansively interpreted in such a manner as to constitute the most comprehensive open meeting law in the nation. At the other extreme, a number of acts have been rendered largely ineffective because of statutory or judicially created exemptions for executive sessions, which permit public "re-runs" after basic issues have been settled in private. See S. Rep. No. 354, 94th Cong., 1st Sess. 7 (1975); Ga. Code §23-802 ("[P]rovided, however, that before or after said public meetings, said bodies may hold executive sessions privately. . . ."); Selkowe v. Bean, 109 N.H. 247, 249 A.2d 35 (1968). See Note, Open Meeting Statutes: The Press Fights for the "Right to Know," 75 Harv. L. Rev. 1199, 1204 (1962).
58. Other provisions dealing with ex parte communications are discussed at pp. 539-557, supra. The bill passed the Senate 94-0 and passed the House by a vote of 390-5.
59. The Act covers all agencies, as defined in 5 U.S.C. §552(e), headed by a collegial body of two or more members, a majority of whom are appointed by the President with the advice and consent of the Senate. 5 U.S.C. §552b(a)(1).

meeting, announce that it is closed, make available a statement of the reasons for the closing, and make public a list of all nonmembers who will attend.

If the majority votes to close the meeting, a full verbatim transcript or electronic recording of the meeting is required. Any portion of the transcript or recording which does not fit within one of the exemptions must be promptly released to the public. This requirement, which goes beyond state open meeting legislation, was one of the most controversial provisions in the Act, and several exceptions to the full transcript requirement were included in the final version of the Sunshine Act.[60]

Seven of the ten exemptions from the Act's open meetings requirement parallel exemptions of the FOIA. Under these seven exemptions, a meeting may properly be closed if it will involve matters which (1) are vital to the national defense or foreign policy; (2) are concerned with the internal personnel rules and practices of the agency; (3) are specifically exempted from disclosure by another statute; (4) concern trade secrets and confidential commercial or financial information; (5) would constitute a clearly unwarranted invasion of personal privacy; (6) would disclose investigatory records compiled for law enforcement purposes under certain limited circumstances; or (7) relate to bank or financial institution examination reports. Three exemptions which do not closely parallel FOIA exemptions permit the closing of meetings if matters will be discussed which (1) involve accusing any person of a crime, or formally censuring any person; (2) would frustrate implementation of a proposed agency action if prematurely known; or (3) concern the agency's participation in formal rulemaking or litigation.[61]

When a meeting is announced to be closed and a person wishes to attend, the Act creates a cause of action to enjoin the closing. The court may enjoin the meeting pendente lite and the burden of proof to support the closing is on the agency. Within sixty days after a closed meeting the agency may be sued for equitable relief and for access to the transcript of the closed meeting. Any person may sue to enforce the Act's requirements. Unlike the FOIA, a Sunshine Act plaintiff may obtain an injunction barring future violations of the Act. In ruling on whether an agency has justifiably invoked one of the exemptions, a court may review portions of the meeting transcript that have not been publicly released.

Open meetings of executive branch advisory committees are required by the 1972 Federal Advisory Committee Act, 86 Stat. 770, 5 U.S.C. App. I. The Act regulates the creation, composition, and functioning of advisory committees. It requires that their meetings be open to the public unless the subject matter falls within specified exemptions; originally, the exemptions were those in the FOIA, but amendments in 1976 provided that the Sunshine Act's exemptions from its open meeting principle should also apply to advisory committees.[62]

---

60. If an agency votes to close a meeting pursuant to Exemption Eight (bank reports), Nine (a) (information likely to lead to financial speculation), and Ten (adjudicatory proceedings or litigation matters), it may elect to keep minutes rather than a transcript or a recording. 5 U.S.C. §552b(f)(1).

61. 5 U.S.C. §552b(c). For a lengthier discussion of the ten Sunshine Act exemptions, see Note, Government in the Sunshine Act: Opening Federal Agency Meetings, 26 Am. U.L. Rev. 154, 172-195 (1976).

62. Sections 5(b) and 5(c) of the Federal Advisory Committee Act provide that the

b. Assessments of the Open Meeting Principle

Although it is difficult to publicly oppose "open government" in the "post-Watergate" era, disputes exist concerning the appropriate limits. Such disputes center on the applicability of open meeting laws to subordinate agencies or subcommittees which may be solely designed as recommendatory bodies, the point in the decisionmaking process at which a meeting may be said to occur, and the appropriateness of particular enforcement mechanisms, and the subject matter and scope of exemptions.[63]

Consider the following evaluation:[64]

> The basic argument for open meetings is that public knowledge of the considerations upon which governmental action is based is essential to the democratic process. The people must be able to "go beyond and behind" the decisions reached and be apprised of the "pros and cons" involved if they are to make sound judgments on questions of policy and to select their representatives intelligently. The presence of outside observers is an invaluable aid in making such information available, for official reports, even if issued, will seldom furnish a complete summary of the discussion leading to a particular course of action. Even though only newspaper reporters and a few interested citizens actually are present, the benefit of granting access to governmental meetings will inure to a far larger segment of the population, because those who do attend will pass on the information obtained. It is further argued that decisions which result in the expenditure of public funds ought to be made openly so that the people can see how their money is being spent; publicity of expenditures further serves to deter misappropriations, conflicts of interest, and all other forms of official misbehavior. Several other considerations support the principle of open meetings. Government will be more responsive to the governed if officials are able to ascertain public reaction to proposed measures. Public meetings also may operate to provide officials with more accurate information; individual citizens will be able to correct factual misconceptions, par-

---

membership of advisory committees shall "be fairly balanced in terms of the points of view represented and the functions to be performed," and that their advice and recommendations will "not be inappropriately influenced . . . by any special interest." Senator Lee Metcalf and a private citizen brought suit challenging the composition of the National Petroleum Council, a committee created to advise the Secretary of the Interior on petroleum policy, as violative of these provisions, because 140 of the council's members were officers or employees of petroleum companies. In Metcalf v. National Petroleum Council, 553 F.2d 176 (D.C. Cir. 1977), the court held that plaintiffs lacked standing to sue.

63. Comment, Government in the Sunshine Act: A Danger of Overexposure, 14 Harv. J. Leg. 620 (1977).

A number of state open meeting laws provide for criminal penalties. In Florida, where there has been some confusion as to whether the state open meeting act is applicable to chance gatherings where official business is mentioned, two city commissioners were arrested and tried after they met in a public restaurant for lunch and discussed golf, weather, and current city business. They were acquitted, Little & Tompkins, Open Government: An Insider's View, 53 N.C. L. Rev. 451 (1975).

64. Note, Open Meeting Statutes: The Press Fights for the "Right to Know," 75 Harv. L. Rev. 1199, 1200-1203 (1962).

ticularly in local government where the public is apt to have greater knowledge of the issues involved. Then too, as people better understand the demands of government and the significance of particular issues, they will be better prepared "to accept necessary, and perhaps difficult and unpalatable, measures essential to the public good." Finally, open meetings foster more accurate reporting of governmental activities. Even when meetings are closed, some hint of what occurs generally reaches the press; but such reports are often incomplete and slanted according to the views of the informant. To restrict the press to such sources of information is a disservice both to the public, which is misled, and to the officials, who may be judged on the basis of these distorted reports.

Granting the virtue of open meetings in general, substantial objections can be made to enacting the principle as a legal requirement. Publicizing proposed governmental action may benefit citizens whose interests are adverse to the general community or harm individual reputations. In some cases, particularly when sharply conflicting interests must be accommodated, freedom from the pressure of public opinion may be desirable; the delegates to the Constitutional Convention, for example, felt constrained to work in secrecy. Even in less unique circumstances "there is something to be said for open covenants, unopenly arrived at." One public official has remarked that "there are many details, ramifications and opinions that no sound administrator ... would care to express in public," and it appears that officials are often reluctant to request information at open meetings lest they create a public image of ignorance.[65] In addition, public officials are prone to waste time making speeches for the benefit of an audience, while in a closed meeting they "are less on their dignity, less inclined to oratory." If the meeting is for preliminary consideration of action, there are additional objections. An open meeting requirement will tend to disadvantage subordinate officials by publicizing their disagreement with policies that they must administer. And publicity of proposals put forth during preliminary discussions may frustrate ultimate agreement, for an official hesitates to abandon a view that he has publicly advocated. A final objection to an open meeting requirement arises from the tendency of the press toward "sensational" reporting. All too frequently newspaper stories are distorted by the bias of the reporter or his paper. Even when there is no bias, newspapers prefer to emphasize as "newsworthy" only "controversial matters about which there is some conflict or ... those items which tend to make legislators appear substantially less than bright." It has even been contended that the need for "right to know" laws has been exaggerated, as "editorials and news articles on star chamber sessions and the like have long been an easy, inevitably irrefutable, and popularly accepted part of every experienced, and frequently cynical, news editor's bag of tricks." Although these

---

65. A Letter From Chief Editorial Writer of the Chicago Sun-Times to the Harvard Law Review, Nov. 28, 1961, states: "[I]t is not so much an unwillingness to express public views that accounts for the desire for secrecy as it is the need to cover up just plain ignorance that so many public officials have. That is the basis for the one argument for secret meetings that might have some validity.... In a secret meeting a public official can honestly confess ignorance of a subject and seek enlightenment from his fellow committee members and witnesses. He would not be able to bring himself to do this in a public meeting and such reluctance might have an adverse effect on the proceedings."

arguments cannot be ignored, they do not compel the conclusion that a legal requirement of open meetings is untenable. Some have urged that the benefits of requiring that all governmental activity be done openly outweighs any disadvantages that may result; perhaps a more rational approach would be to seek to devise a legal standard affording the fullest possible degree of openness while recognizing the interests promoted by governmental secrecy.

Notes and Questions

1. Given similar exemptions, is the case for open meetings stronger than the case for public disclosure of agency documents, or the reverse?

2. Given the recent enactment of the Government in the Sunshine Act, there is as yet no judicial gloss on its provisions. Would you expect that open meeting litigation to be as voluminous as FOIA litigation? Which interests are likely to benefit sufficiently from open meetings in order to initiate litigation to enforce the Sunshine Act's requirements? Will we see "Reverse Sunshine" litigation?

Consider the remarks of Representative McCloskey in the House debates on the Act:

> ... But, by and large, the ones who will be taking advantage of this bill's provisions will be corporate and other special interests attempting to stave off what they deem to be unfavorable Government action. We have seen too many cases where agency action was unnecessarily protracted due to long, drawn-out court battles. This bill gives the special interests just one more forum in which to fight the agency.[66]

3. Does it make any sense to limit the open meeting principle to collegial multimember agencies, such as the FTC or CAB, while ignoring the number of federal agencies headed by a single person?

4. What forms of discussion among agency members constitute a "meeting" for purposes of the Act?

Should the Act apply when two out of the FTC's five members confer about agency business when they meet in the corridor? When they plot how to engineer a given result at the next formal meeting of the commission? When they attend a trade association luncheon together and discuss agency policies with association officials?

Would your answers to the above questions differ if the incidents involved three commissioners rather than two?

State courts have struggled with similar questions under state statutes. An expansive view was taken in Bigelow v. Howze, 291 So.2d 645 (Fla. 1974). In *Bigelow*, two of five county commissioners traveled to another state to investigate and report on the ability of two firms to do a reappraisal of county property values. While in the other state, the two commissioners agreed in private they would support the awarding of the contract to one of the firms. This was held to constitute

66. 122 Cong. Rec. H7875 (daily ed. July 28, 1976).

a nonpublic "meeting" in violation of Florida's open meeting statute. Compare Dayton Newspapers, Inc. v. City of Dayton, 28 Ohio App. 95, 274 N.E.2d 766 (Ct. App. 1971), where a newspaper publisher and its reporter brought an action against city commissioners for a permanent injunction enjoining the commissioners from denying plaintiffs access to any meetings of the city commissioners. The relevant ordinance provided that "[a]ll meetings of the Commission shall be public." After considering various definitions of the term "meeting," the court considered the propriety of informal executive sessions:

> The present issue . . . concerns gatherings of commissioners when they confer together and with each other; and when they collaborate in doing what may be called their "homework." It is important that they do so freely and without restraint. Like all who have the responsibility of making important decisions, they need an opportunity to express, exchange and test ideas, to deliberate freely, off the record, and without the restraint of outside influence. Freedom of discussion and the exchange of ideas is essential to an understanding of a problem. It cannot be satisfactorily accomplished under a spotlight or before a microphone.
>
> Such a procedure is widely and necessarily practiced in various branches of government. After an open public trial, the jury is required to deliberate in privacy. A grand jury, whose duty is investigative, must proceed in strict secrecy, for vital and evident reasons. Ours, like any multiple court, regularly withdraws from the public courtroom to deliberate uninterruptedly in chambers.

5. Will broad interpretations of the term "meeting" simply force the "real" decisionmaking underground, leaving public meetings an empty ritual? How can Sunshine Act plaintiffs ascertain whether this is indeed happening? Do the principles developed in the *Morgan* litigation, pp. 760-766, supra, bar discovery on this question? In any event, what relief can the courts provide? Compare the analogous question under FOIA whether broad disclosure requirements will simply lead administrators to avoid committing important matters to written form.

6. Why does the Sunshine Act require that a verbatim transcript be kept of all agency meetings governed by the Act? Consider again the comments of Representative McCloskey:

> [The verbatim recording or transcript requirement] is simultaneously the bill's most onerous and its most useless provision. It is onerous because of the tremendous expense involved in meeting this requirement — not only the costs of the recording equipment or stenographer, but the costs of transcribing the verbatim record, reviewing it to see if any portions of it can be made public, and, if so, making the necessary deletions in the transcript. It is useless because, under the act, these transcripts, made at considerable expenses, will never be made publicly available if the meeting was legally closed. . . .
>
> This provision will undermine the goals of the two principal planks of Federal information policy, the Freedom of Information Act and the Privacy Act. If these transcripts are in existence, their disclosure will undoubtedly

be the object of a significant amount of Federal Court litigation. One way or another, some of the information in those transcripts will become public — and the protections provided for individuals contained in the Privacy Act, and for various types of exempt matters in the Freedom of Information Act, will be eroded.[67]

Note also that the courts will be required to examine transcripts in camera, raising all of the problems with in camera review discussed under the FOIA. However, is there any other way to ensure that the Act's requirements will be met?

7. Do the above questions persuade you that the Sunshine Act and, similarly, the FOIA, are simplistic, largely ineffective, and excessively costly mechanisms for dealing with agency discretion? Or are they nonetheless justified, warts and all?

67. Ibid.

Appendix: Excerpts from the Federal Administrative Procedure Act

Chapter 5, Subchapter II — Administrative Procedure

§551. *Definitions*

For the purpose of this subchapter —

(1) "agency" means each authority of the Government of the United States, whether or not it is within or subject to review by another agency, but does not include —

(A) the Congress;

(B) the courts of the United States;

(C) the governments of the territories or possessions of the United States;

(D) the government of the District of Columbia;

or except as to the requirements of section 552 of this title —

(E) agencies composed of representatives of the parties or of representatives or organizations of the parties to the disputes determined by them;

(F) courts martial and military commissions;

(G) military authority exercised in the field in time of war or in occupied territory; or

(H) functions conferred by sections 1738, 1739, 1743, and 1744 of title 12; chapter 2 of title 41; or sections 1622, 1884, 1891-1902, and former section 1641(b)(2), of title 50, appendix;

(2) "person" includes an individual, partnership, corporation, association, or public or private organization other than an agency;

(3) "party" includes a person or agency named or admitted as a party, or properly seeking and entitled as of right to be admitted as a party, in an agency proceeding, and a person or agency admitted by an agency as a party for limited purposes;

(4) "rule means the whole or a part of an agency statement of general or

particular applicability and future effect designed to implement, interpret, or prescribe law or policy or describing the organization, procedure, or practice requirements of an agency and includes the approval or prescription for the future of rates, wages, corporate or financial structures or reorganizations thereof, prices, facilities, appliances, services or allowances therefor or of valuations, costs, or accounting, or practices bearing on any of the foregoing;

(5) "rule making" means agency process for formulating, amending, or repealing a rule;

(6) "order" means the whole or a part of a final disposition, whether affirmative, negative, injunctive, or declaratory in form, of an agency in a matter other than rule making but including licensing;

(7) "adjudication" means agency process for the formulation of an order;

(8) "license" includes the whole or a part of an agency permit, certificate, approval, registration, charter, membership, statutory exemption or other form of permission;

(9) "licensing" includes agency process respecting the grant, renewal, denial, revocation, suspension, annulment, withdrawal, limitation, amendment, modification, or conditioning of a license;

(10) "sanction" includes the whole or a part of an agency —

(A) prohibition, requirement, limitation, or other condition affecting the freedom of a person;

(B) withholding of relief;

(C) imposition of penalty or fine;

(D) destruction, taking, seizure, or withholding of property;

(E) assessment of damages, reimbursement, restitution, compensation, costs, charges, or fees;

(F) requirement, revocation, or suspension of a license; or

(G) taking other compulsory or restrictive action;

(11) "relief" includes the whole or a part of an agency —

(A) grant of money, assistance, license, authority, exemption, exception, privilege, or remedy;

(B) recognition of a claim, right, immunity, privilege, exemption, or exception; or

(C) taking of other action on the application or petition of, and beneficial to, a person;

(12) "agency proceeding" means an agency process as defined by paragraphs (5), (7), and (9) of this section;

(13) "agency action" includes the whole or a part of an agency rule, order, license, sanction, relief, or the equivalent or denial thereof, or failure to act; and

(14) "ex parte communication" means an oral or written communication not on the public record with respect to which reasonable prior notice to all parties is not given, but it shall not include requests for status reports on any matter or proceeding covered by this subchapter.

§552. *Public information; agency rules, opinions, orders, records, and proceedings*

(a) Each agency shall make available to the public information as follows:

(1) Each agency shall separately state and currently publish in the Federal Register for the guidance of the public —

(A) descriptions of its central and field organization and the established places at which, the employees (and in the case of a uniformed service, the members) from whom, and the methods whereby, the public may obtain information, make submittals or requests, or obtain decisions;

(B) statements of the general course and method by which its functions are channeled and determined, including the nature and requirements of all formal and informal procedures available;

(C) rules of procedure, descriptions of forms available or the places at which forms may be obtained, and instructions as to the scope and contents of all papers, reports, or examinations;

(D) substantive rules of general applicability adopted as authorized by law, and statements of general policy or interpretations of general applicability formulated and adopted by the agency; and

(E) each amendment, revision, or repeal of the foregoing.

Except to the extent that a person has actual and timely notice of the terms thereof, a person may not in any manner be required to resort to, or be adversely affected by, a matter required to be published in the Federal Register and not so published. For the purpose of this paragraph, matter reasonably available to the class of persons affected thereby is deemed published in the Federal Register when incorporated by reference therein with the approval of the Director of the Federal Register.

(2) Each agency, in accordance with published rules, shall make available for public inspection and copying —

(A) final opinions, including concurring and dissenting opinions, as well as orders, made in the adjudication of cases;

(B) those statements of policy and interpretations which have been adopted by the agency and are not published in the Federal Register; and

(C) administrative staff manuals and instructions to staff that affect a member of the public;

unless the materials are promptly published and copies offered for sale. To the extent required to prevent a clearly unwarranted invasion of personal privacy, an agency may delete identifying details when it makes available or publishes an opinion, statement of policy, interpretation, or staff manual or instruction. However, in each case the justification for the deletion shall be explained fully in writing. Each agency shall also maintain and make available for public inspection and copying current indexes providing identifying information for the public as to any matter issued, adopted, or promulgated after July 4, 1967, and required by this paragraph to be made available or published. Each agency shall promptly publish, quarterly or more frequently, and distribute (by sale or otherwise) copies of each index or supplements thereto unless it determines by order published in the Federal Register that the publication would be unnecessary and impracticable, in which case the agency shall nonetheless provide copies of such index on request at a cost not to exceed the direct cost of duplication. A final order, opinion, statement of policy, interpretation, or staff manual or instruction that affects a member of the public may be relied on, used, or cited as precedent by an agency against a party other than an agency only if —

    (i) it has been indexed and either made available or published as provided by this paragraph; or

    (ii) the party has actual and timely notice of the terms thereof.

(3) Except with respect to the records made available under paragraphs (1) and (2) of this subsection, each agency, upon any request for records which (A) reasonably describes such records and (B) is made in accordance with published rules stating the time, place, fees (if any), and procedures to be followed, shall make the records promptly available to any person.

(4)(A) In order to carry out the provisions of this section, each agency shall promulgate regulations, pursuant to notice and receipt of public comment, specifying a uniform schedule of fees applicable to all constituent units of such agency. Such fees shall be limited to reasonable standard charges for document search and duplication and provide for recovery of only the direct costs of such search and duplication. Documents shall be furnished without charge or at a reduced charge where the agency determines that waiver or reduction of the fee is in the public interest because furnishing the information can be considered as primarily benefiting the general public.

(B) On complaint, the district court of the United States in the district in which the complainant resides, or has his principal place of business, or in which the agency records are situated, or in the District of Columbia, has jurisdiction to enjoin the agency from withholding agency records and to order the production of any agency records improperly withheld from the complainant. In such a case the court shall determine the matter de novo, and may examine the contents of such agency records in camera to determine whether such records or any part thereof shall be withheld under any of the exemptions set forth in subsection (b) of this section, and the burden is on the agency to sustain its action.

(C) Notwithstanding any other provision of law, the defendant shall serve an answer or otherwise plead to any complaint made under this subsection within thirty days after service upon the defendant of the pleading in which such complaint is made, unless the court otherwise directs for good cause shown.

(D) Except as to cases the court considers of greater importance, proceedings before the district court, as authorized by this subsection, and appeals therefrom, take precedence on the docket over all cases and shall be assigned for hearing and trial or for argument at the earliest practicable date and expedited in every way.

(E) The court may assess against the United States reasonable attorney fees and other litigation costs reasonably incurred in any case under this section in which the complainant has substantially prevailed.

(F) Whenever the court orders the production of any agency records improperly withheld from the complainant and assesses against the United States reasonable attorney fees and other litigation costs, and the court additionally issues a written finding that the circumstances surrounding the withholding raise questions whether agency personnel acted arbitrarily or capriciously with respect to the withholding, the Civil Service Commission shall promptly initiate a proceeding to determine whether disciplinary action is warranted against the officer or employee who was primarily responsible for the withholding. The Commission, after investigation and consideration of the evidence submitted, shall submit its findings and recommendations to the administrative authority of the agency concerned and shall send copies of the findings and recommendations to the officer or employee or his representative. The administrative authority shall take the corrective action that the Commission recommends.

(G) In the event of noncompliance with the order of the court, the district court may punish for contempt the responsible employee, and in the case of a uniformed service, the responsible member.

(5) Each agency having more than one member shall maintain and make available for public inspection a record of the final votes of each member in every agency proceeding.

(6)(A) Each agency, upon any request for records made under paragraph (1), (2), or (3) of this subsection, shall —

(i) determine within ten days (excepting Saturdays, Sundays, and legal public holidays) after the receipt of any such request whether to comply with such request and shall immediately notify the person making such request of such determination and the reasons therefor, and of the right of such person to appeal to the head of the agency any adverse determination; and

(ii) make a determination with respect to any appeal within twenty days (excepting Saturdays, Sundays, and legal public holidays) after the receipt of such appeal. If on appeal the denial of the request for records is in whole or in part upheld, the agency shall notify the person making such request of the provisions for judicial review of that determination under paragraph (4) of this subsection.

(B) In unusual circumstances as specified in this subparagraph, the time limits prescribed in either clause (i) or clause (ii) of subparagraph (A) may be extended by written notice to the person making such request setting forth the reasons for such extension and the date on which a determination is expected to be dispatched. No such notice shall specify a date that would result in an extension for more than ten working days. As used in this subparagraph, "unusual circumstances" means, but only to the extent reasonably necessary to the proper processing of the particular request —

(i) the need to search for and collect the requested records from field facilities or other establishments that are separate from the office processing the request;

(ii) the need to search for, collect, and appropriately examine a voluminous amount of separate and distinct records which are demanded in a single request; or

(iii) the need for consultation, which shall be conducted with all practicable speed, with another agency having a substantial interest in the determination of the request or among two or more components of the agency having substantial subject-matter interest therein.

(C) Any person having a request to any agency for records under paragraph (1), (2), or (3) of this subsection shall be deemed to have exhausted his administrative remedies with respect to such request if the agency fails to comply with the applicable time limit provisions of this paragraph. If the Government can show exceptional circumstances exist and that the agency is exercising due diligence in responding to the request, the court may retain jurisdiction and allow the agency additional time to complete its review of the records. Upon any determination by an agency to comply with a request for records, the records shall be made promptly available to such person making such request. Any notification of denial of any request for records under this subsection shall set forth the names and titles or positions of each person responsible for the denial of such request.

(b) This section does not apply to matters that are —

(1)(A) specifically authorized under criteria established by an Executive order to be kept secret in the interest of national defense or foreign policy and (B) are in fact properly classified pursuant to such Executive order;

(2) related solely to the internal personnel rules and practices of an agency;

(3) specifically exempted from disclosure by statute (other than section 552b of this title) provided that such statute (A) requires that the matters be withheld from the public in such a manner as to leave no discretion on the issue, or (B) establishes particular criteria for withholding or refers to particular types of matters to be withheld;

(4) trade secrets and commercial or financial information obtained from a person and privileged or confidential;

(5) inter-agency or intra-agency memorandums or letters which would not be available by law to a party other than an agency in litigation with the agency;

(6) personnel and medical files and similar files the disclosure of which would constitute a clearly unwarranted invasion of personal privacy;

(7) investigatory records compiled for law enforcement purposes, but only to the extent that the production of such records would (A) interfere with enforcement proceedings, (B) deprive a person of a right to a fair trial or an impartial adjudication, (C) constitute an unwarranted invasion of personal privacy, (D) disclose the identity of a confidential source and, in the case of a record compiled by a criminal law enforcement authority in the course of a criminal investigation, or by an agency conducting a lawful national security intelligence investigation, confidential information furnished only by the confidential source, (E) disclose investigative

techniques and procedures, or (F) endanger the life or physical safety of law enforcement personnel;

(8) contained in or related to examination, operating, or condition reports prepared by, on behalf of, or for the use of an agency responsible for the regulation or supervision of financial institutions; or

(9) geological and geophysical information and data, including maps, concerning wells.

Any reasonably segregable portion of a record shall be provided to any person requesting such record after deletion of the portions which are exempt under this subsection.

(c) This section does not authorize withholding of information or limit the availability of records to the public, except as specifically stated in this section. This section is not authority to withhold information from Congress.

(d) On or before March 1 of each calendar year, each agency shall submit a report covering the preceding calendar year to the Speaker of the House of Representatives and President of the Senate for referral to the appropriate committees of the Congress. The report shall include —

(1) the number of determinations made by such agency not to comply with requests for records made to such agency under subsection (a) and the reasons for each such determination;

(2) the number of appeals made by persons under subsection (a)(6), the result of such appeals, and the reason for the action upon each appeal that results in a denial of information;

(3) the names and titles or positions of each person responsible for the denial of records requested under this section, and the number of instances of participation for each;

(4) the results of each proceeding conducted pursuant to subsection (a)(4) (F), including a report of the disciplinary action taken against the officer or employee who was primarily responsible for improperly withholding records or an explanation of why disciplinary action was not taken;

(5) a copy of every rule made by such agency regarding this section;

(6) a copy of the fee schedule and the total amount of fees collected by the agency for making records available under this section; and

(7) such other information as indicates efforts to administer fully this section. The Attorney General shall submit an annual report on or before March 1 of each calendar year which shall include for the prior calendar year a listing of the number of cases arising under this section, the exemption involved in each case, the disposition of such case, and the cost, fees, and penalties assessed under subsections (a)(4)(E), (F), and (G). Such report shall also include a description of the efforts undertaken by the Department of Justice to encourage agency compliance with this section.

(e) For purposes of this section, the term "agency" as defined in section 551(1) of this title includes any executive department, military department, Government corporation, Government controlled corporation, or other establishment in the executive branch of the Government (including the Executive Office of the President), or any independent regulatory agency. . . .

[§§ 552a (dealing with protection of individual privacy) and 552b (dealing with open government meetings) are omitted.]

§553. Rule making

(a) This section applies, accordingly to the provisions thereof, except to the extent that there is involved —

(1) a military or foreign affairs function of the United States; or

(2) a matter relating to agency management or personnel or to public property, loans, grants, benefits, or contracts.

(b) General notice of proposed rule making shall be published in the Federal Register, unless persons subject thereto are named and either personally served or otherwise have actual notice thereof in accordance with law. The notice shall include —

(1) a statement of the time, place, and nature of public rule making proceedings;

(2) reference to the legal authority under which the rule is proposed; and

(3) either the terms or substance of the proposed rule or a description of the subjects and issues involved.

Except when notice or hearing is required by statute, this subsection does not apply —

(A) to interpretative rules, general statements of policy, or rules of agency organization, procedure, or practice; or

(B) when the agency for good cause finds (and incorporates the finding and a brief statement of reasons therefor in the rules issued) that notice and public procedure thereon are impracticable, unnecessary, or contrary to the public interest.

(c) After notice required by this section, the agency shall give interested persons an opportunity to participate in the rule making through submission of written data, views, or arguments with or without opportunity for oral presentation. After consideration of the relevant matter presented, the agency shall incorporate in the rules adopted a concise general statement of their basis and purpose. When rules are required by statute to be made on the record after opportunity for an agency hearing, sections 556 and 557 of this title apply instead of this subsection.

(d) The required publication or service of a substance rule shall be made not less than 30 days before its effective date, except —

(1) a substantive rule which grants or recognizes an exemption or relieves a restriction;

(2) interpretative rules and statements of policy; or

(3) as otherwise provided by the agency for good cause found and published with the rule.

(e) Each agency shall give an interested person the right to petition for the issuance, amendment, or repeal of a rule.

§554. *Adjudications*

(a) This section applies, according to the provisions thereof, in every case of adjudication required by statute to be determined on the record after opportunity for an agency hearing, except to the extent that there is involved —

(1) a matter subject to a subsequent trial of the law and the facts de novo in a court;

(2) the selection or tenure of an employee, except an administrative law judge appointed under section 3105 of this title;

(3) proceedings in which decisions rest solely on inspections, tests, or elections;

(4) the conduct of military or foreign affairs functions;

(5) cases in which an agency is acting as an agent for a court; or

(6) the certification of worker representatives.

(b) Persons entitled to notice of an agency hearing shall be timely informed of —

(1) the time, place, and nature of the hearing;

(2) the legal authority and jurisdiction under which the hearing is to be held; and

(3) the matters of fact and law asserted.

When private persons are the moving parties, other parties to the proceeding shall give prompt notice of issues controverted in fact or law; and in other instances agencies may by rule require responsive pleading. In fixing the time and place for hearings, due regard shall be had for the convenience and necessity of the parties or their representatives.

(c) The agency shall give all interested parties opportunity for —

(1) the submission and consideration of facts, arguments, offers of settlement, or proposals of adjustment when time, the nature of the proceeding, and the public interest permit; and

(2) to the extent that the parties are unable so to determine a controversy by consent, hearing and decision on notice and in accordance with sections 556 and 557 of this title.

(d) The employee who presides at the reception of evidence pursuant to section 556 of this title shall make the recommended decision or initial decision required by section 557 of this title, unless he becomes unavailable to the agency. Except to the extent required for the disposition of ex parte matters as authorized by law, such an employee may not —

(1) consult a person or party on a fact in issue, unless on notice and opportunity for all parties to participate; or

(2) be responsible to or subject to the supervision or direction of an employee

or agent engaged in the performance of investigative or prosecuting functions for an agency.

An employee or agent engaged in the performance of investigative or prosecuting functions for an agency in a case may not, in that or a factually related case, participate or advise in the decision, recommended decision, or agency review pursuant to section 557 of this title, except as witness or counsel in public proceedings. This subsection does not apply —

(A) in determining applications for initial licenses;

(B) to proceedings involving the validity or application of rates, facilities, or practices of public utilities or carriers; or

(C) to the agency or a member or members of the body comprising the agency.

(e) The agency, with like effect as in the case of other orders, and in its sound discretion, may issue a declaratory order to terminate a controversy or remove uncertainty.

§555. Ancillary matters

(a) This section applies, according to the provisions thereof, except as otherwise provided by this subchapter.

(b) A person compelled to appear in person before an agency or representative thereof is entitled to be accompanied, represented, and advised by counsel or, if permitted by the agency, by other qualified representative. A party is entitled to appear in person or by or with counsel or other duly qualified representative in an agency proceeding. So far as the orderly conduct of public business permits, an interested person may appear before an agency or its responsible employees for the presentation, adjustment, or determination of an issue, request, or controversy in a proceeding, whether interlocutory summary, or otherwise, or in connection with an agency function. With due regard for the convenience and necessity of the parties or their representatives and within a reasonable time, each agency shall proceed to conclude a matter presented to it. This subsection does not grant or deny a person who is not a lawyer the right to appear for or represent others before an agency or in an agency proceeding.

(c) Process, requirement of a report, inspection, or other investigative act or demand may not be issued, made, or enforced except as authorized by law. A person compelled to submit data or evidence is entitled to retain or, on payment of lawfully prescribed costs, procure a copy or transcript thereof, except that in a nonpublic investigatory proceeding the witness may for good cause be limited to inspection of the official transcript of his testimony.

(d) Agency subpenas authorized by law shall be issued to a party on request and, when required by rules of procedure, on a statement or showing of general relevance and reasonable scope of the evidence sought. On contest, the court shall sustain the subpena or similar process or demand to the extent that it is found to be in accordance with law. In a proceeding for enforcement, the court shall issue an order requiring the appearance of the witness or the production of the evidence or data within a reasonable time under penalty of punishment for contempt in case of contumacious failure to comply.

(e) Prompt notice shall be given of the denial in whole or in part of a written application, petition, or other request of an interested person made in connection with any agency proceeding. Except in affirming a prior denial or when the denial is self-explanatory, the notice shall be accompanied by a brief statement of the grounds for denial.

§556. Hearings; presiding employees; powers and duties; burden of proof; evidence; record as basis of decision

(a) This section applies, according to the provisions thereof, to hearings required by section 553 or 554 of this title to be conducted in accordance with this section.

(b) There shall preside at the taking of evidence —

(1) the agency;

(2) one or more members of the body which comprises the agency; or

(3) one or more administrative law judges appointed under section 3105 of this title.

This subchapter does not supersede the conduct of specified classes of proceedings, in whole or in part, by or before boards or other employees specially provided for by or designated under statute. The functions of presiding employees and of employees participating in decisions in accordance with section 557 of this title shall be conducted in an impartial manner. A presiding or participating employee may at any time disqualify himself. On the filing in good faith of a timely and sufficient affidavit of personal bias or other disqualification of a presiding or participating employee, the agency shall determine the matters as a part of the record and decision in the case.

(c) Subject to published rules of the agency and within its powers, employees presiding at hearings may —

(1) administer oaths and affirmations;

(2) issue subpenas authorized by law;

(3) rule on offers of proof and receive relevant evidence;

(4) take depositions or have depositions taken when the ends of justice would be served;

(5) regulate the course of the hearing;

(6) hold conferences for the settlement or simplification of the issues by consent of the parties;

(7) dispose of procedural requests or similar matters;

(8) make or recommend decisions in accordance with section 557 of this title; and

(9) take other action authorized by agency rules consistent with this sub-chapter.

(d) Except as otherwise provided by statute, the proponent of a rule or order has the burden of proof. Any oral or documentary evidence may be received, but the agency as a matter of policy shall provide for the exclusion of irrelevant, im-material, or unduly repetitious evidence. A sanction may not be imposed or rule or order issued except on consideration of the whole record or those parts thereof cited by a party and supported by and in accordance with the reliable, probative, and substantial evidence. The agency may, to the extent consistent with the inter-ests of justice and the policy of the underlying statutes administered by the agency, consider a violation of section 557(d) of this title sufficient grounds for a decision adverse to a party who has knowingly committed such violation or knowingly caused such violation to occur. A party is entitled to present his case or defense by oral or documentary evidence, to submit rebuttal evidence, and to conduct such cross-examination as may be required for a full and true disclosure of the facts. In rule making or determining claims for money or benefits or applications for initial li-censes an agency may, when a party will not be prejudiced thereby, adopt proce-dures for the submission of all or part of the evidence in written form.

(e) The transcript of testimony and exhibits, together with all papers and requests filed in the proceeding, constitutes the exclusive record for decision in accordance with section 557 of this title and, on payment of lawfully prescribed costs, shall be made available to the parties. When an agency decision rests on official notice of a material fact not appearing in the evidence in the record, a party is entitled, on timely request, to an opportunity to show the contrary.

§557. *Initial decisions; conclusiveness; review by agency; submissions by parties; contents of decisions; record*

(a) This section applies, according to the provisions thereof, when a hearing is required to be conducted in accordance with section 556 of this title.

(b) When the agency did not preside at the reception of the evidence, the presiding employee or, in cases not subject to section 554(d) of this title, an em-ployee qualified to preside at hearings pursuant to section 556 of this title, shall initially decide the case unless the agency requires, either in specific cases or by general rule, the entire record to be certified to it for decision. When the presiding employee makes an initial decision, that decision then becomes the decision of the agency without further proceedings unless there is an appeal to, or review on mo-tion of, the agency within time provided by rule. On appeal from or review of the initial decision, the agency has all the powers which it would have in making the initial decision except as it may limit the issues on notice or by rule. When the agency makes the decision without having presided at the reception of the evidence, the presiding employee or an employee qualified to preside at hearings pursuant to section 556 of this title shall first recommend a decision, except that in rule making or determining application for initial licenses —

(1) instead thereof the agency may issue a tentative decision or one of its responsible employees may recommend a decision; or

(2) this procedure may be omitted in a case in which the agency finds on the record that due and timely execution of its functions imperatively and unavoidably so requires.

(c) Before a recommended, initial, or tentative decision, or a decision on agency review of the decision of subordinate employees, the parties are entitled to a reasonable opportunity to submit for the consideration of the employees participating in the decisions —

(1) proposed findings and conclusions; or

(2) exceptions to the decisions or recommended decisions of subordinate employees or to tentative agency decisions; and

(3) supporting reasons for the exceptions or proposed findings or conclusions. The record shall show the ruling on each finding, conclusion, or exception presented. All decisions, including initial, recommended, and tentative decisions, are a part of the record and shall include a statement of —

(A) findings and conclusions, and the reasons or basis therefor, on all the material issues of fact, law, or discretion presented on the record; and

(B) the appropriate rule, order, sanction relief, or denial thereof.

(d)(1) In any agency proceeding which is subject to subsection (a) of this section, except to the extent required for the disposition of ex parte matters as authorized by law —

(A) no interested person outside the agency shall make or knowingly cause to be made to any member of the body comprising the agency, administrative law judge, or other employee who is or may reasonably be expected to be involved in the decisional process of the proceeding, an ex parte communication relevant to the merits of the proceeding;

(B) no member of the body comprising the agency, administrative law judge, or other employee who is or may reasonably be expected to be involved in the decisional process of the proceeding, shall make or knowingly cause to be made to any interested person outside the agency an ex parte communication relevant to the merits of the proceeding;

(C) a member of the body comprising the agency, administrative law judge, or other employee who is or may reasonably be expected to be involved in the decisional process of such proceeding who receives, or who makes or knowingly causes to be made, a communication prohibited by this subsection shall place on the public record of the proceeding:

(i) all such written communications;

(ii) memoranda stating the substance of all such oral communications; and

(iii) all written responses, and memoranda stating the substance of all oral responses, to the materials described in clauses (i) and (ii) of this subparagraph;

(D) upon receipt of a communication knowingly made or knowingly caused to be made by a party in violation of this subsection, the agency, administrative law judge, or other employee presiding at the hearing may, to the extent consistent with the interests of justice and the policy of the underlying statutes, require the party to show cause why his claim or interest in the proceeding should not be dismissed, denied, disregarded, or otherwise adversely affected on account of such violation; and

(E) the prohibitions of this subsection shall apply beginning at such time as the agency may designate, but in no case shall they begin to apply later than the time at which a proceeding is noticed for hearing unless the person responsible for the communication has knowledge that it will be noticed, in which case the prohibitions shall apply beginning at the time of his acquisition of such knowledge.

(2) This subsection does not constitute authority to withhold information from Congress.

§558. Imposition of sanctions; determination of applications for licenses; suspension, revocation, and expiration of licenses;

(a) This section applies, according to the provisions thereof, to the exercise of a power or authority.

(b) A sanction may not be imposed or a substantive rule of order issued except within jurisdiction delegated to the agency and as authorized by law.

(c) When application is made for a license required by law, the agency, with due regard for the rights and privileges of all the interested parties or adversely affected persons and within a reasonable time, shall set and complete proceedings required to be conducted in accordance with sections 556 and 557 of this title or other proceedings required by law and shall make its decision. Except in cases of willfulness or those in which public health, interest, or safety requires otherwise, the withdrawal, suspension, revocation, or annulment of a license is lawful only if, before the institution of agency proceedings therefor, the licensee has been given —

(1) notice by the agency in writing of the facts or conduct which may warrant the action; and

(2) opportunity to demonstrate or achieve compliance with all lawful requirements.

When the licensee has made timely and sufficient application for a renewal or a new license in accordance with agency rules, a license with reference to an activity of a continuing nature does not expire until the application has been finally determined by the agency.

§559. Effect on other laws; effect of subsequent statute

This subchapter, chapter 7, and sections 1305, 3105, 3344, 4301(2)(E), 5362, and 7521, and the provisions of section 5335(a)(B) of this title that relate to hearing examiners, do not limit or repeal additional requirements imposed by statute or otherwise recognized by law. Except as otherwise required by law, requirements or privileges relating to evidence or procedure apply equally to agencies and persons. Each agency is granted the authority necessary to comply with the requirements of this subchapter through the issuance of rules or otherwise. Subsequent statute may not be held to supersede or modify this subchapter, chapter 7, sections 1305, 3105, 3344, 4301(2)(E), 5362, or 7521 or the provisions of section 5335(a)(B) of this title that relate to hearing examiners, except to the extent that it does so expressly.

Chapter 7 — Judicial Review

§701. Application; definitions

(a) This chapter applies, according to the provisions thereof, except to the extent that —
    (1) statutes preclude judicial review; or
    (2) agency action is committed to agency discretion by law.
(b) For the purpose of this chapter —
    (1) "agency" means each authority of the Government of the United States, whether or not it is within or subject to review by another agency, but does not include —
    (A) the Congress;
    (B) the courts of the United States;
    (C) the governments of the territories or possessions of the United States;
    (D) the government of the District of Columbia;
    (E) agencies composed of representatives of the parties or of representatives of organizations of the parties to the disputes determined by them;
    (F) courts martial and military commissions;
    (G) military authority exercised in the field in time of war or in occupied territory; or
    (H) functions conferred by sections 1738, 1739, 1743, and 1744 of title 12; chapter 2 of title 41; or sections 1622, 1884, 1891-1902, and former section 1641 (b)(2), of title 50, appendix; and
    (2) "person," "rule," "order," "license," "sanction," "relief," and "agency action" have the meanings given them by section 551 of this title.

§702. Right of review

A person suffering legal wrong because of agency action, or adversely affected or aggrieved by agency action within the meaning of a relevant statute, is entitled to judicial review thereof. An action in a court of the United States seeking relief other than money damages and stating a claim that an agency or an officer or employee thereof acted or failed to act in an official capacity or under color of legal authority shall not be dismissed nor relief therein be denied on the ground that it is against the United States or that the United States is an indispensable party. The United States may be named as a defendant in any such action, and a judgment or decree may be entered against the United States: *Provided*, That any mandatory or injuctive decree shall specify the Federal officer or officers (by name or by title), and their successors in office, personally responsible for compliance. Nothing herein (1) affects other limitations on judicial review or the power or duty of the court to dismiss any action or deny relief on any other appropriate legal or equitable ground; or (2) confers authority to grant relief if any other statute that grants consent to suit expressly or impliedly forbids the relief which is sought.

§703. Form and venue of proceeding

The form of proceeding for judicial review is the special statutory review proceeding relevant to the subject matter in a court specified by statute or, in the absence or inadequacy thereof, any applicable form of legal action, including actions for declaratory judgments or writs of prohibitory or mandatory injunction or habeas corpus, in a court of competent jurisdiction. If no special statutory review proceeding is applicable, the action for judicial review may be brought against the United States, the agency by its official title, or the appropriate officer. Except to the extent that prior, adequate, and exclusive opportunity for judicial review is provided by law, agency action is subject to judicial review in civil or criminal proceedings for judicial enforcement.

§704. Actions reviewable

Agency action made reviewable by statute and final agency action for which there is no other adequate remedy in a court are subject to judicial review. A preliminary, procedural, or intermediate agency action or ruling not directly reviewable is subject to review on the review of the final agency action. Except as otherwise expressly required by statute, agency action otherwise final is final for the purposes of this section whether or not there has been presented or determined an application for a declaratory order, for any form of reconsideration, or, unless the agency otherwise requires by rule and provides that the action meanwhile is inoperative, for an appeal to superior agency authority.

§705. Relief pending review

When an agency finds that justice so requires, it may postpone the effective date of action taken by it, pending judicial review. On such conditions as may be required and to the extent necessary to prevent irreparable injury, the reviewing court, including the court to which a case may be taken on appeal from or on application for certiorari or other writ to a reviewing court, may issue all necessary and appropriate process to postpone the effective date of an agency action or to preserve status or rights pending conclusion of the review proceedings.

§706. Scope of review

To the extent necessary to decision and when presented, the reviewing court shall decide all relevant questions of law, interpret constitutional and statutory provisions, and determine the meaning or applicability of the terms of an agency action. The reviewing court shall —

(1) compel agency action unlawfully withheld or unreasonably delayed; and

(2) hold unlawful and set aside agency action, findings, and conclusions found to be —

(A) arbitrary, capricious, an abuse of discretion, or otherwise not in accordance with law;

(B) contrary to constitutional right, power, privilege, or immunity;

(C) in excess of statutory jurisdiction, authority, or limitations, or short of statutory right;

(D) without observance of procedure required by law;

(E) unsupported by substantial evidence in a case subject to sections 556 and 557 of this title or otherwise reviewed on the record of an agency hearing provided by statute; or

(F) unwarranted by the facts to the extent that the facts are subject to trial de novo by the reviewing court.

In making the foregoing determinations, the court shall review the whole record or those parts of it cited by a party, and due account shall be taken of the rule of prejudicial error.

Administrative Law Judges

§3105. Appointment of administrative law judges

Each agency shall appoint as many administrative law judges as are necessary for proceedings required to be conducted in accordance with sections 556 and 557 of this title. Administrative law judges shall be assigned to cases in rotation so far as practicable, and may not perform duties inconsistent with their duties and responsibilities as administrative law judges.

§7521. Removal

An administrative law judge appointed under section 3105 of this title may be removed by the agency in which he is employed only for good cause established and determined by the Civil Service Commission on the record after opportunity for hearing.

§5362. Administrative law judges

Administrative law judges appointed under section 3105 of this title are entitled to pay prescribed by the Civil Service Commission independently of agency recommendations or ratings and in accordance with subchapter III of this chapter and chapter 51 of this title.

§3344. Details; administrative law judges

An agency as defined by section 551 of this title which occasionally or temporarily is insufficiently staffed with administrative law judges appointed under section 3105 of this title may use administrative law judges selected by the Civil Service Commission from and with the consent of other agencies.

§1305. Administrative law judges

For the purpose of sections 3105, 3344, 4301(2)(E), 5362, and 7521 of this title the provisions of section 5335(a)(B) of this title that relate to administrative law judges, the Civil Service Commission may investigate, require reports by agencies, issue reports, including an annual report to Congress, prescribe regulations, appoint advisory committees as necessary, recommend legislation, subpoena witnesses and records, and pay witness fees as established for the courts of the United States.

Table Correlating Provisions of the Administrative Procedure Act As Presently Codified in 5 U.S.C. and Sections of the Act as Originally Enacted in 1946

5 U.S.C.	1946 Administrative Procedure Act
§551(1)	Sec. 2(a)
§551(2), (3)	Sec. 2(b)
§551(4), (5)	Sec. 2(c)
§551(6), (7)	Sec. 2(d)
§551(8), (9)	Sec. 2(e)
§551(10), (11)	Sec. 2(f)
§551(12), (13)	Sec. 2(g)
§552(a)-(e)	Sec. 3
§533(a)	Sec. 4
§553(b)	Sec. 4(a)
§553(c)	Sec. 4(b)
§553(d)	Sec. 4(c)
§553(e)	Sec. 4(d)
§554(a)	Sec. 5
§554(b)	Sec. 5(a)
§554(c)	Sec. 5(b)
§554(d)	Sec. 5(c)
§554(e)	Sec. 5(d)
§555(a)	Sec. 6
§555(b)	Sec. 6(a)
§555(c)	Sec. 6(b)
§555(d)	Sec. 6(c)
§555(e)	Sec. 6(d)
§556(a)	Sec. 7
§556(b)	Sec. 7(a)
§556(c)	Sec. 7(b)
§556(d)	Sec. 7(c)
§556(e)	Sec. 7(d)
§557(a)	Sec. 8
§557(b)	Sec. 8(a)
§557(c)	Sec. 8(b)
§558(a)	Sec. 9
§558(b)	Sec. 9(a)
§558(c)	Sec. 9(b)

5 U.S.C.	1946 Administrative Procedure Act
§559	Sec. 12
§701(a)	Sec. 10
§701(b)(1), (2)	Sec. 2(a)-(g)
§702	Sec. 10(a)
§703	Sec. 10(b)
§704	Sec. 10(c)
§705	Sec. 10(d)
§706(1), (2)	Sec. 10(e)
§3105	Sec. 11 (1st sentence)
§7521	Sec. 11 (2d sentence)
§5362	Sec. 11 (3d sentence)
§3344	Sec. 11 (4th sentence)
§1305	Sec. 11 (5th sentence)

Table
of Cases

Italics indicate principal cases

Index